The Manambu Language of East Sepik, Papua New Guinea

The Manambu Language of East Sepik, Papua New Guinea

Alexandra Y. Aikhenvald
Research Centre for Linguistic Typology
La Trobe University

with the assistance of
Jacklyn Yuamali Ala and Pauline Agnes Yuaneng Luma Laki

OXFORD
UNIVERSITY PRESS

OXFORD
UNIVERSITY PRESS

Great Clarendon Street, Oxford OX2 6DP

Oxford University Press is a department of the University of Oxford.
It furthers the University's objective of excellence in research, scholarship,
and education by publishing worldwide in

Oxford New York

Auckland Cape Town Dar es Salaam Hong Kong Karachi
Kuala Lumpur Madrid Melbourne Mexico City Nairobi
New Delhi Shanghai Taipei Toronto

With offices in

Argentina Austria Brazil Chile Czech Republic France Greece
Guatemala Hungary Italy Japan Poland Portugal Singapore
South Korea Switzerland Thailand Turkey Ukraine Vietnam

Oxford is a registered trade mark of Oxford University Press
in the UK and in certain other countries

Published in the United States
by Oxford University Press Inc., New York

First published 2008

This publication has been supported by La Trobe University
http://www.latrobe.edu.au

British Library Cataloguing in Publication Data

Data available

Library of Congress Cataloging in Publication Data

Data available

Typeset by SPI Publisher Services, Pondicherry, India
Printed in Great Britain
on acid-free paper by
CPI Antony Rowe, Chippenham, Wiltshire

ISBN 978-0-19-953981-9

1 3 5 7 9 10 8 6 4 2

Contents

Preface

This is a grammar of Manambu, a language of the Ndu family, which is, in terms of numbers of speakers, the largest language family of the Sepik area of New Guinea. Manambu is spoken by about 2,500 people in five villages—three of which, Avatip, Malu, and Yambon, are sufficiently big to appear on most maps of Papua New Guinea. I started studying the language in 1995, as part of my work on classifiers, genders, and noun classes. I was interested in learning a language with shape-based genders. Alan Rumsey was teaching a field methods course at the ANU, with Pauline Agnes Luma Laki as a consultant. I came along to the course, and then carried on working with Pauline for more than ten years afterwards—this is how my voyage of discovery started. I have since worked with several dozen speakers of Manambu, mostly in Avatip. Pauline Agnes Luma Laki and myself are currently engaged in preparing a comprehensive dictionary of the language.

This grammar contains an analysis of the Manambu language, starting from a brief characterization of the language and its speakers, then going on to phonology, morphology, syntax, discourse organization, and semantics. The analysis is cast in terms of a cumulative typological framework of linguistic analysis—which employs 'the fundamental theoretical concepts that underlie all work in language description and change' (Dixon 1997: 128) and in terms of which significant typological generalizations are postulated; this has come to be called 'basic linguistic theory'. I have avoided employing any transient formalisms. This grammar is part of genuine documentation of the Manambu language in its varied facets.

Every chapter of the grammar includes a presentation of the facts of the language interwoven with arguments for their analysis within a typological framework. No attempt has been made to separate pure 'description' from theoretical interpretation—which would not be a productive task. A typological perspective for each phenomenon is crucial for the analysis given here.

Detailed exemplification is provided for every grammatical point. Most examples come from texts, and a few from spontaneous—or carefully directed—conversation. An additional objective was to convey as much of the Manambu culture as possible through using naturally occurring examples. I avoid using elicited sentences; elicitation was limited to lexicon and to paradigms.

English glosses are kept as close as possible to the glosses and explanations offered by my consultants. Readers should be warned against trying to draw conclusions concerning Manambu grammar and semantics from study of the translations.

Examples, tables, diagrams, figures, charts, and footnotes are numbered separately within each chapter. Footnotes are also numbered separately for each chapter. The orthography used in the examples from languages other than Manambu, and language names, follows that of the sources (unless indicated otherwise).

This grammar can be used as a sourcebook for further typological studies, and as a model for further grammars of languages of the Ndu and of other families of the New Guinea area. It is far from being the last word on Manambu—the grammar is intended to provide a sound systematic foundation for further studies, reanalyses, and reinterpretations.

It is my hope that this book will encourage linguists to go out into the field and document languages threatened by extinction (before it is too late to do so). Nothing can compare with the intellectual excitement of working out the grammatical system of a previously undescribed language.

Acknowledgements

I never planned to work on a Papuan language—until I decided I needed to know more about shape-based genders for my work on classifiers, genders, and noun classes. I am grateful to Alan Rumsey for introducing me to Pauline Agnes Luma Laki in 1995. Pauline adopted me as her younger sister, and has since been my closest collaborator. My warmest thanks go to her.

This grammar would not have been written without the self-sacrificing help, and wonderful linguistic insights, of Jacklyn Yuamali Benji Ala—whom Pauline lovingly called 'angel without wings' (*pǝp tǝ-ma:r-na angel*). She spent hours helping me with transcriptions, translations, explanations, and at the same time cooking, cleaning, looking after her children, and telling the most wonderful and sophisticated stories. Her help and dedication could never be sufficiently acknowledged.

I owe an eternal debt of gratitude to my Manambu friends and family. I am grateful to James Sǝsu Laki, Joel Yuakalu Luma, David Yagenmas Takendu, Leo Luma Yambwi, John Sepaywus, Jamis Katalu Angi Balangawi, Kǝmbwiyat, and Kulanawi Yuakaw, for sharing their insights and histories with me. Paul Kat Badaybæg and John Sepaywus were my main teachers of the Manambu history and lore. Catie Teketa:y, Jennie Kudapa:kw, Lowai, the late Wimali Yabukwi, Gemaj, Yuawalup, Maguniway, Yipawal, Sawsepali, Tagwatakw, Gaiawalimæg, Walinum, Ester Yuaya:b, and Ñatabi did not just tell stories and sing women's songs to me—they shared their warmth and friendship, and made me feel part of the village.

Piurkaramb, Leo Kalangas, and Waliaundemi, of Malu, and Aulapan, Seplawan, and Yukwaygab, of Yawabak, shared with us stories of the Manambu past. In Malu I was privileged to meet Duamakwa:y—the oldest man in the Manambu community. Jennie Kudapa:kw, Yuawalup, and Catie Teketa:y spent hours helping me with transcriptions and translations. Kawidu (or Rex) was a most patient and insightful teacher, who never tired of correcting my mistakes. And he was also the greatest canoe guide I ever had—he took us everywhere and patiently explained what was what. Ken Nayau shared with me his linguistic observations about Manambu. The late Eric Yuamalen, and his wife Martha Pambwi, taught me things no one else could. The intuitions of these natural linguists helped put the grammar into shape.

I learnt a lot—both as a linguist, and as a person—from so many more people. Dameliway, or simply Damel, has been the warmest friend I have had for years, as was her sister Motuway. Gemaj—my classificatory mother—told us the most remarkable stories, and looked after me as only a mother could. And Karkamb's (Nelly's) smile would always make the whole house joyful. Nelma's energy and wit brightened our days. Dora and Janet, my classificatory sisters, were towers of strength in every way—always full of love and friendship, as was their mother, Lowai. I greatly enjoyed the company of so many more—not least, Lucy Leo and Ludi (Leo Yambwi's wives) with whom I could only communicate in Tok Pisin. Luke Ala (Jager), Jacklyn Yuamali's husband, was a remarkable host, and a warm friend.

Some of my best friends, and dedicated teachers, were children. During my two stays in Avatip, I learnt more from Jacklyn Yuamali's Tanina (8 in 2001–2, and 11 in 2004) than from many adults. Her wit, energy, intelligence, and linguistic intuitions are unsurpassable. By the time she was 11, she could tell stories almost as well as her grandmother Gemaj. Her little sister Kerryanne, whom I first knew as a 3- and then as a 5-year-old, was a great help—as a non-stop talker, and also as an 'assistant nurse' (one of the duties I assigned her: helping me perform first-aid on other people). Celestin and Stevie (Karkamb's children) were always at hand if I had a question to ask. Jennie Kudapa:kw's son Ryan, Damel's son Alonso, Gaia's daughter Sylvia, and, of course, ever-smiling Simona, the daughter of Teketa:y and Kawidu, were a source of joy, and most patient and thorough teachers. Janet's daughter Joana (Zoana) and Jacklyn's baby Jemima taught me a lot about how children acquire Manambu and Tok Pisin. I will always miss my Manambu family.

Pauline Laki, Albert Yuamuk, Damel, Patrick, Kawindu, Iraman, Leo Yambwi, Maguniwai, and especially Piurkaramb were instrumental for our trip to Swakap (Swagup). Thanks to Piurkaramb, we were immediately adopted into Martin Kumwau's family. I am immensely grateful for Martin's and his wife's hospitality, and for endless hours of patient work on the Gala language he spent with me, together with Peter, Luke, and Bukakoinben.

I greatly enjoyed talking to all the Manambu people I met outside the village, in Port Moresby, Wewak, and Canberra—especially Ruth (Nebekaru), Joel Apikuñ Luma (Pauline Laki's elder brother), Mejikay, Jibudam, Ñidewi, Kila, Elizabeth, Paul, and so many more. And, of course, always cheerful Wanita, Ruth's and Joel Yuakalu Luma's daughter! Pauline Laki's children, Cassie, Salome, and Kelvin, will always be special to me, just like children of my own.

Thanks are also due to Pius Bonjui, himself a Iatmul (from Korogo), the head of the Papua New Guinea branch of ABC radio in Melbourne. Pius organized an interview for Pauline Laki on the program *Lingua Franca*—as a result, many people could hear a Manambu mourning song and her explanations of the Manambu name ownership. And thank you to Martin Lawrence, the creator of *Lingua Franca*, for introducing me to Pius in the first place.

Having a respected anthropologist—Simon Harrison—disentangle the intricacies of the Manambu culture was a great advantage for me, as a linguist. I am very grateful to him. I was also fortunate to be in touch with Ross Bowden, an expert on the Kwoma culture, with Colin Filer, an expert on the Sepik cultures in general, and with Angela Mandie Filer, a sociologist and herself a Kwoma. Contact with Laurie Bragge, an ex-District Officer in the Ambunti area—whose knowledge of the ethnohistories of the Sepik people is truly unsurpassable,— was precious. Paul Roscoe, an expert on Ndu cultures, and Ulrike Claas, an expert on the Sepik area, provided valuable references and feedback. I would like to acknowledge my debt to them.

Various people read through drafts of various chapters and commented on them. I am particularly grateful to Matthew Dryer, Nicholas Evans, Bill Foley, Spike Gildea, John Hajek, Darja Hoenigman, Gerd Jendraschek, Edit Moravcsik, Andrew Pawley, Vera Podlesskaya, Alan Rumsey, Hilário de Sousa, and Tonya Stebbins. Gerrit Dimmendaal's expertise in phonology and phonetics was instrumental in helping Pauline Laki and myself work out the Manambu vowel system. I greatly profited from frequent interaction with Andrew Pawley, on various problems in Papuan and Oceanic linguistics. The information on dogs in New Guinea provided by Jack Golson was invaluable. I also benefited from animated discussions and information on Iatmul, from Gerd Jendraschek, and from other members of RCLT—Seino van Breugel, Oliver Iggesen, Mark Post, and Sheena Van Der Mark.

I would like to acknowledge help and advice from experts in Papuan languages—Alan Rumsey, Lise Dobrin, Eva Lindström, Karl Franklin, Les Bruce, Darja Hoenigman, and also Lila San Roque, Ngawae Mitio, Carol Priestley, John Roberts, Tida Syuntaro, Borut Telban, Ken Sumbuk, and Lourens de Vries. The late Otto Nekitel supported this work, and we still mourn him.

I will always be grateful to Tom Dutton—a remarkable teacher of Tok Pisin, and a friend. I owe a special debt of gratitude to my friends and colleagues in the Summer Institute of Linguistics at Ukarumpa and Wewak, for their hospitality and their willingness to share information and ideas—René van den Berg, Steve Parker (with whom I could also share ideas about the Arawak family), Bob and Selma Bugenhagen, as well as Ken Nayau and Robin and Marva Farnsworth. Cindi and Jim Farr are and will always remain my very special friends—words will never be enough to express my gratitude to them.

Invaluable comments on almost every page came from R. M. W. Dixon, without whose constant encouragement, enthusiasm, criticisms, and support this grammar would never have eventuated.

A debt which can never be over-estimated is to Professor Michael Osborne, who welcomed the Research Centre for Linguistic Typology to La Trobe University and, while he was Vice-Chancellor, inspired us to create an intellectual atmosphere of the highest quality, commencing in 2000 and continuing until 2007. This grammar was written within that stimulating ambience.

List of Plates

List of Charts, Schemes, and Tables

Organization and Cross-references

This grammar has been written as an integrated whole. To understand what follows one needs to have digested what precedes. Chapter 1 provides a quick overview of the main points of the Manambu grammar. Later chapters deal with a particular grammatical topic each.

Chapter 3 discusses the ways in which grammatical relations are expressed. This chapter is basic for understanding the rest of the grammar. Chapter 2 contains a detailed discussion of phonology; it is not necessary to read to understand the rest of the grammar. Chapter 4 gives an overview of all the word classes, and Chapter 11 concentrates on the organization of verbal morphology, giving a preview of Chapters 12–17. Chapters 18 and 19 deal with complex clauses. Chapter 20 draws together the structure of clausal constituents, clauses, and sentences, and discusses the principles and functions of constituent order and of order of grammatical words within each constituent. Issues in semantics are addressed in Chapter 21. Those interested in cultural background and historical and comparative problems are advised to focus on Chapters 1 and 22.

Examples are numbered separately for each chapter. Examples from texts at the end of the grammar are referred to with the letter T followed by the number of the text and the sentence (that is, T2.40 refers to sentence 40 of Text 2).

All the examples and texts are supplied with an interlinear morpheme gloss, and then translated into English. Homophonous morphemes are differentiated by their glosses. The symbol '+' is used to indicate fused morphemes, e.g. *taba-* is glossed as 'hand+LK', its underlying form being *ta:b* 'hand' (with the long vowel shortened when the linker is added) and *-a-* 'linker'. Portmanteau morphemes are glossed with ':', for instance, *mæy* 'come:IMPV'. All grammatical morphemes are glossed in small caps while lexical morphemes are in lower case. Pronominal prefixes are shown as 1sg, 3pl, in lower case. For polysemous morphemes, different translations in glosses correspond to different meanings.

Cross-references are of two kinds:

- Those preceded by § refer to chapter and section number: for instance, §11.1 refers to section 1 of Chapter 11;
- Those beginning with a number refer to examples in the grammar: for instance, 11.1 refers to example 1 in Chapter 11.

Abbreviations and Conventions

Here and passim '-' stands for any morpheme boundary, that is, a boundary between a root and an affix, or between two roots. The symbol '=' indicates a boundary between a root and a clitic, or an affix and a clitic, or two clitics (see Chapter 2). The symbol ´ indicates a primary stress, and ` a secondary stress (obligatory on enclitics). Stress is marked on each example in Chapter 2 ('Phonology') and in other chapters only if relevant to the discussion.

Manambu has a certain amount of variation between allophones (discussed in Chapter 2). Many variants depend on the age of the speaker. Examples reflect the recurrent individual variants which also appear in the Vocabulary at the end of the grammar (e.g. *kamna:gw, kamna:* 'food', *numa, nəma* 'big'). Examples throughout the grammar are given in their phonological representation. Conventions of transcription are addressed in Chapter 2. Loans and code-switches from Tok Pisin and English are italicized in each example throughout the grammar (in Chapter 22, Tok Pisin words are italicized and English words are underlined).

Abbreviations

A	transitive subject	COMPL.VB	completive generic verb
ACC	accusative		
ACT.FOC	action focus	COND	conditional
ADDR	addressee	CONF	confirmation marker
ADJ	adjective		
ADV	adverb	CONN	connective
ALL	allative	COP	copula
ANAPH	anaphoric	COTEMP	cotemporaneous
APPR	apprehensive	CP	complex predicate
APPROX	approximative	CS	copula subject
ASS	associative plural	CURR.REL	current relevance
AUG	augmentative	CUST	customary
AUX	auxiliary	DAT	dative
BAS	basic cross-referencing	DEM	demonstrative
CA	common argument	DEM.PROX.ADDR	demonstrative referring to object close to addressee
CAUS	causative		
CC	copula complement		
CLIM	climatic		
COLL	collective	DEP	dependent
COM	comitative	DER	derivation
COMPAR	comparative	DES	desiderative
COMPL	completive aspect	DIR	directional
COMPL.DS	completive different subject	DIR.SP.REP	direct speech report
COMPL.SS	completive same subject		

DIST	distal	P	past
DS	different subject	p	person
du	dual	pl, PL	plural
E	English	POSS	possessive
EMPH	emphatic	PRED	predicative marker
EP	epenthetic	PRES	present
EXPR	expressive	PROH	prohibitive
fem, FEM	feminine	PROH.EXTRA	extra strong prohibitive
FOC	focus	PROH.GEN	general prohibitive
FOC.M	focus marker	PROH.STR	strong prohibitive
FR	frustrative	PROX	proximal
FUT	future	PUNCT	punctual
HAB	habitual	PURP	purposive
IMM.SEQ	immediate sequence	PURP.DS	different subject purposive
IMPV	imperative		
INCOMPL	incompletive	PURP.SS	same subject purposive
IND.SP.REP	indirect speech report	REACT.TOP	reactivated topic
INSTR	instrument	REC	reciprocal
INT	intensive	RED	reduplication
INTERJ	interjection	REP	repetition
INTO	intonation	REP.SEQ	repeated sequencing
IRR	irrealis	S	intransitive subject
itr	intransitive	SEQ	sequencing
LENGTH	expressive lengthening	sg	singular
LK	linker	SS	same subject
LOC	locative	SUBJ	subject cross-referencing
MANIP	manipulative		
masc	masculine	SUBJ.NP	subject non-past cross-referencing
MOM	momentaneous		
NAT	natural phenomena	SUBST	substitutive case
NEG	negative	SUP.VB	support verb
NEG.SUB	subordinate negator	TERM	terminative
NOM	nominal cross-referencing	TP	Tok Pisin
NOM.ACT	action nominalization	tr	transitive
NP	noun phrase	TRANS	transitivizer
O	object	TRANSP	transportative
OBJ	object case	UNF	unfulfilled
OBL	oblique marker	VB	verb
OPT	optative	VOC	vocative
ORD	ordinal	VT	versatile tense

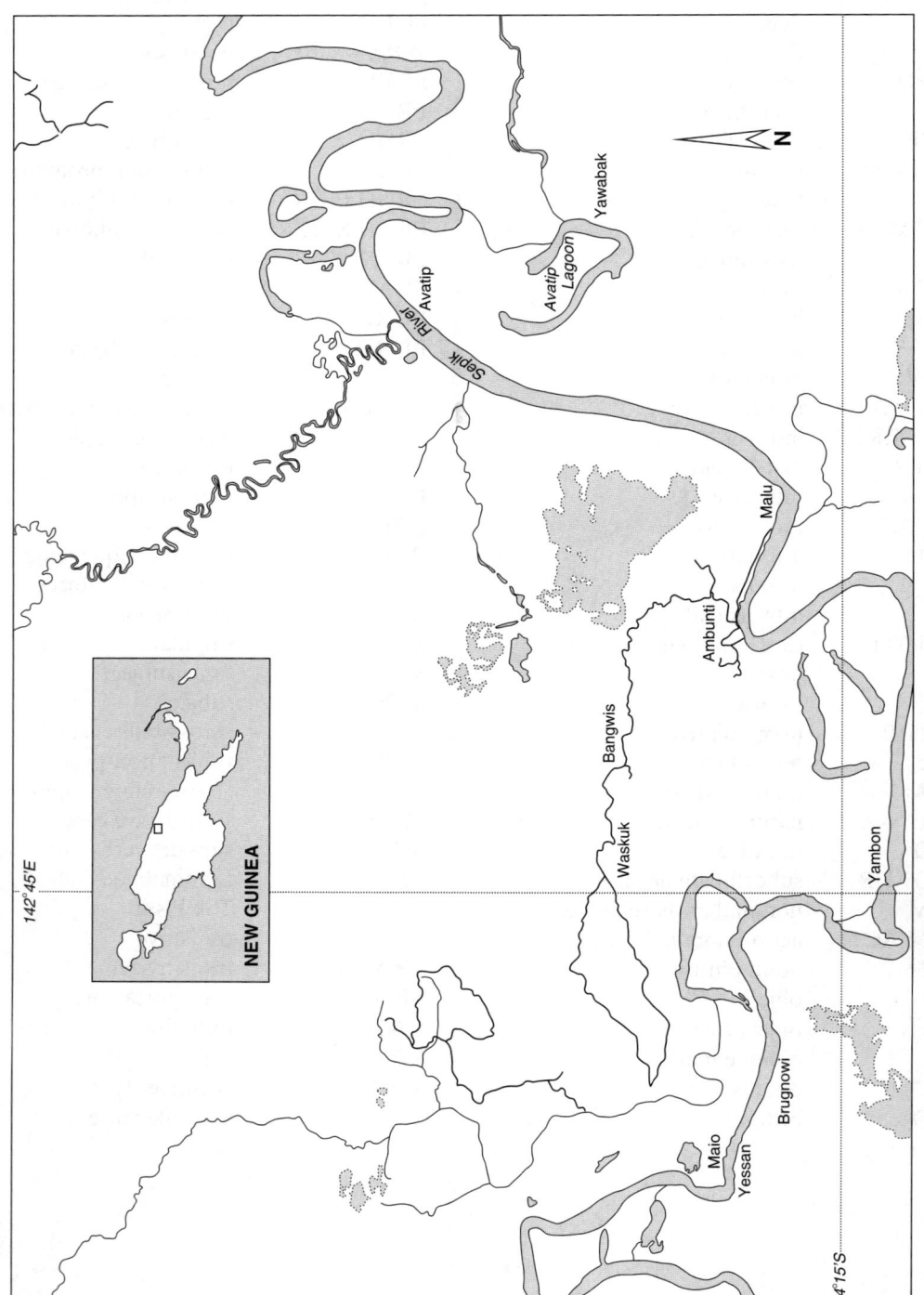

MAP 1.   Location of Manambu villages

1

Introduction: The Language and its Speakers

Manambu belongs to the Ndu language family, and is spoken by about 2,500 people in five villages: Avatip, Yawabak, Malu, Apa:n, and Yambon (Yuanab) in East Sepik Province, Ambunti district. About 200–400 speakers live in the cities of Port Moresby, Wewak, Lae, and Madang; a few people live in Kokopo and Mount Hagen.

1.1 LINGUISTIC TYPE

Manambu is synthetic, with elements of fusion, and predominantly suffixing. The imperative marker *a-* is the only fully productive prefix (§13.2.1), while the causative-manipulative prefix *kay-* occurs with a limited number of verbs (§16.2.1). The infix *-ka-* marks intensive forms of non-agreeing adjectives (§4.3).

Manambu has twenty consonants and nine vowels. There is a series of simple voiced and voiceless bilabial, apico-dental, and dorso-velar stops (just like in other Ndu languages). Voiced and voiceless bilabial and dorso-velar stops also have a labialized counterpart. All the voiced stops and the voiced fricative *j* are prenasalized in word-initial, intervocalic, and word-final positions. Vowel length is contrastive. Long vowels *a:* and *æ:* are a recent innovation: older speakers still pronounce these as sequences of identical short vowels interrupted by a glottal stop. Syllable structure is (C)(C)V(C). Stress is movable and contrastive. Long vowels tend to be stressed (Chapter 2).

Open classes are nouns and verbs. Nominal categories include case, three numbers, and two genders in the singular. Grammatical relations are expressed with verbal cross-referencing and with nominal case marking. Manambu has nine case forms, more than any other Ndu language. The subject case is formally unmarked. The same form marks locative and a definite and fully involved object. Another form expresses direction and instrument. The dative case marks beneficiary and maleficiary, and also has an aversive meaning, 'for fear of'. The terminative case means 'on the very edge of', and 'up until'. Two cases mark 'means of transportation'. The substitutive case means 'instead of'. The comitative case meaning 'together with' is a major device for coordinating noun phrases. Its additional meanings are locative 'along (e.g. a road)' and temporal 'while'. Case markers may attach to verbal roots: the objective-locative case marks completive aspect, dative case marks purpose, instrumental case derives deverbal adverbs, and substitutive case marks dependent clauses meaning 'instead of doing something'.

Verbal categories include personal cross-referencing fused with tense, aspect, mood (imperative-permissive, and irrealis), and modalities (optative, purposive, desiderative, and two frustratives). The subject (A/S) is always cross-referenced on the verb. A second argument—direct object, beneficiary, location, time, manner, or instrument—can be cross-referenced if it is more topical than the subject. A copula complement, a speech report, and a comitative constituent are never cross-referenced. Members of word classes other than verbs take cross-referencing enclitics when they occupy the predicate slot (Chapters 3–4). This is unlike most other Ndu languages which cross-reference only the subject.

A small closed class of agreeing adjectives has three members, 'big', 'small', and 'fine'; these agree in gender and number with the head noun. About sixteen non-agreeing adjectives—which cover semantic types such as value, dimension, colour, and age—share a number of properties with nouns. Adverbs and time words are semi-closed classes which share a few properties with nouns. Word class-changing derivations are limited.

A striking property of Manambu is its gender system. Two genders, masculine and feminine, are assigned to nouns according to their referents' sex and also shape and size. That is, a large house is masculine, and a small house feminine. Genders are covert in the sense that, rather than being marked on the noun itself, they appear on the agreeing modifiers, verbs, and adverbial demonstratives, and in possessive constructions. The feminine gender is both formally and functionally unmarked (Chapter 5).

Three numbers—singular, dual, and plural—are marked on the agreeing modifiers, verbs, and in possessive constructions. Plural and dual are marked on most kinship terms and on a few nouns with a human referent. Associative non-singular (X and his/her associates) is restricted to just personal names (Chapter 6). The choice between five types of possessive construction depends on the type of possessive relationship, of possessee, and of possessor (Chapter 8).

The system of demonstratives is unusually intricate. Three demonstrative roots, *kə-* 'proximate demonstrative: near speaker', *wa-* 'proximate demonstrative: near addressee', and *a-* 'distal demonstrative', are used in nominal demonstratives, in manner adverbial demonstratives, and in reactivated topic demonstratives. Nominal demonstratives express either spatio-temporal deixis or 'current relevance'. The latter are derived from the former with the suffix *-na-* 'current relevance', indicating that the object of pointing is being talked about, or is of immediate or ongoing importance to the speakers. Spatio-temporal demonstratives distinguish gender and number, and may also distinguish either three additional degrees of distance, or five directions. 'Current relevance' demonstratives distinguish five directions, and two additional degrees of distance, but no number or gender. Reactivated topic demonstratives refer predominantly to an S/O constituent (Chapter 10).

Negation is marked differently depending on aspect, tense, mood, and modality. Non-habitual negative indicative clauses have no person marking. All dependent clauses are negated differently from main clauses. Three prohibitives differ in their illocutionary force.

Manambu has a productive system of verbal compounds (they can be alternatively analysed as one-word serial verbs: Chapter 15). They express manner, aspectual and sequential meanings, and function as valency-changing devices. Many are lexicalized and have idiomatic meanings.

Verbs divide into several subclasses depending on whether they can occur with directional markers, and which directional markers they occur with. INHERENTLY DIRECTIONAL VERBS include the six basic verbs *war-* 'go upwards', *da-* 'go downwards', *væki-* 'go across (away from the speaker)', *væra-* 'go across (towards speaker)', *wula-* 'enter, come in, come in a direction from the Sepik River', and *waku-* 'go out (including motion in direction away from the Sepik River)'. These do not take any further directional specifications. Their roots are the base for directional markers on other verbs, and on demonstratives. INTRINSICALLY DIRECTIONAL VERBS include four roots which must take directional suffixes, each of which corresponds to an inherently directional verb. The majority of verbs are OPTIONALLY DIRECTIONAL. They combine with bound forms consisting of *sə-* followed by a directional marker. Copula verbs, the general motion verbs *yi-* 'go' and *ya-* 'come', and ingestive and stative verbs do not combine with any directionals. Directionals also have a valency-increasing effect. Directionals on verbs and on demonstratives have similar origins, but display subtle differences in their semantics (Chapter 16).

Manambu has a semi-productive causative-manipulative prefix *kay-* which causativizes a limited set of intransitive verbs. When applied to transitive verbs, it indicates a special physical effort and the intensity of action. There is no passive. Instead, Manambu employs transitivity-neutralizing constructions which involve clause chaining, and are ambiguous as to their status as biclausal or as monoclausal. A reciprocal marker *awarwa* has an associative meaning 'together with'. Reflexive meanings are expressed with a variety of means none of which involves a verbal derivation (§16.2).

Ten polyfunctional verbs can each be used as an auxiliary or as a support verb, and also as a copula verb (Table 4.1, and Chapter 17). Auxiliary verb constructions express aspectual, positional, and modal meanings. There are also a variety of idiomatic complex predicates. Body part constructions—expressing emotional, mental, and physical states—are a special subtype thereof.

Clause linking in Manambu is achieved through a variety of means. The major strategy is clause chaining via medial dependent clauses. In most cases this involves switch-reference (that is, marking of dependent clauses may be sensitive to whether their subject (A/S) is the same as that of the following clause or not). The tense and extent of action expressed in a medial clause is determined by its relationship to the action of a subsequent dependent clause or a main clause. There are also causal clauses, and 'unlikely condition' clauses. Other clause-linking devices include juxtaposition of a dependent clause and a main clause (this is a preferred manner of indicating conditional meanings); clause linking via a case marker 'instead' and a suffix 'like', and clause linking involving connectives.

Relative clauses are similar to main clauses in most properties; they are negated like dependent clauses. Speech reports—direct, indirect, and 'semi-direct'—are highly frequent. They express a wide variety of meanings, including desire, fear, and reason. Manambu has no complement clauses as a special clause type; instead, medial and other dependent clauses are co-opted as complementation strategies (Chapters 18 and 19).

Constituent order in Manambu tends to be verb final. It is often motivated by discourse pragmatics. Word order within constituents depends on their type. For instance, quantifiers can precede the noun head or follow it depending on the referent's topicality. Chapter 20 offers a comprehensive analysis of the principles of ordering words and constituents, and also of the structure of constituents, and of clauses. An argument, or the predicate, can occur in a highlighting focus construction. A focused constituent appears marked as a non-verbal predicate head with the appropriate person markers, and the rest of the clause remains as it was. Highlighting focus constructions may appear biclausal. A focused noun phrase has the makings of a full verbless clause, since it contains the non-verbal cross-referencing markers. However, it is not a full clause because it cannot be negated separately. Highlighting focus constructions are an instance of grammar-in-the-making, similar to transitivity-neutralizing constructions involving clause chaining (§19.9 and §20.3).

Manambu has a highly elaborate verbal and nominal lexicon. Typologically unusual semantic groups of verbs cover eating, drinking, and chewing, perception, and speech. Highly specific terms coexist with highly generalized ones. A general noun *ma:gw* 'whatever, whatchamacallit' and a general verb *məgi-* 'do whatever' are an option, if one cannot think of the right term, or prefers to be non-specific. In the Manambu tradition, knowledge—tantamount to monetary riches—is viewed in terms of lexicon, especially the totemic names (which are nouns). The issue of name ownership acquires particular importance at name debates (*saki*). Multiple 'names'—each belonging to a different clan—result in multiple synonymy. The totemic names are used as address terms, as an integral part of Manambu speech etiquette, where the traditional patterns coexist with newly acquired Western imports.

In terms of the etymological make-up of its lexicon and grammar, Manambu is a central member of the Ndu family. There are a number of loans from other languages of the area, mostly Western Iatmul. Similarities between Manambu and the neighbouring Kwoma are contact induced. All the speakers of Manambu are proficient in Tok Pisin and many also in English, and code-switching is pervasive. Signs of incipient language obsolescence look ominous—however, a strong opposition to language loss gives room to hope that the language will live.

1.2 THE MANAMBU: THE PRESENT AND THE PAST

The Manambu occupy five villages in the Ambunti District in the East Sepik Province of Papua New Guinea (see Map). They live mostly on the Sepik River (Manambu *ñab*, cf. Kwoma *nabagey*[1]), and more precisely, on its section between the Hunstein Mountain range and the Washkuk Hills. Avatip is the major village in terms of population, of physical size, of ceremonial significance, and of military exploits. We return to this in §1.2.2 and §1.4.

The Manambu and the neighbouring Kwoma have been fortunate, in terms of attracting high-quality anthropological research. Useful and highly informative accounts of the Manambu culture in Newton (1971), Bragge (1990), and especially Harrison (1983, 1985a–b, 1987, 1990a–b, 1993) contain anthropological analysis and innumerable insights into the cultural and cognitive patterns of Manambu ritual and everyday life over the years. This is why this and the following sections are limited to a very brief sketch of cultural background, with just the information necessary for understanding the grammar which follows.

1.2.1 Environment and subsistence

The Sepik River is the centrepiece of the Manambu environment. It is also the major point of reference in spatial orientation: positions of objects and locations of territories are conceptualized in terms of their position with respect to this river (see Chapters 10 and 16 for the marking of spatial orientation on demonstratives and on verbs). Greetings (§21.5.1–4) are also centred around the direction in which the river flows. Trying to understand the Manambu language without having the river near at hand is an almost insurmountable task. The Sepik River is the largest river system in Papua New Guinea (with a catchment of 77,700 square kilometres). It varies in its width between three or four metres and 700 metres, and frequently shifts its course. Mudbanks appear where the river curves, lined with wild sugarcane and reed. The inland terrain is full of swampy forest with sago palm—an important food source—in its understorey. The average rainfall in the Sepik area is over 1,500 mm (250 in the Ambunti District: see Ryan

---

[1] The origin of the Manambu name for the Sepik River requires further investigation. It is somewhat similar to one of the names for the Sepik River in Kwoma, *nabagey* (Bowden 1997: 139), which, according to Bowden, 'derives from the Mayo language; it is the name speakers of the Maio-Yessan dialect of Mayo at Yesan and Maio villages give the Sepik'. The name for 'Sepik River' in Western Iatmul is *avɨsak* (Gerd Jendraschek, p.c.). The general term for 'river' in Ambulas is *kaabélé*, and is related to the Manambu name *kabəl* 'Screw River'.

1972: 1033). A sharp division of seasons affects the patterns of newly introduced agriculture (also see Harrison 1990a: 12–16).

The dry season, called *ñakamali* in Manambu, lasts from May until about September; then the river is usually low, and the fish supply variable. The wet season, *kwayugw* (this could be a frozen plural form: see §6.1), spans October to April; during this time the river rises and may flood the villages. Then some people move to temporary dwellings on higher ground. Cemeteries tend to be located on higher ground because of the floods. The Sepik River carries floating tree trunks and becomes really dangerous, fast flowing, and swollen. There is no shortage of fish, and mosquitoes are highly active.

The lifestyle of the Manambu can be characterized as sedentary hunting and also gathering, with some agriculture. Traditional subsistence involved fishing (done by women), occasional hunting (by men), and exploitation of the sago palm (also see Lewis 1923). Sago (a powdery starch made from the processed pith of the sago palm *Metroxylon sagu*) is the most important food and the source of starch (the various ways in which sago can be prepared include raw sago, fried sago pancakes, baked sago, sago pudding, and 'sago starch', consisting of sago powder mixed with boiling water). Sago production is a joint work of men and of women, and is arduous. People living along the Sepik River tend to acquire up to one-third of their sago supplies in exchange for fish and tobacco from 'dry-land' people (Allen et al. 2002: 51).

Small gardens are made on levee banks parallel to rivers; the food which comes from gardening includes sweet potatoes, yams, taro, perennial bananas, and nowadays also squashes, pumpkins, cucumbers, papaya, snake beans, and tomatoes, alongside spinach-like leafy vegetables. Coconut is an important food product, used in cooking. Further fruit and vegetables include corn, sugarcane, watermelon, breadfruit, and the ever-present betelnut, which still plays an important role in rituals.

Growing tobacco goes back a long way (see Behrmann 1922: 192–3, on its importance in Malu, and also Zöller 1891: 184–5). This is one of the cash crops, which now also include peanuts, coffee, cocoa, and vanilla. Crops in gardens tend to be planted once before fallowing, between May and July (see Allen et al. 2002: 51, for further data on the agricultural system of the Ambunti area in the East Sepik Province).

Yam gardens are planted in the beginning of the dry season, and harvested at the beginning of the wet season. Cultivation, harvesting, and consumption of yams is regulated by complex ceremonies which survive until nowadays. An elaborate 'first-fruits' ceremony involves the whole village, and is performed by initiated men. If a woman sees—let alone tastes—the yams prior to the ceremony, her life is believed to be in danger. In the 1980s, each village used to hold 'an especially complex version' of the yam ceremony, 'which inducts novices into the second of three male initiatory grades' (Harrison 1990a: 15). It appears that such ceremonies are hardly ever held nowadays. Gardening is shared by all: men clear the garden sites and fence them, and women are responsible for the weeding. Everyone in the village is involved in the planting process.

Villagers keep chickens and ducks, and occasionally a pet cassowary. Nowadays, the number of pigs kept is limited by newly introduced religious restrictions: many Manambu belong to the Seventh Day Adventist Church and do not consume pork and fish without scales (such as the eel), or chew betelnut. Fishing is mostly done in lagoons surrounding the villages; this is the women's job. Dried fish is exchanged for goods (and nowadays also sold for money) at a market in the town of Maprik.

European tools available nowadays include metal axes and bush knives, and store-bought fish-hooks and fishnets (see Hatanaka and Bragge 1973–4, on the spread of steel axes in the Sepik area after the establishment of a government station at Ambunti in 1924; also see

Townsend 1968: 99–101). Some people own shotguns. Traditional bows and arrows are the matter of the past, as are stone axes. Nevertheless, some people still keep and treasure them. Dress patterns are European. But grass skirts and traditional male ornaments are worn on ceremonial occasions—such as the name debate and the yam ceremony.

We now turn to the locations, and the internal structure of the villages.

1.2.2   The Manambu villages

The Manambu are river people; they contrast themselves to jungle-dwellers, or 'dry-land' people (see §1.4). The major Manambu settlements are spread along the banks of the Sepik River. The Sepik River, however, is prone to changing its course. As a result, a whole village may have to relocate. This has happened several times in recent history and who knows how many times before.

The 'mighty and formidable Avatip' colourfully described by Townsend (1968: 135–6) was located on the main river. Its subsequent location is described by Newton (1971: 64) as follows:

From east to west, the largest village of the Manambu was formerly Avatəp, inland on a large lagoon. This no longer exists. After World War II the Avatəp people moved to their site at Yentshanggei, on the Sepik, which, even more recently, has overflowed to a new offshoot a few miles east, Labunggei. A former offshoot, Yau'mbok, founded before 1914 by refugees from a German punitive expedition,[2] remains on the eastern shore of the lagoon.

In the late 1970s, when Simon Harrison conducted his fieldwork, Avatip was located at Lapanggai and Yentschanggai. The areas of Lapanggai and Yentschanggai have since then been flooded, and the whole village gradually relocated back to the banks of the Sepik River (see Map). Plate 1 shows the site of Yentschanggai—now completely flooded. Hence the differentiation between the modern *kula-təp* (new-village) and the previous site, referred to as *a-d-a-wula təp* (DEM.DIST-masc.sg-LK-INLAND village) 'that big village located inland'. Yawabak still remains where it was when Newton saw it, on a lake.

The Malu village was, according to Newton (1971: 64), 'formerly on the lower slopes of a ridge on the south bank of the river, and was near the camp of the Berlin expedition of 1910–1912 . . . it has moved to the north bank since 1945. A little further upriver is Apa:n, a hamlet of Malu. Further still is Kamandjau, founded since 1945, a hamlet of the next big village Yambun.' Malu and Apa:n are located exactly where Newton places them (also see Harrison 1990a: 16–17). Kamajau is claimed to be an offshoot of Malu (also see Harrison 1990a: 16–17), and is now scarcely populated.

According to Bowden (1997: xx), the Malu village moved across to where it is now after the establishment of the Ambunti patrol post in 1924, and the suppression of traditional warfare in the area by the Australian government. Prior to that, all river villages adjacent to the Washkuk Hills were located on the south side of the Sepik, as a precautionary measure against surprise attacks by the Kwoma, since the Kwoma—'dry-land people'—did not use canoes and could not cross the Sepik without the help of river people.

The Yambon village is called Yuanab [Yuana:ᵐb] in Manambu. The name Yambon which appears on official maps is said to be an abbreviation of *Yabujədu* [Yambunjendu], the name of the site of the village at the time of early European contact. Yambon/Yuanab also moved to the north bank (after the *Yabujədu* site was bombed by Allied air forces in the Second World War; see Newton 1971: 64).

---

[2]   But see §1.4 for a different account of this by Harrison (1990a: 25–6); further information is in Claas (2007).

Avatip is the largest of the villages (population over 1,000 people); Malu (with Apa:n) is the second largest (over 600), and Yuanab is the third largest (about 400 people). The estimated population of Yawabak is about 350. (These approximate figures were supplied by Joel Yuakalu Luma; government census figures for 1978 are given in Harrison 1990a; more recent official census figures, for 2000, have not been available to me.)

Each of the three communities has a strong sense of separate identity, and tends to be endogamous. Avatip is the largest, and ritually and traditionally the most important one. Malu and Yuanab are said to have been founded about seven/eight generations ago as offshoots of Avatip—this explains why Malu story tellers consistently say 'we are really (from) Avatip' (also cited by Bragge 1990: 38). Yawabak is a very recent offshoot of Avatip, and those from Yawabak call themselves 'real Avatip' (*Avatip tru*). As Harrison (1990a: 17; 1993: 29–30) pointed out, Avatip 'was militarily the most powerful river-village known to the Manambu, and has a kind of metropolitan status among them'.[3]

Overt warfare between the Manambu people is traditionally forbidden (Harrison 1993: 30). There is, however, a certain amount of rivalry between people from Avatip and those from Malu, accompanied by land disputes to do with access to fishing lagoons and sago palms. The existing differences between Avatip and Malu are mostly lexical (see §22.6.1). Harrison (1990a: 17) reports occasional political feuds between Malu and Yuanab, and their political alliances with Avatip rather than with each other (despite their geographic proximity). Newton (1971: 65) mentions that 'as well as their ancestral home, Malu was regarded by the Yambun [Yuanab] as their religious centre, and much of their ceremonial was carried out there, especially initiation'.

The Manambu variety spoken at Yuanab is phonologically divergent from both Malu and Avatip. People from Yuanab are sometimes looked upon as outsiders by those from Avatip, and from Malu. Some 'accuse' them of being Iatmulized; others point out that they are not 'true Manambu' because of the fact that many Gala had escaped from the Manambu and the Kwoma, and had settled in Yuanab (§1.4.1). The Yuanab variety is likely to have absorbed substrata from languages other than Manambu, and the Yuanab people may in fact have shifted to Manambu within the past 180 years or so (see §1.5 and Bragge 1990).

The Yuanab people were more receptive to early missionary and anthropological work than those from Malu and Avatip. When Robin and Marva Farnsworth (SIL) started their activities in the early 1960s, they were allowed to stay in Yuanab rather than in any other village (see §1.7). This explains why, in their 'Organized phonology data' (*c.*1981), Yuanab (that is, Yambon) is given as 'major village'. (Note, however, that their major collaborator, Ken Nayau, comes from Avatip.) According to the Farnsworths, the anthropologist Douglas Newton also spent most of his time in Yuanab (disrupting their missionizing activities). His account of the Manambu mythology, initiation practices, and history combines information from Yuanab and from Avatip. Harrison's fieldwork was conducted mostly in Avatip, as was mine.

Nowadays, additional cultural differences between the villages are created by their different Christian affiliations. People at Yawabak are overwhelmingly Seventh Day Adventists (SDA),

---

[3] This 'metropolitan' status of Avatip is reflected in the transparent etymology of its name: *Ap-a-təp* (bone-LK-village) 'main village'. According to Bowden (1997: xx), the name of Malu 'comes from the mountain on the south side of the Sepik at the base of which it was located before European contact' (also see Bragge 1990: 38). *Yaw-a-bak* (yaw.tree-LK-field) is 'field of trees called *yaw*' (the explanation of this is *yaw-adəka tə-da-l-a tamiy-al* (yaw.tree-ONLY stand-3plSUBJ.VT-3fem.sgBAS.VT-LK area-3fem.sgNOM) 'it is an area where only yaw trees stand'. The etymology of Yuanab is unclear; the name of *Apa:n* may be linked to *apa:n, apan* 'old masculine'.

those in Yuanab are Presbyterians, and those in Malu are mostly Catholic. Avatip is home to at least five Christian denominations: Catholics, Methodists (Wesleyans), Seventh Day Adventists (SDA), Presbyterians, and Apostolic ('One way') Church. In day-to-day life, the major split amounts to a binary division between those 'who sit in church' on Saturday (as do the SDAs) or on Sunday (as do all the rest).

Avatip, Malu, and Yawabak still have ceremonial houses which serve as men's clubs and where rituals are performed (see §1.3). Yuanab has none of these—this is said to be due to the missionaries' efforts. We now turn to the internal structure of the villages and houses within them.

1.2.3   Dwelling patterns: the structure of villages

Within the villages, the Manambu live in traditional houses shared by several households (called *tǝnǝb*, lit. fireplace). The houses belonging to the same patrilineal clan cluster together in 'enclaves' (*yarǝg*). The organization of enclaves was described by Harrison (1990a: 29) for the 'old' Avatip; it remains essentially the same.

Towards the back of each enclave are located the houses (*wi*), and in front of them, close to the river shore, stand small ceremonial houses (*sa:y*) for the clan's uninitiated men and boys, or the subclan's larger ceremonial house, *kara:b*. Traditionally, *kara:b* (also known as *haus tambaran* in Tok Pisin) used to be located in front of *sa:y*. In the modern-day Avatip each enclave has just one ceremonial house.

A ceremonial men's house has been—and continues to be—the centre of men's social life, and of men's rituals, including initiation, and mortuary feasts. The enclave, and all the ceremonial houses, bear the names of a totemic ancestor of the clan they belong to.

Ceremonial houses in Avatip, Malu, and Yuanab were described by Newton (1971: 65–6); also see Behrmann (1950–1: 323) and Harrison (1990a). Behrmann (1950–1: 323) reports that, at the time of his expedition in 1912–13, Avatip had two ceremonial houses. These ceremonial houses followed the middle Sepik pattern: they used to be 'two-storey buildings with pitched rooves and a triangular gable at either end and, like those of the Iatmul, were considered female'. The houses were smaller than those of the middle Sepik; in Malu they were little larger than dwelling houses. Nowadays, ceremonial houses are even smaller than dwelling houses. Unlike dwelling houses, they are not on stilts.

The 'old' Avatip (that is, the village site as it used to be before the last move) used to have ten ceremonial houses. Only some of them made their way to the new villages. John Sepaywus gave the following reason for not building new large ceremonial men's houses in the 'new' village: 'there are no ceremonial-house makers' (*kara:b kur-du ma:* (man's.house make-man NEG): see §19.2.3). This does not necessarily imply lack of able-bodied men, their reluctance to do the job, or shortage of appropriate wood. I suspect that the reason is deeper than that.

McCarthy (1963: 51) praised the Sepik ceremonial houses as 'monuments to their art and building ability', 'probably the best in New Guinea'. In his words, 'these men's houses took a long time to build not because of any lack of energy on the part of the river people, but because of a shortage of essential material. The great posts had to be wet with the blood of an enemy before they could be placed on the ground.' And efforts by the colonial administration to stop these traditional practices were not always successful. Recounting his first experience in Avatip in 1930, McCarthy (1963: 51–2) reports:

The sternness of the Government did not stop the building programme. The Sepik was content to wait. I noticed at Avatip that two post holes remained unfilled while the other eighteen posts were upright. Two heads were needed to 'blood' the remaining posts and the delay continued for several months. Then one day I noticed that the two posts were in place. The village had a festive air as the building was got under way—and soon completed. A swift raid on the timid unfortunates of the interior had been carefully planned and carried out. There had been no reports of a killing but the river people controlled the channels to the lake country inside and so evidence was impossible to get.

Had the evidence been possible to obtain, the District Officer G. W. L. Townsend would have personally punished the offenders—this is how he succeeded in stopping head-hunting practices. We return to this in §1.4.2.

The 'new' Avatip has a number of ceremonial houses, which are perhaps not as impressive architecturally as the ones described by Behrmann (1922), Newton (1971: 64–80), and Harrison (1990a). But their spiritual and ceremonial value remains—and this is what counts in Manambu culture. Plate 2 illustrates a large ceremonial house at Avatip in 1912 (from Behrmann 1950–1: 323). Plate 3 illustrates a ceremonial house (*Warman-kara:b*, belonging to Nabul and Maliau clans) in modern Avatip, where a name debate took place on 8 October 2004. In front of the ceremonial house there is a ceremonial mound (*təpwi*) (see Harrison 1990a: 91) on which the listeners-participants are sitting. (Women and children are out of earshot.)

Avatip has two paths which connect the enclaves: a path located closer to the river for the use of initiated men (*du-a-ya:b* man-LK-path, 'men's path'), and a path further away from the river for the rest (*takwa-ya:b* woman+LK-path, 'women's path'). I was told that this used to be a way of protecting women from attackers arriving by canoe.

Nowadays, men (initiated or not) use the 'men's path', while the 'women's path' is for everybody; occasionally, women would walk on the men's path. Older women would avoid walking on the men's path and passing through ceremonial houses. There is no men's path and women's path in Malu, Yawabak, and Yambon. In Malu, this can be explained by the geography of the place: houses occupy a narrow stretch of land, and there is really no space for two roads. The absence of the two roads in Yawabak and Yambon is perhaps due to the higher impact of Christianity there.

The modern village has at least three markets which serve as centrepieces for the village-wide gossip network, and where betelnut, fruit, and vegetables are sold. Stores in the village are owned by the locals, and sell basic 'Western' (*wali*) goods such as sugar, flour, soap, and pencils. These stores are purely functional, and do not have a role of 'social clubs'. People have a strong preference for shopping in stores owned by members of their own clan.

The spaces between houses and the villages themselves are kept clean—with grass being cut or even mowed, and every bit of rubbish swept away. This is said to be done 'for fear of snakes'. But many confess that the major reason is a fear of *sangguma* (euphemistically called *təp-a ja:p* 'village-LK thing'), a powerful magic for which the Sepik peoples are especially notorious (see Ryan 1972: 29–30, and Bowden 1987). This is something one does not discuss out loud—but which is often blamed as the source of many types of misfortune.

1.2.4 Houses and their structure

The houses—placed high on stilts—face the river (see Plate 4). Unused utensils are kept underneath the house, together with chickens, ducks, and dogs (if there are any). The inside of the house is highly structured (also see Harrison 1990a: 31–2). A household tends to consist of classificatory brothers and their families (including elderly dependants). The family of a genealogically senior brother occupies the part closer to the front of the house (*taga-wi*). The most junior brother's family is at the back of the house (*baga-wi*).

According to Harrison (1990a: 31), houses used to be much bigger than they are nowadays, and all the men of a lineage would live in one house (a clan would consist of two lineages). I have not encountered a house with more than four households in it. There is, however, space for privacy: each person, or each couple, has their own sleeping mat and a (usually store-bought) mosquito net.

Traditionally, the central space of the house used to be reserved for adult men, while sides of a house were women's and children's areas. Each wife used to have (and still has) a cooking space by a side-wall. It is not considered appropriate for a man to eat squatting together with his wife and children.

When a woman menstruates, she must avoid the central part of the house, and may not use the front door. She has to stay in her area by the wall, and go in and out of the house through a hatch in the wall. The expression for female menstruation is *mala-wia:m rə-na* (side+LK-house+LK+LOC sit-ACT.FOC+3fem.sgBAS.VT) 'she sits at the side of the house'. A woman is not supposed to sit in front of the front post of the house facing the front door.

As we will see in §1.3, clans are patrilineal. Residence after marriage is patrilocal. The few men who live in their wives' villages (this is known as uxorilocal residence) are looked upon as funny exceptions. The structure of the village, and of the living space within each house, used to reflect the major principles of social organization—kinship and ritual seniority (Harrison 1990a: 32 ff.).

An aside is in order. The dwelling patterns described here hold only for those Manambu who live in the villages. City-dwellers follow the patterns of mainstream New Guinea life (see Gewertz and Errington 1999; and also Gewertz 1983). The Manambu proudly acknowledge that there are no Manambu 'squatters' in any city in Papua New Guinea—all the Manambu who live in diaspora have jobs, and none live in urban slums. (This is in contrast to the Iatmul who form large 'squatter' communities in major cities, including Wewak.)

The outmigration of the Manambu creates a substantial diaspora in urban centres. Gewertz and Errington (1999) report cases where urbanized people sever their links with their 'backward' grass-roots families. In other cases, representatives of the diaspora maintain close links with their 'home' in the villages. Many refer to their native villages as 'home', even if they have spent most of their lives in Port Moresby. The urban Manambu offer material support to their families—not infrequently paying school fees, providing medicine, and also material goods such as radios, batteries, and even solar panels. Since the urban Manambu speak mostly Tok Pisin and English, their participation in village life results in an increase of Tok Pisin and English in the villagers' lives.

The urban Manambu often facilitate the 'brain-drain' out of the villages, by helping gifted youngsters make their way into urban life. On the other hand, they also play a role in perpetuating mortuary rituals; and many of them take ardent interest in language maintenance and culture transmission, and in community-based language programmes. They are thus contributing to language revival, and survival, and the undying prestige and intellectual—and material—value of traditional knowledge. We return to this in §22.6.2.

We now turn to a brief description of major features of social organization, kinship, and totemic name ownership.

TABLE 1.1   Manambu clans and subclans

CLAN GROUP	SUBCLAN
Wulwi-Ñawi	Maliau
	Ñakau
	Nagudəw
	Sarak
	Wankau
	Nawik
Gla:gw	Yimal
	Makəm
	Gabak or Yalakugabak
	Vali:k
	Wapanab
	Wargab
Nabul-Sablap	Nabul
	Sablap

1.3   SOCIAL ORGANIZATION, KINSHIP, AND NAME OWNERSHIP

1.3.1   Clan membership, kinship, and mortuary ritual

The Manambu divide into three exogamous clan groups. The largest ones are *Gla:gw* and *Wulwi-Ñawi* which, according to Harrison (1990a: 42–3), account for about 44 per cent and 49 per cent of the population respectively. Gla:gw is associated with earth and 'dark' things. Members of the Gla:gw clan group are said to have darker skin than the Wulwi-Ñawi, and are referred to as *gla-səp* 'dark-skin'. The name *gla:gw* is derived by some from *gla-gu* 'dark water'; others simply associate it with the root *gəl* 'dark' (as mentioned in §6.1, it probably contains a fossilized plural marker -*gw*).

In contrast, the Wulwi-Ñawi clan group is associated with light, sun, and moon. Members of this clan group are said to have lighter, reddish skin, and are referred to as *ñiki-səp* 'red-skin', a term which is also used to refer to white people—an alternative for white people being *wali-du* 'east-man', 'man from the east', or *wama-səp* 'white-skin'. Not surprisingly, the few white people adopted into the Manambu system—e.g. Simon Harrison and myself—belong to the Wulwi-Ñawi group. The totems of the Wulwi-Ñawi include sun, moon, and stars, and also white birds (such as *sawən* 'white pelican'). This seems to be common knowledge throughout the region: an Ambunti store owned by a Manambu man from the Wulwi-Ñawi group (subclan Ñakau) is referred to as a 'San-mun' (sun-moon) store.[4]

The third clan group is *Nabul-Sablap*, the middle clan (it is described as *ñəd-əm tə-na-d* (middle-LK+LOC stand-ACT.FOC-3masc.sgBAS.VT) 'stands in the middle').

A list of subclans of each clan is given in Table 1.1.

---

[4] Laurie Bragge (p.c.) points out the similarity between the Gla:gw and the Iatmul moiety Niamei, and between Wulwi-Ñawi and the Iatmul Niaui. This is corroborated by the existing marriage patterns: Nelma, a Iatmul lady from the Niamei group living in Avatip, has married a man from the Maliau subclan of the Wulwi-Ñawi group.

Two additional clans, *Ambasarak* of the Wulwi-Ñawi group and *Kambuli*, of the Gla:gw group, were mentioned by Harrison (1990a: 70–3); they do not appear to be recognized nowadays. The name *Sarambasarak* was said to be a now dispreferred alternative to Sarak. Not every subclan is nowadays represented in each village (Yuanai, an interpreter and carrier for Walter Behrmann mentioned in §1.4.2, is known to be the last representative of the Maliau subclan in the Malu village).

The clan groups used to have specialized hereditary functions. The Gla:gw own the lagoons surrounding Avatip and control fish; they used to own two of the four initiatory rituals in the men's cult promoting the abundance of fish. The most economically important types of fish are their totems. The Wulwi-Ñawi used to own the rituals to do with the growing of yams which are their totems. Nabul-Sablap own the Sepik River and possess the sorcery of making it flood. This is reminiscent of the myth about two brothers who carved the Sepik River making it flow (the elder brother Kwalgudəmi, from Sablap clan, and the younger brother Təwij, from Sarak clan; told by Pauline Yuaneng Luma Laki). Further information on rituals, and associated cosmology, is in Harrison (1990a: 44–52). Most clans have a hereditary ritual 'officer' named *səbuk* [səmbuk] who has major authority in ritual issues, such as totemic name ownership to which we return below.

Clans are strictly exogamous: that is, marrying a member of the same clan group is an absolute taboo. A man can marry several women (not infrequently, sisters). Having more than one wife is a status symbol: only a wealthy man can afford this. Despite the impact of Christianity, polygamy still survives nowadays.

The classificatory kinship system is of Omaha type (Harrison 1993). Consequently, everyone's link to everyone else is defined in terms of the way(s) in which people are related to each other, and in terms of their subclan membership.

Traditional financial exchanges—payments—reinforce and help maintain these links. Each descent group (clan and subclan) possesses hereditary magical and ritual powers, and constitutes a basic political and ritual unit within the society, arranging marriages, debts, and credits (Harrison 1990a: 34–5). Important relationships exist between husbands of female members of the subclan, their sons and daughters, and daughters' husbands. Harrison (1990a: 34–5) calls these 'the subclan's allies'. They contribute to bride wealth payments of the subclan. The closest allies of each subclan are the children of its female members, called 'sister's children' (*gabəra:w*) by the men of the subclan, and 'children' (*ñanugw*) by all the women of their mothers' generation (or any subsequent generation). The general term used by all is *gabəraw-ñanugw*, 'sisters' children'.

When a sister's child dies, his or her mother's agnatic relatives organize a mortuary feast, *Kəkətəp* (lit. eating for last time: §21.1.1). This is planned and carefully organized during the few months after the death has occurred, and involves a wake for several days in the house of the deceased, accompanied by rituals performed in the men's house and in the house where the feast is held, and by singing of mourning songs by older women (also see Harrison 1990a: 35).[5] The mother's agnatic relatives receive a large mortuary payment which invariably includes shell valuables, and also largish quantities of money.

---

[5] After someone has just died, the relatives congregate in the house of the dead person, and weep and sing mourning songs, *gra-kudi*, over the (covered) dead body. This continues until the body is buried the next day. Other relatives come and cook for the mourners. Relatives who were particularly close to the deceased—for instance, a sister of a deceased man, or a mother of a deceased child—wear a piece of black string or wool on their wrists, ankles, and neck for up to a year, as a mark of mourning. A black string is associated with mourning to such an extent that Yuamali called a pot to which she had attached a black string so as not to confuse it with other people's pots 'a pot in mourning' (see example 4.19).

How the money and other valuables are to be divided is often the subject of discussion and also grievances; that is, European-introduced realities also play an important role in traditional ritual. This may also account for the vitality of Kəkətəp as opposed to initiation and other ceremonies which are falling into disuse. Kəkətəp provides a social glue which nurtures social networks and interactions among the villagers, most importantly inside the village as much as outside it: most Manambu, no matter whether they live in towns or in the villages, insist on having their say—and their share—in mortuary payments. The social importance of Kəkətəp helps maintain the basic knowledge of the kinship system, and the outline of the ritual itself.

Mortuary payments terminate the alliance established with sisters' children. Another alliance-related transaction is payment of bride wealth which inaugurates the beginning of an alliance. The payment is smaller than the mortuary payment, and is less socially important. In Harrison's (1990a: 35) words, 'it is not so much wealth that men seek from the marriages of their sisters and daughters; what they want are sons- and brothers-in-law owing them a lifelong debt and allegiance.' The bride price goes to the woman's agnatic relatives, who redistribute it to those members of their subclan who had contributed to their own bride prices. Bride price accounts for a network of mutual debts and obligations between people.

1.3.2 Name ownership and name debates

Monetary wealth and gain are generally perceived as secondary to the subclans' major patrimony: the names of its totemic ancestors, considered to be the source of the magic powers of the subclan. Subclans' totems include animals, plants, ritually important objects, ceremonial houses, shamanic spirits, and supernatural beings. Each subclan owns stretches of land known as *wa:gw* 'totemic area'.

Different positions of the sun during the day are owned as subclans' totems (see Harrison 1990a: 54), and so also are the sectors of the heat haze which surrounds the villages each afternoon. Each subclan owns between 1,000 and 2,000 names; a few names are occasionally shared between subclans.

This gives a total of the maximum of over 25,000 names for all the subclans. Harrison (1990a: 59) estimates the overall number of names as 'some thirty-two thousand ... a figure compatible with Bateson's estimate that an erudite Iatmul man "carries in his head between ten and twenty thousand names" (Bateson 1958: 222)'. Men nowadays do not have this extent of knowledge.

A child acquires a name within a few months of its birth. The father may name the child himself; otherwise, a senior member of the subclan does it. A patrilineal name is given only once—this is known as the 'main' name (*ap-a-sə* bone-LK-name), in contrast to all other names, *səgliak*. Sisters' children (sons and also daughters: Pauline Yuaneng Luma Laki, p.c.) are expected to name children of their mother's subclans. A 'namer' of a person establishes a particularly strong link with them, and the name comes to 'contain the person's Spirit or life-force'. Harrison (1990a: 60) reports: 'some older and more conservative men were for this reason unwilling to give me their genealogies, for fear that by writing down their names, their life-force might be trapped in my note-books and taken away to Australia when I left.' Sorcery is assumed to act upon the victim through their name. Names are owned and inherited patrilineally, but are also 'loaned' to sisters' children.

Being well versed in totemic names belonging to different clans is valued most of all. In day-to-day life, this knowledge is reflected in the correct and creative use of 'address terms'—totemic names belonging to the addressee's father's, and also mother's, subclans (*wayəpi*, *way*). By themselves they form a typologically unusual subclass of nouns (see §4.1.2). The totemic names are used in traditional song styles. Their knowledge is pivotal for name debates, *saki*.

Many of the important rituals—such as male initiation involving scarification (described by Newton 1971 and Harrison 1990a: 84–113)—are not practised any longer. One reason for this could be the fact that head hunting, formerly an important way in which a man would prove his manhood, is no longer possible (see §1.4.2 on how the Australian colonial administration put a stop to this custom). The rules for female seclusion accompanying the first menstruation appear to be relaxed. Many people learn about these cultural practices from the existing literature—basically, from Harrison (1990a), a highly valued source. But some taboos are still going strong. So, a woman who has seen bamboo flutes during the mortuary ritual is bound to become blind, it is said. And this is an explanation given for Ñatabi's blindness.

The ritual of the name debate, however, lives on, albeit not exactly in the elaborate form documented by Harrison (1990a). A full-scale name debate would last for over 24 hours non-stop, and would start with song cycles connected with the subclan's origin myths. A description of a full name debate is in Harrison (1990a: 159–67). Nowadays debates tend to be shorter, about 10–12 hours.

A name debate between the Sarak and the Wagau subclans of the Wulwi-Ñawi clan group was held on 8 October 2004, at the ceremonial house Warman (itself the property of Maliau and Nabul subclans). The object of dispute was the name *Kiginəbək*; this name and its feminine equivalent *Kiginəbəkəbər* was won by the Wagau clan. The Sarak clan was awarded another name, *Kəgidəmi* and its feminine counterpart *Kəgidəminəbər*, as a 'compensation'. The debate was opened by the Councillors of Avatip. The whole ceremony was very impressive: each orator would take a bunch of crotons and, swinging himself rhythmically, would present arguments in favour of his subclan's totemic ownership of the name, starting with genealogies, and finishing with resounding *Kiginəbək wun-adəwun* (Kiginəbək I-1masc.sgNOM) 'I am Kiginəbək'. Particularly spectacular performances—such as those by John Sepaywus, Paul Badaibæg, and Kulanawi Yuakaw—were accompanied by loud cries of appreciation.

The debate ended with what Harrison (1990a: 166) called 'a purely ceremonial display'—each side sang their song cycles, and women, dressed up in their grass skirts (kept for such occasions only), came up to the men dancing and serving them food.[6]

The end of the ceremonial part was marked with exchange of bunches of croton leaves. After having eaten, the men got together again, in small groups, 'playing politics', so as not to offend any of the participants, as John Sepaywus explained to me later (*politics nay-di* (politics play-3plBAS.VT)).

The name debates are now held less frequently than before, perhaps once every two years at most. They attract 'knowledgeable' big men from all the Manambu villages. The time chosen for name debates tends not to coincide with the Christmas and New Year period when the village is full of urban Manambu. The villagers make sure there are no 'tourists' around and that a name debate is not an 'attraction'.

A name debate is not just about a name, or the rights to use it. It is about exclusive rights to one's clan's totemic areas and history, including genealogies, and, consequently, the group's identity. The term *saki* 'name debate ritual' has a broad meaning, and is better translated as

---

[6] Women and children were not allowed to sit together with the men, watching the debate. I was invited to sit with the men, so that I could record and take pictures: as someone explained, a white woman is not the same as a local woman, and she must know what is going on.

'totemic ritual'. It also appears in *saki-təp*, a term for totemic villages (see §1.5) (and may well be related to the directional *saki-* 'ACROSS' (see §16.1), as in *wa-saki-maːj* (tell-ACROSS-story) 'traditional story transmitted from one generation to another' (e.g. Text 2, at the end of this grammar)). Knowing and 'owning' a name implies knowledge of one's ancestors, and one's connections with them. This has been fully addressed by Harrison (1990a), and I will not go any further.

Important orators—big men—and especially hereditary big men with exceptional ritual knowledge (*səbək*) used to be in charge, and even now tend to occupy positions of power. For instance, John Sepaywus, the *səbək* of the Maliau clan, was for many years a Councillor of Avatip; that is, a major official representing the community on the Ambunti Local Government Council. These people used to have the major say in ritual affairs, and in organizing warfare, and intergroup alliances. It was not until the advent of the Australian administration that the villages acquired their 'heads', *luluai* (the government official for the village), and two assistants, *tultuls*. Even then, a big man—rich in knowledge and importance—would tend to be the *luluai*, as was Lumawandem, one of the most respected orators and experts, and the father of Pauline Agnes Yuaneng Luma Laki, Joel Yuakalu Laki, and Leo Yabwi Luma.

We now turn to the ways in which the Manambu used to interact with their neighbours, and to their contact with Europeans. In §1.5, we address the prehistory of the Manambu.

1.4 RELATIONSHIPS WITH NEIGHBOURS AND RECENT HISTORY

1.4.1 Indigenous neighbours and traditional warfare

The Manambu, the 'river people', are surrounded by jungle-dwellers who do not live on the river banks and are known to the Manambu as *nəb-ə-du* (dry.land-LK-people).[7] The latter include a variety of groups, such as the Kwoma, the Kaunga, the Ierikai, and the Garamambu. The Manambu despise the 'dry-land people': the reasons given are that they do not use canoes, build houses directly on the ground, and live deep in the forest like animals (see Harrison 1993: 33). They are also wary of their sorcery (also see Bowden 1987). In the past, the dry-land people have been a frequent target of Manambu head-hunting raids. The tactic used against the dry-land people involved surrounding a hamlet at night, and then destroying it at dawn.

As Roscoe (1996: 662) puts it, 'the condition of village unity in the Sepik is more a military logic of defence than a symbolic logic of personhood or a structural logic of opposition'. That is, warfare was a matter of necessity, and of survival. Harrison (1993: 33–4) reports how the Avatip people almost decimated the Kaunga (see §1.5.1) some time during the nineteenth century, and, as a result, gained access to well-drained alluvial plains, with extensive stands of sago palm, good hunting territories and good areas for yam planting.

But material gain was never the only motive. Warfare used to be one of the major ritual preoccupations of the men's cult. Harrison (1993: 80–3) describes the ways in which men were socialized for aggression, being encouraged to stage mock gang-fights among men of different age grades. (Nowadays, 'men of different age-grades play out their rivalries mainly in football matches': 81.) Real wars, and head-hunting raids, used to play an important cultural role. A man returning from a successful raid with trophies—enemy heads—would be greeted by his mother's brother (*awaːy*) in a ceremony similar to *Naven* described by Bateson (1958).

---

7 The term *nəb* is nowadays also used in the meaning of 'foreign land', and *nəbədu* is used to mean 'foreigner'.

Killing an enemy would be celebrated in front of the ceremonial house of the killer's subclan, and accompanied with a dance. The head would be buried under the mound in front of the ceremonial house; or hung from a tree outside the village; after the flesh had decomposed, skulls would be painted and hung in the ceremonial houses (see Harrison 1993: 82, for further details). People with successful homicides attached special tassels to their lime spatulas (used to mix lime with ginger and mustard seeds with betelnut before chewing) indicating the number of people killed. They also were entitled to wear a pubic apron made of flying fox skin (men who had never killed did not wear any pubic covering, and used to bind their foreskins with fibre thread). In ceremonies, people who had committed homicides wore black face-paint. (This is why, in T2.45, Sesawi and Kamkudi, both experienced warriors, paint their faces black.) Killers enjoyed prestige in the community; they were real men who had proved their manliness. The more people they had killed the higher their status: a man who killed the most people would enter the village first (see examples 10.148–9). Women would prefer to marry such fighters— this is why Harrison (1993: 82) suggests that 'to some extent, the competition between men for the status of homicides was, implicitly, competition for women'. And the reason for the homicide was often nothing but a quest for 'status'.

With the advent of Australian colonial administration, head-hunting raids were stopped. When the Second World War started, the Manambu men saw this as an opportunity to earn 'brownie points' as brave homicides by killing newly acquired 'traditional enemies'— the Japanese invaders. These homicides were celebrated with traditional ceremonies (Harrison 1993: 83). And there are still a few villagers who proudly paint their faces black on ceremonial occasions. We return to this in the next section.

The dry-land people often fought back, and the result was a prolonged military conflict. One such instance—documented in oral histories—involves the Gəñap wars (see §21.5.4), fought at the end of the nineteenth century, according to Harrison's (1993: 67) estimate. Another war which features prominently in the folk memory involved the Gala.

The Gala (see §1.5.1) are said to have been aggressive 'dry-land people' who used to be nasty to the Kwoma, to whom the Avatip Manambu were politically allied. According to John Sepaywus, the Gala used to live around the Ambunti mountain (Makəmawi). Sick and tired of the Gala attacks, the Manambu and the Kwoma managed to overpower the Gala who fled to their present location, Swakap. One group of the Manambu, the clan Vali:k, is claimed to have descended from the surviving Gala. This story is recounted in Text 2, at the end of the grammar.[8] According to Paul Badaybæg, some of the remaining Gala settled in Yuanab.

The exact timing of the Gala war is hard to ascertain. Ross Bowden (p.c.) estimates that it could have happened in the early nineteenth century. Laurie Bragge (p.c.) reports that one of his Kwoma consultants used to 'have a carving mallet which he said belonged to the Nggala and which came from the wreckage of the stockade after the raid'. That is, the war was still fresh in folk memory. However, in Text 2, John Sepaywus says that the number of descendants of the founder of the Vali:k clan (claimed to be the only Gala who had survived the wars) 'has already surpassed two hundred seventy' (T2.65).

Military attacks from the Gala are not entirely a matter of the remote past. My consultants Yuawalup and Lowai (both in their sixties) recall how they used to fear Gala attacks when they were little girls. This is consistent with Newton's (1971: 33) account of Gala raids on

---

[8] Other versions of the same story were told by a variety of speakers including Walinum, Paul Badaybæg, Piurkaramb, and appeared in English translation in Harrison (1993: 45); and, in Manambu, English, and Tok Pisin, in Takendu (1977). The Kwoma version of the Gala war is recounted by Bragge (1990: 38). Alternative names for the Gala in Manambu accounts are Sәruali-Mәgunay and Mukun Kapar. The Kwoma refer to them as Kompom Nggala (Bragge 1990: 38).

their neighbours, including the Iatmul-speaking village of Brugnowi located near Yuanab, where half a dozen people were killed in 1953.[9] After that, administration officers took control.

There were no doubt more wars, and more peoples became extinct, or were absorbed into Manambu-speaking communities. The existence of multiple substrata may explain why Manambu is so linguistically complex.

Other important traditional enemies of the Manambu used to be their downriver neighbours—the Western Iatmul, or the Ñaula. There are numerous accounts of warfare with the Ñaula (see Harrison 1993: 38–40). Fights used to take place on the river, in canoes. The major military techniques involved ambushes, 'with a small force of two canoes lying in hiding among the dense stands of reeds and wild sugar-cane along the banks of the Sepik, and coming out to attack a party on their way to the fishing lagoon on some other expedition'.

We can recall, from §1.2.2, that before the Australian government had succeeded in banning the traditional warfare, all river villages adjacent to the Washkuk Hills were located on the south side of the Sepik, as a precautionary measure against surprise attacks by the Kwoma (who could not cross the river, since they were not so proficient in canoes). That is, the Manambu themselves were highly wary of a possible surprise attack from any quarter. This is one of the reasons why the 'women's road' in Avatip is further away from the river than the 'men's road': the men could defend themselves, the women could not.

Despite the traditional enmities, there was—and to some extent still is—a certain amount of cooperation between the Manambu and the Western Iatmul in traditional matters. Harrison (1993: 44) reports that 'when the last full scale scarification ceremony was held in Avatip in 1936, inducting novices into the first stage of male initiation', men from Yuanab, Malu, Japandai (Western Iatmul), and Sengo came to help. A long-term contact with the Iatmul involved trading spells and incantations in rituals (see §22.3). The Kwoma of the village of Bangwis are a traditional trade partner of the Avatips, and there used to be a special Kwoma–Manambu pidgin used for trade (Bowden 1997; also see §22.2.3). These partnerships were reflected in traditional patterns of multilingualism, now close to extinction. Only some old people know Kwoma and Western Iatmul—the languages of their erstwhile partners in trade.

Further facets of the traditional warfare, the ceremonial significance of head hunting, and trade patterns of the Manambu and their neighbours are discussed in Harrison (1993). We now turn to the encounters with Europeans, and their consequences.

1.4.2　Relationships with outsiders

The first people from the outside world that the Sepiks had contact with could have been Malay bird of paradise shooters (Ryan 1972: 1034). The first Europeans to ever set foot on the Manambu lands were Germans.

Official German interest in New Guinea began in 1884 and lasted until the First World War. The acquired colony included two distinct areas—the north-eastern portion of the mainland then known as Kaiser Wilhelmsland, and the Bismarck Archipelago. Kaiser Wilhelmsland included the Sepik Basin. Dr Otto Finsch (1839–1917), a German ornithologist and ethnographer, was commissioned by the German New Guinea Company (Neuguinea-Kompanie) to lead an expedition up the north-eastern coast of New Guinea, whereby he discovered the

---

[9] These accounts were confirmed by Laurie Bragge and Ulrike Claas (p.c.).

entrance to the Sepik River which he named *Kaiserin Augusta Fluss* in 1885 (Ryan 1972: 404; also Townsend 1968: 75).

The first recorded contact of the Manambu with Europeans took place in 1886, and then again in the second half of 1887, when the members of the New Guinea Company Scientific Expedition under the leadership of Dr Schrader, Mr Hollrung, Mr Schneider, and Mr Hunstein sailed up the Sepik River on board the steamer *Samoa* (Zöller 1891: 367–8; Hahl 1980: 126; and a full account in Claas 2007: 38–40). Zöller (1891: 367) reports that the members of the scientific expedition had stayed in a camp at Malu between 22 August and 7 November. Dr Schrader collected 157 words from Malu and Yambon—this, together with further materials collected from Tsenapian and, apparently, Kwoma, formed the basis for 'Kaiserin-Augusta-Fluss languages' to which we return in §1.7.

A further notable encounter[10] of the Malu people with Europeans took place during the Kaiserin-Augusta-Fluss-Expedition (1912–13), under the direction of District Officer Mining Engineer (Bergassessor) A. Stollé, with Dr Walter Behrmann (1882–1955), later professor of geography at the University of Frankfurt am Main, in charge of the geographical part, and Dr Richard Thurnwald (1869–1954) in charge of the ethnographic research (he continued his work after the outbreak of the First World War until taken prisoner in 1915) (Hahl 1980: 142; Roesicke 1914: 507). The major results are published in Behrmann (1922); this includes a fascinating description of art, customs (including the traditional greeting *kəpəyay*—see §21.5.3), and lifestyle of the Manambu from Malu.

During our visit to Malu, one of Behrmann's interpreters and carriers, Yuanai (his picture is in Behrmann 1922: 178), excited particular interest among the Manambu of today because he was the last member of the Maliau clan in Malu. The other interpreter, Dangwan, was personally known to the oldest living man in the Manambu community, Duamakwa:y, from Malu (who was old enough to shave when he knew Dangwan: see examples 7.23, 9.33, and 21.7).

A certain aura of mystery surrounds the feats of the expedition: Bragge, Claas, and Roscoe (2006) report that some of the so-called 'scientific men from European and U.S. museums . . . took to stealing skulls and even whole skeletons' that 'river villagers installed in their so-called reception huts or, if overmodeled in clay, in their spirit houses'. There are even rumours that some Germans had 'commissioned head-hunting and even hunted heads themselves'. In particular, Adolf Roesicke is reported to have accompanied a Korogo (that is, Iatmul) war party against Malu, 'shot a woman, and brought her head back to the camp to celebrate the kill' (Bragge, Claas, and Roscoe 2006: 103–4). These claims are difficult to substantiate; it is possible that Roesicke happened to be travelling with the Korogo people when they encountered and beheaded a Malu woman. Another, alternative, version of the event could have been that the Melanesian personnel of the expedition—to whom the name 'German' was also applied—had taken, or commissioned the taking of, heads: for them, 'the foreign military resources had opened up new possibilities' (Bragge, Claas, and Roscoe 2006: 104).[11]

The materials published by Behrmann are still valued—despite the fact that the villagers cannot very well read his 1922 book (in German, and in Gothic script), and have to rely on makeshift translations. Leo Kalangas and other men from the Malu village are currently trying

----

[10] In her exhaustive study, Claas (2007: 38–40) reports a few further instances of contacts with Europeans, including the Hamburger Südsee Expedition which was on the Sepik between 23 May and 6 June 1909 with a stop in Malu, and the German-Dutch border expedition in 1910 during which several ships went past the Manambu area.

[11] This is what Bragge, Claas, and Roscoe (2006) call 'military brokerage'.

to use the information provided by Behrmann (1922), in their territorial disputes with the neighbouring Kwoma. There is no more warfare between the Kwoma and the Manambu; but relationships are still somewhat strained.

As mentioned above (§1.2.2; Newton 1971: 64), the encounter between the Manambu and the German explorers in 1910–12 was not uniformly peaceful. According to Clune (1951: 281) who visited Avatip in 1940, the people from Avatip resented the presence of W. Behrmann 'charting the river' and 'fired arrows at the invader, who responded with machine-gun fire. After the first shock of hearing this strange noise, the head-hunters replied with more arrows. The German, to make sure that they'd depart once and for all, shelled Avatip with pom-pom guns, using solid shells with no fuse, seven inches long and two inches in diameter. After that, the Germans surveyed in peace.' As a result, the greatest curio in the village was a pom-pom shell, which was shown to Clune by the Malu people.[12]

Between 1886 and 1914, contacts between Sepik River dwellers and Europeans were rather intensive: Bragge, Claas, and Roscoe (2006: 102) report that, in the thirty years between 1886 and 1914, 'the number of foreign visitors [including all outsiders, that is Melanesian police, carriers etc—A.A.] to the Sepik River was well over a thousand, implying an extensive encounter rate between visitors and villagers'. With the advent of Australian control, this traffic slowed down. By that time, the Avatip people had already acquired a reputation for their hostility towards outsiders. Townsend (1968: 100) reports:

... In 1919, the *Siar* [an Australian vessel—A.A.], mounting a two-pounder gun, had thrown several shells into Avatip village because of its bad reputation and had distributed a number of small Union Jacks to other villages as a mark of friendship. Perhaps Avatip men were naturally hostile, or maybe they resented not getting a flag, but their next visitor, and the only one until we came, was at once stabbed. He was a man named Fritsch, a German recruiter for the Neu Guinea Compagnie who took his launch up the River in early 1921. One of his two crewmen was killed and he and the other wounded but they managed to hide in the engine-room from where he shot several spearmen with a rifle.

In response to that, the Australian Naval and Military Expeditionary Force, then administering New Guinea, organized a punitive expedition against the village (see Rowley 1958: 202–3; Harrison 1990a: 25–6). As a result, half a dozen villagers were shot dead, and the villagers abandoned Avatip for many months, living in isolated bush camps in small groups. Some returned to the village and rebuilt it; others settled in Yawabak (on the Walmaw lagoon). It was during this time that the Avatip men were taken as indentured labourers, returning after two years with some knowledge of Tok Pisin and of the new colonial order. One of these was appointed *luluai* (the government official in the village), and two others were appointed *tultul* (*luluai*'s assistants) (see §1.3.2).

The Australian colonial administration was established in what became Ambunti in 1924 (Townsend 1968: 101). This saw the end of traditional head-hunting practices: Townsend, then the District Officer of the Ambunti District, was 'primarily responsible for the "pacification" of the region, and his several public hangings of men convicted of head-hunting halted warfare almost overnight' (Bragge, Claas, and Roscoe 2006: 109). The way this was done is described by Townsend himself (1968); for the analysis of the consequences for the Manambu and the Middle Sepik peoples in general, see Harrison (1993) and Bragge, Claas, and Roscoe (2006).

During the Second World War, Avatip men resisted the Japanese as best they could. Towards the end of 1944, a small contingent of Japanese soldiers was stationed in Yentschanggai. The

---

[12] This incident was never mentioned by Behrmann himself; whether it had really happened is impossible to tell.

village was occasionally bombed by the Japanese, with no one hurt (Harrison 1990a: 26; Kukelyabau and Kaplenau, p.c.). Kukelyabau, now in her late sixties, told a heart-breaking story about her whole family fleeing into the bush at the sight of a Japanese war plane (see example 18.33). As pointed out by Harrison (1993: 83), the Japanese were conceptualized as traditional enemies of the Avatip; and a number of invaders were ambushed and killed. As mentioned above, the old men who killed Japanese still paint their faces black and wear the homicide regalia during ceremonies.

Avatip men supported the Australian guerrilla forces; until today, they proudly point out that they had never supported the Japanese as did some Iatmul leaders (see Gewertz 1983: 137). This is not to say that the Iatmul did not suffer horrendously at the hands of the invaders: ninety-six men and one woman were massacred in 1944 by native people from other Sepik villages, following Japanese orders, in the Iatmul village of Timbunke. Convinced that what had happened at Timbunke might happen to them, Avatip men decided to take the offensive. After two days of fasting to appease their ancestors' spirits, each Avatip man took his stone axe, singled out a Japanese soldier, and attacked (Curtain 1978: 21). Kaplenau, who was a young man then, reports that at the end of the Japanese occupation, the Avatip managed to capture their commander and proudly carried him—alive and tied up upside down on a pole like a pig—all the way to Wewak.

Intensive evangelization started in the 1950s when a Catholic church was built in Yentschanggai. The Avatip rebelled against the Catholic influence, and burnt down the church, thus acquiring a bad reputation among the missionaries. We will see, in §1.7 below, that the Summer Institute of Linguistics missionaries worked almost exclusively in Yuanab, known among the Manambu as more 'open' to outside influences. Nowadays, as we saw in §1.2.2 above, most Manambu are Christianized—which does not normally stop them from performing such rituals as the mortuary Kəkətəp.

A primary school was established at Yentschanggai in 1961. Since then, most children have acquired some level of education. They may attend secondary school in Ambunti, and many go to Brendi high school in Wewak. The Manambu people are among the most successful New Guineans—many have well-paid jobs as highly ranked army officers, members of the diplomatic corps, policemen, public servants, and teachers (see Harrison 1990a: 28 for further observations).

1.5   LINGUISTIC AFFILIATION AND PREHISTORY

1.5.1   The Ndu language family

The New Guinea region is the most linguistically diverse and complex area in the world, with over 1,000 languages spoken in an area of about 900,000 square kilometres. About 300 to 400 languages spoken there belong to the Austronesian family. Other, non-Austronesian, languages are often referred to as 'Papuan' (see Foley 1986: 1–3; Aikhenvald and Stebbins 2007). The term 'Papuan' is a rough denomination which covers over sixty genetically unrelated language families and a fair number of isolates in the area.

Manambu is a member of the Ndu language family, one of the few well-established Papuan families. In terms of number of speakers, the Ndu family is the largest in the Sepik area. It consists of at least six languages spoken by over 100,000 people along the course of the middle Sepik River and to the north of it (Laycock 1965; Aikhenvald 2004b). Other members of the family are:

1. ABELAM-WOSERA dialect continuum with over 40,000 speakers, in the Maprik District of the East Sepik Province. This includes the following dialects: Maprik, Wingei, Wosera, West Wosera (including Hanga Kundi, Kwasengen, Pukago, Banwingei). Wendel (1993: 1–5) argues that West Wosera is a separate language group. However, this may well be a continuum of dialects, some of which are mutually intelligible (Wilson 1976, 1980; Manabe 1981).

2. BOIKIN (also known as Boiken, Nucum, Yangoru, and Yengoru) is spoken by over 30,000 people in the area of the Yangoru District of the East Sepik Province. Dialects include Yangoru, Kubalia, Central, Nagum, Kunai dialect, Island and Coastal dialects (see a preliminary survey in Freudenburg 1976). Laycock's (1965) work is centred on Kwusaun Boikin, while Freudenburg (1970, 1975, 1979) is based on Yangoru Boikin.

3. IATMUL is a dialect continuum spoken by about 50,000 people in the East Sepik Province, with important minorities in towns such as Wewak and Madang. The four varieties of Iatmul include Western Iatmul (or Ñaula), Central Iatmul (Palimbei), Eastern Iatmul (Waliyakwi), and Northern Iatmul (Maligwat). Mutual intelligibility of the dialects varies. A full list of villages is in Jendraschek (forthcoming). (Burui, Maligwat, and Gaikundi, listed as separate Ndu languages on the Ethnologue website, are among the Iatmul dialects.)

   A number of varieties used to be grouped under the name of 'Sawos' languages (Laycock 1965: 144; 1973: 27); of these, Sengo, Burui, Kwaruwi Kundi, and also Gaikundi appear to be members of the Iatmul continuum. Koiwat—listed as a separate language in the Ethnologue and spoken in the villages of Koiwat, Kamangaui, Seraba, and Paiambit—is lexically close to Boikin; whether or not it is a separate language requires further study. The notion of 'Sawos' is not a linguistic term: it is a Iatmul word used to refer to their trade partners north of the Sepik River. A reliable reappraisal of the languages covered by 'Sawos' is in Staalsen (1975).

4. YELOGU or KAUNGA is reported to have about 200 speakers. It is spoken in two villages, Biananumbu and Ambuken (also see Laycock 1965; 1973: 87, 91). The language is also known by the name of Buwiyamanabu, or Buiamanambu; this is 'a government corruption of the Kaunga name Buwiyamanabu' (see Bowden 1997: xx–xxii, on the precontact history and settlement of the Yelogu people, and their contacts with the Kwoma).

5. GALA, or NGALA, is spoken by about 150 people in Swakap (or Swagup), at a junction of a black-water river running between the Sepik and a point a few miles up the April River. The place was marked under the name of Kara on Behrmann's maps (Newton 1971: 33).[13] Newton also reports that the place was called Nggala, and was later renamed Swagup after the names employed by its neighbours. Different Gala 'wards' claim different places of origin: one claims to have come from far up the Sepik, and two others claim to have come from the Hunstein mountains, from the south-east. Their presence in the Washkuk Hills is corroborated by Kwoma and Manambu accounts of the Gala wars (see §1.4.1).

   A number of innovations are shared by Manambu and Gala (see §22.1). These may be partly accounted for by contacts between Gala and Manambu prior to the Gala wars and their subsequent expulsion from the area of the Washkuk Hills.

A preliminary grouping partly corresponding to the Ndu family was established by Kirschbaum (1922) (who used the term *Tuo* language, after the term for 'man' in Boikin). Linguistic affinity between Abelam and Iatmul was acknowledged by Loukotka (1957: 29).

---

[13] The name [ⁿgala] is phonetically inaccurate inasmuch as the Gala language does not have word-initial prenasalization of velar stops.

The limits of the Ndu family were established by Laycock (1965), who decided to rename the family using the word for 'man' in Iatmul and Manambu. However, most of his materials are superficial and contain mistakes (see §22.1, for some examples), due to insufficient time spent with each group, and questionable fieldwork methodology. Consequently, his internal classification and reconstructions require revision (see Aikhenvald forthcoming b; and §22.1).

Other putative genetic affiliations between Ndu and languages of the Sepik area are entirely unsubstantiated (further discussion is in §22.2).

1.5.2   The varieties of Manambu

The varieties of Manambu spoken in Malu, Avatip, and Yuanab show a few differences which do not impede mutual intelligibility. This is no doubt due to the fact that the existing settlements are fairly recent: according to Harrison (1993: 29), Avatip was founded only about 'six or seven generations ago'. The few differences between the varieties of Avatip (also spoken in Yawabak), Malu (also spoken in Apa:n), and Yuanab are discussed in §22.6.1 where we look at dialect mixing.

The major phonological feature setting the Yuanab variety apart from both Avatip and Malu is the lack of distinction between the lateral and the rhotic. (This feature is also shared with Gala; see above on the possible Gala substratum in Yuanab.)

Apart from a few lexical differences between Malu and Avatip, the Malu variety does not distinguish negative forms of *ya-* 'come' and *yə-* 'go', while the Avatip variety does: Avatip *ma: yæy* 'does not/did not come', *ma: yə* 'does not/did not go'; Malu *ma: yə* 'does not/did not come/go'. There is a difference in speech prosody between the two—the general opinion among the language-conscious speakers of the Avatip variety is that those from Malu 'stretch our language' (*ñan-a təp-a kudi lagu-dana* (we-LK+fem.sg village-LK language stretch/pull-3plSUBJ.VT+3plBAS.VT) 'they stretch our village language', that is, their words sound longer than ours).

The same expression applies to the speakers of Iatmul, or Ñaula—which also correlates with the fact that words in Iatmul are longer than in Manambu because Iatmul retains the word-final vowels which Manambu has lost (see §22.1).

1.5.3   Origins and putative prehistory

According to the Manambu tradition, they originated in the ancestral village called Asiti whose site lies between Avatip and the Western Iatmul village of Japandai. Its offshoots were Maukabu and Garaikwali. In an oral history recorded by Bragge (1990: 38) in the early 1970s, Kwatauwi/Vivigamei reports:

When Asiti overpopulated they made Mogumbo [Maukambu] and Garakoli [Ngarakwali] villages nearby. They stayed there a long time and through many fights, and the waterways silted up and left Asiti, Mogumbo and Garakoli too far inside...[When] Yabsit came and started Avatip...we divided the people to set up Malu and Avatip. Big brother in Avatip, small brother in Malu...all the clans were represented in both places. Malu is the name of the mountain, but the people are Avatips.

Bragge (1990: 49) calculates that the approximate date of establishment of Avatip and Malu could be between 1860 and 1870. This only partly agrees with Harrison's (1993: 30) observations that 'Asiti was abandoned at the end of the eighteenth century or early in the nineteenth'; he estimates dates of founding of Avatip and Malu as 'some seven generations ago' (1993a: 17). An old lady in Avatip (who died in the early 1970s) appeared to have been only four generations removed from Asiti.

The story of Yuanab appears to be more intricate. According to some (Harrison 1993: 30), after the foundation of Avatip, some colonists moved upriver and established the village of Malu; others migrated still further upstream and settled there with an autochthonous people to form the village of Yuanab. This is corroborated by oral histories collected by Bragge (1990)—the origin stories collected by him among the Yuanab people 'tell of the wandering ancestors gathering together' and acquiring a new language—Manambu—for them to use. Nauwi Sauinambi (a Kwoma man from Bangwis) reports that 'Yambon [Yuanab] came from up near Swagup and Alakai, some came from Garamambu. They did not paddle canoes' (Bragge 1990: 37).

This suggests that the Yuanab people originally consisted of a number of groups—not necessarily all speaking one language—'forced together into a simple village situation by the Manambu threat' (37). This 'language shift' is dated by Bragge (1990: 48) as having occurred in about 1830. Originally, the Yuanab-dwellers were 'dry-land' people, only recently 'converted' to be river people. This may explain a somewhat aloof attitude of the people of Avatip and Malu to those from Yuanab. And we can recall, from §1.4, that, according to Paul Badaybæg, after the Gala wars some of the Gala people hid in Yuanab: this points towards some kind of Gala substratum in Yuanab. After the end of the Səruali Məgunay—that is, Gala—war (see §1.4), the Malu people are said to have destroyed Yuanab, with only two or three people surviving.

An alternative version is that the Yuanab people abandoned their village and went off to bush camps. The next waves of migration to Yuanab came from a Iatmul (Ñaula) speaking village of Japandai in the early twentieth century (Bragge 1990: 41–6); as a result of arguments between the new arrivals and the Yuanab people, an armed conflict erupted; the Malu people came to help and took the Yuanab people 'up to their present village site and set them up there' (41). It may have been at that stage that Yuanab 'acknowledged its position as a Manambu village'.

The presence of varying substrata is probably what accounts for more pronounced dialectal differences between Yuanab and the rest than between, say, Malu and Avatip.

In the absence of written documents, dating of historical events has to rely on genealogies, and the information obtained can be contradictory. We saw that the dates for the Səruali Məgunay wars vary from early to late nineteenth century. All we can say with assurance is that the major migrations of the Manambu into more or less their present location within the area of Ambunti mountain took place in the nineteenth century.

What do we know about their more remote history? According to the tradition, the three clans of the Manambu came from three mythical ancestral villages, called *saki-təp* (totemic.ritual.village).[14] The totemic ancestors of the Gla:gw lived near the Yentschang-gai/Lapanggai areas. The totemic ancestors of the Wulwi-Ñawi lived in a village far to the east—which, according to some, is the reason why the Wulwi-Ñawi totemically own the eastward areas, including Australia and places the white people come from, as well as the 'white people's objects'. The word for 'east' is *wali*, also used for 'white people'. The totemic ancestors of the Nabul-Sablap lived further to the west, in the direction of the sea (and perhaps

---

[14] Young Manambu men—orators in training—equate the three ancestral villages, Asiti, Maukabu, and Garaikwali—with the three mythical villages from which the three clan groups had originated. This is the way in which ethnohistory-in-the-making is now evolving.

even on the coast). They are the ones who 'carved' the Sepik River, whose source remains in their ancestral village (also see Harrison 1990a: 45).

This may imply that, historically, the Manambu could have consisted of at least three groups merged together, one of which used to be located towards the coast. This may also explain a few curious similarities between Manambu and Oceanic languages (see §22.3). But nothing can be stated with full assurance.

Different subclans of the Manambu, and sometimes even the same subclan in different villages, claim different migration routes. The Nagudəu of Avatip say that their ancestors came from far up the Screw River, in the direction of the Abelam; while the Nagudəu of Yuanab describe their ancestral 'home' as the south-west shore of Lake Chambri (Newton 1971: 64). This is similar to the ways in which different Gala 'wards' claim different places of origin (see §1.5.1). This may well reflect various layers of population mix and perhaps subsequent language shifts and unknown substrata, which may be held responsible for the linguistic complexity of modern Manambu.

The question of an overall proto-home of the Ndu people remains open. There are indications of the migrations of some of the Ndu-speaking peoples (Gala) from the north-east towards the Washkuk Hills. According to Roscoe (1994: 74), 'it does seem probable that the early Sepik-Ramu population spawned the ancestors of the Ndu-speaking groups now spread across the lands from the Middle Sepik to the northern mountains and that these proto-Ndu arrived first in the Middle Sepik region, quite possibly in what is now the Sawos territory'. However, the exact route of migration is impossible to ascertain, until more archaeological and linguistic studies of the surrounding groups are undertaken.[15] The story about two Manambu brothers carving the Sepik River may suggest the arrival of the Ndu people by water before the recession of the inland sea, rather than on foot. (The Middle Sepik River is thought to be the remnant of a vast inland sea which is believed to have reached its maximum extent between about 5000 and 6500 BC, and was infilled by about 1000 BC: Chappell 2005: 535–6; Paul Roscoe p.c.) Roscoe (1994: 74; p.c.) points out that 'the balance of evidence suggests that the Ndu presence in the Middle Sepik is ancient rather than recent and that the ancestors of the Abelam and Boiken began moving north many hundreds of years ago'.

That is, the proto-home of at least some Ndu peoples could have been the Middle Sepik area. This requires further study.

1.6 LINGUISTIC SITUATION

Currently, Manambu—called by the speakers 'village language' (*təp-a kudi*) or Manambu language (*Mana:bə kudi*)—is the main language of the five villages on the Sepik River. It is used in most homes, especially by older generations (50–80 years of age), and during traditional ceremonies, such as name debates and the mortuary feast (§1.3.1). At present, there are no Manambu monolinguals; just a few old ladies, including Gemaj (see Plate 6) are more comfortable speaking Manambu than Tok Pisin.

Children's early socialization starts in Tok Pisin (see §22.4). Most parents in the villages speak to their children in Manambu as well as Tok Pisin; however, Tok Pisin is the preferred

---

[15] Errors in Foley's (2005a) linguistic data invalidate his conclusions concerning the interrelationships between the languages of the Sepik area (§22.2.1).

means of communication between children of all ages. A few women in Avatip come from other areas of New Guinea, and communicate with their peers, and children, in Tok Pisin. This enhances the frequency of Tok Pisin, and now also of Papua New Guinea English. Most church services are conducted mostly in Tok Pisin, with inserts from Papua New Guinea English, and from Manambu. I attended several SDA church meetings which were mostly in Manambu; later on I was told that this was done 'for my sake'.

Most Manambu who live in towns maintain the language as a means of home communication. However, their children tend to be proficient just in English, with little knowledge of Tok Pisin, and even less of Manambu. When these children go back to the village, during school holidays, the amount of English in the villages soars.

That is, the overall degree of intrusion of Tok Pisin and English into village life looks threatening—no wonder many older people complain that the language is doomed and bound to go (this is comparable to the situation in Taiap described by Kulick 1992). We return to the prospects for the survival of the language in §22.6.

Traditional multilingualism now survives mostly in the folk memory. As we saw in §1.4, the Iatmul (*Ñaula*) used to be traditional trade partners of a number of the Manambu clans (see Harrison 1990a: 69–72). These links were based on (a) trade exchange, and (b) shared cultural practices. Within Manambu clans traditional initiation ceremonies and debates (thoroughly described by Harrison 1990a) involved 'trading' incantations and spells in the closely related (but far from mutually intelligible) Iatmul. Representatives of older generations—especially men who achieved high degrees of initiation—used to have a very good knowledge of this language. A Iatmul influence is reflected in the special 'shadowy' style in traditional songs (see §22.3). Younger people know much less Iatmul.

Further language knowledge involved traditional trade partners. Older people used to know the languages of their neighbours and trade partners, especially Kwoma (also see Bowden 1997: xx). This knowledge is drastically diminished among the younger generation. This gradual disintegration of traditional multilingual patterns, and the increase in knowledge of the main lingua francas—Tok Pisin, and English—is a worrying sign of traditional language endangerment on a global scale (see Aikhenvald 2002b).

Avatip has a primary school (years 1–7), currently with 245 students and 12–13 teachers (a few of them from other communities: for instance, one is an Arapesh). The headmaster, Leo Yabwi Luma, is highly competent and proficient in Manambu language and lore. Most schooling is in Papua New Guinea English together with Tok Pisin. A Manambu vernacular language programme is under way. Manambu alphabetization materials are created by teachers themselves. Plate 5 features Tanina Ala displaying one of the posters relating to a story about 'mother pig' used in the Avatip school in 2002–3. The primary school in Yawabak (years 1–3) currently has a vernacular teaching programme; and apparently so does a primary school in Malu.

A major problem for teaching Manambu at school is the existing orthography. The orthography proposed by SIL missionaries was primarily based on the Yuanab variety which distinguishes just one liquid *r* rather than *r* and *l* as in Malu and Avatip (Farnsworth and Farnsworth 1975). The orthography distinguishes all the other consonant phonemes (digraph *ny* is used for the palatal *ñ*). The orthography distinguishes only four vowels rather than nine (see §2.1.2). The vowels are written as *a* for /a/, *uw* for /u/, *iy* for /i/, and *aa* for either /a:/ or a sequence /aʔa/ (see §2.1.2, on how older speakers pronounce long vowel *a:* as a sequence of identical vowels interrupted by a glottal stop). The symbol *i* is used for ə. People complain that this writing system is bulky—and avoid writing Manambu.

Alternative orthographies have been emerging spontaneously over the years. One exemplar of this is a story by an elder, Daniel Takendu (1977). The writing system is basically phonetic: some automatically prenasalized consonants are written as such (*d* as *nd*, *b* as *mb*, and so on), and some are not; *i* is used for ə, and also for *i*, and a double vowel is used for long *a*:. Palatal *ñ* is written as *ny*. Double consonants appear in stressed syllables. Most enclitics and some suffixes are written as independent words.

The way Manambu was written in Takendu's story about the Gala war (1977: 3) is illustrated in 1.1 (the first line of a story about the Gala war). The second line represents the phonological transcription adopted throughout this grammar.

1.1 *Anndi*   *Ambunti* *wandanandi*   *tipaam,*   *Makimawi*
    a-də   Abunti   wa-dana-di   təp-a:m   Makəmawi
    DEM.DIST-pl Ambunti say-3plSUBJ.VT-3plBAS.VT village-LK+LOC Makemawi-
    annd   *sumbuk*   *si*
    -a:d   səbək   sə
    3masc.sgNOM ritual.officer name
    'In that village that they call Ambunti, there is Makemawi (Ambunti mountain), (this is the) name of a ritual officer'

The orthography used in the primary school programme in Avatip (see Plate 5) combines features of Takendu's (1977) with those of Farnsworth and Farnsworth's (1975) proposals (that is, *iy* for *i*, and *uw* for *u*, as in *duw* 'man' rather than *du*). Enclitics are written as separate words. The sequence of a labialized consonant *gw* followed by a schwa ə is marked as *gu*. Prenasalized stops are sometimes written as simple stops (as in *baal* /ba:l/ 'pig'), and other times as sequences with a nasal, as in *kwarimbaam* /kwarba:m/ 'in the jungle' and *giramb* /grab/ 'afternoon'. A sample with a corresponding phonological transcription and gloss is in 1.2 below:

1.2 *wun* *amaay* *baal awun*   *wun* *kwarimbaam* *kwakwanaun*
    wun amæy ba:l-awun   wun kwarba:m   kwa-kwa-na-wun
    I   mother pig-1fem.sgNOM I   bush+LK+LOC stay-HAB-ACT.FOC-1fem.sgBAS.VT
    wun *nyanugw* *aliy* *tinawun*   *wun* *nyi* *gaan* *si*   *akis*
    wun ñanugw a:li tə-na-wun   wun ñə ga:n sə   akəs
    I   children four have-ACT.FOC-1fem.sgBAS.VT I   day night sleep NEG.HAB
    kwakwanawun
    kwa-kwa-na-wun
    stay-HAB-ACT.FOC-1fem.sgBAS.VT
    'I am mother pig, I live in the bush, I have four children, I never sleep day and night'

Perceived inconsistencies and the unwieldiness of the orthographic conventions suggested by the Farnsworths are a matter of concern for many literate Manambu. There is currently an interest in developing a new, community-based, orthography.

The importance of such orthography approved by a consensus of well-respected Manambu cannot be underestimated: if people start writing their language, this may ultimately diminish the expansion of Tok Pisin into functional domains reserved for Manambu. For the time being, the Manambu language is considered 'difficult to write'.

Throughout this grammar, all the examples are presented in the phonological transcription based on the analysis in Chapter 2.

1.7 WHAT WE KNOW ABOUT THE MANAMBU LANGUAGE

The first records of the Manambu language by Europeans go back to the second half of 1887, when the members of the New Guinea Company Scientific Expedition under Schrader, Hollrung, Schneider, and Hunstein sailed up the Sepik River on board the steamer *Samoa* (Zöller 1891: 367–8; Hahl 1980: 126). Zöller (1891: 367) reports that the members of the scientific expedition had stayed in a camp at Malu between 22 August and 7 November. Dr Schrader collected '68 words from Zenáp-dialects, 26 words of Mangi-dialects spoken to the west from it, 132 words from the Malu dialect, 25 words of the neighbouring Yamboni-dialect [Yambon, or Yuanab, variety], and a further 12 words from a village which lies further down the river "in the grasshills"' (Zöller 1891: 367–8). We have no information on the nature of this first contact, or the ways in which the language data were collected. The combined wordlist was published by Zöller (1891: Appendix, item 18), under the heading *Augustafluss* (Sepik River). It is presented in Appendix 1.1. As shown in the Appendix, sixty-seven words and expressions are recognizably Manambu, and are presumably from the Malu dialect.

Seventeen words in the list are identifiable as Western Iatmul. I hypothesize that they belong to what Zöller calls 'Yamboni-dialect', and perhaps reflect a dialect of Western Iatmul spoken where Brugnowi is located now (next to Yuanab/Yambon). Six of these are shared between Iatmul and Manambu. Five words are similar to Kwoma: this may have been the language from a Grass Hills village. A further sixty-eight are problematic. Six words are identifiable as Chenapian (note that the materials on Chenapian, published in Laycock and Z'graggen 1975: 744, are extremely limited). What is meant by 'Mangi-dialect' remains a mystery.

Zöller's materials are quoted in Schmidt (1902: 70), under the heading of *Sprachen vom Augustafluss*, that is, *Languages of the Sepik*. He points out the impossibility of making any definite pronouncements based on the limited data available, and notes the presence of repetition in the colour terms *nüggi-nüggi* 'red' *(ñiki-ñiki* lit. blood-blood) and *laggi-galagi* 'yellow' (lit. *laki-ka-laki* ginger-INTENSIVE-ginger, 'green'); these forms, still in use in Manambu, are discussed in §4.3.3 below.

Behrmann (1922: 178) mentions the greeting *kubiaai* (kəpəyay), but does not provide any wordlist. Adolf Roesicke (1914), also a member of the expedition, collected vocabularies, part of which he cites to illustrate the fact that the language spoken 'from Támbunum to Jāmānŭm and Tschébandei' (which is identical with Iatmul) is relatively similar to another language, spoken in 'Awatíb, Mālu and Jambŭn' (that is, Manambu) (508–9). The Manambu part of this illustrative list is given in Appendix 1.1.[16]

Malu as a group of languages distinct from Iatmul was recognized by Loukotka (1957: 29–30): 'Málu. Un petit groupe de langues vers l'ouest. Le *Málu* est parlé dans un village du même nom sur le Sepik [Kluge 1938: 176], le *Tuo* dans un autre village de la même région [Schmidt 1901; 1902], l'*Ambunti* dans un autre village encore et l'*Awatib* aussi dans un village /pour les deux: néant/.'[17]

---

[16] The full vocabulary has not been located so far. Ulrike Claas (p.c.) suggests that it must have been destroyed during the Second World War.

[17] Málu. A small group of languages towards the west. Málu is spoken in a village with the same name on the Sepik River [Kluge 1938: 176], Tuo (is spoken) in another village of the same region [Schmidt 1901; 1902], Ambunti (is spoken) in one other village, and Awatip is also (spoken) in one village /for both: nothing/.

The first missionaries of the Summer Institute of Linguistics to set foot in the Manambu villages were Janet Dodson (later Allen) and Phyllis Walker (later Hurd) (1962–3). They produced a sketch of Manambu phonology (Allen and Hurd 1972) based on the Yuanab variety (also quoted in Pike 1964). Pauline Yuaneng Luma Laki recalls their visit to her house in Avatip in the early 1960s: they were the first white people she had ever seen, and the experience was scary. They were then replaced by Robin and Marva Farnsworth (1963–80),[18] who worked mainly in Yuanab (though their major collaborator, Ken Nayau, is from Avatip). (The first survey wordlist collected by Robin Farnsworth in Yuanab [Yambon] is dated 31 December 1964.)

Robin Farnsworth authored a number of papers (1966, 1975, 1976) on Manambu pronouns and demonstratives, phrases and clauses, and translation problems. Farnsworth and Farnsworth produced a grammar sketch (1966), and 'Essentials for translation' (n.d.), as a prerequisite for their translation work, in addition to an orthography proposal (1975) and phonology data (1981?). Marva Farnsworth compiled a number of collections of stories (e.g. 1971, *Nyana maaj* 'our speech'), and a draft wordlist (n.d.), in addition to a few booklets for literacy work and stories (mostly biblical). The Bible, *God diki lapa nyig* (lit. God his banana leaf), was published by the SIL, Ukarumpa, in 1979, and dedicated in 1980. On the request of the Manambu people, a revision of this preliminary translation started in 2001, with the help of Marva and Robin Farnsworth, and their major collaborator Ken Nayau; it is currently being undertaken by several groups of Manambu themselves, including Ken Nayau.

The phonological analysis of Manambu (based on the Yuanab variety) by Farnsworth and Farnsworth (1981?) is similar to that in Allen and Hurd (1972): it postulates three vowel phonemes (*i*, *a*, and *a:*), whose allophones (ə, ɨ, and *u*; we will see in §2.1.2 that ə, *u*, and also *æ* are in fact distinct phonemes) depend on the consonantal environment. This over-parsimonious analysis resulted in the creation of a complicated orthography (§1.6). The grammatical analysis is mostly cast in a rather inscrutable tagmemic framework; many of the paradigms are partial.

A sketch grammar of Manambu by Laycock (1965: 120–31) contains some partial pronominal paradigms and is on the whole very shallow. The materials obtained, and the fieldwork methodology, are problematic: the sketch is based on a short span of work with a consultant who worked as a medical assistant at the Ambunti hospital, while 'a previous informant . . . was dismissed after one morning's work as unsatisfactory'. Despite the statement that both consultants were from Malu, the wordlist contains a number of Yuanab features, which may be due to dialect mixing. His claim that there are no dialectal differences between Avatip, Malu, and Yuanab [Yambon] is incorrect (see §22.6). The language is said to have three vowels, *a*, ə, and ʌ. In his 1991 paper, Laycock postulated the existence of a long vowel *a:* for all the Ndu languages, including Manambu.

Harrison (1990a) and (1993) contain a wealth of lexical items, phrases, and sentences in Manambu, in addition to incisive observations about such aspects of Manambu semantics as the concept of *mawul* 'insides; location of emotions' and *kayik* 'image, shadow' (§21.4).

---

[18] I am grateful to René van den Berg for providing me with these dates.

1.8 BASIS FOR THIS STUDY

This reference grammar is based on a corpus of over 1,500 pages of transcribed texts, notes, and conversations, from over fifty speakers, male and female, including three children (during the period between 1995 and 2004). About 95 per cent of the materials come from the speakers in Avatip, and the rest are from Malu and Yawabak. All the texts were transcribed and translated with the assistance of linguistic consultants.

Texts include traditional tales (genre termed *gabu-ma:j*), traditional stories about historical events which are passed on from one generation to another (*wa-saki-ma:j* and *blajaya-ma:j*), life stories, and stories about recent happenings and developments, and various songs (mourning songs *gra-kudi*, and laments about foiled marriages *namay* and *sui*). Three sample texts have been included at the end of the grammar. Other stories will be available as a web-accessible resource in the near future.

The materials were collected during field sessions, and then transcribed and translated. Elicitation was used very sparingly, and as much as possible was through Manambu. It was employed to complete paradigms, and check hypotheses. Speakers were presented with a putative sentence, or a description of a situation in Manambu, rather than asking them to translate a sentence from Tok Pisin or English. Participant observation played a considerable role in discovering the ways in which the language is used. The Manambu— especially the women—are patient and dedicated teachers, always eager to offer corrections and new ways of saying things, providing additional invaluable linguistic information. The linguistic insights of such natural linguistic analysts as Jacklyn Yuamali Benji Ala, Pauline Agnes Yuaneng Luma Laki, Jennie Kudapa:kw, Patricia Yuawalup, Katie Teketay, David Takendu, and James Katalu Balangawi helped us unfold the beauty and intricacy of the Manambu language. Throughout this book, I make occasional observations on how Manambu relates to other Ndu languages (based on the few published sources, and the unpublished documents made available to me through the generosity of the SIL at Ukarumpa).

APPENDIX 1.1. EARLY DOCUMENTATION OF MANAMBU

This Appendix features two early wordlists of Manambu. Wordlists of Augustafluss language(s) compiled by Zöller (1891: 444–529; item 18) are reproduced in Table A1.1. Manambu words are in bold; words identified as Iatmul words are in italics; * marks words identifiable as Kwoma, and words identifiable as Chenapian are underlined. Words both in bold and in italics are the ones shared by Manambu and Iatmul. The third column contains corresponding words in recent sources on Manambu, Iatmul, Kwoma, and Chenapian. Words which are not in bold or italic, are not underlined, and have no asterisk come from an unidentified source.

Chenapian data are from Laycock and Z'graggen (1975: 744); Iatmul data are from Gerd Jendraschek (p.c).

Table A1.2 contains a sample wordlist of Malu (Mălu) collected by A. Roesicke (1914: 509). The remainder of the vocabularies collected by Roesicke (whose existence was mentioned by Roesicke 1914: 508) have not been located and are believed to have been lost.

TABLE A1.1 'Sepik language', or 'Augustafluss': from the wordlist of 29 languages from the area of German New Guinea Company and 16 languages from British New Guinea

GERMAN (WITH ENGLISH TRANSLATION)	AUGUSTAFLUSS (SEPIK RIVER) 'LANGUAGE'	COMMENTS
2. 'Acht (Zahl)', 'eight (number)'	Tschelagowuk; Uondenommu	*Nommu* appears to be a Chenapian form (see 43 below)
3. Ahnenbild/ancestral image	Gaudiguam	
4. Alles, Alle/everything, all	Ambo*	Kwoma *abo*; cf. Manambu *aba:b*
7. Arm/arm	Andip, Nasgob	
8. Armband/armband, bracelet	Au, Nasgub	
9. Asche/ashes	Queihiph*	Kwoma *keyihapa now* 'ash'
10. Auge/eye	Nou; *Minni*; **Melle**; Jinna	cf. Manambu *məl*; the form **melle** could be either Kwoma (*miyi*) or Manambu (see §22.3); Iatmul *mini* 'eye'
11. Axt (Beil)/adze (hatchet)	Gabugabi; Gu; **Kurla**	cf. Manambu *kul* 'adze, axe'
13. Banane/banana	**Lab**; *Labu*	cf. Manambu *lap*; Iatmul *lavu*
14. Bart/beard	Jegu	
17. Baum/tree	**Mondób**	similar to Manambu *man-ta:b* 'legs-arms'
18. Bein (Schenkel)/leg(thigh)	Zoo	
20. Betelnuss/betelnut	Mena	
21. Bett (Lager)/bed (camp)	Magen	
24. Blatt/leaf	**Njink**	Manambu *ñəg* 'leaf'
30. Bogen/bow	**Am**	Manambu *am* 'bow'
32. Brotfrucht/breadfruit	**Kaam**	Manambu *ka:m*
34. Brust/breast	*Munja*; Mu; **Mui**	Manambu *məñi*; Iatmul *muña*
35. Calebasse (Flasche)/gourd (flask)	Jaab; *Jabo**; Jabi	cf. Kwoma *wapa, wiyopu* 'gourd'?
36. Canoe (Boot, Schiff)/canoe (boat, ship)	**Wal**: Siau	Manambu *val*
40. Donner/thunder	**Tombo; Tombe**	Manambu *təb* 'sky' (also used to refer to thunder)
43. Drei/three	Kobuck; <u>Nommu</u>; **Mongul**	Manambu *mugul*; Iatmul *kupuk*; Chenapian *nəmu* 'three' (Class IV)
44. Du/you (sg)	**Men**	Manambu *mən*; Iatmul *min* 'you masculine'
46. Ei/egg	Kokóbira apadschu	

No.	Gloss	Forms	Notes
48.	Eins (Zahlwort)/one (numeral)	<u>Uarra</u>; **Nak**; *Ketta*	Manambu *nak* 'one'; Iatmul *kìta* 'one'; Chenapian *kwara* 'one (class II)', *gwara* 'one (class V)'
53.	Erde (Staub, Schmutz)/ground (dust, dirt)	**Kob**	cf. Manambu *kəp* 'ground, earth'
54.	Essen/eat	**Djangui; Bei**	cf. Manambu *jaguy* 'yam soup'; *bəy* 'be tasty'
56.	Felderschmuck (auf dem Kopfe)/feather ornament (on the head)	Tubbu; Ju jui	
60.	Feuer/fire	Üm; Njir; Ji nje; **Njie**	cf. Manambu *yi*
62.	Finger/finger	Nassimbi; Anna	
63.	Fisch/fish	Jara; **Bao; *Kami***	Manambu *kami*: 'fish'; Iatmul *kami* 'fish'; Manambu *bau* 'scaly mudgroper'
64.	Fischnetz/fishnet	Jea	
65.	Fischspeer/fish spear	Minja	Manambu *mij* 'forkspear'
71.	Frau/woman	*Taua*	cf. Iatmul *takwa*
74.	Frucht/fruit	Papatap	
75.	Fünf/five	Uondo; **Taambem**	Manambu *taba:b* 'five'
76.	Fuss/foot	Zoejahoa: Agebei	
81.	Gelb/yellow	**Laggi galaggi**	Manambu *laki-ka-laki* 'green, yellowish'
84.	Geschenk/gift	Köbe	
89.	Gibt's nicht (Verneinung)/there is none (negation)	Nu	
92.	Grille/cricket	**Laudai**	cf. Manambu *laday* 'cricket'
93.	Gross/big	Tschimbi	
98.	Halsband/neck-band	Krisch	
99.	Hand/hand	Annier	
102.	Haus/house	Ui; Ja	Manambu *wi* 'house'
104.	Heute/today	**Pavir**	Manambu *papər* 'a little later'
109.	Hobeleisen (beliebter Tauschartikel)/plane-iron (favourite object of exchange)	Be tatabaran	
110.	Holz/wood	Au	
111.	Hören/hear	<u>Namuwinekem</u>	this is likely to be a Chenapian word with 2nd person masc. prefix *na(n)*-
112.	Huhn/rooster	**Tabuk**	Manambu *tapwuk* 'rooster'

(cont.)

TABLE A1.1 *Continued*

German (with English translation)	Augustafluss (Sepik River) 'language'	Comments
113. Hund/dog	*Uarra*; *Asche	Iatmul *wara*; cf. Kwoma *as(a)*
119. Ich/I	*<u>Nun</u>	cf. Kwoma *no* 'we'; Chenapian *an* 'I'
124. Kakadu/cockatoo	Ueigan; Meem	
131. Kind/child	**Jane**; Jemab	cf. Manambu *ñan*
133. Klein/small	Pao	
134. Knie/knee	Zoewú; Zobar	
136. Kokospalme/coconut palm	**Toppan**	cf. Manambu *təp*; Iatmul *təpma* 'coconut'
137. Kokosnuss/coconut	*Tõbma*; **Toppan**	cf. Manambu *təp*; Iatmul *təpma* 'coconut'
140. Kopfhaar/head hair	Tauen abon; **Kau**	cf. Manambu *ka:u* 'sharpness, strength'
144. Lachen/laugh	Benaui; Banazakken	
151. Löffel/spoon	Uare	cf. Manambu *wuti* ?
152. Mädchen/girl	*Taua*	Iatmul *takwa* 'woman'
159. Messer/knife	**Arreb**; Jakass	Manambu *arəp* 'bush knife'
161. Mond/moon	Uamo; Moábo	
163. Morgen (Gegensatz zu heute)/tomorrow (in opposition to today)	**Tschir**	Manambu *sər*, pronounced by older people as *šir*
165. Mund/mouth	Samoa; Jei; **Undi**	cf. Manambu *kundi* 'mouth'
166. Muschel/shell	Udi; Kritsch	
171. Nase/nose	Ussun	
172. Naßhornvogel/hornbill	Mon ama = du heisst/you are called	
173. Nein/no	Uondeharrüs; **Ambali**	cf. Manambu *aba:li* 'nine'. The Manambu word for 'nine' (German *neun*) may have been mistaken for 'no' (German *nein*)
178. Ohr/ear	Uen; **Uan**; Uabo	Manambu *wa:n* 'ear'
179. Ohrring/earring	Gaal; Gallaan	
180. Osten/east	Tschaar	
184. Penis/penis	Mab; Moa; Tschik	
185. Perlen/beads	Wakap; Ambo; **Geiteck**	Manambu *gaytək*
186. Pfeife (Flöte)/pipe (flute)	Djabir; Jambkor; **Tegemi**; Dangur	Manambu *təkəmi* 'tree seeds'

187.	Pfeil/arrow	**Nübbi**	Manambu *nəbi* 'arrow'
189.	Plantage/plantation	Amnú	
193.	Regen/rain	Mabbessi	
194.	Rock (der Frauen)/skirt (for women)	Quar	
195.	Rot/red	Bab; **Nüggi-nüggi**; Dschui	Manambu *ñiki-ñiki* 'red'
197.	Ruder (Paddel)/rudder (oar)	Jei; Ungor	
198.	Sack/bag	**Kojambi**; **Uar**; **Quajembi**	Manambu *kwasabi* 'stringbag'; *wa:r* 'large stringbag'
199.	Sago/sago	*Naa*; *Naau*; Szaga	Manambu *na:gw*; Iatmul *nau*
205.	Schlafen/sleep	Bassanei	
208.	Schlecht/bad	Kuitoga	
211.	Schwarz/black	**Glarangil**	Manambu *gla-ka-gəl* 'black'
213.	Schwein/pig	**Mbal**; Hu	Manambu *ba:l* 'pig'
217.	Sechs/six	Tschergagelag; Uonarra; **Ambun**	Manambu *abun* 'six'
219.	Sehen/see	**Wau**	Manambu *vau* 'may I see'
221.	Setz dich her!/sit down here!	**Arrembana** = sich setzen (sit down)	Manambu *a rə-bana* (then sit-1plSUBJ.VT+3fem.sgBAS.VT) 'Then we sit'
223.	Sieben/seven	Uondenüs; **Ambiti**; Tschelaweli	Manambu *abəti* 'seven'
227.	Sonne/sun	Jaban; **Njie**; **Niö**; Njir; Uang	Manambu *ñe*; Iatmul *nya* 'sun'
229.	Speer/spear	Djambaang-neidi	
234.	Sterne/star	Uiam; Tungüi	
240.	Tabak/tobacco	**Gagi kiger** = rauchen (smoke); Goram	Manambu *yaki kə-kər* 'I want to smoke'
243.	Tanzen/dance	**Baang** = Tanz	Manabu *ba:gw* 'dance, ceremony'
244.	Taro/taro	Nük; **Maei**; Nomsei	Manambu *ma:y* 'taro'
245.	Taube/pigeon	Kewam	
248.	Tochter/daughter	**Dege niana**	Manambu *də-kə ñan-a* (he-OBL+fem.sg child-3fem.sgNOM) 'it is his daughter'
251.	Topf/pot	Nauara	
253.	Trinken/drink	**Djangui**	Manambu *jaguy* 'yam soup'
254.	Trommel/drum	**Rambu**	Manambu *ra:b*; Iatmul *rabu* 'slit drum'
255.	Tuch (Zeug)/fabric (material)	Bokop; Obo: **Zewatambi**	Manambu *səp-a-tabi* (skin-LK-clothes) 'clothes' (*p* realized as *v*, *s* as *ts*)
256.	Vagina/vagina	Hui; Szie	
261.	Vier/four	*Einak*; **Ali**; <u>Hauus</u>	Manambu *a:li*, Iatmul *aynak*; Chenapian *howis* 'four (Class II)'

(cont.)

TABLE A1.1 *Continued*

GERMAN (WITH ENGLISH TRANSLATION)	AUGUSTAFLUSS (SEPIK RIVER) 'LANGUAGE'	COMMENTS
262. Vogel/bird	**Uabbi**	Manambu *wapi*
265. Wade/calf of the leg	Aglip, Zobar	
269. Wasser/water	Jo; *Gu*; Ob	Manambu *gu*; Iatmul *gu* 'water'
270. Weg/way	**Jamb**; Nangur	Manambu *ya:b* 'road'
272. Weinen/cry	Ssintoei; Bedjiei	
273. Weiss/white	Adampäg; **Wamjauam**; Maimboan	cf. Manambu *wamakawam*
288. Wurzel/root	**Mench**	Manambu *mæj* 'root'
289. Yams/yams	Ye; Babeigi	
290. Zähne/teeth	Deu; Uok; Big; *Nimbi*	Manambu *wuk* 'tooth'; Iatmul *nəbi* 'tooth'
292. Zehn/ten	Uondo; *Tambebelli;* **Tambetti**	Manambu *tabəti;* Iatmul *tabavli* 'ten'
295. Zuckerohr/sugar cane	Jo; **Meingui**	Manambu *mayñgwi* 'sugar cane'
296. Zunge/tongue	Taueng; *Tegát*	Iatmul *tɨgat* 'tongue'
299. Zwei/two	Bussi; **Vetti**; *Virla*	Manambu *viti,* Iatmul *viʜɨʜɨk* 'two'; Chenapian *bisi* 'two' (Class III)

TABLE A1.2 Extract from the Mắlu wordlist (given by Roesicke 1914)

GERMAN/ENGLISH	MÁLU	MODERN MANAMBU	Comments
Fliegender Hund/flying fox	kumbuí	kəbwi	
Vogel/bird	uắbi	wapi	
Kasuar/cassowary	mĕntĕ	məd	Final vowel lost in Modern Manambu has been recorded by Roesicke
Mann/man	t	du	The absence of final vowel in Roesicke's notation is unexplained
Frau/woman	tắgō	ta:kw	Final vowel lost in Modern
Haar/hair	nămpe	nab	Manambu has been recorded by Roesicke
Nase/nose	tăắm	ta:m	
Speer/spear	vâi	væy	
Beil/adze	kŭol	kul	No such form attested
Schlitztrommel/slit drum	rámbu	rab	Final vowel lost in Modern
Tantrommel/drum to dance with	kángo	ka:gw	Manambu has been recorded by Roesicke
Bejahung/affirmation	ắi	ayey	Slightly different
Verneinung/negation	măắm	ma:n	Slightly different
Stehlen/steal	lugŭ	luku (kur)	*luku* is part of a complex predicate which can be used on its own as a result of ellipsis
Pflanzen/plant	kándi	ka-di	'they plant'

2

Phonology

Manambu is more complex in its phonology than most other Ndu languages. It has a large inventory of phonemes (twenty-one consonants and nine vowels), contrastive stress, and an array of phonological processes.[1] Most loans are assimilated to the Manambu phonology. Morphophonological processes relevant for nouns are discussed in §4.1.1, and those relevant for verbs in §11.3. Examples throughout the grammar are given in their phonological representation. The phonological sequences *yə* and *wə* are rendered as *yi* and *wu*, to reflect their most frequent surface realization.

2.1 SEGMENTAL PHONOLOGY

Consonants and their realizations are discussed in §2.1.1. We discuss the vowel system in §2.1.2. In §2.1.3 we discuss unusual phonetic segments restricted to interjections and baby talk.

2.1.1 Consonants

The Manambu consonant phonemes are listed in Table 2.1. IPA symbols are given in brackets, if different from those adopted here. The labialized stops are written with a superscript ᵂ in this chapter, but simply as pw, bw, kw, and gw in the grammar chapters that follow.

A. STOPS

All stops in the three sets—bilabial, apico-dental, and dorso-velar—have voicing distinctions. Labial and dorso-velar stops can be either simple or labialized.

The following examples illustrate their occurrence in various positions in different morpheme types (see F below, on Phonotactic restrictions):

> *p*: *pa:t* 'young person', -*pə́k* 'comparative', *kəpəyáy* 'traditional greeting', *Sablápp* 'name of a clan', -*yakə́p* 'non-durative frustrative';
>
> *pʷ*: *pʷipʷi* 'pig's bladder', *jupʷi* 'buttocks', *má:pʷ* 'yellowish possum';
>
> *b*: *bas* 'first', -*baná* 'first person plural subject', *kʷasabí* 'stringbag', *ya:b* 'road', *ta:b* 'hand', -*abá:b* 'together, too', -*b* 'terminative case';
>
> *bʷ*: *bʷi* 'hot to the point of boiling', *kəbʷi* 'flying fox', *wusabʷi* 'water (in childbirth)';
>
> *t*: *təná* 'she has', -*ta* 'first person dual subject series', *kʷatiyáu* 'may I give (to you)', *væt* 'heavy';
>
> *d*: *da:n* 'go down', -*daná* 'third person plural subject series', *adá* 'sit down!', *sa:d* 'fashion; way', -*d* 'third person singular masculine basic series';

---

[1] A statement of Manambu phonemes by Allen and Hurd (1972) is based on the Yuanab variety. Differences between their analysis and mine are addressed when necessary.

TABLE 2.1 Consonant phonemes in Manambu

	bilabial	labiodental	apico-dental	apico-alveolar	postalveolar	lamino-palatal	dorso-velar	glottal
Voiceless non-labialized stops	*p*		*t*				*k*	
Voiceless labialized stops	*pʷ*						*kʷ*	
Voiced non-labialized stops	*b*		*d*				*g*	
Voiced labialized stops	*bʷ*						*gʷ*	
Voiced fricative		*v*						
Voiceless fricatives				*s*				*h*
Voiced affricate					*j (dʒ)*			
Lateral Trilled rhotic			*l* *r*					
Nasals	*m*		*n*			*ñ (ɲ)*		
Glides	*w*					*y (j)*		

k: *kamí:* 'fish', *-ku* 'same-subject switch-reference marker', *taká-* 'put down', *-adəka* 'only', *væk* 'pot', *-nak* 'first person imperative';

kʷ: *kʷasá* 'small', *-kʷa* 'third person singular feminine imperative', *sakʷár sakʷár* 'happy, proud', *takʷ* 'market';

g: *ga:n* 'night', *war-gáy* 'in case he/she/they go up', *lagú-* 'pull', *Yuanəg* 'female name', *-mæg* (derivational formative in female personal names, e.g. *Payan-mǽg*);

gʷ: *gʷalugʷ* 'clan', *gʷa:l* 'paternal grandfather; ancestor; grandchild', *ba:gʷ* 'music, performance', *-Vgʷ* 'plural for kinship and a few other nouns'.

Each labialized stop constitutes one unit, both acoustically and in terms of their production (so, *kʷ* cannot be interrupted with a ə, unlike a heterosyllabic consonant sequence *k-w*). Each counts as one onset consonant in terms of syllable weight (§2.4.2).

B. Allophonic Variation in Voiceless Stops

All stops have allophonic variations word-finally and in the intervocalic position. Word-finally, *p* and *pʷ* are pronounced as unreleased, as in [kəp˺] 'just, on one's own', unless the final syllable is long; in *pa:p* 'wound' *p* has a normal release. Word-final unreleased stops are an additional criterion for a phonological word boundary (see §2.5).

Intervocalically, *p* is pronounced as a bilabial fricative ɸ (which, for some speakers, alternates with a very slightly voiced β), e.g. *ap* 'bone', [aˈβar] 'to a bone' (cf. the place name [Aβaˈtəp˺] 'main village, village of bone' (*ap* 'bone, main', *-a-* 'linker', *təp* 'village'); *sop* 'soap' (a loan word from Tok Pisin), [soˈβar] 'with soap, to soap'; *pasi-tuá* (tie, fasten-1sgSUBJ+3fem.sgBAS.P) 'I tied it up', [a-ˈβas] (IMPV-fasten) 'tie!' (a loan from Tok Pisin *pas-im* 'fasten, tie'). This allophone does not occur if the word contains another labial consonant, e.g. *ap-a-ka-áp* (bone-LK-AUG-bone) 'bony, thin', *apawúl* 'type of evil spirit'. In the coda of a non-final CVC syllable, *p* undergoes very light fricativization in rapid speech, e.g. [kuprap˺] 'bad' may be pronounced as [kuɸrap˺].

Voiceless stops *k* and *p* undergo weakening (or lenition) in an intervocalic position. Then, *k* is realized as a slightly voiced very short *g*, e.g. *aká* 'here' is pronounced as [aˈgːa], *də-kó-k* (3masc.sg-POSS-DAT) 'to him' as [ⁿdə-ˈgːə-k], and *kusədák atà* as [kusidˈagːata] 'they having finished then'. In rapid speech, *k* can disappear altogether before *u* in a syllable without primary stress, if the preceding and at least one following syllable also contain *k*: *krakù-taká-* (bring and put down) may be pronounced as [krau-taˈka] (see §2.6, for the loss of *k*).

The apico-dental *t* in intervocalic position is pronounced as a quick tap in normal to rapid register, e.g. *kətók* 'like' is pronounced as [kərók]. In slow speech register, it is realized as a stop.

In non-word-initial intervocalic position the labialized dorso-velar *kʷ* may display pre- and post-labialization: [ˈta:kʷ] 'woman' may be pronounced as [ˈta:ʷkʷ]. (This is not the case in a word-initial position, and after a CVC syllable, e.g. [kʷaˈsa] 'little' and [kajˈkʷap] 'lazy'.) In rapid speech, if a word contains two labialized dorso-velars, the second one may be pronounced as a simple stop, e.g. [Səkʷiˈsakw, Səkʷiˈsak] 'male name'. Before the vowel *i*, the labialized bilabial stop occasionally appears in free variation with a sequence of a non-labialized stop and vowel *u*, as in [pʷiˈpʷi, puipˈui] 'pig's bladder'.

C. Affricate and Fricatives

The voiced postalveolar affricate *j* (IPA *dȝ*) and the voiceless apico-alveolar fricative *s* are illustrated below:

j: *jau!* 'let it be; don't worry', -*jə́bər* 'always', *glajəpís* 'little black ants', *ma:j* 'story';

s: *samasá:m* 'a lot', -*sap* 'transportative case', *asəkí* 'bad cold', *sa:d* 'manner', *ma:s* 'betel-nut'.

With older speakers (over 60), the fricative *s* has a palatal allophone [ʂ] in the word-initial position followed by *i*, as in [ʂir] 'tomorrow' and [ʂi] 'name; who?' Younger speakers pronounce these words as [sər] and [sə].[2]

Two further fricatives have a restricted distribution. The voiced labiodental fricative *v* is found only in the word- and root-initial position, as in *val* 'canoe', *væs* 'grass', *yakə̀-væki-n* (throw-go.across-SEQ) 'throwing across' (a verb compound: see §15.2). In all other positions, it has the same allophones as *p*, e.g. *və-* 'see', *ap!* (IMPV+see) (pronounced as ['apˀ]) 'see!', *vya-* 'hit', *avi!* [a'βi] 'hit!', *ayvul* ['ajβul] 'hot water'. Native speakers identify *p* and *v* as different phonemes despite the fact that their allophones coincide in pronunciation. The two are distinguished in a very slow register: 5-year-old Kerryanne repeated ['ajβul] 'hot water' very slowly for me as ['ajvul].

The glottal fricative is restricted to the word-initial position in pronominal clitics and a few cliticizable words. It optionally occurs before the vowel *a*, and usually disappears in normal and rapid speech, e.g. *(h)aká* 'here it is', *(h)al* 'it (feminine) is here'. Since *h* before *a* is not automatic (cf. *adá* 'sit down!', not **hada*; *akí* 'news', not **haki*) it should be considered a separate—albeit marginal—phoneme.[3]

D. PRENASALIZATION OF VOICED STOPS AND AFFRICATE

All the voiced stops and the voiced affricate *j* share one feature: they are prenasalized in the word-initial, intervocalic, and word-final position; that is, *bal* 'pig' is pronounced as [ᵐbal], *ya:b* 'road' as [ya:ᵐb], *ab* 'head' as [aᵐb], *abawapʷi* 'headdress, hat' as [aᵐbawa'pʷi], *Juli* 'Julie' as [ⁿ̃dʒ'uli] and so on. Word-initially, the voiced affricate *j* is not prenasalized if the next syllable contains a nasal or another prenasalized stop, e.g. *jágər* 'garfish' is pronounced as ['dʒaᵑgər] and not as **['ⁿdʒaᵑgər].[4]

The velar stop *g* is not prenasalized word-initially if either the coda or the next syllable contain a nasal consonant. That is, *ga:m* 'song, shout' is pronounced as [ga:m] and not as **[ᵑga:m], and *ga:n* 'night' is pronounced as [ga:n] rather than **[ᵑga:n]. The initial *g* is prenasalized very little if there is a nasal consonant in the next but one syllable within one phonological word, e.g. [ᵑgaᵐb-ə-'ma:dʒ] (old-LK-story) 'story' and [⁽ᵑ⁾gaⁿdʒi-n] 'rubbing'. If a nasal consonant is further away from the first syllable containing *g*, it does not affect the degree of its prenasalization, e.g. [ᵑgaⁿdʒi-ᵐba'na] 'we rub (something)'. In a word-medial and word-final position, *g* is always prenasalized, e.g. [ku'ᵑgaᵐb] 'owl', [War'ᵑgaᵐb] 'a Manambu clan', [waraᵑga'ⁿdu] 'ancestor'. The presence of another prenasalized stop in a word does not affect the prenasalization of the word-initial *g* in [ᵑgaⁿdʒi-'tua] 'I rub (something)', [ᵑga:ⁿdʒ] 'small pelican-like white bird', and [ᵑga'ᵐbi] 'creeper plant similar to vanilla'. This shows that prenasalized stops are not underlyingly nasal.[5]

---

[2] Allen and Hurd (1972: 40) pointed out the existence of a voiceless fronted alveolar affricate [ts] as an allophone of *s* word-initially. This allophone, marginally present in the Yuanab variety, is not found in the Avatip variety.

[3] Allen and Hurd (1972) did not include this phoneme in their statement.

[4] Allen and Hurd (1972: 40) report that in the Yuanab variety, *j* is pronounced as a voiceless prenasalized unaspirated alveopalatal affricate [ⁿtʃ] word-medially, and as a voiceless aspirated alveopalatal affricate [tʃʰ] word-finally. I have not observed this allophonic variation.

[5] There is no prenasalization of voiced stops in a handful of loans from English, e.g. ['mabəl] from *marble*. This, and the phoneme *o* as in *pato* 'duck', are the few features of loan phonology in Manambu.

E. Nasals, Lateral and Vibrant

Three nasal phonemes—the bilabial nasal *m*, the apico-alveolar *n*, and its palatal counterpart *ñ*[6]—are found in:

> *m*: *ma:m* 'elder sibling', *-məná* 'second person singular masculine subject series', *ñáməs* 'younger sibling', *-Vm* 'locative/accusative case';
>
> *n*: *nasə-nás* 'counting', *nak* 'one', *-na-* 'tense marker', *Maná:b* 'autodenomination of the Manambu', *sa:n* 'money, shell valuable', *-n* 'sequencing suffix';
>
> *ñ*: *ñab* 'Sepik River', *ñan* 'child', *-ñəná* 'second person singular feminine subject series', *gə́ñər* 'later', *ka:ñ* 'bamboo flute'.

The apico-alveolar lateral *l* and vibrant *r* do not have any significant allophonic variants. Examples are:

> *l*: *la:n* 'husband', *-lək* 'because of', *baláy* 'tail (e.g. of a crocodile)', *ya:l* 'womb, belly', *-l* 'third person singular feminine basic cross-referencing',
>
> *r*: *rəná* 'she sits', *-rəb* 'fully; right away', *Ñáura* 'Iatmul', *sar* 'fowl', *-Vr* 'allative case'.

The Yuanab variety of Manambu differs from other varieties in that it has just one liquid phoneme (*r* and *l* are not distinguished: the phonetically predominant variant is *r*, but *l* is also heard), so, for instance, *Ñaura* 'Iatmul' is pronounced as either *Ñaura* or *Ñaula*.[7]

Bilabial glide *w* and palatal *y* occur in any position (the status of diphthongs and of vowel sequences is discussed in §2.2).

> *w*: *wa-* 'speak', *-wən* 'first person singular feminine basic cross-referencing', *æywán* 'some, a few', *kaw* 'hole';
>
> *y*: *ya:b* 'road', *yarákara* 'OK', *-yakə́p* 'non-durative frustrative', *karyà-kə-tuá* 'I will bring', *-ga:y* 'if'.

F. Phonotactic Restrictions on the Occurrence of Consonants

The bilabial labialized stops p^w and b^w can only occur word-finally and if followed by *i*. The phonological status of syllables p^wə and b^wə is problematic. If a p^w or a b^w is followed by ə, the resulting sequence may be pronounced as p^wə or as *pu*, or as b^wə or *bu*. That is, a word like $b^w uyab^w i$ can be phonologically represented as either $b^w əyab^w i$ or as *buyab^{w}i*. Two voiced labialized velar consonants cannot occur in adjacent syllables (cf. §6.1).

Consonantal phonemes display certain restrictions on their occurrence in various morpheme types. The phonemes b^w, p^w, *v*, and *h* do not occur in affixes. The phonemes *v* and *h* occur only in the root-initial position, and b^w does not occur at the end of roots. Historically, all labialized stops in Manambu are innovations.[8] The phoneme g^w occurs in just one suffix, *-(V)g^w* 'plural marker' which corresponds to Wosera *-(n)gu* and Abelam *-gu* (Wilson 1980: 46). In this Manambu morpheme, g^w comes from a sequence of *g* and a shortened *u*. The phoneme

---

[6] Allen and Hurd (1972: 41) postulate an additional phoneme, bilabial labialized voiced nasal m^w; this phoneme also appears in Farnsworth (n.d.). This does not occur in our data, in any variety of Manambu (e.g. *ma:r* 'wind'; Farnsworth n.d. $m^w ar$; *ma:n* 'bird of paradise' Farnsworth n.d. $m^w aan$). This could have been an allophone of *m* before a long vowel in the language as it was spoken in the 1960s. Laycock (1965: 120–1), in his statement of Manambu phonemes, does not include any labialized consonants.

[7] Only occasionally do speakers of the Avatip variety replace *l* with *r* and vice versa (e.g. *nawurəm* rather than *nawuləm* 'in a line; lining up').

[8] These phonemes are absent from other Ndu languages, e.g. Iatmul (Staalsen 1966; Jendraschek forthcoming) and Wosera-Abelam (Wilson 1980; Wendel 1993).

TABLE 2.2   Vowel phonemes in Manambu

	SHORT VOWELS			LONG VOWELS		
	front	central	back	front	central	back
high	i		u	iː		uː
middle		ə				
low	æ	a		æː		aː

k^w occurs in a few suffixes, including the habitual -k^wa- (this may go back to a grammaticalized verbal root: §12.3) and third person imperative -k^wa(-) (§13.2.1).

2.1.2   Vowels

The phonological system of Manambu vowels is given in Table 2.2. It is unusually large for a language of the Ndu family some of whose representatives have been tentatively described as having a 'vertical' vowel system with no phonological distinction between front and back vowels. Gala is the only other Ndu language with a vowel system of comparable complexity.[9]

An interesting feature of the system is that the long low vowel is back, while its short counterpart is phonologically central.

A. SHORT VOWELS are exemplified below:

i—*wi* 'house', *yawí* 'work', *di* 'shit', *yi* 'fire', -*di* 'third person plural';

u—*du* 'man', *mu* 'crocodile', *yu* 'greensnail shell', *kurən* 'doing', *kalún* 'having put on shoulder', *sui* 'laments', -*ku* 'same-subject completive switch-reference marker';

ə—*səp* 'skin', *gə́ñər* 'later', *nəkə́r* 'cool', -*yakə́p* 'non-durative frustrative', *sə* 'name', *ñə* 'sun';

æ—*amə́y* 'mother', *væs* 'grass', *vyæjə́n* 'putting in line', *bæy* 'mat; feast', *væk* 'clay pot', *yæj* 'frying pan', *vægán* 'putting inside (bag or basket)', *æm* 'share', *yæy* 'appendix', *mæy* 'come', -*yæy* 'instead of' (substitutive case);

a—-*adəka* 'only', *watáːy* 'having said', *akráy* 'bring!', *akwatáy* 'give (to non-third person)!', *am* 'measure', *rəná* 'she sits'.

[9] Other languages of the Sepik area vary in the size of their vowel inventories. Laycock (1965: 120) described the Yuanab variety of Manambu as having three vowels *a*, *ə*, and *ʌ*. (Later, he amended this system, introducing vowel length as a phonologically distinctive feature, without going into detail: Laycock 1991.) In their analysis of the same variety, Allen and Hurd (1972) distinguished three vowels (albeit somewhat different from Laycock 1965): high vowel *i* (with front [i], central [ɨ], and back [u] allophones); mid-vowel *a* with allophones [e], [ə] and [o]; and *aa*, which they described as a 'complex nucleus of low vocoids separated by glottal stop'. Such a system would be typologically highly unusual since it lacks a phonological distinction between front and back vowels. Front and back allophones of individual vowels are viewed as determined by adjacent consonants. A number of other Ndu languages have been analysed as having a similar 'vertical' vowel system, lacking a phonological distinction between front and back vowels (see the analysis of Iatmul by Staalsen 1966: 69; Foley 1986, and Aikhenvald forthcoming b). A radically different analysis of Iatmul is in Jendraschek (forthcoming). The vowel system in Table 2.2 does not, however, appear to be restricted just to the Avatip and Malu dialects of Manambu. Our data show that the modern Yuanab variety has a system much more similar to that of Avatip and Malu than to Iatmul (as analysed by Staalsen). This casts doubt on the reality of a 'vertical' vowel system in Manambu. Farnsworth and Farnsworth (1966) use a five-vowel orthographic system for the Yuanab variety of Manambu, distinguishing *a*, *e*, *i*, *i*, *u*.

The contrast between *æ* and *a* is illustrated by the following pairs: *ayakətáy*! 'throw and go!' versus *ayakətǽy* 'throw and come!'; *anáy* 'play' versus *nǽynadí* 'they play'. The phonemes *ə* and *æ* contrast in *aməy* 'basket of a fish-trap type'—*amǽy* 'mother', and *Yabunməlí* 'woman's name'—*Yabunmælí* 'man's name'. The phonemes *ə* and *a* contrast in *nəb* 'stranger, enemy' versus *nab* 'head hair'; the phonemes *æ* and *a* contrast in *æm* 'share' and *am* 'measure'. That schwa is a fully-fledged phoneme (rather than an epenthetic element) is clear from the fact that it can take stress, just like any other vowel. (The instances where an epenthetic schwa is required are discussed in §2.2.1) The long *a:* and *æ* contrast in *mæy* 'come' versus *ma:y* 'go'.

The vowel *e* occurs in Tok Pisin loans and code-switches, e.g. *les* 'lazy', *save* 'know'.

B. Long Vowels

A phonological distinction between short and long vowels is not totally unexpected in a Ndu language. Laycock (1991) argued that for Abelam the difference between central *ə* and *a* is better described as difference in length; Wendel (1993: 38) also analysed the difference between *ə* and *a* in Hanga Kundi in terms of vowel quantity, and not vowel quality. However, three pairs of short and long vowels (one of which involves a fronted vowel) have not been documented for any other language of the family.

Examples of long vowels are:

æ:—*mæ:j* 'rope', *yæ:p* 'cane', *yæ:y* 'paternal grandmother';
a:—*ta:kw* 'woman', *wa:ñ* 'be alive', *agá:j*! 'rub!', *ma:s* 'betelnut', *ya:pʷ* 'breath', *ya:l* 'belly, womb', *-ma:r-* 'subordinate negator', *-ta:y* 'cotemporaneous sequencing marker';
i:—*Vali:k* 'name of a clan', *yi:n* 'going'.

The long vowel *u:* occurs in a limited number of words, e.g. *wu:* 'ton fruit' and *su:* 'edible cane'. The length contrast between *a* and *a:* can be illustrated with: *sa:r* 'a fly'—*sar* 'fowl'; *ta:kw* 'woman'—*takw* 'calendar; market'; *na:gw* 'sago'—*nagw* 'tree trunk'; *na:k* 'for grandchildren'— *nak* 'one'; *ña:p* 'tusk'—*nap* 'strap'; *wa:r* 'type of stringbag, bilum'—*war-* 'go up'; *wa:m* 'white cockatoo'—*wam* 'shell'; *ba:p* 'line (of people)'—*bap* 'moon'.

The phonemes *æ* and *æ:* contrast in *yæy* 'appendix' versus *yæ:y* 'paternal grandmother'. The phonemes *a:* and *æ:* contrast in *ma:j* 'story' versus *mæ:j* 'rope' (and *məj* 'fork spear'), *mæ:r* 'plate' and *ma:r* 'wind', and in *ya:pw* 'breath' and *yæ:p* 'cane'. Of all the long vowels, *a:* is the most frequent in terms of number of words it occurs in.

Older speakers of Manambu sometimes pronouce the long *a* as a sequence of two identical vowels *a* separated by a glottal stop, e.g. older speaker: *ma'a* ['ma?a], younger speaker *ma:* ['ma:] 'no'; older speaker *ka'añ*, younger speaker *ka:ñ* 'bamboo'; older speaker *ma'an*, younger speaker *ma:n* 'bird of paradise'. The same has been noted for just one instance of the long *æ:*—older speakers tend to say *mæ'ær*, while younger speakers say *mæ:r* 'plate'. The same older speaker can pronounce some words either way. This variation indicates that development of phonemic vowel length and loss of the intervocalic glottal stop could be a recent phenomenon in Manambu.[10] Long vowels occur only in stressed syllables; in unstressed syllables, they undergo reduction as a result of stress shifts (in approximately 15–20 per cent of roots) (§2.3.2). Long vowels other than *a:* do not occur in suffixes, or root-initially. Only *i:* and *u:* can occur root-finally.

---

[10] Alternatively, these can be considered rearticulated vowels. In their description of the Yuanab variety, Allen and Hurd (1972) consistently treated the long vowel *a:* as a sequence of identical vowels separated by a glottal stop.

C. ALLOPHONIC VARIATION

The low front [æ] is in free variation with [ɛ] and [e], as in *bæy*, *bɛy*, *bey* 'mat; feast'. If followed by a palatal glide *y*, it may alternate with back low vowel [a:], e.g. variants *amæy* and *ama:y* 'mother'; and *bæy*, *ba:y* 'mat; feast'. However, not every long *a:* followed by *y* alternates with *æ*: *awá:y* 'mother's brother' is never pronounced as *[aw'æy]. The vowel *a* is sometimes pronounced as [æ] following the palatal glide *y* in an unstressed syllable, e.g. *vyabadə́l* 'hit him is what we did' is sometimes heard as [vyæᵐbaⁿd'əl]. This is restricted to rapid speech by younger people.

The phoneme ə has the following additional allophones depending on whether it is preceded or followed by a glide.[11]

> /ə/ > [u] if preceded or followed by a labial consonant, e.g. *nakamúy*, *nakamə́y* 'one', *Manábə kudí*, *Manábu kudí* [ma'naᵐbə ku'ⁿdi, ma'naᵐbu ku'ⁿdi] 'Manambu language', *wəká*, *wuká* 'this here', *mə́ya*, *máya* 'really', *nəmá*, *numá* 'big', *ñámǝs*, *ñámus* 'younger sibling', *tǝkwaná*, *tukwaná* 'she stays';

or

if the adjacent syllable contains the vowel *u*, e.g. *tǝkú*, *tukú* 'having been', *rǝku*, *ruku* 'having sat'; an alternative pronunciation in this context is *rǝuku*, *tǝuku*.

/ə/ > *i* if preceded by *y* in an unstressed syllable: *yǝná*, *yiná* 'she goes/is'.

These processes apply within a phonological word (see §2.3.4, under II). Speakers vary as to how distinctively they pronounce ə as *u* or as *i* under these conditions: for instance, the same speaker pronounced a name once as *Tabamǝy* and then as *Tabamuy*. If the vowel ə is stressed, the vocalic realization *u* is more frequent, e.g. [ab'un] (rather than [ab'ən]) 'six', [wun] 'I' (rather that wə́n), but [abǝtí] 'seven' (see §10.6).

The underlying allophones of ə can be distinguished from *u* and *i* by the lack of variation: if *u* or *i* is an allophone of ə it will have variants with ə as shown below, while forms with phonemically distinctive *u* and *i* do not have such variants, e.g. *du* 'man', *di* 'shit'.

If the first syllable of a disyllabic word contains *u*, the vowel ə in the second syllable is also pronounced as *u*, especially in rapid register and if stressed, as in *mugúl*, *məgwə́l* [mu'ⁿgul, mə'ⁿgʷəl] 'three, few'. In a number of minimal pairs *u* and *əw*, and *i* and *əy*, do contrast, e.g. *mu* 'crocodile; the day after tomorrow', *məw* 'base of'; *mi* 'tree', *mír* 'upwards', *mə́yir* 'really'; *yi* 'fire', *ayə́i* 'yes'. The contrast between *i* and *æy* is corroborated by the pair *mi* 'tree' versus *mæy* 'come'; and between *i* and ə by *yi* 'fire' versus *(ma:) yə* '(not) go', *(ma:) ki* '(not) die' versus *(ma:) kə* '(not) eat'. Phonemes *i*, ə, and *æi* contrast in *yi* 'fire' versus *(ma:) yə* '(not) go' versus *(ma:) yæi* '(not) come'. (The latter two tend to be neutralized in the Malu variety.) Phonemes *i* and *u* contrast with other vowels, e.g. *kədí* 'these', *kadi* 'they paddle', and *kudí* 'language, mouth'. Optional rounding applies to unstressed *a* in normal register in the context of a labial nasal, e.g. [samas'a:m, sạmạs'a:m] 'many'.

Vowels *æ*, *æ:*, *i:*, and *u:* never occur in suffixes. The vowel ə never occupies a root-initial position. We will also see, in §2.3.2, that ə often occurs as a product of vowel reduction in an unstressed syllable. In addition, the vowel ə can be inserted automatically to break unauthorized consonant clusters (see §2.2.1).

---

[11] This allophonic variation of the central vowel ə is reminiscent of that in other Ndu languages, especially Iatmul and Hanga Kundi, and agrees with the analysis by Allen and Hurd (1972).

2.1.3   Unusual phonetic patterns

Unusual sounds and sound alternations have been attested in interjections and onomatopoeia, and in baby talk. INTERJECTIONS may contain a voiceless apico-alveolar affricate *tʃ*, as in *tʃa!* 'Hey (attention getter)', *tʃe!* 'a shout of disgust, or to avert danger: e.g. a baby trying to jump into the fireplace'. This alternates with the alveopalatal fricative *ʃ*, the fricative *s*, and the palatalized fricative *ṣ*, all in *tʃa, sa, ṣa, ʃa* 'Hey (attention getter)'. The interjection *sa!* 'Don't do it, stop!' does not display this allophony.

All these interjections are also unusual in that they are the only instances of independent phonological words with CV structure, as are the interjections *ma!* 'expression of disgust and surprise' (said in reaction to a cat's attempt to sleep in a mosquito net) and *wa!* 'surprise'. The latter has an alternant *way!* The interjection *wayéy, wayáy* meaning 'oh dear, oh God' contains the vowel *e* in free alternation with *a*—this alternation is not found anywhere outside interjections. The most unusual interjection is [wuu↗ aaa↘] 'expression of support and approval', with intonation going up and down, and each vowel being considerably longer than a normal long vowel.

Interjections used to call animals have unusual sounds: an alveolar click (repeated three times) is used to summon a dog; *ps ps ps* is used for a cat or a baby. All interjections are unusual in having a triplicated CV structure, e.g. *ti ti ti* used to call chickens and ducks, or a quadruplicated CVC structure, e.g. *yaw yaw yaw yaw* 'calming a baby'. Syllabic nasal [m̩] is found in two interjections: the conversation sustainer *m̩m̩* (pronounced with the mouth closed) and the warning marker *m̩ʔm̩* 'yes, I can see the danger of what you are saying'. The latter also contains a glottal stop, and is characterized by a falling intonation. The expression *diu diu diu diu* 'calling puppies' has no prenasalization in the alveolar stops.

Onomatopoeia (which form a separate word class—see §4.5) are phonologically and phonetically unusual in several respects:

(i)   they may contain long consonants, e.g. *sərr* 'sound of making canoe fall into water';
(ii)   they may contain unusual vowel nuclei, e.g. *ou* in *rou rou rou* 'roaring sound';
(iii)   they may have an unusual CCV*m* structure (not found in words of other kinds), e.g. *prəm prəm*, alternating with *brəm brəm* 'sound of a drum'; or CVCCVC structures not attested elsewhere, e.g. *kədran kədran* 'imitiating a cassowary speaking, or when summoning a cassowary' (pronounced with a prenasalized *d* [kəᵈⁿdran]);
(iv)   a vowel can undergo unusual lengthening, as in *wu:::* 'sound of person crying'.

An onomatopoeia can sound like any other word, e.g. *krəján* 'screeching sound', *kuíkuíkuí* 'the noise of a gouria pigeon', *pəkaká:u pəkaká:u* 'rooster singing'. Onomatopoeia tend to be repeated two to five times; other types of grammatical words can also be repeated, albeit less frequently (§9.2).

The bilabial trill ʙ appears in one word in baby talk: *ʙu* 'water'. A salient property of baby talk is CV-CV reduplication, e.g. *didi* 'poo', for *di* 'shit', and *yæ-yæ:y* 'paternal grandmother' for *yæ:y*. Vocative forms derived mostly from kinship nouns and personal names (but potentially formed on any noun used to refer to an addressee) are phonetically unusual. They are marked with a ə plus an off-glide *y*, or with *ay*, or just with *a*. The final syllable undergoes lengthening, e.g. *Walúp*, vocative *Walupá:y!* (also see §2.7). When ə undergoes such lengthening in a vocative form, it is pronounced as *e:*, e.g. *Máli*, vocative *Maliyée:(y)*. Stress moves to the last syllable. The vowel ə undergoes word-final lengthening in farewelling expressions where it is also pronounced as *e:* but remains unstressed. Depending on the distance and the insistence of the one who is calling, the duration of a lengthened ə varies. It is always longer than that of a phonemically long vowel, e.g. *yara adákwə:::* 'stay weeeeell'.

Another instance of a lengthened ə appears in responses from afar. For instance, *ya-kna-dəwunək* becomes *ya-kna-dəwuneek* 'I will come!', and *Yuanəg* 'personal name' sounds as *Yuaneeg!* The vowel *i* can be lengthened in monosyllabic words, to express prolonged action, e.g. *yin* 'going', *yi:::n* 'having gone for a long time, on and on'. In each case, the duration of the lengthened *i* is considerably longer than that of a long vowel.

2.2 SYLLABLE STRUCTURE

2.2.1 Syllable types

Syllable patterns in Manambu are (C)(C)V:(C). CV(:) syllables are basic in the sense that they appear in any position in a phonological word, e.g. *wa-ji-ná* 'she laughs', *ma:* 'no', *a-sə-kí* 'bad cold'. There are no restrictions on syllable onsets in CV(:) syllables. Syllables consisting of just a vowel are found in word-initial and word-medial positions, e.g. *a* 'connective; that feminine singular', *a-wúk* 'listen!', *du-a-má:gw* (man-LK-sibling) 'brother', *Yu-á-kalu* 'male personal name', *I-ra-mán* 'male personal name'.

CV(:)C syllables are found in the following positions in a phonological word:

(i) Word-finally, as *Yuanə́g* 'female personal name', *samasa:m* 'a lot', *æywan* 'a few', and in monosyllables such as in *ma:m* 'older sibling', *rak* 'fish scale'. Then, there are no restrictions on either onset or coda.

(ii) Word-initially and word-medially, if the resulting word-internal CC sequences conform to the types of structures in subsections A–C below.

V(:)C syllables occur word-finally, as in *rək* 'joke', *ar* 'lake', *ap* 'look; try!', *ak* 'eat!'. Consonant clusters in structures #V(:)C$_1$C$_2$V(:), e.g. *akráy* 'bring!' and *astakə́r* 'meet!' are preferably analysed as sequences V(:)-C$_1$C$_2$V(:) rather than V(:)C$_1$-C$_2$V(:). When asked to dictate these words syllable by syllable or to speak very slowly, speakers consistently syllabify them as *a-kráy, a-sta-kə́r*. Note that there is a morpheme boundary between *a-* 'imperative prefix' and the rest of the word.

A syllable onset can consist of two consonants. The allowed consonant sequences include:

I. A non-labialized voiced bilabial stop *b*, or a non-labialized velar stop as C$_1$, and a rhotic, or a lateral as C$_2$, as in <u>br</u>ak 'to you two', <u>bl</u>a-tuá 'I speak'; <u>gr</u>a:l 'she cried', <u>kr</u>ay-kə-tuá 'I will bring', a<u>kr</u>áy! 'bring', <u>gl</u>a:gw 'Manambu clan group', <u>kl</u>ay 'here'. The resulting sequences are: *br, bl, gr, gl, kr*, and *kl*.

II. The fricative *s* as C$_1$ and the voiceless apico-dental stop *t* as C$_2$, as in *stakə́r ma:* '(I, you, he/she) won't meet'. This sequence, *st*, is also found in loans from Tok Pisin, e.g. *státi tə-* (start have) 'start'.

III. The fricative *v* as C$_1$ and the glide *y* as C$_2$ as in *vya-* 'kill, hit'.

In a sequence of two adjacent CV(:)C syllables, an epenthetic ə is not required if an allowed consonant sequence is produced, e.g. *də<u>br</u>ə́m* 'perfect', *sta<u>kr</u>ád* 'he met' (see I above); or if the bilabial nasal *m* is followed by either an apico-dental nasal *n*, the voiceless non-labialized velar stop *k* or voiced dental *d*, e.g. *ka<u>mn</u>á:g^w* 'food', *nə<u>mn</u>ə́m* 'itchy', *ka<u>mk</u>áw* 'hairy yam', *da<u>md</u>á:m* 'spider' (that is, the sequences *mn, mk*, and *md*); or if the apico-dental nasal is followed by a stop or a fricative, as in *góngən* 'tremble',[12] *banvál* 'back of canoe' (that is, *ng* and *nv*); or if a rhotic, a liquid, or a glide is followed by any consonant, as in *kawardá* 'he lifted (something)', *wəlpə́m* 'completed, finished', *górgər* 'tiny' (as of a baby), *kaykətə́k-* 'hold on, hang on'.

All other types of clusters involving two stops, or a stop and a fricative, or a stop and an affricate, require that an epenthetic *ə* be inserted, as in *wukə-kú* (hear-COMPL.SS) 'having heard', compare *war-kú* (go.up-SS) 'having gone up'; *gwaj* 'spin', *gwaj-ə-kə-tuá* 'I will spin (something)'; *gwaj-ə-wayə́k* 'do not ever spin' (strong imperative), *gwaj-ə-dá gwaj-ə-dá* 'the one who spins all the time'.

A cluster involving a non-labialized voiceless velar stop as C_I and a nasal as C_2 only occurs in the sequence of morphemes *-k-* 'future' and *-na* 'focus on activity', as in *wa-kna-wən* 'I will tell', *kwa-kna-wən* 'I will stay'—cf. *kwakə-na-wən* 'I look for' where *kə* belongs to the root of the verb 'look for', and *-na* is 'focus on activity'. The *ə* in the second syllable of *kwakə-na-wən* 'I look for' cannot be reduced to *ø*; however, [kwakə-na-wən] is acceptable as alternative pronunciation of *kwa-k-na-wən* 'I will stay', in slow register. The only cluster of three consonants involves a rhotic or a lateral as C_I preceding the sequence of morphemes *-kə* 'future' and *-na* 'focus on activity', e.g. *war-kə-na-wən* or *war-k-na-wən* (go.up-FUT-ACT.FOC-1fem.sgBAS.VT) 'I will go up', *vəl-kə-na-wən* or *vəl-k-na-wən* 'I will cut'. This creates an instance of a phonetic VCC syllable. Phonological syllables of VCC structure do not exist.

A word-final sequence of two consonants always requires an epenthetic schwa, e.g. *jə́məs* 'James'. If a cluster which does not require an epenthetic *ə* occurs word-finally, an *ə* is inserted, as in *wukə-bərbər* (listen-2duBAS.VT) 'you two are listening'; *bər* 'you two'; 'they two' (but *brak* 'to you two', and not **bərak*). On a morpheme boundary, an optional epenthetic vowel may appear even if the emerging cluster does not require an epenthetic *ə*, e.g. *wukə-ñən-kək, wukə-ñənə-kək* (hear-2fem.sg-PURP.DS) 'for you to hear'; *vya-gur-kək, vya-gurə-kək* (hit-2pl-PURP.DS) 'for you to hit'.

2.2.2   Vowel sequences and diphthongs

The V-glide and glide-V sequences can be considered VC and CV syllables. Examples are *a-wáy* 'maternal uncle', *amáy* 'mother', *ma:y* 'go', *yæ:y* 'paternal grandmother', *waywáy* 'maybe', *nakamáy* 'one, only one'. If these are considered diphthongs, the disadvantage would lie in the otherwise unnecessary increase in the number of vowel nuclei.

Vowel sequences (some of which are separated by morpheme boundaries) are:

- *a-u*, and *a:-u*, as in *wá-u* 'may I talk?', *ká:u* 'platoon, group; be angry', *já:u* 'let's'. In a word-final position in rapid to normal speech *a-u* can be pronounced as a VC syllable *aw*, e.g. [ká:w] 'platoon, group'. But a V-glide syllable cannot be pronounced as a vowel sequence, e.g. *káw* 'hole', not [*kau*];
- *u-a*, as in *du-a-ma:gw* 'sibling', *-tua* 'first person singular subject series', *Yu-a-ya:b* 'female name';
- *u-i*, as in *su-i* 'lament';
- *ə-i*, as in *məir* 'really'.

A sequence *ə-i* requires insertion of a phonetic glide, as in ['mə-y-ir] 'really' (this is the way this word is transcribed in the subsequent chapters, for ease of pronunciation). The sequence

---

[12] The velar stop after *n* is pronounced as voiced, so that it is impossible to establish whether the root contains a voiceless *k* which has undergone voicing or a voiced *g* (compare rule A2 in §2.6).

ə-a results in vowel fusion (see A4 and B2 in §2.6 below). There are no sequences of identical vowels (see 2.1.2 above, on the generational variation between *a:* and a sequence of identical vowels).

Sequences *əw-ə* are realized as [ŭə] or [ŏə], e.g. in *ləw-ən* with variants [lŭən, lŏən] 'snap', *nəwək* 'another one' with [nŭək]. In an unstressed syllable, *əw* can be pronounced as *ŏw*, as in *məw-mi, mŏw-mi* 'base of a tree' (from *maw* 'base' and *mi* 'tree').

2.3 STRESS

2.3.1 Stress assignment

Manambu has movable stress realized in the increased intensity of the vowel. Similarly to other languages of the Sepik area, there are no pitch or tone contrasts. In disyllabic words stress tends to fall on the last syllable, as in *kətá* 'now', *sarák* 'towards a fly; a name of a clan', *mugúl* 'three', *kudí* 'language'. Alternatively, it may fall on the first syllable, as in *yára* 'be well, OK', *jáu* 'let it be', *jágər* 'garfish', *gə́rgər* 'tiny'. The few minimal pairs include *ákəs* 'habitual negation' and *akə́s* 'catch!'; *gəñə́r* 'to tail, with tail' and *gə́ñər* 'later'.

In trisyllabic words, stress falls on the penultimate syllable, as in *gərpáw* 'wild cat', or on the last syllable, as in *yabənáy* 'greeting; be well' (to a woman of the Maliau clan), *nawidú* 'comrade, mate', *kʷasabí* 'a stringbag'. If a word longer than two syllables contains one CVC syllable, this syllable is stressed, e.g. *arawús*, or *arawə́s* 'throw away', *ayakəsád* 'throw downwards' (unless it combines with a stress-shifting suffix, e.g. *yakəsaprán* 'throwing towards the speaker' which contains a stress-shifting suffix *-ən*). In a word consisting of more than three syllables, the main stress does not go beyond the antepenultimate syllable.

Long vowels are typically stressed, e.g. *kamná:gʷ* 'food', *kəkəpá:t* 'food', *yá:kya* 'OK'. A stressed vowel can be optionally lengthened, e.g. *kupráp, kuprá:p* 'bad; poor (thing)'. Most suffixes are stressed on their last syllable, e.g. *val* 'canoe', *valasáp* 'by canoe', *valá:m* 'on a canoe'; *gəngənəkwayík!* 'do not shiver (by any means)!' When a stress-shifting suffix is attached to the root, the root loses its stress, and a long vowel in a root undergoes reduction (see §2.3.2).

Suffixes can have the same segmental make-up and differ just in their stress. The allative-instrumental suffix *-Vr* is stressed, e.g. *kwaráb* 'bush', *kwarbár* 'to bush', *tabák* 'half, side', *tabəkə́r* 'towards a half, side'. It is homophonous with adverbial suffix *-ər* which is unstressed, e.g. *ta:y* 'before, in front', *táyər* 'previously'; *məy* 'very; real', *mə́yir* 'really'; *gəñ* 'last, tail', *gə́ñər* 'later'. The two prefixes (a fully productive second person imperative *a-* and the causative *kay-*, of limited productivity) are not stressed and do not affect the stress placement in a word.

There is one main stress per word. In multimorphemic words with over four syllables, the secondary stress appears on the root, e.g. *kwatiyà-kə-na-dəmən-ə́k* (give.to.nonthird.p-FUT-ACT.FOC-2masc.sgBAS.VT-CONF) 'you will give (something to me)'. A secondary stress occurs on the final syllable of the suffix *-dəka* 'only', e.g. *mən-ádəkà* 'you masculine only'.

2.3.2 Stress shift

Stress shift typically takes place in compounding and as the result of the addition of stressed suffixes. Long vowels become shortened when unstressed, as in *ba:n* 'back', *ban-vál* 'back of canoe'; *ma:l* 'side', *malə-vál* 'side of canoe'; *ta:m* 'nose', *tam-a-vál* 'nose of canoe'; *ta:kw* 'woman', *takw-a-ñán* 'girl' (woman-child); *ya:l* 'womb, belly', *yalá:m* 'in the womb'; *sa:r*

TABLE 2.3   Phonological structure of verbal and non-verbal roots

	VERBAL ROOT	NON-VERBAL ROOT
CVC	yes: *wuk-* 'hear', *war-* 'go up', *gər-* 'scratch', *taw-* 'put up'	yes: *wuk* 'tooth', *məl* 'eye'
CV	yes: *wa-* 'speak', *kə-* 'eat', *kwa-* 'stay'	yes: *ñə* 'day, sun', *mu* 'crocodile'
CCV~CVC	yes: *bla-* 'talk' (*a-bəl* 'talk!'), *gra-* 'cry' (*a-gər* 'cry!')	—
CV(C)V	yes: *waku-* 'go out', *wula-* 'come inside'	yes: *yanu* 'magic', *ka:u* 'platoon'
CVCVC	rare: *kaykət-* 'hold onto'	yes: *pusəp* 'rubbish', *yanan* 'grandchild'
VC	—	yes: *ar* 'lake', *a:s* 'dog'
V	—	no, except for closed classes

'fly', *sar-á-k* 'towards fly' (allative case). Long vowels get shortened if a root undergoes full reduplication and the second part is stressed, as in *sa:d* 'way', *sadə-sá:d* 'every way'.

In compounds the final root is stressed. If a stressed affix is added to such compounds, the vowel *a* in the first component is shortened to *ə*, e.g. *ban-vál* 'back of canoe', *bən-val-á:m* 'at the back of canoe'. Additional vowel alternations in nominal and verbal roots are discussed in §4.1.1 and §11.3.

2.4   PHONOLOGICAL STRUCTURE OF MORPHEMES AND SYLLABLE WEIGHT

2.4.1   Phonological structure of verbal and non-verbal roots

The differences in phonological structure between verbal and non-verbal roots in Manambu are summarized in Table 2.3.

While verbal roots can have CCV structure, nominal roots cannot. CCV verbal roots alternate with CVC. The root 'speak' appears as *bla-* in *bla-tua* 'I spoke'. Forming a second person imperative (§13.1) involves adding prefix *a-* and deleting the final vowel: on this principle, the imperative of *bla-* should be *abl. This form is phonologically impossible since Manambu does not allow more than one consonant in the coda position (see §2.2.1). An epenthetic *ə* 'breaks up' the word-final cluster, resulting in *a-bəl*.

Verbal and non-verbal roots differ in further features. Very few verbal roots contain an underlying long vowel (e.g. *pa:kʷ-*, *pakʷ-* 'be hidden', *ti:-* 'carry on one's head). (A vowel in a verbal root can undergo lengthening in certain morphological contexts: §11.3.)

More nouns than verbs have roots consisting of more than one syllable. Verbs of more than two syllables are typically polymorphemic, e.g. *kay-balak-* (CAUS-turn.upside.down) 'turn upside down like a canoe'; *kay-blakə-sada-* (CAUS-turn.upside.down-DOWN) 'turn upside down downward'. Some contain a fossilized derivational element, as in *kay-kwatu-* (CAUS/MANIP-?) 'empty into a heap; pour out'. Only affixes (e.g. the imperative prefix *a-*) and members of closed

TABLE 2.4   Syllable-weight-sensitive suffixes

WITH LIGHT VERB ROOT	WITH HEAVY VERB ROOT	MEANING
1. *-ta-taká*	*-taká*	immediate sequence (§18.5)
2. *-yakə-yakə́p*	*-yakə́p*	non-durative frustrative (§13.6)
3. Root reduplication-*a:k*	*-ək*	same-subject purposive (§13.4.1)
4. *-kə-kə́k*	*-kə́k*	different-subject purposive (§13.4.2)
5. *-kə-kə́b*	*-kə́b*	different-subject 'as soon as' (§18.6)
6. *-kə(-kə-)*	*-kə-*	future (§12.2)

classes (e.g. the distal demonstrative *a*) can consist just of a vowel.[13] Having different phonological possibilities for verbs and other classes is not uncommon among non-Austronesian languages of the New Guinea area. For instance, in Hua (East Central Highlands family) verb stems always end in a vowel; nouns have hardly any constraints (Haiman 1983). Furthermore, unlike non-verbal roots, verb roots can be heavy or light. Verb forms also have iambic stress patterns.

2.4.2   Syllable weight and evidence for iambic stress in verbs

Two syllable 'weights' can be distinguished. A light syllable has a CV structure and can be said to contain one mora. A heavy syllable contains two morae and has a CVC, or a CCV ~ CVC structure. Six verbal suffixes have different form depending on whether they attach to a monomoraic verb root or to a heavy multimoraic root: this can be monosyllabic, or contain more than two syllables. Since hardly any verb root has an inherent long vowel, the issue of the correlation between morae and long vowels remains open. See Table 2.4.

All syllable-weight-sensitive suffixes (except for future) are stressed on the last syllable and produce forms which consist of two syllables or more. (Words of four syllables or more require a secondary stress: see §2.3.1.)

Suffixes 1–3 attach directly to a verb root (which cannot take person markers). The resulting forms are not inflected for person (§3.1; §11.1.1). In the examples below, the syllable-weight-sensitive suffixes are underlined. Suffixes 1–2 undergo CV or CVCV reduplication if combined with a light verb root. Examples with light roots are *wa-tà-taká* (speak-RED-IMM.SEQ) 'spoke and', *kə-tà-taká* 'ate and', *kwa-tà-taká* 'stayed and'; *wa-yakə̀-yakə́p* (come-RED-FR) 'speak in vain', *kwa-yakə̀-yakə́p* 'stay in vain'. (That a root consisting of a labialized stop and a vowel counts as light constitutes an additional piece of evidence in favour of monophonemic status of labialized stops: see §2.1.1.) Examples with heavy monosyllabic verb roots of CVC structure are *wàr-taká* 'went up and', *gə̀r-taká* 'scratched and', *wàr-yakə́p* 'go up in vain'; of two syllables and polysyllabic compounds are *wulà-taká* 'came in and', *ka-sapwì-taká* 'opened and'; *kwakə̀-yakə́p* (look.for-FR) 'look for in vain', *kaykə̀tə̀-yakə́p* 'hold on to something in vain'. Roots

---

[13] Suffixes typically consist of either a single consonant, or a CV, VC, or a CVC syllable. Disyllabic suffixes are very few (see Table 2.4, for some examples).

with CCV~CVC structure count as heavy, e.g. *blà-taká* 'spoke and', *grà-taká* 'cried and', *vyà-taká* 'hit and', *grà-yakɨ́p* 'cry in vain'. That is, Manambu displays the phenomenon of 'onset moraicity'.

The same-subject purposive suffix (3 in Table 2.4) requires full reduplication of a light verb's root, e.g. *kə-ká:k* 'so that (same subject) should eat', *kwa-kwá:k* 'so that (SS) should stay', *sə-sá:k* 'so that (SS) should plant'.[14] With a heavy root, the form is *-ək*, as in *kaykət-ə́k* 'so that (SS) should hold on to', *war-ɨ́k* 'so that (SS) should go up'. (With CCV~CVC roots, the form is *-a:k*, as in *blá:k* 'so that (SS) should speak'.)

Suffixes 4–5 attach to verb root followed by person markers, and undergo CV reduplication if the verb root is light, e.g. *və-tù-kəkɨ́k* (see-1sg-PURP.DS) 'for me to see, so that I see', *və-tù-kəkɨ́b* (see-1sg-AS.SOON.AS) 'as soon as I saw'. The resulting forms are partially inflected for person (§3.1; §11.1.1). Unreduplicated allomorphs are used with heavy roots, e.g. *wàr-tu-kɨ́k* 'for me to go up', *wàr-tu-kɨ́b* 'as soon as I went up', *wakù-tu-kɨ́k* 'for me to go out', *wakù-tu-kɨ́b* 'as soon as I went out', *blà-tu-kɨ́k* 'for me to speak'; *blà-tu-kɨ́b* (speak-1sg-AS.SOON.AS) 'as soon as I spoke'. If a verb stem consists of a sequence of CV-CV roots it is treated as heavy (each of the roots on their own would be light), e.g. *wa-yà-tu-kɨ́k* (say-come-1sg-PURP.DS) 'so that I carry on saying'. The future marker (6 in Table 2.4) attaches to the verb root and is followed by person markers (§12.2); the resulting forms are fully inflected for person. Examples with light root involve full reduplication of the suffix, e.g. *wa-kɨ́-kə-tuà* (say-FUT-FUT-1sgSUBJ.VT+3fem.sgBAS.VT) 'I will say it'. The unreduplicated form *-kə-* occurs with heavy roots, as in *wàr-kə-tuá* 'I will go up', *blà-kə-tuá* 'I will speak it', *kaykətə̀-kə-tuá* 'I will hold onto it'.

Each of the verb forms containing suffixes discussed here has an iambic stress pattern. They can be seen as consisting of two feet each with an unstressed (light) syllable followed by a stressed (heavy) one. The additional syllable created by reduplicating the initial CV of a CVCV or CVC suffix or the initial CVCV of a CVCVC suffix serves to satisfy the requirement that a multisyllable verbal word containing a monomorphemic suffix of heavy syllable structure be divided into two feet of equal length (this agrees with the average length of a preferred phonological word in Manambu: see §2.5.1). The iambic stress principle is restricted to verbs, and thus provides an additional point of phonological differentiation between verbal and non-verbal roots.[15]

2.5 PHONOLOGICAL WORD

2.5.1 General properties

The main criterion for a phonological word is stress (Dixon and Aikhenvald 2002). Most frequent types include CV(:)C and CV(:)CV(:). A phonological word cannot contain more than one long vowel. A word of a CV structure tends to contain a long vowel, e.g. *yi:* 'fire', *wu:* 'ton fruit', *ma:* 'again; negative'. (There are a few exceptions, e.g. *sə* 'name; who?'). Otherwise, it tends to cliticize to another word, as does *lə* 'she' (see §2.5.3). Or the vowel may be optionally

---

[14] In contrast, the dative-aversive case marker *-Vk*, formally reminiscent of the same-subject purposive (see §7.11), can attach to a monosyllabic noun without reduplication, e.g. *sə* 'name', *sa:k* 'for/for fear of name'.

[15] The iambic principle does not apply if a suffix is of structure *-CV(:)y* (e.g. *-ta:y* 'cotemporaneous sequencing': §18.4; *-ga:y* 'unlikely condition': §18.8), or *-CVr* (e.g. *-kər* 'desiderative': §13.5). That it does not operate with the suffix *-lək* 'because' (§18.7) may be due to the fact that this suffix is a product of a recent grammaticalization of a free form *alək* 'this is why, because'.

lengthened, e.g. *mi, mi:* 'tree, up', *mu, mu:* 'crocodile'. A major class of exceptions with no optional vowel lengthening is interjections, e.g. *tsa, sa!* 'attention getter' (see §2.1.3).

Additional phonotactic restrictions determine the boundaries of a word:

(i) The labiodental fricative *v* pronounced as such appears only word-initially (then it does not have [β] as a possible allophone: see §2.1.1).

(ii) Only low vowels (with the exception of the long *æ:*) occur in the word-initial position.

(iii) No phonological word consists of CəCə.

(iv) In a monosyllabic monomorphemic phonological word, if C_1 and C_2 have the same place of articulation, the coda (C_2) cannot be more voiced than the onset (C_1). That is, words like **pab* and **tad* are not well formed. (This does not apply to *ta:d* 'he stands/stood' which consists of two morphemes, the root *tə-* and the suffix *-d* '3masc.sgBAS.VT/P').

(v) A phonological word of more than one syllable cannot contain a sequence of CV-VC (see §2.2.1). How this is avoided can be seen in the treatment of loans from Tok Pisin. An imperative of the verb *rausə-*, a loan from Tok Pisin *rausim* 'throw out, get out', should be **a-raus*. To avoid such an unacceptable structure, this form is pronounced as *a-rawús*, or *a-rawə́s*, with the word-final syllable becoming a glide-V sequence. Along similar lines, a native Manambu verb, *yakə-saula-* 'throw-inside something or inland', yields the imperative form *a-yakə-sawə́l*, and not **a-yakə-saúl*.

Further tokens of phonological word boundaries include unreleased stops (see §2.1.1), prenasalization (D in §2.1.1), and allophonic variation in the pronunciation of ə (C in §2.1.2).

A preferred phonological word in Manambu does not exceed three syllables in length. We can recall that most words over four syllables require a secondary stress (see §2.3.1). Its intensity varies from speaker to speaker; however, the fact that some people tend to write words like *kwatiyà-kə-na-dəmə́n* (give.to.nonthird.p-FUT-ACT.FOC-2masc.sgBAS.VT) 'You (man) will give (something to me)' as *kwatiya kənadəmən* or as *kwatiya kəna dəmən* reflects the native speakers' attempt to 'conform' to the length limitations of a preferred phonological word. A few four-syllable-long phonological words may not require a secondary stress, e.g. *yará-kara* (fine-AFFIX) 'well'.

Phonological and grammatical word coincide in most cases. As expected (Dixon and Aikhenvald 2002), reduplication and compounding constitute the instances of mismatches whereby one grammatical word may consist of more than one phonological word—see §2.5.2. Two or three grammatical words form one phonological word in the case of some noun phrases, and if a word contains a cliticizable morpheme—see §2.5.3.

2.5.2 When one grammatical word corresponds to more than one phonological word

Instances of one grammatical word forming several phonological words include (Ia) nominal and verbal compounds, (Ib) full reduplication of simple roots, and (Ic) reduplication in compounds.

(Ia) COMPOUNDING. Disyllabic and trisyllabic nominal compounds (see §9.3) form one phonological word, e.g. *du-tá:kw* (man-woman) 'people', *mæn-tá:b* (leg-hand) 'arms and legs', *bap-a-tá:kw* (moon-LK-woman) 'lady moon', *takw-a-ñán* (woman-LK-child) 'girl', *məw-mí* (base-tree) 'base of a tree' (this consists of *maw* 'base' with a reduced vowel (see §4.1.1) and *mi* 'tree'), *rək-a-sə́p* (dry-LK-skin) 'dry skin; a person with dry skin' (see A6 in §2.6, on consonant simplification in such compounds). Verb-noun compounds (which are nouns) follow the same principle, e.g. *kiya-dú* (die-man) 'dead man; name of a Manambu football team' (see §19.2.2). The stress typically falls on the final syllable. A compound of three syllables or more may form two phonological words, e.g. *kamí kamná:g^w* (fish food) 'foodstuff' (the free form of 'fish' is *kami:*), *babáy dú* (maternal.grandparent man) 'maternal grandfather'. Alternatively, such a compound may form one word, and have its main stress on the last syllable of the second component. Then, the first component retains a weaker secondary stress on the erstwhile stressed syllable, e.g. *vyakətà-yakə́* (good/beautiful-FULLY) 'very beautiful (e.g. woman)'.

These compounds form one grammatical word since no other constituent can intervene between their components. That case inflections go at the end of these compounds does not provide conclusive evidence for grammatical wordhood since case markers always occur at the end of a noun phrase (§7.1).

A verb compounded with one or two directional markers (§16.1.1) forms one grammatical word: it takes a single set of inflections, and no other constituent can intervene between the components. Directional compounds form one phonological word if the resulting combination is two or three syllables long, e.g. *wa-sakí-n* (speak-across-SEQ) 'speaking across; telling traditional lore', *yakə-sú-n* (throw-up-SEQ) 'throwing upwards'. If the resulting combination contains four or more syllables, each directional acquires an independent stress, as in *yakə-sakí-salá-n* (throw-across.away-across.inwards-SEQ) 'throw across away and inwards at the same time'. A non-stressed prefix does not affect the phonological wordhood, despite the fact that the resulting word becomes four syllables long, e.g. *a-yakə-sú* (IMPV-throw-up) 'throw upwards!' Verb compounds consisting of several verb roots form one phonological and one grammatical word, e.g. *kui-taká-* (give-put) 'give out, hand out' (see §§15.1–2).

(Ib) FULL REDUPLICATION OF SIMPLE ROOTS. If a verbal, an adjectival, or a nominal root undergoes full reduplication and the resulting structure is four syllables long, it is treated as two disyllabic phonological words in terms of stress assignment, e.g. *kwasá-kwasá* (small-RED+fem.sg) 'very small', *wukə́-wukə́-k* (hear-RED-PURP) 'in order to hear'. The stress on the last phonological word is the same as the non-reduplicated form in isolation, e.g. *kwasá* 'small (fem.sg)'. A sequence of five syllables resulting from reduplication is divided into a trisyllabic word and a disyllabic one, as in *səmi-ká-səmí* (long-INT-long) 'very long' (compare the non-reduplicated form *səmí* 'long'). A longer form will be divided into a sequence of two trisyllabic words, as in *kaykətə́-kaykətə́k* 'in order to hold'. A form two or three syllables long will be treated as one phonological word with a single stress, e.g. *da-dá-k* 'in order to go down', *kur-kur-ə́k* 'in order to do', *təp-a-tə́p* (village-LK-village) 'every village'. That these forms constitute one grammatical word is corroborated by the fact that they take one marker of inflection, e.g. the purposive *-k* in reduplicated verbs, and gender and number marking in reduplicated adjectives, e.g. *k^wasa-k^wasa-də* 'small-RED-masc.sg'. (Inherently reduplicated disyllabic words have one stress, e.g. *damdá:m* 'spider'; cf. *da:m* 'spider'.)

(Ic) REDUPLICATION IN COMPOUNDS. A verb-verb compound, or one of its components, can undergo full reduplication (see §15.1 on the properties of verb-verb compounds). Then, the principle of preferred phonological word applies; for instance, the second component of the compound *və-səmə́l-* (see-dummy.root) 'look for' can be reduplicated; the resulting form consists of two phonological words: *və-səmə́l-səmə́l-* 'look everywhere'. If both components undergo full reduplication, and the initial compound contains more than two syllables, the last vowel of the first component is dropped. The reduplicated components form separate phonological words. So, full reduplication of *kui-taká-* produces two phonological words *kui-ták-kui-taká-* (give-put-give-put) 'give away repeatedly, or of many agents', and not *kui-taká-kui-taká; and that of *kiya-yakɔ́-* (die-throw) 'die irrevocably' produces *kiya-yák-kiya-yakɔ́-* 'die irrevocably, or of many subjects'. No other kind of compound can undergo full reduplication (see §12.8.2; §15.5).

2.5.3   When two or three grammatical words form one phonological word

This includes noun phrases and complex predicates which may form one phonological word (I) and phonological words containing clitics (II).

(I) A modifier-head noun phrase consists of two grammatical words, since other adjectives can intervene between the two, and the adjective can take gender and number agreement, e.g. *kʷasá ñán* (small+fem.sg child) 'small female child', *kʷasa-dɔ́ ñán* (small-masc.sg child) 'small male child'. Yet, if such an NP consists of two or three syllables, it is pronounced as one phonological word, with the stress on the last component, as in [kula ˈmaːdʒ] (new word) 'new word', [kʷasa-ˈɲan] 'small child', [kə-ˈɲan] (this.fem.sg child) 'this female child'. In slow deliberate register these can be pronounced as two words, e.g. [kʷaˈsa ˈɲan], [kˈə ˈɲan]. If an NP consists of more than three syllables, each component receives an independent stress and forms a phonological word on its own. The stress falls on the same syllable as it would if each word were pronounced in isolation, e.g. *kulá kamnáːgʷ* (new food) 'raw food', *ñáura kudí* 'Iatmul language', *kʷasá gərgɔ́r ñán* (small+fem.sg tiny child) 'a tiny little child', *adawúr dú* (DEM.DIST+masc.sg+up man) 'man up there; God'. This agrees with the preferred length of a phonological word in Manambu.

A complex predicate consisting of a monosyllabic nominal and a support verb (see §17.2) can be pronounced as one phonological word, or as two. The compound *bas sə* 'ask' (lit. first plant/put) is a typical example. In slow deliberate speech it can be stressed on the second, inflected, component, or on both, that is, *bás sətuá* 'I ask' in slow speech register and *bassətuá* or *basətuá* in normal speech register (see A6 in §2.6 on the reduction of a sequence of identical consonants). The two components are distinct grammatical words, since the connector *ata* 'then' can intervene between the two and the imperative prefix *a-* occurs on the second component, as in *bás ás!* 'ask!'

(II) Two or even three grammatical words form one phonological word if at least one of them is cliticizable. All such clitics can be either added to a host, or occur as independent phonological words in slow register. They vary in the choice of hosts, and whether they are procliticized or encliticized to it. All enclitics may acquire a secondary stress (independently of the length of the phonological word they are in) and potentially may be pronounced as independent words in very slow register. They also undergo phonological processes discussed under B in §2.6.

(a) Encliticizable pronominal subject markers occur with non-verbal words in the predicate slot (see §§3.1–2; Table 3.4). Some are monosyllabic, and some disyllabic. In slow speech they may be stressed and separated by a short pause; some speakers optionally insert the glottal fricative *h* in front of these clitics. (These enclitics and the cliticizable morphemes *ata* and *aka* discussed under (e) below are the only instances where this phonetic *h* occurs.) Very slow register is illustrated in 2.1a.

2.1a á:s   (h)adi
    dog 3plNOM
    'They are dogs; dogs are'

Normal register is shown in 2.1b: note the secondary stress on the enclitic. The pronunciation in 2.1c reflects normal to rapid speech—note the absence of the secondary stress.

2.1b á:s=adì
    dog=3plNOM
    'They are dogs; dogs are'

2.1c á:s=adi
    dog=3plNOM
    'They are dogs; dogs are'

In normal to rapid speech, a stressed vowel sequence *ə-a* on a clitic boundary results in vowel fusion: *ə + a → a*: (see B2 in §2.6). Pronunciation in slow register (without vowel fusion) is shown in 2.2a; in 2.2b, the same example is pronounced with normal speed, and the vowel fusion takes place:

2.2a ñən-a-kə́   sə́=al
    you.fem-LK-OBL name=3fem.sgNOM
    'It is your name'

2.2b ñən-a-kə́   sá:l
    you.fem-LK-OBL name+3fem.sgNOM
    'It is your name'

(b) A few particles consisting of CV where V is either a short vowel or a schwa tend to cliticize to the preceding phonological word. The emphatic particle *ya* (see §4.5.3) has low selectivity and can be encliticized to any constituent. It always has a secondary stress, e.g. *yawí=yà* 'work really', *akúr=yà* 'do get!' This particle is more frequent in the speech of those who frequently code-switch into Tok Pisin, and could well be a loan from Tok Pisin *ya* 'exclamatory or emphatic particle'. The adverb *bə* 'already' is either procliticized to the following verb, as in *bə̀=yanád* 'he has already left', or encliticized to the preceding adverbial or demonstrative, e.g. *atá=bə̀* 'then-already', or to a sequence of procliticized personal pronoun, an adverbial or a demonstrative, e.g. *lakábə̀* (*lə=aka=bə* 'she=FEM.SG.DIST.DEM.REACTIVATED.TOPIC=already) 'she the one here already'. This is an instance of one phonological word consisting of three grammatical words. In each case, *bə* takes a secondary stress. A non-clitic equivalent of *bə* is *bəta:y* 'already'.

(c) Pronouns *lə* 'she' and *də* 'he' (see §10.1) are optionally procliticized to the following stressed word in normal to rapid speech, e.g. *lə-atá* 'she then' becomes *latá* (see B2 in §2.6), *lə-a* (she-DEM.DIST.fem) 'she that one' becomes *la(:)*, and *də-ada* (he-DEM.DIST.MASC.REACT.TOPIC) 'he new topic S/O' becomes *dadá*. The few extant nouns of Cə structure procliticize to the verb in complex verbs (see §4.2), e.g. *sə=kʷá-* (sleep=lie) 'sleep, be asleep' is pronounced as one phonological word. We saw, in §2.1.2, that *ə* is pronounced as *u* if preceded or followed by a labial consonant within a phonological word. That *sə=kʷá-* can be pronounced as *su=kʷá-* shows that this sequence is treated as one word in its stress placement and also in the allophonic variation. If this same construction is discontinuous (for instance, to express an afterthought), *sə* acquires its own stress, as in *bəta:y kʷa-na, sə* (already lie-ACT.FOC+3fem.sgBAS.VT, sleep) 'she is already lying, asleep' (see (I) in §7.2).

(d) A monosyllabic negative form of the verb (see §14.1) cliticizes to the negator *ma:* in normal to rapid speech register if the negation and the verb are contiguous, e.g. *má: rə* 'not sit', *má: tə* 'not have/be/stand'. The construction *má: kwə* 'not stay' can be alternatively pronounced either as *má: kw*, or as *má: ku*. If the sequence is interrupted, the verb forms an independent phonological word, as in *ma: nəbay tə* (not yet have:NEG) 'I/you/he/she/etc. do not have (it) yet'.

(e) Two disyllabic words tend to procliticize to the following verb, or encliticize to the preceding verb: *(h)aká* 'here (feminine singular); reactivated topic', *(h)atá* 'then'. When cliticized, they retain a secondary stress on their final syllable, as in *atà=wá:d* 'then he said', *kusəlál=akà* 'it (feminine) is finished here'. The sequence *aká-n-akà* (DEM.DIST.REACT.TOP.fem.sg-PRED-REACT.TOP.fem.sg) 'this topical; here it is, this is how it is' can occur on its own; at the end of a story it cliticizes to the final verb, e.g. *kusə́-l=akànaka* (finish-3fem.sgBAS.VT=DEM.DIST.REACT.TOP.fem.sg-PRED-REACT.TOP.fem.sg) 'it is now finished'. This is an instance of three grammatical words realized as one phonological word. The form *ata* procliticizes to a second person imperative with a subsequent fusion of identical vowels (see B3 in §2.6), as in *ata ada* (then sit.IMPV) 'sit, stay, wait' which is pronounced as [ata:ⁿdá] or [ataⁿda], *ata-n aw* (thus-PRED IMPV+speak) 'speak thus' which is pronounced as [ata'naw].

(f) The demonstrative *kləm* 'here (feminine singular)' can procliticize to *ma:n* 'negation', forming one word *kləmá:n* 'here not; it is not here' (the consonant reduction of sequence of identical consonants is addressed in B1 in §2.6 below).

(g) Monosyllabic adverbial modifiers encliticize to an adjective or a verb they modify, e.g. *vyákata=məy* (good=very) 'very good', *máya=kəp* (go=just) 'just go!' Very occasionally, a monosyllabic object gets procliticized to the verb, e.g. *áy yi-kná-d* (IMPV+'do' go/say-FUT-3masc.sgBAS.VT) becomes [ayikn'aⁿd] 'he will say: "do!"' (e.g. the cooking)'. In the two farewell formulae, the manner adverb *yara* 'well' procliticizes to the imperative verb, as in *yara=má:y* (well=go.IMPV) 'goodbye' (literally, go well: said by the person who is staying). In the response by the person who is going, *yara* procliticizes to the imperative of the verb 'stay' and the two identical vowels undergo vowel fusion (B3 under §2.6 below), as in *yaradákʷ* (from *yara=adákʷ* well=stay.IMPV) 'stay well' (§21.5).

Special phonological processes apply on the boundary of cliticizeable morphemes. If a clitic forms a phonological word with a root, the main stress does not shift, and long vowels do not undergo reduction: compare *tá:kw=a* 'it is a woman' and *takwá:k* 'to a woman'. This constitutes evidence in favour of special status of clitic-containing words in Manambu (see Aikhenvald 2002c, for a cross-linguistic perspective).

2.6 PHONOLOGICAL PROCESSES

Phonological processes occur on (A) affix boundaries within a phonological word and on (B) clitic boundaries within a sequence of clitics, or between a cliticized morpheme and its host. The epenthetic glide insertion (C1) occurs on any boundary, be it a suffix boundary or a clitic boundary.

A. PHONOLOGICAL PROCESSES OCCURRING ON AFFIX BOUNDARIES WITHIN A WORD

A1. RHOTIC DISSIMILATION. The second of the two contiguous rhotics undergo dissimilation in the word-final syllable (which does not contain a long vowel). The majority of examples involve the suffix -(V)*r* 'allative/instrumental' added to a stem ending in *r*, the suffix undergoes dissimilation *r→l*, as in *jágər* 'garfish', allative *jagrə́l* 'to garfish'; *ar'* lake', allative *arál*; *tágər* 'type of croton', allative *tagrə́l*; *yipə́r* 'tulip (Gnetum gnemon tree and edible leaves)', allative *yiprə́l*. This dissimilation also applies to loans, e.g. *kar* 'car', allative *karal*. (Urban speakers of Manambu occasionally use forms like *arar* 'to the lake', instead of *aral*.[16])

This process does not apply if the word does not end in *r*, such as -*rəb* 'completely, fully', e.g. *gra-rə́b gra-k-ná* (cry-FULLY cry-FUT-ACT.FOC+3fem.sgBAS.VT) 'she will cry her eyes out'. Neither does it operate if the last syllable contains a long vowel, as in *kwarə́b* 'jungle', allative *kwarbá:r* 'to the jungle', *rə-* 'sit, live', *rərá:k* 'sit (in vain)'. It does not apply if the first rhotic is part of a cluster, as in *jabr-a:r* (boat-LK+ALL) 'to/with a boat', formed on *jabər* 'boat'.

The rhotic dissimilation optionally applies within one loan root containing two *r*'s in adjacent syllables: in rapid register the Tok Pisin import *sarere* 'Saturday' can be pronounced as [sarele], and *sárərəy-a-ñə́* (Saturday-LK-day) 'day of Saturday' comes out as *sárələy-a-ñə́* (see C1, on the epenthetic glide *y* on a suffix boundary). A sequence of *r* and *l* is simplified to *r* in normal to rapid speech, e.g. *war-lə́-k* (go.up-3fem.sg-COMPL.DS) 'after she had come up' is pronounced as [warə́k], and *ka-war-lá* (get-UP-3fem.sgSUBJ.P+3fem.sgBAS.P) 'she took (something) up' is pronounced as [kawaˈra].

A2. VOICING OF VELAR AND LABIAL STOP. This very common process occurs optionally at a suffix boundary, and between components of a compound. A voiceless velar stop *k* and labial *p* become voiced if preceded by a voiced consonant (including a nasal or a rhotic). Voiced stops are prenasalized, and sequences of *n-ᵑg* and *n-ᵐb* subsequently get simplified to *ᵑg* and *ᵐb*. Examples are *jar-kañ* (hollow.of?-bamboo) 'rifle' → [jargañ],[17] *kur-mən-kəb* (do-2masc.sg-AS.SOON.AS) 'while you keep doing' → [kurməᵑgəb]; *ata-n-pək* (thus-PRED-like) 'like this' → [ataᵐbək].

A3. LOSS OF A VOICELESS VELAR STOP. We saw in §2.1.1 that *k* undergoes lenition in intervocalic position. Within a suffix, the stop in an intervocalic position is often elided, as in the suffix -*dəka* 'only' (§9.2) which undergoes contraction to -*da* in normal to rapid speech register, e.g. *tab-á-dəkà* (hand-LINK-ONLY) 'only hands; bare-handed, carrying nothing' realized as [tabˈada]. The elision does not occur in a non-final syllable, as in *də-kə-də* (3masc.sg-OBL-3masc.sg) 'his'. Some innovative speakers avoid a sequence of two adjacent *kə* syllables by inserting a rhotic in the first one, e.g. *wa-tu-kəkək* (say-1sg-PURP.DS) '(for speaker) to leave' becomes either *wa-tu-kər-kək* or *wa-tu-krə-kək*; *wapa-kəkəb* (leave-REP.SEQ) 'having left many times' becomes either *wapa-kərkəb* or *wapa-krəkəb*.

In fast speech, the final *k* of a suffix is often lost, e.g. *rə-na-wun-ək, rə-na-wun-ə* (sit-ACT.FOC-1sgBAS.VT-CONF) 'I am sitting', *rə-da:-k, rə-da:* (sit-3pl-COMPL.DS) 'after they sat'. The

---

[16] A form *arar* only occasionally occurs with older speakers who are exposed to innovative Manambu. In just one instance, the rhotic dissimilation affected the *l* in the non-final syllable: **a-l-ər* (DEM.DIST-FEM.SG-ALL) 'to there' was pronounced as *ar-əl*, by Ñatabi, possibly by analogy with *akrəl* 'where to' (this highly idiosyncratic interrogative consists of the interrogative *ak-* followed by two occurrences of the allative *-r* which undergo regular dissimilation). A distal rhotic assimilation in an O-V structure is found occasionally, e.g. *abra wa-də-bər, abra wa-də-bəl* (DEM.DIST+3du+DEM.DIST say-3masc.sgSUBJ.P-2duBAS.P) 'he said about them two'. That is, for these speakers a kind of 'rhotic harmony' operates within a phonological phrase.

[17] A similar voicing occurs within the word *kamkaw* 'hairy yam', often pronounced as [kamgau] (but note that [g] is not prenasalized). (This can also be pronounced as [kamakau]. This is presumably the original form, and is the way it was recorded in Farnsworth n.d.) It does not happen word-internally elsewhere: for example, the personal name Kamkudi (see Text 2) is never pronounced as *[Kamguⁿdi].

intervocalic *k* is not lost in a CVC word: *aka* 'here; feminine singular distal demonstrative reactivated topic' does not become *a.[18]

The only instance of word-final loss of the labialized voiced *gw* is the high-frequency word *kamna:g*^{w} 'food' which is frequently pronounced as [kamn'a:], or even [kam'na] (see §21.1.1).

A4. VOWEL LOSS ON SUFFIX BOUNDARY. If a suffix ending in an *ə* is followed by a suffix starting with *-a*, *ə* is elided, e.g. *də-kə-aba:b* (3masc.sg-OBL-TOO) 'he too' becomes *dəkaba:b*.

A5. LOSS OF CONSONANT LABIALIZATION. If a final labialized stop of a root is followed by a suffix starting with *-u*, the consonant loses its labialization, e.g. *kalak*^{w} 'stop' + *-u* '1st imperative' > *kalaku* 'may I stop?'

A6. REDUCTION OF SEQUENCE OF IDENTICAL CONSONANTS, AND HAPLOLOGY. Manambu has no long or geminated consonants, or sequences of identical consonants. These are reduced, as in *-y-y* > *y* in *nay-yi-nay-ya-n* (play-go-play-come-SEQ) becoming *nayinayan* 'playing going back and forth'; *-w-w* > *w*, as in *yakraw-wa* 'thunder-comitative' > *yakrawa* 'with thunder'. This is similar to the process B1.

If the first component of an adjective-noun compound ends in a nasal, and the second component contains a prenasalized stop, the two merge into one prenasalized stop, as in *apan-du* (old:masc-man) 'old man' pronounced as [apa^{n}du] rather than [apan^{n}du]. Note that if a suffix starting with [^{n}d] is attached to a root ending in *n*, an epenthetic *ə* is inserted, as in [səbən-ə^{n}d] (return-3masc.sgBAS.VT) 'he returns' (not *[səbə^{n}d]. This shows that the boundary between the components of a compound is phonologically different from a typical root-suffix boundary.

If two identical syllables occur on a morphological boundary, one of these is lost, as in *wukə-kraki-* (hear-bring across) 'recognize by hearing' becoming *wukraki-* and *kiya-yakə* (die-throw) 'die fully' becoming *kiyakə-*. This process of haplology is not obligatory: some speakers, including Duamakwa:ydəmi, the oldest living Manambu man, say *kiya-yakə-*.

A7. FURTHER FAST SPEECH PHENOMENA. In fast speech, occasional syllable simplification has been attested in one highly frequent compound with two adjacent syllables containing labial consonants: *gabu ma:j* (traditional story) 'tale', is pronounced as [gama:j]. (This may well be an idiosyncratic process, since it is attested only in this word in this meaning; the same word is now also used in the meaning of teacher: then, it is always pronounced as *gabu ma:j*.) Some speakers from Malu pronounce *tənəb* 'fireplace' as *təb*.

C-C consonant clusters which do not require an epenthetic *ə* (see §2.2.1) may undergo resyllabification on a suffix boundary. A sequence *r-k* is perfectly acceptable; nevertheless, some speakers pronounce the sequence of suffixes *-gur-kək* (-2pl-PURP) 'for you to do' as [ŋgrukək]. A sequence *-i -yi* in compounds becomes *i:*, as in (slow speech) *væki-yi-n* (go.across-go-SEQ), (rapid speech) *væki:n* 'crossing all the way'. The reactivated topic pronoun *ada* (DEM.DIST.REACT.TOP+masc.sg) 'that one mentioned' shortens to *da* if followed by a clitic, e.g. *da=bə* (DEM.DIST.REACT.TOP+masc.sg=already) 'that one mentioned already'.

---

[18] The variant *nə* 'one' as in *nə... nə* 'one ... another' of the number 'one' (whose form is *nak*) could be a shortened form of the indefinite pronoun *nəkə* 'another, other' which is semantically very similar (see §10.3).

B. Phonological Processes on Clitic Boundaries Within a Phonological Word

B1. Reduction of sequences of identical consonants. A sequence of identical consonants on the boundary between a clitic and its host is reduced to a single consonant, e.g. *kləm* 'here (feminine singular)' = *ma:n* 'negative' → *kləmá:n* 'here not' (§2.5.3, II). A complex verb consisting of an adverb and a verb undergoes similar simplification: what is *bás sətuá* 'I ask' in very slow speech register becomes *basətuá* in normal speech register. Cf. A6, for a similar process on suffix boundary.

B2. Vowel elision on clitic boundary. A sequence of -ə = -a becomes -a, e.g. *lə ata* → *lata* 'she then', *sə abər* → *sabər* 'these are two names' etc. A similar rule applies on a suffix boundary (see A4). However, the difference between A4 and B2 is that B2 is optional: a proclitic like *lə* can be pronounced as a separate word, and then vowel elision will not take place (as shown in 2.1b, 2.1c). There is no such option for a suffix boundary where vowel elision is always obligatory.

The vowel elision does not apply with the cliticizable *a* 'third singular feminine' which occurs on non-verbal predicate heads, e.g. *só=á* (name=3fem.sg.NOM) 'it is a name' (not *sa).

B3. Vowel fusion and simplification on clitic boundary. A sequence of two identical vowels across a clitic boundary undergoes fusion and subsequent simplification, e.g. *a = a* → *a*, as in *kusədá=aká* → [kusədákà] 'he finished thus'. This process is very frequent in rapid speech, e.g. *də-kə-də=a-də ra:w* (he-OBL-masc.sg=DEM.DIST-masc.sg maternal.nephew) 'that maternal nephew of his' is pronounced as [də-kə-da-də ra:w]. A sequence *ata=adak^w* (then=stay) 'stay then' becomes [atadakw].

B4. Further fast speech phenomena. A posture verb preceded by another verb in a sequencing form -*n* 'doing at the same time as' (§18.2) can be pronounced together as one phonological word, and then the final -*n* of the first verb is elided: *wuká-n rə-na-wún* (listen-SEQ sit-ACT.FOC-1sgBAS.VT) 'I am sitting listening; I am listening' is pronounced, in fast speech, as [wukárəna-wun]; and *wapá-n napa-kú* (leave-SEQ COMPL.VB-COMPL.SS) 'having left for good, having fully completed leaving' becomes [wapànapakú]. A sequence of two verbs one of which is monosyllabic may also result, as in *dá:-n adá* (sit-SEQ stay.IMPV) 'sit down' pronounced as [dá:n-dà]. (A year-old baby repeatedly reproduced this command as *dandá*, which for her was a way to refer to a chair: see §13.2.2.)

C1. Epenthetic glide *y* is inserted on any boundary, breaking a sequence of *i* and *a*, as in *saki-ab* 'name debate-too' > [saki-y-ab]; *tami=ad* (area=3masc.sg.NOM) 'it is an area' > [tami-y-ad], and *aki=ata* 'news then' > [aki-y-ata].

2.7 INTONATION PATTERNS

Falling intonation is characteristic of the end of a declarative clause. Interrogative intonation contour involves rising intonation on the last word of a clause (marked with ↗) with high pitch on the clause as a whole and an additional rising pitch on the last syllable, as in:

2.3 akə   səkər waku-kə-na-dəmən↗?
    what.fem.sg time go.out-FUT-ACT.FOC-2masc.sgBAS.VT
    'What time will you go out?'

In a rhetorical question, the sharp rise can be preceded by a falling intonation on the first word (marked with ↘):

2.4 ñən↘   agula↗?
    you.fem.sg why
    'What are you here for?

Commands have a slightly rising intonation, as in 2.5–6:

2.5 pəsəpa:m   atak↗
    rubbish+LK+LOC IMPV+put
    'Put (this) into the rubbish!'

2.6 da-n   ada↗
    go.down-SEQ sit.IMPV
    'Sit down!'

A combination of falling and rising intonation is characteristic of first person imperative clauses, often used as a marker of turn taking in discourse:

2.7 wa↘u↗
    speak+1sgIMPV
    'May I talk?'

Vocative intonation involves slight rise on the last syllable of the vocative and simultaneous lengthening of vowel in the last syllable of the vocative forms (restricted to kinship terms and personal names).

2.8 Maliye:::↗
    'Mali!'

Farewelling intonation is similar, with the proviso that it involves slight rise and then slight fall on the last syllable (note that its vowel is often lengthened):

2.9 yaradákwə::: ↗↘
    well+stay.IMPV
    'Stay well' (said by someone who is leaving as a farewell formula)

Exclamatory clauses involve a sharply falling intonation contour, especially if they include interjections expressing surprise, e.g. *wa*↘ 'Wow, oh dear'.

A further pattern in complex sentences which involve sequences of clauses involves rising intonation on the completive medial verb (see Chapter 18). The final verb of the first clause is repeated in the subsequent medial clause. A different-subject medial clause is shown in 2.10. Clause-final falling intonation in 2.10 is shown with ↘.

2.10 adiya   yə-na-di↘   [short pause] yə-da-k↗   ata
     DEM.DIST.REACT.TOP.pl go-FOC-3plBAS.VT   go-3pl-COMPL.DS then
     wa-d↘
     say-3masc.sgBAS.P
     'They went. Them having gone, he said'

A short pause only appears if some time is supposed to have elapsed between the time of the first sentence, and of the second one. A medial verb may form one phonological phrase with the final verb in the preceding main clause if no time is understood to have elapsed between the two sentences. In 2.11, this is signalled with square brackets around the sequence of two verbs: *yə-dì yə-kú*. The last (stressed) syllable of *yə-kú* is pronouncd with more intensity than the last (stressed) syllable of *yə-dì*.

2.11 adiya   [yə-dì   yə-kú]↗   ata   wa-di↘
      DEM.DIST.REACT.TOP.pl go-3plBAS.P go-COMPL.SS then say-3plBAS.P↗
      'They went. They went, having gone, they said'

This same intonation pattern also appears in Tok Pisin when spoken by the Manambu. This pattern has been observed with medial verbs marked with some sequencing morphemes (e.g. cotemporaneous sequencing *-taːy*), but not others (the immediate sequencing *-taka,* the temporal overlap *-(kə)kəb,* and the sequencing *-ən*). Juxtaposed dependent clauses have a distinctive intonation contour with the pitch going high up on the last syllable of the predicate (see §19.1).

Grammatical Relations

Understanding grammatical relations in Manambu is pivotal for understanding its grammar. A member of any major word class can head an intransitive predicate, or be a modifier in an NP. A verb as head of either transitive or intransitive predicate takes tense- and topicality-sensitive verbal cross-referencing suffixes, to mark subject (A/S) and non-subject. In contrast, if a member of most other classes is head in an intransitive predicate, it takes person-marking enclitics (§3.1). Grammatical relations are also marked by cases on nouns, on subject-non-subject basis (§3.2), and through a set of demonstratives, on an absolutive basis (§3.3).

3.1 CROSS-REFERENCING

Nouns, adjectives, adverbs, verbs, and most closed subclasses (see Chapter 10) can head an intransitive predicate. Only a verb can be head of a transitive predicate. In the indicative mood, all Manambu verbs can cross-reference one or two arguments. One of these has to be the subject—A or S. A non-subject argument can also be cross-referenced if it is more topical than the subject, independently of the verb's transitivity.

This is how it works. In 3.1, the S=A ambitransitive verb 'know' is used intransitively. The suffix -na- 'action focus' indicates that the focus is on the fact of knowing, and not on what is known. The subject (S), 'I', is cross-referenced on the verb. The cross-referencing suffixes employed are in Table 3.1.

3.1 bə   laku-na-**wun**
    already know/understand-ACT.FOC-1fem.sgBAS.VT
    'I know (already), I am knowledgeable'

This same verb can be used transitively, with an object. The object in 3.2 is not topical—that is, it is not something to be further deployed in the discourse. The subject (A) is the only participant cross-referenced on the verb:

3.2 (wun) a   yarək bə   laku-na-**wun**
    I   DEM.DIST+fem.sg news already know/understand-ACT.FOC-1fem.sgBAS.VT
    'I already know that news'

If a constituent other than the subject is more topical than the subject, both are cross-referenced on the verb. In 3.3–4 the object is topical, and it is cross-referenced in the second position on the verb, with the same markers as the ones used for the S/A in 3.1–2 (Table 3.1). The subject is also cross-referenced, but with a different set of markers (Table 3.2). Person marking on the verb can occur together with a full NP. Since the NP is optional, it is in parentheses.

3.3 (də wun-a:m) laku-**da-wun**
    he I-LK+OBJ know-3masc.sgSUBJ.VT-1fem.sgBAS.VT
    'He knows me'

3.4 (a-də   ma:j wun) laku-**tua-d**
DEM.DIST-masc.sg story I   know-1sgSUBJ.VT-3masc.sgBAS.VT
'I have understood it (e.g. a long story)'

An oblique can be cross-referenced on the verb, if topical. The destination, 'road', is the topic of 3.5, and is cross-referenced in the second position on the intransitive verb 'go'. The road is in the allative case (§7.5).

3.5 (wun) a-də   yaba:r   yi-**tua-d**
I   DEM.DIST-masc.sg road+LK+ALL go-1sgSUBJ.VT-3masc.sgBAS.VT
'I went towards that road' (that we are talking about)

The choice of an argument or an oblique to be cross-referenced on a verb depends on the topicality of this argument (or oblique), and also on the verb's semantics. Out of context, 3.6 could be understood as 'I finished that work (we were talking about)' (then, the object 'work' would be cross-referenced), or as 'I finished that work at that (topical) time' (then, 'time' would be cross-referenced), or as 'I finished that work in that (topical) way' (then 'way, manner', of feminine gender (§5.2.1), would be cross-referenced). The cross-referenced constituent can be overtly expressed, but does not have to, inasmuch as it is retrievable from the context:

3.6 a   yawi kusə-**tuə-l**
DEM.DIST+fem.sg work finish-1sgSUBJ.P-3fem.sgBAS.P
'I finished that work (we were talking about)'
'I finished that work at that (topical) time'
'I finished that work in that (topical) way'

Example 3.7 also has two meanings—differentiated only by the context.

3.7 ñap-a-ta:kw   Dora kui-la-bər
mother's.sister-LK-woman Dora give.to.third.p-3fem.sgSUBJ.VT-3duBAS.VT
'Aunt Dora gave (us) these two (Malay apples)'
'Aunt Dora gave (Malay apples) to the two (girls)'

Topical constituents which can be cross-referenced in the second position include time, location, destination, and manner. The following can never be cross-referenced:

(a) A copula complement—see 3.8 and 3.9. The copula subject is always cross-referenced; the second position can be occupied by location, manner or time.

3.8 a-bər   ñədi   kwakuli <u>tə-bər</u>
DEM.DIST-du children:DU orphan become/be/stand-3duBAS.VT
'Those children became orphans'

3.9 a-bər   ñədi   kwakuli <u>tə-brə-di</u>
DEM.DIST-du children:DU orphan become/be/stand-3dusUBJ.P-3plBAS.P
'They became orphans at those times, or in those ways, or in those places'

(b) The second argument of verbs of 'becoming' or 'turning into':

3.10 lə aka bə   məd   <u>patiaku-l</u>
she here already cassowary turn-3fem.sgBAS.P
'She has then already turned into a cassowary'

(c) Nominal components of complex verbs (§7.2), e.g. *gu* 'water' in *gu yaku-* 'wash in water, bathe'; *məl* 'eye' in *məl və-* (eye see) 'see with eyes'; or *wapruku-* 'be overfull', as 3.11. Here, 'house' (of masculine gender) is the subject:

3.11 brə-kə-də   wi   miyawa sa:n-a-dəka   wapruku-d
3du-OBL-masc.sg house all   money-LK-ONLY overfill-3masc.sgBAS.P
'Their whole house was overflowing with money'

(d) A constituent marked with a transportative, substitutive, or comitative case—see §§7.7–9.
(e) A speech report—see §19.5.

Ellipsis of noun phrases, frequent in speech, makes the exact reference of cross-referenced participants highly context dependent. Statistically, some participants tend to be cross-referenced more often than others. For instance, the addressee of the verb *wa-* 'say' is more often cross-referenced than the message. This has to do with the fact that *wa-* is frequently used to frame direct speech reports which can never be cross-referenced. A form *wa-kə-tua-di* (say-FUT-1sgSUBJ.VT-3plBAS.VT) can mean 'I will tell (something) to them', or 'I will tell them, e.g. stories', depending on the context.

A form *kur-məna-dəwun* (do/make-2sgSUBJ.VT-1masc.sgBAS.VT) is more likely to mean 'you did (something) to me', than 'you created or made me', if the story from which this example comes is not a creation myth. With the verb 'give', the overall frequency of cross-referencing either the 'recipient' or the 'gift' is the same (this goes against the frequently discussed preference, among the languages of the world, to mark the recipient rather than the 'gift' of 'give').

In contrast to verbs, non-verbal predicates cross-reference just the subject, with cross-referencing enclitics listed in Table 3.4.

Table 3.1 features the 'basic' set of cross-referencing markers used for

(i) the subject, if no other, more topical, constituent is to be cross-referenced—as in 3.1–2;
(ii) the more topical constituent other than the subject—as in 3.3–5.

In situation (ii), the subject is cross-referenced with a special set of cross-referencing suffixes as listed in Table 3.2. A marker from this set is always followed by a marker from the 'basic' set. The relevant verbal cross-referencing sets distinguish what we call 'versatile tense' (employed for present, recent past, and in future contexts—see §12.2). The tense distinction is neutralized in dual and plural of the basic set. The non-tense-sensitive suffixes in the subject set are the ones used in partially inflected verbal forms (where only the subject is expressed: see §11.1.1).

The two sets of personal markers are similar, but not identical. The versatile tense basic set differs from its past counterpart only in the feminine singular forms. The versatile tense subject markers differ from their past tense counterpart in the quality of the final vowel in all the forms except for first and third person plural where the present–recent past set has an extra syllable *-na*.

The basic sets differ from the subject sets in first person (all numbers). The subject set has no gender distinctions in first person. The basic sets are easily segmentable: they contain gender-number markers *-d-* 'masculine', *-l/ø-* 'feminine' in the singular, and number markers *-bər-* 'dual' and *-di-* 'plural', in dual and plural forms respectively.

All other forms are similar to personal pronouns featured in Table 3.3. The basic set shows more similarities with the personal pronouns than the subject set. The first person markers in the subject sets are not related to the personal pronouns at all.

TABLE 3.1   Verbs as heads of predicate: basic set of cross-referencing suffixes

PERSON/GENDER	SG		DU	PL
	VERSATILE	PAST	VERSATILE/PAST	VERSATILE/PAST
1 fem	*-wun*	*-l-wun*	*-bər-an*	*-di-an*
1 masc	*-də-wun*			
2 fem	*-ñən*	*-lə-ñən*	*-bər-bər*	*-di-gwər*, *-di-gur*
2 masc	*-də-mən*			
3 fem	*-ø*	*-l*	*-bər*	*-di*
3 masc	*-d*			

Person-marking enclitics whose only role is to cross-reference the subject of a verbless clause with a non-verb as a predicate head are given in Table 3.4. The segmental make-up of the markers is almost identical with the basic cross-referencing set in Table 3.1.

The difference lies (a) in that the markers in Table 3.4 are enclitics and the ones in Table 3.1 are suffixes (see §§2.5–6 on the differences between these), and (b) in the existence of free variants of first and third person singular feminine forms. The vowel *a* in the forms in Table 3.4 can be considered a kind of linker; note its absence with the suffixes.

Example 3.12 illustrates an adjective, and 3.13 an adverb as head of intransitive predicates.

3.12 a-di   ja:p   kuprap=adi
     DEM.DIST-pl thing bad=3plNOM
     'These things are bad'

3.13 yabi:b-yabi:b=ad
     quickly-quickly=3masc.sgNOM
     'It (the way he is moving) is very quickly'

In 2.1–2 nouns were used as predicate heads. These same enclitics mark focused constituents, in highlighting focus constructions (see §20.3).

The choice between cross-referencing just the subject or also an additional participant on a Manambu verb is largely independent of the verb's transitivity: both transitive and intransitive verbs can cross-reference one or two arguments.

Importantly, the number of arguments cross-referenced correlates with the grammatical categories of the verb. The option of either one or two cross-referencing positions is available for independent positive indicative declarative and interrogative clauses, positive and negative habitual declarative and interrogative clauses, relative clauses, and dependent juxtaposed clauses (both negative and positive). See examples 3.1–10 above. Such forms are fully inflected for person (see §11.1.1; Table 11.1). Only one cross-referencing position is available for all these clauses if the verb contains the action focus marker *-na-*. Causal clauses and all different-subject medial clauses also cross-reference just the subject (with the non-tensed suffixes in Table 3.2). The imperative has its own paradigm of subject cross-referencing (see §13.2). All these forms are partially inflected.

TABLE 3.2   Verbs as heads of predicate: subject set of cross-referencing suffixes

PERSON/GENDER	SG			DU			PL		
TENSE	VERSATILE	PAST	NON-TENSED	VERSATILE	PAST	NON-TENSED	VERSATILE	PAST	NON-TENSED
1	-tua-	-tuɐ-	-tu-	-ta-		-tɐ-	-bana-		-ba-
2 fem	-ñɐu-	-ɐuɐñ-	-ñɐu-	-bra		-brɐ-	-gwura-, -gura-		
2 masc	-mɐu-	-ɐuɐu-	-uɐu-						
3 fem	-la-	-ɐ-	-ɐ-l-				-dana-		-da-
3 masc	-da-	-ɐp-	-ɐp-						

TABLE 3.3   Personal pronouns

	Sɢ	Dᴜ	Pʟ
1	*wun*	*an*	*ñan*
2 fem	*ñən*		*gwur*
2 masc	*mən*	*bər*	
3 fem	*lə*		*dəy, day*
3 masc	*də*		

No cross-referencing is found in negative declarative non-habitual clauses, in positive completive and customary aspects and in a variety of non-declarative forms including prohibitive, desiderative, and frustrative, and all same-subject medial clauses. These forms are uninflected. See a summary in Table 11.1.

The number of cross-referencing positions on the verb only marginally relates to mood, modality, polarity, and aspect. Most of the verbal forms which accept one cross-referencing position or take no cross-referencing are non-declarative. Most negative forms take no cross-referencing at all.

The number of cross-referencing positions is independent of the verb's transitivity. It depends on the pragmatic properties of the non-subject constituent, and not so much the lexical properties of the verb itself. This is partly reminiscent of Ugric and Samoyedic languages.

There, a special verbal conjugation (called 'objective') is used for transitive verbs if the object is definite or topical. A transitive verb with an indefinite object appears in the 'subjective' conjugation (see, for instance, Moravcsik 1983 on Hungarian and Nikolaeva 1999 on Northern Khanty). Different sets of cross-referencing suffixes in Menya, an Angan language from Morobe Province, Papua New Guinea (Whitehead 1991), mark more topical, and less topical, subjects. However, in neither case is there a complete analogy with the Manambu system.

The marking of A/S as the only cross-referenced constituent ('basic' marking set) is the same as the marking of the second argument if it is more topical than the subject. This may seem reminiscent of split ergativity whereby, under certain conditions, the S constituent (the only

TABLE 3.4   Person marking on non-verbs as heads of predicate

	Sɢ	Dᴜ	Pʟ
1 fem	=*awun*, =*al-wun* as free variants	=*ab(ə)r-an*	=*adiy-an*
1 masc	=*adə-wun*		
2 fem	=*añən*, =*al-ñən* as free variants	=*abər-bər*	=*adi-gwər*, =*adi-gur*
2 masc	=*adə-mən*		
3 fem	=*all-ø*	=*abər*	=*adi*
3 masc	=*ad*		

argument of an intransitive verb) is marked in the same way as the O (the second argument of a transitive verb).[1] However, the Manambu pattern is only superficially similar to this, since:

(a) the basic cross-referencing set marks A/S and also O, a locative, a manner, or a time constituent, that is, it is hardly comparable with a 'real' ergative/absolutive system, with an opposition between S/O and A; and

(b) the occurrence of the marking is conditioned by the topicality of the participant and only partly by its grammatical function (we can recall that some relations, such as copula complement, or comitative, are never cross-referenced).

The closest analogy to the Manambu system comes from Alamblak (Sepik Hill: Bruce 1984: 184–8, 216–30). Here, an argument additional to the subject can be cross-referenced on the verb 'if it can be thought of as a crucial participant in the situation' (219). Just as in Manambu, the second argument marker follows the marker of the subject. However, unlike Manambu, the same set of markers cross-references both arguments, and there are no special sets for non-verbal predicates. It is not clear whether there are any types of arguments which can never be cross-referenced. Sare (or Kapriman), also from the Sepik Hill family, does not have this feature (Sumbuk 1999). Is this similarity between Manambu and Alamblak a simple coincidence? Or, given that some Manambu subclans claim their origins to be in the area of Chambri lake— to the south of which Alamblak is spoken (see §1.5.3)—could this be an areal feature? The question remains open. Also see §§22.2–3, where we return to the issue of areal diffusion.

We conclude that, though marking the pragmatic status of constituents through variation in cross-referencing patterns on the verb is not unprecedented, no other system we know of is fully comparable with the way Manambu verbs mark their participants.

3.2 GRAMMATICAL RELATIONS MARKED ON NOUN PHRASES

Cases in Manambu mark grammatical relations on a basic nominative-accusative principle. Only definite and completely affected objects are marked with the -*Vm* case 'accusative/ locative' (see §7.3 for a hypothesis concerning the motivation for this case syncretism). Table 3.5 summarizes the principles of dependent marking on nouns, and how these correlate with the marking on verbs as heads of predicates.

Table 3.5 shows that grammatical functions covered by the second-position cross-referencing suffixes only somewhat overlap with the ones covered by cases. The case syncretism does not fully coincide with the syncretism of meanings available for the basic cross-referencing set when it refers to a non-subject constituent. We can recall that this may refer to location (for which three cases are available: a location can be unmarked, marked with a locative case or the terminative case); to an object (one case available), or to an instrument or manner (one case available). This illustrates one-to-many correspondences in the relationship between cross-referencing on the verb and case marking on nouns. Case meanings below the thick line in Table 3.5 do not have a cross-referencing correlate: these constituents are not cross-referenced.

An object marked with the accusative/locative case is likely to be a topic, and is cross-referenced more often than an unmarked O, in terms of textual frequency. However, this is not a

---

[1] Instances whereby a language has an ergative pattern of marking grammatical relations depending on the topical continuity of S/O include Asheninca Campa (an Arawak language from Peru: Payne and Payne (2005) showed how a split intransitive pattern marks the main story line, or foregrounded actions). In Yagua (Peba-Yagua) and Pajonal Campa (Arawak), S is marked like O to highlight some new information (but not a new participant) (Dixon 1994: 211).

TABLE 3.5   Head marking and dependent marking in Manambu: a comparison

HEAD MARKING	GRAMMATICAL FUNCTION	DEPENDENT MARKING	GRAMMATICAL FUNCTION
first position cross-reference	A/S	-ø case	A/S time; manner; location
second position cross-referencing	topical non A/S	-*Vm* accusative-locative case	definite completely affected O; locative/time
		-*Vk* dative-aversive case	second/third argument; beneficiary; maleficiary; any dangerous circumstance or participant
		-*Vr* allative-instrumental case	allative/instrumental
		-*Vb* terminative case	terminative (to the point, to the brim)
		-*wa*	comitative
		-*Vsap*, -*Vsay*	transport
		-*yæy*	substitutive

steadfast rule: if another constituent is more topical than the O, then it will be cross-referenced. We saw in 3.7 above that, with the verb 'give', either the gift or the recipient can be cross-referenced, depending on their topicality. Only the 'gift' can be marked with accusative/locative, while the recipient is always marked with dative.

In 3.14, the place which is the topic of the stretch of discourse is cross-referenced on the verb (with the feminine gender form). The indefinite direct object, unmarked for case, is not.

3.14 a-də   jagər   vyapra-tua-l
      DEM-masc.sg garfish shoot-1sgSUBJ.VT-3fem.sgBAS.VT
      'I shoot that garfish (in this place we are in now)'

Alternatively, a completely affected O marked with the accusative/locative case may be less topical than the subject, especially if the verb is marked with the action focus -*na*-. In 3.15, the angry man is determined to exterminate the moon who, as he thinks, is responsible for his wife's menstruation. The moon is marked for case and is the topic of the story, but is not cross-referenced: the action focus -*na*- shows that the focus is on the action and it is more important than the O.

3.15 bap-a:m   vya-kə-na-dəwun
      moon-ACC/LOC hit-FUT-ACT.FOC-1masc.sgBAS.VT
      'I will kill the moon'

TABLE 3.6 Case marking and cross-referencing of O

Cross-referencing O on the verb	Case marking of O	Example
yes	yes	3.3
yes	no	3.4
no (no other non-subject constituent cross-referenced)	no	3.2
no (another non-subject constituent cross-referenced)	no	3.14
no	yes	3.15

Table 3.6 lists the examples illustrating the correlations between case marking and cross-referencing of O.

We conclude that cross-referencing on verbs and case marking on nouns follow different principles. Verbs distinguish between subject and (topical) non-subject, while nouns operate on a principle reminiscent of nominative-accusative. In addition, nouns distinguish a rather large number of forms for non-core participants. We return to the discussion of cases in Chapter 7.

3.3 'REACTIVATED TOPIC' DEMONSTRATIVES

There are three series of demonstratives marking 'reactivated topic'—*kə*- series 'proximal to the speaker', *wa*- series 'proximal to the hearer', and *a*- series 'distant from both' (discussed in detail in §10.2.3). These always agree in gender and number with the S/O argument. They are employed to bring an already established topic 'back to action', if it has not been mentioned for some time. Consider 3.16, said to 5-year-old Kerryanne who was running around at a local market, to remind her of the existence of her mother and myself (whom she ought to be following):

3.16 abra   yi-na-bər
     DEM.DIST.REACT.TOP+dual go-ACT.FOC-3duBAS.VT
     'Those two are going!' (I am reminding you of them; or else you will be left behind)

If an O constituent is a reactivated topic, it is obligatorily cross-referenced on the verb (using the basic set in the second cross-referencing position). In 3.17, the bundle of sago established as a topic in the previous stretch of discourse is mentioned again. Since it is topical, it is also cross-referenced on the verb:

3.17 na:gw ada   ka-war-la-d
     sago   DEM.DIST.REACT.TOP+masc.sg carry-go.up-3fem.sgSUBJ.VT-3masc.sgBAS.VT
     'She has carried up that previously mentioned sago'

With the ditransitive verb 'give', a reactivated topic marker refers to the recipient rather than the gift if it is more animate than the gift, unless the gift is more topical. Example 3.18 comes from a story about a man (the topic of the whole story) who was considered dead by his relatives. In the previous stretch of text the flying fox who had been looking after the man tells him that his relatives were arranging a mortuary feast for him. The man has not been mentioned for a paragraph or so. Then, it turns out that the preparations for the mortuary feast for the man are under way at the man's house. The man is thus 'brought back' into the text as the reactivated topic. The mortuary feast, in the O function in 3.18, is the gift; the 'reactivated topic demonstrative', and the cross-referencing on the verb, refer to the man:

3.18 maja:n   ada_   kui-da-d
      mortuary.feast DEM.DIST.REACT.TOP+3masc.sg give.to.third.p-3plsUBJ.P-3masc.sgBAS.P
      'They were giving mortuary feast to him (the reactivated topic)'

We will see, in §10.2.3, that a reactivated topic demonstrative can refer to the S of an ambitransitive verb used intransitively. It can also refer to a location, as in 10.68. The content of a direct speech report is never referred to with such a demonstrative. The problem of whether the reactivated topic demonstrative forms one NP with a noun it refers to or not is discussed in §10.2.3.

The predominantly absolutive (S/O) basis for the reactivated topic markers agrees with a cross-linguistic tendency for a correlation between the S/O function and topicality (Du Bois 1987). That a demonstrative should operate on an absolutive basis is hardly surprising—in Dyirbal and a few other languages, an NP including a nominal demonstrative may only occur in S or O function (Dixon 2003: 83, 94–99; Aikhenvald and Dixon forthcoming). Reactivated topic demonstratives provide a strong criterion for S (see, for instance, the discussion of polyfunctional verbs and their argument structure in §4.2.2). The subject of a verbless clause or head of non-verbal predicate is hardly ever referred to with the reactivated topic demonstrative (the implication of this is that it is not treated on a par with S arguments).

3.4 GRAMMATICAL RELATIONS IN MANAMBU: A SUMMARY

Cross-referencing on the verb and case marking on nouns in Manambu operate on different principles. The choice of cross-referencing depends on the tense-aspect-mood and polarity, and on the presence of a participant more topical than the subject. Case marking is reminiscent of a nominative-accusative system, with the occurrence of the object case depending on the definiteness and the degree of involvement of the O. Systems of this kind are cross-linguistically attested (see Aikhenvald 1994 for a brief survey).

Cross-referencing on the verb is more unusual. It follows a subject-non-subject principle. The subject of a verb, be it A or S, always has to be cross-referenced. Any non-subject constituent—with the exception of copula complement, transportative, comitative, and substitutive constituents, and speech reports—can be cross-referenced. (This is reminiscent of Alamblak, from the Sepik Hill family.) The same, 'basic', marking is used for cross-referencing the subject (A/S) with no other topical constituent; and for cross-referencing a topical non-subject. In addition, all of the A/S of all verbs are marked in the same way. The subject of a non-verbal predicate head acquires a somewhat different marking, and does not distinguish tense.

In addition, three series of demonstratives marking 'reactivated topic' operate on an absolutive basis, marking gender and number agreement with the topical S/O argument which is then highly likely to be cross-referenced on the verb.

The three ways of marking grammatical relations allow for a highly elaborate way of specifying the topicality of participants and the involvement and definiteness of the object.

A historical note is in order. The dependent marking on nouns appears older than the unusual system of verbal cross-referencing. Cases for core arguments are a shared feature of Ndu languages, while the personal marking of two arguments on verbs appears to be a Manambu innovation also shared with Gala. Iatmul has only subject cross-referencing which appears to be a relatively recent innovation.

4

Word Classes

Open word classes in Manambu are nouns (§4.1) and verbs (§4.2) Two subclasses of adjectives are discussed in §4.3, and §4.4 focuses on the semi-closed class of adverbs. A brief overview of closed classes is in §4.5.

4.1 NOUNS

All nouns have grammatical categories of gender (Chapter 5), number (Chapter 6), and case (Chapter 7). Syntactically, a noun can be both head and dependent in possessive constructions (Chapter 8), head and modifier in an NP, and head of predicate (see §4.3 and §4.4). Derivation and compounding are discussed in Chapter 9. The types of noun phrases and their features (including word order) are addressed in Chapter 20, within the context of other multiword constituents.

Nouns divide into a number of subclasses, in terms of their morphophonological properties (§.4.1.1) and in terms of semantics and correlating grammatical properties of their referents (§4.1.2).

4.1.1 Morphophonological subclasses of nouns

Nouns fall into overlapping subclasses depending on (A) whether the root vowel is alternating or not, and (B) what type of linker it takes.

(A) Vowel alternations in alternating noun roots are as follows.

(i) A long vowel *a:* is often shortened to *a* if a stressed suffix is added, e.g. *ba:n* 'back', *ban-vál* 'back of canoe' (see §2.3.2).

(ii) In about 30 per cent of nouns, the unstressed root vowel *a* or *a:* is shortened to *ə*, as in *takwa-ñán* (woman+LK-child) 'girl', *takwa-ñən-pə́k* 'like a girl', *ñən-a-wa* (child-LK-COM) 'with child'; *tak* 'seed', *tək-ə-mí* 'seed of a tree'; *rak* 'scale', *rək-ə-kamí* 'scale of fish'; *mutam* 'face', *mutəm-a karab* (face-LK men's.house) 'in front of men's house'; *ma:r* 'wind', *mər-ə́m* 'in wind'; *wa:r* 'big stringbag', *wər-ə́m, wur-ə́m* 'in a big stringbag'; *ma:gw* 'generic noun; whatever', *məg-ə́m* 'in whatever'.

(iii) In one noun, *æ* becomes *ə* if the root is unstressed: *væy* 'spear', *vəyír* 'to spear, with spear' further contracted to *ví:r*. The vowel *i* in *yi* 'fire' undergoes reduction to *yə* (other nouns ending in *i* are not alternating, e.g. *wi* 'house').

Non-alternating roots undergo no change, as in *takw* 'market', *takw-a:r* (market-LK+ALL) 'to market'. The information on whether a noun belongs to an 'alternating' class or not has to be supplied in the dictionary.

(B) Type of linker is determined by the noun, and has to be specified in a dictionary. A root requires a vocalic linker, if it is used as:

- a prehead modifier in a noun phrase, e.g. *samasama sa:n* (many/much+LK money) 'much money', *kul-a kamna:gw* (new/raw-LK food) 'raw food'; a part of a compound, e.g. *du-a-ñan* (man-LK-child) 'boy', *takwa ya:b* (woman+LK road) 'female road'; or in reduplication, e.g. *nak-a-nak* (one-LK-one) 'one by one';[1]
- with most case markers (see §7.1),
- as argument of a postposition (§4.5.2) and
- with a number of other affixes, such as *-pək* 'like', e.g. *wun-a-pək* (I-LK-like) 'like me'; or intensive *-ka-*, e.g. *wam-a-ka-wam-a wapwi* (white-LK-INT-white-LK clothing) 'very white clothing'.

The linker is required in a relative clause preposed to the noun it 'modifies', e.g. *luku kur-na-d-ə du* (steal do-ACT.FOC-3masc.sgBAS.VT-LK man) 'a man who steals' (see §19.2.1).

The derivational suffixes which do not require the linker include the numeral suffix *-kərəb* 'together, -some', as in *vəti-kərəb* 'two together, twosome' (see §10.6.1). Coordinating compounds do not require the linker, e.g. *awáy-mamǽy* 'relatives responsible for bringing up a child' (lit. 'maternal uncle (and) mother's sister'). Of the four possessive constructions, one does not require a linker, while all others do, e.g. *wun sə* (I name) 'my name' (and see §8.1).

The information on the presence or absence of a linker has to be specified for each suffix and construction type. If a verb is used as a modifier of NP, the linker is predictable. A verb form ending in a vowel requires no additional linker, e.g. *kiya-na ta:kw* (die-ACT.FOC+3fem.sgBAS.VT woman) 'a dying woman'. A verb form ending in a consonant can only be used as a modifier if it takes personal cross-referencing. The linker for the cross-referencing endings is *ə* for third person, and *a* for other persons, e.g. *kiya-na-d-ə du* (die-ACT.FOC-3masc.sgBAS.VT-LK man) 'a dying man'.

If a non-verb ends in a vowel, it does not require a linker, e.g. *numa ta:kw* (big+fem.sg woman) 'big woman'; but *vyakat-a ta:kw* (good-LK woman) 'good woman'; *kamí:* 'fish', *kamí:k* 'for fish'; *kwasabí* 'stringbag', *kwasabí:m* 'in stringbag'. For non-verbs which do not end in a vowel, the linker (either *ə* or *a*) has to be supplied as dictionary information. The following possibilities are distinguished.

I. THE LINKER *a* is attested with about 40 per cent of nouns and with most adjectives and modifiers from closed classes, e.g. *val-a ma:j* (canoe-LK story) 'story of a canoe, canoe story'; *val-a:r* (canoe-LK+INSTR) 'with a canoe'; *samasama sa:n* (much+LK money) 'a lot of money'; *Luway* 'personal name', *Luway-a:k* 'to Luway'. Personal pronouns (all but third person singular and dual discussed below) take the linker *-a*, e.g. *wun-a ma:m* (I-LK+fem.sg elder.sibling) 'my elder sister'.[2] An epenthetic *y* appears before the linker *-a* following the root-final *i* (see §2.6), as in *wi* 'house', *wiy-a-m* 'in a house'; *tami:* 'area', *tamiy-a kudi* (area-LK language) 'language of the area'. Newly introduced place names can occur with *a* or without a linker, e.g. *Mosbi:m*, *Mosbiy-a-m* 'in (Port) Moresby'.

---

[1] The linker as a marker of a modifier in an NP helps determine constituency boundaries. For instance, in the NP [*adul-a təp*]*-a-kə-di* (DEM.DIST+masc.sg+INSIDE-LK village-LK-POSS-pl) 'those belonging to that inland village', the demonstrative *adul-a* 'that inland (village)' is a modifier to 'village'—this is indicated by the presence of the linker. A headless possessive construction 'derived' from an NP is discussed in §8.2. The linker is absent in *adawəl təp-a-kə-di* (DEM.DIST+masc.sg+INSIDE village-LK-POSS-pl) which means 'there-inland those from the village' and is an ellipsed clause rather than one NP.

[2] The agreeing adjectives *kwasa* 'small' and *nəma* 'big' do not occur without the final *a*. Here, the linker can be considered part of the root (see §4.3).

II. THE LINKER ə is required by about 60 per cent of nouns, e.g. *ñəd* 'middle', *ñəd-ətəp* (middle-LK village) 'middle of the village'; *nagər* 'fishing net', *nagər-ə-l* 'to a fishing net'; *ka:m* 'hunger', *kam-ə-k* 'for hunger'. A word ending in the monomorphemic gender marker *-d* 'masculine singular' receives the linker ə, e.g. *nəma-d-ə təp* (big-masc.sg-LK village) 'a big village'.

Nouns which end in *ay*, *æy*, or *a:y* take the linker ə; and the resulting sequence of *y* and ə is pronounced as *i* (in agreement with §2.1.2), e.g. *amæy* 'mother', *amæyik* 'to mother'; *asa:y* 'father', *asayik* 'to father'; *vəti* 'two', *vətiyik* (two-LK-DAT) 'for the two'. If a word ending with a labialized consonant takes the linker ə, it is pronounced as *u* in rapid speech, e.g. *Manab* 'the Manambu', *Manab-ə kudi* or *Manamb-u kudi* (Manambu-LK language) 'the Manambu language'; *gwalugw* 'clan', *gwalugw-ə-gwalugw-ə-r* or *gwalugw-u-gwalugw-u-r* (clan-LK-clan-LK-ALL) 'from clan to clan; to every clan'.

One noun, *mi*, takes the linker *a*, in its meaning 'tree', as in *miyá:r* 'to tree', *miyá:m* 'in tree'. If used without a linker, it means 'up', e.g. in *mi:r* 'upwards', *mi:m* 'up'. Few nouns, e.g. *ya:b* 'road' and some newly introduced place names, can occur with either linker, e.g. *yabəm*, *yaba:m* 'on the road' without any difference in meaning.

III. A SPECIAL LINKER *-kə-* is used with third person singular and dual pronouns, e.g. *də* 'he', *də-kə ma:j* (he-OBL+3fem.sg story) 'his story', *də-kə wukən* 'with him', *də-kə-m* '(on) him', *dəkadəka* 'only he'. The interrogative *sə* 'who' also takes the linker *-kə-*: see §10.4.

Third person plural pronouns take the linker *a* and no marker *-kə-*, e.g. *dəy-a:m* 'them'. The linker *-kə-* provides a convenient way of distinguishing the two meanings of the pronoun *bər* 'second person dual; third person dual', in *brə-kə-d-ə ñaj* (3du-LK-masc.sg-LK paternal.uncle) 'paternal uncle of the two of them'. In contrast, the dual pronoun *bər* takes a linker *a-*, as in *bra-d-ə ñaj* (2du+LK-masc.sg-LK paternal.uncle) 'paternal uncle of the two of you'.

The origin of the linker morphemes is often straightforward. Proto-Ndu disyllabic nouns whose final syllable ended in a stop lost their final vowel in Manambu, e.g. Proto-Ndu **ta:kwa*, Manambu *ta:kw* (cf. Gala *dokwa*, Iatmul *ta:kwa*) 'woman'; Proto-Ndu **kəpwa*, Manambu *kəpw* (Gala *kubua*, Yelogu *kəpwa*) 'ground', Proto-Ndu *ñiga* (as in Iatmul *ñiga*), Manambu *ñəg* 'leaf', Proto-Ndu **səpa*, Manambu *səp* 'skin', Proto-Ndu **la:pu*, Manambu *lap* 'banana', Proto-Ndu **muña(:)*, Manambu *məñ* 'breast', Proto-Ndu *ta:ba*, Manambu *ta:b* 'hand'. The final vowel loss also occurred in monosyllabic nouns containing a stop or a glide and the vowel *a*, e.g. Proto-Ndu **ña*, Manambu *ñə* 'sun, day', Proto-Ndu **ya*, Manambu *yi* 'fire'. The lost final vowel, typically *a*, appears as a linker, as it does in these words. However, not every linker *a* in Manambu corresponds to a 'lost' vowel; for instance, *tikál* 'tongue' takes the linker *a*; but there is no evidence that any other Ndu language had a final *a* in this word, cf. Gala *dakál*, Iatmul *təgat*. The origin of the linker in these cases requires further comparative study, as does the origin of the linker *-kə-*.

4.1.2 Semantically and grammatically determined subclasses of nouns

Nouns fall into several grammatical subclasses according to their morphological possibilities which correlate with semantic properties of their referents. These classes may overlap. As a result, a noun can belong to more than one class.

Nouns with ANIMATE and with INANIMATE referents differ in the principles of gender assignment. The gender assignment of animate nouns is by sex and also by shape and size of the referent. In the gender assignment of inanimate nouns shape, size, and some other parameters (such as degree and quantity) play a role. The semantics of genders distinguishes mass and count nouns—see §5.2. Vocatives are typically formed on nouns with an animate referent and on personal names. These restrictions are tendencies rather than steadfast rules: any noun referring to an addressee, if called, or spoken to, can acquire a vocative form, e.g. *bal-a* (pig-VOC) 'oh pig!', *amæy-a* 'oh mother!' Vocatives never form part of a clause, and are separated from the clause by a pause (see §2.7 on the specific vocative intonation and vowel lengthening).

BODY PART and ORIENTATION TERMS—such as *ya:l* 'belly', *mutam* 'face', *ma:l* 'side', *ñəd* 'middle'—differ from other nouns in that they appear in part–whole possessive constructions (see §8.1), e.g. *yala-wi* (belly+LK-house) 'inside the house'.

INHERENTLY LOCATIONAL nouns, e.g. *tami:* 'area', *ñab* 'the Sepik River', may occur unmarked for locative or directional case (see Chapter 7). The body part noun *ya:l* 'belly, stomach' behaves as an inherently locational noun with respect to human referents: siblings or twins are often referred to as those who *ya:l nə waku-bər* (belly one go.out-3duBAS.P) 'came from one belly'. Place names can also be unmarked for locative case, as in 4.1:

4.1 Swakap yi-dana
    Swakap go-3plSUBJ.VT+3fem.sgBAS.VT
    'They went to Swakap'

Nouns referring to MEANS OF TRANSPORT take the 'transportative' cases -*Vsay* and -*Vsap*, e.g. *val-a-say*, *val-a-sap* (canoe-LK-TRANSP) 'by canoe' (§7.7).

INHERENTLY TEMPORAL NOUNS refer exclusively to time spans and are often unmarked for case (cf. §7.2 and §21.2.1), e.g. *nəbəl* 'today'; *sər* 'tomorrow'. Temporal nouns form locative, terminative, dative, and comitative cases, and can be modified by a numeral, e.g. *jayib nak* (moment one) 'one moment' (unlike adverbs). Examples 4.2–4 illustrate case marking on temporal nouns. A noun marked with the locative case refers to a defined point in time (4.4), while an unmarked temporal noun refers to the stretch of time (4.3). Along similar lines, *nagəs* means 'the day before yesterday', and *nagəs-ə-b* (the.day.before.yesterday-LK-TERM) means 'lately, exactly up until recently').

4.2 sər-a:k   kamna:gw-a
    tomorrow-LK+DAT food-3fem.sgNOM
    'This is the food for tomorrow'

4.3 nəbəl væra-k-na-di
    today come.back-FUT-ACT.FOC-3plBAS.VT
    'They will come back today (any time today)'

4.4 nəbəl-a:m   væra-k-na-di
    today-LK+LOC come.back-FUT-ACT.FOC-3plBAS.VT
    'They will come back later on today (that is, a part of today which is later than now)'

Temporal nouns are less noun-like than prototypical nouns because they cannot be modified by adjectives, or be possessors or possessees in possessive NPs. Similarly to other nouns, temporal nouns may form coordinate compounds, e.g. *sər-mu:* (tomorrow-the.day.after.tomorrow) means 'within the next few days'. Just like other nouns, they can be coordinated using the comitative, e.g. *sər-a-wa mu:* (tomorrow-LK-COM day.after.tomorrow) 'tomorrow and the day after'.

A small set of NON-INFLECTING nouns which take no case marking are mostly loans, e.g. *lotu* 'church', *stori* 'talking' (from Tok Pisin *lotu*, *stori*), e.g. *stori rə-na-dian* (talking sit-ACT.FOC-1plBAS.VT) 'we sit talking', *lotu ma: rə* (church NEG sit:NEG) '(he) does not go to church'.

Two nouns with GENERIC REFERENCE, *məwi* 'things like that' and *ma:gw* 'whatsitsname, whatever' (see A.III in §20.1.1 and §21.3.1), stand apart from other nouns because of their semantics.

The noun *ma:gw* can replace any noun if the speaker does not recall the exact term. (The general verb *məgi-* 'do whatever' is related to this: §21.3.2.) The generic noun *məwi* is unusual in that it follows a noun it modifies (all other noun and adjective modifiers are preposed to the head noun), as in *yawi məwi* (work things.like.this) 'work and other things of that nature; things like work', *wi məwi* 'things like houses'. This position is similar to that of quantifiers and numerals (§§10.5–6).

KINSHIP NOUNS form a closed subset. They always have a human referent. Some have a fixed gender: *ñaj* 'paternal uncle' and *awa:y* 'maternal uncle' are always masculine, and *amæy* 'mother' and *yawus* 'paternal aunt' are always feminine. Others have variable gender, e.g. *ma:m* 'elder sibling' and *ñamus* (or *ñaməs*) 'younger sibling'. Only kinship terms have an obligatory overt number marking (§6.1).

PERSONAL NAMES are a culturally salient subclass (see §1.3.2, §21.5.4). These always have a human or an important referent, and a fixed gender. As demonstrated by Harrison (1990a), names are conceived of as valued possessions of a clan, and using a name belonging to another clan is tantamount to stealing property.

Names cannot be pluralized, or occur as heads of possessive NPs. They have specific sets of gender-sensitive derivational affixes (see §5.3). They occur as postnominal modifiers in appositional NPs (see §20.1.1, on the noun phrase structure), e.g. *wun-a ma:m Pakənabər* (I-LK+fem.sg older.sibling NAME) 'my elder sibling Pakənabər'; and can form associative plural (§6.2.2). Any object considered a totem of a clan or of a subclan can be used as a personal name. This is why names constitute a potentially open class and also overlap with terms of address. Nowadays, names from Tok Pisin and English are making their way into the language—e.g. *Jəmos* 'James', *Jemima* (pronounced as [Jemi'ma]), *Paulina* 'Pauline', *Pol* 'Paul'. They have the same syntactic properties as the original Manambu names. Most nouns or even noun phrases can be used as personal names, e.g. *Saun* 'white pelican; female name', *Gwarabi* 'mango; male and female name', *Ñəd-ə-wi* (middle-LK-house) 'middle of the house; female name'. When used as such, they share all other properties of personal names.

TERMS OF ADDRESS (Manambu *wayəpi* or *way, wa:y*) are a typologically unusual subclass of nouns. In the Manambu tradition, every clan possesses a set of terms for culturally important objects, alongside the clan's 'own' personal names. Natural objects, flora, and fauna are also divided between clans as their totems. The names of entities and objects which belong to a particular clan are used for addressing and farewelling members of this clan (see Harrison 1990a: 76–7). It is considered proper style to address and farewell a person using address terms and totems of their father's and of their mother's clans. Address forms are widely used in traditional song genres (laments *namay* and *sui*, and mourning songs *gra-kudi*).

For instance, *saun* 'white pelican' is a totem of the Maliau clan, and *məd* 'cassowary' is a totem of the Sarak clan. Consequently, when addressing (especially when greeting) someone belonging to the Maliau clan, one can address them as *saun*, and when addressing a person from the Sarak clan one can address them as *məd*. The moon is a totem for the clan of Ñakau, and so anyone belonging to this clan can be addressed as *bap* 'moon'. Since crotons are a totem of their clan, every Yimal clan member can be addressed as *bəutagər* 'croton'.[3]

In addition to the names of totems, each clan has a set of their own address-only terms. Some can be identified as lexical items referring to totems: so, *apwi*, an address term for someone from the Sarak clan, is also a 'shadowy style' word for cassowary (see §22.3). Others do not appear to have any identifiable lexical source (at least within the Manambu language).

---

[3] A full list of clans and their totems is outside the scope of this grammar (and is a matter of contention among the Manambu speakers themselves).

Address terms can be gender sensitive; for instance *yabən, yaban* is a term of address for men of the Maliau clan, and *yabənay* is its correspondent for women. The form *yabənay* is also a name for the Iatmul clans which are totemically the same as the Maliau clan; this term has no other meaning in Manambu. The same address term can be used for men and for women: for instance, *tapwuk* 'chicken', *gawi* 'eagle', and *wudəb* 'spirit' can be used to address both men and women from the Nabul clan.

Address forms are illustrated in 4.5–6. In 4.5 a cassowary (who has shed her skin and become a beautiful young woman) is addressed in the way appropriate for a member of the Sarak clan, to which she belongs, since the cassowary is its totem. This is said by a man who has just stolen and hidden her skin, and is going to marry the cassowary-woman.

4.5 mæy-a   Apwi   Manab ñən-a   səp
    come.IMPV-VOC cassowary:SARAK address you.fem-LK+fem.sg skin
    kəka
    DEM.PROX.REACT.TOP.fem.sg
    'Come, the one of Sarak clan, your skin is here'

In 4.6, two different address forms are used to one person. The more address forms one knows and uses, the more elaborate one is as a speaker, and the addressee is likelier to listen to what one has to say.

4.6 a-kamal   ya   akrəl   Yaban
    IMPV-come.back EMPH where.to address.masc:MALIAU
    yi-k-na-dəmən-ək   mæy-a   Jamal
    go-FUT-ACT.FOC-2masc.sgBAS.VT-CONF come.IMPV-VOC address:MALIAU
    'Do come back, where are you going, Yaban (the one of the Maliau clan), come, Jamal'

The address forms such as the ones shown in 4.5–6 can be used as vocatives. They can also be heads of intransitive predicates and copula complements: to say that someone is of the Vali:k clan, one can say: *kanukaraki-a* (death.adder-3fem.sgNOM) 'she is (to be addressed as) "death adder" (a totem of the Vali:k clan)'. They are not used in any other function, and can be considered a marginal subclass of nominals, restricted in their morphological and syntactic possibilities.

The general 'goodwill' address term *kəp*, plural *kəpugw* 'my dear' stands apart from all other address terms. It is used exclusively as a term of address in farewells, greetings, and expressions of best wishes, and is noun-like only in the way the plural is derived (see §6.1). It can be considered a defective noun (see §21.2.2). (Since it cannot be modified, or used as an argument, its gender is impossible to establish: see §5.2.)

DEVERBAL ACTION NOMINALIZATIONS are derived via CV/CCV and CVCV reduplication of the verbal root (the choice depends on the root structure; further discussion of nominalizations, their argument structure and meanings is in §§9.1.1–2). They can occur in the S function, as in 4.7 ('be difficult') and 4.8 ('finish').

4.7 də-kə-m   kawar-kawar suan   yi-na
    he-OBL-ACC/LOC go.up-RED   difficult go-ACT.FOC+3fem.sgBAS.VT
    'It is difficult (for her) to get him out'

4.8 Avatəp-a-wa   warya-wari ata   kusə-kwa,   wun-a:b
    Avatip-LK-COM fight-RED   then   end-IMPV.3p+fem.sg I-LK+TERM
    'Let the fight with Avatip be over as far as I am concerned'

Nominalizations cannot be heads of possessive constructions, or be modified by adjectives. They are used as complementation strategies—see §19.8. Unlike other nouns, but just like verbs, nominalizations can be modified by nouns in local cases, e.g. *təp-a kudir nas-ə-nas* (village-LK language+ALL count-LK-count) 'counting in the village language', but not by adjectives. A nominalization can modify a noun, e.g. *tabu-tabu wa:l* (escape-RED rain) 'a passing rain, lit. a rain running away'. Nominalizations do not take any verbal morphology.

A subclass of NOMINALS can occur only as copula complements, e.g. *bwiyabwi* 'heat' (copula *na-*) and *suan* 'difficulty' (copula *yi-*). These also include terms for weather and times of day, e.g. *katəlam* 'dawn', and onomatopoeia, e.g. *rou rou rou* 'growling sound' (both occur with the copula *na-*). Unlike other nouns (except for the address term *kəp*) the gender of these nominals is impossible to establish, since they cannot be heads of NPs or arguments other than copula complements.

They cannot take any nominal (or other) morphological markers. Just a few can be used as modifiers. For instance, the form *səpisəpi* 'drizzle, drizzly' typically occurs with a copula *na-*, as in *səpisəpi na-k-na* (drizzle BE:NAT-FUT-ACT.FOC+3fem.sgBAS.VT) 'it will drizzle'. It can also be used as a modifier to the only noun with which it is semantically compatible: *səpisəpi wa:l* (drizzle rain) 'drizzling rain', and as a modifier to a verb, as in *wa:l səpisəpi væker-na* (rain drizzle fall-ACT.FOC+3fem.sgBAS) 'the rain is falling in a drizzly way'.

This is a potentially open class, since it comprises loans like *bisi* 'busy', *isi* 'easy', *stati* 'start', *save* 'know, knowledge' (from Tok Pisin *bisi, isi, stati,* and *save*) or *les* 'lazy, unwilling' (from Tok Pisin *les*). These always occur as copula complements, with a copula/support verb *yi-* or *tə-* (see §17.2.2), e.g. *stati tə-na-wun* (start 'stand'-ACT.FOC-1sgBAS.VT) 'I start', *ma: save tə* (NEG know 'stand':NEG) '(I/you/she/he, etc.) don't know', and 22.35. They never occur as verbs, despite the fact that, as we will see in §4.2, Manambu is not averse to borrowing verbs.

NOUNS OF PHYSICAL STATES are similar: they typically occur as copula complements, with polyfunctional verbs (see §4.2.2 and §17.2), e.g. *ka:m* 'hunger' (copula *yasa-/yasə-*), *nəkər* 'cold' (copula *tay-*). However, most of them can also take the dative case, be heads of possessive constructions, and occur with derivational suffixes, e.g. *sadəka* (sleep+ONLY) '(process of sleeping) only'. A few can occur with more than one polyfunctional verb with a meaning difference, e.g. *sə* 'sleep' with the copula *yasa-/yasə-* means 'be sleepy', and with the copula *kwa-* means 'sleep, be asleep'. These nouns can be assigned variable gender depending on the 'degree' of quality they express (masculine gender goes with a stronger degree, and feminine gender with a weaker degree—see §5.2).

A number of deverbal aspectual forms (e.g. *-jəbər* 'customary aspect': §12.7) and modal forms (e.g. desiderative *-kər* (§13.5) and frustrative *-p* and *-(ya)kəp* (§13.6)) appear to be more nominal than verbal. First, they do not take any verbal cross-referencing or verbal sequencing suffixes. Secondly, to express tense, or to be used in a non-main clause, these forms have to occur as complements of the support verb *tə-* 'be, stand', as illustrated in 4.9.

4.9 <u>və-kəta-kəp</u> tə-k-na-d
    see-try-FR   be/stand-FUT-ACT.FOC-3masc.sgBAS.VT
    'He will be trying to see in vain'

4.10 ga:m ata sə-na   sə-p sə-p sə-p tə-ku
    call then put-ACT.FOC+3fem.sgBAS.VT put-FR put-FR put-FR be/stand-COMPL.SS
    'She called, having then called many times in vain (she stepped and went up onto the dry land)'

These forms do not have any nominal grammatical categories, and cannot occur in any syntactic function other than a copula complement. Since they express essentially verbal categories and have verbal argument structure, we will consider them in the chapters dealing with verbal morphology (Chapters 11–13).

<h2 style="text-align:center">4.2   VERBS</h2>

4.2.1   Verbal grammatical categories

Verbs are an open class. They constitute the most complicated part of the Manambu grammar, from the point of view of both the richness of grammatical categories, and of morphophono-logical complexity. That verbs are an open class is corroborated by the facility Manambu appears to have in adopting verbs as loans. We saw in §4.1.2 that verb roots are often borrowed as nominals, and then used as copula complements. Verbal roots can also be borrowed as verbs, and then take all the appropriate verbal morphology. It is hard to determine whether these are established loans, or occasional nonce loans, e.g. *a-pas* (IMPV-tie) 'tie!', *pasi-tua* 'I tied' (from Tok Pisin *pasim* 'tie'), *a-tik* (IMPV-tick) 'tick!' Whether to borrow a verb as a verb, or as a nominal employed as a copula complement of the verb *tə-*, is often speaker's choice (see Aikhenvald forthcoming c). The Tok Pisin verb *kamap* 'take place, occur, get up' is frequently used as a full verb in Manambu, e.g. *kamapə-d* 'he got up, (it) happened'. The same root can be borrowed as a copula complement of the verb *tə-*, as in *kamapə ta:d* (get.up 'stand'+3masc.sgBAS.VT) 'He got up (became fine)'. Loan verbs integrated into the language and used by most speakers include *sali-* 'send' (Tok Pisin *salim*), *laiki-* 'like' (Tok Pisin *laikim*), *puti-* 'put' (Tok Pisin *putim*), *paini-* 'find' (Tok Pisin *painim*), and *lukauti-* 'look after' (Tok Pisin *lukautim*) (despite the attempts of the proponents of 'pure' Manambu to get rid of them).

Verbal categories include personal cross-referencing, action focus, tense, aspect (Chapter 12), moods and modalities (Chapter 13), and verbal negation (Chapter 14). Verb compounding is employed for valency increase, and to express an array of aspectual and directional meanings—see Chapter 15. Verbs take a set of directional affixes (see §16.1). A non-productive transi-tivizing prefix derives a morphological causative (see §16.2). Verbs—unlike any other word classes—can occur in the predicate slot of subordinate clauses (without requiring a support verb: see Chapters 18 and 19). Verbs fall into at least five classes depending on root type and vowel alternations in non-stressed syllables within the verbal paradigm. These are discussed in §11.3.

4.2.2   Semantically and grammatically determined subclasses of verbs

Verbs fall into several transitivity classes—see A below. Polyfunctional verbs are a special subclass—see B. The verb 'give' forms a class on its own—see C. A small class of weather verbs is discussed under D, and complex verbs consisting of a verbal root and a non-verbal component are under E.

A few other verbs display unusual grammatical and semantic features. These include ingestive verbs *kə-* 'consume (eat, drink, smoke)' and *jə-* 'chew'; verbs of speech; generic verbs; and verbs of perception. These are discussed in §§21.1–3. Verbs can be classified with respect to how they combine with directional markers—see §16.1.1. Further, minor properties of various semantic subclasses of verbs will be discussed throughout the grammar as appropriate.

A. In terms of TRANSITIVITY CLASSES, Manambu has strictly intransitive, transitive, and ditransitive verbs. Strictly intransitive verbs include motion verbs, e.g. *yi-* 'go', *ya-* 'come', *gəp-* 'run', *tabu-* 'escape', posture verbs, e.g. *kwa-* 'stay', *rə-* 'sit', and a few others, such as *gra-* 'cry', *warsam(a)-* 'be angry', and *kawi-* 'come ashore'.

Over 80 per cent of verbs are S=A ambitransitives, e.g. *laku-* 'know, understand', used intransitively in 3.1 and transitively in 3.2; other such verbs include *kə-* 'consume (food, drink, smoke)', *jə-* 'chew', and *wukə-* 'hear, understand'. A few verbs can be used only transitively, e.g. *yi-* 'say, speak' and *kur-* 'do, make, get'.

As shown in §3.1, an O can be either unmarked for case, or marked with the accusative-locative -(*V*)*m*. The direct object of verbs with somewhat negative overtones takes the dative marking. This agrees with one of the meanings of the dative case as a 'maleficiary' marker (§7.4). For instance, the S=A ambitransitive verb *yaga-* 'be scared' takes the O in dative case, e.g. *kaykak yaga-na* (ghost+DAT be.scared-ACT.FOC+3fem.sgBAS.VT) 'she is scared of a ghost'. In its meaning 'be worried about someone', the polysemous verb *wukə-* 'hear, obey, feel, worry' takes the object in dative, as in 4.11 and 21.19.

4.11 də-kə-k   wukə-na-wun
    3masc.sg-OBL-DAT   worry-ACT.FOC-1fem.sgBAS.VT
    'I am worried about him'

The verb 'see' is unusual in the case marking for its O constituent. It is unmarked if the object seen is indefinite or not completely seen. If the verb has an atelic meaning, 'see' (by chance), the object is in the dative case, as in the first line of 4.12. And it is marked with the accusative-locative if the object is fully seen and the action is telic, rather than atelic—that is, if the verb *və-* means 'look', as in the second line of 4.12. (The accusative-locative case marks the object of this verb in its newly acquired meaning 'read': see §21.1.2.)

4.12 [brə-kə-k   və-tuə-k]   [wun-a:m   və-ku]   [ata wa-bər]
    3du-OBL-DAT   see-1sg-COMPL.DS   I-LK+ACC/LOC see-COMPL.SS   thus say-3duBAS.P
    'After I'd seen the two of them, having looked on and on (lit. going) at me, they said thus'

Strictly transitive and ambitransitive verbs differ from intransitive verbs in their derivational possibilities. Intransitive verbs can form causative compounds with the verb *taka-* 'put' as V₂ (see §15.3.1 on its applicative-like meaning). The prefix *kay-* (limited in productivity) derives a strictly transitive verb from an intransitive verb, e.g. *wiy-* 'be broken', *kay-wiy-* 'break by hand, e.g. nuts'. If used with an ambitransitive verb, *kay-* has a different effect—for instance, it may imply a special effort or an unusually large object, e.g. *tapu-* 'hold, carry', *kay-tapu-* 'hold, carry (an unusually large bundle)' (see §16.2). Most verbs derived with the prefix *kay-*, or causatives with *wa-* 'say' as V₁ are strictly transitive, e.g. *kay-napwi-* 'unwrap (e.g. a parcel)', *kay-puti-* 'take off' (see §15.3.2 and §16.2.1 for further discussion).

Verbs of speech, perception, and giving, and most intransitive verbs (e.g. 'die' or 'stand up'), differ from other verbs in terms of (a) whether they combine with directional markers at all, and (b) what the semantic effects are—see §16.1.

Verbs which are both S=A and S=O ambitransitives include all the generic verbs (§§21.1-3), *təp-* 'close', *kaykwa-* 'spill something intentionally (transitive); capsize (intransitive)', *wuka-* 'drop or spill unintentionally; fall', *wula-* 'enter; make enter', *səluku-* 'forget something; be forgotten', *gwaj-* 'turn (the handle); turn (by itself)', *rali-* 'untie something; untie (by itself)', *kusə-* 'finish' (4.13-14).

4.13 [wun-a   gabu-ma:j]   bu   kusə-na
     I-LK+fem.sg traditional-speech already finish-ACT.FOC+3fem.sgBAS.VT
     'My story is already finished'

4.14 ada   kusə-ta-d
     DEM.DIST.REACT.TOP.masc.sg finish-1duSUBJ.VT-3masc.sgBAS.VT
     'We have finished it (a long story)'

The verb *kusə-* is used intransitively as a euphemism in lieu of 'die', with a human subject.

An ambitransitive verb may have somewhat different meanings when used transitively and when used intransitively: transitive *kaja-* means 'open by moving apart (legs, book), move (e.g. fingers)'; the same verb used intransitively means 'disperse'. The transitive verb *wapa-* means 'leave, abandon'; the same verb used intransitively means 'be full, not want any more', as in *ya:l wapa-na* (belly leave/be.full-ACT.FOC+3fem.sgBAS.VT) 'he was full'.

The class of S=O ambitransitives appears to be expanding. Transitive verbs such as *kasapwi-* 'open ' and *yi-pa:kw-* 'hide' are used intransitively by innovative speakers, much to the annoyance of the traditionalists. A form *yi-pa:kwə-d* (go-hide-3masc.sgBAS.P) normally means 'he hid (something)'; whereas for innovative speakers it can also mean 'he became hidden'. An intransitive verb can occasionally be used transitively: *kiya-* 'die' was used to mean 'kill' in an angry outcry at a misbehaving child:

4.15 ka-l   kiya-kiya-kə-tua-ñən-ək
     DEM.PROX+fem.sg-3fem.sgNOM die-die-FUT-1sgSUBJ.VT-2fem.sgBAS.VT-CONF
     'This one! I will well and truly kill you!'

Extended intransitives form a small subclass of intransitive verbs. These have an obligatory second argument which is unmarked for case and cannot be cross-referenced on the verb. One such verb, *patiaku-* 'turn into (something)', was illustrated in 3.10. The second argument can be obligatory; for instance, *yaku-* 'wash' is typically used with the unmarked instrumental argument *gu* 'water', as in *gu yaku-na-wun* (water wash-ACT.FOC-1sgBAS.VT) 'I wash, bathe' (lit. 'I wash (with water)'). Or it can be optional, as is the case with *wapruku-* 'be overflowing': this verb can be used intransitively, as in *ya:l bu wapruku-na* (belly already be.overflowing-ACT.FOC+3fem.sgBAS.VT) '(I am) very full, lit. belly is already overflowing'; or with an unmarked instrument, as in 3.11 ('overflowing with money').

Ditransitive verbs are a small class which includes *wa-* 'say, tell', *səmaka-* 'show', *yapi-* 'buy, sell, pay', *kalipa-* 'learn, teach', and a loan verb *sali-* 'send' (from Tok Pisin *salim* 'send'), the third argument being recipient. The verb *taka-* 'put' has a location as a third argument. All of these except 'show' and 'put' can be used as transitives and as A=S ambitransitives. The verb *wa-* 'say' has the speech content (as object) and the recipient as its arguments. It can be used transitively, with just the recipient as the second argument. If the speech content is a direct speech report, it cannot be cross-referenced. Direct speech report constructions are discussed in §19.5. The verb 'give' is a class of its own, both in terms of form and of semantics. See C below.

Transitivity of verbs is neutralized in what look like complex sentences consisting of a verb in the completive, cotemporaneous, or manner sequencing form and one of the three polyfunctional verbs (*tə-* 'stand', *rə-* 'sit', *kwa-* 'stay', also used as positional verbs); see §17.5. Pervasive use of sequencing constructions with a copula where the verb's transitivity is neutralized may be one of the reasons why the class of S=O ambitransitives is currently expanding.

B. POLYFUNCTIONAL VERBS: COPULA VERBS, SUPPORT VERBS, AND AUXILIARIES

Manambu has ten verbs which can each be used in two or three of the following functions—as copula verbs, as support verbs, and also as auxiliaries. Five of them are also used as lexical verbs. A summary of these verbs and their functions is in Table 4.1.

When used as COPULA VERBS, they head the predicate of copula clauses which involve two arguments but cannot be considered either transitive or intransitive (see Dixon 2002b for a typological overview of copulas, and §20.1.3). In Manambu, the relationship between the two arguments of a copula clause—the copula subject and the copula complement—covers identity, attribution, location, and possession. Their choice depends (a) on the meaning of the copula construction, and (b) on the semantic type of copula complement. Further meanings typically associated with copula clauses can also be expressed with verbless clauses or non-verbal predicate heads—we return to this in §20.1.3.

When these polyfunctional verbs occur as AUXILIARIES in complex predicates, they impart an aspect or modality specification to the whole construction, and take further tense, aspect, mood, and modality inflections (see §§17.1–4).

Some also occur as SUPPORT VERBS with uninflected verbs, carrying tense, aspect, mood, and modality inflections. Such uninflected verbs include completive, completive-intensive, and customary aspects, desiderative and frustrative modality, and a few other categories detailed in Table 11.1. Loan verbs typically require a support verb, e.g. *stati tə-* (start SUPPORT.VERB) 'start'. Support verbs are similar to the so-called 'light verbs' (see a definition in Matthews 1997), used to construct verbal expressions with accompanying nouns or with borrowed verbal roots (see Haig 2001: 213 on similar use of 'do' in Kurmanjî and Zazaki, both Iranian). See §17.2 for details. In addition, some polyfunctional verbs appear in lexicalized complex predicates—see §17.3.

Five of the polyfunctional verbs can also be used as independent lexical verbs. These are positional verbs 'stand', 'sit', and 'stay', and the verbs *kur-* 'do, take, get' and *yi-* 'say; go'. These have a full range of grammatical forms including imperatives. The other five verbs do not have a full range of grammatical forms—for instance, they cannot form imperatives.

Each of the ten verbs featured in Table 4.1 can be considered polysemous and multifunctional. The regularity of their multiple functions points towards the appropriateness of a polysemy, rather than a homonymy, analysis. But can we decide which of the uses is primary? We address this issue in §17.2.

When these verbs are employed as copula verbs, their copula subject shares all syntactic and morphological properties with subjects (A/S) of other sorts, including cross-referencing on the verb and case marking. It behaves like an S in terms of its ability to control agreement with the 'reactivated topic' deictic marker (operating on an S/O basis)—see §3.3. Copula complements are different from any other argument in that they (i) never take any case marking and (ii) are never cross-referenced on the verb (see §7.2). All copula clauses show the expected relational meanings—identity, attribution, and location. One copula (*tə-*) is also used to express possession and 'becoming'. See discussion below.

The verbs *na-* 'be (of physical states; natural phenomena)', *tay-* 'be (of climatic states)', *yasa-/yasə-* 'be (of physical states, e.g. hunger, thirst)', *say-* 'be (of some states, e.g. shame)', and *yæy-* 'be (of smells)' occur with a restricted set of formally unmarked nouns or nominals, and can be interpreted in either of two ways. They may be viewed either as copula existential verbs with the corresponding nouns and nominals in the copula complement (CC) slot, or as support verbs for such nouns and nominals. We can recall, from §4.1.2, that many nominals can only occur as CC of such verbs. The copulas *na-*, *tay-*, and *yasa-/yasə-* allow the option of having a zero

TABLE 4.1   Copula verbs, auxiliaries, and support verbs in Manambu

FORM	As COPULA VERB	As SUPPORT VERB	As AUXILIARY VERB	As OPEN-CLASS VERB
1. *tə-*	'become', 'be', 'exist (optional overtone of vertical position) (in a location)', 'have'	with most uninflected verbs (§17.2.1) with loan verbs (§17.2.2) with various nominals (§§17.2.3–4)	anterior aspect (§17.1.1) transitivity-neutralizing construction (§17.5)	positional verb 'stand; be (in vertical or standing position)'
2. *rə-*	'be in/at', 'exist (overtone of horizontal position)'	with nominals in lexicalized complex predicates (§17.3)	durative aspect (§17.1.1) transitivity-neutralizing construction (§17.5)	positional verb 'sit; be (in horizontal or sitting position)'
3. *kwa-*	'be in/at', 'exist (in general, or in multiple locations); become and remain'	with nominals in lexicalized complex predicates (§17.3)	prolonged durative (§17.1.1) transitivity-neutralizing construction (§17.5)	positional verb 'stay'
4. *yi-*	'do, be (with some abstract terms)'	with some nominals in lexicalized complex predicates (§17.3)	no	'say'; 'go'
5. *kur-*	'do, get, become (fully)'	with nominals in lexicalized complex verbs (§17.3)	imminent modality (§17.1.2)	'do, take, get'
6. *na-*	'be (of physical states; natural phenomena)'	with various nominals; ideophones and onomatopoeia (§17.2.3); uninflected completive aspect (§12.6; §17.3)	no	no
7. *tay-*	'be (of climatic states)'	with nominals to do with climatic states		
8. *yasa-/yasə-*	'be (of physical states, e.g. hunger, thirst)'	with nominals to do with physical states		
9. *say-*	'be (of some states, e.g. shame)'	with nominals to do with other states		
10. *yəy-*	'be (of smells)'	with 'smell'		

subject cross-referenced with 3fem.sg (formally and functionally unmarked: §5.2.3). We return to these in §17.2.

A nominal part of the predicate containing a support verb shares morphological and syntactic properties with copula complements. Both are formally unmarked, cannot be negated or questioned separately from the verb they precede, and have a fixed position in a clause (they can only be separated from it by the connective *ata* or the reactivated topic demonstratives).

The major difference is semantic: when used as copula verbs, the multifunctional verbs listed in Table 4.1 reflect one or more of the relational meanings typically associated with copula clauses (see §20.1.3 and Dixon 2002b). When used as support verbs, they are effectively mere 'placeholders' for the inflectional categories which cannot be expressed otherwise.

The verbs listed under 6–10 can be seen as primarily support verbs with a strong semantic and partially syntactic similarity to existential copulas. A broken line separating columns 2 and 3 for these verbs in Table 4.1 reflects this indeterminacy in their status.

We will now discuss the polyfunctional verbs in Table 4.1 one by one.

1. The copula *tə-* in the meaning of 'become' was illustrated in 3.8–9. It is used as a support verb with uninflected frustratives in 4.9–10. It can also be used as an existential verb as illustrated in 4.16–17; then it occurs with either a locative, or a reactivated topic demonstrative.

4.16 alək   apawəl kəta bəum   tə-na-di
     this.is.why spirit   now haze+LOC stay-ACT.FOC-3plBAS.VT
     'This is why spirits are now staying in a haze' (and are invisible to us)

4.17 kayik   ada   tə-na-d
     ghost/spirit DEM.DIST.REACT.TOP.masc.sg stand-ACT.FOC-3masc.sgBAS.VT
     'The ghost is (there)!' (said, in fear, by Tanina, then 8 years of age)

The verb *tə-* can also be used in the meaning of 'have', as in 4.18. Its second argument is similar to the copula complement in that it is not cross-referenced on the verb. If a reactivated topic demonstrative occurs in such a construction, it agrees in gender and number with the subject of *tə-* and not with the possessed entity. This indicates that the subject of *tə-* behaves like an intransitive subject (S) no matter whether the verb is used with one argument, or with two.

4.18 nəma   kabak   adika   tə-na-di
     big+fem.sg money(lit.stone) DEM.DIST.REACT.TOP+plural have-ACT.FOC-3plBAS.VT
     'Now they (mentioned again) have a lot of money'

The verb *tə-* also occurs in idiomatic collocations. When preceded by a body part noun in dative case it refers to something wrong with this particular body part, e.g. *ab-aːk tə-* (head-LK+DAT be/stand/have) 'be not quite right in one's head' (see §17.2.3).

2. The copula *rə-* 'sit' can be used as an existential verb; then it requires either a locative or a reactivated topic demonstrative (just like the copula *tə-*), as in 4.19.

4.19 makən   rə-na   væk aka
     mourning sit-ACT.FOC+3fem.sgBAS.VT pan DEM.DIST.REACT.TOP.fem.sg
     rə-na
     sit-ACT.FOC+3fem.sgBAS.VT
     'The pan "in mourning" (that is, a pan with a string of black wool on it) is (here)!'

This same verb also means 'sit', e.g. *təkər-ə-m rə-k-na-wun* (stool-LK-LOC sit-FUT-ACT.FOC-1fem.sgBAS.VT) 'I will sit on a stool'.

The choice between *tə-* and *rə-* as existential verbs is partly determined by the nature of the copula subject. Similarly to many languages of Papua New Guinea (see Aikhenvald 2000: 166–9 for an overview), the verb *tə-* 'stand' is used with referents which are prototypically vertical—humans, spirits, animate beings, and trees. The verb *rə-* 'sit' is used with large, squat, inanimate referents, such as 'pan' in 4.19. This is reminiscent of classificatory verbs—see §17.2.3 for arguments against the analysis of Manambu copula as purely classificatory. The verb *tə-* can optionally replace *rə-* as an existential. Both *tə-* and *rə-* have one suppletive imperative *ada*.

The copula *rə-* 'sit' can take the adjective *yara* 'well' as its copula complement, e.g. *yara rə-na-wun* 'I am fine'; as well as a number of nouns marked with the locative case, e.g. *stua-m rə-* (store-LOC sit) 'be for sale in a store' (see §17.2.3).

3. The copula *kwa-* 'stay' is used with some adjectives and nouns as copula complement, e.g. *yara* 'well', as in 4.20, an answer to a conventional question 'are you fine'? The use of *kwa-* as an auxiliary is discussed in §17.2.1; its use in lexicalized complex verbs is addressed in §17.3.

4.20 yara kwa-na-wun
    well stay-ACT.FOC-1fem.sgBAS.VT
    'I am fine'

4. The copula *yi-* occurs with a few abstract nouns, such as *suan* 'difficult' in 4.7 and 13.80, and some onomatopoeic-like expressions, e.g. *krəsakrəs* (scratchy) in 4.21. Similarly to the polyfunctional verbs discussed so far, *yi-* can be interpreted as a support verb as well as an existential copula. Unlike the verbs under 6–10 below, *yi-*can also be used as an open-class verb.

4.21 wun-a kwa:l krəsakrəs yi-na
    I-LK throat 'scratchy' be-ACT.FOC+3fem.sgBAS.VT
    'My throat is scratchy'

This same verb is used with the nominal *səkulək* 'cooking' to mean 'cook'. This construction can be used without a second argument ('do the cooking') or with a second argument ('cook something'). However, just as with the verb *tə-* in the meaning 'have', this second argument is not an object: it cannot be cross-referenced or referred to with the reactivated topic demonstrative.

The verb *yi-* in combination with *kwasək* (possibly, a dative case form of the adjective *kwasa* 'small') means 'be unwilling to do something, or be tired of someone or something' (*kwasək* can be replaced by Tok Pisin *les*, as in 22.35). It takes an additional, non-O, NP argument in the dative case, as in 4.22. Or it can occur with a postposed irrealis complement clause, as in 13.81. This behaviour is somewhat unusual in Manambu (where the matrix verb tends to be sentence final: see §20.2 on discourse motivations for the constituent order).

4.22 lə-kə-k kwasək yi-na-wun
    3fem.sg-OBL-DAT unwilling be-ACT.FOC-1fem.sgBAS.VT
    'I am fed up with her'

The copula *yi-* has the same form as the intransitive verb *yi-* 'go' and the transitive verb *yi-* 'say, speak' (see §21.1.3 on the syntactic differences between speech verbs in Manambu). These three verbs share all forms, except the imperative: as we will see in §13.1, the verb 'go' has a suppletive imperative *ma:y*, while the verb 'say' and the copula share a regular imperative *a-y*. Given that, cross-linguistically, the verb 'say' often becomes a copula, we hypothesize that the two could be linked in Manambu. The component *yi-* as V$_1$ in a few compound verbs (§15.2.3), e.g. *yi-pa:kw-* 'hide something' (where *pa:kw-* means 'be hidden'), is also likely to be connected to the verb 'say'.

5. The verb *kur-* occurs as a copula verb in the meaning of 'become fully, reach, arrive to be something', as in 4.23. Its copula complement is always a noun.

4.23 du-a-ñan   ata   <u>kurə-d</u>
     man-LK-child then become.fully-3masc.sgBAS.P
     'He then reached the stage of being a boy'

This verb is also used as a transitive lexical verb meaning 'do, make, get, take, procure', e.g. *yawi kur-* (work do-) 'work, do a job'. With a same-subject purposive lexical verb, it forms an imminent construction, 'be about to' (§17.1.2), as in *kiya-k kur-* (die-PURP.SS do/get-) 'be about to die'.

As mentioned above, the remaining five verbs are inherently ambiguous in their status: they can be equally well interpreted either as existential verbs, or as support verbs each used with a limited number of nominals. For each of these, the 'experiencer' can be optionally added; this is why it is in brackets. Without the overt subject, 4.24 means 'it is hot' (in general); 4.25 means 'it is cold' (in general), and examples at 4.26 refer to an unspecified experiencer (also see §17.2).

6. The copula or support verb *na-* takes physical states, natural phenomena, ideophones, and expressives as its complements (also see 4.81).

4.24 (wun) bwiyabwi na-na
     (I)   hot   BE:NAT-ACT.FOC+3fem.sgBAS.VT
     'It is hot', 'I am hot'

7. The copula or support verb *tay-* occurs with nouns which refer to climatic states:

4.25 (wun) nəkər tay-na
     (I)   cold   BE:CLIM-ACT.FOC+3fem.sgBAS.VT
     'It is cold', 'I am cold'

8. The copula or support verb *yasə-/yasa-* occurs with nouns referring to physical states and desires. These include *ka:m* 'hunger', *gu* 'water', and *kwa:l* 'neck' (Yuanab dialect) meaning 'feel thirsty', *sə* 'sleep', *wus* 'urine', *di* 'shit', and *ñiki* 'blood' (for 'feeling reckless').

4.26a (wun) ka:m   yasə-na
      (I)   hunger BE:DESIRE-ACT.FOC+3fem.sgBAS.VT
      'I am hungry'

   Unlike any other polyfunctional verb, it can occur with purposive and desiderative verbs:

4.26b (wun) yaki   kə-kər   yasə-na
      (I)   tobacco consume-DES BE:DESIRE-ACT.FOC+3fem.sgBAS.VT
      'I want to smoke'

4.26c (lə) kurə-k   yasə-na
      (she) do-PURP.SS BE:DESIRE-ACT.FOC+3fem.sgBAS.VT
      'She is displaying signs of having sexual desire'

4.26d kiyak   ñiki   yasə-na
      die+PURP.SS blood BE:DESIRE-ACT.FOC+3fem.sgBAS.VT
      'Do you feel reckless enough to be going to die?'

The subject properties of experiencer in such constructions are discussed in §20.1.4.

9. The copula or support verb *say-* occurs with nouns referring to two mental and physical states—'shame' and 'pins and needles':

4.27 wap   say-na-wun
     shame BE:FEEL-ACT.FOC-1fem.sgBAS.VT
     'I feel ashamed'

10. The copula or support verb *yæy-* occurs with 'smell'. The source of smell (e.g. flower) can be optionally specified; otherwise the construction can have a generic reference: 'there is a smell'.

4.28 (maway) ya:m   <u>yæy-na</u>
     (flower) smell be-ACT.FOC+3fem.sgBAS.VT
     'There is a smell (of a flower)'

The polyfunctionality of the copula, support, and auxiliary verbs is in line with a few other verbs with generic and abstract meanings (but without copular functions). These include *sə-* 'call, make', *ka-* 'take', *ku-* 'put, do', and also the general 'replacement' verb *məgi-* 'do whatever'. Many of these take part in forming lexicalized complex predicates—see §17.3.

C. THE VERB 'GIVE' forms a subclass on its own. This strictly ditransitive verb has two stem forms whose choice depends on the person of the recipient. A few languages across the world, including some from Papua New Guinea (mostly, but not exclusively, the Highlands: Comrie 2003), display a similar pattern.

If the recipient is first or second person (any number or gender), the form is *kwatiya-*, e.g. *mən-a:k kwatiya-kə-tua* (you.masc-LK+DAT give.to.nonthird.p-FUT-2sgSUBJ.VT+3fem.sgBAS.VT) 'I will give you this (thing)'. The stem alternant in the imperative and the non-future negative is *kwata:y* or *kwəta:y*, e.g. *wun-a:k a-kwata:y!* (I-LK+DAT IMPV-give.to.nonthird.p) 'give (something) to me' (see §11.3.2). A first person dual recipient is illustrated in 4.29:

4.29 [ña-nə   kə-kwa-gura-di   bal] an-a:k
     day+LK-day eat-HAB-2plSUBJ.VT-3plBAS.VT pig 1du-LK+DAT
     kwatiya-kwa-na-digwur-ək?
     give.to.nonthird.p-HAB-ACT.FOC-2plBAS.VT-CONF
     'The pigs you eat day in day out, do you give (them) to the two of us?'

If the recipient is third person, the form is *kui-*, e.g. *lə-kə-k a-kui!* (3fem.sg-OBL-DAT IMPV-give.to.third.p) 'give to her', and 4.30. The stem alternant in the non-future negative is *kwa:y*, e.g. *ma: kwa:y* 'did not give' (see §11.3.2).

4.30 adiya   səbənə-n kui-da-di   a-di
     DEM.DIST.REACT.TOP+pl return-SEQ give.to.third.p-3plSUBJ.P-3plBAS.P DEM.DIST-pl
     kamna:gw
     food
     'They gave these types of food back (to them)'

The form *kui-* 'give to third person recipient' can be considered functionally unmarked, for the following reasons. First, it is consistently used in reciprocal constructions, no matter what the person of recipient is. In 4.31, the speaker is talking about us giving, or offering, the mortuary feast to each other; yet, the third person recipient form is used.

4.31 kəkətəp   awarwa kui-na-bran
     mortuary.feast REC   give.to.third.p-ACT.FOC-1duBAS.VT
     'We give the mortuary feast to each other'

Secondly, the third person recipient form is used for recipients in general, in the meaning of 'giving away', as in 4.32.

4.32 a-bər   *marasin* kui-kwa-na-bər   kui-ta:y
     DEM.DIST-du medicine give.to.third.p-HAB-ACT.FOC-3duBAS.VT give.to.third.p-COTEMP
     'They used to give medicine (to people), giving (and giving)'

A third person recipient form is used in generic statements, even if these obviously include a non-third person. Eight-year-old Tanina was worried about me not eating the banana I was given, and giving everything away instead. She was sitting next to me, and I had offered the banana to her. That is, by using *kui-* in 4.33, she had subsumed herself (first person) under a generic set of recipients covered by this form. (Syntactically, this is an example of a desubordinated cotemporaneous clause: see §19.9.) A similar example is in T2.1.

4.33 Sasa kur-ta:y   kui-ta:y   kur-ta:y   kui-ta:y
     Sasha get-COTEMP give.to.third.p-COTEMP get-COTEMP give.to.third.p-COTEMP
     'Sasha (keeps) getting (things) (and) giving (them away), getting (things) (and) giving (them away)'

Thirdly, the form *kui-* is the one that occurs in verb compounded structures whose meaning is only partially predictable, e.g. *kui-taka-* (give.to.third.p-put-) 'send, give away (e.g. money)', *kui-tay-taya-n* (give.to.third.p-TO.SIDE-TO.SIDE-SEQ) 'give back and forth (e.g. in a situation of exchange)'. This same form also occurs in idiomatic collocations, e.g. *mawul nəma kui-* (inside big+fem.sg give.to.third.p-) 'be happy', and *səp kui-* (skin give.to.third.p-) 'get used to'.

In spontaneous speech, many speakers employ *kui-* for a non-third person recipient, where one would expect *kwatiya-*. Teketay is a very lively story teller and a gifted natural linguist. She used *kui-* and *kwatiya-* for non-third person interchangeably, as shown in 4.34. The 'aberrant' use of *kui-* is underlined.

4.34 ka-di   təp   a-di   japə-wa   kur-ku   ya-ku,
     sow-pl coconut DEM.DIST-pl thing+LK-COM get-COMPL.SS come-COMPL.SS
     ñan-a-k   <u>kui-ku,</u>   kə   ñan ata
     we.pl-LK-DAT give.to.third.p-COMPL.SS DEM.PROX+fem.sg child then
     kur-k-ñəna
     get-FUT-2fem.sgSUBJ.VT+3fem.sgBAS.VT
     'Having got these coconuts with those things, having come, having given to us, then you will get this child'

Later in the same story, she used *kwatiya-* for a first person recipient (4.35), and then, a few sentences later in the same story, she used *kui-*, for the same recipient (4.36):

4.35 wun kwatiya   ma: [PAUSE] kə   ñan
     I   give.to.nonthird.p:NEG NEG   DEM.PROX+fem.sg child
     'I won't give (you), this child'

4.36 ñan kə   ñan, <u>kui</u>   ma:, ñən-a:k
     we DEM.PROX+fem.sg child give.to.third.p:NEG NEG, you.fem-LK+DAT
     'We won't give this child, to you'

Similar examples are not infrequent (see, e.g. 13.50). However, it is notable that the form *kwatiya-* is hardly ever used instead of *kui-*. We can hypothesize that a tendency to replace the restricted and functionally marked form *kwatiya-* 'give to non-third person' with a more widely used and functionally unmarked form *kui-* 'give to third person' is indicative of the incipient breakdown of the system, ultimately increasing the overall frequency of the functionally unmarked *kui-* over *kwatiya-*, which is more restricted in the contexts in which it occurs.

Comparative evidence, from other languages of the Ndu family, does not fully support this. The only other language in the family with a distinction between 'give to third person' and 'give to non-third person' is the Abelam-Wosera dialect complex.[4] The Proto-Ndu form for 'give' is **kwa(:)y/kwəy*.

The two forms in Abelam-Wosera are: *tiyaa* 'give to non-third person' and *kwayee* 'give to third person'. The Manambu *kui-* (negative *kwa:y*) and the Abelam *kwayé* 'give to third person' are reflexes of the Proto-Ndu 'give', while the Manambu *kwatiya-* (negative and imperative (-)*kwata:y*) can be interpreted as a combination of *kwa(y)* 'give' and the cognate of Abelam *tiyaa* 'give to non-third person'. That is, the Manambu 'give to non-third person' goes back to a compound verb. The component -*tiya* in *kwatiya-* is likely to be an archaic cognate between Manambu and Abelam-Wosera, lost from other Ndu languages. Sound correspondences between Manambu and Abelam-Wosera support this, making it unlikely for this form to be a borrowing. (We saw in Chapter 1 that there is a certain amount of trade contact between the Manambu and the Wosera people through barter markets; there is hardly any bilingualism, or any substantial linguistic contact.) However, the compound itself can be interpreted as a Manambu innovation. That some people still prefer to replace the new formation *kwatiya-* with the old form *kui-* may reflect the fact that this innovation is not yet fully established in the language. An additional complicating factor in the 'acceptance' of this innovation is the lack of support from neighbouring languages with which Manambu is, or has been, in trade or other contact in recent times: neither Iatmul (also Ndu) nor Kwoma-Washkuk (which is not demonstrably related to Ndu languages) distinguish the third–non-third recipient forms of 'give'. Iatmul has one form *kwi-* 'give' (Staalsen and Staalsen 1973), which is a direct reflex of Proto-Ndu **kwəy*, while Kwoma has a form *ha* (Bowden 1997).

The form *kui-* is unusual and perhaps archaic in one additional way. Unlike other verbs in the language, it does not have to take the suffix -*kwa-* 'habitual' in the negative form. As we will see in §12.3, the habitual aspect marked with -*kwa-* is likely to be the result of recent grammaticalization of the verb *kwa-* 'stay'. Two options are thus available for 'give' in past habitual; there is no semantic difference between the two. The regular form, *kui-kwa-* '(not) give habitually', is shown in 4.37.

4.37 də-kə-k   sa:n   akəs   kui-kwa-na-d
     he-OBL-DAT money   NEG.HAB give.to.third.p-HAB-ACT.FOC-3masc.sgBAS.VT
     'He never used to give him money; he never gave him money'

The non-habitual declarative form, *kui-*, with the habitual negator *akəs* is shown in 4.38:

4.38 akəs   kui-l   ka:b   yiyi   ta:l
     NEG.HAB give.to.third.p-3fem.sgBAS.P selfish AUX:RED stay+3fem.sgBAS.P
     '(She was bad), she never gave (children anything), she was selfish'

---

4 Laycock (1965: 166) did not register the distinction of the two forms for 'give' in Manambu. The Abelam-Wosera *tiya* form is erroneously interpreted as 'give to me', while the form *kway* is said to be used with second person recipient. This goes against all other sources for Abelam-Wosera (e.g. Kundama, Wilson, and Sapai 1987).

The other verb, *kwatiya-* 'give to non-third person', is always marked with *-kwa-* in habitual negative constructions, as in:

4.39 brak   akəs   kwatiya-kwa-na-dəwun
     2du+DAT NEG.HAB give.to.nonthird.p-HAB-ACT.FOC-1masc.sgBAS.VT
     'I never give you two (anything)'

If indeed the original compound form *kwatiya-* is a recent innovation, its grammatical regularity in the formation of the negative habitual (in itself, a recent form) confirms its recent origin.

D. METEOROLOGICAL VERBS are a small subclass. They take one obligatory argument—the weather or time condition in the subject slot. Two verbs unequivocally belong to this class: *ja-* 'rain', used exclusively with the subject *wa:l* 'rain', and *va-* 'fall (night)', used only with *ga:n* 'night', as in 4.40–1:

4.40 wa:l ja-na
     rain be.rain-ACT.FOC+3fem.sgBAS.VT
     'It is raining'

4.41 ga:n aka   va-na
     night DEM.DIST.REACT.TOP.fem.sg fall:night-ACT.FOC+3fem.sgBAS.VT
     'It was getting dark'

The subject *ga:n* 'night' controls gender agreement with the reactivated topic demonstrative in 4.41; this shows that it behaves like an intransitive subject (S). We will see in §5.2.1 that nouns referring to time are normally feminine. These verbs cannot take any cross-referencing other than third person; neither can they occur in imperative, form part of any verbal compound, or take a directional suffix.

They can cross-reference time, location, or manner if it is topical, in the second cross-referencing position, as in 4.42:

4.42 nəma   wa:l ja-la   səkər
     big+fem.sg rain be.rain-3fem.sgSUBJ.VT+3fem.sgBAS.VT+LK time
     'time when big rain fell'

The verb *ja-* is not used in any other context; unlike *va-* which also occurs in an idiomatic collocation *agur va-* 'snore'. Whether or not it is the same *va-* is an open question.

The verb *kusə-* meaning 'finish, end' is an S=A and S=O ambitransitive (see 4.13–14, and 4.8). When used with *ga:n* 'night' in the subject slot, it means 'completely fall (of night)':

4.43 ga:n bə   kusə-na
     night already finish-ACT.FOC+3fem.sgBAS.VT
     'It is dark, the night has completely fallen'

In some ways it behaves similarly to the two meteorological verbs when used in this context—it cannot form an imperative, or be used with a non-third person subject. Unlike meteorological verbs, it can combine with the verb *-ya-* 'come' in V$_2$ slot, conveying the meaning of a prolonged gradual process, as in 4.44:

4.44 ga:n bə   kusə-ya-na
     night already finish-come-ACT.FOC+3fem.sgBAS.VT
     'It is slowly and gradually getting dark'

This is a slightly unusual meaning of a -*ya*- compound (see §15.3.1): these typically refer to durative action. It is not clear whether the two meanings of the verb *kusə*- are an instance of polysemy or of homonymy. Only comparative evidence (hitherto unavailable) may help us make an informed decision.

E. COMPLEX VERBS consist of a non-verbal component (typically, a noun referring to a body part or a state) and a lexical verb. Many such verbs describe a physical condition, e.g. 4.45:

4.45 səp   ji-na
    skin be.tired-ACT.FOC+3fem.sgBAS.VT
    '(I, or another person) am/is/are tired'

Some complex verbs contain an adverb. e.g. *bas sə*- (first plant-) 'ask', or a component not used anywhere else, e.g. *luku kur*- (? do-) 'steal'. Some of the verbs in such constructions are not used anywhere else, e.g. *ji*- 'be tired'. Others are, e.g. *sə* 'plant' in *bas sə* 'ask', *ga:m sə* 'serenade, shout', or *kwa*- 'stay' in *sə kwa*- (sleep stay) 'be asleep, sleep'. See §17.3. Complex verbs which involve body parts allow variation in their cross-referencing. An alternative to 4.45, 'skin is tired', is 4.46:

4.46 səp   ji-na-wun
    skin be.tired-ACT.FOC-1fem.sgBAS.VT
    'I am tired' (lit. skin I-am-tired)

The semantic motivation for this is similar to that in copula clauses involving physical states like cold or hunger (§17.4): the subject is likelier to be cross-referenced if it is focused—if I am really insistent about the fact that **I** am fed up and can't take any of it any longer, I am likelier to use the second construction. No such option is available for complex verbs which do not contain a body part term, e.g. *sə kwa*- 'sleep' (see §17.4 and §20.1.4).

The last issue to be addressed in this section is the multiple class membership for two types of derived verbal forms: reduplicated forms and customary activity forms with the suffix -*jəbər*. These can occur either as copula complements, or nominal parts of complex predicates with support verbs, or as inflected verbs. (We can recall, from B above, that a non-verbal part of a predicate with a support verb is morphologically and syntactically similar to a copula complement.) The reduplicated form *rəpərəp* 'equal, identical' (reduplicated form of *rəp* 'be enough') is a copula complement in 4.47 (see §6.2.3 on this construction type called 'argument elaboration construction', or 'inclusory construction').

4.47 Yuakalu-wa   nabi rəpərəp   tə-na-bran
    Yuakalu-COM year be.enough:RED have/be-ACT.FOC-1duBAS.VT
    'Yuakalu and I are the same age' (lit: 'with Yuakalu we two are same age')

In 4.48, *rəpərəp* 'equal, identical' is an inflected verb:

4.48 mutam rəpərəp-na-bərbər
    face   be.enough:RED-ACT.FOC-2duBAS.VT
    'You two look the same' (lit. 'you are same face-wise')

In addition, reduplicated forms of stative verbs can modify a nominal in the copula complement slot, as in 4.49.

4.49 rəpərəp   kwa:m tə-na-bər
    be.enough:RED crazy have/be-ACT.FOC-3duBAS.VT
    'They two are equally crazy' (talking about two children shouting like mad)

In 12.17 and 12.33–4, a verb inflected with -*jəbər* 'customary aspect' requires a support verb *tə-*, while in 12.37–9 it is an inflected verb. There is no meaning difference between these two. It appears, however, that innovative speakers are more likely to treat these forms as inflecting verbs than traditional speakers. As the language evolves, this may result in the expansion of the class of inflecting verbs. Interestingly, this development does not affect modal forms (the two frustratives and the desiderative) which never take any verbal cross-referencing markers and always occur as copula complements if tense needs to be expressed (see the end of §4.1.2).

4.3 ADJECTIVES

Adjectives fall into two classes: a small class of three underived 'agreeing' adjectives, two of which refer to dimension, and one to value; and a smallish semi-open class of about sixteen 'non-agreeing' adjectives some of which are derived. These cover value, dimension, age, and colour.

4.3.1 Agreeing and non-agreeing adjectives

The three agreeing adjectives differ somewhat in their agreement properties, and agreement marking. The two dimension adjectives, *nəma* 'big' and *kwasa* 'small', agree with the head noun in gender and number when used as modifiers, e.g. *nəma-də du* (big-masc.sg man) 'big man', *nəma taːkw* (big+fem.sg woman) 'big woman', *kwasa-də du* (small-masc.sg man) 'small man', *kwasa taːkw* (small+fem.sg woman) 'small woman'; and also when used as copula complements, e.g. 4.50. Agreement markers are in bold.

4.50 vəti-kərəb   məd-a   ñən-wa   məy-a ñan ata nəma-**bər**
     two-together cassowary-LK child-COM real-LK child then big-du
     tə-**bər**
     stand/be-3duBAS.P
     'Both the cassowary child and the human child (lit. real child) became grown up'

In contrast, the value adjective *yara* 'fine, well-behaved' agrees in gender with the noun only when used as a modifier in a noun phrase, e.g. *yara-l amæy* (fine-fem.sg mother) 'nice mother', *yara-də du* (fine-masc.sg man) 'good, well-behaved man', *ñən-a-di yara-di ñanugw* (you.fem.sg-LK-pl fine-pl children) 'your fine children'. Unlike with the two dimension adjectives, the feminine marker is -*l* and not Ø. Other agreement markers are the same: -*d*(ə) 'masculine singular', -*bər* 'dual', and -*di* 'plural' (listed in Table 5.1). The agreeing adjectives share gender and number agreement with modifiers from closed classes (§4.5), and also with verbs (see §5.1); these agreement forms are the same as the ones used in the basic series of agreement (Table 3.1 and Table 5.1). When used as a copula complement, *yara* does not agree in gender and appears zero marked, as in 4.20.

The two dimension adjectives can be used on their own without the NP head. Then, if used in the feminine form, they have two meanings: that of an adjective with the omitted head noun, as in 4.51, or that of an adverb, as in 4.52.

4.51 kwasa-pək-a   vya-kə-bana
     small-COMPAR-3fem.sgNOM kill-FUT-1plSUBJ.VT+3fem.sgBAS.VT
     'It is the smaller one that we will kill'

4.52 wayway kwasa sǝluku-la,   wau   ya?
      perhaps little forget-3fem.sgSUBJ.P+3fem.sgBAS.P speak+1sg.IMPV EMPH
      'Perhaps, she forgot a little, may I speak now?'

The two meanings are disambiguated by the context. Example 4.52 could have meant 'perhaps she forgot a little story'. The comparative meaning of the suffix -*pǝk* in 4.51 shows that *kwasa* here is an adjective: this suffix has a comparative meaning ('more') only when used with an adjective (see Tables 4.2 and 4.3.)

If a modifying adjective modifies either a noun in the function of a copula complement, or another modifier, some ambiguity may arise, but it is almost always resolved by the context. A sentence *kwasa gǝrgǝr-a* (small+fem.sg tiny-3fem.sgNOM) can have two meanings—'she is a little bit tiny' and '(she is) a tiny little one'. The first reading was judged as strange; this sentence was used in the second sense.

Along similar lines, an exclamation *nǝma kwa:m!* (big+fem.sg crazy) could mean two things—'hugely crazy' and 'crazy big one!' This sentence was said by Yuamali to her daughter Kerryanne who was behaving as if she were the same age as her younger sister, the baby Jemima. And in this context the sentence had the second meaning. The sentence *kwasa sǝmi-pǝk a-ku-su!* (small+fem.sg long-COMPAR IMPV-put-UP) meant 'put on (a shirt that is) a little longer (than another one)', and not 'put on (a shirt that is) small and longish', in the context of Yuaneng trying T-shirts of different length. This second reading would have been perfectly appropriate in another context.

Note that ambiguity arises only if the order is agreeing adjective-other modifier-noun: *nǝma kru ta:kw* (big+fem.sg fat woman) can mean either 'big fat woman' or 'very fat woman; woman with a lot of fat'. If the order is modifier-agreeing adjective, the agreeing adjective can only be interpreted as a modifier to the other modifier, as in 4.53:

4.53 kru   nǝma   (tǝ-na)   ta:kw
      fat   big+fem.sg (have/be-ACT.FOC+3fem.sgBAS.VT) woman
      'a woman (who has) lots of fat'

If an agreeing adjective is used to modify a modifier, only the functionally unmarked feminine singular form is acceptable (cf. §5.2.3).

All three agreeing adjectives undergo full reduplication; the meaning is intensity, e.g. *yara-yara-di du-ta:kw* (fine-fine-pl man-woman) 'very fine people', *nǝma-nǝma-di du* (big-big-pl man) 'very big men', *kwasa-kwasa-di ja:p* (small-small-pl thing) 'tiny little things'. The reduplicated form *kwasa-kwasa* has an additional meaning of 'slowly, little by little', as in 4.54, or 'carefully', as in *kwasa-kwasa ma:y* (small-small go+IMPV) 'go carefully'.

4.54 gu   ata   kǝlǝ-d,   kwasa-kwasa
      water then go.down-3masc.sgBAS.P little.fem.sg-little.fem.sg
      'Water receded then, little by little'

When used as an adverbial modifier to verbs and to nouns referring to gradable properties, *kwasa* has an additional meaning of 'almost', e.g. as in *kwasa kiya-k tǝ-na-wun* (little.fem.sg die-PURP have/stand-ACT.FOC-1fem.sgBAS.VT) 'I was almost going to die' and *kwasa jǝpwas* (little+fem.sg initiated.man) 'an almost initiated man'.

The headless *nǝma* is used in the meaning of 'loudly' with verbs of speech, as in *nǝma yi-tukwa* (big+fem.sg speak-PROH) 'do not speak loudly'. To refer to shouting at the top of one's voice, one can change the gender on *nǝma*: in agreement with the meaning of 'intensity and unusual size' associated with the masculine gender (as in 5.13), *nǝma-d(ǝ)yi-tukwa* (big-masc.sg speak-PROH.GEN) means 'do not speak very loudly'. There are no such extensions for *yara*.

The combination of *kwasa* 'small, little bit' with *nəma* 'big' means 'a little bit big; a little bit bigger', e.g. *kwasa nəma-pək-a wi* (little+fem.sg big+fem.sg-COMPAR-LK house) 'a house that is a little bigger (than another house)'. If we reverse the order, we obtain an idiomatic expression, *nəma kwasa*, as in *nəma kwasa kwa-* (big little stay-) 'spread the news'. In contrast, *yara* does not co-occur with either of the dimension adjectives.

The two agreeing dimension adjectives, 'big' and 'small, little', have a few further extensions of meaning. The adjective *nəma* often means 'serious, grave', e.g. *nəma apaw va:l* (big+fem.sg old.fem mistake) 'a serious breakage of a taboo'. Especially in combination with 'old', 'big' means 'real, really big in a metaphorical sense', as in *nəma apaw tenkyu* (big+fem.sg old.fem thankyou) 'really big thankyou'. Both adjectives are ambiguous between comparative size and comparative age when used with human referents. With other referents (including high animates, such as dogs and pigs) they refer just to size.

All other adjectives show no agreement in gender or number with the head noun; these cover dimension, e.g. *gərgər* 'tiny', value, e.g. *vyakət* 'good, good-looking', *kuprap* 'bad', colour, and few other semantic domains (see Table 4.3). Many non-agreeing adjectives can be considered zero derivations of corresponding nouns, e.g. *səmi* 'length; long'; *təpwi* 'width; wide' (this is also a term for a ritual bench); *kru* 'fatness; fat'. Colour adjectives rather transparently correspond to a noun whose referent has that prototypical colour, e.g. *wa:m* 'white cockatoo', *wam-a* 'white'; *gəl* 'dark raincloud', *gla* 'dark, black'; *ñiki* 'red', *ñiki* 'blood'; *væs* 'grass', *væs-a* 'yellow, green (colour of grass)'.

Two colour adjectives contain roots not attested anywhere else in the language: *wəla-ka-wal* 'light, white, transparent' and *wasə-ka-was* 'yellow' which contain the intensive -*ka*- and appear to be fully reduplicated (see under 5 in §4.3.2). In conversation, one frequently hears colour terms borrowed from English, e.g. *blu* or *bəlu* (and even an intensive derivation *blu-ka-blu* 'very blue; blue like a sky'), and *grin* 'green'.

Speakers found it difficult to agree on the term for 'brown': *juwi-ka-juwi* is reportedly used in the Yuanab variety (based on *juwi* 'a type of tree with brownish-reddish berries'), and rejected as incorrect by others, from both Avatip and Malu. Those prefer to refer to 'brown' as *səpkətək* 'like skin'; and to 'green' as *væs kətək* 'like grass', instead of a derivation *laki-ka-laki* 'green' based on *laki* 'ginger'.

A few working sessions with a colour chart revealed an interesting tendency. Both old and young (5- to 10-year-old) speakers had to use a term for a natural phenomenon displaying an appropriate colour, if they judged the colour terms in Manambu unsatisfactory. So, a very black colour was termed as *ga:n-ad* (night-3masc.sgNOM) 'it is night', and a bluish-greenish colour as *su:-ad* (edible.cane-3masc.sg) 'it is edible cane'; bright yellow was described as *wulək vya-kwa-dana-l aka* (lightning hit-HAB-3plSUBJ.VT+ 3fem.sgBAS.VT-3fem.sgNOM DEM.DIST.REACT.TOP+fem.sg) 'this is how the lightning usually strikes'.

Yet not every non-agreeing adjective is derived from a noun: for instance, the two value adjectives *kuprap* 'bad' and *vyakət* 'good' have no corresponding noun; neither do the size adjective *gər* 'tiny', the age adjective *kul(a)*, or the 'intensive property' adjective *məy* 'real' (see §21.2.4).

An agreeing dimension adjective always precedes a non-agreeing one within a noun phrase, as in *kwasa ñiki ñan* (little+fem.sg red child) 'little pink baby', and 4.55 (the NP, in the copula complement function, is in square brackets). This example also illustrates the absence of gender and number agreement on the adjective *kru*.

4.55 [məy-a nəma-nəma   væk-a-kru væk-a-kru] ata   ta:l
     real-LK big-RED+fem.sg   pot-LK-fat pot-LK-fat then stay+3fem.sgBAS.P
     a   tami:
     DEM.DIST+fem.sg area
     '(The moon) then became very big and well and truly fat like a pot in that area'

The adjective 'old, useless' has two forms—*apan* 'masculine' and *apaw* 'feminine'; gender agreement is obligatory in noun phrases and with copula complements, e.g. *apan du* (old:masc man) 'old man; old men', *apaw ta:kw* (old:fem woman) 'old woman; old women'. These adjectives have no number agreement (unlike the three agreeing adjectives). In all other properties (see §4.3.2) they pattern with non-agreeing adjectives. The root 'old' is probably related to the noun *ap* 'bone; foundation', and also appears in a non-agreeing adjective *apar* 'adult, experienced'.

There are no productive word class-changing derivations which would form nouns or verbs from adjectives, or adjectives from verbs. The only exception is the verb *vyakanaku-* 'correct, improve' which is related to an adjective *vyakət* 'good' via a nonce derivation.

The class of non-agreeing adjectives can be considered semi-open, because it accepts loans: besides the colour terms mentioned above, one hears *nupela* 'new' (from Tok Pisin *nupela*), instead of *kula*, and *lapun* 'old' (Tok Pisin *lapun*) instead of *apan* 'old (masculine)' and *apaw* 'old (feminine)'.

In summary, adjectives in Manambu share a number of features with nouns, and have some properties of their own. Syntactically, non-agreeing adjectives are more 'noun-like' than agreeing adjectives.

4.3.2   Adjectives in comparison with nouns and verbs

Table 4.2 features a comparison of morphological and syntactic properties for nouns, verbs, and adjectives. We saw, in §3.1, that members of any word class can head a one-place predicate in declarative and interrogative main clauses. Then, verbs use verbal sets of person marking (Tables 3.1–2), while other word classes use the 'nominal set' (Table 3.4). Only verbs can head a predicate in a non-declarative clause, or in a temporal or conditional subordinate clause. Other word classes require a copula/support verb in these contexts. Any word class can be focused (see §§11.1–2 and §20.3). The differences between verbal and non-verbal roots were summarized in Table 2.3. Only verbal roots have unpredictable vowel alternations (see §11.3).

1. NEGATION is marked differently for verbal and non-verbal heads of a predicate; these also differ in how tense distinctions are expressed. See §§14.1.1–2, for a discussion.

2. COMPOUNDING is productive for verbs, and is used to express a number of meanings, including aspectual, valency changing, manner, sequencing, and complete involvement, e.g. *kə-yakə-* (eat-throw) 'eat fully, eat up', *vægru-yakə-* (get.together-throw) 'get together (all people)' (see §15.3). Verb-noun compounds can be considered functional equivalents of relative clauses if the noun is not specific, e.g. *kiya-du* (die-man) 'dead man', *kiya-d-ə du* (die-3masc.sgBAS.P-LK man) 'a/the man who died'—see §19.2.2. Noun compounding is extremely productive, e.g. *ap-a-təp* (bone-LK-village) 'Avatip (the main village)' (see §9.3).

Agreeing adjectives cannot be part of a compound. Other adjectives can form nominal-like compounds, e.g. *væk-a-kru* (pot-LK-fat) 'fat as a pot' in 4.55, or *wi-a-kru* (house-LK-fat) 'thick,

TABLE 4.2 Morphological properties and syntactic functions of adjectives, verbs, and nouns

MORPHOLOGICAL PROPERTY	VERBS	AGREEING ADJECTIVES	NON-AGREEING ADJECTIVES	NOUNS
1. Negation - §14.1	'verbal system'	'non-verbal' system		
2. Compounding	productive (§15.2)	none	some like verbs, some like nouns	productive (§9.3)
3a. Partial reduplication	aspect marking (§12.8.2)	none		
3b. Full reduplication	intensive aspect (§12.8.2); modality (§13.4); nominalizations (§9.1.1)	intensive	intensive with some	distributive ('every')
4. Semantics of *-pək*	'like'	comparative	comparative (most)	more or less, like
5. Infix *-ka-* 'intensive'	no	no	yes (most)	some

SYNTACTIC FUNCTION	VERB	AGREEING ADJECTIVES	NON-AGREEING ADJECTIVES	NOUN
6. Modifier to a verb	no	yes	yes (some)	no
7. Modifier to another adjective	no	yes	no	
8. Copula complement	no	yes (two of three: agreement with the subject); no (one of three)	yes (no agreement)	
9. Head of NP and argument	no	yes		
10. Modifier in NP		[yes]		
11. Modification by *məy* 'real; very'	adverb *məyir*	adjective+*məy* 'very ADJ'	*məy-a* + ADJ 'real ADJ'	*məy-a* NOUN 'real NOUN'

wide as a house'. The adjective *vyakət* 'good' is unusual in that it forms a compound with *-yakə* 'throw' as a second component, as if it were a verb, e.g. *vyakəta-yakə nəb-a ta:kw* (good-throw young.female-LK woman) 'very beautiful young woman'.

3. REDUPLICATION can be partial only for verbs (see §9.1.1 and §12.8.2). Just one noun has a partially reduplicated form: *jija:p* 'things, belongings' formed on *ja:p* 'thing'. Full reduplication results in different meanings with different word classes. WITH VERBS, full reduplication marks:

(i) action nominalizations, e.g. *nas(ə)-* 'count (verb)', *nasənas* 'counting (noun)' (§§9.1.1–2);
(ii) intensive, continuous, or durative aspectual meanings (§12.8.2).

Full reduplication of a NOUN has distributive meaning, as in *nabi-nabi* (year-year) 'every year', *təp-a-təp* 'every village', *gwalugw-u gwalugw-u ma:j* (clan-LK clan-LK story) 'story which goes from one clan to another', *sad-ə-sad* (manner-LK-manner) 'various ways; every way', *tamiy-a-tami:* (area-LK-area) 'every area, every place'. In a reciprocal construction, full reduplication conveys the meaning of 'to one another', as in 4.56.

4.56 awarwa rək   kur-na-bran   kajal-kajal
      REC   joke make-ACT.FOC-1duBAS.VT brother's.wife-brother's.wife
      'We make jokes to/about each other, from brother's wife to brother's wife' (an explanation of joking relationship with one's brother's wives) (also see 5.16)

WITH ALL AGREEING ADJECTIVES, full reduplication has intensive meaning, e.g. *kwasa-kwasa-di kami* (little-little-pl fish) 'very small fish', *kwasa-kwasa-di gwalugw* (little-little-pl clan) 'very small clans'; *nəma-nəma-di kami:* (big-big-pl fish) 'very big fish'. Some non-agreeing adjectives can also undergo full reduplication, with the same intensive meaning, e.g. *a-di vyakət-vyakət-a ta:kw* (DEM.DIST-pl good-RED-LK woman) 'those very good women', *ñiki-ñiki ñan* (red-RED child) 'a very pink baby', *gər* 'small', *gər-gər* 'tiny'. Other non-agreeing adjectives derive intensive forms via full reduplication and the infix *-ka*—see 5 below.

The non-agreeing adjective *kula* 'new, raw (food)' has a partially unpredictable meaning, when reduplicated: *kulakul* means 'naive, unknowing (e.g. about a person who has come somewhere for the first time)'.

4. SEMANTICS OF *-pək* 'MORE OR LESS, COMPARATIVE' varies depending on the class of its host word (see further discussion in §9.2). With nouns, verbs, some non-agreeing adjectives (and also numerals, pronouns, adverbs) the suffix *-pək* 'approximative' means 'about; more; more or less like this', e.g. *vətiy-a-pək* (two-LK-like) 'more or less two'; *takwa ñan-a-pək* (woman+LK child-LK-like) 'someone who is more or less like a girl'. With the agreeing dimension adjectives, this suffix implies comparison. The standard of comparison is not overtly expressed, and the idea of comparison is understood from the context, as in 4.51.

The suffix *-pək* has comparative meaning with non-agreeing adjectives referring to value, size, and age, e.g. *apar-pək-a ñan* (adult-COMPAR-LK child) 'an older child', *vyakət-pək-a val* (good-COMPAR-LK canoe/car) 'a better car (than other cars)', *səmi-pək-a wapwi* (long-COMPAR-LK clothing) 'a piece of clothing longer than another one'. It is hardly ever used with colour adjectives.

5. THE INFIX *-ka-* 'INTENSIVE' is used with most non-agreeing adjectives, and also with some nouns. The root of an adjective or of a noun undergoes full reduplication, and the infix (which requires a linker) is inserted between the two reduplicated parts, e.g. *pa:p* 'short', *papa-ka-pa:p* 'very short'; *kru* 'fat', *kru-k(u)a-kru* 'very fat'; *væs* 'yellow, green (colour of grass)', *væsə-ka-væs* 'very yellow'; *gəl* 'black', *gla-ka-gəl* 'very black'; *səmi* 'long', *səmi-ka-səmi* 'very long'; *təpwi*

'broad', *təp(w)i-ka-təpwi* 'very broad';[5] *juwi-ka-juwi* 'brown' (Yambon dialect: Farnsworth and Farnsworth 1966). This process also applies to loans, e.g. *blu* 'blue', *blu-ka-blu* 'very blue'. The adjective *kuprap* 'bad' forms an irregular derivation *kəprə-ka-kuprap* 'very bad'.

Adjectives which can take *-ka-* cannot undergo full reduplication without it. The only exception is the adjective *kuprap* 'bad': an alternative intensive form of *kuprap* involves an echo compound *kuprapə-saprap* 'really bad' (§9.3). Adjectives which undergo full reduplication (see 4 above) cannot take *-ka-*; these include *vyakət* 'good', *ñiki* 'red', and a few others.

An additional connotation of the *-ka-* derivation with adjectives involves 'all over, everywhere'. To refer to a sequence of samples of black colour on a colour chart, 10-year-old Celestin explained:

4.57 kə-lə-m   karya-rəb   gəl-a-ka-gəl-adi
     DEM.PROX-fem.sg-LOC carry-FULLY black-LK-INT-black-3plNOM
     'Right up until here they are all black all over'

A few nouns also occur fully reduplicated with the infix *-ka-*. Some of these formations are used as non-agreeing modifiers only, e.g. *səp* 'skin', *səp-ə-ka-səp* (skin-LK-INT-skin) 'skinny, thin, flat'; *ap* 'bone', *ap-a-ka-ap* 'very thin; bone-like';[6] *laki* 'ginger', *laki-ka-laki* 'green as ginger' (also see §9.1.2). Other such formations have an intensive meaning, e.g. *ya:l* 'stomach, belly', *yal-a-ka-ya:l* (stomach-LK-INT-stomach) 'stomach and nothing else, empty stomach', as in 4.58; and the nominal *suan* 'hard', e.g. *suan-ə-ka-suan* (hard-LK-INT-hard) 'very hard'.

4.58 yala-ka-yala:m   rə-tukwa
     stomach+LK-INT-stomach+LK+LOC sit-PROH.GEN
     'Don't stay on an empty stomach'

6. MODIFIER TO A VERB is a syntactic function typical for three agreeing adjectives (see §4.3.1 and examples there). Non-agreeing dimension adjectives can modify verbs directly, e.g. *səmi rə-* (long sit-) 'stay for a long time'. Alternatively, a non-agreeing adjective may be adverbialized (see §4.4):

4.59 səmir   yi-kə-na-wun
     far+DER go-FUT-ACT.FOC-1fem.sgBAS.VT
     'I will go far'

Value and age adjectives can be used as modifiers only if they form one NP with the noun *sa:d* 'manner, way', e.g. *kuprapə sa:d* 'bad way; badly'. Nouns cannot be used as modifiers to verbs, with a possible exception of *sa:d* 'way'.[7]

7. MODIFIER TO ANOTHER ADJECTIVE is a syntactic function restricted to the two agreeing dimension adjectives, e.g. *kwasa səmi* (little+fem.sg long) 'a little far, long', *nəma kru* (big+fem.sg fat) 'very fat' (see example 4.52 and the discussion there).

8. COPULA COMPLEMENT is a syntactic function which verbs do not have (they have to be nominalized to be used this way). All nouns and adjectives can be copula complements; unlike non-agreeing adjectives, the two agreeing dimension adjectives agree in gender and number

---

[5] The loss of labialization in the first part of the reduplicated word is optional.

[6] *Ap-a-ka-ap* can be pronounced either as [apaˈkaːp] or as [apakaˈap], with a highly unusual sequence of identical vowels.

[7] We can recall (§3.1) that 'manner' can be cross-referenced on the verb in second position, if topical, e.g. *akatawa sa:d suku-kə-tua* (thus way write-FUT-1sgSUBJ.VT+3fem.sgBAS.VT) 'I will write (it) this way'. Manner words are feminine (§5.2.1).

with the subject; see examples in §4.3.1. The value adjective *yara* 'fine' does not agree with the subject when used as copula complement.

9. HEAD OF NP is a syntactic function limited to nouns and adjectives. Verbs have to be nominalized to be used as arguments. The resulting nominalizations are used in a limited range of functions (see §9.1.1). We can recall, from §4.1, that deverbal nouns can be heads of noun phrases, but cannot be modified or possessed. A few verbs can be nominalized with the syllable-structure-sensitive suffix *-ka:u*, e.g. *kakəl-* 'exceed, win', *kakəl-ka:u* 'competition' (see §9.1.2).

In contrast, any noun or adjective can be head of an NP, and be used as an argument. Heads of possessive NPs of the types discussed in §8.1 are mostly nouns.

10. A member of any word class can be MODIFIER IN AN NP. The structure of NPs (with special attention to the variable positioning of possessives, quantifiers, and modifiers from closed classes) is discussed in §20.1.1. Only rarely can an NP contain two non-agreeing adjectives. The few available examples involve a dimension adjective and a colour adjective; dimension precedes colour, as in *gərgər ñikiñiki ñan* (tiny red:RED child) 'tiny pink baby' (said ironically to a 3-year-old crying as if she were a baby).

We saw in §4.3.1 above that the two agreeing dimension adjectives can occur together (but then the meanings are slightly idiosyncratic). The third agreeing adjective, *yara* 'fine', hardly ever co-occurs in a noun phrase with any other adjectival modifiers. The agreeing adjectives occur further away from the head of a noun phrase than non-agreeing adjectives; this is a feature they share with other modifiers from closed classes—e.g. demonstratives or indefinites—which have the same gender and number agreement patterns and marking (see §5.1 and §§10.2–3).

11. MODIFICATION BY *məy* 'REAL; VERY' provides an additional criterion for distinguishing between the three major word classes in Manambu. The non-agreeing adjective *məy* 'real' occurs preposed to nouns, with the meaning 'real', e.g. *məy-a ma:j* (real-LK story) 'real story'. Like any prehead modifier, it then takes a linker. It occurs postposed to an adjective in the predicate slot with the meaning of 'very', e.g. *kwasa məy* (little+fem.sg real) 'very small, very little', *vyakət-a məy* (good-LK very) 'very good'. When it appears preposed to an adjective in any function, its meaning is 'really', e.g. *məy-a kwasa-di du-ta:kw* (real-LK little-pl man-woman) 'really small people', *məy-a nəma-di kəp* (real-LK big-pl land) 'really big stretches of land', *məy-a vyakət-a* (real-LK good-LK) '(something) really good'.

This same adjective occurs with nouns, in the meaning of 'real', e.g. *məy-a du* (real-LK man) 'real man (that is, not a spirit or an animal in disguise)', *məy-a ta:kw* 'real woman'. In contrast, a verb can only take the adverb *məyir* 'really', as in *wun məyir ma: la:kw* (I real+ALL NEG know:NEG) 'I really do not know' (also see §21.2.4). The meaning 'very' with verbs is covered partly by intensifying reduplication (see §12.8.2), and partly by *-yakə-* compounds (see §15.3).

In summary: the two adjective subclasses differ in a number of properties, and yet have enough properties in common (especially 4–11, and also 1, 9, and 10) to justify being assigned to one major word class. Agreeing adjectives show similarities to modifiers from closed classes (§4.5), while non-agreeing adjectives—most of which are derived from nouns—are noun-like.

4.3.3 Semantics of adjectives

Table 4.3 summarizes the correlations between the semantic types cross-linguistically associated with adjectives (see Dixon 2004) and other word classes.

TABLE 4.3 Semantic types of adjectival concepts and word classes in Manambu

SEMANTIC TYPE	WORD CLASS	MEMBERS	DERIVATION
1. Dimension	agreeing adjectives	nəma 'big', kwasa 'small, little'	underived
	non-agreeing adjectives	səmi 'long; tall (about a person)'	noun səmi 'length'
		paːp 'short (refers to both animates and inanimates)'	noun paːp 'shortness'
		təpwi 'wide'	noun təpwi 'width'
		gawun 'narrow'	noun gawun 'thorn; small stick'
		kru 'fat'	noun kru 'fatness'
		apakaap 'thin'	noun ap 'bone'
		gər, gərgər 'tiny'	?
2. Age	non-agreeing adjectives	badi 'young (man)'	badi 'young (man)'
		naubadi 'young (man)'	naubadi 'young (man)'
		nəbə- 'young (woman)'	only in compound nəbə-taːkw 'young woman'
		kula 'new, fresh, raw'	?
		apan 'old (masc); worn out'	from ap 'bone'?
		apaw 'old (fem); worn out'	from ap 'bone'?
3. Value	agreeing adjective	yara- 'fine, well-behaved'	?
	non-agreeing adjectives	vyakat 'good'	?
		kuprap 'bad'	?
4. Colour	non-agreeing adjectives	wama 'white'	noun waːm 'white cockatoo'
		gla- 'black'	noun gəl '(dark) cloud'
		laki-ka-laki 'green'	noun laki 'ginger'
		ñikiñiki 'red'	noun ñiki 'blood'

Verbs are used to express some dimension concepts, e.g. *kau-* 'be deep' and *vərvər-* 'be shallow'; value, such as perfect or strange; physical properties, human propensity, qualification, e.g. *rəp-* 'be enough', and position. Adverbs are used for speed, while difficulty is covered with nominals. Similarity is expressed with postpositional structures (see §4.5.2 on *kətək* 'like'). Quantification is marked with quantifiers (§10.5). Ordinal and cardinal numbers are a special class (§10.6.1). An exception is *ta:y* 'first' which is an adverb.

4.4 ADVERBS

Adverbs form a semi-open heterogeneous class of over forty members. They do not have any grammatical categories characteristic of other word classes. Their major syntactic function is to modify verbs. Unlike manner arguments, adverbs are never cross-referenced on the verb.

Many underived adverbs are monosyllabic, e.g. *kəp* 'just', *ma:k* 'personally, in person', *bə* 'already', *ma:* 'again', *ta:y* 'first, preceding', the reflexive-emphatic *ka:p* 'oneself, by oneself' (4.63; §16.2.4). Some are disyllabic, e.g. *(ma:) nəbay* 'not yet', *walba:b* 'close', *wayway* 'maybe', *jaujay* 'in a sloppy, incorrect way', and arguably also the reciprocal marker *awarwa* (in itself, the comitative case form of the noun *awar* 'side, sideways direction': see §16.2.4). A few adverbs come from nouns, e.g. *sək* 'far', from *sək* 'long distance'; *ma:k* 'in person', from *ma:k* 'face, person' (as in 4.69), or *gañ* 'last', related to *gəñ* 'tail' (4.60-2).

4.60 Səsawi **ta:y**, də **gañ** ata   yi-bər
      Sesawi first   he last   then   go-3duBAS.P
      'Sesawi went first, he (Kamkudi) last'

The alternative form of the same adverb is *gəñ* 'last' which coincides with the noun 'tail', and could be a back formation from the noun in its use as modifier, where it also means 'last', e.g. *gəñ-a ta:kw* (tail-LK woman) 'last/non-first wife'.

Adverbs may contain derivational suffixes which have the same segmental make-up as case markers. The suffix *-Vb* is similar to the terminative case *-Vb* and is used to derive adverbs from some nominals (which are typically used as copula complements), e.g. *kwam-a:b* (crazy-LK+TERM) 'by mistake, not thinking', *sək-a:b* (far-LK+TERM) 'far, from afar, to a far point', from noun phrases, e.g. *kwasa-məy-a-b* (little+fem.sg-very-LK-TERM) 'little by little; a little bit', from nouns, e.g. *ta:l* 'past', *tal-a:b* 'long time ago', and from other adverbs, e.g. *kəp* 'still, yet, just' (see §21.2.2), *kəpa:b* 'in case', *awar* 'one-sidedly', *awar-ə-b* 'in turn'.

This same formative occurs in some adverbs which do not appear to be derived (synchronically), e.g. *waya:b* 'in very recent past; just now'; *səmsəma:b* 'no way'. This formative also occurs in *nakamib* 'together', from *nak, nakaməy* 'one'. The meaning of this suffix is hardly predictable; similarly to the terminative case, it is stressed.

The suffix *-Vr* is similar to the allative-instrumental case *-Vr*. Unlike the case suffix, it is not stressed. It is used to derive adverbs from nouns, e.g. *gə́ñər* 'later' (cf. *gəñ* 'tail'; *gəñər* 'to tail; with tail'), from some non-agreeing adjectives, e.g. *səmir* 'along' (from *səmi* 'long') and *pápər* 'a little later' (from *pa:p* 'short') and from underived adverbs, e.g. *ta:y* 'before, in front, ahead', *tá:yir* 'previously; towards the front'; *məy* 'very', *mə́yir* 'really'.

This same formative appears in a few other adverbs, such as *japwár* 'conveniently', *yapwur* 'quickly'. Note that the allative-instrumental case forms are reminiscent of adverbs in their semantics and usage, especially if repeated, as in *ab-á-r ab-á-r* (head-LK-ALL head-LK-ALL) 'head first'. The adverb *kukə́r* 'after, later' is also used as a postposition (see §4.5.2). A few inherently repeated adverbs are derived from verb roots, e.g. *pakwúr pakwúr* (hide+ALL hide+ALL) 'in a secretive way' (from *pa:kw-* 'be hidden').

A formative -*Vk*, similar to the dative case marker -*Vk*, appears in *madək madək* 'especially, namely'. The comitative -*wa* appears to derive adverbs with the meaning of 'all the referents' from a few nouns, e.g. *mi:* 'tree; high', *miy-awa* 'together; whole', *təp* 'village', *təp-awa* 'the whole village' (see §7.9). A few derivational formatives occur on numbers (see §10.6.1) deriving adverbs, e.g. -*kərəb* 'together', as in *vəti-kərəb* 'two together'. The formative -*ta:y* in *bəta:y* 'already' may be cognate to the verbal cotemporaneous sequencing suffix -*ta:y* (§18.4). This adverb is unusual in that it can occur with the verbal confirmation marker -*ək*, *beta:yək* 'right now, already' (see §12.5). A few adverbs typically occur repeated, e.g. *yapwur yapwur* 'quickly', or reduplicated, e.g. *səmsəma:b* 'no way', *wayway, wəywəyau* 'maybe', and *rəka:rək* 'properly'. The adverbial derivational suffixes (none of which is productive, or semantically predictable) are the only adverb-specific morphological property.

A few frequently used forms containing the suffix -*ən* 'manner sequencing' are on the way towards becoming grammaticalized as adverbial manner modifiers (see §19.9). Examples include *yi:n* (go+SEQ) 'all along', as in *ñikiñiki yi:n kələb say-na-di* (red go+SEQ DEM.PROX+fem.sg+TERM finish-ACT.FOC-3plBAS.VT) 'red (colour) all along (the sheet) finishes here', *kray-in* (bring-SEQ) 'up until', and *səbən-ən* (return-SEQ) 'back', as in *səbən-ən a-kray* (return-SEQ IMPV-take) 'take (it) back!' However, they have hardly any of the morphological properties of the adverbs outlined in Table 4.4. They cannot be considered bona fide members of the class of adverbs despite their meanings and can be treated on a par with verbal forms, with one proviso: they cannot be negated independently.

All three agreeing adjectives can be used adverbially (that is, to modify a verb, or an adjective)—see 4.53 above. The agreeing value adjective *yara* 'fine' forms part of a derived adverb *yara-kara* (which contains a formative not found anywhere else in the language).

Just like verbs, nouns, and adjectives, all adverbs can be heads of intransitive predicates. Most adverbs can be modifiers in noun phrases. They do not require a linker, e.g. *bas wari* (first fight) 'fighting for the first time', *ta:yir ñaj* (early+ADV father's.brother) 'the father's brother (who was here) earlier', *ta:y ta:kw* (early/preceding woman) 'first wife' (also see 4.77, 'previous hole'), *miya-wa du* (tree+LK-COM man) 'all the men; all men together' (also see 15.100).

Table 4.4 features a comparison of morphological properties and syntactic functions of adverbs with the three other major word classes—nouns, verbs, and adjectives (see Table 4.2).

1. NEGATION. If an adverb is the head of an intransitive predicate, it is negated just like a noun or an adjective in the same function: the negator *ma:* is placed after the predicate head (which has no person markers); and no tense distinctions are made, e.g. *sək ma:* (far NEG) 'it is not far'—as a general statement which can refer to present, past, or future. If tense has to be expressed, then a verbal negative construction with the copula (most often *tə-*) is used. See §§14.1.1–2.

2. COMPOUNDING is typically not found with adverbs—a property they share with agreeing adjectives. Just occasionally does an adverb form a compound, e.g. *ab-a-gañ* (head-LK-last) 'very last'.

3. REDUPLICATION of adverbs has an 'intensive' meaning, e.g. *ka:p* 'alone, by oneself' (also used as a reflexive marker: §16.2.4), *kapə-ka:p* 'really alone', and also as in 4.61:

TABLE 4.4 Morphological properties and syntactic functions of adverbs in comparison with other major word classes

MORPHOLOGICAL PROPERTY	ADVERB	COMMENTS
1. Negation: §§14.1.1–2	'non-verbal system'	similar to nouns and adjectives
2. Compounding	none	similar to agreeing adjectives
3. Reduplication	intensive	similar to most adjectives
4. Semantics of *-pək*	'like' (restricted in use)	similar to verbs and nouns, different from adjectives
5. Infix *-ka-* 'intensive'	very rare	different from adjectives, similar to verbs

SYNTACTIC FUNCTION	ADVERB	COMMENTS
6. Modifier to a verb	yes	similar to adjectives
7. Modifier to an adjective	no	similar to nouns, verbs, and non-agreeing adjectives
8. Copula complement	yes	similar to nouns and adjectives
9. Head of NP and argument	no	similar to verbs
10. Modification by *məy* 'real, very'	adverb *məyir*; or adjective *məy*	similar to verbs similar to nouns and adjectives

4.61 ata væsə-ta:y   ata ya:l,   də-kə   kukə-b,   lə gəñ-gəñ,
      thus step-COTEMP thus go+3fem.sgBAS.P he-OBL+fem.sg after-TERM she last-last
      də tay-tay
      he first-first
      'Thus stepping she went, right after (behind) him, she the very last, he the very first'

4. Semantics of *-pək* 'like' when it occurs with adverbs is similar to that with nouns and verbs, e.g. *miy-a-wa-pək* (tree-LK-COM-LIKE) 'as if all, like it were all', *yabib-a-pək* (quickly-LK-LIKE) 'as if it were quick'. This suffix is not used with most monosyllabic and disyllabic adverbs.

5. THE INFIX *-ka-* 'INTENSIVE' is used with just two adverbs: *ka:p* 'on one's own', *kapə-ka-ka:p* 'absolutely on one's own', and *kəp* 'just; for nothing', *kəp-ə-ka-kəp* 'well and truly for nothing'.

6–7. An adverb can MODIFY a verb, as shown in 4.63; this is a function adverbs share with adjectives. An adverb can modify a nominal copula complement, but not an adjective.

8. An adverb can be a copula complement, e.g. *kəp kwa-na-d* (just stay-ACT.FOC-3masc.sgBAS.VT) 'he just stays, stays for nothing'. Some such constructions have idiomatic meanings, e.g. *ma:k kwa-* (in.person stay) 'be born'.

9–10. Just like a verb, an adverb cannot be head of an NP or an argument. An adverb can be modified by *məyir*—just like a verb, e.g. *məyir yapwur yapwur ma:j bla-kwa-na* (real+ADV quickly quickly talk speak-HAB-ACT.FOC+3fem.sgBAS.VT) 'she speaks really fast'. This is the only instance of an adverb modifying another adverb. One adverb, *gañ* 'last', can be modified by *məy-* 'real, very', just like a noun or an adjective, as in 4.62:

4.62 ada   gañ kwa:d   məy-a-gañ
      DEM.DIST.REACT.TOP+masc.sg last stay+3masc.sgBAS.P real-LK-last
      'Then he stayed there last, really last (the very last)'

As shown in Table 4.4, adverbs share some properties with nouns and adjectives, and some with verbs. Adverbs can be positioned anywhere in a clause (unless they modify a noun, in which case they precede that noun). A clause can contain up to three adverbs in the corpus collected, as shown in 4.63 (adverbs are in bold):

4.63 a-di   təp   **ka:p aba:b bə**   kiya-di
      DEM.DIST-pl village alone all   already die-3plBAS.P
      'Those (of) the village already all died by themselves'

This is a unique syntactic property of adverbs: a clause or an NP cannot contain more than two modifiers of other sorts. Some connectives are connected with demonstratives (see §4.5.3).

4.5 CLOSED CLASSES

Closed classes in Manambu include (a) personal pronouns (Table 3.3 and §10.1); (b) demonstratives (§10.2); (c) indefinites (§10.3); (d) interrogatives (§10.4); (d) quantifiers, e.g., *sama:sam* 'many, much' (§10.5); and (e) numerals (§10.6). All of these, with the exception of demonstrative and interrogative adverbs, are similar to nominals in most properties. They differ in the amount of nominal morphology they take; in their position within a noun phrase; and in their syntactic functions (whether they can be heads of intransitive predicates, copula complements, or modifiers). Demonstrative and interrogative adverbs do not take nominal cross-referencing sets when they head a predicate.

Further closed classes are modal verbs, postpositions, emphatic particle, connectives, hortative, interjections, and onomatopoeia.

4.5.1 Modal words

Modal words are a small closed class, which consists of two members, *bənak* and *nəbə* 'be able to, can'. Both form a complex predicate with an inflected verb in the indicative mood (see §20.1.2). They are not inflected, cannot be negated, or questioned, or appear in a command; neither do they appear in any of the modalities discussed in Chapter 13. Both have an epistemic meaning of a potential. The form *bənak* appears to be rarer than *nəbə* and is always followed by a verb inflected for person, number, and gender of the subject, as in 4.64. It occurs clause-initially.

4.64 bənak   val   suku-kə-tua
      capable canoe carve-FUT-1sgSUBJ.VT+3fem.sgBAS.VT
      'I can carve a canoe'

The form *nəbə* does not have to occur clause-initially. It always precedes the inflected verb. It can be accompanied by a verb inflected for third person singular feminine (basic set). Such a form can have a generic subject, as in *papər nəbə val* (a.little.later.on able see+3fem.sgBAS.VT) 'one can see later'. The use of feminine cross-referencing here goes together with the functionally unmarked character of feminine in Manambu—see §5.2.3. Depending on the context, such an expression can be understood as 'we', or 'you'.

When Tanina said to me *sər nəbə kwatiya-l* (tomorrow able give.to.nonthird.p-3fem.sgBAS.VT) 'one can give (this to me) tomorrow', it was clear from the context that I was the giver. Similarly, 5.27 refers to two people ('us') writing together. The referent of the subject can be specified, by adding an NP, as in 4.65, or a personal pronoun, as in 4.66.

4.65 papər   Jagər nəbə val
     little.later Jager able see+3fem.sgBAS.VT
     'A little later Jager can see (what's wrong with the machine)'

4.66 bər   nəbə wula-l
     you.two able come.in-3fem.sgBAS.VT
     'The two of you can come in'

This construction does not appear to be used with first person singular subject. The second alternative is to employ a verb form fully inflected for person, number, and gender. Then, there are no restrictions as to the person of the subject—the first person subject is shown in the first clause of 15.53.

In summary: the modal words form one complex predicate with an inflected verb (allowing for two options of inflection). They cannot take any inflection themselves, or be used in any other syntactic function, and can only occur in positive declarative clauses. (The negative counterpart would be a copula clause with *suan yi-* (as in 4.7).) This makes them different from any other word class in the language.

4.5.2   Postpositions

Postpositions form a small closed class, of three members: *kətək* 'like; similarly', e.g. *du kətək* 'like a man', *wukən* 'together with', and *kukə-* 'behind'. All of them follow their nominal argument. No other constituent can intervene between them. The third person pronouns and the interrogative *sə* 'who' do not take the oblique marker *-kə-* when used as postpositional arguments of the first two, e.g. *də kətək* (he like) 'like him'.

The three postpositions differ in a number of properties. The postposition *kətək* 'like; similarly' does not require a linker on the noun, as shown in 4.67:

4.67 nənəm   sakə-lə-d   [bal kətək]
     smoking.grid+LK+LOC smoke-3fem.sgSUBJ.P-3MASC.SGBAS.P pig like
     'She smoked him on a smoking grid like a pig'

The suffix *-pək* 'like, almost like' implies comparative likeness, while *kətək* implies just about full similarity; to express complete similarity, the suffix *-rəb* 'straight, fully' is used (see the discussion in §9.2). A noun phrase containing *kətək* is syntactically an oblique which cannot be cross-referenced in the second position; it can head a predicate or occupy the copula complement slot, e.g. *du kətək-al* (man like-3fem.sgNOM) '(she) is/was like a man'; but cannot be used as a modifier or as an argument of a verb. This postposition may have an approximative meaning, as in *nabi mugul a:li kətək* (year three four like) 'about three or four years of age'. A somewhat archaic variant of *kətək* is *kaytək*.

The postposition *wukən* 'together' (homonymous with the sequential form *wukə-n* (hear-SEQ.MANNER) 'hearing, understanding, feeling') does not require a linker on the noun it governs. It marks the second subject participant in the argument elaboration ('inclusory') construction (§6.2.3), as in 4.68 and 6.38.

4.68 an   [Aulapan wukən] Sarak-abran
    we.du Aulapan with   Sarak-1duNOM
    'The two of us, Aulapan and I, are of the Sarak clan'

It can also mark an oblique participant which is not cross-referenced, e.g. 'with his mother' in 4.69:

4.69 ata wukə-ku   gra-dian   [də-kə   amæy wukən]
    then hear/feel-COMPL.SS cry-1plBAS.P he-OBL+fem.sg mother with
    də-kə   ma:k və-ma:r-ku   ata gra-dian
    3masc.sg-OBL+3fem.sg person see-NEG.SUB-COMPL.SS then cry-1plBAS.P
    'Then feeling sorry (for the missing boy) we (all) cried, together with his mother, not having seen him in person (and suspecting the worst), we then cried'

It can occur on its own if the noun is recoverable from the context, as in 4.70:

4.70 wukən a-kray
    with IMPV-bring
    'Bring (glasses) with you!'

The postposition *wukən* is similar in meaning to the comitative case (see §7.9). The difference is the degree of participation: if all the participants are equally involved, comitative is used. If not, *wukən* is preferred. A speaker said 4.71, rather than 4.72, because an 11-year-old, however smart, could not be an equal participant in an adult women's job of going to a market to sell and buy things.

4.71 maketar   lə-kə   wukən yi-k-na-bran
    market+ALL she-OBL with go-FUT-ACT.FOC-1duBAS.VT
    'We two will go to the market, (me) with her (11-year-old girl)'

4.72 lə-kə-wa   yi-k-na-bran
    she-OBL-COM go-FUT-ACT.FOC-1duBAS.VT
    'We two will (go to the market), (me) with her'

Younger speakers who frequently code-switch with Tok Pisin replace *wukən* with its synonym, the Tok Pisin code-switch *wantaim*, e.g. *mən-a wantaim*, *mən wukən* 'with you (masculine)'. Some use *wukən* in the context where a comitative is expected; 4.73 is an example of *wukən*—spontaneously produced by Janet and addressed to her daughter, Joana—where a double comitative construction (§7.9 and §6.2.3) would have been more appropriate for a traditional speaker.

4.73 yi-k-ñəna,   [təp-a   kudi   wukən] [wali
    speak-FUT-2fem.sgSUBJ.VT+3fem.sgBAS.VT village-LK language with   white.people
    kudi   wukən]
    language with
    'You will speak, (in) the village language together with the white people's language'

The argument of this postposition, rather than the whole NP, can be focused (§20.3):

4.74 [[Kay-a-wa   Harold-ad]_FOCUS   wukən] kwa-tuə-l
     Kay-LK-COM Harold-3masc.sgNOM with   stay-1sgSUBJ.P-3fem.sgBAS.P
     gabu-ma:j-a
     traditional-story-3fem.sgNOM
     'This is the story of me staying together with (focused) Harold and Kay'

Just like *kətək*, an NP containing this postposition can occur in the predicate slot. It cannot occupy the copula complement slot, or be used as a modifier or an argument of the verb unless it occurs as part of the argument elaboration construction, as in 4.71–2.

The postposition *kukə-* 'at the back of; behind; after' is only superficially similar to the other two postpositions. The root *kukə-* takes three local cases: locative, with the meaning 'behind', as in *də-kə kuk-ə-m rə-d-ə du* (he-OBL behind-LK-LOC sit-3masc.sgBAS.VT-LK man) 'a man sitting behind him'; allative, with the meaning of 'towards the direction of behind something', as in 4.75; and terminative, meaning 'exactly behind something', as in 4.61 above. It always requires a linker. In these respect it is noun-like (however, it is not used as a noun, 'back').

4.75 [ñan-a   kuk-ə-r]   ya-n   væki-n   tə-na-di
     we.pl-LK back-LK-ALL come-SEQ go.across-SEQ stand-ACT.FOC-3plBAS.VT
     '(Soldiers) were coming across towards behind us'

An NP containing *kukə-* can modify a noun. [*Yuajan kuk-ə-b-a*] *du* (Yuajan:female.name behind-LK-TERM-LK man) means 'male (son) (born) after Yuajan'; this was used to describe the sequence of children, by Gemaj. This example also shows that the spatial meaning 'behind' is extended to temporal, 'after' (also see 13.43).

Any of the case forms of *kukə-* can be used without an argument, that is, similarly to a locative adverb. Sometimes the argument of *kukə-* can be recovered from the context, as in the mother's answer to my question why the baby was crying, under 13.43 ('she wants to go out after (her)'). No such argument is 'recoverable' in 4.76—this is an example of an adverbial-like use of *kukə-*:

4.76 wun kəka-n-aka   bla-tuə-l   kuk-ə-m
     I   DEM.PROX.REACT.TOP-PRED-REACT.TOP talk-1sgSUBJ.P-3fem.sgBAS.P back-LK-LOC
     'Here (I am), this is what I said afterwards'

Just like any other adverb (Table 4.4), a case-marked form of *kukə-* can be used as a modifier of a noun, e.g. *kukər ñan* (behind+ALL child) 'last child', *kukə-səbuk* (back-high.degree.of.initiated.man) 'the most senior of simbuks' (also used for 'high priest', in Bible translation).

Unlike any other postpositions, but similarly to body part terms, *kukə-* can appear in part–whole possessive constructions, as in *kukə-tag* (back-tank) 'back of the (water)tank', *kukə-ab* 'back of the head', *kukə-təkər* (back-chair) 'back of the chair', *kukə-wi* 'back of the house' combining the reference to the back part of something and to the spatial orientation. This construction type is typical for body part and spatial orientation terms: compare *mutam* 'face', *mutəm-a-wi* (face-LK-house) 'in front of the house', *mutəm-a-təkər* 'in front of the chair', *ma:l* 'side', *mal-a-wi* (side-LK-house) 'side of the house', and so on. (The question of what is the head in these constructions is addressed in §8.1.2.)

The only difference between body part terms and *kukə-* is that *kukə-* does not occur on its own, and can only take the three locational cases. In addition, a part–whole construction with *kukə-* cannot be paraphrased with any other possessive construction (§8.1.2). That is, *mutəm-a-wi* (face-LK-house) 'in front of the house' can be rephrased (with a change in meaning) as *wi lə-kə mutam* (house 3fem.sg-OBL+fem.sg face) 'the front, or the face, of the house'; while *kukə-wi* cannot be paraphrased in the same way.

Occasionally, *kukə-* can occur in the headless possessive construction marked with the possessive suffix *-kə-*, as in 4.77:

4.77 a-də   [taːy   kaw] væ-ku,   [kukə-kə-də   kaw] ata
      DEM.DIST-masc.sg before hole dig-COMPL.SS back-POSS-masc.sg hole then
      væ-brə-d
      dig-3dusUBJ.P-3masc.sgBAS.P
      'Having dug the first hole, having put up the fence, having come there, then they dug the next hole (lit. the hole belonging to the back), having stood up the fence'

Similarly to a noun, the form *kukə-* appears in a few modifier-noun compounds (see §9.3), e.g. *kukə-yaːb* (back-road) 'sideroad'. Some of these are somewhat unpredictable in meaning: *kukə-məl və-* (back-eye see) means 'look back' (as in 21.15).

Two analytic options arise. We can consider *kukə-* a special kind of 'bound' body part and orientational noun, since it shares a number of syntactic properties with them, but never occurs on its own. Or we can consider it a special word class: a bound noun which forms the base for the spatial postpositions 'behind', and shares similarities with the two other postpositions, *kətək* 'like' and *wukən* 'with' which have no corresponding bound noun forms. Both analyses are adequate. I opt for the second one simply because of the syntactic similarities between the postpositional structures.

In summary: postpositions form a heterogeneous class. They appear to be a Manambu innovation, given that other Ndu languages appear not to have any postpositions.

4.5.3 Particles and connectives

The emphatic particle *ya* is a class on its own. As shown in §2.5.3, it is a clitic with low selectivity; it tends to cliticize to a contrastive constituent. It can only go at the end of a constituent, and may be considered a criterion for constituency. It often accompanies a command or a permissive form—similar to a command directed to oneself, as in 4.52; in each case, *ya* makes the command or the request more urgent. The particle *ya* shows formal and semantic similarity to the emphatic *ya* in Tok Pisin. Since, in Manambu, *ya* is frequent in spontaneous discourse but hardly ever appears in traditional planned narratives, it could be originally a Tok Pisin loan (but is not recognized as such by the speakers).

The hortative particle *jau* 'don't worry; let it drop; you may do it' is a class on its own. *Jau* often occurs stogether with an imperative in the same clause, and has a tinge of permission, as in 4.78 which is an invitation to eat one's fill:

4.78 jau   ak
      don't.worry IMPV+eat
      'Eat now, don't worry or feel restrained'

Very occasionally, it occurs with the prohibitive *tukwa*, as in *jau tukwa*, lit. 'don't let it drop', in the meaning of 'there is no reason to drop this; this is important; there is no reason to say *jau*'.

Jau is semantically similar to Tok Pisin *maski* 'let it drop; it is all right'; the two can occur together, reinforcing each other. When Motuway came across the picture of recently deceased Wimali, she exclaimed *jau maski*, as a way of saying 'oh dear, let it drop!' The adverb *jaujay* 'in a sloppy, incorrect way' could be related to *jau*.

Connectives are a smallish heterogeneous class:

(a) The clause connective *ata* 'then' is used to mark sequences of clauses in discourse, indicating that the clause or the sentence is part of a larger paragraph (see §19.6). It typically precedes the verb and never occurs on the first sentence in a text (see 4.8, 4.10, and 4.12).

When used in the predicate slot or as part of predicate focus, it takes the predicate marker *-n* (see §10.2.3, on how it also occurs with reactivated topic demonstratives), as in 4.79:

4.79 ata-n   aw
     then-PRED IMPV+speak
     'Speak up then', lit. 'it is then that you must speak'

(b) The clause connective *alək* 'because of this; this is why' is a result of grammaticaliza-
    tion of *a-* 'distal demonstrative; anaphoric demonstrative' and the suffix *-lək* 'because'
    (see §19.6). It tends to occur at the beginning of a main clause. Alternatively, it may
    appear in combination with the completive same-subject form of the verb *tə-* 'stay,
    stand', *tə-ku*; the meaning is 'this is why something happened; and so'. The combi-
    nation *alək tə-ku*, or *alək tu-ku* is a fixed expression, frequently pronounced as one
    phonological word. No other constituent intervenes between the components. It is on
    the way towards becoming a grammaticalized connective 'this is why', an alternative to
    alək—see §19.6.

(c) The connective *aw* 'and then; but; and...and' introduces referents and may have an
    adversative meaning. When repeated, it refers to alternating actions, as in *aw yi-n aw
    ya-n* (and.then go-SEQ and.then come-SEQ) 'on the one hand coming, on the other hand
    going'. Unlike *ata, aw* cannot occupy the predicate slot. Unlike *ata* and *alək, aw* can link
    non-main clauses, and noun phrases. See further discussion in §19.6. The connective *a*
    'then' has a similar meaning.

Two further connectives, (d) *wa* 'and' and (e) *o* 'or', link noun phrases (see §20.1.1). The disjunctive *o* is a borrowing from Tok Pisin, and is reinforced by the influence of Papua New Guinea English; it can occasionally coordinate main clauses (see §19.6).

4.5.4   Interjections and onomatopoeia

Interjections are a small class of forms which are often phonologically unusual (see §2.1.3). Some are CV monosyllables, e.g. *ʧa!* 'Hey (attention getter)', *ʧe!* 'a shout of disgust; or to avert danger', *sa!* 'attention getter'. An example of disyllabic interjection is *wayey!* 'oh dear'. Numerous interjections occur repeated, e.g. *ps ps ps* used to call a cat or a baby, *ti ti ti ti* to call chickens and ducks. An example of a quadruplicated CVC structure is *yaw yaw yaw yaw* 'calming the baby', and of a quadruplicated CVV structure—*diu diu diu diu* 'calling puppies'.

Interjections cannot be possessed or modified; they typically form one-word clauses. A direct speech report—framed with the verb *wa* 'say'—may contain an interjection, typically at the beginning of the report (see §19.5). A direct speech report can consist just of an interjection, e.g. *ata wa-bər m̥ʔm̥* (then say-3duBAS.P 'beware!') 'then they two said *m̥ʔm̥* meaning: beware!' Interjections are easily borrowed; nowadays, one hears *sit!* (from English *shit*) as an expression of annoyance.[8]

Onomatopoeia and expressives form a smallish potentially open class. They are often phonologically unusual (see §2.1.3). Onomatopoeic expressions typically imitate sounds, e.g. *sərr* 'sound of making canoe or another heavy object fall into water', *rou rou rou* 'roaring sound (e.g. of wind)'; *prəm* or *brəm brəm* 'sound of a drum'; *wu:::* 'sound of person crying'. They can imitate animals' talk, e.g. *kəndran kəndran* 'imitating a cassowary speaking, or when summoning a cassowary', *kuíkuíkuí* 'the noise of a guria pigeon', *pəkakáu pəkakáu* 'rooster singing'. A few forms which imitate natural phenomena other than sound are similar to onomatopoeia in their form and function. These include reference to colour *sər sər sər* 'very white', and *sək sək sək* 'very dark (as a raincloud)' (17.34); shape, e.g. *pukəpuk pukəpuk* 'bulging'; and movement with accompanying sound, e.g. *tən tən tən* 'movement (e.g. of many turtles)', as in 4.80 and 17.32–3.

4.80 aw   gwa:s wiya:m   tən tən tən, tən tən tən yi-di
     then turtle house+LK+LOC (onomatopoeia)   go-3plBAS.P
     'Then turtles went within the house tən tən tən, tən tən tən'

Just like ideophones, onomatopoeia and expressives cannot be possessed or modified, and are often repeated several times. Unlike ideophones, they occur as complements of the copula *na-* (see §4.2, and Table 4.1), used for most natural phenomena (see further discussion in §17.2.3), e.g. 12.82, T2.25, and 4.81:

4.81 ata   prəm, prəm, prəm, prəm na:d
     then sound of drum   BE:NAT+3masc.sgBAS.P
     'Then (the drum) sounded prəm, prəm, prəm, prəm'

An onomatopoeic expression can form a direct speech report framed by *wa-* 'say', to reproduce animal sounds, e.g. *tapwək pəkaka:u ata wa:d* (rooster cockadoodledoo then say+3masc.sgBAS.P) 'rooster said: "Cock-a-doodle-doo" ' (see §19.5). An onomatopoeic expression can be used as a manner modifier. With the verb 'cry', it imitates the sound of crying, e.g. *wuu gra-n rə-di* (wuu cry-SEQ sit-3plBAS.P) 'they kept crying wuu'. In these instances onomatopoeic expressions can be considered a type of manner modifier. They are not obligatory, and are never cross-referenced. Extensive use of onomatopoeia is characteristic of highly proficient and expressive story tellers.

4.5.5 'Pro-sentences'

Pro-sentences are a closed class of forms each of which can form a sentence on its own. The pro-clause *ayəy* 'yes' is used as confirmation of a previous statement; or to provide a positive answer to a question. For instance, if I ask 4.82:

---

[8] While in the village in 2001–2, I spontaneously used two Russian interjections—*briš'*, to shoo a cat, and *kiʃ* to shoo birds. The members of Yuamali's household liked them so much that when I came back in 2004, I was told that the best way to get rid of a cat is to shout [ᵐbrəš'] at the top of your voice.

4.82 gu   bəta:y   yaku-na-ñən?
      water   already wash-ACT.FOC-2fem.sgBAS.VT
      'Have you washed yet?'

the answer *ayəy* would mean 'yes, I have'. If I ask 4.83:

4.83 ñən   sə   ma: ku?
      you.fem.sg sleep NEG sleep:NEG
      'You didn't sleep?'

an answer *ayəy* would mean 'no, I didn't'.[9] This form can be replaced with an interjection *ah* accompanied with a characteristic facial gesture consisting of a slight raise of eyebrows, half-closed eyes, and an optional backward head tilt.

The pro-sentence *ya:k*, or *ya:kya* (which probably consists of *ya:k* and the emphatic particle *ya*) means 'OK, fine' and is a marker of the end of a discourse paragraph, and a pause filler. A combination of *ya:kya* as direct speech report slot of the verb *wa-* 'say' and the verb 'say' means 'agree; finish doing something' (see §19.5). Speakers who frequently code-switch with Tok Pisin or English replace *ya:kya* with *orait*.

The two declarative negators *ma:* 'non-habitual' and *akəs* 'negative habitual' can be used as pro-sentences, that is, as negative answers to questions. A negative can be replaced with a facial gesture, consisting in a side-to-side head movement. In terms of the verbal form they occur with, each may be considered a class on its own (see §§14.1–2). The desiderative-purposive negator *ata* (see §14.3) is not used as a pro-sentence.

The greeting *kəpəya:y* is a class on its own (see §21.5.3). Syntactically, this is used only as a greeting, that is a vocative form. It may be related to the address form *kəp*, plural *kəpugw*, discussed in §4.1.2 above.

4.5.6   Word class assignment of loans and code-switches

Most loanwords and code-switches fit squarely into the system of word classes in Manambu: nouns are borrowed as nouns, and verbs are borrowed either as inflected verbs, or as nominals used exclusively in the copula complement function (see §4.1.2).

Adjectives, such as *grin* 'green', *blu* 'blue', *rait* 'right', and *lapun* 'old', are borrowed as non-agreeing adjectives. Some borrowings and code-switches behave in the same way as the Manambu words they 'translate'. *Orait* and *okey* are functional equivalents of *ya:kya* 'OK', and belong to the same class. The same applies for the English *yes* which occasionally replaces *ayəy*.

The word class assignment for other loans is problematic. The borrowed numeral 'one', *wanpela* (from Tok Pisin *wanpela*), and the borrowed quantifier *planti* (Tok Pisin *planti* 'many') differ from their indigenous counterparts in that they precede the head noun, while the Manambu word follows it, as is the case with *nak* 'one', e.g. *wanpela ta:kw* (one:TP woman), *ta:kw nak* (woman one) 'one woman' (see Aikhenvald forthcoming c). Or the Manambu word may either precede or follow the head noun (see §10.5), e.g. *planti ta:kw* (many woman), *ta:kw samasa:m, samasam-a ta:kw* (woman many, many-LK woman) 'many women'. These borrowed quantifiers can be considered special subclasses of quantifiers.

---

[9] Some speakers accept *ma:* 'no' rather than *ayey* as an affirmative answer to 4.83.

There are yet other terms in the process of making their way into the language whose word class assignment remains problematic. Semantically, the Tok Pisin loanword *mas* 'must' is a modal. However, unlike any other modal term, it occurs with the imperative, as in *lə mas laku-kwa* (she 'must' know-IMPV.3p+fem.sg) 'she must know (this)' (13.22). One will have to wait until the bulk of these are fully integrated into the language to see how they are treated.

5

Gender Marking, Semantics, and Agreement

Manambu is among the few languages of the world where the gender assignment involves animacy and sex, and also correlates with the shape and size of the referent. 'Shape-based' gender assignment appears to be an areal feature of the Sepik area (a somewhat similar system has been described for Alamblak by Bruce 1984; also see Aikhenvald 2000: 276–8 for a discussion of Manambu in a typological perspective).

Manambu gender is, by and large, 'covert': that is, it is not marked on the noun itself. Two genders, masculine and feminine, are distinguished in singular. They are realized through agreement within a noun phrase and on the predicate.

5.1 GENDER AND NUMBER AGREEMENT: CONTEXTS AND FORMS

Agreement in gender and number is obligatory within noun phrases and on the predicate.

5.1.1 Agreement contexts

WITHIN A NOUN PHRASE, gender and number agreement is obligatory with the following prehead modifiers:

- agreeing adjectives *kwasa* 'small', *numa* or *nəma* 'big', and *yara* 'fine' (§4.3.1);
- adjective 'old' (§4.3.1);
- all demonstratives (except for the 'current relevance' *-na-* series) (§10.2);
- indefinite pronouns used as modifiers (§10.3); and
- interrogative *akə* 'where, belonging to where' (§10.4).

Any of these modifiers can be used without a nominal head (see §4.3 and especially 4.51). Outside an NP, gender agreement is marked on reactivated topic demonstratives (see 3.16–18 in §3.3). These are always used without any nominal head. The headless indefinite pronoun *nəwək* '(an)other one' takes no agreement marking (§10.3).

No number (or gender) agreement is marked on quantifiers, ordinal, and cardinal numbers (which can occur in a prehead or in a posthead position: see §§10.5–6).

The only exception is the cardinal numeral 'one, only one' which optionally takes a gender agreement marker. Its masculine form is *naka-də-məy*, and its feminine form is *naka-məy*. They do not have any non-singular forms (see §10.6.1). The feminine *nakaməy* is also used in counting. This is consistent with the functionally unmarked status of feminine gender in Manambu (see §5.2.3). The adverb *nak-a-l-əb* (one-LK-fem.sg-TERM) 'together' (of a group consisting of women only, or of a mixed group) also contains a feminine marker. It can, however, be used to refer to any group of people, almost interchangeably with its synonym *nakamib* 'together' (see §10.6.1). The interrogative prehead modifier *agw-* 'which, what sort of?' does not require gender or number agreement (see §10.4).

TABLE 5.1   Gender and number agreement forms

SINGULAR FEMININE	SINGULAR MASCULINE	DUAL	PLURAL
-l, -ø	*-d*	*-bər*	*-di*

Possessive constructions with specific possessor (see §8.1) require agreement in gender and in number with the possessee marked on the pronominal possessor, as in *ñən-a-də ma:m* (you.fem.sg-LK-masc.sg older.sibling) 'your elder brother', and in 5.1. If the possessor is expressed with a noun phrase, agreement in gender and number with both possessor and possessee is realized on the possessive marker, as in 5.1. The direction of agreement is indicated with arrows.

5.1 amæy   lə-kə-də   du-a-ma:gw
     mother fem.sg-OBL-masc.sg man-LK-generic.noun
     'the mother's brother'

Constructions with headless and associative POSSESSION always mark gender and number of the possessee, e.g. *təp-a-kə-di* (village-LK-POSS-pl) '(those) of the village', *mən-a-kə-l* (you.masc.sg-LK-POSS-fem.sg) 'yours (feminine thing)'. Personal pronouns distinguish three numbers, and two genders in second and third person singular. As shown in §10.4, the interrogative pronoun *sə* takes double gender marking when used as predicate head (10.82) or is marked for highlighting focus, as in 10.83.

VERBS AND OTHER WORD CLASSES in the predicate slot distinguish three numbers and two genders in second and third person singular throughout the indicative cross-referencing paradigm in basic and subject sets, and in nominal cross-referencing (see Tables 3.1–4 and 3.6).

In addition, two genders are distinguished in first person in the basic set and in nominal cross-referencing. Imperative distinguishes three numbers, and masculine and feminine genders in third person (but not in second person) (§11.1). Two genders are distinguished in second and third person singular in different subject medial clauses (see §18.1).

No gender or number is expressed in negative declarative non-habitual, admonitive, frustrative, completive, desiderative, customary, forms with a derivational suffix *-dəka* 'only' or *-rəb* 'fully', same-subject medial completive, cotemporaneous medial, immediate sequence medial, conditional medial, and manner sequencing.

5.1.2   Gender and number agreement forms

Gender and number agreement markers are given in Table 5.1 The same markers, except for feminine singular, are uniform throughout all the agreement contexts.[1] Table 5.2 summarizes the complex distribution of the two singular feminine agreement markers, depending on the locus of gender agreement.

For some forms—namely, in the nominal cross-referencing paradigm—the two feminine singular alternants are in free variation. The choice depends on the speaker's preference. It

---

[1] The first and second person singular, dual, and plural basic and nominal cross-referencing forms contain gender markers preposed to number markers, e.g. *-di-an* (pl-1plBAS.VT) 'first person plural basic', *-də-wun* (masc.sg-1sgBAS.VT) 'first person singular masculine basic'.

TABLE 5.2   Feminine gender agreement forms and agreement loci

AGREEMENT LOCUS	FEMININE SINGULAR -*L*: EXAMPLES

NP: agreeing adjective
demonstratives with directional affixes and
discontinuous demonstratives
headless case-marked demonstratives (see
§10.2)
    associative possession
 	
    headless possession
    others
	yara- 'fine; good' (§4.3.1)
	a-l-a-wur (DEM.DIST-fem.sg-LK-UP) 'that one up'
	a-l-ay (DEM.DIST-fem.sg-DIST) 'that one far away'
	kə-lə-m (DEM.PROX-fem.sg-ACC/LOC) 'here; on
	    this one'
	təp-a-kə-l taːkw (village-LK-POSS-fem.sg woman)
	    'a woman belonging to the village'
	wun-a-kə-l (I-LK-POSS-fem.sg) 'mine' (fem. thing)
	nak-a-l-əb (one-LK-fem.sg-TERM) 'together'
	akə-l 'where/which (feminine)'—Table 10.7.

V: basic cross-referencing general past all
persons in singular
subject cross-referencing third person sg
nominal cross-referencing all persons sg
second and third person singular in medial
    different subject completive
    different subject purposive
causal and cotemporaneous medial clauses
third sg optative marked with -*kwa*-
	Table 3.1
	
	Table 3.2
	Table 3.4
	
	See §18.3
	See §13.4.2
	See §§18.6–7
	See §13.2.3

AGREEMENT LOCUS	FEMININE SINGULAR ∅: EXAMPLES

NP: agreeing adjective
    demonstratives as modifiers
    reactivated topic demonstrative
    interrogative
    indefinite
    agreeing form of the numeral 'one'
    constructions with specific possessor
	kwasa- 'small', *numa-* 'big' (§4.3.1)
	a 'that one (feminine)'
	aka 'that one topical (feminine)'
	akə- 'which; where' (§10.4)
	nəkə- 'another; other' (§10.3)
	nakaməy 'one' (feminine) (§10.6.1)
	wun-a takw-a-ñan (I-LK+fem.sg woman-LK-
	    child) 'my daughter'

V: basic cross-referencing present-recent
past all persons singular
    nominal cross-referencing all persons sg
    third person singular imperative
	Table 3.1
	
	Table 3.4
	See §13.2

appears, however, that more traditional speakers would say 5.2a, while others would prefer 5.2b (which may well be described as a product of assimilation of *l-n*).

5.2a kwasa   ñan-alñən
    small+fem.sg child-2fem.sgNOM
    'You are a small child'

5.2b kwasa   ñan-añən
    small+fem.sg child-2fem.sgNOM
    'You are a small child'

If two feminine markers occur together in one grammatical word, the form marked with *-l* occurs non-word-finally. This is the case in the highlighting focus construction (see §20.3, especially examples 20.87–9). The *-l*/ø distribution in demonstratives (except for reactivated topic demonstratives) is governed by a similar principle: if there is a segmental morpheme following the agreement marker, the *-l* form is used, e.g. *a* 'that one feminine', but *a-l-a-wur* (DEM.DIST-fem.sg-LK-UP) 'that one feminine which is up' (a full set of forms is under §10.2).

In possessive constructions, the ø form is used on the possessor or the possessive marker if it is not used on its own, that is, headlessly, e.g. *wun-a takwa-ñan* (I-LK+fem.sg woman+LK-child) 'my daughter', with a ø feminine agreement; but *wun-a-kə-l* (I-LK-POSS-fem.sg) 'mine' when used on its own.

In third person singular non-indicative verbal forms, the alternant ø appears only at the end of a grammatical and phonological word, while the alternant *-l* appears if followed by another marker—as in the different-subject purposive *kur-lə-kək* (do-3fem.sg-PURP.DS) 'for her to do', or different subject completive *kur-lə-k* (do-3fem.sg-COMPL.DS) 'after she has done'.

Consider gender marking in third person imperative (§13.2.1), and in the optative (§13.2.3). The third person singular feminine imperative is marked with *-kwa-* and ø feminine singular, e.g. *kiya-kwa-d* (die-IMPV.3p-masc.sg) 'may he die', *kiya-kwa* (die-IMPV.3p+fem.sg) 'may she die'. The third person feminine optative expressing an unfulfilled desire is 'derived' from the imperative with the suffix *-əu*, as in *kiya-kwa-d-əu* (die-IMPV.3p-masc.sg-OPT) 'may he die, I wish he'd died'. The feminine form of this contains an *-l* alternant: *kiya-kwa-l-əu* (die-IMPV.3p-fem.sg-OPT) 'may she die, I wish she'd died'. Similarly, if a nominal predicate is in predicate focus (both marked with nominal cross-referencing), the non-final form has to be *-l*, as in 5.30. The same principle applies for the agreement forms of gender-sensitive interrogative *akə-* 'where' (see Table 10.7): if it is used as predicate head (that is, the gender marker occupies the final position), the form is *akəl* 'where is she?', and if it is used as a modifier (that is, followed by another word), the form is *akə* as in *akə ta:kw* (where+fem.sg woman) 'where is the woman?'

We conclude that the two alternants for feminine singular can be, at least partly, considered allomorphs in complementary distribution, following different rules within an NP, and on a verb.

Etymologically, the agreement markers are transparently related to the corresponding third person pronouns. The third person singular feminine is *lə* and masculine *də*. This is consistent with an almost-universal historical scenario whereby agreement typically arises via grammaticalization of personal pronouns (Aikhenvald 2000: 391–8; Heine 2001).[2]

5.1.3 Additional gender and number forms

Gender forms of second person pronouns differ from those in Tables 5.1–2. As shown in Table 3.3, the second person singular feminine pronoun is *ñən*, and its masculine counterpart is *mən*.

---

[2] The form *-bər* 'dual' has three additional meanings—that of second person dual (Table 3.1 and §10.1), and of plural marker on kinship terms (§6.1) and associative plural on personal names (§6.2.2). Synchronically, these can be considered homonyms; their etymological correlates and historical development are discussed in Aikhenvald (forthcoming b).

The age adjective 'old' is unusual in its agreement forms, which are restricted to singular only. The two gender forms are *apan* 'old (masculine)' and *apaw* 'old (feminine)', e.g. *apan du* (old:masc man) 'old man', *numa apaw va:l* (big+fem.sg old.fem mistake) 'big old woman-type mistake'. The root *ap* is probably related to the noun *ap* 'base, bone' also used in *ap-a-sə* 'first or main name' and *apar-du* 'headman, chief man', *apar-ta:kw* 'main woman'. The feminine form is used if the adjective 'old' has any non-singular referents (see 5.23).

5.1.4   Functions of gender and number agreement

Gender and number agreement plays an important role in tracking referents in discourse. A verbal form with no person marking can always be disambiguated with a gender-sensitive pronoun: a command *a-war* (IMPV-go.up) 'go up' can refer to a man, or a woman, but once a gender-sensitive pronoun is used, no problem arises, as in *mən a-war* (you.masc.sg IMPV-go.up) 'you (man), go up!'

Gender agreement helps determine boundaries of constituents. In 5.3, gender shows that 'I' is the possessor of 'village', and not of 'child'. If 'I' were the possessor of 'child', 5.4 would have been appropriate.

5.3 [wun-a   təp-a]   ñan   numa-d-ad
    I-LK+fem.sg village-LK child big-masc.sg-3masc.sgNOM
    'The child (son) of my village is big'

5.4 [wun-a-də   [təp-a   ñan]] numa-d-ad
    I-LK-masc.sg village-LK child big-masc.sg-3masc.sgNOM
    'My village-son is big'

In noun phrases gender and number agreement provides a strong criterion for determining the head (see §8.1 for a discussion of 'headship' in possessive constructions). Gender assignment helps disambiguate polysemous nouns—see the next section.

5.2   HOW TO CHOOSE A GENDER: SEMANTICS, AND MARKEDNESS RELATIONSHIPS

5.2.1   The semantics of gender choice

Gender assignment in Manambu is determined by the semantics of a noun referent. Quite a few nouns have a preferred gender, whose choice is by and large determined by the inherent properties of prototypical referents of a noun. In general, small and roundish referents are feminine, and longish and biggish ones are masculine.

Gender assignment goes along the following lines.

A. GENDER ASSIGNMENT TO HUMANS is based on their sex: that is, *du* 'man', *asa:y* 'father', and *awa:y* 'maternal uncle' are always masculine, and *amæy* 'mother', *ta:kw* 'woman', *ñap* 'mother's sister' are always feminine (see Table 6.1, for a list of kinship terms). Gender assignment to kinship nouns is fixed (hybrid nouns are exceptions).

Hybrid nouns—such as *ma:m* 'older sibling' and *ñaməs* 'younger sibling'—are also assigned genders depending on the sex of the referent—that is, *wun-a ma:m* (I-LK+fem.sg older.sibling) means 'my elder sister', and *wun-a-də ma:m* (I-LK-masc.sg older.sibling) means 'my elder brother'.

The choice of gender of the hybrid noun *ñan* 'child' is determined by the gender of the referent. The sex of the referent may be disambiguated with the help of compounds with 'man' and 'woman' (see §5.3). Or it can be determined by size: 'small child' or 'baby', *kwas-a ñan* (small-LK+fem.sg child), is feminine because it is small. Similarly to what happens in many languages (see Aikhenvald 2000), gender assignment to 'babies' partly follows the same principle as for non-human animates (see B). We will see in G below how variable gender assignment of nouns *du* 'man', *ta:kw* 'woman, wife', and *la:n* 'husband' accounts for jokes and metaphorical extensions.

B. GENDER ASSIGNMENT TO HIGHER ANIMATES is based on their size, and on their sex. Large animals and dogs belong to the masculine gender, and smaller animals and dogs belong to feminine gender. A big dog (*a:s*), a big pig (*ba:l*), or a big wild fowl (*sar*) will be masculine, and a small one would be feminine. If the sex is known, it 'overrides' the size-based assignment: a small tom-cat was referred to with masculine gender, because his sex was known.

Names for young animals are feminine (unless they are unusually big). In just a few cases, gender assignment is based on mythological principles: the preferred gender for *məd* 'cassowary' is feminine, because cassowaries are conceived of as mythical women.

For lower animates, such as insects, the use of masculine gender can be associated with their quantity (see E below). For instance, *ka:l* 'mayfly' is masculine because these insects (considered a great delicacy) usually come in large groups. If a lower animate has a characteristic shape, it is assigned a gender in agreement with it: a turtle, *gwa:s*, is feminine because it is round, and the crocodile, *mu*, is masculine because it is long. So are most snakes, e.g. *kabay* 'snake', *kanukaraki* 'death adder', and *kanu* 'taipan'. Most lower animates are feminine, e.g. *wakuli* 'mouse, rat', *jataw* 'small bat', *japal* 'bigger bat', *kwa:j* 'another bigger bat', *kəbwi* 'flying fox'.

A few insects have a fixed gender which is not semantically motivated. The following insects are small in size, and are feminine: *sa:r* 'fly', *sa:m* 'bee', *da:m*, *damda:m* 'spider'. Others are also small and are masculine, e.g. *waw* 'blue fly', *ba:b* 'wasp', *paba:n* 'large black ant'. Some insects which appear in largish quantities are typically treated as plural, e.g. *mapa-jəpis* 'little red ants', *gla-jəpis* 'little black ants'.

C. GENDER ASSIGNMENT TO INANIMATES is almost uniformly based on their size and shape. Long and/or large objects are treated as masculine, and small and/or round ones as feminine. *Val* 'canoe' is masculine if big, and feminine if small. *Vəy* 'spear' is masculine due to its inherent long shape and size; it is feminine when it is used to refer to a small spear or a shotgun. The same principle operates for body parts, e.g. *ta:b* 'hand, arm' (masculine), 'small finger' (feminine); *wuliñ* 'big nail' (masculine), 'small nail' (feminine). A house of usual size is referred to as feminine; an unusually big house is masculine—so, the Manambu people who have visited England agreed that Buckingham palace is a 'masculine type' house because it is big. Along similar lines, skyscrapers are 'masculine', and so are big men's houses (*kara:b*).

When asked about how big the Malu village is, 5.5 was produced. The implication was that it is a big village, but not huge—that is, big enough to be called 'big', but not sufficiently so to warrant masculine gender agreement.

5.5 Malu numa   təp-al   numa-də   təp   ma:
     Malu big+fem.sg village-3fem.sgNOM big-masc.sg village NEG
     'Malu is a big village (feminine), it is not a huge village (masculine)'

To refer to a longish distance, one says *numa sək-al* (big+fem.sg distance-3fem.sgNOM) 'it is quite far away'. If the same noun refers to a very long distance, it is 'reclassified' as masculine, e.g. *numa-də sək-ad* (big-masc.sg distance-3masc.sgNOM) 'it is very far away'.

Some inanimate referents have a 'typical' shape and size—just like the lower animates in B above. For instance, *ar* 'lake', *ab* 'head', *ya:l* 'stomach; womb', *kwati* 'knee', and *kabak* 'stone' are typically round, and hence assigned to the feminine gender. The polysemous word *mawul* 'inside; mind, spirit' (see §21.4) is typically feminine, as shown in 5.6:

5.6 də-kə   mawul ata   kuprap ta:l
    he-POSS+fem.sg inside then bad   become+3fem.sgBAS.P
    'His spirit became bad (that is, he got into a bad mood)'

But if a referent which is typically feminine is particularly big, it can be assigned masculine gender. In texts, change in gender is used to indicate increasing size—as is the case in 5.7, from a story about a woman impregnated by a snake; her belly gets bigger and bigger, and becomes really huge—then it is 'masculine'.

5.7 ya:l ata   numa   məy ta:l   tə-lə-k   a
    belly then big+fem.sg very become+3fem.sgBAS.P become-3fem.sg-COMPL.DS then
    numa-də   ya:l adəka
    big-masc.sg belly DEM.DIST.REACT.TOP+masc.sg
    '(Her) belly then became very big (feminine), having become (big), here is a very big (masculine) belly'

Referents with preferred masculine gender include *bagwa-kwal* 'necklace', *kwasabi* 'stringbag', *wa:r* 'bigger stringbag', and the loan *trausis* 'trousers': all these are typically long. However, a tiny baby's trousers can be referred to with feminine gender, as in 5.8:

5.8 ñən-a   trausis ka-l
    you.fem-LK+fem.sg trousers DEM.PROX+fem.sg-3fem.sgNOM
    rə-la
    sit-3fem.sgSUBJ.VT+3fem.sgBAS.VT
    'It is here that your (tiny) trousers are sitting'

Gender is often used metaphorically to describe unusual situations which involve inanimate objects and body parts (also see G below). 'Head' is usually feminine because of its round shape, but it is treated as masculine when a person has a headache: the speaker explained that the head then feels heavy and unusually big—as shown in 5.9:

5.9 ab-ad   kagəl yi-na-d
    head-3masc.sgNOM pain go/say-ACT.FOC-3masc.sgBAS.VT
    'It is (my) head that is aching'

All trees are treated as masculine due to their height and vertical stance, and their fruit is feminine regardless of the shape, e.g. *mi:* 'tree' and *ma:s* ' betelnut tree' are masculine, and *təkəmi* 'fruit' and *ma:s* 'betelnut fruit' are feminine.

D. GENDER ASSIGNMENT TO NOUNS DENOTING NATURAL PHENOMENA

Nouns which refer to natural phenomena are assigned feminine gender if the extent of the phenomenon is not complete, or the completeness is not in focus; otherwise they are assigned masculine gender.

For instance, *ga:n* 'night' is feminine, unless it implies complete darkness: *ga:n-al* (night-3fem.sgNOM) means it is somewhat dark (typically used for 6–7 p.m.); *ga:n-ad* (night-3masc.sgNOM) 'big night' means complete darkness. *Gəl* 'raincloud' is assigned feminine gender if clouds are few, and masculine gender if they cover the whole sky (also see 'big masculine night' in T3.40, at the end of the grammar).

Some natural phenomena are assigned a gender which correlates with their customary shape or size. Rainbow (*walimaudi*) is masculine because it is long; and sun is feminine because it is round. However, if the sun is really hot, it is referred to with the masculine gender to reflect its intensity, as in 5.10:

5.10 numa-də   ñə ada   sə-na-d
    big-masc.sg sun DEM.DIST.REACT.TOP+masc.sg shine-ACT.FOC-3masc.sgBAS.VT
    'The sun is shining very strongly'

Physical states are treated similarly: for instance, *ka:m* 'hunger' is usually feminine (as in 4.26a), unless it is very intense; then it triggers masculine agreement. If an onomatopoeia (whose typical function is a copula complement) refers to an unusually loud sound, the copula acquires masculine agreement (as in 4.81).

E. GENDER ASSIGNMENT TO MASS NOUNS AND TO NOUNS COVERING 'EXTENT'

Nouns referring to time spans (*səkər* 'time', *ñə* 'day', *wik* 'week' (a loan from Tok Pisin)), manner (*sa:d* 'manner; way'), and language or voice (*kudi*) are feminine. The term for year, *nabi*, is masculine, because 'a year is so long' (James Laki, p.c.). The term for month, *bap*, literally 'moon', is feminine: we return to the 'femininity' of the moon in F below.

Gender assignment of mass nouns and of any noun whose meaning involves extent, or degree, depends on the quantity and the extent. For instance, a usual way of saying that something is rather expensive is *numa kabak-a* (big+fem.sg stone-3fem.sgNOM) 'it is big money'. The way of phrasing that something is extremely expensive is *numa-də kabak-ad* (big-masc.sg stone-3masc.sgNOM) 'it is huge money'.

Along similar lines, gender agreement on the verb in 5.11 indicates that the elder brother put a small ('feminine') quantity of hair on top of his sibling's head:

5.11 ab-a-yuwi   ma:m   kləm sə-də-l
    head-LK-hair elder.sibling here put-3masc.sgSUBJ.P-3fem.sgBAS.P
    'The elder brother put some hair here'

In contrast, masculine gender agreement on the possessive marker and on the verb indicates that in 5.12 the hawk plucked a lot of her plumage to give to her adoptive son:

5.12 abakapi   lə-kə-də   yuwi   ada
    hawk(fem) 3fem.sg-POSS-3masc.sg plumage/hair DEM.DIST.REACT.TOP+masc.sg
    gwa-la-d
    pluck-3fem.sgSUBJ.VT-3masc.sgBAS.VT
    'The hawk plucked her plumage'

The head noun does not have to be present. An order to speak up is:

5.13 numa-də   aw
    big-masc.sg IMPV+speak
    'Speak loudly!' (lit. speak big-masculine)

We will see, in §5.3, that the noun *asa:y* 'father' can accompany the adjective 'big' as a kind of augmentative; such combinations—with countable and with uncountable nouns—are always masculine. Example 5.14 was said by Tanina (then 8 years of age), when she saw a big bowl of water (full to the brim).

5.14 numa-də   asa:y gu-ad
     big-masc.sg father water-3masc.sgNOM
     'It is a huge amount of water'

Mass and uncountable nouns are often feminine, e.g *səp* 'skin'. If they are assigned masculine gender, this implies unusually large quantity, e.g. *ñiki-al* (blood-3fem.sgNOM) 'there is (some) blood', *ñiki-ad* (blood-3masc.sgNOM) 'there is a lot of blood'. This is similar to the gender assignment of lower animates (see B above)—5.15 implies that mosquitoes are coming into the house in huge quantities.

5.15 kəpi   ada   wula-na-d
     mosquito DEM.DIST.REACT.TOP+masc.sg come.in-ACT.FOC-3masc.sgBAS.VT
     'Mosquito comes in (masculine)'

A similar example is in 15.26: the fact that 'all the people' finished or died as a set is expressed through using masculine singular agreement on the predicate 'finish completely'.

Masculine gender is assigned to large objects and prolonged actions: so, *ma:j* 'story' is masculine if it is long, and feminine if it is short—see F below on how genders can be associated with cultural importance.

F. Gender Assignment by 'Association'

If the choice of a gender depends on the noun's meaning, a gender can be assigned based on association by an important property (see Dixon 1972: 306–12, 1982: 178–83; Aikhenvald 2000: 23–4).

In Manambu society, descent is strictly patrilineal, and so the *gwalugw* 'patrilineal clan' is masculine. (Morphologically, *gwal-ugw* is the plural form of *gwa:l* used for 'father's child (female or male) and father's father'; see §6.1). All the clan names are masculine; however, a small clan can be assigned feminine gender (especially if clans are being compared by their size, as in 6.3).

Masculine gender associated with large size and extent acquires the overtone of cultural importance, where appropriate. A story, *ma:j*, requires masculine agreement, no matter how long it is, if it is a traditional story. If it refers to a casual story or a biography of someone it is likely to be feminine. Similarly, *ba:gw* 'performance, dance' is masculine only when it refers to a traditional act. This extension of masculine gender, from size to 'importance', goes together with the male dominance of Manambu culture: women are denied access to highly valued traditional knowledge, as well as active participation in traditional activities such as the yam ritual or name debates (see Harrison 1990a).

Association with 'male' and 'female' determines gender assignment of culturally important objects. The notion of *ja:m* 'a set of hereditary magical and ritual powers' is personified as a named female spirit, the role of which is to punish incest and violation of the principles of exogamy (Harrison 1990a: 32). Each group has a *væy*, its ancestor, literally 'spear'. The connotations of *væy* are masculine and phallic (which goes together with its prolonged, 'masculine', shape), while *ja:m* is represented as a womb. Together *væy* and *ja:m* 'signify the "male" and "female" aspects of a group's social identity' (Harrison 1990a: 33). This agrees with the assignment of masculine and feminine genders to these lexemes. Along similar lines, *kara:b* 'large ceremonial house' and *sa:y* 'ceremonial house for uninitiated men' are both masculine.

It is traditionally believed that human bones (*ap*) are formed from father's semen and transmitted agnatically. In contrast, blood (*ñiki*) derives from mother's womb blood and is transmitted by matrifiliation (Harrison 1990a: 33). Consequently, *ap* 'bone' is assigned masculine gender, while *ñiki* is usually feminine (unless it comes in large quantities: see E). The noun *ap* also carries the connotations of centrality and importance, another corollary of masculine gender. Thus, speakers derive the name of Avatip, considered the most important of the four Manambu villages, from *ap-a təp* (bone-LK village) 'the strong, large, central village' (lit. the bone-village).

Mythological association plays a role in gender assignment of celestial bodies. Moon (*bap*) is feminine, because it is conceived as a mythological woman; an alternative, endearing, name for it is *bap-a-ta:kw* (moon-LK-woman) 'lady moon'.[3] Similarly, stars (*kugar*) are conceptualized as women belonging to the Wulwi-Ñawi clan group (associated with sun, moon, and light).

However, one needs to be careful in determining a primary and a secondary reason for gender assignment. Both *væy* 'spear' and *ap* 'bone' could well be assigned masculine gender based on their longish size and shape. Similarly, *ya:l* 'womb, belly'—which is typically feminine— is associated with women; but it is also conceived as 'round' in shape. Moon and stars are mythological women, but they are also roundish in their shape. Which comes first—gender choice by shape, or by mythology? Which one is contingent upon the other?

We can recall that *ab* 'head' is feminine, due to its round shape, and despite its perceived importance for mental processes. This may imply that shape was also primary in the gender assignment of 'spear', 'bone', 'womb; belly', 'moon', and 'star', and that the cultural extension to masculinity or femininity is a later development. Synchronically, however, we are faced with multiple semantic parameters in gender assignment. Different criteria converge and reinforce each other in gender assignment.

G. METAPHORICAL EXTENSIONS AND JOKES

A noun with a human referent is assigned a fixed gender, depending on the sex of a referent. As a joke, a man can be referred to with feminine gender, and a woman with masculine gender, depending on their 'shape' and 'size'. A smallish fat woman-like man can be treated as feminine, e.g. *numa du* (big+fem.sg man) 'fat round man'. And a largish woman can be ironically referred to with a masculine gender form, e.g. *kə-də numa-də ta:kw* (DEM.PROX-masc.sg big-masc.sg woman) 'this (unusually) big woman'. This is comparable to Dyirbal where the word *yara* 'man' can be used with the feminine class marker, instead of masculine, to point out the female characteristics of a hermaphrodite (see Dixon 1972: 306–12, 1982: 178–83).

Gender is manipulated in other, more culturally specific, jokes. Classificatory sisters-in-law (that is, brothers' wives, *kajal*) are potential co-wives; they are in a joking relationship (see 4.56). One way of greeting a brother's wife is by saying:

---

[3] The moon is held responsible for women's menstruation: it is said to inflict 'moon sickness' upon women. Interestingly, in other societies, e.g. among the Vaupés Indians of north-west Amazonia, Moon is also held responsible for female menstruation; but, since Moon is a mythical male, it is said to have sexual intercourse with women when they menstruate.

5.16 ñən   wun-a   ta:kw-añən   wun ñən-a
you.fem.sg I-LK+fem.sg wife-2fem.sgNOM I   you.fem.sg-LK+fem.sg
la:n-adəwun
husband-1masc.sgNOM
'You (feminine) are my wife, I (masculine) am your husband (feminine)' (said by a woman
to a woman)

Such pronouncements are typically accompanied by roars of laughter. There is a gender
mismatch: masculine gender is cross-referenced on the predicate of the second clause ('I am
your husband'), but the agreement on the possessive 'your' is feminine. The 'correct' way to say
'I am your husband' is *ñən-a-də la:n-adəwun* (you.fem.sg-LK-masc.sg husband-1masc.sgNOM).
The feminine cross-referencing here is part of the joke—a woman saying 5.16 presents herself
as a kind of female husband.[4]

A similar example comes from Harrison (1990a: 31). He describes a joking reaction of the
Manambu people to a long-term uxorilocal marriage (marriages in the Manambu culture
are virilocal). A man is said to behave like a woman (by living in the woman's village), and
a woman like a man (by taking him to live at her place). In 5.17, 'woman'—who is 'like a
husband'—triggers feminine gender agreement on the demonstrative and on the focus marker.
The agreement on the predicate of the two clauses is masculine.

5.17 a   ta:kw-a   la:n-ad   kra-n
DEM.DIST.fem.sg woman-3fem.sgNOM husband-3masc.sgNOM take.as.wife-SEQ
kray-da
carry-3masc.sgSUBJ.VT+3fem.sgBAS.VT
'It is that (feminine) woman who is (masculine) the husband, she married (him) and
fetched him away'

Once again, the gender mismatch, together with using masculine gender for a woman, emphasizes the grotesqueness of the culturally inappropriate situation.

Chart 5.1 summarizes the principles of gender assignment for different semantic groups of
noun referents in Manambu.

An important function of gender is distinguishing polysemous nouns. For instance, since
nouns referring to time are feminine, *ga:n* is feminine in the meaning of 'night-time'. If this
same noun refers to darkness as a natural phenomenon, its gender can be either masculine or
feminine, depending on the extent of darkness (see E). As we have seen, gender assignment
is predominantly semantic. Deverbal action nominalizations are perhaps the only instance of
morphological gender assignment: they are always feminine.

As in most gender languages, most nouns are assigned to a gender class. One defective noun,
the greeting *kəp*, plural *kəpugw* (see §4.1.2) 'be well', does not belong to a gender class, because
it is only used as a vocative and never as argument or NP head. Nominals which are only used
as copula complements, such as *katelam* '(be) dawn', or *wakuwakw* '(be) just about dawn', are
also outside the gender system, because they never occur in a context where they would trigger
gender agreement; the default feminine singular agreement is used.

---

[4] Alan Rumsey (p.c.) pointed out a similarity to the Naven ritual described by Bateson (1958); cf. also Houseman
and Severi (1998).

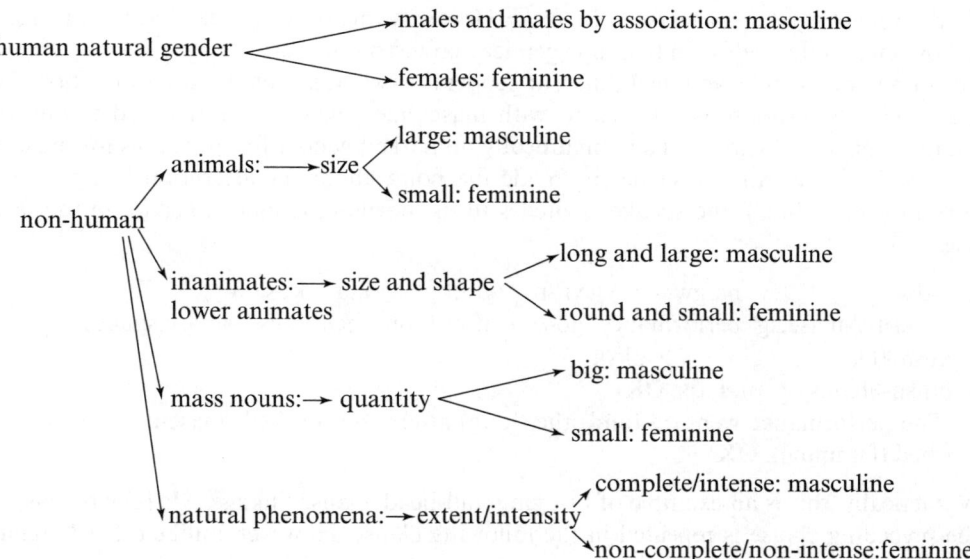

CHART 5.1   Gender assignment in Manambu

5.2.2   Mismatches in gender agreement

The same noun can trigger agreement with different genders within the same clause. In 5.16, the predicate is marked as masculine and the possessor as feminine, and yet the two refer to the same person. In 5.17, the same participant—a woman—triggers feminine agreement on a demonstrative and a focus marker, and masculine agreement on the verb.

Gender mismatches are not restricted to grotesque joking contexts. In texts and in conversations, if the subject has a human referent, agreement on the predicate always follows its sex: masculine for male, feminine for female. But if a male is particularly small, that is, a child, it can be reclassified as feminine, by its size. The feminine gender agreement, however, is likely to be restricted to a noun phrase. In 5.18, David Takendu was talking about himself as a little child:

5.18 [kwasa   ñan]   tə-dəwun
     small+fem.sg child be-1masc.sgBAS.P
     'I was (masculine) a small (feminine) child'

Along similar lines, 5.19 was said about a 5-year-old boy:

5.19 a   kə   kuprap   kləm
     then DEM.PROX+fem.sg bad/poor   DEM.PROX+fem.sg+LOC
     kwa-k-na-d
     stay-FUT-ACT.FOC-3masc.sgBAS.VT
     'Then this (feminine) poor (one) will stay (masculine) here'

A similar example is in 20.99. These examples indicate that gender agreement within a noun phrase, and on the predicate, may operate on somewhat different principles. Agreement in noun phrases tends to be variable depending on semantic principles other than sex (that is, size), while the verbal agreement tends to be fixed. However, this is not a steadfast rule: in 10.18 a little boy refers to himself with feminine gender marked on the verb.

The same noun can be assigned different genders in two adjacent clauses. In the first clause in 5.20, *gra:b* 'afternoon' is referred to with masculine gender, since it lasted a long time, and a lot happened during it. The semantically unmarked gender for *gra:b*—as for most time nouns—is feminine. And, after having made the point about the afternoon being long and important ('masculine'), the speaker switches to its 'normal', feminine, gender in the second clause.

5.20 a-də   ba:gw   yi:-n   gra:b   ata   kusə-d
      DEM.DIST-masc.sg performance go-SEQ afternoon then finish-3masc.sgBAS.P
      kusə-lə-k   ya:kya
      finish-3fem.sg-COMPL.DS OK
      'The performance went on (and) the (long) afternoon finished (masculine). Having fin-
      ished (feminine), OK'

Syntactically, this is an example of bridging 'tail-head' clause linkage, whereby the last verb of the preceding clause is repeated in the following clause. However, unlike other languages, Manambu does not require verbatim repetition in 'tail-head' linkage: we return to this in §20.4.1.

5.2.3 Markedness relations

There are two main types of markedness—formal and functional. A term in a system is formally unmarked if it has zero realization or a zero allomorph. If all of the terms in a system except one are used only in specified circumstances and the remaining term is used in all other circumstances, then this term is said to be functionally unmarked (cf. Dixon 1994: 56–7; Aikhenvald and Dixon 1998).

We have seen (Table 5.2) that feminine gender is formally unmarked in a number of contexts: feminine has two agreement forms, ø and -*l*, while masculine gender is always marked, and the agreement form is always -*d*.

The following evidence indicates that feminine is also functionally unmarked, independently of the context and of agreement form—that is, whether it is ø or -*l*.

A. The feminine form is used for a referent whose gender, or size and shape, are unknown. If they are known, then semantic principles outlined in §5.2.1 apply. The generic noun *ma:gw* 'whatever; don't remember what' often triggers feminine gender (unless the speaker has a long or big object in mind). An abstract noun triggers feminine agreement if the action is not particularly intense or does not refer to an exceptional realization of a state. For instance, *ka:m* 'hunger' is feminine when referring to a normal state of hunger. It is only when hunger is exceptionally strong that it triggers masculine agreement.

To ask 'what is it?', a feminine agreement form is used—unless one knows what to expect:

5.21 agwa ja:p-a?
      what thing-3fem.sgNOM
      'What is it?'

If something serious is suspected, then the masculine agreement form can be used in such a question: 5.22 was asked as a reaction to a very loud commotion in the backyard. Gemaj suspected that something serious must have happened (it turned out to be a snake).

5.22 agwa ja:p-ad?
what thing-3masc.sgNOM
'What is it (this loud noise)?'

The non-agreeing adjective 'old' which distinguishes two gender forms in the singular does not have a plural form. Then the feminine form *apaw* is used as a general form, as in 5.23.

5.23 numa apaw-adi ñəg
big+fem.sg old:fem-3plNOM mosquito.net
'Mosquito nets are truly/largely old'

A group of referents of different sex (for animates), shape, and size (for inanimates) requires agreement with non-singular numbers, where gender is neutralized. Coordinate compounds whose referent is inherently non-singular require non-singular agreement on modifiers. Just occasionally, they can trigger singular agreement. Then, if the last noun has inherent gender, it determines the agreement. In 5.24, the masculine agreement on the possessor is determined by the inherent gender of *asa:y* 'father'.

5.24 ñən-a-də amæy asa:y vəvak
2fem.sg-LK-masc.sg mother father see+RED+DAT
'(You) want to see your parents (lit. mother-father)'

B. The feminine agreement form is used with a number of non-prototypical controllers, including action and object nominalizations in the predicate slot: see 4.7–8. A purposive form as a complementation strategy (in the function of the subject of a verbless clause: 5.25) and a copula complement (5.26) requires feminine agreement.

5.25 təp-a:r yiya:k numa ja:p-a
village-LK+ALL go+RED+DAT big+fem.sg thing-3fem.sgNOM
'To go to the village is a big thing'

5.26 təp-a:r yiya:k suan yi-na
village-LK+ALL go+RED+DAT difficult go-ACT.FOC+3fem.sgBAS.VT
'To go to the village is hard'

And we saw, in 4.65–6, that in modal constructions with *nəbə* 'be able' (§4.5.1) the verb is in the third person feminine form, no matter what gender and number the S or A is. A similar example is 5.27.

5.27 nəbə ya:n suku-l
able come+SEQ write-3fem.sgBAS.P
'One can carry on writing' (referring to the two of us writing together)

The feminine agreement form is used with loans with abstract meaning, e.g. *numa apaw tenkyu* (big+fem.sg old+fem.sg thankyou) 'thank you very much, a very big thankyou' (lit. big old thankyou).

C. The feminine form is the one consistently used in highlighting focus constructions—as shown in 5.28 (see further discussion in §20.3):

5.28 Swakap-a:r yi-ba-l-a
Swakap-LK+ALL go-1plSUBJ.P-3fem.sgBAS.P-3fem.sgNOM
'It is (the case) that we went to Swakap'

Generic statements—often used for phatic communication—always require feminine agreement, as in 5.29 which is almost like a fixed expression.

5.29 aka-n   aka
     DEM.DIST.REACT.TOP+fem.sg-PRED   DEM.DIST.REACT.TOP+fem.sg
     'Here it is, this is how things are'

Example 5.30 illustrates a summarizing phrase which can be roughly translated as 'this is how things are, this is it'. The distal demonstrative *a* is in a highlighting focus construction (this pronoun is typically used for textual deixis: §10.2).

5.30 al-al
     DEM.DIST.fem.sg+3fem.sgNOM-3fem.sgNOM
     'This is how it is' (lit. it is that, that is that)

The same principle applies to adjective forms. The feminine agreement form of the adjective 'old', *apaw*, is used in generic statements: 5.31 is a general comment about old people who had lived all their adult lives outside the village:

5.31 apaw   apaw   tə-ku   təp-a:r   yiya:k   vyakət ma:
     old.fem old.fem become-COMPL.SS village-LK+ALL go+RED+DAT good   NEG
     'Having become very old, it is not good to go to the village'

D. The feminine, rather than the masculine, form of agreeing adjectives and agreeing closed classes is used as a default form in a number of grammatical contexts where the gender agreement is not required.

The feminine form of AGREEING ADJECTIVES is used when agreeing size adjectives appear in adverbial functions, e.g. *kwasa* (small+fem.sg) 'a little; almost', *numa* (big+fem.sg) 'in a big way' (also see 4.52 and discussion there), and in idiomatic expressions such as *numa kwasa kwa-* (big small stay-) 'spread the news'.

The feminine form of the INDEFINITE *nəkə-* 'other, another' appears in the distributive headless adverbial *nəkəm nəkəm* (another.fem.sg+ACC/LOC another.fem.sg+ACC/LOC) 'bit of everything; in a random way'.

The feminine form of the INTERROGATIVE *akə-* 'which, where' is used in the formation of a general locational interrogative *akəm* (which.fem.sg+LOC) 'where'. This form is also used to enquire about the location of a singular object belonging to the feminine gender, and in a complex construction to express the meaning *akəm tə-ku* (which.fem.sg+LOC stay-COMPL.SS) 'where from' (see §10.4). (See §6.2.4 on plural agreement with *sə* 'who' to enquire about someone whose sex is unknown.)

The feminine form of GENDER-SENSITIVE DEMONSTRATIVES is used in adverbial demonstratives, such as *kləm* (DEM.PROX+fem.sg+LOC) 'here', *aləm* (DEM.DIST+fem.sg+LOC) 'there'. The feminine form of the PROXIMATE DEMONSTRATIVE *kə* is used in negative interjections *kal* or *ka* (DEM.PROX+fem.sg+3fem.sgNOM) 'no! not that!' (pronounced with falling intonation and high intensity of the vowel).

The feminine form of the CARDINAL NUMERAL *nakaməy* 'one, only one' (§10.6.1) is used in counting, e.g. *nakaməy, viti, mugul, a:li* 'one, two, three, four'. It often replaces the masculine form *naka-də-məy* in noun phrases (even when counting men). The adverb *nakamib* (one.fem.sg+ADV) 'together' is based on the feminine form *nakaməy*.

E. The final piece of evidence in favour of the unmarked character of the feminine gender comes from child language acquisition. Kerryanne, when she was 3, would use the feminine gender to refer to any unknown object or person, independently of their apparent sex or size attributes. When looking at the photos of a white man and a boy (both obviously male), she would invariably ask: *Ka-l?* (DEM.PROX+fem.sg-3fem.sgNOM) 'This feminine one is (what)?'

Statistically, feminine agreement forms are more frequent than masculine, due to the fact that nouns of quite a few semantic groups, e.g. time and manner, are typically feminine. The feminine gender in Manambu shows an almost perfect match between a functionally and a formally unmarked category. In the few instances where both gender forms are equally marked and there is no formally unmarked choice (as in the case of the adjective 'old'), the feminine form is still unmarked functionally. The agreeing adjective *yara-* 'fine' is an exception. It has two gender forms, each of which is formally marked. The formally unmarked form *yara* is used adverbially as well as in the copula complement function, rather than the formally marked feminine singular *yara-l*. This conforms to the general tendency in the language to match the two kinds of markedness.

Most Ndu languages have the markers *d* 'masculine' and *l* 'feminine', also found in personal pronouns in all languages except Gala. Gala and Manambu share ø as a feminine marker, e.g. Gala *ki* 'she', *kir* 'he' (related to Proto-Ndu *kə* 'proximal demonstrative', attested in Manambu in this function). I hypothesize that the ø-marking in feminine forms is a Manambu-Gala innovation, and that the forms containing -*l* are more archaic than the zero-marked ones.

5.3 OVERT GENDER MARKING

Natural gender can be marked on a noun with a human referent, to disambiguate hybrid nouns (i.e. nouns which can denote either male or female). Lexemes *ta:kw* 'woman' and *du* 'man' are used to disambiguate the hybrid noun *ñan* 'child', e.g. *takwa-ñan* (woman+LK-child) 'girl', *du-a-ñan* (man-LK-child) 'boy'.

The root *du* 'man' also occurs in one kinship term, *du-a-ma:gw* (man-LK-generic.noun) 'brother'. Its female counterpart is *jukwar* 'sister' (which is non-segmentable, and does not have any overt gender marker). The same construction can also be used with animate nouns assigned a fixed gender because of their shape (see B under §5.2.1), e.g. *gwa:s* 'turtle', *du-a gwa:s* 'male turtle', *takwa gwa:s* 'female turtle'. Gender reference of a few hybrid kin terms can be disambiguated via a compound with the second element -*du* 'man' or -*ta:kw* 'woman', e.g. *yanan* 'grandchild', *yanan-ta:kw* 'granddaughter', *yanan-du* 'grandson'; *babay* 'maternal grandparent', *babay-du* 'maternal grandfather', *babay-ta:kw* 'maternal grandmother'.

A semantically redundant gender marking component -*ta:kw* 'woman' appears with some kinship nouns with feminine reference: e.g. *ña:p* and *ñap-a-ta:kw* 'mother's sister' are used interchangeably. Along similar lines, *ti:d* is 'co-wife; woman of the same clan and generation as ego'. The term *tidə-ta:kw* has the same meaning but appears to be used in not quite so usual contexts: a rare and archaic form *tidə-takwa:gw* (co.wife-woman+PL) was used to refer to stars as my potential 'co-wives', since stars belong to the same clan group as the one I was adopted into (also see F in §5.2.1).

Heads of noun phrases containing the noun *asa:y* as an augmentative marker are always masculine, e.g. *numa-də asa:y wuk* (big-masc.sg father tooth) 'huge big tooth', or *asa:y wuk* (father tooth) 'huge tooth', and 5.14. That is, *asa:y* in such noun phrases can be considered tantamount to an overt gender and augmentative marker.

Vocatives distinguish masculine and feminine forms whose choice depends on the gender of the addressee, e.g. *yaban* 'Maliau clan: greeting, masculine addressee'; *yabənay* 'Maliau clan: greeting, feminine addressee'. The latter form is also used as a denomination of a clan group of the Iatmul with which the Maliau have long-standing ties.

Personal names often contain formatives which identify them as feminine or masculine. Male names often contain *-du* 'man' as their last component, as in *Yuakalu-du, Dəmiyawi-du, Duamakwai-du, Kawi-du.* Female names contain *-ta:kw* 'woman', as in *Ñamamayra-ta:kw, Saun-ta:kw, Yuwasəpa-ta:kw, Ganvala-ta:kw.* Frequently, names come in pairs, e.g. *Kapavala-du* (male), *Kapavala-ta:kw* (female). (In actual interaction names are shortened, and the final syllable dropped; as a result, a shortened name *Kapaval* can refer to a man or to a woman.)

Other formatives which occur in male names include

-bædi, as in *Saun-bædi, Wali-bædi*;
-dəmi, as in *Kwalgu-dəmi, Kasa-dəmi*;
-duí, as in *Kipam-duí, Sagi-duí, Wali-duí*;
-gab, as in *Kwaləkə-gab, Səpər-gab, Kabə-gab*;
-kəban, as in *Maji-kəban, Madaw-kəban, Təpwi-kəban*;
-nakwan, as in *Yəma-nakwan*;
-məli, -mæli, as in *Saunəgə-mæli, Win-məli, Yapun-məli, Tujə-məli*;
-nəbuk, as in *Way-nəbək, Yua-nəbək, Kwaru-nəbuk.*

Feminine formatives in personal names include:

-kay, as in *Kwarawijəba-kay, Wakənaw-kay, Gwarabi-kay*;
-mæg, as in *Payan-mæg, Gabalmæg, Yuamali-mæg*;
-(n)əbər, as in *Saunəgə-nəbər, Manwalaku-nəbər, Kulamakway-nəbər*;
-wali, as in *Paka-nəbər-wali, Kapamada-wali.*

In each of these the final formative can be omitted, if the form is shortened.

Many names do not have any special suffixed formatives, e.g. female names *Yuanəg, Vakərgay, Walimuk, Yapikudi*; and male names *Yuasasəg, Apikuñ, Lumawadəm.* A female name can end in *-du*, e.g. *Abasadu.*

Some personal names appear to be derived from common nouns (whose referents are totemic creatures) using one of the formatives listed above, e.g. masculine names *Mepe-nakwan* from *məp* 'totemic rooster'; *Yapun-məli* from *yapun* 'totemic bird (Wapanab clan)'; *Saun-napan* from *saun* 'pelican', and its female counterpart *Saun-ta:kw*; *gwarabi* 'mango' and the female name *Gwarabi-kay.*

Some names have a female counterpart in *-nəbər* and a male counterpart in *-mæli*, e.g. female *Saunəgə-nəbər*, male *Saunəgə-mæli.* A few others have *-mæg* in feminine forms and *-mæli* in masculine, e.g. female *Payan-mæg*, male *Payan-mæli*; female *Yali-mæg*, male *Yali-mæli*; female *Yavi-mæg*, male *Yavi-mæli*; male *Kasakun-mæli*, female *Kasakun-mæg.* Some female names have two male counterparts, with different gender-marking suffixes, e.g. female *Gəmajə-nəbər*, male *Gəmajə-du* and *Gəmajə-bædi.*

A female formative can be added to a male name (which already contains one of the formatives). Here is an example. A name debate was held in Avatip on 8 October 2004 concerning the ownership of the male name *Kigi-nəbək.* It was decided that the Wagau clan had won the ownership of this name, and of its female counterpart, *Kigi-nəbək-əbər.* The rival Sarak clan was granted the male name *Kəgi-dəmi*, and its female counterpart *Kəgi-dəmi-nəbər.*

At least some of these names could be of Iatmul origin (see Harrison 1990a), as are, perhaps, masculine and feminine formatives other than the transparently Manambu *-du* 'man' and *-ta:kw* 'woman'. Personal names in Manambu are a prized and often disputed possession of a clan, or a clan group (§1.3.2). Knowledge of personal names is highly valued, and not easily parted with, or even transmitted. This makes the study of the origin, and internal structure, of personal names a highly sensitive issue. In the present situation of encroaching cultural obsolescence, their full study may gradually become impossible.

6

Number

Manambu distinguishes singular and non-singular numbers expressed via agreement (outlined in §5.1) and also on the head noun. A non-singular number can be associative (that is, denoting the set by association with its central member: see Moravcsik 2003 for a typological perspective), or non-associative. Either of these can be dual or plural. See Chart 6.1.

The singular number is the least formally marked. Associative non-singular is marked on the head noun which can only be a personal name. Non-associative non-singular is marked on some nouns, which include kinship terms and a few others. All of dual, plural, and singular are expressed through agreement.

We first discuss number marking on head nouns (§6.1). Then, we look at agreement patterns and discuss markedness in number agreement (§6.2).

6.1 NUMBER MARKING ON NOUNS

Associative non-singular is invariably marked with the suffix *-bər* on a personal name (no matter whether it is borrowed or traditional), e.g. *Tanina-bər* (Tanina-ASS) 'Tanina and whoever is with her'; *Yuayabə-bər* (Yuaya:b+LK-ASS) 'Yuaya:b and whoever is with her'. An associative non-singular form can have a dual or a plural reference—these are disambiguated by number agreement (§6.2).

Non-associative plural and dual are marked on most kinship nouns as shown in Table 6.1.[1] The first-named plural form is preferred by traditional speakers (see §22.6.1).

The noun 'child' has an irregular dual form. Nouns other than kinship terms which have been attested with a plural marker in the corpus are listed below the thick line. These are *pa:t* 'youngster', and a body part term *kudi* 'mouth'. The vocative address form *kəp* 'an endearing farewell/hello' has a plural *kəp-ugw* used if addressed to more than one person.

The plural markers are *-bər* (with an optional linker), and *-Vgw*: the vowel is *-a* if the noun requires the linker *-a* or *-u*, with a variant *ə*, realized as *u* (in agreement with the rule in C under §2.1.2) for nouns which require the linker *ə*.

When kinship terms form a compound referring to a kin group, only the last term takes the plural marking, e.g. *ñaməs-ma:m* (younger.sibling-elder.sibling) 'younger and elder siblings (one of each)'; *ñaməs-mam-əgw* 'younger and elder siblings (many)'.

The semantics of dual and plural is straightforward (also see §6.2). We discuss additional features of number marking below.

A. OVERT NUMBER MARKING AND POLYSEMOUS NOUNS. If a noun on which an overt plural can be formed has two meanings, just one meaning is likely to be retained in the plural form.

The noun *ta:kw* means both 'wife' and 'woman'. The plural can be formed on it only if it means 'wife', as in 6.1 (see §21.2.2). Agreement markers are underlined throughout this chapter.

---

[1] The kinship system is of Omaha type; also see Harrison (1993).

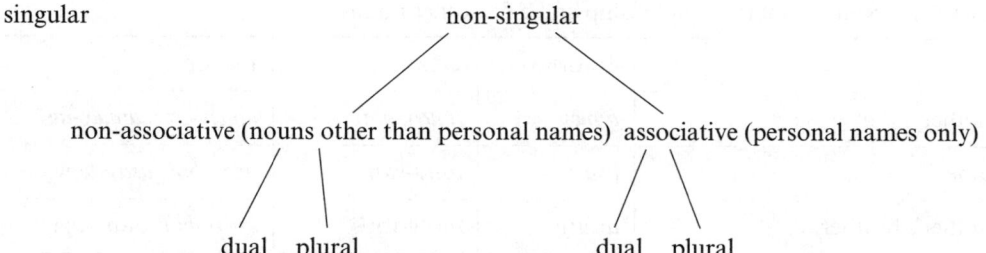

singular   non-singular

non-associative (nouns other than personal names) associative (personal names only)

dual plural   dual plural

CHART 6.1 Number system in Manambu

6.1 a-<u>di</u>   mən-a-<u>di</u>   takwa:gw-<u>adi</u>   yi-na-<u>di</u>
  DEM.DIST-PL you.masc-LK-PL woman+LK+PL-3plNOM go-ACT.FOC-3plBAS.VT
  'It is those wives of yours that are going by' (as a joke, to a man, indicating a group of
  marriageable relatives)

If the noun *ta:kw* appears on another kinship term as an overt feminine 'gender marker' (see
§5.3), it can also be pluralized, as in *tidə-takwa:gw* (co.wife+LK-woman+LK+PL) 'women-co-
wives'. Such an expression, seemingly redundant, is used to refer to totemic co-wives who are
not obviously women—for instance, to stars, or female turtles.

    The noun *kudi* has two meanings: 'speech, language, noise' and '(the outside of) mouth'. The
second meaning is very restricted: it appears in compounds, e.g. *səp-a-kudi* (skin-LK-mouth)
'lip', *kudi-gu* (mouth-water) 'saliva', and in fixed expressions, e.g. *kudi nak* (mouth one) 'one
mouthful; a little bit'. A general term for mouth is *day*. The plural *kudi-ugw* only occurs in the
first sense, with a collective meaning ('lips and mouth'), and has an archaic feel to it. In 6.2,
the speaker chose to accompany it with *day*, stressing the fact that the character washed the
whole mouth:

6.2 kudi-ugw day   jan-ku
  mouth-PL mouth wash-COMPL.SS
  'After she has washed the whole of her mouth'

    A similar principle applies to the noun *gwal-ugw*. The noun *gwa:l* has two meanings:
'grandchild' and 'paternal grandfather'. The plural *gwal-ugw* is used for both; it also has the
meaning 'clan'. Only in the first two meanings does *gwal-ugw* always trigger plural agreement.
The 'double plural' formation *gwal-ugw-ə-bər* (grandfather-PL-LK-PL) has only been attested in
the meaning of 'many paternal grandfathers' (see B below). The noun *gwalugw* 'clan', though
etymologically a plural form, can have a singular referent, as in 6.3. The clan in question is
considered small—and is accorded feminine gender, realized in agreement on demonstratives
and on possessives:

6.3 aw   <u>a</u>   wulwi ñawi <u>kwasa</u>   gwalugw
  then DEM.DIST+fem.sg Wulwi Ñawi small+fem.sg clan
  <u>kəka</u>   Maliau wa-<u>dana</u>   wun-a-<u>kə</u>
  DEM.PROX.REACT.TOP+fem.sg Maliau say-3plSUBJ.VT+3fem.sgBAS.VT I-LK-OBL+fem.sg
  gwalugw <u>aka</u>-n   <u>aka</u>
  clan   DEM.DIST.REACT.TOP+fem.sg-PRED DEM.DIST.REACT.TOP+fem.sg
  'Then here is a small clan belonging to Wulwi Ñawi (clan group), this is my clan'

    A dual reference for *gwalugw* in the meaning of 'clan' is illustrated in 6.4, while 6.5 illustrates
plural agreement.

TABLE 6.1   Number marking in kinship and a few other nouns

	SINGULAR	DUAL	PLURAL
mother	*amæy*	*amæy-vəti*	*amæy-bər, amæy-ugw*
father	*asa:y*	*asay-vəti*	*asay-bər, asay-ugw*
mother's brother	*awa:y*	*away-vəti*	*away-bər, away-ugw*
mother's elder sister	*ñap*	*ñap-vəti*	*ñap-bər, ñap-agw*
mother's younger sister	*mamæy*	*mamæy-vəti*	*mamæy-bər, mamæy-ugw*
father's sister	*yawus*	*yawusə-vəti*	*yawəs-bər*
father's younger brother	*ñaj*	*ñajə-vəti*	*ñaj-ugw*
father's elder brother	*ñasap*	*ñasapa-vəti*	*ñasap-bər, ñasap-agw*
father's mother	*yæy*	*yæy-vəti*	*yæy-bər*
father's sister's child	*kagrəs*	*kagrəs-vəti*	*kagrəs-ugw*
co-wife	*ti:d*	*ti:d-vəti*	*tid-i:gw*
mother's brother's child	*ra:w*	*rawa-vəti*	*raw-agw*
grandchild; father's father	*gwa:l*	*gwal-vəti*	*gwal-ugw, gwal-ugw-bər*
mother's parents	*babay*	*babay-vəti*	*babay-bər, babay-ugw*
ancestors	*warag*	*waraga-vəti*	*waraga-bər, warag-agw*
elder sibling	*ma:m*	*mam-vəti*	*mam-ugw, mam-ugw-bər*
younger sibling	*ñamus*	*ñamusə-vəti*	*ñamus-ugw, ñamusə-bər*
sister (of male ego)	*jukwar*	*jukwar(a)-vəti*	*jukwar-agw*
brother (of female ego)	*du-a-ma:gw*	*du-a-ma:gw-vəti*	*du-a-magwə-bər*
husband's mother's brother	*ya:w*	*ya:w-vəti*	*ya:w-bər, yaw-əgw*
husband's mother	*yawəl*	*ya:wəl-vəti*	*yawəl-bər, yawəl-ugw*
mother's brother's wife	*batay*	*batay-vəti*	*batayə-bər*
wife's brother	*wawəs*	*wawusə-vəti*	*wawus-ugw*
wife	*ta:kw*	*ta:kw vəti*	*takw-a:gw*
husband	*la:n*	*la:n vəti*	*lan-ugw*
son's child	*yanan*	*yanan-vəti*	*yanan-ugw*

TABLE 6.1   *Continued*

	SINGULAR	DUAL	PLURAL
daughter's child	*na*	*na:-vəti*	*na:gw*
youngster	*pa:t*	—	*pat-əgw*
mouth	*kudi*	—	*kudi-ugw*
child (age and status group); child of someone	*ñan*	*ñədi*	*ñan-ugw*

6.4 nəma-<u>bər</u> gwalugw viti-a-<u>bər</u>   kə-<u>bər</u>   viti gwalugw
    big-DU   clan   two-LK-3plBAS.VT DEM.PROX-DU two clan
    'Big clans are two, these two clans'

6.5 kə-<u>di</u>   wulwi ñawi gwalugw a-<u>di</u>
    DEM.PROX-PL Wulwi Ñawi clan   DEM.DIST-PL
    'These are clans belonging to the Wulwi Ñawi clan group'

In summary, plural formation provides an additional mechanism for differentiating various meanings of polysemous nouns. We will now discuss further morphological features of number marking.

B. DUAL MARKING. All the dual forms of kinship nouns (except for 'child': see E below) contain the numeral *viti, vəti* 'two'. Unlike noun phrases consisting of a noun and a numeral, they

(a) form one phonological word and one grammatical word, since no other constituent can intervene between the two, and
(b) do not allow alternative ordering of components. For instance, in 6.4 the number 'two' can appear before and after the head noun (see §10.6.1 for the discussion). Such alternative ordering is impossible for a dual form of a kin term. Kin terms marked for dual require dual agreement on any agreeing constituent, for example:

6.6 bər   awuk,   kə-<u>bər</u>   nəkə-<u>bər</u> amæy-vəti
    you.du IMPV+hear DEM.PROX-DU other-DU mother-two/DU
    'You two listen, these other two mothers!'

In contrast to the irregular dual form of the noun 'child', the dual forms of kinship nouns do not combine with the number two: *ñədi viti* (child+DU two) 'two children' is perfectly acceptable, while **amæy-vəti viti* (mother-two/DU two) is not. A noun phrase *amæy viti-viti* (mother two-two), with a different phonological and grammatical structure, would mean 'each two mothers' and is an example of a distributive noun phrase with a numeral.

C. ALTERNATIVE PLURAL FORMS, with the marker *-bər*, and also with *-Vgw*, have been attested for most nouns (see Table 6.1). Two nouns, *mam-ugw-bər* (elder.sibling-PL-PL) and *gwal-ugw-bər* (grandfather-PL-PL), have double plural markers. In each case, the first form in the third column of Table 6.1 is the most frequent one, and also the one judged correct by many speakers. What are the factors that may condition the choice of *-bər* or of *-Vgw* as a plural marker, and the appearance of the seemingly aberrant 'double plural'?

Both markers have cognates in other Ndu languages. The plural marker *-bər* marks plural with kin terms in Abelam *-béré* 'pluralizer' (Wilson 1980: 36), and the irregular plural marker *-mbri* in Western Wosera (Wendel 1993: 57–8). The plural marker *-Vgw* has its cognates in Western Wosera *-(n)gu*, Abelam *-gu* (Wilson 1980: 46), where it is also restricted to kinship nouns. In Manambu, the marker *-Vgw* is somewhat more productive than the marker *-bər*. (Also see §22.1.)

For most kin terms listed in Table 6.1, the additional, 'second-named', plural is *-Vgw*. Most terms have the *-Vgw* form as their only form. The only noun for which the alternant with *-Vgw* does not exist is the noun *duama:gw* '(female ego's) brother'. This gap may have to do with a tendency to avoid the occurrence of two labialized consonants in adjacent syllables within one word (see A6 in §2.6).

For nouns with the plural *-Vgw* as the 'second-named' plural form, the instances of the *-Vgw* plural occur if a preceding noun, within the same noun phrase, or a paragraph, exhibits the same number marking. In 6.7, the speaker tells a story about the origin of the Manambu people. He first uses a traditional form *asay-bər* 'fathers':

6.7 ñan-a-<u>di</u> asay-bər kwa-ku,   a   ñan kəka
we-LK-PL father-PL stay-COMPL.SS then we   DEM.PROX.REACT.TOP+fem.sg
kwa-bana
stay-1plSUBJ.VT+3fem.sgBAS.VT
'After our fathers had stayed (here), we are living here'

He then goes on to list thirteen generations of his Manambu ancestors, *gwalugw*, literally, paternal grandfathers, and concludes:

6.8 kə-<u>də</u>   təp   asay-ugw aka-n
DEM.PROX-masc.sg village father-PL DEM.DIST.REACT.TOP+fem.sg-PRED
aka   ñan mam-ugw   <u>day</u> ñamus-ugw   tənəb
DEM.DIST.REACT.TOP+fem.sg we elder.sibling-PL they younger.sibling-PL fireplace
kə<u>də</u>ka-n   a<u>dəka</u>   kə-di
DEM.PROX.REACT.TOP+masc.sg-PRED DEM.DIST.REACT.TOP+masc.sg DEM.PROX-PL
kukə-tənəb-adi   day kə-<u>di</u>   Yima:l
after-fireplace-3plNOM they DEM.PROX-PL Yima:l
'The fathers of this village are like this, we (belong) to the elder siblings' fireplace, they (belong) to the younger siblings' fireplace here, they are later fireplaces, these (members of the clan of) Yimal'

The use of the *-Vgw* form on 'father' in 6.8 is likely to have been influenced by the previously occurring term *gwal-ugw*, in a very similar meaning, as a kind of 'echo effect'. Notably, within the same story the speaker is also talking about sibling relationships—and the plural forms of the two words for 'sibling' involve *-Vgw*.

The echo effect has also been noticed in spontaneous conversation: once the speaker chooses to use an innovative form with the *-Vgw* plural, they are likely to carry on applying the same marker to other kin terms within the same noun phrase, or clause. For instance, Tanina asked me about my *asay-ugw* (father-PL) 'fathers, relatives of father's generation', and then lamented the fact that I have no living *asay-ugw* nor *mamay-ugw* (maternal.aunt-PL) 'maternal relatives'. For both terms, a more traditional option is the *-bər* plural.

The traditional 'first-named' plural for *gwa:l* 'grandchild; father's father' is *gwalugw*—this is shown in 6.9–10, both from historical accounts of the Manambu wars and migrations. In 6.9 *gwalugw* is used as a synonym for *warag* 'ancestor' in the collective sense, and *asay-bər* 'fathers'.

6.9 warag   gwal-ugw   asay-bər <u>adiya</u>   raːn   və-ku
    ancestor grandfather-PL father-PL DEM.DIST.REACT.TOP+pl sit+SEQ see-COMPL.SS
    'Having seen ancestors, that is, grandfathers, fathers being (there)'

In 6.10, *gwal-ugw* 'paternal grandfathers' and *warag-agw* 'ancestors' (both marked with -*Vgw* plural) follow each other: the second one is a specification for the first one.[2]

6.10 təp   yi-n   gər-ku,   ñan-a-<u>di</u> gwal-ugw   warag-agw ya-n
     village go-SEQ establish-COMPL.SS we-LK-PL grandfather-PL ancestor-PL come-SEQ
     kar-<u>da</u>-l
     bring-3plSUBJ.P-3fem.sgBAS.P
     'Having established the village, our grandparents, ancestors kept bringing (people) here'

If the noun 'ancestors' had been used on its own, the preferred form would have been *waragə-bər*.

However, as we saw above (6.3–5), the term *gwalugw* also means 'clan'. A sentence *a-di-awur gwal-ugw-adi* (DEM.DIST-PL-UP grandfather-PL-3plNOM) is potentially ambiguous—it can mean either 'These are the clans that are up there', or 'These are your grandfathers (paternal ancestors) up there'. This sentence was a comment on stars who are supposed to be my ancestors (since I was adopted into the clan group associated with sun, moon, and stars). That is, the ambiguity was resolved by context.

However, to avoid potential misunderstandings, and to differentiate the meaning 'clan' from the meaning 'numerous paternal grandfathers', some speakers opt for an additional plural marker, -*bər*, on *gwalugw*, in the meaning of 'many paternal grandfathers', as in 6.11:

6.11 tayir   ñan-a-<u>di</u> warag-<u>agw</u> gwalu-gwə-bər
     before we-LK-PL ancestor-PL grandfather-PL-PL
     'Before (having stayed in the village called Asiti, they then stayed in Avatip) our ancestors, paternal grandfathers'

That is, the double plural marking is a result of a tendency towards disambiguating two meanings of *gwal-ugw*—that of a plural, and that of a singular noun 'clan'. The double plural form *mam-ugw-bər*, used by innovative speakers, has a similar motivation: *mam-ugw* (elder.sibling-PL) tends to acquire a collective meaning, of 'elder siblings as a group'. To ensure the individuated plural reading of *mam-ugw*, the additional plural marker -*bər* is added.[3]

D. PLURAL MARKING ON NON-KINSHIP TERMS involves the marker -*Vgw* in three cases ('mouths', 'youngsters', and the address term *kəp*). We saw, in C above, that the marker -*Vgw* is more frequent and productive than its synonym -*bər* with kinship nouns. That it is an archaic retention, and not an innovation, is corroborated by the fact that the noun *kudi* in its plural form *kudiy-ugw* means 'mouths', while in the singular it is much more often used to mean 'language, noise', and the meaning 'mouth' survives in a handful of compounds and fixed expressions. That more nouns could take the overt plural -*Vgw* in the previous stages of the language is supported by the existence of a few other nouns which, in all probability, go back to plural forms: the name *Glaːgw* 'clan group associated with darkness' is transparently related

---

  [2] The authors of the history accounts often used the Tok Pisin word *tumbuna* in lieu of both *gwal-ugw* and *warag-agw*.
  [3] The form *ñamusə-bər* was attested as an 'echo effect' of *mam-ugw-bər*, within the same clause.

to *gəl* 'black, blackness, dark cloud'. The term *kwayugw* 'wet season' could also be a frozen plural form.

E. IRREGULAR NUMBER MARKING ON 'CHILD'. The word for 'child' has an irregular dual form, *ñədi*, and a plural form *ñan-ugw*. This word has two meanings, that of a kinship term, 'child (of someone)', and that of an age group, 'child, young person; non-initiated man'. Dual and plural forms are usually employed in both meanings. Dual agreement is illustrated in 6.12, and plural agreement in 6.13.

6.12 aw   wun kə-bər   kwasa-bər ñədi-ə-k   wa-ku
      then I   DEM.PROX-DU small-DU child:DU-LK-DAT say-COMPL.SS
      'After I told (them) about these two small children (of mine)...'

6.13 wun-a-di ñan-ugw dəy-a-də   asa:y-a:b ata stakra-tuə-d
      I-LK-3pl child-PL they-LK-masc.sg father-TOO then meet-1sgSUBJ.P-3masc.sgBAS.P
      'Then I met the father of my children, too'

The dual form often occurs followed by a seemingly redundant number 'two', *viti*, as in *takwa-ñədi viti* (woman+LK-child:DU two) 'two girls'. The term for 'twins', *kisa-ñədi* (?-child:DU), also typically occurs with the number 'two': *kisa-ñədi viti* 'two twins'. This term only exists in a dual form, and refers to twins only. The form *viti* here has not yet been grammaticalized into a dual marker: first, it does not form one phonological word with *kisa-ñədi*, and secondly, it can be preposed to *kisa-ñədi* (the constituent order in numeral phrases and its motivation are discussed in §10.6.1 and §20.1.1).[4] If the singular form *ñan* 'child, young people' has a collective referent, it can trigger plural agreement. We return to this in the following section.

6.2 NUMBER AGREEMENT

Number is marked on prehead modifiers (which include adjectives, demonstratives, and indefinite pronouns), possessives (see §8.1.1), and on predicates. See §5.1.1, and Table 5.1.

Number agreement is the only means of disambiguating the number of a countable referent. In 6.14, the number agreement shows that we are talking about two roads—one for men, one for women:

6.14 kə-bər   wa-tua-bər   ya:b kəp kwa-na-bər
      DEM.PROX-DU say-1sgSUBJ-3duBAS.P road still stay-ACT.FOC-3duBAS.VT
      'The two roads I am talking about are still there'

Number agreement—just like gender agreement in 5.3–4—helps determine boundaries of constituents. In 6.15 number agreement shows that 'I' is the possessor of 'village', and not of 'children'. If 'I' were the possessor of 'children', 6.16 would have been appropriate.

6.15 [wun-a təp-a]   ñan-ugw-adi   nəma-di-adi
      I-LK   village-LK child-PL-3plNOM big-PL-3plNOM
      'It is the children of my village who are big'

6.16 [wun-a-di [təp-a   ñan-ugw-adi]] nəma-di-adi
      I-LK-PL   village-LK child-PL-3plNOM big-PL-3plNOM
      'It is my village-children who are big'

---

4 The English loan *twins* triggers dual agreement, as in *twins-abər* (twins-3duNOM) 'the (two) were twins', but does not occur with *vəti* 'two'.

Just like gender, number agreement helps track referents in discourse. And it can also differentiate meanings of nouns with uncountable referents—see below.

6.2.1   Number agreement with mass and collective referents

Manambu does not have any restrictions on number agreement with countable and with uncountable nouns. Depending on whether the referent is countable, or mass (i.e. uncountable), the non-singular agreement has different meanings.

With countable referents, non-singular number agreement always implies a non-singular referent. Uncountable referents trigger singular agreement, as in 6.17. Here the mass noun 'water' triggers masculine agreement because of its large quantity.

6.17 gu ata kələ-d
  water then dry-3masc.sgBAS.P
  'Then the water (large quantity) dried'

In 6.18, the quantity of money is not particularly large; and this is why 'money' triggers feminine agreement.

6.18 sa:n ata kray-də-l
  money then bring-3masc.sgSUBJ.P-3fem.sgBAS.P
  'He then brought (some) money'

Non-singular agreement with uncountable nouns implies different varieties of a mass refer-ent. So, for instance, *a səkər* (DEM.DIST-fem.sg time) means 'that time, that time frame', and *a-di səkər* (DEM.DIST-pl time) means 'those (many various) times; periods of time'. Similarly, *a sa:n* means 'that money', and *a-di sa:n* refers to 'those (different kinds of) money from different sources'. This is similar to the meaning of plural in English 'different monies', to refer to different sums of money coming from different sources. In 6.19, *sa:n* 'money' refers to monies that were acquired at different times.

6.19 wa-di   akə-m kur-bra-di   luku kur-bra-di
  DEM.PROX.ADDR-PL where-LOC get-2duSUBJ.P-3plBAS.P steal get-2duSUBJ.VT-3plBAS.VT
  sa:n-adi
  money-3plNOM
  'Where did you get these (monies) from, they are stolen monies'

Along similar lines, *kamna:gw* 'food' usually refers to food in general. In 6.20, however, it refers to two portions of food. This is why the agreement on the modifiers and on the predicate is dual:

6.20 abrəka   bər-abər kamna:gw-abər a-na-wur
  DEM.PROX.REACT.TOP+du 2du-3duNOM food-3duNOM DEM.DIST-ANAPH-UP
  ñəg-a-m   rə-na-bər
  mosquito.net-LK-LOC sit-ACT.FOC-3duBAS.P
  'Those two portions of your (dual) food are up there (previously mentioned) in the mosquito net'

In 4.30, *kamna:gw* 'food' refers to different kinds of food, and is cross-referenced on the verb with a plural object marker. If a mass noun occurs in a noun phrase with the generic *məwi* 'things like this, things of similar nature' (which is countable: §20.1.1), the noun phrase requires plural agreement:

6.21 an-a-<u>di</u>   saːn   məwi   adiya
     1du-LK-PL money things.like.that DEM.DIST.REACT.TOP+pl
     kusə-k-na-<u>di</u>
     finish-FUT-ACT.FOC-3plBAS.VT
     'Money and things like this belonging to the two of us might come to an end'

A locational noun can be used metonymically, to refer to its inhabitants—this is why the noun *təp* 'village' triggers plural agreement on the predicate in 17.11.

Natural phenomena which occur simultaneously trigger singular agreement. In 6.22, 'thunder' and 'lightning' are part of the same phenomenon; they are linked with the comitative. That it was a strong thunderstorm is reflected in the masculine gender agreement on the verb:

6.22 yakrawa   wulək   ata   daːd
     thunder+COM lightning then come.down+3masc.sgBAS.P
     'Then a thunderstorm came down'

We will see in §7.9 that a double comitative construction implies that the participants, or the participating phenomena, occurred simultaneously. During a thunderstorm, thunder is heard following the lightning; but during a cyclone torrential rain and wind always go together. That they are part of the 'package' is reflected in the singular agreement on the verb, in 7.73.

A non-singular agreement would have implied several occurrences of a thunderstorm, or a cyclone. If a double comitative construction involves human participants, the agreement is always non-singular:

6.23 asay-wa   amæy-wa   abra   maː yi-bər
     father-COM mother-COM DEM.DIST.REACT.TOP+du again go-3duBAS.P
     'Father and mother together went off again'

The same principle applies to human participants in comitative argument elaboration constructions (see §6.2.3).

A countable noun accompanied by the quantifier *samasaːm* 'many, a lot of' may trigger singular agreement if conceived of as a collective, uncountable, unity. In the first line of 6.24 women are looked upon as individual countable entities, hence plural agreement on the predicate head. In the second line adult women folk are viewed as a crowd—hence singular agreement. Since the crowd is big, the agreement is masculine:

6.24 miyawa   taːkw-ab   samasaːm-<u>adi</u>, ñan-a-wa   atawa tə-<u>di</u>,
     all.together woman-TOO many-3plNOM we-LK-COM thus stay-3plBAS.P
     apar taːkw ada   samasaːm-ad
     adult woman DEM.DIST.REACT.TOP+masc.sg many-3masc.sgNOM
     'All the (kidnapped) women were numerous, this is how they stayed with us; the crowd of adult women was big'

Following the same principle, the plural form *ñan-ugw* 'children' can have a collective referent if it describes an age group. Then it triggers feminine agreement on the adjective, as shown in 6.25 (this is Yuamali's description of 'baby talk'):

6.25 kwasa   ñan-ugw-aːk   bla-kwa-dana
     small+fem.sg child-PL-LK+DAT talk-HAB-3plSUBJ.VT+3fem.sgBAS.VT
     maːj-a
     speech-3fem.sgNOM
     'This is the speech one uses to talk to small children'

However, the agreement on the predicate tends to be plural, as in 6.26:

6.26 kwasa   ñan-ugw mabəl-a   næy-kwa-dana
      small+fem.sg child-PL marble-3fem.sgNOM play-HAB-3plSUBJ.VT+3fem.sgBAS.VT
      'It is with marbles that small (singular) children play (plural)'

Agreement in noun phrases tends to be variable depending on semantic principles other than sex (that is, size), while the verbal agreement tends to be more fixed. This is comparable to agreement mismatch found in gender in §5.2.2. Examples 5.18–19 and 6.25–6 show that, with respect to children who are small (and hence should be treated as 'feminine'), the feminine form *kwasa* 'small' is effectively becoming functionally unmarked, especially if children are not individuated.

Nouns with uniquely identifiable referents cannot form plurals, or trigger plural agreement. Most such nouns, however, have an additional meaning compatible with non-singular reference. The noun *ñə* has no plural in the meaning of 'sun'; if it occurs in a construction with plural agreement, it can only mean 'day', e.g. *a-di ñə* (DEM.DIST-PL day) 'those days'. The noun *bap* in its meaning 'moon' is uniquely identifiable. If it occurs in a construction with plural agreement, it may mean 'month', e.g. *a-di bap* (DEM.DIST-PL moon) 'those months'. In addition, *bap* 'moon' is the totem of the Wulwi-Ñawi clan group. And the construction *a-di bap* (DEM.DIST-PL moon) may also mean 'those who belong to the moon clan, or to the Wulwi-Ñawi clan group' (that is, those who can be addressed as *bap*: see §4.1.2).

This is similar to the meanings of non-singular agreement morphology with place names and clan names. It typically refers to people from that place, or those belonging to that clan. In 6.8, *day kə-di Yima:l* (they DEM.PROX-PL Yima:l) means 'these members of the Yimal clan, these Yimals', and not *these Yimal clans. (This latter reading makes no sense because there is just one Yimal clan.) Similar examples are under 6.27–8. Along similar lines, dual agreement on the predicate in 4.68 refers to the two members of the Sarak clan (and does not imply the existence of two Sarak clans).

6.27 kə-di   Apatəp ar-a:m   tə-di   du
      DEM.PROX-PL Avatip lake-LK+LOC stay-3plBAS.P man
      'Those (men from) Avatip, people who were on the lake'

6.28 kə-bər   Maliau-abər   kəbra   yi-na-bər
      DEM.PROX-DU Maliau-3duNOM DEM.PROX.REACT.TOP+DU go-ACT.FOC-3duBAS.P
      'It is these two (people of) the Maliau clan that are going by'

The generic term for 'clan' as the predicate head also has 'inclusive' meaning—that is, *gwalugw nak-abran* (clan one-1plNOM) means 'we two belong to one and the same clan'. If the NP *gwalugw nak* (clan one) heads an NP which triggers non-singular agreement, this NP refers to people belonging to the same clan, and not to several occurrences of the same clan, as in *kə-bər gwalugw nak* (DEM.PROX-DU clan one) 'those two belonging to the same clan'.

The semantics of non-singular agreement with clan names and place names is a criterion for considering them as special subclasses of nouns (see §4.1.2).

6.2.2 Agreement with associative non-singular

The associative non-singular (invariably marked with the suffix -*bər*) is a category marked on personal names only (in agreement with the predictions by Moravcsik 2003). An associative can refer to two people—the bearer of the name, and one more person, as in 6.29. This is indicated through dual agreement.

6.29 Nelma-bər a<u>bra</u>   waku-na-<u>bər</u>
  Nelma-ASS DEM.DIST.REACT.TOP+du go.out-ACT.FOC-3duBAS.VT
  'Nelma and one person associated with her are going out' (referring to Nelma and her son)

Alternatively, an associative may refer to more than two people—the bearer of the name, and whoever is with them, as in 6.30, where the associative plural form heads a predicate:

6.30 Celestin-bər-<u>adi</u>
  Celestin-ASS-3plNOM
  'These are Celestin and others with him' (referring to Celestin, his mother, his brother, and his sister)

A similar example is in T2.63: here, the noun 'Sabray and those belonging to him' triggers plural agreement on a modifier and on the predicate, and is also modified by a clan name with plural reference (see end of §6.2.1). If there is no agreeing constituent present, the reference of the associative non-singular could be ambiguous between dual and plural. This ambiguity is typically resolved by context: in 6.31, everyone knew that Leo was going to come with a group of people (and not just one more person).

6.31 Leo-a-brak   kap-ən   rə-k-na-<u>bran</u>
  Leo-LK-ASS+LK+DAT wait-SEQ sit-FUT-ACT.FOC-1duBAS.VT
  'We two will sit waiting for Leo and whoever is with him'

The associative non-singular is always used to refer to a group of people closely associated with each other—such as family members, or work partners—rather than a disparate group who happen to be together at one time.

The name bearer is the most 'salient' member of the group. This can be in terms of seniority—for instance, Nelly's family can be referred to as *Neli-abər* (Nelly-ASS) 'Nelly and others', and Ester's family as *Esta-bər* (Ester-ASS) 'Ester and others', if one talks about something a mother is responsible for (such as going to church).

In another instance, a child may be more prominent than the mother—so, in 6.30, Nelly's family was referred to as Celestin (her eldest son) and others, because he had come in first carrying her heavy load.

Kawidu and Luke were referred to as *Kawidu-abər* 'Kawidu and whoever is with him' because the speaker was waiting for Kawidu rather than for his mate Luke. Piur and his extended family were referred to as *Piur-bər* 'Piur and others' simply because Piur was the only one everyone knew really well. We will see, in §6.2.3 below, that associative plural shares semantic similarities with argument elaboration constructions, inasmuch as the choice of the 'head' noun is concerned.

6.2.3 'Argument elaboration' constructions and number agreement

The argument elaboration (or inclusory) construction (identified in numerous languages of the Pacific area: see Dixon 1988: 157–61; Lichtenberk 2000; Dixon forthcoming) consists of two components: a cover term which is often a pronoun, and the participants themselves. Argument elaboration constructions are used to coordinate nouns with human or high animate referents.

Manambu has two kinds of argument elaboration constructions, whose choice largely depends on the degree of the involvement of the participants.

1. JUXTAPOSED CONSTRUCTIONS are marked via juxtaposition of a non-singular pronoun and one or both participants. The constituent order is fixed. Agreement can be dual, as in 6.32, where there are two referents both covered by the third dual person pronoun *bər*. The verb agrees in person with the non-singular pronoun. In the following examples, argument elaboration constructions are in square brackets.

6.32 [bər   ñan asa:y] ata ka:p   kwakuli ya-n   tə-bər
     they.two child father then by.oneself orphan come-SEQ stay-3duBAS.P
     'The two of them, father and child, then became destitute (after the cassowary woman left them)'

If there are more than two participants (any of which may or may not be plural), the pronoun is plural, and so is the agreement, as in 6.33 and the last line of 6.38:

6.33 [ñan wun Lumawadəm   Məkaytaman] atawa da-dian
     we   I   Lumawandəm Məkaytaman thus   go.down-1plBAS.P
     'This is how we, including me, Lumawandəm and Məkaytaman, went downriver'

The cover pronoun can be omitted if recoverable from the context. In 6.34, it is clear from the dual agreement on the verb that Lumawandəm, the *luluai* ('chief') of the Avatip village, did not remain on his own. The context makes it clear that Lumawandəm remained there with the whole village. Only one participant is listed.

6.34 aw a   [Lumawadəm] kwa-br̩ə-l
     then then Lumawandəm stayed-3dusUBJ.P-3fem.sgBAS.P
     'Then Lumawandəm and (the village) stayed'

Alternatively, both, or all, participants can be listed, as in 6.35. The dual agreement shows that we are going to complete the activity together. The pronoun *an* '1du' could be optionally inserted.

6.35 [wun Kerryanne] yapi-na-br̩an
     I   Kerryanne buy-ACT.FOC-1duBAS.VT
     'Kerryanne and I are doing the shopping'

In all such constructions, the personal pronoun precedes other participants (unlike, for instance, in formal English). A construction of this type implies equal participation of all players.

2. COMITATIVE-MARKED CONSTRUCTIONS are composed of a non-singular pronoun (dual or plural) followed by a noun marked with comitative. Number agreement on the verb shows how many participants are involved.

6.36 bər   abra   kəp-a:r   war-na-bər   [bər
     they.two DEM.DIST.REACT.TOP+du ground-LK+ALL go.up-ACT.FOC-3duBAS.VT they.two
     tapwuk-a-wa   yayib]
     rooster-LK-COM wallaby
     'The two went up to the ground (from the river), the two: wallaby with the rooster'

   The pronoun can be omitted: the person and the number of participants are retrievable from the agreement on the verb, as in 4.47 ('with Yuakalu we-two are same age'='Yuakalu and I are the same age'), and in 6.37.

6.37 gra-kə-dana-di   [də-kə   takwa-wa]
      cry-FUT-3plSUBJ.VT-3plBAS.VT 3masc.sg-OBL+3fem.sg woman+LK-COM
      'They all cried, (them) including his wife'

In constructions like this, comitative can be replaced by the postposition *wukən* 'together' (see §4.5.2), as in 4.68 ('we two with Aulapan' meaning 'Aulapan and myself') and 6.38. The NP consisting of a head noun+postposition can be moved before the pronoun, as in the second line:

6.38 aw   [bər   Tubəki wukən] ata   kwa-yi-kwa-bər   [roselyn wukən
      then they.two Tubəki together then stay-go-HAB-3duBAS.P Roslyn   together
      bər]   ata   kwa-yi-kwa-bər   [dey amæy   asa:y]   ka:p   ata
      they.two then stay-go-HAB-3duBAS.P they mother father by.themselves then
      kwa-yi-kwa-di
      stay-go-HAB-3plBAS.P
      'The two of them, (my mother) and Tubəki (Roslyn) stayed (back in the village), the two (including Roslyn) stayed, them all including my father and mother stayed by themselves'

Such freedom is not allowed in comitative constructions. The use of the postposition *wukən* as a substitute for comitative is a characteristic feature of innovative speakers who frequently code-switch with Tok Pisin (also see 4.73).

An alternative construction involves the adverb *nakamib* 'together', as shown in 6.39. The verbal agreement shows that two people are involved:

6.39 [Sasa nakamib] su   ku-su-jəbər
      Sasha together   shoe put-UP-CUST
      'They two (including Sasha) always wear shoes'

Argument elaboration constructions of the first type imply equal participation of all the players. The comitative-marked participant in argument elaboration constructions with the comitative is somewhat backgrounded. So, in 6.36 the rooster is less focused than the wallaby (whose fate is the topic of the stretch of discourse). In 6.37, 'his wife' is just one additional participant. In 6.38, Tubəki, a younger sister, is obviously less important than mother and father—the topic of the stretch of text. And 6.39 was an ironic comment about baby Jemima trying to wear her new shoes all the time, and not about Sasha.

However, the two argument elaboration constructions are very close in meaning, to the extent that the two can follow each other in discourse. This is the case in 6.38: the speaker starts with a comitative-marked argument elaboration construction, and then uses the juxtaposed argument elaboration structure. The situation described is the same. Argument elaboration constructions can be considered a subtype of noun coordination—see §20.1.1.

6.2.4 Markedness in the number system

Dual and plural are quite transparent in their semantics. Plural agreement always signals a plural referent, and dual agreement indicates that there are just two participants. There is just one exception. A noun phrase with the numeral *mugul* 'three; few' can trigger dual agreement, if the numeral *mugul* means 'few (two or three)', as in 6.40. The same principles apply, no matter whether the head noun has an animate referent or not.

6.40 kə-<u>bər</u>   laulap   mugul   kə-di
     DEM.PROX-DU banana three/few eat-3plBAS.P
     'After they have eaten a few (two or three) bananas . . . '

If a noun phrase with *mugul* refers to exactly three entities, the agreement is plural: 6.41 is about having exactly three classificatory mothers.

6.41 kə-<u>di</u>   amæy   mugul tə-da-l-a
     FEM.PROX-PL mother three   have-3plSUBJ.P-3fem.sgBAS.P-3fem.sgNOM
     'This is how they had these three mothers'

Dual agreement with *mugul* in the meaning of 'a few' suggests that, at an earlier stage, the dual number in Manambu could have had the meaning of 'paucal', referring not necessarily exactly to two entities, but rather to a small number of entities. The forms and semantics of dual agreement in Ndu languages are considered in Aikhenvald (forthcoming b).

Plural agreement is used in a variety of further contexts. Plural agreement is the unmarked choice in content questions if the speaker has no idea about the sex or the quantity of people they are asking about, as in 6.42.

6.42 sə   kulapu-na-<u>di</u>
     who clean-ACT.FOC-3plBAS.VT
     'Who cleaned (the path)?'

Along similar lines, the question in 6.43 contains a plural form of 'child', and yet the answer could be in the singular—that is, the plural is used as a kind of cover term for all numbers. This choice may also have to do with the semantics of the interrogative quantifier *kas* which implies a non-singular quantity.

6.43 də-kə-m   ñan-ugw kas?
     he-OBL-LOC child-PL how.many/much
     'How many children does he have?'

A final piece of evidence in favour of plural being less marked functionally than dual comes from mistakes and slips of the tongue. It is not infrequent for any speaker to mistake dual participants for plural. In 6.44, the speaker is talking about two people. She first uses dual, and then refers to them with plural; later on she corrects herself again.

6.44 abra   waku-<u>bər</u>,   waku-di   waku-<u>bər</u>
     DEM.DIST.REACT.TOP+du go.out-3duBAS.P go.out-3plBAS.P go.out-3duBAS.P
     'The two went out, (many) went out, two went out'

Mistakes like this are always 'in favour' of plural. It is as yet too early to say that the dual is on its way out. However, these examples may indicate that within non-singular numbers, plural is less functionally marked than the dual.

7

Case Marking

7.1 FORMATION OF CASES: AN OVERVIEW

Manambu has a system of nine case forms. One can distinguish nine cases each corresponding to a form. By their functions and meanings, one can distinguish eighteen cases. At the end of this chapter, we argue for an intermediate solution.

Core cases mark grammatical relations on a basic object–non-object principle (see §3.2). Table 3.5 summarizes the principles of dependent marking on nouns, and how these correlate with the cross-referencing of arguments on verbs as heads of predicates. All cases, except for the comitative, can only be marked once per NP. Case markers occur on the head of an NP (which is, in most instances, also the last word in the NP; the few exceptions include comitative, and NPs with cardinal numbers, such as 'three' in 7.50, and quantifiers: see §§10.5–6; §20.1.1). Case-marked forms, and Ø-marked nouns, are underlined throughout this chapter. Some cases can occur on verb stems and forms: see §7.11.

Case markers attach to a linker whose choice depends on the subclass of nouns (§4.1.1). The sequence of linker -a and the V in accusative-locative, dative, and allative-instrumental cases results in a long vowel a:. If the linker is ə, the V of the case marker disappears. Third person singular and dual pronouns and the interrogative sə 'who' take the oblique marker -kə- as a linker (homophonous with the possessive marker -kə- discussed in §8.2).

7.2 FUNCTIONS OF A NOUN UNMARKED FOR CASE

A noun unmarked for case appears as (A) A/S and copula subject, (B) copula complement, (C) the second argument of verbs of 'turning into'; (D) object; (E) manner; (F) locations; (G) purpose; (H) instrument; and also (I) nominal component of complex verbs. Topics and afterthoughts also appear unmarked, no matter what function they are in.

A. Subjects (A/S and copula subjects) do not receive any formal marking, as shown in 4.16–17, 4.35–6, and 7.1 below. All subjects are cross-referenced on the verb (see §3.1). Their subject properties (including behaviour in clause chaining) are summarized in §20.1.4.

B. Copula complements are also formally unmarked (see §7.9, for one exception); unlike other non-subject arguments, they are never cross-referenced on the verb, as shown in 3.8–9 and 7.1 (also see discussion of copula verbs under B in §4.2.2).

7.1 [brə-kə-bər amæy asa:y kiya-brə-k] kwakuli_CC ya-n tə-bər
3du-POSS-3du mother father die-3du-COMPL.DS orphan come-SEQ stay-3duBAS.VT
'After their mother and father died, the two came to be orphans'

C. The second argument of the verbs of change of state and turning into is formally unmarked and not cross-referenced on the verb, as illustrated in 3.10, 7.2, and 15.116.

7.2 <u>ta:kw</u>₂nd.argument sawəl-na   ya
     woman   be.transformed-ACT.FOC+3fem.sgBAS.VT   EMPH
     '(The mango) turned into a woman'

These verbs are similar to copula verbs in that their second argument (which denotes a kind) is obligatory and cannot be cross-referenced on the verb itself.

D. An object can be formally unmarked if it is indefinite, non-referential, or generic, as in 3.14, 4.31–2, and 7.3, or its complete involvement in the activity is not in focus, as in 4.29–30 and 4.34–6. A topical object can be cross-referenced in the second position (see §3.1).

7.3 wun <u>wali-kamna:gw</u>   akəs   kə-kwa-na-wun
     I   white.people-food NEG.HAB eat-HAB-ACT.FOC-1sgBAS.VT
     'I never eat white people's food'

In idiomatic expressions the object is always unmarked, as in T1.4 and 7.16, *bap və-* 'menstruate', literally 'see moon'. The object of the verb *nay-* 'play' is always unmarked, e.g. *politics nay-* 'play politics', *təpətəpəka:u nay-* (diving play) 'play at diving'; it cannot be cross-referenced.

If the focus is on the activity (and this is marked with action focus *-na-*), the object is likely to be unmarked:

7.4 [wun-a-di *kaukau*]   bə   luku kur-na-di
     I-LK-pl   sweet.potato already steal get-ACT.FOC-3plBAS.VT
     'They already stole my sweet potatoes'

This is in contrast to 3.15 and 7.17 where the case-marked referents are completely involved in the activity (see §7.3). Personal pronouns and proper names are usually case marked, unless the grammatical relations are clear from the context. An example like 7.5 or 10.64 is unusual (it was a cry of surprise by Gemaj when she realized I was carrying water into the house):

7.5 wun <u>ñən</u> ma: və
     I   you NEG see+NEG
     'I didn't see you!'

E. A noun referring to the manner in which an action is performed appears unmarked for case, as in 7.6. The manner is the topic, and so it is cross-referenced on the verb in the second cross-referencing position. Manner is typically feminine (see §5.2.1).

7.6 <u>sad-ə-sa:d</u>   kur-lə-l
     way-LK-way   got-3fem.sgSUBJ.P-3fem.sgBAS.P
     'It was in a variety of ways that she (cassowary) got him (the human child)'

In 7.7, the crocodile surfaces in different form, disguised as different beings. These forms are what this stretch of the text is about, which explains the feminine cross-referencing on the verb.

7.7 [kwasa-də   <u>ñan</u> <u>mu</u>]   ata   <u>gwa:s</u> <u>karu</u>   <u>ba:u</u>
     small-masc.sg child crocodile then turtle mudgroper scaly.mudgroper
     adawur   war-də-l
     DEM.DIST+masc.sg+UP come.up-3masc.sgSUBJ.P-3fem.sgBAS.P
     'Having come up as a fish, he came up as a baby crocodile, in the form of a turtle, a small fish, a big fish, in these forms he came up'

The semantics of the 'manner' oblique is reminiscent of the second argument of verbs with the meaning 'turn into' (under C above). While the second argument of such verbs is obligatory (that is, a sentence like 7.2 would be ungrammatical without it), form and manner in 7.6–7 are optional.

F. Nouns referring to location, direction, and provenance can occur unmarked for case. This is typical for inherently locational nouns and place names (see §4.1.2), as in 4.1, 7.8, and 13.34, or if the direction is obvious, as in 4.56.

7.8 [atabək-ə   ta:kw] [kə-də   təp]   ma: ku
    that+like-LK woman DEM.PROX-masc.sg village NEG stay:NEG
    'There are no women like this (in) this village'

A noun which is not inherently locational can occur without locative marking if it obviously refers to a location, as in 7.9 ('nose' of a canoe):

7.9 tapwuk <u>ta:m</u> yayib   malə-m   abra
    rooster nose tree.kangaroo stern+LK-LOC DEM.DIST.REACT.TOP+du
    yi-na-bər
    go-ACT.FOC-3duBAS.VT
    'The rooster on the nose (of the canoe), the tree kangaroo on the stern, the two went'

An unmarked noun can refer to direction, as in 7.10, and to provenance 'from', as in 7.11, if these meanings are recoverable from the context and the verbs have directional semantics.

7.10 [nəkə-də   <u>tama:y</u> nak] ada
     other-masc.sg point   one DEM.DIST.REACT.TOP.masc.sg
     wula-na-d
     come-ACT.FOC-3masc.sgBAS.VT
     '(Onto) another point, one (more bandicoot) comes in'

7.11 alək   <u>wi</u>   waku-dian
     this.is.why house go.out-1plBAS.VT
     'This is why we went out (of) the house'

Inherently temporal nouns often occur unmarked, as in 4.3.

G. Nouns expressing purpose can be unmarked if the purpose meaning is clear from the context, as in 7.12a; in this cases dative case would be expected, as in 7.12b (see §7.4).

7.12a <u>na:gw</u> ma: yə
     sago   NEG go:NEG
     'One didn't go for sago' (during the Japanese occupation)

7.12b nagwə-k   yi-kwa-na-di
     sago+LK-DAT go-HAB-ACT.FOC-3plBAS.VT
     'They used to go for sago'

Nominalizations in *-ka:u* occur unmarked (see §9.1.2):

7.13 <u>kakəl-ka:u</u> yi-k-na-bər
     surpass-NOM go-FUT-ACT.FOC-3duBAS.VT
     'They two were about to go for races'

H. Instruments can occur unmarked if the instrumental meaning is clear from the context, as in 7.14:

7.14 <u>ta:b</u> kaykətə-n
hand hold/lean-SEQ
'Holding (him with) a hand'

A formally unmarked noun can be used to describe a property of an inanimate entity, as in 17.63–4, e.g. *day yi vər-k-na* (mouth fire burn-FUT-ACT.FOC+3fem.sgBAS.VT) 'Mouth will burn' (lit. burn in terms of fire) (if you eat hot pepper).

Functions E–H correspond to oblique arguments, none of which is required by the verb's argument structure.

I. Nominal components of complex verbs are always unmarked and never cross-referenced on the verb. As shown in §4.1.2, these nominal components are often body parts, e.g. *səp* 'skin' in *səp ji-* and *səp sakwi-* both meaning 'be fed up', or states, e.g. *ka:m* 'hunger', as in *ka:m yas-* 'feel hunger', and *sə* 'sleep' as in *sə kwa-* 'be asleep' and *sə yasa-* 'feel sleepy'. Other nouns include *gu* 'water' in *gu yaku-* (water wash) 'bathe; wash oneself', *sua:l* 'lie, story' in *sua:l kur-* (lie do) and *sua:l taka-* (lie put) 'tell a lie', and *yanu* 'magic' in *yanu bla-* (magic talk) 'cast a magic spell'. (Similar constructions, e.g. *gu ya:ku-* 'wash', are attested in Iatmul: Gerd Jendraschek, p.c.)

The nominal component cannot be cross-referenced on the verb. Unlike any other argument, it cannot be questioned, focused, or negated separately. One cannot ask 'what is she putting', and receive a reply 'a lie'; one cannot say 'it is a lie that she is putting'. This is because it is not part of the verb's argument structure. Further analysis of complex verbs is in §17.3.

Topics and afterthoughts occur unmarked, no matter what functions they are in. In 4.35, 'child' is an afterthought, and is separated from the rest of the clause with a pause. Case markers are mutually exclusive with derivational suffixes *-dəka* 'only', *-rəb* 'fully', *-pək* 'like', and *-kərəb* 'together', as in 10.147. (See §9.2.)

The functions and meanings of formally unmarked nouns in Manambu are summarized in Table 7.1. Zero-marked nouns vary in terms of their functions discussed above and (1) how obligatory they are; (2) whether they can or cannot be cross-referenced on the verb; (3) whether they can alternate with a case-marked noun; and (4) whether they can be replaced with an unmarked personal pronoun.

We conclude that zero-case marking in Manambu has nine different meanings and functions corresponding to the contexts A–I outlined here. Nouns in contexts A–E can be considered zero marked for case since zero is in paradigmatic contrast to segmental marking. In contrast, nouns in contexts F–H are better considered as formally unmarked since there is an underlying case form which can be omitted thus producing a surface zero (location can be marked with locative case, purpose with dative, and instrument with allative-instrumental). Not all case markers can be omitted: there are no unmarked comitatives, transportatives, or substitutives. Components of complex verbs are not special grammatical relations.

7.3 ACCUSATIVE-LOCATIVE CASE

The accusative-locative case has two major functions discussed below.

A. DIRECT OBJECTS AND RECIPIENTS are marked with the accusative-locative case under the following conditions.

TABLE 7.1 Polysemy of zero case marking on nouns

FUNCTION	1. OBLIGATORY	2. CROSS-REFERENCING ON THE VERB	3. ALTERNATION WITH A CASE-MARKED FORM	4. SUBSTITUTION WITH UNMARKED PRONOUN	EXAMPLES
A. A/S; CS	yes	obligatory (§3.1)	no	possible	7.1, 4.16–17
B. Copula complement	yes	no	no	possible	7.1, 3.8–9
C. Second argument of 'turn into'	yes	no	no	rare	7.2, 3.10
D. Object	yes	possible (§3.1)	yes	possible	7.3, 3.14, 4.31–2
E. Manner	no	possible (§3.1)	no	no	7.6–7
F. Location	no	possible (§3.1)	yes	no	7.8–11, 4.1
G. Purpose	no	possible (§3.1)	yes	no	7.12a, 7.13
H. Instrument	no	possible (§3.1)	yes	no	7.14
I. Component of complex verb	yes	no	no	no	4.45–6

(i) If a direct object is inherently definite and referential, it is likely to be case marked. Personal pronouns are typically case marked, as shown in 7.15 (7.5 is highly unusual).

7.15 <u>wun-a:m</u>   mən   karda   ma: ta:y
I-LK+ACC/LOC you:masc bring+DOWN NEG first
'You will not carry me down first'

(ii) If the direct object is completely involved in the action, or completely affected by it, it is likely to be case marked. In 3.15 and T1.8, the man is planning to exterminate the moon, that is, to fully kill her. The moon is marked with the accusative-locative. In contrast, 'moon' in the object function in an idiomatic expression, as in 7.16, is unmarked.

7.16 yala-wa   tə-ta:y   akəs   <u>bap</u>   və-kwa-na-di
belly+LK-COM stand-COTEMP NEG.HAB moon see-HAB-ACT.FOC-3plBAS.VT
'When one is pregnant (lit. with a belly) one does not menstruate (that is, see the moon)'

In 7.17, the object is completely involved: the spirit is known to eat children up completely:

7.17 dakul wapi <u>du-a-ñanugw-a:m</u>   kə-da:-di
spirit bird man-LK-children-LK+ACC/LOC eat-3plSUBJ.P-3plBAS.P
'The spirit birds ate up male children'

In all these instances the accusative-locative case is in paradigmatic opposition with a zero-marked object. We now consider verbs which allow for a choice between accusative-locative, dative, and zero marking for their second argument.

(iii) The accusative-locative case with perception 'see' and 'hear' (see §21.1.2) and 'find, look for' indicates telic action whose result was achieved. In 7.18, the verb *kwakə-* with an accusative-marked object means 'find'.

7.18 [wula-l-a]   [a   <u>takwa:m</u>]
come.in-3fem.sgBAS.P-3fem.sgNOM DEM.DIST+fem.sg woman+LK+ACC/LOC
kwakə-ku
look.for/find-COMPL.SS
'It is that she came in, after having found that woman'

This verb with an unmarked object refers to atelic action, as in 7.19. Here it means 'look for'.

7.19 [ñanugw <u>amæy</u>] kwakə-ya-bana
children mother look.for-come-1plSUBJ.VT+3fem.sgBAS.VT
'We are looking and looking for the children's mother'

This same verb with an object marked by dative case has a frustrative overtone of 'looking for and not finding', as in 7.20:

7.20 [a-də   <u>kiyak</u>]   kwakə-n   tə-la
DEM.DIST-masc.sg key+LK+DAT look.for-SEQ stay-3fem.sgSUBJ.VT+3fem.sgBAS.VT
'She is constantly looking for the key (without finding it)'

Verbs of perception, *və* 'see, look' and *wukə-* 'hear, listen', show comparable alternations. A generic object of 'see' is unmarked, as in 7.16. Its O is marked with dative, if the object has not been seen completely, or intentionally looked at. If the object is fully seen and the action is volitional and/or telic (meaning 'look', or 'see well'), the object is marked with accusative-locative—see 4.12. In 7.21 the object is definite and completely seen and the action is volitional:

7.21 [[a   wəpak-a:m]   və-ku]   a-də
     DEM.DIST+fem.sg type.of.tree-LK+ACC/LOC see-COMPL.SS DEM.DIST-masc.sg
     yabəm   yi-tukwa
     road+LK+LOC   go-PROH.GEN
     'Having seen the tree (whose leaf I put on the ground), do not go on that road'

In the non-volitional meaning 'see, notice', and 'look around for', the object is marked with dative, as in 7.22 (also see 7.28). In 7.22 the head of the village is the topic, and this is why he is cross-referenced on the verb:

7.22 [ta:y waku-də   yibun-miya:k]   ata   və-brə-d
     first go.out-3masc.sgVT stick-tree+LK+DAT   then see-3dusUBJ.P-3masc.sgBAS.P
     'Then the two looked around for the number one chief (of the village)'

This meaning of the dative case is consistent with its overtone of future projection: see §13.7. As shown in §21.1.2, verbs *və-* 'see, look, try, experience' and *wukə-* 'hear, listen, miss, feel sorry, obey' are polysemous. Body parts *məl* 'eye' and *wa:n* 'ear' are used to differentiate their meanings to do with perception: *məl və-* can only mean 'see, look', and *wa:n wukə-* means 'hear, listen'. The body parts cannot be cross-referenced on the verb; and a limited number of constituents can intervene between the body part and the perception verb. The verbs remain transitive—that is, they can take an object (either case marked or not). These collocations are similar to complex verbs, and the zero-marked body parts behave like nominal components in complex verbs (see under I in §7.2). In its meaning of 'experience', the verb *və-* takes an unmarked object, as in 7.23 and 21.7.

7.23 mən   bə   wasa-yuwi   və-dəmən   wasa-yuwi   ma:
     you.masc.sg already cheek+LK-hair see-2masc.sgBAS.VT cheek+LK-hair NEG
     və
     see+NEG
     'Did you shave yet (have a beard) or did you not shave (when you met Dangwan)?'

The verb *wukə-* with the dative object means 'listen to, try to hear', as in T3.27–8 ('the snake sat listening for man's name' (trying to hear it)). This verb with an object in the accusative-locative may mean 'listen to, obey':

7.24 [atabək-ə   japə-m]   wukə-tukwa
     like.this-LK thing+LK-ACC/LOC listen-PROH.GEN
     'Do not listen to/obey things like this'

Dative and accusative-locative alternations are also attested with verbs of affect, such as verb *vya-* 'hit, kill'. With an accusative-locative object it implies strong hitting and especially killing (that is, hitting the victim until they die, as in 3.15 and T1.8). In 7.25, the mother asks the child if anyone has attempted to hit her just slightly, and so the object is in dative case. The mother knows that no one has hit the child, and the child is crying for no reason at all.

7.25 sə-kə-lal   ñən-a:k   vya-na
     who-OBL-fem.sg+3fem.sgNOM you.fem.sg-LK+DAT hit-ACT.FOC+3fem.sgBAS.VT
     'Who is it who hit at you?'

(iv) The accusative-locative case can mark a number of other arguments, including the third
     argument of ditransitive verbs if it is topical and includes all the recipients, as in 7.26;
     or if the beneficiary or maleficiary is fully affected, as in 7.34 ('for us' in first line).

7.26 Gala <u>Waskuka:m</u>   ta:kw kra-di
     Gala Washkuk+LK+ACC/LOC wife marry-3plBAS.P
     'Gala married Washkuk (Kwoma) women' (lit. Gala married women from/of Washkuk)

If the 'gift' is permanent possession, the recipient is marked with accusative-locative case. The alternative is dative case (which is typically used to mark recipients: see §7.4, and 7.36). Example 7.27 is a way of referring to a man's father by birth:

7.27 <u>wun-a:m</u> wus kui-də   asa:y
     I-LK+LOC penis give.to.third.p-3masc.sgBAS.VT father
     'the father who gave me penis' (lit. penis on me)

This is similar to 7.30 and T1.32 (see below).

In summary: the accusative-locative case marking on NPs indicates complete involvement and/or complete affectedness of a second or third argument in the action. The argument is most often the object, but can also be a recipient or a possessor. The use of this case correlates with definiteness and animacy, and also focuses on the completion and telicity of the action and its result (rather than the action itself).

B. OBLIQUES IN THE FUNCTION OF LOCATION AND DIRECTION are marked with the locative case, as shown in 7.21, 7.28, and 7.32 (see §7.2 on unmarked location).

7.28 ga:n [də adəda   <u>gu-a:m</u>   tə-na-də
     night he DEM.DIST+masc.sg+DOWN water-LK+LOC stay-ACT.FOC-3masc.sgBAS.VT
     du] wujəmowr [[a-də   val-a:k]   və-ku]   ata
     man water.spirit DEM.DIST-masc.sg canoe-LK+DAT see-COMPL.SS then
     warə-d
     come.up-3masc.sgBAS.VT
     'At night the man, the water spirit who lives in water, having noticed the canoe, came up'

Locative is also used in constructions of provenance, 'from'; these are biclausal structures, as in 7.29. Note that while locative case marks location and allative case (§7.5) marks direction, there is no special ablative case to express provenance. In each of its purely locative uses including this one, the -*Vm* case can be replaced with the terminative case if the exact point in time or space is implied (see §7.6).

7.29 [akəm   tə-ku]   ya-na-d
     where+LOC stay-COMPL.SS come-ACT.FOC-3masc.sgBAS.VT
     'Where is he coming from?' (lit. 'Where having stayed he come?')

The locative case is used with an inherently temporal constituent, if the whole duration of time is in focus, or an exact point in time referred to, as in 4.4.

The locative case is also used to mark complete lack of possession, as in 7.30, or complete involvement, as in 7.34 ('for us'). The possessor completely affected by the 'possession' of, say, a sickness, as in T1.32, is also marked with locative.

7.30 <u>wun-a:m</u> ma:s   ma: ku
     I-LK+LOC betelnut NEG stay:NEG
     'I have no betelnut'

The locative contrasts with the allative whose main meaning is 'direction towards' (see 7.49 in §7.5). However, the difference goes beyond that. The allative case indicates direction which has not yet been reached, as in 7.31.

7.31 ada   war-na-d   də-kə-r
      DEM.DIST.REACT.TOP.masc.sg go.up-ACT.FOC-3masc.sgBAS.VT he-OBL-ALL
      'Here he is climbing onto it (and never got there)'

In contrast, if the action is completed and the destination reached, the locative case is used:

7.32 war-də-l   [a   məd   lə-kə
      go.up-3masc.sgSUBJ.P-3fem.sgBAS.VT DEM.DIST+fem.sg cassowary she-OBL+fem.sg
      məñ-a:m]
      breast-LK+LOC
      'He (the man's head) went up onto the cassowary's breast (and stayed there)'

Using the locative rather than the allative case implies complete coverage of the destination. In 7.33, hot water was poured all over the woman's skin, which is marked with locative. A similar example is in 7.41 ('jump over you-locative').

7.33 adika   [lə-kə   səp-a:m]
      DEM.DIST.REACT.TOP+pl she-OBL+fem.sg skin-LK+LOC
      kaykwata-taka-lə-di
      pour-put-3fem.sgSUBJ.P-3plBAS.VT .
      'She poured (quantities of hot water) all over her body'

A locative-marked NP, 'bad way', is used in the predicate slot, in a 'completive' meaning of 'it will be absolutely bad for us'.

7.34 ñəd-ə-ñəd-ər   yi-kə-kə-bana   ma: ñan-a:m
      middle-LK-middle-LK+ALL go-FUT-FUT-1plSUBJ.VT+3fem.sgBAS.VT no we-LK+LOC
      kuprap-ə sad ata   kuprap-ə sadəm
      bad-LK   way then bad-LK   way+LK+LOC
      'If we get into the middle (of the rainbow), then it will be bad for us, it will be absolutely bad (for us)'

Summing up: the accusative-locative case in Manambu can mark (i) obligatory arguments as well as (ii) obliques. In (i), it is in opposition to zero-marked nouns and to nouns marked with dative case. In (ii), it is in opposition to allative and to terminative cases. What the two uses have in common is the meaning of complete involvement of a non-subject constituent (object, recipient, possessor, location, or direction) and the focus on result. This agrees with the way in which the same marker is used on verbs. We return to this in §7.11.

7.4 DATIVE-AVERSIVE CASE

The dative case, marked with -*Vk*, has a wide variety of functions covering (A) addressee and beneficiary; (B) purpose and destination; (C) cause and reason; (D) 'lest, for fear of'; and (E) bodily states. We saw in §7.3 (7.20, 7.22, 7.25, and also T3.28) that dative can mark the second argument of a number of verbs if the argument is not completely affected or the action is atelic. Dative obligatorily marks the second argument of a number of verbs discussed under (F) below.

The dative case is highly polysemous. However, to simply say that the dative case always marks an object which is not primarily affected would be a simplification. An argument or an oblique marked with the dative case can be cross-referenced on the verb. The aversive meaning of -*Vk* can be easily shown to 'derive' from a more general meaning of the dative as a marker of second argument of verbs to do with emotions, such as fear. If a dative-marked noun is used in isolation, it may acquire aversive reading depending on its semantics. The dative marker could be cognate to the future and purposive markers -(*V*)*k*——we return to this in §7.11.

A. ADDRESSEE, OR BENEFICIARY OF DITRANSITIVE VERBS, is marked with dative, as shown in 7.35–6. Also see examples of 'give' in §4.2.2.

7.35 də [də-kə   takwa:k]   ata wa-də-l
     he he-POSS+fem.sg woman+LK+DAT here say-3masc.sgSUBJ.P-3fem.sgBAS.P
     'He spoke like this to his woman'

In 7.36, the topical addressee (not the object 'shown') is cross-referenced on the verb, since the story is about the man.

7.36 ata də-kə-k   nəkə   yawi səmaka-dana-d
     then he-OBL-DAT other+fem.sg work show-3plSUBJ.VT-3masc.sgBAS.VT
     'Then they showed him another work'

Dative case marks beneficiary—that is, person for whom the action is being done:

7.37 də-kə-də   yanu ada   bla-də-di
     he-OBL-masc.sg magic DEM.DIST.REACT.TOP+masc.sg speak-3masc.sgSUBJ.P-3plBAS.VT
     [a-də   ñənək]
     DEM.DIST-masc.sg child+LK+DAT
     'Then he performed his magic for that child'

B. PURPOSE AND DESTINATION marked with dative case are illustrated in 7.38–9. Example 4.2 illustrates the dative case on a temporal noun ('for tomorrow').

7.38 wun-aba:b yawi:k   yi-na-dəwun
     I-TOO   work+DAT   go-ACT.FOC-1masc.sgBAS.VT
     'I too am going to work'

7.39 daya-di   sər   yi-kə-dana-di   [ñan də-kə
     they-3plNOM tomorrow go-FUT-3plSUBJ.VT-3plBAS.VT child he-OBL+fem.sg
     bagwə-k]
     ceremony+LK-DAT
     'Tomorrow it is them who will go up for the ceremony for (the death of) the child'

   When I asked why Avatip women were so keen on smoking large quantities of fish, the answer was *sana:k* (money+LK+DAT) 'for money'. The purpose of hunting or fishing is usually marked with dative:

7.40 kədika   væki-di   [kə-də   mu-a:k]
     DEM.PROX.REACT.TOP+pl go.across-3plBAS.P/VT DEM.PROX-masc.sg crocodile-LK+DAT
     'These (people) went across for this crocodile (to fetch the trapped crocodile)'

A nominal component of a complex verb 'do cooking' can be marked with dative, as in 17.44. This is the only case this form can take.

C. CAUSE AND REASON are also marked with dative. A fight between two women broke out in front of our house in Avatip. I asked a young boy what was happening. His short answer was *du-a:k* (man-LK+DAT), meaning 'because of a man (they are fighting)'.

'Purpose' and 'reason' are often hard to distinguish. The form *agw-a japə-k* in 7.41 means both 'for what purpose' and 'why, for what reason'. An alternative is *agw-a:k* (which-LK+DAT) 'why, what for'—see §10.4.

7.41 bər   ñən-a:m   agw-a-japə-k   sarə-bər-kək
     3du you.fem-LK+LOC   which-LK-thing+LK-DAT   jump-3du-PURP.DS
     'Why/what for would they two be jumping over you?'

Along similar lines, 7.42 can be interpreted as 'crying because of his mother (since she hit him)', or 'about his mother (because he misses her)', or 'for his mother (for her to come)'.

7.42 a-də   kwasa-də   ñan-a:b   ata   gra-d   [də-kə
     DEM.DIST-masc.sg small-masc.sg   child-too   then cry-3masc.sgBAS.P   he-OBL+fem.sg
     amæyik]
     mother+LK+DAT
     'That small child too cried for his mother'

D. AVERSIVE 'LEST, FOR FEAR OF' is another meaning of the dative case:

7.43 a-rabə-tak   waw-a:k
     IMPV-cover-put.down   fly-LK+DAT
     'Cover yourself for fear of flies'

Women worried about me standing underneath a coconut palm would shout: *təp-a:k*! (coconut-LK+DAT) 'for fear of coconut; beware of coconut!' When walking on a path for the first time, I was warned: *wukəl, diyak* (careful, shit+LK+DAT) 'be careful, (beware) of (dog's) shit!' We will see, in F that the second argument of the verb *yaga-* 'be afraid of' takes dative case.

E. BODILY STATES AND DESIRES are marked with dative case. We saw in §4.2.2 that the verb *tə-* preceded by a body part or a body state noun in dative case refers to something wrong with this particular body part, e.g. *aba:k tə-* (head+LK+DAT be, stand, have) means 'be not quite right in one's head'; and *kamək tə-* 'be hungry', as in 7.44. The verb *kwa-* 'stay' is used in a similar way, as in 7.75.

7.44 [kamək   tə-kə-dana]   agw-a:r
     hunger+LK+DAT   stand-FUT-3plSUBJ.VT+3fem.sgBAS.VT   which/what-LK+INSTR
     kə-kə-dana-di
     eat-FUT-3plSUBJ.VT-3plBAS.VT
     'When they are hungry, how will they eat (sago)?'

By itself, *kamək* (for hunger), is easily understood as '(he/she/they) is/are hungry'. The verb 'say' accompanied by a noun with an inanimate referent in dative case is interpreted as 'wanting' (see §19.5, on speech reports), or intention, as in 7.45a.

7.45a [amæy wun gu-a:k]   wa-də-k
      mother I   water-LK+DAT say-3masc.sg-COMPL.SS
      'After he said: "Mother, I am thirsty" . . .' (lit. I for water)

A headless possessive in dative case can have a similar meaning. A little boy desperately wanted to get hold of his brother's bow and arrow. This was phrased as:

7.45b [wun-a-brək] wa:d
      I-LK-du+DAT   say+3masc.sgBAS.P
      'He said he wanted the two of mine' (lit. he said, for the two of mine, i.e. bow and arrow)

F. DATIVE MARKING OF THE SECOND ARGUMENT is a feature of a number of verbs of emotions, the verbs *yaga-* 'fear', *bas sə-* 'ask', *kapə-* 'wait', *sa:l yi-* 'be short of something', *warsama-* 'be cross at someone/something', *suguya-* 'help', *kaləpa-* 'teach', and a few others:

7.46 də-kə-k   kapə-n   kwa-na-wun
     he-OBL-DAT wait-SEQ stay-ACT.FOC-1fem.sgBAS.VT
     'I am waiting for him'

The object of *wukə-* 'hear, worry about' in the meaning of 'worry about, be sad about' is marked with dative case—see 4.11. The objects of verbs of liking—including *məyakw kwa-* 'like' and its equivalent, a Tok Pisin borrowing *laiki-* (in 7.47b), a complex verb *mawul war-* (inside go.up-) in 7.47c, and *mawul kur-* (inside get) in 7.71—are marked with dative.

The polyfunctional verb *yasa-/yasə-* 'be of physical state' (see Table 4.1) can occasionally occur with its copula complement in dative case. 7.47a–c are used as synonyms:

7.47a agw-a   kamnagwə-k   yasa-na-dəmən
      which-LK food+LK-DAT be.of.physical.state-ACT.FOC-2masc.sgBAS.VT
      'What food would you like?'

7.47b agw-a   kamnagwə-k   laiki-na-dəmən
      which-LK food+LK-DAT like-ACT.FOC-2masc.sgBAS.VT
      'What food would you like?'

7.47c agw-a   kamnagwə-k   mawul war-na-dəmən
      which-LK food+LK-DAT inside   go.up-ACT.FOC-2masc.sgBAS.VT
      'What food would you like?'

The dative case also marks theme for verbs of speech—that is, what the talk is about, as in 7.48.

7.48 mən-a:k   təp-a   du   wa-dana-dəmən
     you.masc-LK+DAT village-LK man say-3plSUBJ.VT-2masc.sgBAS.VT
     'Village people talk about you'

The dative case marker -*Vk* occurs on a few adverbs (see §4.4). The etymologically dative form of the distal demonstrative *alal*, *alək*, means 'this is why, for this reason'. We will see in §18.7 that this form has grammaticalized as a causal marker -*lək* 'because of' on the verb.

7.5 ALLATIVE AND INSTRUMENTAL CASES

The same form, -*Vr*, has two different meanings and functions—allative ('towards') and instrumental.[1] In 7.49 'direction' of motion marked by allative is contrasted to location marked by locative.

7.49 [makaw   samasa:m ar-a:m   tə-na-di]   [an   ar-a:r
     telopia.fish many   lake-LK+LOC stay-ACT.FOC-3plBAS.VT 1du lake-LK+ALL
     yi-tək]
     go-1duIMPV
     'There are many telopia-fish in the lake. Let us two go to the lake'

We saw under B in §7.3 above that locative can also mark direction with an implication that the destination was fully reached, and also that the whole location was involved. Allative has no such implications (see 7.31, in contrast to 7.32, with a locative-marked constituent). Allative

---

[1] -*r* in the allative-instrumental is often subject to the process of rhotic dissimilation detailed in A1 in §2.6.

is used with directional nouns, such as *mapa-taba:r* (right-hand+LK+ALL) 'to the right', *aki-tabar* (left-hand+LK+ALL) 'to the left', and with demonstratives, e.g. *alə-da:r* (DEM.DIST.fem.sg-DOWN+ALL) 'that small (one) downwards'. It is very rarely used with animate nouns. Allative with time nouns refers to a future time span, as in 7.50:

7.50 [ña:r   mugul] kwa-ku   yi-k-na-bran
       day+LK+ALL three   stay-COMPL.SS go-FUT-ACT.FOC-1duBAS.VT
       'Having stayed for about three days, we will go away'

In its second meaning, the -*Vr* case is typically used with nouns with inanimate referents used as instruments, e.g. *mæn-ər* (foot-LK+INSTR) 'on foot', and:

7.51 də wa:j mij-a:r   vya-də-l
       he eel   fish.spear-LK+INSTR kill-3masc.sgSUBJ.P-3fem.sgBAS.P
       'He killed an eel with a spear'

The instrumental of *kudi* 'language' means 'in a language', as in 7.52.

7.52 [təp-a   kudi-r]   atəta wa-u
       village-LK language-INSTR how   say-1sgIMPV
       'How am I to say (this) in the village language?'

The -*Vr* case with non-locational inanimate nouns has a preferential instrumental reading: *sana:r* (money+LK+ALL) normally means 'with money' rather than 'towards money'. A few nouns allow for multiple interpretations. The word *kabak* has two meanings, 'stone' and 'lot of money'; the form *kabak-ər* can be understood either as 'towards a stone; into a stone'; 'with a stone', or 'with a lot of money' (but hardly as 'towards a lot of money').

This case is often used with locational nouns used as a means for reaching a destination:

7.53 asay-wa   da-lwun   Sambri-r   val-a:r
       father-COM go.down-1sgBAS.P Chambri-ALL/INSTR canoe-LK+INSTR
       'I went down with my father, towards the Chambri lakes, on a canoe'

The form *Sambrir* is ambiguous: it can mean 'via the Chambri lakes', or 'towards the Chambri lakes'. This indeterminacy can be resolved only by context, or with an appropriate question. We will see in §10.4 that question words distinguish allative (*akrəl* 'where to?') and instrumental (*akə-r* (what/where-INSTR) 'with what, which way?' and *agw-a:r* (which/what-LK+INSTR) 'with what thing, how?') (as in 7.44).

The instrumental case with means of transport is synonymous with the transportative cases (see §7.7), e.g. *val-a-r*, *val-a-sap*, *val-a-say* 'by canoe, by car'.

Synchronically speaking, allative and instrumental are better analysed as homonymous cases rather than two meanings of one, polysemous, case. We saw in §7.3 that locative and allative are in a paradigmatic opposition. In contrast, instrumental case is not in any paradigmatic opposition to other cases; it is almost synonymous with transportative cases when used on a small group of nouns describing means of locomotion or of reaching a destination. In addition, allative and instrumental meanings are marked differently in the interrogative system. The -*Vr* form occurs on verb roots with the meaning of manner (§7.11).

The instrumental-allative polysemy is uncommon cross-linguistically. It is attested in a couple of Australian languages (Dixon 2002a: 168). A formal connection between instrumental and allative is a feature of various languages of the Sepik area, including a number of Ndu languages and Kwoma (see Aikhenvald forthcoming b).

7.6 TERMINATIVE CASE

The terminative case, marked with -*Vb*, has the meaning 'exactly on the dot or reaching the point; to the brim'. In 7.54, a speaker was commenting on how small an Amazonian Indian was compared to me:

7.54 kələb   tə-na,   ñən-a:k
     DEM.PROX+fem.sg+TERM be/have-ACT.FOC+3fem.sgBAS.VT you.fem-LK+DAT
     sagwa:b   tə-na
     shoulder+LK+TERM be/have-ACT.FOC+3fem.sgBAS.VT
     'She is up to here, she is up to your shoulder'

Terminative case has similarities with the locative case, with a subsequent change in meaning: 7.55 is a variant of 7.29, but the meaning is 'where exactly?'[2]

7.55 [akəb   tə-ku]   ya-na-d
     where+TERM stay-COMPL.SS come-ACT.FOC-3masc.sgBAS.VT
     'Where exactly is he coming from?' (lit. 'Where exactly having stayed he come?')

Locative and terminative are contrasted in 7.56: the rooster is instructing the rock wallaby exactly what part of the canoe he wants to be on:

7.56 [mən   ya:n   maləm   ada],   [wun ya-n   tama:b
     you.masc come+SEQ steer+LK+LOC stay.IMPV I   come-SEQ nose+LK+TERM
     ta:u]
     stay+1sgIMPV
     'On the way there, you stay on the stern, let me stay exactly on the nose (of a canoe)'

The terminative case contrasts with the unmarked form of the noun in 7.57a and 7.57b. The verb 'reach' is transitive.

7.57a kwati ma: nəbay kakəl
      knee NEG yet   reach:NEG
      '(Water) has not reached the knees yet'

7.57b gu   kwatiyib   bu   kakəl-na
      water knee+LK+TERM already reach-ACT.FOC+3fem.sgBAS.VT
      'Water has already reached knees; is exactly knee-high'

Terminative case can also express direction, as in 7.58:

7.58 [kə-də   təp-a:b]   yi-di
     DEM.PROX-masc.sg village-LK+TERM go-3plBAS.VT
     'They went up until this village'

With the noun *ma:j* 'talk', it has the meaning of 'following the words exactly', as in 7.59; the expression *majəb* is often used to mean 'using someone's exact words'. With temporal nouns, it implies exact time frame (§4.1.2).

7.59 [də-ka   majəb]   wukə-ku
     3masc.sg-OBL+DEM.DIST.fem.sg word+LK+TERM listen-COMPL.SS
     'Having obeyed his words exactly'

    [2] Laycock (1965) erroneously treated -*b* case in Manambu as an ablative.

A suffix of the same form appears in manner adverbs (§4.4), where it is often accompanied by reduplication, e.g. *məy-a-məy-a:b* (real-LK-real-LK+TERM) 'for real, fully well and truly'.

7.7 TRANSPORTATIVE CASES

Two transportative cases occur with a limited group of nouns, and are similar in their meanings. The markers are *-Vsap* and *-Vsay*; both are used with nouns referring to means of locomotion or of reaching a destination. Their meaning overlaps with the instrumental *-Vr* (see §7.5). The form *-say* appears to be more frequent than *-sap*. See 7.60–1.

7.60 <u>gu-jabra-sap</u>   ya-na-wun
water-boat+LK-TRANSP come-ACT.FOC-1fem.sgBAS.VT
'I come by water-raft'

7.61 [a   kiya:l   brəka   amæy] ata
DEM.DIST+fem.sg die+3fem.sgVT 3du+LK+fem.sg+DEM.DIST.fem.sg mother then
<u>kar-asay</u>   ya:l
car-LK+TRANSP come/go+3fem.sgBAS.VT
'That dead mother of them two then came by car'

The sentence in 7.61 is followed by 7.62, where the meaning 'by car' is marked with the allative-instrumental. This shows similarity in meanings of the allative and the transportative:

7.62 [kar-a:l   waku-n]   ata pəuna-l   *matəmat-ə-m*
car-LK+ALL go.out-SEQ then appear-3fem.sgBAS.VT cemetery-LK-LOC
'Going out by car, she appeared at the cemetery'

The marker *-say* can also be used with locations such as waterways used as means of getting from one place to another, as in 7.63:

7.63 alawur   Kabla-say   da:d
DEM.DIST.fem.sg+UP Screw.River+LK-TRANSP go.down+3masc.sgBAS.VT
'He went down from up there via Screw River'

Both markers can be used with other means of getting from one place to another: one can say *yab-ə-say* or *yab-ə-sap* 'by road', *nəb-ə-say* or *nəb-ə-sap* 'by dry land'. With some words, only *-say* was considered acceptable and produced spontaneously: *pətakau-say* (ladder-TRANSP) was judged to be synonymous with *pətakaur* (ladder+INSTR) 'by ladder'; but **pətakau-sap* was rejected. The marker *-say* was also used on an interrogative, in 7.64; *-sap* was judged strange in this context. The answer was: with a ladder. An alternative would have been *agw-a:r* (what/which-LK+INSTR) 'with what, how?'

7.64 wun <u>akə-say</u>   da-u
I   what/where-TRANSP go.down-1sgIMPV
'How (lit. with which means) shall I go down?'

Neither case can occur on personal pronouns or demonstratives. There is a lookalike *-sap* used with one word, *yanu* 'magic'; *yanu-sap* means 'by way of or through magic'. Whether the two are related or not is an open question. According to the intuition of some speakers, they are homonyms.

7.8 SUBSTITUTIVE CASE

The substitutive case *-yæy* means 'instead of something; in the absence of something or someone', as shown in 7.65–7.

7.65 mən-a-yæy   tabək-ə-m   aka kunay   nugway   kənay
  you.masc-LK-SUBST side-LK-LOC then spear.grass type.of.grass DEM.PROX.ANAPH
  tə-na-di
  stand-ACT.FOC-3plBAS.VT
  'In your absence, on the other side spear grass and another type of grass have grown there'

7.66 kijap-ə-yæy   ñab-a:r   waku-bər
  protein.food-LK-SUBST Sepik.river-LK+ALL go.out-3duBAS.VT
  'In the absence of protein food they went out (to fish) in the Sepik River'

In 7.67, the case marker appears in a headless possessive structure, 'instead of hers':

7.67 lə-kə-di-yæy   Sirunki adika   nənəm
  she-OBL-pl-SUBST Sirunki DEM.DIST.REACT.TOP.pl smoking.grid+LK+LOC
  taka-lə-di
  put-3fem.sgSUBJ.P-3plBAS.P
  'Instead of her (own fishes), Sirunki put those (previously mentioned) on the smoking grid'

In 7.68 a substitutive form occurs as head of predicate in an elliptical clause; no other case form can be used this way.

7.68 kad-ad   wun-a   ñamus-ə-yæy-ad
  DEM.PROX+masc.sg-3masc.sgNOM I-LK+fem.sg younger.sibling-LK-SUBST-3masc.sgNOM
  'This one, he is instead of my younger sibling'

When used on verbal stems, it has a similar meaning—see §7.11.

7.9 COMITATIVE CASE

The comitative case marked by *-wa* is unlike other cases in a number of ways. It marks (a) relations of nouns within an NP, alongside two non-core clausal functions: (b) an associated participant and (c) location 'along something'. It can also (d) mark the copula complement of *tə-* 'have, be, become, stand'. It appears to have developed into (e) a derivational suffix meaning 'all together'. And there appears to be a link between the comitative marker *-wa* and the connective *wa* (mentioned in §4.5, and §20.1.1). We discuss these uses of the comitative one by one.

The major grammatical difference between the adnominal comitative and the comitative used for clausal functions is the placement of the case marker. The marker of coordinating comitative within an NP occurs on the first constituent in an NP. If the comitative marks a clausal function, it occurs on the last word of the NP, like other case markers discussed so far. Adnominal comitative can be marked twice within an NP, expressing simultaneity and 'togetherness' of the participants.

The comitative marker *-wa* attaches to the linker, just like any other case. The only anomaly is the comitative formed on *sə* 'who': the comitative is *səka:wa* 'with whom?' rather than **sə-kə-wa*, as would be expected following the analogy of *də* 'he', *də-kə-wa* 'with him'.

A. COORDINATING COMITATIVE is the most common means of coordinating two nouns within one NP. Three options are available here:

A1. COMITATIVE MARKED ONCE IN AN NP is used to coordinate any two nouns whose referents are closely linked together, e.g. as co-participants in a story, such as *tapwuk-a-wa yayib* (rooster-LK-COM rock.wallaby) 'rooster and rock wallaby', *wajə-wa sakibag* (eel+LK-COM wild.taro) 'eel and wild taro', *ñanugw-ə-wa ta:kw* (children-LK-COM woman) 'women and children', or *Yəsan-a-wa Mayau* (Yessan-LK-COM Maio) 'people from Yessan and from Maio' (representatives of one group live next door to each other and speak the same language). The expression *sər-a-wa mu:* (tomorrow-LK-COM day.after.tomorrow) means not just 'tomorrow and the day after', but can refer to 'next few days' as a whole. In contrast, a list of disparate entities does not require a coordinator.

A coordinating comitative requires dual or plural agreement on the possessive, e.g. *Wargab-a-wa Wapanab dəya-kə-di a:s* (Wargab.clan-LK-COM Wapanab.clan they-OBL-pl dog) 'dog (names) belonging to the Wargab and the Wapanab clans (lit. Wapanab and Wargab their names of dogs)', and on the verb, as in 7.69. (Another example of agreement of coordinate comitatives with demonstratives, 'his (two) bow and arrow', is in 7.71).

7.69 [a   takwa-wa   lə-kə   ñan] ata kwa-bər
      DEM.DIST+fem.sg woman+LK-COM she-OBL+fem.sg child then stay-3duBAS.VT
      'The woman and her child then stayed (there)'

If more than two nouns are coordinated, there are two options: the second and the third nouns can be juxtaposed to the comitative marked noun, as in 7.70.

7.70 [Kuimag-a-wa   Sirunki Lai] ata   ya-di
      Kuimag-LK-COM Sirunki Lai then come-3plBAS.VT
      'Kuimag, Sirunki, and Lai came then'

Alternatively, the connective *wa* can be used, e.g. *Elizabet-a-wa Paul wa brə-kə ñan Sandra* (Elizabeth-LK-COM Paul and 3du-OBL+fem.sg child Sandra) 'Elizabeth, Paul, and their daughter Sandra'. The latter option is dispreferred by older and more traditional speakers. In each case, the plural agreement on the verb indicates that the coordinate NP is one constituent.

There are no restrictions on the function of an NP containing a coordinating comitative of types A1 and A2. Example 7.71 is an example of an adnominal comitative on the first word of the two NPs, and the dative and the accusative-locative at the end of the respective NPs.

7.71 də-ka   mawul kur-də-l
      3masc.sg-OBL+fem.sg+DEM.DIST inside get-3masc.sgSUBJ.P-3fem.sgBAS.P
      a-də   kuprapə ñan adəka   [də-kə-bər
      DEM.DIST-masc.sg bad/poor child DEM.DIST.REACT.TOP+masc.sg he-OBL-du
      am-a-wa   nəbi:k]   [...] aw də-kə-wa   warya-k,   [a-bər
      bow-LK-COM arrow+LK+DAT   then he-OBL-COM fight-PURP.SS DEM.DIST-du
      ama-wa   nəbiya:m]   lagu-də-kəb
      bow+LK-COM arrow+LK+LOC pull-3masc.sg-AS.SOON.AS
      'The poor boy took a liking to his (his brother's) bow and arrow, so he was going to fight him, having pulled bow and arrow (off him)'

This is the closest Manambu comes to 'double case' (that is, two cases marked within the same noun phrase); note that the case markers go onto different words within an NP constituent. Coordinate comitative NPs are pronounced as one intonation unit, without a pause. The word order is fixed, and the NP cannot be split.

A2. COMITATIVE IN COMITATIVE-MARKED ARGUMENT ELABORATION CONSTRUCTIONS was discussed in §6.2.3. The major difference between such constructions with and without comitative is the equality of participation: the comitative-marked participant is somewhat backgrounded (see 6.37–9). For innovative speakers highly proficient in Tok Pisin, the comitative postpositions *wukən* 'with, together' (as in 4.69–70 and 7.72) and *nakamib* (as in 6.39) are synonymous with the comitative.

A comitative-marked inclusory construction can be in any case function. The case marker goes onto the cover pronoun, as shown in 7.72. This is in contrast to most other types of NP:

7.72 kusə-də-k aw [an-a:k wun-a-wa Yuakalu wukən]
die-3masc.sg-COMPL.DS then we.two-LK+DAT I-LK-COM Yuakalu together
an-a:k kapə-n tə-da-l aka
we.two-LK+DAT wait-SEQ stay-3plSUBJ.P-3fem.sgBAS.P DEM.DIST.REACT.TOP.fem.sg
'After he died, that time they waited for us two, me and Yuakalu'

The word order within the NP is fixed, just as in A1 above.

A3. DOUBLE COMITATIVE occurs in an NP consisting of two nouns marked with the comitative referring to one participant or event which can be in any function in a clause. Saying *təp-a-wa kapayawi-a-wa kə-k-na-wun* (coconut-LK-COM sweet.potato-LK-COM eat-FUT-ACT.FOC-1sgBAS.VT) means 'I will eat coconut and sweet potato together' referring to eating them simultaneously (with shaved coconut spread on the sweet potato). In 7.73, *mərə-wa*[3] *wala-wa* (strong.wind+LK-COM rain+LK-COM) 'hurricane; strong wind and heavy rain happening simultaneously' triggers singular agreement on the verb. That *wa:l* 'rain' is the head of the construction is corroborated by the choice of the weather verb *jə-* 'to rain' (see §4.2.2) which can only be used with 'rain', and not with any other phenomenon:

7.73 [mərə-wa wala-wa] ata ja:d
strong.wind+LK-COM rain+LK-COM then fall.of.rain+3masc.sgBAS.P
'Then there was (lit. rained) a heavy rain with simultaneous wind'

If the two participants are animate, the agreement on the verb is non-singular, as in T3.52 ('Oselo and the snake the two together died that night'). This is not an inclusory construction: the double comitative is one NP, and the 'two together' is another. There is an intonation break between the two NPs.

A double comitative construction can consist of any nouns, e.g. *amæy-ə-wa ñənə-wa* (mother-LK-COM child+LK-COM) 'mother and child together', and even of pronouns: when I showed a picture of myself with Kulanawi, his reaction was: *ñən-a-wa wun-a-wa!* (you.fem-LK-COM I-LK-COM) 'you and me together!' A double comitative construction does not allow any other case morphology on the same NP.

B. COMITATIVE AS ASSOCIATED PARTICIPANT is an oblique, meaning 'together with'; it is never cross-referenced on the verb. Unlike adnominal comitative, the marker of the comitative of associated participant goes on the head of an NP. The comitative-marked NP can be placed before the verb or after it depending on its topicality: in 7.74 it is postposed to the verb.

---

[3] The ə in the sequences ə-w and ə-y may not be pronounced at all in normal speech register.

7.74 [wun-a-də   asa:y] ma: wa-na-d   [wun dada:k
     I-LK-masc.sg father no say-ACT.FOC-3masc.sgBAS.VT I   go.down:RED+PURP
     mən-a-wa]
     you.masc-LK-COM
     'No, my father said no for me to go down with you'

Comitative on nouns with inanimate referents marks a concomitant object: *kwara-wa naya-d*
(grass.skirt+LK-COM play-3masc.sgBAS.VT) means 'he (a transvestite boy) played with a grass
skirt on' (also see 14.105). Similarly, a comitative on a noun denoting weather condition implies
'at the same time as'. Damel gave the following explanation for her visiting our house rather
than going to work in the garden:

7.75 [wala-wa   yawi kur-ku]   ata   barək   kwa-kər
     rain+LK-COM work do-COMPL.SS NEG.DES fever+LK+DAT stay-DES
     'I don't want to get fever after having worked during the rain'

  The comitative also marks a participant in an inherently reciprocal action, such as 'mixing,
putting together' in T3.20 and fighting ('with him') in 7.71 (third line).
  If a clause contains an oblique comitative, and the subject is acting alone, the verb acquires
singular cross-referencing, as in 7.76: the man is going to fight with the moon, but there is no
indication that the moon will fight back.

7.76 wun lə-kə-wa   warya-k   yi-k-na-dəwun-ək
     I   she-OBL-COM fight-PURP.SS go-FUT-ACT.FOC-1masc.sgBAS.VT-CONF
     'I will go to fight with her'

Dual or plural agreement is required if the participants act together, as in 7.77.

7.77 [də-kə-də   asa:y] [nəkə-də   du-a-wa]   [asa-wa]   ata yi-di
     he-OBL-masc.sg father other-masc.sg man-LK-COM dog+LK-COM then go-3plBAS.VT
     'His father with another man, with a dog then went'

  The placement of the comitative and the presence of intonation break in between the NPs
and enumerating intonation in 7.77 show that this is not an instance of coordinating comitative.
  Comitative often indicates reciprocal activity, without the overt reciprocal marker *awarwa* as
in 7.78. The form *awar-wa* is in itself a comitative form of *awar* 'side, sideways direction' (also
see §§4.4, 16.2.4).

7.78 də-kə-wa   karkwas   tə-na-bran
     he-OBL-COM quarelling have-ACT.FOC-1duBAS.VT
     'I am quarrelling with him' (lit. we-two with him are quarrelling)

The reciprocal often warrants using comitative on each of the participants to stress that the
action is mutual, as in 7.79. This 'double' comitative is different from the double comitative
construction in A3 above in that it consists of two NPs separated by a pause. In 7.79, they are
coordinated with the connective *wa* 'and' (also see 16.93b).

7.79 awarwa kurnaka-di,   [Malikəban tənəb-a-wa]   wa [Kamimali
     REC   offer-3plBAS.VT Malikeban household-LK-COM and Kamimali
     tənəb-a-wa]
     household-LK-COM
     'They made ritual offers to each other, the household of Malikeban with the household
     of Kamimali'

C. PERLATIVE is an oblique, with the meaning of 'along or throughout a location', as in 7.80. The mother complained that her baby was breastfeeding while we were walking along the road. 'Road' and 'breast' do not form one NP (there is an intonation break between the two, and semantically they do not belong together).

7.80 yabə-wa   məñ   aka   kə-na
      road+LK-COM breast DEM.DIST.REACT.TOP.fem.sg eat-ACT.FOC+3fem.sgBAS.VT
      'She is now breastfeeding (lit. eating breast) along the road'

A village submerged under water was described as:

7.81 kə-də   təp   gu-a-wa   ra:d
      DEM.PROX-masc.sg village water-LK-COM sit+3masc.sg
      'This village is covered with water throughout'

This meaning is obviously linked to 'together with', or 'during', as in 'during the rain' in 7.75.

D. COPULA COMPLEMENT of the verb *tə-* 'have, be, become, stand' takes the comitative case in a few expressions to do with the acquisition of a bodily state, e.g. *yala-wa tə-* (belly+LK-COM be) 'become pregnant' (as in 7.16), and *məñ-a-wa tə-* (breast-LK-COM be) 'acquire breasts (of a young girl); become adult'.

E. DERIVATIONAL MEANING of the comitative was mentioned in §4.4. A few nouns marked with the comitative can be used as adverbial-like modifiers, with the meaning of 'all together', e.g. *du-a-wa* (man-LK-COM) 'all the men', *təp-a-wa* (village-LK-COM) 'the whole village', *wiya-wa* (house+LK-COM) 'the whole household'. The meaning is transparent in all these cases, except for one quantifier: *mi* 'tree' derives *miya-wa* (tree+LK-COM) 'all together, the whole of', as in *miya-wa gu ayakw* (tree+LK-COM water IMPV+wash) 'wash/bathe the whole body!' (also see 6.24 and 16.50). Such forms can modify the action of the verb, as in 7.82. In this example, *təp-a-wa* can also be interpreted as a modifier to the subject 'they'. The form *təp-a-wa* does not form one NP with 'they', because it is an afterthought (separated from the rest of the clause with a pause).

7.82 dəy   nagwə-k   adiya   ya-kə-na-di   ya,
      they sago+LK-DAT DEM.DIST.REACT.TOP+pl come-FUT-ACT.FOC-3plBAS.VT EMPH
      təp-a-wa
      village-LK-COM
      'They will be coming to fetch sago, as a whole village'

Unlike any other adverbs, such derived comitatives can be used in S (7.83) or O (7.84) function.

7.83 təp-a-wa   ada   kusə-na-d
      village-LK-COM DEM.DIST.REACT.TOP+masc.sg end-ACT.FOC-3masc.sgBAS.VT
      'The whole village then came to an end (died out)'

7.84 [a   təp]   təp-a-wa   kwakə-da-l   ma:
      DEM.DIST.fem.sg village village-LK-COM search-3plSUBJ.P-3fem.sgBAS.P no
      'They searched that village through and through the village—nothing'

A noun in the form of a derivational comitative cannot be modified, and cannot be referential. There is a clear semantic link between the derivational comitative and other meanings of the comitatives, especially the locative 'throughout' (as in 7.81).

The comitative marker occurs on two demonstrative adverbs, *kətawa* 'like this; along here' (10.47), *atawa*, and *akətawa* 'like that' (see §10.2.2).

Of all the cases in Manambu, the comitative is the most complex semantically. It can be used to coordinate nouns within an NP, to mark two oblique functions (concomitant participant and perlative locative), and one core function (copula complement), and has developed into a derivational marker.

7.10 SUMMARY: HOW MANY CASES DOES MANAMBU HAVE?

Manambu has nine case forms (including zero). Each has a number of meanings and functions, and is in opposition to others. There are two ways of interpreting this system. We can distinguish nine cases each corresponding to one form (this can be called a 'lumper' approach). Or we can distinguish eighteen cases, going strictly by their function (this can be called a 'splitter' approach). Table 7.2 contrasts a 'lumper' and a 'splitter' approach, with a summary justification for either.

The coordinating comitative on NP level is used to link constituents of an NP and does not mark any grammatical relations; this is why it is not treated on a par with other cases here. The terminative, two transportative and substitutive cases are semantically and functionally straightforward, and constitute one case each. (As shown in Table 3.5, a form marked with these cases, except for terminative, cannot be cross-referenced on the verb.)

A 'lumper' approach has two advantages—it is economical and allows us to capture a notable semantic and syntactic connection between different case meanings and uses, which include

(i) ø marking for copula complements and for the second argument of verbs 'turn into' (which may be viewed as a variety of copula verbs of 'becoming');
(ii) the -*Vm* 'accusative-locative case' which has a shared meaning of complete involvement of the O argument, the locative, or another argument completely affected by the action;
(iii) the -*Vk* 'dative-aversive' case where the common syntactic core is marking arguments which are not prototypical or not completely affected objects; and
(iv) the -*wa* 'comitative case' which has a variety of meanings all of which can be captured under the umbrella notion of 'accompaniment'.

A 'splitter' approach allows us to separate different meanings and functions of the same form. It is appropriate when two or more meanings of a form have little in common semantically or syntactically or both.

Putting together the advantages of both approaches, we judge it most reasonable and economical to postulate the following system of thirteen cases:

ø-case for subjects;
ø-case for copula complements;
ø-case for objects;
ø-case for manner;

-*Vm* 'complete involvement of an argument (most often locatives and O arguments)';
-*Vk* 'dative case for third arguments and not fully affected second arguments; aversive and purposive';
-*Vr* 'allative case';
-*Vr* 'instrumental case';
-*wa* 'comitative case';

TABLE 7.2   Polysemous cases in Manambu: two approaches

LUMPER: AS MANY CASES AS THERE ARE FORMS		SPLITTER: AS MANY CASES AS THERE ARE FUNCTIONS	
CASE	MOTIVATION	CASE	MOTIVATION
-ø 'subject, copula complement, second argument of 'turn into', object, unmarked manner, location, purpose, instrument, component of complex verbs'	• one form • analysis with too many meanings assigned to ø morpheme is not economical	A. A, S, and CS	• a unified category of subject (see §20.1.4); • always cross-referenced on the verb (Table 3.1).
		B. copula complement	• special grammatical relation; not cross-referenced on verb
		C. second argument of 'turn into'	grammatical relation different from others; can be put together with B
		D. unmarked O	contrast with -Vm case
		E. unmarked manner	no other case form available; grammatical relation different from others
-Vm 'accusative-locative'	• marks both core and oblique clausal arguments; • shared meaning of complete involvement of O/Locative	-Vm 'locative'	• marks an oblique • in paradigmatic opposition to allative
		-Vm 'accusative/completely involved second argument'	• marks a core argument • in paradigmatic opposition to ø-object
-Vk 'dative-aversive'	• marks arguments which can be considered not fully affected and not prototypical objects; • dative and aversive distinguishable by context and semantics of nouns	-Vk 'dative'	• marks third argument of ditransitive verbs and second argument of verbs low in transitivity
		-Vk 'aversive'	• has distinctive semantics; occurs on nouns on their own

TABLE 7.2 *Continued*

LUMPER: AS MANY CASES AS THERE ARE FORMS		SPLITTER: AS MANY CASES AS THERE ARE FUNCTIONS	
CASE	MOTIVATION	CASE	MOTIVATION
-Vr 'allative-instrumental'	• one form marks obliques; • ambiguity with locations	*-Vr* 'allative'	• means 'direction'; • is in opposition to locative
		-Vr 'instrumental'	• means 'instrument'
-wa 'comitative'	• plausible semantic link between the four meanings	*-wa* 'with'	• marks an oblique
		-wa 'copula complement'	• marks a core argument
		-wa 'perlative along'	• in opposition to locative and allative
-Vb 'terminative'		n/a	
-sap 'transportative'			
-say 'transportative'			
-yæy 'substitutive'			

-*Vb* 'terminative case';
-*sap*, -*say* 'two transportative cases',
-*yæy* 'substitutive case'.

7.11 CASE MORPHOLOGY ON VERBS

Nominal case suffixes (with the exception of the terminative, transportative, and comitative cases) can occur on verbal roots. None of the zero-case morphology applies to verbs: a verb root cannot occur on its own. The resulting forms differ in their status. In addition, all case morphology can occur on headless relative clauses (see §19.2.1). Relative clauses in Manambu have all the tense-aspect and person marking of the main clause (they differ from main clauses in how they are negated). An example of a headless relative clause marked with a comitative is *kui-kwa-na-di-a-wa* (give.to.third.p-HAB-ACT.FOC-3plBAS.VT-LK-COM) 'with those who usually give'. These look like instances of case marking on what is homonymous with an inflected main clause verb.

The marker -*Vm* 'complete involvement of a second participant' is reminiscent of -*Vm* 'accusative-locative' whose meaning involves completeness of involvement of an argument, or an oblique. The marker -*Vm* occurs on verbal and other roots (see §12.6) indicating completion of an action, or total achievement of a state, as in *kuprap-ə-m* (bad-LK-LOC) 'it is totally bad', 7.34, and in 7.85:

7.85 də-kə-də   ñan   wukəmar-ə-m
     he-LK-masc.sg child forget-LK-LOC
     '(I) completely forgot his son'

A completive form of *rəp* 'be enough', *rəp-ə-m* 'fully enough', is often used in the meaning of 'this is perfect; this is fine'. The completive form can only be used as a copula complement of *na-* 'copula for abstract states' (see §12.6).

Dative -*Vk* case on a verbal root has same subject purposive meaning (see §13.4.1 and §19.4.1), as in 7.76 where such forms are used as purpose complements to verbs of motion.

This same form is used in a construction with the auxiliary *kur-* 'do' in its imminent meaning, e.g. *kiya-k kur-* (die-PURP.SS get/do) 'be about to die' (§17.1.2).

The instrumental -*Vr* appears on a few verbal roots, in a function of manner adverb, as in *væs-ə-r mæy* (walk-LK-INSTR come.IMPV) 'come by stepping' (see Aikhenvald forthcoming g, for further discussion). It also occurs in one lexicalized V-V compound *nas-ə-kəta:-r* (count-LK-try-INSTR) 'by counting (when talking about the number of people or days)'.

The substitutive case -*yæy* on a verb can serve as a sequencing marker with the meaning 'instead of, rather than' (§19.3, and examples 19.36–7 and T3.40).

Using cases on verbal roots does not nominalize them. The resulting forms are less pro-totypically verbal: -*Vm* and -*Vk*- marked verbs belong to the group of uninflected aspectual modal forms, and the combination of verb root plus -*Vr* case can be considered similar to a manner adverb. The verb forms marked with the substitutive -*yæy* can be same subject (with no special subject marking) or different subject (and then the subject is marked on them: see §18.1 for the discussion of this as a general principle in Manambu). The phenomenon of verbal case as exponent of clausal meanings, and as clause-linking device, is widespread in Australian languages (Dixon 2002a: 237–8) and in a number of languages from other parts of the world. The discussion of Manambu verbal case in typological perspective is in Aikhenvald (forthcoming d).

8

Possession

Manambu distinguishes five major kinds of possessive noun phrases whose choice depends mainly on the semantics of a noun and that of the possessive relationship—see §8.1. Predicative possession and the ways of cross-referencing the possessor on the verb are discussed in §8.2.

8.1 POSSESSIVE NOUN PHRASES, THEIR FUNCTIONS AND SEMANTICS

8.1.1 Possessive noun phrases

Manambu has five types of possessive noun phrases: (A) part–whole NPs; (B) NPs with juxtaposed components; (C) NPs with a linker; (D) NPs with pronominal possessive marker; and (E) associative possessive NPs.

Table 8.1 contrasts these in terms of (i) semantic relationship between nouns; (ii) restrictions on type of possessee; (iii) restrictions on possessor; (iv) focusing of possessor, possessee, or the possessive relationship; (v) whether the possessor or the possessee can consist of a noun plus a modifier; (vi) whether the head can be omitted; (vii) whether multiple possessors are possible; and (viii) whether a possessive NP can be discontinuous. What all the constructions have in common is that the possessed noun is invariably the head. We will see in §8.1.2 that most nouns can occur in any of the five constructions, with meaning differences (Table 8.2). Manambu has no strictly defined possession classes for nouns, with one exception. No nouns other than body and plant parts can occur in part–whole NPs (type A); body and plant parts can occur in constructions B–E.

A. PART–WHOLE NPs consist of a body or plant part, or of a spatial term, plus the linker followed by the 'whole', or the 'possessor'. The possessor is generally inanimate, and the first component constitutes its inherent part, e.g. *yala wi* (belly+LK house) 'the inside (lit. belly) of a house', *baga wi* (back+LK house) 'back part of the house, backyard'; *tama val* (nose+LK canoe) 'prow, front part or nose of a canoe'; *ñəd-ə ñab* (middle-LK Sepik.river) 'middle of the Sepik River'; *tək-ə mi* (seed-LK tree) 'fruit of a tree; medicine'; *səp-a lap* (skin-LK banana) 'banana skin', *kui-a lap* (flesh-LK banana) 'flesh of banana'; *ab-a məñ* (head-LK breast) 'nipple; upper part of the breast'.

The same construction is used to express spatial relations and orientation, e.g. *mutəm-a kara:b* (face-LK man's.house) '(at) the front of the man's house'; *api ñəg* (top mosquito.net) '(on) top of the mosquito net'; *mada ñəg* (bottom/testicles+LK mosquito.net) 'underneath mosquito net'.

The noun *məw* 'reason of, base of' forms a similar construction with another noun, e.g. *məw mi:* 'base of a tree', *məw ñab* 'main part of the river', *məw təp* 'main part of the place; main place'. These constructions can be pronounced as one phonological word (with one stress on the last component) if they do not exceed three syllables (see §2.5.1 on the preferred phonological word). Some are used as personal names, e.g. female names *Ñəd-ə-wi* (middle-LK-house) 'middle of the house' and *Jib-ə-da:m* (design-LK-spider) 'spider's design'.

Table 8.1 Possessive noun phrases

TYPES	SEMANTIC RELATIONSHIP	RESTRICTIONS ON POSSESSEE	RESTRICTIONS ON POSSESSOR	FOCUS	CAN POSSESSOR OR POSSESSEE CONTAIN A MODIFIER?	OMISSION OF HEAD	MULTIPLE POSSESSORS	CAN THE NP BE DISCONTINUOUS?
A. Part–whole constructions with linker	part–whole; spatial relations	inanimate: body and plant parts and spatial terms	none	n/a	no	no	no	no
B. Juxtaposition		none	none		either can	(yes)	yes (only two)	yes
C. Juxtaposition with linker	possession and association in general		non-specific referent		no	no		
D1. Possessor is a pronoun		none			possessee only	yes	no	
D2. Possessor is a noun and there is a pronominal possession marker			specific referent	possessor or possessive relation	either can		yes (two or more)	no
E. Associative	association		none	n/a			no	

These possessive constructions cannot be discontinuous or contain more than one possessor. Neither the possessor nor the possessed can consist of a noun plus a modifier. The possessed noun is the head of the construction, since it determines gender and number agreement. A noun phrase *nəma-də tama-val* (big-masc.sg nose+LK-canoe) 'big nose (front part) of a canoe' means 'big nose of a canoe', not *'nose of a big canoe'. The 'possessor' can be omitted: instead of saying *gala-taba:m atak* (the.fork.like.part+LK-hand+LK+LOC IMPV+put) 'put (the medicine) in the fork-like part of the hand (between fingers)', one can say: *gal:am a-tak!* 'put (it) in the fork-like part'.

B. POSSESSIVE NOUN PHRASES WITH JUXTAPOSED COMPONENTS have no restrictions on the animacy of the possessor or of the possessed. The meaning of the construction covers a broad semantic range, from possession proper to association with the possessor. A possessor—which precedes the possessed—can be a noun or a pronoun with a specific referent, e.g. *ta:kw ya:b* '(a) woman's road', *Yuaya:b amæy* 'Yuaya:b's mother', *jagər sa:p* (garfish character) 'character or image of a garfish', *bal ya:m* (pig smell) 'smell of a (dead) pig', *wun amæy* 'my mother'.

These constructions can never be treated as compounds. Either the possessor or the possessed can consist of noun phrases with a modifier, e.g. [*kə-də təp*] *wa:ñ* (DEM.PROX-masc.sg village line) 'the line of this village', *wun* [*kwasa ñan*] (I small+fem.sg child) 'my small child'. The possessor can be a coordinate NP, e.g. [*mərə-wa wa:l*] *pəpli* (wind+LK-COM rain noise) 'loud noise of [rain and wind]'.

The possessed noun is the head, since it determines the gender and number agreement. In 8.1, the feminine cross-referencing on the possessive NP (in brackets) indicates agreement with the feminine noun *wa:ñ* 'genealogical line' (the feminine gender is used here because the line is small).

8.1 alək   [[kə-də   təp]   wa:ñ]-al
    this.is.why DEM.PROX-masc.sg village(masc) line(fem)-3fem.sgNOM
    'This is why this is the line of this village'

A possessive NP of this type can be discontinuous, as in 8.2 where the adverb *kwasa* 'a little' intervenes between possessor and possessed. (That *kwasa* is indeed an adverb and not a feminine singular agreement form of the adjective *kwasa* 'small' is corroborated by the fact that 'I' has a male referent in this example, and 'head' triggers masculine agreement on the predicate because of the headache which makes it feel big and heavy, similarly to 5.9 in §5.2.1.)

8.2 [wun kwasa ab]   la:n-ad
    I   little head ache-3masc.sgNOM
    'My head aches a little'

Multiple and embedded possessors (not more than two) are allowed, e.g. *amæy asa:y təp* (mother father village) 'village of [mother and father]', *Yuakalu wi væs* ([[Yuakalu [house]] [grass]]) 'grass of the house belonging to Yuakalu'. There are no examples of multiple possessees (e.g. 'our mother and father') in the corpus; I suspect that this does not occur. Speakers who often code-switch with Tok Pisin use Tok Pisin-like juxtaposed possessive constructions more frequently than others. The surface parallel between juxtaposed structures in Tok Pisin and in Manambu is illustrated in 8.3. The Tok Pisin forms are underlined.

8.3 aw   kə-da   kələm
    then DEM.PROX+fem.sg-DOWN DEM.PROX+fem.sg+LK+LOC
    rə-k-na-d,   [skul bilum] ya [Tanina skul kwasabi]
    sit-FUT-ACT.FOC-3masc.sgBAS.VT school stringbag EMPH Tanina school stringbag
    'Then it should be here, down here, school stringbag, Tanina's school stringbag'

The possessed noun can be occasionally omitted: 8.4 was an answer to my question to Yipawal 'where is your house?' Since Yipawal is a woman, it would have made no sense for her to refer to herself with masculine gender, so the gender agreement on the demonstrative must be with the unstated head—here, the house.

8.4 wun ka:d
    I   DEM.PROX+masc.sg
    'My (house) is this one'

C. POSSESSIVE NOUN PHRASES WITH A LINKER have no restrictions on the animacy of possessor or possessed. Just as in type B, the meaning of the construction covers a broad range, from possession proper to an association with the possessor. Unlike the type A, the possessor precedes the possessed and typically has non-specific reference, e.g. *takwa ya:b* (woman+LK road) 'female road', *du-a ya:b* (man-LK road) 'male road'; *təp-a kudi* (village-LK talk) 'the village language' (Tok Pisin *tok ples*). The possessor cannot have an inherently definite referent; as a consequence, pronouns and proper names do not occur in these constructions.

Possessive constructions with a linker often lexicalize, e.g. *ab-a-wapwi* (head-LK-dress) 'head-dress, hat'; *ap-a-sə* (bone-LK-name) 'first name', *taba-ñə* (hand+LK-sun) 'wrist watch'. They are similar to the part–whole constructions in that if they contain no more than three syllables, they form one phonological word (in agreement with §2.5.1). That is, they can be realized as compounds, depending on the number of syllables they contain (also see §9.3).

Possessive constructions of type A can form part of a type B construction (Possessor-Possessed), as in 8.5. This describes a post belonging to a location (back) within the house:

8.5 [[baga-wi-a]ₐ.ₚₒₛₛ   kwa:t]ᵦ.ₚₒₛₛ
    back+LK-house-LK post
    'post of the back of the house'

The possessed noun is the head of the construction since it determines number and gender agreement, as shown in 8.6. The head cannot be omitted, and multiple possessors are not acceptable. A possessive NP with a linker cannot be discontinuous; neither the possessor nor the possessed can consist of a noun plus a modifier.

8.6 a-bər   ab-a-wapwi   viti-abər
    DEM.DIST-du head-LK-dress two-3duNOM
    'Those hats (lit. headdresses) are two'

D. NPs WITH PRONOMINAL POSSESSIVE MARKER are of two kinds: either possessor is a personal pronoun or possessor is a noun and there is an additional pronominal marker of possession.

D1. If the possessor is a personal pronoun, the pronoun itself serves as a possession marker. Agreement in gender and number is always marked on the pronoun (see §5.1.1). Third person singular and dual (non-plural) pronouns, and the interrogative *sə* 'who?' take the oblique marker -*kə*- (same as the one in case formation: §7.1).

8.7 aw   wun-a-di away-bər-adi
    then I-LK-3pl mother's.brother-PL-3plNOM
    'Then they are my mother's brothers'

These constructions are preferred to possessive constructions with juxtaposition (type B above) if the possession or the possessor are in contrastive focus (which one is in focus is usually clear from the context). A modifier can intervene between the possessor and the possessed, as in 8.8.

8.8 [ñən-a-də   kwasa-də   ñan] akə-d
   you.fem.sg-LK-masc.sg small-masc.sg child where-masc.sg
   'Where is your little son?'

An additional advantage of using an NP with pronominal possessive is the fact that it allows the speaker to distinguish gender and number of the possessed noun: *wun ñan* (I child) can mean 'my son' or 'my daughter', while *wun-a ñan* (I-LK+fem.sg child) can only mean 'my daughter'. A possessive NP with a linker cannot be discontinuous, or contain multiple possessors.

D2. Possessor is a noun with a specific referent, of any semantic group. Then, the possessive relationship or the possessor is in focus, as in 8.9 and in 5.1. In 8.9, the story teller is concerned with getting the name of that particular focused man right:

8.9 [[a-də   karya-də-də   du] də-kə-də   sə]
   DEM.DIST-masc.sg bring-3masc.sgSUBJ.P-3masc.sgBAS.P man he-OBL-masc.sg name
   Kamkudi-ad
   Kamkudi-3masc.sgNOM
   'The name of that man brought in by him was Kamkudi'

Example 8.9 shows that the possessor can be expressed with an NP containing one or two modifiers. The possessee is usually expressed with just one noun.

Such possessive constructions may express a relationship of 'belonging' somewhere, or being from somewhere, as in 8.10. The whole construction is in contrastive focus. Swakap is contrasted to other locations to which the Gala people escaped (see §1.4.1).

8.10 Yuanab [[Swakap dəya-di   du]-adi]FOCUS kwa-na-di
    Yuanab Swakap 3pl+LK-3pl man-3plNOM stay-ACT.FOC-3plBAS.VT
    'In Yuanab (that is, Yambon), it is the men from Swakap (not anywhere else) who stay'

Multiple possessors are possible, as shown in 8.11:

8.11 Ambunti [karabə   sa:d]   [[Ñakau dəya-di nəbək]
    Ambunti man's.house+LK name+3masc.sgNOM Ñakau they-pl mountain
    [dəya-də   sa:d]]
    they-masc.sg name+3masc.sgNOM
    'Ambunti is the name of a man's house, (it is) the name of the mountain belonging to the Ñakau clan'

Noun phrases with a pronominal possessive marker can be used without a head (see 7.45b and 7.67). There are no examples of discontinuous possessive NPs of this type.

E. ASSOCIATIVE POSSESSIVE NPs consist of a possessor + suffix *-kə-* + gender and number agreement marker followed by the possessed noun, as in *kwarba-kə-l ta:kw* (jungle+LK-POSS-fem.sg woman) 'woman belonging to the forest', *təp-a-kə-di du-ta:kw* (village-LK-POSS-pl man-woman) 'village people'. Associative possessive constructions indicate origin in terms of a clan or a country, e.g. *sablap gwalugw-ə-kə-də du* (Sablap clan-LK-POSS-masc.sg man) 'man from Sablap clan', *Ostrelia-kə-l ta:kw* (Australia-POSS-fem.sg woman) 'woman from Australia', or belonging to a particular place, as in 8.12. The associative possessor is a type of gender-sensitive modifier (see §5.1.1; Table 5.2). The possessor can be a complex NP with a modifier:

8.12 [[nəkə-di wi-a]-kə-di   pusi] kamna:gw luku   kur-kwa-na-di
    other-pl house-LK-POSS-pl cat   food   stealing do-HAB-ACT.FOC-3plBAS.VT
    'Cats from other houses keep stealing food'

It may indicate a loose association with the 'possessor': *ab-a-kə-l* (head-LK-POSS-fem.sg) 'the one to do with head' was used to refer to hair cream. A big plate of food leftovers from the day before yesterday was referred to as *nagəs-ə-kə-də* (the.day.before.yesterday-LK-POSS-masc.sg) 'the one from the day before yesterday'. An associative possessive noun phrase cannot be discontinuous, or contain multiple possessors. An associative possessive construction often appears with its head noun omitted:

8.13 təp-a-kə-di:k   aki   wa-u
     village-LK-POSS-pl+DAT news   say-1sgIMPV
     'May I tell the news to the villagers (lit. those belonging to/from the village)?'

In narratives, a headless associative NP with a pronominal possessor often refers to what the story is about. The expression *lə-kə-l aka* (she-POSS-fem.sg DEM.DIST.REACT.TOP.fem.sg) 'this is its story' is a typical ending of a story.

A headless associative NP can contain a personal pronoun as a modifier to the omitted head, as in 8.14. The second occurrence of a headless associative NP in this example appears in the predicate slot. Then, number and gender are effectively marked twice: once with gender-number suffix *-di* 'plural' agreeing with the omitted head noun of a possessive NP ('people'), and once with gender-number-person enclitic *-adi* 'third person plural nominal predicate':

8.14 [dəy [gla:gw-ə-kə-di]ASS.POSS] [kəp-a-kə-di-adi]PRED.SLOT
     they Gla:gw-LK-POSS-pl   ground-LK-POSS-pl-3plNOM
     'They (the people) of the Gla:gw clan group are those (people) of the ground'

When the head of a D2 possessive construction is omitted, it is rather similar to a headless associative E type construction (see, for instance, 8.9). This similarity is superficial, for three major reasons.

First, in D2 constructions, the marker *-kə-* occurs only on third person singular and dual pronouns. In contrast, the associative *-kə-* occurs on any pronoun, e.g. *mən-a-kə-l* (you.masc-LK-POSS-fem.sg) 'your (man's) round (feminine) (thing)'. A third person plural pronoun with *-kə-* is shown in 8.15b.

Secondly, the feminine agreement form of the pronominal marker is different: it is ø for D2 possessive constructions, and *-l* for associative constructions, as illustrated in 8.15b.

And thirdly, the semantics of the two when used as modifiers is subtly different: the D2 construction in 8.15a implies possession while the associative construction in 8.15b indicates any kind of link.

8.15a [Gala dəya   wa:ñ] kənay   Yuanaba:m
      Gala 3pl+LK+fem.sg line   DEM.PROX.ANAPH Yuanab+LK+LOC
      kwa-na
      stay-ACT.FOC+3fem.sgBAS.VT
      'The genealogical line of the Gala stays here (mentioned) in Yuanab'

8.15b [[mugul rə-di   du] dəya-kə-l   wa:ñ] anay
      few   sit-3plBAS.VT man 3pl+LK-POSS-fem.sg line   DEM.DIST.CURR.REL
      kwa-na
      stay-ACT.FOC+3fem.sgBAS.VT
      'The line linked to those few men who are few is there'

The marker of associative possession *-kə-* can acquire independent stress, if it occurs together with a word longer than three syllables, unlike the linker. The differences between D2 and E constructions suggest that, synchronically, the oblique marker *-kə-* which occurs on singular possessive pronouns and the associative marker *-kə-* which can occur on any pronoun or a noun are different morphemes. Diachronically, they may well be related.[1]

There is an additional, marginal possessive structure, so far attested with only two nouns, *təp* 'village' and *kəp* 'land'. The forms *təp-a-ba* (village-LK-POSS) and *kəp-a-ba* (land-LK-POSS) mean 'belonging to the village' and 'belonging to the land; the one from this place', as in *kəp-a-ba du* (land-LK-POSS man) 'man of the land, belonging to this place' and *təp-a-ba du* (village-LK-POSS man) 'villager, someone who lives in a village (as opposed to a jungle-dweller)'. Synchronically, this is best treated as a derivational suffix with limited productivity. Historically, this suffix is cognate to a regular possession marker *-ba* in Gala.

8.1.2   Possessive noun phrases in Manambu: a comparison

The five possessive constructions in Manambu differ in their semantic and syntactic properties, and only partly in the semantics of possessor and possessee. There is no binary division into inalienably and alienably possessed nouns based on the semantics of the possessee. Only body parts and spatial orientation terms can participate in type A, 'part–whole', constructions, which is the closest Manambu gets to expressing inalienable possession.

Body parts and some spatial terms can also take part in any other construction (subject to semantic compatibility). Just about any other noun can occur in constructions B–E. Table 8.2 illustrates different meanings of possessive NPs A–E with a body part noun, *kui* 'flesh, meat', and B–E with a non-body part noun *ya:b* 'road'.

Constructions C with body parts are uncommon, but possible. Body parts as possessed nouns acquire different extensions in various possessive constructions. For instance, a type A construction *mæn-a bal* (leg-LK pig) means only 'pig's leg (as its body part, or as a dish)'; while a type B construction *bal mæn* (pig leg) may mean 'pig's leg' if compared to legs of other animals, or it may mean 'the way in which a pig trots', as in *bal mæn-a:r væsə-na-di* (pig leg-LK+INSTR walk-ACT.FOC-3plBAS) 'they walk in pig trot; trotting like pigs'.

Constructions A and C share one further feature: depending on the overall number of syllables in a construction, they can be treated as compounds (that is, as one phonological word each).

In two instances, distinctions between types of possessive constructions are neutralized. If a construction of type B consists of two nouns, and a cluster formed by the final consonant of the first and the initial consonant of the second is not acceptable (see §2.2.1), the linker is inserted. Consider *karab-ə sə* (man's.house-LK name) 'name of a man's house'. 'Man's house' has a specific referent; nevertheless, the underlying construction of type B has a surface similarity to the construction C, simply because a cluster *-b-s* would have been unacceptable on a boundary between two words in an NP. The two constructions can be distinguished by their further properties outlined in Table 8.1.

Secondly, if the third person singular head of a D2 possessive construction is omitted, the resulting structure can be easily confused with a headless associative possessive. The ways of distinguishing these were outlined at the end of the preceding section.

---

[1] Speakers of the Malu variety appear to extend the linker *-kə-* to all third person pronouns. Walter Behrmann's highly valued book was referred to as [*kə-di Germani*] *dəya-kə buk* (DEM.PROX-pl Germany 3pl+LK-POSS+fem.sg book) 'the book associated with those German (members of the expedition)'. This could be an innovation reflecting the levelling of the two formally similar construction types.

TABLE 8.2   Possessive noun phrases A–E with the noun *kui* 'flesh, meat' and *ya:b* 'road'

TYPE OF CONSTRUCTION	FORM	MEANING	FORM	MEANING
A. Part–whole	*kui-a bal* (flesh-LK pig)	'piece of pork'	n/a	n/a
B. Juxtaposition	*bal kui* (pig flesh)	'pig's meat, pork' (contrasted to other types of meat)	*du ya:b* (man road)	'road of a man'
C. Juxtaposition with linker	*bal-a kui* (pig-LK flesh)	'pig's meat in general'	*du-a ya:b* (man-LK road)	'road for men; road where only men go'
D1. Pronominal possessor	*də-kə-də kui* (he-OBL-masc.sg meat)	'his (large quanitity: masculine) meat'	*də-kə-də ya:b* (he-OBL-masc.sg road)	'his road'
D2. Pronominal possession marker	*bal də-kə-də kui* (pig he-OBL-masc.sg meat)	'the meat of the pig'	*du də-kə-də ya:b* (man he-OBL-masc.sg road)	'the road of the man'
E. Associative possession	*kui-a-kə-də ja:p* (meat-LK-POSS-masc.sg thing)	'thing associated with meat'	*yabə-kə-də ja:p* (road-POSS-masc.sg thing)	'thing associated with road'

Both possessors and possessed nouns can be relativized in all constructions except A and C. When possessor is relativized, the difference between the types of possessive NPs is neutralized, and the possessor bears no marking, as in *ta:kw kiya-də du* (wife die-3masc.sgBAS.P man) 'a man whose wife died' (lit. wife he-died man)—see §19.2.1 (19.15).

8.2   PREDICATIVE POSSESSIVE CONSTRUCTIONS AND POSSESSOR CROSS-REFERENCING

Any possessive construction can head a predicate (just like any noun phrase)—see examples 8.1–2, 8.7, and 8.14. Two constructions are used for predicative possession par excellence.

8.2.1   Verb 'have'

The polyfunctional verb *tə-* 'have, be, stand' marks predicative possession (see §4.2.2 on further functions of this verb used as a copula and a support verb, as an auxiliary, and as a stance verb). It can only be omitted in negative possessive constructions. This verb can be used with any noun, as illustrated in 8.16 (a common noun 'money'), 8.17 (a body part), and 8.18 (a kin term).

8.16 nəma   kabak   tə-na-di
     big+fem.sg money (lit. stone) have-ACT.FOC-3plBAS.VT
     'They have big money'

The second argument of *tə-* in the meaning 'have' can be cross-referenced on the verb, as in 8.17. This distinguishes *tə-* 'have' as a transitive verb from its other uses (we can recall that a copula complement is never cross-referenced).

8.17 ñən   nəma-də   ta:m tə-ñəna-d
     you.fem big-masc.sg nose have-2fem.sgSUBJ.VT-3masc.sgBAS.VT
     'You have a big nose' (said a willy wagtail to hornbill)

8.18 du-a-ñan   nak ata   tə-bər
     man-LK-child one then have-3duBAS.VT
     'Then they had one boy'

An idiomatic possessive expression *ja:p kal kiya-ku tə-* (thing DEM.PROX+3fem.sgNOM die-COMPL.SS have) 'be rich, have many possessions' refers to ownership of material goods.

In negative possessive clauses, *tə-* is frequently omitted: 8.19b is a version of 8.19a:

8.19a dəy kami: ma: tə
     they fish   NEG have:NEG
     'They do not have fish; they have no fish'

8.19b dəy kami: ma:
     they fish   NEG
     'They do not have fish; they have no fish'

In fixed expressions, like the one in 8.20, the verb 'have' is never used (see §21.5):

8.20 wun ma:j ma:
     I   story NEG
     'I have nothing else to say; everything is clear'

8.2.2   Identification construction

An alternative to a predicative possessive construction with 'have' is identification construction whereby the possessor is the subject of a non-verbal clause, and the possessed noun occupies the predicate slot. These constructions tend to be employed if the possessive relationship is conceived of as a permanent one, as, for instance, belonging to a clan—e.g. Wargab in 8.21:

8.21 dəy-a-də   kara:b   Waikab-ad   Wargab-ad
     they-LK-masc.sg men's.house Waikab-3masc.sgNOM Wargab-3masc.sgNOM
     'Their men's house is Waikab, it belongs to the Wargab clan'

Place names and clan names in general can be used metonymically, to refer to people from a place, or belonging to a clan. Such use is normally reflected in non-singular agreement on modifiers, as in 6.8, *day kə-di Yima:l* (they DEM.PROX-pl Yima:l) which can only mean 'these members of the Yimal clan', and not *these Yimal clans (see §6.2.1). Similar examples are under

6.27–8 and 4.68. In 8.22, the agreement on the predicate and on the demonstrative is singular, because the referents belonging to the two villages are one each:

8.22 Malu bə   yi-na,   Avatəp kəka
     Malu already go-ACT.FOC+3fem.sgBAS.VT Avatip DEM.PROX.REACT.TOP.fem.sg
     '(The one from) Malu is already gone, the one from Avatip is here'

This sentence would not make sense if Malu and Avatip were to refer to the villages. Along similar lines, the term for 'house' is often used in such 'inclusive' meaning. If a noun phrase *wi nak* (house one) heads an NP with a non-singular agreement, it can only be understood as referring to people belonging to one house (see §6.2.1). Structures like 8.21 can be analysed as having metonymically used clan names or place names as predicates of verbless clauses.

Other possessed nouns can be used in the predicate slot in the same construction type. By themselves, these nouns do not have any metonymical reading. The identification construction is used to describe permanent ownership, as in 8.23:

8.23 bal-adəmən-ək   a:s-adəmən   təp-adəmən
     pig-2masc.sgNOM-CONF dog-2masc.sgNOM coconut-2masc.sgNOM
     'You have a pig, you have a dog, you have a coconut (they are an intrinsic part of your household)'

In name debates, experienced orators enumerate the names of their ancestors, and then finish by saying 8.24. This implies full ownership, and, what's more, identification between the possessor and the possessed.

8.24 wun-adəwun
     I-1masc.sgNOM
     'They are mine' (lit. 'it is me')

These possessive structures are negated in the same way as any non-verbal clause: the negator *ma:* appears in the predicate clause and there is no personal cross-referencing (see §14.1):

8.25 mən   ma:
     you.masc NEG
     'You do not have (this), or: this does not belong to you'

Neither in 8.23 nor in 8.24 can an unmarked possessor be head of an NP producing the same meaning—that is, *bal* on its own cannot mean 'having a pig'. This is unlike clan names and place names in structures like 8.21: a noun *gwalugw* 'clan' or *wi* 'house' can be used in the meaning of 'people belonging to a clan', or 'people belonging to a house'.

The frequent use of 'have' in Manambu could have been influenced by Tok Pisin *gat* 'have'. However, we have not observed any generational differences in the use of 'have'. In contrast, identification constructions, especially the ones like 8.23–5, are more frequent in special circumstances—either in traditional stories (8.25), or in name debates (8.24). This suggests that they are archaic.

8.2.3   Possessor cross-referencing on the verb

Since the possessed noun, and not the possessor, is the head of any possessive noun phrase in that it controls agreement on the modifiers and on the predicate, the possessor cannot normally be cross-referenced on the verb. It can be cross-referenced occasionally, if in contrastive focus, as in 8.26 (the possessive construction here is of D2 type). The cross-referenced possessor is underlined.

8.26 [wun-a   kui]   kə-kwa-dana-<u>wun</u>
     I-LK+fem.sg meat eat-HAB-3plSUBJ.VT-1fem.sgBAS.VT
     'They used to eat <u>my</u> flesh' (lit. they used to eat me (on) my flesh) (said the turtle)

As shown in §7.3, under (iv), the locative-accusative -*Vm* case can mark a third argument of ditransitive verbs, if the beneficiary or recipient is fully affected, or the gift is permanent (as in 7.27). Examples like 7.26 ('The Gala married women from/of Washkuk', or 'belonging to Washkuk') and 8.27 can be considered instances of possessor raising since the possessor is treated as the object:

8.27 [kə   a:b]   vya-ləpa-də-l   [a
     DEM.PROX.fem.sg head hit-BREAK-3masc.sgSUBJ.P-3fem.sgBAS.P DEM.DIST.fem.sg
     takwa:m]
     woman+LK+ACC/LOC
     'He smashed the woman's head' (lit. he head-smashed that woman)

In 7.26 and in 8.27, the possessor ('Washkuk' and 'woman' respectively) does not form one noun phrase with the possessed ('woman' and 'head', respectively). The possessive relationship is understood from the context; and the locative-accusative case indicates the complete affectedness of the possessor in each case. This 'possessor raising' is available for body part possession only.

Derivation and Compounding

Manambu has a few derivational mechanisms which change word class (§9.1) and a number of those which do not (§9.2). Nominal compounding is discussed in §9.3.

9.1 WORD CLASS-CHANGING DERIVATIONS

Fully productive action nominalizations are derived through full reduplication of the verb's root. These are discussed in §9.1.1, in the light of other functions of reduplicated verbal root. Non-productive deverbal nominalizations and a partially productive adjectivizing derivation are addressed in §9.1.2. There are no morphological means for deriving a verb from a noun. One adjective, *vyakət* 'good, beautiful', is related to a verb *vyakanaku-* 'correct, improve' via a unique process. (Neither has cognates in other Ndu languages.)

9.1.1 Full reduplication of verbal root and its functions

Full reduplication of verbal root is a productive means of deriving action nominalizations, e.g. *war-* 'go up', *warwar* 'going up'; *nas(ə)-* 'count', *nasənas* 'counting' (see §2.2.1 on the insertion of *ə* to break an unauthorized consonant cluster); *kawar-* 'take up', *kawar-kawar-* 'carrying and going up'; *yawi kur-* (work do) 'work (verb)', *yawi kur-kur* 'doing work (noun)'.

If a root ends in *-u* and undergoes full reduplication, the final vowel is reduced to *-w* and, if it follows a stop, is realized as labialization of the last consonant, as in *waku* 'go out', *wakuwakw* 'going out'. If a verb root has a structure CVC_1C_2V, and C_2 is *y*, the final vowel is dropped and *y* becomes *i*, as in *warya-* 'fight', *warya-wari* 'fighting'. Monosyllabic roots with the vowel *a* acquire the shape *CaCə* when reduplicated, e.g. *da-* 'go down', *da-də* 'going down', *ra-* 'cut', *ra-rə* 'cutting'. Nominalizations are stressed on the last syllable; whether they form one phonological word depends on the syllable count (see §2.5). Nominalizations can occur in S or O function, as obliques and as part of complex predicates (see §4.1.2). They cannot be part of a possessive NP or be modified. All nominalizations have the verb's argument structure and argument marking (their A/S is Ø marked, as in 9.1 and 9.4, and their O can be unmarked, as in 9.2–3, or marked with accusative-locative case following the principles in §7.2, e.g. 4.7).

But is every reduplicated verb a nominalization? We will see below that the reduplicated forms differ in their semantics and in their syntactic possibilities depending on their function and the type of additional marking they take. The broad meaning 'action nominalization' appears to be fully applicable to some combinations of form and function of reduplicated verb root, and only partly so to others. We will use this term here for convenience. At the end of this section we return to the problem of whether all these can be analysed as one category.

I. NOMINALIZATIONS UNMARKED FOR CASE are used as S in 4.7–8 and 9.1; and as O in 9.2. They cannot be used as A.

9.1 [kasan war-war]   vyakət-a
     peanut go.up-RED good-3fem.sgNOM
     'Peanuts are coming up fine' (lit. Peanuts going up is fine)

Deverbal nominalizations in O function are employed as complementation strategies, with the verb 'know', as in 9.2, and 'finish', as in 4.8.

9.2 [na:gw kə-kə]   bər bəta:y   laku-bra
     sago   eat-RED 3du already know-3duSUBJ.VT+3fem.sgBAS.VT
     'They were eating sago, they already knew how to eat sago' (lit. they already knew sago eating)

'Peanuts coming up' in 9.1 and 'sago eating' in 9.2 are different from possessive constructions of type B (§8.1.1), for two reasons. First, given the right pragmatic circumstances, another possessive construction (types C–E) can replace a B-type possessive construction. In contrast, no possessive construction can be used instead of an action-nominalization structure. Secondly, an object of a nominalization can take the accusative-locative case if fully affected, as in 4.7. In all of 9.1–2 and 4.7–8 nominalizations are employed as complementation strategies (see IX in §19.8).

An action nominalization can occur in the predicate slot, as in 9.3 (predicate is focused: see §20.3).

9.3 kə   lap   kwa:j   kə-kə-l-a
     DEM.PROX+fem.sg banana flying.fox eat-RED-3fem.sgNOM-3fem.sgNOM
     'This is the way of eating of bananas by flying fox'

As can be seen from these examples, nominalizations are assigned feminine gender, in accordance with its functionally unmarked character (see §5.2.3).

Nominalizations are frequently used as modifiers to nouns, e.g. *vya-vy-a ta:b* (hit+LK-RED-LK hand) 'right hand, lit. hitting hand', *wusau-wusau səp* (itch-RED skin) 'itchy skin', *væt-ə-væt-əj əpis* (bite-LK-RED-LK ant) 'an ant that bites a lot'. An alternative interpretation for these constructions as analogous to relative clauses is in §19.2.2.

II. DATIVE-AVERSIVE-MARKED NOMINALIZATIONS are used to mark a purpose, or a goal expressed with what translates as a clausal complement. These are used where one expects the dative-aversive case, as in 9.4 and 13.81–2.

9.4 kapə-n kwa-na   [nəkə-di ñanugw ya-ya:k]
     wait-SEQ stay-ACT.FOC+3fem.sgBAS.VT other-pl children come-RED+DAT
     'She is waiting for the other children to come' (lit. she is waiting for other children coming)

The dative-aversive marked nominalizations are used with a variety of expressions with negative meaning, such as 'forbid, refuse', literally, 'say no', as in 9.5, or 'feel shame', as in 9.6.

9.5 [mən   kapə-ka:p da-da:k]   ma: wa-na-wun
     you.masc self+LK-self go.down-RED+DAT no say-ACT.FOC-1fem.sgBAS.VT
     'I forbid you to go down fully on your own' (lit. I say no to you going by yourself)

9.6 [kə-ka:k]   də wap   sayid
     eat-RED+DAT he shame feel+3masc.sgBAS.VT
     'He felt ashamed to eat'

This is in line with the aversive meaning of the -*Vk* case. The nominalizations are also used in a more clearly aversive, 'for fear of', sense, as in 9.7:

9.7 [ankəl səp kagəl <u>yi-ya:k]</u>   marasin-al
     nettle skin sore GO-RED+DAT medicine-3fem.sgNOM
     'Nettle is a medicine against sore skin' (lit. nettle is a medicine for fear of skin going sore)

Dative-aversive-marked nominalizations are used in yet another sense—that of future projection, as in 9.8.

9.8 [lə-kə-də   ñan kiya-kiya:k] atawa kurə-d
     she-LK-masc.sg child die-RED+DAT thus do-3masc.sgBAS.P
     'It (the cat) was acting like this (as a premonition) for her little boy dying'

We saw that a nominalization unmarked for case can be used with the expression 'be hard' in 4.7 where the difficulty is not limited to the future. If a future difficulty is implied, a dative-aversive-marked nominalization is employed:

9.9 [apawəl bəu-m   tə-na]   [[alək   suan
     spirit   haze-LOC stay-ACT.FOC+3fem.sg.BAS.VT this.is.why hard
     yi-na-wun]   [apawəl-a:m   <u>və-væk]]</u>
     go-ACT.FOC-1fem.sgBAS.VT spirit-LK+ACC see-RED+DAT
     'A spirit is in a haze, this is why it is hard for me to (try and) see the spirit (in future)'

The dative-aversive nominalization can be considered a type of complementation strategy (§19.8). Unlike other complementation strategies, they often follow the inflected verb. This same form is also used in clauses introduced with *kəpa:b* 'in case'—see §13.7.

Dative-aversive nominalizations can be derived from any verb, with the exception of verbs of *Cəl/r* structure. So, the verb *bəl-/bla-* 'talk' forms a nominalization *blabəl* 'talking'; but not **blabək*; the same-subject purposive *bla:k* is used instead (see §13.4). Such gaps in the paradigm of dative-aversive nominalizations show that their morphological possibilities do not fully coincide with those of nominalizations discussed at I above. This could be an argument in favour of analysing them as a separate category.

III. TERMINATIVE CASE-MARKED NOMINALIZATIONS marked with *Vb* can only be used with the polyfunctional verb *tə-* as support verb. The meaning of the construction is 'to be on the brink of doing something; to do just so':

9.10 ñən-a-də   majan   <u>kui-kuib</u>   tə-na-dian
      you.fem-LK-masc.sg funerary.ritual give-RED+TERM have/be-ACT.FOC-1plBAS.VT
      'We are about to offer you a funerary rite (because we thought you were dead)'

The support verb can be omitted, if its subject is coreferential with that of a juxtaposed clause:

9.11 [kuprap-ə du taba:m   rə-ku]   [ya:n] [rə-tua
      bad-LK   man hand+LK+LOC sit-COMPL.SS come+SEQ sit-1sgSUBJ.VT+3fem.sgBAS.VT
      aka   <u>kiya-kiya:b]</u>
      DEM.DIST.REACT.TOP.fem.sg die-RED+TERM
      'Sitting in the bad man's hands, having come, here I sit, on the brink of dying'

The meanings of -*Vb* with nominalizations agree with the general semantics of the terminative case (see §7.6). Noun phrases marked with terminative case are typically used as obliques, unlike nominalizations with the same marking.

IV. NOMINALIZATIONS AS PARTS OF COMPLEX PREDICATES with the verb *tə*- 'be, stand, have' as a support verb have an intensive and habitual meaning, as in 9.12. Compare 9.12a, with an inflected verb, and 9.12b, with a nominalization as part of a complex predicate.

9.12a day-a:k   warsamad
     they-LK+DAT be.angry+3masc.sgBAS.VT
     'He is angry at them'

9.12b day-a:k   warsam-warsam tə-na-d
     they-LK+DAT be.angry-RED   be-ACT.FOC-3masc.sgBAS.VT
     'He is very angry at them'

The verb *bla* means 'speak; say magic spells'; a person who keeps saying magic spells is called *yanu bla-bəl tə-kwa-na-d-ə du* (spell say-RED stand/have-HAB-ACT.FOC-3masc.sgBAS.VT-LK man). Similarly, *wukəmar* means 'forget', *wukəmar wukəmar tə*- means 'be forgetful'.

The meaning of a reduplicated nominalization may be only partially predictable: for instance, reduplicated *rəp* 'be full, satisfied' within a complex predicate means 'equal, same as', as in 4.47.

An analytical problem arises here. At the end of §4.2.2 we mentioned multiple word class membership of fully reduplicated verbal roots. Most of them can be used as inflected verbs (in which case they are interpreted as intensive aspect forms: see §12.8), and also as parts of complex predicates. This was illustrated with examples 4.47–8; also see 9.13a–b:

9.13a a-di   pato wali-wali   tə-na-di
     DEM.DIST-pl duck walk.around-RED be-ACT.FOC-3plBAS.VT
     'Those ducks keep wandering around'

9.13b a-di   pato wali-wali-na-di
     DEM.DIST-pl duck walk.around-RED-ACT.FOC-3plBAS.VT
     'Those ducks are wandering around all the time'

For dynamic verbs, like *wali*- 'wander around', there appears to be a subtle difference: nominalizations as parts of complex predicates refer to an atemporal action that keeps repeating, while inflected verbs describe something that is happening either right now or at some particular time (this is why the action focus marker is preferred in examples like 9.13a–b). For stative verbs there is no such difference.

In addition, a reduplicated verb root can occur as part of a complex predicate with support verbs other than *tə*- 'be, stand', with the basic meaning of action nominalization. The noise of rolling is described in 9.14, and this warrants the use of the polyfunctional verb *na*- 'be (of natural phenomena, including noise)':

9.14 təməl-təməl ata   na:l
     roll-RED   then be:NAT+3fem.sgBAS.VT
     'There was a noise of (him) rolling and rolling'

The reduplicated root triggers feminine agreement, like any nominalization in S function. Examples like 9.14 are infrequent; nevertheless, they point towards a different nature of reduplicated verb roots with a support verb and verbal nominalizations.

V. EMPHATIC NOMINALIZATIONS are used as manner modifiers to a semantically similar (or the same) verb, as in 9.15.

9.15 <u>wukə-wuk</u> wukə-tua
      hear-RED   hear-1sgSUBJ.VT+3fem.sgBAS.VT
      'I am just listening' (not saying anything; lit. listening I listen)

The emphatic nominalization constructions often have a frustrative connotation: in 9.16 there is an overt contrast between 'just hearing' and 'really talking'.

9.16 <u>wukə-wuk</u> wukə-na   yi-yi   suan yi-na
      hear-RED   hear-ACT.FOC+3fem.sgBAS.VT talk-RED hard go-ACT.FOC+3fem.sgBAS.VT
      'She does hear (understand) (the language), talking is difficult' (lit. hearing she hears, talking is difficult)

A nominalization containing a different, but semantically similar, root can modify a verb, denoting a manner in which the action is performed, as in 9.17:

9.17 <u>væsə-væs</u> ma:y
      step-RED   go.IMPV
      'Go by stepping carefully'

Just occasionally can a reduplicated verb root be used to modify a verb of a different semantic group, as in 9.18:

9.18 wiya:m   aw   təməl-təməl aw   təməl-təməl ata   gra:l
      house+LK+LOC in.turn roll-RED   in.turn roll-RED   then   cry+3fem.sgBAS.VT
      'At home she then cried in turn rolling and rolling (lamenting her drowned son)'

VI. NOMINALIZATIONS IN NEGATIVE CONSTRUCTIONS as predicate heads are a means of expressing negative obligation. This is consistent with a typologically widely attested pattern whereby non-verbal forms are used to express curt commands and strong prohibitions (Aikhenvald forthcoming a). In 9.19, the mother was trying to explain to her baby daughter that one does not breastfeed while walking along the road:

9.19 yabə-wa   məñ   <u>kə-kə</u>   ma:
      road+LK-COM breast eat-RED NEG
      'One does not breastfeed while walking' (lit. There is no breastfeeding along the road)

Such negative statements can refer to something that has not happened yet (as in 9.19 said before the girl had started breastfeeding—see 7.80), or to something that has already occurred.

The position of the negator is congruent with its position in clauses with a non-verbal predicate (see §14.1.2). However, an additional problem arises here. We will see in §14.3.3 that the negative form of the reduplicated intensive aspect of a verb coincides with the reduplicated verb stem, that is, a nominalization. In negative future, the negator is postposed to the negative form of an inflected verb, making a construction like 9.20 (and in T1.7) inherently ambiguous between (a) a negated nominalization as a means of expressing negative obligation; and (b) a negative future of the intensive aspect.

9.20 lə   wun-a   takwa:m   və-və   ma:.
     she I-LK+fem.sg wife+LK+ACC/LOC see-RED NEG
     (a) 'She (the moon) is not to see my wife'
     (b) 'She (the moon) will not be intensively staring at my wife'

This ambiguity can be resolved by the context. Interestingly, both readings are possible in the humorous story from which the example 9.20 is taken. The story is about a naive newly wed young man who had no idea that women menstruate, literally, 'see moon', once a month. He decides to stop the moon from seeing his wife by killing the moon (cf. 3.15), and says 9.20.

The reduplicated forms discussed in I–V cannot be negated independently (see §14.1.3). For instance, a reduplicated deverbal nominalization as part of a complex predicate (IV above) is negated in the same way as any other clause containing the support verb *tə-* 'stand, be, have'.

9.21 wukəmar-wukəmar akəs   tə-kwa-na-wun
     forget-RED   NEG.HAB stand-HAB-ACT.FOC-1fem.sgBAS.VT
     'I am never forgetful'

The differences in semantics and functions of reduplicated verb root discussed in I–VI are summarized in Table 9.1.

Just like with cases (§7.10), one may wish to follow a 'lumper' approach, and consider all instances of reduplicated verbs in Manambu as essentially one category with six different functions. The fact that six different functions are in a complementary distribution as to the additional marking and syntactic functions of the reduplicated root is a strong argument in favour of this approach.

Alternatively, one can follow a 'splitter' approach, and distinguish several semantic and functional categories expressed with homophonous forms: (i) deverbal action nominalization: structures I–III and VI; and (ii) non-inflected verb with intensive-habitual meanings: IV and V. Once used as head of predicates, deverbal action nominalizations are reinterpreted as a modality (§13.7).

The meaning differences between reduplicated verb root in constructions I–III and in IV are substantial. In addition, the reduplicated verb root as part of a complex predicate in IV can be replaced with an inflected verb form containing the same reduplicated verbal root, as shown in 9.13a–b. Reduplicated verb roots as parts of complex predicates may well be considered a special grammatical form of a verb, which is only superficially similar to nominalizations discussed under I–III. The two analytic alternatives are equally valid.

9.1.2   Other nominalizations and an adjectivizing derivation

Non-productive action nominalizations involve the syllable-weight-sensitive suffix *-ka:u* 'action nominalization': it requires that the root it combines with should contain at least one light and one heavy syllable (in the sense of §2.4.2). This suffix has been attested with one disyllabic root *kakəl* 'surpass, exceed'; the resulting form *kakəl-ka:u* (surpass-NOM.ACT) means 'races, competition' (as in 9.22). All other roots this suffix occurs with consist just of one heavy syllable (of CVC structure); they have to undergo full reduplication. The resulting forms are *gəp-ə-gəp-ə-ka:u* (run-LK-run-LK-NOM.ACT) 'running around', *təp-ə-təp-ə-ka:u* (dive-LK-dive-LK-DER) 'diving up and down', and *pakw-ə-pakw-ə-ka:u* (hide(intr)-LK-hide(intr)-LK-NOM.ACT) 'hiding; hide and seek'. A possible exception is *rali-rali-ka:u* (untie-untie-DER) 'game of untying (grass skirt)', as in *kwa:r rali-rali-ka:u nayi-di* (grass.skirt untie-untie-NOM.ACT play-3plBAS.P) 'they played

TABLE 9.1 Meanings and functions of reduplicated verb root

TYPE	ADDITIONAL MARKING	FUNCTION	MEANING	FURTHER FEATURES	ANALYTIC DIFFICULTIES
I	ø	S/O, predicate, modifier	action nominalization		n/a
II	Dative-aversive -*Vk*	Purpose, future projection, complementation strategy	purpose, goal, object of fear, complementation strategy	same meanings as those of dative-aversive case (§7.4)	when desubordinated, analysed as a modality (§13.4; §13.7)
III	Terminative -*Vb*		'be on the brink of doing something; do/be just so'	same meanings as those of terminative case (§7.6)	unlike terminative case forms on nouns, never used as an oblique
IV	ø	Part of complex predicate	intensive and habitual	similar to inflected verb with reduplicated root (intensive aspect: §12.8)	have nothing in common with nominalizations; perhaps belong to different categories
V	ø	Modifier to same, or similar, verb	emphatic 'really'	similarity to verb roots used as modifiers	
VI	ø	Negated predicate head	negative obligation	negated in the same way as any non-verb in predicate slot	ambiguous with future negative form of inflected verb with reduplicated root (intensive aspect: §12.8)

at untying grass skirts'. The formative *-ka:u* in *pətəka:u* 'ladder' may also be related to this morpheme. All the *-ka:u* derivations refer to a kind of game, or process. These nominalizations cannot take case marking (see 7.14). They are freely used as heads of predicates as in 9.22, and express unmarked purpose, as in 7.14. With the verb 'play' they refer to the game played, as in 9.23.

9.22 nəbəl maket-a:m   <u>kakəl-ka:u-a</u>
today market-LK+LOC surpass-NOM.ACT-3fem.sgNOM
'Today at the market there was a "competition" (to get fish first)'

9.23 gəp-ə-gəp-ə-ka:u   təp-ə-təp-ə-ka:u   nayi-di
run-LK-run-LK-DER dive-LK-dive-LK-DER play-3plBAS.VT
'They played at running around (and) diving up and down'

Unlike any other object it can never be cross-referenced on the verb. In these properties, it is reminiscent of the nominal component of complex verbs.

The suffix *-kay* derives an object nominalization from one root, *yabər-* 'fan (somebody)', producing *yabrəkay* 'fan'. Two suffixes occurring with one root each derive adverbs: *-sap* as in *yanu-sap* (magic-DER) 'by magic' (this suffix is homophonous with one of the transportative case markers: §7.7) and *-naral* as in *takwanaral* (woman+DER) '(row or sit in a canoe) in a woman's fashion (for a man)'.

The infix *-ka-* 'intensive' accompanied by root reduplication is partly a word class-changing derivation (see Table 4.2, and §4.3.2). It derives non-agreeing adjectives with intensive meaning from numerous non-agreeing adjectives, e.g. *səmi* 'long', *səmi-ka-səmi* 'very long'. A few nouns take this infix, and the result is, in many cases, a non-agreeing adjective, e.g. *laki* 'ginger', *laki-ka-laki* 'green; ginger colour'. Some nouns refer to colours when used as modifiers, e.g. *wa:m* 'white cockatoo; white colour'. When used with the infix *-ka-*, these are used only as non-agreeing adjectives, e.g. *wama-ka-wa:m* (white+LK-INT-white) 'very white'. Further examples are in §4.3.2.

The infix *-ka-* when applied to nouns does not always derive an adjective: as mentioned in §4.3.2, this derivation with *ya:l* 'stomach' results in *yala-ka-ya:l* (stomach+LK-INT-stomach) 'empty stomach', as in 4.58.

9.2 NON-WORD CLASS-CHANGING DERIVATIONS

Manambu has a few adverb-specific derivational suffixes (§4.4) and derivational formatives occurring on personal names (§5.3). Verbal formatives whose status is ambiguous between derivational suffixes and parts of compounds are discussed in §15.2.4.

Manambu has one non-word class-changing derivational suffix, a collective marker *-ja:y* which applies just to nouns. This suffix has a fairly specific meaning: it defines a peer group or a generation-based group of people, e.g. *nəbə-takwa-ja:y* (marriageable-woman+LK-COLL) 'young marriageable women', *naubadi-ja:y* (young.man-COLL) 'young men', *du-a-ñanugw-ə-ja:y* (man-LK-children-LK-COLL) 'a peer group of little boys', *takw-a-ñanugw-a-ja:y* (woman-LK-children-LK-COLL) 'a peer group of little girls'. This suffix is also used with kinship terms, e.g. *amay-brə-ja:y* (mother-pl-COLL) 'peer group of classificatory mothers', *asay-brə-ja:y* 'peer group of classificatory fathers', *jukwar-ugwə-ja:y* 'peer group of siblings', *ñaju-gwu-ja:y* 'peer group of paternal uncles', *away-bra-ja:y* 'peer group of maternal uncles'.

To refer to an exclusive group, the suffix *-ja:y* appears infixed in between the reduplicated parts of a fully reduplicated noun, as in *takwa-ja:y-ta:kw* (woman+LK-COLL-woman) 'a group of women only', *ñanugw-a-ja:y-ñanugw* 'a group of children only', and *du-a-ja:y-du* (man-LK-COLL-man) 'a group of men only'.

Forms containing this suffix have plural reference and require plural agreement. The suffix itself requires a plural form of a noun it occurs with (if the noun has one). If the plural form of a noun is archaic and restricted in usage, it cannot occur with *-ja:y*, e.g. *tidə-takwa-ja:y* (co.wife+LK-woman+LK-COLL) 'peer group of co-wives' (i.e. women of the same clan who are either married to the same man, or are eligible to marry men from the same clan), but neither **tid-igw-ja:y* nor **takwagwa-ja:y* (though the archaic forms *tidi:gw* 'co-wives' and *takwa:gw* 'wives' exist and occur in songs).

Note that *-ja:y-* follows the plural marking in the forms above. This may be considered as an exception to an oft-quoted tendency to place inflectional markers (such as plural) after derivational markers. However, as shown in §6.1, number marking on nouns themselves in Manambu is highly restricted and quite irregular. It can be argued that plural on nouns is a derivation, and not an inflection.

A collective form marked with *-ja:y* can modify a personal pronoun, as in 9.24; or occur in S and in an oblique function, as in 9.25.

9.24 [ñan   kwasa-ñanugw-a-ja:y]   nay-ək   waku-dian
     we.pl small.fem.sg-children-LK-COLL play-PURP go.out-1pl.BAS.VT
     'We as a group of little children went out to play'

9.25 karabə-m   du-a-ja:y-du   kwa-na-di
     men.house+LK-LOC man-LK-COLL-man stay-ACT.FOC-3plBAS.VT
     'A group of only men stay in men's house'

A suffix of the same segmental form occurs on the command marker *jau* 'let it drop' (Tok Pisin *maski*) resulting in the adverb *jau-ja:y* 'any old way, carelessly'. It appears impossible to decide whether the two *ja:y* are indeed instances of the same affix, or different affixes.

The unstressed non-productive derivational suffix *-kara* occurs with *yara* 'all right'; the resulting form is *yara-kara* 'well'.

Four further suffixes appear to form one morphological system. They can combine with any word class (that is, they are low in selectivity), displaying somewhat different properties depending on the word class they occur with. Their properties are summarized in Table 9.2.

All these suffixes require a linker (see §4.1.1). Third person singular and dual pronouns require the linker *-kə-*, just as with case markers. One grammatical word cannot take more than one of these suffixes—this is an argument in favour of them forming one morphological system. However, they can occur on different words within one NP, as shown in 9.34 below (similarly to the way in which one noun phrase can contain two cases which occur on different words within one noun phrase, as in 7.71, where one is comitative and the other dative). We discuss them one by one.

1. The suffix *-dəka* 'only, just, exactly' can occur with members of any word class, with the basic meaning 'only, just', e.g. *takwa-dəka təp* (woman+LK-ONLY village) 'village of women only', *mən-a-dəka* (you.masc-LK-ONLY) 'you only, just you'. A noun marked with *-dəka* can occur in any function. In 9.26, *-dəka* occurs on an O and on a deictic adverb 'like that'. The suffix is pronounced as *-da* in rapid register (see §2.6).

The suffix *-dəka* 'only' is unstressed. When it is added to a noun or a verb, the stress moves to the antepenultimate position, e.g. *a:s* 'dog', *asá-dəka təp* (dog+LK-ONLY+LK village) 'village of only dogs'.

TABLE 9.2   Properties of non-word class-changing suffixes with low selectivity

SUFFIX	-dəka 'only'	-rəb 'fully'	-aba:b, -a:b 'too'	-pək 'more or less'
Selectivity	any word class, same meaning			any word class, meaning difference
Scope	grammatical word			grammatical word or clause
Verb form	non-inflected (root) form		n/a	inflected form
Noun form	root form; occasionally inflected form	root form	inflected form	inflected form
Can be case marked		no		yes
Can take inflections when in predicate slot		no		yes

9.26 [atawa-dəka   aka   kəp   məkəmək] [lə-kə-də
      like.that-ONLY   DEM.DIST.REACT.TOP.fem.sg simply be.silent   she-POSS-masc.sg
      ñan-a-dəka   karya-ku   mapi:m]
      child-LK-ONLY carry-COMPL.SS breast+LOC
      'Just like that, silent, after she was carrying just her son on her breast . . .'

The form *taba-dəka* (hand+LK-ONLY) 'hands only, carrying nothing' can be used in any function, including a manner modifier, or even as an elliptical greeting, in the meaning of 'give me your hand to shake, let's shake hands' (a more conventional way of saying the same thing is *ta:b kuru* (hand get+1sgIMPV) 'may I take (your) hand'—see §13.2). Only occasionally can this suffix appear on a case-marked noun, as in *ganər-dəka* (night+LK+INSTR-ONLY) 'only/just by night'.

The suffix *-dəka* can occur on the first of a sequence of nouns repeated for expressive purposes (§9.3), e.g. *ganə-dəka ga:n* (night+LK-ONLY night) 'only night after night (and never in daytime)'. This suffix occurs on the indicative positive form of the verb root, with the meaning of 'do just this', e.g. *waji-dəka* (laugh-ONLY) '(he is) just laughing' (§12.8.1).

It can also occur on a nominal component of a complex verb, especially if its verbal component is clear from the context, e.g. *sa:-dəka* (sleep+LK-ONLY) '(we will) only (do) sleeping'.

2. The suffix *-rəb* 'fully, totally' occurs on uninflected forms of nouns and verbs and is not compatible with any other inflections. A noun marked with *-rəb* can occur in any function except A. In 9.27, it occurs on a noun in an oblique function; in 9.28 it appears on a pronoun ('right there').

9.27 ñəd-ə-ñəd-ə-rəb   adi:d
      middle-LK-middle-LK-FULLY go.down.IMPV
      'Go down right in the middle (of a ladder)'

The suffix *-rəb* is used in lieu of a superlative, e.g. *kwasa-rəb* in 9.28. An elder sister is teaching her younger sister how to shoot birds, and she is telling her to hit the really small one.

9.28 ata [kə   kwasa-rəb]_{NP}   a-rəb   avi
      then DEM.PROX+fem.sg small+fem.sg-FULLY DEM.DIST+fem.sg-FULLY IMPV+hit
      '(Can I hit it, said (the younger sister), no! (said the elder sister), that is a big one), you hit this the smallest one (or: a really small one), right there'

Along similar lines, *nəma kudi-rəb* (big+fem.sg language/voice-FULLY) means 'in a really loud voice'. A headless adjective *nəma-rəb* (big+fem.sg-FULLY) 'really big one' was used to refer to a very big teacup.

This same suffix is also used to express full identity with another entity. Yuamali's reaction to a list of cognates between Manambu and Gala was *ñan-a kudi-rəb* (we-LK language-FULLY) '(this is) our language fully!' Similarly, Kulanawi said to me that his son's name was Michael, and added 9.29. A similar example is in 9.31.

9.29 ñən-a-də   ñan sa:-rəb
      you.fem-LK-masc.sg child name+LK-FULLY
      'It is exactly like your son's name'

Just like *-dəka*, *-rəb* attaches only to the indicative positive stem of a verb (see §12.8.1).

With personal pronouns, *-rəb* may be used somewhat idiomatically to refer to a person's wishes. This is the only instance where a form with *-rəb* takes nominal cross-referencing in a non-verbal clause, as in *ñən-a-rəb-a* (you.fem-LK-FULLY-3fem.sgNOM) 'it is up to you (lit. it is fully you)'.

3. The suffixes *-aba:b*, *-a:b* 'also' are used with members of any word class, and can attach to an inflected noun or a verb. There are no restrictions on the syntactic function of a noun. In 9.30, *-aba:b* goes onto the inflected verb in the form of predicate focus. That is, *-aba:b* can have a whole clause in its scope:

9.30 <u>kar-da-kə-məna:l-aba:b</u>
      carry-down-FUT-2masc.sgSUBJ.VT+3fem.sgBAS.VT+3fem.sgNOM-TOO
      'It is the case that you took her down, too'

Within a clause, *-aba:b* and *-a:b* more often attach to a constituent than to the inflected verb. The difference between the two suffixes is subtle: *-a:b* is preferred when numerous additional possibilities are enumerated, that is, when there is more than one additional participant in the clause. In contrast, *-aba:b* tends to be used when there is just one additional participant. In 9.31 *-a:b* (underlined) occurs with enumerated body parts, and *-aba:b* (bold and underlined) adds one extra body part (line 3) or participant (line 5):

9.31 [a-bər   lə-kə-bər   ñədi   abakapi <u>məla:b</u>   ma: tə]   [abakapi
      DEM.DIST-du   she-POSS-3du   child:du hawk   eye+LK+TOO   NEG have:NEG hawk
      <u>ta:ma:b</u>   ma: tə]   [abakapi lə-kə-di   <u>yuwi-a:b</u>   ma tə]
      nose+LK+TOO   NEG have:NEG hawk   she-POSS-pl feathers-TOO NEG have:NEG
      [<u>lə-aba:b</u> <u>dəg-a-ta:maba:b</u>   tapwuk dəg-a-rəb]   [du-a-ñan
      she-TOO beak-LK-nose+LK+TOO chicken beak-LK-FULLY man-LK-child
      takwa-ñan   kə-bər   də-kə-bər   <u>barbar-a:b</u>   a-bər   tapwuk
      woman+LK-child DEM.PROX-du he-POSS-3du beard+LK-ALSO DEM.DIST-du chicken
      lə-kə-bər   <u>barbar-a-rəb</u>]   **[<u>lə-ka:ba:b</u>**   tapwuk lə-kə   ab-a-pək
      she-POSS-du beard-LK-FULLY she-POSS+TOO chicken she-POSS+fem.sg head-LK-LIKE
      ta:l]]
      stay+3fem.sgBAS.VT
      'Her two children did not have hawk's eyes either, they did not have hawk's nose either, they did not have hawk's feathers either. This, too, the beak, too, is fully like a chicken's beak, both (for) boy and (for) girl; their beards too are fully like chicken's beards. She, too, got the head like (that) of a chicken.'

This example also shows that the linker *-kə-* can occasionally be omitted (as in *lə-aba:b* in the third line). These are the only suffixes with long vowels. Given that they do not trigger vowel shortening in nouns with a long vowel as would be expected for suffixes, such as *ta:m* 'nose', it is possible that these are better treated as clitics (note that they do not acquire secondary stress).

The suffix *-aba:b* 'also' is probably etymologically related to the quantifier *aba:b* 'all' (see 4.63 and §10.5).

4. The suffix *-pək* has somewhat different meanings depending on the class of word it attaches to. As shown in Table 4.2 (§4.3.2), it means 'like' when used with verbs, 'more or less; like' when used with nouns and other nominals, and is a comparative marker when used with adjectives. The standard of comparison is not stated; a comparison is implied, as in 4.51 and 9.32 (a continuation of 9.28):

9.32 ya:kya, [a   kwasa-pək-al]CLEFT.O
    OK,   DEM.DIST+sg.fem   small+fem.sg-MORE-3sg.femNOM
    vya-lə-l
    hit-3fem.sg.SUBJ.PAST-3fem.sg.BAS.P
    'OK, it was a smaller one (?or the smallest one) that she hit'

When used with nouns and pronouns, *-pək* means 'more or less, like', as in 9.33. This was a question to the oldest living Manambu man, Duamakwa:y, to determine how old he was at the time of Behrmann's expedition (see §1.4.2):

9.33 a-də   Dagwan   laku-mənə-l   sə-kə-pək
    DEM.DIST-masc.sg   Dangwan   know-2masc.sgSUBJ.P-3fem.sgBAS.P   who-POSS-like
    tə-ku   laku-mənə-d
    be-COMPL.SS   know-2masc.sgSUBJ.P-3masc.sgBAS.P
    'At the time when you knew Dangwan, who were you like (in terms of size and age) when you knew him?' (lit. having been like who you knew him?)

One grammatical word can contain only one suffix of the four suffixes contrasted in Table 9.2; but in a noun phrase, one suffix can go onto its head and another one can attach to its end, as in 9.34. The suffix *-pək* typically attaches to the end of an NP, or a clause, as we will see below.

9.34 təb-ə-dəka   kudi-pək   wa-kwa-na
    sky-LK-ONLY   language/voice-LIKE   say-HAB-ACT.FOC+3fem.sgBAS.VT
    'It (earthquake) sounds just like the language/voice of thunder'

With the connective *atan* 'then', *-pək* means 'like this, this is how' (§10.2.2). With a numeral, *-pək* means 'more or less, approximately', as in 9.35:

9.35 akwur   lə-kə-k   vitiya-pək
    IMPV+get   she-OBL-DAT   two+LK-APPROX
    'Give her two (Malay apples) or so'

A noun or a pronoun accompanied by *-pək* can occur in the predicate slot and take personal cross-referencing, as in 9.36.

9.36 wun aw   mən-a-pək-awun-ək
    I   then   you.masc-LK-LIKE-1fem.sgBAS.VT-CONF
    'Then I am like you'

A noun with the suffix *-pək* can take further case suffixes, e.g. *Malu-pəka:r yi-di* (Malu-LIKE+LK+ALL go-3plBAS.VT) 'they went a distance like (the one) from here to the Malu village'.

When used with a verb, the suffix *-pək* implies comparison of activity. It then has a whole clause in its scope—see 14.117, §19.3, and examples there. The suffix *-pək* does not qualify as a case marker: it can occur with cases and also, unlike any case-marked forms, a form marked with *-pək* can head a predicate. Unlike other derivational suffixes described here, it is polyfunctional, being used as a derivational suffix 'like', as a means of clause combining, and as a comparative marker on adjectives.

Further non-word class-changing derivations include reduplication of nouns. Full reduplication of nouns has distributive meaning (also see §4.3, and Table 4.2), as in *ña-ñə* (day+LK-day) 'every day, day in day out', *bap-a-bap* (moon-LK-moon) 'month after month', *təp-a-təp* 'every village', *gwalugwə gwalugwə ma:j* (clan+LK clan+LK story) 'story which goes from one clan to another', *tamiy-a-tamiy* (area-LK-area) 'every area, every place', *wi(y)-a-wi* (house-LK-house) 'every house', and *nəb-a-nəb* 'various strangers'. Such nouns can be used in any function, and take case markers.

The reduplicated form of *ga:n* 'night' is irregular: *ganap-ganap* 'every night'. The time noun *ganbab* 'early in the morning' undergoes repetition rather than reduplication, in order to acquire a distributive meaning, as in *ganbab ganbab* 'every early morning'. The noun *gra:b* is repeated in the locative case form: *grabəm grabəm* 'every afternoon'. Time nouns denoting relative time (tomorrow, yesterday, etc.) cannot be reduplicated.

The noun *sə* 'name' has an irregular reduplication pattern: *say-si* '(call) each (person or house) by name'. This pattern is reminiscent of that discussed in §12.8 (also see §16.1, on *kətay-kəti* 'look around and around'). In both *kətay kəti* and *say-si*, reduplication involves repeating all the syllables of the form after its main occurrence, with the vowel of the last syllable lost and *y* changed to *i*.

If a noun has a unique referent, it acquires an intensive meaning when reduplicated, as does *ñəd* 'middle' in *ñəd-ə-ñəd* 'the very middle' (see 9.27 and 7.34). As shown in §4.3.2, reduplicated adjectives also have intensive meaning, e.g. *kwam* 'crazy', *kwam-a-kwam* 'very crazy'; *yara* 'fine', *yara-yara* 'very good'.

The reduplication of closed word classes produces intensive or distributive meaning, e.g. adverbs *məya-məya:b* 'really really; indeed'; *səmsəma:b* 'well and truly (not) at all' (*səma:b* 'not at all': see §14.6); *kəp* 'just', *kəp-a-kəp-a ma:j* (just-LK-just-LK talk) 'words for nothing, useless talk'. When the number 'one' is reduplicated, its meaning is idiosyncratic: *nak-a-nak* (one-LK-one) 'not many; each individually' (also see §10.6.1; cf. Iatmul *kita* 'that one', *kita kita* 'one each; each per unit': Gerd Jendraschek, p.c.). The indefinite determiner *ka:p* 'on its own; alone' can be reduplicated in the intensive meaning 'all alone' (*kapə-ka:p*).

Inherently reduplicated roots are found in every word class except for verbs, e.g. *ñauñau* (*tə*) 'smash', *ləkiləki* 'soft', *nəmnəm* 'tired', *məkmək*, *karkar* 'quietly' (noun-like complements); adverbs *rəka:rək* 'properly', *apar apar* 'not properly', *madək madək* 'especially, namely', and *rəka:rək* 'properly'; and quantifiers *samasa:m* 'a lot', and *aba:b* 'all'.

Among one-off derivational formatives is the formative *-b* which derives the lexeme *ganəb* 'morning' from *ga:n* 'night', and *-ab* which derives the time noun *ganba:b* 'early in the morning' from *ganəb* 'morning'. (This noun undergoes repetition rather than reduplication, to acquire a distributive meaning, as in *ganbab ganbab* 'every early morning'.) The formative *-b* may well be cognate with the terminative case *-Vb* which is used as a derivational device on adverbs (§4.4).

9.3   COMPOUNDING

Manambu has a number of patterns of nominal compounding. Some noun phrases can be realized as one or more than one phonological word depending on their syllable length. They differ from compounds in the number of grammatical words they form, and their semantic compositionality. A compound always forms one grammatical word and tends to be semantically non-compositional. We saw in §2.5, that a modifier-head noun phrase or a possessive noun phrase (types A and C in §8.1.1) consisting of two or three syllables is pronounced as one phonological word. Examples are: *kula-má:j* (new-word) 'new word', *kwasa-ñán* 'small child', *yala-wí* (belly+LK-house) 'the inside of a house', *məw-mí* 'base of a tree', *taba-yí* (hand+LK-fire) 'wrist watch'. They can be pronounced as two phonological words in slow deliberate register. Similar structures are pronounced as several phonological words if more than three syllables long.

Possessive noun phrases and adjective-noun noun phrases which start their life as phono-logical compounds become true morphological compounds once (i) their meaning becomes non-compositional (that is, the meaning of the whole is no longer a simple combination of the meanings of the parts), and (ii) they form one grammatical word. This is the case with possessive NPs of type A: these include personal names, e.g. *Ñəd-ə-wi* (middle-LK-house) 'middle of the house', and of type C, e.g. *ab-a-wapwi* (head-LK-dress) 'hat' and *ap-a-təp* (bone-LK-village) 'Avatip'. These are discussed under types (1) and (2) below.

In terms of morphological relationship between components and their word class, com-pounds are of the following types:

1. 'GENITIVE' COMPOUNDS consist of two nouns, one in a genitive, possessive, or associative relationship to the other. Structurally, these correspond to possessive constructions of types A and C in §8.1.1. The meaning is non-compositional to a varying extent. Examples include *məw-təp* (base-village) 'main village; an alternative name for Avatip', *ap-a-naːgw* (bone/remainder-LK sago) 'sago fibre left over from washing sago; sago pith', *nagwə-gar* (sago+LK-field) 'field or grove of sago; where sago palms are', *təp-a-kudi* (village-LK-language) 'village language, Manambu', *nəb-ə-du* (dry.land-LK-man) 'people of the jungle, strangers (a general term for those who do not traditionally live on the Sepik River and are thus potential enemies: see Harrison 1993 for a discussion of this notion)'. Place names are often compounds of this kind, e.g. *Yawa-bak* (tree.species+LK-field) 'field of tree.species'.

Ad hoc expressions, like *nəbəl-a-gaːn* (today-LK-night) 'tonight, the night of today', *nagwə-yaːb* (sago+LK-road) 'road to sago or with sago', or *məgwə-ñan* (whatever+LK-child) 'child to do with whatever we were talking about previously', straddle the boundary between NPs and compounds and are inherently ambiguous, given the immense productivity of N-N structures described in §8.1.1.

Fixed collocations can be problematic as to whether they are compounds or noun phrases. Examples like *təp-a-jaːp* (village-LK-thing) 'village thing, to refer to sorcery'; *gu-jabər* (water-ship) 'water-raft'; *tənəb-ə-baw* (fireplace-LK-ash) 'ashes from a fireplace'; and *yarəg-a-du* (household-LK-man) 'man of (the same) household' can each be described as referring to a unitary culturally significant concept, and hence better treated as compounds. The latter two instances are more than three syllables long and are often pronounced either with a secondary stress, or as two phonological words.

A particular N-N combination can be fully semantically transparent and be on the way towards developing into a term. For instance, *tək-ə-mi* (seed-LK-tree) 'fruit or seed of a tree' is the preferred way of referring to any kind of pill. Similarly, *təp-a-sə* (village-LK-name) 'village name' is a term for traditional name, and *wali-sə* (white.person-name) means 'Christian or given name' (referring to name given at baptism and different from the traditional, or 'village', name and not just 'name of/for a white person').

A component of a compound can develop a special meaning limited to just this context: *ap-a-* (bone-LK) has the meaning of 'main, true', as in the name of *apa-təp*, that is, Avatip, the main village; and other expressions, such as *ap-a-nagudaw* (bone-LK-Nagudaw) 'a true member of Nagudaw clan'.

2. ADJECTIVE-NOUN COMPOUNDS are fairly productive, e.g. *kula-təp* (new-village) 'new village; term referring to the new location of Avatip and the villages which are relatively recent compared to Avatip'; *rək-a-səp* (dry-LK-skin) 'dry skin; a person with dry skin; term referring to any old person'. Just as with type 1 compounds, some are ambiguous with noun phrases, e.g. *kula-kamnaːgw* (new/fresh-food) 'fresh food' as opposed to dry food.

Adjective-noun compounds often contain *məya-* 'real' whose exact meaning depends on the second component of a compound: *məy-a-məy-a-kayik* (real-LK-real-LK-image/ghost) means 'carving; picture (or any man-made image of a human or animal)'; *məy-a-naːgw* (real-LK-sago) refers to cultivated sago; *məy-a-kamnaːgw* (real-LK-food) refers to protein foods and also traditional foods considered 'strong', such as sago (see §21.2.4).

The noun *wali* used as a modifier frequently occurs in compounds to refer to white people's imports, e.g. *wali-kamnaːgw* (white.person-food) 'non-traditional food stuff', *wali-yaki* (white.person-smoke) 'store-bought tobacco', *wali-naːgw* (white.person-sago) 'biscuit', *wali-sə* 'Christian name' (see above). This term is often extended to refer to any object acquired after contact, e.g. *wali-kamiː* (white.person-fish), to refer to a type of fish reportedly from Indonesian waters which has been invading the waters of the Sepik for the last twenty-five years. Some of these compounds develop very specific meanings, e.g. *wali-kudi* (white.person/east-language) used to refer to any 'white man's language', that is, both Tok Pisin and English, but now mostly used to refer to Tok Pisin (*Inglis kudi* being the term for English). The compound *wali-nəb* (white.person-dry.land) 'dry-land-dweller of white person type; white person' is a way of referring to white people. (This has a morpheme-per-morpheme cognate in Iatmul (Gerd Jendraschek, p.c.), and could have been calqued from Iatmul.)

The status of a compound as type 1 or type 2 may be indeterminate if the first component can be used as either a noun or an adjective. This is the case with compounds containing *wali* 'white person; something to do with white person; eastern (wind); something coming from the east', and a few others, e.g. *kaykwap-a taːb* (lazy-LK hand) 'left hand', literally, 'lazy-hand or hand of a lazy one'.

3. COORDINATE COMPOUNDS consist of two nouns typically without the linker referring to a new referent which can be defined by the two conjoined referents as its major representatives, e.g. *du-taːkw* (man-woman) 'people', *mæn-taːb* (leg-hand) 'arms and legs', *amæy-asaːy* (mother-father) 'parents', *væy-kaːd* (spear-shield) 'arms'. If the first component contains a long vowel, it gets shortened, e.g. *awaːy* 'mother's brother', *away-mamæy* (lit 'maternal.uncle-mother.and.her.sisters') 'relatives responsible for bringing up a child'. The first component of some coordinate compounds can take the comitative marker, e.g. *am-a-wa nəbi* (bow-LK-COM arrow) (as in 7.71) or *am-nəbi* 'bow and arrow'. Possibly, *du-taːkw* (man-woman) 'people', *mæn-taːb* (leg-hand) 'arms and legs' were influenced by Tok Pisin *man-meri* 'people' and *lek-han* 'arms and legs'. (However, compounds of similar structure have been attested both in related Ndu languages and in the neighbouring Kwoma and Yessan-Mayo.) The compound *kami-kamnaːgw* (fish-food) 'foodstuff' has a generic noun as its second component.

4. SYNONYMOUS COMPOUNDS are structurally and semantically similar to coordinate compounds. They consist of two near-synonyms, or nouns from the same semantic field, both with non-human referents. The compound describes either a group of linked referents, or one referent with pronounced features of both components. The linker is obligatory, e.g. *kamkaw-a-ñan* (hairy.yam-LK-smooth.white.yam) 'yams as a group'; *ar-a-ñab* (lake-LK-river) 'lake'; *apwi-məd* (cassowary.vocative.term-cassowary) 'mature female cassowary'; *dəg-a-taːm* (beak-LK-nose) 'nose'.

5. GENERIC-SPECIFIC COMPOUNDS are somewhat similar to constructions with noun classifiers in Australian and in Mayan languages. They consist of a noun 'woman' or 'man' followed by a specific noun. With hybrid nouns, they serve to disambiguate the sex of a referent (see §5.3), as in *takwa-ñan* (woman+LK-child) 'girl', *du-a-ñan* (man-LK-child) 'boy', *gwaːs* 'turtle', *du-a gwaːs* 'male turtle', *takwa gwaːs* 'female turtle'. They can also combine with some specific

nouns whose referents are inanimate, or non-human; then they indicate species, as in *du-a-mæj* (man-LK-thread) 'strong natural fibre for making stringbags' and *du-a-kabay* (man-LK-snake) 'type of dangerous snake'. The term *du-a-ma:gw* (man-LK-generic.noun) 'brother' also belongs to this type. These are similar to GENDER-IDENTIFYING COMPOUNDS containing nouns 'man' and 'woman' as their second component, as in *babay-du* 'maternal grandfather', *babay-ta:kw* 'maternal grandmother', *yanan-ta:kw* 'daughter's daughter', *yanan-du* 'daughter's son', and *bap-a-ta:kw* (moon-LK-woman) 'lady moon' (note that moon is always feminine: see §5.2.1).

6. ORDER AND SIZE COMPOUNDS contain *asa:y* 'father' and *amæy* 'mother' as their first component. The term 'father' denotes large size, as in *numa-də asa:y wuk* (big-masc.sg father tooth) 'very big tooth', or *asa:y wuk* 'huge tooth', *numa-də asa:y na:b* 'very long hair' and so on (also see §5.2.1 and 5.14). The term *amæy* refers to order in the compound *amæy ta:kw* (mother wife) 'first wife', and perhaps also to prominence, as in *amæy ta:b* (mother hand) 'thumb'. There is no linker between the components.

7. ECHO COMPOUNDS involve nouns with non-human referents, and have the meaning of 'things of the same nature as the component which serves as base of echo alliteration' (cf. Yip 1998: 237–8, for an outline of this phenomenon), e.g. *ar-sar* (lake-ECHO.REDUPLICATION) 'lake and so on; lake and waterways'; *mij-ma:j* (ECHO.REDUPLICATION-talk) 'all kinds of small talk'. Echo compounds of adverbs and one adjective have intensive meaning, e.g. *kuprap* 'bad', *kuprapə-saprap* 'really bad', *walba:b* 'near, close', *walba:b kalba:b* 'very close' (or *waləb* 'close', *waləb kaləb* 'very close'), and *sakwər* 'happy', *makwər sakwər* 'very happy', and so do noun-like complements, such as *waygər* (with auxiliary) 'complain', *waygər saygər* 'complain a lot'; *kaygən* '(be) silent', *kaygən saygən* 'be really silent'. The only example of an inherently echo compound is the noun-like complement *sauləy pauləy* 'be in great numbers', as in 9.37:

9.37 du-ta:kw   sauləy.pauləy   yi-di
      man-woman   in.great.numbers go-3plBAS.VT
      'People were in great numbers'.[1]

8. COMPOUNDS INVOLVING CLOSED WORD CLASSES include a Postposition-Noun combination *kukə-məl* (at.back-eye) '(look) sideways', and a Numeral-Noun combination *viti-kisa-ñədi* (two-?-child:du) 'twins'.

9. VERB-NOUN COMPOUNDS consist of a verb root plus a noun. The structure of the compounds is similar to that of relative clauses (see §§19.2.2–3): the noun can be S, O, oblique, or A (the latter is not so frequent), *rə-tami:* (sit-area) 'area where one lives; living area', *kiya-du* (die-man) 'dead man', *bra-təp* (scrape-coconut) 'coconut for scraping', *bla-ma:j* (speak-speech) 'talk'. A compound can consist of a subject of a weather verb + the weather verb's root + noun root, as in [*wa:l ja*]-*səkər* (rain fall-time) 'time of rainfall'.

This compounding type is extremely productive and is widely used to coin terms, such as *kusu-ja:p* (wear-thing) 'clothing', *gra-kudi* (cry-language) 'mourning, crying; term for mourning songs', *kiya-du* 'dead man; used as name of a Manambu football team in Avatip'. The term *səkwa-mawul* (carve-state.of.mind/inside) 'state of mind of a carver' was suggested by David Takendu as a term meaning 'patience'. The first component of such compounds can consist of

---

[1] Echo compounds are attested in other Ndu languages; the examples given by Wendel (1993: 92) from Hanga Kundi (Wosera), involve verbs, unlike Manambu where verbs do not follow this pattern. Similar examples are given by Staalsen and Staalsen (1975) in their dictionary of Iatmul, e.g. *walanga salanga* 'relatives'. Gerd Jendraschek discovered further echo compounds, e.g. *wapuk sapuk* 'stories' (pronounced as *wapuchapuk*). The number of echo compounds in Manambu is too restricted to warrant any meaningful generalizations.

a complex verb in its root form and a noun, as in *sə-kwa-ja:p* (sleep-HAB-thing) 'sleeping gear', *sə-kwa-wi* (sleep-HAB-house) 'house for sleeping'.

In just one instance, the verb root in a Verb-Noun compound appears with a formative unique to this compound: *bla-ja-ya-ma:j* (speak-?-come?-talk/story) 'story; something to tell' (see §15.3). This compound is not functionally equivalent to a relative clause.

A morphological type of a compound is hard to determine if part of it is not used anywhere else. Examples include *saw-na:gw* (?-sago) 'wild sago', *səp-a-tabi* (body-LK-?) 'clothes; body cover', *asə-kami:* (?-fish) 'catfish', and *ñəg-a-ñam* (leaf-LK-?) 'leafy vegetable'. Sometimes a part of a compound is no longer used in Manambu itself, and comparison with related languages may provide a clue. This is the case with *gab-ə-ma:j* (?-LK-story) 'traditional story; teacher', often pronounced as *gama:j*. The first component is cognate to Iatmul *gabu-* 'talk, discuss' (Staalsen n.d.b; Jendraschek, p.c.); that is, originally this form must have been a type 9 compound. Along similar lines, the term *gai-na:gw* (?-sago) 'sago starch' probably contains the element *gai* cognate to the term for 'house, household' throughout the Ndu family. Terms *gai-du* (Gai-man) and *gai-ta:kw* (Gai-woman) are used to refer to the Wosera, and especially the Abelam in whose language *gai* is a term for 'house, village'.

The modifier *nawi* 'mate, one of the same kind, peer group', as in *nawi-du* (mate-man) 'man of the same age; mate' and *nawi-ta:kw* 'woman of the same age, peer group', never occurs on its own; as a result, the structural type of compound is difficult to determine. Unlike other components of compounds, *nawi* can be reduplicated without reduplicating the noun. The reduplication imparts collective meaning, as in *nawi-nawi-du* 'all male peer group', *nawi-nawi-ta:kw* 'all female peer group'. In combination with 'child', the reduplicated form *nawi-nawi* requires the plural *ñanugw* 'children', as in *nawi-nawi-ñanugw* 'all children peer group'. The agreement on the verb is also plural:

9.38   [nawi-nawi-ta:kw] ata   aban taka-di
       peer-peer-woman   then   pact   put.down-3plBAS.VT
       'All peer group women then conspired together'

Compounds can have a complex internal structure. Attested combinations involve type 2 and type 9, e.g. *gla-[kusu-wapwi]* (black+LK-wear-clothes) 'black clothes' (for instance, as a type of clothing worn under mourning); type 2 and type 5, as in *[ñiki-səp-]a-du* (red-skin-LK-man) 'white man'; or type 2 and type 3, e.g. *nəb-ə-[du-ta:kw]* (inland-LK-man-woman) 'people who live inland' (a term used to refer to those who do not traditionally live on the Sepik River: §1.4.1).

Closed Classes

Closed word classes are personal pronouns (§10.1), demonstratives (§10.2), indefinites (§10.3), interrogatives (§10.4), quantifiers (§10.5), and numerals (§10.6). Most of them share some properties with nouns but do not take the full range of noun morphology discussed in Chapters 4–9. This justifies their recognition as separate classes. An overview of their morphological and syntactic features is in §10.7.

10.1 PERSONAL PRONOUNS

Personal pronouns are given in Table 3.3 (repeated here). They distinguish three numbers—singular, dual, and plural—and two genders in second and in third person singular. There is a clear etymological connection between independent pronouns, the two sets of tense-sensitive verbal cross-referencing markers, and cross-referencing enclitics employed with non-verbal predicates (listed in Tables 3.1–2 and 3.4). Grammaticalization of personal pronouns as cross-referencing markers appears to be relatively recent.

Personal pronouns share most properties with nouns. Just like nouns, they take the approximative suffix -pǝk in the meaning 'like', e.g. wun-a-pǝk (I-LK-APPROX) 'more or less like me'. A pronoun can occur in apposition with a noun or a noun phrase, e.g. wun ñǝn-a ñamǝs (I you.fem-LK+fem.sg younger.sibling) 'me, your younger sister'. However, it cannot be modified by adjectives or relative clauses, or head a possessive NP (see type D2 in §8.1.1, for possessive constructions employed with a pronominal possessor).

All non-singular personal pronouns participate in argument elaboration ('inclusory') constructions (see §6.2.3; examples 6.32–3) as cover terms. A direct object expressed with a personal pronoun tends to be case marked, unless the grammatical relations are fully clear from the context (as in 7.5, in §7.2).

Non-third person pronouns stand apart from third person pronouns in the following ways:

(i) First and second person pronouns always have an animate (preferably human) referent, as a speech act participant. Third person pronouns may refer to any entity.

(ii) Third person non-plural pronouns take the oblique marker -kǝ- (see §4.1.1; this form is homophonous with the possessive marker -kǝ- discussed in §8.2) to form cases expressed with a non-ø suffix, e.g. dǝ-kǝ-k (he-OBL-DAT) 'to him', dǝ-kǝ-wa (he-OBL-COM) 'with him', and to combine with each of four suffixes discussed in §9.2. The linker is also obligatory if a pronoun is used as an argument of a postposition (see §4.5), e.g. dǝ-kǝ kukǝr (he-OBL after) 'after him'.

(iii) Third person pronouns take all case markers, while first and second person pronouns do not occur with transportative cases.

(iv) First and second person pronouns occur in identification constructions (see §8.2.2) whereby the notional possessor is the subject of a verbless clause, and the possessed noun occupies the predicate slot. Such constructions with personal pronouns imply full ownership and complete

TABLE 3.3   Personal pronouns

	SG	DU	PL
I	*wun*	*an*	*ñan*
2 fem 2 masc	*ñən* *mən*	*bər*	*gwur*
3 fem 3 masc	*lə* *də*		*dəy, day*

identification between the possessor and the possessed. An orator would enumerate the totemic names belonging to their clan, and then summarize his speech by saying 8.24 or 10.1:

10.1 ñan-adiyan
     we-1plNOM
     'These are ours' (lit. '(these) are us')

(v) Only third person pronouns are used as pronominal possessive markers in possessive noun phrases of type D2, used if possessor is a noun with a specific referent (§8.1.1).

(vi) Only a third person pronoun can be used as a modifier in noun phrases which contain a functionally unmarked distal demonstrative. The agreement in gender and number with the head noun is obligatory. The meaning of these combinations is akin to that of a definite article with emphatic overtones, 'that very one' (see §20.1.1 on NP structure). This is a way of referring to a previously mentioned important participant. Example 10.2 comes from a story about a man who encountered a woman in the jungle.

10.2 [la   ta:kw] vyakət-a ta:kw   ma:, kuprap-ə ta:kw-al
     she+DEM.DIST.fem.sg woman good-LK woman NEG bad-LK   woman-3fem.sgNOM
     'That previously mentioned woman is not a good woman, she is a bad woman (she is an evil spirit)'

Three clauses later, the woman is mentioned again; she is an important participant—the one who is going to bring misfortune to the man. A noun phrase which contains a personal pronoun in an article-like function, a distal demonstrative, and an indefinite pronoun is in 10.3:

10.3 [də a-də   nəkə-də   du] ata ya:d   kwarba:r
     he DEM.DIST-masc.sg other-masc.sg man then go+3masc.sgBAS bush+LK+ALL
     'That very one (previously mentioned important participant) other man then went to the bush'

Such sequences of a personal pronoun and a demonstrative do not belong to two separate NPs, because there is no pause between them, and the two are often pronounced as one phonological word.

These six features point towards the existence of subtle grammatical distinctions between first and second person pronouns (that is, speech act participants) and third person pronouns (non-speech act participants). We return to this distinction in §19.5.4, on speech report techniques.

A fully reduplicated pronoun has an emphatic meaning roughly translatable as 'oneself', e.g. *ñən-a-ñən* 'you (feminine) yourself, really you, as for you', *wun-a-wun* 'I myself; really me, as for me'. A fully reduplicated singular third person pronoun requires the oblique marker *-kə-*, as in *də-kə-də-kə* (he-OBL-he-OBL) 'he himself'. As is typical for *VkV* syllables (process A3 in §2.6), the middle syllable *-kə-* is elided in normal to fast speech, and one frequently hears *də-də-kə* 'he himself' (as in 10.10, 10.11, and 10.15). Interestingly, the oblique *-kə-* does not occur on third person dual pronouns (10.4)—we can recall that the linker *-kə-* is obligatorily used with any non-plural non-reduplicated third person pronoun.

This emphatic meaning of full reduplication is a specific feature of pronouns as a word class. An emphatic pronoun can occur in any function in a clause. In 10.4, it is used to mark possessor, and in 10.5 it marks addressee.

10.4 bər-brə-kə   ñan   kaytək   wuna:k   kur-kwa-na-bər
      3du-3du-OBL+fem.sg child   like   I+LK+DAT   do-HAB-ACT.FOC-3duBAS.VT
      'They used to treat me like their own child'

10.5 wun-a-wuna:k   akəs   wa-kwa-na-d
      I-LK-I+LK+DAT   NEG.HAB   speak/tell-HAB-ACT.FOC-3masc.sgBAS.VT
      'He never talks to me myself'

In 10.15, it marks the A and the O. The two meanings of an emphatic reduplicated personal pronoun—that of emphasis and that of ownership—may not be distinguishable, as in 10.6:

10.6 də-kə-də-ka   ta:kw   ma:
      he-LK-he-LK+DEM.DIST+fem.sg wife   NEG
      'He himself had no wife' (lit. 'His own wife did not (exist)', or 'As for him, there was no wife')

When a reduplicated pronoun appears in the predicate slot, it does not take any personal cross-referencing. As shown in 10.7, it can take the confirmation marker *-ək*:

10.7 wun-a-wun-ək   kəka   rə-tua
      I-LK-I-CONF   DEM.PROX.REACT.TOP.fem.sg   sit-1sgSUBJ.P+3fem.sgBAS.VT
      'It is me myself, I am here sitting'

Reduplicated personal pronouns translate into Tok Pisin with a particle *yet* (as in *em yet* 'he himself', *yu yet* 'you yourself'). Speakers who frequently code-switch into Tok Pisin employ the particle *yet* (underlined), as in 10.8. This was corrected as 10.9, by another speaker:

10.8 ñən <u>yet</u> væn   rə-ñən-ək
      you yet see+SEQ   sit-2fem.sgBAS.VT-CONF
      'You yourself are sitting looking'

10.9 ñən-a-ñ   væn   rə-ñən-ək
      you.fem-LK-you.fem see+SEQ   sit-2fem.sgBAS.VT-CONF
      'You yourself are sitting looking'

Some speakers from Malu village employ both a reduplicated personal pronoun and the Tok Pisin particle *yet*:

10.10 dədə-kə   *yet* məy-a-məy-a   ap-a-nagudaw-ad
       he(+LK)+he-OBL   yet real-LK-real-LK   bone-LK-nagudaw-3masc.sgNOM
       'He himself is a very true member of real Nagudaw clan'

This phenomenon whereby native and borrowed grammatical forms appear together is known as lexical/grammatical parallelism (see Hajek 2006 for Tetun Dili; Aikhenvald forthcoming c). This is how foreign forms make their way into the language, in a situation which appears to disfavour a downright replacement of native forms with foreign insertions.

The semantic analogy between the reduplicated personal pronouns must have contributed to an extension of reduplicated pronouns to mark reflexive, as in 10.11 which describes a suicide. Such examples are rare.

10.11 dədə-kə   vya-səpa-ku   ada
      he(+LK)+he-OBL hit-hit.body-COMPL.SS DEM.DIST.REACT.TOP.masc.sg
      kiya:d
      die+3masc.sgBAS.P
      'Having hit himself, he died'

An alternative to emphatic personal pronouns as markers of co-referential possession is the adverb *ka:p* 'own', as in *kapa kagrəs* (own+LKnephew) 'one's own nephew'. Further ways of expressing reflexive meanings are discussed in §16.2.4.

10.2 DEMONSTRATIVES

Manambu has three demonstrative roots, *kə-* 'proximate demonstrative: near speaker', *wa-* 'proximate demonstrative: near addressee', and *a-* 'distal demonstrative (far from both)'. These roots occur in nominal demonstratives also used as spatio-temporal demonstratives (§10.2.1), in manner adverbial demonstratives (§10.2.2), and in reactivated topic demonstratives (§10.2.3). Of all demonstratives, only nominal demonstratives distinguish additional distance (as shown in Table 10.1 below) and directions.

10.2.1 Nominal demonstratives

All nominal demonstratives can be used as prehead modifiers and as heads of NPs. When they occupy the predicate slot, they take nominal cross-referencing enclitics (like most other non-verbs; but unlike reactivated topic demonstratives discussed in §10.2.3).

The three stems of nominal demonstratives are deployed in the 'reactivated topic' demonstratives. Just two of them, *kə-* 'close to speaker' and *a-* 'distal', are used in adverbial demonstratives.

Nominal demonstratives mark either spatio-temporal deixis or 'current relevance'. The latter are derived from the former with the suffix *-na-* 'current relevance'. This indicates that the object of pointing is being talked about, or is of immediate or ongoing importance to the speakers.

Two spatio-temporal demonstratives, *kə-* and *a-*, can also be used for substitution anaphora (in the sense of Dixon 2003: 63–4). The distal demonstrative *a* can also be used similarly to a definite article. Given the variety of its uses not directly related to 'pointing', the distal demonstrative can be considered functionally unmarked.

Spatio-temporal demonstratives distinguish obligatory gender and number; they may also distinguish either three additional degrees of distance, or five directions. 'Current relevance' demonstratives distinguish five directions, and two additional degrees of distance.

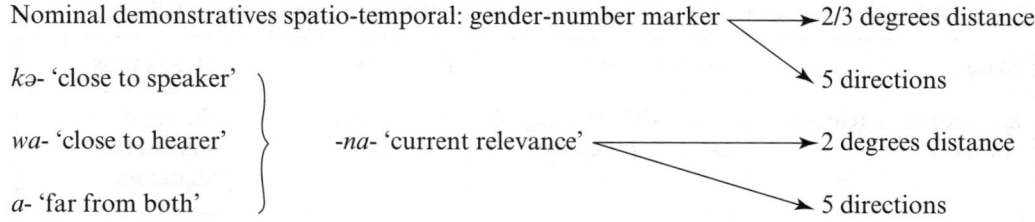

SCHEME 10.1   Nominal demonstratives, their structure and categories

Scheme 10.1 shows the structure of the two types of nominal demonstratives and the categories which can be expressed in each.

Spatio-temporal demonstratives take the same cases as nouns (§7.1), with two differences:

- the accusative–locative case with nouns always has a locative reading with demonstratives; and
- there are no examples of the transportative cases with a nominal demonstrative.

In contrast, 'current relevance' demonstratives do not take cases at all—the same form refers to an argument or an oblique in any function.

Nominal demonstratives are employed in the function of local adverbial demonstratives (Dixon 2003: 69). Spatio-temporal demonstratives without a directional specification are always marked with locational cases when they refer to locations, e.g. *kə-lə-m* (DEM.PROX-fem-LOC) 'here', *kə-lə-r* (DEM.PROX-fem-ALL) 'towards here', *wa-lə-m* (DEM.PROX.ADDR-fem-LOC) 'here (close to addressee)', *a-lə-m* (DEM.DIST-fem-LOC) 'there', and so on. Those with directional specification tend to take cases, but do not have to, e.g. *a-l-ə-da-m* (DEM.DIST-fem.sg-LK-DOWN-LOC) 'there underneath', *a-l-ə-da* (DEM.DIST-fem.sg-LK-DOWN) 'there underneath'.

We first discuss (A) spatio-temporal demonstratives and their usage, and then (B) 'current relevance' demonstratives. In (C), we compare directional meanings distinguished in demonstratives and in verbs. Types of orientation, or frames of reference, prevalent in the Manambu speech communities are addressed under (D).

A. SPATIO-TEMPORAL DEMONSTRATIVES refer to relative distance in space or in time and distinguish either (i) two or three additional degrees of distance, or (ii) five directions. The demonstratives which distinguish additional distance are in Table 10.1. The spatio-temporal demonstratives unmarked for additional distance are discussed in A1. Those with segmental marking for additional distance are considered in A2.

The choice of a feminine gender marker in spatio-temporal demonstratives is governed by the following principle: if there is a segmental morpheme following the agreement marker, the *-l* form is used, e.g. *a-l-əm* (DEM.DIST-fem.sg-LK+LOC) 'there' (see §5.1.2), *a-l-a-wur* (DEM.DIST-fem.sg-LK-UP) 'that one feminine which is up' (see A3 and Table 10.2). Otherwise, the feminine form is ø, e.g. *a* 'that one feminine'.

All the demonstratives have spatial uses; some can also refer to time. The proximal and distal demonstratives unmarked for additional distance—discussed in A1—can be used for textual deixis, that is, anaphora of different kinds. The 'proximal to addressee' demonstrative can be used to imply a speaker's detachment, and also mark empathy with the hearer, in a narrative. It cannot be used to refer to time. A summary is in Table 10.1. Demonstratives are underlined throughout this section.

TABLE 10.1   Nominal spatio-temporal demonstratives distinguishing additional distance

STEM	GENDER/NUMBER	DISTANCE	OTHER USES
kə- 'proximal' (close to speaker)	fem.sg *-ø/-l-*; masc.sg *-d*, dual *-bər*, pl. *-di*	*ø* 'proximal'	time and substitution anaphora
	fem.sg *-l-*; masc.sg *-d-*; dual *-bər*, pl. *-di*	*-ay* 'further from speaker'	time
		-awi 'even further from speaker'	—
wa- 'proximal to addressee' (close to addressee)	fem.sg *-ø*; masc.sg *-d*, dual *-bər*, pl. *-di*	*ø* 'proximal to addressee'	detachment or empathy
	fem.sg *-l-*; masc.sg *-d-*; dual *-bər*, pl. *-di*	*-ay* 'further from hearer'	address term
a- 'distal' (far from both speaker and addressee)	fem.sg *-ø*; masc.sg *-d*, dual *-bər*, pl. *-di*	*ø* 'far from speaker and hearer'	substitution and textual anaphora time
	fem.sg *-l-*; masc.sg *-d-*; dual *-bər*, pl. *-di*	*-ay* 'further from speaker and hearer'	time
		-awi 'very far indeed'	—

A1. SPATIO-TEMPORAL DEMONSTRATIVES UNMARKED FOR ADDITIONAL DISTANCE consist of a demonstrative stem followed by a gender-number marker.

(i) SPATIO-TEMPORAL USES. In its spatio-temporal use, the demonstrative *kə-* refers to an object close to the speaker, as in 6.6, 6.8, and 10.12. In 6.6 the demonstrative is used to address the two mothers, 'these two of you (close to me)'. In 10.12, the two instances of headlessly used *kə-* refer to two different girls, both sitting next to the speaker (accompanied with pointing).

10.12 [kə   nəma   tə-ku]   kə-l-ək
      DEM.PROX.fem.sg big+fem.sg become-COMPL.SS DEM.PROX-fem.sg-LK+DAT
      kui-lə-di
      give.to.third.p-3fem.sgSUBJ.P-3plBAS.P
      'After this one (girl) has become big, she has given them (her clothes) to this one'

This same demonstrative can be considered the semantically unmarked 'proximate', since it often indicates proximity of the object to both speaker and addressee. This is the case in 6.8, where *kə-də* (this-masc.sg) refers to 'this village where we are now', that is close to both speaker and hearer. In contrast, the demonstrative *wa-* 'close to the addressee' is used to stress the fact that the object is close to the addressee (and not so close to the speaker), as in 10.13. The locative form of the proximate demonstrative *kə-* in 10.13 refers to a location close to the speaker, but not to the addressee.

10.13 <u>wa-də</u>   waːr   <u>kə-l-əm</u>   a-kaytak
DEM.PROX.ADDR-masc.sg large.string.bag DEM.PROX-fem.sg-LK+LOC IMPV-attach
'Put this (close to you/your) stringbag here'

This demonstrative can combine reference to spatial proximity and possessive relationship: in 10.14, *wa-də* 'this masculine close to you' refers to a child belonging to a mother and thus 'close' to her, as an addressee. The man is giving orders to his two wives with their respective children.

10.14 ñən   Sirunki <u>wa-də</u>   ñən-a-də   ñənwa   Lai
you.fem.sg Sirunki DEM.PROX.ADDR-masc.sg you.fem.sg-LK-masc.sg son+COM Lai
ata   sər   yi-kə-dian,   <u>a-də</u>   bagwək   Ñən
then   tomorrow go-FUT-1plBAS.VT DEM.DIST-masc.sg dance+LK+DAT you.fem.sg
Kayak <u>wa-də</u>   ñan kur-ku   adakw
Kayak DEM.PROX.ADDR-masc.sg son get-COMPL.SS stay.IMPV
'You, Sirunki, we will go tomorrow together with this (close to you) son of yours to that dance. You, Kayak, having got this (close to you, that is, your) son, stay'

This form (zero-marked for additional distance) can also be used in a slightly derogatory sense, referring to something belonging to the addressee the speaker wishes to have nothing to do with. In 10.15 the main character, Kuimagan, is rebuking one of his two wives who had taken a wrong road and is thus responsible for a disaster that had happened to her son. Kuimagan does not want to have anything more to do with the wretched boy. He refers to the boy as 'this-close to you':

10.15 <u>alək</u>   wuka   <u>wa-də</u>
DEM.DIST+fem.sg+LK+DAT DEM.PROX.ADDR.REACT.TOP+fem.sg DEM.PROX.ADDR-masc.sg
ñan   ada   bə   ñən-ñən-a
child DEM.DIST.REACT.TOP+masc.sg already you.fem-you.fem-3fem.sgNOM
dədə-kə   kuprap wa-ñəna-d
he(+LK)+he-OBL bad   say-2fem.sgSUBJ.VT-3masc.sgBAS.VT
'This is why here (close to you), this-close-to-you boy, you yourself made him himself (be) in a bad way'

A similar example is in the last line of 10.29 where the speaker uses this same demonstrative to refer to the Swakap people for whom he has hardly any respect. Another reason for using the 'close-to-listener' demonstrative there is that the speaker knew that the Swakap people were of particular interest to me as a listener.

The distal demonstrative *a-* can be used to refer to an object which is close to neither speaker nor addressee, as in 10.16. Here, the proximal demonstrative *kə-* is contrasted to the distal *a-*:

10.16 <u>kə-də</u>   du   maː, <u>a-də</u>   du-ad
DEM.PROX-masc.sg man NEG DEM.DIST-masc.sg man-3masc.sgNOM
'It is not this man, it is that man'

Only *kə-* and *a-* stems are used for temporal reference. The zero-marked proximal demonstrative refers to an ongoing stretch of time, e.g. *kə wik* (DEM.PROX+fem.sg week) 'this week now', *kə-də nabi* (DEM.PROX-masc.sg year) 'this year now'; *a wik* (DEM.DIST+fem.sg week) 'that (last) week'. And the zero-marked distal demonstrative refers to past, e.g. *a-də nabi* (DEM.DIST-masc.sg year) 'that (past) year'. (Demonstratives discussed under A2 below refer to more remote stretches of time.)

(ii) ANAPHORIC USES. As a marker of participant anaphora, the demonstrative *kə-* 'close to speaker' refers to a topical referent just mentioned or previously discussed, as in 6.4–5 (there, the demonstrative *kə-* 'close to speaker' refers to the clans talked about). A similar example is 10.17: it is the beginning of a story about a group of Japanese who tried to escape after the war into the Sepik area, and how they were massacred by the combined forces of the Manambu and the Iatmul. We were discussing this event before the beginning of the story: this explains the anaphoric use of the demonstrative in the first line:

10.17 kə-di   *Japanese* [*war* kusə-lə-k]   [1945 kusə-lə-k],
      DEM.PROX-pl Japanese war finish-3fem.sg-COMPL.DS 1945 finish-3fem.sg-COMPL.DS
      [aw   day *sampela* tabu-ku]   [kə-də   du   ta:kw   [gus
      then   they some   escape-COMPL.SS DEM.PROX-masc.sg man woman paddle
      ka:n]   ñab-a-rəb   war-di]
      paddle+SEQ river-LK-FULLY go.up-3plBAS.P
      'These Japanese (we have just talked about), after the war had finished, after it finished in 1945, then after some of them had escaped, these people went straight up the Sepik River paddling'

The proximal demonstrative *kə-* is never used cataphorically (that is, to mark forwards anaphora). It can only be used for textual anaphora when it modifies the noun *ma:j* 'story'.

The distal demonstrative *a-* is most frequently used for substitution anaphora, as in 10.14, where 'to that dance' refers to a dance mentioned in the preceding clause. It is never used with a new referent, and tends to occur with definite referents only, especially the ones to be deployed as topics of a whole text. In 10.18, the demonstrative refers to previously mentioned foodstuff which Sirunki had brought with her:

10.18 [[amæy, wun ka:m   yasa-na-wun],   wa-də-k],
      mother I   hunger feel-ACT.FOC-1fem.sgBAS.VT say-3masc.sg-COMPL.DS
      [a-di   krayi-lə-di   kamna:gw] ata
      DEM.DIST-pl bring-3fem.sgSUBJ.P-3plBAS.P foodstuff   then
      kui-lə-d
      give.to.third.p-3fem.sgSUBJ.P-3masc.sgBAS.P
      'After the small child had said: "Mother, I am hungry", she gave him the foodstuff she'd brought'

The distal demonstrative is also used as a marker for definite (that is, uniquely identifiable) referents, as in 10.19, where Kuimagan addresses his two wives as 'the (lit. those) two women':

10.19 [a-bər   ta:kw,   awuk,   wun-a   majək]
      DEM.DIST-du woman IMPV+listen I-LK+fem.sg speech+LK+DAT
      '(Kuimagan thus said) "The two women, listen to my speech"'

As similar example is in 10.3 where the demonstrative is accompanied by a third person pronoun. Unlike the proximal demonstrative, the distal demonstrative can be used for textual anaphora (but not for cataphora of any kind). The distal demonstrative, but not the proximal one, can be used as a modifier in a headless relative clause, as in 10.20.

10.20 [a   wa-ñəna]   a
      DEM.DIST+fem.sg say-2fem.sgSUBJ.VT+3fem.sgBAS.VT DEM.DIST+fem.sg
      wukəmar-tua
      forget-1sgSUBJ.VT+3fem.sgBAS.VT
      'That what you said—that I forgot'

It is instructive to compare the use of *kə* 'close to speaker' and *a* 'distal' as anaphoric markers. If one referent is mentioned more recently than the other, it is referred to with the proximal demonstrative, and the other one with the distal, as in 10.21.

10.21 aw   kəta [a-di   də-kə   wa:ñ] [kə-də   du
      then now   DEM.DIST-pl 3masc.sg-OBL+fem.sg line   DEM.PROX-masc.sg man
      də-kə   wa:ñ]
      3masc.sg-OBL+fem.sg line
      'Then now (here are) those lines (of descendants) of his (first mentioned a few clauses back), the line (of descendants) of this man (just mentioned)'

If there are two equal alternatives, the least important one is likely to be referred to with the distal demonstrative, and a more important one with the proximal. In 10.22, Kuimagan is giving his two wives instructions on what to do. They are supposed to encounter two roads (introduced in 10.22a). The roads are anaphorically referred to with the distal demonstrative (in 10.22b). Then he introduces a tree *wəpak* whose leaf he was going to place on the road which the women are not to follow (10.22c, same as 7.21). The tree is anaphorically referred to with the distal demonstrative, and so is one of the roads—the one that the women should not take. The correct (and thus the more important) one is referred to with the proximal demonstrative in 10.22d.

10.22 a. [ñəd-ə-yabəm   yabə-bra   viti] nak aki-tabar
          middle-LK-road+LK+LOC road+LK-3duNOM+LK two one left-hand+LK+ALL
          kwa-kna-d,   nak mapa-tabar
          stay-FUT+ACT.FOC-3masc.sgBAS.VT one right-hand+LK+ALL
          kwa-kna-d
          stay-FUT+ACT.FOC-3masc.sgBAS.VT
          'In the middle of the road there are two roads, one will be on the left hand, one will be on the right hand (side)'
       b. a   a-bər   ya:b aki-taba:r   yi-na-d-ə
          then DEM.DIST-du road right-hand+LK+ALL go-ACT.FOC-3masc.sgBAS.VT-LK
          ya:b a   wun-a-dəka gaga-mi   kur-ku
          road DEM.DIST+fem.sg I-LK-ONLY   leaf+LK-tree get-COMPL.SS
          təpə-saki-kə-tua-d
          close-ACROSS.AWAY-FUT-1sgSUBJ.VT-3masc.sgBAS.VT
          'As for those two roads, the road going to the right, then/so just I, having got a leaf (of *wepak* tree) closed it off'
       c. [[a   wəpak-a:m]   və-ku]   a-də
          DEM.DIST+fem.sg type.of.tree-LK+LOC see-COMPL.SS DEM.DIST-masc.sg
          yabəm   yi-tukwa
          road+LK+LOC go-PROH.GEN
          'Having seen the tree (whose leaf I put on the ground), do not go on that road'
       d. kə-də   mapa-taba   yabə-rəb   ma:y
          DEM.PROX-masc.sg left-hand+LK road+LK-STRAIGHT go.IMPV
          'Go straight on this one on the left hand-side'

The two anaphoric demonstratives can have the same referent, as in 10.23. The proximate demonstrative is more expressive, and used to draw the hearer's attention to this very village we are talking about.

10.23 [kə-də   təp],   [a-də   numa-də   saki   təp]   ata
      DEM.PROX-masc.sg village DEM.DIST-masc.sg big-masc.sg name.debate village then
      ma: rəpə-d
      again submerge-3masc.sgBAS.VT
      'This very village, that village of big name debates, submerged again'

The two demonstratives have a number of additional uses. The demonstrative *kə* 'close to speaker' as predicate head (usually as functionally unmarked feminine) occurs in the meaning of emphatic 'no', as in 10.24 and 14.41. This is similar to how one can exclaim 'what on earth is that!' as a token of negative reaction or amazement. Whenever it is used in a negative meaning, an alternative—that is, the correct 'solution'—is usually suggested (see §14.6).

10.24 sə-kə-də   wi-ad   wa-lə-k
      who-OBL-masc.sg house-3masc.sgNOM   say-3fem.sg-COMPL.DS
      ka!   ñən!   an-a-də   wi-ad
      DEM.PROX+3fem.sgNOM you.fem we.du-LK-masc.sg house-3masc.sgNOM
      'After she'd said: "Whose house is it?", (they said) "That??? (meaning No!) Yours??? It is our house." '

The distal demonstrative *a-* is used as a connective 'then, so' in its functionally unmarked feminine form, as in the second line of 10.22b. The dative feminine form of the distal demonstrative is used as a sentence connective *alək* (DEM.DIST.fem.sg+LK+DAT) 'this is why' (see 4.16, 10.15, 10.36, and §19.6).

Within a narrative, the 'close to hearer' demonstrative can occasionally be used to refer to a previously mentioned referent, to indicate empathy with the audience, and to encourage their attention whenever the narrator may feel that their attention is slipping away. In 10.25, the two women, the protagonists of the story, are referred to in this way: Maguniway, the narrator, used it as a device to make sure we, the audience, were listening:

10.25 [wa-bər   ta:kw   na:gw yaku-ta:y]   tə-brə-k
      DEM.PROX.ADDR-du woman sago   wash-COTEMP stay-3du-COMPL.DS
      'After these two women (close to you—so do listen) had stayed washing sago . . . '

This is reminiscent of the attention-getting use of this same demonstrative marked for additional spatial distance—see A2 below (e.g. 10.30).

The less formally marked nominal demonstratives have more functional and semantic extensions (and thus may be considered functionally unmarked) than those which receive additional formal marking for distance—see A2. This agrees with a tendency of correlating formal and functional markedness, a pervasive feature of the Manambu grammar.

A2. SPATIO-TEMPORAL DEMONSTRATIVES MARKED FOR ADDITIONAL DISTANCE consist of a demonstrative stem followed by a distance marker and then by a gender-number marker. All of these are used for spatial, and some also for temporal reference.

The form *kə-* 'close to speaker' + *-ay* 'additional distance' refers to objects close to the speaker, but somewhat further away than *kə-* 'proximate; close to speaker', and often also visible. The Ambunti mountain (called Makəmawi) towering over the Sepik River and perfectly visible from Avatip was referred to as *kə-d-ay nəbək* (DEM.PROX-masc.sg-DIST mountain) 'this distant mountain'.

However, an object referred to with the proximate demonstrative marked for additional distance may not be visible from where the speaker is located; yet it can be conceptualized as being within the 'close' range. In 10.26 Aulapan referred to the stream close to Yawabak (where the story was told), but not visible from the place we were sitting, as *kə-d-ay bəyib* (DEM.PROX-masc.sg-DIST stream). In the second clause of this example, the whole area is anaphorically referred to with the distal demonstrative *a*, unmarked for additional distance:

10.26 [waku-də-k   kə-d-ay   bəyib   Baljəb-ə-m],   orait,
go.out-3masc.sg-COMPL.DS DEM.PROX-masc.sg-DIST stream Baljəb-LK-LOC all.right
[a-l-ə-m   waku-ku   ra:d]
DEM.DIST-fem-LK-LOC go.out-COMPL.SS sit+3masc.sgBAS.P
'After he had emerged on this-further-away stream Baljəb, all right, (his adversary) stayed there having emerged'

The form *a-* 'distal' + *-ay* 'additional distance' refers to objects considerably further away from both speaker and addressee than those referred to with a simple *a* 'distal demonstrative'. In 10.27, from the same story as 10.26, *alayir* refers to a location very far from Yawabak:

10.27 a-lə-da   kawawa   a-l-ayir
DEM.DIST-fem.sg-DOWN hole+LK+COM DEM.DIST-fem.sg-DIST+LK+ALL
waku-d
go.out-3masc.sgBAS.P
'He emerged via that hole down below (going) towards over there (a remote location)'

The *kə-* and *a-* stems with the additional distance marker *-ay* refer to future and past time respectively, e.g. *kə-l-ay wik* (DEM.PROX-fem.sg-DIST week) 'next week', *kə-d-ay nabi* (DEM.PROX-masc.sg-DIST year) 'next year', *a-l-ay wik* (DEM.DIST-fem.sg-DIST week) 'week before last', *a-d-ay nabi* (DEM.DIST-masc.sg-DIST year) 'year before last'.

The form *wa-* 'close to addressee' + *-ay* often implies that the referent is closer to the addressee than to the speaker, but not in close proximity to either. When we went to visit Damel at her house, I asked Mali which of the two fireplaces belonged to Damel. Damel's fireplace was in the other end of the house, and somewhat closer to me than to Mali, so she said:

10.28 lə-kə   tənəb   wa-l-ay   aka
she-OBL+fem.sg fireplace DEM.PROX.ADDR-fem.sg-DIST DEM.DIST.REACT.TOP.fem.sg
'Her fireplace is here further away from us both but closer to you'

In his story about the Swakap people and how they went to live with the people at Yuanab (Yambon), the narrator used *wa-d-ay* (DEM.PROX.ADDR-masc.sg-DIST) 'this close to addressee further away' twice because the place where I was sitting was slightly closer to the direction where Yuanab is:

10.29 yi:n   wa-d-ay   Yuanab
go+LENGTH+SEQ DEM.PROX.ADDR-masc.sg-DIST Yambon
rə-dana   ta:miy a   təp
sit-3plSUBJ.VT+3fem.sgBAS.VT area DEM.DIST.fem.sg village
aka   wula-dana,
DEM.DIST.REACT.TOP.fem.sg enter-3plSUBJ.VT+3fem.sgBAS.VT

wa-də-ay		rə-na-di	Yuanab-a-wa	nakamib
DEM.PROX.ADDR-masc.sg-DIST		sit-ACT.FOC-3plBAS.VT	Yambon-LK-COM	together
wa-di	Yuanab	Swakap-adi		
DEM.PROX.ADDR-pl	Yambon	Swakap-3plNOM		

'Having gone on, they (the Swakap people) entered that-closer-to-you but far away area where the Yambon people live, those-closer-to-you but far away stayed (in) that village together with the Yambon people, these-close-to-you Yambon people are the ones from Swakap'

The form *wa-* 'close to addressee' + *-ay* is used as an address term for a familiar interlocutor, e.g. *wa-l-ay* (DEM.PROX.ADDR-fem.sg-DIST) 'hey you (woman), you here (close to addressee)', *wa-d-ay* (DEM.PROX.ADDR-masc.sg-DIST) 'hey you (man), you here (close to addressee)'. An example is under 10.30 where the mother was calling to her baby daughter, trying to stop her playing with her mother's food:

| 10.30 | wun-a | kami:-a, | kaykətə-tukwa | wa-l-ay! |
| | I-LK+fem.sg | fish-3fem.sgNOM | hold-PROH.GEN | DEM.PROX.ADDR-fem.sg-DIST |

'It is my fish, do not hold (onto it), hey you here!'

Such an address form can be optionally accompanied by *ñan* 'child' (if referring to a woman or a non-initiated man). That is, it is somewhat conventionalized.

The proximal demonstrative *kə-* accompanied by the marker of very remote distance *-awi* is used to refer to objects more remote than the ones referred to with *kə-* + *-ay* 'distance', and yet conceived as not too remote from the speaker. Two proximal demonstratives marked for additional distance within the same sentence in 10.31 illustrate this idea of 'relative' remoteness. The narrator is vehement about a particular clan having no right to the piece of land beyond the Ambunti mountain, quite far away (beyond visibility range, referred to as *kə-l-ay* (DEM.PROX-fem.sg-DIST) 'this-distant'), and far up the Sepik River (*kə-l-awi* (DEM.PROX-fem.sg-VERY.DIST) 'this-very distant'):

10.31	kə-l-ayim-a:b,		dəy-a	tami:	ma:,
	DEM.PROX-fem.sg-DIST+LOC-TOO		3pl-LK+fem.sg	area	NEG
	kə-l-awi-a:b				
	DEM.PROX-fem.sg-VERY.DIST-TOO				

'In this (distant place), it is not their land; in this very distant place, too'

The distal demonstrative *a-* accompanied by the marker of very remote distance *-awi* is used to refer to extremely remote objects, e.g. *a-l-awi təp* (DEM.DIST-fem.sg-VERY.DIST village) 'a village very far away'—as I was told, such a village would be somewhere 'over the horizon'. The source (headwaters) of the Sepik River was referred to as *alawi*. In 10.32 (continuation of 10.31), this demonstrative refers to a village located very far away from the deictic centre (the outskirts of the Malu village), next to the Yessan (which is beyond Ambunti and further inland). The unmarked distal demonstrative in 10.32 is used anaphorically (referring to the village mentioned before).

10.32	a	təp	a-l-awi		yəsanawa,	Pulwunawi
	DEM.DIST.fem.sg	village	DEM.PROX-fem.sg-VERY.DIST		Yessan+LK+COM	Brugnowi
	wa-dana,		a	təp		
	say-3plSUBJ.VT+3fem.sgBAS.VT		DEM.DIST.fem.sg	village		

'That (mentioned) village (is) that very distant one, alongside the Yessan, they call it Brugnowi, that village'

TABLE 10.2 Nominal spatio-temporal demonstratives distinguishing direction

STEM	GENDER/NUMBER	DIRECTION
kə- 'proximal'	fem.sg *-l-*; masc.sg *-d-*; dual *-bər*; pl. *-di*	-*wur* 'up' -*d(a)* 'down'
wa- 'proximal to addressee'	fem.sg *-l-*; masc.sg *-d-*; dual *-bər*; pl. *-di*	-*aki* 'across' -*aku* 'outwards'
a- 'distal'	fem.sg *-l-*; masc.sg *-d-*; dual *-bər*; pl. *-di*	-*wula* 'inside, away from the Sepik River'

The demonstrative *wa-* 'close to addressee' does not distinguish this extra degree of distance.

A3. SPATIO-TEMPORAL DEMONSTRATIVES DISTINGUISHING DIRECTION consist of a demonstrative stem followed by a gender-number marker and then by one of five directionals: see Table 10.2.

These demonstratives are used for spatial deixis, indicating location of an object with respect to the speaker ('relative' frame of reference: Levinson 2003). Gemaj said 10.33, showing me the stars up in the sky (who are supposed to be the totemic ancestors of the clan group I was adopted into):

10.33 <u>kə-di-a-wur</u>   kugar gwalugw-adi
       DEM.PROX-pl-LK-UP star   ancestors-3plNOM
       'These stars up (in the sky/above us) are ancestors'

Or it can indicate the location of an object with respect to an important landmark ('absolute' frame of reference). Within the Sepik area, this is invariably the Sepik River itself, as in 10.27 (location downstream) and in 10.34. The previous location of Avatip is further away from the river (since it has been flooded after the river had changed its course). This 'old' village is remote from the present one, and this is why the distal demonstrative is used.

10.34 a-d-a-wula   təp   də-kə-də   sə   Təpayaburman
       DEM.DIST-masc.sg-LK-INLAND village masc.sg-OBL-masc.sg name Tepayaburman
       'The name of that (big) village inland is Tepayaburman'

Along similar lines, as we were walking along a path parallel but not close to the river, Kerryanne told me to walk on the other side of the path (to avoid mud) which was 'inland' from the Sepik River (*kə-l-a-wulam*: DEM.PROX-fem.sg-LK-inland+LOC). The lake (which is where the Yawabak village is located) is considered as being in an 'outward' direction from the Sepik River, as shown in 10.35:

10.35 <u>kə-l-aku</u>   ar-a:l   waku-waku-k   tabu-a
       DEM.PROX-fem.sg-OUTWARDS lake-LK+ALL go.out-RED-PURP forbidden-3fem.sgNOM
       'It was forbidden to go out to the lake in the outward direction' (during an air raid)

A reference point with respect to which the direction is determined can be established within a narrative. The man raised by a flying fox and two birds lives up the tree; his mother, the flying fox, allows him to marry a woman who is underneath the tree by saying 10.36. A woman had requested to marry *a-d-a-wur du* (DEM.DIST-masc.sg-LK-UP man) 'that man up there'.

10.36 alək   kə-l-a-da   ta:kw-a   də
DEM.DIST+fem.sg+LK+DAT DEM.PROX-fem.sg-LK-DOWN woman-3fem.sgNOM he
kə-də   ñan-a-də   ñan   kra-kwa-d
DEM.PROX-masc.sg we-LK-masc.sg child marry-IMPV.3p-masc.sg
'Thus, may he this son of ours marry this woman down below (focused)'

One often hears these demonstratives in conversations where different directions are useful for disambiguating classificatory relatives in the same relationship to the speaker. For instance, if I am sitting in a house in a company of classificatory sisters, I may well refer to one as *kə-l-aki ñamus* (DEM.PROX-fem.sg-ACROSS.AWAY younger.sibling) 'this younger sister sitting across from me', and to the other as *kə-l-a-wula ñamus* (DEM.PROX-fem.sg-LK-INLAND younger.sibling) 'this younger sister sitting closer to the part of the house further away from the Sepik River than me'.

The 'close to speaker' and the distal demonstratives are often used anaphorically, exactly as in (ii) under A1 above. In 10.37, Katalu announced that the story he was about to tell was to deal with the previously mentioned place up the river:

10.37 nəbəl a-l-a-wur   ka   bla-ma:j-a
today DEM.DIST-fem.sg-LK-UP DEM.PROX.fem.sg+3fem.sgNOM tell-story-3fem.sgNOM
'Today this is it, the story about that (area) up the river'

We have seen that specifications of additional distance and of direction are not compatible within one demonstrative. As a result, two demonstratives often occur together in one NP—one specifying the direction, and the other additional distance. The surface order is always that illustrated in 10.38: direction first, distance second. No other constituents can intervene between the two demonstratives.

10.38 [a-di-a-wur   a-di-ay   warag]   asay-bər
DEM.DIST-pl-LK-UP DEM.DIST-pl-DIST ancestor father-PL
vya-war-da-l   ma:j-a
hit-go.up-3plsSUBJ.P-3fem.sgBAS.P story-3fem.sgNOM
wa-kə-tua
tell-FUT-1sgSUBJ.VT+3fem.sgBAS.VT
'I will tell a story (focused) about how those far away ancestors from upriver, fathers, fought and went up'

This is the only technique available for combining information about additional distance and direction in one NP.

B. THE 'CURRENT RELEVANCE' DEMONSTRATIVES distinguish either (i) two degrees of distance (B1), or (ii) five directions (B1). A 'current relevance' demonstrative refers to an object which is being talked about, or is known or important to the speakers. It tends to be mentioned just prior to referring to it with a demonstrative; but more often than not it is part of information shared by the speech act participants.

B1. THE 'CURRENT RELEVANCE' DEMONSTRATIVES DISTINGUISHING ADDITIONAL DISTANCE are in Table 10.3.

The 'far from both speaker and addressee' 'current relevance' demonstrative distinguishes a further degree of distance—'very distal'. In contrast to the spatio-temporal demonstratives discussed in A, the proximate *kə*- does not have this distance specification.

The morpheme *-ay* has different meanings with spatio-temporal and with 'current relevance' demonstratives. With the former it has a meaning of 'further from speaker; or hearer; or both' (depending on the choice of the stem). With 'current relevance' demonstratives it is like a

TABLE 10.3   'Current relevance' demonstratives distinguishing additional distance

STEM	'CURRENT RELEVANCE' MARKER	DISTANCE
kə- 'proximal'	*-na-*	*-ay* 'close to speaker'
wa- 'proximal to addressee'	*-na-*	*-ay* 'close to hearer'
		-awi 'very far indeed'
a- 'distal'	*-na-*	*-ay* 'far from speaker and hearer'
		-awi 'very far indeed'

'placeholder' which obligatorily accompanies the marker *-na-* 'current relevance'. It is in a paradigmatic opposition with *-awi* 'very far indeed (from both speaker and hearer)', but only for the stems *kə-* and *a-*. 'Current relevance' demonstratives often have a locational meaning; but can also be used as prehead modifiers, e.g. *kə-na-y kə-l-ay ñan* (DEM.PROX-CURR.REL-DIST DEM.PROX-fem.sg-DIST child) 'this mentioned further away female child', and also 10.40. A 'current relevance' demonstrative can occur with time words: *a-na-y nabi* (DEM.DIST-CURR.REL-DIST year) means 'that (past) year we are/were talking about', and *kə-na-y nabi* (DEM.PROX-CURR.REL-DIST year) refers to 'this (present) year we are/were talking about'.

'Current relevance' demonstratives are semantically complex. The 'current relevance' marker *-na-* shows that it has been previously mentioned, or talked about, or that it is something the speaker has in mind. And a demonstrative stem indicates the position of the object with respect to the speaker or the hearer or both. The 'relevant' referent may occur in the previous stretch of discourse, as in line five of T3.43: *a-na-y* (DEM.DIST-CURR.REL-DIST) 'that mentioned' refers to the place visited by the character where he claims to have killed all the snakes. The place was overtly mentioned two clauses earlier.

Or the demonstrative may refer to an object or a place interlocutors can both see at the same time, and/or have just been talking about, as in 10.39. The fireplace is closer to the speaker than to the addressee.

10.39 wun-a   wuti   kə-na-y   rə-na
I-LK+fem.sg spoon DEM.PROX-CURR.REL-DIST sit-ACT.FOC+3fem.sgBAS.VT
'My spoon is sitting here (on the fireplace we have just been cleaning together)'

Spatio-temporal demonstratives and 'current relevance' demonstratives can occur together in one NP, as in 10.40, and always in this order: a current relevance demonstrative with no gender or number specification occurs first and a spatio-temporal one comes next. The two complement each other, since the 'current relevance' demonstrative here does not convey information about the gender of the noun or the additional distance.

10.40 ñan kə-na-y   kə-d-ay   numa-də   wi-a:m
we   DEM.PROX-CURR.REL-DIST DEM.PROX-masc.sg-DIST big-masc.sg house-LK+LOC
kwa-n   yawi kur-na-dian
stay-SEQ work do-ACT.FOC-1plBAS.VT
'We are working staying in this-previously-mentioned (talked about) this-further-away big house'

Alternatively, a spatio-temporal and a 'current relevance' demonstrative can refer to the same location—in 10.41 it is the sky. The fact that the moon's location appears to be close to us and has just been talked about is reflected in the use of *kə-na-y* 'this/here-previously mentioned'. The fact that it is up there in the large (and hence 'masculine') sky far away is reflected in the use of *a-d-a-wur* 'that masculine up there'.

10.41　bap-a-ta:kw　　　aka　　　　　　　　　　　war-na
　　　　moon-LK-woman　DEM.DIST.REACT.TOP.fem.sg　go.up-ACT.FOC+3fem.sgBAS.VT
　　　　kə-na-y　　　　　　　　　a-d-a-wur　　　　　*mun*
　　　　DEM.PROX-CURR.REL-DIST　DEM.DIST-masc.sg-LK-UP　moon
　　　　'Lady moon is now going up, here previously mentioned (in the sky (masculine)) up there, the moon'

Or a 'current relevance' demonstrative can be added to a spatial demonstrative, to make sure the addressee realizes that the object pointed at is the one under discussion. Example 10.28 was rephrased as 10.42:

10.42　lə-kə　　　　　　　tənəb　　　wa-l-ay
　　　　she-OBL+fem.sg　fireplace　DEM.PROX.ADDR-fem.sg-DIST
　　　　wa-na-y　　　　　　　　　　　　　　aka
　　　　DEM.PROX.ADDR-CURR.REL-DIST　DEM.DIST.REACT.TOP.fem.sg
　　　　'Her fireplace is here further away from us both but closer to you, the fireplace close to you we have been talking about'

B2. THE 'CURRENT RELEVANCE' DEMONSTRATIVES DISTINGUISHING DIRECTION are in Table 10.4
　　These are used similarly to spatial demonstratives distinguishing direction. Example 10.43 is Gemaj's answer to the question whether there is moonlight outside (so as to help me decide whether to take a torch with me or not). The question was: *bap-a-ta:kw təba:m tə-na?* (moon-LK-woman sky+LK+LOC have/be-ACT.FOC+3fem.sgBAS.VT) 'is the lady moon in the sky?'

10.43　bap　kə-na-wur　　　　　　　　bəum　　　tə-na
　　　　moon　DEM.PROX-CURR.REL-UP　haze+LOC　have/be-ACT.FOC+3fem.sgBAS.VT
　　　　'The moon is up there (location we are talking about) in the haze'

A location or an object referred to with the 'current relevance' demonstrative may not be overtly mentioned at all—it is enough for it to be in the focus of people's attention. A mother used to say 10.44 to her baby daughter to stop her from going into a corner of the house where the food was stored (located downriver with respect to the Sepik River's course), believing that the girl should be scared of imaginary mice:

TABLE 10.4　'Current relevance' demonstratives distinguishing direction

STEM	'CURRENT RELEVANCE'	DISTANCE
kə- 'proximal'	*-na-*	*-wur* 'up'
		-d(a) 'down'
wa- 'proximal to addressee'	*-na-*	*-aku* 'outwards'
		-aki 'across'
a- 'distal'	*-na-*	*-wula* 'inside, inland'

TABLE 10.5   Directional markers with verbs and with demonstratives

MEANING	DIRECTIONALS WITH INHERENTLY DIRECTIONAL VERBS	DIRECTIONALS WITH DEMONSTRATIVES
down	-*d*(*a*)	-*d*(*a*) (cf. *da*- 'go down')
up	-*u*-/-*war*	-*wur*- (cf. *war*- 'go up')
across away from speaker	-*aki*-	-*aki*
outwards from speaker	-*aku*-	-*aku*
across towards speaker	-(*a*)*pra*-/-(*a*)*par*	—
towards speaker or inland	-*wula*-/-*wəla*-/-*wul*	-*wula*- (cf. *wula*- 'come in')
sideways away from speaker	-*tay*-	—
sideways towards speaker	-*tæy*-	—

10.44   wakuli   <u>wa-na-d</u>   rə-na
   mouse   DEM.PROX.ADDR-CURR.REL-DOWN   sit-ACT.FOC+3fem.sgBAS.VT
   'A mouse is sitting here-close-to-you in the mentioned (downstream) location!'

'Current relevance' demonstratives are subtly different from anaphoric demonstratives. Anaphoric demonstratives provide a relationship between a pronoun and 'another element, in the same or in an earlier sentence, that supplies its referent' (Matthews 1997: 18), and 'are used for reference to something earlier . . . in discourse'. 'Current relevance' demonstratives state that the referent is within the discourse (being mentioned, or talked about), or within the frame of attention of the participants in a situation. Their scope is thus broader than simple anaphora, though the analogy between the two is striking.

C. DIRECTIONAL DISTINCTIONS IN NOMINAL DEMONSTRATIVES AND IN VERBS (see Tables 10.5 and 16.1) share a number of similarities, but are rather different. (In the majority of cases, verbal directional markers do not attach directly to the verbal root: they appear on a dummy root *sə*-.)

Directional markers on verbs and on demonstratives distinguish directions upward (marked somewhat differently), downward, across, outwards, and inwards (all marked similarly). In addition, directionals with verbs also distinguish motion towards the speaker (absent from demonstratives), and two types of motion sideways. These differences can be accounted for by the fact that directionals on verbs are inherently associated with motion, while with demonstratives they refer to location in space.

While directionals on demonstratives always have spatial reference, those on verbs can be extended metaphorically and acquire idiosyncratic meaning, e.g. 'talk-across away from speaker' means 'to tell a traditional story', and 'die-across away from speaker' means 'half-die, almost die'. This is discussed in §16.1. In that same section we look at how directional markers can be used, or avoided, on verbs, and on demonstratives, within one clause.

D. Frames of reference in Manambu are of three basic kinds.

Intrinsic frame of reference (that is, reference from the perspective of the ground object) is employed for describing positions of objects within an enclosed space (e.g. top of mosquito net), as in 10.45:

10.45 wun-a   aba-wapwi   <u>kə-lə-m</u>   api-ñəg-a:m
      I-LK+fem.sg   head+LK-dress   DEM.PROX-FEM.SG-LOC   top-mosquito.net-LK+LOC
      rə-na
      sit-ACT.FOC+3fem.sgBAS.VT
      'My hat is here on top of the mosquito net'

It can also be used to describe the location of one landmark relative to another, as in 10.46.

10.46 Makəmawi də-kə-də   bunər   Waskuk
      Makemawi 3masc.sg-OBL-masc.sg back+LK+ALL   Washkuk
      wa-dana-di   nəbək-adi
      say-3plSUBJ.VT-3plBAS.VT   mountain-3plNOM
      'The so-called Washkuk mountains are at the back of the Ambunti mountain'

There is a preference for describing locations inside the house using the intrinsic frame of reference. But this is not always so: in 10.44, the 'downwards' location of the place with the imaginary mice reflects the position of this part of the house as 'downriver' with respect to the Sepik River.

We saw, in A2 and in B above, that directional demonstratives can be used within relative frame of reference (10.33) and within absolute frame of reference whereby a relevant landmark (most often, the Sepik River) is established within the context (10.34–5). Out of context, a form like *a-l-a-da* (DEM.DIST-fem.sg-LK-DOWN) can mean either 'downriver' or 'downwards (from where we are)', or 'underground'. The frame of reference is largely determined by the speaker's choice.

Nowadays, cardinal directions are used more and more, especially by people exposed to Western-style schooling. The terms include *wali* 'eastward direction; easterly wind; East; also used for white people (who supposedly came from the East) and all things associated with them (see §9.3)'; *yabun* 'westward direction, westerly wind; West', *yuwagwadian* 'North', and *awkup(w)* 'South' (cf. Harrison 1990a: 12–13). These are often replaced by the Tok Pisin terms.

Relative frame of reference (left and right) is also used—as illustrated in 10.22a, b, and d above. It is impossible to decide whether this pattern results from a Western influence or not.

In summary: the system of nominal demonstratives in Manambu is typologically unusual in a variety of ways:

  (i) The language has three demonstrative stems ('close to speaker', 'close to hearer', and 'distal') which can take either two or three additional distance specifications, or five additional direction specifications.
 (ii) Additional distance and directions are mutually exclusive.[1]
(iii) The language distinguishes between spatio-temporal demonstratives and 'current relevance' demonstratives. The latter cannot take gender-number or case, and have fewer distance distinctions than the spatio-temporal ones.

---

[1] In his study of demonstratives in Manambu, Farnsworth (1966) confused spatio-temporal demonstratives distinguishing distance with those distinguishing direction and with the 'current relevance' ones.

TABLE 10.6   Adverbial demonstratives

DEMONSTRATIVE STEM	MANNER	OTHER
kə- 'close to speaker'	*kə-ta-wa* 'like this (pointing)' *kə-kətawa* 'exactly like this'	*kə-ta* 'now' *kə-ta-* 'like this' (bound)
a- 'distal'	*a-ta-wa* 'like that' (pointing and textual deixis)	*a-ta* 'thus; then'
a- 'distal' and *kə-* 'close to speaker'	*a-kə-tawa* (variant: *akatawa*) 'like this (textual anaphora)'	—

(iv) There is no special set of local adverbial demonstratives: locative forms of spatio-temporal demonstratives and all 'current relevance' demonstratives are regularly used to indicate location.

(v) Only two of the three demonstrative stems ('close to speaker' and 'distal') can refer to time as well as to space.

(vi) Only two of the three demonstrative stems ('close to speaker' and 'distal') are used for substitution anaphora. The 'distal' demonstrative is also used for textual anaphora. The third stem can be used to establish empathy with the addressee, or the audience, and to transmit the speaker's negative attitude to a participant.

(vii) Nominal demonstratives are not used for cataphora.

10.2.2   Manner adverbial demonstratives

Manambu has two sets of manner demonstratives, based on two of the stems found in nominal demonstratives: *kə-* 'close to speaker' and *a-* 'distal': *kətawa* 'this way, like this', and *atawa* 'that way, thus, like that'.[2] These forms can be used for pointing, and can also be used anaphorically and cataphorically. Table 10.6 features these, and other forms which can be considered as adverbial demonstratives (at least etymologically). The origin of the formative *-ta-* is unknown. The formative *-wa* could be related to the comitative case marker *-wa* (§7.9).

All manner demonstratives are used as adverbs. Only *atawa* and *akatawa* can modify the noun *sa:d* 'manner' (and its equivalents in Tok Pisin *kain, pasin* which occur as a result of code-switching). The demonstratives *ata-* and *kəta-* in combination with *-pək* 'like' are often used as prehead modifiers (see 10.58–60).

Manner demonstratives and the form *ata* 'thus' share a number of properties which *kəta* 'now' does not have:

(i) When either of these heads is a predicate, or is part of predicate focus, it takes the predicative marker *-n*, as in 4.79.

(ii) The forms *kətawa*, *atawa*, and *ata* can be used for cataphora.

(iii) Manner demonstratives *atawa*, *akətawa*, and *ata* can also be used as interrogatives meaning 'how?' This is rather unusual typologically.

---

[2] Very occasionally, a word-initial *h* is inserted, just as in *ata(n)* (§4.5) and even in distal demonstratives. This is best considered as an idiosyncratic feature characteristic of some speakers.

The demonstrative *ata* differs from other manner demonstratives in a variety of ways. Unlike *ata*—which is used cataphorically, especially with speech reports—the forms *kətawa*, *atawa*, and *akətawa* can be used for substitution and textual anaphora. Unlike the manner demonstratives, *ata* (i) cannot be used for pointing; (ii) cannot modify the noun *sa:d* 'way, fashion' (see note 7 in Chapter 4); and (iii) is often used as a connective between clauses, sentences, and paragraphs, as in 4.8 and 4.10 (also see §19.6).

Only the proximal manner demonstrative has a reduplicated form *kə-kətawa* 'exactly like this'. Unlike *kəta* and *ata*, the manner demonstratives can take the suffix -*dəka* 'only'. In its interrogative use as 'how?' *ata* can be repeated, e.g. *ata ata*, or replaced with its near-synonym *atəta* (see §10.4); such repetition has not been attested for other manner demonstratives used as interrogatives.

The form *ata* is also used as negator for purposives and desideratives (see §14.3). Whether we are faced with polysemy or homonymy (especially for the second use of *ata* as negator) is an open question. A comparative study of Ndu languages may shed light on this issue.

Unlike *ata*, *kəta* 'now' is just a temporal adverb (see §4.4). The form *kəta-* 'like this' only occurs as a bound form, with the suffix -*pək* (see 10.59 below, and discussion there).

Both *kətawa* and *atawa* can be used for pointing, typically indicating the way in which something is to be done. If the action is happening close to the speaker, *kətawa* is used, as in 10.47; otherwise, *atawa* is preferred, as in 10.48.

10.47 mæn   viti-kərəb   kətawa   yi-la
       leg/foot two-together   like.this   go-3fem.sgSUBJ.VT+3fem.sgBAS.VT
       'She went putting two feet together, like this' (showing)

10.48 agwa-japək   atawa   kur-na-dəmən
       what-thing+LK+DAT   like.that   do-ACT.FOC-2masc.sgBAS.VT
       'Why have you acted like that (against your younger brother?)'

The form *kətawa* can also be used for pointing to a non-static location, as in 10.49:

10.49 kətawa   ma:y
       like.this go.IMPV
       'Go like this way, like this' (pointing the way to go)

Kətawa often refers anaphorically to the manner or way in which something is done. In 10.50, it refers to the way Gemaj as a little girl was dressed up, for the two white men to take her picture. They are telling her to go down (to the river) in exactly the way she was dressed:

10.50 kətawa   adi:d
       like.this go.down.IMPV
       'You go down like this (dressed as you are now)' (said the two men)

In 10.51, this same form refers to the way in which a woman looked around the spirit's hut, summarizing the manner and the direction of her gaze (she looked across).

10.51 kətawa   kətaki   və-lə-l
       like.this look.ACROSS   see-3fem.sgSUBJ.P-3fem.sgBAS.P
       'Like this she looked across'

The demonstrative *atawa* is used in a similar way, 'summarizing' the manner and location:

10.52 nəkə-də   nənəm   w̲ə̲d̲i̲y̲a̲   bal, nəkə-də   na:n
other-masc.sg grid+LK+LOC DEM.PROX.ADDR.REACT.TOP+pl pig other-masc.sg grid
bal, nəkə-də   na:n məd   kui, nəkə-də   nan du   kui,
pig, other-masc.sg grid cassowary meat other-masc.sg grid man meat
nəkə-də   nan ab   kui nəkə-də   nan məd   kui, a̲t̲a̲w̲a̲
other-masc.sg grid possum meat other-masc.sg grid cassowary meat like.that
rə-k-na-di
sit-FUT-ACT.FOC-3plBAS.VT
'On one grid here (next to you) is pork, on one (another) grid pork, on another grid
cassowary meat, on another grid human flesh, on another grid possum meat, on another
grid cassowary meat, like that they will be sitting there'

Both proximal and distal manner demonstratives can be used for textual anaphora and
cataphora. If the stretch of text to which the demonstrative refers follows it immediately, *kətawa*
is used:

10.53 nəkə   wa-saki-ma:j   k̲ə̲t̲a̲w̲a̲ wa-na
other.fem.sg say-ACROSS-story like.this say-ACT.FOC+3fem.sgBAS.VT
'Another story (which goes across generations) goes like this (the story follows)'

If the stretch of text does not follow immediately, *atawa* is preferred. It is also a preferred
option of referring to a long chunk of text, almost as a summary 'thus'. Example 10.54
summarizes a discussion of how an ugly man could not get himself a wife, and was jealous
of his friends:

10.54 a̲t̲a̲w̲a̲-dəka   dəy adika   tə-də-di
like.that-ONLY they DEM.DIST.REACT.TOP+pl stay-3masc.sgSUBJ.P-3plBAS.P
'Just like that he was with respect to them (his friends)'

The two manner demonstratives can be used in the alternating meaning, 'this way' and 'that
way', as in 10.55.

10.55 nəkə-də   ga:n k̲ə̲t̲a̲w̲a̲ kwa-na-d,   nəkə-də   ga:n
other-masc.sg night like.this stay-ACT.FOC-3masc.sgBAS.VT other-masc.sg night
a̲t̲a̲w̲a̲   kwa-na-d
like.that stay-ACT.FOC-3masc.sgBAS.VT
'One night he stayed like this (asleep), another night he stayed like that (awake)'

The reduplicated proximal demonstrative means 'exactly like this'. It is used in the same way
as *kətawa*. Its cataphoric use is illustrated in 10.56:

10.56 aw   wali-nəb   ma:j k̲ə̲k̲ə̲t̲a̲w̲a̲   wa-kwa-na-dian
then white.person-dry.land talk exactly.like.this say-HAB-ACT.FOC-1plBAS.VT
hap past faiv   orait, ñan-a   ma:j a̲k̲a̲
'half past five', alright we-LK+fem.sg talk DEM.DIST.REACT.TOP.fem.sg
takwtakw   a̲k̲a̲   na-k-na
daylight.dawning DEM.DIST.REACT.TOP.fem.sg BE.NAT-FUT-ACT.FOC+3fem.sgBAS.VT
'Then in the white man's language we used to say exactly like this: "Half past five", all
right, in our language it is "daylight would be dawning"'

The manner demonstrative *a-kə-tawa*, and its free variant *akatawa* 'like this', is used only
for textual anaphora. The difference between *akətawa* and *atawa* is that *akətawa* has a generic

overtone of 'this is how things are', as in 10.57. Using *atawa* would have implied the actual working of the story, while *akətawa* refers to the general story line:

10.57 a   stori   ak<u>ə</u>tawa   yi-na
 DEM.DIST.fem.sg story   like.this.ANAPH   go-ACT.FOC+3fem.sgBAS.VT
 'That story goes (in summary) like this'

This demonstrative as a predicate head typically summarizes a narrative, or a stretch of discourse: *akatawa-n-a* (like.this.ANAPH-PRED-3fem.sgBAS.VT) 'this is it, this is how it is'.

We saw above that *ata* can also be used as a cataphoric manner demonstrative, especially when introducing speech reports, as in the last clause in 4.12 (see §19.5 on speech reports).

Ata cannot occur with a suffix, except for *-pək* 'like; more or less'; then it takes the predicative focus form *ata-n*. The resulting form, *atabək* (*ata-n-pək*) 'like this/that, more or less this/that way' (see under A2 in §2.6, on the consonant fusion and voicing in this environment), is used anaphorically and cataphorically, both as an adverb and as a modifier. In 10.58, this refers to a type of beautiful magical woman not found in the village:

10.58 <u>atabək-ə</u>   ta:kw   ma:
 thus+PRED+LIKE-LK woman   NEG
 'There was no woman like that (in the village)'

As mentioned above, *kəta-* in the meaning 'like this (proximate)' occurs in an idiomatic form accompanied by the predicative *-n* and *-pək* 'like', as shown in 10.59 (where it modifies the noun 'boy's house-men's house'):

10.59 a-di   ma:j [k<u>ə</u>tabək-a   say-karab<u>ə</u>m
 DEM.DIST-pl story like.this+LIKE-LK boy.house-men.house+LK+LOC
 rə-da-kəkəb]   wa-da-di   ma:j-adi
 stay-3pl-AS.SOON.AS say-3plSUBJ.P-3plBAS.P story-3plNOM
 'Those stories are the stories told as soon as people sit down in a boy's house and men's house like the one here (we are sitting in)'

This form is employed to anaphorically or cataphorically refer to something near at hand to the speaker. It can also refer to present time, meaning 'like now'; this is reminiscent of the meaning of *kəta* 'now' as an independent word, e.g. *kətabək-ə ñakamali* (like.this/like.now-LK dry.season) 'in dry season like this/like now', *kətabək-ə gra:b-a* (like.this/like.now-LK afternoon-3fem.sgNOM) 'it is afternoon like this/like now'). Some speakers occasionally use the form *a-kətabək* 'like this':

10.60 akəs   kə-kwa-na-wun-ək   a-di   <u>akətabək-ə</u> kəkəpa:t
 NEG.HAB eat-HAB-ACT.FOC-1sgBAS.VT-CONF DEM.DIST-pl like.this-LK   food
 'I never eat the (previously mentioned) foods like this (like type of food offered to me)'

This form could have resulted from an analogy between forms like *atawa* 'like that' and *akatawa, akətawa* 'like this'.

Ata has a number of other, non-demonstrative functions: it is extremely frequent as a sentence and paragraph sequencing device, as in 4.8, 4.10, 4.12, 10.3, 10.14, and 10.18. A combination of *ata* with the verb 'say' marked with the cotemporaneous sequencing suffix *-ta:y*, *atawa:tay*, has undergone reinterpretation as an adverb meaning 'thus, and so'.

To conclude: the forms *ata* 'thus, then' and *kəta* 'now; like this' have a certain degree of parallel usage. We can hypothesize that at a certain stage in the history of the language they were in a paradigmatic relationship as a distal and a proximal manner demonstrative. This relationship can still be seen (a) in the uses of *atabək* 'like that' and *kətabek* 'like this' (10.58–60), and (b) in the uses of *atawa* 'like that' and *kətawa* 'like this' shown above.

10.2.3 'Reactivated topic' demonstratives

The three demonstrative stems—*kə-* 'proximal (to the speaker)', *wə-* 'proximal to the addressee', and *a-* 'distal'—mark reactivated topic, within the following structures:

Demonstrative stem-gender/number agreement marker -*əka* (pronounced in normal to rapid register as *a*, in agreement with A3 under §2.6, see §3.3), e.g. *kə-d-əka*, normal to rapid speech *kə-d-a* (DEM.PROX-masc.sg-REACT.TOP) 'this one masculine'; *kəka*, underlying form *kə-Ø-əka* (DEM.PROX-fem.sg-REACT.TOP) 'this one feminine'.

Reactivated topic demonstratives, and the ways in which they operate, were introduced in §3.3. Their major function is to reintroduce or re-establish a previously established topic, especially if it has not been mentioned for some time. (Additional examples are under 3.16–18.) They typically refer to S/O argument, and always agree in gender and number with the S/O argument, and constitute the major instance of an absolutive pattern in the language. As mentioned in §3.3, reactivated topic demonstratives provide a strong criterion for S—see, for instance, the discussion of copula subject in §4.2.2.

The choice of the demonstrative stem depends on the distance of the referent. In 10.61, the narrator, John Sepaywus, is telling about the origin of the people of cassowary's feathers; he then reminds the audience of the fact that these people are in fact the Kwoma (in S function). He then goes on talking about the Kwoma and their totemic links with cassowaries.

10.61 Kum   <u>adika</u>   kwa-na-di
       Kwoma DEM.DIST.REACT.TOP+pl stay-ACT.FOC-3plBAS.VT
       'The Kwoma are the ones who stay there'

A similar example is under 10.11 (where the S of the verb 'die' is referred to with a reactivated topic pronoun).

If a verb is strictly transitive, its A can never be referred to with a reactivated topic demonstrative. If a verb is ambitransitive and is used intransitively (with only one, the S, cross-referencing position filled), the S can be referred to with the reactivated topic demonstrative, as in 10.62. The rooster is reintroduced as a topic (his appearance is important for this stretch of the text because his singing implies that the night is over):

10.62 tapwuk <u>ada</u>   ma: pəkaka:u
       rooster DEM.DIST.REACT.TOP+masc.sg again 'cockadoodledoo'
       <u>ada</u>   wa-na-d
       DEM.DIST.REACT.TOP+masc.sg say-ACT.FOC-3masc.sgBAS.VT
       'The rooster then (said) "cock-a-doodle-doo" again, he said again'

We can recall, from §3.3, that if an O constituent is a reactivated topic, it is obligatorily cross-referenced on the verb (using the basic set in the second cross-referencing position), as in 10.63 (an offer to tell yet another story), and in 10.64 (the reactivated topic is a personal pronoun: the speaker stresses that what she is talking about is herself and how she got taken into a strange place) (a similar example, with *wuka*, is under 10.15).

10.63 nak <u>ada</u>   suku-kə-tua-d
       one DEM.DIST.REACT.TOP+masc.sg create/record-FUT-1sgSUBJ.VT-3masc.sgBAS.VT
       'I will tell one (future topic: story)'

10.64 wun <u>aka</u>   nəkə-də   du   nəb-ə-du
       I   DEM.DIST.REACT.TOP.fem.sg other-masc.sg man   dry.land-LK-man
       kray-da-wun-ək
       bring-3masc.sgSUBJ.VT-1fem.sgBAS.VT-CONF
       'Another man, a jungle-dweller (lit. dry-land man), has just brought me (future topic)
       (here)'

If the verb 'say' is used transitively, the addressee can be referred to with the reactivated topic
demonstrative, if appropriate. In 10.65, the underlined form refers to the participants close to
the speaker who were to fight the enemy from then on throughout the narrative:

10.65 <u>kədiya</u>   wa-tua-di
       DEM.PROX.REACT.TOP+pl say-1sgSUBJ.VT-3plBAS.VT
       'I told these (people)'

The content of a direct speech report is never referred to with a reactivated topic demonstrative (or cross-referenced). An NP object of the verb 'say' can be referred to this way (see
10.69).

We saw in 3.18 that a reactivated topic marker refers to the recipient rather than the gift of
the ditransitive verbs 'give' if it is more animate than the gift. This is, however, not a steadfast
rule. After he had announced that he would tell us the names of men's houses in the Avatip
village in its previous location (see 10.68), John Sepaywus added 10.66. The names are the
topic of the whole paragraph; they are referred to with the reactivated topic demonstrative and
cross-referenced on the verb 'give':

10.66 dəy-a-di   sə   <u>adiya</u>   kui-kə-tua-di
       they-LK-pl name DEM.DIST.REACT.TOP+pl give.to.third.p-FUT-1sgSUBJ.VT-3plBAS.VT
       'I will give (everyone) their (topical) names' <names follow>

If the gift is more topical in a given paragraph than the recipient, it can be referred to with
the reactivated topic demonstrative. In 10.67, 'banana' is re-established as a topic: this is what
the flying fox used to give to her adopted son (whose topicality has already been established),
and it is the banana she gave him again. The second occurrence of 'give' cross-references the
recipient, as a means of further clarification.

10.67 lau-lap   <u>aka</u>
       ripe-banana DEM.DIST.REACT.TOP.fem.sg
       kui-la
       give.to.third.p-3fem.sgSUBJ.VT+3fem.sgBAS.VT
       kui-la-d
       give.to.third.p-3fem.sgSUBJ.VT-3masc.sgBAS.VT
       'She gave (him) the (topical) banana (then), she gave him (it)'

A location can also be referred to with a reactivated topic demonstrative. In 10.68, John
Sepaywus once again enumerates the names of men's houses in the Avatip village in its previous
location. This is something we had been talking about on and off during that morning, and the
reactivated topic demonstrative is used to 'bring them back' as important topics. The other
'reactivated topic' is the old 'inland' village itself—that is, a location.

10.68 a-di   kara:b   [INTO.BREAK] <u>adəka</u>
DEM.DIST-pl   men's.house   DEM.DIST.REACT.TOP+masc.sg
[[a-də-wula   təpa:m]   a-di   kwa-di   kara:b]
DEM.DIST-masc.sg-INLAND   village+LK+LOC   DEM.DIST-pl   stay-3plBAS.VT   men's.house
<u>adiya</u>   ma: nasə-kə-tua-di
DEM.DIST.REACT.TOP+pl   again   enumerate-FUT-1sgSUBJ.VT-3plBAS.VT
'Those men's houses, those men's houses which stay in that (topical) inland village, I will enumerate them (topical) again'

In 10.54, a cross-referenced constituent referred to with a reactivated topic demonstrative is someone with respect to whom the action is performed. Examples of this sort indicate that the reactivated topic demonstratives operate predominantly, but not exclusively, on an S/O basis. Alternatively, they can be described as operating on a non-A basis. As illustrated in 10.68, a clause can contain two occurrences of reactivated topic demonstratives, but never more than that.

The reactivated topic demonstratives do not appear to form one NP with the noun they refer to. They agree with this noun in gender and number, but can never take any cases or suffixes or be arguments of postpositions. There can be an intonation break between a demonstrative and an NP it refers to (as in 10.68)—something atypical for an NP. Within a clause, they tend to occur immediately preceding the verb (or the complex adverb+verb, as in 10.68). If the constituent they refer to has a contrastive overtone, they follow it, as in 10.62. We will see, in §20.1.1, that Manambu is not averse to split NPs; however, they are never split between clauses.

In terms of spatial reference, the demonstrative stems employed in reactivated topic demonstratives have similar overtones to the nominal spatio-temporal demonstratives (§10.2.1, under A). In 10.69, the 'close to addressee' demonstrative is used to refer to the names of men's houses which were enumerated for my (addressee's) benefit (just as in 10.25 above).

10.69 a-də-wula   təp-a-kə-di   <u>wudiya</u>   bə
DEM.DIST-masc.sg-INLAND   village-LK-POSS-pl   DEM.PROX.ADDR.REACT.TOP+pl   already
wa-tua-di,   tabati   ya:kya,   <u>aka</u>
say-1sgSUBJ.VT-3plBAS.VT   ten,   OK,   DEM.DIST.REACT.TOP+fem.sg
kusə-na
finish-ACT.FOC+3fem.sgBAS.VT
'I have already told the ones (names) of the away-from-the-Sepik River village, the (topical ones) for you (close to you), ten (of them), OK, it is finished'

The last occurrence of *aka* (DEM.DIST.REACT.TOP+fem.sg) in *aka kusə-na* combines reference to the O ('story') and to the action of telling itself: it supplies an aspectual overtone of 'here and now; ongoing action' to a verb marked with action focus. Similar examples are under 10.56 and 10.78. We return to this in §12.1 and in §12.8.3 (C).

When reactivated topic demonstratives appear as predicate heads, they take the predicative marker *-n* followed by *-a-* and by gender-number agreement marker *-əka*, e.g. *kəka-n-aka* (DEM.PROX.REACT.TOP.fem.sg-PRED-REACT.TOP.fem.sg) 'this feminine singular (reactivated topic) is', often used as a summary statement, 'this is how it is, this is how things are'. Its distal demonstrative counterpart is often used in a similar way, meaning 'so, this is how it is':

10.70 aw   [kə-l-əm   ñan vara-ku],
      then DEM.PROX-fem.sg-LK+LOC we   come.back-COMPL.SS
      aka-n-aka   *kamap*-adian
      DEM.DIST.REACT.TOP.fem.sg-PRED-REACT.TOP.fem.sg appear-1plBAS.VT
      'Then having come back here, this is how things are, we appeared (again) (to start
      fighting)'

In 10.71 (the end of Sepaywus's recital of the names of men's houses in Avatip), a plural
reactivated topic demonstrative heads the predicate. The gender and number agreement with
the subject is thus marked twice.

10.71 [a-di   [a-də-wula   təpa]-kə-di   kara:b]
      DEM.DIST-pl DEM.DIST-masc.sg-INLAND village-LK-pl men's.house
      adika-n-adika
      DEM.DIST.REACT.TOP+pl-PRED-REACT.TOP.pl
      'The men's houses belonging to that village inland are those ones (topical)'

To conclude: reactivated topic demonstratives agree with a cross-linguistic tendency for
preferred argument structure whereby a topical element is never introduced in the A function. They are typologically quite unusual in that they combine reference to the constituent's
topicality, its grammatical relation, and its position in space. The latter makes them somewhat
redundant, given that they often occur in the same clause as nominal demonstratives with the
same spatial reference.

10.3 INDEFINITES

Manambu has two indefinites, with the meaning 'other, another'. The agreeing modifier fem.sg.
nəkə, masc.sg. *nəkə-də*, dual *nəkə-bər*, plural *nəkə-di* 'another, other' (see §5.1.1) refers to
another, additional and different, participant, e.g. *nəkə ña* (another+fem.sg day) 'next day,
another day' and in 10.53 ('another story'). It can refer to 'one' and 'another' (members of a
pair), as in 10.55, or to several choices, as in 10.52. This example contains six occurrences of
nəkə corresponding to the number of smoking grids in the spirit's house. This pronoun can
also refer to an indeterminate location or time, or referent: *nəkə ña* (another+fem.sg day) can
mean 'next day, another day' (then its synonym is *kwapək* 'next day'). Or it can mean 'some
other day, whenever'. This same pronoun may refer to additional objects, e.g. 'two more plates'
as in 10.72.

10.72 nəkə-bər plet   viti akray!
      other-du plate two IMPV+bring
      'Bring two more plates!' (lit. two other plates)

The pronoun 'other, another' carries with it a distinct overtone of something undesirable
and potentially dangerous. In 10.3 above, 'another man', or a 'stranger' is a trespasser. A
similar example is 8.12 (the gist of it is that other people's cats are strangers and do nothing
but damage).

The feminine locative form of the INDEFINITE *nəkə-* 'other, another', *nəkəm*, means 'half-
heartedly; not fully':

10.73 gura:m   [və-tua   məl] nəkə-m
     you.pl+LK+ACC/LOC see-1sgSUBJ.VT+3fem.sgBAS.VT eye other-LOC
     və-tua-digur-ək
     see-1sgSUBJ.VT-2plBAS.VT-CONF
     'I see you (with) the eye that sees (you) not very well'

This form can be repeated as *nəkəm nəkəm* (another.fem.sg+LOC another.fem.sg+LOC) 'bit of everything; in a random way'. In 10.74 it is used as modifier to the noun, and in 10.75 as a manner modifier to the verb. In 21.44, repetition of *nəkəm* means 'wherever'.

10.74 a-di   kamkaw ñan, nəkəm   nəkəm   kəkəpa:t a-bər   bə
     DEM.DIST-pl yam   tuber other+LOC other+LOC food   DEM.DIST-du already
     rəpəm   na:n   kə-kwa-na-bər
     be.enough+LOC be.NAT+SEQ eat-HAB-ACT.FOC-3duBAS.VT
     'They two used to eat those yams and tubers, bit of every kind of food, having got enough (of these)'

10.75 nəkəm   nəkəm   kur-kwa-na-bər
     other+LOC other+LOC do-HAB-ACT.FOC-3duBAS.VT
     'They two kept pottering around (do this and that in a random way)'

The pronoun *nəkə-* is usually employed as a prehead modifier; only occasionally can its head be omitted. In contrast, the indefinite *nəwək* '(an)other one' is used only as a head. It can be modified with nominal demonstratives, but, unlike any other nominal, does not take case marking. It can have a singular referent, as in 10.76. It is in O function, but is not marked for case.

10.76 a   kusə-lə-l,   kwasa   maw nəwək
     DEM.DIST.fem.sg finish-3fem.sgSUBJ.P-3fem.sgBAS.P little+fem.sg base another.one
     wukə-bana
     hear-1plSUBJ.VT+3fem.sgBAS.VT
     'That one (story) is finished, we are listening to another one (as) a little base (for it)'

This pronoun can also have a non-singular referent. The number value of its referent can be recovered from the context.

10.77 [kə-di-ay   nəwək]   və-kə-tua-di
     DEM.PROX-pl-DIST another.one see-FUT-1sgSUBJ.VT-3plBAS.VT
     'I will see these other ones further away'

Unlike *nəkə-* which refers only to third person, *nəwək* can refer to any person. In 10.78, *nəwək* refers to 'others among us': the personal reference is obvious from the marking on the verb.

10.78 ñan bə   abak   kwa-na-dian,   nəwək   manək
     we already head+LK+DAT stay-ACT.FOC-1plBAS.VT another.one leg+LK+DAT
     kwa-na-dian,   aba:b aka   barək
     stay-ACT.FOC-1plBAS.VT all   DEM.DIST.REACT.TOP.fem.sg fever+LK+DAT
     kwa-na-dian
     stay-ACT.FOC-1plBAS.VT
     'We already have headache (lit. stay to head), others (of us) have sore leg, (we) all are feverish'

Speakers who frequently code-switch with Tok Pisin employ *narapela* 'other' to cover both *nəkə-* and *nəwək*. The meaning of 'someone; one…another' can be achieved by using the numeral 'one' (see §10.6). Repetition of a noun has a distributive indefinite meaning, e.g. *agək* 'one of the two sides', *agək agək* 'one side to the other', *tabək* 'end of, side', *tabək təbək* 'one side and another'.

10.4   INTERROGATIVES

Content questions are marked with a question word and slightly rising intonation, while polar questions are marked by intonation only. Interrogative clauses are discussed in §20.1.3. A question word does not have a fixed position in a clause; like any constituent, if it is in contrastive focus it tends to occupy the clause-initial position and acquire focus marking.

Interrogatives form a heterogeneous class in terms of their meanings, syntactic function, focus marking, and grammatical categories. Interrogatives include nouns, adjectives, adverbs, and quantifiers. There are no interrogative verbs. Manambu employs the following interrogative stems:

   (i)   *sə-* 'who; whose';
  (ii)   *agwa-* 'what, which';
 (iii)   *akə-* 'where; belonging to where; when';
  (iv)   *akrəl* 'where to';
   (v)   *agula* 'what's up; what for; why';
  (vi)   *ata, ata ata, atəta, atawa, atətawa, atətaka, kətətaka* 'how'; and
 (vii)   *kas* 'how many/much; which (by number)'.

(i) The pronoun *sə* 'who' has human reference, and can be used as an argument, as head of predicate, and as a possessive modifier ('whose'). It takes all cases, except for transportatives and substitutive. Unlike nouns, it cannot take any modifier. As shown in §7.1, this form behaves similarly to third person non-plural personal pronouns in that it takes a linker *-kə-*, as shown in 10.79 (see §7.9 on the form of the comitative with 'who').

10.79 ñən   sə-ka:wa   kwa-na-ñən-ək,   kə-də
       you.fem   who-OBL+COM   stay-ACT.FOC-2fem.sgBAS.VT-CONF   DEM.PROX-masc.sg
       təpa:m
       village+LK+LOC
       'Who are you staying with, in this village?'

Unlike a personal pronoun, it cannot be reduplicated. A constituent in a medial completive clause can be questioned, as in 10.80 and 9.33. This is one of the properties of these clauses which differentiates them from other types, especially relative and conditional clauses (see Chapter 19). The interrogative 'who' in 10.80 is in dative case, required by the verb 'ask' (lit. 'first plant'):

10.80 mən   sə-kə-k   bas   sə-ku   karya-məna
       you.masc who-OBL-DAT   first   plant-COMPL.SS   bring-2masc.sgSUBJ.VT+3fem.sgBAS.VT
       'Who did you ask when you brought her here?' (lit. having asked who did you bring it (here)?)

When used as a possessive modifier, *sə* takes the oblique marker *-kə-* and agrees in gender and number with the possessee, as in 10.81.

10.81 kə-də   nəbək   [sə-kə   gwalugw dəy-a-də
DEM.PROX-masc.sg mountain who-OBL+fem.sg clan   they-LK-masc.sg
nəbək]-ad
mountain-3masc.sgNOM
'Whose clan does this mountain belong to?' (lit. this mountain whose clan's mountain is
it?)

This pronoun can have masculine or feminine singular reference, as in 10.82: the speaker
cannot see whether the person behind the door is a man or a woman. The gender and number
reference is established via agreement on the predicate.

10.82 ñən   sə-kə-l-al   o mən   sə-kə-d-ad
you.fem who-OBL-fem.sg-3fem.sgNOM or you.masc who-OBL-masc.sg-3masc.sgNOM
'Who are you-woman, or who are you-man?'

If the speaker is not sure whether the actor was a man or a woman, or how many people
there were, plural agreement is preferred, as in 6.42.

If the pronoun 'who' is used as predicate head, as in 10.82, or is marked for focus, as
in 10.83, it appears in a form reminiscent of an associative NP (as illustrated in 8.12–14),
characterized by a gender-number marker -*l*- 'feminine', -*d*- 'masculine', -*bra*- 'dual', and -*di*-
'plural', followed by a nominal predicate cross-referencing enclitic.[3]

10.83 sə-kə-d-ad   vya:d
who-OBL-masc.sg-3masc.sgNOM hit+3masc.sgBAS.P
a. 'Who is it who hit him?'
b. 'Who is it he hit?'

The two readings of 10.83 have to be disambiguated by the context; the ambiguity results
from the fact that focused constituents do not distinguish case.

(ii) The pronoun *agwa*- 'what, which' is used as a non-agreeing modifier to a noun with a non-
human referent, especially to the noun *ja:p* 'thing': *agwa ja:p* means 'what?', and can be used
as A, S, O, and head of predicate, e.g. 10.84.

10.84 agwa ja:p kur-na-ñən   aləm
what thing do-ACT.FOC-2fem.sgBAS.VT DEM.DIST+fem.sg+LK+LOC
'What are you doing there?'

The form *agwa ja:p* marked with dative case means 'why, for what (material) reason or
purpose?', as in 10.85:

10.85 mən   Apatəp agwa japək   da-na-dəmən
you.masc Avatip what thing+LK+DAT go.down-ACT.FOC-2masc.sgBAS.VT
wuna:wa   warya-k
I+LK+COM fight-PURP.SS
'You, a man from Avatip, for what purpose have you come down to fight with me?'

---

[3] A similar construction with *agwa*- 'what, which' marked for 'double gender' was described by Farnsworth and
Farnsworth (1966), based on the Yambon variety, e.g. *agwa-l-al-a* (what-fem.sg-fem.sg-3fem.sgNOM) 'What sort of
thing is it (feminine)?'; *agwa-d-ad* (what-masc.sg-3masc.sg.NOM) 'What is it (masculine)?'; *agwa-da-di ha-di* 'What are
they (plural)?'; and *agwa-da-bər* 'What are they (dual)?' (the last form apppears highly dubious). No such forms were
recognized as grammatical by any of the speakers I worked with.

The combination *agwa ja:p* is very frequent. In informal discourse, the noun *ja:p* 'thing' can be used in the meaning of 'what', e.g. *ja:p-al?* (thing-3fem.sgNOM) 'what is it?' as a synonym of *agwa ja:p-al?* (what thing-3fem.sgNOM) 'what is it?' The form *agwa-* can modify other nouns, e.g. *agwa kudi* 'what language?', *agwa ma:j* 'what talk/stories are there, what's the gossip?' It can co-occur with adjectival modifiers, e.g. *agwa kwasa-kwasa-di ma:j bla-dana-di?* (what small-small-pl story talk-3plSUBJ.VT-3plBAS.VT) 'what little stories are they telling?' In 10.86, *agwa* modifies a non-agreeing adjective 'good' used as head of predicate. Of all interrogatives, only *agwa* can occur in exclamations, as exemplified in 10.86.

10.86 <u>agwa</u> vyakət-al
      what   good/beautiful-3fem.sgNOM
      'What a beautiful (woman) it is!'

The form *agwa-* can be used as head only in non-core functions—that is, marked with dative (*agwa:k*) meaning 'why, what for', as in 10.87, with locative (*agwa:m*) meaning 'in what location?', with instrumental (*agwar*) meaning 'with what; how', and with comitative (*agwawa*) meaning 'with what', as in 10.88.

Agwa:k is very similar in meaning to *agwa japək* (in 10.85); the difference is that the latter presupposes a longer statement of reason or purpose, and may imply a material object as a reason, while the former is more abstract and is often used in rhetorical questions:

10.87 a   <u>agwa:k</u>   atawa wa-ñəna-dəwun-ək
        then   what+DAT thus   say-2fem.sgSUBJ.VT-1masc.sgBAS.VT-CONF
        'Then why did you say thus to me?!'

10.88 <u>agwawa</u>   kə-kər
      what+COM   eat-DES
      'What am I to eat (sago) with?'

Similarly to nominal demonstratives, *agwa* takes the accusative-locative case only in the locative meaning. Unlike any other word class, the allative-instrumental case with *agwa* has only instrumental meaning. Note that there is a special interrogative word with an allative meaning, *akrəl* 'where to' (see (iv)).

(iii) The pronoun *akə-* 'where, belonging to where' is used as a modifier to a noun whose location is being questioned, and as predicate head. If it is used as a modifier, the noun is either the subject of a verbless clause, a temporal or a locative oblique, or the possessor. The pronoun always takes gender and number agreement. Its feminine singular agreement forms vary depending on whether it is used as head or as a modifier. The masculine singular agreement is, as expected, *-də*, the dual is *-bər*, and the plural is *-di*. This pronoun is only used with third person reference.

TABLE 10.7   Agreement forms of *akə-* 'where'

SYNTACTIC FUNCTION	FEMININE AGREEMENT FORM	EXAMPLE
predicate head	*-l*	*akə-l* (T1.20)
modifier	*-ø*	*akə* (in 10.89, 10.91)

This pronoun refers to the location of a participant in space, as in T1.20: a man has come to fight the moon but cannot find her. *Akə-* can be extended to have a temporal sense: *akə səkər* (where.fem.sg time) is the only way of saying 'when', as in 10.89.

10.89 <u>akə</u>   səkər ap   yi-bər?
      where.fem.sg time   bone go/get-3duBAS.VT
      'When did they two grow up' (lit. 'get bone')

In 10.90, the masculine singular interrogative *akə-də* is used to refer to a bamboo, in an elliptical sentence. The bamboo is masculine because it is long:

10.90 wun asa:y a-d-a-wur   kañək   wa-na-d
      I   father DEM.DIST-masc.sg-LK-UP bamboo+LK+DAT say-ACT.FOC-3masc.sgBAS.VT
      <u>akə-də</u>   ka:ñ?
      where-masc.sg bamboo
      'My father told me about that bamboo up (i.e. told me to fetch it). Bamboo which is where?'

In 10.91, this interrogative refers to a possessor (here, a locality). This is the preferred way of asking where a person is from:

10.91 <u>akə</u>   tami-kə-l   ta:kw-a?
      where.fem.sg area-POSS-fem.sg woman-3fem.sgNOM
      'What (lit. where) area's woman (is she)?'

The form *akə-* can take one transportative case, *-say*, as in 7.64. If the question focuses on the location, and not on the participant in a location, the locative or the terminative case form is used, as in 10.92:

10.92 a-di   kway   <u>akəm</u>   kur-ñəna-di
      DEM.DIST-pl shrimp where+LOC get-2fem.sgSUBJ.VT-3plBAS.VT
      'Where did you get those shrimp?'

Either terminative or locative case can be used in asking about the source, as in 7.29, 7.55, and 10.93:

10.93 oh, vyakət-a ta:kw, [<u>akəm</u>   tə-lə-k]
      oh good-LK woman where+LOC be/stand-3fem.sg-COMPL.DS
      karya-məna
      bring-2masc.sgSUBJ.VT+3fem.sgBAS.VT
      'Oh, (what) a beautiful woman, where did you bring her from?' (lit. 'while she was staying where, did you bring her from?')

When focused, *akə-* behaves similarly to reactivated topic demonstratives used as predicate heads: the *akə-* form takes a linking marker followed by *-aka* (glossed here as focus marker). Unlike reactivated topic demonstratives, the marker is *-m-* (not *n*) for all forms, except *akəm* (where+LOC) which does not take any marker (cf. *-n-* in *aka-n-aka* in 10.70). Focused forms of interrogatives—unlike those for reactivated topic demonstratives—are not used as predicate heads. Forms marked with the transportative *-say* and with the terminative *-Vb* do not occur in the focus position at all.

As is always the case with focused constituents, focused locative interrogatives appear clause-initially. In 10.94, a masculine singular form of *akə-* is a modifier in contrastive focus. As is typical for a focused element, it is in the clause-initial position. The implication of the rhetorical question in 10.94 is that there is no territory belonging to the cassowary's son.

10.94 <u>akə-də-m-aka</u>   kuprap-ə məd-a   gaba-ñan
where-masc.sg-PRED-FOC.M bad-LK   cassowary-LK traditional-child
də-kə-də   gəlbay-ad
he-POSS-masc.sg territory-3masc.sgNOM
'This is the territory of the bad legendary son of cassowary who is from where (lit. 'where-being-focused')?'

The focused forms of *akə-* can take additional case markers: locative, as in 10.95, and allative, as in 10.96. Then they take a 'linker' *n*.

10.95 <u>akəm-aka-nəm</u>   titiya-ku   ya-n
where-FOC.M-LK+LOC walk.around-COMPL.SS come-SEQ
kwa-na-ñən-ək?
stay-ACT.FOC-2fem.sgBAS.VT-CONF
'You stayed after you walked around exactly where?'

10.96 <u>akəm-aka-nər</u>   yi-na?
where-FOC.M-LK+ALL go-ACT.FOC+3fem.sgBAS.VT
'Where exactly did she go to?'

(iv) The interrogative *akrəl* 'where to' is used to ask about the direction of motion, as in 10.97. Note that the questioned direction is part of a medial clause: a questioned constituent can be in the main clause, or in a medial completive clause.

10.97 oh, [wun-a-bər rawa-viti   abra   bə   <u>akrəl</u>
oh, I-LK-du   mother's.brother's.child-du DEM.DIST.REACT.TOP.du already where.to
yi-brə-k]   vya-da-bər
go-3du-COMPL.DS hit-3plSUBJ.P-3duBAS.P
'Oh, they killed my two nephews after they had already gone where?'

Given that *akrəl* 'where to', discussed below, cannot occupy a focus position, the focused interrogative *akəm-aka-nər* (where-FOC.M-LK+ALL) 'exactly where to?' can be considered its suppletive focus form. The etymology of *akrəl* is not fully clear. This form appears to contain the root *akə-* 'locative interrogative' followed by *-Vr* which could be the allative marker; the final *-l* could well be another instance of the allative marker which has undergone rhotic dissimilation (A1 under §2.6). A similar allative form has been occasionally heard for the proximate demonstrative *krəl* (DEM.PROX+fem.sg+ALL) 'to here' (see 12.18).

(v) The interrogative *agula* 'what's up; what for; why' is used to enquire about someone in general, and often has negative overtones. When a mentally deranged woman came into our house and sat down, no one was pleased to see her. The mistress of the house asked her, in an annoyed tone of voice:

10.98 <u>ñən   agula?</u>
you.fem what's.up/why
'What are you about? Why are you here?'

Similarly, a man was behaving in a peculiar way trying to hide from what he thought was an evil spirit; his wife came in and said: *mən agula?* (you.masc what's.up/why) 'what's happening? what's wrong with you?' This same form is used to question the reason of something unpleasant, or unusual. Another example is under 10.99. This was said to a child who was crying out of spite, and not because anyone did anything to her:

10.99 <u>agula</u>   gra-na-ñən?
      what's.up/why cry-ACT.FOC-2fem.sgBAS.VT
      'Why on earth are you crying?'

The etymology and the structure of *agula* is obscure. It probably contains the root *agwa-* 'what, which' and an additional formative.

(vi) The ways of questioning the manner in which something has been performed are *ata*, *ata ata*, *atəta* 'how'. The form *ata* is polysemous with the manner demonstrative discussed in 10.2.2. Both *ata* and its repeated version *ata ata* are used to question someone's physical state, as in 10.100, speech reports, as in 10.101 (see §19.5), and names, as in 10.102:

10.100 mən   <u>ata</u>   <u>ata</u>
       you.masc how how
       'How <u>are</u> you? What's happening to you?'

10.101 <u>ata</u>   <u>ata</u>   wa-na?
       how how say-ACT.FOC+3fem.sgBAS.VT
       'What did she say?'

10.102 <u>ata</u>   *marasin*   sə?
       how medicine name
       'What's the name of the medicine?'

The difference in meaning between *ata* 'how' and *ata ata* is that of emphasis: *ata ata* can be translated as 'exactly what?' It is often used as an elliptical question, e.g. *ata ata* 'what (did you say)?' The form *ata* is not used in such elliptical sentences. When *ata* occurs as predicate head or as part of predicate focus, it takes the predicative *-n*, as in 10.103. The repeated form *ata ata* cannot head a predicate or be focused.

10.103 a-də   wa:y sə   <u>ata-n-ad,</u>   ma:?
       DEM.DIST-masc.sg magic name how-PRED-3masc.sgNOM again
       'What's the name of the magic again?'

The interrogative *atəta* 'how' is used similarly to *ata* and *ata ata*, in the meaning of 'how', as in T1.22 (first line), from a story about a man who got upset about the moon making his wife menstruate and decided to kill the moon. Both *ata* and *ata ata* were used in other versions of T1.22. Unlike *ata*, *atəta* is not used in non-interrogative clauses. Unlike both *ata* and *ata ata*, it is not really used to question speech reports—it is used to question the manner of saying things, including a word or an expression to be used, as in 13.10.

This form often occurs with the same-subject purposive, as in 10.104, and also with the desiderative, as an emphatic way of stating how impossible it is to do something:

10.104 ma:j <u>atəta</u> wukə-k
       talk how   hear-PURP.SS
       'How (am I to) hear the story (if children are screaming)?'

Similarly to *ata* in 10.102, *atəta* can be used as a modifier, 'which kind of; how':

10.105 ñən   <u>atəta</u> gwalugw?
       you.fem how   clan
       'What clan do you belong to?'

Just like *ata*, *atəta* can head a predicate or be in focus; then it takes the predicate marker *-n*, as in 10.106:

10.106 ñən   atəta-n-añən-ək
         you.fem how-PRED-2fem.sgNOM-CONF
         'How are you? What's the matter with you?'

The form *atəta* is etymologically connected with *ata*; possibly, it is the result of fusion of the repeated *ata ata*. However, synchronically, these are different forms.

Three other forms are occasionally used in the meaning of 'how', as full synonyms of *atəta*: *atətawa*, *atətaka*, and *kətətaka* (the two latter ones were used by a speaker of the Malu variety).[4]

Two adverbial manner demonstratives can occasionally acquire interrogative meanings, *atawa* 'thus, like that' (10.107) and *akətawa* 'like this' (10.108), with very similar meanings. Note the form of the negator in this clause: we return to the use of non-main clause negator in questions in §14.5.

10.107 atawa   və-ma:r-ñəna-l
         how/like.that see-NEG.SUB-2fem.sgSUBJ.VT+3fem.sgBAS.VT-3fem.sgNOM
         'How come you didn't see her?' (lit. 'how did it happen that you did not see her?')

10.108 akətawa   kə-k-na-wun-ək
         how/like.this eat-FUT-ACT.FOC-1sgBAS.VT-CONF
         'How will I eat (uncooked food)?'

The form *akətawa* in its interrogative use can occur with the locative case, in the same meaning, *akətawa-n-əm* (how/like.this-PRED-LK+LOC) 'how, in what way?'

This polysemy between interrogatives and demonstratives is unique to adverbial manner demonstratives, and not attested for nominal demonstratives. None of the forms discussed here is used to enquire about degree—see 10.112 below.

(vii) The interrogative quantifier *kas* 'how many/much; which (by number)' is always postposed to the noun it quantifies, as shown in 10.109 and 6.43 (countable referent) and in 10.110 (uncountable referent):

10.109 ñən   ñan-ugw kas?
         you.fem child-PL how.many/much
         'How many children do you have?'

10.110 ñə   kas   tə-na?
         sun how.many/much stay/have-ACT.FOC+3fem.sgBAS.VT
         'What time is it?' (lit. How much sun is there?)

This quantifier is often used without an accompanying noun where it is obvious from the context, as in 10.111:

10.111 də-kə-k   kas   yapi-kə-tua-d?
         he-OBL-DAT how.many/much sell/pay-FUT-1sgSUBJ.VT-3masc.sgBAS.VT
         'How much shall I pay for him?'

It never occurs in a focus construction. It can be used to enquire about size, with a size noun, as in 10.112, and about the relative order, as in 10.113.

10.112 səmi   kas?
         length how.many/much
         'How long (is the stretch of cloth)?'

---

[4] Farnsworth and Farnsworth (1966) report the use of *akata* in the meaning of 'how'; none of my consultants used this form.

Motuway, who was sitting next to me chatting at a prayer meeting, missed the number of the verse the preacher told everyone to read; she then asked (see 19.104 for *kas* in a reported question):

10.113 vers   kas   wa-na-d
         verse how.much/many say-ACT.FOC-3masc.sgBAS.VT
         'Which verse (by number) did he say?'

Unlike any other interrogative (but similar to a noun), *kas* can be reduplicated yielding a distributive meaning, as in 10.114:

10.114 kas-ə-kas   yapi-kwa-na-di?
         how.much/many-LK-how.much/many sell/pay-HAB-ACT.FOC-3plBAS.VT
         'For how much do they sell each of these?' (referring to cucumbers, sold individually at
         a local market)

A questioned constituent can be part of the main (final) clause, or of medial completive clause (§18.3; also see example 9.33). Within a main clause, two constituents can be questioned, as in 10.115.

10.115 akrəl   sə-kə-m   vyak?
         where.to who-OBL-ACC/LOC hit+PURP.SS
         'Where are you going to hit whom?'

Two constituents in a medial clause cannot be questioned simultaneously; neither can one constituent in the main clause, and one in the medial clause. That questions are a separate clause type, different from declarative clauses, is corroborated by the way in which they are negated (as shown in 10.107); see §14.5.2 and also §20.1.3.

10.5 QUANTIFIERS

Quantifiers are a closed class of a couple of dozen members, covering the semantics of quantity and arrangement. Quantifiers refer to large quantity; these include *samasa:m* 'many', *æywan* 'quite a few (less than *samasa:m*)', and its synonym *mæyək* 'many' in the Malu variety. Two frequently used quantifiers with the meaning of 'all' are *miyawa* 'all' and *aba:b* 'all, all together'. Speakers who frequently code-switch with Tok Pisin also use the quantifier *sampela* 'some', as in 10.17.

These quantifiers can be used as modifiers to nouns, to verbs, and as heads of predicate. When used as modifiers to nouns, a quantifier can either precede or follow the noun, depending on its discourse status. A newly introduced or a non-topical referent is followed by the quantifier, as in 10.116. Once the referent has been established, the quantifier precedes it. We will see in §10.6 that numerals operate on a similar principle. In the very beginning of a story (10.116) the speaker states that her foster father used to do a lot of work.

10.116 də yawi samasa:m kur-kwa-na-d
         he work much   do-HAB-ACT.FOC-3masc.sgBAS.VT
         'He used to do a lot of work'

She then goes on to describe exactly what he did, and finally says 10.117.

10.117 samasam-a yawi kur-kwa-na-d
         much-LK   work do-HAB-ACT.FOC-3masc.sgBAS.VT
         '(He) used to do a lot of the work (mentioned already)'

Unlike numerals (but similarly to non-agreeing adjectives), the quantifiers take a linker when used as preposed modifiers within NPs. Similarly to numerals (e.g. 7.50), they do not take case markers, even when used as posthead modifiers (the case marker then goes onto the noun head). The only quantifier which can only be used postposed to the head is the interrogative *kas* 'how many/much' (§10.4).

All quantifiers can be used with countable and uncountable referents, except for *aba:b* 'all' which is preferred with countable referents. Its counterpart with uncountable and collective referents is the quantifier *miya-wa* (tree+LK-COM) 'all, whole' (this contains the comitative in a derivational function (§7.9, under E) and does not take any additional linker), e.g. *aba:b-a du-ta:kw* (all-LK man-woman) 'all the people (one by one)', *miyawa du-ta:kw* 'all the people as a group' (10.123); *miyawa tǝp* 'the whole village (as a group)'. An NP of the form ?*aba:b-a tǝp* is barely acceptable.

The quantifier *aba:b* 'all' can be used headlessly, as in 10.78. A preacher addressed his congregation by saying *vyakǝt-a ganǝb aba:b* (good-LK morning all) 'good morning all (of you)'. A frequent headless use of this quantifier may be due to calquing from Tok Pisin *olgeta* 'all'.

We saw in §7.9 (under E) that the comitative case can derive nouns with quantificational meanings, such as *tǝpawa* (village+LK+COM) 'the whole village; all villagers together'.

The number agreement of a verb or an agreeing modifier with an NP containing a quantifier depends on the countability of the referent, and the degree of individualization: if *samasam-a du-ta:kw* (many-LK man-woman) 'many people' is treated as one non-differentiated group, agreement is singular; if they are to be discussed as a set of groups, or individuals, agreement is plural. Quantifiers modify nouns and verbs. Quantifiers as modifier to verbs are illustrated in 10.118–19, and T3.43 (*miyawa* 'all').

10.118 samasa:m kwa-bana-lǝk
      much   stay-1plSUBJ.VT+3fem.sgBAS.VT-because
      'Because we stayed there as numerous (people) (there was not enough food)'

10.119 ata ma: ata samasa:m wukǝ-l
      then again then lot   worry-3fem.sgBAS.P
      'Then she worried a lot again'

In 10.120, a quantifier modifies a copula complement (and acquires an intensifying meaning). This is the only way of intensifying a copula complement, e.g. *nǝkǝr samasa:m tay-na* (cold much BE.NAT-ACT.FOC+3fem.sgBAS.VT) 'it is very cold'.

10.120 kǝ   jaguy   bæy samasa:m ada
      DEM.PROX.fem.sg yam.soup tasty much   DEM.DIST.REACT.TOP+masc.sg
      yi-na
      go-ACT.FOC+3fem.sgBAS.VT
      'This yam soup was very tasty'

In 10.121, a quantifier heads a predicate: it then takes nominal cross-referencing, as do most non-verbs in this slot (see §3.1).

10.121 bǝ   æywan-adian
      already many-1plNOM
      'We were already numerous'

The form *samasa:m* has an inherently reduplicated form; the component *sam-* appears in a compound *sam-a-ja:p* (all-LK-thing) meaning 'all', used as a modifier to a verb, as in 10.122.

10.122 du-ta:kw   bə   <u>sam-a-ja:p</u>   <u>kamapə-na-d</u>
man-woman already many-LK-thing come.up-ACT.FOC-3masc.sgBAS.VT
'People already appeared in big quantity'

Two further quantifiers—less frequently used than the ones discussed above—with the meaning 'many' appear to be just prehead modifiers, e.g. *kəb* in 10.123 and *səp-* in 10.124 (this latter form may be related to *səp* 'body'):

10.123 miyawa <u>kəb-a</u>   du-ta:kw   kətəkətun tə-də-d
all   many-LK man-woman cut+SEQ have-3masc.sgSUBJ.P-3masc.sgBAS.P
'He cut up all the many people'

10.124 a-də   təp <u>səp-a</u> du-ta:kw   yana-n ata
DEM.DIST-masc.sg village all-LK man-woman burn-SEQ then
da-k-na-dian-ək
go.down-FUT-ACT.FOC-1plBAS.VT-CONF
'(We) all the people of that village would have gone down burning (if we hadn't escaped)'

As shown in §4.3.1, the two agreeing adjectives, *kwasa* 'small' and *nəma* 'big', can be used adverbially, with a quantifying meaning '(a) little' and 'a lot'. See 10.125 and 4.52:

10.125 kwasa   o nəma,   gu   yaku-na-ñən?
small.fem.sg or big.fem.sg water wash-ACT.FOC-2fem.sgBAS.VT
'Have you washed a little, or a lot?'

Note that neither *kwasa* nor *nəma* in 10.125 are modifiers to *gu* 'water', the unmarked argument of *yaku-* 'wash' (see §7.2): this noun in this function cannot be further modified, and an intonation break (marked with a comma) between *nəma* and *gu* indicates that they do not form one NP.

Using *kwasa* 'small; a little' is the only way of referring to a small quantity of either countable or uncountable referents. We will see, in §10.6.1 below, that the numeral *mugul* 'three' can also be used to mean 'a few' (with countable nouns). The adjective *numa* 'big' can be used as a quantifier only with uncountable referents (with countable referents, it is a size adjective).

There is also a subtle difference between *numa* 'big, a lot' and *samasa:m* 'much' with uncountable referents: *numa gu* 'big water; a lot of water' refers to one big lot of water, while *samasam-a gu* (much-LK water) refers to large quantities of water which may be used for washing, or drinking, at several different times. In addition, only an agreeing size adjective can modify a noun or an agreeing modifier—that is, one can only say *numa kru tə-na ñan* (big+fem.sg fat have-ACT.FOC+3fem.sgBAS.VT child) 'a child who has a lot of fat', but not *samasam-a kru (much fat). That is, the size adjective quantifies the amount of a noun (10.126a, 10.127a: masculine gender refers to intensity and large quantity: §5.2.1), while the quantifier quantifies the intensity of the verbal action and number of times it is performed (10.126b, 10.127b). The size adjective and the quantifier *samasa:m* are contrasted in the following pairs of examples:

10.126a <u>numa-də</u>   yi-tukwa
big-masc.sg go/say-PROH.GEN
'Do not talk in a loud (voice)'

10.126b <u>samasa:m</u> yi-tukwa
a.lot   go/say-PROH.GEN
'Do not talk a lot'

10.127a [numa-də   sə]   sə   kwa-na
   big-masc.sg sleep sleep stay-ACT.FOC+3fem.sgBAS.VT
   'She is sleeping a deep sleep; she is sleeping deeply'

10.127b samasa:m sə   kwa-na
   a.lot   sleep stay-ACT.FOC+3fem.sgBAS.VT
   'She sleeps a lot (in times, and quantity)'

In addition to quantifiers, Manambu has a couple of dozen words referring to units and arrangements, e.g. *pui* 'parcel' (e.g. *na:gw pui nak* (sago parcel one) 'one parcel of sago'), *tan* 'measure, bundle' (as in *ñapwi tan nak* (firewood bundle one) 'one bundle of firewood'), *bæy* 'flat bundle, used for mats and limbum', *tukwi* 'heap, pile', *jibəl* 'arrangement of fish on a string', *pərəgabi* 'a small string of things, especially fish', *gwas* 'a big string or bundle', *bak* 'crowd', *sə* 'bundle (as of banana)', and *sa:y* 'bundle (of leaves)', exemplified in 10.128.

10.128 [tuay   sa:y   tabəti] ji-də-di
   coconut.leaves.for.burning bundle ten   bind-3masc.sgSUBJ.P-3plBAS.P
   'They bound ten bundles of coconut tree leaves (to be used as torches)'

   These quantifiers are not numeral classifiers since they only optionally occur with numbers. Their choice is determined by the ways in which the object is arranged and put into a particular shape or form, rather than by its intrinsic properties (see Aikhenvald 2000: 114–19). Nouns whose meaning is inherently shape or form based can be used as arrangement quantifiers, e.g. *yap* 'string; objects strung on a string', *dab* 'layer; layered objects', *tabək* 'side, half'. These straddle the boundaries between nouns and quantifiers.

10.6 NUMERALS

Numerals form a largish albeit closed class of non-agreeing modifiers. Numerals one to ten form one phonological and grammatical word each, while all other numerals consist of more than one word. Speakers vary in their competence with respect to numbers higher than twenty. We discuss numerals from one to ten, and those higher than ten, in §10.6.1 and §10.6.2.

10.6.1 Numerals from one to ten

Numerals from one to ten are given in Table 10.8, together with an indication of their additional meanings and composition (for numbers over four).

   Numerals 'one', 'two', and 'three' differ from other numerals in that they have meanings additional to counting. Numeral 'one' stands apart from other numerals in a number of properties outlined in A below. Numbers 'two' and 'three' are discussed in B and C respectively. Words for 'five' and 'ten' contain the term for 'hand, arm'.

   Numbers 'two' to 'ten' can be employed as prehead or posthead modifiers; their position in a noun phrase depends on whether the noun referent is newly introduced or already established, and whether it is focused on. Just as with quantifiers (§10.5), a newly introduced referent is followed by the numeral. In contrast, number 'one' always follows the noun.

   Numerals one to ten form one grammatical word. Numerals one to four are underived. Number five contains the root for 'hand', *ta:b-*, and the formative *-a:b*, which could be cognate to *-a:b* 'too', or to *aba:b* 'all' (see §22.1 on this being a possible calque from Kwoma). Ordinal

TABLE 10.8   Numerals from one to ten

NUMBER	FORM	ADDITIONAL MEANINGS	COMPOSITION
1	*nakaməy, nak, nə*	'alone'; 'single'; 'another'; indefinite	n/a
2	*viti*	dual marker with some kin terms	n/a
3	*mugul*	few	n/a
4	*a:li*	—	n/a
5	*taba:b*	—	*ta:b* 'hand'+ *a:b* 'too'
6	*abun*	—	*a:b* 'too'+ *n* 'one?'
7	*abəti*	—	*a:b* 'too'+ *viti* 'two'
8	*abumugul*	—	*a:b* 'too'+ *mugul* 'three'
9	*aba:li*	—	*a:b* 'too'+ *a:li* 'four'
10	*tabəti, tabati*	—	*ta:b* 'hand'+ *viti* 'two'

numbers can be formed on cardinal terms from 'two' to 'ten', using the suffix *-yay* attached to the linker, as in *viti-a-yay* (two-LK-ORD) 'second', *mugul-a-yay* 'third', and so on. Ordinal numbers are non-agreeing modifiers, similar to quantifiers and cardinal numbers 'two' to 'ten', in that they occur postposed to a new or non-topical referent, as in 10.129:

10.129 kad   təp   mugul-a-yay mugul-a-yay-əm
DEM.PROX+3masc.sgNOM village third-LK-ORD three-LK-ORD-LK+LOC
rə-bana   aka-n-aka
sit-1plSUBJ.VT+3fem.sgBAS.VT DEM.DIST.REACT.TOP.fem.sg-PRED-REACT.TOP.fem.sg
'This is a third village; it is (the case) that we settled in the third village'

Ordinal numerals occur preposed to a topically established or definite referent (see §20.2):

10.130 a   mugul-a-yay wiya:r   yi-lə-1
DEM.DIST.fem.sg three-LK-ORD house+LK+ALL go-3fem.sgSUBJ.P-3fem.sgBAS.P
aka
DEM.DIST.REACT.TOP.fem.sg
'It is that she went to that third house'

An ordinal numeral can be used without a nominal head, and it can then take the appropriate case marker, as in 10.129. This is in contrast to cardinal numbers which do not take case marking.

All numbers can be used in counting, as in 'one, two, three', and as modifiers; the number 'one' is unique in that the form used for counting (or number recital) is different from forms used in most other contexts.

A. NUMBER 'ONE' has three forms. The form *nakaməy* has two uses: it occurs in counting 'one, two, three', as shown in 10.131—an incitement for the two children who are diving to come up again:

10.131 nakaməy viti   mugul a:li, taba:b, a-war-əy
one   two   three four   five   IMPV-go.up-VOC
'One, two, three, four, five—up you go!'

As mentioned in §5.1.1, *nakaməy* can be used as a prehead modifier meaning 'only one, one (of many)'. Then it optionally takes an infixed gender agreement marker: *naka-də-məy* means 'only one (masculine)', and *naka-məy* 'only one' is feminine. This refers to one turtle out of many in 10.132:

10.132 <u>nakamǝy-a</u>   gwa:s aka   ya-na
       one.single.fem-LK turtle DEM.DIST.REACT.TOP.fem.sg come-ACT.FOC+3fem.sgBAS.VT
       'One single turtle (out of many) came'

In 10.133, the masculine form refers to the only child:

10.133 wun-a-dǝ   *nak-a-dǝ-mǝy-a*   du-a-ñan   adǝka
       I-LK-masc.sg one-LK-masc.sg-very-LK   man-LK-child DEM.DIST.REACT.TOP+masc.sg
       tǝ-na-d
       stand-ACT.FOC-3masc.sgBAS.VT
       'My only son (about whom we are talking again) is standing (here)'

This form is the only one in the language to distinguish two gender forms, but no number forms. The use of *nakamǝy* in counting goes together with the functionally unmarked character of the feminine gender. These forms are likely to be compounds consisting of *nak-* 'one', *-a-* 'linker', followed by the gender marker (*-d(ǝ)* 'masculine', ø 'feminine'), and *mǝy* 'real; very'.

The two further forms, *nak* and *nǝ*, are both used as posthead modifiers and are almost synonymous: one can refer to children of the same mother (or to those who belong to the same maternal clan) as *ya:l nak waku-di* or *ya:l nǝ waku-di* (belly one come.out-3plBAS.VT) 'they came out of the same belly'. Both *jayǝb nak* and *jayǝb nǝ* mean 'one moment, quickly, instantaneously'. In enumerating objects one by one, the form *nǝ* appears to be somewhat preferred. Both *nak* and *nǝ* can mark indefinite and newly introduced referents. In 10.134, from the very beginning of a story, the speaker introduced the referent as *ta:kw nak* (woman one) 'a woman'. A variant *ta:kw nǝ* is also used in the same function.

10.134 ta:kw   <u>nak</u> lǝ-kǝ-di   ñan-ugwǝwa   kwa:l
       woman one she-OBL-pl child-PL+LK+COM stay+3fem.sgBAS.P
       'One woman lived with her children'

However, there are a number of differences between *nak* and *nǝ*, along the following lines:

1. The numeral *nak*, but not *nǝ*, can be used without a nominal head, as in:

10.135 kudi   <u>nak</u> ak   wa-di   <u>nak</u> ata ka:l
       mouthful one IMPV+eat say-3plBAS.P one then eat+3fem.sgBAS.P
       ' "Eat one mouthful!", they said, she then ate one (mouthful)'

It can also head a predicate, which is not the case for *nǝ*, and can have a meaning of 'same (as previous)', as in 10.136:

10.136 ma:j   <u>nak-al</u>
       word/talk one-3fem.sgNOM
       'This is the same word'

2. The numeral *nak* (but not *nǝ*) often has the meaning of 'another, one more'. In 10.137, Walinum volunteers to tell another short story. *Nak* 'another one' is used headlessly; it can have the same meaning as a modifier.

10.137 wun-a   kwasa   ma: <u>nak</u> aka
       I-LK+fem.sg small+fem.sg again one DEM.DIST.REACT.TOP.fem.sg
       wa-kǝ-tua
       tell-FUT-1sgSUBJ.VT+3fem.sgBAS.VT
       'I will tell another little one of mine again'

This use of *nak* is reminiscent of the use of the indefinite *nəkə* 'another', illustrated in 10.3 and 10.52. It is possible that forms *nak*, *nə*, and *nəkə* are etymologically related. In rapid casual speech, *nəkə* can be pronounced as *nə* (in agreement with A3 under §2.6), e.g. rapid speech *nə ja:p nə ja:p kur-ku*, normal speech *nəkə ja:p nəkə ja:p kur-ku* (another.fem.sg thing another.fem.sg thing get-COMPL.SS) 'having taken one thing and another'. Unlike both *nak* and *nə*, *nəkə* is an agreeing prehead modifier.

3. The numeral *nak* can be used in opposition to other numbers, while *nə* is not used this way. An example is under 10.138—a description of what happens during warfare:

10.138 du   <u>nak</u> akəs   kiya-kwa-na-d   dəy <u>viti</u>, <u>mugul</u>, <u>a:li</u>, ata
        man one NEG.HAB die-HAB-ACT.FOC-3masc.sgBAS.VT they two three   four then
        kiya-kwa-na-di
        die-HAB-ACT.FOC-3plBAS.VT
        'One man never dies, two, three, four die'

The form *nə* is only occasionally used in opposition to another number, but never more than one, as in 10.139:

10.139 bap   <u>nə</u> tə-kə-na-dəwun-ək   o bap   <u>viti</u> tə-ku
        month one stay-FUT-ACT.FOC-1masc.sgBAS.VT-CONF or month two stay-COMPL.SS
        ya-k-na-dəwun-ək
        come-FUT-ACT.FOC-1masc.sgBAS.VT-CONF
        'I will stay (away) for one month, or I will come back having stayed (away) two months'

4. Only *nak* and not *nə* can undergo full reduplication. A reduplicated form *nak-a-nak* (one-LK-one) has two meanings: 'one by one', as in 10.140, and 'few, not too many', as in 10.141.

10.140 <u>nak-a-nak</u>   kur-ta:y   səpur-taka-bana
        one-LK-one get-COTEMP shell-put-1plSUBJ.VT+3fem.sgBAS.VT
        'Having got (peanuts) one by one we shell them'

10.141 wurəbi-adi   kə-di,   <u>nak-a-nak</u> adiya
        large.mosquito-3plNOM DEM.PROX-pl one-LK-one DEM.DIST.REACT.TOP+pl
        'These are large mosquitoes, they are few' (since this is dry season)

This same form can be used adverbially, meaning 'one by one', as in 21.4. These uses may well have resulted from a Tok Pisin influence: cf. Tok Pisin *wan wan* 'few'; *wanpela wanpela* 'one by one'. Nowadays they are part of everyday usage. The final *k* can be elided in fast speech.

5. The form *nak* is strongly preferred to *nə* in complex numbers higher than ten (see §10.6.2).

In its use as a marker of newly introduced referents, the numeral 'one' is influenced by a similar usage of the number 'one', *wanpela*, in Tok Pisin. Young speakers, especially children and teenagers whose major language of communication is Tok Pisin, display a peculiar pattern of code-switching, introducing a new referent, for example *wanpela ta:kw* (one:TP woman) and then correcting this to *ta:kw nak* (as in 10.134). Some speakers even use both Tok Pisin and Manambu lexemes in this same function, as shown in §22.4 (*wanpela du nak* (one:TP man one) 'a man'). This is unusual since the Tok Pisin numeral does not go into the same slot as its Manambu correspondent, but rather keeps the Tok Pisin linear order. In most instances, a Tok Pisin number occurs together with a Tok Pisin word, as in *wanpela taim* (one time) 'once' (see Aikhenvald forthcoming c).

As shown in §5.1.1, the root *nak* occurs in two other forms, *nak-a-l-əb* (one-LK-fem.sg-TERM) 'together' (of a group consisting of women only, or of a mixed group) and its synonym *nakamib* 'together' (which is most likely derived from *nakaməy* and the terminative case frequently employed in deriving adverbs)—see 16.106.

Unlike other numbers, 'one' has the adverb *ta:y* 'first' in lieu of a corresponding ordinal number, as in 4.61, 13.15, and T2.47. An alternative term is an adverb *bas* 'firstly', as in *bas yawi waku-n* (first work go.out-SEQ) 'going out to work for the first time'. The term for last is *gañ*. Further terms involving the idea of being first or last include *gəm* 'first pregnancy', *kə-təp-ə məñ* (eat-close-LK breast) 'last child', *amay ta:kw* (mother woman/wife) 'first wife', *gəñ-a ta:kw* (last-LK wife) 'non-first wife'; *ap-a sə* (bone-LK name) 'first name' (of the many names one has), as contrasted to *səgliak* 'any name other than the first one'. The term *kukə-səbuk* (late-sibuk) 'the latest/most senior of all initiated men (*simbuks*)' was suggested as a term for 'first priest'.

B. NUMBER 'TWO' has an additional, non-numerical, meaning. We saw in Table 6.1 that the numeral *viti* or its cliticized version *-vəti* marks dual on several kin terms.

Case marking on NPs provides a way of distinguishing *viti* as a dual marker and *viti* as number two (also see B in §6.1). When the number 'two' acts as a number, it does not take case marking—we saw in 7.50 that this is a general property of numbers. This is shown in 10.142.

10.142 [asa:k   viti] yaga-na
       dog+LK+DAT two be.afraid-ACT.FOC+3fem.sgBAS.VT
       'She is afraid of two dogs'

In contrast, a noun marked for dual takes case marking:

10.143 də-kə-bər jukwar-a-vəti:k   wapa-ku
       he-POSS-du sister-LK-DU+DAT leave-COMPL.SS
       'Having left his two sisters . . .'

The number 'two', when reduplicated, has a somewhat idiomatic meaning of 'muddled', as in 10.144—this was Kawindu's explanation for a mess up in local flights:

10.144 ma:j viti-viti tə-na-bər
       story two-two have-ACT.FOC-3duBAS.VT
       'They two tell muddled stories' (lit. have two stories each?)

C. Number 'three' as a cardinal number has an additional, non-numerical quantifying meaning of 'a few, several'. Whether *mugul* is used in a numerical meaning or not is usually clear from the context. In 7.50, we were leaving exactly three days later. In 10.131 and 10.138, *mugul* is one of the numbers used in counting. In 10.145, *mugul* 'few' is contrasted to another quantifier—it cannot possibly mean 'three'.

10.145 *orait*   mugul æywan ma:, mugul-a-bə   da-di
       alright few   many NEG few-LK-already go.down-3plBAS.P
       'OK, (there were) few, not many, few people went down (river)'

When an ordinal number is formed on 'three', its meaning is always strictly numerical, as in 10.130. A noun phrase with the quantifier *mugul* 'few' can trigger dual agreement, if the number of referents is about two, as in 6.40. Or it can trigger plural agreement, if there are more than two referents, as in 10.146. If *mugul* means 'three', agreement is always plural.

10.146 gurawa   mugul-a bal-adi,   wun samasa:m-adi
       you+LK+COM few-LK pig-3plNOM I   many-3plNOM
       'There are few pigs with you, I, (my pigs) are many'

The non-numerical quantifier usage of *mugul* suggests that its numerical meaning is relatively recent. This is corroborated by the data from other Ndu languages: while terms for 'one' and 'two' are relatively stable throughout the family, the terms for numerals from three onwards vary. The Iatmul form for 'three' can also mean 'few' (Jendraschek forthcoming). (The two forms equally reconstructible for Proto-Ndu 'three' are *məgəl and *kəp(w)ək; their reflexes are scattered across the family: see Aikhenvald forthcoming b.)

Numerals 'two' and 'three' can take the derivational suffix *-kərəb* 'together', as in *viti-kərəb* 'two together' and *mugul-a-kərəb* 'three together' (but not *a few together). Both numbers have a strictly numerical meaning in such derivations (see 10.47). A derivation containing *-kərəb* can be used to refer to humans, as in T3.52 (where it modifies a pronoun, 'they two, two of them together'). It can modify a noun with a non-human referent, as in 10.147. This is an example of a split noun phrase:

10.147 <u>viti-kərəb</u>   avæs   mæn
       two-together IMPV+step foot
       'Step with two feet together!' (while walking on a narrow log in lieu of a bridge)

Just like any numeral, a derivation marked with *-kərəb* can be used as a posthead modifier, as in 10.47, or as a prehead modifier. In the latter case, the noun takes a modification marker, e.g. *viti-kərəb-a ta:kw* (two-together-LK woman) 'two women together' (e.g. two co-wives).

Numbers from 'two' to 'ten' can occur with the approximative suffix *-pək* 'more or less', e.g. 9.35, and with *-rəb* 'fully' (see §9.2.1). If combined with either suffix, the number *mugul* has a strictly numerical meaning, 'three'. The number 'one' does not combine with any suffixes.

10.6.2 Numerals higher than ten

Table 10.9 features numerals from eleven to twenty, with translations and a gloss. We have seen that numerals from one to ten are uniform for all speakers. The larger the numeral, the more variability there is. The third column of Table 10.9 features numbers from eleven to twenty produced by several 8- to 9-year-olds. The forms different from those used by traditional speakers are in bold.

For ten and twenty, there are special counting terms for money (traditionally used for shell valuables): *mi nak* (literally, stick one) or *jələg nak* (literally, string one) 'ten (valuables)', and *mi-vəti* or *jələg vəti* 'twenty valuables'.

All numerals higher than ten are noun phrases. Numerals from eleven to fourteen consist of 'ten' followed by the word *mæn* 'leg', and then a numeral one to four: *tabəti mæn nak* 'eleven' (lit. both hands one on one leg?), *tabəti mæn vəti* 'twelve', *tabəti man mugul* 'thirteen', and *tabəti man ali* 'fourteen'. 'Fifteen' is formed with 'ten' and the form *man* followed by *-əb* 'all?' (this could be the same morpheme as in *tab-ab* 'five'), *tabəti manəb* (literally, two hands (and) all the leg).

Numbers from sixteen to nineteen are formed on fifteen, followed by *nəmnəm* (not used anywhere else in the language), and then followed by numbers one to four, e.g. *tabəti manəb nəmnəm nak* 'sixteen'.

Young speakers regularize the system, by forming all numbers from eleven to nineteen in the same way (and avoiding the rare form *nəmnəm*). The term for 'twenty', *du-a-mi nak* (man-LK-tree one), refers to the number of fingers and toes on one person. This is reminiscent of the form for 'twenty' in Boiken, *du mi napʌ* (man stick one), which also involves *mi*, and also Iatmul *kita*

TABLE 10.9   Numerals from eleven to twenty

TRADITIONAL MANAMBU	TRANSLATION AND GLOSS	YOUNGER SPEAKERS	TRANSLATION AND GLOSS
tabəti mæn nak	11 (ten(=hand+two) leg one)	*tabəti mæn nak*	11 (ten(=hand+two) leg one)
tabəti mæn vəti	12 (ten leg two)	*tabəti mæn vəti*	12 (ten leg two)
tabəti mæn mugul	13 (ten leg three)	*tabəti mæn mugul*	13 (ten leg three)
tabəti mæn a:li	14 (ten leg four)	*tabəti mæn a:li*	14 (ten leg four)
tabəti mænəb	15 (ten leg+also)	**tabəti mæn tabab**	15 (ten leg five)
tabəti mænəb nəmnəm nak	16 (ten leg+also add one)	**tabəti mæn abun**	16 (ten leg six)
tabəti mænəb nəmnəm vəti	17 (ten leg+also add two)	**tabəti mæn abəti**	17 (ten leg seven)
tabəti mænəb nəmnəm mugul	18 (ten leg+also add three)	**tabəti mæn abumugul**	18 (ten leg eight)
tabəti mænəb nəmnəm ali	19 (ten leg+also add four)	**tabəti mæn abali**	19 (ten leg nine)
du-a-mi nak	20 (man-LK-tree one)	**du-a-mi**	20 (man-LK-tree)

du-mi (one man-?stick). (In other Ndu languages, such as Gala, the term for 'twenty' is 'one person': *lua-nok*.)

Table 10.10 features numbers from twenty-one onwards. Numbers from twenty-one to twenty-nine are given in full. They consistently involve *du-a-mi* 'twenty', a connector *sa:p* (not found anywhere in the language except for complex numerals), and then a lower number from one to nine.

Numbers for the multiples of ten have alternative forms. The forms in the first column are the ones accepted by a majority of knowledgeable male speakers. These are twenty-based and involve (formally unmarked) multiplication, and addition marked with either *sa:p* or with *nəmnəm*. So, the term for thirty is 'twenty plus ten'; forty is 'two twenties'; fifty is 'two-twenty plus ten'; sixty is 'three twenties'; seventy is 'three twenties plus ten'; eighty is 'four twenties'; ninety is 'four twenties plus ten'; and one hundred is 'five twenties'. The connector for twenties is *sa:p*, and *nəmnəm* is a connector for units (one to nine).

Such a twenty-based system is found in the dialect of Iatmul described by Staalsen (n.d.b), e.g. *dumi kuvuk* (twenty three) 'sixty'. Similar forms appear in the dialect of Korogo (Jendraschek, p.c.), e.g. *ndumi kuvuk* 'sixty', *du-mi taba nak* (man-? hand one = five). The numbers in Gala also partially operate on the same, vigesimal, basis, e.g. *lua-nok waja-fit* (man-one = twenty ten (=hand-two)') 'thirty'.

Speakers are fairly consistent in the forms for numbers up until twenty-nine. From thirty onwards, there is a certain amount of confusion which cuts across dialectal boundaries. The numbers in Table 10.10 appear to be the most accepted ones (this system was partially described by Farnsworth and Farnsworth n.d.).

Some speakers use *du-a-mi mugul* (twenty (man-LK-tree three)) for 'thirty'. This parallels Iatmul *ndu-mi kuvuk* (man-? three) (note that in Iatmul the term for twenty is *du-mi kita* (man-? one)) (Jendraschek, p.c.). Forms containing units are *duami mugul sa:p nak* (twenty three plus one) 'thirty one', *duami mugul sa:p viti* (twenty three plus two) 'thirty two', and so on. For the same speakers, 'forty' is *duami a:li* (twenty four), reminiscent of Iatmul *ndu-mi ainak* (man-?

TABLE 10.10   Numerals from twenty-one onwards

NUMBERS	GLOSS	TRANSLATION
duami nak sa:p nak	20 (man-LK-tree one) 'plus' one	twenty-one
duami nak sa:p viti	20 (man-LK-tree one) 'plus' two	twenty-two
duami nak sa:p mugul	20 (man-LK-tree one) 'plus' three	twenty-three
duami nak sa:p a:li	20 (man-LK-tree one) 'plus' four	twenty-four
duami nak sa:p taba:b	20 (man-LK-tree one) 'plus' five	twenty-five
duami nak sa:p abun	20 (man-LK-tree one) 'plus' six	twenty-six
duami nak sa:p abəti	20 (man-LK-tree one) 'plus' seven	twenty-seven
duami nak sa:p abuməgəl	20 (man-LK-tree one) 'plus' eight	twenty-eight
duami nak sa:p aba:li	20 (man-LK-tree one) 'plus' nine	twenty-nine
duami nak sa:p tabəti	20 (man-LK-tree one) 'plus' ten	thirty
duami nak sa:p tabati nəmnəm nak	20 plus ten 'plus' one	thirty-one
duami nak sa:p tabati nəmnəm viti	20 plus ten 'plus' two	thirty-two
duami viti	20 two	forty
duami viti sa:p tabəti	20 two plus ten	fifty
duami mugul	20 three	sixty
duami mugul sa:p tabəti	20 three plus ten	seventy
duami a:li	20 four	eighty
duami a:li sa:p tabəti	20 four plus ten	ninety
duami taba:b	20 five	hundred

four), fifty is *duami taba:b* (twenty five) (cf. Iatmul *ndu-mi tamba nak* man-? hand one); sixty is *duami abun* (twenty six); seventy is *duami abəti* (twenty seven), eighty is *duami abumugul* (twenty eight), and ninety is *duami aba:li* (twenty nine). Each of these forms has a parallel in Iatmul of Korogo where doublet forms were also attested, e.g. *du-mi ainak* (man-? four) and *du-mi viti* (man-? two) 'forty', *du-mi sila kita* (man-? ? six) and *du-mi kuvuk* (man-? three) 'sixty', and so on.

The alternative term for 'hundred' in Manambu is *duamir duamir tabəti* (twenty+INSTR twenty+INSTR ten), which is somewhat similar but not fully parallel to Iatmul *du-mi taba vli* (man-? hand two=ten) (Jendraschek, p.c.).

Another alternative form for forty was *duamir duamir a:li* (twenty+INSTR twenty+INSTR four). This was discarded as an error by most speakers who said that this means 'row of twenties'. Another alternative is *duamir viti* (twenty+INSTR two) 'forty'. In 10.149 below, *duami viti* and *duamir viti* were used interchangeably. Occasionally, a forty-based system was attested, as in *duamir nə sa:p tabəti mæn nak* (twenty+INSTR one and ten leg one) 'fifty-one' (lit. one forty and eleven). This was used by just one speaker (who had used *duami viti* and then *duamir viti* for 'forty' in the previous sentence, in 10.149). Since the term in Tok Pisin almost always accompanies such lengthy numbers, there are hardly ever any misunderstandings.

The following forms have been cited for numbers over 100:

duami tabəti (twenty ten) '200',
duami tabəti mana:b (twenty ten leg+TOO) '300',
duamir duamir duami nak (twenty+INSTR twenty+INSTR twenty one) '400',
duamir duamir duami nak mana:b (twenty+INSTR twenty+INSTR twenty one leg+TOO) '500',
duamir duamir duami nak mana:b nəmnəm nak '600';
duamir duamir duami nak mana:b nəmnəm viti '700';

duamir duamir duami nak mana:b nəmnəm mugul '800';
duamir duamir duami nak mana:b nəmnəm a:li '900', and
duamir duamir duami nak mana:b nəmnəm taba:b '1000'.

Numbers over 100 are hardly ever used.

The Manambu people are 'number-proud'. Knowledge of high numbers is considered a valuable token of expertise in the language. At present, Tok Pisin numbers (which are easier to handle and to remember) are used in everyday life, especially those from eleven onwards. Higher numbers occur in traditional stories, or when a speaker wishes to display their expertise, especially if the context involves traditional counting contexts. These include counting one's ancestors, counting the number of enemies killed in battle, and counting shell valuables. In 10.148, from the story about how the Vali:k clan was founded (similar to Text 2), high numbers are used to compare the prowess of the two men.

10.148 yi-da-k   Səsawi paki   duami mugul sa:p tambəti
       go-3pl-COMPL.DS Səsawi number twenty three plus ten

       vya-də-di   du, Kamkudi duami a:li sa:p abali
       kill-3masc.sgSUBJ.P-3plBAS.P   man Kamkudi twenty four plus nine

       vya-də-di   du, pakiya-nas   ata wa-bər
       kill-3masc.sgSUBJ.P-3plBAS.P   man number+LK-count   then say-3duBAS.P

       'Having gone (to fight), number of people killed by Səsawi is 70, number of people killed by Kamkudi is 89, this is how they counted'

High numbers, whenever they are used, are likely to be accompanied by translations into Tok Pisin, since the speakers are never confident that their audience really understands these. In 10.149, the speaker made sure he translated the numbers; however, he himself used two different forms for 'forty':

10.149 duami viti vya-da-di   vya-ku   wali kudir
       twenty two hit-3plSUBJ.P-3plBAS.P   hit-COMPL.SS white language+INSTR

       wa-kwa-dana-di   adika,   fotipela-adi
       say-HAB-3plSUBJ.VT-3plBAS.VT REACT.DEM.DIST+pl forty:TP-3plNOM

       vya-da-di,   təp-a-majib   ñan aka
       hit-3plSUBJ.P-3plBAS.P   village-LK-talk+LK+TERM we REACT.DEM.DIST+fem.sg

       duamir   viti
       twenty+INSTR   two

       'They killed forty (people), having killed them; in white language (Tok Pisin) we say about them, they are forty, in the village language we (say) "forty"'

Numbers higher than ten are postposed to the head noun, or occur in split noun phrases (as in 10.148), or without a head noun, as in 10.149. Manambu has a word for number, *paki*; the verb for counting *nas-* can also mean 'enumerate', or 'list' (as in 10.68). A full account and an attempt to reconstruct the Proto-Ndu numbers is in Aikhenvald (forthcoming b).

10.7 CLOSED CLASSES: AN OVERVIEW

Closed classes in Manambu differ in terms of several major parameters: (i) whether they can occur as heads of noun phrases; (ii) whether they can occur as prehead or as posthead

TABLE 10.11 Properties of closed classes: a comparison

	HEAD OF NP	MODIFIER		CASE MARKING	OVERT NUMBER AND GENDER
		prehead	posthead		
Personal pronouns	yes	yes (possessive NP only)	no	yes	no
Demonstratives	yes	yes	no	yes (not all)	yes
Indefinite *nǝkǝ-*	rare	yes	no	yes	yes
Indefinite *nǝwǝk*	yes	no	no	no	no
Quantifiers	yes	yes	yes	no	no
Numbers 1–4	yes	yes: 2–4	yes: 1	no	no

modifiers, (iii) whether they can take case marking; and (iv) whether they allow overt marking of number and gender. These are partly summarized in Table 10.11.

Further grammatical subclasses can be established within each particular class. We saw above that reactivated topic demonstratives behave differently from any other demonstratives (or any other classes in the language) in that they take a predicative marker *-n* followed by *a*-gender-number-*ka* when focused or when used as predicate heads. Current relevance demonstratives have no gender and number marking, in contrast to spatio-temporal demonstratives which do.

11

Predicate Structure and Verb Root Types

Verbs are the most complicated part of the Manambu grammar, both in terms of the wealth of their categories, and of the array of root alternations (see §4.2.1). In §11.1, I discuss verbal categories and verb structure. The structure of non-verbal predicates is addressed in §11.2. An overview of verbal root types in terms of their alternations is in §11.3.

11.1 VERBAL CATEGORIES AND VERB STRUCTURE

11.1.1 Inflected and uninflected verbs

Each verb can occur in one of two types of form:

- INFLECTED—those which take personal cross-referencing, and
- UNINFLECTED—those which do not take any personal cross-referencing (though they may take other affixes).

Inflected verb forms can be either

- FULLY INFLECTED, that is, allow for cross-referencing of one or two arguments (see Tables 3.1–2), or
- PARTIALLY INFLECTED, that is, allow for cross-referencing just one argument which is always the subject—A or S (see Table 3.1).

The number of arguments cross-referenced on a fully inflected verb does not depend on the verb's transitivity: the A/S argument always has to be cross-referenced and a non-subject argument is only cross-referenced if it is more topical than the subject (see §3.1). The categories which require FULLY INFLECTED, PARTIALLY INFLECTED, and UNINFLECTED verb forms are summarized in Table 11.1. (Numbers of sections where each category is described are in brackets.)

The distribution of fully inflected, partially inflected, and uninflected forms to some extent correlates with clause types. Most non-main (or dependent) clauses contain partially inflected and uninflected verbs (see Chapter 19 and Table 19.1, and §20.1.3). So do main clauses marked for non-declarative mood and modality values, and non-habitual declarative negative clauses.

FULLY INFLECTED verb forms are the most complex of all. They allow the expression of categories which cannot be expressed in partially inflected or uninflected verbs.

Only fully inflected main-clause verbs can be within the scope of highlighting focus introduced at §3.1. The pragmatic implications of highlighting focus constructions in Manambu are discussed at some length in §20.3. And see §14.5 for the ways in which a verb in highlighting focus is negated.

TABLE 11.1 Categories of fully inflected, partially inflected, and uninflected verbs

FULLY INFLECTED VERBS: CROSS-REFERENCE ONE OR TWO ARGUMENTS DEPENDING ON THE PRESENCE OF ACTION FOCUS -na-: SCHEME 11.2		PARTIALLY INFLECTED VERBS: CROSS-REFERENCE ONE ARGUMENT: SCHEME 11.3		UNINFLECTED VERBS: NO ARGUMENT CROSS-REFERENCING	
MAIN CLAUSE	NON-MAIN CLAUSE	MAIN CLAUSE	NON-MAIN CLAUSE	MAIN CLAUSE	NON-MAIN CLAUSE
• positive declarative and interrogative clauses (§12.1–2) • positive and negative habitual clauses (§12.3) • irrealis (§13.3)	• juxtaposed dependent clauses (§19.1) • relative clauses (§19.2)	• imperative (§13.2) • different-subject purposive (§13.4.2)	• different-subject completive medial (§18.3) • causal (§18.7) • temporal overlap sequencing (§18.6) • different-subject purposive (§13.4.2 and §19.4.1)	• negative declarative non-habitual (§14.1) • completive (§12.6) • customary (§12.7) • with suffix -rəb 'fully' (§9.2; §12.8.1) • with suffix -dəka 'only' (§9.2; §12.8.1) • same-subject purposive (§13.4.1) • desiderative (§13.5) • frustrative (§13.6) • prohibitive (§14.4)	• same-subject completive medial clauses (§18.3) • cotemporaneous medial clauses (§18.4) • immediate sequence medial clauses (§18.5) • manner sequencing (§18.2) • same-subject purposive (§13.4.1 and §19.4.1) • desiderative (§19.4.2) • unlikely condition (§18.8)

(i)   causative-manipulative prefix *kay-* (§16.2)
(ii) verbal root(s) (see Chapter 15 on verb compounding)
(iii) one or two suffixal directional markers (see §16.1).

SCHEME 11.1   The structure of a verb stem

11.1.2   The structure of verbal predicate

All verbal markers occur on a verb stem. The structure of the verbal stem is in Scheme 11.1.

The verb stem must include (ii), that is, there has to be at least one verbal root (which can undergo reduplication: see §12.8.3). Manambu has numerous types of verb compounding, covering sequences of subactions, valency changing, and aspectual meanings, such as 'incomplete action', 'action to perfection', and 'completion'. The aspect markers which have grammaticalized from compounded verbal roots can be reduplicated (see §15.2 for a discussion of their meanings). This is unlike aspect markers discussed in Chapter 12.

Positions (i) and (iii) are optional. A verbal stem can also contain one, or maximally two, directional markers, whose form varies somewhat depending on the verb (see §16.1).

We saw, in §3.1, that if a verb takes the action focus *-na-*, no constituent other than the subject can be cross-referenced on it. The structure of a fully inflected verb with and without the action focus marker is given in Scheme 11.2. Numbers of sections of Chapter 12 dealing with every specific category are in brackets. Verbal stem and subject (A/S) cross-referencing are the only obligatory components of a fully inflected verb—in the sense that a verb form could not exist without them. Others can be added if a particular meaning is to be expressed.

An example of a longish fully inflected verb is in 11.1. The verb stem here contains a causative-manipulative prefix *kay-*, two compounded verb roots (see §15.3.2), and two directionals (§16.1.4). This is followed by the habitual, the future, the action focus marker, the non-A/S 'basic' cross-referencing marker, and the confirmation marker. Numbers above example 11.1 correspond to the positions in the stem structure and the verb structure:

---

1. Verbal stem
2. *-kwa-* 'habitual aspect' (§12.3)[a] or *-tu-* 'complete involvement of S/O' (§12.4)
3. *-kə-* 'future' (§12.2)[b]

---

either

4a. A/S marked with the subject set of tense-sensitive cross-referencing markers (§12.1.1)
5a. non-A/S marked with basic set of tense-sensitive cross-referencing markers if it is more topical than A/S (§12.1.1)

or

4b. *-na-* 'action focus' (§12.1.2)
5b. A/S marked with the basic set of tense-sensitive cross-referencing markers (§12.1.1)
6. *-ək* 'confirmation marker' (§12.5)

SCHEME 11.2   The structure of a fully inflected verb

[a] The habitual aspect requires the versatile tense cross-referencing markers.
[b] The future is not compatible with the habitual; it requires the versatile tense cross-referencing markers.

1. Verbal stem
2. A/S marked with the subject set of non-tense-sensitive cross-referencing markers (Table 11.2)
3. Marker of different-subject purposive (§13.4.2), different-subject completive (§18.3), temporal 'as soon as' (§18.6), or causal (§18.7)

SCHEME 11.3   The structure of a partially inflected verb

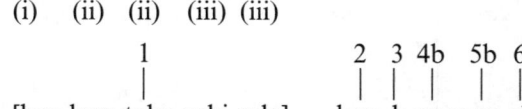

11.1 [kay-kwa-taka-saki-sala]stem-kwa-k-na-wun-ək
MANIP-stay-put-ACROSS-INWARD-HAB-FUT-ACT.FOC-1fem.sgBAS.VT-CONF
'I will be pouring (liquid) by moving it side to side (across and inward)'

A partially inflected verb is much simpler. There is a basic difference between imperatives as partially inflected verbal forms, and all other uninflected verbs. The imperative obligatorily takes either the prefix *a*- which triggers changes in the verb stem, or a special set of imperative-only suffixes (see §13.2). A second person imperative is in 11.2, and a third person imperative is in 11.3:

11.2 atak
IMPV+put
'put (it down)!'

11.3 taka-kwa-d
put-IMPV.3p-masc.sg
'may he put (it down)!'

A non-imperative partially inflected verb has just three positions, as shown in Scheme 11.3. All of these are obligatory, if the given meaning is to be expressed.
An example is under 11.4:

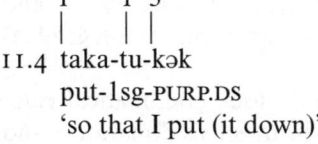

11.4 taka-tu-kək
put-1sg-PURP.DS
'so that I put (it down)'

Non-tensed and tense-sensitive subject cross-referencing markers are listed in Table 11.2 (repeated from Table 3.2). They are in part identical. The main difference lies in the absence of final vowel in first and second person singular non-tensed forms. In dual and plural, the non-tensed cross-referencing markers are identical with those denoting remote past tense.

The structure of an uninflected verb is straightforward: a suffix marking a category of an uninflected verb attaches directly to the stem. In 11.5, the desiderative suffix *-kər* attaches to a verbal stem with positions (i) and (ii) filled:

11.5 [kay-kwa-taka]stem-kər
MANIP-stay-put-DES
'(I/you/(s)he/we/they want to pour'

The negative declarative non-habitual stands apart from other verb forms in the language. For some verbs it coincides with the verb's root, e.g. *kə*- 'eat', *ma: kə* (NEG eat+NEG) 'do(es) not

TABLE 11.2   Non-tensed subject cross-referencing set in partially inflected verbs compared with past and non-past subject cross-referencing in inflected verbs

PERSON/ GENDER	SG			DU			PL		
TENSE	NON-PAST	PAST	NON-TENSED	NON-PAST	PAST	NON-TENSED	NON-PAST	PAST	NON-TENSED
1 fem/masc	-tua-	-tuə-	-tu-	-ta-		-tə-	-bana-		-ba-
2 fem	-ñəna-	-ñənə-	-ñən				-gwura-, -gura-		
2 masc	-məna-	-mənə-	-mən	-bra		-brə-			
3 fem	-la-	-lə-	-lə-				-dana-		-da-
3 masc	-da-	-də-	-də-						

eat'. For other verbs, it is marked with root alternation, e.g. *wa-* 'say', *ma: wə* (NEG say+NEG) 'do(es) not say' (see §11.3). The corresponding negative future coincides with the verb root, e.g. *kə ma:* 'will not eat', *wa ma:* 'will not say'. (But note that the negator is placed after the verb root—see §14.1.1.)

Uninflected verbs used in main clauses—with the exception of the negatives and the prohibitives—require a support verb if they head the predicate of a non-main clause, or if additional tense, aspect, or mood/modality specifications are to be provided. Such forms include completive aspect (§12.6), customary aspect (§12.7), same-subject purposive (§13.4.1), desiderative (§13.5), frustrative (§13.6), and also verbs marked with suffixes -*rəb* 'fully' and -*dəka* 'only' (§9.2; §12.8.1).The support is normally *tə-* 'be, have, stand'. The only exception is the completive aspect which requires *na-* 'copula for abstract states'. This is a feature uninflected verbs share with nominals, and with deverbal nominalizations (see §9.1.1, and §17.2.1). Reduplicated verbs and forms of the customary aspect (see 4.47–8, and §12.7, §12.8.2) can be used either as inflected or as uninflected verbs.

Manambu presents a clear example of dependencies between various grammatical categories. Gender, number, and person distinctions are neutralized in negative declarative and prohibitive clauses; so are all aspect and modality meanings—just as predicted by Aikhenvald and Dixon (1998). All the modalities, aspects, and tenses are distinguished in positive declarative main clauses.

Habitual forms behave differently from non-habitual ones: when they are negated, there is no neutralization of person, number, and gender. And there is no habitual imperative—the habitual meaning (and marking) does not occur in commands. Along similar lines, a verb marked with the suffix -*tu-* 'complete involvement of S/O' does not occur in imperatives, or in any uninflected verbs. In contrast to the habitual, a verb marked with -*tu-* cannot be negated.

No aspect or modality categories can be marked in imperative clauses—this is typologically quite common. Non-indicative moods and modalities, and aspectual meanings—such as habitual, customary, or completive—are mutually exclusive. This may reflect the fact that the choice of aspect depends on mood, and on modality. This type of dependency requires further investigation.

We will see in §14.5 and in Chapter 18 that relative clauses and juxtaposed sequencing clauses can be distinguished from main clauses only by the ways in which they are negated. That more formal distinctions in clause types are made in negative than in positive polarity appears to contradict the general spirit of dependencies between grammatical systems. In addition, Manambu has one imperative construction, and three ways of marking prohibitive. These features are typologically unusual.

11.2   THE STRUCTURE OF NON-VERBAL PREDICATE HEADS

Non-verbal predicate heads are simpler in structure than verbs: they can only take nominal cross-referencing enclitics (listed in Table 3.4), and the confirmation marker. This is shown in Scheme 11.4.

Non-verbal predicate heads include nouns, adjectives, adverbs, and members of most closed classes. In addition, there are a few special cases.

First, reactivated topic demonstratives, and manner demonstratives and interrogatives (§10.2.2, §10.2.3, and §10.4), take the predicative marker -*n*, and do not occur with any person markers. Of these, only manner demonstratives can take the confirmation marker, e.g. 11.6:

11.6   akətawa-n-ək
       like.this-PRED-CONF
       'It is really like this (as far as the speaker is concerned)'

And secondly, we can recall, from §10.2.3, that reactivated topic demonstratives contain a predicate marker -*n*- when focused or when used as predicate heads. Again, no person enclitics can be used.

When an agreeing adjective ('small' or 'big'—see §4.3.1) or any other agreeing modifiers from closed classes occur in the predicate slot, they also take subject agreement marking. This results in what can be seen as redundant double agreement in gender with the same constituent, as shown in 11.7:

11.7   numa-d-adəwun
       big-masc.sg-1masc.sgNOM
       'I (man) am big'

The agreeing adjective *yara* 'fine' is not used as a predicate head. Further examples of non-verbal predicates are in 3.12–13; also see T3.8 ('I am Oselo').

Just like a fully inflected verb, a non-verbal predicate can be within the scope of highlighting focus. Then, the non-verbal predicate head is marked—for the second time—with non-verbal person markers. An example is under 11.8. Square brackets mark the boundaries of a clause with a non-verbal predicate as its head, 'it is a man'. Curly brackets indicate that the clause is within the scope of highlighting focus—see §20.3.

---

1. Stem
2. Subject marked with the nominal cross-referencing enclitics
3. -*ək* 'confirmation marker' (§12.5)

SCHEME 11.4   The structure of a non-verbal predicate

11.8 {[du-ad]-ad}
　　　man-3masc.sgNOM-3masc.sgNOM
　　　'It is the case that it is a man'

   Clauses with non-verbal predicates are negated differently from verbal clauses (see §14.1.2, and §20.1.3). If a speaker wishes to express tense, aspect, mood, and modality distinctions in a clause headed by a non-verbal predicate, or make it into a dependent clause, the only option is for the non-verbal form to be used as the complement of the support verb *tə-*. The copula then carries all the required specifications, as in 11.9 and 11.10.

11.9 wun [du   tə-kər]
　　　I   man be-DES
　　　'I want to be a man'

The copula complement and the copula verb carrying the desiderative inflection are in square brackets in 11.9.

11.10 [kwakuli tə-brə-k]   brə-kə-də   ñaj
　　　orphan   be-3du-COMPL.DS 3du-OBL-masc.sg paternal.uncle
　　　kəda   wa-də-bər
　　　DEM.PROX.REACT.TOP+masc.sg say-3sgmascSUBJ.P-3duBAS.P
　　　'Since they two were orphans, this paternal uncle said to them two'

   The first clause is in square brackets in 11.10.

Non-verbal predicates share this property with uninflected verbs (see §4.2.2; and also §§12.6–7, and §17.2).

11.3   ROOT ALTERNATIONS IN VERBS

About 50 per cent of verbs have one form in all the morphological contexts. The remainder of verbs have a number of root alternations discussed here. These are independent of the semantics of the verb or its transitivity. First, we outline a number of automatic alternations characteristic of all verbs (§11.3.1), and then discuss types of verbs with specific root alternations (§11.3.2).

11.3.1   Automatic alternations in verbs

Automatic alternations always take place on the boundary between the verbal root and the suffix. They include the following.

1. When the second person imperative prefix *a-* is added to the verbal root, the final vowel of the root is deleted. If the final vowel is *u*, it leaves its traces in the consonant labialization, e.g. *waku-* 'go out', *a-wak^w*! '(you) go out'. The deletion of a final vowel in forming a negative non-future form of a disyllabic root has a similar effect, e.g. *laku-* 'know', *ma: la:k^w* 'did not/do not know'.

2. A linker vowel *ə* occurs after a stop, or a fricative, if a suffix starts with a consonant (including the bilabial glide) as in the following examples (the linker vowel is underlined): *gwaj* 'spin', *gwaj-ə̲-kə-tua* 'I will spin (something)'; *gwaj-ə̲-wayək* 'do not ever spin' (strong

prohibitive), *gwaj-ə-n* (spin-LK-SEQ) 'while spinning, spinning', *gwaj-ə-dəka gwaj-ə-dəka* 'the one who only spins all the time'. (This agrees with the patterns of consonant clusters: see §2.2.1.)

The linker vowel also appears before the prohibitive *tukwa* (which forms a phonological word on its own; see §14.4), e.g. *gwaj-ə tukwa* 'do not spin', and occasionally before the postposed negator *ma:* (which then marks negative future: see §14.1.1), e.g. *gwaj-ə ma:* 'will not spin'.

As mentioned at the end of §2.2.1, a phonological word of more than one syllable cannot contain a sequence of CV-VC. As a result, automatic alternations occur (see §2.2.3), e.g. an imperative of the verb *rausi-*, a loan from Tok Pisin *rausim* 'throw out, get out' yields *a-rawə́s* (rather than an incorrect **a-raus*), with the word-final syllable becoming a glide-V sequence, and a form like *yakə-saula-* 'throw-inside something or inland' yields the imperative form *a-yakə-sawə́l*, and not **a-yakə-saúl*.

11.3.2 Other root-specific alternations in verbs

Non-automatic root alternations occur in verbs of a variety of types listed below.

A. MONOSYLLABIC VERBS consist of CV, with the root vowel either *ə* or *a*. (The few verbs with a root vowel *u* do not occur without directionals, e.g. *ku-* as in *ku-su-* 'put on; dress'; *ku-sada* 'put downwards'.) Examples are *ka-* 'paddle', *ra-* 'cut', *wa-* 'speak, say', *kə-* 'eat, drink', *jə-* 'chew', *rə-* 'sit; copula'. When these verbs take a suffix and the resulting form is monosyllabic, the root vowel is lengthened, as in *wa:d* (say+3masc.sgBAS.P) 'he said'; *ja:l* (chew+3fem.sgBAS.P) 'she chewed'. Note that the verbs with vowel *a* and with *ə* are then regularly homophonous: *ra:l* (sit/cut+3fem.sg.BAS.P) means 'she sat' and 'she cut'.

The verbs *yi-* 'go' and *ya-* 'come' also become homonymous when the resulting form is monosyllabic, as in *ya:l* (go/come+3fem.sg.BAS.P) 'she went'; 'she came'. These are not ambiguous if the form is not monosyllabic, e.g. *rə-na* (sit-ACT.FOC+3fem.sgBAS.NP) 'she is sitting' and *ra-na* (cut-ACT.FOC+3fem.sgBAS.NP) 'she is cutting', *yi-na* (typically pronounced as *yə-na*) (go-ACT.FOC+3fem.sgBAS.NP) 'she is going' and *ya-na* (come-ACT.FOC+3fem.sgBAS.NP) 'she is coming'.

When such verbs take the second person imperative prefix *a-*, the root vowel is deleted, as in *aw* 'speak, say!', *aj* 'chew!' This often creates homonymy between verbs with vowel *a* and *ə*, so *ak* means 'paddle!' and 'eat!' But in fact such homonymy is not all that pervasive, since many monosyllabic verbs of posture and motion have suppletive imperatives. For example, *ar* can only mean 'cut!', because the positional verb *rə-* 'sit' (also used as a copula: see Chapter 17) has a suppletive second person imperative *ada* which it shares with another monosyllabic verb, *tə-* 'be, have, stand'. Examples of monosyllabic verbs with suppletive second person imperatives (see §13.2) are *kwa-* 'stay/lie', imperative *adakw*; *yi-* 'go', imperative *ma:y*; *ya-* 'come', imperative *mæy*; *da-* 'go down', imperative *adi:d*. The verb *yi-* is used as a copula and in the meaning 'say' forms a regular imperative *ay* 'say!'

When the permissive (first person imperative) suffix *-u* (see §13.2) is added to a monosyllabic verb with a root vowel *ə*, this vowel becomes *a*, as in *kə-* 'eat, drink', *kau* 'may I eat, drink'. Permissive forms of monosyllabic verbs with root vowels *ə* and *a* are consistently homophonous, and have to be distinguished by the context, e.g. *kau* 'may I paddle/drink'; similarly, *yau* (go/come+1sgIMPV) 'may I come/go'.

Negative declarative non-future forms of these verbs involve reduction of the root vowel, that is, *a* to *ə*, e.g. *da-* 'go down', *ma: də* 'did not/do not go down'. Such forms of verbs of CV structure distinguishable only by their vowel become homophonous: *ma: kə* means both 'did not/do not paddle' and 'did not/do not eat'.

The verbs 'go' and 'come' have the same negative form in the Malu variety (*ma: yə* 'did not/do not go/come'), but are distinguished in the Avatip variety: *ma: yə* 'did not/do not go' and *ma: yæy* 'did not/do not come'.

The monosyllabic verb *kwa-* 'stay, lie' has a somewhat irregular negative form: *ma: ku* or *ma: kw(ə)*, depending on the speaker (meaning 'did not/do not stay/lie'). Declarative non-future negative constructions do not form one phonological or grammatical word: they can be discontinuous, e.g. *ma: nəbay kə* (NEG yet eat:NEG) 'has/have not eaten yet' (see §14.1.1).

When a monosyllabic verb with a vowel *a* undergoes reduplication, the second reduplicand contains *ə*, as in *wa-* 'say', *wa-wə* 'saying', *ya-* 'come', *ya-yə* 'coming'.

Monosyllabic verbs require a formative *-k-* in the strong prohibitive (§14.4.1 and D below), e.g. *wa-k-wayik* 'do not ever say', *kə-k-wayik* 'do not ever eat'.

We saw, in §2.2.3, that monosyllabic roots of CV structure are 'light' in terms of their syllable weight; consequently, they require an additional syllable when combined with the syllable-weight-sensitive suffixes *-taka* 'immediate sequencing' and *-yakəp* 'frustrative' (also see §15.2.5 for similar phenomena in the choice of the allomorphs for the incompletive *-pəsa*).

B. NUMEROUS DISYLLABIC VERBS OF CVCV STRUCTURE AND VERBS OF CVC STRUCTURE have vowel alternations in the negative non-future form. Their negative non-future form also involves dropping the verb-final vowel, e.g. *waku-* 'go out', *ma: wa:kʷ* 'did not/do not go out'. The first syllable vowel *a* undergoes compensatory lengthening, as in *wajə-* 'laugh', *ma: wa:j* 'did not/do not laugh', *gaji-* 'rub', *ma: ga:j* 'did not/do not rub'.

A syllabic vowel *ə* or *i* becomes *a:*, for example *gər-* 'scratch', *ma: ga:r* 'did not/do not scratch'; *kwatiy-* 'give to non-third person', *ma: kwata:y* 'did not/do not give to non-third person'. The first syllable vowel *u* becomes *a:*, as in *suku-* 'write, carve', *ma: sa:kw* 'did not/do not write/carve', *wukə-* 'hear, understand', *ma: wa:k* 'did not/do not hear/understand'; or *wa:*, as in *kusə-* 'finish', *ma: kwa:s* 'did not/do not finish', *kur-* 'get, do', *ma: kwa:r* 'did not/do not get/do'. A sequence *ui* becomes *wa:*, as in *kui-* 'give to third person', *ma: kwa:y* 'did not/do not give to third person'.

All these verbs also drop their final root vowel in forming second person imperative, e.g. *a-wakʷ* 'go out!', unless they contain the vowel *-i* or *-u* in their second syllable, e.g. *wali-* 'go round', *a-wali* 'go round!', *ma: wali* 'did not/do not go round', *ku-su-* (put-UP) 'put on; dress', *a-ku-su* 'put (clothing) on', *ma: ku-su* 'did not/do(es) not put on'.

Negative declarative non-future forms may appear in negated subordinate clauses, e.g. *kui-* 'give to third person', *kwa:y-mar-ən* (give.to.third.p.NEG-NEG.SUB-SEQ) 'by not giving to third person' (see §14.1). This shows that the vocalic alternations in negative non-future forms cannot be accounted for by the fact that the resulting form is monosyllabic.

Verbs of the structure CVC and CCV form second person imperatives of the form *a-CəC*, and if their consonants are the same, the imperatives are homophonous, e.g. *gra-* 'cry', imperative *agər* 'cry!'; *gər* 'scratch', imperative *agər* 'scratch!' Note that their negative forms are different: *ma: gər* 'did not/do not cry' versus *ma: ga:r* 'did not/do not scratch'.

C. VERBS WHICH CONTAIN A FINAL SYLLABLE *-ya* drop it in second person imperative and in negative declarative non-future. The vowel *i* is lengthened in the negative form, e.g. *kiya-* 'die', *aki* 'die!', *ma: ki:* 'did not/do not die', *vya-* 'hit, kill', *avi* 'hit/kill!', *ma: vi:* 'did not/do not hit/kill'. The vowel *u* is realized as *wi* in the imperative and in the negative form, e.g. *guya-* 'vomit', *agwi* 'vomit!', *ma: gwi:* 'did not/do not vomit'. When reduplicated, the second reduplicand has the shape *Ci* or *Cwi*, as in *vya-vi* (hit/kill-RED) 'hitting, killing' and *guya-gwi* 'vomiting'.

D. A NUMBER OF VERBS TAKE THE FORMATIVE *-k-* IN COMBINATION WITH THE MARKER OF THE STRONG PROHIBITIVE *-way* AND *wayik* (§14.5). These include monosyllabic verbs (A above) and a few verbs of CVC structure, e.g. *gaj-ə-k-wayik* 'do not ever rub', *butə-k-wayik* 'do not ever fold'. The origin of this formative requires further etymological analysis.

In addition, a number of disyllabic roots may undergo optional reduction of their second syllable, e.g. *yasa-* and *yasə-* 'be: of feelings', and *-təka* and *-təkə-* 'do incompletely' (see 15.38 and discussion there).

In summary: monosyllabic (CV) verbs form one consistent class in terms of root alternations. The information on whether any of the other verbs belongs to an alternating class or not needs to be given in a dictionary.

Verbal Categories in Positive Declarative and Interrogative Clauses

In this chapter we discuss verbal categories of positive declarative and interrogative clauses shared with relative and juxtaposed sequencing clauses (see §§19.1–2). None of these categories, except root reduplication (§12.8) and the customary aspect (§12.7), can be expressed in most medial clauses (Chapter 18). Forms discussed in §§12.6–7 and §12.8.1 are uninflected (unlike the rest of the forms discussed here). Further aspectual meanings are expressed with verb compounding (§15.3) and complex predicates (§17.1.1).

12.1 NON-FUTURE TENSES AND ACTION FOCUS

12.1.1 Non-future tenses

Fully inflected verbs can occur with cross-referencing suffixes which also mark either past or the 'versatile' tense. The latter has a wide range of meanings covering recent past (yesterday or a couple of days ago), near future, and present. The past refers to what happened a few days ago or earlier than that. These suffixes are listed in Tables 3.1–2 (see also Table 11.2).

Past tense is typically used in stories and accounts of the past. An example is under 12.1. The verb in the first main clause cross-references two arguments (the second argument is O which is highly animate and topical). The verb in the second clause cross-references one argument: there is no argument more topical than the A/S.

12.1 [wa-ku],　　　[Kuimagan Lai ata　yata-də-d]　　　　　　　　　[yata-n
say-COMPL.SS Kuimagan Lai then carry-3masc.sgSUBJ.P-3masc.sgBAS.P carry-SEQ
tə-də-k],　　　　　　[Sirunki aka　　　　　　　　　wula-l]
have-3masc.sg-COMPL.DS Sirunki DEM.DIST.REACT.TOP.fem.sg go.inland-3fem.sgBAS.P
'Having said (this), Kuimagan then carried Lai, as he was carrying him, Sirunki went into the bush away from the river'

A reactivated topic demonstrative may combine reference to an S/O and to the action itself, as in 10.69. It supplies an aspectual overtone of 'here and now; ongoing action' to a verb marked with action focus. Similar examples are under 10.56 and 10.78.

The versatile tense may refer to an ongoing event, as in 12.2; or to an event that took place just recently, as in 12.3.

12.2 wun-a　　　yi-n　　yi-tua
I-3fem.sgNOM go-SEQ come-1sgSUBJ.VT+3fem.sgBAS.VT
'As for me, I am going away'

12.3 [kuprap-ə ya:b-ad],　　　　təpə-yakə-tua-d
bad-LK　　road-3masc.sgNOM be.closed-FULLY-1sgSUBJ.VT-3masc.sgBAS.VT
'It is a bad road, I have closed it off'

The recent past reference of the versatile tense can be highlighted by the temporal adverb *bə* 'already':

12.4 [wun ka:m   yasa-lə-k],   [də-kə-di   kamna:gw-a:b bə
       I   hunger feel-3fem.sg-COMPL.DS he-POSS-pl food-TOO   already
       kə-tua-di]
       eat-1sgSUBJ.VT-3plBAS.VT
       'Having felt hunger, I have already eaten his foodstuffs'

The versatile tense can also refer to immediate future, as in T3.8 where Osəlo is about to kill all the snakes. Versatile tense forms are also used in generic statements, for example, about psychological states. These involve the polysemous word *mawul* 'the inside; spirit' (see §21.4), e.g. *mawul samasa:m tə-na* (inside much be-ACT.FOC+3fem.sgBAS.VT) 'she frets, worries, feels sorrow or concern' (lit. she has much inside).

The versatile tense cross-referencing, and not the past tense cross-referencing, is used with the future and with the habitual aspect (which has an additional past tense marking). In terms of functional markedness, the versatile tense can be considered the unmarked choice. Formally speaking, both past and versatile tense are marked.

12.1.2 Action focus

The action focus marker *-na-* indicates that the activity itself rather than any of the participants is in focus; in clauses which contain the action focus marker there are no participants more salient or topical than the subject. In fact, other participants are often backgrounded.

The action focus is often used in clauses describing actions which take place one after another, as in 12.5 (the forms are underlined). All the actions are happening at the same time as the speech act itself, with the exception of the last clause where the action is immediately preceding the time of speech act.

12.5 [mən-a-də   gu   kəda
       you-LK-masc.sg water DEM.PROX.REACT.TOP+masc.sg
       da-na-d]   [wun wun-a-də   ñənwa   [an
       go.down-ACT.FOC-3masc.sgBAS.VT I   I-LK-masc.sg child+COM we.du
       karya-ta-d-ə]   gu-a:m   kə-na-bran]
       bring-1dusUBJ.VT-3masc.sgBAS.VT-LK water-LK+ACC/LOC drink-ACT.FOC-1duBAS.VT
       [laka,   wun sə-kwa-tami: ma:] alək
       fem.sg+DEM.DIST.REACT.TOP.fem.sg I   sleep-lie-area NEG thus
       aka   væra-na-wun-ək
       DEM.DIST.REACT.TOP.fem.sg come.in-ACT.FOC-1sgBAS.VT-CONF
       'This (topical) water of yours is flowing. My son and I we are drinking the water we brought, this is how it is, I have no place to sleep, this is why I have come in here'

The recent past reference is often emphasized by the adverb *bə* 'already', as in 12.6.

12.6 kamna:gw bə   kə-na-d?
       food   already eat-ACT.FOC-3masc.sgBAS.VT
       'Has he eaten yet?'

As mentioned above, traditional stories are usually cast in past tense. However, vivid accounts of actual events are often cast in the versatile tense, with the action-focus marker employed to focus the audience's attention on the event itself.

This is illustrated in 12.7, from a story about how the Avatip men had killed the Japanese invaders during the Second World War. At the very beginning, the speaker establishes the past time frame. As soon as he starts talking about the action itself, he switches to versatile tense (first line of 12.7).

This was followed by a sequence of actions which describe the attack, each marked with action focus. The sequence was interrupted once (lines 6–7), by the speaker bringing the audience back to the time frame of the narrative, and saying: 'this was the time when we the fathers were also young'. Here, the verb form is in bold. It is also in highlighting focus, and this is why it is marked with an additional set of nominal enclitics. (The feminine cross-referencing here refers to the time of event: 'time' in Manambu is inherently feminine.) After this insertion, the speaker goes back to his lively narration using action-focused terms:

12.7 adiya   <u>vya-bana-di</u>.   Vya-ba-k,   ya:kya
     DEM.DIST.REACT.TOP+pl hit-1plSUBJ.VT-3plBAS.VT hit-1pl-COMPL.DS OK
     Adiya   bə   aba:b kusəm   nak-a:ḅ ma: yə. Ya:kya
     DEM.DIST.REACT.TOP+pl already all   finish+COMPL one-TOO NEG go OK
     kusə-n   tə-lə-k   du   adiya
     finish-SEQ be-3fem.sg-COMPL.DS man DEM.DIST.REACT.TOP+pl
     <u>pəkə-na-di</u>   klawur   war-ku   kə-də
     jump.up-ACT.FOC-3plBAS.VT DEM.PROX.fem.sg.UP go.up-COMPL.SS DEM.PROX-masc.sg
     Amibag ada   <u>ya-na-d</u>   Amibag
     Amibag DEM.DIST.REACT.TOP+masc.sg come-ACT.FOC-3masc.sgBAS.VT Amibag
     ada   kaykətə-da-na-d   [asay-bər
     DEM.DIST.REACT.TOP+masc.sg hold.on-go.down-ACT.FOC-3masc.sgBAS.VT father-PL
     ñan-aba:b badi **kwa-ba-l**-a]   nak-a-nak ñan-ugw
     we-too   young stay-1plSUBJ.P-3fem.sgBAS.P-3fem.sgNOM one-LK-one child-PL
     ata   adiya   <u>war-na-di</u>   pək-ə-man pək-ə-man
     then DEM.DIST.REACT.TOP+pl go.up-ACT.FOC-3plBAS.VT jump-LK-leg jump-LK-leg
     adiya   <u>war-na-di</u>   *orait*.
     DEM.DIST.REACT.TOP+pl go.up-ACT.FOC-3plBAS.VT alright
     'We strike at them. After we'd struck, OK. They are all already finished, not one escapes (lit. went), OK, (this) having finished, men jump up. Having done up here, this Amibag is coming, Amibag is meeting up (with them). This was (time) when we the fathers too were young. One by one young boys each goes up, hurriedly (lit. jump-leg) they go up. All right'

Taken out of context, a form marked with action focus can have a wide range of temporal references, from present to recent past to near future, just like any versatile tense. So, a form *rə-na-wun* (sit-ACT.FOC-1sgBAS.VT) may mean 'I am sitting down', or 'I have just sat down', or 'I am about to sit down'. Action focus does not make the verb intransitive and is thus not a valency-changing device: as shown in examples 3.2 and 12.8, a verb marked with action focus can take an object. Example 12.8 describes the event which triggers the developments in the rest of this story:

12.8 [a-də   də-kə-də   last ñan] ada   ta:kw
     DEM.DIST-masc.sg he-OBL-masc.sg last child DEM.DIST.REACT.TOP+masc.sg woman
     ada   <u>kra-na-d</u>
     DEM.DIST.REACT.TOP+masc.sg take-ACT.FOC-3masc.sgBAS.VT
     'That last son of his got married' (lit. took a wife)

As we saw under D in §7.2. the object of a verb marked with action focus is likely to be unmarked for case. Such objects have either a generic reference, or their full involvement in the activity is irrelevant, as in 3.2, 7.4, and 12.8. This agrees with the general meaning of the action focus.

The action focus marker occurs with versatile tense cross-referencing markers. We can recall, from Scheme 11.2 and §3.1, that it can only occur with basic A/S cross-referencing. It is thus mutually exclusive with a non-subject constituent more topical than the subject. This follows from the meaning of action focus: the action itself is more important than the participants, and the topicality of participants is not an issue. Action focus is incompatible with the highlighting focus marking (see §20.3).

12.2 FUTURE

The future in Manambu is marked with the suffix *-kə-*, followed by versatile tense cross-referencing markers. The future marker can occur with the action focus marker provided the action—rather than the participants—is focused on. Past markers do not occur with the future. The future marker may be etymologically connected with the same-subject purposive *-k*, different-subject purposive *-kək*, or the dative-aversive case *-Vk* (see §7.4, §13.4).

The future form usually refers to an action or state subsequent to the speech act, as in 12.9. Here, the object ('key') is the topic of a stretch of a story about how the hen and the hawk do not get along because of a key the hen had lost. The key is masculine because it is long and thin, and the house is feminine, because it is small.

12.9 kə   wiya-kə-də   ki   ada
     DEM.PROX.fem.sg house+LK-POSS-masc.sg key DEM.DIST.REACT.TOP+masc.sg
     kwatiya-kə-tua-d
     give.to.nonthird.p-FUT-1sgSUBJ.VT-3masc.sgBAS.VT
     'I will give you that (topical) key of this house'

In 12.10, the action focus marker is used, since the important point is what the participants are going to do:

12.10 an   kwa-kə-na-bran,   səkulək yi-ku,   a   mən-a-pək
      we.du stay-FUT-ACT.FOC-1duBAS.VT cooking go-COMPL.SS then you.masc-LK-LIKE
      mu   ya-k-na-bran
      the.day.after.tomorrow coming-FUT-ACT.FOC-1duBAS.VT
      'We two will stay, having cooked, then, like you, we will come the day after tomorrow'

As shown in §2.4.2, light monosyllabic verb roots have an option of marking future with the reduplicated *-kə-kə-* (Table 2.4). The existence of two allomorphs depending on the syllable weight of the verb root was discussed in §2.4.2. An example is at 12.11.

12.11 na:gw sau-n   yi-kə-kə-bana
      sago fry-SEQ go-FUT-FUT-1plSUBJ.VT+3fem.sgBAS.VT
      'We will go straight away after having fried sago'

However, the marker *-kə-* can occasionally occur with a light verb root. The two options are in free variation, as shown in 12.12.

12.12 nəkə   maːj abaːb <u>wa-kə-kə-tua,</u>   alək a
other+fem.sg story too say-FUT-FUT-1sgSUBJ.VT+3fem.sgBAS.VT so   then
lə-kə-l-al   <u>wa-kə-tua</u>
fem.sg-POSS-fem.sg-3fem.sgNOM tell-FUT-1sgSUBJ.VT+3fem.sgBAS.VT
aka   <u>wa-kə-kə-tua</u>
DEM.DIST.REACT.TOP.fem.sg tell-FUT-FUT-1sgSUBJ.VT+3fem.sgBAS.VT
'I will tell another story straight away. So it is (life story) I will tell, I will tell (it)'

The reduplicated -kə- is never used with the verb kə- 'consume (eat, drink, smoke)': so, a form like *kə-kə-kə-bana (eat-FUT-FUT-1plSUBJ.VT+3fem.sgBAS.VT) is ungrammatical, and kə-kə-bana would always be used instead in the meaning of 'we will eat (it)'. This may also be due to a rule of loss of a voiceless velar stop discussed at A3 in §2.6.

The future is homophonous with irrealis (§13.3). In positive clauses, the two meanings are distinguished solely by context. But, as we will see in §13.3, the future and the epistemic, or irrealis, meanings are formally distinguished under negation: ku-sada ma: means 'she won't put', and akəs ku-sada-k-la means 'she might not have put; she would not have put' (§14.1.1 and §14.3.1). This suggests that synchronically there are two morphemes -kə-: one is marking future, and the other one marking irrealis (§13.3).

An example of an irrealis form is at 12.13. This was said as an explanation for why the little girl woke up in tears. A future interpretation would not make sense here.

12.13 yigən və-kə-na
dream see-FUT-ACT.FOC+3fem.sgBAS.VT
'She must have seen a (bad) dream'; *'She will see a bad dream'

A future and an irrealis in a main clause can be ambiguous: for instance, 12.14 can mean 'she will put (the purse) inside the bag', or 'she might have put (the purse) inside the bag':

12.14 bəgam   ku-sada-k-la
bag+LK+LOC put-DOWN-FUT-3fem.sgSUBJ.VT+3fem.sgBAS.VT
(a) 'She will put (the purse) inside the bag'
(b) 'She might have put (the purse) inside the bag'

The overtones of future and irrealis in juxtaposed clauses are discussed in §19.1.

12.3 HABITUAL ASPECT

The habitual aspect is the only aspect which consistently combines with a fully inflected verb. It can co-occur only with the versatile tense cross-referencing, and has the following properties:

- It has two forms: non-past tense marked with the suffix -kwa, and past marked with -yi-kwa-. The semantic distinction is that of non-past versus past—this is in contrast to the difference between the past tense and 'versatile' tense in non-habitual clauses which covers recent past, recent future, and present, and is also used in vivid narratives.
- The non-past habitual can occur with the action focus marker, as shown in 12.17.
- The habitual is negated with the particle akəs which, unlike the non-habitual declarative negator, occurs with a fully inflected verb. The same categories can be expressed in positive and in negative habitual clauses. In contrast, negative declarative non-habitual clauses

require the negator *ma:* accompanied by a non-inflected form of the verb with no person, gender, or number distinctions (§§14.1–2).

- The habitual aspect does not combine with future: a future habitual meaning can only be expressed with a complex predicate involving the verb *kwa-* 'stay' (12.20–1).

The habitual marker could be etymologically related to the polyfunctional verb *kwa-* 'stay' (see §17.1.1 on its use as auxiliary in aspectual complex predicates with the meaning of prolonged durative). Synchronically, however, the habitual differs from verb compounding structures since (i) it is negated in a unique way, (ii) its past form involves an additional marker *-yi-*, and (iii) it only takes the versatile tense cross-referencing markers.

The past habitual marker could be related to the verb *yi-* 'go' or the copula verb *yi-* (the two are distinguished in the ways they form imperative: see §4.2.2), or to neither of these.

Unlike the verb *kwa-*, the habitual does not form an imperative, or combine with any further modality specifications. The irregular negative habitual form of the verb 'give' was illustrated in 4.38 (also see 4.37, for a regular one).

The habitual aspect describes usual activities, as in 12.15. The versatile tense form refers to activities not restricted to any time frame, and is frequent in generic statements, with or without the action focus marker:

12.15 mi:ya-bər   yap-ə-m   ji-ku   ñan-ugw ata
      log+LK-3duNOM rope-LK-LOC tie-COMPL.SS child-PL then
      nay-kwa-na-di   gaydua:m
      play-HAB-ACT.FOC-3plBAS.VT swings+LK+LOC
      'Having tied two logs on the rope, children play on the swings'

Along similar lines, 12.16 states what the snake used to do. Fish are the topic, and this is why they have to be cross-referenced on the verb:

12.16 kami: də kə-kwa-da-di
      fish   he eat-HAB-3masc.sgSUBJ.P-3plBAS.P
      'He (the snake) used to eat fish'

In a vivid narrative about her experience living with an Australian couple, the speaker used the non-past habitual marked with action focus, so as to highlight what her foster parents used to do:

12.17 Harold, də kamna:gw-a:b kə-jəbər tə-kwa-na-d   a-di
      Harold he food-TOO   eat-CUST be-HAB-ACT.FOC-3masc.sgBAS.VT DEM.DIST-pl
      gwaj,   *painepol*, laulap, də *frut* məwi   samasa:m
      sugar.cane pineapple banana he fruit things.like.that a.lot
      kə-kwa-na-d   də-kə   takwa:wa   Key wukən.
      eat-HAB-ACT.FOC-3masc.sgBAS.VT he-OBL+fem.sg woman+LK+COM Kay together
      rəka:rək ñan kaytək wun-a:k   ata kur-kwa-na-bər
      correctly child like I-LK+DAT then do-HAB-ACT.FOC-3duBAS.VT
      'Harold, he always used to eat food, too, those sugarcane, pineapple, banana, he used to eat things like fruit, together with his wife Kay. They then treated me correctly, like (their) child'

The past habitual refers to usual activities restricted to the time before the speech act, which are no longer relevant for the present. The usual activities described in 12.18 ended just after Australians occupied the Sepik area:

12.18 aw   krəl   da-yi-kwa-di
then   DEM.PROX+fem.sg+ALL   go.down-HAB.PAST-HAB-3plBAS.P/VT
'They then used to go down the river here'

In 12.19 the past habitual—used in a relative clause—refers to something that is no longer there (we will see in §14.5 and §19.2 that relative clauses have all the specifications of a main clause, unless negated; in cases like this one they can be distinguished from juxtaposed main clauses by intonation only).

12.19 ata   [kwa-yi-kwa-da-di   kara:b]
then   stay-HAB.PAST-HAB-3plSUBJ.P-3plBAS.P   men's.house
adiya   akatawa sa:d   kəta ma:
DEM.DIST.REACT.TOP+pl+EMPH   like.this   fashion   now   NEG
'Those (reactivated topic) men's houses in which they used to stay were like this. Now they are no longer there'

A negated form of the habitual aspect is illustrated in 7.16 (also see §14.2). A future habitual meaning can be expressed by a complex predicate consisting of the lexical verb marked with the sequencing manner suffix -n and the verb kwa- 'stay' marked for future, as in 12.20. Such examples may have an additional connotation of 'staying in a place' (rather than moving), due to the primary meaning of the verb 'stay'.

12.20 ñən   a-kəs,   wun [kurən   kwa-kə-tua]
you.fem.sg IMPV-get I   take.care+SEQ stay-FUT-1sgSUBJ.VT+3fem.sgBAS.VT
'You get (shrimp), I will keep taking care (of the baby)' or
'You get (shrimp), I will stay taking care (of the baby) (rather than move)'

If the context excludes the connotation of 'staying in a place', the reading of such constructions is habitual. In 12.21, the sorceress is expected to keep going back and lighting a fire. There is no connotation of 'staying'—the verb kwa- has a purely habitual meaning.

12.21 yi   [taka-n kwa-kə-na]
fire   put-SEQ stay-FUT-ACT.FOC+3fem.sgBAS.VT
'She will keep lighting a fire'

The habitual marker can occur with the root kwa- 'stay' in one grammatical word, e.g. *walimǝudi waku-n kwa-kwa-da sǝkǝr* (rainbow go.out-SEQ stay-HAB-3masc.sgSUBJ.VT+ 3fem.sgBAS.VT time) 'the time when the rainbow usually stays having come out'. Without a future marker, the verb kwa- in combination with a verb marked with a sequencing -n describes a sequence of actions—see §18.2.

Etymologically, the habitual could well be related to the Wosera -*kwa* 'vivid present' (Wilson 1980: 68). No other Ndu language appears to use a habitual aspect marker of this shape.

12.4   COMPLETE INVOLVEMENT OF S/O

The suffix -*tu*- 'all' indicates complete involvement of S or O. That an affix referring to plurality or complete coverage of participants operates on an absolutive basis is not uncommon cross-linguistically (Dixon 1994: 55). This suffix does not occur together with the habitual.

In 12.22 and 12.72, the suffix marks complete involvement of numerous S.

12.22 a-di   kwasa-kwasa   jəpis paba:n   mədi   ata
DEM.DIST-pl small+fem.sg-small+fem.sg ant   black.ant centipede then
<u>vækər-tu-na-di</u>
fall-MANY-ACT.FOC-3plBAS.VT
'Those tiny ants, black ants, centipedes all fell (into the fire)'

In 12.23, -*tu*- indicates that all the O were involved:

12.23 na:gw <u>vya-wuta-tu-lə-di</u>
sago   hit-break.in.two-MANY-3fem.sgSUBJ.P-3plBAS.P
'She broke all the (branches) of sago palm'

The suffix -*tu*- refers to S of an ambitransitive verb, thus showing that it is used intransitively, as in 12.24. We can recall, from §7.2, that *gu* in examples like 12.24 is part of a complex ambitransitive verb and not its object. Not surprisingly, -*tu*- in 12.24 refers to people who washed themselves fully, and not to the water:

12.24 gu   ata   <u>yaku-tu-di</u>
water then wash-MANY-3plBAS.VT/P
'Then they washed (fully)'

The suffix -*tu*- is often used with verbs of affect. It is likely to be cognate to the Wosera suffix -*to*- 'all' (Wilson 1980: 63).

12.5 CONFIRMATION MARKER

The confirmation marker -*ək* stresses that the action or state has taken place or is happening. This marker occupies the very last place within an inflected verb (see Scheme 11.2) and occurs on verbs, and on non-verbal predicates (see Scheme 11.3), provided these have a first or second person subject (as in 12.25–7), or first or second person object (as in T3.8). That is, this suffix can only be used with speech act participants. In 12.25, the confirmation marker goes onto a nominal head of predicate and onto the verb in a following clause.

12.25 [takw-a-ñən-ək]   [wiya:m   rə-na-ñən-ək]
woman-LK-2fem.sgNOM-CONF house+LK+LOC stay-ACT.FOC-2fem.sgBAS.VT-CONF
'You are indeed a woman, (this is why) you are indeed staying at home'

When we arrived at Yuanab and asked an old lady whether she had been to church yet, she answered:

12.26 bəta:y-ək
already-CONF
'Already indeed! (that is, I have already!)'

In 12.5 ('I have come'), the confirmation marker co-occurs with the action focus, and in 10.60 it occurs on a verb marked with habitual aspect.

The confirmation marker can occur with future, provided the point in time is defined, as in T3.7 and T3.40 ('today you will die'). The confirmation marker occurs in rhetorical questions, as in 12.27, but not in information questions:

12.27 ñən   ata ata kur-ñən-ək?
      you.fem.sg how how do-2fem.sgBAS.VT-CONF
      'What (on earth) have you done!'

The confirmation marker is not compatible with negation.

12.6   COMPLETIVE ASPECT

Completive aspect is marked with the suffix -*Vm*, the same as the locative case (see the discussion at §7.11). Its meaning conveys completion of an action or total achievement of a state. As was shown in §7.11, this marker can attach to a verbal root, as in 7.85, 12.7 (second line), and 12.28.

12.28 a-də   təp ada   bə
      DEM.DIST-masc.sg village DEM.DIST.REACT.TOP+masc.sg already
      kusə-pakwəm
      finish-EVERYTHING+COMPL
      'In this village everything was completely over'

This same marker occurs on adjectives in the predicate slot, as in 12.29:

12.29 kuprap-ə-m
      bad-LK-COMPL
      'It is irredeemably bad'

To be used in dependent clauses or to take further person or modality expressions, the completive form requires the support verb *na-* 'copula for abstract states'. This is in contrast to other uninflected verbs, which are used with the functionally unmarked support verb *tə-* 'be, stand'. The support verb occurs in main clauses if the tense and person, number and gender specifications are required:

12.30 sa:l   yi: ma:, kwasa-kwasa   ja:p rəpəm
      short.of go NEG small+fem.sg-small+fem.sg thing be.enough+COMPL
      na-dəmən
      BE:NAT-2masc.sgBAS.VT
      'You won't be short (of anything), you are fine as far as small things are concerned'

The support verb is obligatory in subordinate clauses—see the second clause in 12.31. In the first clause of 12.31 the copula is omitted, since this is a main clause, and no extra specifications are required: they are clear from the context.

12.31 [ata apək-ə-m   aka   səkwari:m]
      then side-LK-LOC DEM.DIST.REACT.TOP.fem.sg scrape.earth+COMPL
      [səkwari:m   səkwari:m   səkwari:m   səkwari:m
      scrape.earth+COMPL scrape.earth+COMPL scrape.earth+COMPL scrape.earth+COMPL
      na-lə-k],   a-də   agwa-ja:p kəp səkwarak
      BE:NAT-3fem.sg-COMPL.DS DEM.DIST-masc.sg what-thing earth scrape.earth+PURP.SS
      səkwara-ñən-ək
      scrape-2fem.sgBAS.VT-CONF
      'Then she (the cassowary) completely scraped the earth (with her foot shuffling it like a dog trying to hide rubbish, after she had completely scraped it and scraped it and

scraped it and scraped it, (the woman asked), "You are scraping earth to scrape what kind of earth away?" '

Some nominal-like forms containing formative -*Vm* which cannot be omitted occur as complements of the copula *na-* 'be: natural phenomena or abstract state'. These could be instances of fossilized completive, e.g. *katelam na-* 'be light (of daylight)', *karyam na-* 'be almost light' (of daylight), *tugwam na-* 'be clear, have clear vision'.

The completive aspect cannot be used in commands; nor is there any form which can be used instead. One reason for this gap is semantic: it focuses on the full completion of the action, and commands in Manambu do not convey such meanings. The other reason is formal: the completive aspect is an uninflected verb used as copula complement of the 'abstract state' copula *na-*. This copula does not have an imperative, and hardly ever occurs in commands of any sort.

12.7 CUSTOMARY ASPECT

The customary aspect is marked with the suffix -*jəbər*, and means 'usually, always or continuously do'. It can head the predicate of an independent clause without a copula, if person, number, gender, or additional aspect meanings do not have to be specified, as in 12.32 and 6.39.

12.32 də   mərəwa   wa:l ada   ja-jəbər
3masc.sg wind+LK+COM rain DEM.DIST.REACT.TOP+masc.sg rain-CUST
'Rain with wind was falling customarily and continuously'

In 12.17, 'he always used to eat', the customary form appears in the copula complement slot. As expected, the copula, *tə-*, carries all the grammatical markers. A similar example is at 12.33.

12.33 lə   tapwuk wuka   kaw rəpa-jəbər
she hen   DEM.PROX.ADDR.REACT.TOP.fem.sg hole scrape-CUST
tə-na
be-ACT.FOC+3fem.sgBAS.VT
'The hen is always scraping a hole (in the ground, looking for a key she'd lost)'

Unlike the habitual and the completive aspects, the customary aspect can occur in negative and prohibitive constructions. In all such cases it has to occur with the copula *tə-*.

12.34 yaki   kə-jəbər tə-tukwa
smoke eat-CUST be-PROH.GEN
'Don't keep smoking!'

A verb marked with the customary aspect can be used as a modifier to an inflected verb:

12.35 a-də   ka:gw kur-jəbər warə-d
DEM.DIST-masc.sg drum get-CUST go.up-3masc.sgBAS.VT/P
'He went up always clinging (lit. getting) to the drum'

If a verb carrying the marker of the customary aspect heads the predicate of a dependent clause, the copula *tə-* is used—this is a typical property of an uninflected verb:

12.36 [də ata kətay   və-jəbər   tə-ta:y]   ka:gw ata
he then look.around see-CUST stay-COTEMP drum then
sa:d
produce.sound+3masc.sgBAS.VT/P
'Then he, keeping looking around, sounded the drum'

However, unlike any other uninflected verb, verbs marked with customary aspect offer an option of taking a medial clause marker directly. Examples 12.37–8 illustrate a number of medial clause markers used this way:

12.37 və-jəbər-ta:y   laku-kə-tua-di
see-CUST-COTEMP understand-FUT-1sgSUBJ.VT-3plBAS.VT
'Having seen (these words) all the time, I will understand them'

12.38 [a   yawi kusə-jəbra-lə-k]   kamna:gw ata gəñər
DEM.DIST+fem.sg work finish-CUST-3fem.sg-COMPL.DS food   then later
kə-kwa-na-di
eat-HAB-ACT.FOC-3plBAS.VT/P
'After her having always finished the job (building the house), they eat food later'

Examples like 12.37–8 are characteristic of speakers of all generations. It is unlikely that they are a recent innovation. In male songs about foiled marriages, verbal forms marked with *-jəbər* function as fully inflected verbs, taking person, number, and gender marking. Example 12.39 comes from Harrison (1983: 62).

12.39 Magadəmi rə-jəbrad   pətaka:u
(name)   sit-ALWAYS+3masc.sgBAS.VT/P ladder
'The ladder Magadəmi is there'

Such examples are not found in everyday speech. We can hypothesize that, in the past, verbs with the marker *-jəbar* could have been fully inflected, similarly to the compound verbs with aspectual meanings discussed in §15.3.

12.8 EXPRESSING INTENSIVE, CONTINUOUS, AND REPEATED ACTIONS

Intensive and continuous actions can be marked in a variety of ways, including

(i) one of the derivational suffixes discussed in §9.2—see §12.8.1;
(ii) reduplication of the verb root—see §12.8.2, and
(iii) repetition of the verb—see §12.8.3.

12.8.1 Derivational suffixes *-rəb* 'fully' and *-dəka* 'only' on verbs

Verb roots carrying one of the two derivational suffixes, *-rəb* 'fully' and *-dəka* 'only', are uninflected (see Table 11.1). They differ from all other uninflected predicates in two ways. First, they cannot be used as copula complements. Secondly, they often form one constituent with an inflected form of the same verb root. The two derivational suffixes cannot co-occur in one predicate. Neither can they co-occur with any of the aspectual, confirmation, or modality markers discussed here, or in Chapter 13.

I. An uninflected verb marked with the derivational suffix *-rəb* 'fully' can head a predicate, as in 12.40–1:

12.40 [nəkər-ə-k   məy-a   kiya-rəb]
      cold-LK-DAT real-LK die-FULLY
      '(I) really fully died of cold'

Example 12.41 was the way little Stevie described the light colours on a colour chart which for him were subsumed under 'very white':

12.41 wama-ka-wa:m-adi,   akatawa yi-rəb
      white+LK-DER-white-3plNOM   thus   go-FULLY
      'They are very white, all the way going this way'

As mentioned above, a verb root marked with *-rəb* often forms one constituent with an inflected form of the same verb root. No constituent except for the connective *ata* 'then' and a reactivated topic pronoun can intervene between the inflected and the uninflected components of a predicate. This justifies treating constructions consisting of *-rəb* and an inflected verb as complex predicates. The meaning is intensive, 'fully, straight away', as in 12.42, with a transitive verb, and 12.43, with an intransitive one.

12.42 wapa-rəb   wapa-tuə-l   wun-a-kə   yawi
      leave-FULLY leave-1sgSUBJ.P-3fem.sgBAS.P I-LK-POSS+fem.sg job
      'I left my welfare job fully straight away'

12.43 gra-rəb   ata   gra:l
      cry-FULLY then cry+3fem.sgBAS.P
      'Then she cried strongly straight away'

In 12.44, the suppletive imperative form of the verb 'go' appears as the inflected component accompanying the uninflected form marked with *-rəb*:

12.44 yi-rəb   ma:y
      go-FULLY go.IMPV
      'Go straight away!'

The order of components is fixed. It can only be reversed, if the root + *-rəb* form is an afterthought separated from the main clause with a pause, as in 12.45. A normal constituent order is in 12.46.

12.45 kiya-k-na-ñən   [PAUSE] kiya-rəb
      die-FUT-ACT.FOC-2fem.sgBAS.VT   PAUSE   die-FULLY
      'You will die, die straight off (if you come near the door and fall out of the house)'

12.46 kiya-rəb   kiya-k-na
      die-FULLY die-FUT-ACT.FOC+3fem.sgBAS.VT
      'She will die straight off (if she falls out of the window)'

We can recall, from §9.2 and Table 9.2, that *-rəb* also occurs on nouns and adjectives, with similar meanings. Constructions consisting of verb root + *-rəb* and followed by an inflected form of the same verb are unique to verbs—there is no similar structure for nouns or adjectives.

II. A verb marked with the derivational suffix *-dəka* 'only' means 'do only and non-stop', e.g. *bla-dəka* 'talk non-stop'. A verb marked with *-dəka* can be repeated to express continuous and persistent activity, e.g. *paku* 'hide', *paku-dəka paku-dəka* 'hide continuosly', *bla-dəka bla-dəka* 'talk continuously', *vætə-dəka vætə-dəka* 'bite continuously', *wasupu-dəka wasupu-dəka* 'gossip non-stop, do nothing but gossip'. Such repeated forms can head the predicate, as in 12.47.

12.47 akatawa <u>yakə-dəka</u> <u>yakə-dəka</u> yawa   kamnagəwa
      thus   throw-ONLY throw-ONLY fire+LK+COM food+LK+COM
      'Thus (he was) just throwing and throwing, food into fire'

The uninflected verb marked with *-dəka* can be repeated more than once, if the action was taking place over an extended period of time. This is a special property of the suffix.

12.48 [dəy-adi   væse-n   adiya   tə-na-di]   <u>tə-dəka</u>
      they-3plNOM walk-SEQ DEM.DIST.REACT.TOP+pl stay-ACT.FOC-3plBAS.VT stay-ONLY
      <u>tə-dəka</u> <u>tə-dəka</u> <u>tə-dəka</u> grab   tə-da-k,   mərəwa   wa:l
      stay-ONLY stay-ONLY stay-ONLY afternoon stay-3pl-COMPL.DS wind+LK+COM rain
      ata   təmələ-d
      then make.noise-3masc.sgBAS.P
      'As for them, they went on walking, only went on, only went on, only went on, only went on, after the afternoon fell on them, a storm sounded'

Alternatively, one or two occurrences of a verb marked with *-dəka* can be accompanied by an inflected form of the same root, to express persistence and continuity of an activity, as in 12.49–50:

12.49 <u>suku-dəka</u> <u>suku-dəka</u> suku-na-wun
      write-ONLY write-ONLY write-ACT.FOC-1sgBAS.VT
      'I am writing, writing, writing only'

This is somewhat similar to the constructions with a verb marked with *-rəb* and followed by an inflected form of the same verb, illustrated in 12.42. The difference is that the verb itself, marked with *-rəb*, is not repeated, while the verb marked with *-dəka* is.

The order of components in V+*-dəka* constructions is fixed, and no constituent can intervene between components. The meaning is that of increased intensity. So, Israel, with its current political situation of constant fighting, was referred to as 12.50. Many Manambu people strongly believe that they are descendants of one of the tribes of Israel; consequently they have very pronounced feelings in support of this country.

12.50 <u>warya-dəka</u> <u>warya-kwa-dana-də</u>   təp
      fight-ONLY fight-HAB-3plSUBJ.VT-3masc.sgBAS.VT village
      'a place where one does nothing but fighting all the time'

In 12.51, a similar construction expresses a strong prohibition:

12.51 gəñər <u>ya-dəka</u>   <u>ya-k-wayik</u>!
      later come-ONLY come-EP-PROH.STRONG
      'Later do not you dare come any more!'

A form marked with suffix *-dəka* can be used as the predicate of a subordinate clause, as in 12.52. Here, it is used on the generic completive verb *napa-* (§18.9) used exclusively in medial clauses:

12.52 [gu   yaku-n   <u>napa-dəka</u>]   da-k-na-wun
      water wash-SEQ do.after-ONLY go.down-FUT-ACT.FOC-1sgBAS.VT
      'I will go down only after I have washed'

Examples like 12.51 and 12.44 show that the meanings conveyed by the suffixes -*rəb* 'fully' and -*dəka* 'only' are not incompatible with imperatives and prohibitives. We saw in 12.34 that the customary aspect can also occur in commands and prohibitions.

This is in contrast to the completive and the habitual aspect, which cannot occur in commands. However, positive and negative commands with a habitual meaning can be expressed through using the customary aspect (as in 12.34). That is, an apparent gap in the paradigm of the habitual aspect can be said to be filled through using another form. This is in contrast to the completive aspect which cannot be used in commands.

12.8.2   Reduplication of the verb root

Reduplication of the verb root can be either (A) full, or (B) partial. Full reduplication of the root is fully productive, while partial reduplication is not.

A. FULL REDUPLICATION OF THE VERB ROOT

The meaning of full reduplication of a verbal root can be intensive (as in 12.53, 12.55–7, and 12.59), continuous (as in 12.58), or durative (as in 12.54). A verb which consists of three syllables or fewer can undergo full reduplication. (See §11.3.2 under C, on the reduplication of verbs containing a syllable *ya* and explaining how the verb *vya-* 'hit, kill' becomes *vya-vi-* when reduplicated.)

If a verb root has more than three syllables, the last syllable undergoes omission, as in *sapeyakə-* 'open mouth', *sapeya-sapeyakə-* 'open mouth really wide' in 12.53.

12.53 sapəya-sapəyakə-n   rə-k-na-di
       RED-open.mouth-SEQ   sit-FUT-ACT.FOC-3plBAS.VT
       'They will stay with their mouths wide open (in surprise)'

The same principle applies to full reduplication of compounds, with one difference. If a verbal compound containing more than three syllables undergoes full reduplication, only the vowel of the final syllable—rather than the whole syllable—undergoes deletion, as in *kui-taka-* (give-put) 'transmit', *kui-tak-kui-taka* 'transmit many times or to many recipients', *kiya-yakə* (die-throw) 'die completely; die (all S)', *kiya-yak-kiya-yakə-* 'die completely many times, or many S', *kapə-* 'wait', *kapə-yakə-* 'wait all the time', *kapə-yak-kapə-yakə-* 'wait and wait for a long time'. These are illustrated in 12.54–5.

12.54 war-ku   ma:j   ata
       go.up-COMPL.SS   speech   then
       kui-tak-kui-taka-ba-l
       give.to.third.p-put:RED-give.to.third.p-put-1plSUBJ.P-3fem.sgBAS.P
       'Having gone up, we transmitted the news to many people'

12.55 kiya-yak-kiya-yakə-ku   tə-di
       die-FULLY:RED-die-FULLY-COMPL.SS   stay-3plBAS.P
       'After all of them fully died they stayed (this way)'

We recall, from §2.5.2 that such reduplicated compounds consist of two phonological words (they form one grammatical word).

Full reduplication of a three-root compound is illustrated in 12.56. The reduplicated compound verb consists of three components: *yi-* 'go', *səwul-* 'turn into, change', and *yakə-* 'throw; do fully'. As expected, the final vowel of the third root is deleted.

12.56 yi-səwul-yak-yi-səwul-yakə-ku,   ata   rə-di
       go-turn.into-FULLY:RED-go-turn.into-FULLY-COMPL.SS then sit-3plBAS.P
       'After all of them turned (into ginger leaves), they stayed (there)'

Some innovative speakers tend to reduplicate CVCVCVCV structures of verbal compounds
with the verb *-taka* as second component without syllable omission, as in 12.57:

12.57 a-di   kui-taka-kui-taka-tu-di   ja:p
       DEM.DIST-pl give.to.third.p-put-give.to.third.p-put-1sgSUBJ.P-3plBAS.P thing
       'things I was giving or passing on many times'

Some inherently reduplicated roots, e.g. *kusiya-kusiyakə-* 'dance (with hands up)', appear
to have undergone a similar process of omission. Occasionally, omission of the final vowel
occurs in shorter roots, e.g. *yi-gaji-* (go/say-rub) 'rub something onto surface', *yi-gaji-gaji-* 'rub
something fully' (as in 15.128), with a variant *yi-gaj-gaji-*, with the same meaning. (Note that
only the second root is reduplicated; we will see below that in such verbal compounds, *yi-* is
never reduplicated.)

An additional instance of vowel omission occurs in a few compounds whose second
component of CVCV structure imparts an aspectual meaning to the compound, and is
not used on its own, e.g. *vya-jika-* (hit-PROPERLY) 'hit properly' and *vya-jik-jika-* means 'hit
really hard'; *ləpa-təka-* (chop-DO.INCOMPLETELY) 'chop incompletely', *ləpa-tək-təka-* (chop-
RED-DO.INCOMPLETELY) 'chop a bit' (see §15.3.1).

Verbs with variable stem and ə in the non-negative indicative form allow for variation when
reduplicated. For instance, *təp-* 'close' may occur as *təp-* or as *tap-* —see the third line of
12.58 below, *taka-táp-taka-təpə-kú* 'having shut well'. The form with a non-schwa vowel is
preferred if the root is stressed, as is the case in *taka-tap-taka-təpə-ku* which divides into two
phonological words: *taka-táp taka-təpə-kú*.

12.58 wula-n   japukap-a:m   japukap-a:m
       come.in-SEQ underneath.the.house-LK+LOC underneath.the.house-LK+LOC
       səmən-səmənə-ku   vyakəta-yakə kəp-ad,   a-də
       cement-RED-COMPL.SS good-FULLY   ground-3masc.sgNOM DEM.DIST-masc.sg
       wiya:m   ata   ta:d   lə taka-tap-taka-təpə-ku
       house+LK+LOC then stand+3masc.sgBAS.P she put-close:RED-put-close-COMPL.SS
       kaigən kwa:l
       silent stay+3fem.sgBAS.P
       'Having come in, having continuously cemented the underneath part of the house, it was
       very good ground, he stayed in the house, she, having shut the door really well, stayed
       silent'

Reduplicands with an omitted vowel, like the ones under 12.54–6 and the middle line of 12.58,
may warrant an alternative analysis. We may prefer to consider the underlying form of verbs of
CVCV structure (*yakə-* 'throw', *taka-* 'put') as CVC accompanied by a linker vowel required if
the root is followed by a suffix. This would make the reduplication rules seem easier—that is,
we would not have to postulate the process of vowel omission.

However, this analysis involves additional complications in how we represent the verb root
structure: for every root one would need to know what the linker vowel is. This 'linker' vowel is
often different from an automatic linking ə which appears on the boundary between the root
and a verbal suffix and whose only function is to break an unauthorized consonant cluster (see
§11.3.1). Also, such analysis would not account for the fact that the final vowel of a reduplicated

disyllabic verb, or of a reduplicated disyllabic component of a compound, is not omitted: we have forms like *yakə-yakə-* (throw-FULLY) 'throw fully', and *kur-yakə-yakə-* 'get (rubbish out) completely and fully' in 12.65, and not **yak-yakə* or **kur-yak-yakə*.

A reduplicated root can occur within a fully inflected verb. Alternatively, a reduplicated root can occur as a copula complement of the verb *tə-* 'be, stand, have', as in 4.47 and 9.12b. That is, a fully reduplicated root can be treated as inflected or as uninflected, with a subtle difference in meaning. Only an inflected reduplicated verb can have continuous meaning, as in 12.59, while an uninflected reduplicated verb tends to refer to repeated actions (see 9.13a–b and discussion there).

12.59 ata   wa-ta:y   a   tə-tə-bər
        thus say-COTEMP DEM.DIST+fem.sg stay-RED-3duBAS.VT/P
        'This is how they two lived (for a long time)'

A fully reduplicated verb root may have overtones of gradual completion of an event, or state, as in 12.60–1:

12.60 yi: kiya-kiya-də-kək   yi-lə-k   a   yak
        fire die-RED-3masc.sg-PURP.DS go-3fem.sg-COMPL.DS DEM.DIST+fem.sg OK
        'After she went to the fire to make sure it was gradually dying and dying, then it was OK'

12.61 wukə-wukə-ta-d
        hear-RED-1duSUBJ.VT-3masc.sgBAS.VT
        'We keep understanding him, we gradually understand him'

Full reduplication often marks intensive and all-encompassing activity, as in 12.62, 12.56, and the third line of 12.58.

12.62 a-di   takwa:k   væn   tə-kər
        DEM.DIST-pl woman+LK+DAT see+SEQ stay-DES
        kabəl-kabəl-dana-d
        surround-RED-3plSUBJ.VT-3masc.sgBAS.VT
        'They (men) surrounded (the men's house) fully, being on the lookout for women'

As shown above, a directional compound can undergo full reduplication, like any other verb, as in 12.63. The meaning is that of intensive and continuous activity:

12.63 adiya   ma: kə-də   dəpu-nagwum
        DEM.DIST.REACT.TOP+pl again DEM.PROX-masc.sg inside+LK-sago+LK+LOC
        saula-saula-di
        make.sound+INSIDE-make.sound+INSIDE-3plBAS.P
        'Those (mentioned dogs) again kept on barking in the direction of the inside part of the sago trunk (where the Gala man was hidden)'

Verb compounds can also undergo full reduplication. Either of its components can be reduplicated on its own, without reduplicating the other one. (Compounds whose first or second component has undergone full reduplication are not used as copula complements.)

If the first component of a compound is reduplicated, it expresses continuity and intensity of the sub-action referred to by the reduplicated component. In 12.64 (where the verb *ya-* 'come' as second component in a compound marks continuous action), the speaker comments on the generosity of an Australian official and his wife, who would buy all sorts of things and:

12.64 ata   <u>kui-kuya-brə-di</u>
      then give.to.third.p-RED+come-3duSUBJ.P-3plBAS.P
      'Then they gave (all the things) to everyone time and time over'

Reduplication of a second component has an intensive rather than a continuous meaning. For instance, *kur-yakə-yakə-* (do/get-FULLY-FULLY) in 12.65 means 'get (things out) completely and fully; clean completely and fully'. Full reduplication of this compound would have yielded a form *kur-yak-kur-yakə-* ambiguous between 'get (things out) completely and fully', 'get (things out) many times completely', or 'get many things (out) completely'.

12.65 a-də   dəg <u>kur-yakə-yakə-ku</u>   a-di   wuk-a:m
      DEM.DIST-masc.sg nose get-FULLY-FULLY-COMPL.SS DEM.DIST-pl tooth-LK+LOC
      tə-di   pusəp   də-kə   wa:n də-kə   ta:m
      stay-3plBAS.VT rubbish he-OBL+fem.sg ear he-OBL+fem.sg nose
      <u>kur-yakə-yakə-ku</u>   ata <u>kur-yakə-yakə-də-d</u>
      get-FULLY-FULLY-COMPL.SS then get-FULLY-FULLY-3masc.sgSUBJ.P-3masc.sgBAS.P
      'Having fully cleaned the nose (lit. having got (things out) of his nose completely and fully), having cleaned the rubbish out of his teeth, ears, and the inside of the nose, he cleaned him (the Gala man) completely'

Along similar lines, *kə-yakə-yakə-* in 12.66 means 'they completely finished eating'. If the whole compound were reduplicated, the resulting form *kə-yak-kə-yakə-di*, would have been ambiguous between 'they completely ate many things', 'they repeatedly ate many things', or just 'they fully ate many things'.

12.66 <u>kə-yakə-yakə-ta:y</u>   yi-di
      eat-FULLY-FULLY-COTEMP go-3plBAS.VT/P
      'Having finished eating completely they went away'

As will be seen in §15.2, some of the second components impart what can be seen as manner or aspectual markers. They differ from aspect markers discussed in this chapter in that they can undergo reduplication and then impart intensive meaning, just like verbs. Similar examples, where the second component in a compound is not used on its own, and its reduplication indicates the intensity and diligence of the manner of action, are *və-səməl-* (see-?) 'look for', and *və-səməl-səməl-* 'look carefully'; *vætə-pæy-* 'bite and pick', *vætə-pæy-pay-* 'bite by picking relentlessly'; *vya-təpul-* 'kill by smashing', *vya-təpul-təpul-* 'kill by smashing strongly' (see §15.5).

Full reduplication of a second component in a cause-effect compound expresses the repetition of the sub-action, as in *vya-təməl-* (hit-roll/make.noise) means 'make something roll by hitting it', and *vya-təməl-təməl-* means 'hit something in all directions' (as in 15.24a–b).

Of all directional markers in compounds, only the motion marker *-tay* '(move) back and forth' can be reduplicated, in the meaning of 'repeatedly back and forth', as in 12.67 which describes the good neighbourly relations of giving back and forth:

12.67 awarwa <u>kui-tay-tayan</u>   tə-kwa-dian
      REC   give.to.third.p-BACK.FORTH-BACK.FORTH+SEQ stay-HAB-1plBAS.VT
      'We have been and are giving (things) to each other back and forth'

As an expressive device, both first and second component can be reduplicated separately. In 12.68, the reduplication of the first component, 'hit', implies continuous hitting, and the reduplication of the second component *-taka* 'put' implies intensive knocking the victims down:

12.68 ata   vya-vi-taka-taka-də-di
     then hit-RED-put-RED-3masc.sgSUBJ.P-3plBAS.P
     'Then he hit (mothers of all little spirits) down many times intensively'

If both components are reduplicated separately, vowel omission does not apply.

A special variety of full reduplication is the 'go-come' reduplication. The verb root undergoes full reduplication, its first occurrence is accompanied with -*yi*- 'go', and its second occurrence is followed by -*ya*- 'come'. The resulting meaning is that of 'erratic movement back and forth, here and there', as in 12.69. This is different from deliberate and directional back-and-forth movement achieved through reduplicating the directional -*tay*-. Compare 12.69 and 12.70:

12.69 ata   kwakə-yi-kwakə-ya:d
     then look.for-go-look.for-come+3masc.sgBAS.P
     'Then he looked (for his mother) here and there and back and forth'

12.70 ata   wa-tay-tay-a-bər
     then say-BACK.FORTH-BACK.FORTH-LK-3duBAS.VT/P
     'Then the two spoke back and forth (as in a dialogue)'

There are a number of restrictions on reduplication in compounds. If the first component of a compound belongs to a closed class, and the first component is a verb from an open class, the first component cannot be reduplicated (§15.5). There are no such restrictions concerning reduplicating the second component, e.g. *yi-gaji*- (go/say-rub) 'rub something onto surface', *yi-gaji-gaji*- 'rub something fully' (as in 15.128), but not **yi-yi-gaji*-. Monosyllabic verbs of motion *yi*- 'go' and *ya*- 'come' hardly ever undergo intensive reduplication (they can be reduplicated as a means of deriving an action nominalization, just like any other verb—see §9.1.1). The verb -*ya* 'come' grammaticalized into a marker of prolonged action in V₂ position (as in 12.64) cannot be reduplicated, unless the whole verb is also reduplicated, e.g. *tukwi-ya-yak-tukwi-ya-yakə*- (break-come-FULLY-break-come-FULLY) 'keep on breaking fully'. We return to this in §15.5. Neither type of full root reduplication is compatible with partial root reduplication addressed below.

B. PARTIAL REDUPLICATION OF THE VERB ROOT

This process applies to limited groups of verbs. We distinguish (i) root-initial and (ii) root-final partial reduplication. Partial reduplication has iterative meaning (in all cases but one).

(i) ROOT-INITIAL PARTIAL REDUPLICATION is limited to a few verbs involving motion. Root-initial partial reduplication is rather unusual phonologically. It involves—almost exclusively—verbs beginning with a labial consonant followed by a short vowel. The first CV sequence is reduplicated and accompanied by *y* insertion. If it contains the vowel ə, the vowel undergoes lowering to *a*. The reduplicated syllable acquires a secondary stress, e.g. *balák*- 'be turned upside down', *bày-balák*- 'be turned upside down over and over again', *pəsɔ́*- 'go around (e.g. a cape)', *pày-pəsɔ́*- 'go round many times'.

We can recall, from §2.4.2, that Manambu has a number of suffixes which are sensitive to the moraic structure of a syllable, and take different form depending on whether a verbal root consists of a light CV syllable (one mora), or a heavy CVC or CCV syllable (two morae). Following the same principle, we can hypothesize that the root-initial partial reduplication operates in terms of morae rather than of syllables: a light syllable (e.g. *ba* in *balak*- and *pə* (phonetically realized as *pu*) in *pəsə*-) is made heavy by the addition of a glide *y*. A verb with root-initial reduplication can take derivational prefixes and appear in compounds, e.g. *kay-pay-pəsən* (CAUS-RED-go.round+SEQ) 'make go round and round; go round and round forcefully', *yi-pay-pəsən* (go-RED-go.round+SEQ) 'go and keep going round and round; go on and on', *kay-bay-balak-ən* (CAUS-RED-turn-SEQ) 'overturn something many times', *jabə-* 'spit', *væte-jay-jabə-* 'bite and spit out'. A similar pattern is illustrated in 15.102 (see §15.5), *vya-jik-jika-* (hit-PROPERLY:RED-PROPERLY). An alternative pattern for the components *-jika-* 'do properly' is *vya-ji-jika-* 'hit really properly'.

This reduplication pattern whereby the first reduplicand has to be 'heavy' is reminiscent of the irregular reduplication pattern of the noun *sə* 'name': *say-si* '(call) each (person or house) by name' (see §9.2).

Root-initial partial reduplication applies to one verb which can be the second component of verb compounds, the form *-ba:gw-* 'do incessantly' which is not used as an independent verb. Such reduplication only takes place when *-ba:gw-* combines with verbs of motion. The meaning is iterative: *gəpə-bay-bagwə-d* (run-do.incessantly-RED-3masc.sgBAS.VT/P) 'he is running all over the place in every direction'. This same suffix combines with verbs of other semantic groups, e.g. *kə-ba:gw-* 'eat incessantly', *yaku-ba:gw-* 'wash incessantly'; then, it does not undergo reduplication (see §15.3.1 for further examples of *-ba:gw-*).

One other, rather unusual, instance of a morpheme-initial partial reduplication involves the verb *wukəma:r* 'forget' which is a lexicalized compound consisting of *wukə-* 'remember, think' and *-ma:r-* 'dependent clause negator' (see §14.5). Partial reduplication of the second syllable *mar* as *may* marks complete extent of 'forgetting something', as in 12.71 and 14.159. (This is an example of an anterior complex predicate—see §17.1.1.)

12.71 bə   wukə-may-marə-n   ata   tə-lwən
      already hear-NEG.SUB.RED-NEG:DEP-SEQ then stay-1fem.sgBAS.P
      'I have already completely forgotten about it'

Similarly to other examples of morpheme-initial partial reduplication, the form *-mar-* contains an initial labial consonant. However, unlike all other examples, there is no motion involved. This is the only instance of partial reduplication with intensive meaning.

(ii) ROOT-FINAL PARTIAL REDUPLICATION applies to verbs of affect, such as hitting and cutting. The second syllable undergoes reduplication. The syllable can be of CV structure, *vya-ləp-* 'hit and break; cut (cross-wise)', *vya-ləpa-pa* 'cut, hit, or chop all many times', as in 12.72, or CVC structure, as in 12.73, *patəp-* 'cut (e.g. rope)', *patəp-təp-* 'cut many times', as in 12.73. In a trisyllabic root, the last CVCV sequence gets reduplicated, as in *kətək-* 'cut' and *kətək-təka-* 'cut bit by bit'.

12.72 vækər-tu-da-k   vya-təpul-ku
      fall-MANY-3pl-COMPL.DS hit.SMASH-HIT-COMPL.SS
      vya-ləpa-pa-də-di
      hit-chop-RED-3masc.sgSUBJ.P-3plBAS.P
      'After all of them fell down, having smashed them he hit and chopped them up many times'

12.73 ata   lagu-n   kray-ku,   ya:kya, aka
      then pull-SEQ bring-COMPL.SS OK   DEM.DIST.REACT.TOP.fem.sg
      patəp-təp-ə-də-l
      cut-RED-LK-3masc.sgSUBJ.P-3fem.sgBAS.P
      'Then having brought it (snake) by pulling it, OK, he cut it many times'

In summary: morpheme-initial and morpheme-final partial reduplication are similar in their meanings; yet they follow different principles. The former applies to verbs of motion, and the latter to verbs of affect. The former can be described as sensitive to the moraic structure of heavy versus light syllables, and the latter operates simply in terms of syllables. Both kinds of partial reduplication appear to be restricted to syllables involving a labial consonant.

12.8.3 Repetition of the verb

Repetition of an inflected verb features prominently in expressing intensity and repetition of actions and states. We identify the following conventionalized techniques.

A. REPETITION OF A SEQUENTIAL FORM OF THE VERB MARKED WITH THE SUFFIX -*n* indicates a repeated action done little by little and simultaneous with that of the main verb, as in 12.74–5. The verb is repeated twice. If a root is monosyllabic, it does not undergo lengthening as is normally the case when the suffix -*n* attaches to it (as in 12.80 below). The two instances of repeated forms are often pronounced as one phonological word: *kənkən* is pronounced as /kən gən/ undergoing an ad hoc voicing assimilation (under the influence of the preceding nasal). A usual sequential form of *kə* 'eat' is *ka:n* 'eating', with vowel lengthening (see similar forms under (C) below).

Just before we went off to Swakap, embarking on a long and exhausting journey, Yuaya:b brought us a few sticks of sugarcane to keep us going and said:

12.74 kən   kən   kə-gura-di
      eat+SEQ eat+SEQ eat-2plSUBJ.VT-3plBAS.VT
      'You are going to keep eating (these) little by little'

Similarly, in 12.75 the narrator refers to the fact that the two people had just brought the ladder made of rope up into the house by tying it up bit by bit:

12.75 waya:b   kə-də   pətaka:u ji-n   ji-n
      recently DEM.PROX-masc.sg ladder tie-SEQ tie-SEQ
      kawar-bra-d
      carry+UP-2duSUBJ.VT-3masc.sgBAS.VT
      'Just recently you two carried this ladder up by tying it repeatedly bit by bit'

A similar example is in 14.113 ('eating and eating and eating').

B. REPETITION OF INFLECTED COMPOUND VERB IN COMBINATION WITH DIFFERENT DIRECTIONALS is a way of expressing a sequence of movements in different directions. Operating a pump torch involves pressing it 'in and out', and this was described as 12.76:

12.76 kay-bətuku-səwəlan   kay-bətuku-saku-n
      MANIP-pump-INSIDE+SEQ MANIP-pump-OUTWARDS-SEQ
      kay-bətuku-tua-d
      MANIP-pump-1sgSUBJ.VT-3masc.sgBAS.VT
      'I pump it pumping it in pumping it out'

C. REPETITION OF A VERBAL FORM IN A SEQUENTIAL CONSTRUCTION WITH THE SAME VERB IN THE MAIN CLAUSE indicates gradual achievement of the verb's action or state, as in 12.80–1. The closest analogy is English 'going, going...gone'. The reactivated topic demonstrative refers to the action as a whole, and can appear either before the main clause, or after it. The whole is pronounced as one intonation unit—which shows that it can no longer be analysed as multiclausal:

12.77 <u>kusə-n</u>   kusə-n   kusə-lə-l   aka
     finish-SEQ   finish-SEQ   finish-3fem.sgSUBJ.P-3fem.sgBAS.P   DEM.DIST.REACT.TOP+fem.sg
     'It (the story) is slowly coming to an end and is now finished'

12.78 təpə-taka-n   təpə-taka-n   aka
     be.closed-put.down-SEQ   be.closed-put.down-SEQ   DEM.DIST.REACT.TOP+fem.sg
     təpə-taka-tua
     be.closed-put.down-1sgSUBJ.VT+3fem.sgBAS.VT
     'I am slowly closing (the door) and have closed it'

D. REPETITION OF A VERBAL FORM IN A SEQUENTIAL CONSTRUCTION WITH A COPULA VERB IN THE MAIN CLAUSE marks an action that continually goes on and on, as in 12.79.

12.79 təpa:m   kwa-na-di   du   akatawa <u>titiya-n</u>   <u>titiya-n</u>
     village+LK+LOC   stay-ACT.FOC-3plBAS.VT   man thus   go.round-SEQ   go.round-SEQ
     tə-kwa-na-di
     stay-HAB-ACT.FOC-3plBAS.VT
     'Men who are in the village go round and round like this'

The instances of repetition discussed under A–D above can be considered at least partially grammaticalized, since their meaning is somewhat idiosyncratic.

    Besides this, any inflected verb, within a main or a subordinate clause, can be repeated more than twice in a fully iconic meaning. The verb is typically repeated two, three, five, seven, or ten times (but hardly any other number of times), depending on the length of time of the action the speaker is trying to express. In 12.80, the form *ta:n* 'by staying' is repeated three times, to indicate a considerable length of time:

12.80 ka-war-tu-kəb   atawatay ta:n   ta:n   ta:n   ya:kya
     carry-UP-1sg-COMPL.DS+TERM   thus   stay+SEQ   stay+SEQ   stay+SEQ   OK
     'As soon as I brought (my family) up there, having stayed (for some time), OK (I then left)'

In 12.81, this same form *ta:n* 'by staying' is repeated seven times—indicating that the ceremony went on for a very long time. The repeated forms belong to different intonation units.

12.81 waku-ku,   ba:gw   adiya   tə-na-di   <u>ta:n</u>
     go.out-COMPL.SS   ceremony   DEM.DIST.REACT.TOP+pl   have-ACT.FOC-3plBAS.VT   stay+SEQ
     <u>ta:n</u>   <u>ta:n</u>   <u>ta:n</u>   <u>ta:n</u>   <u>ta:n</u>   <u>ta:n</u>   napa-ku   sə
     stay+SEQ   stay+SEQ   stay+SEQ   stay+SEQ   stay+SEQ   stay+SEQ   COMPL.VB-COMPL.SS   sleep
     ata   kwa-di
     then   stay-3plBAS.VT/P
     'Having gone out, they held a ceremony, after they held it (for a very long time), they went to sleep'

A complement of a support verb (see Chapter 17) can also be repeated, but no more than three times, as in 12.82, 9.14, and T2.25 (fourth line: 'eyes bulging out').

12.82 <u>təməl</u>   <u>təməl</u>   <u>təməl</u>   ata   na:l
      roll/make.noise roll/make.noise roll/make.noise then BE:NAT+3fem.sgBAS.P
      'There was a noise of (him) rolling and rolling'

Tok Pisin shares the principle of repetition as a marker of intensive and prolonged action and state with Manambu. The influence of Tok Pisin may have contributed to the productivity of this phenomenon in Manambu (which could well reflect an areal feature).

13

Mood and Modality

13.1 OVERVIEW

Of all the modal forms discussed here, only irrealis is fully inflected. Imperative is partially inflected, employing a special set of subject markers. Different-subject purposive is partially inflected with the non-tensed subject markers listed in Table 11.2. All other modalities are uninflected. A summary is at §13.8. None of the modal forms is compatible with the verbal categories discussed in Chapter 12.

13.2 IMPERATIVE

The imperative is the main means of marking directive speech acts, including orders and requests. The subject of the imperative is marked with affixes listed in Table 13.1. The resulting forms are partially inflected. Second person imperative is unusual in that it does not distinguish number or gender. As we will see in 13.3–5 below, number and gender meanings can be disambiguated through personal pronouns. First person imperative distinguishes three numbers, but no genders; and third person imperative distinguishes two genders in the singular and no genders in dual or plural, just as expected.

The imperative paradigm is formally heterogeneous. The formal aspects of second, first, and third person imperative are discussed in §13.2.1, and their semantics in §13.2.2. Optative modality formed on imperative is featured in §13.2.3.

13.2.1 Formal aspects of imperative

The second person form of imperative is by far the most frequent in conversations. Second person imperative is the only form marked with a productive prefix in Manambu (the other prefix, *kay-* 'transitivizer; manipulative', is not productive). This is accompanied by the loss of root-final vowel in many disyllabic verbs (except for those ending in a vowel other than *a* or *ə*) and in all monosyllabic verbs, e.g. *kə-* 'eat', *ka-* 'paddle', imperative *ak*; *taka-* 'put', imperative *a-tak*; *wukə-* 'hear, understand', imperative *a-wuk*; but *rali-* 'untie', imperative *a-rali*; *kusu-* 'put on', imperative *a-kusu*; *kisi-yi-* (get-go) 'keep getting', *a-kisi-yi*! 'keep getting' (see §11.3.2). The stress in the second person imperative falls on the root. There is a certain amount of inter-speaker variation: innovative speakers occasionally omit the root-final *i* in imperatives of disyllabic verbs, while traditional speakers do not do this. For instance, an imperative of *væki-* 'go across' would be *a-væk* 'go across!' for an innovative speaker, and *a-væki* for a traditional speaker.

Verbs of the structure CCV undergo final vowel deletion. A schwa is inserted between the two consonants to avoid unauthorized clusters, as in *gra-* 'cry', *a-gər* 'cry!', *bla-* 'speak', *a-bəl* 'speak!'; *kra-* 'get; marry', *a-kər* 'marry!' (as in 13.4).

TABLE 13.1 Imperative cross-referencing

PERSON/GENDER	SG	DU	PL
1	-*u*	-*tǝk*	-*nak*
2		*a-*	
3masc	-*kwa-d*	-*kwa-bǝr*	-*kwa-di*
3fem	-*kwa*		

The second person imperative of *wa-* 'say' is *áu* or *áw*—that is, after the final vowel deletion *w* can be vocalized as *u*. The imperative of *kui-* 'give to third person' is *a-kwí*, with the stress on the second vowel, and the first vowel becoming a glide. The imperative of *kwatiyá-* 'give to non-third person' is *a-kwatáy*, with an irregular vowel change in the last syllable.

Suppletive second person imperative (mentioned in §11.3.2) is found with frequently used verbs of stance and motion (some of which also occur as copulas in copula clauses). The second person imperative of *rǝ-* 'sit' and of *tǝ-* 'stand; have' is *ada*. The second person of *kwa-* 'stay' is *adakw*. Other forms from the imperative paradigm of all these verbs are regular, e.g. *rau* 'let me sit, may I sit', *rǝ-kwa-d* 'let him sit'; *tau* 'let me stand, let me have', *tǝ-kwa-d* 'let him stand, let him have'. A list of these verbs is in Table 13.2.

The two stance verbs also used as copulas, *rǝ-* and *tǝ-*, share one second person imperative form, as shown in 13.1 and 13.2. The two are distinguished in all other forms.

13.1 da:n <u>ada</u>
go.down+SEQ sit.IMPV
'Sit down!'

13.2 rasǝ-n <u>ada</u>
stand.up-SEQ stand.IMPV
'Stand up!'

TABLE 13.2 Verbs with suppletive second person imperatives

VERB ROOT	SECOND PERSON IMPERATIVE
rǝ- 'sit; stay, copula'	*ada*
tǝ- 'stand, be, have, copula'	
kwa- 'stay, copula'	*adakw*
yi- 'go'	*ma:y*
ya- 'come'	*mæy*
da- 'go down'	*adi:d*

The verb *yi-* has a suppletive imperative *ma:y* in its meaning 'go'. When the same form is used as a copula and in the meaning 'say', the imperative is *ay* (see §4.2.2).

Verbs with stative meanings, e.g. *rəp-* 'be enough', *warsam(a)-* 'be angry', cannot form a second person imperative; neither can such copulas as *na-* 'be (of abstract states)', *tay-* 'be (of climate states)', *yasalə-* 'be (of physical states)', *say-* 'be (of some states, e.g. shame, pins and needles)', and *yæy-* 'be (of smells)'. Verb compounds with the second component *ya-* 'come' do not form second person imperatives.

Unlike the second person imperative, the corresponding first and third person forms can be formed on any verb, including statives.

The formation of first person imperatives is straightforward (see §11.3.2 under A, on the vowel lengthening in monosyllabic roots): the markers listed in Table 13.1 attach to the stem. These do not appear to be etymologically related to each other. Third person imperatives contain the suffix *-kwa* accompanied by gender and number markers employed throughout the language—the masculine singular *-d*, dual *-bər*, and plural *-di*. Feminine singular form is ø. It is realized as *-l* if followed by the optative suffix *-əu* (§13.2.3). This distribution of the feminine singular allomorphs—whereby ø occurs at the end of a word, and *-l* occurs if followed by a vowel—is consistent with §5.1.2 and Table 5.2.

The distinction between three subsets of imperatives—first, second, and third person—is neutralized under negation. We discuss the prohibitives (or negative imperatives), and their correlations with person, in §14.4.

The second person imperative prefix *a-* has cognates in Iatmul and in Boiken (Freudenburg 1970: 79). The origin of first person imperative markers is obscure. The marker of first person dual, *-tək*, may be etymologically related to the first person dual subject marker of the subject series, *-ta* or *-tə*. The first person plural suffix *-nak* does not seem to have any correlates elsewhere in the language (*n* could be cognate to *-n* in first person plural pronoun *ña-n*). The etymology of the third person imperative marker *-kwa* may be related to the jussive *-ku* in Ambulas and/or to the formative *-kwa-* in *yékwak*, an additional marker of third person imperative in Ambulas (Wilson 1980: 168–9). Another potential cognate is *-kwa* in just one second person imperative form in Iatmul: *ya-kwa* (come-IMPV) 'come!'

13.2.2   Semantics of imperative

In addition to formal differences, the three person forms of imperative differ in their semantics. Second person imperatives are typically used for orders (A); first person imperatives often have permissive overtones (B); and third person imperatives tend to combine these two meanings (C). These differences are likely to be due to universal correlations between person value and the meaning of a command with it. The three persons share just one non-command function (D).

A. SECOND PERSON IMPERATIVES are typically used for commands and orders. They are extremely frequent in Manambu discourse. Commands are addressed to people of any age, and especially to children. Such was the frequency with which the baby Jemima (15 months) kept hearing 13.1 that she started using this construction as a name for chair and bench, in a slightly reduced form *dandá*.

If the speaker deems it necessary, the gender and the number for the addressee of second person imperative can be supplied by a personal pronoun, as in 13.3–4. In 13.3 the imperative is formed on a complex predicate (in square brackets) consisting of the main verb marked with the manner suffix *-n* and the auxiliary *kwa-* 'stay' (which has a suppletive imperative *adakw*).

13.3 ñən   [kurə-n   adakw]
     you.fem take.care-SEQ stay.IMPV
     'You (feminine) stay looking after (the baby)'

Constituent order in imperative clauses is similar to that in declarative clauses. The O can follow the verb if it is an established topic, as in 13.4:

13.4 mən   akər   kə   ta:kw   Kamkudi
     you.masc IMPV+marry DEM.PROX.fem.sg woman   Kamkudi
     'You marry this woman, Kamkudi!'

A topically established subject can occasionally follow the verb, as in 13.5:

13.5 adakw   bər
     stay.IMPV you.du
     'You two stay!'

Two second person imperatives can follow each other in one sentence, expressing two concomitant actions, as in 13.6:

13.6 ma:y   gur   awakw
     go.IMPV you.pl IMPV+go.out
     'Go, you (plural) go out'

Any imperative form can be accompanied by the hortative *jau* 'don't worry; you may do it' (see §4.5), as in 4.78 and 13.7, with the meaning of letting something happen:

13.7 jau   a-war
     don't.worry IMPV-go.up
     'Go up (into the house) without any restraint'

Similar examples, with other persons, are at 13.17 and 13.23. Just like any other command, second person imperative often occurs followed by the emphatic particle *ya*, to make a command sound more urgent (see §4.5, and also 13.14).

B. FIRST PERSON IMPERATIVES have slightly different meaning overtones depending on the number value. First person singular imperative has permissive meaning, and is often used for mild requests.

13.8 kwasa   wiya:r   yau
     small+fem.sg house+LK+ALL go+1sgIMPV
     'May I go to the toilet; let me go to the toilet'

13.9 bas sau
     first plant+1sgIMPV
     'May I ask' (lit. 'first plant')

The first person imperative has a permissive meaning when used in content questions implying first person's intention, as in 13.10.

13.10 təp-a   kudir   '*marasin*'   atəta wau
      village-LK language+ALL 'medicine' how say+1sgIMPV
      'How shall I say "medicine" in Manambu (lit. the village language)?'

In yes-no questions, the implication is that of the speaker's intention to be confirmed by the addressee. After we came back from a tiring trip to Yawabak, Dora took a limbum leaf and asked me:

13.11 <u>yabru</u>
fan+1sgIMPV
'Shall I fan (you) (to cool you off)?'

This same form occurs in general statements of intention without any implication of permission, as in 13.12. Note the person marker *-mən* rather than the expected *-dəmən*: this may indicate an emergent new non-declarative form.

13.12 mæy-a   ata wun-a:m kaykətə-mən   <u>krayu</u>
come.IMPV-VOC then I-LK+LOC hold.onto-2masc.sgBAS.VT take+1sgIMPV
'You come (said the hawk to the man), you hold on to me, and I shall take you (there)'

A command to a second person can be echoed by a command to a first person, as in 13.13. Here, the tree kangaroo is telling his mate and himself who is going to occupy what seat on a canoe. The tree kangaroo is not asking for permission—he is stating what he is going to do.

13.13 [mən   ya:n   maləm   ada]   [wun ya:n
you.masc come+SEQ side/stern+LK+LOC sit/stand.IMPV I   come+SEQ
tama:b   <u>ta:u</u>]
nose+LK+TERM stand+1sgIMPV
'You come and sit/stand at the stern; let me stand at the nose (of a canoe)'

The two positional verbs used here ('sit' and 'stand') share one second person imperative; but have different forms in other persons.

First person non-singular (dual and plural) forms of imperative are usually employed as hortatives ('let's do something') as in 13.14. The emphatic particle *ya* makes the command sound truly urgent.

13.14 [[aməy taka-n] wapa-ñən]   [yi-tək   ya]
basket put-SEQ leave-2fem.sgBAS.VT go-1duIMPV EMPH
'You put the basket (to collect shrimp) and leave it, and (then) let's two of us go'

As illustrated in 13.13, first person singular imperative can occur with first person singular pronoun if it is contrastive: the tree kangaroo contrasts himself to his companion on the canoe. Non-singular first person pronouns can be used in a similar way. We can recall that with second person imperatives, second person pronouns have a somewhat different function of disambiguating number and gender of the addressee.

C. THIRD PERSON IMPERATIVE is used for commands and instructions with reference to a third person, as shown in 13.15. There are no semantic differences between singular and non-singular numbers; and an overt subject NP can be supplied, if necessary.

13.15 adaku   təpwi:m   tə-na-d-ə
DEM.DIST+masc.sg+OUTWARDS opening+LOC stay-ACT.FOC-3masc.sgBAS.VT-LK
ma:s   ta:y sər   ma:m   <u>war-kwa</u>   puku-n
betelnut.tree first tomorrow elder.sibling go.up-IMPV.3p+fem.sg pick-SEQ
<u>da-kwa</u>   ñamus   ata <u>war-kwa</u>
go.down-IMPV.3p+fem.sg younger.sibling then go.up-IMPV.3p+fem.sg
'Tomorrow may the elder sister climb up the betelnut tree standing there in the outward direction in the opening, having picked (the nuts), may she go down, then may the younger sister climb up'

Third person imperative can have permissive overtones, of letting something happen by itself, as in 13.16—an instruction on how to take sore throat lozenges.

13.16 kəmarki-tukwa   dayim   kurə-n   kwa:n
swallow-PROH.GEN mouth+LOC get-SEQ stay+SEQ
yi-kəta-kəta-kwa
go-AROUND?-AROUND?-IMPV.3p+fem.sg
'Do not swallow (it), having got (it in your mouth) with it staying (there) let it dissolve'

In 13.17, the elder sister was urged not to bother the baby while the baby was eating: the overtone of 'letting her be' is emphasized by the use of *jau* 'don't worry; let it be':

13.17 kamna:gw jau   <u>kə-kwa</u>
food   don't.worry   eat-IMPV.3p+fem.sg
'Let her eat food!'

Or a third person imperative can express permission, as in 13.18:

13.18 kə-də   nabi-dəka ñan-a-wa da-n   yawi <u>kur-kwa</u>
DEM.PROX-masc.sg year-ONLY we-LK-COM go.down-SEQ work do/get-IMPV.3p+fem.sg
'Let her be allowed to work with us down there for only this year!'

Descriptions of what was traditionally allowed are also cast in third person imperative. In 13.19, Saosepali tells her audience that, traditionally, only initiated men were allowed to sit on a bench. This is cast in third person imperative. In the last line, a negative obligation is expressed using a nominalization—see §9.1.1 and §14.3.3.

13.19 də-kə-dəka   təkər-əm   <u>rə-yi-kwa-d</u>   təkər-əm
he-OBL-ONLY bench-LK+LOC sit-go-IMPV.3p-masc.sg bench-LK+LOC
rə-kwa-na-d,   ta:kw-al   təkər-əm   rə-rə   ma:
sit-HAB-ACT.FOC-3masc.sgBAS.VT woman-3fem.sgNOM bench-LK+LOC sit-RED NEG
butə-kə-na   ñiki
form.clot.haemorrhoid.like-FUT-ACT.FOC+3fem.sgBAS.VT blood
'Only he (the initiated man) could sit on the bench, he used to sit on the bench, as for woman, she was not to sit on the bench, or else her blood would clot like a haemorrhoid'

A traditional blessing (performed by blowing lightly on the person, the process called *wurəbasawəl-*) is accompanied by asking the blesser's spirit to ensure the addressee is cured if they are sick. This also involves a third person imperative (also see Harrison 1993: 108):

13.20 wun-a-də   kayik   ba:r   <u>kusə-kwa</u>   yara <u>kwa-kwa-d</u>
I-LK-masc.sg spirit/image illness end-IMPV.3p+fem.sg well stay-IMPV.3p-masc.sg
'My spirit, may the illness end, may he (the patient) be well'

Third person imperative occurs with modal words discussed at §4.5.1 with an overtone of 'ought to', or 'must', as in 13.21:

13.21 a   nəbə asa:y-a:b   <u>wukə-kwa-d</u>
then able father-TOO understand/know-IMPV.3p-masc.sg
'(I will tell the father that a man wanted to marry you two), then the father too must know'

The Tok Pisin borrowing *mas* 'must' can occur with third person imperative in the meaning of strong obligation. Paul Kat said 13.22 to Sepaywus, explaining why he had to tell me the story of the Gala wars:

13.22 lə *mas* laku-kwa
     she must know-IMPV.3p+fem.sg
     'She must know'

Third person imperatives differ from first and second person imperatives in some of their non-command meanings—we discuss these in the next subsection.

D. THE NON-COMMAND MEANING OF IMPERATIVES—shared by forms of all persons—is that of consequence and indirect causation. The first clause expresses the cause, and the second clause—cast in imperative—expresses the result. The first clause can also contain an imperative, as in 13.23. Such a combination of two clauses is the only natural way of expressing the notion of 'feeding someone':

13.23 jau, kə-di rək-a-kija:p-ə-rəb kwatiyau
     don't.worry DEM.PROX-pl dry-LK-protein.food-LK-FULLY give.to.nonthird+1sgIMPV
     ak
     IMPV+eat
     'Don't worry, let me give you these real pieces of dry meat/fish, (so that) you eat' (meaning 'let me feed you with these pieces of dry meat/fish')

A sentence consisting of several clauses the last of which contains an imperative—as in 13.24—is the most natural way of saying 'get her to come':

13.24 [wun-a ta:kw aləm kwa-lə-k]
     I-LK wife DEM.DIST+fem.sg+LOC stay-3fem.sg-COMPL.DS
     [wa-yakə-gur-ək] ya-kwa
     say-throw-2pl-COMPL.DS come-IMPV.3p+fem.sg
     'Get my wife to come from there' (lit. My wife having stayed there, you order (lit. say-throw) her: may she come)

Third and second person imperative in direct speech reports is a widespread means of expressing causation. '"May his throat be wet", he said (and) gave him water' in T2.34 is a functional equivalent of 'he made (or let) him drink water'. Along similar lines, 13.25 is the most natural way of rendering the meaning of 'tell your wife to bring sago':

13.25 mən-a takwa:k wa-mən-ək na:gw
     you.masc-LK+fem.sg wife+LK+DAT say-2masc.sg-COMPL.DS sago
     kapra-kwa
     bring.across.to.speaker-IMPV.3p+fem.sg
     'Tell your wife to bring sago across to me' (lit. After you have told your wife, may she bring sago across to speaker)

Manambu has a morphological causative with limited productivity, and a syntactic causative which is infrequent and has strong implications of forceful causation—see §16.2.2. Marking causation with the help of imperative, as illustrated in 13.25, helps fill an existing gap.

   A sequence of a non-imperative and an imperative form is a way of expressing one action following another as its consequence, without any forceful causation, as in 13.26.

13.26 waku-məna asa:y və-kwa-d
     go.out-2masc.sgSUBJ.VT+3fem.sgBAS.VT father see-IMPV.3p-masc.sg
     'You go out, (so that) father may see you'

A direct speech report marked with imperative may have the meaning of consequence, as in 13.27: the girl who has been abducted against her will leaves kitchen ashes behind on the path so that her brothers could come to her rescue by following the ashes (see §19.5).

13.27 waku-lə-l,   ya:b bau   yakə-n   mæn væsə-n,
go.out-3fem.sgSUBJ.P-3fem.sgBAS.P road ashes throw-SEQ leg   step-SEQ
wun-a   wayika:m   <u>ya-kwa-bər</u>   vən   vən   wa-ku
I-LK+fem.sg footprint+LK+LOC come-IMPV.3p-du see+SEQ see+SEQ say-COMPL.SS
'She went (out of the house), throwing ashes on the road, (every time) she made a step, so that her two brothers could come following her footprints (lit. having said, may they two come (following) my footprints)'

Unlike any other imperative form, third person imperative can be used in maledictions: the exasperated mother who said 13.28 did not wish her daughter dead. A third person imperative here expresses her anger at the recalcitrant child:

13.28 <u>kiya-kwa</u>   kwasa-kwasa wula-ma:r-ən
die-IMPV.3p+fem.sg little-little   enter-NEG.SUB-SEQ
'May she die, having nearly missed (being hit by a lid)'

This usage is similar to that of third person imperative forms in optatives discussed in §13.2.3.

As is the case in many languages, second person imperative forms occur in leave-taking formulae (see §21.5.2). The second person general prohibitive of *wa-* 'say', *wa-tukwa*, has an additional meaning of 'say it again, I couldn't agree more' (§21.1.3). Note that the strong prohibitives, *-way* and *-wayik*, with this same verb do not have such overtones—see §14.4.

First person singular imperative of the verb *wa-* 'say, speak' (*wa:u* 'may I say; let me say') and also of *bla-* 'talk' mark turn-taking in public speaking, and in story telling. The second person imperative of the verb *wukə-* 'hear, listen' (*awuk* 'hear, listen!') is used as an attention-getting device in public speaking, including the name-debating ceremonies, and oratories during funerary ceremonies.

A number of devices can be used instead of commands, with weaker or stronger illocutionary force. These command strategies are discussed in §19.9.

13.2.3   Optative modality

The optative modality is used to express wishes, hoped for and often difficult to accomplish. Optative can be formed on first and third person imperative with the marker *-əu*. This same marker can occur on the irrealis forms discussed in §13.3 with a similar meaning (examples 13.29–40). Second person irrealis accompanied with the marker *-əu* is used to fill in the gap in the optative paradigm formed on the imperative. The marker *-əu* triggers the allomorph *-l* of the third person feminine form (see §5.1.2). The first person singular imperative marker *-u* is realized as *-əw* before the optative *-əu*, as in 13.30.

The optative refers to actions in present and in future, but not in the past. On a particularly hot and windless day Mali expressed a wish that:

13.29 ma:r <u>vya-kwa-l-əu</u>
wind hit-IMPV.3p-fem.sg-OPT
'I wish the wind could blow'

The optative can be accompanied by an interjection: *ša* 'attention getter; oh dear' or *šay* 'oh dear', as in 13.30–1.

13.30 šay papər vyakat-a ma:j <u>wukəw-əu</u>
oh later good-LK story hear+1sgIMPV-OPT
'I wish I could hear good news later'

In 13.31, Gemaj, fed up with waiting for a plane to come, exclaimed:

13.31 ša a   balus yabi:b <u>da-kwa-l-əu</u>
oh DEM.DIST.fem.sg plane quickly go.down-IMPV.3p-fem.sg-OPT
'Oh, I wish the plane could descend quickly!'

The optative can be used in maledictions, without implying an actual wish. A mother, exasperated by annoying behaviour of a child, may exclaim 13.32, without actually wishing the child dead. This is a more expressive version of 13.28.

13.32 məy-a-məyab   <u>kiya-kwa-l-əu</u>
real-LK-real+LK+TERM die-IMPV.3p-fem.sg-OPT
'May she well and truly die!'

Optative cannot be negated; a negative form of the irrealis (§13.3) is used instead. That is, the subtle distinction between optative and irrealis is neutralized in negative constructions. This agrees with the principle of dependencies between grammatical systems whereby fewer categories may be distinguished in negative than in positive clauses (Aikhenvald and Dixon 1998).

13.3 IRREALIS

In our discussion of the future in §12.2, we pointed out that, in non-negative main clauses, it is homophonous with a form termed irrealis. As shown in 12.13–14, a verb form marked with future -*kə*- can have a wide array of epistemic meanings, referring to something that is probably happening, or might happen, or might have happened. Whether a form marked with -*kə*- has an irrealis or a future meaning is often determined by the context (they are differentiated under negation). In 13.33, a future meaning is highly unlikely: on hearing a cry, a woman suspects it could be her baby daughter crying:

13.33 wun kwasa   ñan <u>gra-k-na</u>
I   small.fem.sg child cry-IRR-ACT.FOC+3fem.sgBAS.VT
'Perhaps my little daughter is crying'

The irrealis form is used in warnings, as in 13.34. I was told not to go and bathe in the flooded and muddy Sepik River, because:

13.34 <u>piñu-k-ñəna</u>   karki
slip-IRR-2fem.sgSUBJ.VT+3fem.sgBAS.VT mud
'You might slip in the mud'

The irrealis form is often used in juxtaposed clauses with counterfactual meanings (see §19.1, and further examples there). An example of a counterfactual use of irrealis in an independent clause is at 13.35 (continuation of 10.124). Kukelyabau is talking about a fire during the Second World War when a plane (the first one she'd ever seen) crashed into the village: as soon as the plane went down, the villagers left their houses; had they not done so, they would have perished in the fire:

13.35 [də da-də-lək]   [alək   wi   waku-dian]   [ya:k] [wi
he go.down-3masc.sg-BECAUSE this.is.why house go.out-1plBAS.P OK house
waku-ba-l]   [alək   kə-də   təp   wa:ñ-al
go.out-1plSUBJ.P-3fem.sgBAS.P this.is.why DEM.PROX-masc.sg village line-3fem.sgNOM
wuli-n   kwa-bana]   [kə-də   təp-a   du
multiply-SEQ stay-1plBAS.VT+3fem.sgBAS.VT DEM.PROX-masc.sg village-LK man
ta:kw   wa:ñ alək   taka-n kwa-na-di]   [ta:l
woman line this.is.why put-SEQ stay-ACT.FOC-3plBAS.VT before
kusə-kə-na-di]   ta:l   kiya-kə-na-di,   akəs
finish-IRR-ACT.FOC-3plBAS.VT before die-IRR-ACT.FOC-3plBAS.VT NEG.IRR
kwa-kə-na-di
stay-IRR-ACT.FOC-3plBAS.VT
'Since it (plane) went down, this is why we left our houses. OK. We left our houses, this is why there is a line (of descendants) in this village. We are multiplying, we men and women of this village. This is why we stay creating descendants (lit. putting line). Before we would have finished, we would have died, we would never have been here'

In positive clauses, the future and the irrealis meanings are distinguished solely by context. Under negation, however, the future and the epistemic meanings are distinguished formally: future negation involves the negator *ma:* postposed to the uninflected root, while irrealis negation involves *akəs* with a fully inflected verb, as shown in the last two lines of 13.35 (see further discussion in §§14.2–3). Another example is at 13.36, where irrealis forms appear in a counterfactual conditional construction, both in the dependent clause and in the main clause:

13.36 [mən   an-a-də   ñaj   tə-kə-məna]
you.masc 1du-LK-masc.sg father's.brother be-IRR-2masc.sgSUBJ.VT+3fem.sgBAS.VT
[an-a:k   atawa   akəs   kurə-k-məna-bran]
we.du-LK+DAT like.that NEG.IRR do/get-IRR-2masc.sgSUBJ.VT-1duBAS.VT
'If you had been our uncle, you would not have acted like this to us'

Irrealis forms can be used as command strategies. Their illocutionary force is milder than that of prohibitives—they sound more like a strong wish than a proper order, as in 13.37–8:

13.37 kap   akəs   da-k-na-ñən
alone NEG.IRR go.down-FUT-ACT.FOC-2fem.sgBAS.VT
'May you not go down alone (to the toilet at night)'

13.38 wa:l   sər   akəs   ja-k-na
rain tomorrow NEG.IRR fall-FUT-ACT.FOC+3fem.sgBAS.VT
'May it not rain tomorrow!'

To express a desire for something hardly attainable, the optative marker *-əu* is attached to the irrealis form. Such forms only occur in main clauses. Third person feminine marker preceding *-əu* is *-l*, just like with the optative discussed in §13.2.3. In 13.39, the speaker wished the frog could frighten her naughty daughter and keep her quiet for a few minutes:

13.39 kra kra kra wa-k-na-l-əu
kra kra kra say-FUT-ACT.FOC-3fem.sgBAS.VT-OPT
'(I wish) (the frog) could say kra kra kra'

Optative irrealis forms are negated with *akəs*, just like the irrealis forms in 13.35–6. In 13.40, Mali wished that it should not rain on us when we go to Swakap, notwithstanding black clouds gathering on the horizon:

13.40 wa:l <u>akəs</u>   <u>ja-k-na-l-əu</u>
          rain NEG.IRR fall-FUT-ACT.FOC-3fem.sgBAS.VT-OPT
          'I wish it did not rain!'

The difference in meaning between 13.38 and 13.40 is subtle: the desire in 13.40 is likely to be less attainable than that in 13.38. This agrees with general overtones of the optative marker in Manambu.

13.4   PURPOSIVE

The purposive modality is used in main and in dependent clauses to express intention and purpose. It distinguishes same-subject (§13.4.1) and different-subject forms (§13.4.1). Same-subject forms are uninflected verbs, and different-subject forms are partially inflected. This accords with the general principle operating throughout the language: that same-subject verbs are not marked for subject, and different-subject verbs are (see Table 11.1, and Chapter 18). In §13.4.3, we compare the 'same-subject' and 'different-subject' purposive in terms of how they are used.

13.4.1   Same-subject purposive

The same-subject purposive is marked with suffix -*(V)k*. This form is homonymous with the completive different subject sequencing suffix -*k* (§18.3). However, the latter is partially inflected, and never occurs in independent clauses. An etymological connection of the two markers with the dative case -*Vk* is tenuous.

We can recall, from §2.4.2 and Table 2.4, that the same-subject purposive suffix is sensitive to the syllable weight of the verb root. With a light root, it is formed by root reduplication and the suffix -*a:k*, while heavy roots take the suffix -*ək*, e.g. same-subject purposive *ya-ya:k*; another example of a monosyllabic verb is at 13.45. If the resulting form is monosyllabic, the vowel is lengthened, as in *bla-* 'speak', *bla:k*. If the suffix attaches to a root ending in *u*, the sequence of -*u-(V)k* can be pronounced either as -*uk* or as -*wək* (as in *waku-* 'go out', *wakuk*, *wakwək* in 13.43). The positive same-subject purposive forms of monosyllabic verbs are ambiguous with dative-aversive-marked nominalization (§9.1.1 and §13.7). However, they are negated differently (see §14.3).

The same-subject purposive in a main clause indicates that the subject (A/S) of the purposive is the same as the speaker, as in 13.41:

13.41 wun <u>warya-k</u>
          I   fight-PURP.SS
          'I am going to fight'

Same-subject purposive can be used to refer to the intentions of the addressee, as in 13.42:

13.42 wuk   <u>janə-k</u>
          tooth wash-PURP.SS
          'Are you going to brush your teeth?'

Same-subject purposive with third person implies that the intended action has not been caused by any external agent—that is, the person intends to act of their own free will. In 13.43 the mother provides an explanation for the baby's tears:

13.43 babay   waku-na,   kukə-b   wakwək
maternal.grandparent go.out-ACT.FOC+3fem.sgBAS.VT after-TERM go.out+DAT/PURP
'Granny (mother's mother) is going out, she (the baby) is intending to (go) after (her)'
(but I am not letting her, and so she is crying)

To head a dependent clause other than a purpose complement (discussed further on in this section), the same-subject purposive has to be used as copula complement of the copula *tə-* — this is typical for an uninflected verb:

13.44 [awa:y   væki:k   tə-d-ə]   ña:l
mother's.brother go.across+PURP.SS be/have-3masc.sgBAS.VT-LK day+3fem.sgNOM
'It is the day when uncle was going to go off'

It is also used in a series of main clauses if there is no change in subject, as in 7.71.

Same-subject purposive marks a purpose complement of any verb if this is semantically appropriate. It then indicates that the subject of the matrix verb and that of the purpose-marked verb are identical. This is shown in 7.76 and 19.43–4.

Same-subject purposive can also be used as a complementation strategy with the verb 'say' if the subject of the verb expressing purpose is coreferential with the subject of 'say', as in 19.57 (see further examples in §19.5.4; and §19.8).

We will see, in §13.4.2, that different-subject purposive is used in the only clear type of indirect speech report in Manambu—indirect commands. However, in generic statements containing indirect commands, if the reporter is involved in the required activity, the same-subject purposive is used, as in 13.45.

13.45 [kə-də   vækər-d-ə   mi jija:k]
DEM.PROX-masc.sg fall-3masc.sgBAS.VT-LK tree tie+PURP.SS
wa-na
say-ACT.FOC+3fem.sgBAS.VT
'She told (us, including the speaker) to tie this long reclining piece of wood'

Same-subject purposive also occurs as part of complex predicate expressing an imminent action—see §17.1.2 and examples there.

Same-subject purposive is used in main and in dependent clauses, and also as part of complex predicates, with similar frequency. Synchronically, one can argue that the same-subject purposive in dependent clauses, and the purposive in main clauses, are different homophonous forms, for three reasons:

- First, the same-subject purposive in dependent clauses and the uninflected purposive in main clauses are semantically different: there is no same-subject requirement in main clauses, and the purposive in dependent clauses does not have any special implications concerning the agency of the intended action (as does the purposive in independent clauses in 13.43).
- Secondly, they are also syntactically different: the uninflected purposive can occur as copula complement (as in 13.44), and there are no such options for the same-subject purposive complement.
- And thirdly, the main clause purposive verb does not have any 'same-subject' constraint.

Diachronically, the purposive in dependent clauses is undoubtedly the source for both forms. We hypothesize that the erstwhile subordinate same-subject purposive clause has acquired the status of main clause through regular ellipsis of the main clause, in the spirit of a process described at length by Blake (1993, 1999) and Dixon (2002a) for Australian languages; see also Dixon (1972: 68, 145) for the purposive *-ɲgul/-li* in Dyirbal in dependent and in main clauses.

The process of desubordination is clearly at work in other areas of Manambu grammar (see §19.9). We will see in §13.7 that at least some instances of modal uses of dative-aversive case-marked nominalizations also involve desubordination.

13.4.2   Different-subject purposive

Different-subject purposive is a partially inflected form. It is marked with a non-tensed subject marker (Table 11.2) followed by the suffix *-kək* or *-kəkək*, whose choice depends on the syllable weight of the root (see §2.4.2 and Table 2.4). The allomorph *-kəkək* is used with light monosyllabic verb stems of CV structure, e.g. *və-tu-kəkək* (see-1sg-PURP.DS) 'for me to see, so that I see', *wa-mən-kəkək* (say-2masc.sg-PURP.DS) 'for you (man) to say, so that you say' (also see 15.114b). This allomorph is occasionally pronounced as *-kərkək* by innovative speakers who avoid a sequence of two adjacent *kə* syllables by inserting a rhotic at the end of the first one (see A3 in §2.6).

The other allomorph, *-kək*, appears with heavy roots, e.g. *waku-tu-kək* (go.out-1sg-PURP.DS) 'for me to go out, so that I go out', *kur-tu-kək* (do/get-1sg-PURP.DS) 'for me to get, so that I get', and also in compound verbs, e.g. *rə-yi-tu-kək* (sit-go-1sg-PURP.DS) 'for me to keep sitting, so that I keep sitting'. As a result of tendency towards lenition of *k* in intervocalic position (see §2.1.1 and §2.6), *-kəkək* can be pronounced as *-kək* in rapid speech.

Different-subject purposive is most frequently used in non-main clauses, marking a purpose complement whose subject is different from that of the main clause, as in 13.46–7. The purposive verb can be preposed or postposed to the main clause (see §20.2, on constituent order).

13.46 ma:m   ada   kaw væ-yi-na-d
      elder.sibling DEM.DIST.REACT.TOP+masc.sg hole dig-go-ACT.FOC-3masc.sgBAS.VT
      <u>da-bər-kəkək</u>
      go.down-3du-PURP.DS
      'The elder sibling was digging a hole for them two to go down'

As shown in 13.47, the main clause and a purposive clause can share an object. Their subject is different. The object ('pig') belongs to both 'kill' and 'cut'.

13.47 wun alakum   waku-ku
      I   DEM.DIST+fem.sg+OUTWARDS+LOC go.out-COMPL.SS
      vya-tua   bal <u>ra-də-kəkək</u>
      kill-1sgSUBJ.VT+3fem.sgBAS.VT pig cut-3masc.sg-PURP.DS
      'I, having gone out across there in the direction away from the river, have killed a pig for him to cut'

The main clause can follow the purposive clause if the action of one clause has no temporal relationship with the other. Example 13.48 comes from Gemaj's account of how white men came to take a picture of her, and of the village, when she was a girl:

13.48 wi   aka   piksa   <u>kur-da-kək</u>
       house DEM.DIST.REACT.TOP.fem.sg picture do/get-3pl-PURP.DS
       tə-na
       be-ACT.FOC+3fem.sgBAS.VT
       'That house (topical) was there for them to take a picture'

Different-subject purposive marks the verb in indirect commands. This is the only clear type of indirect speech report in Manambu; as we will see in §19.5, other speech reports are either direct or semi-direct (also see Aikhenvald 2008). The different-subject purposive is used if the 'reporter' is not involved in the activity (otherwise the same-subject purposive is used: see 13.45). The person shift in the verb 'stay' shows that this is an example of indirect speech:

13.49 [galəb-a   takwa:k   a-di   ñan-ugw kurən   <u>kwa-da-kəkək</u>]
       childcare-LK woman+LK+DAT DEM.DIST-pl child-PL do/get+SEQ stay-3pl-PURP.DS
       wa-də-k
       say-3masc.sg-COMPL.DS
       'After he told the childcare women to stay taking care of those children (the parents went off to the lake)'

In 13.50, the subject of indirect command is first person:

13.50 [kui-lə-di   buk   kədika   ana:k
       give.to.third.p-3fem.sgSUBJ.P-3plBAS.P book DEM.PROX.REACT.TOP+pl 1du+LK+DAT
       <u>və-tə-kəkək</u>]   ata   wa:l
       see-1du-PURP.DS then say+3fem.sgBAS.P
       'She told us to see (i.e. read) these books she gave (us)'

A purposive clause as a complement of the verb *wa-* 'say' is the only way of forming a different-subject complement clause for the concept of 'wanting': we will see in §13.5 below that the desiderative—which is the major means of expressing the idea of wanting something—cannot imply anyone other than the speaker (also see §19.8).

13.51 də dəy-a:k   wa-də-di   <u>ya-da-kəkək</u>   də-kə-k
       he they-LK+DAT say-3masc.sgSUBJ.P-3plBAS.P come-3pl-PURP.DS he-OBL-DAT
       'He wanted them to come to him' (lit. he said for them to come to him)

Different-subject purposive clauses are used as complementation strategies with verbs of asking (see §19.8), as in 13.52.

13.52 Melbournar   <u>ya-mən-kəkək</u>   bas   mən-a:k
       Melbourne+LK+ALL come-2masc.sg-PURP.DS first you.masc-LK+DAT
       sə-na-bran
       plant-ACT.FOC-1duBAS.VT
       'We two are asking (lit. first planting) you to come to Melbourne'

Different-subject purposive can be used in main clauses whose subject is different from that of a preceding clause. This is in contrast to examples like 7.71 where the same-subject purposive is used to describe the intention of the same person as the one mentioned in the preceding text. In 13.53 the cassowary is asking about a participant who has just been mentioned as a different subject. The use of different subject is due to the change of speaker.

13.53 [tə-də-k]   [yi:n]   ya:kya [də agwa-japək   sa:l
stay-3masc.sg-COMPL.DS go+SEQ OK   he_i what-thing+LK+DAT be.short.of
yi-də-kəkək]
be/go-3masc.sg_i-PURP.DS
'After he'd stayed (like that), going on, this was OK. What is he going to be short of?
(asked the cassowary)'

Given that different-subject purposive retains a different subject meaning in examples like
13.53, we can assume that this use results from desubordination of erstwhile different-subject
clauses.

Alternatively, the different-subject purposive in a main clause may imply intention to do
something following the speaker's order, as in 13.54, and 19.10a:

13.54 ñən   təp-a:r   da-ñən-kəkək
you.fem village-LK+ALL go.down-2fem.sg-PURP.DS
'(I want) you to go down to the village'

When the order-giver is different from the speaker, it is explicitly stated and cast as an indirect
command, as in 13.55:

13.55 ñən   təp-a:r   da-ñən-kəkək   wa-na
you.fem village-LK+ALL go.down-2fem.sg-PURP.DS say-ACT.FOC+3fem.sgBAS.VT
'She tells you (or she wants you) to go down to the village'

We recall, from 13.43–4, that the same-subject purposive is used to express the speaker's
intention to do something of their own free will. That is, same-subject and different-subject
purposive thus show parallelism in their meanings in main clauses, and in subordinate clauses.

13.4.3   Same-subject and different-subject purposive: a comparison

Throughout this section, we saw that same-subject and different-subject purposive share a
number of properties. The two are marked with suffixes which could well be etymologically
related. They differ in form depending on the syllable weight of the root (Table 2.4).

In terms of their semantics, same-subject purposive and different-subject purposive parallel
each other. We will see, in §14.3, that they are negated somewhat differently. Different-subject
purposive is more often used in non-main clauses than the same-subject purposive. The process
of desubordination is likely to account for the uses of both same-subject and different-subject
purposive in main clauses.

The two forms differ in a number of ways. A different-subject purposive can only occur
in purposive complements, while same-subject purposive can occur in any dependent clause
as a copula complement (as illustrated at 13.44). Only the same-subject purposive takes part
in forming complex predicates (§17.1.2). This is a feature it shares with the desiderative -*kər*,
discussed in the next section.

13.5   DESIDERATIVE

Desiderative is an uninflected verb form marked with the suffix -*kər*. The major meaning of
desiderative in main clauses is the desire to perform an activity, as in 13.56.

13.56 ñən   yi-kər   dəyawa?
      you.fem go-DES they+LK+COM
      'Do you want to go with them?'

A similar example is at 11.9, said ironically by a woman; other examples are in T1.30, T2.12, and T3.45. A clause containing a direct speech report with a desiderative-marked verb is a conventional way of reporting other people's desires and intentions. An example is at 13.57—this was said about a 15-month-old child who could not yet talk:

13.57 di   yi-kər   wa-na
      shit go-DES   say-ACT.FOC+3fem.sgBAS.VT
      'She wants to shit' (lit. she says (I) want to shit)

In 13.58, from a letter, the same construction 'say Verb-desiderative' is used to refer to the wishes of a second person:

13.58 [təp-a:r   Apatəp-a:r   yi-kər   a
       village-LK+ALL Avatip-LK+ALL go-DES DEM.DIST+fem.sg
       wa-mənə-l]   [klay   August bap   məyir
       go-2masc.sgSUBJ.P-3fem.sgBAS.P   DEM.PROX+fem.sg+DIST August month really
       yi-kər   wa-ku]   wun-a:k   yabi:b   aw
       go-DES say-COMPL.SS   I-LK+DAT quickly IMPV+say
       '(Suppose) you want to go to Avatip (lit. you say go-desiderative), if you really want to go this (coming) August, tell me quickly'

Desiderative in a main clause with non-volitional predicates implies that something is to happen, as in 13.59–60. A purposive would be inappropriate in either of these instances, because—unlike desiderative—it implies controlled and volitional activity.

13.59 təb gəl   war-na   wa:l ja-kər
      sky blackness go.up-ACT.FOC+3fem.sgBAS.VT rain fall-DES
      'Sky is becoming black (lit. sky blackness is rising), it is about to rain'

13.60 ñə   nak tə-kər   aka   walba:b tə-na
      hour one stay-DES   then close stay-ACT.FOC+3fem.sgBAS.VT
      'It is almost one o'clock' (lit. it is almost staying going to become one o'clock)

Desiderative can be used to express purpose, as in 12.62 ('They (men) surrounded (the men's house) fully, looking-desiderative for women'), and in 13.61. The same-subject purposive would have been possible here, but with a difference in meaning: purposive implies definite intention very likely to succeed, while the desiderative indicates that there is no reason to believe that the intention will be successful. In both 12.62 and 13.61 the intended action had indeed failed: the villagers were unable to get sago because they were attacked. That is, desiderative may have slightly frustrative overtones.

13.61 dəy a-də   təp-a   du ta:kw nagw-ək   yi-kər aban
      they DEM.DIST-masc.sg village-LK man woman sago-LK+DAT go-DES arrangement
      taka-na-di
      put-ACT.FOC-3plBAS.VT
      'These people (lit. man woman) of that village made arrangements to go get sago'

Desiderative also occurs in complex predicates consisting of an inflected form of the verb *kur-* 'do, get' preceding the desiderative, with the meaning of impending intention. This is very similar to a complex predicate consisting of *kur-* and same-subject purposive, as in 17.15–16. The difference in meaning is consistent with the difference between the purposive and the desiderative: the woman's death in 17.16 is imminent and cannot be prevented; while the intended actions (of cats) in 13.62 can. Once again, the desiderative in a dependent clause implies that the intention is not bound to be realized. (Also see §17.1.2.)

13.62 [pusi kə-kər kur-da-lək]   væga-tua-di
cat   eat-DES do/get-3pl-BECAUSE put.inside.bag-1sgSUBJ.VT-3plBAS.VT
'Because cats might be about to eat (the foodstuffs) I put (the foodstuffs inside the basket)'

Just like the same-subject purposive, the desiderative can head a dependent clause; then it has to take the polyfunctional verb *tə-* as support verb, as is typical for any uninflected verb. Examples are at 13.63–4—semantically similar but not identical with 13.44. The speaker said 13.63 on Friday—this is an example of future projection, corroborated by the future and potential meaning of *nəbə* 'able, can' (see §4.5).

13.63 [fonde yi-kər tu-ku]   nəbə va:l   sa:n
Monday go-DES be-COMPL.SS able see+3fem.sgBAS.P money
'On Monday, after (you) are about to go, one can see about money'

This example has an overtone of indeterminacy to do with something that might, or might not, happen in the future. (The hesitation and indeterminacy is also characteristic of the attitude of the people to any mention of money: they do not mind accepting it as a present, but feel shy discussing anything to do with it.)

Example 13.64 was said to describe a picture from the same album as 13.44. The difference was that in 13.44 the uncle was shown as embarking on a canoe, while the picture described by 13.64 only showed us preparing for an impending trip.

13.64 [yi-kər tə-da-l]   ñə-a
go-DES be-3plSUBJ.P-3fem.sgBAS.P day-3fem.sgNOM
'This is the day they were about to go'

In summary, same-subject purposive implies controlled activity and intention which is bound to come to fruition. In contrast, the desiderative expresses non-controlled activities (such as time and weather) and activities which are desirable but may or may not take place.

A clause with a desiderative can be used as a complementation strategy, as in 13.65. This describes a prohibition on marrying women from the same clan as oneself:

13.65 [awarwa   ta:kw kra-kər] a   nəma   apaw
each.other woman take-DES DEM.DIST+fem.sg big.fem.sg old.fem.sg
va:l-a
taboo-3fem.sgNOM
'Wanting to marry each other's women is a big strong (lit. old) taboo'

The desiderative marker may, or may not, be related to the purposive. Its most likely cognate is the Iatmul marker *-kit*, which functions as an indirect object case on nouns and as a verbal purposive (Brugnowi dialect: Staalsen n.d.a).

13.6 FRUSTRATIVE

Frustrative indicates that the action was done to no avail—that is, the desired result was not achieved. Frustrative is an uninflected verb, but, unlike other uninflected verbs, frustrative makes a distinction between durative and non-durative action. Durative frustrative is marked with the suffix -*p* on the verb stem and repetition of the frustrative form. This indicates that the action which failed to achieve the result took place over a lengthy period of time—as in 13.66. The form can be repeated from two to five times, but hardly ever more than that. The more times the form is repeated, the lengthier the failed attempt is supposed to be. The repeated frustrative-marked verbs form one intonation unit, and no other constituent can intervene between them.

A clause containing a frustrative form is typically accompanied by another clause indicating either why the action failed, as in 13.66, or what was done after it failed, as in 13.67 and T3.31.

13.66 <u>lagu-p</u> <u>lagu-p</u> <u>lagu-p</u> suan yi-na
pull-FR pull-FR pull-FR difficult go-ACT.FOC+3fem.sgBAS.VT
'(He) pulled and pulled and pulled (the canoe out of mud) in vain, it was hard'

Like any uninflected verb, the durative frustrative can only occur in a dependent clause as a copula complement of *tə-*, as in 13.67 and T3.29. Then there is only one copula no matter how many times the durative frustrative form is repeated—this is an argument in favour of treating the durative frustrative as one predicate, and not as repetition of several predicates:

13.67 [də asa:y war-də-l wiya:r] [kapə-n <u>rə-p</u> <u>rə-p</u>
he father go.up-3masc.sgSUBJ.P-3fem.sgBAS.P house+LK+ALL wait-SEQ sit-FR sit-FR
<u>rə-p</u> <u>rə-p</u> tə-ku] [oh wa-ku] kəda
sit-FR sit-FR be-COMPL.SS oh say-COMPL.SS DEM.PROX.REACT.TOP+masc.sg
da:d
go.down+3masc.sgBAS.P
'The father went up into the house, having sat and sat and sat and sat waiting in vain, having said, "oh", he went down'

The non-durative frustrative is marked with -*yakəp*. This form contains no indication as to how long the frustrated attempt had lasted. The form is usually not repeated. We can recall, from §2.4.2, that -*yakəp* is syllable-weight sensitive. If a verb root has a CV(C)V, a CVC, or a CCV/CVC structure, the form of the marker is -*yakəp*, as in *kwakə-yakəp* (look.for-FR) 'look for in vain', *kayketə-yakəp* 'hold onto something in vain', *gra-yakəp* 'cry in vain'. If a verb consists of a CV, the frustrative suffix undergoes initial CVCV reduplication, as in *ya-yakə-yakəp* (come-RED-FR) 'come in vain', *və-yakə-yakəp* 'look in vain; be unable to see'. The verb *və-* 'see' is unusual in that it has an alternative non-durative frustrative form *və-kətakəp*—this is illustrated below. This alternative form fits in with the iambic stress pattern characteristic of weight-sensitive suffixes—see §2.4.2.

13.68 <u>və-yakə-yakəp</u> væ:n rə-da-l
see-RED-FR see+SEQ sit-3plSUBJ.P-3fem.sgBAS.P
'They looked in vain and sat looking'

13.69 <u>və-kətakəp</u> aka bə waku-na
see-FR DEM.DIST.REACT.TOP.fem.sg already go.out-ACT.FOC+3fem.sgBAS.VT
'She looked (to see where the husband was) in vain, and she has already gone out'

In 13.70, the frustrative of the verb 'say' refers to calling in vain—there was no answer. The action of calling and getting no answer is repeated in different clauses, to show that this was done twice.

13.70 ka:m   kədiya   bəta:y   nugu-tua-di,
      breadfruit DEM.PROX.REACT.TOP+pl already collect-1sgSUBJ.VT-3plBAS.VT
      wa-də-l,   wa-yakə-yakəp, wa-də-l
      say-3masc.sgSUBJ.P-3fem.sgBAS.P say-RED-FR   say-3masc.sgSUBJ.P-3fem.sgBAS.P
      wa-yakə-yakəp, ya:kia, ada   ga:m   san
      say-RED-FR   OK   DEM.DIST.REACT.TOP+masc.sg serenade plant+SEQ
      ada   kwa-na-d
      DEM.DIST.REACT.TOP+masc.sg stay-ACT.FOC-3masc.sgBAS.VT
      'He said to her, "I have already collected the breadfruit", he said in vain (there was no answer), he said to her, he said in vain, OK, he called, and he stayed that way'

If a verb contains -*ya* 'come' as the last syllable, the frustrative -*yakəp* is 'shortened' to -*kəp*, as in 13.71. Such haplology is unusual.

13.71 kwakə-yi-kwakə-ya-kəp   ma:, səbənə-n ya:d
      look.for-go-look.for-come-FR NEG   return-SEQ go/come+3masc.sgBAS.P
      'He looked for her this way and that way in vain, nothing, he went back'

Like any uninflected verb, a frustrative -*yakəp* can only be used in a dependent clause as a copula complement:

13.72 [a   wun-a:k   kwakə-yakəp tə-ku]   [wun-a-di ja:p   buti-ku]
      then I-LK+DAT look.for-FR be-COMPL.SS I-LK-pl   thing pack-COMPL.SS
      kaula-n   ata   yi-pakwu-di   dəy-a-di   japəwa
      enter-SEQ then go-hide-3plBAS.P they-LK-pl thing+LK+COM
      'Having looked for me in vain, having packed my things, by entering (inside the bush) they hid them together with their things'

The two frustrative markers may well be etymologically related: they share the formative -*p*. We can hypothesize that -*yakə*- in -*yakəp* could be related to -*yakə*- 'do fully' (see §15.3.1), and that -*kəta*- in *və-kətakəp* could be linked to -*kəta*- 'try', as in *kə-kəta* 'try eating'. However, these hypotheses require further substantiation.

Unlike the other modal forms discussed so far, neither of the frustratives can be negated.

13.7   NOMINALIZATIONS MARKED WITH DATIVE-AVERSIVE CASE

We saw in §9.1.1 (under II) that deverbal nominalizations marked with the dative-aversive case -*Vk* express a variety of modal meanings to do with future projection, unrealized wishes, weak probability, or events to be prevented from happening. When used in the predicate slot, these nominalizations behave like any uninflected verb; examples are at 13.73–5.

13.73 sər   dəy ya-ya:k
      tomorrow they come-RED+DAT
      'They would like to come tomorrow (but won't be able to)'

In 13.74, the first occurrence of dative-aversive-marked nominalization expresses a wish. This is a typical meaning of the dative-aversive case (see §7.4). The second occurrence of dative-aversive-marked nominalization is ambiguous: we recall, from §13.4.1, that these forms are used in lieu of same-subject purposives with monosyllabic verbs. This is why the form *kwakwak* (as in T3.40, third line, and 13.74) can be interpreted either as a dative-aversive nominalization, meaning 'might stay', or as same-subject purposive, meaning 'going to stay'. The ambiguity can be resolved by the context, and under negation (see §14.3).

13.74 [kə   karya-da   val   lagu-su-lagu-su-ək]
      DEM.PROX.fem.sg carry-3masc.sgSUBJ.VT+3fem.sgBAS.VT canoe pull-UP-RED-RED-DAT
      [wa-ku],   [da-brə-k],   [adəka
      say-COMPL.SS go.down-3du-COMPL.DS DEM.DIST.REACT.TOP+masc.sg
      wa-na-d],   [wun kwa-kwa:k   gur-awa]
      say-ACT.FOC-3masc.sgBAS.VT I   stay-RED+DAT you.pl-LK+COM
      'Having said "We might pull this canoe which he brought up onto the shore", they two came down, and he said: "I might/am going to stay with you"'

Dative-aversive case-marked nominalizations may express weak probability, both in questions and in statements. In 13.75, a grandmother is desperately looking for her two grandchildren, asking in every men's house in Avatip village:

13.75 wun-a-bər na: viti kə-l-ə-m   kwa-kwa:k?
      I-LK-3du grandchild two DEM.PROX-fem.sg-LK-LOC stay-RED+DAT
      'Are my two grandchildren perhaps here?'

After a younger sister refused point blank to let her estranged paternal uncle stay in her house, her brother asks her, without much hope:

13.76 [agwa ata wa-na-ñən-ək]   [a   jau
      what then say-ACT.FOC-2fem.sgBAS.VT-CONF DEM.DIST+fem.sg let.it.be
      nəkə-də   wiya:r   war-war-ək?]
      other-masc.sg house+LK+ALL go.up-RED-DAT
      'What are you saying then, let it be, (is he) to go to another house perhaps?'

Nominalizations are also used in rhetorical questions:

13.77 aw   kəta sə   kui-kui-k   eh?
      then now who give.to.third.p-RED-DAT eh?
      'Then now (after everything bad he did to us), who is going to give him (things), eh?'

Dative-aversive-marked nominalizations are used as clausal complements in contexts which would require the dative-aversive case on a noun phrase. These include verbs with a negative meaning, e.g. 'feel shame', as in 9.6, 'say no', or 'forbid, refuse', as in 9.5 and 13.78 (cf. also 10.35), 'forget', as in 13.79, 'be difficult', as in 9.9 and 13.80, and 'be unwilling' (lit. go for little), as in 13.81.

13.78 [mən   titiya:n   təta:k]   ma: wa-na
      you.masc walk.around+SEQ be+RED+DAT NEG say-ACT.FOC+3fem.sgBAS.VT
      'She forbids you to walk around' (lit. she says 'no' to you walking around)

As can be seen from examples such as 13.79–81, a dative-aversive-marked nominalization can precede or follow the main (inflected) verb.

13.79 kəp wukəmar-yake-tuə-l   buk   yapi-yapi-k
      just forget-FULLY-1sgSUBJ.P-3fem.sgBAS.P copy.book buy-RED-DAT
      'I just forgot to buy a copy-book'

13.80 su   <u>ku-su-ku-su-k</u>   suan   yi-na
      shoe put-UP-RED-UP-DAT difficult go-ACT.FOC+3fem.sgBAS.VT
      'It is hard (for her) to put shoes on'

13.81 kwasək   ya:d   yawi <u>kur-kur-ək</u>
      little+LK+DAT go+3masc.sgBAS.P work do/get-RED-DAT
      'He is unwilling to do the job' (lit. go for little to do work)

Dative-aversive case-marked nominalizations mark the second argument of the verb of fear (cf. also 9.7).

13.82 yaga-na-wun,   [a-də   wiya:r   <u>war-war-ək</u>]
      be.afraid-ACT.FOC-1fem.sgBAS.VT DEM.DIST-masc.sg house+LK+ALL go.up-RED-DAT
      'I am afraid of going up to that house'

This is a way of marking any clausal argument with an apprehensive meaning. In 13.83, it is a complement of the verb 'see':

13.83 nəkə-di   ta:kw   adiya   pakwu-n væ-n   tə-di
      other-pl woman DEM.DIST.REACT.TOP+pl hide-SEQ look-SEQ stay-3plBAS.P
      [day-a-di   du   <u>ya-ya:k</u>]
      they-LK-pl man come-RED+DAT
      'Other women were hidden looking secretly, lest their men might come'

In juxtaposition to another clause, a dative-aversive-marked nominalization may refer to something ominous and unpleasant—as in 13.84–5, and 9.8:

13.84 [wa:l væker-ga:y <u>vækər-vækər-ək</u>] [alək   val-a:m   rabə-taka-nak]
      rain   falls-IF   fall-RED-DAT   that's.why canoe-LK+ACC cover-put-1plIMPV
      'If it rains, in case it rains (lit. against raining), let's cover the canoe'

13.85 ma:y   waləb <u>tə-ta:k</u>   luku   kur-k-na-di
      garden close have-RED+DAT stealing do-IRR/FUT-ACT.FOC-3plBAS.VT
      'If one has a garden close (to the village), they might steal (vegetables from it)'

A dative-aversive nominalization on its own may have an apprehensive meaning, just like dative-aversive case forms (see §7.4):

13.86 <u>kiya-kiya-k</u>
      die-RED-DAT
      '(Do not go there) lest you die!'

The aversive use of dative-aversive-marked nominalizations in main clauses is another instance of desubordination of verb forms which are predominantly used in dependent clauses.

In all the cases discussed above, dative-aversive case-marked nominalizations occupy the second argument slot of a verb. They can also occupy the S slot of a non-verbal predicate with a negative meaning, as shown in 13.87. This sentence states a convention concerning men's road and women's road in Avatip. (A corresponding positive statement would require a ø-marked nominalization: see §9.1.1.) A noun phrase marked with dative-aversive case cannot be used this way. Examples like 13.87 offer an argument in favour of considering fully reduplicated verbs marked with the suffix -*k* as separate modal forms which are homonymous, rather than polysemous, with a dative-aversive (-*Vk*) case form of a deverbal action nominalization.

13.87 kəta-n-ab   [ñan-a-də   təp   ta:kw   du-a-yabər   yi-ya:k]
      now-PRED-TOO we-LK-masc.sg village woman man-LK-road+LK+ALL go-RED+DAT
      vyakət ma:
      good   NEG
      'Now, too, it is not good for a woman to go on a man's path in our village'

What I call dative-aversive-marked nominalizations are obligatorily used in an additional type of dependent conditional clause introduced by the adverb *kəpa:b* 'in case' (most probably, terminative case of *kəp* 'just'). The meaning of such clauses is 'in case VERB' as in 13.88. Unlike the examples above (especially 13.84–5), the verb does not have to have any negative connotations.

13.88 kusu-n   ap   kəpa:b   rəpə-rəp-ək
      wear-SEQ IMPV+see in.case be.enough-RED-DAT
      'Try it (dress) on, just in case it fits' or 'to see if it fits'

Such forms are identical to dative-aversive nominalizations. However, like any non-main clause forms they require a suffixed negator *-ma:r-*, albeit in a somewhat different form (see §14.3 and §14.5.1). The ways in which nominalizations are negated are discussed in §14.3.3. This is an argument in favour of the reduplicated verbs marked with *-k* in 'in case' clauses being special modal forms, homonymous with other, seemingly identical, forms.

13.8 SUMMARY

Manambu is rich in modal forms. The imperative mood has three person sub-paradigms which differ from each other in their form, function, and semantics. The optative modality can be formed on imperative, and on the irrealis.

The pervasive problem in distinguishing tenses and modalities in Manambu is that of polysemy versus homophony. We have already discussed similar problems with cases, and will return to the same problem in the lexicon, in Chapter 21. The irrealis forms are homophonous with future, and can only be formally distinguished under negation. Same-subject purposive is homophonous with dative-aversive case-marked nominalizations of light monosyllabic verbs; again, the two are negated differently.

Dative-aversive case-marked nominalizations are used in main clauses, and as clausal complements. Their lookalikes express condition in dependent clauses meaning 'in case (something happens)'—that these are different forms can only be seen in the ways they are negated.

The use of same- and different-subject purposives in main clauses involves the process of desubordination. The same process appears to be at work with dative-aversive case-marked nominalizations used in an apprehensive meaning, that is, as warnings.

The desiderative modality is relatively unproblematic in terms of its semantics. In contrast, frustrative offers a choice between durative and non-durative, absent from any other modality. Frustrative is the only modality which cannot be negated.

14

Negation

Manambu has a highly complicated system of negation. The choice of a negative form correlates with the tense, aspect, mood, and modality value of the clause, and with clause type. We saw above that negation is often the only means of distinguishing otherwise homophonous verb forms, and clause types.

14.1 NEGATION OF DECLARATIVE NON-HABITUAL CLAUSES

All declarative non-habitual clauses are negated with the negator *ma:*. Just as in positive clauses, verbal predicates differ from non-verbal predicates in what tense distinctions are expressed under negation (see §12.1). Negation of verbal predicates (including copulas) is discussed in §14.1.1. In §14.1.2 we look at how non-verbal predicates are negated.

The verbal negator *ma:* (variants: *ma:n, ma'an, ma'a*) has clausal scope, and is also used as a pro-clause meaning 'no'. The forms *ma:* and *ma'a* are in free variation; and so are *ma:n* and *ma'an* (see §2.1.2). The variants *ma:* and *ma:n* are in free distribution in most instances, with the variant *ma:n* found only with traditional and older speakers. The only noted difference between the two is discussed under §14.1.2 (example 14.15). Additional uses of the negator *ma:* are discussed in §14.6. See the discussion in §14.1.3.

14.1.1 Negation of verbal predicates

The general negator *ma:* negates a verbal predicate of a declarative non-habitual clause. All person, number, and gender distinctions are neutralized on the verb. We recall, from Chapters 11 and 12, that positive clauses distinguish the past and the versatile tense (which covers near future, present, and recent past), and also action focus and future. Of these, only future and non-future are expressed in non-habitual negative clauses. This is shown in Scheme 14.1.

In negative clauses, person cross-referencing suffixes which distinguish tense, and the action focus marker, are omitted. The non-future tense in negative clauses is expressed by preposing the negator to a special negative form. This form is often the same as the verb's root, as in *wali-* 'go round', *ma: wali* 'does not/did not go round'. About 50 per cent of verbs undergo vowel changes described in §11.3.2. These changes are only partially predictable, e.g. *gra-* 'cry', *ma: ga:r* 'does not/did not cry'; *gər-* 'scratch', *ma: ga:r* 'does not/did not scratch'; *kur-* 'do/get', *ma: kwa:r* 'does not/did not do/get'. The origin of these alternations requires further investigation.

Future tense in negative clauses is marked by postposing the negator *ma:* to the verb root, as in *gra ma:* 'will not cry', *kur ma:* 'will not work'. Neutralization of person, number, and gender in negative clauses is not unusual: similar examples can be found, for instance, in some Balto-Finnic languages (see Aikhenvald and Dixon 1998). That positive and negative clauses have different tense distinctions is rather unusual.

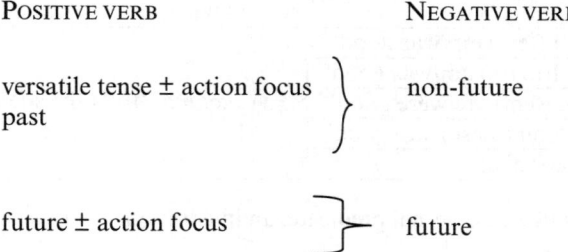

Positive verb — Negative verb

versatile tense ± action focus
past — non-future

future ± action focus — future

SCHEME 14.1   Verbal categories in positive and in negative declarative non-habitual verb

The complete involvement of S/O (§12.4) and confirmation marker (§12.5) are not compatible with negation.

Examples of a negative non-future are at 14.1–2 (also see 7.5, 7.8, 7.12a, 7.30, 7.57a, and T3.31). The past versus non-past reference can be disambiguated with a temporal adverb.

14.1 kəta <u>ma:</u> tə
now   NEG have/be.NEG
'Now this (custom) does not exist'

14.2 aw   də lə-kə-k   <u>ma:</u> səma:k   a   lə-kə
then he she-OBL-DAT NEG show.NEG DEM.DIST+fem.sg she-OBL+fem.sg
məd-a   səp
cassowary-LK skin
'Then he did not show her cassowary skin to her'

Non-future negative structures form two phonological and grammatical words. The negator and the verb do not have to be contiguous—see §14.1.3, on the types and functions of discontinuous non-future negatives.

Future negation is illustrated in 14.3–4; the future and the non-future negation of the same verb are contrasted in 14.3. (Further examples are at 7.15 and T3.43.) Unlike in non-future negation, no constituent can intervene between the verb and the negator. The two form one phonological word (they remain two grammatical words, and neither is a clitic), and this is why a linking ə is required in 14.3:

14.3 [ma: ra:p]   [rəpə   ma:]
NEG be.enough/fit.NEG be.enough/fit.NEG.FUT NEG
'It (the T-shirt) does not fit, it won't fit!'

14.4 [walimaudi-ad]   [wa:l ja   ma:]
rainbow-3masc.sgNOM rain fall.NEG NEG
'There is rainbow, there will be no rain'

Grammatical relations in negative clauses are marked in the same way as in positive clauses. If the referent of the subject is not clear from the context, it can be expressed with an overt NP, as in 7.5. The uninflected customary aspect (§12.7) can occur in negative clauses as a complement of the copula tə-. This is illustrated in 14.5.

14.5 yaki   kə-jəbər <u>ma:</u> tə
smoke eat-CUST NEG be.NEG
'One (or any other person) does not smoke (all the time)'

POSITIVE	NEGATIVE
vyakət-a-(l)wun 'I (fem) am/was good'	
vyakət-a-də-wun 'I(masc) am/was good'	
vyakət-a-ñən 'you (fem) are/were good'	*vyakət ma:* 'I/you/he/she etc. is/was not good'
vyakət-a-də-mən 'you (masc) are/were good'	
vyakət-a-d 'he is good' etc.	

SCHEME 14.2   Negation of a non-verbal predicate: an illustration

A verb marked with a derivational suffix *-rəb* 'fully' (§12.8.1) can occur in a negative clause only if accompanied by the negative form of the same root (see examples of such structures in positive polarity in 12.42–3). An example is at 14.6. One character is trying to convince another to cut off his wife's breast and put it into a yam soup to make it taste better, assuring him that:

14.6 [kiya-saki-ku]   [kwasa rə-ku]   [rapə-k-na]
      die-ACROSS-COMPL.SS little   stay-COMPL.SS stand.up-FUT-ACT.FOC+3fem.sgBAS.VT
      [kiya-rəb   kiya   ma:] kwasa kiya-k-na
      die-FULLY die   NEG little   die-FUT-ACT.FOC+3fem.sgBAS.VT
      'Having half-died, having stayed for a little while, she will get up, she won't fully die, she will die a little bit'

The verbal derivational suffix *-dəka* 'only' and the completive aspect (see §12.6) do not occur in negative clauses.

14.1.2   Negation of non-verbal predicates

Non-verbal predicates do not distinguish tenses or aspects characteristic of verbs. To negate a non-verbal predicate, the negator *ma:* is postposed to the non-verb stripped of nominal cross-referencing markers. Person, gender, and number distinctions are neutralized under negation—just as in negative forms of verbal predicates. A negated non-verbal predicate does not distinguish tense (just like its positive counterpart). And the negator can only occur postposed to the predicate head—this is unlike verbal negative structures where the position of the negator (and the form of the verb) distinguish non-future and future constructions. That is, postposition of the negator to the negated predicate has different meanings depending on whether we are dealing with a verb or with a non-verbal predicate head. Scheme 14.2 shows how all person, number, and gender distinctions are neutralized once a non-verbal predicate is negated.

Consider 14.7. In the negative structure, the head of predicate 'man' does not take any nominal cross-referencing markers, while in the positive structure it takes the nominal cross-referencing for third person singular masculine. The positive and the negative forms are underlined. Both the negative and the positive non-verbal predicates are tense neutral. Similar examples are at 10.2, 10.16, and 10.31.

14.7 [a-d   kə-də   təp-a-kə-də   du   ma:]
      DEM.DIST-masc.sg DEM.PROX-masc.sg village-LK-POSS-masc.sg man NEG
      [a-d   adaki   rə-na-d-ə
      DEM.DIST-masc.sg DEM.DIST+masc.sg+ACROSS sit-ACT.FOC-3masc.sgBAS.VT-LK
      nəbək   Turu wa-dana-d-ə   nəbək-əm
      mountain Turu call-3plBAS.VT-3masc.sgBAS.VT-LK mountain-LK+LOC

aləm rasə-ku vara-d-ə
DEM.DIST+fem.sg+LOC grow.up-COMPL.SS come.across-3masc.sgBAS.VT/P-LK
du-ad]
man-3masc.sgNOM
'That is (was, will be) not a man from this village; that is a man who had grown up across there, on the mountain called Turu, and had come across'

The same negative structure is used for negating existence of something, as in 14.8 and 10.58, or lack of possession, as in 8.20, 10.6, and 14.9.

14.8 nəkə sə <u>ma:</u>
other+fem.sg name NEG
'There is no other name (for this bird)'

14.9 bər yawi-kur-tami: <u>ma:</u>
you.two work-do-area NEG
'You have no area to do work'

An alternative to a non-verbal negative possessive structure is a negative version of a clause containing a positional verb *kwa-* 'stay', as in 7.8 ('there are no women like this (in) this village') and 7.30 ('I have no betelnut'). The implication is of negating 'living', or 'staying', or 'being on someone'—that is, implying a temporary lack of possession. This is in contrast to structures like the one in 14.9 which imply permanent lack of possession, or of existence.

Negative attributive verbless clauses have the same structure, as in 13.87, 14.7, and 14.10–12.

14.10 [kə mən-a ar <u>ma:</u>] [kə
DEM.PROX.fem.sg you.masc-LK+fem.sg lake NEG DEM.PROX+fem.sg
mən-a-də nagwə-ga:r <u>ma:</u>]
you.masc-LK-masc.sg sago+LK-field NEG
'This is not your lake, this is not your sago field'

We can recall, from §11.2, that when agreeing adjectives ('small' or 'big') or any other agreeing modifiers from closed classes occur in the predicate slot, they mark agreement with the subject. In positive clauses, this results in what can be seen as redundant double agreement in gender with the same constituent. In negative clauses the verbal cross-referencing is omitted so that only one agreement marker remains—see 14.11–12 (an example of a positive clause with 'double' agreement is at 11.7).

14.11 [ñən təp-a-kə-l <u>ma:</u>], [kwarəb-a-kə-l-añən]
you.fem village-LK-POSS-fem.sg NEG bush-LK-POSS-fem.sg-2fem.sgNOM
'You are not from a village, you are a bush-lady' (said the man to his cassowary-wife)

14.12 [mən kwasa-d <u>ma:</u>] [numa-d-adəmən]
you.masc.sg small-masc.sg NEG big-masc.sg-2masc.sgNOM
'You (man) are not small, you are big'

In 14.13, a reduplicated adjective *səmi* 'far' heads the negative attributive clause. The reduplicated form has the same meaning in a positive and in a negative clause. This is unlike reduplicated verbs—we will see in §14.3.3 that negating a reduplicated verb root results in a modal meaning.

14.13 kə təp səmi-səmi <u>ma:</u>
DEM.PROX.fem.sg village far-far NEG
'This village is not very far'

All non-verbal predicates are negated in the same way, no matter whether they take nominal cross-referencing or not in positive polarity. The predicate marker is obligatory with manner demonstratives—which do not take nominal cross-referencing—when they appear in the predicate slot of a positive clause (see §10.2.2); it is omitted from negative clauses:

14.14 akətawa ma:
      like.this NEG
      'It is not like this'

Different types of verbless clauses with non-verbal forms as predicate heads are neutralized under negation (see §20.1.3 on clause types). This agrees with the spirit of dependencies between grammatical systems: we expect fewer distinctions in negative clauses than in corresponding positive clauses.

   The variant *ma:n* of the general negator appears to be required under one condition: if a negated clause with a non-verbal predicate is in highlighting focus and the predicate takes nominal cross-referencing. (It is possible that *ma:n* is morphologically complex and consists of *ma:* followed by the predicative marker *-n*.) This is illustrated with 14.15, from a story about a grandmother desperately looking for her grandchildren who were nowhere to be found.

14.15 [kə-lə-m   ma:n-a]   [kə-lə-m   ma:n-a]
      DEM.PROX-fem.sg-LOC NEG-3fem.sgNOM DEM.PROX-fem.sg-LOC NEG-3fem.sgNOM
      'It is the case that they were not here, they were not there'

This construction has only occurred in one traditional story. I recorded it three times, with different speakers. Each stretch in square brackets in 14.15 was pronounced as one word, and repeated twice with a fixed singing intonation. I suspect that focusing clauses with non-verbal negative predicates is not a productive process, and that 14.15 is a one-off, archaic structure. We will see, in §14.5, that focus structures in negative clauses with verbal predicates involve dependent negation.

   Tense, or aspect, can be expressed in a negative clause headed by a non-verb. The non-verbal form has to be used as the complement of the copula *tə-* 'be' (this form retains its root form *tə* when negated). In 14.16, the speaker says that she was not a big girl when the Second World War came. The non-verbal component, 'big girl', is a copula complement of *tə-* which forms a non-future negative construction:

14.16 [wun a   ñə   numa   ñan ma: tə],   [war
      I   DEM.DIST.fem.sg time/sun big.fem.sg child NEG be.NEG war
      ya-də-l]]
      come-3masc.sgSUBJ.P-3fem.sgBAS.P
      'At that time I was not a big girl, (time when) the war came'

   In 14.17, a negated copula clause with the adjective *kuprap* 'bad' as the copula complement forms a future negative construction:

14.17 kamna:gw kuprap tə   ma:
      food   bad   be.NEG NEG
      'Food won't be (or become) bad'

   A similar example is in T3.43. Copula constructions with the copula *tə-* and an adjective as copula complements are ambiguous: they may mean either 'be ADJECTIVE' or 'become ADJECTIVE'; this ambiguity is resolved only through context. For instance, while in 14.17 either reading is acceptable, in 14.18 only the 'be' reading makes sense: the speaker was trying to persuade her mother to let her go and work in Australia, telling her that Australia is not all that far away.

14.18 [wun-a   amæy] [ata ma:] [wukə-tukwa]   [ata wa-tuə-l]
      I-LK+fem.sg mother then again worry-PROH.GEN then say-1sgSUBJ.P-3fem.sgBAS.P
      [səmi tə   ma:]
      far stay.NEG NEG
      ' "My mother", (I said) then again, "don't worry", then I said, "it is not far away" '

To be used in a negative dependent clause, a non-verbal predicate has to be transformed into a copula complement of the same copula *tə-*, which is marked with a dependent clause negator, as shown in 14.19. We return to the negation of dependent clauses in §14.5.

14.19 [na:gw tə-ma:r-lə-k]   nagwək   aka
      sago   be-NEG.SUB-3fem.sg-COMPL.DS sago+LK+DAT DEM.DIST.REACT.TOP.fem.sg
      yi-na-wun
      go-ACT.FOC-1fem.sgBAS.VT
      'If/after there is no sago, I am going to go and fetch sago'

We will see, in §14.1.3, that there is a certain amount of freedom in word order within non-future negative constructions, including those involving copulas.

14.1.3   Contiguity in non-future negative constructions, and the scope of negation

In future negative constructions, the verb and the negator are always contiguous, and form one phonological word. In non-future negative constructions, contiguity is not required. Then the order of the negator and the verb cannot be reversed: the negator has to precede the negative verb.

The only form which obligatorily intervenes between the negator and the negated verb is the adverb *nəbay* 'yet, already', as in 14.20. Any other order is ungrammatical (see 14.20a).

14.20 də ma: nəbay yæy
      he NEG yet   come.NEG
      'He has not come yet'

14.20a?? *də nəbay ma: yæy
      he yet   NEG come.NEG
      'He has not come yet'—???

The following types of constituents may intervene between the negator and the negative verb form. The effect is focusing on the intervening constituent. As mentioned in §20.3, individual constituents hardly ever occur in highlighting focus in negative constructions. Changing their position in a clause is one way of focusing them.

1. The adjective *yara* 'well, fine' used adverbially can intervene between the negator and the negated verb, as in 14.21a where 'well' is in focus.

14.21a wun ma: yara la:kw
       I   NEG well know.NEG
       'I do not know (this) well (contrary to what you may expect)'

In 14.21b, 'well' is not in focus:

14.21b wun yara <u>ma:</u> <u>la:kw</u>
      I   well NEG know.NEG
      'I do not know (this) well'

2. The object can intervene between the negator and the negated verb, as in 14.22–3, with the object in highlighting focus:

14.22 man-ta:b <u>ma:</u> ap   tə
      foot-hand NEG bone/force have.NEG
      '(His) hands and feet had no strength'

14.23 kəta wun ma: brə-kə-m   wukəmar
      now I   NEG 3du-OBL-ACC forget.NEG
      'Now I haven't forgotten these two (white people) (despite the fact that we lost touch)'

3. The copula complement can intervene between the negator and the negated verb. In 14.24, the narrator stresses that people and *apawul* spirits are not friendly because of a number of misunderstandings—in contrast, they fear each other:

14.24 alək   ñan-awa   <u>ma:</u> kapawi tə
      this.is.why we-LK+COM NEG friend be.NEG
      'This is why (they) are not friends with us (they are scared of us)

4. The subject can intervene between the negator and the verb. An example of the A of *tə-* 'have' is at 14.25—this is what a speaker said about her siblings:

14.25 takwa-dəka   du-a-ma:gw   <u>ma:</u> ñan tə
      woman+LK-ONLY man-LK-'thing' NEG we have.NEG
      '(We are) just women, we (in contrast to others) do not have brothers'

In 14.26, *gu* 'water', in the S function, intervenes between the negator and the verb:

14.26 <u>ma:</u> gu   rə
      NEG water sit.NEG
      'There was no water (in contrast to what was expected)'

5. An oblique in a locative, or an allative case, can intervene between the negator and the verb, as in 14.27–8, and T3.14:

14.27 [yæj   kə-na-wur   tənəb-a:m   rə-na]
      frying.pan DEM.PROX-CURR.REL-up fireplace-LK+LOC sit-ACT.FOC+3fem.sgBAS.VT
      [<u>ma:</u> wiya:m   rə]
      NEG house+LK+LOC sit.NEG
      'The frying pan is up there (in previously mentioned location) on the fireplace, it was sitting in the house (contrary to what the character expected)'

14.28 <u>ma:</u> ña:r   krakw
      NEG sun+LK+ALL take+OUTSIDE
      '(The two brothers) did not take (their new sister) out into the sun' (contrary to what would be expected)

6. A part of complex predicate marked with the sequential *-n* (see §17.1.1 and §16.2.3) can intervene between the negator and a posture verb, as a means of focusing on the lexical verb:

14.29 ñan [Malu kwa-na   nagwəm]   ma: væn   rə
      we   Malu stay-ACT.FOC+3fem.sgBAS.VT sago+LK+ACC NEG see+SEQ sit+NEG
      'We did not sit watching the sago that was staying at the Malu village'

Examples like 14.21–9 are common to all generations of speakers of all levels of proficiency.
In most such cases, the intervening word does not exceed two syllables. An exception is at
14.24—but note that it comes from a story by an elderly man who was trying his best to be as
elaborate as possible.

Only highly elaborate speakers allow a whole clause to intervene between the negator and
the verb. Examples are at 14.30 and 14.31.

14.30 a-də   a:s ma: [ya:n   brə-kə-k   ma:k] ta:k
      DEM.DIST-masc.sg dog NEG come+SEQ 3du-OBL-DAT face put.NEG
      'That dog did not show his face by coming to them two' (contrary to what they expected)

In 14.31, two constituents intervene between the negator and the negated verb—the adverb
nəbay (for which this is the only possible position) is placed close to the negator, and followed
by a dependent clause 'like I stay'. The spirit of a dead woman refuses to give her living husband
the food she eats in the world of the dead:

14.31 mən-a:k   kə-di   kami: a-di   kwa:y kwatiya   ma:,
      2masc.sg-LK+DAT DEM.PROX-pl fish DEM.DIST-pl shrimp give.to.nonthird.p NEG
      mən   [ma: nəbay [wun kwa-tua-pək]   ku]
      you.masc NEG yet I   stay-1sgSUBJ.VT+3fem.sgBAS.VT-LIKE stay.NEG
      'I won't give you these fish, those shrimp, you are not yet in the same state as I am
      (contrary to what you may think)'

There is an intonation break between *ma: nəbay* 'not yet' and the rest. This is not surprising:
ma: nəbay behaves like a fixed expression.

If a multiword complex predicate consists of an inflected auxiliary and an uninflected part
(see Chapter 17), the uninflected part of the complex predicate intervenes between the negator
and the inflected part. This is shown in 14.32.

14.32 də væy ma: warya-n   tə
      he spear NEG quarrel/fight-SEQ have+NEG
      'He hadn't fought with spear'

To focus the uninflected part of the complex predicate, this has to be preposed to the negator.
Note that the uninflected part of the complex predicate cannot follow the negative form of the
auxiliary—this is in contrast to uninflected verbs which are not part of complex predicates
(§17.1–2). In 14.33, the speaker focuses on the fact that she had never ever *seen* European-type
long hair (she had heard of this, but this was her first-time visual experience):

14.33 wun tala:b væ-n ma: tə   nab [ñən-a
      I   before see-SEQ NEG have.NEG hair you.fem-3fem.sgNOM
      tə-na-pək]
      have-ACT.FOC+3fem.sgBAS.VT-LIKE
      'I have never before seen hair like you have'

Complex predicates consisting of a nominal and a verb are negated just like other complex
predicates in 14.32: the whole complex predicate follows the negator, as in 14.34–5:

14.34 wun <u>ma:</u> səkulək yə
      I   NEG cooking do/go
      'I didn't do the cooking'

14.35 wun kə   təpa:m   <u>ma:</u> jəbə   kwa:r
      I   DEM.PROX village+LK+LOC NEG image do/get+NEG
      'I didn't learn to write (lit. get image) in this village'

The position of negator and the effect of reversing the order of the nominal, or the dependent-marked verb, and the negated verb help differentiate superficially similar complex verbs containing auxiliaries (as in 14.33–5) and sequencing structures (as in 14.29).

In none of the examples discussed above does the change in the position of the negator affect the scope: the negator consistently has the whole clause within its scope. There is just one exception. The adverb *məyir* appears to be unique in that the scope of negation differs depending on its position in a clause. In 14.36, *məyir* 'really' precedes the negator, and the verb is within the scope of negation.

14.36 a-di   ma:j nəkə-di du-ta:kw   məyir <u>ma:</u> la:kw
      DEM.DIST-pl story other-pl man-woman really NEG know.NEG
      'Other people really do not know those stories'

In 14.37, this same adverb intervenes between the negator and the verb. Either the verb or the adverb can be understood as being within the negator's scope. The ambiguity is resolved by context.

14.37 a-di   ma:j nəkə-di du-ta:kw   <u>ma:</u> məyir la:kw
      DEM.DIST-pl story other-pl man-woman NEG really know.NEG
      'Other people do not really know those stories' or 'Other people really do not know those stories'

Manambu has no negative pronouns. The numeral 'one' in its indefinite meaning is used in negative clauses, meaning 'not one', as in 12.7 (*nak-a:bə ma: yə* (one-TOO NEG go) 'not one escapes'), and T3.14 where the form *nakaməy* 'single one (feminine)' is used.

If a constituent other than the predicate is to be negated, it has to form an independent non-verbal clause negated by *ma:*. To say 'not only in Avatip' one literally says 'only in Avatip—no', as in 14.38. The non-verbal negative clause is in square brackets.

14.38 nəbəl wun-a-də   təp-a:m   Apatəp-a:m   [wun-a-də   təp-a-dəka
      today I-LK-masc.sg village-LK+LOC Avatip-LK+LOC [I-LK-masc.sg village-LK-ONLY
      ma:] [[ñan təp   mugul a:li manab   təp-a-kə-di]   titiya-n
      NEG] [[we   village three four Manambu village-LK-OBL-pl go.round-SEQ
      tə-kwa-bana-di]   ya:b yal-a-təp-a:m
      stay-HAB-1plSUBJ.VT-3plBAS.VT road inside-LK-village-LK+LOC
      kwa-na-bər   ya:b-abər
      stay-ACT.FOC-3duBAS.VT road-3plNOM
      'Now in my village, Avatip, not only in my village, (lit. only in my village—no), in our three or four Manambu villages, there are two roads by which we keep going round'

A negative non-verbal clause can occupy the same position as a noun phrase. For instance, the word for 'bald' is *nab ma: tə-* (hair NEG have). How this term was used is shown in 14.39 (an example of the argument elaboration construction: §6.2.3). That *ma:* 'negator' forms one constituent with *nab* 'hair' and not with the verb *tə-* 'have' is evident from the form of the verb: it is inflected as a positive, and not as a negative verb. A negative form of *tə-* is shown in 14.40—this sentence was used to describe a girl who is not bald, but whose hair had been shaved because of lice. (Constituency is indicated with square brackets.)

14.39 [an   Bob wukən] [nab ma:] tə-na-bran
      we.two Bob together hair NEG   have-ACT.FOC-1duBAS.VT
      'We two, Bob and I, are bald' (lit. we have there-is-no hair)

14.40 nab [ma: tə]
      hair NEG have.NEG
      'She has no hair'

Negating one constituent as a separate non-verbal clause produces the effect of strong contrast. One sister is saying to the other: 'We two will eat that sago with coconut', and the younger sister replies 14.41:

14.41 ka!   təp-a:wa   ma:, bal-awa
      DEM.PROX+3fem.sgNOM coconut-LK+COM NEG   pig-LK+COM
      kə-kə-ta
      eat-FUT-1duSUBJ.VT+3fem.sgBAS.VT
      ' "That? (meaning: no way!), not with coconut, we will eat (sago) with pork!" '

A similar example is at 10.145 ('few, not many, few people went down (river)').

As we will see in §14.6, the negator *ma:*—unlike any other negator—can be used as a complement of the verb *wa-* 'say' with the meaning of 'forbid, negate, refuse'. This is illustrated in 9.5, 13.78, and 14.42. In such constructions the verb *wa-* remains inflected as required. The second occurrence of 'say no' is negated in the last line of 14.42.

14.42 alaku   [ma: wa-k-na-bər],   wun-a:k
      DEM.DIST+fem.sg+OUTWARDS NEG say-FUT-ACT.FOC-3duBAS.VT I-LK+DAT
      jama-jama-k   ma: awakw   bər   [[ma:] wa] ma:!
      get.fire-RED-DAT no, IMPV+go.out they.two NEG   say.NEG NEG
      ' "Across there they will refuse (say no) to me getting fire." "No, go out, they won't refuse" '

This example also illustrates another usage of *ma:*—that of a general negative pro-clause. We return to this in §14.6. Inherently negative lexemes (see §14.6) co-occur with clausal negator *ma:*. They do not have the same scope effects as does *ma:*. Neither do other negators.

14.2 NEGATION OF HABITUAL CLAUSES

Habitual clauses (which require the verb in habitual aspect marked with the suffix *-kwa-* 'present', *-yikwa-* 'past': see §12.3) are negated with the negator *akəs* which occurs with the verb in habitual aspect (marked with the suffix *-kwa-*). Unlike the general negator, *akəs* co-occurs with fully inflected verbs, as in 14.43–4, 10.5, and 10.60. The negative habitual refers to what is typically not done.

14.43 ñən   akəs   kə-kusə-kwa-na-ñən
      you.fem NEG.HAB   eat-finish-HAB-ACT.FOC-2fem.sgBAS.VT
      'You never eat (things) up'

The copula *tə-* is obligatorily used to express a habitual non-occurrence involving a non-verbal predicate head:

14.44 yabi:b   <u>akəs</u>   kuprap   <u>tə-kwa-na-di</u>
       quickly NEG.HAB bad   stay-HAB-ACT.FOC-3plBAS.VT
       'They do not become bad quickly'

We can recall, from §4.2.2, that the verb *kui-* 'give to third person' is quite unusual in that it has two alternative forms of the negative habitual. Unlike other verbs in the language, it does not have to take the suffix *-yikwa-* 'past habitual' in the past negative form. Two options are thus available for 'give' in past habitual; there is no semantic difference between the two. The regular form, *kui-kwa-* '(not) give habitually', is shown in 4.37 and 14.45:

14.45 <u>akəs</u>   kui-yikwa-l   də-kə   ta:kw
       NEG.HAB give.to.third.p-HAB.PAST-3fem.sgBAS.P he-OBL+fem.sg wife
       'She never used to give (them food), his wife'

The alternative non-habitual declarative form, *kui-*, with the habitual negator *akəs*, is shown in 4.38 and 14.46. Within the same story, 14.45 and 14.46 follow each other.

14.46 ñaj   ta:kw kuprap-al   <u>akəs</u>   kui-d
       paternal.uncle wife   bad-3fem.sgNOM NEG.HAB give.to.third.p-3masc.sgBAS.P
       'Paternal uncle's wife was bad, she never gave (children food)'

A negative construction containing the negator *akəs* and an inflected verb forms two grammatical and two phonological words. A habitual negative construction with *akəs* does not have to be contiguous. In 9.21 the copula complement precedes the construction of *akəs* followed by an inflected verb, and in 14.44 the copula complement is positioned between the negator and the inflected verb. The effect of inserting a constituent between *akəs* and the inflected verb is essentially the same as that in constructions with the non-future negative structures involving the declarative non-habitual negator *ma:* (see §14.1.3 above): the inserted constituent is in highlighting focus.

In fact, any constituent, except for subject or object, can intervene between *akəs* and the inflected verb. In 14.47 *gus* 'paddle' is part of a complex predicate involving a typical instrument (see §7.2).

14.47 wun <u>akəs</u>   gus   <u>ka-kwa-na-wun</u>
       I   NEG.HAB paddle paddle/row-HAB-ACT.FOC-1fem.sgBAS.VT
       'I never paddle'

In 14.48, a series of dependent clauses intervenes between the negator and the inflected verb: these clauses contain information which is contrary to what is expected of the river-dwellers:

14.48 aday   a   yabwiyim
       DEM.DIST+masc.sg+DIST DEM.DIST.fem.sg soft.wood.tree+LOC
       rə-na-də   gawi   ñan alək   yaga-ta:y,
       sit-ACT.FOC-3masc.sgBAS.VT white.breasted.eagle we   this.is.why be.afraid-COTEMP
       kami: <u>akəs</u>   kur-ən   kə-kwa-na-dian   <u>akəs</u>   gu   waku-n
       fish   NEG.HAB get-SEQ eat-HAB-ACT.FOC-1plBAS.VT NEG.HAB water go.out-SEQ
       ara:m   yata-n   <u>yaku-kwa-na-dian</u>
       lake+LK+LOC carry-SEQ wash-HAB-ACT.FOC-1plBAS.VT
       'This is why being afraid of the white-breasted eagle over there sitting on that soft wood tree we never get fish and eat it, never wash going out to the lake and carrying (things)'

In contrast to *ma:* 'declarative non-habitual negator', the habitual negator *akəs* does not occur with *nəbay* 'yet'. An anterior complex predicate involving the habitual form copula *tə-* and a sequential form of a verb is preceded by *akəs* as shown in 14.49 (a non-habitual negated anterior complex predicate is at 14.32). Any alternative ordering of *akəs* and the inflected verb in such structures appears contrived.

14.49 *antibiotic* <u>akəs</u>   kur-ən   <u>tə-kwa-na-wun</u>
      antibiotic NEG.HAB do/get-SEQ have-HAB-ACT.FOC-1sgBAS.VT
      'I have never been taking antibiotics'

The negators *ma:* and *akəs* share some similarities in terms of contiguity in negative constructions; but are not identical in their properties. Unlike *ma:*, the negator *akəs* is not used to negate non-verbs on their own—that is, without a copula (see 14.44). Consequently, it is not used to negate a nominal constituent in the way *ma:* is employed (see 14.41). Neither is it used as a complement of the verb *wa-* 'say'. The negator *akəs* can be used elliptically, meaning 'never': in its second occurrence in 14.50, 'never' is an elliptic clause recapitulating the previous clause:

14.50 [lə ñan-a-kə   kwa:s <u>akəs</u>   <u>yakə-sada-kwa-na-bər</u>]
      she we-LK-POSS+fem.sg salt   NEG.HAB throw-DOWN-HAB-ACT.FOC-3duBAS.VT
      [<u>akəs</u>], [sama:b <u>akəs</u>   <u>yakə-sada-kwa-na-bər</u>]
      NEG.HAB no.way NEG.HAB throw-DOWN-HAB-ACT.FOC-3duBAS.VT
      'This salt of ours they would never throw (into their food), never, never ever would they throw (salt in their food)'

The general non-habitual negator *ma:* and the habitual negator *akəs* are both used as proclauses in elliptical replies—see 14.51 and 14.42.

14.51 <u>ñən</u>   yaki   <u>kə-kwa-na-ñən?</u>   <u>akəs</u>
      you.fem smoke eat-HAB-ACT.FOC-2fem.sgBAS.VT NEG.HAB
      ' "Do you usually smoke?" "Never!" '

Further similarities and differences between *ma:* and *akəs* are addressed in §14.6.

The same negator, *akəs*, is used to negate irrealis in main clauses, and in counterfactual conditional clauses, and to negate the optative mood—this is the topic of the next section.

14.3 NEGATION OF NON-INDICATIVE MODALITIES

All of the non-indicative modalities discussed in Chapter 13 can be negated, with the exception of the frustrative. Irrealis and optative, on the one hand, and same-subject purposive and desiderative, on the other, are negated in the same way (§§14.3.1–2). Different-subject purposive is negated in the same way as any verbal predicate in a non-main clause—see §14.3.2 and §14.5. The negation of nominalizations as predicate heads is addressed in §14.3.3.

14.3.1 Negation of irrealis and optative

We mentioned in §13.3 and in §12.2 that future and irrealis modality (both marked with the suffix *-kə-*) are formally distinguished by the way in which they are negated. While the negative future consists of a verb root followed by the negator *ma:* (see §14.1.1), the negative irrealis is formed with the negator *akəs* (same as the habitual negator discussed in §14.2) followed by a fully inflected verb. The negative irrealis consists of two independent grammatical and phonological words.

The negative irrealis can be used in main clauses without an overtly stated condition, and in main clauses (also known as apodosis) in conditional sentences. Examples in main clauses include 13.35, and 14.52–3. The negative irrealis typically refers to something that could have happened but did not.

14.52　aka　　　　　　　　　　　kəp　akəs　　rasə-k-na
　　　　DEM.DIST.REACT.TOP.fem.sg　just　NEG.IRR　get.up-IRR-ACT.FOC+3fem.sgBAS.VT
　　　　'Then (the war) would not have arisen by itself (without provocation)'

In 14.53 a positive future form is contrasted to a negative irrealis. The future reading of 'I will do' is determined by the context: an irrealis meaning is not appropriate here since this is what the man is determined to do.

14.53　a-rəb-a:b　　　　　　　ata　rəka:rək　kur-kə-tua
　　　　DEM.DIST.fem.sg-FULLY-TOO　then　correctly　do/get-FUT-1sgSUBJ.VT+3fem.sgBAS.VT
　　　　akəs　　jaujay　　　　kur-kə-tua
　　　　NEG.IRR　in.sloppy.way　do/get-IRR-1sgSUBJ.VT+3fem.sgBAS.VT
　　　　'Then in a straight way too I will treat (lit. do) her correctly, I would never treat her in a sloppy way'

A negative irrealis form in a main clause can express mild commands and wishes, as in 13.37–8. The irrealis in 14.54 expresses a strong wish:

14.54　akəs　　kus　tə-kə-k-na-ñəna!
　　　　NEG.IRR　cold　have-IRR-IRR-ACT.FOC-2fem.sgSUBJ.VT+3fem.sgBAS.VT
　　　　'May you well and truly not get a cold!'

A negative irrealis in a conditional sentence expresses a counterfactual event—something that could have happened under a counterfactual condition expressed with a verb marked for future or irrealis. A clause expressing condition (also known as protasis) is juxtaposed to the main clause (see §19.1 on juxtaposed clauses).

Examples with a positive clause expressing counterfactual condition with irrealis are at 13.36 and 14.55. In 13.36, we know that the man did not behave as a good uncle ought to have behaved; hence the irrealis reading of the juxtaposed conditional clause. Similarly, in 14.55, we know from the story that the magic woman did not give us her magic—if she had, we would have had a lot of money (which we do not have).

14.55　[[la　　　　　　　yanu　kway-ma:r-lə-lək]　　　　　　　　　　　　yawi　suan
　　　　she+DEM.DIST.fem.sg　magic　give.to.third.p.NEG-NEG.SUB-3fem.sg-BECAUSE　work　hard
　　　　yi-na-dian]　　　　　　[yanu　kui-k-la]
　　　　go-ACT.FOC-1plBAS.VT　magic　give.to.third.p-FUT-3fem.sgSUBJ.VT+3fem.sgBAS.VT
　　　　sa:n-aba:b　akəs　　kusə-k-na-di,　　　　　　　sa:n,　sa:n-aba:b　akəs
　　　　money-TOO　NEG.IRR　finish-FUT-ACT.FOC-3plBAS.VT　money　money-TOO　NEG.IRR
　　　　'Since she did not give magic, we work hard. Had she given magic, money too would have never finished, money, money too, never'

We will see, in §14.5, that the distinction between negative future and negative irrealis is neutralized in dependent clauses: the marking -*ma:r-kə*- (NEG.SUB-FUT/IRR) is used for both.

That is, whether the condition is counterfactual or not can only be decided in the context of a whole sentence. The form of the verb in a main clause may provide additional clues.

For example, 14.56 is ambiguous as to whether the condition is counterfactual or not: the main clause form is ambiguous between irrealis and future. Inserting a time word—such as *sər* 'tomorrow' or *nal* 'yesterday'—would have disambiguated this sentence.

14.56 [væki-maːr-k-la]
    go.across-NEG.SUB-FUT/IRR-3fem.sgSUBJ.VT+3fem.sgBAS.VT
    [da-k-na-wun]
    go.down-FUT/IRR-ACT.FOC-1sgBAS.VT
    'If she does not go across, I will go down (to meet her)' or
    'If she had not gone across, I would have gone down (to meet her)'

In contrast, 14.57 can only have a counterfactual reading because of the negative irrealis form in the main clause.

14.57 [væki-maːr-k-la]   [akəs
    go.across-NEG.SUB-FUT/IRR-3fem.sgSUBJ.VT+3fem.sgBAS.VT NEG.IRR
    da-k-na-wun]
    go.down-FUT/IRR-ACT.FOC-1sgBAS.VT
    'If she had not gone across, I would not have gone down (to meet her)'

And 14.58 is not counterfactual since the main clause contains a non-irrealis form:

14.58 [ganəb   sə   kwa-maːr-kə-tua,]
    morning sleep lie-NEG.SUB-FUT-1sgSUBJ.VT+3fem.sgBAS.VT
    [sik   tə-kwa-na-wun]
    sick be-HAB-ACT.FOC-1sgBAS.VT
    'If I do not sleep (the next) morning, I usually am sick'

An adverb, a copula complement, or the object of 'have' can intervene between the irrealis negator and the inflected verb, as shown in 14.54 and 14.59. In contrast to the habitual negator *akəs* (see, for example, 14.48) inserting more than one-word constituents between the irrealis negator and the verb results in unnatural expressions.

14.59 Simon Harrison də-kə-də   buk   akəs   kuprap
    Simon Harrison he-OBL-masc.sg book NEG.IRR bad
    tə-kə-k-na-di
    be/become-IRR-IRR-ACT.FOC-3plBAS.VT
    'Simon Harrison's book would not have got bad (if we had proper storage space)'

Just as with discontinuous constructions involving the habitual negator *akəs*, the effect is that of focusing on the constituent which is placed after the negator.

Just like the habitual negator *akəs* in 14.50, the irrealis negator can be used elliptically if the irrealis value is immediately recoverable from the context—this was illustrated in 14.55. However, it cannot be used as a negative response (unlike the habitual negator in 14.51).

The irrealis negator *akəs* is also used to negate the optative modality formed on irrealis, as in 13.40. Another example is at 14.60: this is a very strong wish for the unwanted guest not to turn up:

14.60 akəs   ya-kə-na-d-əu
    NEG.IRR come-IRR-ACT.FOC-3masc.sgBAS.VT-OPT
    'May he not come!!!'

Negative optative constructions are rare in discourse. They cannot be discontinuous, and do not occur in non-main clauses (we recall, from §13.2.3 and §13.3, that the positive optative does not occur in non-main clauses either). The optative modality formed on first and third person imperatives cannot be negated (see §14.4 for negative imperatives).

Are the two morphemes with the same shape—*akəs* 'habitual negative' and *akəs* 'irrealis negator'—the same morpheme or different morphemes? Synchronically speaking, they are better considered as distinct, given that the conditions of their use, their meanings, and syntactic properties are different. Diachronically speaking, the question remains open. It is not uncommon for irrealis and habitual to be expressed with the same morpheme—as, for instance, English *would*. However, since analogy is not a proof, the question concerning any etymological link between the two forms with the shape *akəs* remains open until more comparative data become available.

14.3.2   Negation of same-subject purposive and of desiderative

The same-subject purposive in main clauses and the desiderative are negated with the particle *ata* which obligatorily precedes the modal form, and forms an independent phonological and grammatical word. The negator *ata* is not used on its own as a pro-clause or a negative response. The constituent order is fixed: the negator always precedes the verb.

Examples of the negative desiderative are 14.61–2, and the first line of 14.65. The negative desiderative is an uninflected verb (just like the positive desiderative), so person, number, and gender of the subject are not expressed on the verb. If necessary for disambiguation, a personal pronoun can be supplied, as in 14.61.

14.61 wun day-a-wa   ata   kə-kər
      I   they-LK-COM NEG.DES eat-DES
      'I do not want to eat with them'

Example 14.62 is ambiguous: it is a suggestion to a second person, and at the same time a generic statement:

14.62 ñam   yawi kur-tukwa   səp kuprap ata   tə-kər
      sun+LK+LOC work do/get-PROH.GEN skin bad   NEG.DES become-DES
      'Do not work in the sun, you don't want your skin to get bad'

The same negator is used with the same-subject purposive in main clauses:

14.63 ñən   ata   vækər-ək
      you.fem NEG.DES fall-PURP.SS
      'You are not going to fall down'

The negator *ata* does not have to be contiguous with the desiderative or the purposive. A part of a complex predicate, as in 14.64–5, or a copula complement, as in 7.75, can intervene between the negator and the verb, if focused. This is similar to the behaviour of the negators *ma:* 'general non-habitual negator' and *akəs* 'habitual negator'.

14.64 wun ata   sə   kwa-kər
      I   NEG.DES sleep stay-DES
      'I don't want to sleep'

Example 14.65, from the same story as 14.35 above, contains a complex predicate:

14.65 [[[an   skul   <u>ata</u>   rə-kər] [an   <u>ata</u>   jəbə   <u>kur-ək</u>]]   wa-ku]
      we.two school NEG.DES sit-DES we.two NEG.DES image do/get-PURP.SS say-COMPL.SS
      abra   tabu-na-bər
      DEM.DIST.REACT.TOP+du run.away-ACT.FOC-3duBAS.VT
      'Having said, "We do not want to study (lit. sit school), we do not want to learn (lit. get image)", the two ran away (from school)'

Neither the negative desiderative nor the negative same-subject purposive occur in non-main clauses. Neither can be negated if used other than as main clause predicates—a different structure has to be used instead.

For instance, neither of the complex predicates involving the auxiliary *kur-* 'do/get' (illustrated in 13.62 and §17.1.2) can be negated using *ata*. The predicates are negated using *ma:* 'general non-habitual negator' as a separate pro-clause, as illustrated in 14.66–7. There is an intonation break and a short pause before *ma:* which is indicative of a clause boundary.

14.66 kamna:gw kə-kər   kur-də-l   kə-kər
      food   eat-DES do/get-3masc.sgSUBJ.P-3fem.sgBAS.P eat-DES
      kur-də-l   [PAUSE] <u>ma:</u>
      do/get-3masc.sgSUBJ.P-3fem.sgBAS.P [PAUSE] NEG
      'He was about to eat food, was about to eat—nothing' (meaning: he could not get himself to eat)

14.67 kaja-k   kur-də-l   [PAUSE] <u>ma:</u>
      open-PURP.SS do/get-3masc.sgSUBJ.P-3fem.sgBAS.P [PAUSE] NEG
      'He was about to open (the basket)—nothing' (meaning: he could not open it)

The negative pro-clause negates the whole clause—that is, the desiderative or the same-subject purposive component of the complex predicate cannot be negated separately.

Same-subject purposive in non-main clauses cannot be negated either. The only way of expressing negative same-subject purpose is by using the general non-habitual negator *ma:* as a separate pro-clause.

14.68 [an-a:k   <u>vya:k</u>   (war-na-d)   [PAUSE] <u>ma:</u>
      1du-LK+DAT hit+PURP.SS say-ACT.FOC-3masc.sgBAS.VT [PAUSE] NEG
      'He came up to hit us—no'

A same-subject purposive used in a main clause can be negated with a pro-clause *ma:* following the verb form, in an admonitive sense, as in 14.69 where a mother berates her daughter for not looking after others.

14.69 <u>kur-takak</u>   ma:!
      do-put+PURP.SS NEG
      'You are not going to look after others (you ought to)'

Just as in 14.67–8, the whole clause is within the scope of *ma:*. There is no other straightforward way of negating the same-subject purposive without negating the whole clause. To achieve this effect, the clause has to be rephrased.

In contrast, the different-subject purposive can be negated, using the dependent clause negator *-ma:r-*, in both main and non-main clauses. We can recall, from §13.4.2, that different-subject purposive in a main clause implies that something is to be done following the speaker's order. The same holds for the negative different-subject purposive, as shown in 14.70.

14.70 mən   laku-ma:r-mən-kəkək
you.masc know-NEG:SUB-2masc.sg-PURP.DS
'I don't want you to know' (lit. You are not to know on speaker's order)

An example of a different-subject purposive in a non-main clause is at 14.71.

14.71 [mən   laku-ma:r-mən-kək]   mən-a:k   wa: ma:
you.masc know-NEG:SUB-2masc.sg-PURP.DS you.masc-LK+DAT tell.NEG NEG
'I will not tell you so that you shouldn't know'

It is possible that the negator *ata* used to be able to occur with different-subject purposive. Such examples appear in Harrison's (1983) collection of archaic songs about foiled marriages, e.g. *ata* can also be used, apparently, without an implication of another participant (song 8, p. 48):[1]

14.72 gra-kə-tua-di   ata   wukə-ñən-kək
cry-FUT-1sgSUBJ.VT-3plBAS.VT NEG.DES hear-2fem.sg-PURP.DS
'I will cry about these, you won't hear'

The negator *ata* is homophonous with the interrogative *ata* 'how' (§10.4) and the manner demonstrative *ata* 'thus, then' (§10.2.2). We saw in §10.4 that the manner demonstrative and the manner interrogatives are likely to be related. But is the negator *ata* related to these, and if we assume that it is, how can a negative and a manner/interrogative meaning be connected to each other?

On the surface, the negative meaning and usage of *ata* appear to be pretty independent from the interrogative and manner use of the same form, and its derivatives, such as *atawa* 'thus', *ata ata*, *atəta* 'how'. However, a certain amount of evidence in favour of a link between these lies in the ways in which interrogative clauses are used with a negative meaning. Examples are 10.104 (*ma:j atəta wukə-k* (talk how hear-PURP.SS) 'How (am I to) hear the story (if children are screaming)' meaning 'I am not going to hear the story'), and 14.73:

14.73 [[wanəb yi-da:-k]   sə   kwa-kwə ma:] [sə   kwa-kər ata   ata]
noise   go-3pl-COMPL.DS sleep lie-RED NEG sleep lie-DES how how
'When they make noise, there is no sleeping, how am I going to sleep' (meaning: I am not going to sleep)

We will see in §14.6 below that questions are often used in lieu of negative statements and commands. We can hypothesize that *ata* developed a meaning of negative intention out of its interrogative use. No Ndu language appears to have an interrogative or a negator of this shape, or function.

14.3.3 Negation of nominalizations

Deverbal nominalizations which consist of a reduplicated verbal root are negated like any non-verb, with a postposed negator *ma:*. However, as shown in §9.1.1 (see (VI)), negated nominalizations most often imply negative obligation, or a taboo, as in 9.19, 13.19, 14.74, and 14.97.

[1] Farnsworth and Farnsworth (1966) suggest that the negation of *də yi-kər* (he come-DES) 'he wants to come' is *də kwasək yi-na-d* (he small+DAT come-ACT.FOC-3masc.sgBAS.VT) 'he does not want to come'. However, these are clearly different construction types, and the structure with *kwasək* is simply a lexical expression of 'not wanting to do something'.

14.74 Apatəp-a-wa   warya-k   kə-də   bæyib-ər   [war-war ma:]
      Avatip-LK-COM fight-PURP.SS DEM.PROX-masc.sg stream-LK+ALL go.up-RED NEG
      'There is a prohibition against going up this stream to fight with the Avatip people'

Negated nominalizations can be used in lieu of negative commands, and as a means of berating someone who has done something they should not have done, as in 9.20 and 14.75:

14.75 atawa kur-kur ma:
      thus   do-RED NEG
      'You shouldn't have acted like this' (lit. there is no doing that way)

A negated nominalization may also be used to straightforwardly negate an action no matter whether good or bad. This is shown in 14.76, a description of what happened to a Gala man who had survived the attack of the Avatip people, and hid in a hollow of a sago tree (the continuation of this is 14.22). He was so weak that:

14.76 yi:n   bə   ya   məl kuprap man-ta:b bə   kap   [yi-yə ma:]
      go+SEQ already EMPH eye bad   leg-hand already on.its.own go-RED NEG
      'By and by (his) eye (became) bad, (with) his body (lit. legs and hands), he already could not walk on his own' (lit. there was no walking on his own)

A similar example is the first clause of 14.73—the speaker was complaining that there is no sleeping while children are making noise, not that one should not sleep when there is noise.

The meaning of a nominalization under negation is determined entirely by the context. The meaning of 'negative obligation' is the most frequent one. And this is the reason why the negation of nominalizations is considered within this section. However, this reading makes little sense in a context like that in 14.76—then the meaning is 'lack of action'.

And, as we saw in §9.1.1 (at VI), an additional problem may arise. The negative form of the reduplicated intensive aspect of a verb may coincide with the reduplicated verb stem, that is, a nominalization. In negative future, the negator is postposed to the negative form of an inflected verb, making constructions like 9.20 and T1.15 inherently ambiguous between (a) negated nominalization as a means of negative obligation; and (b) negative future of the intensive aspect. Just as in 9.20, both readings make sense in the given context of a comic story about a newly wed young man who had no idea that women menstruate, literally, 'see moon', once a month. He decides to stop the moon from seeing his wife by going and fighting her (cf. 3.15 and 7.76). T1.15 is what his relatives tell him: it is your own moon, and there is no point in fighting her.

However, such negative constructions are only ambiguous if the subject is second person (the addressee), or a generic 'one', or a third person. Example 14.77 is not ambiguous—this can only refer to the future. As shown in §12.2, future often has the meaning of 'being able to'. In this example, the man is not refusing to pay the bride price, he has no means of paying it. The story from which 14.77 comes was told by a traditional speaker, and this explains the use of negator *ma:n*; the form *ma:* would have been equally acceptable:

14.77 wun-a-dəka [yapi-yapi ma:n]
      I-LK-ONLY   buy-RED NEG
      'I by myself won't pay the bride price' (lit. 'buy (wife)')

A potential ambiguity in the context of non-first person may be resolved by context: in the first clause of 14.73 the negated reduplicated verb cannot have a future intensive meaning, because there is no future reference: the speaker was complaining about what was happening in the house in general and the night before in particular.

Deverbal nominalizations marked with the dative-aversive case whose modal meanings are discussed in §13.7 are negated just like any other nominalizations, or non-verbal predicate heads, by postposing the general negator *ma:*. This is shown in 14.78–9:

14.78 wun kə-lə-m   [kwa-kwak   ma:]
      I   DEM.PROX-fem.sg-LOC stay-RED+DAT NEG
      'I am not going to stay here; there is no probability that I will stay here'

14.79 du-ta:kw   dəy-a:m   [və-væk   ma:]
      man-woman   they-LK+LOC see-RED+DAT NEG
      'People are not to see them' (spirits) (since the spirits live in a totemic haze after a conflict with people)

Example 14.80 is a confirmation question: the mother wanted to make sure her baby daughter was not interested in eating any more food:

14.80 ñən   [kə-ka:k   ma:]?
      you.fem eat-RED+DAT   NEG
      'You are not going to eat, are you?'

Monosyllabic verbs have homonymous forms for dative-aversive-marked nominalizations and same-subject purposive—this is discussed in §13.7. The two are negated differently: a nominalization is negated as in 14.80, and the same-subject purposive is negated with the marker *ata* (as shown in §14.3.2).

Negated dative-aversive nominalizations can be used in an admonitive sense, as in 14.81–2. This is quite unlike the negated nominalizations illustrated in 14.74–5.

14.81 kamna:gw æm   sə-sa:k   ma:
      food   share plant-RED+DAT NEG
      'Why don't you share food among yourselves, you ought to share food'

A similar construction can be used ironically:

14.82 kad   kiya-kiya:k ma:
      DEM.PROX+3masc.sgNOM   die-RED+DAT NEG
      'This one, he is not going to die' (said about a selfish man who knows how to look after himself)

Instances of modal uses for the dative-aversive nominalizations (see 13.74–86) can be negated in a somewhat different way: the negator *ma:* is postposed to the nominalization but there is a pause which indicates that *ma:* is a negative pro-clause negating the clause as a whole. A dative-aversive nominalization in the apprehensive sense of 'lest' (13.86) is likely to be negated:

14.83 kiya-kiya-k [PAUSE] ma:
      die-RED-DAT   NEG
      'Beware lest you die—no (you won't die)' (there is nothing to fear)

This is similar to how any clause can be negated; the meaning is that of an emphatic statement or command (see 14.152–4 in §14.6 below). We return to further functions of the pro-clause *ma:* in §14.6.

As mentioned in §13.7, the predicate of the conditional 'in case' clause looks exactly like a dative-aversive-marked nominalization. But, being a part of a non-main clause, it is negated differently. This is the topic of §14.5.1.

14.4   NEGATIVE IMPERATIVE

Manambu has several negative imperatives (or prohibitives) whose use correlates with person, and with the strength of a prohibition. There is no first person prohibitive—in other words, there is no negative equivalent of first person imperative (§13.2). The negative imperatives fall into two broad classes: (i) non-first person negative imperatives which can refer to second or third person (§14.4.1) and (ii) specifically third person negative imperatives (§14.4.2). We discuss these one at a time. Unlike negative non-future forms, the formation of negative imperatives always involves simple (that is, positive) verb stem (§11.1.2).

14.4.1   Non-first person negative imperatives

There are three forms with negative imperative meaning, used predominantly with second person reference, and also sometimes with third person reference: the general negative imperative marked with the suffix -*tukwa*, and two strong prohibitives, -*way* 'strong' and -*wayik* 'extra-strong'.

A. THE GENERAL PROHIBITIVE is marked with the suffix -*tukwa* forming one phonological word with the root (and therefore requires an automatic ə after a verb root ending in a consonant to avoid non-authorized consonant clusters). It always bears a secondary stress on its final syllable, e.g. *wukə́-tukwà* (hear/listen-PROH.GEN) 'do not listen', *bas sə́-tukwà* 'don't ask'.

Unlike any other verbal affix, -*tukwa* can be used with the free form *jau* 'let it drop, let it be', as in *jau tukwa*, lit. 'don't let it drop', in the meaning of 'there is no reason to drop this; this is important; there is no reason to say *jau*' (see §4.5). Such structures are not frequent, and may be analysed as 'echo constructions', because they appear as a reaction to someone saying *jau* in the first place. The form *jau*, frequent with positive imperatives, is otherwise not used in prohibitions.

Just occasionally, *tukwa* may be used as a prohibitive 'don't' on its own. This is found in abrupt elliptical speech. These usages may well be an innovation, due to the fact that -*tukwa* is disyllabic and requires secondary stress. Alternatively, they may reflect an older usage, and perhaps even provide justification for tracing -*tukwa* to an independent verb—see the end of this section. No other prohibitive can be used this way.

The general negative imperative typically refers to second person, as shown in 14.84–6, and also 4.58, 13.16, 14.18, and 14.62.

14.84 wali   kudi   yi-tukwa
       white.men language go/say-PROH.GEN
       'Do not speak white man's language!'

Since the negative imperative does not encode person distinctions, a pronoun can be added for disambiguation, as in 14.85, and 14.86.

14.85 mən   kaykətə-tukwa
       you.masc. hang.on/touch-PROH.GEN
       'Don't you touch (my bow and arrow)'

The personal pronoun can follow the verb, if contrastive, as in T3.7. A general prohibitive is often accompanied either by an instruction on what to do instead of what is being prohibited (as in 14.93), or by a statement of the consequences, as in T3.7 and 14.86 (a continuation of

14.6). This is similar to the situation described for Dyirbal and other Australian languages by Dixon (1972: 112).

14.86 mən   alək   mawul wukə-tukwa,   aka   bə
      you.masc.sg this.is.why inside worry-PROH.GEN DEM.DIST.REACT.TOP.fem.sg already
      kiya-na,   wa-ku   ma:, rapə-k-na
      die-ACT.FOC+3fem.sgBAS.VT say-COMPL.SS NEG stand.up-FUT-ACT.FOC+3fem.sgBAS.VT
      'This is why don't you worry (lit. you inside don't worry), having said "She has died already", no, she will get up'

A prohibitive can be formed on complex predicates, including physical and mental state constructions (discussed in Chapter 17), as in 14.86 and 14.87a. The corresponding declarative constructions are at 14.87b and 14.87c: the difference between these two is in the focus on the experiencer in 14.87c.

14.87a mawul war-tukwa
       inside go.up-PROH.GEN
       'Don't get excited'

14.87b (wun) mawul   war-na
        I   inside/mind go.up-ACT.FOC+3fem.sgBAS.VT
        '(I) am excited' (lit. my inside goes up)'

14.87c (wun) mawul   war-na-wun
        I   inside/mind go.up-ACT.FOC-1fem.sgBAS.VT
        'I am excited' (lit. I go up (with respect to) my inside)'

The prohibitive in 14.87a may be interpreted as having third person reference, with a literal translation 'may the inside not get excited', or as having second person reference, 'may you not get excited with respect to your inside'. Such constructions are hardly ever used in positive imperatives. They cannot form second person imperatives, because non-volitional verbs and states are mutually exclusive with second person imperative (see §13.2.1–2). Theoretically, they could form third person imperatives—that is, a construction like 14.87d would be grammatically acceptable, but culturally questionable. It is in fact not culturally appropriate to be in a state describable as 'inside goes up': this state covers excitement, anger, and further uncontrollable strong feelings which are considered improper:

14.87d mawul war-kwa
       inside go.up-IMPV.3p+fem.sg
       'May (second/third person) be excited'—?

We will see in §20.1.4 that *mawul* here is not a direct object: under no circumstances can it be cross-referenced on the verb. We return to the concept of *mawul* in §21.4.

A general prohibitive can be directed at humans and high animates. In Mali's family, it is not uncommon to address inanimate objects with a general prohibitive. In 14.88, Mali was berating her cooking pots for being lazy and not getting the food cooked quickly enough:

14.88 kwas-ək   yi-tukwa
      small-LK+DAT go/say-PROH.GEN
      'Don't be unwilling!'

And Tanina, her eldest daughter, instructed a piece of watermelon which was rolling off the edge of the floor:

14.89 <u>piñu-tukwa</u>
    slide-PROH.GEN
    'Don't slide!'

No positive imperative was used this way. Neither can any other prohibitive be addressed to an inanimate object.

Unlike the other two non-first person negative imperatives, the general *-tukwa* hardly ever has obviously non-second person reference. The interpretation of examples in 14.86–87a as having a third person addressee is possible, but unlikely: they are obviously addressed to a person, and not to their inside. A prohibition marked with *-tukwa* can occasionally be addressed at a third person—an inanimate force, as in 14.90:

14.90 wa:l <u>ja-tukwa</u>   an   yi-ya:k
    rain rain-PROH.GEN we.du go-RED+DAT
    'May the rain not fall, we two would like to go' (to a ceremony)

When used in the direct speech report slot, a *-tukwa* prohibitive is a way of marking negative purpose, with non-first subject reference. This is a usage not attested with any other prohibitives:

14.91 [wukəmar-wukəmar-tukwa] wa-na-wun
    forget-RED-PROH.GEN   say-ACT.FOC-1fem.sgBAS.VT
    'I am telling (you) so that this should not be forgotten (or: so that you should not fully forget)' (lit. I say 'do not fully forget')

As mentioned in §13.2.2, the general prohibitive of *wa-* 'say', *wa-tukwa*, has an additional meaning of 'say it again, I couldn't agree more'. This is an idiomatic usage which is not shared with any of the other prohibitives.

B. THE STRONG PROHIBITIVES are marked with the suffixes *-way* and *-wayik* which form one phonological word with the verb stem to which they attach. Neither suffix can be used on its own, or accompany *jau* 'let it drop, let it be' on its own, unlike the general prohibitive *-tukwa*. All monosyllabic verbs and a few other verbs require a formative *-k-* in the strong prohibitive (see §11.3.2), e.g. *wa-k-wayik* 'do not ever say', *kə-k-wayik* 'do not ever eat'.

The two strong prohibitives differ from the general prohibitive in their illocutionary force. For instance, if a mischievous child is told 14.92a, it is likely that she will pay no attention and wait and see what happens next.

14.92a <u>kur-tukwa</u>   ñən-a-kə-l   ma:
    do/get-PROH.GEN you.fem-LK-OBL-fem.sg NEG
    'Do not take (this), it is not yours'

A parent who is really annoyed and does not want the child to keep on reaching out for what is not hers is likely to shout:

14.92b <u>kur-way!</u>
    NEG-PROH.STR
    'Do not take (this)!!'

On saying this, a parent is likely to get hold of something heavy to throw at the child. The child gets a bit edgy, preparing to start running away; and she is likely to stop what she was doing. If she does not, or the parent is not satisfied with the effect, 14.92c follows:

14.92c <u>kur-wayik</u>!
  NEG-PROH.EXTRA
  'Do not take (this)!!!'

On hearing this, the child is off in a flash—she knows for a fact that the parent is well and truly annoyed, and will hit her if she does not disappear.

The two strong prohibitives are similar in their behaviour. We saw above that the general prohibitive is very often accompanied by a statement of what may happen otherwise, as shown in 14.86 and 14.93 (partly repeated from 7.21):

14.93 [[a   wəpak-a:m]   və-ku]   a-də   yabəm
  DEM.DIST+fem.sg type.of.tree-LK+LOC see-COMPL.SS DEM.DIST-masc.sg road+LK+LOC
  <u>yi-tukwa</u>   kə-də   mapa-taba   yabə-rəb   ma:y
  go-PROH.GEN DEM.PROX-masc.sg right-hand+LK road+LK-FULLY go.IMPV
  'Having seen the tree (whose leaf I put on the ground), do not go on that road, go straight onto the road on the right-hand side'

In contrast, a strong prohibitive often occurs unaccompanied by such statements. Strong and extra-strong prohibitions are likely to occur on their own—they are so strong that the addressee is supposed to be aware of the consequences anyway. Or the consequences of disobedience may be such that the speaker does not want to stress them. Example 14.94 is a strongish prohibition: a bush boy has to wear a grass skirt at all times.

14.94 akətawa kwa:r   <u>ləpa-way</u>
  like.this grass.skirt break-PROH.STR
  'Don't you ever undo (break) your grass skirt'

In 14.95, the spirit instructs the woman to never ever look inside her stringbag. She disobeys and the consequences are disastrous—her little son becomes a monster:

14.95 kə-də   wurəm   səmərab kəta-d
  DEM.PROX-masc.sg string.bag+LK+LOC never.ever look.DIR-DOWN
  <u>və-k-wayik</u>   də-kə-m   kaja-saki-n-a:b   <u>və-k-wayik</u>
  look-EP-PROH.EXTRA he-OBL-LOC open.up-ACROSS.AWAY-SEQ-TOO look-EP-PROH.EXTRA
  'Never ever look down into this stringbag, do not ever look by opening it sideways'

A reason for the prohibition, but not the consequence, can be stated; however, this has only been attested with the strong, but not the extra-strong, prohibitive:

14.96 [kə   mi: <u>vəl-way</u>]   [wun-a   ta:kw kə-na-wur
  DEM.PROX.fem.sg tree cut-PROH.STR I-LK+fem.sg woman DEM.PROX-CURR.REL-UP
  ñan   kur-ən   rə-na]
  child do/get-SEQ sit-ACT.FOC+3fem.sgBAS.VT
  'Do not cut this tree, my wife is sitting up there having a baby'

Either of the strong prohibitives can be accompanied by an inherently negative form *səmərab, səma:b,* or *səmsəma:b* 'never ever', as in 14.95 (see §14.6). Neither can have an inanimate addressee, in contrast to the general prohibitive. Strong prohibitives are not used with verbs of mental states—the general prohibitive is preferred in such contexts (14.86-7).

Either of the strong prohibitives may refer to a third person, much more frequently so than the general prohibitive *-tukwa.* We also saw, at 14.90, that *-tukwa* may be used with a non-human third person agent. In contrast, a third person with either of the strong prohibitives always has a human referent. In 14.97, the third person is explicitly stated, and in 14.98 it was understood from the context. A taboo stated with a negated nominalization in 14.97 is reinforced with the prohibitive, to make sure the audience understands the strength of the ban.

14.97 [du-a-ñanugw   və-və   ma:] [du-a-ñanugw   və-k-wayik]
man-LK-children see-RED NEG man-LK-children see-EP-PROH.EXTRA
'Boys are not to see (girls in seclusion at the time of their first menstruation), boys should not see (them) under any circumstances'

14.98 ya-k-wayik
come-EP-PROH.EXTRA
'He should not come in' (accompanied with a sign reference to an unwanted guest)

A strong prohibitive can be used as an apprehensive—meaning 'lest', 'or else', as in 14.99. This expresses the prohibition not to cook the manioc and the white hairy yam together:

14.99 a-di   ñan   kamkaw   nakalib kwata-ku   kiya-way
DEM.DIST-pl manioc white.hairy.yam together cook-COMPL.SS die-PROH.STR
'Do not cook manioc and white hairy yam together lest you die' (lit. Having cooked manioc and white hairy yam together may you not die!)

A similar example with an extra-strong prohibitive -*wayik* is at 14.100.

14.100 dəb-a:m   ata kwa-l   [wali   kamna:gw
fence-LK+LOC then stay-3fem.sgBAS.P white.person food
kə-lə-k]   [kuprap tə-k-wayik]
eat-3fem.sg-COMPL.DS bad   stay-EP-PROH.EXTRA
'She sat inside the fence (that is, in a ritual enclosure, having her first menstruation), having eaten white people's food, she might be sick'

Apprehensive usages of the strong prohibitives express a highly undesirable consequence of a previously finalized action described with a dependent clause.

Either of the two strong prohibitives can be used as a causative strategy, mirroring the similar usages typical of the positive imperatives (see §13.2.2, examples 13.23–5):

14.101 wun-a:k [kə-lə-m   səkulək ay]   wa-k-wayik
I-LK+DAT DEM.PROX-fem.sg-LOC cooking IMPV+do say-EP-PROH.EXTRA
'Do not you tell me to cook here!' or 'Don't make me cook there!'

The properties of the two strong prohibitives and of the general prohibitive are contrasted in Table 14.1.

Table 14.1 shows that, besides the differences in the strength of a prohibition (illustrated in 14.92a–c), the three prohibitives differ in their morphosyntactic properties, and in actual usage.

Languages of the world tend to have fewer prohibitives than they have positive imperatives (Aikhenvald forthcoming a); there are, however, a few languages where more distinctions are expressed in negative than in positive commands. Manambu is one such example: there are three prohibitives, with just one positive counterpart. The positive imperative is richer than the negative imperatives in just one respect: first person imperative only exists in the positive polarity. However, the seeming scarcity of positive imperative forms is compensated for by a large array of command strategies—see Table 19.5 in §19.9.

The etymology of the three prohibitives is unknown—there are no clear cognates of any of these in any of the Ndu languages. We hypothesize that the form -*tukwa* may be derived

TABLE 14.1   The properties of three non-first person prohibitives: a comparison

PROPERTIES	GENERAL PROHIBITIVE	STRONG PROHIBITIVE -*way*	EXTRA-STRONG PROHIBITIVE -*wayik*
Person reference	second, rarely third	either second or third	
Inanimate addressee or non-human third person	yes	no	
Statement of consequences	often	hardly ever	
Occurrence with inherently negative lexemes	rare	frequent	
Apprehensive	no	yes	
Causative strategy	no	yes	

from a third person imperative of the verb *tə*- 'be, have, stand', *tə-kwa* (stand/be/have-IMPV.3p+3fem.sg) 'let it stand/be/have'. (Note that, as shown in §2.1.2, *təkwa* is an alternative realization of *tukwa*.) This etymology is corroborated by typological analogy—non-infrequently, prohibitives come from expressions like 'stop, let it be, leave it' (Heine and Kuteva 2002; Aikhenvald forthcoming a; and similar developments suggested in Dixon 1972: 112).

The strong prohibitive marker -*way*- is homonymous with the inherently reduplicated form *wayway* 'maybe, posssibly'. The component *way*- also occurs in the interjection *wayay, wayey* 'oh dear'; but any etymological connection with the prohibitive is dubious.

The formative -*ik* in -*wayik* may well be related to the confirmation marker -*ək* (see §12.5; and note that ə is pronounced as [i] in the context of a palatal glide *y*: see §2.1.2), given that the strong negative imperative -*way* differs from -*wayik* in the degree of strength, or 'assertiveness'.

14.4.2   Third person negative imperatives

Manambu has two specifically third person negative imperatives. One of these is well established in the language, and the other appears to be a recent innovation. Unlike the negative imperatives discussed in §14.4.1, which may be addressed to either second or third person but bear no gender or number markers, the third person negative imperatives cross-reference gender and number of the third person.

The third person imperative used by all generations is marked with the suffix -*ba* which follows the third person personal cross-referencing markers, e.g. *ya-də-ba* (come-3masc.sg-3pPROH) 'he should not come'; *ya-bər-ba* (come-3du-3pPROH) 'they two should not come'; *ya-da-ba* (come-3pl-3pPROH) 'they should not come'. Its meaning is that of strong prohibition and negative obligation directed at third person. The referent of third person is always human, just as with the strong prohibitives discussed in §14.4.1. In its illocutionary force it is comparable to the extra-strong prohibitive -*wayik*, with an additional overtone of negative obligation. This is illustrated in 14.102–3.

14.102 yabi:b kamna:gw <u>kə-lə-ba</u>   ta:y *marasin* kə-ku   kamna:gw
quickly food   eat-3fem.sg-3pPROH first medicine eat-COMPL.SS food
ata kə-kwa
then eat-IMPV.3p+fem.sg
'She is not to eat food quickly (or straight away), having eaten the medicine first, let her eat food then'

14.103 Ambuntim   ta:n   yawi <u>kur-da-ba</u>
Ambunti+LOC stay+SEQ work do-3pl-3pPROH
'While in Ambunti they should not work'

Unlike any other command, negative or positive, a third person negative imperative can occur marked as highlighting focus. A girl strongly prohibits her paternal uncle and his children from coming into the house, since they had mistreated herself and her brother when they were little. Her statement contrasts with what her brother has to say.

14.104 [kə   wun-a   wiya:r-ab   war ma:] [du nak-ab
DEM.PROX.fem.sg I-LK+fem.sg house+LK+ALL-TOO go.up NEG man one-TOO
<u>ya-də-ba-l</u>]   [wa-də
come-3masc.sg-3pPROH-3fem.sgNOM DEM.PROX.ADDR-masc.sg
mala-wiya:r-a:b   <u>yi-də-ba-l</u>]
side+LK-house+LK+ALL-TOO go-3masc.sg-3pPROH-3fem.sgNOM
'He is not going to go up to this house of mine, it is the case that not even one man is to come up (into the house). It is the case that he must not go to this side of the house close to you' (said the girl to her brother)

An alternative form of the *-ba-* third person negative imperative contains an additional syllable *-kə-* between the person-gender-number marker and the suffix *-ba-*. An example is in 14.105: the bush baby (referred to in 14.94) is not to take off his grass skirt, under any circumstances. The negative imperative is in highlighting focus: what he is not to do is contrasted to what other boys do—that is, wash naked.

14.105 [kwa:r rali:n   da:n   gu   <u>yaku-də-kə-ba-l</u>]
grass.skirt untie+SEQ go.down+SEQ water wash-3masc.sg-?-3pPROH-3fem.sgNOM
[kwara-wa   yaku-kwa-d]
grass.skirt+LK-COM wash-IMPV.3p-masc.sg
'It is the case that he is not to wash having untied the grass skirt, he should wash with grass skirt (on)'

The two alternatives, with and without *-kə-*, appear to be identical in meaning and use. The absence of *-kə-* in forms quoted in 14.102–4 can be explained as a result of intervocalic *-k-* lenition (see A3 in §2.6). The only problem with this explanation is that in all clear cases of intervocalic *-k-* lenition, *k* is invariably supplied in careful speech register. In contrast, the two alternative forms of the third person negative imperative occur in all speech registers. The third person negative imperative is rare in discourse. Young and innovative speakers know the forms, but hardly ever use them.

What they use instead is an innovative third person imperative construction consisting of the verb stem followed by the dependent clause negator *-ma:r-* and then by third person imperative markers (listed in Table 13.1). Such commands do not have a strong overtone of negative obligation—their meaning is that of a negative command to third person. A mother told her eldest daughter not to let a younger daughter wear dirty trousers to church:

14.106 <u>kusu-ma:r-kwa</u>
        wear-NEG.SUB-IMPV.3p+fem.sg
        'May she not wear (this)'

A wish that an unwanted guest should not come was spontaneously phrased as:

14.107 <u>ya-ma:r-kwa-d</u>
        come-NEG.SUB-IMPV.3p-masc.sg
        'May he not come!'

Such forms can also be used to express indirect causation, as in 14.108. This was said as an explanation of why I had to use a hairclip:

14.108 lə-kə   nab kay-gwaj-ən   tə-na-d
        she-OBL+fem.sg hair MANIP-wrap-SEQ stay-ACT.FOC-3masc.sgBAS.VT
        <u>væker-ma:r-kwa-d</u>
        fall-NEG.SUB-IMPV.3p-masc.sg
        'It (hairclip) wraps her hair, so that (the hair) should not fall down'

These forms are used in everyday speech by speakers of all ages—but they are condemned by some speakers, especially those puristically oriented, as 'non-existent' and 'wrong'. Given that older and traditional speakers consider them wrong, I hypothesize that they constitute a recent innovation. We will see, in §14.5.3 below, that the subordinate negator *-ma:r-* can be used in main declarative clauses if they refer to a wish, or if the clause is in focus. The meaning of 'wish' is consistent with the third person command; and it is likely that third person imperative markers were added to the *-ma:r-* form by analogy.

One cannot exclude, however, that this seemingly innovative negative imperative is in fact an archaic form. We will also see, at the end of §14.5, that the negator *-mar-ék* marks negative commands in Wosera (Wilson 1980: 164–5). If the markers in Manambu and Wosera are related, the negative imperative use of Manambu *-ma:r-* may be a retention rather than an innovation.

14.5   NEGATION OF DEPENDENT CLAUSES, QUESTIONS, AND FOCUS STRUCTURES

Dependent clauses are negated with the negator *-ma:r-* which follows the verb stem. If the verb stem undergoes vowel changes in a non-future negative form (as outlined in §11.3.2), the non-future negative form is preferred, e.g. *kur-* 'do/get', negative *ma: kwa:r* 'do(es) not/did not do/get', dependent negative *kwa:r-ma:r-, kəl-* 'dry (of water)', *ma: ka:l* 'do(es) not/did not dry', negative dependent *ka:l-ma:r-* (also see the first line of 14.55, with the form *kwa:y-* 'negative non-future give.to.third.person'). There is a tendency to reduce either the root vowel, or the affix vowel, so as to avoid having two long vowels in one phonological word (in agreement with §2.5.1). That is, variants *kwar-ma:r-* (rather than *kwa:r-ma:r-*) and *ka:l-mar-* (rather than *ka:l-ma:r*) are not uncommon.

However, many speakers use a non-negative form, as is the case in a headless relative clause in 14.122. Those who prefer the negative form are typically innovative 'big men'; while women, who are more traditional speakers, tend to use the non-negative form.

The negative dependent marker *-ma:r-* is used in three basic contexts: to negate the predicate of a variety of types of dependent clause (§14.5.1), to negate the predicate of questions (§14.5.2), and in independent clauses, among them the ones expressing wishes and laments (§14.5.3). That the three clause types are negated in the same way indicates similarities in their underlying structure.

The marker *-ma:r-* is compatible with the future and the non-past habitual *-kwa-* (see 14.58, 14.118, and 14.124) in juxtaposed clauses, causal clauses, and relative clauses. (The action-focus *-na-*, the future, or the optative modality are not used in any of these.) In all other clauses, *-ma:r-* occurs with whatever clause-chaining affixes are appropriate. The negative clauses preserve the same specifications as the corresponding non-negative clauses. That is, different-subject clauses keep their subject cross-referencing in positive and in negative forms (see 14.19, 14.112, and 14.113), and same-subject clauses have none in either (as in 14.111). A non-negative uninflected predicate remains uninflected if negated, as does the manner sequential form (14.109), the cotemporaneous form (14.114), and the immediate sequencing form (14.115).

14.5.1   Negating dependent clauses

A verbal predicate of a dependent clause of any of the types described in Chapters 18–19 is negated with the suffix *-ma:r-*. There are two exceptions: a repetitive clause marked with the suffix *-kəkəb* is never negated; the corresponding meaning is partly conveyed by using habitual negative in a juxtaposed clause, as in 14.124. An irrealis conditional clause marked with *-ga:y* is never negated, and has no simple negative counterpart (see §18.8).

A manner sequential clause whose predicate is marked with the suffix *-ən* is illustrated at 14.109. We will see, in §18.1, that *-(ə)n*-marked clauses have a wide range of meanings, covering time ('while'), as in 14.109, and reason ('as, because'), as in 14.110. The resulting form is uninflected. An *-n* clause can either precede or follow the main clause.

14.109 bra:k   say-si   karab-ə-kara:b
        2du+LK+DAT boyhouse-RED men's.house-LK-RED
        kwakə-ya-tua   kwakə-yakəp [bər ya-ma:r-ən]
        look.for-come-1sgSUBJ.VT+3fem.sgBAS.VT look.for-FR   2du come-NEG.SUB-SEQ
        'I have been looking for you two in each boy house in each men's house, looking in vain, while/as/since you did not come' (lit. you not coming)

14.110 [sə   kwa-ma:r-ən]   wa:n taka-kwa-dian
        sleep stay-NEG.SUB-SEQ ear   put.down-HAB-1plBAS.VT
        'Not sleeping (as we are not sleeping) we keep eavesdropping'

A complex predicate consisting of a verb marked with *-ən* and an auxiliary *tə-* (see §17.1.1) can be negated in two ways, with different meanings. If the auxiliary is negated, as in 14.32–3, this implies anterior reading—implying that something has or has not happened in the past and this is relevant for the moment of speech. Alternatively, the *-ən* form of the verb can be negated, e.g. *səkulək yarakara yi-yə laku-mar-ən ta:l* (cooking well go-RED know-NEG:SUB-SEQ stay+3fem.sgBAS.VT) 'She did not know how to cook properly'. The implication is that of a complete lack of experience whose general relevance goes beyond the moment of speech.

A desubordinated manner sequential clause occurs in questions (in 14.132)—we return to this in §14.5.3.

A negated same-subject completive clause is illustrated in 14.111. A desubordinated same-subject completive clause can be used in a question (at 14.133)—see §14.5.3.

14.111 [də-kə   ma:k və-ma:r-ku]   ata   gra-dian
       he-POSS+fem.sg face see-NEG.SUB-COMPL.SS then cry-1plBAS.VT
       'Not having seen him personally (lit. not having seen his face), we then cried'

A negated different-subject completive clause is at 14.19 and 14.112.

14.112 [kija:p   tə-ma:r-lə-k]   wali-kamna:gw kə ma:
       protein.food have-NEG.SUB-3fem.sg-COMPL.DS white.man-food eat NEG
       'There not being protein food, he won't eat white man's food'

We will see in Chapter 19 that Manambu employs 'tail-head', or bridging, linkage as a device for maintaining discourse coherence. This involves repeating the last verb in a main clause within a dependent completive clause of the following sentence. If the repeated verb is negative, it takes the dependent negator when used in a dependent clause. An example of tail-head linkage involving negation is at 14.113.

14.113 [a-di   təp-a   du-ta:kw-ab   kamna:gw brə-kə-k   ma:
       DEM.DIST-pl village-LK man-woman-TOO food   3du-OBL-DAT NEG
       kwa:y]   [kwa:y-ma:r-da-k]   [pusəp-a-pusəp
       give.to.third.p+NEG give.to.third.p+NEG-NEG.SUB-3pl-COMPL.DS rubbish-LK-rubbish
       {a-di   yakə-da-di   pusəp} {kur-pæsan
       DEM.DIST-pl throw-3plSUBJ.P-3plBAS.P rubbish do/get-INCOMPL+SEQ
       kə-pəsan   yakə-da-di   pusəp} na:gw o
       eat-INCOMPL+SEQ throw-3plSUBJ.P-3plBAS.P rubbish sago or
       {pukə-ya-yi-di   kami:} kə-ya-bər]   [kə-ya-n
       rot-come-go-3plBAS.VT fish   eat-come-3duBAS.P/VT eat-come-SEQ
       kə-ya-n   kə-ya-n]
       eat-come-SEQ eat-come-SEQ
       'Those people (man-woman) from the village did not give these two food, after they did not give them food, the two kept eating all sorts of rubbish, those bits of rubbish which were thrown (away) by them (people), bits of rubbish not fully put together, not fully eaten, sago, or fish which was rotting, they (kept) eating and eating and eating'

A negated cotemporaneous clause is at 14.114. The dependent clause predicate is an uninflected form marked with -ta:y:

14.114 [ñanugw tə-ma:r-ta:y]   amæy   asa:y akəs   wa-kwa-na-di
       children have-NEG.SUB-COTEMP mother father NEG.HAB say-HAB-ACT.FOC-3plBAS.VT
       'When/while they have no children, they do not say mother father (to each other)'

A negated dependent clause containing the immediate sequencing suffix -taka is shown in 14.115:

14.115 də kəp tə-na-d   ta:kw kra-ma:r-taka
       he just stay-ACT.FOC-3masc.sgBAS.VT woman marry-NEG.SUB-IMM.SEQ
       'He just stays not having got married'

A negated clause marked with the suffix (a)lək 'because, this is why', recently grammaticalized from the linker a-lə-k (DEM.DIST-fem.sg-DAT) (see §10.2.1 and §18.7), is shown in 14.116 and 19.76. Tok Pisin code-switches are in italics.

14.116 wun *wori* tə-na-dəwun   [*pas* kwar-ma:r-tu-lək]
       I   worry have-ACT.FOC-1masc.sgBAS.VT letter get.NEG-NEG.SUB-1sg-BECAUSE
       'I am worrying (about Simon Harrison) because I haven't received a letter'

1. Pauline Agnes Yuaneng Luma Laki and Kawindu in the former site of Yentschanggai, now completely flooded.

2. Ceremonial house at Avatip (1910–12) (Behrmann 1950–1: 323).

3. Ceremonial house Warman in modern Avatip during a name debate.

4. A view of the Avatip village (the enclave of the subclan Maliau).

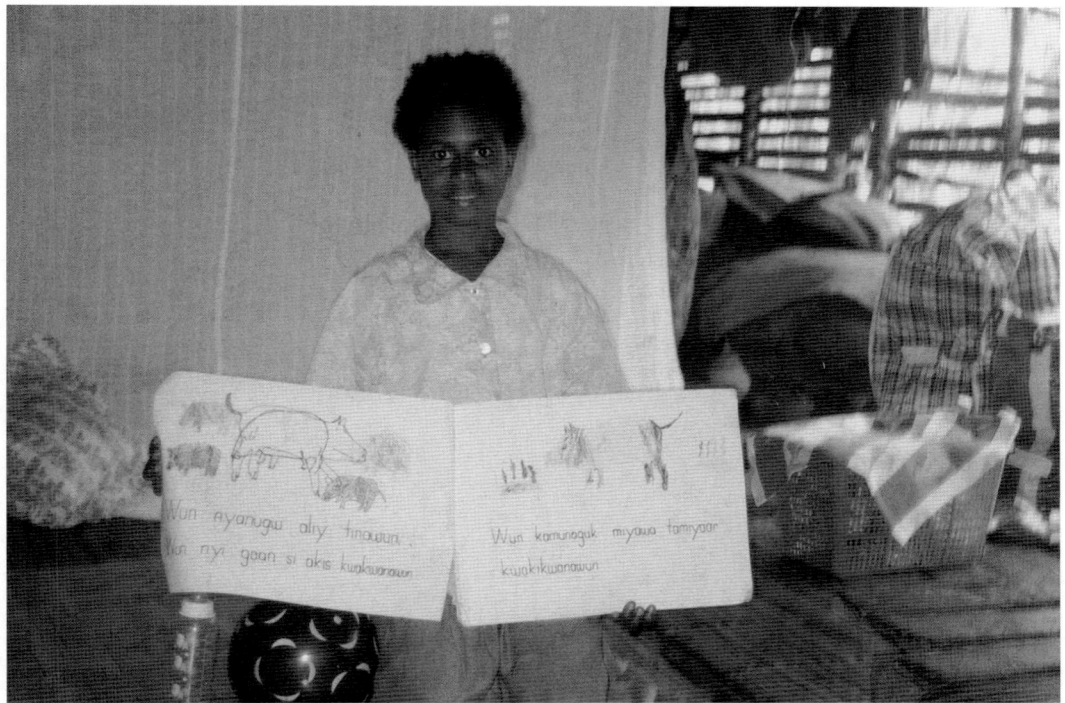

5. Tanina Ala in her home in Avatip displaying a poster used for teaching Manambu in the primary school programme in 2002–3.

6. 'Mothers': Gemaj, Maguniway, and Yipawal relaxing around Gemaj's fireplace.

7. Ester Yuayab and Jacklyn Yuamali Benji Ala explaining the process of 'working' sago.

8. View of the Malu village, from the direction of the Sepik River. Elders from two Manambu villages meet when a delegation from Avatip visited Malu on 2 October 2004.

Different-subject purposive in a dependent clause is negated in the same way as it is negated in a main clause—see 14.70–1. We can recall, from §9.2, that a clause can take the suffix *-pǝk* 'like'; when negated, the verb takes the subordinate negator *-ma:r-* which confirms the status of such clauses as dependent, as in 14.117.

14.117 kwa:m tǝ-ma:r-na-pǝk   mǝkǝmǝk
      crazy   be-NEG.SUB-ACT.FOC+3fem.sgBAS.VT-like silent
      rǝ-na
      sit-ACT.FOC+3fem.sgBAS.VT
      'She sits all quiet as if she is not crazy (said about a child who was unusually quiet)'

Relative clauses share all the categories with positive main clauses; in fact a positive relative clause can only be distinguished from a main clause by the lack of intonation break between the clause and the common argument. Examples of relative clauses—whose predicates are fully inflected verbs—are in curly brackets in 14.113. There are no restrictions on the function of a common argument in either the main or the relative clause. The only type of relative clause whose surface realization differs from a main clause involves relativization of the possessor—see the full discussion in §19.2.

Relative clauses reveal their true nature when they are negated: they require the negator *-ma:r-*, just like any dependent clause. As expected, the action focus does not occur in negative relative clauses, but the habitual *-kwa-* does. A positive relative clause is given at 14.118a and its negative equivalent at 14.118b. Further examples of negated relative clauses are at 14.119–21, and 19.23a–b.

14.118a [sa:n   tǝ-kwa-na-di]   du-ta:kw
       money have-HAB-ACT.FOC-3plBAS.VT man-woman
       'people who usually have money'

14.118b [sa:n   tǝ-ma:r-kwa-di]   du-ta:kw
       money have-NEG.SUB-HAB-3plBAS.VT man-woman
       'people who usually do not have money'

14.119 [na:gw kǝ-ma:r-dana]   maw
       sago   eat-NEG.SUB-3pl.SUBJ.VT+3fem.sgBAS.VT reason/basis
       aka-n-aka
       DEM.DIST.REACT.TOP.fem.sg-PRED-REACT.TOP.fem.sg
       'That is the reason (or the truth) of them not eating sago (in that area)'

14.120 [day tǝ-ma:r-dana-di]   ja:p   kǝdika
       they have-NEG-3plSUBJ.VT-3plBAS.VT thing DEM.PROX.REACT.TOP+pl
       'Here are the things that they do not have'

14.121 ka   a-dǝ   yabǝ-rǝb   ya:l
       DEM.PROX+3fem.sgNOM DEM.DIST-masc.sg road+LK-FULLY go+3fem.sgBAS.VT
       [a-dǝ   tǝpǝ-tay-ma:r-dǝ-dǝ]
       DEM.DIST-masc.sg shut-BACK.FORTH-NEG.SUB-3masc.sgSUBJ.P-3masc.sg.BAS.P
       yabǝr
       road+LK+ALL
       'As for this one, she went straight on that road, that road that he had not blocked'

Any relative clause can be used headlessly, and it is negated in the same way. In 14.122, a headless relative clause is used in A function:

14.122 yawi <u>kur-ma:r-dana-di</u>   luku *moa yet* kur-kwa-dana-di
     work do-NEG.SUB-3plSUBJ.VT-3plBAS.VT steal more yet do-HAB-3plSUBJ.VT-3plBAS.VT
     'Those who do not work steal even more'

Juxtaposed clauses which express condition of different kinds (see Chapters 18 and 19) are another dependent clause type which is segmentally indistinguishable from main clauses unless negated. (Even if not negated, they have a particular intonation contour which indicates their dependency—see Chapter 19.) When negated, they require the dependent negator *-ma:r-* and thus behave just as dependent clauses are expected to. An example is 14.123—a positive juxtaposed clause is contrasted to a negative one. The man is telling his wife what to expect of his trip. Juxtaposed clauses are in curly brackets, and a relative clause is in square brackets.

14.123 {yi-kə-tua}   {məyir tə-kə-tua}
     go-FUT-1sgSUBJ.VT+3fem.sgBAS.VT really be-FUT-1sgSUBJ.VT+3fem.sgBAS.VT
     səbən-kə-na-dəwun-ək
     return-FUT-ACT.FOC-1masc.sgBAS.VT-CONF
     {səbən-ma:r-kə-tua}   {[yi-kə-tua
     return-NEG.SUB-FUT-1sgSUBJ.VT+3fem.sgBAS.VT go-FUT-1sgSUBJ.VT+3fem.sgBAS.VT
     ya:b] məyir tə-ma:r-k-la}   a   səbən   ma:
     road really be-NEG.SUB-FUT-3fem.sgSUBJ.VT+3fem.sgBAS.VT then return.NEG NEG
     'When I go, if I am right (lit. really), I will come back; if I don't come back, if the road which I follow (lit. which I go) is not real, then I won't come back'

The distinction between negative future and negative irrealis is neutralized in dependent clauses: the marking *-ma:r-kə-* (NEG.SUB-FUT/IRR) is used for both. As we saw in 14.56–8, whether the condition is counterfactual or not can only be decided in the context of a whole sentence, and by the form of the verb in a main clause.

As mentioned at the beginning of this section, the habitual or repetitive negative meaning in a dependent clause can be expressed with a negative habitual juxtaposed clause—see 14.124. In positive polarity, a dependent clause would have been likely to be marked with the suffix *-kəb/kəkəb* 'as soon as' (see §18.6).

14.124 {jan-ma:r-kwa-tua}   samasa:m tə-k-na-di
     wash-NEG.SUB-HAB-1sgSUBJ.VT+3fem.sgBAS.VT many be-FUT-ACT.FOC-3plBAS.VT
     'If I do not keep washing (dishes) there will be many (dirty ones)'

That is, any dependent clause is likely to be negated with *-ma:r-*. Confirmation of this principle comes from spontaneously introduced innovations, which arise through adopting code-switches in Tok Pisin to the Manambu system. Consider 14.125. Manambu does not have a one-word equivalent to the Tok Pisin *nogut* 'it is no good that, lest', and the clausal complement of this nonce code-switch was reinterpreted as a dependent clause—which can be seen from the way '(that) you will not see' is negated.

14.125 *nogut*   [və-ma:r-k-ñəna   Kabla:m]
     no.good see-NEG.SUB-FUT-2fem.sgSUBJ.VT+3fem.sgBAS.VT Screw.River+LK+ACC
     'It is no good that you won't see the Screw River'

There is just one exception. As mentioned in §13.7, the predicate of the dependent conditional clause introduced by the adverb *kəpa:b* 'in case' is negated with *-ma:r-*, just as expected. However, the negator is reduplicated: we can recall that in 13.88 and other positive counterparts of examples like 14.126 the verbal root, and not any other morpheme, is reduplicated. The verbal root occurs in its negative form *ra:p* (the positive form is *rəp* 'be enough, fit') (but note that in 14.160 and 18.52 positive forms of the verbal root are used in similar constructions). When reduplicated, the negator loses its long vowel.

14.126 ku-sun   ap   kəpa:b   ra:p-marmar-ək
       put-UP+SEQ IMPV+see in.case fit.NEG-NEG.SUB:RED-DAT
       'Try it on, in case it is not good'

A similar example is at 14.160 below. That is, judging by the way in which they are negated, the 'in case' clauses stand apart from dependent clauses of all other types.

14.5.2 Negating questions

Negation of questions, content and polar, follows essentially the same pattern as that of dependent clauses: the verb is marked with the dependent negation -*ma:r*-. As expected, a non-verbal predicate has to be used as a copula complement of *tə*- which is then negated with -*ma:r*- in order to be able to occur in negative questions. Just as with any instances of the dependent negator -*ma:r*-, the marker usually goes onto a non-future negative stem (see §11.3.2), as shown in 14.130. However, this is only a tendency (cf. 14.133).

The difference between negated questions and negated dependent clauses lies in the presence of interrogative morphemes in content questions (see §10.4) and also in the intonation contour. Questions have a rising intonation, while dependent clauses have intonation contours of their own (we return to these in Chapter 20).

In 14.127, a negative content question is followed by a positive one. Other examples of a negated content question are at 14.128, and 10.107 ('How come you didn't see her?').

14.127 [agwa japək   yi-ma:r-na-d],   kə-də
       what   thing+LK+DAT go-NEG.SUB-ACT.FOC-3masc.sgBAS.VT DEM.PROX-masc.sg
       də-kə-də   awa:y-a:b   akrəl   ya:da?
       he-OBL-masc.sg mother's.brother-TOO where.to go+3masc.sgSUBJ.VT+3fem.sgBAS.VT
       'Why didn't he go, where did this maternal uncle of his go?'

14.128 agwa:k   kray-ma:r-də-l
       what+DAT marry-NEG.SUB-3masc.sgSUBJ.P-3fem.sgBAS.P
       'For what reason didn't he marry her?'

Polar questions are negated in the same way, as shown in 14.129–30.

14.129 ka   amy kwa:y
       DEM.PROX.fem.sg+DEM.DIST.fem.sg basket shrimp
       kwa-ma:r-na?
       stay-NEG.SUB-ACT.FOC+3fem.sgBAS.VT
       'Are there no shrimp in this very basket?'

In 14.130, a negative polar question contains a negated dependent clause. The two are negated in the same way.

14.130 [al-ay   ta:kw   væn   ku-ma:r-ən]   a-di   a:s
       DEM.DIST+fem.sg-DIST woman look+SEQ stay.NEG-NEG.SUB-SEQ DEM.DIST-pl dog
       rəka:rək   kwa:r-ma:r-ñəna
       correctly do/get.NEG-NEG.SUB-2fem.sgSUBJ.VT+3fem.sgBAS.VT
       'As that woman far away was staying without looking, you did not look after the dogs properly?'

However, there are two additional ways of asking a negative polar question. First, many speakers, in particular young and innovative ones, use negative declarative forms, as in 14.131. A similar example is at 14.151 below.

14.131 lə   du-a:k   ma: rə?
       she man-LK+DAT   NEG sit.NEG
       'She didn't get married, did she?'

And secondly, a desubordinated dependent clause can be used as a polar question. Such questions frequently have overtones of counterexpectation. At the name debating ceremony (held on 8 October 2004) I was allowed to sit with the men, record, and take pictures. Dameliway was keeping an eye on me from the women's quarters; she was worried that I could have lost my stringbag, and, at first opportunity, rushed to me with a worried question:

14.132 ñən   kwasabi   ku-su-ma:r-ən?
       you.fem stringbag put-UP-NEG.SUB-SEQ
       'How is it that you are not wearing a stringbag (as I expected you would because you always do)?'

The speaker who said 14.133 was surprised that there was water left in the bucket:

14.133 aw   gu   ata   kusə-ma:r-ku?
       then water thus/then finish-NEG.SUB-COMPL.SS
       'Then the water is not finished (or you haven't finished the water)?'

Only some same-subject and non-switch-reference-sensitive sequencing clauses undergo desubordination. We return to this in §19.9. Positive desubordinated clauses are often used in commands, and in statements, rather than in questions.

That there is a formal connection between questions and dependent clauses comes as no surprise to a typologist. It is well known that in many languages questions, both negative and positive, involve clefts with the surface structure of dependent clauses. That this connection in Manambu reveals itself only under negation is unusual.

14.5.3   The negator -*ma:r-* in independent clauses

The negator -*ma:r-* can negate a fully inflected predicate of an independent clause, albeit rarely, and under marked circumstances. The fully inflected verb takes -*ma:r-* immediately after the stem (see the structure of the inflected verb in §11.1.2) and remains fully inflected.

The most frequent context in which a predicate of an independent clause negated with -*ma:r-* may occur involves focusing a negated clause. This is shown in 14.134. That the verb is in highlighting focus is corroborated by the presence of the nominal cross-referencing enclitics which provide an additional overtone of 'it is the case that'; this is reflected in the translation.

14.134 yanu   tə-ma:r-na-a:l
       magic   have/be-NEG.SUB-ACT.FOC+3fem.sgBAS.VT-3fem.sgNOM
       'It is the case that she did not possess the magic'

The presence of the negator may be the only indicator that the absence of the action of the verb is in focus, as in 14.135.

14.135 nakaləb waku-tə-l   ata   ya-ma:r-ə-l
together go.out-3du.SUBJ.P-3fem.sgBAS.P then come-NEG.SUB-EP-3fem.sgBAS.P
kar-a:l
car-LK+ALL
'It is the case that we went out together, then (it was the case that) she did not come, in
a car'

Typologically speaking, focus constructions are often expressed via cleft clauses which, in
their turn, involve marking part of a clause as dependent. That a dependent clause negator is
used in focused clauses confirms that such clauses may be considered underlyingly dependent.
However, there are no other overt indicators that the clause is desubordinated.

Desubordinated clauses containing fully inflected verbs are also negated with the dependent
clause negator *-ma:r-*. In 14.136, the elliptical answer to the question contains a desubordinated
relative clause:

14.136 akə   səkər nana:u   vya-lə-l?   ñən
what.fem.sg time earthquake hit-3fem.sgSUBJ.P-3fem.sgBAS.P you.fem
ya-ma:r-ñən
come-NEG.SUB-2fem.sgBAS.P
'When (lit. what time) did the earthquake strike? (Time when) you had not come'

In 14.137, what could have been phrased as a causal clause, just like 14.116 and the first
clause of 14.55, was phrased as an independent clause negated with *-ma:r-* followed by the
conjunction *alək* 'this is why' as an afterthought. This was Gemaj's answer to an unstated
question why my sandals were getting loose.

14.137 məy-a kamna:gw kə-ma:r-ñəna   [PAUSE] alək
real-LK food   eat-NEG.SUB-2fem.sgSUBJ.VT+3fem.sgBAS.VT [PAUSE] this.is.why
'You do not eat real food, this is why'

We will see, in §19.9, that same-subject completive forms of the verb *tə-* 'be, have' are
developing into conjunctions which introduce what are treated as dependent clauses containing
fully inflected verbs. That this is really the case is corroborated by the fact that such newly
developed dependent clauses are negated with the dependent negator *-ma:r-*, as shown in
14.138. This is a comment on why a neighbouring group does not have any traditional masks
left:

14.138 sana:k   karabə   ja:p   kui-taka-dana-di
money+LK+DAT men's.house+LK thing give.to.third.p-put-3plSUBJ.VT-3plBAS.VT
[alək   tə-ku   tə-ma:r-na-di]
this.is.why be-COMPL.SS have-NEG.SUB-ACT.FOC-3plBAS.VT
'They gave away the things from men's house for money, this is why they do not have
(them any more)'

Independent clauses can be negated with *-ma:r-* if they express wishes and regrets. Dameliway and myself developed a mutual liking for each other from the very first meeting, at the end
of which she exclaimed:

14.139 oh, walba:b kwa-ma:r-na-dian
oh near   stay-NEG.SUB-ACT.FOC-1plBAS.VT
'Oh (it is a pity that) we do not live close!'

Similarly, an exclamation at 14.140 expresses a wish that:

14.140 wanǝb y<u>i-maːr-na</u>
        noise go/say-NEG.SUB-ACT.FOC+3fem.sgBAS.VT
        'May she not make noise! (meaning I wish she did not make noise)'

Along similar lines, 14.141 expresses a regret concerning the fishing grounds spoilt forever.

14.141 aw   kǝta kǝ   *kamap*-maːr-da   kǝta
        then now   DEM.PROX.fem.sg appear-NEG.SUB-3masc.sgSUBJ.VT+3fem.sgBAS.VT now
        kǝ   vǝ-maːr-bana   a   tayir
        DEM.PROX.fem.sg see-NEG.SUB-1plSUBJ.VT+3fem.sgBAS.VT CONN before
        kǝ   ar   atawa   ma: rǝ
        DEM.PROX.fem.sg lake like.that NEG sit/be.NEG
        'Now this (a variety of fish) does not appear, now we regretfully do not see this! Before
        this lake was not like that'

An independent clause negated with *-maːr-* may also have an irrealis meaning if it occurs
with future marking; this is always mixed with a wish for the thing not to happen:

14.142 [gu   kǝ-ku]   kiya-k-na-wun   [wun-a-dǝ   naka-dǝ-mǝy-a
        water eat-COMPL.SS   die-FUT-ACT.FOC-1sgBAS.VT I-LK-masc.sg one-masc.sg-real-LK
        ñan   vǝ-maːr-kǝ-tua-d]
        child see-NEG.SUB-FUT-1sgSUBJ.VT-3masc.sgBAS.VT
        'Having drowned (lit. eaten water), I will die, oh dear I might not see my only son'

If such a negated form follows a command, it may have an apprehensive meaning 'or else':

14.143 kǝ-di   plet   ajan   a   kamna:gw
        DEM.PROX-pl plate IMPV+wash DEM.DIST+fem.sg food
        kǝ-maːrǝ-kǝ-na-ñǝn
        eat-NEG.SUB-FUT-ACT.FOC-2fem.sgBAS.VT
        'Wash these plates, or else you may not get the food'

The ways in which independent negative clauses marked with *-maːr-* are used to express
meanings covering wishes, regrets, negative irrealis, and undesirable consequences can be
ultimately traced back to the negative focused clauses (as illustrated in 14.134–5): all of these
involve focusing on the non-activity.

The marker *-maːr-* appears to be cognate to the negative imperative *-mar-ék* in Wosera
(Wilson 1980: 164–5). The use of the morpheme *-maːr-* to express wishes is a link between
otherwise hardly comparable meanings of Manambu *-maːr-* and Wosera *-marék*.

14.6 INHERENTLY NEGATIVE LEXEMES AND NEGATIVE PRO-CLAUSES

Manambu has a number of inherently negative forms. These cannot be negated, and occur in
a negative context only.

The adverb *sǝmǝrab*, *samaːb*, *sama:b* or *sǝmsǝma:b* 'never ever' is typically used in negated
clauses as an emphatic negator. It occurs both in declarative clauses which already have the
negator *ma:* as in 14.144 and T3.43, or *akǝs*, as in 14.50, and in commands, as in 14.95 and
14.145. The four forms appear fully synonymous.

14.144 wun ma: la:kw   s̩ms̩ma:b
       I   NEG know.NEG never.ever
       'I do not know anything (about this)'

14.145 <u>sama:b</u>   br̩-k̩-wa   wa-k-wayik
       never.ever 3du-OBL-COM say-EP-PROH.EXTRA
       'Do not ever talk to them two!'

Just occasionally, this adverb can be used as the only negative word in a clause, making the whole clause negative, as in 14.146 (with the predicate in desiderative mood), and in 14.147.

14.146 [wa-tua-d̩   ma:j] <u>sama:b</u>   wuk̩r
       say-1sgSUBJ.VT-3masc.sgBAS.VT speech never.ever listen+DES
       'You never want to listen to what I say (lit. speech said by me)!'

14.147 [<u>sama:b</u>   karya-k̩-m̩na]   k̩-d̩
       never.ever bring-FUT-2masc.sgSUBJ.VT+3fem.sgBAS.VT DEM.PROX-masc.sg
       k̩p-a-tamiya:m   kwa-k̩-na-di
       ground-LK-area+LK+LOC stay-FUT-ACT.FOC-3plBAS.VT
       'Since you will not bring (them in), they will stay on the ground'

A development of an emphatic form in a negative construction into a negation marker is typologically well attested. In Manambu, there is no doubt that this is an innovation. Whether the root *sam-* is etymologically linked to the quantifier *samasa:m* 'many' (§10.5) is an open question.

A number of inherently negative forms are used as pro-clauses, that is, as negative responses. An inherently negative adverb *kapi sapi* 'no way' is used as a negative response and a negative pro-clause. This could well be an alliterative compound based on the root *kapi* cognate to the negator *kupu(k)* found in numerous Ndu languages. Its variants are *sapi kapi* or just *kapi*. I was told that *sapi* can also be used this way, but never found an example.

A proximate demonstrative *k̩* in highlighting focus (*ka, kal* (DEM.PROX+3fem.sgNOM) or *kad* (DEM.PROX+3masc.sgNOM)) can be used as an emphatic negator, as in 10.24, 18.26, 14.41, and 14.148:

14.148 vyau   wa-l̩-k   <u>ka!</u>
       hit+1sgIMPV say-3fem.sg-COMPL.SS DEM.PROX+3fem.sgNOM
       ' "Can I hit (it)?", said (the younger sister), "No!" (said the elder sister)'

This looks like a demonstrative—however, we cannot rule out that this form is in fact a remnant of a Proto-Ndu negator with the velar first syllable, ultimately cognate with *kapi*.

The negator most frequently used as a negative pro-clause is *ma:* 'no'. It is used as a negative reaction to a command, as in 14.42, or just to contradict a statement, as in 14.86. It is also used as a negative response to positive questions, as in 14.149, where it is often accompanied by a negated verb:

14.149 s̩r   ya-k-na-d?   ma:, yæy   ma:
       tomorrow come-FUT-ACT.FOC-3masc.sgBAS.VT No, come.NEG NEG
       ' "Will he come tomorrow?" "No, he won't come" '

To provide a confirmation to a negative question, *ayey* 'yes' is used, as in 14.150 (also see §4.5.5 and 4.83). This can optionally be accompanied by a negated verb:

14.150 ñən   ga:n sə   kwa-ma:r-ñəna?   ayey
      you.fem night sleep stay-NEG.SUB-2fem.sgSUBJ.VT+3fem.sgBAS.VT Yes
      ' "You didn't sleep (last) night, did you?" "No, I didn't (lit. yes)" '

To refute a negative suggestion, *ma:* 'general negator' or *akəs* 'habitual negator' is used, as in 14.151 and 14.51.

14.151 ñən   ma: ya:g? ma:! samasa:m yaga-lwun   wun
      you.fem NEG fear <u>No</u> a.lot   fear-1fem.sgBAS.VT I
      ' "You were not scared (of a plane crash)?" "No, I was scared a lot" '

The desiderative negator *ata* is not used this way. The negator *ma:* is often used to negate a clause as a whole. It is then postposed to the clause and preceded by a short pause, as in 14.66–8 and 14.152–4.

14.152 [[wun yi-ku]   [və-tua   ja:p] və-tua]
      I   go-COMPL.SS see-1SUBJ.VT+3fem.sgBAS.VT thing see-1SUBJ.VT+3fem.sgBAS.VT
      [PAUSE] ma:
      [PAUSE] NEG
      'Having gone I looked at the thing I saw (before)—nothing!'

14.153 məyir laku-n   [PAUSE] ma:
      really know-SEQ [PAUSE] NEG
      'They do not really know' (lit. really knowing—no)'

An interjection may precede the negator, showing that it constitutes a separate clause:

14.154 [æya   vyakət-a sa:d-ad]   [PAUSE] a   ma:
      always good-LK fashion-3masc.sg.NOM [PAUSE] CONN NEG
      'It was not always good way of life' (lit. it is always good way—this was not the case)

The negator *ma:* is often used elliptically in any clause type, as in 14.155–6. The habitual negator *akəs* but not the desiderative negator *ata* can also be used this way—see 14.50 and 14.157.

14.155 [ah, ya: ma:], [ñən   <u>ma:]</u> [adakw] [ñanugw məwi
      ah come NEG   you.fem NEG stay.IMPV children things.like.that
      saku-n   adakw]
      give.birth-SEQ stay.IMPV
      ' "Oh, I won't come", "you—no (won't come), you stay, stay giving birth to children etc." '

14.156 [anay   Swakapa:m   rə-na-di   a-di   Gala]
      CURR.REL+DIST Swakap+LK+LOC sit-ACT.FOC-3plBAS.VT DEM.DIST-pl Gala
      [aw day <u>ma:]</u>
      CONN they no
      'They stayed there at Swakap (previously talked about), those Gala, but they (the other lot)—no (they did not stay, they went across to Yambon)'

14.157 [kəjap-adəka   akəs   kə-kwa-na-bər]   [kə-di
      protein.food-ONLY NEG.HAB eat-HAB-ACT.FOC-3duBAS.VT DEM.PROX-pl
      kəjap   <u>akəs]</u>
      protein.food NEG.HAB
      'Only protein food these two never used to eat, protein food never'

We saw in §14.1.3 that if a constituent is to be negated separately, it has to form a negative clause with the negator *ma:*; see 14.41. The general negator *ma:* can occur as a complement of the verb *wa-* 'say', in the meaning of 'refuse, say no', as shown in 9.5, 13.78, and 14.42.

Like most languages of the world, Manambu has numerous other expressions with negative meanings, such as *wa-təp-* (say-be.closed) 'forbid' and *wukə-təp-* (hear/think-close) 'forget'. However, such terms are not inherently negative because they can be negated just like any other verb (see §15.3, on their structure).

A recently introduced inherently negative term *tabu* 'taboo, forbidden', from Tok Pisin, is often used by those speakers who tend to code-switch. It tends to be accompanied by a negative command in Manambu, as in 14.158 (partly repeated from 14.74).

14.158 [tabu] [war-tukwa]
taboo go.up-PROH.GEN
'It is forbidden, don't go up'

The dependent clause negator *-ma:r* appears to participate in the formation of two verbs, *wukə-mar-* 'forget' (lit. remember/think-NEG.SUB) and *ya:p sə-mar-* (breath plant-NEG.SUB) 'be dead'. Both verbs can be negated, and thus are not inherently negative. There is evidence, however, that *-mar-* in 'forget' and the negator *-ma:r-* may be lookalikes and not cognates. First, the component *-mar-* in the verb 'forget' does not have a long vowel. Secondly, as we saw in 12.71 (§12.8.2), this component undergoes partial reduplication quite different from the reduplication of the negator *-ma:r-*. Another example of such partial reduplication meaning 'fully' is at 14.159:

14.159 kəkətəp kui-ku,   də-kə-m   atawa sa:d
Kəkətəp give.to.third.p-COMPL.SS he-OBL-LOC thus   way
wukə-may-mar-ba-l   aka   ya
think-NEG.SUB.RED-?-1pl.SUBJ.P-3fem.sg.BAS.P DEM.DIST.REACT.TOP.fem.sg EMPH
'Having given (him) the Kəkətəp feast (mortuary feast), this way we have forgotten all about him'

We saw in §14.5.1 that the negator *-ma:r-* can undergo reduplication of a different sort: an example of the reduplicated negator used to negate 'in case' conditional clauses is at 14.126. A similar example is at 14.160, where the verb *wukə-* 'hear, listen, think' is negated this way. The form *wukə-marmar-ək* can mean 'unless/lest I forget', or 'for me not to forget'.

14.160 suku   (kəpa:b) wukə-marmar-ək
write+1sg.IMPV in.case   think-NEG.SUB.RED-DAT
'Let me write it down lest I might not think (of it)'

That the negator *-ma:r-* and the component *-mar-* in what look like verbs with negative meanings are reduplicated differently shows that, at least synchronically, they are different forms.

Despite the wealth of negative constructions in Manambu, additional negative strategies may be employed. As shown in 14.73, questions are often used in negative meanings. In 14.161, a question implies a negative command: the girl was not supposed to drink too much water because there was no place for her to go to the toilet:

14.161 toilet yi-k-ñəna   tami: akəm-a?
toilet go-FUT-2fem.sgSUBJ.VT+3fem.sgBAS.VT area where-3fem.sgNOM
'Where is the place for you to go to the toilet?'

TABLE 14.2   Negators in Manambu: declarative and interrogative clauses

NEGATOR	*ma:*	*akəs*	*ata*	*-ma:r*	*-marmar*
Meaning	1. declarative non-habitual; 2. pro-clauses	1. habitual 2. irrealis 3. optative	1. purposive 2. desiderative	any dependent clause	'in case' dependent clause
Marking of various categories	requires negative verb forms; no person, number, or gender marking	no special negative forms; same marking of person, gender, and number as in positive clauses			

In 14.162, the character is trying to tell the snakes that he and his brother did not cook for them—this is accompanied with ironic intonation.

14.162 gur-a:k   yi-bana   səkulək, a?
       you.pl-LK+DAT go-1plSUBJ.VT+3fem.sgBAS.VT cooking eh
       'Did we cook for you, eh?' (meaning: we did not cook for you)

These negative strategies confirm the connection between questions and negation in Manambu, corroborating an etymological link between the negative and the interrogative *ata* (§14.3).

14.7   SUMMARY

Manambu has a complex system of expressing negation. Only predicates can be negated; and if a non-predicate constituent has to be negated, this is achieved by making it into an independent predicate head. A limited variability of the scope of negation is found with the general negator *ma:* in non-future declarative clauses only. A summary is in Tables 14.2–3.

Numerous categories are neutralized under negation. These include the following.

(i) DEPENDENT CLAUSE TYPES: in positive polarity Manambu has seven types of medial dependent clauses (see §18.1), juxtaposed dependent clauses, and relative clauses; of these, one ('unlikely condition') cannot be negated, and all the rest except for one (the 'in case' conditional clause) are negated in the same way, with the dependent negator *-ma:r-*.

TABLE 14.3   Negators in Manambu: prohibitive clauses

NEGATOR	*-tukwa*	*-way*	*-wayik*	*-(kə)ba-*	*-ma:r-kwa-*
Meaning	general prohibitive	strong prohibitive	extra-strong prohibitive	'must not'	prohibitive
Person value	second or third			third	third
Gender and number marking	none				two genders in singular; dual, plural numbers

This means that a general opposition between main and dependent clause underlies the ways polarity operates in the language.

(ii) PERSON, NUMBER, AND GENDER are neutralized in declarative non-habitual negative clauses.

Negation is instrumental in providing a distinction between relative clauses, juxtaposed clauses, and main clauses. In positive polarity, these types are distinguished by intonation only.

Negation distinguishes future from irrealis forms. The existing link between questions (conceived as underlyingly dependent structures) and dependent clauses surfaces only under negation.

Three prohibitives differ in their strength, and in a number of morphosyntactic properties (see Table 14.1). These correspond to just one positive imperative, and a variety of imperative strategies.

The negation of desiderative involves a marker which is possibly of an interrogative origin. This may have its basis in a tendency to use questions in lieu of negative structures throughout the language.

Verb Compounding

Manambu has a wide variety of compound verbs which can consist of two or three roots. Their meanings include cause-effect, sequence of sub-events, and aktionsart. One or two components can undergo full reduplication (see §12.8.2). Verb compounds form one grammatical and one phonological word. Their components are strictly contiguous: no other element can intervene between them.

The components cannot have separate value of tense, aspect, mood, action focus, modality, or polarity. A compound is marked just once for each of the appropriate categories. All compounds have fused argument structure: that is, they share all the core and peripheral arguments. Two identical verbs cannot occur in one compound.

Compounds account for about 20 per cent of verbs in texts and conversations. The productivity of compounds varies, depending on their type. Components of a compound always occur in a fixed order. The only exception in the corpus is the pair *taka-təp-* (put-close) 'prevent (from seeing), block' and *təpə-taka-* (close-put) 'cover (the surface of something); prevent from seeing': these only partly overlap in their meanings (see §15.3 (A7 and A8)).

All these properties are typical of one-word serial verb constructions, of a kind similar to those found in other languages of the Sepik area (e.g. Yimas and Alamblak), and elsewhere (e.g. Olutec in Central America and Dâw in Amazonia: a comprehensive typological account is in Aikhenvald 2006a). What sets the Manambu verb compounds apart from canonical one-word serial verbs is their composition, and their semantics.

A number of components in verb compounds provide manner, aspect, and other specifications to the major component, but are not used in the language on their own (e.g. *-jika-* 'do properly', *-maki-* in *gra-* 'cry', *gra-maki-* (cry-do.a.lot) 'cry a lot'). These nonce roots are treated as verb roots rather than as derivational suffixes only for the sake of a unified analysis of verb compounding structures. When more information on the lexicon of other Ndu languages becomes available, we may be able to confirm, or refute, our assumptions about their verbal origins.

The semantic link between the independent verb and the same form in a compound is often obscure. For instance, the verb *yakə-* means 'throw', and the compounded root *-yakə-* means 'do fully'—the formal match is perfect, but the semantic link is not. The verb *ya-* means 'come'. The form *-ya-* in compounds has two meanings. One, 'coming; (do) while coming', is transparently related to the verb 'come', and the other, 'carry on doing', is not. We are faced with the problem of differentiating polysemous stems from homonyms—a pervasive puzzle throughout Manambu.

All these features are atypical for serial verbs (see an exhaustive account in Aikhenvald 2006a). The meanings of many compounds are idiomatic and do not follow any straightforward semantic rules. Even those compounds which can be considered productive display restrictions on one or both components. Some verbs hardly ever occur in compounds. One verb, 'see', has a suppletive form when it occurs as second component in compounding. This feature is reminiscent of 'combining forms' described in derivational morphology (Aikhenvald 2007), and is atypical of serial verbs. This is why I prefer to analyse Manambu verb sequences as lexicalized compounds rather than as bona fide serial verbs.

In terms of their composition, Manambu compounds divide into SYMMETRICAL and ASYMMETRICAL (cross-linguistically, this distinction is encountered in serial verbs, and other multi-verb constructions: see Aikhenvald 2006a; Amha and Dimmendaal 2006).

(i) SYMMETRICAL COMPOUNDS consist of two components, from large open classes, whose semantic relationship is that of sequence of sub-actions, manner, or cause-effect. Each has restrictions on the nature and/or the transitivity of one of the components. See §15.2.

(ii) ASYMMETRICAL COMPOUNDS consist of a verb from a largish open class ('major' verb) followed by a root from a closed class ('minor' verb) which provides a meaning to do with aspect, aktionsart, extent of action, and valency increase, as in *kə-kusə-* (eat-finish) 'finish eating, eat up', *kə-kəta-* (eat-try) 'try eating'. See §15.3.

An alternative structure, whereby a 'minor' verb from a closed class precedes the 'major' verb, is restricted to two 'minor' verbs—*wa-* 'say' and *yi-* 'go'. Given the restrictions on these constructions, we cannot exclude the option of their alternative analysis as prefixes.

Asymmetrical compounds whose second component is the verb *-yi-* 'go' or *-ya-* 'come' which provides aspectual specification do not occur in the imperative. To be used in a command, they have to be rephrased with a biclausal structure.

Verb compounds may consist of a symmetrical compound within an asymmetrical one; or of two asymmetrical compounds. They can never contain more than three verb roots. See §15.4. The effects of verb root reduplication in compounds are summarized in §15.5 (also see §12.8.2).

Some directionals can be analysed as a subtype of verb compounds—see §16.1.

Verb compounds differ from complex predicates consisting of an uninflected form of the major verb and an inflectable auxiliary. Unlike compounds, complex predicates form one grammatical construction (with one tense, aspect, modality and polarity value), but consist of two grammatical and phonological words—this is the topic of Chapter 17.

15.2 SYMMETRICAL COMPOUNDS

Symmetrical compounds belong to three broad types: sequencing (§15.2.1), manner (§15.2.2), and cause-effect (§15.2.3). Semantically non-compositional idiomatic compounds, including those with nonce roots, are discussed in §15.2.4.

15.2.1 Sequencing compounds

Sequencing compounds describe a sequence of related sub-actions. They consist of two components, one of which (typically, the second one) is a posture verb, a verb of specific motion, often with a directional specification, or an inherently directional verb. The order of components is iconic in that it reflects the sequence of sub-actions. The timing of sub-actions may overlap, so the term 'sequencing' is an approximation. We will see, in §15.3, that general motion verbs *yi-* 'go' and *ya-* 'come' form asymmetrical compounds whereby they impart directional and aspectual meanings to the compound. Neither of them occurs in sequencing compounds (the only possible exception, *yi-pay-pəsə-* (go-RED-go.round(?)+SEQ) 'go and keep going round and round' with the root which does not occur on its own is discussed in §16.2.1).

In terms of transitivity of components, any combination is possible. We discuss each of these one at a time. Combinations A–C are more frequent than D.

A. Two INTRANSITIVE VERBS IN A SEQUENCING COMPOUND share their S, e.g. *væsə-piñə-* (step-slip) 'step and slip' (15.1), *kaula-rə-* (enter-stay) 'enter and stay', and *pakwə-rə-* (hide-stay) 'hide and stay' (15.2). The resulting forms are intransitive. Forms containing compounds are underlined throughout this chapter.

15.1 miya:m   <u>væsə-piñə-tua</u>
      tree+LK+LOC step-slip-1sgSUBJ.VT+3fem.sgBAS.VT
      'I slipped stepping on a tree'

15.2 ta:kw   <u>pakwə-rə-kə-na-l-a:b</u>
      woman hide-sit-FUT-ACT.FOC-3fem.sgBAS.VT-TOO
      'The woman was hiding (and) staying (in hiding) too'

B. A TRANSITIVE V₁ CAN BE FOLLOWED BY AN INTRANSITIVE V₂, as in *yaku-war-* (wash-go.up) 'wash and go up' and *yaku-væs-* 'wash and step' in 15.3. The resulting form is transitive.

15.3 <u>yaku-væsal</u>   nagwək
      wash-step+3fem.sgBAS.P sago+LK+DAT
      'She stepped (out) to wash sago' (lit. she wash-stepped, with respect to sago)

The V₂ of 15.3 can also be interpreted as indicating the goal of V₁. The exact interpretation depends on the context.

C. AN INTRANSITIVE V₁ CAN BE FOLLOWED BY A TRANSITIVE V₂, as in 15.4. The resulting forms are transitive. Sequential compounds are the only type of compound in which the verb 'see/look' appears in the V₂ slot. Its suppletive version *-kəta* is used then, as in 15.4 (repeated from T3.38; also see T3.39) and 15.116 ('stand-look.upward'). This same root means 'try', and occurs in the form *-kəta*, in asymmetrical compounds discussed in §15.3 below; it also occurs as a free-standing directional form of 'see'—see §16.1.

15.4 a   gapəm   ata   <u>rə-kətəwun</u> ra:l
      then big.post+LK+LOC then sit-LOOK   sit+3fem.sgBAS.P
      'She then sat at the house post looking up'

Another example of the bound form *kəta-* as V₂ with a posture verb is *tə-kətakun* 'stand facing outwards', and *tə-kətəwun* 'stand looking upwards' in 15.116.

D. Two TRANSITIVE VERBS can form a sequential compound, as in 15.5. The nominalized compound contains a directional 'up' (§9.1.1):

15.5 amæy   asa:y ma: wa-na-bər   <u>yakə-su-yakə-su-nay-nayi:k</u>
      mother father no   say-ACT.FOC-3duBAS.VT throw-UP-throw-UP-play-play+DAT
      'Mother and father told (us) not to play (with pig's bladder) and throw it up' (lit. said no to throwing up (and) playing)

This compound, just like the ones in 15.8–9 below, allows for an alternative interpretation as a manner compound: 'play by throwing (the pig's bladder) up'. The semantic boundary between purely sequential and manner compounds is not watertight—we return to this in §15.2.2.

Not every verb can occur as V₁ or as V₂ in a sequencing compound. As is the case with any symmetrical compound, two verbs can only occur together if the resulting compound makes sense to speakers—that is, if a sequence of sub-events can be conceived as one unitary event (see Aikhenvald 2006a: 10–11, and Bruce 1988: 29). It makes sense to 'sit looking up', but it would scarcely make sense, in the Manambu context, to 'sew looking up', or to 'sew coming in'—this is not what people do when they sew. This is why compounds like *təpə-kətu 'sew look up' or *təpə-wula 'sew come in' are not grammatical. Some verbs, like verbs of speech, hardly ever occur in sequential compounds (see §21.1.3).

The semantic effects of a directional V_2 in a sequencing compound vary, depending on the semantics of V_1. These are discussed at I–III below. If we were to analyse sequencing compounds in Manambu as serial verbs, this feature would have been highly unusual. Since most compounds are lexicalized, no idiosyncratic feature should appear strange.

I. If V_1 IS A MOTION VERB, an inherently directional verb as V_2 of sequencing compounds typically provides a directional specification to the V_1. Examples are *təməl-væra-* (roll-come.in) 'roll and go out; roll in the inland direction' in 15.6, and *kawar-waku-* (lift-go.out) 'take out (from upper location, e.g. a house)' in 15.7.

15.6 təməl-væra-ku   ya:d
     roll-come.in.direction.to.speaker-COMPL.SS come+3masc.sgBAS.P
     'He came having rolled and come inland'

15.7 [[kə-də   wiya:m   kwa-na-di   du   ta:kw]
     DEM.PROX-masc.sg house+LK+LOC stay-ACT.FOC-3plBAS.VT man woman
     ka-war-waku-da-k]]   [və-ku]
     bring/carry-up-go.out-3pl-COMPL.DS see-COMPL.SS
     'Having seen that people staying in this house were taking (things) up and outside (he said)'

A sequence of a directional and an inherently directional verb is the only way of marking two directions—'up' and 'outside'—in one predicate. We will see in §16.1.5 that the directional suffixes and bound forms 'up' and 'outside' never occur in one word (see also §16.1.2).

An inherently directional V_1 can be interpreted as indicating direction of a motion verb in V_2 slot, or as providing manner modification to it. Examples 15.8 and 15.9 can be translated either as (a) or as (b).

15.8 [[gəpə-wula:k   kurə-n] kaulak,   a   mayər]
     run-go.inside+PURP.SS do-SEQ get.in+PURP.SS DEM.DIST+fem.sg garden+LK+ALL
     'He aimed to enter that garden, being about to (a) run inside or (b) go inside by running'

15.9 Kamagab də-kə   yibən nak a   gəpə-væki:d
     Kamagab masc.sg-OBL+fem.sg harbour one then run-go.across+3masc.sgBAS.P
     'Then Kamagab (a) ran and went across or (b) went across by running to his one harbour'

Both interpretations are equally valid—the semantic boundary between manner and sequencing is quite fluid (see 15.5). The exact interpretation is determined by the context.

Sequencing verb compounds with a directional verb as V_2 are ambiguous. They can be interpreted as expressing real sequences of actions. Alternatively, the directional component may be seen as a simple marker of the direction of action. This ambiguity is rooted in the generic character of the semantics of inherently directional verbs. We return to this in §16.1.2.

That the directional follows the main verb accords with the general suffixing tendency of the language.

II. If V₁ IS NOT A MOTION VERB, an inherently directional V₂ provides directional or locational specification to it. And there is a certain amount of ambiguity. The compound in 15.10 can either mean 'play outside' or 'play and go outside (at the same time)'.

15.10 ñədi   viti   <u>nay-waku-bər</u>
      child:du two play-go.out-3duBAS.VT/P
      'Two children were playing outside' or 'Two children played and went outside'

Along similar lines, *vya-waku-* (hit-go.out) means 'kill outside', 'kill and go outside', or 'kill while going outside', *kamna:gw kə-waku-* (food eat-go.out) means 'eat outside', 'eat and go outside', or 'eat while going outside', and *kə-da-* (eat-go.down) may mean 'eat while being in a downward direction', 'eat and go down', or 'eat while going down' (here the order is not fully iconic).

The context may help—in 15.11, it suggests a locational reading: the character was drifting downstream when he killed the garfish:

15.11 [ada   jagər <u>vya-da-ku</u>]
      DEM.DIST.REACT.TOP+masc.sg garfish kill-go.down-COMPL.SS
      'Having killed that garfish down(stream) (he went inland)'

And in 15.12, the context leaves both interpretations possible: having sharpened their spears, the villagers went outside the village to assemble their arms for the subsequent warfare:

15.12 ja:p   <u>saki-waku-di-di</u>
      thing assemble-go.out-3plSUBJ.P-3plBAS.P
      'They assembled things going out' or 'They assembled things outside (the village)'

The inherently directional V₂ can simply indicate the direction of the action, as in 15.13, where no 'going across' is implied—the verb 'go across' refers to the direction of the needle. The people who were hiding in the mosquito net were not going anywhere. The other two people outside the net were sewing it up so as to make it a safer hiding place:

15.13 [ñəg-a:m   wula-brə-k]   [a-də   ñəg ata kulkula:r
      net-LK+LOC go.inside-3du-COMPL.DS DEM.DIST-masc.sg net then needle+LK+INSTR
      təpa-væki-brə-d]   [təpa-væki-ku,]   [təkər api:m
      sew-go.across-3duSUBJ.P-3masc.sgBAS.P sew-go.across-COMPL.SS chair top+LOC
      taka-ku]   ada   ra:d
      put-COMPL.SS DEM.DIST.REACT.TOP+masc.sg sit+3masc.sgBAS.P
      'After they went inside the net, the other two then sewed the net across with a needle, having sewn it across, having put (the needle) on top of the bench, he sat (there)'

This usage is reminiscent of directional markers on verbs (see §16.1). The inherently directional verbs, such as *væki-* 'go across and away', *væra-* 'go towards speaker', *wula-* 'enter, go inside or inland', *war-* 'go up' and *da-* 'go down', and verbal directional markers overlap in their functions. An inherently directional verb as V₂ is preferred to a directional marker if V₁ does not imply motion. In 15.13, a speaker could not have said *təpa-saki-* (sew-ACROSS.AWAY) because 'sew' is a stationary activity (people do not move around while they sew: see further discussion in §16.1).

III. If the V₁ IS A POSTURE VERB AND V₂ IS INHERENTLY DIRECTIONAL, the resulting meaning is 'stay (doing something) and move in an upward direction', as in 15.14 below. That the last verb is semantically main is reflected in the translation, and also in the way tail-head linkage operates: we can see, in the second sentence in 15.14, that *war-* 'go up' is repeated, and not the whole compound (unlike in 15.13).

15.14 [ada   ka:n   tə-war-na-d]
      DEM.DIST.REACT.TOP+masc.sg paddle+SEQ stay-go.up-ACT.FOC-3masc.sgBAS.VT

[warən   warən   warən   warən   warən   warən   warən]
go.up+SEQ go.up+SEQ go.up+SEQ go.up+SEQ go.up+SEQ go.up+SEQ go.up+SEQ

[ada   kawi:d]
DEM.DIST.REACT.TOP+masc.sg go.ashore+3masc.sgBAS.VT

'He went upstream paddling (lit. paddling stay-go.up), having gone up (7 times) he went ashore'

That is, the status of the two components of symmetrical verbs is only roughly equal.

Sequencing compounds share semantic similarity with a biclausal sequence of two verbs one of which takes the sequencing suffix *-n* (see §18.2). In rapid speech the formal difference between sequencing compounds and clause sequencing is lost. The manner sequencing structures marked with *-n* form one phonological phrase with the following verb. In rapid speech, they form one phonological word with the verb that follows. So, a sequence *wukə-n rə-na-wun* (hear-SEQ sit-ACT.FOC-1fem.sgBAS.VT) 'I am sitting listening' is pronounced as [wukə́-(n)-rə-na-wun], with elision of *n*. Along similar lines, in a slow register, *waji-nay-* in 15.15a is rephrased as *waji-n nay-* (laugh-SEQ play) in 15.15b. The meaning is the same.

15.15a day ata waji-nayin   kwa:n   gu   yaku-di
       they then laugh-play+SEQ stay+SEQ water wash-3plBAS.VT/P
       'Then they washed themselves keeping laughing and playing'

15.15b day ata wajin   nayin   kwa:n   gu   yaku-di
       they then laugh+SEQ play+SEQ stay+SEQ water wash-3plBAS.VT/P
       'Then they washed themselves keeping laughing and playing'

Semantically, sequencing compounds and manner sequencing structures are rather similar. In the manner sequencing structures (§18.2) the verb marked with the sequencing suffix *-n* often describes the action and precedes the fully inflected verb which provides a directional specification, as in *kurə-n kawar-kə-tua* (get-SEQ bring.up-FUT-1sgSUBJ.VT+3fem.sgBAS.VT) 'I will get it and bring it up' (lit. getting bring up), and *wukə-n karya-kə-tua* (remember/think-SEQ bring-FUT-1sgSUBJ.VT+3fem.sgBAS.VT) 'I will remember it' (lit. thinking bring).

This functional similarity is corroborated by an additional feature. Sequencing structures can be used if a compound cannot be formed. For instance, the imperative of *tə-war-* (stay-go.up) is *ta:n a-war* (stay+SEQ IMPV-go.up) 'staying go up'. The verb *tə-* has a suppletive imperative *ada* not used in compounding.

Compounds in examples like 15.15a occur as a result of surface phonetic realization of general sequencing structure. In due course, they may be indicative of a change in progress, whereby the rapid speech phenomena may give rise to a new grammatical structure.

15.2.2 Manner compounds

Manner compounds consist of a verb which provides manner modification as V_1 and another verb as V_2. Just as in sequencing compounds, there are no restrictions on transitivity of either verb. Transitivity of the whole compound is determined by the second, semantically 'main' verb.

V_I is often a motion verb, e.g. *væs-* 'step' or *gəp-* 'run' (see 15.8–9), e.g. *væsə-waku-* (step-go.out) 'go out by stepping carefully', as in 15.16, or *væsə-war-ən væsə-da-n* (step-go.up-SEQ step-go.down-SEQ) 'moving up and down by stepping'.

15.16 kwasa-kwasa <u>væsə-waku-k-na-wun</u>
　　　 little-little　　step-go.out-FUT-ACT.FOC-1fem.sgBAS.VT
　　　 'I will go out (into the Sepik River) by stepping carefully (so as not to slip)'

V_2 does not have to be a verb of motion. In 15.17 the cassowary (a mythical woman) is trying to tear the head of a man off her breast by twisting it and by stepping on it:

15.17 [væsə-gwajə-lə-d]　　　　　　　　　　　　　ata　wi:d
　　　 step-turn-3fem.sgSUBJ.P-3masc.sgBAS.P　then　break.off+3masc.sgBAS.P
　　　 'She twisted (the man's head off) by stepping (on him), and then (the head) broke off (her breast)'

The compound 'sew-close.up' in 15.18 means 'close up by sewing'. I gave one of my sisters a button-up dress with too much opening. She liked it and said, using a manner compound:

15.18 təpə-wulpi-ku　　　　　ku-su-kə-tua
　　　 sew-close.up-COMPL.SS put-UP-FUT-1sgSUBJ.VT+3fem.sgBAS.VT
　　　 'Having sewn it tightly, I will wear it'

Such manner compounds typically contain two transitive verbs—e.g. *vya-ləpa-* (hit-cut) 'hit and break; cut (cross-wise)' (see 12.72 where it occurs partially reduplicated).

Manner compounds with verb of affect as V_I and an ambitransitive verb as V_2 have distinct overtones of cause-effect. The compound in 15.19 can be understood as either manner or cause-effect:

15.19 ku-su-wapwi væsə-pərki-lwun
　　　 'put'-UP-cloth step-tear-1fem.sgBAS.P
　　　 'I tore (my) dress by stepping on it' or 'I stepped on (my) dress and (it) tore'

We saw in 15.8–9 that sequencing compounds can be interpreted as manner compounds. Both manner and sequencing compounds are similar in meaning to biclausal structures whereby one verb is marked with the manner sequencing marker *-n*—see 12.76 and §18.2. There is, however, no indication that any of the manner compounds result from clause sequencing in rapid speech.

15.2.3　Cause-effect and manner compounds

Cause-effect compounds contain an affect verb, typically *vya-* 'hit, kill', *væsə-* 'step on', or *vætə-* 'bite' as V_I, and an intransitive verb or a transitive verb as V_2. All cause-effect compounds are transitive. The O of V_I is the same as the S/A of V_2. The meaning of the cause-effect compounds is fairly compositional; most of them have an overtone of manner. Examples are *glu-* 'be settled down', *vya-glu-* 'shake (something) down', *prapi-* 'be hollow', *vya-prapi-* 'break something open and make it hollow', *wuta-* 'break (as a coconut falling from a tree)', and *vya-wuta-* (hit-break.in.two) 'hit and break in two' (see 12.23); *kəsək* 'shake (S=A ambitransitive)', *vya-kəsək-* (hit-shake) 'shake off (earth from peanuts) by shaking (them)' (as in 15.20), *wi:-* 'break, split (intransitive)', *væsə-wi:-* 'step on something so that it splits' (as in 15.21), and *təməl-* 'roll' and *vya-təməl-* 'make roll or sound by hitting' (as in 15.24a):

15.20   *kasan*   gwa-n   <u>vya-kəsək-ən</u>   <u>səpər-taka-n</u>   numa   yawi-a
       peanut   snip-SEQ   hit-shake-SEQ   shell-put-SEQ   big.fem.sg   job-3fem.sgNOM
       'Snipping peanuts, shaking (the earth off), shelling them out onto drying surface is a big job'

15.21   ka:m   mænər   <u>væsə-wi:-k-ñəna</u>
       sugarcane   leg+LK+INSTR   step-be.split-FUT-2fem.sgSUBJ.VT+3fem.sgBAS.VT
       'You will step and split sugarcane'

The cause-effect compounds are superficially similar to *kay-* causatives (§16.2.1). The verb *puti-* 'fall off, come out by itself (e.g. a shoe which is too big)' occurs with a *kay-* 'causative/manipulative'. The form *kay-puti-* means 'take something off (e.g. a shoe)'. The compound *vya-puti-* has a somewhat different meaning, 'shake something off by hitting, e.g. dust from a mat or a sheet'. Further comparison of *kay-* derivations and cause-effect compounds is in §16.2.1.

Cause-effect compounds are highly productive, so much so that they can contain the generic verb *məgi-* 'do whatever' in the V₂ slot. An example is at 15.22: the speaker was describing how the defeated Gala man hit a sago tree so that it broke, went inside and stayed there in hiding. There is a multitude of verbs for breaking in Manambu, and the speaker was too eager to finish telling the important story to think of the exact appropriate verb. So he used *məgi-*. That *məgi-* is here replacing a verb of breaking is clear from the context.

15.22   [[rək-a-na:gw tə-də]   a-də   dəpu-nagwəm
       dry-LK-sago   have-3masc.sgBAS.P   DEM.DIST-masc.sg   inside-sago+LK+LOC
       <u>vya-məgi-ku</u>]   [wula:n]   a-də   dəpu-nagwəm
       hit-do.whatever-COMPL.SS   come.inside+SEQ   DEM.DIST-masc.sg   inside-sago+LK+LOC
       ta:d
       stay+3masc.sgBAS.P
       'He having hit the inside of the sago tree so that it whatever-ed (=broke), having entered (the inside), he stayed in the inside'

The generic verb cannot be used in V₁ slot of cause-effect compounds: the 'cause' slot is occupied by one of the three verbs listed above.

In terms of their semantics, cause-effect compounds have a distinct connotation of manner. Compounds such as *væsə-pərki-* 'tear by stepping; step and tear' (15.19), *vya-pərki-* 'tear by hitting, hit and tear', and *vætə-pərki-* 'tear by biting, bite and tear (as one would do to a thread)' differ in the manner in which the result has been achieved.

The second component of a cause-effect compound can be reduplicated. This indicates the repetition or the intensity of the action of the second verb (see §12.8.2, under A). Example 15.20 contains a statement about the hard work involved in picking peanuts, shaking the earth off them, and shelling them. In 15.23, the addressee is first ordered to shake peanuts, and then shake them really strongly, to make sure they come out clean:

15.23   a-<u>vya-kəsək</u>   a-<u>vya-kəsək-kəsək</u>
       IMPV-hit-shake   IMPV-hit-shake-shake
       'Hit and shake (peanuts), hit and shake them many times and strongly'

In 15.24a, the movement provoked by hitting occurred only once, and in 15.24b the man hit a slit drum with a stick in all directions producing a strong noise which went on and on—this is expressed with full reduplication of the second component.

15.24a kəka   səbən-ən   vya-təmələ-l
       DEM.PROX.REACT.TOP.fem.sg return-SEQ hit-roll/sound-3fem.sgBAS.P
       'There was a conflict (lit. hit-roll) again'

15.24b rəbə-jay-ə-r   kəda
       slit.drum+LK-stick-LK-INSTR DEM.PROX.REACT.TOP+masc.sg
       vya-təməl-təmələ-də-d
       hit-roll/sound-roll/sound-3masc.sgSUBJ.P-3masc.sgBAS.P
       'Here he struck (the drum) with a drumstick and it sounded many times'

This pattern of intensive reduplication is also characteristic of asymmetrical compounds (also see examples 12.67–8); we return to this in §15.3 and §15.5.

Most cause-effect compounds are semantically transparent. But they also develop idiomatic meanings. The compound *væsə-blakə-* (step-be.turned) may have a straightforward meaning, of 'step and overturn', as in 15.25a. That *blakə-* 'be turned upside down' is intransitive is shown in 15.25b:

15.25a val   væsə-blakə-ku   bunər   bunər   tə-dian
       canoe step-turn-COMPL.SS back+LK+ALL back+LK+ALL stay-1plBAS.VT
       'Having turned the canoe upside down by stepping on it, we stayed really underneath it (hiding from strange men)'

15.25b val   bə   blakə-na
       canoe already turn.upside.down-ACT.FOC+3fem.sgBAS.VT
       'The canoe has already been turned upside down'

The same compound can be used metaphorically with a meaning 'conquer, exterminate, or raid', as in 15.25c.

15.25c a   təp   sər   væsə-blakə-kə-bana
       DEM.DIST+fem.sg village tomorrow step-turn-FUT-1plSUBJ.VT+3fem.sgBAS.VT
       'We will raid that village tomorrow'

The root *blakə-* 'be overturned' is also attested with the causative prefix *kay-* (see §16.2.1), but without any metaphorical extension: *kay-blakə-* means 'turn something upside down'. This accords with the more generic nature of the causative-manipulative *kay-* as opposed to the specific connotations associated with the first component of cause-effect compounds. We will see, in §16.2.1, that *kay-* can occur with the general verb *məgi-* 'do whatever'.

A metaphorical meaning of the compound *væsə-təkwi-* (step-break) is 'destroy, wipe out', as in 15.26, from a description of the fate of Asiti, one of the three Manambu ancestral villages:

15.26 [a-də   mæməm   bla-n   bla-n   napa-ku]
      DEM.DIST-masc.sg fight+LK+ACC talk-SEQ talk-SEQ COMPL.VERB-COMPL.SS
      [væsə-təkwiya-də-k]   [aba:b-a   du   ta:kw
      step-break-3masc.sg-COMPL.DS all-3fem.sgNOM man woman
      ada-bə   kusə-pakwə-na-d]
      DEM.DIST.REACT.TOP+masc.sg-already finish-DO.ALL-ACT.FOC-3masc.sgBAS.VT
      [gu-a:r   sakra-yakə-d]
      water-LK+ALL fall.into-FULLY-3masc.sgBAS.P
      '(The totemic character) having said his (spell about) fight, having destroyed (Asiti), it is the case that all men and women finished completely, all of them fell fully into water'

Even what looks like a straightforward cause-effect compound may be only partly compositional. The compound *vya-puk-* is composed of the familiar *vya-* 'hit' and *puku-* 'become fat, bulge', often used reduplicated in *puku-puku-* 'bulge, stand out, goggle (eyes)' (see 16.63). The meaning of the compound is 'hit something so that it comes out', e.g. *məlvya-puku-də-d* (eye hit-bulge-3masc.sgSUBJ.P-3masc.sgBAS.P) 'He hit his eye out'. The second component is not a directional verb—and yet it appears to provide a directional-like meaning to the activity of hitting. This brings us to the next issue, that of highly lexicalized idiomatic compounds.

15.2.4 Fully lexicalized idiomatic compounds

A certain amount of unpredictability and lexicalization in symmetrical compounds comes as no surprise (Aikhenvald 2006a). Manambu has a high number of such idiomatic verb compounds. Examples include *vya-vægru-* (hit-meet) 'shake hands on meeting someone', *vatə-jə-* (bite-chew) 'devour', and *taka-rəp-* (put-be.enough) 'compare; size up; fix, tie together'.

In some instances, V_2 can be seen as providing additional specification to V_1 and has the same segmental form as an independent verb in the language. For instance, *vəl-* means 'cut'. The same form is used in a compound *yata-vəl-* (carry-?) 'carry off'. Speakers vary as to whether they accept or reject a connection between the two verbs. The two forms *vəl-* could well be homonyms. An idiomatic lexical compound may contain three roots, as does *wa-karay-kur-* (say-bring-do) 'be hospitable (to someone)'. The verb of speech *wa-* forms a number of idiomatic compounds, such as *wa-tək-* (say-break) 'accuse', *wa-yakə-* (say-throw) 'order' (see §15.3 below). We will see, in §16.1, that combinations of this verb with directionals may also have unpredictable meanings.

Compounds *və-kraki-* (see-carry.across) 'recognize by seeing' and *wukə-kraki-* (hear-carry.across) 'recognize by hearing' are reminiscent of those instances where V_2 provides a directional specification to V_1. However, neither 'see' nor 'hear' can combine with other directional forms of the verb *kər-* 'carry, bring' (there is no **və-krapar-* (see-bring.towards.speaker) or *və-krawul (see-bring.inside)).

The second component of what looks like a compound may not be used on its own—examples include *kə-marki-* (eat/drink-?) 'swallow', *və-səməl-* (see-?) 'look for', *vya-səl-* (hit-?) 'split (firewood)', *wa-jali-* (say-?) 'call', *və-kəka-n tə-* (see-?-SEQ have) 'look after' in 15.27, and *və-və-ka-* (see-see-?-) in *və-və-ka-taka-* (see-see-?-put) 'watch carefully' in 15.28.

15.27 day   də-kə-k   <u>və-kəka-n</u> tə-di
       they he-OBL-DAT see-?-SEQ   stay-3plBAS.VT
       'They look after him'

15.28 məl <u>və-və-ka-taka-n</u> tə-na-dian
       eye see-see-?-put-SEQ   stand/be-ACT.FOC-1plBAS.VT
       'We were watching carefully, guarding (prisoners)'

The bound form *-maki* is used only with the root *gra-* 'cry', as in *gra-maki-* 'cry for pity, or for comfort', as in 15.29, said about a little girl who was crying her eyes out because her mother had just left.

15.29 amæyik   <u>gra-maki-na</u>
       mother+LK+DAT cry-?-ACT.FOC+3fem.sgBAS.VT
       'She is crying for her mother'

The form *-maki-* could be related to the root *makə-n* '(be) in (ritual) mourning' (cf. Iatmul *maki'n* 'mourning, sorrow'); but both formal and semantic connections are tenuous.

A bound root can be inherently reduplicated, as is *-kəta-kəta-* used exclusively with *yi-* 'go', in *yi-keta-keta* meaning 'overcome, disperse, penetrate fully'—see 13.16 and 15.30. Any link between *-kəta-kəta* and *-kəta* 'try; suppletive form of "see, look" ' (see §15.3: 15.40–1) is hard to substantiate.

15.30 [gra:b   kusə-lə-k],   ata wiya:r   wiya:r
      afternoon finish-3fem.sg-COMPL.DS then house+LK+ALL house+LK+ALL
      yi-kəta-kəta-dian
      go-?-?-1plBAS.VT
      'After the afternoon had set in, then we went off (dispersed) each to our own house'

A bound form *-kway* combines with the verb *væsə-* 'step, walk', and the result means 'walk straight away, hurrying'. This form differs from all others in that it is uninflected: in 15.31a it is used as a complement of the copula *na-* 'be (abstract state)', and in 15.31b it is the predicate head with no inflection.

15.31a [væsə-kway   na-n]   yi-na-di
       walk-STRAIGHT.OFF BE:NAT-SEQ go-ACT.FOC-3plBAS.VT
       'They are going straight off, in a hurry'

15.31b bər   væsə-kway
       they.two walk-STRAIGHT.OFF
       'They two (went) off'

In one instance, the second component of a compound involving *vya-* as V_1 appears to be of a nominal origin. The compound *vya-səpa-* 'kill by hitting' is illustrated in 15.32; also see 15.127.

15.32 babay   vya-səpa-la-d
      paternal.grandmother hit-body?-3fem.sgSUBJ.VT-3masc.sgBAS.VT
      '(After our younger brother had gone up the tree) our paternal grandmother killed him'

The morpheme *-səp* may be related to the noun *səp* 'body; person' (this noun takes the linker *a*, which makes it even more similar to the verbal component *səpa*, e.g. *səp-a:m* (body-LK+LOC) 'on body/person'). The verb *vya-səpa-* requires a human or an animate object, which provides circumstantial evidence for the connection.

In terms of their semantics and composition, such idiomatic compounds are impossible to classify as either asymmetrical or symmetrical. A full list of these belongs to a dictionary rather than to a grammar. The ways in which they can combine with other types of verb compounds allow us to group them together with symmetrical, rather than with asymmetrical, structures—see §15.4. Only in some of them can the second component undergo full reduplication. So, the component *-səməl-* in *və-səməl* (see-?) 'look for' can be reduplicated, and *-maki* in *gra-maki-* 'cry for pity or comfort' cannot.

One other compound type—whereby V_1 is a complement of V_2—deserves a mention. This compound has occurred in a relative clause, as a translation from English: *suku-kaləva-di du* (carve/write-teach-3plBAS.VT/P man) 'writing teachers; men who teach how to write'. The rarity of this construction may well be due to the fact that this is a recently introduced calque.

A second component in a compounded verb often provides manner, aspectual, and extent overtones of the main verb. We will see in §15.3 below that many of such components are bound morphemes which do not occur anywhere outside this context.

TABLE 15.1   Minor verbs which follow major verbs in asymmetrical compounds

FORM AND TRANSLATION	MEANING	DISCUSSED IN
-kusə- 'finish'	completion: 'completive; do fully'	A1
*-təkal-pæsa- 'do incompletely'	non-completion of action	A2
*-kəta- 'try'	conative: 'trying'	A3
-yi- 'go'	(a) motion-direction: 'do while going; away'; (b) continuous with repetitive overtones	A4
-ya- 'come'	(a) motion-direction: 'do while coming; towards speaker'; (b) durative	A5
VERB-yi-VERB-ya- 'VERB back and forth'	motion-direction, to and fro	A6
-taka 'put, arrange by spreading'	(a) valency changing; (b) large surface	A7
-təp 'be closed'	(a) do for the last time; (b) stop; (c) do fully	A8
*-baːgw- 'do incessantly'	manner and extent of action	A9
*-pakw- 'do all, affect all (S/O)'	extent of action, participant involvement	A10
*-jika- 'do properly'	extent and fullness of action	A11
*-yakə- 'do fully; very; well and truly'	extent of action	A12

15.3 ASYMMETRICAL COMPOUNDS

Asymmetrical compounds are of two types. The first type consists of a verb from a large open class ('major' verb) followed by a root from a closed class ('minor' verb), which provides a meaning to do with completion, aktionsart, and extent of action. These compounds are numerous, and many of them are quite productive; see §15.3.1, and a summary in Table 15.1 Their make-up is consistent with the predominantly suffixing character of the language.

In compounds of the second type, the verb which provides grammatical specification to the compound precedes the 'major' verb. These are few, and not at all productive—see §15.3.2.

15.3.1 Major verb precedes minor verb

Compounds of this type vary in productivity, semantic transparency, and restrictions on V_1. The minor verbs used in asymmetrical compounds are listed in Table 15.1. The components

which are not used anywhere else in the language are marked with an asterisk. One of these—
-*yakə*- 'do fully'—may be homophonous with a freely occurring verb, *yakə*- 'throw'.

Asymmetrical compounds whose second component is the verb -*yi*- 'go' or -*ya*- 'come'
do not occur in commands. Neither do the markers -*baːgw*- and -*paːkw*-. To be used in a
command, they have to be rephrased with a sequencing structure. The general verb *məgi*- 'do
whatever' has been attested as V₁ only in combination with -*taka*- and -*yakə*-.

As expected in asymmetrical compounds, the minor verb provides a grammatical specification for the major verb—this includes completion of action or lack thereof (A1–2), conative
meaning (A3), motion and direction (A4–6) and aspect marking (A5), changing valency (A7),
phase of action (A8), and manner and extent of action (A9–12). We will now consider the
asymmetrical compounds one at a time.

A1. -*kusə*- 'FINISH' as V₂ in asymmetrical compounds expresses completion, or complete extent,
of an activity. The two meanings are distinguished exclusively by the context—a form *suku-
kusə-ta-di* (write-finish-1dusUBJ.VT-3plVT) can mean either 'we two have written them up', or
'we two have finished writing'. The compound *kə-kusə*- in 15.33 means 'eat up, eat completely'
(but not *stop eating) (a similar example is in 14.43).

15.33 lə   kamnaːgw akəs   kə-kusə-kwa-na
       she   food   NEG.HAB   eat-finish-HAB-ACT.FOC+3fem.sgBAS.VT
       'She never eats food up'

Similar examples are at 15.39b and 15.125. The compound *kawi-kusə*- in 15.34 describes
completing the process of embarking on the shore:

15.34 ata   warə-d,   kawi-kusə-d
       then   go.up-3masc.sgBAS.VT   disembark-finish-3masc.sgBAS.VT
       'Then he went up, and completed disembarking'

With verbs referring to natural phenomena, and describing inherently atelic actions which
cannot be done to completion, -*kusə*- as V₂ means 'stop':

15.35 waːl ja-kusə-k-la   marketaːr
       rain fall.rain-finish-FUT-3fem.sgSUBJ.VT+3fem.sgBAS.VT   market+LK+ALL
       yi-k-na-bran
       go-FUT-ACT.FOC-1duBAS.VT
       'If rain stops, we will go to the market'

Two compounds containing -*kusə*- as V₂ have developed idomatic extensions. The compound *kwa-kusə*- (stay-finish) is a euphemism for *kiya*- 'die'. (The verb *kusə*- 'finish' is frequently used in the same meaning.) The combination of *yi*- 'go' with *kusə*- has a somewhat
idiomatic meaning 'disappear', as in *yi-n yi-kusə-di* (go-SEQ go-finish-3plBAS.VT) 'they went off;
disappeared from sight'. The second component can be reduplicated in another idiomatic compound which involves two occurrences of *yi*-: *yi-kus-kus-yi-di* (go-finish-finish-go-3plBAS.VT)
'they all went off'.

A2. *-*təkal*-*pæsa* 'DO INCOMPLETELY' as V₂ in asymmetrical compounds expresses non-
completion of action. The choice of an allomorph partly depends on the root: a monosyllabic
light root of CV structure requires the allomorph -*təka*-, as in 15.36 and 15.124. Heavy roots
tend to require the allomorph -*pæsa*-, as in 15.37 and 14.113. However, this is not a strict rule:
as can be seen from 14.113, a light verbal root *kə*- 'eat' also takes the allomorph -*pæsa*-, and
heavy roots like *ləpa*- 'cut' (15.127) and *kurpa*- 'miss, drop' occur with -*təka*.

The semantics of 'do incompletely' involves either incomplete coverage of the participant—leaving some grass uncut, as in 15.36; leaving a story half-written, as in 15.37, half-eating the food, or half-doing the job, as in 14.113.

15.36 sər   mayir   yi-kə-ta,
        tomorrow garden+LK+ALL go-FUT-1duSUBJ.VT+3fem.sgBAS.VT
        vəl-təka-ta-l   vəsək
        cut-INCOMPL-1duSUBJ.VT-3fem.sgBAS.VT grass+LK+DAT
        'We two will go to the garden tomorrow, for the grass we two cut incompletely'

15.37 suku-pæsa-ta-də   gabu-ma:j
        write-INCOMPL-1duSUBJ.VT-3masc.sgBAS.VT tradition-story
        ada   suku-kə-ta-d   ma:
        DEM.DIST.REACT.TOP+masc.sg write-FUT-1duSUBJ.VT-3masc.sgBAS.VT again
        'We two will write the half-written story again' (that is, resume writing the story we only half transcribed)

With a verb of motion, this morpheme implies not quite reaching the destination, as in 15.124. With a verb of affect, the meaning of incompletive may imply doing something a bit, but not fully, as in 15.38. This is an introduction to an amendment to a story by another speaker:

15.38 [amæy suku-la-d-ə   gabu-ma:j   kwasa
        mother write/record-3fem.sgSUBJ.VT-3masc.sgBAS.VT-LK tradition-story little+fem.sg
        kurpa-təkə-la]   [aka
        leave.out-INCOMPL-3fem.sgSUBJ.VT+3fem.sgBAS.VT DEM.DIST.REACT.TOP.fem.sg
        wa-kə-tua]
        say-FUT-1sgSUBJ.VT+3fem.sgBAS.VT
        'I will tell the (part) she left out a little bit belonging to the story mother had recorded'

A similar example is at 15.127 (§15.5) where the woman's body was cut, but not completely. The example 15.127 also shows that the incompletive can be reduplicated (see §15.5): the meaning is 'doing many times bit by bit'.

The forms -*kusə*- 'finish, do completely' and -*təka*/*pæsa* 'do incompletely' are in a paradigmatic relationship with each other. They were used as antonyms: for instance, 15.39a (involving -*pæsa*) was suggested as having the opposite meaning to 15.39b (involving -*kusə*).

15.39a [vya-səla-pæsa-lə-di   ñapwiyik]
        hit-?-INCOMPL-3fem.sgSUBJ.P-3plBAS.P firewood+LK+DAT
        da-na
        go.down-ACT.FOC+3fem.sgBAS.VT
        'She has gone down for firewood which has been split incompletely'

15.39b [vya-səla-kusə-lə-di   ñapwiyik]
        hit-?-COMPL-3fem.sgSUBJ.P-3plBAS.P firewood+LK+DAT
        da-na
        go.down-ACT.FOC+3fem.sgBAS.VT
        'She has gone down for the firewood which has been split completely'

Along similar lines, the opposite of *suku-pæsa-ta-də gabu-ma:j* 'half-written story' in 15.37 was given as *suku-kusə-ta-də gabu-ma:j* (write-COMPL-1duSUBJ.VT-3masc.sgBAS.VT tradition-story) 'fully written up story', with an alternative *suku-kusə-yakə-ta-də gabu-ma:j* (write-COMPL-FULLY-1duSUBJ.VT-3masc.sgBAS.VT tradition-story) 'fully and completely written up story'—see A12 and §15.4.

Needless to say, the completive and the incompletive markers cannot occur together in one verb.

A3. *-*kəta* 'try' as V₂ in asymmetrical compounds has a conative meaning of 'trying'. There appear to be no restrictions on V₁; but the most frequently used V₁ involve physical experience, as in 15.40–1.

15.40 [wali-kamna:gw kə-kəta-kə-tua]   [kə-kəta-n va:u]
       white.man-food eat-try-FUT-1sgSUBJ.VT+3fem.sgBAS.VT eat-try-SEQ see+1sgIMPV
       'I will try and eat white people's food, I will see (what it is like) by trying to eat (it)'

15.41 ji-kəta-n   va:u
       tie-try-SEQ see+1sgIMPV
       'I will try to tie (a towel around me) and see (if this will be OK)'

If semantically appropriate, -*kəta* has a connotation of 'trying and doing something carefully', e.g. *a-væsə-kət* (IMPV-step-try) 'Try and step carefully, walk carefully' (the final vowel here undergoes truncation, as is expected in the second person imperative: see §13.2.1).

We will see, in §21.1.2, that the verb *və-* 'see' has two further meanings in Manambu: 'try' and 'experience'. The root -*kəta*- is consistently used as equivalent of *və-* as V₂ in symmetrical compounds (as in 15.4), and in directionals (see §16.1). That is, synchronically speaking, many of the occurrences of -*kəta* can be interpreted as a suppletive form of 'see/look'.

The problematic cases include the form -*kəta*- compounded with *wa-* 'say' as V₁. The meaning of the compound *wa-kəta*- is 'ask carefully, nicely' rather than 'try and ask'. This is similar to the compound *væsə-kəta*- (step-try) 'step carefully'; 'try and step'. The root -*kəta*- does not occur on its own (see §16.1, on how this is used as a directional form of 'see').

A4. -*yi*- 'GO' as V₂ in asymmetrical compounds expresses motion-direction, and means 'do while going; going or doing something away from speaker'. When used with motion verbs or inherently directional verbs, *yi*- as V₂ indicates direction of motion, as in 15.42–3.

15.42 gra-ta:y   gəpi-yi-l,   kukə-b   ata gəpi-yi-l
       cry-COTEMP run-go-3fem.sgBAS.P after-TERM then run-go-3fem.sgBAS.P
       'Crying she ran away (from where she was), after (him) she ran off'

15.43 a-di   ja:p adiya   kraki-yi-lə-di
       DEM.DIST-pl thing DEM.DIST.REACT.TOP+pl 'carry'+ACROSS-go-3fem.sgSUBJ.P-3plBAS.P
       'She took those things away' (from those who gave them to her)

A directional reading is also possible with non-directional verbs, as in 15.44:

15.44 ata   səmaka-yi-lə-di
       then show-go-3fem.sgSUBJ.P-3plBAS.P
       'She then showed them (the traces) (to the people) away from her'

With verbs which are not inherently directional, *yi*- tends to have one of two meanings—

(a) it either refers to 'going along as the action of V₁ is happening' providing additional motion-direction specification, or
(b) it can have a continuative meaning with overtones of repetition.

An ambiguous example is:

15.45 atawa-dəka ata   wa-yi:d
       thus-ONLY then say-go+3masc.sgBAS.P
       'He went talking' or 'He went on talking (saying the same thing time and time again)'

The two meanings can be disambiguated by the context—15.46, from a story about traditional warfare, describes killing without going anywhere. The continuative reading is the only one appropriate here.

15.46 [a   təpa-da-l   ñəg   ata vi:r
       DEM.DIST.fem.sg sew-3plSUBJ.P-3fem.sgBAS.P mosquito.net then spear+INSTR
       vya-yi-da-l]   [vya-yin,   vya-yin,   vya-yin],
       hit-go-3plSUBJ.P-3fem.sgBAS.P hit-go+SEQ hit-go+SEQ hit-go+SEQ
       [vya-da-l   aka]
       hit-3plSUBJ.P-3fem.sgBAS.P DEM.DIST.REACT.TOP.fem.sg
       'They then went on hitting with the spear the mosquito net they had sewn, went on hitting, went on hitting, went on hitting, this is how the hitting was'

In contrast, 15.47 is inherently ambiguous—since the action of 'looking for' involves movement:

15.47 brə-kə-də   ñaj   ada
       3du-OBL-masc.sg paternal.uncle DEM.DIST.REACT.TOP+masc.sg
       kwakə-yi-na-d
       look.for-go-ACT.FOC-3masc.sgBAS.VT
       'Their paternal uncle then kept on looking for them' or
       'Their paternal uncle went looking for them'

If a verb can imply directionality, all three meanings are possible. They can only be disambiguated by the context.

15.48 gwar   ata   taka-yi-da-di
       ointment then put-go-3plSUBJ.P-3plBAS.P
       'They spread the ointment (away, in the direction of all the people outside)'
       'They spread the ointment as they were going'
       'They kept spreading the ointment'

The monosyllabic past tense form of -*yi* as V$_2$ is -*yi:d* and not *ya:d* (see 15.45)—we can recall, from §12.1 and §11.3.2 that when the verbs *yi*- 'go' and *ya*- 'come' are used independently, they share one past tense form *ya:d*. This shows that verbs of motion behave somewhat differently as V$_2$ in verb compounding than they would behave elsewhere. This is comparable to how the verb 'see' has a suppletive combining form in verb compounding. This property of Manambu verb-verb combination distinguishes them from bona fide serial verbs cross-linguistically.

Examples like 15.46 show that V$_1$ is the major verb if 'go' marks continuous action as V$_2$: *vya*- 'hit' is repeated as a summarizing verb in the last clause of 15.46.

The frequency of verb compounds with *yi*- as V$_2$ may have been enhanced by the similar use of directional 'go' in Tok Pisin. Compounds with *yi*- as V$_2$ have some similarities with compounds with *ya*- 'go' in the same slot—this is discussed below.

Like most kinds of verb compounds, -*yi* compounds may acquire unpredictable meaning, e.g. *taka-yi-* (put-go) 'arrange, make arrangements'.

A5. -*ya*- 'COME' as V₂ in asymmetrical compounds has two meanings (a) motion-direction: 'do while coming; motion towards speaker'; (b) durative, referring to prolonged action.

The first meaning is mainly attested with verbs which involve motion, such as *kəl*- 'chase, make escape', *vægru*- 'meet, get together', or *səbən*- 'return'—see 15.49–50.

15.49 kəka   mən-a:k   <u>kəl-ya-na</u>
       DEM.PROX.REACT.TOP.fem.sg you.masc-LK+DAT   chase-come-ACT.FOC+3fem.sgBAS.VT
       'This one (reactivated topic) is coming to chase you; is chasing you coming towards you'

In combination with 'see', -*ya*- refers to the direction of the gaze, as in *tə-kətə-ya-n tə-bər* (stay-'see'-come-SEQ stay-3duBAS.VT) 'they stayed looking (in the direction towards the coming figure)'. The verb 'see' as V₂ appears in its combining form, *kətə*.

A compound with the verb *ya*- in a directional meaning behaves differently from (a) compounds with *ya*- in durative meaning, and from (b) compounds with *yi*- 'go'.

In tail-head repetition, the verb 'come' is repeated, as in the second line of 15.50, and not the V₁, as in 15.46. Alternatively, the whole verb compound can be repeated—an example is in the last sentence of 15.50. In the first sentence, reduplication of the first component of the *ya*-compound expresses the extent and intensity of action (also see §15.5).

15.50 [ma: wa-da-k,   səbən-səbən-ya-di].   [ata <u>væki-yi-di]</u>
       no   say-3pl-COMPL.DS   return-return-come-3plBAS.P   then go.across-go-3plBAS.P
       [<u>væki-yi-ku]</u>,   [kə-di:m   atawa dəya:m   vya-gurə-kək]
       go.across-go-COMPL.SS   DEM.PROX-pl+ACC   thus   they+ACC   hit-2pl-PURP.DS
       'After they'd said no, they (the other lot) went all back coming towards them, then they were going across, after they'd gone across, (I said) "You are going to hit these (people)" '

In their directional usage as V₂ of compounds, 'come' and 'go' behave differently. This may have to do with differences in relative chronology of the grammaticalization of 'come' and 'go' as directionals. We return to this at the end of A6 below.

The verb 'come' as V₂ expresses durative action which goes on and on. Unlike with 'go' as aspectual marker, there are no overtones of repeating the same action over and over again. Any verb, including a copula—except 'come' and 'go' themselves—can occur in the V₁ slot. Examples are at 15.51–2, and 14.113 (*kə-ya-* (eat-come) 'keep eating')

15.51 atawa warya-ta:y   <u>tə-ya-di</u>
       thus   fight-COTEMP   stay-come-3plBAS.P
       'Thus they kept fighting'

15.52 a   məd-a   ta:kw   la:n   nəkə-di du-a:k   luku
       DEM.DIST+fem.sg   cassowary-LK   woman   husband other-pl man-LK+DAT   stealing
       <u>wa-təka-ta:y</u>   <u>vya-ya-də-l</u>
       say-break-COTEMP   hit-come-3masc.sgSUBJ.P-3fem.sgBAS.P
       'The husband of that cassowary woman kept beating her accusing (her) of (having) other men'

Just as with compounds containing -*yi*-, motion verbs with -*ya* as V₂ can be ambiguous: -*ya* may refer to the duration of action, or its direction. The exact interpretation depends on the context—the compound in 15.50 is potentially ambiguous, but the one in 15.53 is not: the little girl was running away from the monstrous man, and not towards him. So, only the durative meaning makes sense here.

15.53 [[wun nəbə kə-kə-tua-digur-ək]   wa-də-k]
     I   able   eat-FUT-1sgSUBJ.VT-2plBAS.VT-CONF say-3masc.sg-COMPL.DS
     a-də   du   wa-də-k]   a   takwa-ñan
     DEM.DIST-masc.sg man say-3masc.sg-COMPL.DS DEM.DIST+fem.sg woman+LK-child
     ata   gəpi-ya-l
     then run-come-3fem.sgBAS.P
     'After he said, I am capable of eating you up, that man having said, that girl kept running'

There is no connotation of 'coming' in compounds which do not involve a motion verb, like the one in 15.54—*ya-* indicates continuity. This is quite unlike compounds with 'go', such as the one in 15.47.

15.54 kwakə-ya-tua-d,   kad
     look.for-come-1sgSUBJ.VT-3masc.sgBAS.VT DEM.PROX+3masc.sgNOM
     yi-pakwə-la-d
     go-be.hidden-3fem.sgSUBJ.VT-3masc.sgBAS.VT
     'I keep looking and looking for it (the key), as far as it is concerned, she hid it'

Along similar lines, *wa-yi-* 'say-go' can mean either 'say and go; speak while going' or 'keep saying (or repeating same thing many times over)' (as in 15.45), while *wa-ya-* 'say-come' can only mean 'keep saying/talking (without repetition)'.

Compounds with aspectual *ya-* as V₂ can describe gradual attainment of a result. An expression *ga:n kusə-ya-na* (night finish/close.up-come-ACT.FOC+3fem.sgBAS.VT) 'night is gradually coming to close up' refers to late afternoon when it just starts getting dark (also see 4.44; when it is completely dark, one says 'night is finished', as in 4.43).

Such compounds can develop somewhat unpredictable meanings: *kwa-ya-* (stay-come) can mean 'stay for a duration of time', but often means 'stay up for a long time (normally, all night) in mourning', or 'stay (all night) worrying', as in 15.55.

15.55 brə-kə-di   du-a-magwu-bər,   lə-kə-di   du-a-magwu-brawa,   ga:n
     3du-OBL-pl man-LK-'thing'-PL she-OBL-pl man-LK-'thing'-PL+LK+COM night
     kwa-ya-di   kwa-ya:n   kwa-ya:n
     say-come-3plBAS.P stay-come+SEQ stay-come+SEQ
     'The brothers of the two, together with her siblings, stayed up all night (in worry), having stayed and stayed (up)'

If -*ya* 'come' as V₂ provides an aspectual meaning, the whole verb has to be repeated in head-tail constructions—this is unlike examples like 15.50 (first line). This indicates that compounds with a directional 'come' and with the aspectual 'come' are synchronically different structures. Also, compounds with -*ya-* behave differently from those with -*yi-*.

The verb *bla-* 'speak' has a specific combining form *blaja-* which only occurs with -*ya-* as a durative marker: *blaja-ya-* (speak-come), as in *blaja-ya-bana ma:j* (speak-come-1plSUBJ.VT+3fem.sgBAS.VT talk) 'our conversation; what we talk about' (also see §9.3).

The two verbs, -*ya-* and -*yi-*, can occasionally occur together in one compound in their aspectual meanings, as in 14.113—*pukə-ya-yi-di kami:* (rot-come-go-3plBAS.VT fish) 'fish which was rotting', to express ongoing duration of a process.

We will see, in §17.1, that the verb *ya-* 'come' also imparts durative meanings in auxiliary constructions, as in 5.27 (*nəbə ya:n suku-l* (able come+SEQ write-3fem.sgBAS) 'One can carry on writing'). But how do we know the verb *ya-* here is the same as the verb 'come', and not its homonym? We don't—and in all likelihood, the two verbs with the same segmental make-up, *ya-*, are lookalikes, at least synchronically. The two *ya-*, 'directional come' and 'aspectual durative', behave differently; only the second one shows a certain degree of lexicalization. Even if the two go back to the same source, the relative chronology of their grammaticalization is different. The development of *ya-* 'come' into a directional marker is plainly more transparent, and more recent.

And, just as with directional compounds involving 'go', the directional compounds involving 'come' are strikingly similar to the constructions involving *go* and *kam* in Tok Pisin. It is probable that the frequency of such compounds in Manambu increased through contact with Tok Pisin. In just one construction, discussed in A6, do *yi-* and *ya-* consistently refer to motion to and fro.

A6. *VERB-yi-VERB-ya-* 'VERB BACK AND FORTH' as V₂ in asymmetrical compounds expresses motion-direction to and fro and every way. This was mentioned in §12.8.2, at A, as the 'go-come' reduplication involving reduplicating a full verb whose first occurrence is accompanied with *-yi* 'go' and the second with *ya-* 'come'. This was illustrated with 12.69 and 13.71.

The movement 'to and fro' is erratic—this is unlike the directional *-tay* involving deliberate direction back and forth (see §16.1). Any verb can be used in this construction—except for *yi-* and *ya-* themselves and verbs of motion—see 15.56–7. In 15.57, *nay-yi-nay-ya-* becomes *nayi-nayan*, following the rules of haplology (see §2.6).

15.56 ata   vya-yi-vya-ya-lə-d
      then   hit-go-hit-come-3fem.sgSUBJ.P-3masc.sgBAS.P
      'She hit him every which way'

15.57 wun ñan   samasa:m   nayi-naya-n   wu: kan
      I   child much   play+go-play+come-SEQ   DEM.DIST-pl ton.fruit eat+SEQ
      napa-ku   ata   væra-tuə-k   ata
      COMPL.VB-COMPL.SS then come.back-1sg-COMPL.DS then
      'As a child I having played back and forth, having eaten those ton fruit, then I would come back'

A 'go-come' construction with a transitive verb may also refer to handling objects of every possible kind, and animacy, as in 15.58–9.

15.58 da-ta:y,   adiya   kami: jagər kur-ta:y,   ata
      go.down-COTEMP DEM.DIST.REACT.TOP+pl fish   garfish get-COTEMP then
      war-di   kur-ən kur-ən   kur-yi-kur-ya-ta:y   ata   war-di
      go.up-3plBAS.P get-SEQ get-SEQ get-go-get-come-COTEMP then go.up-3plBAS.P
      'Having gone down, having got fish of garfish type, they went up, getting, getting, getting this and that, they went up'

15.59 day-a   wa-jəwi-yi-wa-jəwi-ya-ku,   dəya:m   kurə-n
      they-3fem.sgNOM say-be.awake-go-say-be.awake-come-COMPL.SS they+ACC get-SEQ
      karya-da-di
      carry.off-3plSUBJ.P-3plBAS.P
      'Having woken everyone up here and there, they carried them (women) off'

Verbs of motion are not used in the 'go-come' construction. Sequential structures involving 'go' and 'come' in the same clause are used instead, as in *warə-n yi-n warə-n ya-n* 'going up back and forth' and 15.60. In such constructions neither *yi-* nor *ya-* can have an aspectual meaning; the only reading is 'back and forth'.

15.60 ata   <u>gəpə-yin</u>   <u>gəpə-ya-di</u>
       then run-go+SEQ run-come-3plBAS.P
       'Then they ran back and forth'

This same construction is used to describe random multiple actions involving copula clauses with *yi-* as a copula verb, e.g. *sikulək yi-n sikulək ya-n* (cooking go-SEQ cooking come-SEQ) 'cooking non-stop, back and forth'. We saw in §13.2.1 that the verb *yi-* has a suppletive imperative *ma:y* in its meaning 'go'. When this same form is used as a copula and in the meaning 'say', the imperative is *ay*—and the imperative of *sikulək yi-* 'cook' is *sikulək ay* (cooking IMPV+go) 'you cook!'. In the 'go-come' construction the difference between the two verbs *yi-* is neutralized. A 'go-come' construction does not occur in commands of any sort.

What looks like a *yi-ya* 'go-come' construction can be part of an inherently reduplicated verb, e.g. *taka-yi-taka-ya-* 'be very angry, be raging all over the place'. Alternatively, a *yi-/ya-* alternation meaning 'back and forth' occurs in a sequencing structure involving movement, as in *titi-yi:n titi-ya:n* (?-go+SEQ ?-come+SEQ) 'stroll back and forth', *bənawi-yi:n bənawi-ya:n* (dive?-go+SEQ dive?-come+SEQ) 'dive all over the place, back and forth'.

The directional forms of the generic verb *kər-* 'bring, carry' (see §16.1), *karya-* 'bring from afar, take far away', and *kray-* 'bring from close, take to a close-by place' do not occur in the 'go-come' construction either. To express the meaning of 'bringing and taking things back and forth', the two verbs are compounded, as in 15.61. Note, however, that they are compounded in the opposite order from what one finds in 'go-come' construction: the direction 'close' precedes the direction 'away' (see §16.1).

15.61 ata   tamiya-tami: kurə-n   <u>kray-karya-lə-bər</u>
       then area+LK-area get-SEQ bring:close-bring:far-3fem.sgSUBJ.P-3duBAS.P
       'So she (the cassowary) carried the two of them (her children) to and fro in every area'

The go-come construction is not compatible with either *yi-* or *ya-* in their aspectual meaning. Nor can it involve any of the asymmetrical compounds discussed here. We hypothesize that the grammaticalization of 'go' and 'come' in the go-come construction may have proceeded independently from grammaticalization of *yi-* and *ya-* as directionals, and as aspect markers.

The order of components within the 'go-come' construction involves placing a form referring to movement away from the speaker before that referring to movement towards the speaker. We will see, in §16.1, that this is a consistent pattern in Manambu—unlike other languages, such as English where the order would be the opposite, as in 'come and go'.

A7. *-taka* 'PUT, ARRANGE BY SPREADING' as V$_2$ in asymmetrical compounds has two meanings: (a) adding a non-locational participant; or (b) adding a location (typically, a large surface onto which something is put, or spread). The exact meaning of a *-taka* compound is only partially predictable from the meanings of its components.

(a) ADDING AN ARGUMENT. If V$_I$ is intransitive or ambitransitive, *-taka* 'put, arrange by spreading' in the V$_2$ slot, *-taka* 'put' may act as a transitivizer, as in *təp-ə-taka-* (be.closed/close/fence/sew-LK-put) 'close; cover up'. The 'causee' is inanimate, and causation is performed by putting something down. Example 15.62 describes the action of closing up a traditional doorway by putting down planks of wood.

15.62 taga-wi   yarakara təpə-taka-da-l
      front+LK-house well   be.closed-put-3plSUBJ.P-3fem.sgBAS.P
      'They closed the front of the house properly'

A similar example is at 16.40. And 15.63 describes a hole covered or closed with leaves put on top:

15.63 væːn   napa-ku   tak-ə-kaːw təpə-taka-də-k
      dig+SEQ COMPL.V-COMPL.SS tip-LK-hole be.closed-put.down-3masc.sg-COMPL.DS
      taːd
      stay+3masc.sgBAS.P
      'Having dug up (the hole), he covered up (closed) the tip of the hole and it stayed'

Along similar lines, *kwa-taka-* (stay-put) means 'put things down to stay' (e.g. when loading a canoe). The *-taka* component in these examples preserves part of its lexical meaning involving 'putting down' and 'spreading over a surface', as in 15.62–3. Or it may involve just putting something down as in 15.123 ('She came to close off the road that he went on' (by putting a leaf on it)).

This is by no means a rule: *-taka* in *kirapi-taka-* (get.up-put.down) 'make raise' and also 'revive' acts as a simple transitivizer (this word contains a Tok Pisin loan, *kirap* 'get up'), as it does in *kusə-taka-* (finish/be.finished-put) 'finish (everyone off)'—here an ambitransitive verb become strictly transitive.

The verb *-taka* as V₂ usually has a transitivizing effect in compounds containing an intransitive V₁. Yet, the meaning of the compound can be somewhat unpredictable. Examples are *war-taka-* (go.up-put) meaning 'put something around the neck' and *yi-taka-* (go-put) 'produce; conceive a child', as in 15.64.

15.64 aka   bətaːy ñan yi-taka-ku   kurə-n
      DEM.DIST.REACT.TOP.fem.sg already child go-put-COMPL.SS get-SEQ
      rə-lə-d
      sit-3fem.sgSUBJ.P-3masc.sgBAS.P
      'Having already conceived a child (by drinking the urine of a magic man), she was about to give birth'

With a verb involving physical action, such as 'wash', 'put on (clothing)', and 'put on (headdress)' as V₁, adding *-taka* as V₂ introduces a beneficiary. An intransitive verb becomes transitive, e.g. *yaku-* 'wash (oneself)', *yaku-taka-* means 'wash someone else' (as in 15.82). And a transitive verb becomes ditransitive: it acquires an extra argument, a beneficiary.

So, *ku-su* (lit. 'put'-UP) means 'put on (clothing)', and *ku-su-taka-* means 'dress someone else, put clothing onto someone else'. Before her mother had died Yuayaːb had to do everything for her:

15.65 ku-su-taka-n   gu   yaku-taka-n atawa kur-lə-l
      'put'-UP-put-SEQ water wash-put-SEQ thus do-3fem.sgSUBJ.P-3fem.sgBAS.P
      'Dressing (her), washing her, this is how she (Yuayaːb) acted'

The command in 15.66a refers to someone else taking the shoes off the baby's feet—she could not do it herself. If one were commanding the baby to do it herself, one would have said 15.66b, without *-taka*. The verb *kay-puti-* 'take off' is transitive (see §16.2.1), and *kay-puti-taka-* 'take off for someone else' is ditransitive. The overt NPs are omitted, as is often the case in Manambu.

15.66a a-kay-<u>puti-tak</u>
IMPV-MANIP-take.off-put
'Take (her shoes) off for her'

15.66b a-<u>kay-puti</u>
IMPV-MANIP-take.off
'Take (shoes) off'

The compound in 15.67, *ti:-taka-* 'help (someone) carry on head', has a distinct benefactive applicative overtone: V₁ *ti-/ti:-* 'carry on head' in its normal transitive usage appears in the third line, followed by the compound:

15.67 ka-war-ən   aba:m   <u>sada-taka-də-k</u>,
'carry'-UP-SEQ head+LK+LOC put.down-put-3masc.sg-COMPL.DS
ada   ti:-lə-d
DEM.DIST.REACT.TOP+masc.sg carry.on.head-3fem.sgSUBJ.P-3masc.sgBAS.P
<u>ti:-taka-ku</u>,   ji-gu   ata
carry.on.head-put-COMPL.SS chew-water then
kui-də-d
give.to.third.p-3masc.sgSUBJ.P-3masc.sgBAS.P
'After he (the magic man) put (the heavy stringbag) on (her) head by lifting it, she carried it on her head, after he'd helped her carry on her head he gave saliva to him (the boy inside the bag)'

Along similar lines, a combination of the transitive verb *səki-* 'call name' with *-taka* as V₂ means 'bestow a name upon someone or something'. In 15.68a, *səki-* is used on its own, and in 15.68b it appears in a compound—which is ditransitive.

15.68a wun-a-də   sa:d   səki-tua-d
I-LK-masc.sg name+3masc.sgNOM call.name-1sgSUBJ.VT-3masc.sgBAS.VT
'This is my own name I am calling out'

15.68b ta:l-a   səkər a-di   nəma-di val   day-a-di   asæy   du   sə
before-LK time DEM.DIST-pl big-pl canoe they-LK-pl father man name
<u>səki-taka-yi-kwa-da-di</u>
call.name-put-HAB.PAST-HAB-3plSUBJ.P-3plBAS.P
'Those days the owners of the big canoes used to bestow names upon them'

A similar example is at 14.69: a mother berates her daughter for not looking after others. There, the form *kur-taka-* (do-put) is used in the sense 'do/act for others'. The ambitransitive verb *kur-* 'do, get, become' becomes ditransitive, by adding *-taka*. However, this is not the only meaning of the *-taka* compounds—as shown in (b) below.

The compound *warapwi-taka-* (exchange-put) 'exchange (for something)' provides another example of a valency-increasing, applicative-like effect of *-taka* as V₂. The transitive verb *warapwi-* means 'exchange, replace', without specifying what the object being exchanged for is, as in 15.69—a generic statement about what a market is for:

15.69 takwa:m   awarwa warapwi-kwa-dana
market+LK+LOC REC   exchange-HAB-3plSUBJ.VT+3fem.sgBAS.VT
'At a market one makes exchanges'

The Manambu term for stock exchange is *sa:n warapwi-kwa-dana tami:* (money exchange-HAB-3plSUBJ.VT+3fem.sgBAS.VT area), lit. 'area where they exchange money'.

In contrast, *warapwi-taka-* implies that one object was exchanged for another, specifically stated (and obligatory) one, as in 15.70. An old woman stole a magic pot from a boy while he was asleep, and replaced (*warapwi-taka* 'exchange-put') it with a pot which had no magic powers.

15.70 a   ta:kw   væn   rə-ku
      DEM.DIST+fem.sg woman   see+SEQ sit-COMPL.SS
      warapwi-taka-lə-l   a   væk
      exchange-put-3fem.sgSUBJ.P-3fem.sgBAS.P DEM.DIST.fem.sg pot
      'That woman sat and looked, and then she exchanged that pot (with one with no magic powers)'

That is, *-taka* as V₂ is a means of adding an extra participant: the object of exchange. Both objects involved in the exchange can be mentioned in the sentence, as two syntactically equal objects—but note that the two are hardly ever overtly mentioned in one clause since the identity of participants is usually clear from the context:

15.71 [kami: warapwi-taka-ku]   na:gw ata   kur-kwa-na-dian
      fish   exchange-put-COMPL.SS   sago   then get-HAB-ACT.FOC-1plBAS.VT
      'Having exchanged (sago) for fish, then we used to get sago'

This same compound can be extended to changing a situation—as in 15.72, used by a mother to describe how she managed to improve her baby daughter's health by feeding her:

15.72 kamnagwəb   warapwi-taka-tuə-l
      food+LK+TERM   exchange-put-1sgSUBJ.P-3fem.sgBAS.P
      'I changed (her, or her state) just (with) food'

As a second component in compounds, *-taka* acts as a valency-increasing device. However, exactly what participant is added largely depends on the semantics of the verb, and is only partially predictable.

(b) ADDING A LOCATION (TYPICALLY, A LARGE SURFACE ONTO WHICH SOMETHING IS PUT, OR SPREAD). This second meaning of *-taka* as a V₂ is fairly consistent with its meaning as an independent verb—'put, arrange by spreading'. Examples are *taw-* 'put up (e.g. a post)', and *taw-taka-* 'put out or up on a large surface'; *kraku-* 'carry across' and *kraku-taka-* (carry.across-put) 'get and put' (e.g. when loading a canoe: see 15.74); *gwa-* 'pull out' (e.g. bits of grass seeds), and *gwa-taka-* 'pull out (e.g. bits of grass seeds) and put on surface (e.g. floor)', and *səpər-* 'snap something' and *səpər-taka-* 'snap and put', in 15.73.

15.73 gwa-n   napa-ku   galəp   səpər-taka-bana
      pull-SEQ COMPL.VB-COMPL.SS   peanut snap-put-1plSUBJ.VT+3fem.sgBAS.VT
      'Having pulled (peanuts out of the ground) we snap them (off branches) onto surface'

A location does not have to be particularly extended. It can be a plate, or a mat, as in the following pairs: *kətək-* 'cut', *kətək-a-taka-* 'cut and lay it out' (e.g. pieces of watermelon), *rau-* 'peel' and *rau-taka-* 'peel onto surface', *rali-* 'untie, roll', *rali-taka-* 'untie and roll out onto surface'. It can be a piece of paper or a plaster, as in *kaña-* 'be glued', and *kaña-taka-* 'glue, paste over'; *məñər-* 'chip, break off' (like a tooth chips off), *məñər-taka-* 'chip and put' (on a plate, or a lap, as one could do with pieces of melon). Or it may be a hole in the ground, as in *gəp(ə)-* 'bury', *gəpə-taka* 'bury in a particular location (grave)'. A similar example is in 15.67: the compound *sada-taka-* (put.down-put) refers to putting a heavy stringbag onto the woman's head.

With verbs of affect, *-taka* as V₂ may have an overtone of full extent, as in *kaja-taka-* (disperse/move.away-put) 'open up completely' (as when undoing a bandage or pulling a plaster off), *jar-taka-* (put.hand.inside.to.take.someting.out-put) 'take it out completely' (when allowing a child to empty mother's pocket), *kabəl-* means 'surround (something or someone)', and *kabəl-taka-* means 'surround from every possible side or surround everyone'; *takw-* means 'clear garden', and *takwə-taka-* means 'clear the whole space of a garden'. In 15.74, *-taka* as V₂ in *vægru-taka-* (meet-put) has an overtone of doing things all together:

15.74 [Səruali <u>vægru-taka-da-k</u>]   yak [ñan ya:b
      Səruali meet-put-3pl-COMPL.DS OK we road
      <u>kui-tak-kui-takan</u>   napa-ku],   Səruali
      give.to.third.p-put:RED-give.to.third.p-put+SEQ COMPL.VB-COMPL.SS Səruali
      <u>kraku-tak-kraku-taka-ku</u>   [kur-yi-ba-l]
      carry.across-put:RED-carry.across-put-COMPL.SS do-go-1plSUBJ.P-3fem.sgBAS.P
      'After the Səruali (possibly, the Gala: note 8 to Chapter 1) had all met together, OK,
      we, having spread (i.e. prepared) the road, having carried the Səruali and piled them (on
      canoes), we worked as we went along (and we killed them all)'

With the verb *saku-* 'lay an egg; give birth to a child', a *-taka* compound means 'have children or lay eggs one after another'. In 15.75, *saku-* describes the birth of one child, and *saku-taka-* describes having child after child after child:

15.75 [də-kə-m   <u>saku-taka-lə-di</u>   ñanugw sama:sam]
      he-OBL-LOC give.birth-put-3fem.sgSUBJ.P-3plBAS.P children many
      '(She) kept giving birth to many children for him (her man)'

The verb *-taka* as V₂ may have a distinct overtone of 'putting', especially in combination with a V₁ followed by a directional marker, making compounds like the one in 15.76 look like symmetrical compounds (this example is a continuation of 15.5):

15.76 kwasa   məy nay-ku   <u>yakə-su-taka-kə-bana</u>
      little+fem.sg very play-COMPL.SS throw-UP-put-FUT-1plSUBJ.VT+3fem.sgBAS.VT
      'Having played a little bit, we will throw it (pig's bladder) up onto a surface'

A similar example is 15.77—a man carried by a bird put his head on her wings somewhat burying it inside. A similar example is *kraku-taka-* (carry.across-put) 'carry across and put onto surface' in 15.74.

15.77 nak-aba:b ata   ab   pəpa:r   <u>ku-sula-taka-də-l</u>
      one-TOO   then head wing+LK+ALL 'put'-INSIDE-put-3masc.sgSUBJ.P-3fem.sgBAS.P
      'One (man) too put his head onto (its) wings burying it inside'

The same compound was used to refer to threading a needle: Tanina offered to help me when I was fighting with threading a needle in the dark—*ku-sula-taka-u* ('put'-INSIDE-put-1sgIMPV) 'May I thread it?'

The verb *-taka* as V₂ with transitive verbs of affect may imply downward movement—that is, acting as a directional. The location is understood from the context, as it is in 15.78.

15.78 [mi: vəl-ta:y],   <u>vəl-taka-kwa-dana-di</u>
      tree cut-COTEMP cut-put-HAB-3plSUBJ.VT-3plBAS.VT
      'Cutting a tree, they cut it down (to the ground)'

That -*taka* can impart a directional meaning is corroborated by its occurrence with the bound generic verb root *wər-* 'move', as in *wər-taka-* 'move downwards onto a larger surface (e.g. fish from pot to plate)'. This root often occurs with bound directionals, e.g. *wər-saki-* (move-ACROSS) 'turn; translate; pour water (from a bucket to a bucket)', *wər-sada-* (move-DOWN) 'move down'. We return to this in §16.1.

Numerous compounds with a V₁ that has a meaning compatible with a location, and also used with -*taka* as a marker of valency increase, are polysemous. For instance, *kur-taka-* (do-put) may mean 'do for other people' (as in 14.69), or 'take things out (e.g. of a stringbag) and spread on a surface' (e.g. on the floor), or 'assemble' (e.g. a canoe). The compound *sapu-taka-* (cover-put) may mean 'put a headdress on someone else's head' or 'cover a large surface'. The compound *ku-su-taka-* ('put.on'-UP-put) means 'dress someone' as in 15.65. It does not have to—it may mean 'lift up and put', as in 15.79. This is similar to 15.77—the overtone of actual 'putting' is obvious.

15.79 yata-n   krayi:n   ada   yabwi:m
       carry-SEQ 'bring'+close+SEQ DEM.DIST.REACT.TOP+masc.sg large.tree.sp
       ku-su-taka-kə-tua-ñən-ək
       'put'-UP-put-FUT-1sgSUBJ.VT-2fem.sgBAS.VT-CONF
       'Carrying, bringing (you) close, I will put you on top of that (reactivated topic) yabwi tree'

Along similar lines, *təpə-taka-* (be.closed/fence/sew-put) can mean 'close', as in 15.62–3 above. In an appropriate context, the same compound may mean 'sew onto a location':

15.80 *batəna*-yæy   ku-su-wapwi:m   ata   təpə-taka-u
       button+LK-SUBST 'put.on'-UP-clothing+LOC then be.closed/fence/sew-put-1sgIMPV
       'Shall I sew (this: a badge) onto the clothes instead of a button?'

We will see, in A8 below, that *təpə-taka-* may also have an additional meaning (identical to that of *taka-təp-*) 'prevent from seeing; block'.

In each case the exact meaning of a -*taka* compound is determined by the context. And, in addition to that, compounds containing -*taka* as V₂ often develop meanings which are hard to predict from semantics of the components. In 15.81, *vya-taka-* (hit-put) in combination with a direct object *ta:b* 'hand' means 'wave a hand'.

15.81 akətawa rə-dian,   kəp ta:b vya-taka-n,   səmaka-n səbən-ən
       like.this sit-1plBAS.VT just hand hit-put-SEQ show-SEQ return-SEQ
       kwa-ba:-l
       stay-1plSUBJ.P-3fem.sgBAS.P
       'This is how we were, just waving hand, showing (the way) again'

In 15.82, the same compound, *vya-taka-*, means 'hit and put down; shake with downwards movement':

15.82 [yata-ku,   gu   adəka
       carry-COMPL.SS water DEM.DIST.REACT.TOP+masc.sg
       yaku-taka-bana-d]   [yaku-taka-ku],   [ñan-a-ñan-a-di
       wash-put-1plSUBJ.VT-3masc.sgBAS.VT wash-put-COMPL.SS we-LK-we-LK-pl
       səpa:m   tə-na-di   yuwi   ata   gwa-bana-di]
       body+LK+LOC be/have-ACT.FOC-3plBAS.VT feather then pluck-1plSUBJ.VT-3plBAS.VT
       [gwa-ku]   [nak-a-nak   nak-a-nak   vya-taka-ku],   [də-kə   səp
       pluck-COMPL.SS one-LK-one one-LK-one hit-put-COMPL.SS he-OBL+fem.sg body

kulapu-ku],   adəka   ma:

decorate-COMPL.SS DEM.DIST.REACT.TOP+masc.sg again

kapra-bana-d

'bring'+TOWARDS.SPEAKER-1plSUBJ.VT-3masc.sgBAS.VT

'Having carried him, we wash him, having washed him, we pluck the feathers from our own bodies, having plucked (them), having shaken them one by one with downwards movements, having decorated his body, then we bring him in again'

The meaning of *-taka* as V$_2$ is equally unpredictable in a number of compounds involving other verbs as V$_1$—for instance, *wukə-taka-* (hear-put) means 'provide', and *kay-kwa-taka-* (CAUS-stay-put) means 'pour'. The form *kui-taka-* (give.to.third.p-put) may mean 'spread', as in 15.74, 'send around, distribute', as in 15.83, and even 'put on display in a store', as in 15.84.

15.83 kə-di   ñəg   kui-taka-tua-di

       DEM.PROX-pl letter give.to.third.p-put.down-1sgSUBJ.VT-3plBAS.VT

       'I have passed these letters on'

15.84 [a-di   krim   stuam   kui-taka-da-di]

       DEM.DIST-pl cream store+LOC give.to.third.p-put-3plSUBJ.P-3plBAS.P

       [yapi-kə-tua-di]

       buy-FUT-1sgSUBJ.VT-3plBAS.P

       'They put those (hair) creams out on display in the store, I will buy them'

The meaning 'send around, spread' appears in the term *kui-taka-na mæj* (give.to.third.p-put-ACT.FOC+3fem.sgBAS.VT rope) 'a rope used for sending messages or marking days with knots' (traditional Manambu way of marking time).

These compounds allow only third person recipient forms—saying **kwatiya-taka-* (give.to.nonthird.p-put) is ungrammatical. This is an additional argument in favour of considering the third person recipient forms as functionally unmarked (see §4.2.2).

A number of verbs are composed of a nonce root (not attested anywhere else in the language) followed by *-taka*, e.g. *saw-taka-* (?-put) 'adorn, decorate', and *məl sray-taka-* (eye ?-put) 'look closely', *wapu-taka-* (?-put) 'light a fire', *tu-taka-* (?-put) 'tie' (there is a verb *tu-* 'burn'; but the connection is tenuous). These idiomatic constructions are reminiscent of lexicalized compounds discussed under §15.2. Verbs of speech, perception, and ingestion do not occur with *-taka*.

We have seen that in many cases compounds with *-taka* 'put, arrange by spreading' as V$_2$ have developed unpredictable semantic overtones. And yet we can establish a semantic core for *-taka* as V$_2$. This semantic core includes:

(a) adding an argument which can be a direct object, a beneficiary, an object of exchange, or a location; and

(b) imparting the meaning of putting an object onto an extended surface in a downward direction.

Meaning (b) is more functionally unmarked than meaning (a). There are two reasons for this conclusion.

First, most verb compounds with *-taka* as V$_2$ which have meaning (a) also have meaning (b): the context is instrumental in deciding exactly which meaning is appropriate. There are exceptions—for instance, the verb *yaku-taka-* (wash-put) appears to only have the meaning of 'washing someone other than oneself' (as shown in 15.65 and 15.82).

Secondly, *-taka* can be compounded with the general verb *məgi-* 'do whatever' (§21.3.2). The resulting form *məgi-taka-* means 'do whatever with respect to extended surface' (for instance, peeling pawpaw onto a mat), or 'do whatever and put it down' (e.g. pulling a lever down). This form is not used in the meaning of 'do whatever for someone else'—possibly because the number of verbs which occur in V_1 slot with *-taka* adding a beneficiary is limited, and it is unlikely that a speaker would choose to replace such a verb with *məgi-*.

We will see in §21.3.2 that *məgi-* is used either when the speaker cannot readily remember the exact verb, or when there is no verb in the language available for the description of a particular activity. Verbs 'dress', 'put a headdress on', 'wash', etc. are quite specific, very frequent, and hard to forget.

That *-taka* combines directionality with valency increase is not unexpected, in the context of the overall behaviour of directionals throughout the language. We return to this in §16.1.

A8. *-təp(ə)-* 'BE CLOSED; FENCE' as V_2 in asymmetrical compounds has two related meanings (a) cessative, 'do for the last time', and (b) 'stop'; and another meaning (c) 'do firmly'.

Just like most other compounds, numerous compounds with *təp(ə)-* in the V_2 slot have developed meanings not quite predictable from the sum of their components.

Compounds with a verb from most semantic groups in V_1 position and *təp(ə)-* in V_2 position have the cessative meaning of 'never do again; do', e.g. *bla-təp-* 'speak for the last time', *yi-təp-* 'go for the last time', *kui-təp-* 'give to third person for the last time', and 15.85. The transitivity of the compound is always determined by V_1:

15.85 bə   və-təpə-tua-dəmən
      already see-be.closed-1sgSUBJ.VT-2masc.sgBAS.VT
      'It was the last I saw of you'

The verb *təp(ə)-* appears in the term for the mortuary feast *Kəkə-təp* (eat:RED-be.closed), lit. 'eating for the last time' (which involves ritual 'eating' of a relative: see Harrison 1990a: 35). It also occurs in the term for 'last child', *kə-təp-ə-məñ* (eat-be.closed-LK-breast) 'eating breast for the last time', 'last child'. The array of synonyms for 'last child' are in brackets at 15.86:

15.86 a-də   də-kə-də   [*last* ñan] [kə-təp-ə-məñ]
      DEM.DIST-masc.sg he-OBL-masc.sg last child eat-be.closed-LK-breast
      [gəñ   ñan] [kukər ñan]
      last/tail child after   child
      'That last son of his, the one who ate breast for the last time, tail-child, child (who came) after'

The cessative meaning is closely linked with the other meaning of *təp(ə)-* as V_2, 'stop' (an activity). In this meaning, it also does not affect transitivity of the compound. In 15.87, the father tries to stop his two sons pulling at the bow and arrow which belong to one of them:

15.87 [asa:y rasə-ku],   [kur-təpə-ku],   [nəkə-dəwa   kaja-k
      father get.up-COMPL.SS do-closed-COMPL.SS other-masc.sg+COM move.apart-PURP.SS
      kur-də-l],   ma:
      do-3masc.sgSUBJ.P-3fem.sgBAS.P no
      '(After the children had started pulling at each other), the father got up and stopped (them), he was about to separate (the two children)—no (nothing came out of it)'

The meaning of *-təp(ə)-* as V_2 may be ambiguous: in 15.88 it can mean either 'stop killing', or 'hit for the last time'. The context suggests the second reading.

15.88 [aləm   ata amæy <u>vya-təpə-da-k</u>]
DEM.DIST+fem.sg+LOC then mother hit-be.closed-3pl-COMPL.DS
[kusə-lə-k],   ata war-di-ya
finish-3fem.sg-COMPL.DS then go.up-3plBAS.P-EMPH
'Then they hit the mother for the last time, after she'd died (lit. finished), then they went up'

Both 'cessative' and 'stop' reading can be equally appropriate, if the context is sufficiently vague. The gist of 15.89 is that the boy had paid his relatives off and they went away to their village.

15.89 yi:n   [a-di   mi <u>vəl-yakə-da-k</u>]   [sa:n
go+SEQ DEM.DIST-pl tree cut-FULLY-3pl-COMPL.DS money
<u>yapi-təpə-də-k</u>]   [təp-a:r   yi-di]
pay/buy-be.closed-3masc.sg-COMPL.DS village-LK+ALL go-3plBAS.P
'As it went on, after they had cut all the trees fully, after he had paid them for the last time (or: stopped paying them) they went to (their village)'

The verb *-təp(ə)-* as V₂ can also impart the idea of 'preventing, stopping' to a number of compounds, such as *taka-təp-* (put-be.closed) means 'prevent from seeing, close up; cover'. Its variant is *təpə-taka-*. These two appear to be the only examples of permutability of components in a compound, e.g. 15.90, from a story about why the *apawul* spirits cannot be seen by human beings:

15.90 adiya   baw <u>taka-təpə-la-di</u>
DEM.DIST.REACT.TOP+pl+DEM.DIST haze put-stop-3fem.sgSUBJ.VT-3plBAS.VT
'The haze covers them (preventing them from being seen)'

Along similar lines, compound *væsə-təp-* (walk-be.closed) means 'prevent (from getting something, e.g. food)', and *taw-təp-* (stand-be.closed) means 'prevent, stand in the way', as in 15.91:

15.91 [bəta:y bau <u>taw-təpə-lə-k</u>]   [bəum   tə-na-di]
already haze stand-be.closed-3fem.sg-COMPL.DS haze+LOC stand-ACT.FOC-3plBAS.VT
'Already since the haze is preventing (standing in the way), they (spirits) are in a haze'

We will now turn to some idiomatic compounds involving *-təp(ə)-*. The compound *wa-təp-* (say-be.closed) means 'forbid, deprive', as in 15.92–3. This verb is included in the term for the first pregnancy, associated with numerous taboos, *watəp-ə-gəm* (forbid-LK-first.pregnancy), literally, 'the first pregnancy of taboos'. The object of 'forbid, deprive' is in dative case—we can recall from §7.4 that the dative case marks any undesirable non-subjects.

15.92 [japək   <u>wa-təpə-da-k</u>],   [sarmabap ata kwa-bər]
thing+LK+DAT say-be.closed-3pl-COMPL.DS miserable then stay-3duBAS.VT
'Since (uncle and his family) deprived (them) of things, they stayed miserable'

15.93 [[ñən   yi-tukwa]   wa-ku]   [aka
you.fem go-PROH.GEN say-COMPL.SS DEM.DIST.REACT.TOP.fem.sg
<u>wa-təpə-da</u>]
say-be.closed-3masc.sgSUBJ.VT+3fem.sgBAS.VT
' "Don't you go", having said (this), he forbade her (to go)'

The compound *wukə-təp(ə)-* (think-be.closed) means 'forget (completely)' (this differs from *wukə-mar-* (think-NEG?) 'forget (not necessarily completely)'), as shown in 15.94. (Also see §14.6: neither of these can be considered inherently negative lexemes.)

15.94 [a   wukə-təpə-tua
DEM.DIST+fem.sg   think-be.closed-1sgSUBJ.VT+3fem.sgBAS.VT
kwasa]   wa-u
little+fem.sg   say-1sgIMPV
'Let me tell the little bit I had forgotten completely'

The third meaning of *-təp(ə)-* as V$_2$ is 'do firmly'. This meaning can be easily associated with the lexical meaning of this verb—'be closed, fence' and so on. Examples are at 15.95–6. The compound *taka-təp-* in 15.95 is homophonous with *taka-təp-* 'prevent from seeing', in 15.90. Shutting a traditional door involves putting the planks close together firmly.

15.95 [lə   takətap   taka-təpə-ku]   kaigən kwa:l
she   door   put-be.closed-COMPL.SS   silent   stay+3fem.sgBAS.P
'Having firmly shut the door, she sat silent'

15.96 ji-təpə-ku   rə-kwa
tie-be.closed-COMPL.SS   sit-IMPV.3p+fem.sg
'May it (piece of pumpkin) sit (there) covered firmly'

The idiomatic expression *sa:l yi-təp(ə)-* (oath say/go-be.closed) means 'swear a solemn binding oath'. The degree of idiomaticity in *-təp(ə)-* compounds makes them different from grammaticalized compounds. Unlike *-taka* compounds, *-təp(ə)-* does not occur as V$_2$ with the general verb *məgi-* 'do whatever'.

A9. *-ba:gw-* 'DO INCESSANTLY' as V$_2$ in asymmetrical compounds expresses manner and extent of action, as in *yaku-ba:gw-* 'wash all over the place (e.g. sago)', *kə-ba:gw-* 'eat all over the place, eat habitually', *væsə-ba:gw-* 'step all over the place', *vya-ba:gw-* 'hit all over the place', *gəpə-ba:gw-* (run-do.incessantly) 'run around' in 15.97, and *yi-ba:gw-* 'go incessantly'. A similar example is in 18.33. The form *-ba:gw-* can undergo partial reduplication (see §12.8.2); the resulting compound refers to multiple movements in every direction, e.g. *gəpə-bay-ba:gwə-d* (run-RED?-do.incessantly-3masc.sgBAS.VT/P) 'he is running all over the place in every direction'.

15.97 lə-kə-də   la:n   kapə-kap   gəpə-ba:gwə-d
she-OBL-masc.sg   husband   alone+LK-alone   go-do.incessantly-3masc.sgBAS.P
'Her husband was running around all alone'

There are no semantic restrictions on the V$_1$ which can be a stative verb, as in 15.98, or an existential verb, as in 15.99.

15.98 an-a-də   ñaj   an-a:k
we.du-LK-masc.sg   paternal.uncle   we.du-LK+DAT
warsama-ba:gwə-də-bran
be.angry-do.incessantly-3masc.sgSUBJ.P-1duBAS.P
'Our paternal uncle is incessantly angry with us two'

15.99 wun   yabə-rəb   tə-ba:gwə-kə-na-dəwun-ək
I   road+LK-STRAIGHT   be-do.incessantly-FUT-ACT.FOC-1masc.sgBAS.VT-CONF
'I will stay straight on the road incessantly'

There are no examples in the corpus of *-ba:gw-* combining with a copula, or an auxiliary (see Chapter 17). This form does not occur in imperatives.

A10. **-pakw-* 'DO ALL, AFFECT ALL (S/O)' as V₂ in asymmetrical compounds expresses extent of action, participant involvement. This marker can occur with transitive and with intransitive verbs, and it refers both to complete involvement of S/O and the complete degree of activity. In 15.100, it implies that the spirits ate up all the people in the village completely:

15.100 a   təp-a-kə-di   du   ta:kw   miyawa
       DEM.DIST.fem.sg village-LK-POSS-pl man woman   all
       kə-pakwə-da-di
       eat-DO.ALL-3plSUBJ.P-3plBAS.P
       'They ate up all the people of that village'

In 15.26, 15.101, and 15.124 (at §15.4), *-pakw-* refers to the S—indicating that everyone died: *kusə-* 'finish' is a euphemism for 'die':

15.101 [aba:b kusə-da-k,   kusə-pakwə-yakə-da-k]   [a-də
       all   finish-3pl-COMPL.DS finish-DO.ALL-FULLY-3pl-COMPL.DS DEM.DIST-masc.sg
       nakadəməy-a   du   ada   də   warəd]
       single.one+masc.sg-LK man DEM.DIST.REACT.TOP+masc.sg he   go.up+3masc.sgBAS.P
       'After they'd all died, after they completely all died, that single man (reactivated topic) went up'

The form *-pakw-* frequently occurs with verbs to do with killing and dying. It could be considered homonymous with *pa:kw-* 'hide' (see 15.54 and B2 in §15.3.2) (the long vowel is expected to shorten in an unstressed position), but any such link is too far-fetched.

A11. **-jika-* 'DO PROPERLY' as V₂ in asymmetrical compounds refers to proper achievement of an action. There do not appear to be any restrictions on the semantics of V₁; *-jika* does not affect the verb's transitivity.

In her description of a now almost completely forgotten male initiation ritual, Sawsepali described how the mother of the initiand(s) would undergo a ritual beating; the point was to beat her well and truly, until she was covered in blood. Then other female relatives would take her place.

15.102 [ləka   daya   amæy-a:b məy-a kuprap
       she+DEM.DIST.REACT.TOP.fem.sg they+fem.sg mother-too real-LK bad
       vya-jik-jika-da-k],   [ñiki   bakəbak]
       hit-PROPERLY:RED-PROPERLY-3pl-COMPL.DS blood   coming.out
       [aka   waku-na   jukwar amæy]
       DEM.DIST.REACT.TOP.fem.sg go.out-ACT.FOC+3fem.sgBAS.VT sister   mother
       'After they hit their mother too really badly many times, the blood coming out, she (another woman) goes out, (that is) sister (and) mother'

Heron-like birds called *wudəmali* were continuously attacking Yuamali's plantations of sweet potatoes. She managed to trap one bird, and almost killed it, but not quite. The bird was left to die a slow death in the corner of the house, by the front door, so as to teach the whole lot of these birds a lesson not to steal again. The bird spent the whole day in convulsions. Everyone who visited our house that day approved of Yuamali's actions. And Dora, Yuamali's sister, commented:

15.103 kiya-jika-kwa-d
        die-PROPERLY-IMPV.3p-masc.sg
        'May he die properly'

When I was writing down a long story, the comment was:

15.104 suku-jika-n   kwa-ñəna-d
        write/carve-PROPERLY-SEQ stay-2fem.sgSUBJ.VT-3masc.sgBAS.VT
        'You are in the process of writing it properly (lit. staying writing it properly)'

With the verb 'sleep', -jika- refers to proper deep sleep:

15.105 sə   kwa-jika-na-wun
        sleep stay-PROPERLY-ACT.FOC-1sgBAS.VT
        'I have been fast asleep'

A12. *-yakə- 'DO FULLY; WELL AND TRULY' as V$_2$ in asymmetrical compounds refers to an extreme extent of activity or state. This morpheme is homophonous with the verb yakə- 'throw'. The semantic link, between 'throw' and 'do fully; well and truly; very' is tenuous. In addition, any connection between the two was denied by most speakers.

There are no restrictions on the semantics of V$_1$ combining with -yakə- as V$_2$; and we will see in §15.4 that -yakə- frequently attaches to a compound verb in V$_1$ position. We saw in §4.3.2 that the adjective vyakət 'good' is unusual in that it forms a compound with -yakə 'throw' as a second component, as if it were a verb, e.g. vyakəta-yakə takwa-ñan (good-throw/FULLY woman+LK-child) 'very beautiful girl'. Other examples include 15.89 ('cut the tree fully'), 15.101 ('die fully'), 12.3 ('close off completely'), 12.55 ('die completely'), and 15.106.

In terms of its meaning, -yakə- refers to the complete extent of action, but may extend to include complete involvement of any core participant—as in 12.55 where 'everyone died completely' (the verb kiya- 'die' may mean 'die', or just 'faint', as in 15.122). In 15.106 -yakə describes the fact that people went away for good, and that all of them did so.

15.106 [aba:b yi-yakə-da-k]   [mugul rə-di]
        all   go-FULLY-3pl-COMPL.DS few   stay-3plBAS.P
        'After all (people) went off for good, few stayed'

In all the examples mentioned above, -yakə- overlaps in its meaning with -ba:gw-, -pakw-, and -kusə- as V$_2$. We saw, at A2 above, that suku-kusə-yakə-ta-də gabu-ma:j (write-COMPL-FULLY-1duSUBJ.VT-3masc.sgBAS.VT tradition-story) 'fully and completely written up story' was given as an opposite of suku-pæsa-ta-də gabu-ma:j 'half-written story' in 15.37.

Unlike any other V$_2$, -yakə- has a distinct overtone of 'do fully, be well and truly the case', as in 15.107, with an action verb 'glue, mend', and 15.108, with a stative verb 'surpass; take precedence':

15.107 [brə-kə-də   val   kaña-ku]   [kəp kaña-ku   rəka:rək],
        3du-LK-masc.sg canoe mend-COMPL.SS earth mend-COMPL.SS properly
        [kaña-yakə-ku]   [abra   ga:n rasi-na-bər]
        glue-FULLY-COMPL.SS DEM.DIST.REACT.TOP+du night get.up-ACT.FOC-3duBAS.VT
        'Having glued their canoe, having properly glued it with earth, having well and truly mended (it), the two got up at night'

15.108 kami: na:gw ña:n   kamkau   yawi:m   kakəl-yakə-na
        fish   sago   red.yam hairy.yam work+LOC surpass-FULLY-ACT.FOC+3fem.sgBAS.VT
        '(Building a house) well and truly takes precedence over the task of fishing, sago making, yam gardening'

The form -*yakə*- can be used with any verb, including the general *məgi*- 'do whatever'. In 15.109 this refers to touching, or messing with it: the speaker decided not to specify exactly how this was done:

15.109 kəla-wur   kamna:gw   kui-tua   bəta:y
DEM.PROX+fem.sg-UP   food   give.to.third.p-1sgSUBJ.VT+3fem.sgBAS.VT   already
<u>megi-yakə-ku</u>
do.whatever-FULLY-COMPL.SS
'I give (him) this food up there, having already done whatever to it' (that is, touched it)

The suffix -*tu*- 'complete involvement of S/O' (§12.4) can occur together with -*yakə*-, e.g. *kətəkə-tu-yakə-brə-di* (cut-ALL-FULLY-3duSUBJ.P-3plBAS.P) 'they two well and truly cut them all up'. A compound consisting of the verb *wa* 'speak' in V_1 slot and -*yakə*- in the V_2 slot has a somewhat idiosyncratic meaning of 'send, order', as in 15.110.

15.110 [wun-a   ta:kw   aləm   kwa-lə-k]   [wa-yakə-gur-ək]
I-LK+fem.sg   wife   there   stay-3fem.sg-COMPL.DS   say-'throw'-2pl-COMPL.DS
[ya-kwa]
come-IMPV.3p+fem.sg
'After my wife stayed there, you sent her to come' (lit. after you sent her, let her come)'

The second component of a *wa-yakə*- compound can occur twice, as in 15.111: the meaning of the resulting form is 'well and truly; intensively, strongly order (not to)'. The intensive reading may have resulted from the meaning of reduplication (see §12.8.2). Or it may be interpreted as an instance of an extra -*yakə*- 'do fully'. The two interpretations are equally plausible:

15.111 amæy   a   lə   ma: <u>wa-yakə-yakəl</u>   wiya:r
mother   then   she   no   say-'throw'-RED/FULLY+3fem.sgBAS.P   house+LK+ALL
war-warək
go.up-RED+DAT
'Mother, she strongly ordered (them) not to go up into the house'

The verb *wa-yakə*- typically implies a verbal order. Whether this is the same -*yakə*- as in 15.106–8 or a different one, and how it may or may not be related to *yakə*- 'throw' is an open question. We return to the use of *wa-yakə*- as a causative strategy in §16.2.2.

15.3.2   Minor verb precedes major verb

Compounds of the second type are composed of a verb from a closed class ('minor' verb) which provides a valency-changing or an aktionsart specification followed by a verb from an open class. These are summarized in Table 15.2. Such compounds are highly restricted: only two 'minor' verbs, *wa*- 'say' and *yi*- 'go, say', can occur in V_1 slot. The existing combinations with V_2 can be exhaustively listed. Their semantics is only partly predictable.

A valid analytical option would be to analyse these instances of V_1 as prefixes. None of them can occur together with the prefix *kay*- 'causative/manipulative' (see §16.2.1).

Two minor verbs can occur as V_1 in grammaticalized compounds: (B1) *wa*- 'say', and (B2) *yi*- 'go, say'. Neither of these is productive.

B1. CAUSE-EFFECT COMPOUNDS WITH 'SAY' involve four verbs in V_2 slot: *yaga*- 'be scared', *jəwi*- 'be awake', *la:kw*- 'know', and *buti*- 'fold'. Unlike in the cause-effect compounds discussed in

TABLE 15.2 Asymmetrical compounds: minor verb precedes major verb

FORM AND TRANSLATION	MEANING IN COMPOUNDS	DISCUSSED IN
wa- 'say'	causative (four or five verbs)	B1
yi- 'go, say'	(a) causative (one verb); (b) doing fully (one verb); (c) involving surface (one verb)	B2

§15.2 above, the actual meaning of 'saying' is bleached: 'scaring' or 'wakening' does not have to be done by speaking.

The S=A ambitransitive verb *yaga-* 'be scared (of something)' is illustrated in 15.112a where it is used transitively. It can also be used intransitively, as in *yaga-tukwa* (be.scared-PROH) 'don't be scared!'.

15.112a ka:p   da-n   tətak   yaga-lwun
        alone go.down-SEQ   stay+RED+DAT   be.scared-1fem.sgBAS.P
        'I was scared to go down (there) on my own'

In 15.112b, the same verb appears in a compound with *wa-*, with a causative meaning 'scare someone'. The child cried because I was the first white person he had ever seen; I did not have a chance to talk to him—so the causation has nothing to do with a speech act.

15.112b ñan   <u>wa-yaga-ñənalək</u>   gra:d
        child say-be.scared-2fem.sg+BECAUSE   cry+3masc.sgBAS.VT/P
        'Since you scared the child, he cried'

The verb *jəwi* 'wake up, be awake' is strictly intransitive—see 15.113a.

15.113a a   səkər jəwi-tua
        DEM.DIST+fem.sg   time   wake.up-1sgSUBJ.P+3fem.sgBAS.P
        'That time I was awake'

In 15.113b, it is causativized with *wa-* 'say':

15.113b wus   yasa-lə-k   wun-a:m   <u>a-wa-jəwi</u>
        urine feel-3fem.sg-COMPL.DS   I-LK+ACC IMPV-say-be.awake
        'If you want to pee (lit. if it feels like peeing), wake me up'

We saw in 3.1–2 that the verb *laku-* 'know, understand' is S=A ambitransitive. A compound consisting of *wa-* 'say' and *laku-* 'know, understand' is a strictly transitive verb meaning 'give advice (as a parent to the child)', as illustrated in 15.114a and 15.114b:

15.114a [an-a   amæy   lə-kə   <u>wa-laku-majik</u>   wukə-ku]
        we.two-LK   mother she-POSS+fem.sg say-know-speech+LK+DAT   listen-COMPL.SS
        ya-tə-l   aka
        come-1dusUBJ.P-3fem.sgBAS.P DEM.DIST.REACT.TOP.fem.sg
        'Having listened to our mother's advice, here we came'

In 15.114b, this same compound occurs with the purposive suffix (this is a complementation strategy).

15.114b laku-lakub   tə-də-kəkək   <u>wa-laku-tua</u>
        know-RED+TERM   be/stay-3masc.sg-PURP.DS   say-know-1sgSUBJ.VT+3fem.BAS.VT
        'I am giving advice for him to have knowledge'

This verb is quite specific in its meaning: it can only be used to refer to advice given from someone superior to someone inferior—that is, it is not appropriate for an equal member of a peer group.

The fourth verb which occurs with a prefixed *wa-* is an S=A ambitransitive verb *buti-* 'be folded; fold': the strictly transitive verb *wa-buti-* means 'fold forcefully or with care; fold a full length of something, e.g. a long sheet'. It is similar in its meaning to *kay-buti-* (MANIP-fold) 'fold a full length of a big object' (see §16.2.1). In this instance, *wa-* does not really causativize the verb *buti-* (neither does it have any implication of a speech act): it restricts an ambitransitive verb to a transitive use, and adds an implication of full extent of activity and a special manipulative effort. This is in line with the way *kay-* 'causative-manipulative' is used with transitive verbs, but quite unlike all other instances of *wa-* as a putative V_1.

At least one other form may contain a causative with *wa-*. The form *suan* 'difficult' occurs as copula complement of the auxiliary *yi* 'say, go' (see §4.2.2), as in *suan yi-na* (difficult go-ACT.FOC+3fem.sgBAS.VT) 'it is difficult' (see 4.7).[1] The S=O ambitransitive verb *wa-sway-* 'postpone, be postponed, undo the plan', may be related to it (e.g. *wasway-na-dəwun* 'I could not do it'; *wasway-na* 'it was postponed', *a-wasway* 'postpone!', *wasway-bran* 'we postponed').

The class of *wa-* causatives may be bigger, if we include other compounds involving *wa-* 'say'. Under A8 above, we analysed *wa-təp(ə)-* (say-be.closed) 'forbid, deprive' (see 15.92–3) as a subtype of asymmetrical compound with *-təp(ə-)* as V_2, with a somewhat unpredictable meaning. This verb can be equally well analysed as having causativizing *wa-* as V_1 and *-təp(ə)-* 'be closed, fence, ?stop' as V_2. Its somewhat unpredictable meaning 'forbid, deprive' can be easily linked with the meaning of the components: 'make stop, tell to stop'. Similarly, a lexicalized symmetrical-looking compound *wa-tək-* (say-break) 'accuse' can be interpreted as a *wa-* causative with an idiosyncratic meaning. So can *wa-yakə-* (say-throw) 'send, order' (illustrated in 15.110–11), since its meaning is not a sum of the meanings of its components.

The causatives with *wa-* as V_1 form a closed class, whose exact membership is debatable. The semantics of each of the causatives is not quite straightforward. At a first glance, there is nothing wrong with this analysis. It is even corroborated by the fact that *wa-* 'say' is used as a causative strategy with transitive verbs in biclausal structures (see §16.2.2). In addition, verbs of speech are easily grammaticalized as causative markers, both in languages of New Guinea (e.g. Yimas: Foley 1991), and in most other parts of the world (Heine and Kuteva 2002; Aikhenvald 2008). However, a typological analogy is not a proof. We cannot exclude an alternative option: that *wa-* 'causatives' do not contain the verb 'say', but a transitivizing prefix *wa-* with no known etymology.

B2. THE VERB *yi-* 'GO, SAY' occurs as V_1 in three combinations, all with different meanings.

Its CAUSATIVE meaning occurs with one verb: we saw in §4.2.2 that *pa:kw-* 'hide' is intransitive—see 15.115a and 15.2. Its transitive counterpart is *yi-pakw-* 'hide (something)'—see 15.115b and 15.54. This verb is strictly transitive for traditional speakers; innovative speakers can use it as an S=O ambitransitive (see §4.2.2).

15.115a də-kə-k   pakwən   tə-k-na-dəwun-ək
         he-OBL-DAT hide+SEQ stay-FUT-ACT.FOC-1masc.sgBAS.VT-CONF
         'I will stay hidden from him'

---

[1] Possibly, the same root appears in *suyi-* 'be a problem; be difficult', as in *kə-də təp aləb ada suyil* (DEM.PROX-masc.sg village DEM.DIST+fem.sg+TERM DEM.DIST.REACT.TOP+masc.sg have.difficulty+3fem.sgBAS.P) '(people) in this village down there experienced problems'.

15.115b [yu-ku],   [adiyay   wiya:m   ada
        go-COMPL.SS   DEM.DIST+pl+DIST house+LK+LOC   DEM.DIST.REACT.TOP+masc.sg
        bəta:y rəka:rək yi-pakwə-lə-d,   a-də
        already well   go/say-hide-3fem.sgSUBJ.P-3masc.sgBAS.P   DEM.DIST-masc.sg
        kabay]
        snake
        'Having gone off, she already hid him, the snake, very well in the faraway house'

The causativizing effect of *yi-* 'go, say' is reminiscent of the causativizing effect of *wa-* 'say' as V₁. The same verb *yi-* occurs as V₁ in combination with the extended intransitive verb *səwul-* 'turn into, become', imparting an overtone of FULL ACHIEVEMENT. The two are illustrated in 15.116:

15.116 bau yi-səwul-əl   səwəl-ku,   məumiya:m   ata
       haze go-turn-3fem.sgBAS.P turn-COMPL.SS base+tree+LK+LOC   then
       tə-kətəwun   ta:l
       stand-look.upwards stay+3fem.sgBAS.P
       'She fully turned into haze; having turned (into haze), she was standing at the base of a tree looking upwards'

The verb *yi-* combines with a transitive verb *gaji-* 'rub, spread, clean, wipe, squash', forming a compound *yi-gaji-* 'spread, rub'. The resulting meaning difference is quite subtle. The verb *gaji-* describes cleaning, wiping, rubbing, spreading, or destroying (by crushing or dissolving) something which one has not put in there. For instance, the correction fluid was described as *gaji-kwa-dana ja:p* (rub-HAB-3plSUBJ.VT+3fem.sgBAS.VT thing) 'thing they rub or eliminate (things) (with)'. In 15.117, this same verb describes 'rubbing and cleaning one's eyes', and in 15.118 it refers to killing a centipede by squashing it.

15.117 [məl-adi   gaji-ku]   ata wa-na
       eye-3plNOM clean/rub-COMPL.SS then say-ACT.FOC+3fem.sg.VT
       'Having cleaned her eyes she then said'

15.118 [kwasa-də   gərgər mədi   vætə-də-k],   [a-də
       small-masc.sg tiny   centipede bite-3masc.sg-COMPL.DS DEM.DIST-masc.sg
       gajid]
       clean/rub+3masc.sgBAS.P
       'After a teeny weeny centipede bit (him), he crushed that one by rubbing'

A speaker shouted at an annoying child: *gaji-kə-tua-ñən* (squash-FUT-1sgSUBJ.VT-2fem.sgBAS.VT) 'I will squash you!' This same verb is also used to refer to wiping something off—after we'd completed picking peanuts Mali told me to wipe my dirty hands with a towel: *tawəla:r a-gaj* (towel+LK+ALL IMPV-clean/rub/wipe) 'wipe (the dirt off) with a towel!'

The compound *yi-gaj-*, with *yi-* as V₁, implies spreading a specific substance (ointment or water) over the whole surface, as in 15.119 and 15.120.

15.119 [gu   kur-ku]   [ta:b a-yi-gaj]
       water get-COMPL.SS hand IMPV-go/say-spread
       'Having got water, spread (water) on (your) hand (to ease the itching of mosquito bites)'

Note that an ointment in 15.120 is referred to as *yi-gaj-ə-ja:p* 'spreading thing'. This is very different from the term for correction fluid mentioned above ('thing they rub or eliminate (things) (with)').

15.120 də yi-gaji-ja:p   yi-gaji-də-l
       he go/say-rub-thing go-rub-3masc.sgSUBJ.P-3fem.sgBAS.P
       'He spread the (magic) ointment (for attracting women over his body)'

A similar example is at 15.128. It looks as if *yi-* in *yi-gaj-* adds an extra participant to the verb, that is, both an instrument of rubbing and the surface to be rubbed on. This function may be linked together through the use of *yi-* as a causativizing device with the intransitive verb 'hide'. However, the number of examples is so limited, and each use of *yi-* as V₁ so idiosyncratic, that none of these observations is likely to extend beyond speculation.

One can equally well state that *yi-* in all the three verbs discussed here is simply a nonce prefix, and has nothing to do with the verb *yi-* 'say, go'.

15.4 COMBINATIONS OF VERB COMPOUNDS

Symmetrical and asymmetrical verb compounds differ as to how they can be 'nested' within one another. A compound with complex structure typically contains no more than three verb roots.

A symmetrical compound can occupy the V₁ slot of an asymmetrical compound of all types listed in Table 15.1, except for *-təp(ə)-* compounds which are more idiosyncratic than others, e.g. [[*vya-ləpa*]-*yakə*]- (hit-cut-FULLY) 'hit and break fully; cut cross-wise fully', [[*væsə-pərki*]-*ya*]- (step-tear-come) 'keep stepping and tearing', [[*vya-ləpa*]-*taka*]- (hit-cut-put) 'hit and break in a downward direction involving large surface'. Also see 15.39a–b, and 16.40 (*təpə-taka-ya-* (be.closed-put-come) 'keep closing (the road) off').

In 15.121, a sequential compound containing an inherently directional verb *væki-* as its V₂ combines with *yi-* 'go'. The resulting compound has a motion-direction meaning 'do while going' (see A4 above):

15.121 ata   [[kur-væki]-yi]-l   [kur-væki-ku]   [[kə-bər   yagəl
       then do-go.across-go-3fem.sgBAS.P do-go.across-COMPL.SS DEM.PROX-du destitute
       yi-bər]   ñədi   sə   ata   kwa-bər]
       go-3duBAS.P/VT child:du sleep then stay-3duBAS.P/VT
       'She then went on going across and acting like this (collecting wild breadfruit), having done (like this) going across the two destitute children went to sleep'

That *kur-væki-* 'do (and) go across' is the main verb in the compound *kur-væki-yi-* 'went on going across and doing' is corroborated by the fact that just this part is repeated in a completive clause in a tail-head structure in 15.121.

Very occasionally, a V₁ or a V₂ within a cause-effect or a sequential compound can be a compound. Two compounds—one as V₁ and one as V₂—are not attested. In all the attested cases, the second part of the compound V₁ or V₂ is a non-existent root, e.g. [*vya-təpu*]ᵥ₁-*kiya*ᵥ₂- (hit-?-die) 'be killed and die' and *tani*ᵥ₁-[*yi-ba:gw*]ᵥ₂- (turn-go-?) 'turn and go round and round'. One lexicalized compound based on *vya-* 'hit, kill', *vya-təpu-* (hit/kill-?) 'kill', forms a cause-effect compound, as in *vya-təpu-kiya-kwa* (hit-?-die-IMPV.3p+fem.sg) 'Let her be killed and die' (said in annoyance about a particularly nosy and naughty child). This example may have resulted from contraction of a sequential construction with *-n* in rapid speech.

The V₁ slot of an asymmetrical compound can be a compound containing *wa-* or *-yi-* as their V₁, as in 15.122:

15.122 kiya-də-k   [[wa-jəwi]$_{V_1}$-ya]$_{V_2}$-da-d   də ma:
        die-3masc.sg-COMPL.DS   say-be.awake-come-3plSUBJ.P-3masc.sgBAS.P he NEG
        wa:k
        hear+NEG
        '(After he lost consciousness), they kept waking him up, he did not hear'

Asymmetrical compounds containing *kusə-* 'finish' (A1), **-təkalpæsa* 'do incompletely' (A2), *-kəta* 'try' (A3), *-taka* 'put, arrange by spreading' (A7), *-təp* 'be closed' (A8), **-ba:gw-* 'do incessantly' (A9), and **-pakw-* 'do all, affect all' (A10) can occur as V_1 with one of *-yi* 'go' (A4), *-ya* 'come' (A5), and **-yakə-* 'do fully' (A12) as V_2. The form **-jika* 'do properly' (A11) is not attested in complex compounds. An asymmetrical compound V_1 cannot appear in the 'go-come' construction (A6).

Some examples are at 15.123–6 and 15.101 ([[*kusə-pakwə*]-*yakə*]-da-k (finish-DO.ALL-FULLY-3pl-COMPL.DS) 'after they completely all died'). In all such cases, the last verb specifies motion-direction, aspect, or extent of the complex V_1.

15.123 kə-də   yi-na-də   yabəm
        DEM.PROX-masc.sg go-ACT.FOC-3masc.sgBAS.VT road+LK+LOC
        [[təp-ə-taka]-ya]-lə-d
        be.closed-LK-put-come-3fem.sgSUBJ.P-3masc.sgBAS.P
        'She came to close off the road that he went on' (by putting a leaf on it, to make sure no one goes there)

15.124 nəkə   val   aka   bə
        other+fem.sg canoe DEM.DIST.REACT.TOP.fem.sg already
        [[yi-təka]-yakə]-də-l   ma:,   a-də   təp
        go-INCOMPL-FULLY-3masc.sgSUBJ.P-3fem.sgBAS.P   again, DEM.DIST-masc.sg village
        ada   bə   kusə-pakwəm
        DEM.DIST.REACT.TOP+masc.sg already finish-DO.ALL+COMPL
        'He went off already on another canoe but did not quite get there, that village was already completely finished'

15.125 wun-a-də   gwalugw [[vya-kusə]-yakə]-da-di
        I-LK-masc.sg ancestor kill-finish-FULLY-3masc.sgSUBJ.VT-3plBAS.VT
        'Having fought, the man who stayed there, the man called Mukunkapar, my ancestor, killed them all completely'

15.126 səpakudi:m   [[taka-kəta]-yakə]-də-k,   aka
        mouth+LK+LOC put-try-FULLY-3masc.sg-COMPL.DS DEM.DIST.REACT.TOP+fem.sg
        wapi səwulə-l
        bird turn.into-3fem.sgBAS.P
        'After he really tried to put (things) into her mouth, she turned into a bird'

That the verbs *-yi* 'go' (A4), *-ya* 'come' (A5), and **-yakə-* 'do fully' (A12) as V_2 can occur in compound verbs—whether symmetrical or asymmetrical—as grammatical markers goes together with their high productivity. That V_2 and not V_1 marks aspect, motion-direction, and extent accords with the predominantly suffixing character of Manambu.

The forms *-yi-* 'go' (A4), *-ya-* 'come' (A5), and **-yakə-* 'do fully, fully' (A12) as V_2 are the most likely candidates for further development into grammatical markers. We can recall that *-ya-* as an aspect marker may not even be connected with the verb *ya-* 'come', and *-yakə-* 'do fully' does not really have a corresponding full verb in the language. Their status is thus comparable with that of *-kwa-*, a marker of habitual aspect which could have come from grammaticalization of the verb *-kwa-* 'stay', and its past form, *-yi-kwa-*, which may well have come from a combination of 'stay' and 'go'. The only reason why the habitual aspect is considered together with other aspectual categories (§12.3), and *-yi-* 'go' (A4), *-ya-* 'come' (A5), and **-yakə-* 'do fully' (A12) as V₂ are treated on a par with verb compounds, lies in the grammatical properties of the forms: habitual has its own system of negation (§14.2). The habitual marker cannot be reduplicated; neither can *-yi-* 'go' and *-ya-* 'come' in compounds. In contrast, **-yakə-* 'do fully' can—see the following section.

15.5 REDUPLICATION IN COMPOUNDS

We saw in §12.8.2 that both components of a compound verb can undergo full reduplication (see 12.57–8); the meaning is that of intensive and continuous activity, as in *və-səməl-* (see-?) 'look for', *və-səməl-səməl-* 'look for something very carefully', and *vya-təməl-* 'hit-roll', 'make roll or sound by hitting', *vya-təməl-təməl* (hit-roll-RED) 'make roll or sound by hitting many times', as in 15.24b. The first component of a symmetrical and of an asymmetrical compound can be reduplicated, as in 12.64 and the first line of 15.50, where it indicates continuous action. The second component of a symmetrical cause-effect compound can be fully reduplicated, to indicate intensity—as in 15.23.

Any second component of an asymmetrical compound can be reduplicated, except for *-yi-* 'go' and *-ya-* 'come', and the components of the 'go-come' construction. In 15.127, the second component **-təka-* 'do incompletely' undergoes reduplication (accompanied by vowel omission: see §12.8.2): the meaning is 'bit by bit but not fully'.

15.127 [vya-səpa-də-k]   [kiya-lə-k]
      hit-body?-3masc.sg-COMPL.DS die-3fem.sg-COMPL.DS
      [ləpa-tək-təka-ku]   [a-də   væka-rəb
      cut-INCOMPL-INCOMPL-COMPL.SS DEM.DIST-masc.sg pot+LK-STRAIGHT
      ku-sada-də-l]
      put-DOWN-3masc.sgSUBJ.VT-3fem.sgBAS.P
      'Having killed (her), after she'd died, having cut (her body) bit by bit (incompletely) he put her straight into the pot'

Further similar examples are at 12.65–6 (*-yakə-* 'do fully'), and 15.102 (*-jika-* 'properly').

Both components of an asymmetrical compound can be reduplicated separately as an expressive device, e.g. *vya-vy-taka-taka-lə-d* (hit-hit:RED-put.down-put.down-3fem.sgSUBJ.P-3masc.sgBAS.P) 'she hit him downwards really strongly'; also see 12.68. This does not happen with symmetrical compounds.

Compounds with *yi-* as V₁ (see §15.3.2) can occupy the V₁ slot of any asymmetrical compound (except for *-təp* compounds). The verb *yi-gaji-* (go-spread) as V₁ with *-yakə* 'do fully' as V₂ is illustrated in 15.128. The second component, *gaji-*, is reduplicated to express the full extent of 'wiping':

15.128 [kamkaw-a-ñan   kə-ta:y   [[yi-gaji-gaji]ᵥ₁-yakə]ᵥ₂-ta:y]
      hairy.yam-LK-red.yam eat-COTEMP go-rub-rub-FULLY-COTEMP
      [yi-lə-k]   [akatawa-dəka]
      go-3fem.sg-COMPL.DS thus-only
      'Eating yams, wiping (the remains of the food) off fully, going, this is what she did'

We can recall from B in §12.8.2 that -*ba:gw*- 'do incessantly' and -*jika*- 'properly' can undergo partial reduplication, with an iterative meaning. This kind of reduplication is not found with any other kinds of V$_2$ of asymmetrical compounds.

15.6 SUMMARY

Verb compounds in Manambu fall into symmetrical and asymmetrical. The former can express conventionalized sequences of sub-events, manner, and cause-effect. The latter consist of a major verb and a minor verb which specifies its aspect, motion-direction, and extent. The minor verb can also affect the valency of the whole compound. This is the case with -*taka* 'put' as a V$_2$.

Manambu verb compounds vary in how semantically unpredictable they are. Most of the Manambu compounds have to be listed in the lexicon, rather than generated via grammatical rules. Many of them show superficial similarities with English phrasal verbs, or prepositional verbs in German, Estonian, or Hungarian, in that the sum of the meanings of components does not allow us to predict what the compound would mean.

Some compounds could alternatively be analysed as suffixing, or even prefixing structures (see §15.3.2). The V$_1$ in any grammatical compound can consist of a verbal root followed by a directional, e.g. [*yakə-su*]$_{V_1}$-*kəta*$_{V_2}$- (throw-up-try) 'try and throw high up'. This is the topic of the next chapter.

Directionals and Valency-Changing Devices

Marking directionality of action on the verb is a prominent feature of Manambu. We discuss verbal directionals in §16.1, and then contrast them with directionals on nominal demonstratives (discussed in §10.2.1). Directionals are among the many valency-manipulating devices in the language which are discussed in §16.2. Of these, the causative-manipulative derivation is the only semi-productive exclusively valency-changing morphological device in the language. At the end of §16.2, we also look at the expression of reflexive and reciprocal meanings.

16.1 DIRECTIONALS

16.1.1 Formal aspects of directionals

Manambu verbs fall into four categories depending on which directional markers they take, if any. We distinguish four classes of verbs, two closed and two open. The forms and the meanings of the inherently directional verbs, the directional markers with intrinsically directional verbs, and bound directional forms with optionally directional verbs (I–III below) are given in Table 16.1. This table also contains directional forms used with demonstratives (see Table 10.5, which includes some verbal directionals). An etymological connection between the roots of inherently directional verbs, the directional suffixes on intrinsically directional verbs, and bound directionals is apparent. The shared morphemes are in bold. Table 16.2 features the directional suffixes used with intrinsically directional verbs.

I. INHERENTLY DIRECTIONAL VERBS include the six basic verbs *war-* 'go upwards', *da-* 'go downwards', *væki-* 'go across (away from the speaker)', *væra-* 'go across (towards speaker)', *wula-* 'enter, come in, come in a direction from the Sepik River', and *waku-* 'go out (including motion in the direction away from the Sepik River)'. These verbs do not take any further directional specifications. Their roots are the base for directionals on other verbs, and on demonstratives—see Tables 16.1 and 10.5. Inherently directional verbs occur as V_2 within sequencing compounds (§15.2.1) indicating that the action of V_1 was accompanied by, or done at the same time as, movement in a given direction. See §16.1.4.

II. INTRINSICALLY DIRECTIONAL VERBS include the following four roots which must take directional suffixes each of which corresponds to an inherently directional verb and has a corresponding bound directional form:

IIa. *kar-/kra-/*ka-* 'bring, carry' has the allomorphs: *kar-*, *kra-*, and *ka-* in complementary distribution depending on the morphological context (see first column of Table 16.2). The form *ka-* is used with the directional 'up' (all forms except second person imperative), 'across towards speaker' (all forms except second person imperative), and 'away from the Sepik River or inside' (all forms except second person imperative). The form *kar-* is used only with the directional 'downward' (all forms except second person imperative) and in a directional form 'bring from or take to a faraway place'. The form *kra-* is used in all other instances (including all second person imperatives containing a directional).

The root **ka-* never occurs on its own. The root *kra-* with an allomorph *kər-* in a word-final position means 'marry, take as a wife'. It could be related to the allomorph *kra-* of the verb **kar-/kra-* 'bring, take'. The exact nature of the vowel alternation in *kar-/kra-* remains a puzzle.

The bound verbal root *ka-* also occurs with a verb *-sapwi* 'disclose something, with an implication of sudden discovery and outward movement', in *ka-sapwi-* ('move/bring'-disclose) 'open up to disclose something'. Whether this is the same *ka-* as the one which occurs in the intrinsically directional verb *kar-/kra-/*ka-* 'bring, carry' is an open question.

IIb. The form *-kəta-*, also used as a suppletive combining form of the verb 'look' (see §15.2), takes the directional markers to provide directional specifications for *və-* 'see/look'. Note that, since directionals make the verb telic (see §16.1.3), the translation 'look', and not 'see', is appropriate for *və-* with a directional. The resulting forms are independent grammatical and phonological words which cannot head a predicate; they can be classified as adverbs. No free forms other than *ata* 'then' can intervene between the directional and the verb 'see/look' (see 16.56). The form *-kəta*+DIRECTIONAL typically precedes the verb 'look', but can also follow it. The verb 'look' can be ellipsed. The root *-kəta* means 'try' in asymmetrical compounds discussed in §15.3.

IIc. The generic verb *sə-* 'plant; put; call' can occur on its own. And it also appears to occur with several directional suffixes, in *sə-wul(a)-* 'push inside', *sada-* 'put downwards', and *saku-* 'push outwards' (also see 16.44, and further discussion in §16.1.3).

IId. The verb *tə-* 'stand, stay, be' can occur on its own in a variety of functions—as posture verb, as a copula, and as an auxiliary. In its postural meaning it occurs with one directional suffix: *tapra-* means 'stand facing speaker'.

III. OPTIONALLY DIRECTIONAL VERBS include all verbs which imply motion, e.g. *lagu-* 'pull', *yakə-* 'throw', *prapə-* 'be upside down', *blakə-* 'turn downwards', *kur-* 'get', *sə-* 'plant, put, move', and a number of verbs which do not. Directional distinctions, each of which has a corresponding inherently directional verb, are expressed with bound forms consisting of *s-* followed by a directional marker. Three further distinctions are expressed with directional suffixes *-tay* 'sideways away from speaker or reference point', *-tæy* 'sideways towards speaker or reference point', or reduplicated *-tay-tay-* 'back and forth'. These three cannot occur on intrinsically directional verbs. Bound directionals often develop somewhat unpredictable idiomatic connotations, especially with verbs which do not have to imply motion, e.g. *kiya-saki-* (die-across.away.from.speaker) 'half-die', *wa-saki-* (speak-across.away.from.speaker) 'tell a traditional story', *ta-saku-* (hit/move-outward) 'appoint, elect someone', *ku-su-* (put-upwards) 'wear, put on (clothing)'. See §16.1.2. One verb, or one clause, can contain two directionals—see §16.1.4.

A full set of bound directional forms and directional suffixes with the verb *yakə-* 'throw' is shown in 16.1. Also see Table 16.1.

16.1 *yakə-su* 'throw upwards'
    yakə-sada- 'throw down'
    yakə-saki 'throw across away from speaker or reference point'
    yakə-sapra- 'throw across toward speaker or reference point'
    yakə-səwəl- 'throw inside or away from the Sepik River'
    yakə-saku- 'throw in the outward direction'

yakə-tay- 'throw sideways away from speaker or reference point'
yakə-tæy- 'throw sideways toward the speaker or reference point'
yakə-tay-tay- 'throw back and forth'

Bound forms which contain more than two syllables require a secondary stress—in this respect, they are more similar to nominal compounds than to verbal compounds (§2.5). They cannot be considered clitics: we can recall that all clitics in Manambu can be also used as independent words. Their phonological similarity to compounds is corroborated by their etymology: we will see below that bound directionals are likely to be composed of a generic root *sə-* 'put, plant' and the directional suffixes occurring on intrinsically directional verbs. Directional suffixes do not require a secondary stress, unless reduplicated—we can recall, from §2.5, that this is a property of reduplicated morphemes.

All the directionals can be used with the general verb *məgi-* 'do whatever; be or become whatever'. Given its highly general meaning, this verb presents an almost perfect testing ground for establishing the core meanings of the directionals. This verb is S=A and S=O ambitransitive. We will see, at §16.1.3 below, that the bound directional morphemes increase valency making the action telic—as a consequence, if *məgi-* is accompanied by a directional, it has to refer to a transitive and telic action (see 16.58d).

16.2 *məgi-su-* 'do whatever upwards'
    məgi-sada- 'do whatever down'
    məgi-saki- 'do whatever across away from speaker or reference point'
    məgi-sapra- 'do whatever across toward speaker or reference point'
    məgi-səwəl- 'do whatever inside; tuck inside; move away from the Sepik River'
    məgi-saku- 'do whatever in the outward direction, stretch out'
    məgi-tay- 'do whatever sideways away from speaker or reference point'
    məgi-tæy- 'do whatever sideways toward the speaker or reference point'
    məgi-tay-tay- 'do whatever back and forth'

Two monosyllabic verbs, *ta-* 'move, hit' and *ku-* 'put, move' do not occur without directionals, e.g. *ku-su-* (put/move-UP) 'move up; put upwards; put on (clothes)', *ku-sada-* (put/move-DOWN) 'move or put downwards', *ku-saki-* 'put, move across away from speaker', *ku-səwəla-* 'put inside; put on (shoe), put spear in/spear'; *ta-saki-* 'move across away from speaker', *ta-sapra-* 'move across towards speaker'; *ta-saku-* 'appoint, elect someone'. The verb *ku-* also occurs with the verb *-sapwi-* 'disclose, with an implication of sudden discovery and outward movement': *ku-sapwi-* ('put'-disclose) means 'come out of something, e.g. a nose of an animal sticking out of a burrow'.

IV. VERBS WHICH DO NOT COMBINE WITH DIRECTIONALS are copula verbs, positional verbs with the exception of *tə-* 'stand', the general motion verbs *yi-* 'go' and *ya-* 'come', ingestive verbs *kə-* 'consume without chewing (that is, eat, drink, and smoke: §21.1.1)' and *jə-* 'chew', and stative verbs, such as *warsam(a)-* 'be angry'.

INHERENTLY DIRECTIONAL VERBS do not form one class in terms of their transitivity. The verbs *war-*, *da-*, *væki-*, and *væra-* are strictly intransitive. The verb *wər-/wur-* 'bring something up (e.g. from water)' could be related to *war-* 'go up' (interestingly, the Wosera/Ambulas verb *waaré* 'go up; put up, e.g. on neck'—which corresponds to both Manambu *war-* and *wər-*—is S=A ambitransitive). The verb *wula-* 'enter' is an S=O ambitransitive (see §4.2.2).

Four directional markers result from a straightforward grammaticalization of inherently directional verbs:

TABLE 16.1 Inherently directional verbs, and directional markers

Inherently directional verbs	Directional suffixes with intrinsically directional verbs	Bound directionals with optionally directional verbs	Meanings	Directionals with demonstratives and their meanings
war- 'go up; upstream'	-*u* / -***war***	-***su***- / —	'up' / 'up, upstream'	-*wur*- 'up, upstream'
da- 'go down; downstream'	-***d(a)***-	-***sada***-	'down'; 'downstream' (only -*da*)	-*d(a)*- 'down, downstream'
vaki- 'go across away from speaker'	-***aki***-	-***saki***-	'across away from speaker'	-*aki* 'across away from speaker'
vara- 'go across towards speaker'	-***(a)pra***-/-***(a)par***	-***sapra***-/***sapar***	'across towards speaker'	—
wula- 'go inside, away from the Sepik River'	-*wula*-/-*wela*-/-*wul*	-*sawes*-/-*sawel(a)*/-***sawel***; variants -*sula*/-*sul*-; *saula*-	'inside, away from the Sepik River'	-*wula*- 'towards speaker; away and inland from the Sepik River'
—	—	-*saki-sala*-	'to and fro, across away-towards'	—
waku- 'go outside'	-***aku***-	-***saku***-	'outside, outward'	-*aku* 'outwards from speaker'
—	-*tay*-	-*tay*-	'sideways away from speaker'	—
—	-*tey*-	-*tey*-	'sideways towards speaker'	—

Note: The roots of inherently directional verbs and formatives associated with them are in bold.

TABLE 16.2 Intrinsically directional verbs with directional suffixes

IIa. kar-/kra-/*ka- 'BRING, CARRY'		IIb. *kəta- 'LOOK'	IIc. sə- 'PLANT/PUT'	IId. tə- 'STAND'	MEANINGS
[kar-/kra-]	[ka-]				
a-kra-war '2IMPV'	ka-war- 'take up'	kətu 'look up'	—		'up'
kar-da- 'take downwards' a-kra-d '2IMVP'	—	kətad(-) 'look downwards'	sada- 'put down'	—	'down'
kraki- 'take across away from speaker'	—	kətaki 'look around'		—	'across away from speaker'
ka-pra- 'take across towards the speaker' a-kra-par '2IMPV'	—	kətapra-lkətapar 'look towards speaker'		tapra- 'stand facing the speaker'	'across towards speaker'
ka-wəla- 'take away from the Sepik River, inside' a-kra-wul '2IMPV'	—	kətawul(-)	səwəla- 'push inside; make sound towards inside; bark'; ? sewul- 'turn into something'	—	'inside, away, and inland from the Sepik River'
kraku- 'take across outwards'	—	kətaku	saku- 'push outwards; cut across; lay eggs, produce children'	—	'outside, outward'
—		kətay kəti	—	—	'all around'
kray- 'bring from or take to a nearby place'	—	—	—	—	'close by'
karya- 'bring from or take to a faraway place'	—	—	—	—	'far away'

- *war-* 'go up' → *-war* 'upwards' in one intrinsically directional verb *ka-war-* 'take/bring upwards' (Table 16.2);
- *da-* 'go down' → *-da* 'downwards' in intrinsically and optionally directional verbs (Tables 16.1–2);
- *wula-* 'go inside, away from the Sepik River' → *-wəla-* 'inside, away from the Sepik River' in intrinsically and optionally directional verbs (Tables 16.1–2);
- *væra-* 'go across towards the speaker' → *-pra/apar* 'across towards the speaker' in intrinsically and optionally directional verbs (Tables 16.1–2).

The complementary distribution of *v* and *p* was described in §2.1.1. The root vowel *æ* is unstressed. The vowel *æ* changes to ø in the directional suffix and in the bound form if the vowel does not bear the primary stress. An example is *yakə-saprà-daná* (throw-across.to.speaker-3plSUBJ.VT+3fem.sgBAS.VT) 'they throw (it) across towards the speaker'. If the vowel of the directional bears the primary stress its realization is *a*, as in *a-yakə-sapár* (IMPV-throw-across.to.speaker) 'throw across to speaker!'

The directional *-aki* 'across away from speaker' is clearly related to the inherently directional verb *væki-* 'go across away from speaker'. The component *v-* could have arisen by analogy with the initial consonant of *væra-* 'go across towards speaker'. There are no known cognates within the Ndu family, so this remains speculation.

The directional *-aku* 'outward' is related to the inherently directional verb *waku-* 'go out'. As with *-aki* and *væki-*, the component *w-* in *waku* could have arisen by analogy with *wula-* 'enter'. The latter has cognates throughout the Ndu family (e.g. Wosera/Ambulas *wula* 'enter'), while *waku-* does not.

An intriguing pattern emerges from the comparison of the four directionals involving movement towards and away from speaker: this is shown in Table 16.3.

A brief comparison of the forms in Table 16.3 shows that the directionals with the meaning 'away (from speaker)' do not share the initial consonant with the corresponding verb, while the ones with the meaning 'towards speaker' and 'inside, away and inland from the Sepik River, inside' do. The initial consonant is the same for the two pairs—*v*/*p* for 'across' and *w-* for 'away from the Sepik River' versus 'outwards, away from land'. The two pairs look similar to echo compounds (see §9.3).

The directional *-u* which occurs as a directional suffix with *kətu* '(look) upwards' and in bound directional forms does not have a corresponding verb. (A hypothesis that *-u* may be related to *war-* 'go up' is somewhat tentative.)

The complex directional bound form *-saki-sala-* 'to and fro; across away-across towards' does not have an equivalent verb, or a directional suffix. The component *-sala-* (see §16.1.4) is

TABLE 16.3   Directionals involving movement towards and away from speaker

DIRECTIONAL VERB	DIRECTIONAL BOUND FORM	MEANING
v-æra-	*-pl*vra	'across towards speaker'
v-aki-	*-aki*	'across away from speaker'
w-ula-	*-wəla*	'inside, away, and inland from the Sepik River'
w-aku-	*-aku*	'outwards or away from land'

segmentally similar to *-sawəla-*. If stressed, the two have the same form, as in *yakə-saki-salá-n* (throw-across.away-across.towards-SEQ) 'throw to and fro', *a-yakə-saki-sawə́l* (IMPV-throw-across.away-across.towards) 'throw to and fro!', *yakə-sawəlá-n* (throw-inside-SEQ) 'throw inside', *a-yakə-sawəl* (IMPV-throw-inside) 'throw inside!' The two are etymologically related; but exactly how remains an open question. The directional bound form *-solo* 'inside' in West Wosera (Wendel 1993: 62) could be related to either form in Manambu.

THE INTRINSICALLY DIRECTIONAL VERBS are fairly generic in their meanings. Each of these roots has cognates throughout the Ndu family. It is thus likely that the four verbs in Table 16.2 display an archaic pattern whereby the directional markers attach directly to the root as suffixes. The directionals in other Ndu languages tend to have the *s-* formative (see note 3). Two of the four intrinsically directional verbs have additional directional distinctions not found anywhere else. The verb *kəta-* in its fully reduplicated form *kətáy kətí* means 'around; round and round'. This reduplication pattern is reminiscent of the irregular reduplication pattern found with the word *say* 'boy house': *say-si* 'each boy house'. In both *kətáy kətí* and *say-si*, reduplication involves repeating all the syllables of the form after its main occurrence, with the vowel of the last syllable lost and *y* changed to *i* (also see §9.2).

kətáy → *kətáy kət-y* → *kətáy kətí*
say → *say-s-y* → *say-si*

An alternative explanation could go along the lines of a partial reduplication involving *y* insertion, as in *pay-pəsən* (RED-go.round+SEQ) 'go round and round'—this was discussed in §12.8.2.

Another possible analysis of *kətáy kətí* involves deriving it from a sequence of *kəta-*, the suppletive combining form of 'look', and *-tay* 'sideways away from speaker' (with subsequent haplology of two identical syllables *-ta-*, following A6 in §2.6). All these possibilities are equally plausible: whichever way we look at it, the partial reduplication in *kətáy kətí* is somewhat irregular.

The verb 'bring, carry' distinguishes two extra forms: *kray-* 'bring from or take to a nearby place' and *karya-* 'bring from or take to a faraway place'. It is possible that these forms consist of the root *kar-/kra-* and a generic motion verb, either *yi-* 'go' or *ya-* 'come'. The question is, which one of the two? At the moment, we cannot decide.

Another unsolved problem is the vowel *a* in the imperative and negative form of *karya-*: *a-karay* 'bring (from distance)!' and *ma: karay* 'did not/do(es) not bring (from distance)' (compare *a-kray* 'bring (from nearby place)' and *ma: kray* 'did not/doe(es) not bring (from nearby place)'). In addition, the two verbs *kray-* and *karya-* form a compound *kray-karya-* 'carry to and fro' (illustrated in 15.61).[1]

This compound is quite unusual from the Manambu perspective: we can recall that in compounding involving 'go' and 'come', 'go' precedes and 'come' follows, as in the 'go-come' construction discussed in §15.3. And we will see, in §16.1.3, that the directional away from the speaker precedes the one towards the speaker in sequences of directionals, as in *-saki-salan* (across.away-across.inwards) 'to and fro'. The origin of the pair *kray-* and *karya-* remains unknown.[2]

---

[1] The intrinsically directional verbs can occur with some bound directionals—the forms *kra-su-* (carry/bring-UP) 'bring upwards', *kra-sada-* (carry/bring-DOWN) 'carry or push downwards', and *kra-saki-* (carry/bring-ACROSS.AWAY.FROM.SPEAKER) 'carry/bring across away from speaker' are judged as acceptable by some innovative speakers but are hardly ever used. Traditional speakers frown at these. The same holds for *və-su-* 'look up' and *və-sada-* 'look down'. I suspect these are analogical innovations.

[2] Ambulas (Kundama and Wilson 1987: 53, 58) employs *yé* 'go' and *yaa* 'come' in the formation of verbs 'bring', *kure yaa*, and 'take', *kure yé*. Additional complex verbs are *kérae kure yaa* 'bring' and *kérae kure yee* 'take' (p. 53);

BOUND DIRECTIONAL FORMS used with OPTIONALLY DIRECTIONAL VERBS consist of a formative *s-* followed by directional suffixes. This formative is most likely the generic verb *sə-* 'do, make, plant, put, move' followed by a directional suffix. Phonologically, such compounds are only slightly irregular: we have no explanation why the directional *səwəla-* 'inside' has a *ə*, and the directional *sada-* 'down' has an *a* in the first syllable.

This hypothesis is corroborated by the fact that the verb *sə-* is one of the intrinsically directional verbs—see Table 16.2. It takes either one or two directional suffixes—the most uncontroversial instance is *sada-* 'put down', alternatively pronounced as *səda-*; the other two are *səwəla-* or *saula-* 'push inside', and *saku-* 'push outside' (see further discussion in §16.1.2).

Considering bound directional forms as instances of verb compounding involving *sə-* has an additional advantage. The verb *sə-* is transitive, and the bound directional forms have a transitivizing effect on the verb—see §16.1.3.

In addition, the verb *sə-* in the meaning 'move' can also take bound directional forms: *sə-sada-* means 'move down', *sə-su-* 'move up', *sə-saki-* 'move across away from speaker', *sə-sapra-* 'move across towards speaker', and *sə-səwəla-* 'move inside'. (And see 16.61–2, for the adverbial use of *sə-su* (put/plant?-UP) 'a little bit upwards'.) This does not invalidate the hypothesis that bound directionals derive from the verb *sə-*. However, this hypothesis cannot be fully proved at this stage.[3]

The directionals -*tay* 'sideways away from speaker' and -*tæy* 'sideways towards speaker' differ from the bound directionals in a variety of ways, including the following:

(i) they do not have corresponding verb(s);
(ii) they do not occur with intrinsically directional verbs;
(iii) they can be reduplicated (see 12.67 and 12.70); and
(iv) they do not contain the formative *s-* which appears in the directionals used with optional directional verbs.

They are functionally different from other directionals in that they never affect the verb's valency. See Table 16.4 in §16.1.3 and the discussion there. Just like other directionals, they may have idiomatic meanings with non-motion verbs, e.g. *wukə-tay-* (think/hear-SIDEWAYS.AWAY) 'miss, be longing for (someone)'.

Verb compounds with inherently directional verbs as V₂ also have directional overtones: they indicate that something was happening while moving in one of the six directions encoded in inherently directional verbs, e.g. *yakə-su-* 'throw upwards', *yakə-war-* 'throw and go up'; *yaku-saki-* 'wash (e.g. sago) with criss-cross movements', *yaku-væki-* 'wash and go across'. See Table 16.5 in §16.1.3 below.

A comparison of directionals on verbs and on demonstratives shows a number of similarities due to the same origins. Yet, the existing differences show that the two systems have most likely arisen independently of each other as a result of polygrammaticalization of inherently directional verbs, whereby the same set of morphemes grammaticalized in two independent ways. See the discussion in §16.1.5.

---

the verb *kéraa* meaning 'get, take; buy' displays a vowel alternation with *kérae* which is reminiscent of *kray-/karya-*. However, any further comparison is tenuous.

[3] Directional markers documented for Wosera/Ambulas (Wilson 1980; Wendel 1993) bear some similarity to the bound directionals in Manambu, and contain the formative *s-*, e.g. -*sada* 'down', -*sage* 'towards', *sala* 'out', *sawula* 'inside', -*sawuré* 'up' (Wilson 1980: 63). At least some of these are transparently related to verbs such as *wula* 'enter', *wuré* 'go up', *daa* 'go down'. Since Wosera/Ambulas also has a generic verb *sé* with a basic meaning 'make', this may also be an instance of grammaticalized verb compounding shared with Manambu. Iatmul also has bound directionals with the formative *s* (Jendraschek forthcoming).

16.1.2   Directionals: semantics and functions

The general function of directionals is to specify the possible directions of the motion encoded in the verb they occur with. The meanings and functions of bound directionals and of directional suffixes are somewhat different. And the meanings of intrinsically directional verbs tend to differ slightly from their bound directional counterparts. They have many fewer idiomatic extensions. We start with the discussion of bound directionals and the corresponding intrinsic directional verbs, pair by pair. Discussing the directionals in pairs is justified by the way in which most of them pattern (see Table 16.4), and by how they occur together in one verb, or one clause (see §16.1.4). At the end of this section, we contrast the bound directionals and directional suffixes.

A. 'DOWN' AND 'UP'

The directional 'down(wards)' is semantically straightforward. In 16.3, the directional -*sada*- 'down(wards)' describes throwing food downwards from a tree, and then throwing it into fire for cooking purposes. The same directional in 14.50 describes throwing salt into the food. Verbs containing directionals are underlined throughout this chapter.

16.3 [kraki-ku]   [adiya
    carry/bring+ACROSS.AWAY-COMPL.SS   DEM.DIST.REACT.TOP+pl
    yakə-sada-lə-di   kamna:gw] [yi: yakə-sada-n]
    throw-DOWN-3fem.sgSUBJ.P-3plBAS.P food   fire throw-DOWN-SEQ
    [də-kə-də   yi:r   ata   yakə-sada-lə-di]
    he-OBL-masc.sg fire+ALL then throw-DOWN-3fem.sgSUBJ.P-3plBAS.P
    'Having carried (the food) across away (from the reference point) by throwing the foods she had thrown down she threw them down into the fire'

This directional can be used to refer to taking something off, or down, as a skin (but not for taking shoes or clothes off: the verb *kay-puti-* (CAUS-take.off/go.out-) is used then):

16.4 gra-də-k   ata   lapi-sada-lə-l
    cry-3masc.sg-COMPL.DS then take.off-DOWN-3fem.sgSUBJ.P-3fem.sgBAS.P
    a   səp
    DEM.DIST+fem.sg   skin
    'After he (child) cried, she (the cassowary woman) took off the skin (putting it down)'

It is also used to describe pulling or pushing something from shore to the water—the shore is always higher than the river, so this is straightforward:

16.5 lagu-sada-da-k   kwa-də-l
    pull-DOWN-3pl-COMPL.DS stay-3masc.sgSUBJ.P-3fem.sgBAS.P
    'After they'd pulled the canoe to the water, it stood that way'

The form *wa-sada-* 'say-downwards' implies that the addressee is located below the speaker, and so the speech is directed downwards, as in 16.6—the man is standing on a hill and his two wives are down below:

16.6 aka   <u>wa-sada-də-bər</u>   də-kə-bər

DEM.DIST.REACT.TOP.fem.sg say-DOWN-3masc.sgSUBJ.P-3duBAS.P he-OBL-du

takwa:k   vitiyik

woman+LK+DAT two+DAT

'Then he called them directing his speech downwards to his two wives'

The directional forms of verbs of perception, 'see/look' and 'hear/listen', indicate the direction of the gaze, or of the sound, as in 14.95, 'don't look down (into the bag)', and 16.7. In the second line of this example, the form *kətad* 'look (downwards)' appears on its own, without an accompanying verb *və-* 'look'—this is an example of ellipsis. We mentioned in §16.1.1 that the intrinsically directional suppletive forms of 'look' are used adverbially, as modifiers to 'see', and not as verb roots. This is how 'look' differs from all other intrinsically directional verbs (see Table 16.2).

16.7 [abakapi kəka   təp-a:m   kətad-ə   væn]

hawk   DEM.PROX.REACT.TOP.fem.sg village-LK+ACC 'look'+DOWN-LK see+SEQ

[təp-a:m   <u>kəta-d</u>]

village-LK+ACC 'look'-DOWN

'As the hawk was looking down onto the village, it looked down on the village'

Unlike the directional suffix *-da* used with the intrinsically directional verb *kar-/kra-/ka-*, and the corresponding inherently directional verb *da-*, the bound directional *-sada-* does not refer to movement downstream. Neither does the inherently directional verb *sada-* 'put down(wards)' (see §16.1.5).

In 16.8, *kar-da-* (carry/bring-DOWN) refers to carrying the edible mayflies being taken downstream, following the course of the Sepik River. This is an example of a landmark ('absolute') reference. The demonstrative 'there away from the Sepik River' refers to the location of the old Avatip which used to be on the Sepik River before it had changed its course, and now is away from the Sepik River: this is an example of a combination of absolute and relative reference, since the landmark is not stationary or permanent:

16.8 [ka:l   <u>kar-da-da-k</u>]   [da-n]   [Avatəpa:m

mayfly carry/bring-DOWN-3pl-COMPL.DS go.down-SEQ Avatip+LK+LOC

tə-da-k]

be-3pl-COMPL.DS

'having taken the mayflies downstream, having gone downstream, having stayed in Avatip'

The bound directional 'up' is illustrated in 16.9.

16.9 suguya-ku   mada-wurəm   a-yata-su

help-COMPL.SS underneath+LK-string.bag+LK+LOC IMPV-lift-UP

<u>yata-su-ñən-ək</u>   ti:u

lift-UP-2fem.sg-COMPL.DS put.on.head+1sgIMPV

'Having helped, lift the underneath part of the stringbag, after you have lifted it up, I will put it on your head'

In 16.10 this directional describes the movement of spoken word—talking to someone up in the tree. Similar examples are in T2.5 and T2.24 (dogs barking up the tree).

16.10 ada   <u>wa-su-na-d</u>

DEM.DIST.REACT.TOP+masc.sg say-UP-ACT.FOC-3masc.sgBAS.VT

'He called upwards (to his mates)'

This same directional in 15.5 indicates that playing with the pig's bladder involved throwing it upwards. And in T3.27 *wukə-su* (hear/listen-UP) implies a character sitting on the ground and listening to what was happening up there in the house.

The directional *-su* also refers to the movement from water to the shore, as in 16.11:

16.11 [a-bər   [a   val   vya-n   napa-ku]   [lagu-su-ku]
      DEM.DIST-du   DEM.DIST.fem.sg canoe   hit-SEQ   COMPL.VB-COMPL.SS   pull-UP-COMPL.SS
      [vyaguyauta-ku]   [ma: rə-brə-l]]
      chop.up-COMPL.SS   again   stay-3dusUBJ.P-3fem.sgBAS.P
      'After they two had hit the (enemy) canoe, pulled it onto the shore, chopped it up, they
      stayed there again'

This directional is also used to describe putting on a piece of clothing or a hat, using the verb *ku-su-* (put-UP), as in 15.17–18, and 15.65. (We can recall that the verb *ku-* only occurs with bound directionals.)

This does not normally apply to putting on shoes or socks: one says *ku-səwəla-* 'put inside' instead. However, a shoe can be called *ku-su-ma:n* (put-UP-foot) 'footwear, what one puts on foot', by analogy with *ku-su-wapwi* (put-UP-clothes) 'clothes to wear'—that is, *ku-su-* is in the process of being extended to mean 'wear (in general)', presumably, under pressure from Tok Pisin and English.

The verb *ku-su-* is also used in its more straightforward meaning, 'put (something) upwards', e.g. from the ground into a house (as in the second line of 16.53). The same directional *-su-* can be used somewhat metaphorically, for instance, to refer to fever going up, as in *kuyak lə-kə-k sə-su-na-di* (wound she-OBL-DAT plant/put-UP-ACT.FOC-3plBAS.VT) 'wounds are pushing (fever) up for her'.

The directional *kətu* 'look.up' has the same meaning—looking at something higher up than the speaker or the reference point, as illustrated in 16.12. This form is semantically simpler than *-su* since it has no additional extensions.

16.12 ata   kətu   və-lə-d   a?   ada-wur
      then   look.up   see-3fem.sgSUBJ.P-3masc.sgBAS.P   hey?   DEM.DIST+masc.sg-UP
      du-ad?
      man-3masc.sgNOM
      'Then she looked up (on the tree): "Hey? Is there a man up there?"'

The intrinsically directional *ka-war-* 'carry up' describes upward movement in 16.13: houses are on stilts, so carrying someone into a house is always 'up'. In 16.14 this verb refers to bringing fish in from water—this example is parallel to 16.11 (cf. also 15.67).

16.13 [kawi-ku]   [wula-n]   [abra
      come.ashore-COMPL.SS   come.inland-SEQ   DEM.DIST.REACT.TOP.du
      ka-war-da-bər   də-kə   wiya:r]
      carry/bring-UP-3plSUBJ.P-3duBAS.P   he-OBL+fem.sg   house+LK+ALL
      'Having come ashore, coming inside (or inland) they carried the two up into his house'

16.14 [akatawa-ta:y   dəy   kamakaw   kraku-da-k],   [kami:
      like.that+say-COTEMP   they   hairy.yam   carry/bring+OUTSIDE-3pl-COMPL.DS   fish
      ka-war-ən],   [akatawa-ta:y   yapi-yi-di]
      carry/bring-UP-SEQ   like.that+say-COTEMP   sell-go-3plBAS.P/VT
      'After they had taken the yams off, having brought fish (from water), like that they kept
      selling (them)'

And in 16.15, *ka-war-* describes movement upstream.

16.15 kə-di   Ñaura gus   kan   ka-war-da-di
      DEM.PROX-pl Iatmul paddle paddle+SEQ carry/bring-UP-3plSUBJ.P-3plBAS.P
      gusa:r
      paddle+LK+ALL
      '(During the war) these Iatmul took them (the Japanese) upstream paddling, with a
      paddle'

This meaning is shared with *war-* 'go up; go upstream', but not with the bound directional
-su- 'up' or *kətu* 'look up'. A sequencing biclausal construction involving *war-* 'go up' has to
be used instead, as in 15.14 (also see §18.2).

We conclude that the bound directionals 'down' and 'up' are more semantically complex
than the directionals used with 'look'. Neither of these refers to movement downstream or
upstream. In contrast, the intrinsically directional verb 'bring, carry' shares these meanings
with the inherently directional verbs 'go down' and 'go up'.

Formally, the directional markers 'up' and 'down' used with 'bring, carry' are identical with
the corresponding inherently directional verbs. In contrast, the bound directionals, and the
suffixes on 'look' are not. This indicates that, though directionals 'up' and 'down' with the
verb 'carry, bring', and in other instances described here, have a shared origin, they probably
have followed different historical paths.

B. 'ACROSS AWAY FROM SPEAKER OR REFERENCE POINT' AND 'ACROSS TOWARDS SPEAKER OR REFERENCE POINT'

The directional 'across towards speaker or reference point' is straightforward in its meaning
and usage. In 16.16, the sun is shining across in the direction of the reference point—the elder
brother's new headdress:

16.16 atawa   ñə   məgi-sapra-n
      like.that sun do.whatever-ACROSS.TOWARDS-SEQ
      kwar-sapra-də-k
      get/affect-ACROSS.TOWARDS-3masc.sg-COMPL.DS
      'The sun "whatevered" like that across to (the elder brother's headdress), shone across
      to it (lit. affected it)...'

The intrinsically directional verb *kapra-* 'bring towards speaker or reference point' is illustrated in 16.17, from a story about moving from an old location of Avatip to a new one. The
story was told in the new location—so the form *kapra-* refers to bringing things across to where
the speaker and his audience were at the time of the story telling.

16.17 a-di   ja:p kədika   bəta:y adiya
      DEM.DIST-pl thing DEM.PROX.REACT.TOP+pl already DEM.DIST.REACT.TOP+pl
      kapra-da-di
      bring+ACROSS.TOWARDS-3plSUBJ.P-3plBAS.P
      'Those (sacred) things are here, they already brought them across here (where we are,
      from the old location)'

In 16.19 this same verb, *kapra-* 'bring across towards' refers to bringing the wounded man
across to where his relatives were—that is, the point of reference of the story.

The intrinsically directional verb *tapra-* 'stand facing the speaker' is used exclusively with
this directional—see Table 16.2. An example is at 16.18.

16.18 atawa   ñə   atawa   <u>tapra-də-l</u>
like.that sun like.that stand+ACROSS.TOWARDS-3masc.sgSUBJ.P-3fem.sgBAS.P
'The sun was facing us (lit. it was standing across towards us)'

The two directionals meaning 'across' are quoted by speakers as contrasting with each other, e.g. *səmaka-saki-* (show-away.from.speaker) 'show pointing across in the direction away from speaker or reference point', *səmaka-sapra-* (show-towards.speaker) 'show pointing across in the direction of speaker or reference point'. That the two directionals meaning 'across' are in a paradigmatic opposition is corroborated by the fact that they often occur together in one stretch of discourse. Note that the form meaning 'across away' precedes the form meaning 'across towards' (see §16.1.4).

16.19 [ata <u>kətaki</u>   ap]   [a-naki   mayka:r
then look.ACROSS.AWAY IMPV+see DEM.DIST-CURR.REL.ACROSS.AWAY visibly
ta:n   yaku-k-na-di]   [wa-də-k]
stand+SEQ wash-FUT-ACT.FOC-3plBAS.P say-3masc.sg-COMPL.DS
[adiya   <u>kətapar</u>   və-ta-taka,   ya:kya ata kurən
DEM.DIST.REACT.TOP+pl look.ACROSS.TOWARDS see-EP-IMM.SEQ OK   then get+SEQ
<u>kapra-da-d</u>]
bring.ACROSS.TOWARDS-3plSUBJ.P-3masc.sgBAS.P
'After (the relative) had said: "Look across (away from me), they are probably washing across from there standing visibly", on having looked across towards (the men), (here they were), they then took and brought (the injured man) towards (the relatives)'

The directional *-saki* usually means 'across away from speaker', or 'across to the side', if a verb implies motion on the same level as the speaker. An example is at 16.20:

16.20 a-bər   ta:kw abra   brə-kə-m
DEM.DIST-du woman DEM.DIST.REACT.TOP+du 3du-OBL-ACC
<u>wapu-saki-bər</u>   væki:n   agəkər
push-ACROSS.AWAY-3duBAS.VT/P go.across+SEQ side+LK+ALL
'Those two women pushed them two across going across to the side'

In 16.21, the speaker says she'd turned the skirt the right way round (before it was back to front).

16.21 wun-a   ku-su-wapwi
I-LK+fem.sg 'put'-UP-clothing
<u>kay-blakə-saki-tua</u>
CAUS-be.turned-ACROSS.AWAY-1sgSUBJ.VT+3fem.sgBAS.VT
'I have turned my clothing (skirt) across to the right side'

And in 16.22 *-saki* is used in an instruction to a child: she is to pour water into the cup from a bucket. The action is on the same level as the speaker—if a downward direction were implied, as from a bottle into a cup, the verb *wur-sada-* (pour-DOWN) 'pour down' would have been appropriate.

16.22 kap-a:r   gu   <u>wur-sakin</u>   ak
cup-LK+ALL water pour/move-ACROSS.AWAY+SEQ IMPV+eat/drink
'Drink water pouring it into the cup (from the bucket)' (or: 'Drink water having poured it into the cup')

The directional *-saki* is also used to describe something put crosswise on the side, as in 16.23: here, a sign was put on the ground to mark a land claim:

16.23 kə-l-ay   təpə-saki-lalək
      DEM.PROX-fem.sg-DIST be.closed/fence-ACROSS.AWAY-3fem.sg+BECAUSE
      wa-kwa-bana-l-a
      say-HAB-1plSUBJ.VT-3fem.sgBAS.VT-3fem.sgNOM
      'Because here further away (a group) put a mark (or a fence) on the side, we call it (this way)'

The bound directional *-saki* is more frequent and has a broader meaning than its counterpart *-sapra-*. And unlike *-sapra*, *-saki* has a few further idiomatic meanings. One such meaning is 'half, not fully', as in 14.95, *kaja-saki-* (open-ACROSS.AWAY) 'open up crosswise, not fully', and in 14.6, *kiya-saki-* (die-ACROSS.AWAY) 'half-die, not die fully'. The marker *-saki-* 'across, not fully' was illustrated in 10.22b, with *təpə-saki-* (be.closed/fence-ACROSS.AWAY) 'close up halfway, by putting (a leaf) across'. In contrast, *təpə-taka-* (be.closed/fence-put-) means 'close off completely', as illustrated in 16.40, from the same story.

The compound *wa-saki-* (say-ACROSS.AWAY) refers to telling a traditional account of events which is passed across generations and passing information on; this metaphorically directional meaning is shown in 16.24:

16.24 akatawa ñan-a-kə   wa-saki   ma:j aka
      like.this we-LK-OBL+3fem.sg speak-ACROSS.AWAY story DEM.DIST.REACT.TOP.fem.sg
      akatawa-n-a   wa-saki-n   rə-kwa-na-dian
      like.this-PRED-3fem.sgNOM   speak-ACROSS.AWAY-SEQ stay-HAB-ACT.FOC-1plBAS.VT
      'Our traditional story is like this, it is like this that we stay telling stories'

The expression *wa-saki ma:j* (speak-ACROSS.AWAY story) refers to a traditional account of true events, different from a *blajaya ma:j* (speak+come story) 'legend, story'. This same verb *wa-saki-* can also describe transmitting information from one person to another. Or it may mean 'call across', as in 16.25. This is similar to examples like 16.6 ('call downwards'), 16.10 ('call upwards'), and 16.36 ('call outward').

16.25 [wula-lə-k],   [ata wa-saki-də-l],
      come.in-3fem.sg-COMPL.DS then say-ACROSS.AWAY-3masc.sgSUBJ.P-3fem.sgBAS.P
      [ñən   a-war-ay]
      you.fem IMPV-go.up-VOC
      'After she'd come inside (the hiding, from fishing), then he called across to her, "You go up!!"'

Only the context helps decide if the meaning of *wa-saki-* is 'tell a traditional story' or 'say, or call across'. Whether the directional *-saki* is related to the noun *saki* 'name debate' (also used to refer to traditional lore) remains an open question.

The intrinsically directional *kətaki* 'look across' shown in 16.19 is straightforward in its meaning (also see 16.55). So is the intrinsically directional *kraki-* 'take/carry across', as shown in 16.3. We can recall, from §15.2.4, that *kraki-* forms compounds *və-kraki-* (see-carry.across) 'recognize by seeing' and *wukə-kraki-* (hear-carry.across) 'recognize by hearing' (see 16.41). No other form of this intrinsically directional verb forms any compounds of this nature.

The directional meaning 'across away (from the speaker)' has a higher propensity for developing idiomatic meanings than its counterpart, 'across towards (the speaker)'.

C. 'INSIDE, AWAY FROM THE SEPIK RIVER' VERSUS 'OUTSIDE, AWAY FROM LAND' are roughly parallel in their meanings. The directional -*səwəla/-sawəl* describes movement inside something, as in 16.26, or away from the Sepik River, as in 16.27.

16.26 də-kə   ñəga:r   ku-səwəla-taka-da-k
      he-OBL+fem.sg mosquito.net+LK+ALL 'put'-INSIDE-put-3pl-COMPL.DS
      adəka   rə-na-d
      DEM.DIST.REACT.TOP+masc.sg sit-ACT.FOC-3masc.sgBAS.VT
      'After she had put him inside the mosquito net, he (topical) is sitting (there)'

16.27 val   kur-səwəla-ta:y   ata   tə-dian
      canoe get-INSIDE-COTEMP then stay-1plBAS.VT
      'Having put the canoe away from the Sepik River, we stayed (listening to the enemy's aeroplane)'

The verb *ku-səwəl-* can also refer to putting shoes on (since this involves putting feet inside the shoes), and to putting something into someone's lap.

This same directional may refer to the orientation of speech or sound, with an appropriate verb—'bark' in 16.28 and 'hear' in 16.29. Whether the verb 'bark' is related to the homonymous directional is an open question: the form *səwəla-* in 16.28 has been translated both as 'bark' and 'make sound towards inside'.

16.28 a:s ma: krayi:d   səwəla-səwəla-di
      dog again bring+3masc.sgBAS.P bark-INSIDE-3plBAS.P
      'He brought the dogs again, they barked in the direction of the inside (of the sago palm where the Gala man was hidden)'

The directional in 16.29 describes the bird listening to what was happening inside the house of the man she'd saved. His in-laws were debating his mortuary feast thinking he'd died:

16.29 [laka   ñəg-a:m   rə-ku]   [ata
      she+DEM.DIST.REACT.TOP.fem.sg mosquito.net-LK+LOC sit-COMPL.SS then
      wukə-saku   kui-taka]   [[ada,   yi-n   wukə-səwəla-u]
      listen-OUTWARD give.to.third.p-IMM.SEQ stay.IMPV go-SEQ listen-INSIDE-1sgIMPV
      wa-ku],   [aka   yi-na],   [wurən]
      say-COMPL.SS DEM.DIST.REACT.TOP.fem.sg go-ACT.FOC+3fem.sgBAS.VT fly+SEQ
      [Wukə-səwəla-n   tə-lə-k],   [də-kə-də   kəkətəp
      hear/listen-INSIDE-SEQ be-3fem.sg-COMPL.DS he-OBL-masc.sg mortuary.feast
      kui-k],   [wa-ku],   [də-kə-də   kəkətəp
      give.to.third.p-PURP.SS say-COMPL.SS he-OBL-masc.sg mortuary.feast
      kui-k]   [adika
      give.to.third.p-PURP.SS DEM.DIST.REACT.TOP+pl
      bla-saku-sala-na-di   də-kə-di wawusugw]
      speak-OUTWARDS-INWARDS-ACT.FOC-3plBAS.P he-OBL-pl wife's.brother+PL
      'Then she, having stayed in the mosquito net, immediately after having listened to (sounds) outside, (she said), "You stay, I will go and listen to (what is happening) inside", having said this, she went off flying. As she was listening to what was happening inside his wife's brothers were debating as to how to give his mortuary feast, having said (that) they were to give his mortuary feast'

Like most bound directionals, *səwəl-* can develop meanings which are not fully predictable. The verb *təpə-səwəl-* (be.closed/fence-INSIDE) has a pretty straightforward meaning 'enclose something, hide something inside something', as in 16.30.

16.30 kwasa-ñan   nak a-na-wur   ñəg-a:m
      small+fem.sg-child one DEM.DIST-CURR.REL-up mosquito.net-LK+LOC
      <u>təpə-səwəla-u</u>   rə-na
      be.closed/fence-INSIDE-1sgIMPV sit-ACT.FOC+3fem.sgBAS.VT
      'I am hiding one little girl up there (previously mentioned) in the mosquito net' (lit. I will close her off inside-she sits)

Or it can mean 'block, close up', as in 16.31.

16.31 [a-di   yawi war-ku   tə-ku]
      DEM.DIST-pl work go.up-COMPL.SS be-COMPL.SS
      [<u>təpə-səwəla-də-k</u>],   [ata rasə-di   ya]
      be.closed/fence-INSIDE-3masc.sg-COMPL.DS then get.up-3plBAS.VT/P EMPH
      'Having gone up to (do) the work, having done (so), after he had blocked (the way), they rose (against him)'

Note that in 16.31 *təpə-səwəla-* has a meaning 'block' similar to that of *təpə-saki-* in 10.22b, but not in 16.23—this shows the versatility of both bound directional forms, whose meaning is heavily context dependent.

The use of these two directionals with the general verb *məgi-* 'do whatever' is particularly instructive. This directional is frequently associated with tucking things inside—as shown in 16.2, *məgi-səwəl-* means 'put inside', 'tuck inside' (e.g. a sheet underneath a sleeping mat, or a skirt). In 16.32, Mali, forever worried that I may not tuck my skirt properly between my legs when sitting down cross-legged, described herself doing what she considered proper:

16.32 atawa   *skət* <u>məgi-səwəla-ku</u>   kwa-u
      like.that skirt do.whatever-INSIDE-COMPL.SS stay-1sgIMPV
      'I will stay having tucked my skirt inside like that'

The opposite, *məgi-saku-*, implies taking things out and stretching them in an outward direction—a command *a-məgi-sakw!* was used to tell me to stretch my injured leg, and, in a different situation, to stretch a sheet by pulling it outward away from the mat.

Similarly, *wapu-səwəl-* may refer to pushing any object inside any other object. When I was bandaging little Celestin's wound, he was told to help me by tucking one end of the plaster inside and underneath the other one: *a-wapu-səwəl!* (IMPV-push-INSIDE) 'push (it) inside!'

The intrinsically directional verb *səwəla-* means 'push (something) inside'. The verb *səwəl-* 'turn into something' (see 15.116, and §15.3.2) could conceivably be related to this same verb.

The meanings of the intrinsically directional verbs *kaula-/krawul* 'bring inside' and *kətawul* 'look inside' are quite straightforward. Typical examples are at 16.33 and 16.34 (another example is in the second line of 16.53).

16.33 væk <u>akrawul</u>,   səkulək yi-kər
      pot bring.inside.IMPV cooking go/do-DES
      'Bring the pot inside (the pot was left outside to dry after it had been washed), (I) want to cook'

16.34 yi-n   <u>kətawul</u>   və-də-l
      go-SEQ 'look'+INSIDE see-3masc.sgSUBJ.P-3fem.sgBAS.P
      'Having gone, he looked inside (the sago tree)'

The bound directional *-saku-* is the opposite of *-səwəl-*—see 16.32 and comment to it, and also 16.2 and 12.76 (cf. 16.78) which describes operating a pump torch as 'pumping in pumping out'. A palm bending inward from the Sepik River and then outward again was described as:

16.35 <u>tagwu-səwəlan</u>   <u>tagwu-saku-n</u>
      bend-INSIDE+SEQ bend-OUTWARDS-SEQ
      'bending in bending out'

The order of forms containing directionals is iconic, in the sense that it corresponds to the sequence of sub-actions in real life: to operate a pump torch, one presses it inwards and then lets it return outwards. Same with the palm: it was bending away from the river, and then outwards towards the river again.

The directional *-saku-* 'outwards' can be used with the verb of speaking, *wa-*, to describe the direction of calling: from a river bank out to the river, just like other bound directionals in 16.6, 16.10, and 16.25. This is shown at 16.36. There are no metaphorical extensions. This is quite unlike the way *-saki-* 'across away' is used with the verb of speech.

16.36 wun aləm   ta:n   <u>wa-saku-na-dəwun</u>
      I   DEM.DIST.fem.sg+LOC stand+SEQ say-OUTWARDS-ACT.FOC-1masc.sgBAS.VT
      'Standing there, I call (to them) from river bank to the river'

With verbs of perception, *-saku-* implies the presence of a sound coming in an outward direction: in 16.37, the spirit *apawul* is listening to what is happening outside the house:

16.37 a   apawəl lə   <u>wukə-saku-ya-n</u>   ta:l
      DEM.DIST.fem.sg spirit   she listen-OUTWARDS-come-SEQ stay+3fem.sgBAS.P
      'That spirit, she was listening (to the sound outside)'

In 16.20, *wapu-saki-* (push-ACROSS.AWAY) described pushing across away from the reference point; in 16.38, *wapu-saku-* also describes pushing away, but in an outward direction:

16.38 [dəya-kə-di val   bər <u>wapu-saku-dəka</u>   <u>wapu-saku-dəka</u>
      they-POSS-pl canoe 3du push-OUTWARDS-ONLY push-OUTWARDS-ONLY
      <u>wapu-saku-brə-k</u>],   [brə-kə-m   abra:b   ata
      push-OUTWARDS-3du-COMPL.DS 3du-OBL-ACC DEM.DIST.REACT.TOP.du+TOO then
      vya-də-ber,   kə-bər   Malu]
      hit-3masc.sgSUBJ.P-3duBAS.P DEM.PROX-du Malu
      'After these two (Malu men) just pushed and pushed their canoes off, after they'd pushed them off, he (Avatip man) struck the two, these men from Malu'

This same verb *wapu-saku-* may mean 'set out (on a trip)', as in 16.39.

16.39 [val   <u>wur-saki-sala-ku</u>]   [yi-n] Parmali də-kə
      canoe lift-ACROSS.AWAY-INSIDE-COMPL.SS go-SEQ Parmali he-OBL+fem.sg
      təpa:m,   yak də-kə-di kwas mas   kurən
      village+LK+LOC OK he-OBL-pl salt   betelnut get+SEQ
      napa-də-k,   aka   <u>wapu-saku-ku</u>
      COMPL.VB-3masc.sg-COMPL.DS DEM.DIST.REACT.TOP.fem.sg push-OUTWARDS-COMPL.SS
      da-na-dian
      go.down-ACT.FOC-1plBAS.VT
      'Having sorted out the canoe, going, in Parmali's village, OK, we got salt and betelnut, so having set off, we went downstream'

This is an obvious extension of the idea of pushing a canoe away from the shore when sailing off—but the same verb can be used metaphorically to refer to any kind of trip, not necessarily involving waterways. The directional -*saku*- appears in a number of idiomatic combinations—these include *ta-saku*- ('put'/cut-OUTWARDS) 'appoint, choose, elect', *jama-saku*- (extinguish.fire-OUTWARDS) 'light up a fire which is almost extinguished', and *kur-saku*- (do/get-OUTWARD) 'do a job incompletely'. The latter verb is reminiscent of the way -*saki* 'across away' is used to refer to an incomplete action or event, as in *kiya-saki*- 'half-die'.

The verb *saku*- which is, in all likelihood, related to the bound directional -*saku*- has a multiplicity of meanings (see Table 16.2). Two of them, 'cut across' and 'take things off which were put across each other (e.g. dismantle a traditional door by taking the planks off)', can be easily linked to the meaning of the directional 'outward'. The meaning 'give birth; lay eggs (hen)' (see 15.75) is less easily relatable to the directional *saku*-: the semantic link is to do with pushing babies, or eggs, out of the body in the process of giving birth or laying eggs. Interestingly, the equivalent of *saku*- 'give birth' in the Malu variety is *sapwi*- which is reminiscent of the directional verb -*sapwi* 'discover' used in the Avatip variety (see §15.2.4).

The meanings of *kraku*- 'carry in an outward direction' and *kɔtaku* 'look in an outward direction' are straightforward. This agrees with the general principle—that directionals with intrinsically directional verbs have no special extensions. Examples of *kraku*- are at 16.40, 16.14, and 16.53.

16.40 [aw   [kə-də   du   adəka
      then DEM.PROX-masc.sg man DEM.DIST.REACT.TOP.masc.sg
      taka-də-d-ə   wəpak]   [adəka   ma:
      put-3masc.sgSUBJ.P-3masc.sgBAS.P-LK type.of.tree DEM.DIST.REACT.TOP.masc.sg again
      kraku-taka]]   [[kə-də   yi-na-d-ə
      carry.OUTWARD-IMM.SEQ DEM.PROX-masc.sg go-ACT.FOC-3masc.sgBAS.VT-LK
      yabəm]   təpə-taka-ya-lə-d],   [a-də
      road+LK+LOC be.closed-put-come-3fem.sgSUBJ.P-3masc.sgBAS.P DEM.DIST-masc.sg
      kuprapə ya:b adəka   kəp   ta:d]
      bad   road DEM.DIST.REACT.TOP.masc.sg alone stay+3masc.sgBAS.P
      'Then immediately after having carried a leaf put by this man (on the road to block it) again away in an outward direction, she kept closing off the road he went on, only that bad road remained'

The directional *kɔtaku*- 'look across' is shown in 16.41:

16.41 [aka   wukə-kraki-yi-də-l]
      DEM.DIST.REACT.TOP.fem.sg hear-carry.across-go-3masc.sgSUBJ.P-3fem.sgBAS.P
      [kɔtaku   væn] [ata ta:d]
      look.OUTWARDS see+SEQ then stay+3masc.sgBAS.P
      'He recognized her voice as he went, having looked outwards he stayed (looking)'

We will see, at §16.1.4, that an additional form -*sala*- 'inside' occurs in combination with both -*saki* and -*saku*. Very occasionally, this form occurs on its own, as a variant of -*səwəla*- 'inside': for instance, 16.42 was used to describe moving a chair towards the middle of the house from where it was, close to the front door:

16.42 atawa   məgi-sala-l
      like.that do.whatever-INSIDE-3fem.sgBAS.P
      'She whatevered (moved the chair) towards inside'

We return to this in §16.1.4.

D. THE DIRECTIONALS *-tay* 'SIDEWAYS AWAY FROM SPEAKER' AND *-tæy* 'SIDEWAYS TOWARDS SPEAKER' differ from the directionals described in A–C above in that they have no corresponding inherently directional verb. They do not attach directly to the intrinsically directional verb *kər-/ka-* 'carry, bring', nor to the directional *-kəta-* 'look'. See §16.1.3.

The directional meaning of *-tay* 'sideways away from speaker, to the side next to speaker' is illustrated in 16.43. This same command, 'move away to the side', is used to get people to move over within enclosed space—for instance, in a canoe.

16.43 wun-a:k   waləb-kaləb rə-tukwa,   <u>a-sə-tay</u>
     I-LK+DAT near-near sit-PROH.GEN IMPV-plant/move-TO.SIDE.AWAY
     'Do not sit very close to me, move away to the side'

Its counterpart *-tæy* is used much less frequently than *-tay*. It occurs with verbs which involve motion, as in 16.1, or 16.44, and is never reduplicated. It is most probably an innovation.

16.44 <u>a-sə-tæy</u>
     IMPV-plant/move-TO.SIDE.TOWARDS
     'Move to side towards the speaker' (on a canoe)

With verbs of most semantic groups, the directional *-tay* refers to sideways motion. In 16.45, it describes 'hitting the side' of the lower part of the mosquito net:

16.45 [day ñəg   nak-al]   [a   apaw
     they mosquito.net one-3fem.sgNOM DEM.DIST.fem.sg old.fem.sg
     ta:kw-al]   [mada-ñəg-a:m
     woman-3fem.sgNOM underneath+LK-mosquito.net-LK+LOC
     <u>vya-tay-lə-k]</u>   [kwa:d]
     hit-TO.SIDE.AWAY-3fem.sg-COMPL.DS stay+3masc.sgBAS.P
     'They were in one mosquito net, as for the old woman, after she'd been hitting the side of the lower part of the net, he stayed (there)'

It may also refer to moving an object to some distance away, and not necessarily sideways, as shown in 16.46.

16.46 [a   væk kaula-ku]   [gəpi-yi-ku]   [sək-a:m
     DEM.DIST.fem.sg pot bring.INSIDE-COMPL.SS run-go-COMPL.SS far-LK+LOC
     <u>yakə-tay-lə-l]</u>
     throw-TO.SIDE.AWAY-3fem.sgSUBJ.P-3fem.sgBAS.P
     'Having brought the pot inside the house, having gone off running, she threw it (her other pot) away'

The meaning of *-tay* is rather similar to that of *-saki* 'across away from speaker'. We can recall that in 10.22b *təpə-saki-* (be.closed/fence-ACROSS.AWAY) means 'close up halfway, by putting (a leaf) across (the road)'. Later on in the same story, the main character describes this same action as *təpə-tay-* 'close sideways, half-blocking'.

Unlike any other directional, *-tay-* (but not *-tæy*) can be reduplicated (see §12.8.2), with the meaning of 'moving back and forth', as in 12.67 (*kui-tay-tay-* 'give (to each other) back and forth'), and 12.70 (*wa-tay-tay-* 'speak back and forth as in a dialogue'). The reduplicated *-tay-tay* may also mean 'side to side many times'. In 16.47, a tree shakes because of something that feels like an earthquake:

16.47 kə-lawur   mi   agula
       DEM.PROX-fem.sg+UP   tree   what's.up/why
       narkə-tay-tayal-a
       shake-TO.SIDE.AWAY-TO.SIDE.AWAY+3fem.sgBAS.P-3fem.sgNOM
       'Why is it so that this tree up here is shaking many times?'

With the verb of speech *wa-* 'say, speak', *-tay* refers to 'calling out' or 'speaking outwards' in the direction away from speaker. If the directional marker is reduplicated, the resulting verb means 'call in every direction, back and forth', as in 16.48:

16.48 tapwuk pəkaka:u   kwa:s   ata   kui-kwi-kwi-kwi wa-ku,
       rooster cockadoodledoo type.of.pheasant then kui-kwi-kwi-kwi say-COMPL.SS
       ata   wa-tay-taya-ber
       then   say-TO.SIDE.AWAY-TO.SIDE.AWAY-3duBAS.P
       'The rooster (said) cock-a-doodle-doo, the pheasant said kui-kwi-kwi-kwi, they were saying (this) back and forth (echoing each other)'

The reduplicated directional *-tay-tay* can also describe movement from side to side. e.g. *piñu-tay-tayan* (slide-TO.SIDE.AWAY-TO.SIDE.AWAY+SEQ) 'sliding side to side', like a piece of watermelon on a damp plate. We can recall, from §12.8.2, that reduplication often has intensive meaning and describes an action done really well and to completion. The reduplicated directional *-tay-* is no exception: 16.49 was used to refer to girls who were stretching mats on the floor really well:

16.49 kay-nawul-tay-tayan   kwa-di
       CAUS-be.stretch-TO.SIDE.AWAY-TO.SIDE.AWAY+SEQ   stay-3plBAS.VT
       'They are stretching (the mats on the floor) as well as can be (so that there are no folds)'

A similar example is at 16.50: the reduplicated directional describes the full extent of an action of 'surrounding':

16.50 [kə   tami:-a   miyawa
       DEM.PROX.fem.sg   area-3fem.sgNOM   whole
       səlki-tay-tayan]
       surround/tie.around-TO.SIDE.AWAY-TO.SIDE.AWAY+SEQ
       'surrounding this whole area completely'

Similar to other directionals involving movement away from speaker, *-tay-* 'to side away' often forms lexicalized combinations. So, *kui-tay-* (give.to.third.p-TO.SIDE.AWAY) means 'spread (the news); distribute; send', as in *lapañəg kui-tay-tay-* (letter give.to.third.p-TO.SIDE.AWAY-TO.SIDE.AWAY) 'send off letters'. Its other meaning, 'give away; give back and forth', was illustrated in 12.67.

The form *wukə-tay-* (hear/think-TO.SIDE.AWAY) means 'worry (about)'. The directional can be reduplicated, and then the verb acquires an intensive meaning, as in w*ukə-tay-tay-* 'worry a lot (about)'; *taka-tay-tay-* (put-TO.SIDE.AWAY-TO.SIDE.AWAY) 'whinge a lot'; and *yakə-tay-tay* (throw-TO.SIDE.AWAY-TO.SIDE.AWAY) 'mess around; be around', as in 16.51:

16.51 yakə-tay-tayan   tə-gur-alək
       throw-TO.SIDE.AWAY-TO.SIDE.AWAY+SEQ   stay-2pl-BECAUSE
       '(You are not paying attention) because you are messing around'

In each case, the exact meaning of the verb plus directional can only be determined by context. The three directionals meaning 'away from speaker'— *-saki-*, *-saku-*, and *-tay-* —are prone to lexicalization, just like many second components of compound verbs (see §15.2–3). A superficial analogy can be found in English phrasal verbs—'up' typically refers to upward direction, but does not have to in combinations like *put up*, *make up*, etc. The same holds for *down*, *along*, and many others (see Dixon 1982 and 2005). The only puzzle is: why are the forms with the meaning 'away' in Manambu more 'lexicalizable' than others?

This is the only feature *-tay-* 'to side across' shares with bound directionals *-saki-* and *-saku-*. Unlike those, neither *-tay-* nor *-tæy-* affects the verb's valency. We return to further differences between the directional suffixes in §16.1.3.

E. ADDITIONAL DIRECTIONAL FORMS are found with two inherently directional verbs. As we saw in Table 16.2, the verb 'bring, carry' distinguishes two extra forms: *kray-* 'bring from or take to a nearby place' and *karya-* 'bring from or take to a faraway place' (which may well contain the root *kər/kra-* and a generic motion verb, either *yi-* 'go' or *ya-* 'come'). These two verbs are illustrated in 16.52–3. In 16.52, the Avatip man Sesawi brought dogs to the bush to hunt—the verb is *kray-* (this is from a version of T2).

16.52   wun-a-də   *tumbuna* a:s   kray-ku,   kəda
       I-LK-masc.sg ancestor dog bring-COMPL.SS DEM.PROX.REACT.TOP+masc.sg
       kur-taka   lukauti-da-d
       put-IMM.SEQ look.after-3masc.sgSUBJ.VT-3masc.sgBAS.VT
       'My ancestor having brought the dog (to the bush), having got that very (man, that is, the Gala man hidden in the sago palm), looked after him'

He found a starving Gala man, Kamkudi, hidden in the sago tree, and took him away from his hiding to Avatip—the verb is *karya-*:

16.53   [waku-də-k],   [kamna kui-taka],   [karya-ku],
       go.out-3masc.sg-COMPL.DS food   give.to.third.p-IMM.SEQ take.away-COMPL.SS
       [təpa:r   kaula-taka],   [wiya:m   ku-su-də-k]
       village+LK+ALL bring+INSIDE-IMM.SEQ house+LK+LOC put-UP-3masc.sg-COMPL.DS
       [rə-də-k]   [kamna: kui-ya-də-d]
       sit-3masc.sg-COMPL.DS food   give.to.third.p-come-3masc.sgSUBJ.P-3masc.sgBAS.P
       [[[Aləb   ra:n]   ya:kya] yi:n]   [də-kə   səp   kru
       DEM.DIST+fem.sg+TERM sit+SEQ OK   go+SEQ he-OBL+fem.sg skin/body fat
       tə-də-l]   [mayka:r ata
       stay/become-3masc.sgSUBJ.P-3fem.sgBAS.P openly   then
       kraku-də-d]
       bring+OUTWARDS-3masc.sgSUBJ.P-3fem.sgBAS.P
       'After he had gone out (of the sago palm), having given him food, having taken him away (from the hiding) having brought (him) inside (the village), after he had put him up there in the house, after he'd stayed there, he kept giving him food. Having stayed there, OK, (so it) went on, he got fat on his body, then he took him outwards (out of the house) openly'

This example conveniently illustrates different directionals with the verb of carrying—*karya-* 'take away', *kaula-* 'take inside', and *kraku-* 'take outside'. Along similar lines, bringing the children to one's own village in the continuation of 16.56 is described with *kray-*.

In 16.54, *karya-rəb* means 'onwards; going all the way'—this refers to a row on a colour chart which consisted of various shades of black:

16.54 kə-lə-m   <u>karya-rəb</u>   gəl-a-ka-gəl-adi
      DEM.PROX-fem.sg-LOC take.away-FULLY black-LK-DER-black-3plNOM
      '(From) here onwards (lit. taking away) they are all very black'

This is consistent with a general tendency throughout the language, to develop idiomatic extensions with directionals meaning 'away' rather than 'towards', speaker. The two verbs *kray-* and *karya-* form a compound *kray-karya-* 'carry to and fro' (illustrated in 15.61).

Both *kray-* and *karya-* are S=A ambitransitives; this is in contrast to most other directionals (except *-tay* in D above).

The verb 'look' accompanied by an additional directional form *kətay kəti* 'all around, round and round', refers to 'looking around for something': *kətay kəti və-* can mean 'look around (the area) evaluating it' as in 16.55.

16.55 [aləm   rə-ku]   [kətay   kəti
      DEM.DIST+fem.sg+LOC stay-COMPL.SS around around
      və-də-l]   [alək   tu-ku]   [ata
      see-3masc.sgSUBJ.P-3fem.sgBAS.P DEM.DIST+fem.sg+DAT stay-COMPL.SS then
      kətaki   væd,   adaki   nəbəkər,
      see.ACROSS.AWAY look+3masc.sgBAS.P DEM.DIST.masc.sg.ACROSS.AWAY hill+LK+DAT
      Makəmawir]
      Makemawi+ALL
      'Having stayed there, he looked around evaluating it (the area), so he then looked across away (from where he was), to that hill across (away from us), to Makemawi (Ambunti mountain)'

Or it can mean 'watch over and guard something' (then it is synonymous with the verb *jawə-* 'be on guard'). It can be used intransitively, but its meaning has to be telic: while the verb *və-* on its own can refer to either seeing or looking (and see 7.28 and §7.4 on how the telic and the atelic meaning of *və-* can also be distinguished by choosing the case of the object). An example of 'look around to see, inspect' used intransitively is at 16.56: the children of the dead mother inspect the new territory, so as to be able to understand where their mother had brought them:

16.56 [ala-wur   aba:m   tə-ku],   [kətay kəti   ata və-di]
      DEM.DIST.fem.sg-UP head+LK+LOC stay-COMPL.SS around around then see-3plBAS.P
      'Having arrived up there at the end (lit. head), they looked around (inspecting)'

That is, at least some directionals make the action of the verb telic, and effectively add an argument—this and other properties of bound directionals and directional suffixes are addressed in the next section.

16.1.3   Bound directionals and directional suffixes: a comparison

Bound directionals (A–C in §16.1.2) and directional suffixes (D in §16.1.2) share a major semantic function: both provide directional specification to the clause. Yet, they differ in a number of grammatical properties summarized in Table 16.4 and discussed below.

I. VALENCY CHANGING is a property of bound directionals. A strictly intransitive verb with a bound directional has a telic meaning and an obligatory directional specification. There is often a noun phrase specifying the direction of action. An example is at 16.57:

TABLE 16.4 Directional suffixes and bound directionals

PROPERTY	DIRECTIONAL SUFFIXES (D)	BOUND DIRECTIONALS (A–C)
I. Valency changing	no	yes
II. Adverbial usage	no	yes: some
III. Reduplication	yes: only one	no
IV. Lexicalization	yes: for the meaning 'away'	yes: for the meanings 'away across' and 'away outwards'
V. Potential replacement with a partly synonymous directional verb	no	yes

16.57 [a-də   kabay ada   pəkə-da-d
      DEM.DIST-masc.sg snake DEM.DIST.REACT.TOP+masc.sg jump-DOWN-3masc.sgBAS.VT/P
      kəp-aːr]   [pəkə-da-də-k]   wa!
      ground-LK+ALL jump-DOWN-3masc.sg-COMPL.DS wa!
      'That snake there jumped downwards, onto the ground, after he had jumped (there was
      a sound) wa!'

A directional with an intransitive non-motion verb makes it telic, and adds a resultative overtone, as in 16.63 (*puku-su-* (bulge/get.fat-UP) 'get big').

A directional used with an ambitransitive verb of either S=O or S=A type has a different effect: it restricts the verb's transitivity to just its transitive use. We will see, in §16.2, that the causative-manipulative *kay-* may have a similar effect.

The verb *təp-* 'be closed, fence off' is an S=O ambitransitive. With a directional, it is always transitive, as illustrated in 16.23, 16.30, and 10.22b (also see 12.3). The effect of a directional is similar to that of *-taka* 'put' as V₂ in asymmetrical compounds (see 15.62–3). The verb *piñu-* 'slide, slip' is an S=O ambitransitive. If accompanied by a bound directional, it has a transitive meaning: *piñu-sada-tua* (slide-DOWN-1sgSUBJ.VT+3fem.sgBAS.VT) means 'I slide (it) downwards'. The verb 'look' used with a directional means 'look at something; in the direction of something', or 'with a particular purpose'—see examples 16.12, 16.19, 16.34, and especially 16.55–6. If the verb 'say' is used with a directional, the addressee needs to be expressed, as in 16.6, or understood as in 16.10.

The valency-changing or, better, valency-adjusting effect of bound directionals is especially clear with the general verb *məgi-* 'do whatever, happen', which is S=O=A ambitransitive. Without a directional, it can have any transitivity value, depending on what the speaker has in mind. In 16.58a it is used transitively:

16.58a kaməm   məgi-də-d
       breadfruit+LK+ACC do.whatever-3masc.sgSUBJ.P-3masc.sgBAS.P
       'He did whatever to breadfruit' (in the context: grabbed the breadfruit)

Its intransitive use is shown in 16.58b—this example shows that *məgi-* is an S=A ambitransitive:

16.58b yakraw   məgi-da-l
       thunder do.whatever-3masc.sgSUBJ.VT+3fem.sgBAS.VT-3fem.sgNOM
       'It was that (that time) thunder did whatever' (in the context: struck)

An example like 16.58c shows that the verb *məgi-* is also an S=O ambitransitive:

16.58c lə-kə   mæn atawa   məgi-l-a
       she-OBL+fem.sg leg   like.that do.whatever-3fem.sgBAS.P-3fem.sgNOM
       'It is the case that her leg whatevered like that' (in the context: her leg became paralysed)

If accompanied by a directional, *məgi-* has to be transitive, and also refer to a telic action. Examples are 16.16, 16.42 (also see the full paradigm at 16.2), and 16.58d (here the omitted O is the foot).

16.58d [a-məgi-su]   [kə   mæn nəkər nəkər kur-kwa]
       IMPV-do.whatever-UP DEM.PROX.fem.sg foot cold cold get-IMPV.3p+fem.sg
       'Whatever it (the foot) up (in context: put your foot up), may your foot get really cool'

In contrast, the directional suffixes *-tay* 'sideways away from speaker' and *-tæy* 'sideways towards speaker' do not have any such effect: *məgi-tay-* (do.whatever-TO.SIDE.AWAY) may mean either 'move or affect (something) to side', or 'move itself to side'; *piñu-tay-tayan* (slide-TO.SIDE.AWAY-TO.SIDE.AWAY+SEQ) means 'sliding side to side', and may also mean 'make something slide side to side', depending on the context.

That is, one set of directionals affects transitivity, and the other set does not. The inherently directional verbs—each of which corresponds to a bound directional (Table 16.1)—do not affect the verb's valency (see §15.2, and also V below). The morphological make-up of the bound directionals accounts for their valency-changing effect. As mentioned above, they could be composed of the transitive verb *sə-* 'put, plant' followed by an inherently directional verb. We can recall that verbs *sada-* 'put down' and *saku-* 'push outwards' which contain *sə-* as an intrinsically directional verb are transitive.

This corroborates our hypothesis that the transitive verb *sə-* 'put, plant' imparts a transitivizing value to these morphemes.

II. ADVERBIAL USAGE is a property of a few bound directional forms, such as *-su* 'upwards' in 16.59–61 and *-saku* 'outwards' in 16.29. We can recall, from Table 16.1, that the directional *-su* is unusual in that it is not directly relatable to an inherently directional verb, unlike other directionals in the paradigm. In their adverbial usage, the directionals modify the verb, as does the form *wukə-su* (listen-UP) used in the sense of 'lending one's ear' while listening, in 16.59 (repeated from T3.30; a similar example is in T3.27).

16.59 [a   gapum   wukə-su kui-n   aka
       then big.post+LK+LOC listen-UP give.to.third.p-SEQ DEM.DIST.REACT.TOP.fem.sg
       ra:l]
       sit+3fem.sgBAS.P
       'Having gone to another house, she sat on the big post listening to what was above'

The versatile nature of the form *wukə-su* becomes apparent in an adjacent sentence within the same story (T3.31) where this same form occurs as a bona fide verb, *wukə-su:n* (listen-UP+SEQ) 'having listened (to what was above)'. A similar example, with the directional *-saku* 'outwards', is at 16.29 (second line).

A directional verb used adverbially can mark manner, as in 16.60:

16.60 kə   bagula-manəm   <u>yakə-su</u>
       DEM.PROX.fem.sg ankle-foot+LK+ACC throw-UP
       kaykətə-də-l,   a-də   apan   du
       hold.onto-3masc.sgSUBJ.P-3fem.sgBAS.P DEM.DIST-masc.sg old.masc man
       'He held on to (the tree) by throwing this ankle of his foot upwards, that old man'

This is reminiscent of the directionals used with 'look'. But, unlike any other directional, it can be used with the inflected predicate ellipsed, as in 16.8.

The directional -*su* 'up' used with the generic verb *sə*- 'put, plant' in 16.61 has a somewhat idiomatic meaning, 'upwards/upstream a little bit'.

16.61 [Sapaday <u>sə-su</u>   waku-n]   [aləm   taka-də-k]   [wun
       Japanday put-UP go.out-SEQ DEM.DIST+fem.sg+LOC put-3masc.sg-COMPL.DS I
       ata   ya-dəwun]
       then come-1masc.sgBAS.VT
       '(A group from) Japanday having gone out a little bit upstream, established themselves there (lit. put (line)), then I came'

We can recall, from A above, that the directional -*su* 'up' does not refer to the upstream direction—unlike the directional -*war* in *ka-war*- 'bring/take upwards or upstream'. The form *səsu* is unlike other directionals in an additional way—it can be used in a noun phrase, similarly to a postposition, as 16.62.

16.62 wuka-n-aka   *haiskul*
       REACT.TOP.DEM.PROX.ADDR.fem.sg-PRED-REACT.TOP.fem.sg highschool
       tə-lawa   <u>sə-su</u>]
       stay-3fem.sgSUBJ.VT+3fem.sgBAS.VT+COM put-UP
       'Here it is (closer to you), upstream from where the high school is'

Verbal forms marked with directional suffixes -*tay* 'sideways away from speaker' and -*tæy* 'sideways towards speaker' are never used adverbially.

III. REDUPLICATION of a directional is an exclusive property of the directional suffix -*tay* 'sideways away from speaker' (see 12.67, 12.70, 16.47). No other directional, including -*tæy* 'sideways towards speaker', can be reduplicated.

IV. LEXICALIZATION is a property of many directionals, especially those meaning 'across away' and 'outwards'— -*saki* and -*saku*, and -*tay*. A few verb roots only occur accompanied by directionals, e.g. *rəm-su* (?-up) 'come up (plants in a garden); heap up (ground)'.

V. POTENTIAL REPLACEMENT WITH A PARTLY SYNONYMOUS DIRECTIONAL VERB is a property of bound directionals. The directional suffixes do not have this option.

There are two alternatives. The first one is to use a verb compound with an inherently directional verb as V₂. The compound describes something happening while moving in one of the six directions encoded in inherently directional verbs—that is, concomitant motion (also see §15.2.2, examples 15.6 and 15.8–12).

Verb forms with bound directionals do not have an additional movement overtone. In contrast, they indicate the directionality of the action upon an object. They may also imply that the position of an object in space was affected.

The pairs in Table 16.5 illustrate the different semantic effect of verb compounds with inherently directional verbs, and of bound directionals, with the verb *yakə*- 'throw' which implies motion and directionality, and with the verb *yaku*- 'wash' which does not.

TABLE 16.5   Verb compounds and bound directionals: a comparison

COMPOUND WITH INHERENTLY DIRECTIONAL V₂	VERB WITH BOUND DIRECTIONAL
yakə-war- (throw-go.up) 'throw and go upwards or upstream'	*yakə-su-* 'throw something upwards'
yakə-da- (throw-go.down) 'throw and go downwards or downstream'	*yakə-sada-* 'throw something downwards'
yaku-war- 'wash and go upwards or upstream'	*yaku-su-* 'wash in upward direction, e.g. a mount or a heap of sago; wash something that is heaped up'
yaku-da- 'wash and go downwards or downstream'	*yaku-sada-* 'wash in a downward direction; wash something that is located below oneself'
ñam-væki- 'chew and go across'	*ñam-saki-* 'chew with sideways mouth movements'

If a verb does not imply directionality, an inherently directional V₂ may refer to a process, and a bound directional describes reaching a state. An example is at 16.63:

16.63 [ata puku-su-bər]   [pukupuku-warən   tə-brə-k . . .]
      then bulge/get.fat-UP-3duBAS.VT/P bulge/get.fat:RED-go.up+SEQ stay-3du-COMPL.DS
      'Then they two got big. As they were getting bigger and bigger (lit. going up in getting fat) . . .'

A verb can combine with either an inherently directional verb or with a directional, if its meaning is compatible with the idea of concomitant motion or directionality. Directionals do not occur on atelic verbs. So, *kwakə-su-* (look.for-UP) ?? 'look for upwards' is not acceptable; but in an appropriate context it can mean 'find in an upward direction'.

The second alternative is a verb-sequencing construction (which can be considered biclausal: see §18.1). Then, one verb is marked with the sequencing -*n* and the other verb is fully inflected. The meaning of the sequence is that of concomitant actions and manner. An example is at 16.64, underlined.

16.64 a-də   məd-a   ñan ada   pəkə-yi:n
      DEM.DIST-masc.sg cassowary-LK child DEM.DIST.REACT.TOP+masc.sg jump-go+SEQ
      væki-yi:d
      go.across-go+3masc.sgBAS.VT/P
      'That cassowary's son (topical) went across (the hole) by continuously jumping'

If the construction 'jumping he went across' in 16.64 were replaced with a verb plus a directional, *pəkə-saki-* (jump-ACROSS.AWAY), it would be grammatical, but its meaning would have been simply 'jump across in the direction away from reference point'.

Semantic affinity between a directional compound and a corresponding verb of motion is corroborated by examples like 16.65: the verb 'go downstream' in the second clause echoes the directional 'down' in the first clause:

16.65 [laku-sada-də-k]   [da:n   kwa-d]
      pull-down-3masc.sg-COMPL.DS go.down+SEQ stay-3masc.sg.BAS.VT/P
      'After he'd pulled it (canoe) down (from bank), it stayed on water (going) downstream'

The sequencing construction in 16.66 shows that a bound directional imparts a somewhat different meaning to the verb from an inherently directional verb. Here, the directional refers to jumping up, and the inherently directional verb describes concomitant motion:

16.66 <u>pəkə-su-yakə-n</u>   warə-d
jump-up-FULLY-SEQ go.up-3masc.sgBAS.VT/P
'It (the snake) jumped up fully and went up (into the house)'

A verb containing two directionals (see §16.1.4) can be rephrased with a compound, and a sequencing construction, since a compound cannot contain two verbs of motion. So, *pəkə-su-sada-* (jump-UP-DOWN) meaning 'jump up and down in the same place' (see §16.1.4) can be rephrased as *pəkə-warən pəkə-da-n* (jump-go.up+SEQ jump-go.down-SEQ) meaning 'jump while moving up and down (e.g. on a ladder)'.

If an intrinsically directional verb 'carry, bring' requires an additional directional specification, it is likely to be used in a compound with an inherently directional verb as V$_2$: *ka-war-waku-* (carry/bring-UP-go out) in 15.7 can mean 'carry (things) upwards (e.g. to the house) and out', or 'carry (things) upwards and go out'. An alternative is a biclausal sequencing construction, as in 16.67:

16.67 <u>ka-war-ən</u>   <u>karya-tua-di</u>
'bring'-UP-SEQ take.away-1sgSUBJ.VT-3plBAS.VT
'I will take (plates) carrying them up (to the house)'

The verb *karya-* 'take away' develops idiomatic meanings in sequencing constructions, e.g. *wukə-n karya-n* (think-SEQ take.away-SEQ) 'remember, remind'. Just as with bound directionals, the verb implying movement 'away' is more prone to developing idiomatic overtones than its counterpart meaning 'towards'.

We conclude that, synchronically, Manambu has two independent grammatical systems: that of two directional suffixes (neither of which has a corresponding inherently directional verb) and that of six bound directionals (each with a corresponding inherently directional verb). A directional suffix and a bound directional cannot co-occur in one verb. We will now discuss the ways in which bound directionals can appear together.

16.1.4 How directionals co-occur

Two bound directionals can occur on one verb. The following combinations have been attested:

(a) *-su-sada-* (up-down) 'up and down', e.g. *pəkə-su-sada-* (jump-UP-DOWN) 'jump up and down', *yi-su-sada-* 'go up and down';

(b) *-saki-sala-* (across.away-inside) 'back and forth, across and back', as in *sə-saki-sala-* (put/plant-ACROSS.AWAY-INSIDE) 'push back and forth, across and back', *vyajibə-saki-sala-* (pole.forcefully-ACROSS.AWAY-INSIDE) 'pole forcefully across and back', *blakə-saki-sala-* (rock-ACROSS.AWAY-INSIDE) 'rock across and back (as a canoe does)'. This combination can have idiomatic meanings, as in *wur-saki-sala-* (lift-ACROSS.AWAY-INSIDE) 'sort out (a canoe)' (see 16.39), and *san-saki-sala-* (choose-ACROSS.AWAY-INSIDE) 'pick and choose'.
It may also describe reciprocal activities, as in *vya-saki-sala-* 'hit (each other) back and forth', and *wa-saki-sala-* (say-ACROSS.AWAY-INSIDE) 'talk back and forth between each other', as in 16.68:

16.68 abra   awarwa <u>wa-saki-sala-ku</u>
  DEM.DIST.REACT.TOP.du REC say-ACROSS.AWAY-INSIDE-COMPL.SS
  abra   warsama-bər
  DEM.DIST.REACT.TOP.du be.angry-3duBAS.VT/P
  'Those two having talked to each other back and forth got angry'

(c) -*saki-sapra-* (across.away-across.towards) 'back and forth, across away from speaker and back towards speaker', as in *yakə-saki-sapra-* 'throw across away and across towards speaker' (playing ball).

(d) -*saku-sala-* (outwards-inside) 'outwards and inwards', as in *wapu-saku-sala-* (push-OUTWARDS-INSIDE) 'push in and out'. This combination occurs in an idiomatic expression *bla-saku-sala-* 'debate; perform ceremonial talk in men's house', as in 16.29 (last line).

The general verb *məgi-* can occur with any of these directional combinations, e.g. *məgi-saki-sala-* 'do whatever back and forth' (said about a pilot moving gears of a plane in an apparently random way).

An alternative to having two directionals on one verb is using them in two clauses, as in 16.19 (*kətaki...kətapar* 'look across away...look across towards'), or in a sequence of predicates, as *vya-saki-n vya-sapra-n* (hit-ACROSS.AWAY-SEQ hit-ACROSS.TOWARDS-SEQ) 'hit back and forth, fight', *sə-saki-n sə-sapra-n* 'move across away and towards speaker', and 16.35.

A rarely used combination -*væki-vala-* 'go across away-across towards' is attested with verbs of movement, e.g. *pəkə-væki-vala-n* (jump-go.across-go.inside?-SEQ) 'jumping side to side'. This could be based on an analogy to -*saki-sala-*.

The form -*sala-* occurs only in the combinations of directionals—the only exception being 16.42. Occasionally, one hears *məgi-saki-n məgi-sala-n* (do.whatever-ACROSS.AWAY-SEQ do.whatever-INSIDE-SEQ) as a variant of *məgi-saki-sala-* 'do whatever back and forth'. This is, in all likelihood, an analogical formation.

None of the inherently directional verbs takes any further directional markers.

The order of co-occurring directionals deserves a mention. If two directional specifications follow each other within one clause or one word, the order is typically 'far'-'close', similarly to 'go come' constructions (see §12.8.2) and -*saki-sala-*, and not the other way round. It appears that languages of the world have different preferences as to the relative ordering of 'far' and 'close'. For instance, the preferred order in English *this and that, here and there, come and go* is opposite to that in Manambu. But the order in Manambu is reminiscent of Tok Pisin *go kam*. This question requires an in-depth typological investigation.

16.1.5 Directionals on verbs and on demonstratives: similar systems, different pathways

A comparison of bound directionals on verbs, and directional suffixes on demonstratives (Table 10.5), shows a number of semantic and formal similarities. It is apparent that both systems must have developed from inherently directional verbs. Yet, the existing differences show that the systems have most likely arisen independently from each other.

The two systems differ in (a) semantic distinctions; (b) semantics of each of the directionals and their correlations with the meaning of a corresponding inherently directional verb; (c) co-occurrence of directionals with each other; and (d) patterns of lexicalization.

(a) The semantics of directionals is pretty uniform, with the exception of a few idiomatic combinations found with bound directionals on verbs. Just like directional demonstratives,

TABLE 16.6 'Up' and 'down' in bound directionals, directional demonstratives, and inherently directional verbs

UP/DOWN	BOUND DIRECTIONALS ON VERBS	DIRECTIONAL DEMONSTRATIVES	INHERENTLY DIRECTIONAL VERBS
'upwards'	up	up, upstream	up, upstream
'downwards'	down	down, downstream	down, downstream

verbal directionals are a means of marking spatial deixis, indicating direction of activity with respect to the speaker, or a character in a story (this is known as 'relative' frame of reference), or with respect to the most important landmark—the Sepik River (see examples 10.34–5, for the ways in which this can be illustrated with the demonstratives).

The verbal bound directionals fall into three pairs: 'up' versus 'down'; 'across away from speaker' versus 'across towards speaker', and 'inside, away from the Sepik River' versus 'outside, outward'. The directional demonstratives lack the term 'across towards speaker'— the term 'inside, away from the Sepik River' can be used in approximately this same meaning. That is, the system of directional demonstratives is less paradigmatically neat than that of verbal directionals.

(b) The semantics of each of the directionals and their correlations with the meaning of corresponding inherently directional verbs is particularly relevant for the directions 'upwards' and 'downwards'. The correlations are summarized in Table 16.6.

The bound verbal directional 'downward' only refers to 'down' as opposed to 'up'. (It only refers to 'downstream' direction when used with the intrinsically directional verb 'carry/bring'). This is unlike the demonstratives where the downward direction refers both to 'down' and to 'downstream'. The directional 'down' completely overlaps in its meaning with the corresponding inherently directional verb -da- only when it has the same form. To describe the downstream direction of a movement, the inherently directional verb -da- is used in a biclausal sequencing construction.

The bound verbal directional 'up' refers to 'up' as opposed to 'down', rather than to 'upstream'. This is unlike the corresponding inherently directional verb *war-*, and unlike the corresponding demonstrative. The directional can only refer to 'upstream' when used with the intrinsically directional 'carry/bring'—where its form -*war*- is the same as that of the inherently directional verb. The bound verbal directional and the directional on 'look' involves a different morpheme, -*u*. This is the only instance of the verbal directional 'up' and the inherently directional verb 'go up' having the same form.

In all other instances, the meanings of a verbal bound directional and of the directional demonstrative are identical.

The directional 'across away from speaker (or reference point)' may also refer to any faraway distal direction, and is in opposition to the directional 'across towards speaker (or reference point)'. The reference point can be relative, or absolute—and its identity is always clear from the context. The direction 'inside', or 'away from the Sepik River', can also refer to something inside the house, or away from waterways in general.

The direction 'outside, outward' appears to be more limited in scope and in frequency—it typically refers to outward direction, e.g. opening a hand when releasing a pump (12.76), or a palm leaning outward (16.35).

But in each case, a corresponding inherently directional verb (see Table 16.1) has a broader range of meanings—it covers any kind of movement in a given direction.

(c) We saw in §16.1.3 that different verbal bound directionals can co-occur with each other. Directional demonstratives cannot.

(d) Having patterns of lexicalization is a property of verbal directionals. The semantics of directional demonstratives is always straightforwardly spatial, with additional anaphoric meanings (see §10.2.1). And verbs vary in what directionals they take: we distinguish between intrinsically directional verbs (Table 16.2) and optionally directional verbs. Some verbs hardly ever occur with a directional. In contrast, all demonstratives can occur with any directional.

We saw in §16.1.1 above that the directional markers are likely to have grammaticalized from the inherently directional verbs. That they are more restricted in meaning than the corresponding verbs agrees with the general principles of semantic change in grammaticalization. Directionals with demonstratives are closer to inherently directional verbs in their meanings than are bound verbal directionals. They are also semantically more straightforward, and their semantics is not complicated by idiomatic extensions.

All this suggests that directionals in demonstratives are younger. And this is confirmed by comparison with other languages. Manambu shares some of its verbal directionals with its relatives: Iatmul and the Wosera/Ambulas dialect complex (see note 3). Only Iatmul also has directional distinctions in demonstratives.[4]

To conclude: both directional demonstratives and directionals on verbs derive from inherently directional verbs. But the relative chronology of their development is different. Directionality in demonstratives and in verbs is a clear example of polygrammaticalization: the same set of inherently directional verbs grammaticalized slightly differently in different contexts, and not at the same time.

16.2 VALENCY-CHANGING DEVICES

We saw above that directionals increase the verb's valency. Morphological means for marking valency increase are discussed in §16.2.1. In §16.2.2 we discuss causative strategies, all of them biclausal.

There is no passive, or any other valency-reducing derivation. Instead, Manambu employs a 'transitivity-neutralizing' biclausal construction which is functionally similar to a passive—see §16.2.3. Neither the reciprocal nor the reflexive involves a verbal derivation; their marking is dealt with in §16.2.4.

16.2.1 Morphological means for marking valency increase

These include (A) *kay-* 'causative-manipulative' derivation, (B) verb compounding, and (C) bound directional forms.

---

[4] A similar (but simpler) system of directionals was described for Alamblak, from the Sepik Hill family (Bruce 1984: 150–1). Directional (or 'elevational') prefixes occur on verbs, sometimes in conjunction with elevational suffixes. The latter appear on noun phrases (p. 98) in the form of enclitics. Similarly to Manambu, there are two—possibly related—subsystems of directionals-elevationals: a nominal and a verbal one. Given other structural similarities between Manambu and Alamblak, we cannot exclude shared substrata in the creation of both systems (see §22.3, and §3.4, on potential areal diffusional features in Manambu). We need more information on other Sepik Hill languages—including Sare (or Kapriman) and Kaningra—before any sensible hypothesis can be put forward.

TABLE 16.7   Causatives of intransitive verbs marked with prefix *kay-*: some examples

INTRANSITIVE VERB	*kay*-DERIVATION
nawul- 'be stretched; line up'[5]	*kay-nawul-* 'stretch something' (see 16.49)
dapu- 'be wrapped'	*kay-dapu-* 'wrap'
napwi- 'be unwrapped'	*kay-napwi-* 'unwrap'
wi:- 'be broken, break'	*kay-wi:-* 'break (e.g. a nut)'
pərki- 'tear, be torn'	*kay-pərki-* 'tear something, e.g. a dress or piece of paper'
bətuku- 'pump by itself; be blown like a balloon'	*kay-bətuku-* 'pump (something)' (see 12.76)

A. THE CAUSATIVE-MANIPULATIVE DERIVATION

The only semi-productive morphological means of deriving causatives is the prefix *kay-* (pronounced as *ka-* if there is an *a* in the following syllable, or as *ke-*, in rapid speech). This prefix does not occur with ingestive verbs, stative verbs, verbs of bodily states and functions, perception, and motion; most copula and posture verbs, the verb 'give', or with the majority of inherently directional verbs. It derives straightforward causatives from a few dozen intransitive verbs of affect. Some examples are in Table 16.7.

An intransitive verb, and its transitivized counterpart, are illustrated in 16.69a–b:

16.69a ka:p   wi:-na
      by.itself break/split-ACT.FOC+3fem.sgBAS.VT
      'It (e.g. boil or egg) has broken (by itself)'

16.69b ba:d   kay-wi:-na-wun
      egg   CAUS-break/split-ACT.FOC-1fem.sgBAS.VT
      'I broke an egg'

Pairs like 16.69a–b are quite straightforward. But when *kay-* occurs on ambitransitive verbs it has a somewhat different effect. It maintains its function as a valency-changing device since it converts an ambitransitive verb into a strictly transitive. However, it does not make such a verb into a causative. The semantic effect of *kay-* on ambitransitive verbs is that of forceful manipulative and highly volitional action (typically, involving hands or arms as an instrument) which is bound to achieve the needed result. This is why I gloss it as 'manipulative'.

Here are some examples. The verb *rali-* 'untie, undo' is an S=O ambitransitive. Its intransitive use is shown in 16.70a. In 16.70b it is used transitively.

16.70a wun-a   kwa:r   ka:p   rali-na
      I-LK+fem.sg grass.skirt by.itself untie-ACT.FOC+3fem.sgBAS.VT
      'My grass skirt untied by itself'

16.70b kwa:r   ata   rali-də-l
      grass.skirt then   untie-3masc.sgSUBJ.P-3fem.sgBAS.P
      'He then untied her skirt'

In 16.70c, the same verb is used with the prefix *kay-*—the implication is that untying the ropes implies a special effort:

---

[5] This verb can occasionally be used as an S=O ambitransitive.

16.70c ya:n   kə-di   ya:p <u>a-rali</u>   <u>a-kay-rali</u>
       come+SEQ DEM.PROX-pl rope IMPV-untie IMPV-MANIP-untie
       'Come and untie these ropes; untie them with special effort'

The verb *kay-rali-* can also be used for action such as unrolling and disentangling wool. Along similar lines, S=A ambitransitive verb *lagu-* means 'pull', and *kay-lagu-* means 'pull with a special effort; get out by pulling'; *buti-* means 'fold (any length of object); be folded', and *kay-buti-* refers to particularly careful folding of a full length of object; *rapya-* means 'twist something (e.g. a lid or a top of a bottle)', and *kay-rapya-* implies a particularly forceful action to the same effect. This prefix is also used with the strictly transitive intrinsically directional verb 'bring, carry'. A command *a-kay-krakw* (IMPV-MANIP-bring+OUTSIDE) means 'take something outside applying a physical effort, e.g. pulling!', *a-kay-krapar* (IMPV-MANIP-bring+INSIDE) means 'bring something inside applying a physical effort, e.g. pulling!', and so on.

The prefix *kay-* is used with the ubiquitous *məgi-* 'do whatever', an A=S=O ambitransitive (see 16.58a–d). The resulting form *kay-məgi-* 'do whatever with a special effort' is strictly transitive, and is used as a replacement for a verb of affect—such as breaking. The resulting form can refer to any kind of forceful breaking: in 16.71 it replaces the verb *kay-wut-* 'break in two':

16.71 [bay   adika   <u>kay-məgi-ku</u>]
      edible.green DEM.DIST.REACT.TOP+pl MANIP-do.whatever-COMPL.SS
      kə-di-di
      eat-3plSUBJ.VT/P-3plBAS.VT/P
      'They ate the edible greens having whatevered them (broken them into two)'

The exact verb of breaking can always be supplied by a speaker, especially if they are conscious of ambiguity of the 'lazy' verb *məgi-*, as was Teketa:y when she instructed me:

16.72 [kə   təp   <u>kay-məgi-ku</u>]   [akatawa wawək]
      DEM.PROX.fem.sg coconut MANIP-do.whatever-COMPL.SS like.this say+RED+DAT
      vya-prapi-u
      hit-break-1sgIMPV
      'Having "whatevered" this coconut, (it is) to say like this: "I shall split it by hitting"'

The exact meaning of the *kay-* derivation with an ambitransitive verb depends on the verb itself. The manipulative *kay-* on an ambitransitive verb typically imparts a meaning of a special effort involved in performing the activity. So, the verb *gwa-* means 'pull out, take out or off, e.g. sticky bits of grass or thorns off the body'; and *kay-gwa-* refers to the same activity applied to particularly sticky thorns. Similar examples are at 16.70–2. Or it may also involve acting on a particularly massive object: the verb *tapu-* means 'carry', e.g. a smallish heap, as in 16.73a, or a limbum mat full of rubbish, as in 16.73b.

16.73a [væs tukura-ku]   [ata tapu-kə-tua-di]
       grass cover/heap.up-COMPL.SS then carry-FUT-1sgSUBJ.VT-3plBAS.VT
       'Having heaped up (some) grass, I will carry it (in my arms)'

16.73b pəsəp   tapu-taka-kə-tua-di
       rubbish carry-put-FUT-1sgSUBJ.VT-3plBAS.VT
       'I will carry the (limbum mat full of) rubbish putting (it) on extended surface'

The form *kay-tapu-*, containing the manipulative *kay-*, refers to carrying heaps of stuff, e.g. a stack of clothes, or grass, in one's arms.

16.73c [kay-tapu-ku   krayin]   [yakə-kə-tua-di]
MANIP-carry-COMPL.SS bring.towards+SEQ throw-FUT-1sgSUBJ.VT-3plBAS.VT
'Having brought (heaps of rubbish) I will throw them away'

In such cases *kay-* indicates the extent of activity as well as an associated physical effort. Similarly, *buti-* refers to folding anything; and *kay-buti-* describes careful folding of a lengthy object, e.g. a sheet, in its full length. This verb is of particular interest: we can recall, from §15.3.2, that *kay-buti-* is synonymous with *wa-buti-* (say?-fold) 'fold forcefully or with care; fold a full length of something, e.g. a long sheet'. This appears to be the only instance in the language where *kay-* and *wa-* have the same meaning—of a forceful manipulative effort—which transforms an ambitransitive verb into a fully transitive one.

Just like any derivation in Manambu, *kay-* derivations may develop unpredictable meanings, e.g. *kay-kwa-* (CAUS-stay) 'pour' and *kay-wər-* (CAUS-bring.up) 'lift off the top layer of a log'. A few verbs, transitive and intransitive, contain a formative *kay-*, which may or may not be related to the causative-manipulative *kay-*. Their 'root' either does not occur anywhere else in the language, or, if it does, has an unrelated meaning. Examples include *kay-kət-* 'hold onto' (cf. bound verb root *-kəta-* 'look, see'); *kay-gəpə-* 'hold in hand, hug' (cf. *gəpə-* 'run; bury'), *kay-lapə-* 'get dark' (the form *lapə-* does not occur elsewhere).

The transitive verb *kay-pəsə-* 'go around something; turn around something, circumnavigate' contains a root *-pəsə-* which does not occur on its own. This root also appears in a sequencing compound *yi-pay-pəsə-* (go-RED-*go.round+SEQ) 'go and keep going round and round' (this is a very rare instance of a sequencing compound involving the verb *yi-* 'go': see §15.2.1). The three forms, *kay-pəsə-*, *kay-pay-pəsə-*, and *yi-pay-pəsə-* are illustrated in 16.74a–b—this is the way we had to go before we could reach Swakap travelling from Avatip.

16.74a [kay-pəsə-n   yu-ku]   [tu-ku]   [nəkə-də   tama:y ata
CAUS-'go.around'-SEQ go-COMPL.SS stay-COMPL.SS other-masc.sg cape   then
kay-pəsə-kə-gura-d]
CAUS-'go.around'-FUT-2plSUBJ.VT-3masc.sgBAS.VT
'Having gone going around (a cape on a river), having done that, you will go around another point (cape)'

16.74b [tama:y waku-n]   [wamən wula-n]   [atawa   kay-pay-pəsə-n]
cape   go.out-SEQ bay   enter-SEQ like.that CAUS-RED-'go.around'-SEQ
[yi-k-na-dian]   [yi-pay-pəsə-n]
go-FUT-ACT.FOC-1plBAS.VT   go-RED-'go.around'-SEQ
'Going out at one cape, entering a bay, like that going round and round and round (capes) we will go, keeping going round'

The semantic range of *kay-*, from causative to a marker of manipulative effort and multiplicity of O, is somewhat reminiscent of other languages where causative and intensive forms are polysemous (see Aikhenvald forthcoming f, for a typological perspective). This can be conceived as an extension of the meanings associated with direct causation (see Dixon 2000) which implies manipulative effort.

The prefix *kay-* is cognate to a non-productive causative *ke-* in Ambulas (Wilson 1980: 61–2). The examples given by Wilson involve two intransitive verbs, *ke-pulaap-mék* (cause.to-be.broken-past.tense) 'broke (plate)' and *ke-naap-me* (cause.to-collapse-same.actor.partially.consecutive) 'knocked down and...', and one transitive verb, *ke-puti-ye* (cause.to-take.off.skin-same.actor.partially.consecutive) 'took off his own skin and'. The verb *puti* 'throw away; take off (clothes; skin), discard' is transitive or S=A ambitransitive (since it also means 'alight'). Its cognate in Manambu is *puti-* 'take off' (see *kay-puti-* 'take off with effort') above. We can only hypothesize that the Ambulas prefix *ke-* is similar to its Manambu cognate, *kay-*, in its semantics.

B. VERB COMPOUNDING

Both symmetrical and asymmetrical verb compounds may have a valency-increasing effect. In its causative meaning, the prefix *kay-* can be compared with an affect verb as V_1 in symmetrical CAUSE-EFFECT COMPOUNDS discussed in §15.2.3. A *kay-* derivation can occasionally occur as V_2 in such compounds. A number of intransitive verbs can occur either with *kay-* as a causativizing or transitivizing device, or as V_2 of an affect verb in cause-effect compounds.

The semantic difference is to do with the manner of causation. A *kay-* derivation refers to typical and functionally unmarked manner. Examples include *puti-* 'fall off, come out by itself (e.g. a shoe which is too big)' versus *kay-puti-* meaning 'take something off (e.g. a shoe)' (see §15.2.3); *pərki-* 'tear, be torn' versus *kay-pərki-* 'tear something, e.g. a dress or piece of paper'; and *wi:-* 'be broken, break' versus *kay-wi:-* 'break (e.g. a nut, or an egg)'. In contrast, a cause-effect compound specifies the exact manner: *vya-puti-* (hit-fall.off) means 'shake something off by hitting, e.g. dust from a mat or a sheet', *væsə-pərki-* (step-be.torn) means 'tear by stepping' (as in 15.19), *vætə-pərki-* (bite-be.torn) means 'tear by biting', *vya-pərki-* means 'tear by hitting', and *væsə-wi:-* means 'step and split something; split by stepping'.

Some types of causation are not judged applicable. My attempts at using the verb **vætə-wi:-* (bite-break/split) '?split by biting' were rejected: I was told this made no sense because *wi:-* implies breaking or splitting objects that cannot be broken by biting, such as eggs, boils, or coconuts. A compound *væsə-bətuku-* (step-be.pumped) was accepted as a highly dubious alternative to *kay-bətuku-* (CAUS-pump) 'pump (e.g. a pump torch); press' because no one has ever seen, say, a pump torch operated by foot—but one could imagine this.

A *kay-* derivation is thus simply more abstract in terms of manner of action than any of the cause-effect compounds. The idiomatic extensions of *kay-* derivations point in a similar direction.[6] We can recall, from §15.2.3, that the intransitive verb *blakə-* 'be turned upside down' (15.25b) occurs with *væsə-* 'step on' meaning 'turn upside down by stepping' (see 15.25a). This root is also attested with the causative prefix *kay-*, in *kay-blakə-* 'turn something upside down', as shown in 16.75. It is used in a metaphorical sense of 'conquering'. The compound *væsə-blakə-* also has a metaphorical meaning 'conquer, raid, exterminate' (15.25c). It implies exterminating the enemy village—*kay-blakə-* does not have this nuance.

16.75 [warya-k   yi-bana]   [kə-də   təp   nəbəl
       fight-PURP.SS go-1plSUBJ.VT+3fem.sgBAS.VT   DEM.PROX-masc.sg village today
       kay-blakə-kə-bana-d]
       CAUS-overturn-FUT-1plSUBJ.VT-3masc.sgBAS.VT
       'We will conquer today the village with which we are going to fight'

The prefix *kay-* is not necessarily associated with any action done 'with hands' and is not in any paradigmatic opposition with *væsə-* 'step'. This is corroborated by the co-occurrence of

---

[6] Farnsworth and Farnsworth (n.d.) discuss a binary opposition between manner 'by hand', marked with *kay-*, and manner 'by foot' marked with *væsə-*. As has been shown above, the opposition is not binary, given that *væsə-* 'step' is one of three verbs of affect which can mark causation and manner of it in cause-effect compounds. Despite the fact that physical action and effort associated with *kay-* often involves a contrast between hands and arms, the difference between *kay-* and *væsə-* cannot be captured by a simple pair of 'hand' versus 'foot'.

væsə- 'step' and *kay-*. This is shown in 16.76. The meaning is 'conquer and exterminate in raid; wipe from the face of the earth':

16.76 a   təp   [væsə-kay-blakə-kə-bana   təp]
        DEM:DIST.fem.sg village step-CAUS-overturn-FUT-1plSUBJ.VT+3fem.sgBAS.VT village
        wuka   yaki   war-k-na
        DEM.PROX.ADDR.REACT.TOP.fem.sg smoke go.up-FUT-ACT.FOC+3fem.sgBAS.VT
        'That village, the village we are going to exterminate, will go up in smoke next to the addressee'

That is, cause-effect compounds can be considered a valency-increasing strategy.

We now turn to ASYMMETRICAL COMPOUNDS with major verb preceding the minor verb (§15.3.1). The verb *-taka* 'put, arrange by spreading' as V_2 (see A7 at §15.3.1) has a valency-increasing effect. If V_1 is intransitive or ambitransitive, *-taka* acts as a transitivizer, and a resulting verb is strictly transitive, e.g. *təpə-taka-* (be.closed/fence-put) 'close; but not *be closed' (15.62–3). This is somewhat similar to *kay-* with intransitive and ambitransitive verbs.

Unlike *kay-*, *-taka* also has an applicative-like effect. With a verb involving physical action as V_1, *-taka* as V_2 adds a beneficiary, as in *kay-puti-* (CAUS-come.off) 'take something off, e.g. shoes' versus *kay-puti-taka-* 'take something off for someone else, e.g. a child or an elderly person'—see 15.65–6. As a V_2, *-taka* also 'adds' an obligatory object of exchange to the verb 'exchange' (15.70–2). And, in addition, *-taka* as V_2, can add a locative participant to just about any verb as V_1, as in 15.73. This is also an applicative-like extension. The *-taka* compounds are prone to developing idiomatic meanings not predictable from the sum of the meanings of the components (see 15.74–84). That is, *-taka* as a V_2 in compounds can be considered a general valency-increasing strategy, whose meaning goes beyond a causative strategy.

Of the asymmetrical compounds where minor verb precedes major verb (§15.3.2), compounds with *wa-* 'say' and one compound with *yi-* 'go; say' as V_1 have a causativizing effect, e.g. *yaga-* 'be afraid', *wa-yaga-* 'scare'; *jəwi-* 'wake up', *wa-jəwi-* 'wake someone up'; *laku-* 'know', *wa-laku-* 'advise'; and *pa:kw-* 'be hidden', *yi-pakw-* 'hide (something)'. The verb *buti-* 'fold' participates in the derivation *wa-buti-* which is synonymous with *kay-buti-* 'fold a lengthy object carefully'. None of these compounds is productive. And, as mentioned in §15.3.2, both *wa-* and *yi-* in these compounds could be prefixes, homophonous with verbs. The existence of a biclausal causative strategy involving the verb of speech *wa-* suggests, however, that the causativizing *wa-* and the verb *wa-* 'say' have the same origin. This is the topic of §16.2.2.

C. BOUND DIRECTIONALS

We saw in §16.1.3 above that bound directionals affect the verb's valency. But this effect is somewhat different from the other means discussed in A and B above. A strictly intransitive verb with a bound directional has a telic meaning and an obligatory direction (see 16.57).

A directional used with an ambitransitive verb makes it strictly transitive. This is similar to the effect of *kay-* 'causative/manipulative', *-taka* 'put, arrange by spreading' as a V_2, and *wa-* 'say; valency increase marker' in *wa-buti-* 'fold a lengthy object carefully'.

Bound directionals appear to consist of the transitive verb *sə-* 'put, plant' accompanied by directional suffixes. Given that bound directionals follow the main verb's root, they are rather similar to verbal compounds. The transitive verb *sə-* 'make, put, plant' followed by directional suffixes in the V_2 position imparts a transitivizing value to the whole verb. In this way, it behaves just like *-taka* as a V_2, with its valency-changing effect.

We have seen, so far, that Manambu has a variety of ways in which the verb's transitivity can be altered without having to resort to a biclausal construction. Yet none of these ways is fully productive. In each case we may expect unusual semantic extensions, and semantic gaps. Additional, biclausal, strategies for expressing causation are discussed in the next section.

16.2.2 Biclausal causative strategies

Table 16.8 summarizes the meanings and functions of monoclausal and biclausal valency-increasing devices in Manambu. Table 16.9 contains a comparison of valency-increasing devices in Manambu in terms of semantic features outlined by Dixon (2000). These parameters include (i) the properties of the verb, that is, its transitivity and whether it describes action or state; (ii) the ways in which causee is treated—whether they are in control, whether their actions are volitional, and their affectedness; and (iii) the way the causer behaves—whether the causation is direct, intentional, natural, and how much the causer is involved.

Some of the valency-increasing devices in Manambu have additional, applicative-like functions, and other features. These are also included in Table 16.9.

A brief comparison of *kay-* derivations with cause-effect compounds shows that:

 (i) *kay-* derivations imply forceful and direct intentional causation; causee fully affected; achieved with effort; they are used with intransitive and ambitransitive verbs; while
 (ii) cause-effect compounds imply forceful and intentional direct causation; causee fully affected; achieved with effort, manner specified, and are only used if V_1 is transitive and V_2 is intransitive.

A biclausal syntactic causative construction involving the verb *kur-* 'do, make' implies forceful and intentional direct causation which implies something happening to the causee rather than the causee acting willingly. The strategy involves juxtaposition of two fully inflected clauses.

16.77 [rasə-k-na]   [kur-na-ñən]
get.up-FUT-ACT.FOC+3fem.sgBAS.VT do-ACT.FOC-2fem.sgBAS.VT
'You are making her get up' (said by an annoyed mother to an older child who was kicking her sleeping sister)

Direct causation expressed with *kur-* 'make, do' may have to involve physical effort on the part of the causer, as in 16.78—an instruction to a little boy on how to operate a pump torch (cf. 12.76):

16.78 [[kay-bətuku-səwəlan]   [kay-bətuku-saku-n]
CAUS-be.pumped-INSIDE+SEQ CAUS-be.pumped-OUTWARDS-SEQ
[kur-mənə-kəb]]   [ada
go-2masc.sg-AS.SOON.AS DEM.DIST.REACT.TOP+masc.sg
lama-na-d]
burn/light-ACT.FOC-3masc.sgBAS.VT
'Pumping in pumping out, as soon as you had made it (act like this), it (topical) will light up'

Examples like this occur in spontaneous speech, but hardly ever in careful narratives. They may reflect some influence from Tok Pisin *mekim* 'make'.

TABLE 16.8 Valency-increasing devices in Manambu

STATUS	FORM	MEANING
one word	*kay-*	• forceful and direct intentional causation; causee fully affected; • causative meaning with intransitive verbs; 'manipulative' meaning with ambitransitive verbs; • transforms ambitransitive verbs into fully transitive ones • manner of causation unspecified • not fully productive
	cause-effect compounds	• forceful and intentional direct causation; causee fully affected; • typical pattern: V_1 transitive; V_2 intransitive • manner of causation specified
	-taka compounds	• causative with few intransitive and ambitransitive verbs: forceful and intentional direct causation; causee fully affected; causee inanimate; • applicative-like with few verbs
	yi- and *wa-* compounds	• causative with limited number of miscellaneous verbs
	bound directionals	• applicative-like with all verbs (make ambitransitive verbs strictly transitive)
biclausal structures	involving *kur-* 'do'	• forceful and intentional direct causation; causee does not do it willingly
	involving *wa-* 'say'	• verbal order • intentional not forceful indirect causation; may involve a stative verb or an adjective; causee not in control
	involving imperative	• intentional not forceful indirect causation; causer involved; may involve stative verbs
	involving dependent clauses	• indirect causation, causer not involved; overtone of consequence and naturalness

TABLE 16.9 Valency-increasing devices in Manambu and their semantics

MARKING	APPLICATIVE FUNCTION AND OTHER FEATURES	RELATING TO VERB		RELATING TO THE CAUSE				RELATING TO CAUSER		
		action/state	transitivity	control	volition	affectedness	directness	intention	naturalness	involvement
kay- 'caus/manip'	none	action	any	yes	yes	yes	yes	yes	no	yes
cause-effect compounds	none; manner of causation specified	action	intransitive	yes	yes	yes	yes	yes	no	yes
-taka 'put' as V$_2$ in compounds	yes (some); causee inanimate	action	any	yes	yes	yes	yes	yes	no	yes
yi- and *wa-* as V$_1$ in compounds	used with very few verbs	action/state	any	yes	yes	yes	yes	yes	no	yes
bound directionals	applicative-like	action/state					n/a			
biclausal with *kur-* 'do'	none; rare	action	any	no	no	yes	yes	yes	no	yes/no
biclausal with *wa-* 'say'	none; also verbal order	action/state	any	no	no	no?	no	yes	yes	yes
biclausal with imperative	none	action/state	any	yes	yes	yes	no	yes	no	yes
biclausal with dependent clause	none	action/state	any	no	no	no	no	no/yes	no	no

A biclausal causative construction with the verb *wa-* 'say' or *wa-yakə-* (say-'throw') in a fully inflected clause may imply a verbal order, as in 16.79 and 15.110.

16.79 [wa-yakə-məna]   [war-na-dəwun-ək]
      say-'throw'-2masc.sgBAS.VT+3fem.sgBAS.VT go.up-ACT.FOC-1masc.sgBAS.VT-CONF
      'You order me to go up' (lit. you order me—I go up)

A biclausal construction involving *wa-* 'say' can also imply intentional—but not forceful—indirect causation, as in 10.15 (repeated here as 16.80). Kuimagan is rebuking one of his two wives who had taken a wrong road and is thus responsible for a disaster that had happened to her son. However, she did not affect the son in any direct way. The assumption is that the woman had acted intentionally, but not forcefully or directly. These (rare) constructions may involve a stative verb or an adjective. The causee is not in control.

16.80 <u>alək</u>   wuka
      DEM.DIST+fem.sg+LK+DAT DEM.PROX.ADDR.REACT.TOP+fem.sg
      wa-də   ñan ada   bə
      DEM.PROX.ADDR-masc.sg child DEM.DIST.REACT.TOP+masc.sg already
      ñən-ñən-a   də-də-kə   kuprap
      you.fem-you.fem-3fem.sgNOM he+LK-he+LK-OBL bad
      wa-ñəna-d
      say-2fem.sgSUBJ.VT-3masc.sgBAS.VT
      'This is why here (close to you), this-close-to-you boy, you yourself made him himself (be) in a bad way'

Cause and consequence is often expressed as speech report (see §19.5); so a speech report like the one in 16.81 can be considered a causative strategy used for indirect causation. This is the only way of saying 'she made me hold it', or 'she got me to hold it'. There is no speech act involved—'she' refers to a 9-month-old baby who could not talk yet.

16.81 [[a-kaykət] wa-ku]   [kə-lə-m
      IMPV-hold   say-COMPL:SS DEM.PROX-fem.sg-LOC
      ku-səwəla-la]
      put-INSIDE-3fem.sgSUBJ.VT+3fem.sgBAS.VT
      'She put it (the orange here), so that I would hold it' (lit. 'Having said "hold!" she put it here')

We can recall, from §13.2.2, that imperatives in Manambu have non-command meanings of consequence and indirect causation (see 13.24). The first clause expresses the cause, and the second clause—cast in imperative—expresses the result or the effect. The first clause can also contain an imperative, as in 16.82 which is the only way of saying 'make them stay'. Along similar lines, 16.83 is a natural way of expressing the notion of 'feeding someone':

16.82 [kagulu]   [kə-lə-m   rə-kwa-di]
      leave+1sgIMPV DEM.PROX-fem.sg-LOC sit-IMPV.3p-pl
      'I shall make them stay here' (Let me leave (them) so that they stay)'

16.83 [jaw   kui-gur-ək]   [kə-kwa-d]
      don't.worry give.to.third.p-2plBAS.VT-CONF eat-IMPV.3p-masc.sg
      'Give him (the food) to eat; get him to eat the food; feed him' (lit. don't worry, give (food) to him so that he may eat)

Similar examples are at 13.25–7, and 14.108. To express indirect causation, a command may be cast as a speech report, as in T2.34. Kamkudi gives the starving Sisawi some water, to make his throat wet. This is phrased as 'he gave him water, saying: may this-down-there throat of his be wet'. In actual fact, there is no indication Kamkudi had said anything at all—the verb 'say' is used as a makeshift causative marker.

Along similar lines, 16.84 means 'getting her to marry him'. The context of the story indicates that this 'getting' involved more than a simple speech act: the causer did not act directly, but what he did was intentional.

16.84 [[də-kə-k   rə-kwa]   [wa-ku]]
      he-OBL-DAT sit-IMPV.3p+fem.sg say-COMPL.SS
      'After he got her to marry him' (lit. having said may she marry him)' ...

A clause-sequencing structure with the verb expressing reason in a non-final position can also be used to express causation. The causee is not in control, and the result is achieved as a natural consequence. The causation is not direct, but the causer may, or may not, act intentionally—this depends on the type of the verb stating the 'reason'. Example 16.85 is deliberately vague as to whether the man cut the tree intentionally so that someone sitting on top of it should fall down, or whether he just cut the tree without any such intention:

16.85 [vəl-mən-ək]   [vækər-k-na-d]
      cut-2masc.sg-COMPL.DS fall-FUT-ACT.FOC-3masc.sgBAS.VT
      'After you cut (the tree), he (the man on top of the tree) will fall down'

To conclude: none of the valency-increasing morphological devices in Manambu is fully productive. Each has a propensity towards developing unpredictable meanings. As if to compensate for this, Manambu has a wealth of other, syntactic, strategies for expressing causation without increasing the verb's valency.

16.2.3   Transitivity-neutralizing construction

Manambu has no passive, nor any other valency-reducing derivation, like most languages of the area. Instead, however, there is a 'transitivity-neutralizing' biclausal construction.

I briefly mentioned in §4.2.2 that transitivity of verbs is neutralized in structures consisting of a verb in the completive, cotemporaneous, or manner sequencing form and one of the three polyfunctional verbs (*tə-* 'stand', *rə-* 'sit', *kwa-* 'stay', also used as positional verbs). An intransitive or a transitive verb in such constructions focuses on the result of the action, producing what can be thought of as functional equivalent of passive. In 16.86, a transitive verb which contains the causativizing *kay-* is marked with the manner sequencing *-n*. The copula *tə-* 'stand, stay, be' is fully inflected—a literal translation would be 'my hair tied by turning it-stands':

16.86 wun-a-də   nab [kay-gwaj-ən   tə-na-d]
      I-LK-masc.sg hair MANIP-tie.by.wrapping.around-SEQ stay-ACT.FOC-3masc.sgBAS.VT
      v//ker-ma:r-kwa-d
      fall-NEG.SUB-IMPV.3p-masc.sg
      'My hair stays tied and wrapped, so that (the hair) should not fall down' (lit. My hair having tied by wrapping around stands, may it not fall down)

This example is similar to 14.108, where the same construction *kay-gwaj-ən tə-na-d* means '(hairclip) is wrapped, tied around', literally 'having tied stays'. That is, a construction with an inflected copula makes a strictly transitive verb appear as ambitransitive. A similar example is at 16.49. Similarly, in 16.87, *kay-dap-* is a transitive verb meaning 'wrap (e.g. fish into a sago pancake)'. To refer to the result of such action one says:

16.87 kay-dapə-n   rə-na
       CAUS-wrap-SEQ sit-ACT.FOC+3fem.sgBAS.VT
       'It was wrapped' (lit. it stays having wrapped)

In 16.88, an intransitive verb *kaña-* 'be glued' is used in exactly the same construction. This verb does not occur with the causative *kay-*, but it can be causativized with *-taka* 'put' as V$_2$. The construction in 16.88 focuses on the result of sticking on a piece of plaster to cover a wound:

16.88 kaña-n   rə-kwa-na
       be.stuck-SEQ sit-HAB-ACT.FOC+3fem.sgBAS.VT
       'It (piece of plaster) typically sticks' (lit. it keeps sitting stuck)

Transitivity-neutralizing constructions containing a lexical verb marked with the sequencing suffix *-n* can be considered monoclausal complex predicates. The polyfunctional verbs in these complex predicates impart aspectual value to the construction; that is, their function is that of auxiliaries. As we will see in §17.1, the auxiliary *tə-* forms complex predicates with anterior meaning, while the auxiliaries *rə-* and *kwa-* form predicates with durative meanings.

The monoclausal character of such complex predicates is corroborated by the following:

(a) First, no constituent, including the ubiquitous connective *ata* 'then', can intervene between the two verbs.
(b) Secondly, the two verbs cannot be negated separately. The ways in which a complex predicate is negated, and contiguity within negated complex predicates, were discussed in §14.1.3.
(c) Thirdly, none of the three polyfunctional verbs retains its meaning as a positional verb when used in a complex predicate since it cannot take an independent locational argument.

Manner sequencing clauses do not have these features—see the discussion in §18.2.

Transitivity-neutralizing constructions may involve other sequencing markers: see discussion in §17.5. In 16.89, the dependent verb takes the completive same-subject marker. This reflects a sequence of sub-events—that the tomatoes might fall down first and then 'stay':

16.89 [yabə-rəb   vækər-ku]   [rə-k-na-di]   [plastikam
       road+LK-STRAIGHT fall-COMPL.SS sit-FUT/IRR-ACT.FOC-3plVT plastic.bag+LK+LOC
       væaga-ku]   [taka-u]   [rə-kwa-di]
       put.inside-COMPL.SS put-1sgIMPV sit-IMPV.3p-pl
       'They (tomatoes) might fall straight onto the road (lit. having fallen they might stay), I shall place them (into a plastic bag) having put them inside the bag, (so that) they may sit (there)'

A similar example is at 15.96. Two analytic questions arise. First, are all these constructions biclausal or monoclausal? The only argument in favour of a biclausal analysis lies in their similarity to other clause-chaining constructions involving switch-reference. However, similarly to complex predicates discussed above, they tend to be treated as one predicate head, since (a) no constituent can intervene between the two verbs; and (b) the two verbs cannot be negated separately. In addition, the two verbs cannot have separate arguments (they have a fused argument structure). This, and the features (a) and (b) above, show that such constructions are on their way towards being treated as one predicate head. Further evidence in the same direction comes from examples like 16.90.

16.90 [vya-təpul-ku]   [kiya-k-na-d]
    kill-'hit'-COMPL.SS die-FUT-ACT.FOC-3masc.sgBAS.VT
    'He will die being killed' (lit. 'Having killed he will die'?)

This is a threat a speaker made to an annoying rooster who she was threatening to kill.

At a first glance, this example appears ungrammatical. The verb *vya-təpul-* 'kill by hitting, kill' is transitive, and its A is not identical to the S of 'die'. However, same-subject marking is not a slip of the tongue. Constructions like 16.90 result from analogical spreading of transitivity-neutralizing constructions with inflected polyfunctional verbs. Once a verb is used in a sequencing structure immediately preceding the fully inflected verb which states its result, the first verb's transitivity is neutralized. So, 16.90 has the same transitivity-levelling effect as the examples 16.86–9.

The second question concerns a possible analysis of such constructions as passives. From both formal and functional perspective, they are very much like stative agentless passive (see criteria for passives in Dixon 1994: 146–7). The underlying A of the transitive verb cannot be expressed and is irrelevant; the focus is on the resulting state. What was an O of a transitive verb is now the S of the whole construction. The construction is even superficially similar to a *be-* passive in many familiar European languages. And we can recall that all the copulas can be used in the meaning of 'be'.

What makes these constructions different from a prototypical passive is the fact that both transitive and intransitive verbs can be used in them, with a similar effect. We saw this in 16.86–8. There is a certain difference between an intransitive verb and its causativized counterpart used in a transitivity-neutralizing structure, but this difference has nothing to do with the verbs' transitivity value. Example 16.91 illustrates a strictly intransitive verb *pa:kw-* 'be hidden', and 16.92 shows its causative counterpart *yi-pa:kw-* 'hide (something or someone)':

16.91 pakwən   rə-na
    be.hidden+SEQ sit-ACT.FOC+3fem.sgBAS.VT
    'She is being hidden' (lit. hidden she sits)

16.92 yi-pakwə-n   rə-na
    say/go?-be.hidden-SEQ sit-ACT.FOC+3fem.sgBAS.VT
    'She is being hidden (by someone)' (lit. 'Having hidden her she sits')

There is an overtone of someone else's intervention in 16.92; but the 'hidden agent' cannot be stated overtly. And the two constructions—16.91 and 16.92—are often used interchangeably.

Transitivity-neutralizing constructions are very frequent in conversations and in narratives. We hypothesize that as a result of their frequency, more and more transitive verbs are coming to be treated as ambitransitives. Further discussion is in §17.5.

16.2.4 Reciprocal-associative, and reflexives

Neither reciprocals nor reflexives are expressed with a valency-changing verbal derivation. The reciprocal and associative marker *awar-wa* is the comitative of the inherently locational noun *awar* 'side; sideways direction' (see §4.4). Both reciprocal and associative uses are consistent with the meaning of the comitative. We saw in §7.9 that the comitative marks a participant in an inherently reciprocal action, such as 'mixing, putting together' in T3.20 and 'fighting' in 7.71. A comitative can mark a participant involved in a reciprocal activity, with the overt *awarwa* as in 16.93a, or without it, as in 7.78.

16.93a ñan gur-a-wa   awarwa və   ma:
      we   you.pl-LK-COM REC   see.NEG FUT
      'We won't see each other' (lit. we with you plural will not see each other)

An alternative may involve double comitative on both participants, to stress that the action is mutual, as in 16.93b and 7.79. Both 16.93a and 16.93b are statements made by the spirit *apawul* about how they are to become invisible to humans.

16.93b ñan gur-a-wa   ñan-a-wa   awarwa və   ma:
      we   you.pl-LK-COM we-LK-COM   REC   see.NEG FUT
      'We won't see each other at all'

In 7.79, the two comitatives are also conjoined with the noun phrase linker *wa*. In terms of its behaviour and position in a clause, *awarwa* is identical to any adverb or oblique constituent. Its position is preferably before the inflected verb, but can vary, depending on its pragmatic status (see §20.2). The reciprocal *awarwa* is never used with singular A/S.

When used in a clause containing a transitive or ditransitive verb, a reciprocal may indicate that A is identical to O and the action is symmetrical, as in 16.93a–b, and 16.94. Once mentioned in one clause, the reciprocal can be omitted in subsequent clauses:

16.94 [awarwa warapwi-taka-ta:y]   [na:gw warapwi-ta:y]   [yapi-ta:y]   [ata
      REC   exchange-put-COTEMP   sago   exchange-COTEMP buy-COTEMP then
      da-di]
      go.down-3plBAS.P
      'Having exchanged (goods) with each other, having exchanged sago, having bought (things), they went downstream'

Or it may indicate that A is identical to addressee, as in 16.95. Here, the Avatip people swore each other to secrecy.

16.95 awarwa wa-sapwi-wa-sapwi-k   wa-sapwi-tukwa
      REC   say-be.open-say-be.open-DAT say-be.open-PROH.GEN
      'As for disclosing (information) to each other, (he said): "do not disclose it"'

A similar example is at 16.96—'be good to each other, treat each other well'. This is an example of a sequencing form used as a command strategy: this is an instruction to siblings to look after each other properly (which was particularly important since their youngest brother had recently died by drowning):

16.96 awarwa rəka:rək kurə-n
      REC   properly make/do-SEQ
      'You must be good to each other' (lit. 'Doing properly to each other!')

The reciprocal may also state the identity between A and a beneficiary, as in 16.97a–b:

16.97a [awarwa gwar   taka-ku]   [ata adakw]   [wa-bər]
      REC   ointment put-COMPL.SS then stay:IMPV say-3duBAS.P
      'Having applied ointment to each other, they said "Good bye (lit. stay!)"'

16.97b [ban [ñiki   da-na-di   ba:n] <u>awarwa</u> vægətə-ta:y] gwar   atak
       back blood go.down-ACT.FOC-3pl back REC   wipe-COTEMP ointment IMPV+put
       'Apply ointment (on) the back, the back on which blood is streaming down, to each
       other'

A similar example is in 4.31, 'giving mortuary feast to each other'.

The reciprocal with an intransitive verb has an implication of multiple participants, and may imply symmetrical action, as in 16.98. The reciprocal itself does not have to be stated, as in 7.78: the comitative marking makes the reciprocal meaning of 'quarrelling' obvious:

16.98 <u>awarwa</u> *karanki*   tə-na-di
      REC   angry/annoyed have-ACT.FOC-3plBAS.VT
      'They are annoyed with each other'

I was warned not to go out at night by myself, since I would be in danger because:

16.99 təp-a-kə-di   du-ta:kw   <u>awarwa</u> kuprap tə-na-di
      village-LK-POSS-pl man-woman REC   bad   be/stand-ACT.FOC-3plBAS.VT
      'Village people are bad to each other (and I could be affected by sorcery)'

The reciprocal may just state a general symmetrical relationship, 'between themselves', as 16.100 (cf. 7.26). These examples involve a transitive verb, 'take wife; marry':

16.100 Waskuk   Gala <u>awarwa</u> ta:kw kra-di
       Washkuk Gala REC   wife get-3plBAS.P
       'The Washkuk (and) the Gala intermarried between themselves' (lit. took wives (from/between) each other)

A similar example is 4.56. This is an explanation of the joking relationship with one's brother's wives. The distributive noun phrase, *kajal kajal* (sister.in.law (brother's wife) sister.in.law), reinforces the reciprocal meaning. The clause refers to a woman making jokes when face to face with a brother's wife (as in 5.16) who is a woman of the opposite clan group, and is not a potential co-wife.

That is, the reciprocal *awarwa* can mark any kind of symmetrical relationship independently of the verb's transitivity or the semantic roles involved. However, the semantic expectations are somewhat different, depending on the verb's transitivity.

The other meaning of *awarwa* is 'associative; together'. This meaning is in line with the main meaning of the comitative (see §7.9). This meaning is attested both with transitive and with intransitive verbs. Example 16.101 comes from the same story as 16.100—if the Gala had not been nasty to the Washkuk, they would have carried on marrying each other (16.100), and building their 'line' of descendants together (16.101):

16.101 [kəta-n-a:b   bəta:y <u>awarwa</u> wañ ba:p taka-n] [ata kurə-n
       now-PRED-TOO already REC   line row put-SEQ then do/get-SEQ
       kwakə-k-na-di]
       seek-FUT/IRR-ACT.FOC-3plBAS.VT
       'Now, too, having established (lit. put down) a line, a row (of descendants) together already, they would have been seeking to act'

An intransitive verb with *awarwa* as an associative marker is shown at 16.102.

16.102 <u>awarwa</u> atawa   rə-di
       REC   like.that sit-3plBAS.P
       'Like that they stayed all together'

The two meanings—reciprocal and associative—are not readily distinguishable—in 16.103 either reciprocal or associative sounds plausible. Both readings are given at 16.103.

16.103 brə-kə-bər   ta:b   wula:n   <u>awarwa</u> kaña-bər
       3du-POSS-du   hand   enter+SEQ   REC   be.stuck-3duBAS.VT
       'Holding hands (lit. having entered their hands), (a) the two were walking stuck together or (b) were walking stuck to each other'

Often only the context determines if the meaning of *awarwa* is reciprocal or associative. An example is at 16.104. A man was attacked by a crocodile and was saved by another man, Kainu, and a few others. Out of context, *awarwa lagu-* could have meant 'pull each other'. In this context, this can only mean 'pull together': there was no reciprocality involved, just a joint effort:

16.104 [awarwa lagu-ma:r-kə-da]   [kə-da   Kainu
       REC   pull-NEG.SUB-FUT-3plSUBJ.P+3fem.sgBAS.P DEM.PROX-masc.sg Kainu
       akuir   kaula-də-k]
       thigh+INSTR   bring+inside-3masc.sg-COMPL.DS
       [puka-yi-k-na-d]   [akəs   war-k-na-d]
       break-go-FUT-ACT.FOC-3masc.sgBAS.VT NEG.IRR   go.up-FUT-ACT.FOC-3masc.sgBAS.VT
       'If they had not pulled all together, after this Kainu brought him away from the Sepik River by his thigh, it (the bone) would have broken, he would have never come ashore again'

In 16.105, *awarwa lagu-* has both associative and reciprocal meanings. It describes a dispute between two boys: they were both pulling the coveted bow and arrow, away from each other:

16.105 a-bər   am-a-wa   nebiya:m   kəbra   lagu-bər
       DEM.DIST-du   bow-LK-COM   arrow+LK+ACC   DEM.PROX.REACT.TOP.du   pull-3duBAS.P
       <u>awarwa</u>
       REC
       'Those two pulled these two (topical) bow and arrow together each away from the other'

In its associative meaning, *awarwa* is partly synonymous with *nakamib* 'together' (see §10.6.1), and in fact can even be replaced with it. Example 16.106 was used as a synonym of 16.100, in an additional explanation of the relationship between the Washkuk and the Gala:

16.106 <u>nakamib</u>   ta:kw   kra-di
       together   wife   get-3plBAS.P
       'They intermarried among themselves (that is, took wives (from/between) each other)'

Examples like 16.106 bear a distinct similarity to the way *wantaim* 'together, with each other' is used in Tok Pisin. And note that the speaker who said 16.106 as a comment to 16.100 was judged by others as speaking very 'carelessly': his Manambu was peppered with Tok Pisin code-switches.

To express a reciprocal and an associative meaning simultaneously, both *awarwa* and *nakamib* are used. Example 16.107 described us taking a picture of each other all together—the whole big family and neighbours were involved:

16.107 <u>awarwa</u> nakamib kayik   kur-kə-bana
       REC   together picture   get-FUT-1plSUBJ.VT+3fem.sgBAS.VT
       'We will take a picture of each other all together'

The associative has a strong overtone of 'togetherness; being next to each other', especially in the case of inanimate objects, as in 16.108:

16.108 <u>awarwa</u> kwa-di   kamna:gw ka:n
       REC   stay-3plBAS.VT food   eat+SEQ
       'eating foods (which are) next to each other (lying on a smoking grid)'

The reciprocal/associative *awarwa* does not occur with singular subjects. And just like most other adverbs, it can modify a noun. Then, the meaning tends to be associative, with the overtone of 'something shared, joint', as in 16.109–10:

16.109 [<u>awarwa</u>   ma:j] aka   wa-tua
       REC/together story DEM.DIST.REACT.TOP.fem.sg say-1sgSUBJ.VT+3fem.sgBAS.VT
       'I am telling (topical) joint story' (shared by all Manambu groups)

16.110 [<u>awarwa</u>   gwalugw]
       REC/together clan
       və-kraki-və-kraki-al-al
       see-carry.across-see-carry.across-3fem.sgBAS.VT-3fem.sgBAS.VT
       'What it (the story) is is a noticeable sign (symbol) of (our) joint clans'

However, even here the exact meaning entirely depends on the context. So, *awarwa wa:r* (REC boundary/mark) means 'joint boundary; shared boundary'. But *kə-di dəya-di awarwa ta:kw* (DEM.PROX-pl they+LK-pl REC woman) means 'these women who are in a peer group relationship to each other', and not 'women to each other', or 'women together'.

In 16.111, the job of building a house is described as a joint enterprise. Pauline Laki, the author of this story, translated *awarwa ja:p* as 'joint work' and also as 'give and take process'. This indicates the close link between reciprocal and associative meanings of which speakers are acutely aware.

16.111 wiya   yawi a   nəmal   a
       house+LK work DEM.DIST+fem.sg   big+3fem.sgNOM DEM.DIST+fem.sg
       <u>awarwa</u>   ja:p-al
       together/each.other   thing-3fem.sgNOM
       'The work on the house is big, it is a thing one does together (or: to each other')
       Pauline Laki's literal translation: 'enormous task of building is also a give and take process'

All these examples show that associative and reciprocal meanings are intertwined, and not so easy to tease apart. And this is where the reciprocal strategies come into play.

We can recall, from §16.1.4, that two directionals on one verb, *-saki-sala-* (outward-'inward') can have a reciprocal overtone (see 16.68). So can the reduplicated directional *-tay-* 'sideways away from speaker' (see 12.67). Their major meanings have nothing to do with reciprocality. But they are used as reciprocal strategies (with or without *awarwa*) as means of avoiding the associative/reciprocal ambiguity of *awarwa*.

A further note on *awarwa*. The noun *awar* 'side, sideways direction' is an inherently locational noun, and is most often used to indicate location (note that it does not take locative case, which is natural for a locational noun), as in 16.112:

16.112 awar-dəka yi:n   və-kə-tua-d
       side-ONLY go+SEQ see-FUT-1sgSUBJ.VT-3masc.sgBAS.VT
       'I will go and look sideways' (also: in a hidden way)

The expression *awar məla:r* (side eye+LK+INSTR) means 'out of the corner of one's eye, in a secretive way'. When reduplicated, *awar* means 'between (two similar things)', as in 16.113:

16.113 awar awar ñəgawa   rə-na
      side side mosquito.net+LK+COM sit-ACT.FOC+3fem.sgBAS.VT
      'It (bag) is sitting between the mosquito nets'

An alternative to *awar* in 16.113 is the connective *aw* 'then, or' (see §4.5) used when something is located between two different objects, as in 16.114. Senapian was not on the map, but Mali suggested that it should be between Swakap and Ambunti:

16.114 aw   Swakap aw   Ambunti, aw   ñədəm
      then Swakap then Ambunti   then middle+LK+LOC
      rə-k-na
      sit-FUT/IRR-ACT.FOC+3fem.sgBAS.VT
      'It (Senapian) should be between Swakap and Ambunti, in the middle'

An etymological connection between *awar* and *aw* is possible, but tenuous. Had *aw* been anything other than a connective, one could have hypothesized that *awar* is formed of *aw* plus the instrumental *-(a)r*.

In contrast to the reciprocal-associative, there is no dedicated reflexive. The reflexive-emphatic *ka:p* 'alone, by itself' is used as a reflexive strategy. The emphatic meaning (by oneself) and the reflexive meaning are difficult to tease apart—see 16.69a and 16.70a. Both occur in clauses with animate and with inanimate subjects.

Another way of expressing a reflexive-emphatic meaning is with a reduplicated personal pronoun—see §10.1, and especially example 10.11.

An additional emphatic strategy involves the adverb *ma:k* 'in person; face to face; oneself':

16.115 nən-a:m   ma:k   və-kə-tua
      you.fem-LK+ACC in.person see-FUT-1sgSUBJ.VT+3fem.sgBAS.VT
      'I will see you in person'

This form can co-occur with a reciprocal-associative, as shown in 16.116. The referent of *ma:k* can be coreferential with the subject. So far, *ma:k* has not been attested in a purely reflexive meaning.

16.116 awarwa ma:k   ma: və
      REC   in.person NEG see:NEG
      '(We) haven't seen each other in person/ourselves'

17

Complex Predicates

Manambu has a variety of complex predicates which consist of more than one grammatical and phonological word. These include:

(i) complex predicates containing auxiliaries—see §17.1;
(ii) complex predicates containing support verbs—see §17.2; and
(iii) lexicalized complex predicates—see §17.3.

Body part and part–whole clausal constructions (referred to as 'body part constructions' and 'part–whole constructions' for short) share similarities with complex predicates—see §17.4. Transitivity-neutralizing constructions which involve clause-chaining markers (§16.2.3) are semantically akin to aspectual complex predicates; see §17.5. Complex predicates involving repetition of the verb were discussed in §12.8.3. A comparison of complex predicates is in §17.6.

We can recall, from B under §4.2.2, that Manambu has ten polyfunctional verbs used as an auxiliary or as a support verb, and as copulas (see Table 4.1). The bulk of this chapter focuses on discussion of these verbs.

Polyfunctional verbs in (i) and (ii) have a grammatical role to play. Auxiliaries impart aspectual or modal meanings to the whole construction, and also serve as carriers for various inflections. Support verbs simply serve as inflection carriers. A complex predicate can contain not more than one occurrence of the same polyfunctional verb in a grammatical function, and only one non-inflected component. That is, an auxiliary is usually incompatible with a construction already containing the same verb as a support verb. Two support verbs can occasionally occur together (as in 17.36a–b). A nominal component of a complex predicate can never be focused. Some can be questioned—see §§17.2–3. Components of complex predicates are underlined throughout this chapter.

17.1 COMPLEX PREDICATES CONTAINING AUXILIARIES

Auxiliaries are defined as a closed subclass of verbs which (a) form part of one complex predicate in combination with an uninflected verb from a large open class; (b) take all the person, number, gender, aspect, tense, mood, and modality specifications required; and (c) impart a modal or aspectual meaning to the construction. There are no restrictions on the transitivity of the lexical verb.

Complex predicates containing auxiliaries cannot contain stative verbs or non-verbal predicate heads. As we can recall from Table 4.1, four of the polyfunctional verbs are used as auxiliaries. The positional verbs tə- 'stand', rə- 'sit', and kwa- 'stay' mark anterior and durative aspects in complex predicates. (They are glossed as 'stand', 'sit', and 'stay' in their auxiliary and support verb functions throughout this chapter.) Aspectual complex predicates consist of a lexical verb marked with the manner sequencing suffix -n and an auxiliary. Aspectual complex predicates are discussed in §17.1.1. The verb kur- 'do, get, become (fully)' marks imminent modality in combination with the same-subject purposive or the desiderative form of a lexical verb (§17.1.2).

Complex predicates discussed in this section can be used in a main and in a dependent clause. An additional type of complex predicate with temporal meaning is restricted to dependent clauses. It consists of a verb marked with the sequential *-n* and the generic completive verb *napa-* accompanied by the appropriate clause-chaining markers (as in 17.25b)—see §18.9. Modal complex predicates of yet another type consist of one of the two modal verbs both meaning 'be able to, can' followed by an inflected verb. These complex predicates cannot be negated, questioned, or occur in a command; neither can they take any of the modalities discussed in Chapter 13. (See §4.5.1.)

17.1.1 Aspectual and positional complex predicates

Aspectual complex predicates express (A) anterior aspect, (B) durative aspect, and (C) prolonged durative aspect. The polyfunctional verbs which occur in all three aspectual complex predicates are also used as positional verbs. In these constructions, they tend to be bleached of their positional meanings. We will see, under (B), that this bleaching is incomplete, and that positional verbs sometimes retain their meanings to do with 'standing' and 'sitting'. Since their choice does not correlate with the shape or any other inherent property of the referent, they cannot be considered classificatory (see Aikhenvald 2000: 159–66, on classificatory verbs in New Guinea languages).

A. AN ANTERIOR COMPLEX PREDICATE consists of the auxiliary *tə-* preceded by the verb from an open class marked with the sequential *-ən*. It refers to an action which may be completed by the time of speech act, and remains relevant for the present. The focus is on the result of an action, as is the case with other aspectual complex predicates. The action itself may, or may not, extend to the present; it is its result that has to be relevant for the present (as in 12.71, 'I have completely forgotten (it)').

This is illustrated in 17.1, with the verb *və-* 'see/look'. The action of 'seeing/looking' started prior to the timing of the main line of the story, and continues to be relevant for the rest of the story because the people keep looking at what is happening.

17.1 [a-də   və-səmul-də-k]   [day du ta:kw ata <u>væn</u>
     DEM.DIST-masc.sg see-LOOK.FOR-3masc.sg-COMPL.DS they man woman then see+SEQ
     tə-di]
     stand-3plBAS.VT
     'As he had searched (for the missing man), the people (men-women) have been looking'

In 17.2 the hen had started looking for the key and has been doing so ever since:

17.2 a-də   kiya:k   <u>kwakə-n</u>   <u>tə-na</u>
     DEM.DIST-masc.sg key+LK+DAT look.for-SEQ stand-ACT.FOC+3fem.sgBAS.VT
     'She (the hen) has been looking for that key ever since'

An anterior complex predicate can appear in a dependent clause, as in 17.3. Kuimagan keeps holding the baby in his arms while his wife Sirunki goes off into the bush. The action expressed with a complex predicate (*yata-n tə-* (carry-SEQ stand-) 'to have been carrying') started before Sirunki had gone off to the bush, and is continuing while she is in the bush.

17.3 [Kuimagan Lai ata   yata-də-d],   [yata-n
     Kuimagan Lai then carry/hold-3masc.sgSUBJ.P-3masc.sgBAS.P carry-SEQ
     tə-də-k]   [Sirunki aka   wula-l]
     stand-3masc.sg-COMPL.DS Sirunki DEM.DIST.REACT.TOP.fem.sg go.inside-3fem.sgBAS.P
     'Then Kuimagan held Lai (in his arms), as he was carrying him, Sirunki went inside (the
     bush)'

The auxiliary in an aspectual complex predicate can be marked for future and for desiderative modality, as illustrated in 17.4.

In the second line, the form *tə-də-k* (stand-3masc.sg-COMPL.DS) is an example of a head-tail
linkage whereby only the inflected, auxiliary, part of the complex predicate gets repeated (see
§20.4.1):

17.4 [gəñər yi-ku   kədəka   væn   ta:d]
     later go-COMPL.SS DEM.PROX+masc.sg+REACT.TOP see+SEQ stand+3masc.sgBAS.P
     [tə-də-k],   [wun lə-kə-k   væn   tə-kər
     stand-3masc.sg-COMPL.DS I   she-OBL-DAT see+SEQ stand-DES
     ya-na-dəwun-ək]   du   ata wa:d
     come-ACT.FOC-1masc.sgBAS.VT-CONF man then say+3masc.sgBAS.P
     'Having gone off later, he had been looking (at the woman), having been looking (at her),
     "I will come with an intention of keeping on looking at her", the man said'

The ways in which the anterior complex predicate is negated, and the issues of contiguity
in non-habitual negative anterior, were discussed in §14.1.3. Examples 14.32–3 illustrate the
semantic difference between negative anterior constructions with the declarative non-habitual
negator *ma:* preceding the whole construction, or just the auxiliary. If the negator precedes the
auxiliary, this implies negative anterior reading: something has not happened in the past, and
this remains relevant for the moment of speech. If the negator precedes the whole construction,
the implication is a complete lack of experience.

A negative habitual anterior is shown in 14.49—here the habitual negator *akəs* obligatorily
precedes the whole complex predicate. The meaning is 'I have never been taking antibiotics'.
An example of positive habitual anterior is at 12.67.

The intensive (marked via a full reduplication of the verb root) can occur in a complex
predicate with auxiliary (see §12.8.2 and §17.1.2). No modality other than the desiderative has
been attested with any of the aspectual complex predicates. Neither can the customary aspect
discussed in Chapter 12 co-occur with an aspectual complex predicate. The reasons for this are
purely formal. We can recall, from §12.7, that the customary aspect requires *tə-* as a support
verb to carry the necessary person-number-gender inflections (see §12.7 and §17.2), since it is
an uninflected verb. And the same verb used as a support verb and an auxiliary cannot occur
in one complex predicate.

A complex predicate with an auxiliary can occur in a command, albeit rarely. There are no
instances of anterior commands in the corpus. We can recall, from §13.2.1, that the polyfunctional verbs *tə-* and *rə-* share the suppletive imperative *ada*. However, all the examples with *ada*
as part of a complex predicate have a distinct durative meaning, and thus reflect the auxiliary
rə-—see B below.

B. A DURATIVE COMPLEX PREDICATE consists of the auxiliary *rə-* preceded by the verb from an
open class marked with the sequential *-ən*. The focus is on the result of an action, as is the case
with other aspectual complex predicates. A durative complex predicate can have past, non-past,
and future reference—see 17.5–6. Further examples are at 16.88 and 16.91–2.

17.5 Japan-adi   ya-n   rə-di
Japan-3plNOM come-SEQ sit-3plBAS.VT/P
'As for the Japanese, they kept coming'

17.6 wun away-bər   wiya:m   war-ən   rə-k-na-dəwun
I   maternal.uncle-PL house+LK+LOC go.up-SEQ sit-FUT-ACT.FOC-1masc.sgBAS.VT
'I will keep going up to the house of my maternal uncles'

A durative complex predicate can combine with a construction containing the suffix *-dəka* 'only'. We can recall, from §12.8.1, that an uninflected verb marked with *-dəka* can be accompanied by an inflected form of the same root, to express persistence and continuity of an activity, as in 12.50 and 17.7:

17.7 mikuli   wa-dəka   wa-n   rə-na
complaint say-ONLY say-SEQ sit-ACT.FOC+3fem.sgBAS.VT
'She keeps only complaining all the time'

A durative complex predicate occurs in commands, as shown in 17.8 (continuation of 17.1: the younger brother commands the people to keep looking). Note the suppletive imperative *ada* which could belong to either *tə-* or *rə-* (§13.2.1). The durative semantics of the construction indicates that *ada* is a form of *rə-*:

17.8 [væn   ada]
see+SEQ stand:IMPV
'Keep looking'

In the instances discussed so far, the positional verbs *tə-* and *rə-* employed as auxiliaries appear to be bleached of their meanings 'stand' and 'sit' respectively. However, this is not always the case. Some actions have a typical position associated with them. For instance, the verb *kapə-* 'wait' is associated with sitting position, and as a result a durative complex predicate in 17.9 receives an alternative interpretation as 'she is sitting (for a long time) waiting':

17.9 lə-kə   du-a:k   kapə-n   rə-na
she-OBL+fem.sg man-LK+DAT wait-SEQ sit-ACT.FOC+3fem.sgBAS.VT
'She is sitting waiting for her husband' or 'She is waiting for her husband'

The two positional verbs 'stand' and 'sit' preceded by a verb referring to a position in space—such as 'be standing' and 'go down'—each marked with the sequential *-ən*, form complex predicates with positional, rather than aspectual, meanings. As shown in 13.1, *da:n rə-* (go.down+SEQ sit) means 'sit down, be seated'—also see 17.10.

17.10 ada   da:n   rə-na-d
DEM.DIST.REACT.TOP+masc.sg go.down+SEQ sit-ACT.FOC-3masc.sgBAS.VT
sayi:m
boy's.house+LK+LOC
'He (topical) sat down (or was sitting down) in boy's house'

A complex predicate *rasə-n tə-* (stand.up-SEQ stand) often means 'stand up, be standing' (as in 13.2), rather than having an expected anterior reading. The verb *rasə-* often has an anterior reading in its other meanings, 'get up' and 'grow up'. An anterior complex predicate *da:n tə-* (go.down+SEQ stand-) would mean 'have gone down'; in contrast, **rasə-n rə-* (stand.up-SEQ sit) does not make sense since, as I was told, 'one cannot stand up and sit down at the same time'.

The positional semantics of 'sit' and 'stand' appears to be maintained in complex predicates by analogy with copula clauses and constructions with a support verb—see §17.2 (especially examples 17.39–40).

C. A PROLONGED DURATIVE COMPLEX PREDICATE consists of the verb *kwa-* 'stay' preceded by a verb from an open class marked with the sequential *-ən*. It describes an action which goes on for a long time, longer than the one described with the durative complex predicate. In 17.11, a prolonged durative complex predicate describes a situation that persisted for a long time.

17.11 day tayir kə-də   təp   warya-n kwa-di
 they before DEM.PROX-masc.sg village fight-SEQ stay-3plBAS.VT/P
 'Before they, (the inhabitants of) this village, kept on and on fighting'

A specific time frame is stated in T2.41: a prolonged action which involved looking after a captured Gala man took the Manambu man two weeks. Like other aspectual complex predicates, the prolonged durative predicate can occur with future, as in 17.12:

17.12 [ñən a-kəs],   [wun kurə-n   kwa-kə-tua]
 you IMPV-catch I   take.care.of/do-SEQ stay-FUT-1sgSUBJ.VT+3fem.sgBAS.VT
 'You catch (shrimp), I will keep looking (after the baby)'

It is instructive to compare the aspectual complex predicate with prolonged durative meaning with the habitual aspect (§12.3 and examples 12.20–1). We can recall that the marker of the habitual is likely to be etymologically related to the polyfunctional verb *kwa-* 'stay'; however, synchronically habitual is quite different from other aspects, and from any of the verb compounding structures. The habitual aspect does not combine with the durative complex predicates. The habitual aspect does not combine with future: a future habitual meaning can only be expressed with a complex predicate involving the verb *kwa-* 'stay'. That is, 17.12 has an additional meaning 'I will habitually look after the baby' (cf. 12.20). Here, the habitual and the durative meanings can only be disambiguated by context.

An aspectual complex predicate can contain two lexical verbs if they describe aspects of the same action, as in 17.13a, b:

17.13a da:n   warə-n   ta:d
 go.down+SEQ go.up-SEQ stand+3masc.sgBAS.VT/P
 'He has been going up and down'

17.13b da:n   warə-n   kwa:d
 go.down+SEQ go.up-SEQ stay+3masc.sgBAS.VT/P
 'He keeps going up and down'

This is similar to complex predicates with the completive verb *napa-* (§18.9), but not to any other complex predicate, including the imminent modality described in §17.1.2.

17.1.2 Imminent modality

A complex predicate with the meaning of imminent modality consists of the auxiliary verb *kur-* 'do, get' preceded by the same-subject purposive form or by the desiderative form of the lexical verb. If the lexical verb is marked with same-subject purposive, the action expressed by it is on the verge of definitely taking place. A chair which had been pushed was rocking, about to overturn:

17.14 [narək narək tə-na] [blakə-k
rock rock stand/be-ACT.FOC+3fem.sgBAS.VT be.overturned-PURP.SS
kur-na]
do-ACT.FOC+3fem.sgBAS.VT
'(It) is rocking, it is about to overturn'

Along similar lines, 17.15 was a speaker's preamble to what he considered a definitive version of the events:

17.15 aw ñan təp-a ma:j, *sampela* wa-saki-ma:j mau taka-k
then we village-LK story some tell-ACROSS-story basis put-PURP.SS
kur-bana
do-1plSUBJ.VT+3fem.sgBAS.VT
'Then we are about to put down the foundation of our village story, some traditional story'

A complex predicate of a similar structure in 17.16 was used to describe a terminally ill woman:

17.16 kiya-k kur-na
die-PURP.SS do/get-ACT.FOC+3fem.sgBAS.VT
'She is on the verge of dying'

And when I said 17.17 it raised an alarm: I was standing in the part of the house where the floor was rotten, and everyone came to my aid, to save me from imminent danger:

17.17 væker-ək kur-tua
fall-PURP.SS do-1sgSUBJ.VT+3fem.sgBAS.VT
'I am on the verge of falling down'

An alternative construction contains a desiderative form of the lexical verb. The meaning is subtly different: the subject is ready to perform the action expressed by the lexical verb but there is an overtone of future projection, intention, and preparation consistent with the overall meaning of desiderative (also see 13.63–4 in comparison with 13.44).

17.18 an bagw-ə-k yi-kər kur-na-bran
we.du party-LK-DAT go-DES do-ACT.FOC-1duBAS.VT
'We two are intending to go to the party'

The action is not as imminent as in 17.15–17, and in fact can be averted. In 13.62, the speaker explains why she had to put the food inside baskets: the intention of the cats to steal the food has been successfully thwarted, and this is expressed with the imminent complex predicate containing desiderative marking. In 17.19 the angry cat was on the verge of scratching the baby—and since this appeared to be more than just an intention, the same-subject purposive was used. This sounds very much like a warning:

17.19 kay-wusə-k kur-na
CAUS-scratch-PURP.SS do-ACT.FOC+3fem.sgBAS.VT
'She is about to scratch'

The imminent predicate with desiderative modality is used in making statements about how the weather may be about to change, as in 17.20. Such statements can hardly be fully definite and do not have the certainty of the same-subject purposive used in this context. This example contains a complex predicate with a support verb *na-* 'be of natural phenomena' (in curly brackets) as a component of the imminent complex predicate.

17.20 {yipayip <u>na-kər</u>}   ada   <u>kur-na-d</u>
      cooler   BE:NAT-DES DEM.DIST.REACT.TOP+masc.sg do-ACT.FOC-3masc.sgBAS.VT
      '(The sun) is about to get cooler'

Imminent complex predicates are negated with *ma:* 'general non-habitual negator' as a separate pro-clause, as shown in 14.67–8 and 17.21 (see §14.3.2). There is a short pause between the complex predicate and the negator.

17.21 [wa:r   <u>yata-k</u>   <u>kur-lə-l</u>   PAUSE ma:],
      big.stringbag carry-PURP.SS do-3fem.sgSUBJ.P-3fem.sgBAS.P PAUSE NEG
      lə-kə   ap   ma:, ap   ma: tə
      she-OBL+fem.sg strength/bone NEG strength/bone NEG have+NEG
      'She was about to carry the stringbag—no, her strength was non-existent, she had no strength'

The imminent complex predicate tends to occur in non-imperative clauses only, and is not compatible with any further modal meanings.

The verb *kur-* 'do, get' occurs with a dative-marked nominal, to indicate that the subject is about to be in a state expressed by this nominal. Consider 17.22 and 17.23:

17.22 [ga:n kamna:gw ma: kə]   [kamək   kur-na]
      night food   NEG eat:NEG hunger+LK+DAT do-ACT.FOC+3fem.sgBAS.VT
      'She didn't eat food at night. She is about to be hungry'

17.23 day ata nəkər-ək kur-di
      they then cold-DAT do/get-3plBAS.VT/P
      'They then were about to get cold'

This construction may have arisen by analogy with the purposive-marked imminent complex predicate. This appears to be especially plausible in the light of segmental similarity between the same-subject purposive on verbs and dative marking on nouns (the two may well be historically related). Synchronically speaking, it can be analysed as an emergent type of complex predicate with modal meaning.

17.2   COMPLEX PREDICATES CONTAINING SUPPORT VERBS

Complex predicates containing support verbs involve uninflected verb forms and a nominal which need a verbal element to be used as predicate heads. In all instances but one, the support verb can be omitted in a main clause.

17.2.1   Support verbs with uninflected verbs and deverbal nominalizations

The vast majority of uninflected verbs require *tə-* 'stand; be, have' as a support verb to be used in dependent clauses, or to express additional mood and modality specifications, such as imperative or prohibitive (as in 12.34). Examples include desiderative (as in 13.63–4), purposive (as in 13.44), customary (as in 12.34–5), and frustrative (as in 13.67). A similar example, with the desiderative accompanied by a support verb as head of predicate in a dependent clause, is at 17.24.

17.24 [ya-kər   tə-mənə-k]   wula-na-wun-ək
       come-DES be:SUP.VB-2masc.sg-COMPL.DS come.in-ACT.FOC-1fem.sgBAS.VT-CONF
       'I am coming in since you wish to come'

Nominalizations with the terminative case -*Vb* can only be used with the polyfunctional verb *tə-* as support verb (see §9.1.1, and 9.10). The meaning of the construction is 'to be on the brink of doing something'—see 17.25a:

17.25a ñan-a-di kamna:gw kusə-kusəb   tə-na-di
        we-LK-pl food   finish-RED+TERM be:SUP.VB-ACT.FOC-3plBAS.VT
        'Our foodstuffs are on the brink of finishing'

Just occasionally another polyfunctional verb can be used with the terminative-case-marked nominalizations, as in 17.25b. Here, the auxiliary *kwa-* 'stay, lie' adds an overtone of prolonged action: the speaker's mother had been on the point of dying for a long time:

17.25b kiya-k   kusə-kusə-b   kwa-n   napa-ku
        die-PURP:SS finish-RED-TERM stay-SEQ COMPL.VB-COMPL.SS
        'After she had been on the point of dying for a long time (she called me back)'

Deverbal nominalizations as parts of complex predicates with the verb *tə-* 'be, stand, have' as a support verb have an intensive and habitual meaning, as in 9.12b. The meaning of a deverbal nominalization accompanied by a support verb is only partly predictable, as shown in §9.1.1. Synchronically speaking, constructions like the one in 9.12b can be considered a special type of complex predicate with intensive-habitual meaning.

Completive aspect (§12.6) requires the support verb *na-*. Examples are at 12.30–1. Uninflected verbs marked with -*rəb* 'fully' (§9.2; §12.8.1) and with -*dəka* 'only' (§9.2; §12.8.1) do not require a support verb; repetition patterns described at §12.8.1 are used instead.

17.2.2 Support verbs with loan verbs

Loan verbs often head a predicate as part of complex predicates with *tə-* 'have, be, stand' as a support verb, as shown in 17.26a–b. This is the only instance when the support verb cannot be omitted from the main clause.

17.26a aw   1963 *transferred* tə-dian   kəka   *East Sepik*
        then 1963 transferred stand-1plBAS.VT DEM.PROX.REACT.TOP.fem.sg East.Sepik
        'Then in 1963 we were transferred here to East Sepik'

17.26b *understand* ada
        understand stand+IMPV
        'Understand, you!'

The support verb strategy is the only one available for loan verbs whose syllable structure is more complex than (C)CVCV, as in 17.26a–b. Verbs of (C)CVCV structure can be borrowed as inflected verbs, as in 17.27a, or as components in support verb complex predicates, as in 17.27b–c. The two strategies appear to be in free variation, as shown in 17.27a and 17.27b (by the same speaker). Traditional speakers have a slight preference towards using loan verbs in support verb constructions.

17.27a də bas *stati*-də-l   kə   wantok ñiuspepa
        he first start-3masc.sgSUBJ.P-3fem.sgBAS.P DEM.PROX.fem.sg Wantok Newspaper
        'He first started the Wantok Newspaper'

17.27b də bas *stati* tə-də-l
he first start stand-3masc.sgSUBJ.P-3fem.sgBAS.P
'He first started (it)'

17.28 [*resain* tə-ku]   təpa:r   ata yi-lwun
resign have-COMPL.SS village+LK+ALL then go-1fem.sgBAS.P
'Having resigned I went to the village'

17.2.3 Support verbs with nominals, onomatopoeia, and expressives

The polyfunctional verb *tə-* is also used as a support verb with nominals, e.g. *kaigən tə-* 'be quiet', *warsam tə-* 'be angry', *kwa:m tə-* 'be crazy', *bapi tə-* 'be soft, spongy, drenched'. The verb *tə-* is the semantically neutral choice: it does not involve any connotation of 'standing'. The two other positional verbs, *rə-* 'sit' and *kwa-* 'stay', can also be used with these nominals. They then impart aspectual and positional overtones to the construction: *kaigən rə-* means 'be quiet for some time, with an implication of sitting position of the subject', and *kaigən kwa-* means 'be quiet for quite a long time'. Further examples are at 17.39–41.

Nouns marked with dative case take *tə-* as support verb, e.g. *manə-k* (leg/foot+LK-DAT) *tə-* 'have something wrong with one's foot or leg', *yala:k* (belly+LK+DAT) *tə-* 'have something wrong with one's belly', or *ab-a:k tə-* (head-LK+DAT be/stand/have) means 'be not quite right in one's head'. The noun *ba:r* 'fever' occurs in a similar construction with *kwa-* 'stay' as support verb: *barək kwa-* (fever+LK+DAT stay) 'have fever, malaria'. As a joke, other nouns can be used in this construction: an annoyingly talkative woman was once referred to as *majək tə-na ta:kw* (speech+DAT have-ACT.FOC+3fem.sgBAS.VT woman), 'a woman who has something wrong with her talking'. The only exceptions are expressions with the noun *kamək* (hunger+LK+DAT) 'for hunger' which can be used with all three verbs: *kamək tə-* 'be hungry', *kamək rə-* 'be hungry (for some time)', *kamək kwa-* 'be hungry for a very long time'.

The polyfunctional verb *rə-* 'sit' can take the adjective *yara* 'well' as its copula complement, e.g. *yara rə-na-wun* 'I am fine'; as well as a number of nouns marked with the locative case, e.g. *stua-m rə-* (store-LOC sit) 'be for sale in a store', *məwula:m rə-* (mind/inside+LK+LOC sit-) 'stay in one's memory', and the uninflected *lotu* 'church': *lotu rə-* 'go to a church'. It also forms idiomatic collocations, e.g. *du-a-k rə-* (man-LK-DAT sit) 'get married (of a woman)', and *makən rə-* (mourning sit) 'be in mourning' (illustrated in 4.19: the sign of mourning is a black string worn around one's neck, wrists, and ankles; 'pan in mourning' was a nickname given to a pan with a black string tied to it).

The polyfunctional verb *na-* is used as a support verb with nominals referring to physical states, natural phenomena, ideophones, and expressives, as shown in 4.24, 4.81, 17.20 (in curly brackets), and 17.29–32.

17.29 gur-a-di   wa:r   pa:m   na-na-di
you-LK-pl stringbag empty BE:NAT-ACT.FOC-3pl.BAS.VT
'Your stringbags are empty'

17.30 gəngən-dəka   na-na-dəwun
tremble-ONLY BE:NAT-ACT.FOC-1masc.sg.BAS.VT
'I am only trembling'

17.31 [karyam   na-lə-k]   adiya   yi-di
      dawn   BE:NAT-3fem.sg-COMPL.DS   DEM.DIST.REACT.TOP+pl   go-3plBAS.VT/P
      'After it had dawned, they went off'

Onomatopoeia—that is, a replication of an actual sound made by a living thing or an object—with *na-* as support verb are illustrated in 17.32–3. A reactivated topic demonstrative can intervene between the non-verbal component of a complex predicate and the support verb:

17.32 [kian kian kian kian kian   na-ku]   yi-tua
      noise.a.hawk.makes   BE:NAT-COMPL.SS   go-1sgSUBJ.VT+3fem.sgBAS.VT
      'Having sounded kian-kian-kian-kian-kian, I go off' (said the hawk)

17.33 krəjan   aka   na-na
      crackling.noise   DEM.DIST.REACT.TOP.fem.sg   BE:NAT-ACT.FOC+3fem.sgBAS.VT
      'It (shell) made a crackling noise'

Expressives are similar to onomatopoeia in that they appear to iconically reflect a natural phenomenon, without, however, replicating it. They are typically repeated from three to five times. In 17.34 an expressive refers to a very dark cloud.

17.34 [gəl   ata   və-də-k]   [ata   warə-n   sək   sək
      dark   then   see-3masc.sg-COMPL.DS   then   go.up-SEQ   EXPR:black   EXPR:black
      sək   sək   na-də-k]   [kətay
      EXPR:black   EXPR:black   BE:NAT-3masc.sg-COMPL.DS   around
      və-də-l   aka]
      see-3masc.sgSUBJ.P-3fem.sgBAS.P   DEM.DIST.REACT.TOP.fem.sg
      'He had then seen the dark (cloud), as it came, as it became black-black-black-black, he then looked at it (the village)'

In T2.25, the expressive *sər* describes a very white colour of a man's teeth glowing in the dark (as the man was hiding standing in a sago trunk). Neither *sər* 'expressive:white' nor *sik* 'expressive:black' are used in any other function. In 17.35, an expressive used with a support verb *na-* refers to fire bursting higher and higher:

17.35 yi   jigər   jigər   jigər   na-na
      fire   EXPR:go.up   EXPR:go.up   EXPR:go.up   BE:NAT-ACT.FOC+3fem.sgBAS.VT
      'The fire is going up and up and up'

We recall, from §12.8.3, that a verbal root can be repeated to express particularly intensive action, or state, as in 12.82, and T2.25 (third line: 'eyes bulging out'). Such expressives also take *na-* as a support verb.

A complex predicate with *na-* as a support verb cannot form an imperative. To be used in a command, it has to occur with an additional support verb *tə-* or *rə-*. This is the only instance of two support verbs occurring in one complex predicate. The non-imperative equivalent of 17.36a is 17.36b.

17.36a {kərkəm   na-n}   ada
       be.silent   BE:NAT-SEQ   sit/stand.IMPV
       'Keep silent!'

17.36b {kərkəm   na-n}   rə-di
       be.silent   BE:NAT-SEQ   sit-3plBAS.VT/P
       'They kept being silent (in a sitting position)'

As we recall, the verbs *rə-* and *tə-* share a suppletive imperative *ada*. Example 17.36c is also a possible non-imperative version of 17.36a. The difference in meaning between 17.36b and 17.36c is congruent with the difference between aspectual complex predicates involving *rə-* and *tə-*.

17.36c kərkəm   na-n   tə-di
      be.silent BE:NAT-SEQ sit-3plBAS.VT/P
      'They have been silent'

The support verb *na-* can be omitted in main clauses, just like any support verb. There is evidence that native speakers conceptualize the combination of the nominal component and the support verb *na-* as one unit. Consider the following conversation. Five-year-old Kerryanne was not sure how to say 'hot' in Manambu, and so she asked her mother in Tok Pisin with one Manambu insert, *təp-a-kudi* (village-LK-language) 'village language':

17.37a *Mama, hotpela long* təpakudi *em i olsem wanem?*
      'Mama, how is "hot" in the village language?'

Mali's reply included not just the lexical item itself, but also the support verb:

17.37b bwiyabwi na-na
      hot   BE:NAT-ACT.FOC+3fem.sgBAS.VT
      'It is hot'

A nominal requiring *tə-* as support verb would be typically given without a support verb, e.g. *məkəmək* 'be silent'. Further evidence comes from child language acquisition. At the age of 3 Kerryanne had a tendency to overuse *tə-* in lieu of other support verbs (much to the annoyance of her elder sister Tanina). For instance, she would say *bæy tə-na* (taste stand:SUP.VB-ACT.FOC+3fem.sgBAS.VT), instead of *bæy yi-na* (taste 'go':SUP.VB-ACT.FOC+3fem.sgBAS.VT) 'It is tasty'. (At the age of 5 she did not do this any more.)

This, and the fact that the verb *tə-* appears as a support verb in a wider variety of contexts than *na-*, indicates that *tə-* could be considered a functionally unmarked choice of support verb. This is consistent with its use as the least functionally marked copula, 'be', 'have', or 'become' (see 4.16–17; further discussion of copula clauses is in §20.1.3). In neither of these copula contexts is *tə-* straightforwardly associated with the meaning of 'stand' which it has as a positional verb.

Other polyfunctional verbs can occur as support verbs for selected nominals, but not for any verbal forms. These involve *yi-* 'say, go', as in *bæy yi-* 'be tasty', *kagəl yi-* 'be painful', *væt yi-* 'be heavy', *karkwas yi-* 'squabble', *bəkəs yi-* 'quarrel', *kakelka:u yi-* 'be in a competition', *kwasək yi-* 'be unwilling' (see 4.22), and *ka:b yi-* 'be greedy, not giving', illustrated in 4.38.

The verb *yi-* can be used instead of *tə-* as a support verb for loans denoting the process of acquiring a state, as in 17.38.

17.38 *les* yi-na-wun-ək   gu   kəka:k
      lazy 'go'-ACT.FOC-1fem.sgBAS.VT-CONF water consume+RED+PURP
      'I am getting too lazy (unwilling) to drink water'

The verb *kur-* 'do, get' occurs as a support verb in a few instances, e.g. *karkwas kur-* 'squabble', *luku kur-* 'steal'. At least some of these instances can be alternatively analysed as lexicalized complex predicates—see §17.3.

17.2.4 How to choose a support verb for a nominal

The semantic principles behind the assignment of a support verb to particular nominals are not always straightforward. While ideophones, expressives, and descriptions of natural phenomena almost exclusively warrant *na-*, for many nominals referring to physical states the choice appears to be arbitrary, and the support verb has to be remembered. The nominal *wiyaw* 'light and dry' requires the support verb *na-*; and the nominal *væt* 'heavy' goes with *yi-*. The nominal *kərkəm* 'silent' requires *na-*, and its near synonym *məkəmək* requires *tə-*, as shown in 17.40.

Alternatively, *məkəmək* (but not *kərkəm*) can occur in an aspectual complex verb containing either *rə-* or *kwa-*—see 17.39 and 14.117. Both 17.39 and 17.40 have distinct positional overtones.

17.39 ma:j   ma: wə,   məkəmək ra:d
      speech NEG say+NEG silent   sit+3masc.sgBAS.VT/P
      'He did not say anything, he kept silent (in sitting position)'

17.40 ta:b ku-sada-taka-ku   məkəmək ta:d
      hand put-INSIDE-put-COMPL.SS silent   stand+3masc.sgBAS.VT/P
      'Having put his hand (inside a pocket) he stood very still'

Two support verbs can sometimes be interchangeable: *karkwas yi-* and *karkwas kur-* 'squabble' are a case in point. Not so for the nominal *kaigən* 'quiet' which requires the support verb *tə-*, *rə-*, or *kwa-* depending on the subject's position and the aspectual value of the clause, as in 17.41a–c.

17.41a kaigən aka   tə-na
      quiet   DEM.DIST.REACT.TOP.fem.sg stand-ACT.FOC+3fem.sgBAS.VT
      'She is quiet' (position unspecified)

17.41b kaigən aka   rə-na
      quiet   DEM.DIST.REACT.TOP.fem.sg sit-ACT.FOC+3fem.sgBAS.VT
      'She is keeping quiet (sitting)'

17.41c kaigən aka   kwa-na
      quiet   DEM.DIST.REACT.TOP.fem.sg stay-ACT.FOC+3fem.sgBAS.VT
      'She is staying quiet' (long time)

If used in the same clause as *yi-*, *kaigən* can only be interpreted as a modifier to *yi-* in its meaning 'go' as a main verb—see 17.42.

17.42 kaigən aka   yi-na
      quiet   DEM.DIST.REACT.TOP.fem.sg go-ACT.FOC+3fem.sgBAS.VT
      'She is going quietly'
      *'She is quiet'

The nominal component of a complex predicate can be questioned, with *atəta* 'how?' (see §10.4), as illustrated in 17.43a–b.

17.43a ab-a   kagəl yi-na
      head-3fem.sgNOM pain 'go':SUP.VB-ACT.FOC+3fem.sgBAS.VT
      '(My) head aches' (lit. is achy)

17.43b ab-a   atəta yi-na?
head-3fem.sgNOM how 'go':SUP.VB-ACT.FOC+3fem.sgBAS.VT
'Head is what?' (lit. Head is how?), i.e. 'What's the matter with your head?'

This is unlike complex predicates of other kinds, where the non-auxiliary component cannot be questioned. We can recall, from §4.2.2, that copula clauses are structurally similar to support verb constructions; moreover, the copula complement shares features with the nominal component of support verb constructions. The ability of being questioned is one such feature.

An additional complication comes into play. Polyfunctional verbs which form aspectual and modal complex verbs and occur as support verbs also appear in what can be considered lexicalized complex predicates. This is the topic of our next section.

17.3 LEXICALIZED COMPLEX PREDICATES

As we saw in the previous section, the choice of a support verb can be fairly unpredictable. Many support verb constructions are lexicalized. Nominal components of lexicalized complex predicates vary in their status: some are full nouns, and others have few nominal properties. For instance, *səkulək* as in *səkulək yi-* (cook go/do) 'do cooking, cook' cannot head an NP in any function other than purpose. Then it is marked with dative case, as in 17.44:

17.44 ñən   adakw   alədab   səkulək-a:k
you.fem stay:IMPV DEM.DIST+fem.sg+DOWN+TERM cooking-LK+DAT
'You (feminine) stay right down there, for (the purpose of doing) the cooking'

Whether a nominal component in complex verbs is part of the verb's argument structure or not is a difficult question. The meaning of complex verbs is idiomatic to a varying extent. For instance, the verbs *ji-* and *sakwi-* are used only in complex verbs with *səp* 'skin', meaning 'be fed up'. The nominal component *məyakw* is not used anywhere except with the verb *kwa-* 'stay'; the resulting complex verb *meyakw kwa-* means 'like'.

Other complex verbs are semantically transparent. The noun *gu* 'water' in *gu yaku-* (water wash) 'bathe' can be interpreted as the unmarked typical location for 'washing oneself'; *sua:l* 'lie, story' can be interpreted as the object of *taka-* 'put', and *kur-* 'do', in expressions *sua:l taka-* and *sua:l kur-* 'to lie'. The verbs *yaku-* 'wash', *taka-* 'put', and *kur-* 'do' are transitive if used on their own. Complex verbs 'bathe' and 'lie' are intransitive. That is, a nominal component of a complex verb may affect the transitivity of the whole.

Numerous complex predicates consist of a nominal which usually cannot head a predicate on its own, followed by a verb from a closed class. They share the following features:

   (i) they form two independent phonological and grammatical words;
  (ii) their components tend to be contiguous, and only constituents such as *ata* 'then', reactivated topic demonstratives, and adverbs can intervene between them;
 (iii) the order of components can be reversed as a means of marking afterthought;
 (iv) the nominal component cannot be questioned;
  (v) the nominal component or the verb can be ellipsed if clear from the context;
 (vi) it is often the case that the nominal component is not used elsewhere in the language; and
(vii) they are translated into Tok Pisin or English as one verb, and when code-switching takes place they are replaced with a one-word verb.

Lexicalized compounds may include a polyfunctional verb, e.g. *sə kwa-* (sleep lie) 'sleep' (12.5, 12.81), *məyakw kwa-* (? stay) 'like'; *luku kur-* (? do/get) 'steal' (7.4, 13.85), *səkulək yi-* (? go) 'cook' (12.10, 17.44). Or they may include another verb with a generic meaning, e.g. *sə-* 'make, plant', as in *ya:p sə* (breath plant) 'breathe', *bas sə-* (first plant) or *ga:m sə-* (? plant) 'shout, serenade, sing', or *wa-* 'say, speak', as in *mikuli wa-* (17.7), or *taka-* 'put' as in *aban taka-* (? put-) 'agree, conspire' and *api: taka-* (? put) 'yawn'. Or both parts may not be used anywhere else in the language, e.g. *agur væ-* 'snore'.

The nominal component may, or may not, be used in the language in other contexts. For instance, *məyakw*, *luku*, or *səkulək*, *ga:m*, and *aban* are not used anywhere other than in complex predicates. In contrast, the form *bas* 'first' appears as an adverb meaning 'first', e.g. *bas yawi waku-* (first work go.out) 'go out for work for the first time' or *bas-a du* (first-LK man) 'first/most important man'. The nouns *ya:p* 'breath, asthma' and *sə* 'sleep' can be used as ordinary common nouns.

The components of lexicalized complex predicates tend to be contiguous, but this is not a steadfast rule. In 12.81 the connective *ata* 'then' intervenes between components. In the last line of 17.45, a repeated adverb *yapwər yapwər* 'very quickly' and the connective intervene between the components of a lexicalized complex predicate. This is a means of focusing on the adverb: the woman was told to cook quickly, and so quickly she cooked:

17.45 wa-də-k   yapwər yapwər <u>səkulək</u> <u>ay</u>,   <u>səkulək</u> ata
       say-3masc.sg-COMPL.DS quickly quickly cooking IMPV+'go' cooking then
       yapwər yapwər <u>ya:l</u>
       quickly quickly 'go'+3fem.sgBAS.P
       'After he had said: "Cook quickly", quickly she cooked'

In 14.122 two adverbs, both loans from Tok Pisin, intervene between the components of the complex predicate *luku kur-* 'steal'. The speaker was lamenting the fact that people steal food from other people's gardens more and more. The negator tends to be placed between the two components, as in 17.46:

17.46 <u>ya:p</u>   ma: <u>sə</u>
       breath NEG plant+NEG
       '(He) is not breathing'

Alternatively, it can precede the whole predicate (as in the first clause of 17.52), with no noticeable semantic difference.

The nominal component of a lexicalized complex predicate can be ellipsed if the predicate is repeated, as in the following dialogue (a continuation of 17.45). In examples 17.47–50, Ø indicates that the nominal component or the verb has been omitted.

17.47 [ata   wa-də-l],   [ñən   <u>səkulək</u> <u>a-y</u>],
       then say-3masc.sgSUBJ.P-3fem.sgBAS.P you.fem cooking IMPV-'go'
       [wa-de-k]   [aka   kəp   Ø
       say-3masc.sg-COMPL.DS DEM.DIST.REACT.TOP.fem.sg right
       <u>yi-k-na-wun-ək</u>]   [ata wa:l]
       'go'-FUT-ACT.FOC-1fem.sgBAS.VT-CONF then say+3fem.sgBAS.P
       'Then he said to her: "You cook!", after he had said (this), "I will do (cooking)", she then said'

Along similar lines, in 'head-tail' linkage only the verb gets repeated, as in 17.48:

17.48 [səkulək ata ya:l]   [Ø ya:n   napa-lə-k]   [ata
cooking then 'go'+3fem.sgBAS.P   go+SEQ COMPL.VB-3fem.sg-COMPL.DS then
wa:d]
say+3masc.sgBAS.P
'Then she did the cooking. After she had done (cooking), he said'

Or the verb can be omitted, as in 17.49–50. Such ellipsis only occurs in highly colloquial register, and only if the non-verbal component is frequent and not used anywhere else, as is the case with *luku* 'stealing'.

17.49 wun-a-di *kaukau*   bə   luku Ø, miyawa
I-LK-pl sweet.potato already stealing all
'My sweet potatoes (have been) stolen, all of them!'

17.50 luku-dəka   luku-dəka   luku-dəka
stealing-ONLY stealing-ONLY stealing-ONLY
'Stealing, stealing, stealing only' (said about young people stealing sweet potatoes from gardens)

When used without the verb, *luku* may have a more general meaning, 'cheating, being unfaithful', as in 15.52. The non-verbal component can be placed after the verb, as an afterthought—as in 17.51:

17.51 pusi kur-kurək,   luku
cat   do-RED+DAT stealing
'(I put the food into a basket hung on the ceiling) so that cats may not steal it (lit. may not take it, that is stealing)'

This afterthought is here used to avoid potential ambiguity: without *luku* the hearer could have thought that cats were going to get the food (we can recall that *kur-* also means 'get'), and not that they were going to steal it, or to get it stealthily.

Complex verbs whose non-verbal components are not so frequent do not seem to allow such ellipsis. For instance, the lexicalized complex predicate *məyakw kwa-* 'like' is hardly ever reduced to just *məyakw*:

17.52 [ta:kw aba:b də-kə-k   ma: məyakw ku],   [alək   ta:kw ma: kər]
woman too he-OBL-DAT NEG liking   stay:NEG this.is.why woman NEG get+NEG
'Women too didn't like him, this is why he didn't get married'

Some lexicalized complex predicates whose non-verbal component is also used as a noun can occur with manner and quantity modifiers which contain either the same noun, as in 10.127a, or a synonymous adverbial expression such as *kwasa gwadəm* meaning 'fast asleep' in 17.53.

17.53 kwasa gwadəm sə   kwa-na
fast.asleep   sleep stay-ACT.FOC+3fem.sg.BAS.VT
'She is fast asleep'

These examples provide further evidence in favour of lexicalized complex predicates as conceptual units with one, unitary meaning. This is corroborated by the ways in which they get translated into Tok Pisin and English, and also how code-switching operates. The complex predicate *məyakw kwa-* (see 17.52) was replaced with Tok Pisin code-switch *laiki-* by a different speaker: so, *məyakw kwa-na-ñən* (liking stay-ACT.FOC-2fem.sgBAS.VT) 'you like (something or to do something)' was given as equivalent to *laiki-na-ñən* (like-ACT.FOC-2fem.sgBAS.VT).

The class of lexicalized compounds may be extended to include a variety of fixed expressions involving polyfunctional verbs and nouns or adjectives, e.g. *yawi kur-* (work do-) 'work'; *sua:l kur-* (lie do) and *sua:l taka-* (lie put) 'lie', *məwulam rə-* (inside+LOC sit) 'stay in one's memory, be remembered', *yara rə-* 'live OK, be in place', *kəp kwa-* (just stay) 'be messing about, doing nothing', *yara kwa-* 'be OK (or not)'. Some such fixed expressions containing positional verbs can be considered copula clauses with a somewhat unpredictable idiomatic meaning (see §20.1.3). They differ from lexicalized complex predicates, discussed at some length in this section, in that their nominal component can be questioned. One can ask *atəta kwa-na?* (how stay-ACT.FOC+3fem.sgBAS.VT) 'How is she?' and receive an answer *yara kwa-na* 'she is fine', or *kəp kwa-na* 'she is messing about, doing nothing'.

Not so with *məwulam rə-* (inside+LOC sit) 'stay in one's memory, be remembered'. One can say *a ma:j məwulam rə-na* (DEM.DIST.fem.sg story inside+LOC sit-ACT.FOC+3fem.sgBAS.VT) and this means 'I remember that story', literally 'that story sits in my inside' (see §21.4 about *mawul* 'inside' as a location for human emotions and memory). But one cannot ask a question *a ma:j agwam rə-na?* (DEM.DIST.fem.sg story what+LK+LOC stay-ACT.FOC+3fem.sgBAS.VT) 'where does the story sit?' and receive an answer *məwulam rə-na. An appropriate answer to such a question would involve a concrete location, for instance, *bukam rə-na* 'it is in the book/notebook'. Similarly with *dua:k rə-* (man+LK+DAT sit) 'get married (of a woman)': a question *sə-kə-k ra:l?* (who-OBL-DAT sit+3fem.sgBAS.P) always has the meaning of 'Who did she marry?' One can question *yawi* in *yawi kur-* 'work', but not *sua:l* in *sua:l kur-* or its synonym *sua:l taka-* 'lie, tell a lie'.

In such idiomatic constructions the verb itself may be so easily recoverable from the context that it can be omitted in elliptical discourse, as shown in 17.54. A woman says 17.54 to the spirit, and the spirit answers 17.55.

17.54 [ata wa-lə-l],   [wun-a:k sua:l kur-ñən-ək]
      then say-3fem.sgSUBJ.P-3fem.sgBAS.P I-LK+DAT lie   do-2fem.sgBAS.VT-CONF
      'Then she said to her, "You are telling a lie to me"'

17.55 wun sua:l ma:
      I   lie   no
      'I am not (telling) a lie'

There appears to be a continuum between semantically compositional constructions containing polyfunctional verbs, and fully lexicalized idiomatic entities. These idiomatic collocations have to be listed in a dictionary.

We will now turn to the discussion of another set of constructions which show semantic and formal affinity with lexicalized complex predicates.

17.4 BODY PART CONSTRUCTIONS AS COMPLEX PREDICATES

Body part constructions consist of a formally unmarked noun followed by a semantically appropriate verb. The noun is a body part, or a physical or other state with respect to which the process is happening. Such constructions describe states, and thus cannot occur in aspectual and modal complex predicates (§17.1).

Many body part constructions in Manambu are composed of a physical state or a body part nominal followed by one of the polyfunctional verbs listed in Table 4.1, e.g. *ka:m* 'hunger' as in *ka:m yasa-/yasə-* 'feel hunger' and *sə* 'sleep' in *sə yasa-/yasə-* 'feel sleepy' (see other examples in 4.26a–d and 17.56a). The order of components is fixed.

17.56a lə   sə   ma: ya:s
        she sleep NEG BE:DESIRE:NEG
        'She is not sleepy'

The noun *gu* 'water' in combination with *yasa-/yasə-* describes thirst, in the Avatip variety:

17.56b gu   yasa-na
        water BE:DESIRE-ACT.FOC+3fem.sgBAS.VT
        '(I) am thirsty'

In the Yuanab variety, the body part term *kwa:l* 'throat' is used instead: *kwa:l yasa-* means 'be thirsty'.

They may also contain verbs other than polyfunctional verbs to do with feelings, e.g. *ji-* and *sakwi-* 'be fed up' (always used with *səp* 'skin, body': see 4.45), or *yaga-* 'be scared'. The verb *war-* 'go up' is often used with *mawul* 'inside', to indicate a state of excitement (as in 14.87), or a physical state, as in 17.57a. The experiencer is not cross-referenced on the verb. It can be supplied if necessary: in 17.57a 'I' appears in brackets since it is optional. The bodily states typically belong to the functionally unmarked feminine gender, and this explains the feminine cross-referencing on the verb:

17.57a (wun) dəpugwəl war-na
        (I)   hiccup   go.up-ACT.FOC+3fem.sgBAS.VT
        'Hiccup (or burp) appears' (lit. goes up)

The verb *waku-* 'go out' is used with *wa:gw* 'sweat' as in 17.58a. Again, the experiencer is not cross-referenced, and is optional.

17.58a (ñən) wa:gw waku-na
        you.fem sweat go.out-ACT.FOC+3fem.sgBAS.VT
        '(You) come out in sweat; sweat is coming out on you'

As mentioned in §17.2, the body part components in such constructions are similar to the nominal parts of lexicalized complex predicates. They are formally unmarked and are never cross-referenced on the verb. The nominal component does not affect the verb's transitivity; and so it is likely not to be part of the verb's argument structure.

All constructions involving body parts allow for variation in their cross-referencing. An alternative to saying 4.45, 'skin is tired', is 4.46, '(I) am skin-tired'. Along similar lines, an alternative to 17.57a is 17.57b and to 17.58a is 17.58b. This property is not found with complex predicates of any other sort.

17.57b (wun) dəpugwəl war-na-wun
        (I)   hiccup   go.up-ACT.FOC-1fem.sgBAS.VT
        'I hiccup (or burp)' (lit. 'I go up in hiccuping/burping')

17.58b wa:gw waku-na-ñən
        sweat go.out-ACT.FOC-2fem.sgBAS.VT
        'You come out in sweat; sweat is coming out on you'

The difference between the two pairs is pragmatic. The experiencer is more likely to be cross-referenced if focused—if the speaker is focusing on their own state or that of their interlocutor, they are more likely to use the b-version. In 17.59a, the speaker is talking about his own urgent desire, focusing on himself. In the second line, he rephrases the statement about his desire to have a shit by using a desiderative with an overt pronoun:

17.59a wun <u>di</u>   <u>yasa-na-dəwun</u>   wun di   yi-kər
     I   faeces BE:DESIRE-ACT.FOC-1masc.sgBAS.VT I   shit go-DES
     'I feel like having a shit, I want to shit'

An alternative would have been 17.59b, from a dialogue—which is a normal way of stating one's need:

17.59b ñən   akrəl?   <u>di</u>   <u>yasa-na</u>
     you.fem where.to shit BE:DESIRE-ACT.FOC+3fem.sgBAS.VT
     ' "Where are you (going)?" "I feel like having a shit" (lit. shit feels)'

Note that no such option is available for complex verbs which do not contain a body part term, e.g. *sə kwa-* 'sleep'.

When a body part construction is used in a dependent clause, the bodily state is cross-referenced on the verb, and the construction requires different subject marking—despite the fact that the same person may be experiencing the state and performing subsequent actions, as in 17.60. In a main clause, an experiencer in body part constructions can be either back-grounded, as in 17.57a, 17.58a, or 17.59b, or foregrounded, as in 17.57b, 17.58b, and 17.59a. A dependent clause does not allow this option: the experiencer is always backgrounded. This is in line with a generally backgrounded character of information within dependent clauses.

Take 17.60. The main clause foregrounds 'me', the experiencer, who is cross-referenced on the polyfunctional verb 'be:desire'. Once in a dependent clause within a head-tail linking structure, the experiencer is backgrounded, and not cross-referenced on the verb of feeling. A different subject sequencing marker is typically required:

17.60 [ka:m   yasa-na-wun],   [ka:m   yasa-lə-k]
     hunger BE:DESIRE-ACT.FOC-1fem.sgBAS.VT hunger BE:DESIRE-3fem.sg-COMPL.DS
     [wa-tua]
     say-1sgSUBJ.VT+3fem.sgBAS.VT
     '**I** am hungry, after I felt hunger (lit. after hunger felt), I am telling (my uncles to feed me)'

We return to the problem of subjecthood in body part constructions in §20.1.4.

Body part constructions often involve terms denoting physical locations of mental states. The most frequent one is *mawul* 'inside', e.g. *mawul war-* (inside go.up) 'be excited, angry', *mawul wukə-* (inside think) 'worry' (see 14.86–7), *mawul taka-* (inside put) 'agree, be agreeable to', *mawul wa-* (inside say) 'think'. Another one is *ya:l* 'belly', as in *ya:l gra-* (belly cry) 'be angry' (see further discussion in §21.4). Similar constructions involve physical concepts, such as being itchy, as in 17.61a–b, or full, as in 17.62a–b. As in the examples above, the difference between versions a and b here lies in the focus on the experiencer. Examples with third person cross-referencing allow for an impersonal reading.

17.61a <u>səp</u>   <u>wusau-k-na</u>
     skin be.itchy-FUT-ACT.FOC+3fem.sgBAS.VT
     'Skin will be itchy (for I/you, or a person in general)'

17.61b wun <u>səp</u>   <u>wusau-k-na-wun</u>
     I   skin be.itchy-FUT-ACT.FOC-1fem.sgBAS.VT
     'I will be itchy in my skin (that is, my skin will be itchy)'

17.62a <u>ya:l</u>   <u>wapruku-na</u>
  belly overflow-ACT.FOC+3fem.sgBAS.VT
  'Belly is overfull' (that is, I am very full)

17.62b <u>ya:l</u>   <u>wapruku-na-wun</u>
  belly overflow-ACT.FOC-1fem.sgBAS.VT
  'Belly is overfull' (that is, **I** am very full)

In 17.61b and 17.62b, 'I' cannot be interpreted as possessor of the body part because of the potential pause between 'I' and the body part atypical for possessive NPs.

To describe properties of inanimate entities, a similar construction type is used. Then, only third person can be cross-referenced, as in 17.63–4:

17.63 [təb <u>gəl</u>   <u>war-na</u>]   [wa:l ja-kər]
  sky blackness go.up-ACT.FOC+3fem.sgBAS.VT rain rain-DES
  'Sky is becoming black (lit. Sky goes up in terms of blackness), it is wanting to rain'

17.64 day   <u>yi</u>   <u>vər-k-na</u>
  mouth fire burn-FUT-ACT.FOC+3fem.sgBAS.VT
  'Mouth will burn' (lit. 'burn in terms of fire') (if you eat hot pepper)

The semantic function of *gəl* in 17.63 and *yi* in 17.64 is similar to manner, or instrument. Formally unmarked body part terms such as *məl* 'eye' and *wa:n* 'ear' can be used in a similar meaning with verbs of perception, to stress their telic perceptual meanings. We will see, in §21.1.2, that *və-* 'see' also means 'try' and 'experience', while *wukə-* has a wide range of meanings from 'hear' and 'listen' to 'obey' and 'worry'. In 17.65 *və-* can only refer to 'looking', and in 17.66 *wukə-* only refers to 'listening' (see §21.1.2):

17.65 məl ap
  eye IMPV+see
  'Look!'

17.66 wa:n a-wuk
  ear IMPV-hear/listen
  'Listen!' (lit. 'ear listen')

Functionally, 'eye' and 'ear' in 17.65–6 are similar to other nominal components of complex verbs, e.g. *gu* 'water' in *gu yaku-* (water wash) 'bathe; wash oneself', and *yanu* 'magic' in *yanu bla-* (magic talk) 'cast a magic spell'.

Just like with other complex predicates, very few elements can intervene between the components of such constructions. Body part constructions are more semantically predictable than lexicalized complex predicates, and their components can be used on their own. Similarly to complex predicates of other types, they consist of two grammatical words (which are also two phonological words) in one predicate slot and form somewhat idiomatic collocations.

17.5 TRANSITIVITY-NEUTRALIZING CONSTRUCTIONS INVOLVING CLAUSE CHAINING

Transitivity-neutralizing constructions involving clause-chaining markers (§16.2.3) are similar in structure and meaning to the aspectual complex predicates discussed in §17.1.1 above. They consist of a verb with a switch-reference-sensitive clause-chaining marker followed by one of the three positional polyfunctional verbs: *tə-* 'stand', *rə-* 'sit' or *kwa-* 'stay'.

In 17.67, the dependent verb is marked as completive. The meaning of the whole construction is akin to the anterior meaning of complex predicates with verb *tə-* discussed in §17.1: the bags have been overflowing with money, and the fact that they remained in this state was relevant for the story as a whole:

17.67 wapwi-wa wapwi-wa <u>wapruku-ku</u>   <u>tə-di</u>
bag-COM   bag-COM   overflow-COMPL.SS stand-3plBAS.VT/P
'The bags have been overflowing (with money)' (lit. having overflowed with money they remained (this way))

If the action of the dependent clause is described as prolonged and overlapping with the main clause, the cotemporaneous sequencing marker *-ta:y* is used, as in 17.68:

17.68 kwarəb <u>yisəwul-ta:y</u>   <u>ta:d</u>   mi:r war-ən
bush   turn.into-COTEMP stand+3masc.sgBAS.VT/P up   go.up-SEQ
'He was turning (into a wild bird) in the bush, going upwards (to tree tops)' (lit. 'As he was turning (into a wild bird) he stood going upwards')

As shown in §16.2.3, the dependent verb can be marked for different subject, as in 17.69, if the two actions are closely related and the O of the first verb is identical to the S of the second verb.

17.69 <u>yi-pakwə-də-k</u>   də ata <u>ra:d</u>
go-be.hidden-3masc.sg-COMPL.DS he then sit+3masc.sgBAS.VT/P
'He stayed (in a sitting position) hidden' (lit. 'he having hidden (him) he sat')

The choice of the polyfunctional verb partly depends on the duration of the ensuing result, and partly on the position of the S. In 17.69, the connotation is that the man was in hiding for some time in a sitting position. If the duration had been irrelevant, the verb *tə-* would be used, as in 17.70.

17.70 adula   təpam   <u>yi-pakwu-da-k</u>
DEM.DIST.INLAND+masc.sg village+LK+LOC go-be.hidden-3pl-COMPL.DS
<u>ta:d</u>
stand+3masc.sgBAS.VT/P
'He stayed hidden in the inland village' (lit. After they had hidden him in the village inland, he stayed)

The verb *kwa-* 'stay' is used in similar structures to describe prolonged resulting state, as in 17.71.

17.71 yi-n   wula:-n   a   təpa:m   <u>rə-ku</u>
go-SEQ enter-SEQ DEM.DIST.fem.sg village+LK+LOC sit/live-COMPL.SS
<u>kwa-dana</u>
stay-3plSUBJ.VT+3fem.sgBAS.VT
'Having gone in and out (lit. gone and entered) they remained in that village' (lit. 'having lived in that village they stayed')

As shown in §16.2.3, on the surface these constructions appear to be biclausal. Yet, they tend to be treated as one predicate head since the two verbs cannot be negated separately, and have a fused argument structure. Their semantics is very similar to that of aspectual complex predicates. They are best considered as emergent complex predicates.

17.6 COMPARISON OF COMPLEX PREDICATES

Table 17.1 contrasts the major types of complex predicates (CP) in terms of the following criteria:

1. TYPES OF INFLECTED VERB: polyfunctional verbs are used in complex predicates containing auxiliaries and support verbs, while lexicalized complex predicates and body part constructions can contain other verbs. This agrees with the major property of polyfunctional verbs: their ability to be used as grammatical markers.

TABLE 17.1   A comparison of complex predicates (CP)

PROPERTY	CP CONTAINING AUXILIARIES	CP CONTAINING SUPPORT VERBS	LEXICALIZED CP	BODY PART CONSTRUCTIONS
1. Types of inflected verbs	polyfunctional verbs *tə-*, *rə-*, *kwa-*, *kur-*	polyfunctional verbs *tə-*, *na-*, *rə-*, *kwa-*, *kur-*, *yi-*	polyfunctional verbs *tə-*, *rə-*, *kwa-*, *kur-*, *yi-*, and some other verbs	all polyfunctional verbs plus other verbs
2. Other restrictions on verbs	any verbs other than stative verbs and non-verbal predicate heads	none		
3. Role of the inflected verb	the auxiliary is inflected, and imparts aspectual and modal values; carries inflection	carries inflection	a nominal and a verb form one lexical unit	provides lexical meaning to construction
4. Combination with other CP	CP with support verb *na-* Lexicalized CP	CP with auxiliary (if support verb is different from auxiliary)	CP with auxiliaries	none
5. Omission of inflected verb	no	yes (except loan verbs)	yes	no
6. Strict order of components	yes	yes	no	yes
7. Variation in cross-referencing depending on focus	no			yes
8. Questioning a component separately	no	yes, with nominals only	no	no

2. OTHER RESTRICTIONS ON VERBS refer to the fact that complex predicates with auxiliaries cannot be formed on stative verbs, or involve non-verbal predicate heads. This sets them apart from other complex predicates.
3. ROLE OF THE INFLECTED VERB as a grammatical marker for complex verbs with auxiliaries and complex verbs with support verbs sets these apart from lexicalized CP and body part constructions which are largely idiomatic collocations.
4. COMBINATION WITH OTHER CPs reflects the restriction on co-occurrence of CPs with same polyfunctional verbs, and other restrictions.
5. OMISSION OF INFLECTED VERB is a property of most CPs with support verbs and lexicalized CPs.
6. STRICT ORDER OF COMPONENTS, or lack thereof, is a property of lexicalized CPs.
7. VARIATION IN CROSS-REFERENCING DEPENDING ON FOCUS is a unique property of body part constructions.
8. QUESTIONING A COMPONENT SEPARATELY is a unique property of some CPs containing support verbs.

Table 17.1 shows that we can distinguish at least four types of complex predicates, in terms of these properties. In addition, complex predicates with support verbs may divide into additional subclasses, with CPs containing loan verbs set apart from the rest by the restriction on the omission of the support verb in main clauses. Unlike any other complex predicates, aspectual complex predicates can contain two lexical verbs.

A certain amount of unpredictability in the choice of support verbs brings them close to lexicalized idiomatic complex predicates.

18

Clause Linking and Dependent Clauses

18.1 CLAUSE LINKING AND DEPENDENT CLAUSES: AN OVERVIEW

Clause linking in Manambu is achieved using a variety of means. The major strategy is 'clause chaining' via medial dependent clauses which in most cases involves switch-reference marking. Other clause-linking devices are considered in Chapter 19. Further issues of semantics of clause linking are addressed in Aikhenvald (forthcoming g).

Neither dependent medial clauses nor dependent clauses of any other sort can be considered core arguments, or complements, of the main clause. They are akin to peripheral arguments in that they provide temporal, conditional, locative, and manner specification to the main clause. That is, they cannot be considered embedded clauses in the way complement clauses would be. Their further affinity with peripheral arguments is corroborated by the fact that their marking may involve one case and the suffix 'like' also used on nouns and noun phrases (§19.3).

Clause chaining via medial dependent clauses is a feature Manambu shares with numerous New Guinea languages, including those within the Ndu family. Clause-chaining constructions have the following properties.

(i) They occur in a sentence which contains one or more dependent clauses whose predicate is not a fully inflected verb, and one main clause. The main clause can contain a verb with any tense, aspect, or mood specification.

(ii) Dependent clauses may be sensitive to whether their subject (A/S) is the same as that of the following clause or not. That is, they may be switch-reference sensitive. Within clause-chaining constructions, canonical switch-reference is defined as 'an inflectional category of the verb which indicates whether or not its subject is identical with the subject of some other verb' (Haiman and Munro 1983: ix). Unlike in a number of other switch-reference languages, the identity of the subjects in Manambu is controlled by an adjacent, and not necessarily by the main, clause within the sentence.

(iii) Dependent clauses tend to precede the main clause. Only one dependent clause can occur postposed to the main clause. This preference for a non-final position of dependent clauses justifies calling them 'medial clauses'. In contrast, the position of juxtaposed dependent clauses (§19.1) and relative clauses (§19.2) is fixed in a sentence. Only some dependent medial clauses can be employed as complementation strategies (see §19.8).

Table 18.1 contains a summary of medial clause markers, their semantics, and correlations with switch-reference marking. The same-subject medial clauses feature uninflected verbs, while different-subject medial clauses contain partially inflected verbs (see Table 11.1). Non-switch-reference-sensitive medial clauses may contain an uninflected verb, or a fully inflected verb.

All medial clause markers are mutually exclusive, with the exception of -ta:y 'cotemporaneous' which can combine with -kəb 'as soon as'. Medial clauses of types 1–5 express temporal relations. Of these, type 1 can also express manner, and type 2 can be interpreted as expressing

TABLE 18.1 Medial clause types and their markers

MARKING	SWITCH-REFERENCE	SEMANTICS	VERB TYPE	CAN HEAD A PREDICATE	CAN BE NEGATED OR REPEATED	OCCURS WITH COMPLETIVE VERB *napa-*
1. -*n* (§18.2)	n/a	simultaneous; manner	Uninflected	yes	yes	yes
2a. -*ku* (§18.3)	SS	(i) temporal completive 'after'	Uninflected	no		
2b. -*k* (§18.3)	DS	(ii) reason	Partially inflected	no		
3. -*ta:y* (§18.4)	SS	cotemporaneous 'before, during and after'	Uninflected	yes		
4. -*taka* (§18.5)	SS	immediate sequence	Uninflected	no		
5. -*kəb* (§18.6)	DS	as soon as: little temporal overlap	Partially inflected	yes		
5a. -*ta:y-kəb* (§18.6)	SS	the action that started before the action of the following clause and overlaps with it	Uninflected	no		no
6. -*lək* (§18.7)	n/a	causal	Fully inflected	no	no	
7. -*ga:y* (§18.8)	SS	unlikely condition	Uninflected	no		

reason. Type 5a is the only complex marker. Type 6 expresses a causal relationship (§18.7), while type 7 expresses unlikely condition (§18.8). Medial clauses with the completive auxiliary *napa-* used exclusively in temporal clauses are considered at §18.9.

The unlikely condition clause (type 7) differs from other dependent clauses in that it cannot be negated; the verb marked with *-ga:y* has to be repeated in the next clause. Neither the causal clause nor the unlikely condition clause can occur with the completive verb *napa-*.

The tense and extent of action expressed in a medial clause is determined by its relationship to the action of a subsequent dependent clause or a main clause within the clause chain. The following options are overtly marked:

- the action of the dependent clause overlapping with that of an adjacent or a main clause: sequencing marking *-n* (§18.2);
- the action of the dependent clause fully completed before the start of the action of an adjacent or a main clause: completive marking *-ku* (SS) or *-k* (DS) (§18.3);
- the action of the dependent clause started before that of an adjacent or a main clause and overlapping with it: cotemporaneous marking *-ta:y* (§18.4);
- the action of the dependent clause completed and immediately followed by that of an adjacent or a main clause: immediate sequence marking *-taka* (§18.5);
- the action of the dependent clause immediately followed by that of an adjacent or a main clause, with a possible short temporal overlap between the two: marking *-kəb* 'as soon as' (§18.6).

Such fine-grained distinctions in temporal relationships between clauses are characteristic of other Ndu languages, such as Iatmul (see Staalsen 1972) and Ambulas (Wilson 1980: 72–4; also see Roberts 1988, 1997).

The only switch-reference-sensitive medial markers which form a same-subject/different-subject pair are the completive markers *-ku* and *-k*. Other markers do not have paired forms, similarly to Iatmul and to Ambulas. The cotemporaneous and the immediate sequence marker require that the subject of the clause they mark be the same as that of the subsequent clause. This requirement may be understood as a consequence of topical continuity of same-subject participants in such situations.

In contrast, the markers with the meaning 'as soon as (little temporal overlap)' and 'same time as: consecutive overlap' do not have the topical continuity requirement. Consequently, their subjects do not have to be the same as those of a following clause.

We will now discuss the semantics and the properties of each of the medial clause types one at a time. Medial clauses can be embedded within one another and form a clause chain—this is addressed in §18.10. In each section, dependent verb forms under discussion are underlined.

18.2 SEQUENCING *-n*

The sequencing medial clause marker *-n* is the most general of all medial clause markers, in terms of its semantics and usage. It indicates that the action of the dependent clause is simultaneous with that of an adjacent or a main clause, or shows a significant degree of temporal overlap with it. In 18.1, the event of the clause marked with *-n* is simultaneous with the main clause: as one road goes off to the left, another comes in on the right.

18.1 [nak aki-taba:r   <u>væki:n</u>]   [nak mapa-taba:r
one left-hand+LK+ALL go.off+SEQ one right-hand+LK+ALL
værad]
come.in+3masc.sgBAS.P
'One (road) going off to the left, one comes in on the right'

In 18.2, the actions of the clauses marked with -*n* are simultaneous; they significantly overlap
with the action of a subsequent clause, marked with the completive -*k*:

18.2 [yi-ku],   [a-də   na:gw {<u>yaku-n</u> <u>yaku-n</u>   <u>yaku-n</u>}] [karya-n]
go-COMPL.SS DEM.DIST-masc.sg sago wash-SEQ wash-SEQ wash-SEQ bring-SEQ
[væk-a:m   væsə-brə-k]   [tə-də-k],   [ata
pot-LK+LOC store-3du-COMPL.DS stand-3masc.sg-COMPL.DS then
wa-brə-d]
say-3duSUBJ.P-3masc.sgBAS.P
'Having gone, as they washed-washed-washed that sago, as they brought (it), having
stored it in a pot, it having stayed, then they said to him'

Repetition of the verb *yaku-* 'wash' marked with -*n* in 18.2 iconically reflects repetition of
the action (see §12.8.3, and examples there). The three occurrences of *yaku-n* are pronounced
as one intonation unit and belong to the same clause—this is why they are in curly brackets
(similar examples are at 12.77–9). No other medial verb form can undergo such repetition.

In 18.2, the subject of the simultaneous clause marked with -*n* is the same as that of the
subsequent clause (marked with the completive -*k*). Not so in 18.3. In the third clause, the
sequential form with -*n* is repeated four times. There is an intonation break between the second
and the third clause which is indicative of a clause boundary. The vowel of the verb in the
second clause is lengthened, iconically reflecting the distance to be travelled:

18.3 [an   yi-kə-ta   aka],   [<u>yi:n</u>],   [<u>yi-n</u>
we.du go-FUT-1duSUBJ.VT+3fem.sgBAS.VT DEM.DIST.REACT.TOP.fem.sg go+SEQ go-SEQ
<u>yi-n</u>   <u>yi-n</u>   <u>yi-n</u>], [ñəd-ə-yabəm   yabə-bra   viti]
go-SEQ go-SEQ go-SEQ middle-LK-road+LK+LOC road+LK-3duNOM+LK two
'This is how we two will go, as (we) go, as (we) go-go-go-go, in the middle of the road
there are two roads'

As can be seen from 18.3 and numerous other examples, 'simultaneity' of the dependent
clause is only one of the meanings of the sequencing suffix -*n*. Its general implication is that
the event was concomitant to some other event—as in 18.3 where the characters were not
necessarily walking simultaneously with the two roads appearing in front of them. Similar
examples of concomitant events are at 14.105 and 14.109 (where the dependent clause follows
the main clause), and T1.33. In 14.110, the second clause marked with -*n* has additional
overtones of reason ('since/as/while you did not come or were not coming').

Clauses marked with -*n* often reflect sequence of actions, as in 18.4—a suggestion by Tanina
that she should, as always, take my microphone down the stairs and put it down in the sun, so
that its solar panel could be recharged:

18.4 [<u>kar-da-n</u>]   [taka-u]
bring-DOWN-SEQ put.down-1sgIMPV
'Shall I take it down(stairs) and put it down?'

Here, the action of the dependent clause clearly has to precede that of the main clause. The two form a closely knit sequence. A dependent clause marked with -*n* can refer to a process which leads up to the result stated in the main clause, as in 18.5:

18.5 [wun <u>warə-n</u>]   ñən-a-pək   tə-k-na-wun
     I   go.up-SEQ   you.fem-LK-LIKE become-FUT-ACT.FOC-1fem.sgBAS.VT
     'I will grow to be like you' (lit. I going up will be like you)

Similar examples are 16.22, 18.6, and 16.19. All of these have an additional implication of manner. Example 16.22 was an instruction to the little girl to drink water from a cup, and not straight from the bucket where the water was stored. Example 18.6 refers to the way of obtaining food.

18.6 [kamna:gw <u>yapi:n</u>]   [kə-kwa-d]
     food   buy+SEQ   eat-IMPV.3p-masc.sg
     'May he eat having bought/buying food' or 'May he eat through buying food (rather than growing his own)'

A one-word clause marked with -*n* is akin to an adverbial modifier. In 18.7, the dependent clause can be translated as 'being hidden', or 'in a secret way'.

18.7 [də <u>pakwə-n</u>]   kə-kər
     he be.hidden-SEQ eat-DES
     'He wanted to eat (stolen food) being hidden (himself)' (or 'in a secret way')

The -*n* marked forms of positional and motion verbs are often used to modify other verbs in adjacent clauses, as in 18.8: here, the sequencing form of the verb *səbən*- 'return, come back' means 'back'. A similar example is in the penultimate line of T2.40.

18.8 <u>səbənə-n</u>   akəs   kui-kwa-na
     come.back-SEQ NEG.HAB give.to.third.p-HAB-ACT.FOC+3fem.sgBAS.VT
     'She never gives (things) back'

Along similar lines, *yi:n* (go+SEQ) in 18.9 does not involve going anywhere—the meaning of this form is 'on and on', and it is used to describe continuous crying for the drowned boy.

18.9 [gra-n gra-n   napa-ku]   [ga:m   sə-dəka   sə-dəka],
     cry-SEQ cry-SEQ COMPL.VB-COMPL.SS shouting plant-ONLY plant-ONLY
     [a   *fondey*-a   ñə yi:n,   ga:n kusəm]
     DEM.DIST.fem.sg Thursday-LK day go+SEQ night finish+COMPL
     '(We) having cried and cried, calling only, that Thursday. (As we went crying and calling) on and on, the night finished'

These forms are being reinterpreted as adverbs; we return to the grammaticalization and reinterpretation of medial verbs in §19.9.

Speakers of Manambu tend to offer sequencing forms marked with -*n* as citation forms of verbs, e.g. *væsə-n* (step-SEQ) 'to step', *væs kapə-n* (grass cut-SEQ) 'to cut grass'. These forms can be used as S in verbless clauses, as in 18.10a–b, and 15.20:

18.10a [gu <u>tu:n</u>   səkulək yi:n]   samasama yawi-a
      water fetch.water+SEQ cooking go+SEQ   a.lot+LK   job-3fem.sgNOM
      'Fetching water and cooking is a lot of work'

18.10b [wiyugw <u>saku-n</u>]   aka-n-aka
       door   push.outside-SEQ REACT.TOP.DEM.DIST.fem.sg-PRED-REACT.TOP.fem.sg
       'This is how is (done) opening (lit. pushing outside) a (traditional) door'

Or they can head the predicate of a verbless clause, and take the appropriate nominal cross-referencing:

18.11a væs   <u>kapə-n</u>-a
       grass cut-SEQ-3fem.sgNOM
       'This (activity) is cutting grass'

A similar example in negative polarity is at 18.11b:

18.11b na:gw kurən   kə   tami: ma:
       sago get+SEQ DEM.PROX.fem.sg area NEG
       'There is no place to get sago in this area'

They can also mark clausal complements of a transitive verb (as in 18.12) or of a ditransitive verb (18.13) (see §19.8):

18.12 [[a   ja:p <u>kurə-n</u>] ma: wa-kə-bra]   [aw   agwa
       DEM.DIST.fem.sg thing do-SEQ   no say-FUT-3duSUBJ.VT+3fem.sgBAS.VT then which
       jap   kə-bər-kəkək]
       (thing) eat-3du-PURP.DS
       'Then if they would refuse doing this thing, then what are they to eat?'

18.13 [*family* <u>kulapu-n</u>]   [<u>vyakanaku-n</u>] atawa *skul*
       family keep.tidy-SEQ improve-SEQ   thus   school
       kui-yikwa-lwun
       give.to.third.p-HAB.P-1fem.sgBAS.P
       'Keeping the family tidy, improving (things), thus I taught (them to do)' (lit. gave school)

Sequencing forms marked with -*n* can be used on a par with noun phrases, similarly to action nominalization. An example is at 18.14.

18.14 [kur-ma:r-kə-bra-di   yawi adiya]   [ñapwi
       do-NEG-FUT-3duSUBJ.VT-3plBAS.VT work DEM.DIST.REACT.TOP+pl firewood
       məwi   yi-n <u>kur-ən</u> <u>karya-n</u>] [gu məwi   <u>tu:n</u>
       things.like.that go-SEQ get-SEQ bring-SEQ water things.like.that fetch.water+SEQ
       wiya:r   <u>kawarə-n</u>] [kə jap   atawa akwər]
       house+LK+ALL carry.up-SEQ this thing thus IMPV+do
       'The work they won't do, things like going getting carrying firewood and things like that, fetching water (and) carrying it up to the house and things like that, do these things! (she usually kept telling them)'

The sequencing forms are not really noun-like in any other way. Unlike action nominalizations (see §9.1.1), the sequencing forms cannot take any cases, be part of an NP, or occur with modifiers. And we can recall, from §17.1.1, that the sequential form -*n* is also used in aspectual complex predicates. This is also the citation form (cf. 16.108). There is no doubt that it is a verbal form, and the most polyfunctional of all medial verb forms in the language. As it occurs in a wide variety of contexts, it can be considered the least functionally marked.

18.3   COMPLETIVE *-ku* 'SAME SUBJECT'/*-k* 'DIFFERENT SUBJECT'

The completive medial markers *-ku/k* indicate that the action of the dependent clause was fully completed before the start of the action of an adjacent or a main clause. An example of same subject in the dependent and the main clause is at 18.15, and of different subject at 18.16.

18.15 [vya-ku]   [kə-kə-bana-bər]
      kill-COMPL.SS eat-FUT-1plSUBJ.VT-3duBAS.VT
      'Having killed (them) we will eat them two'

18.16 [ata wa-tuə-k]   [kə-di   ñan-ugw asa:y ata wa:d]
      thus say-1sg-COMPL.DS DEM.PROX-pl child-PL father thus say+3masc.sgBAS.P
      'After I'd said thus, the father of these children said thus'

The use of same or different subject is frequently triggered by an adjacent clause which may itself be a dependent clause. An example is at 18.17. Switch-reference in clause chaining helps keep track of who did what to whom—this is especially important in the case of third person participants. The subject of the first clause in 18.17 is the same as that of the second clause. But the subject of the main clause is different from that of the following clause which happens to be the main clause.

18.17 [də-kə-də   ñan gu   kə-ku]   [kiya-də-k]   [ata
      he-POSS-masc.sg child water consume-COMPL.SS die-3masc.sg-COMPL.DS then
      gra:d]
      cry+3masc.sgBAS.P
      'After/because his[i] son[j] had died after/because he[j] drowned (lit. consumed water) he[i] (father) cried'

This example highlights the inherent ambiguity of the completive medial clauses—they may express temporal sequence and also reason. The completive verb construction is used as a means of disambiguation—see §18.9.
    A chain of clauses with subject change is often much longer than this. Example 18.18 is a rather typical lengthy clause chain. Further examples include T2.4–5 and T2.13–17.

18.18 [ata a-di   məd   day-a-di   məd-a   sap kay-puti-ku]
      then DEM.DIST-pl cassowary they-LK-pl cassowary-LK skin CAUS-take.off-COMPL.SS
      [taka-da-k]   [rə-da-k]   [day adiya   bəta:y
      put.down-3pl-COMPL.DS stay-3pl-COMPL.DS they DEM.DIST.REACT.TOP+PL already
      məy-a ta:kw patiaku-ku]   [tə-di]
      real-LK woman turn.into-COMPL.SS stay-3plBAS.P
      'Then after those cassowaries took off their cassowary skins, after they put them down, they (the skins) stayed (there), after they (cassowaries) then having turned into real women, they (cassowaries) stood (there)'

A dependent medial clause can be postposed to the main clause, as is the second clause in 18.19. This clause has the same subject as the main clause, and forms one intonation unit with it. We return to this later on in this section. A pause separates second and third clause. Note that the subject of the third clause is the same as that of the subsequent, fourth, clause.

18.19 [abra   da-bər]   [da-ku]   [PAUSE]
      DEM.DIST.REACT.TOP+du go.down-3duBAS.P go.down-COMPL.SS [pause]
      [ka-war-taka   wiya:m],   [ñəg   ka-sapwi-də-k]
      bring-UP-IMM.SEQ house+LK+LOC mosquito.net bring-open-3masc.sg-COMPL.DS

'The two went down, having gone down; immediately on carrying them up (into the house), after he opened the mosquito net [after they went inside the net, the other two then sewed the net across with a needle, having sewn it across, having put (the needle) on top of the bench, he sat (there)]'

That is, switch-reference is a powerful means for tracking referents (see Roberts 1988, 1997). Further examples of different-subject completive are at 7.1, 7.72, 17.31, and 19.31, and of same-subject completive are at 7.18, 7.21, 7.28, 14.111, 14.142, 17.28, and 19.3. Examples 17.4, T2.4–5, and T2.13–18 illustrate lengthy clause chains where the subject change is marked with switch-reference-sensitive suffixes.

If a clause marked as same subject is followed by another clause also marked as same subject this implies that there is no subject change, as in 18.20.

18.20 [[sər   yi-kə-bana]   <u>wa-ku</u>]   [val   <u>kur-ku</u>]
      tomorrow go-FUT-1plSUBJ.VT+3fem.sgBAS.VT say-COMPL.SS canoe get-COMPL.SS
      [adiya   yi-di]
      DEM.DIST.REACT.TOP+pl go-3plBAS.P
      'Having said: "We will go tomorrow", having got the canoe, they went'

In contrast, if two clauses—each carrying different-subject completive marker and identical person markers—are consecutive, the subject does not have to change. This is in fact a means of linking two dependent completive clauses. Consider 18.18 above: second clause 'after they put' and third clause 'after they'd stayed (that way)' are both marked for different subject because their subjects are different from that of the following clause 'having changed into'. This is particularly obvious if the same clause is repeated, either slightly rephrased, as in 18.21, or verbatim, as in T3.37.

18.21 [kar-da-n]   [taka-də-k   ya:m],   [numa-də   ya:m
      bring-DOWN-SEQ put-3masc.sg-COMPL.DS fire+LK+LOC big-masc.sg fire+LK+LOC
      taka-də-k],   [təp-a   du-ta:kw   ata   wa-di]
      put-3masc.sg-COMPL.DS village-LK man-woman then say-3plBAS.P
      'After he'd put (the snake) into the fire bringing it down, after he put (it) into a big fire, village people then said ("What a big snake!")'

The second clause of 18.21 is an infrequent example of a non-verb-final order in a medial dependent clause.

In contrast, a sequence of two clauses each marked for different person of different subjects implies that the subjects are indeed different, as in 17.4 (second and third clauses). Alternatively, if the cross-referencing is the same, but participants are different, at least one of them tends to be stated with an overt NP. In T3.37, the main character, a woman, is the subject of the first clause—hence the feminine singular cross-referencing. The subject of the third clause is different from that of the first clause, but, since night is feminine (see §5.2), it also requires feminine cross-referencing. To indicate that the two 'feminine' participants—'night' and 'woman'—are different, 'night' is overtly stated.

We will see, in §20.4.2, that a clause chain can be interrupted by *ya:kya* or *ya:k* 'all right, OK' whose major function is to indicate that a certain time has elapsed between the actions of the two adjacent clauses. Such interruption also allows the speaker to regain their breath.

Just as in many languages with switch-reference, establishing what counts as same and as different subject is not always straightforward. If the subject of the first clause is part of a (non-singular) subject of the subsequent clause, the two subjects tend to be treated as same. In

18.22, the subject of the first clause is the son, and the subject of the third, final clause is the son and his mother. The medial dependent clauses are marked for same subject.

18.22 [də-a:b-a   kamna:gw kə-ku]   [də-ab-a   gu
      he-TOO-3fem.sgNOM food   consume-COMPL.SS he-TOO-3fem.sgNOM water
      kə-ku]   [ata rə-bər]
      consume-COMPL.SS then stay-3duBAS.P
      'After he (son: not anyone else) too had eaten food, after he (son: not anyone else) too had drunk water, they two (son and mother) then stayed (there)'

Not so in T2.13: Sesawi who had struck the slit gong was among those Avatip men who got together and went off to fight the Gala hiding on top of a tree. Yet his association with his fellow villagers was not as close as that of a mother and a son; hence different-subject marking.

Two quite different referents may acquire same-subject marking if they take part in a closely knit event (see Reesink 1983, on similar phenomena in other Papuan languages). In 18.23, the subjects of the second and the third clause are different—yet they are marked as if they were the same since the sub-events happened almost simultaneously, and the second clause was the direct reason for the third clause: the narrator looked around scared as she had heard the sound of something exploding:

18.23 [ar waku-n]   [pou   na-ku],   [wun
      lake go.out-SEQ sound.of.explosion BE:NAT-COMPL.SS I
      aka   kətaki   və-ku]   [ata wa-lwun]
      DEM.DIST.REACT.TOP.fem.sg look.ACROSS.AWAY see-COMPL.SS then say-1fem.sgBAS.P
      'Going out to the lake, noise of explosion having occurred, I having looked across away (to see what's happening), then said'

We can recall, from §17.4 (especially example 17.60) that body part constructions expressing feelings or states within dependent clauses require different-subject cross-referencing even though the experiencer is the same person. Once in a dependent clause, the experiencer is backgrounded, and not cross-referenced on the verb of feeling. A different-subject sequencing marker is then required. A typical example is at 18.24—the same people felt thirsty, went down to the lake, and drank water:

18.24 [gu yasa-lə-k],   [a-də   gu ata da-ku]
      water BE:DESIRE-3fem.sg-COMPL.DS DEM.DIST-masc.sg water then go.down-COMPL.SS
      [tə-ku],   [ra:n kə-brə-d]
      stand-COMPL.SS sit+SEQ consume-3dusSUBJ.P-3masc.sgBAS.P
      'Having felt thirsty (lit. after water felt), having descended onto water, having done so, they two drank it sitting'

However, body part constructions can be treated as containing the same subject in terms of switch-reference, if the subject is highly topical, as is the pronominal subject *wun* in 18.25:

18.25 [wun ya-tua-l-a]   [wun-a   ta:kw atawa bap
      I   come-1sgSUBJ.VT-3fem.sgBAS.VT-3fem.sgNOM I-LK+fem.sg wife this moon
      və-la-lək],   [alək ya:l gra-ku]
      see-3fem.sg-BECAUSE this.is.why belly cry-COMPL.SS
      [ya-na-dəwun-ək]
      come-ACT.FOC-1masc.sgBAS.VT-CONF
      'It is the case that I have come, because my wife saw the moon (that is, menstruated), this is why having become angry (lit. belly having cried), I am coming'

In 18.26, *məl* 'eye' appears in a body part construction with *pukə-puk pukə-puk* 'bulge and bulge' (see §12.8.3, on the function and meaning of repetition here). The character, who had been hiding in a hollow sago tree, is the topic of this stretch of discourse: he had just been found by an enemy, and is asking the enemy to kill him straight away (this is from a different version of Text 2, told by another speaker). The reactivated topic marker *adəka* in the third clause refers to the topical participant, the subject of 'say':

18.26 [məl pukə-puk <u>pukə-puk</u> <u>na-ku</u>]   [wa-ku],
     eye   bulge-RED bulge-RED BE:NAT-COMPL.SS say-COMPL.SS
     [adəka   wa:d],   [wun-a:m   avi   ya],
     DEM.DIST.REACT.TOP+masc.sg SAY+3MASC.SGBAS.P I-LK+ACC/LOC IMPV+kill EMPH
     [vya-səpa-mənə-k]   [kiyau]   [də ka!]
     hit-body?-masc.sg-COMPL.DS die+1sgIMPV he   DEM.PROX+3fem.sgNOM
     'His eyes bulging out, (he) saying, he (topical) said: "Kill me, after you'd hit me to death may I die". He, "that?" ' (meaning: no way)'

The completive dependent clause has here an additional, recapitulative, function. The same-subject completive form of the dependent verb appears after the main verb, forming one intonation unit with it, indicating the completion of the action of the main verb. Such completive dependent forms never express causal meanings. An example is at 18.27. Curly brackets indicate that the inflected verb in the main clause forms one intonation unit with the verb in the following same-subject dependent clause.

18.27 [tə-də-k],   [kula:r a-də   na:gw ata
     stand-3masc.sg-COMPL.DS axe   DEM.DIST-masc.sg sago   then
     {vya-pravi-də-d],   [vya-pravi-ku]},
     hit-be.hollow-3masc.sgSUBJ.P-3masc.sgBAS.P hit-be.hollow-COMPL.SS
     [waku-də-l]
     go.out-3masc.sgSUBJ.P-3fem.sgBAS.P
     'After he (Kamkudi) had been (there), after he (Sesawi) completed splitting that sago (tree) open (lit. hit open—having hit open), he (Kamkudi) went out (of the sago tree) at that (time)'

A similar example is at the penultimate clause of T2.40 (*kur-ku yi-ku* get-COMPL.SS go-COMPL.SS). We will see, at §19.5, that such recapitulating constructions are particularly frequent with speech reports, e.g. *wa-tua wa-ku* (say-1sgSUBJ.VT+3fem.sgBAS.VT say-COMPL.SS) 'I said' (lit. I said saying) (e.g. 19.74). One additional function of this repetition is to stress that a speech act actually took place: speech reports in Manambu are used in a wide variety of meanings not all of which involve a speech act.

Alternatively, the same-subject form of the verb *tə-* 'stand, be' can be used in the meaning of 'after that', literally, 'having been (like that)'. This form often follows a dependent clause, as in second and third clauses in 18.24—note that the sequence of verbs {*da-ku tə-ku*} (go.down-COMPL.SS stand-COMPL.SS) are pronounced as one intonation group. A similar example is at 18.28: the recapitulating *tə-ku* occurs twice:

18.28 [atawa warə-d   yawi] [a-di   yawi {war-ku]
     thus   go.up-3masc.sgBAS.VT work DEM.DIST-pl work go.up-COMPL.SS
     [tə-ku]}   [təpə-saula-də-k]   [ata rasə-di   ya]
     stand-COMPL.SS be.closed-INSIDE-3masc.sg-COMPL.DS then get.up-3plBAS.P EMPH
     {[rasə-ku]   [tə-ku]}   [væra-ku]   [ta:y   a
     get.up-COMPL.SS stand-COMPL.SS go.across.towards.speaker-COMPL.SS before then

kə	ta:miya	a	kə-di	Maliau
DEM.PROX.fem.sg	area+3fem.sgNOM	then	DEM.PROX-pl	Maliau

kələb	vələ-n	kar-da-da-l]
DEM.PROX+fem.sg+TERM	cut-SEQ	carry-DOWN-3plSUBJ.P-3fem.sgBAS.P

'Thus he went up (to do) work, having gone up to do work, having been (thus), after (the enemy) had blocked (his way), then they got up (against the enemy), having got up, having been (thus), after they'd gone across here, before as far as all this area is concerned, these people from the Maliau clan cut and carried (sago) down up until here'

The form *tə-ku* operates almost like a connective 'thus, and so'. We will see, in §19.6, that this form is indeed in the process of grammaticalizing as part of a connective: *alək tə-ku* (DEM.DIST.fem.sg+DAT stand-COMPL.SS) is used as a clause linker meaning 'and so, as a result'. It is pronounced as one phonological word.

18.4   COTEMPORANEOUS CLAUSE MARKED WITH *-ta:y*

Cotemporaneous clauses indicate the action of the dependent clause which started before that of an adjacent or a main clause and overlaps with it. The suffix *-ta:y* could be related to the adverb *ta:y* 'before' (§4.4).

A dependent clause marked with *-ta:y* in 18.29 describes an action which started before that of the main clause, and continued after the action of the main clause had started, overlapping with it:

18.29 [kə-ta:y]   [wa-na-bər]
      eat-COTEMP   say-ACT.FOC-3duBAS.VT
      'They two talk while eating' (they started eating before they started talking)

Yuaneng instructed Benji to put on a shirt we'd just given him as a present, and to come back to show us:

18.30 [ku-su-ta:y]   [væra-k-na-dəmən]
      put-UP-COTEMP   go.towards.speaker-FUT-ACT.FOC-2masc.sgBAS.VT
      'You will come (to us) having put (the shirt) on and wearing it'

The ancestors of the Makem clan have been killing fish and eating it on their own without telling their relatives from Avatip. The killing of the fish has obviously started prior to them not telling the other lot about it (first clause of 18.31a). In 18.31b (which follows 18.31a in the same story), killing fish had started before 'eating on their own'; the effect of *-ta:y* in the first clause is that they kept killing and eating the fish:

18.31a [kə-di   Makəm   dəy-a-də   warag-a-du
       DEM.PROX-pl Makem.clan they-LK-masc.sg ancestor-LK-man
       alaki   nəma   ar   kami: vya-ta:y],   [ma: wa-sapwi
       DEM.DIST+fem.sg+ACROSS big.fem.sg lake fish kill-COTEMP NEG say-open:NEG
       Apatəp du-a:k]
       Avatip man-LK+DAT
       'The ancestors of the Makem clan having been killing fish across there on a big lake, did not disclose (this) to the man from Avatip'

18.31b [dəy   vya-ta:y]   kapə-ka:p   kə-da-l
     they kill-COTEMP alone+LK-alone eat-3plSUBJ.P-3fem.sgBAS.P
     'Killing fish they ate it (fish) on their own'

It is instructive to compare the three medial clause types we have discussed so far, in terms of their semantics—which is not always easy to render in a translation into English (let alone Tok Pisin).

We can recall, from 18.7, that [*də pakwə-n*] *kə-kər* (he be.hidden-SEQ eat-DES) means 'He wanted to eat (stolen food) being hidden (himself)' (or 'in a secret way'). If a completive form is used, [*də pakwə-ku*] *kə-kər* (he be.hidden-COMPL.SS eat-DES) would mean 'He wanted to eat (stolen food) after having hidden (himself)'. With a cotemporaneous form, the meaning would be subtly different again: [*də pakwə-ta:y*] *kə-kər* (he be.hidden-COTEMP eat-DES) means 'He wanted to eat (stolen food) having been hidden (before he ate, or before he expressed his desire) and staying hidden while eating'.

With an example like 18.32a–b, the difference is rather more illustrative (compare 18.8):

18.32a səbən-ku   akəs   kui-kwa-na
      come.back-COMPL.SS NEG.HAB give.to.third.p-HAB-ACT.FOC+3fem.sgBAS.VT
      'Having come back she never gives (things)'

18.32b səbən-ta:y   akəs   kui-kwa-na
      come.back-SEQ NEG.HAB give.to.third.p-HAB-ACT.FOC+3fem.sgBAS.VT
      'As she is coming back, she never gives (things)'

The cotemporaneous *-ta:y* has an overtone of action or state stretching over time, as in 14.114, 12.37, and T3.43. Two clauses marked with *-ta:y* can be juxtaposed, with a sequential effect, as in 18.33. This is a description of the way of life of the Manambu people hiding in the bush during the Japanese occupation of Avatip:

18.33 [məy-a sə   ma: ku]   [amay-bər   səkulək yi-da-kərəb]
     real-LK sleep NEG stay+NEG mother-ASS.PL cooking 'go'-3pl-AS.SOON.AS
     [ganganək   da-ta:y]   [ñan-a:m   kur-ta:y]   [ata
     night+night+LK+DAT go.down-COTEMP we-LK+ACC/LOC get-COTEMP then
     kray-da-dian   kwarba:r]   [waku-n]   [adaku
     bring-3plSUBJ.P-1plBAS.P bush+LK+ALL go.out-SEQ DEM.DIST+masc.sg+OUTWARDS
     atawa-ta:y   kwa-ba:gwə-dian]
     then+say-COTEMP stay-do.incessantly-1plBAS.P
     '(We) did not really sleep. As mothers were cooking, every night going down taking us they would take us to the bush (to hide)'

The verb or a sequence of verbs each marked with *-ta:y* can be repeated to describe an action that goes on and on, as in 18.34, and T1.29. This is congruent with the general meaning of repetition (see §12.8.3).

18.34 [ñən-a-di   ñan-ugw aw   wun kədəka   {vya-ta:y]
     you.fem-LK-pl child-PL then I   DEM.PROX.REACT.TOP+masc.sg kill-COTEMP
     [kə-ta:y]}   {[vya-ta:y]   [kə-ta:y]}   [ata kə-kə-tua-di]
     eat-COTEMP kill-COTEMP eat-COTEMP then eat-FUT-1sgSUBJ.VT-3plBAS.VT
     'Your children I will eat, killing-eating killing-eating' (said the man taunting a snake)

A sequence of verbs marked with *-ta:y* in 18.34 is pronounced as one intonation group (marked with curly brackets). This is reflected in the English translation with a dash (killing-eating) These verbs share not only the subject, but other arguments as well. Such juxtaposed clauses form a clause union, similarly to above.

Repeated cotemporaneous forms are often used as the only predicates in a clause (see §19.9 on desubordination). The semantic effect is that of an action which keeps repeating itself, as in 4.33—a comment on me getting things and giving them away. Similarly, Celestin commented on my habit of washing my teeth every time I ate anything:

18.35 {kə-ta:y   jan-ta:y}   {kə-ta:y   jan-ta:y}
       eat-COTEMP wash(part)-COTEMP eat-COTEMP wash(part)-COTEMP
       'Eating-washing eating-washing'

This is an example of a desubordinated clause—a dependent clause used on its own.

Just like the same-subject completive form, the cotemporaneous form may have a recapitulating function, adding the meaning of 'keeping on and on' to the main clause. Then, the same verb as that of the main clause occurs in the cotemporaneous form postposed to it, forming one intonation group with it (as in 4.33 'getting and giving').

Cotemporaneous forms can, just occasionally, head the predicate, taking the nominal cross-referencing—just like a sequential -*n* (example 18.11a). The meaning is that of repetitive action.

18.36 gu   tu-ta:y-ad
       water fetch-COTEMP-3masc.sgNOM
       'He kept fetching water'

Alternatively, one or several cotemporaneous dependent verbs can be used with *tə-* 'stand' as support verb. The meaning is that of an action that started before the moment of speech and keeps going on and on. In 18.37, such a construction with four dependent verbs occurs in a main clause, and in 18.38 it is used in a dependent completive medial clause. They share all arguments. In terms of their intonation, they do not differ from other -*ta:y*-marked clauses.

18.37 [waku-ta:y]   [ya-ta:y]   [wula-ta:y]   [pakwu-ta:y]   [ata
       go.out-COTEMP come-COTEMP   go.inside/inland-COTEMP be.hidden-COTEMP then
       tə-dian]
       stand-1plBAS.P
       'We kept on going out, coming, going inland, being hidden'

18.38 [[wun kəka   adaki   *ailanem*
       I   DEM.PROX.REACT.TOP.fem.sg   DEM.DIST+masc.sg+ACROSS.AWAY island+LK+LOC
       na:gw yaku-ta:y]   tə-ku]   [kətaki   və-tu-di]
       sago   wash-COTEMP stand-COMPL.SS look.ACROSS.AWAY see-1sgSUBJ.P-3plBAS.P
       'As I had been washing sago on and on across there on an island, I looked across here'

As mentioned in §17.5, such structures can be analysed as complex predicates with a repetitive meaning whose action had started before the speech act. Their meaning is much more straightforward than that of aspectual complex predicates (§17.1.1): the anterior, durative, or prolonged durative meaning of the aspectual complex predicates arises from putting together the -*n*-marked verb form accompanied by the appropriate auxiliary. In contrast, the repetitive meaning of 18.37–8 is inherent to the cotemporaneous form.

If the position, or duration of action, is to be specified, another positional verb can be used as a support verb with a cotemporaneous form, e.g. *rə-* 'sit' as in 18.39 where the character is in a sitting position.

18.39 [na:gw sau-ta:y]   [rə-na]
sago   fry-COTEMP sit-ACT.FOC+3fem.sgBAS.VT
'She is sitting frying sago on and on' (she had started frying sago before the moment of the narrative)

Examples 18.37–9 illustrate dependent verb forms heading a predicate and requiring a support verb—just like any uninflected verb form would, if used in a dependent clause, or if person, number, gender, and tense specifications are required.

Similarly to the same-subject completive forms, cotemporaneous forms may become grammaticalized. The form *wa-ta:y* (say-COTEMP) 'that way; lit. having been saying' is a case in point. In 18.40, *wa-ta:y* has nothing to do with any speech act; just like *təku* 'thus' discussed at the end of §18.3, it operates as a connective:

18.40 [ata rə-ta:y]   [kə-ta:y]   [ata wa-ta:y   tabu-dian]
then sit/live-COTEMP eat-COTEMP then say-COTEMP escape-1plBAS.P
'Then living (and) eating, that way we escaped (the Japanese)'

Similar examples are at 12.59 and 18.33. The form *ata wa-ta:y* is often pronounced as one word—see §19.6. This grammaticalization path is not surprising given the frequency and the breadth of meaning of the verb *wa-* 'say'—we return to this in §19.5.

18.5   IMMEDIATE SEQUENCE CLAUSE MARKED WITH -*taka*

The medial clause suffix -*taka* is one of the four suffixes which are sensitive to the syllable weight of the root and trigger iambic stress pattern (§2.4.2). The suffix has two allomorphs: -*taka* with heavy roots and -*ta-taka* with light (CV) roots. This suffix requires the same subject as the main clause. It indicates that the action of the dependent clause has been completed and is immediately followed by that of an adjacent clause. In 18.41, the sorcerer opened the stringbag with the baby in it the very moment he got hold of the bag. This idea of the 'very moment' is captured by -*taka*:

18.41 [də a-də   du yata-taka]   [wa:r   ada
he DEM.DIST-masc.sg man carry-IMM.SEQ string.bag DEM.DIST.REACT.TOP+masc.sg
kaja-saki-ku]   [ketad
open.by.moving.apart-ACROSS.AWAY-COMPL.SS look.DOWN
və-də-d]
look-3masc.sgSUBJ.P-3masc.sgBAS.P
'The man opened the stringbag he had carried and looked down into it' (lit. 'he that man immediately on carrying (the stringbag) having opened the stringbag by moving the sides apart, looked down (into the bag) (and put a spell onto the baby that was inside)'

Other examples are at 18.19, 16.19, and 16.29. A clause marked with -*taka* can be postposed to the main clause, as in 14.115.

Just as with the completive same-subject clauses (e.g. 18.20), a sequence of -*taka* clauses share their subjects. An example is in T1.3.

A -*taka* clause which is postposed to the main clause and contains the same verb as the main clause has a recapitulative function, as in 18.42. The two verbs form one intonation unit, and there is no intonation break between them. This is similar to the behaviour of a same-subject completive clause (see 18.27).

18.42 [yi-n,   yi-n,   yi-n,   ñəd-ə-yabər   ata   {waku-di],
       go-SEQ go-SEQ go-SEQ middle-LK-road+LK+ALL then go.out-3plBAS.P
       [waku-taka]}
       go.out-IMM.SEQ
       'Going going going onto the middle of the road they went out immediately on going
       out'

Unlike cotemporaneous clauses and sequencing clauses marked with *-n*, *-taka* clauses cannot
head a predicate. They hardly ever occur desubordinated (that is, without a main clause), and
are much less frequent in texts and conversations than medial clauses of other types.

18.6 TEMPORAL OVERLAP MARKED WITH *-kəb* 'AS SOON AS'

The medial clause suffix *-kəb* is sensitive to the syllable weight of the root, and triggers the
iambic stress pattern (§2.4.2). The suffix has two allomorphs: *-kəb* with heavy roots and *-kə-
kəb* with light (CV) roots. A variant of *-kə-kəb is -kərəb* (see A3 at §2.6). This suffix requires
different subject; consequently the resulting verb is partially inflected. It indicates that the
action of the dependent clause is immediately followed by that of an adjacent or a main clause,
with a possible short temporal overlap between the two. In 18.43, as the Gala people were
eating fish (first clause), as soon as the Avatip people had approached them (second clause,
marked with *-kəb*), the Gala started carefully putting together pieces of limbum palm leaves
(to hide the fish), and gave the Avatip people just coconuts to eat:

18.43 [kə-ta:y],   [Apatəp du   væki-da-kəb],   [rəka:rək bæy
       eat-COTEMP Avatip man go.across-3pl-AS.SOON.AS properly limbum.palm
       taykət-kəta-ta:y]   [təp-a-rəb   kui-da-di]
       join.two.pieces-RED-COTEMP coconut-LK-FULLY give.to.third.p-3plSUBJ.P-3plBAS.P
       'As they were eating, as soon as the Avatip men came across, they having carefully joined
       (pieces) of limbum (to hide the fish), gave them nothing but coconuts'

A similar example is at T2.15: after the Avatip people had come (to fight the Gala fugitives
hiding on top of the tree), as soon as the Avatip people cut the tree (marked with *-kəkəb*), while
the Gala people were throwing spears down from the tree, they (the Gala people) hit the shields
of the Avatip men. Further examples are at 10.59, 12.80, and 16.78.

Adjacent clauses marked with *-kəb* may have different subjects, if the verbs are next to each
other as in 18.44 (clauses 4 and 5), or same subjects (as in clauses 5 and 6) if they are not.

18.44 [kur-ta:y]   [ya:kya] [kaula-ta:y]   [ñam
       get-COTEMP OK   carry+INSIDE/INLAND-COTEMP sun+LK+LOC
       taka-da-kəb]   [rə-da-kəkəb]   [kwas-a-məy səpər-da-kəb]
       put.down-3pl-AS.SOON.AS stay-3pl-AS.SOON.AS small-LK-very dry-3pl-AS.SOON.AS
       [dəy-a-di   kwas-a-kwasa-di beg-a:m   væga-ta:y] [kur-ta:y] [tami-a-tami:
       they-LK-3pl small-LK-small-pl bag-LK+LOC put-COTEMP get-COTEMP area-LK-area
       kwas-a-ñan-ugw   ata   tamiya-tamia:m   dəy-a-di   kapa
       small-LK-child-PL then area+LK-area:LOC they-LK-3pl own+LK
       yarəg-əm   ata   kwa-ta:y] [næy-kwa-na-di]
       village.area-LK+LOC then stay-COTEMP play-HAB-ACT.FOC-3plBAS.VT
       'As they (children) collect (the seeds), OK, as they carry them inland (from the river), as
       soon as they put them (on the ground), as soon as they (seeds) stay (there), as soon as

they (seeds) dry a bit, as they (children) put them (seeds) into their tiny little bags (and) get them, little children from every area having been staying in their own village area, usually play (with these seeds)'

Only if adjacent clauses contain the same verb, as in 18.44, are the subjects the same. Note that they have to be different from those of the next clause. The constituent in slashes / / in the first clause in 18.45 is a complex predicate with a prolonged durative meaning (§17.1.1).

18.45 [ñan-a təp-a:m   walimaudi /waku-n   kwa-də-kəkəb/]
     we-LK village-LK+LOC rainbow   come.out-SEQ stay-3masc.sg-AS.SOON.AS
     [waku-n   təb-a:m   atawa kwa-də-kəkəb]   a   wa:l
     come.out-SEQ sky-LK+LOC thus   stay-3masc.sg-AS.SOON.AS DEM.DIST+fem.sg rain
     ja-səkər
     fall-time
     'In our village as soon as the Rainbow keeps coming out and stays in the sky, that is the time of rain'

This is similar to the behaviour of the different-subject completive -k in adjacent clauses: 18.43 is similar to 18.18, and 18.44 is reminiscent of 18.21.

Unlike other medial clause markers, -kəb can combine with -ta:y 'cotemporaneous'. The sequence -ta:y-kəb and its variant -ta:y-kərəb (always in this order) has the same subject as the following clause, and refers to the action that started before the action of the following clause and overlaps with it. The subject is the same, because -ta:y is the same-subject marker:

18.46 [abakapi wuka   da-ta:y-kərəb]   [ñan-ugw
     hawk   DEM.PROX.ADDR.REACT.TOP.fem.sg go.down-COTEMP-AS.SOON.AS child-PL
     adiya   kə-la-di]
     DEM.PROX.ADDR.REACT.TOP.pl eat-3fem.sgSUBJ.VT-3plBAS.VT
     'The hawk as soon as she has descended here (close to you: she'd started descending before the moment of narrative), ate up the children (of the chicken)'

A similar example is in T3.8. The medial verb forms marked with -kəb can head a predicate, as shown in 18.47.

18.47 nəkə   kəkəpa:t nəkə   kəkəpa:t
     other+fem.sg foodstuff other+fem.sg foodstuff
     kui-də-kəb-ad
     give.to.third.p-3masc.sg-AS.SOON.AS-3masc.sgNOM
     '(This was) as soon as he'd given (them) various sorts of foodstuff'

This is the only circumstance when it occurs desubordinated.

18.7   CAUSAL CLAUSES MARKED WITH -*lək*

The predicate of causal clauses takes the suffix -*lək* which is not switch-reference sensitive. This suffix is a product of recent grammaticalization of the (functionally unmarked) distal demonstrative feminine dative *a-l-ək* 'for that feminine'. We can recall, from §7.4, that causal meaning is congruent with the meaning of the dative case. The form *alək* 'this is why' is also used as a clausal connective (see §19.6).

The causal medial forms differ from all other medial forms. They can be considered fully inflected, because they occur with main clause tensed subject cross-referencing for A/S (see

Table 11.2). However, unlike the inflected verbs in main clauses, no second argument can be cross-referenced. Alternatively, the lack of second argument cross-referencing can be understood as Ø-cross-referencing which corresponds to feminine singular basic non-subject. This agrees with the functionally unmarked character of the feminine singular choice.

This is understandable, from a historical perspective: the second position after the tensed subject cross-referencing is 'occupied' by the 'reason' marking. We can conceive of the Ø-cross-referencing as reflecting the 'reason'.

Unlike other medial clauses, dependent causal clauses can contain verbs marked with the habitual aspect (as in T1.24), and with the action focus, as in 18.48.

18.48 [wañ   wuli-yi-n   kwa-na-lək]   [wun-a
      line   multiply-go-SEQ   stay-ACT.FOC+3fem.sgBAS.VT-BECAUSE   I-LK+fem.sg
      kəp-a:m   vyakət-a   wa-na-dəwun]
      land-LK+ACC/LOC   good-3fem.sgNOM   say-ACT.FOC-1masc.sgBAS.VT
      'Because the (genealogical) line keeps getting bigger and bigger, I say about my land "It is good"'

Some speakers use non-tensed subject markers—rather than tensed ones—in causal clauses, thus making them more similar to other dependent clauses. An example is at 14.116—Kulanawi said *kwar-ma:r-tu-lək* (get.NEG-NEG.DEP-1sg-'BECAUSE) 'because I did not get (a letter)' using the non-tensed form -*tu*- rather than -*tua* (SUBJ.VT) or -*tuə* (SUBJ.P). This is in contrast to 18.49 where a more frequent tensed form is used.

18.49 [wun   ga:n   səkər   yawi   kur-tua-lək],   [alək   wun   ña   səkər
      I   night   time   work   do-1sgSUBJ.VT-BECAUSE   this.is.why   I   day+LK   time
      lapa:m   kaytakawə-n   tə-k-na-wun]
      banana.palm   hang-SEQ   stay-FUT-ACT.FOC-1fem.sgBAS.VT
      'Because I work at night, this is why at day time I will keep hanging on the banana palm' (said the flying fox)

Uninflected verbs in causal clauses require a support verb. Causal clauses are negated with the suffix -*ma:r*, just like all other dependent clauses—see 14.55 and 14.116 (this example contains a causal clause postposed to the main clause). Desubordinated causal clauses are ungrammatical.

A causal medial clause is compatible with the connective *alək* 'this is why' in the main clause—as shown in 18.49. We return to clause linking involving connectives in §19.6.

18.8   UNLIKELY CONDITION -*ga:y*

A medial clause marker -*ga:y*, with the meaning of unlikely condition, 'if, in an (unlikely) case', requires the same subject as that of the following clause and forms an uninflected verb. Medial clauses marked with -*ga:y* take part in a construction involving the root form of the verb with the suffix -*ga:y* followed by the same verb in whatever form is appropriate. In 18.50, it is rather unlikely that we might have to go away; the -*ga:y* form is followed by future. The first clause is a juxtaposed dependent clause, and is marked with intonation (see §19.1):

18.50 [sər   yi-ga:y   yi-kə-kə-bana]   *stuam*
      tomorrow   go-COND   go-FUT-FUT-1plSUBJ.VT+3fem.sgBAS.VT   store+LOC
      [jijap   yapi-k-na-dian]
      various.things   buy-FUT-ACT.FOC-1plBAS.VT
      'If (in an unlikely situation) we go tomorrow, we will buy various things in the store'

In 18.51, the -*ga:y* form appears in a dependent medial clause and consequently is followed by a dependent completive medial verb marked for different subject:

18.51 [wa-su-ga:y   wa-su-da-k]   [yabi:b   wukə-nak]
call-UP-COND   call-UP-3pl-COMPL.DS   quickly   listen/hear-1plIMPV
'Just in case they call up (to the house where we are), let's quickly listen'

In 13.84, the -*ga:y* form is followed by a dative-aversive-marked nominalization. No other constituent can intervene between the verb marked with -*ga:y* and the other verb. A -*ga:y* form cannot be negated. It can be used in a negative construction: 18.52 is an example of the 'unlikely condition' marker occurring in the same clause as a dependent conditional clause introduced by the adverb *kəpa:b* 'in case' (see §13.7 and §14.5.1). We can recall, from §14.5.1 (especially example 14.126), that such dependent conditional clauses are negated with a reduplicated dependent clause negator -*marmar*-. This same negator appears in 18.52:

18.52 [kəpa:b ya-ga:y   ya-marmar-ək]   alək   samasama kamn:agw
in.case come-COND come-NEG.SUB:RED-DAT this.is.why much+LK   food
səkulək   yi-tukwa
cook   go-PROH.GEN
'Just in case if they do not come, this is why do not cook a lot of food'

'Unlikely condition' clauses are rare in all genres of texts, and in conversations. We will see in §19.1 how other conditional meanings are expressed.

18.9   GENERIC COMPLETIVE VERB *napa*-

The completive auxiliary *napa*- forms a complex predicate with a verb marked with the sequencing suffix -*n*. No other constituent, including *ata* 'then', can intervene between the two components. The order can never be reversed: clauses containing *napa*- are strictly verb final. They cannot be negated. A clause containing *napa*- can be postposed to the main clause (see 17.25b).

Using the completive auxiliary is a way of emphasizing that the activity or part of it has been finished. This strong overtone of 'over and done with' associated with *napa*- was corroborated by the paraphrases by some consultants. When helping me transcribe a variety of Manambu narratives, Jennie Kudapa:kw consistently rephrased all the occurrences of *napa*- with *wapa*- 'leave, stop'. In her own speech, she used *napa*- and *wapa*- as synonyms. (A cognate could be *naap* in Wosera/Ambulas, meaning 'fall'.)

Medial clauses containing complex predicates with the completive verb *napa*- have only temporal meaning. This is in contrast to completive-marked dependent clauses (§18.3) which may have a causal meaning: 18.53 refers to temporal sequence, and not to cause-effect, while 18.17 is ambiguous. Complex predicates are in slashes.

18.53 [də-kə-də   ñan /kiya-n napa-də-k/]   [səbən-ən
he-POSS-masc.sg child die-SEQ COMPL.VB-3masc.sg-COMPL.DS return-SEQ
napa-ku]   makən   ata   ra:d
COMPL.VB-COMPL.SS in.mourning then sit+3masc.sgBAS.P
'After/*because his$_i$ son$_j$ had died, after/*because he$_i$ came back, he$_i$ (father) sat in mourning'

A vast majority of clauses containing *napa-* are marked with the completive medial clause suffixes *-ku* (SS)/*-k* (DS). Further examples are at 12.81, 16.11, 16.39, 17.48, 18.9, and T2.13, 33, 35, and 37.

Other medial clause affixes—with the exception of the unlikely condition marker *-ga:y* and the causal *-lɔk*—also occur, but less frequently. In 18.54, a complex predicate with the completive verb *napa-* appears in an immediate sequence clause marked with *-taka*: the focus is on the completion of the action of eating food followed by washing:

18.54 [a-di   kur-da-di   kamna:gw-adi] /kan   napa-taka/
      DEM.DIST-pl get-3plSUBJ.P-3plBAS.P food-3plNOM   consume+SEQ COMPL.VB-IMM.SEQ
      [gu   {ya-ku}   [tə-ku}],   ya:kya, [adiya
      water come-COMPL.SS stand-COMPL.SS OK   DEM.DIST.REACT.TOP+pl
      yi-k-na-di]
      go-FUT-ACT.FOC-3plBAS.P
      'As for those foods they brought on just having eaten them, after they'd entered the water, OK, they went off'

In 18.55 (a version of the story of the Gala war, similar to that in Text 2), *napa-* is used with *-ta:y* 'cotemporaneous'. The Gala people who were hiding on top of a tree would have got food and eaten it down below; this process would be started and completed with some temporal overlap with the action of climbing back up the tree, to hide:

18.55 [kamna: məwi   /kurə-n kan   napa-ta:y/]
      food   things.like.that get-SEQ consume+SEQ COMPL.VB-COTEMP
      [war-da-di]
      go.up-3plSUBJ.P-3plBAS.P
      'As they have been getting food and things like that (and) eating they climbed up (the tree where they were hiding)'

Just like aspectual complex predicates (see the end of §17.1.1), a complex predicate with a completive verb can contain two lexical verbs if they describe aspects of the same action, as in 18.54. Alternatively, the lexical verb can be repeated as in 18.9. A complex predicate with a completive verb cannot contain complex predicates of any other sort. A whole *napa-* clause can never be repeated.

18.10   CLAUSE CHAINING AND SENTENCE STRUCTURE

In a language with extensive clause chaining a sentence contains one main clause and a series of dependent medial clauses each of which specifies relative tense with respect to the main clause or to the adjacent clause. The resulting structure can be dauntingly lengthy and complex. The head-tail linkage between sentences ensures coherence of the text itself, and enables the listener to keep track of the sequence of subevents. Thus, the sub-events are presented as a chain structure—each one connected to the next. T2.3–7 are a prime example of such a chain. The average number of medial clauses per sentence is two to three, as in Texts 1–3. An unusually long sentence with five medial clauses (all same subject) is in 18.56, from one of the numerous versions of the story of Gala wars told by Walinum, a highly proficient story teller.

18.56 [rəka:rək kur-ku],   [bæy   kətəkə-ku],   [a
      carefully look.after-COMPL.SS limbum.leaf cut-COMPL.SS DEM.DIST+fem.sg
      bæyim   taka-ku]   [a-də   dəg kur-yakə-yakə-ku]
      limbum.leaf+LOC put-COMPL.SS DEM.DIST-masc.sg nose get-FULLY-FULLY-COMPL.SS
      [[a-di   wuk-a:m   tə-di   pusəp] də-kə   wa:n
      DEM.DIST-pl tooth-LK+LOC stay-3plBAS.VT rubbish he-OBL+fem.sg ear
      də-kə   ta:m kur-yakə-yakə-ku]   [ata
      he-OBL+fem.sg nose get-FULLY-FULLY-COMPL.SS then
      kur-yakə-yakə-də-d]
      get-FULLY-FULLY-3masc.sgSUBJ.P-3masc.sgBAS.P
      'Having looked after him properly, having cut limbum palm leaf, having put (him) onto
      the limbum leaf, having fully cleaned the nose (lit. having got (things out) of his nose
      completely and fully), having cleaned the rubbish out of his teeth (lit. which was staying
      in his teeth), ears, and the inside of the nose, he cleaned him completely'

A lengthy chain is often interrupted by *ya:kya*, or its variant *ya:k* 'OK, all right', or Tok
Pisin *orait*, as in T2.17. We return to the use of *ya:kya* in §20.4.2.

Other Dependent Clauses and Further Features of Clause Linking

We will now discuss clause-linking devices other than clause chaining via medial dependent clauses (see Aikhenvald forthcoming g, on their semantics). These include: juxtaposition of a dependent clause and a main clause (§19.1); relative clauses (§19.2); clause linking via a case marker 'instead' and a suffix 'like' (§19.3); purposive and desiderative clauses (§19.4); speech reports (§19.5); clause linking involving connectives (§19.6); and juxtaposition of main clauses (§19.7).

Manambu does not have complement clauses as a type on their own. Some types of medial dependent clauses, juxtaposed clauses, purposives, desideratives, speech reports, and nominalizations can be used as complementation strategies—see §19.8. Dependent clauses can be used as main clauses. This phenomenon, known as desubordination, is addressed in §19.9, together with grammaticalization and reinterpretation of 'medial' verbal forms.

Table 19.1 features a comparison of dependent medial clauses, juxtaposed dependent clauses, relative clauses, and main clauses in terms of their constituent order, predicate head possibilities, and tense, aspect, and moods expressed. Relative clauses are more similar to juxtaposed clauses than to clauses of the other two types.

A constituent in a medial completive clause can be questioned, as in 10.80 and 9.33. This is a special property of these clauses which sets them apart from all other dependent clause types, especially relative and conditional clauses (see §10.4).

19.1 JUXTAPOSITION OF A DEPENDENT CLAUSE AND A MAIN CLAUSE

Juxtaposed clauses are a type of dependent clause with no segmental marking. Juxtaposed clauses are preposed to a main clause. They mark absolute tense (unlike medial dependent clauses whose tense is relative to that of the main clause). All aspect and tense distinctions of main clauses can be expressed. Similarly to dependent clauses in general, and unlike main clauses, juxtaposed clauses are negated with the subordinate negator -ma:r-. Uninflected aspectual and modal forms require a support verb to be able to be used in juxtaposed clauses.

A striking feature of juxtaposed clauses is their rising intonation contour with the pitch going up on the last syllable of the predicate. This intonation contour may be the only feature that distinguishes positive juxtaposed dependent clauses from juxtaposed main clauses discussed at §19.7. Juxtaposed clauses are strictly verb final.

Juxtaposed clauses often express condition. Examples with a positive clause expressing counterfactual condition via irrealis marking are at 13.35–6 and 14.55–7 (also see §13.3 and §14.3.1 on irrealis in positive and in negative clauses). Examples expressing real condition are 14.58, 14.123–4, and 18.12. As shown in 14.56, whether the condition is counterfactual or not may depend on the context, given the inherent ambiguity between irrealis and future. Example 19.1 may have either of three meanings: 'if I had gone, I would have told you (the secret)',

TABLE 19.1 Main clauses versus dependent clauses: some distinguishing features

PROPERTY	MAIN CLAUSES	DEPENDENT MEDIAL CLAUSES	JUXTAPOSED DEPENDENT CLAUSES	RELATIVE CLAUSES
1. Constituent order	verb-final tendency; some freedom		strictly verb final: little freedom	
2. Position	not fixed; sentence final tendency		fixed	
3. Predicate head	any word class	only verbs		
4. Uninflected modal and aspectual forms	modal and aspectual forms head the predicate	modal and aspectual forms require support verb		
5. Clausal negation	future negation; past negation; habitual negation expressed	suffix -ma:r- 'dependent clause negation'		
6. Tense	absolute: present/recent past; remote past; future	relative tense meaning fused with dependent clause marking in all clauses	absolute: present/recent past; remote past; future	
7. Habitual aspect	yes	none	yes	
8. Imperative	regularly expressed	none		
9. Juxtaposition with clauses of same type	yes			no
10. Grammatical relations	same as in main clauses			marking of possession differs from main clauses
11. Generic completive verb	not used	used	not used	
12. Focus	any constituent can be focused	any constituent except the predicate can be focused	no constituent can be independently focused	

'if I go, I will tell you (the secret)', or 'when I go, I will tell you (the secret)'. In the actual context, the second reading was the most appropriate: the speaker had not yet gone, was not sure if she was going, and telling the secret depended on her going to another village and learning the details:

19.1 [wun yi-kə-tua]   [ñən-aːk
      I   go-FUT-1sgSUBJ.VT+3fem.sgBAS.VT you.fem-LK+DAT
      wa-kə-tua]
      say-FUT-1sgSUBJ.VT+3fem.sgBAS.VT
      'If I go, I will tell you (the secret)'

That is, a real-condition reading is appropriate in 19.1. This is in contrast to *-gaːy* 'unlikely condition' (§18.8) which always has a conditional reading. Similar examples are at T3.23 and T3.25.

Alternatively, a juxtaposed clause may have a purely temporal meaning. An example is at 19.2: we know that it is not conditional because of the context of the story: the man is bound to hit the road to go back home. This example shows that a juxtaposed clause can be postposed to the main clause, just like most other dependent clauses.

19.2 [atawa saku-ku]   [kə-də   waːr   səmərab
      thus   put/create-COMPL.SS DEM.PROX-masc.sg string.bag never.ever
      kaja-saki-wayik]   [yabaːr   yi-kə-məna]
      open-ACROSS.AWAY-PROH.EXTRA road+LK+ALL go-FUT-2masc.sgSUBJ.VT+3fem.sgBAS.VT
      'Having put (the mangoes together), do not ever half-open the stringbag as you go onto the road'

A similar example is in the first clause of T3.43. Here, the juxtaposed clause cannot possibly have a conditional reading.

A juxtaposed clause does not have to be contiguous with the main clause: in 19.3 a cotemporaneous clause intervenes between a juxtaposed clause and a main clause. This same example shows that a juxtaposed dependent clause can itself contain a medial clause. The 'relative tense' of the medial clause is determined by the absolute tense of the juxtaposed clause.

19.3 [[wula-ku]   sə   kwa-kə-məna]   [[kə-də
      enter-COMPL.SS sleep lie-FUT-2masc.sgSUBJ.VT+3fem.sgBAS.VT DEM.PROX-masc.sg
      tə-na-d-ə   gwarabim] wudika
      be-ACT.FOC-3masc.sgBAS.VT-LK mango+LOC DEM.PROX.ADDR.REACT.TOP+pl
      wur-yakə-taːy]   [yi-k-na-di]
      fly-FULLY-COTEMP go-FUT-ACT.FOC-3plBAS.VT
      'If you sleep having entered (mosquito net or house), these (topical) close to you on the mango tree which is staying here will go away flying off'

Juxtaposed clauses are similar to main clauses in most ways, except negation. No such clauses have been documented in related languages. This clause type may constitute a recent innovation.

19.2 RELATIVE CLAUSES

Relative clauses (see Table 19.1) involve an inflected verb—see §19.2.1. An alternative relativization strategy is verb-noun compounding—see §19.2.2. The two are compared in §19.2.3.

19.2.1   Relative clauses with an inflected verb

Relative clauses in Manambu are restrictive. The main clause and the relative clause must have an argument in common. The shared argument can be stated in the main clause, but does not have to be. It is not stated in the relative clause. Headless relative clauses are treated on a par with any other constituents of the main clause. A relative clause typically follows the demonstrative and precedes an adjective within an NP (see §20.1.1).

Relative clauses share properties with a main clause: the predicate can be an inflected or a partially inflected verb. Similarly to other dependent clauses, no predicate head other than a verb can be used in a relative clause. Uninflected verbal forms and non-verbal predicate heads require a support verb (typically, *tə-* 'stand/be') (see §17.2).

Relative clauses are strictly verb final. All tenses, aspects, and modalities can be expressed. Unlike medial dependent clauses, but similarly to juxtaposed dependent clauses, no constituent within a relative clause can be independently focused. The predicate of a relative clause can have one or two cross-referencing positions (following the same principles as in the main clauses: see Chapter 3). It always requires the linker -*ə* after a word-final stop. The last cross-referencing position agrees with the common argument. Relative clauses are negated with the dependent clause negator -*ma:r-*, just like other dependent clauses.

Relative clauses have no special segmental marking. Monosyllabic verbs have a somewhat special form in relative clauses. We can recall, from §11.3.2, that when monosyllabic verbs consisting of CV, with a root vowel either *ə* or *a*, take a suffix and the resulting form is monosyllabic, the root vowel is lengthened. And the verbs with vowel *a* and with *ə* are then homophonous, e.g. *rə-* 'sit', *ra-* 'cut', and *ra:d* (sit/cut+3masc.sgBAS.P) 'he sat/cut'. When such verbs appear in relative clauses, they do not undergo vowel lengthening and there is no homophony, e.g. *rə-d-ə du* (sit-3masc.sgBAS.VT/P-LK man) 'man who sits/sat', *ra-d-ə du* (cut-3masc.sgBAS.VT/P-LK man) 'man who cut(s)'. The reason lies in the syllabic structure: since a relative clause is in the modifier slot to a noun, it requires a linker (see §4.1.1), and this linker adds an extra syllable to a monosyllabic verb. Consequently, its root vowel remains unaltered.

As we saw in Table 19.1, relative clauses are similar to juxtaposed dependent clauses. However, they lack a special rising intonation contour; instead they tend to form one phonological phrase with the common argument. If used headlessly (as in 14.122 and T2.67) they have the same phonological properties as any headless NP.

Any core or peripheral argument, including locative, temporal, instruments, associated arguments, and possessors, can appear as a common argument (CA) in a relative clause. There are very few restrictions on the function of the common argument in a main clause. Only the argument of the three postpositions *kətək* 'like; similarly', *wukən* 'together with', and *kukə-* 'behind' cannot be relativized on. This appears to go against the hierarchy established by Keenan and Comrie (1977): according to the hierarchy, if a language can relativize on a possessor, it is expected to relativize on the argument of an adposition. A tentative explanation is offered at the end of this section.

The CA in A function in a relative clause and the S function in the main clause is shown in 19.4. A similar example is at 14.122 (where a headless relative clause contains the CA in A function, which is also in the A function in the main clause).

19.4 a   [brə-kə-m   yaku-ya-l   ta:kw-a:b]   [a
        then 3du-OBL-OBJ wash-come-3fem.sgBAS.P woman-TOO then
        kiya-na   ya]
        die-ACT.FOC+3fem.sgBAS.VT EMPH
        'Then, the woman, too, who kept washing you two, has indeed died'

In 19.5 the CA is in S function in the relative clause, and S in the main clause. A similar example is in T1.31: the CA is the S of the relative clause, and the A of the main clause ('(We)-the people who stay on the earth see the moon').

19.5　[dəy-a-də　　　　　ta:y waku-d-ə　　　　　　　yibun-mi] [tayir
　　　they-LK-3masc.sg first go.out-3masc.sgBAS.VT-LK shore-tree first+ADV
　　　ñaj　　　　　tə-də-l-pək]　　　　　　　　　　　[ata　wa:d]
　　　father's.brother stay-3masc.sgSUBJ.P-3fem.sgBAS.VT-like then say+3masc.sgBAS.P
　　　'Their chief (lit. shore-tree) who appeared (lit. went out) first, (being a chief) like father's brother (who was here) before, then said'

In 19.6 the common argument is itself the head of a non-verbal predicate. A similar example is in T1.26 ('this is the moon who keeps shining all over this earth'), and at 14.118a–b.

19.6　[væra-d-ə　　　　　　　　　　　　　du]-ad
　　　come.across.towards-3masc.sgSUBJ.VT/P-LK man-3masc.sgNOM
　　　'It is a man who is coming across towards (us)'

In 19.7 the common argument is an O in the relative clause and S in the controlling clause. Note that the relative clause occurs together with an adjective 'small' in the same NP preceding the adjective:

19.7　[[kwatiya-tua　　　　　　　　　　kwasa　　　lapa-ñəg]
　　　give.to.nonthird.p-1sgSUBJ.VT+3fem.sgBAS.VT small.fem.sg banana+LK-leaf
　　　kray-ku]　　　[mən-a-mən-a　　　　taba:m　　　tə-kwa]
　　　bring-COMPL.SS you.masc-LK-you.masc-LK hand+LK+LOC stay-IMPV.3p+fem.sg
　　　'After you have brought the small book (lit. banana leaf) I gave you (to the village), may it stay in your hand' (that is, do not let your sister get it)

In 18.14, the first clause of 16.40 and in the third line of T1.4, the CA is the O in both relative clause and main clause. In 19.45, it is the O of the relative clause and a location in a main clause. In 18.56 ('having cleaned [...] the rubbish which was staying in his teeth'), the CA is the S of the relative clause and the O of the main clause. This is also an example of a relative clause within a dependent clause. A similar example is at 19.8: the CA is S of the relative clause (with an aspectual complex predicate which has a transitivity-neutralizing effect: §16.2.3 and §17.1.1), and O of the main clause:

19.8　[a-də　　　　　　təpə-taka-n　　　rə-d-ə　　　　　　　kaw] ma: və
　　　DEM.DIST-masc.sg be.closed-put-SEQ sit-3masc.sgSUBJ.VT-LK hole NEG see:NEG
　　　'He (the human child) did not see the hole which had been covered up' (lit. 'stayed closed')

The first line of T1.4 illustrates relativization on the addressee. The CA is in A function in the main clause. A CA can be a nominal component of a lexicalized complex predicate NOUN-DAT *rə-* 'for (noun) sit' meaning 'marry (a man)', as in 19.9:

19.9　[də lə-kə-də　　　　　la:n-ad]　　　　　　　[rə-la-də
　　　he she-OBL-masc.sg husband-3masc.sgNOM sit-3fem.sgSUBJ.VT-3masc.sgBAS.VT
　　　du-ad]
　　　man-3masc.sgNOM
　　　'He is her husband, the man whom she married' (lit. the man for whom she sat)

In 19.10a the CA is a locative, and in 19.10b it is a source 'from'. A similar example is the Manambu term for stock exchange *sa:n warapwi-dana tami:* (money exchange-3plSUBJ.VT+3fem.sgBAS.VT area), lit. 'area where they exchange money' mentioned at A7 in §15.3.1. Also see the penultimate line of 16.40, and T3.19.

19.10a ata [wa-də-di   a-di   mi:] [an-a-də
       then say-3masc.sgSUBJ.P-3plBAS.P DEM.DIST-pl tree we.du-LK-masc.sg
       kə-də   rə-ta-d-ə   təp] [nəbəkəm
       DEM.PROX-masc.sg sit-1duSUBJ.VT-3masc.sgBAS.VT-LK village hill+LK+LOC
       grələm   tə-na-di   mi] vəl-grəkək
       side+LK+LOC stand-ACT.FOC-3plBAS.VT tree cut-2pl+PURP.DS
       'You are to cut those trees he talked about, the trees which stand on the side of the hill, (in) this village of ours where we live'

19.10b [ta:y waku-l   wiya:r]   ata ya:d
       first go.out-3fem.sgBAS.P house+LK+ALL then go+3masc.sgBAS.P
       'He went towards the house from which she'd gone out before'

In 19.11, the CA is an oblique with a temporal meaning in both relative clause and the main clause.

19.11 ñən-a-də   asa:y [Tani ma:k kwa-la-d-ə   nabi]
      you.fem-LK-masc.sg father Tani person stay-3fem.sgSUBJ.P-3masc.sgBAS.P-LK year
      kiya:d
      die+3masc.sgBAS.P
      'Your father died the year (when) Tanina was born (lit. person stayed)'

The CA can be the second argument of the extended intransitive verb 'say' (see §19.5.5 on its argument structure):

19.12 [Asiti wa-na-d-ə   təp] [alədam
      Asiti say-ACT.FOC-3masc.sgBAS.VT-LK village DEM.DIST+fem.sg+DOWN+LK+LOC
      rə-na-d]
      sit-ACT.FOC-3masc.sgBAS.VT
      'The village called Asiti is down there'

In 14.119 the CA is an oblique with a causal meaning, and in 19.13 it is an oblique indicating 'manner':

19.13 [[a-di   dəb-a:b   kwa-da-di   səkər] [a-bər
       DEM.DIST-pl fence-TOO stay-3plSUBJ.P-3plBAS.P time DEM.DIST-du
       du-a-yaba-wa   takwa-ya:b   tə-bra]   sa:d]
       man-LK-road+LK-COM woman+LK-road stay-3duSUBJ.VT+3fem.sgBAS.VT way
       [tə-bra   maw] [lə-kə-l
       stay-3duSUBJ.VT+3fem.sgBAS.VT basis 3fem.sg-OBL-3fem.sg
       laku-tua]
       know-1sgSUBJ.VT+3fem.sgBAS.VT
       'I know the essence (lit. base) of their staying, the way in which those two women's road and men's road stayed, at the time when they (women) stayed in ritual enclosure'

And 19.14 illustrates the possessee, 'dog', as a common argument; it is the S of the main clause:

19.14 [a-də   wiya:m   sə   kwa-na-d-ə   du]
DEM.DIST-masc.sg house+LK+LOC sleep stay-ACT.FOC-3masc.sgBAS.VT-LK man
[də-kə-də   a:s bə   kiya:d]
he-OBL-3masc.sg dog already die+3masc.sgBAS.P
'The dog of that man who is sleeping in the house has already died'

The argument structure and the marking of arguments in relative clauses is the same as that in main clauses, unless the CA is the possessor closely associated with the possessee. Such possessees include kinship relations, as in 19.15, body parts, as in 19.16, and physical states, as in 19.17a–b. Then, the possessee is zero marked and preposed to the predicate of the relative clause followed by the CA. That is, 'men whose wives died' are literally 'wife they-died men', 'man whose hand you shook' is 'hand you-shook man', and 'boy whose fever goes up' is 'fever he-goes up boy':

19.15 [ta:kw kiya-di   du] [du kiya-di   ta:kw] [sarmabap-adi]
woman die-3plBAS.P man man die-3plBAS.P woman destitute-3plNOM
'Men whose wives died, women whose husbands died are destitute' (lit. wife they-died men, man they-died woman)

19.16 [ta:b kur-ñəna-d-ə   du]-a:k   [væn ap]
hand shake/get-2fem.sgSUBJ.VT-3masc.sgBAS.VT-LK man-LK+DAT see   IMPV+see
'Look at the man whose hand you shook' (lit. hand you-shook man)

19.17a [ba:r war-na-d-ə   ñan] [ada
fever go.up-ACT.FOC-3masc.sgBAS.VT-LK child DEM.DIST.REACT.TOP+masc.sg
tə-na-d]
stand-ACT.FOC-3masc.sgBAS.VT
'Here is the boy whose fever has gone up'

19.17b [ya:p   war-na   takwa-ñan]-al
asthma/breath go.up-ACT.FOC+3fem.sgBAS.VT woman+LK-child-3fem.sgNOM
'She is a girl with asthma' (lit. asthma she-goes up girl)

A similar relative clause construction occurs whenever a connection between the possessor and the possessee can be conceived as close enough and culturally acceptable. That is, 19.18a was judged possible, but 19.18b was treated as contrived, the reason being that children do not really own mice or rats:

19.18a a:s kiya-d-ə   ñan
dog die-3masc.sgBAS.P-LK child
'a child whose dog died' (lit. dog he-died child, or child dead with respect to dog)

19.18b ?wakuli   kiya-d-ə   ñan
mouse/rat die-3masc.sgBAS.P-LK child
'a child whose mouse died'?

The possessor in 19.15–18 can be in any function in a main clause. Its function in a relative clause is the subject (S, as in 19.15, 19.17–18) or the object (as in 19.16): this function is indicated by the person, number, gender, and tense markers on the predicate of the relative clause. The possessees in the relative clauses in 19.15–18 are ambiguous as to their syntactic functions: they can be considered part of the S in 19.15, 19.17–18, and part of O in 19.16.

This creates an unusual clause type, only found in relative clauses involving relativization of possessor.

From a semantic point of view, the phenomenon of 'extraction' of an inalienably possessed noun and change in its argument status is akin to the phenomenon known as double object construction. For instance, in Tariana (Arawak: Aikhenvald 2003: 156–7) if a possessive construction containing a body part or any inalienably possessed item is in a non-subject function in a clause, both possessor and the possessee acquire the non-subject case marking and are treated as objects. In constructions known as 'external possession', the possessor is coded as a 'core grammatical relation of the verb and in a constituent separate from that which contains' the possessee (see Payne and Barshi 1999: 3).

We have just seen that in Manambu, relative clauses involving possession with a close link between the possessor and the possessee have the surface structure of either double subject or double object. And the relativization in Manambu appears to go against the NP accessibility hierarchy proposed by Keenan and Comrie (1977): the hierarchy predicts that if a language allows relativization on possessors, it should also allow relativization on arguments of adpositions. However, the analysis above suggests that in Manambu possessors need to be transformed into either a subject or an object (depending on the function of the possessive construction in the main clause), before they can be relativized. Possessors as such cannot be relativized on. That is, relativization in Manambu does in fact conform to the hierarchy suggested by Keenan and Comrie.

If there is a close association between the process and the result, the 'associated result' can also be relativized on. This is illustrated in 19.19: the man looked into the house and saw the fire lit by the woman (CA is O in the relative clause and in the main clause), and also saw what literally translates as 'the smoke that she was cooking'—that is, the smoke associated with, or coming from, her cooking:

19.19 [a   apaw   ta:kw   aka
       DEM.DIST.fem.sg old.fem.sg woman   DEM.DIST.REACT.TOP.fem.sg
       sakə-na   yi] [səkulək yi-la   yaki]
       light-ACT.FOC+3fem.sgBAS.VT   fire cooking go-3fem.sgSUBJ.VT+3fem.sgBAS.VT smoke
       [a   kətawul və-da]
       then look.INSIDE see-3fem.sgSUBJ.VT+3fem.sgBAS.VT
       'He saw inside (the house) the fire lit by that old woman, the smoke of her cooking (lit. cooking she-do smoke, or the smoke associated with her doing cooking)'

Along similar lines, 19.20 literally translates as 'these are the pictures which they spoke at a name debate called "saki"', meaning 'these are the pictures to do with (that is, taken at the time of) a name debate "saki"':

19.20 [saki   bla-dana   kayik]-adi
       name.debate speak-3plSUBJ.VT+3fem.sgBAS.VT picture-3plNOM
       'These are the pictures of them speaking at the name debate "saki"' (lit. name debate they-speak pictures)

There are no grammatical restrictions on the nature of an associated participant.

Since any core argument can be relativized on, ambiguity may arise: 19.21 allows for two interpretations—since both participants, the man and his companion, are marked with the same third person singular masculine cross-referencing:

19.21 kə-də   də-kə-də   *poroman*   [a-də   vya-k
       DEM.PROX-masc.sg   he-OBL-masc.sg   companion   DEM.DIST-masc.sg   hit-PURP.SS
       kur-də-d-ə   du-a:k]   ata
       do/get-3masc.sgSUBJ.VT-3masc.sgBAS.VT-LK   man-LK+DAT   then
       wa-də-d   wun   mən-a:m   vi   ma:
       say-3masc.sgSUBJ.VT-3masc.sgBAS.VT   I   you-LK+ACC/LOC   hit:FUT   NEG
       'This companion of his said to that man <u>who</u> was about to hit him: "I won't hit you" ' or
       'This companion of his said to that man <u>whom</u> he was about to hit: "I won't hit you" '

In the context of the story, only the second reading is appropriate. If the common argument and the core argument(s) of the main clause require different gender and number marking, no ambiguity arises—see 19.28.

Overt expression of participants in a relative clause is an alternative way of disambiguating the role of the CA. A clause *kwa-na-d-ə wi* (stay-ACT.FOC-3masc.sgBAS.VT-LK house) is ambiguous: adding an additional argument allows us to disambiguate between 'a house that stays (is located) on a hill' and 'a house where someone stays':

19.22a [nəbəkəm   kwa-na-d-ə   wi]-ad
        hill+LK+LOC   stay-ACT.FOC-3masc.sgBAS.VT-LK   house-3masc.sgNOM
        'It is a house that stays (is located) on a hill'

19.22b [du   kwa-na-d-ə   wi]-ad
        man   stay-ACT.FOC-3masc.sgBAS.VT-LK   house-3masc.sgNOM
        'It is a house where a man stays (lives)'

Any relative clause can be used without a head. If the head is omitted, the verb takes the case marking which the common argument would have taken had it been there. In 14.122 the headless relative clause, '(people) who do not work', is in the A function of a main clause, and in T2.67 ('those we were talking about') it is in S function. A dative case-marked headless relative clause is illustrated in 19.23a. The omitted common argument is in the O function in the relative clause, and in the function of second argument of the complex verb 'ask' which requires dative marking:

19.23a gəñər bas   sə-kə-tua-di   [a-di
        later first plant-FUT-1sgSUBJ.VT-3plBAS.VT   DEM.DIST-pl
        laku-mar-tua-di:k]
        understand-NEG.SUB-1sgSUBJ.VT-3plBAS.VT+DAT
        'I will ask later about (the ones) I do not understand'

If the CA had not been omitted, it would have taken the dative case:

19.23b gəñər bas   sə-kə-tua-di   [a-di
        later first plant-FUT-1sgSUBJ.VT-3plBAS.VT   DEM.DIST-pl
        laku-ma:r-tua-di   majək]
        understand-NEG.SUB-1sgSUBJ.VT-3plBAS.VT   word+LK+DAT
        'I will ask later about words I do not understand'

And in 19.24a the omitted CA is an S in the relative clause. In the main clause it is a location, marked with the comitative case (see §7.9). Since the CA is omitted, the case marking goes onto the verb.

19.24a [a   væk   rə-lawa]   mæy
        DEM.DIST.fem.sg   pot   sit-3fem.sgSUBJ.VT+3fem.sgBAS.VT+COM   come.IMPV
        'Come by the (area) where that pot sits'

If the CA had not been omitted, the sentence would be:

19.24b [a   væk rə-la   tamiya-wa]   mæy
DEM.DIST.fem.sg pot   sit-3fem.sgSUBJ.VT+3fem.sgBAS.VT   area+LK-COM come.IMPV
'Come by the area where that pot sits'

This is how what looks like a fully inflected verb can take a case marker (see §7.11, for the discussion of case marking on verbs). A similar example is in T3.43, with a headless relative clause *ata wa-tua-di-a-wa* (then say-1sgSUBJ.VT-3plBAS.VT-LK-COM) 'with those (the words) which I was saying'.

We can recall, from 19.7–8, that a relative clause follows a demonstrative and precedes an adjective modifying a common argument. This same order holds if the CA is omitted, as in 19.25. The CA is the O function in both relative and main clause:

19.25 [a   wukəmar-tua]   kwasa
DEM.DIST.fem.sg forget-1sgSUBJ.VT+3fem.sgBAS.VT little+fem.sg
aka   wa-kə-tua
DEM.DIST.REACT.TOP.fem.sg tell-FUT-1sgSUBJ.VT+3fem.sgBAS.VT
'I will tell that little (bit of a story) which I forgot'

A headless relative clause in an elliptical sentence looks exactly like a main clause would look. A speaker heard a woman shout from the next-door house, and asked *Sə-kə-l-al*? (who-OBL-fem.sg-3fem.sgNOM) 'Who is this?' Gemaj answered 19.26:

19.26 anaki   wiya:m   rə-na
DEM.CURR.REL+ACROSS.AWAY house+LK+LOC sit-ACT.FOC+3fem.sgBAS.VT
'(It is the one who) lives in previously mentioned the house across from us (meaning our next-door neighbour Esther-Yuaya:b)'

An alternative interpretation for this clause could have been 'She lives in previously mentioned the house across from us'; but this interpretation would not have made sense under the circumstances. That is, a headless relative clause—if it is not negated—can sometimes be distinguished from a main clause by context only. If it is negated, it takes the dependent clause negator -*ma:r*- which a normal main clause does not take (except under special circumstances: §14.5.3). In addition, all relative clauses, including headless ones, can be used as complementation strategies—see §19.8.

Relative clauses are very common in every genre of Manambu. An alternative strategy is verb-noun compounds.

19.2.2   Verb-noun compounds as a relativization strategy

Verb-noun compounds consist of a verb root followed by a noun. A schwa (ə) appears at the end of verb roots ending in a stop to break up unlawful consonant clusters (see §2.2.1). Verb-noun compounds form one grammatical and phonological word (see §9.3), and behave like nouns—that is, they can have the same array of syntactic functions as any other noun, and can be inflected for case. The noun can be the S of the verb, as in *kiya-du* (die-man) 'dead man', *wusau-səp* (be.itchy-skin) 'itchy skin', *tabu-wa:l* (run-rain) 'quickish rain', and *pusa-mi* (rot/be.broken-tree) 'broken tree' (T2.57). Or it can be an A, e.g. *væt-ə-jəpis* (bite-LK-ant) 'an ant that bites'. It can also be an O, as in *bra-təp* (scrape-coconut) 'coconut for scraping', *walaku-ma:j* (advise (lit. say-know)-talk) 'advice', or *taka-təpə-tami:* (put-be.closed-area) 'closed up area'. It can also be a locative, e.g. *rə-tami:* (sit-area) 'living area', *yi-ya:b* (go-road) 'road to go'; or a temporal, e.g. *yi-nə* (go-day) 'day of going', *ja:-səkər* (rain-time) 'time of rain'; or an instrument, as in *yaku-bi:r* (wash-foam) 'foam used for washing'; or an associated participant in general, e.g. *vya-yanu* (kill-magic) 'magic to do with killing', *væki-yanu* (go.across-magic) 'magic to do with going across (a river)', and *ñam-kamna:gw* (chew-food) 'chewed food mothers used to give to their babies'.

That is, a transitive verb can be compounded with a noun in A function, in O function, or even in a locative function. The function of a noun is determined by its semantics and prototypical role. Consider the following set:

- *kur-du* (do/get-man) means 'man who makes (something); workman' (rather than *a man made), since a man is a prototypical agent;
- *kur-ja:p* (do-thing) means 'thing done, thing to do' (rather than *a thing that makes) because things are hardly ever agentive;
- *kur-tami:* (do/get-area) means 'area of doing/getting (something)', because an area is a prototypical location; and
- *kur-ñə* (do/get-day) means 'day/time of doing', because a day is a temporal noun.

Along similar lines, *yakwiya-asa:y* (adopt-father) means 'adoptive father; father who adopted a child', and *yakwiya-ñan* (adopt-child) means 'adopted child; child who was adopted': in the Manambu society fathers do not get adopted by children.

The verb can be reduplicated, and then the meaning is that of intensification, in agreement with the general semantics of reduplication (§12.8.2), e.g. *wusau-wusau səp* (itch-RED skin) 'very itchy skin', *tabu-tabu wa:l* (run-RED rain) 'a quick rain, a rain which passes quickly', *væt-ə-væt-ə jəpis* (bite-LK-RED-LK ant) 'an ant that bites a lot', *vya-vya yanu* (hit-RED magic) 'magic to do with killing a lot'. Following the requirements for the length of an optimal phonological word (see §2.5), these compounds are pronounced as two words. They remain one grammatical word.

A verb-noun compound can itself be a common argument of a relative clause and a main clause, as in 19.27–8:

19.27 [an-a   amæy   wa-lə-l]   [wa-laku-majəb]
      1du-LK+fem.sg mother say-3fem.sgSUBJ.P-3fem.sgBAS.P say-know-talk+LK+TERM
      [ya-ta   aka]
      go-1dusUBJ.VT+3fem.sgBAS.VT DEM.DIST.REACT.TOP.fem.sg
      We are going (now) exactly by the words of advice said by our mother'

The verb in a verb-noun compound can take an additional noun phrase object, as in 19.28: here, 'man' is the object of *warya-* 'fight' which in its turn forms a compound with *yanu* 'magic'.

19.28 aw [abakapi a-di   kui-lə-di   [du
      then hawk   DEM.DIST-pl give.to.third.p-3fem.sgSUBJ.P-3plBAS.P man
      warya-yanu]] [mawula:m   kwa-yakə-di]
      fight-magic.spell inside+LK+LOC lie-FULLY-3plBAS.VT
      'Then those magic spells for fighting men given by the hawk really stayed in (his) mind'
      (lit. inside)

Or a verb in a verb-noun compound can have an overt subject (if the noun in the compound is in some other function), as in 19.29. Here, 'I' is the subject of *yi-* 'go' compounded with *tami:* 'area'. In the examples below, the compounds are underlined.

19.29 [wun y̲i̲-tami: ma:] [sə-kwa-tami: ma:]
　　　I　go-area NEG　sleep-stay-area NEG
　　　'I do not have a place to go to, I do not have a place to sleep'

An overt argument can be a location, as in 19.30.

19.30 [[Apatəp-a:m y̲i̲-d̲u̲] wudiya　　　　　　　Yuanab
　　　Avatip-LK+LOC go-man DEM.PROX.ADDR.REACT.TOP+pl Yuanab
　　　kwa-na-di]
　　　stay-ACT.FOC-3plBAS.VT
　　　'The men who went to Avatip are here (close to you) (at) Yuanab'

The verb itself can be complex, e.g. *yawi-kur-tami:* (work-do-area) 'area to do work' in 14.9, *sə-kwa-tami:* (sleep-stay-area) in 19.29, *gu yaku-swap* (water wash-soap) 'soap for washing (with water)', and *tugwam na-tami:* (clearing BE:NAT-area) 'area of clearing in the jungle' in 19.33.

Whether a complex verb forms one phonological word with the noun or not depends on the number of syllables in the resulting form. If the resulting form consists of more than four CV syllables, or two CVC and one CV syllable, it is realized as two phonological words. Then, the boundaries of phonological and grammatical words coincide. Otherwise, it forms one phonological word regardless of grammatical word boundaries.

A compound may even involve a verb in a clause-chaining construction which contains the sequencing suffix *-n*, as in 19.31. The construction is in curly brackets, together with its directional argument. It consists of three phonological and grammatical words.

19.31 [abakapi lə-kə-di　yanu　　ata kui-lə-di]　　　　　　　　　[du
　　　hawk　she-OBL-pl magic.spell then give.to.third.p-3fem.sgSUBJ.P-3plBAS.P man
　　　v̲y̲a̲-̲y̲a̲n̲u̲] 　{ñaba:r　　　　surə-n　v̲æ̲k̲i̲-̲y̲a̲n̲u̲}　　　　　　[du
　　　fight-magic.spell Sepik.river+LK+ALL jump-SEQ go.across-magic.spell man
　　　v̲y̲a̲-̲v̲y̲a̲-̲y̲a̲n̲u̲,　　　gawi v̲y̲a̲-̲y̲a̲n̲u̲,　　aba:b ata
　　　kill-RED-magic.spell eagle kill-magic.spell all　　then
　　　kui-lə-di],　　　　　　　　　[lə lə-ka　　　　　abakapim
　　　give.to.third.p-3fem.sgSUBJ.P-3plBAS.P she she-OBL+3fem.sgNOM hawk+ACC/LOC
　　　v̲y̲a̲-̲y̲a̲n̲u̲　　aba:b ata　kui-yakə-lə-k]　　　　　[ñamus
　　　kill-magic.spell all　then give.to.third.p-FULLY-3fem.sg-COMPL.DS younger.sibling
　　　ma:m　　ata kwa-bər]
　　　elder.sibling then stay-3duBAS.P
　　　'The hawk then gave (the siblings) her magic spells, she gave them all the spells, a spell of killing men, a spell to do with going across river by jumping, spell to do with killing a lot of men, magic spell of killing eagles, after she'd fully given her own magic of killing the hawk, the elder and the younger siblings remained (with this knowledge)'

The overt arguments of verbs in verb-noun compounds can be case marked as necessary—a locational argument is marked with locative case in 19.30, direction is marked with allative in 19.31. An object can be zero marked (as in the second line of 19.31), or marked with the accusative-locative case, as in the penultimate line of 19.31 (see §7.3, for the discussion of case marking for objects).

The order of constituents is fixed: nothing, not even the ubiquitous *ata* 'then', can intervene between the compound and the overtly marked argument. Only one argument can be overtly expressed: one cannot say *wun ñaba:r yi-tami:* (I Sepik.river+LK+ALL go-area) ? 'area for me to go to the river'. Verb-noun compounds cannot be negated (since they are nouns).

19.2.3   Relative clauses and verb-noun compounds: a comparison

Table 19.2 summarizes the formal differences between the relative clauses and the verb-noun compounds.

Relative clauses and verb-noun compounds are similar in their functions—which is to provide further specification for an argument of a clause. Yet there is semantic difference between them.

A noun modified by an inflected relative clause has to have a specific referent. In contrast, the referent of a noun in a verb-noun compound has to be generic. So, a noun-verb compound *kara:b kur-du* (man's.house do/get-man) is best translated as 'maker of man's house', and a relative clause *kara:b kur-d-ə du* (man's.house do/get-3masc.sgBAS.VT/P-LK man) as 'a man who makes or has made a man's house'. And a compound *bra-təp* (scrape-coconut) is a general term for 'coconut for scraping'; if I am talking about a specific coconut I am going to scrape, I will say *bra-kə-tua təp* (scrape-FUT-1sgSUBJ.VT+3fem.sgBAS.VT coconut) 'the/a coconut I will scrape'—using a relative clause.

Along similar lines, the generic term *yakwiya-asa:y* means 'adoptive father', and is a compound. And the generic term *kui-wus asa:y* (give.to.third.p-penis father), a term for blood father, is also compound. However, in 19.32, when talking about his parentage, James Katalu was specific about the identity of his two fathers—the blood father, and the adoptive father. As a consequence, he used a relative clause rather than a verb-noun compound to refer to both parents.

TABLE 19.2   Relative clauses with inflected verbs and verb-noun compounds

PROPERTY	RELATIVE CLAUSES WITH INFLECTED VERBS	VERB-NOUN COMPOUNDS
1. Position of verb	strictly verb-final clauses: all arguments precede the verb	verb-noun
2. Inflectional status of verb	Verb inflected as in a main clause (also see Table 18.1)	bare verbal root
3. One phonological and grammatical word with an argument	never	yes
4. Can be negated	yes	no
5. Can contain more than one overt argument	yes	no
6. Can be lexicalized	no	yes
7. Overt arguments and verb strictly contiguous	no	yes

19.32 [wun-a:m   wus   kui-d-ə   asa:y] Yuadabwi
      I-LK+ACC/LOC penis give.to.third.p-3masc.sgBAS.P-LK father Yuadabwi
      [wun-a:m   yakwiya-d-ə   asa:y] Balagawi
      I-LK+ACC/LOC adopt-3masc.sgBAS.P-LK father Balagawi
      'The father who created me (lit. gave me penis) is Yuadabwi, the father who adopted me
      is Balagawi'

A generic statement concerning the cassowary's son's living habits involves verb-noun compounds—he never stays in closed-up areas preferring clearings in the jungle.

19.33 [ta:y   taka-təpə-tamia:m   akəs   kwa-kwa-na-d]
      before put-be.closed-area+LK+LOC NEG.HAB stay-HAB-ACT.FOC-3masc.sgBAS.VT
      [və-də-k   kət:ay kəti] [tugwam na-tamia:m
      see-3masc.sg-COMPL.DS around around clearing BE.NAT-area+LK+LOC
      kwa-kwa-na-d]
      stay-HAB-ACT.FOC-3masc.sgBAS.VT
      'Before he never used to stay in closed area. Having looked around, he would stay in an
      area of clearing'

In contrast, in 19.34, the central character stayed on a specific clearing he had just found:

19.34 [tugwam na-lə-l   tamia:m]   ata
      clearing BE.NAT-3fem.sgSUBJ.P-3fem.sgBAS.P area+LK+LOC then
      ra:d
      stay+3masc.sgBAS.P
      'He then stayed in the clearing'

The generic meaning of a noun in a compound structure agrees with a general principle: nouns in compounds are typically non-referential and non-specific (see Mithun 1984; Aikhenvald 2007).

As mentioned in §9.3, verb-noun compounds are productive, and new ones are always being coined spontaneously. Scolding her daughter for being clumsy, a mother exclaimed 19.35:

19.35 gu   kaykwa-tami:-al   a
      water spill-area-3fem.sgNOM eh
      'Is this the area for spilling water?'

In addition, they often get lexicalized, and acquire somewhat unpredictable meanings. So, *gra-kudi* (cry-language) is not just 'language with which people cry'; it is a term for 'mourning songs', and *wa-saki-ma:j* (say-ACROSS.AWAY-talk) refers to traditional stories which are transmitted across generations. Similarly, *ku-su-ja:p* (put-UP-thing) is a generic term for 'clothing', *ku-su-mæ:n* (put-UP-leg) is a generic term for 'footwear', and *sə-kwa-ja:p* (sleep-stay-thing) is used for 'sleeping gear'. Such compounds frequently become names. For instance, *kiya-du* 'dead man' is used as the name of a Manambu football team in Avatip whose members live not too far from a local cemetery.[1]

In contrast, relative clauses do not undergo lexicalization. This does not mean that they cannot give rise to names—for instance, we used to refer to the blind Ñatabi as *məl kusə-na yawus* (eye close/finish-ACT.FOC+3fem.sgBAS.VT father's.sister) 'blind father's sister', lit. 'father's

---

[1] A reduplicated verb used in a verb-noun compound developed a somewhat idiosyncratic meaning in *vya-vya ta:b* (hit+LK-RED+LK hand) 'right hand, lit. hitting hand'. This can be alternatively interpreted as a deverbal nominalization used as a modifier to another noun (§9.1.1).

sister whose eyes finished', and to a sickly girl in the village as 19.17b. Each of these coinages is, however, more of an occasionalism than a fixed expression, as is the case with verb-noun compounds.

19.3 CLAUSE LINKING VIA CASE MARKER 'INSTEAD' AND SUFFIX 'LIKE'

Of all case markers which can attach to verbs only the substitutive case -*yæy* 'instead, rather than, in exchange for' is uncontroversially used to link clauses. There are two options. If the case marker attaches to the verbal root, the subject of the dependent clause is the same as that of a main clause, as in 19.36.

19.36 [məy-a-mæja:r   yati-yæy] [wali-mæja:r   wa:r
       real-LK-thread+INSTR knit-SUBST white.man-thread+INSTR string.bag
       yati-na]
       knit-ACT.FOC+3fem.sgBAS.VT
       'Instead of knitting with real thread (made of tree bark), she has knitted a stringbag with wool (lit. white people's string)'

If the subjects are different, the substitutive case marker attaches to the verb inflected with main clause subject marker (in versatile tense). The case marker occupies the second cross-referencing position. Examples are 19.37 and T3.40.

19.37 [ñən   kiya-ñəna-yæy]   [də-kə-m
       you.fem die-2fem.sgSUBJ.VT+3fem.sgBAS.VT-SUBST he-OBL-OBJ
       vya-təpul-kə-ñəna-d]
       kill-hit-FUT-2fem.sgSUBJ.VT-3masc.sgBAS.VT
       'Instead of you dying, you will kill him'

   In T3.40, the substitutive clause has the meaning 'in exchange for' (*wun-a-di ñan-ugw vya-məna-yæy wun-aba:b aka ya-na-wun-ək* (I-LK-pl child-PL kill-2masc.sgSUBJ.VT+3fem.sgBAS.VT-SUBST I-TOO DEM.DIST.REACT.TOP.fem.sg come-ACT.FOC-1fem.sgBAS.VT-CONF) 'in exchange for you killing my children, I too have come here (to kill you)'. Examples of the substitutive case -*yæy* as a clause-linking device are rare in texts and in conversations. I have never heard a negated substitutive clause used; nor are there any examples of negated substitutive clauses in the corpus.

   Clauses linked with -*pək* 'like' are not that scarce. We saw in §9.2 that the suffix -*pək* 'like' can be used with most word classes, with somewhat different meanings. It is used on a fully inflected verb if one activity or state is compared to another. Examples are at 14.31, 14.33, 19.5, and 19.38–42. In 9.38 and 14.117, -*pək* is used on a negated clause, in a slightly different meaning 'as if'. The use of the dependent clause negator -*ma:r*- confirms the dependent clause status of the -*pək* clause. There are no restrictions on tense and aspects, or the occurrence of any main clause complex predicate, in clauses marked with -*pək*. Just as in any dependent clause, uninflected verbs require a support verb.

19.38 [tami: tə-ma:r-na-pək]   rə-na
       space be/have-NEG.SUB-ACT.FOC+3fem.sgBAS.VT-LIKE sit-ACT.FOC+3fem.sgBAS.VT
       'She sits (over there) as if there were no space'

A clause marked with -*pək* can occur with *tə*- 'stand/be/have' as a support verb, as in 19.39.

19.39 kə   ñan-al   [ñan tə-na-pək]
       DEM.PROX+fem.sg child-3fem.sgNOM child have-ACT.FOC+3fem.sgBAS.VT-LIKE
       tə-na
       stay-ACT.FOC+3fem.sgBAS.VT
       'It is this girl (who) is as if she had a child'

In 19.40, a *-pək* clause follows an NP argument also marked with *-pək*. This shows a similarity between the *-pək* clause and any oblique argument marked with *-pək* 'like'. The *-pək* clause itself occurs in a chain with a completive same-subject clause:

19.40 [wun-a-pək] [a   yi-tua-pək]   [rəka:rək yu-ku]   ma:y
       I-LK-LIKE   then go-1sgSUBJ.VT+3fem.sgBAS.VT-LIKE carefully go-COMPL.SS go.IMPV
       'Like me, like I went, go having gone carefully'

A *-pək* clause can itself be complex: in 19.41 it contains a same-subject completive clause. In his story about how he and his mates ran away from school when they were little, David Takendu compared this event to the flight of Jews from Egypt:

19.41 [a-di   *ju* *igipt* wapa-ku,   tabu-da-l-pək]
       DEM.DIST-pl Jew Egypt leave-COMPL.SS escape-3plSUBJ.P-3fem.sgBAS.P-LIKE
       atabək-al
       thus+PRED+LIKE-3fem.sgNOM
       'Like Jews escaping (from) Egypt having left (it), that is how it was'

In contrast to juxtaposed clauses, a clause marked with *-pək* can head a predicate of a verbless clause:

19.42 wa-kwa-bana-pək-al
       say-HAB-1plSUBJ.VT+3fem.sgBAS.VT-LIKE-3fem.sgNOM
       '(This is) like the way we usually speak'

19.4 PURPOSIVE AND DESIDERATIVE CLAUSES

19.4.1 Purposive clauses

The predicate of a purposive clause takes purposive modality, distinguishing same-subject purposive (uninflected) and different-subject purposive (partially inflected)—see §13.4. The marker of same-subject purposive *-Vk* and the marker of different-subject purposive *-kək* (or *-kəkək*, with light verb roots) are similar to the dative case marker *-Vk* on nouns. The markers may well be related. However, synchronically speaking, *-Vk* on nouns behaves differently from *-Vk* on verbs: seemingly the same marker can attach directly to a monosyllabic noun+linker, while to be used with a monosyllabic verb it requires the root to be reduplicated. So, the noun *sə* 'name' and the verb *sə-* 'put, plant' combine with *-Vk* yielding different forms: *sa:k* (name+LK+DAT) 'for name' and *səsa:k* (put/plant+RED+PURP) 'so that (same subject) puts or plants' (also see §2.4).

Same-subject purposive forms of monosyllabic verbs are homophonous with dative-aversive-marked nominalization (§9.1.2 and §13.7). They can be easily distinguished by the ways in which they are negated (see §14.3).

The same-subject purposive marks a purpose complement of any verb if this is semantically appropriate, indicating that the subject of the matrix verb and that of the purpose-marked verb are identical—see 7.76, 16.75, T1.8, T1.12, and T1.14. Another example is at 19.43:

19.43 [kamna:gw kəka:k]   [*hat* tə-na-d]
food   eat+RED+PURP.SS hard have/be-ACT.FOC-3masc.sgBAS.VT
'It was hard for him to eat food'

Same-subject purposive clauses cannot be negated: the negative pro-clause *ma:* has to be used, as in 14.67 and 14.68.

A purposive clause can precede the main clause, as in 19.43, or follow it, as in 19.44. The order of constituents depends on pragmatics (see Chapter 20). The second line of 19.44 shows that a purpose clause can appear with a completive clause as its matrix clause. Their subjects are the same. And the subject of the completive clause is, in its turn, the same as that of the main, fully inflected clause:

19.44 [a-di   ñə abəti kusə-lə-k]   [nagwək
DEM.DIST-pl day seven finish-3fem.sg-COMPL.DS sago+LK+DAT
yi-kə-bana]   [nag:w yaku-k]   [au nak ma:
go-FUT-1plSUBJ.VT+3fem.sgSUBJ.P sago wash-PURP.SS then one again
vya-ku]   [kəka:k]
kill-COMPL.SS eat+RED+PURP.SS
'After those seven days finished, we will go (to fetch) sago, to wash sago, having killed one (pig) again, for (us) to eat'

The matrix clause for a purposive clause can be a relative clause, as in 19.45. The common argument is the O of the relative clause and a location in the main clause.

19.45 [[wi   kurə-k]   kulapu-tua]   [tami: mi
house do-PURP.SS clean-1sgSUBJ.VT+3fem.sgBAS.VT area   tree
aka   bə   war-dana]
DEM.DIST.REACT.TOP.fem.sg already go.up-3plSUBJ.VT+3fem.sgBAS.VT
'(In) the area which I cleaned to make a house trees have already grown'

Different-subject purposive forms are partially inflected, exactly like other different-subject forms. A different-subject purposive clause can precede or follow the main clause—see 13.51, 13.55, and 19.46.

19.46 [lə kəka-n-aka   ga:m
she DEM.PROX.REACT.TOP.fem.sg-PRED-REACT.TOP serenade
sə-na]   [wa:j ya-lə-kəkək]
plant-ACT.FOC+3fem.sgBAS.VT eel   come-3fem.sg-PURP.DS
'She here is calling, so that the eel should come'

A matrix clause for a different-subject purposive clause can be a dependent clause, as in 13.49 where it is employed as a complementation strategy. We return to this in §19.8.

Different-subject purposive clauses are negated with a dependent clause negator *-ma:r-* (see 14.71), unlike same-subject purposive clauses. This is a crucial difference between same-subject and different-subject purposive clauses (see §13.4.3).

19.4.2   Desiderative clauses

A desiderative form in a dependent clause always requires the same subject as that of the main clause. Similarly to the same-subject purposive, desiderative is an uninflected verb. Desiderative can express purpose, as in 12.62, 13.57–8, 19.47, 19.102, and T3.45. While the same-subject purposive would have implied definite intention, the desiderative indicates a certain insecurity. The desire expressed in 19.47 does not mean that the expedition will eventuate:

19.47 [kapayawi-k   yi-kər] [war-na]
      sweet.potato-DAT go-DES go.up-ACT.FOC+3fem.sgBAS.VT
      'She has come up (into the house) wanting to go and get sweet potatoes'

We will see in §19.8 that desiderative clauses are used as complementation strategies with verbs of negative desire, such as 'be unwilling' (in 19.102). Manambu has no verb meaning 'want'. The idea of wanting something is most frequently expressed as a speech report (using the verb *wa-* 'say') accompanied with a desiderative clause (this is also the case in many other languages of New Guinea and Australia: see Aikhenvald 2008, for discussion and references).

    Unlike purposive clauses, desiderative clauses always have to be preposed to the main clause. If they appear postposed, they typically form an independent clause juxtaposed to another main clause. A short pause indicates a clause boundary in 19.48:

19.48 [mæy   yi-tək]   [PAUSE] [ka:m   kə-kər] [və-tua]
      come.IMPV go-1duIMPV pause   breadfruit eat-DES see-1sgSUBJ.VT+3fem.sgBAS.VT
      [ka:m   samasa:m ra:d]
      breadfruit a.lot   sit+3masc.sgBAS.VT
      'Come, let's go, (I) want to eat breadfruit, I saw there is a lot of breadfruit'

Just like purposive clauses, desideratives can be used within dependent clauses, as in T3.45. Neither purposives nor desideratives can head the predicate of a verbless clause. Desiderative in dependent clauses cannot be negated—if they have to be, a desiderative clause has to be rephrased as a main clause, which may be cast as a speech report.

    A comparison of purposive and desiderative clauses is given in Table 19.3.

    Dative-aversive-marked nominalizations can also be used to express purpose and have the implications of same subject (see, for instance, T2.8: 'to wash sago'). Their syntactic and semantic properties are considered in §13.7. Similarly to purposive and desiderative clauses,

TABLE 19.3   Purposive and desiderative clauses

PROPERTIES	PURPOSIVE (DS)	PURPOSIVE (SS)	DESIDERATIVE (SS)
1. Verb type	partially inflected	uninflected	
2. Negation	like any dependent clause	with a negative pro-clause	cannot be negated
3. Position	preposed or postposed to main verb		strictly preposed to main verb
4. Constituent order	strictly verb final		

they are employed as complementation strategies in a variety of meanings, all congruent with the basic meanings of the dative-aversive case—see §19.8.

19.5 SPEECH REPORTS

19.5.1 Speech report constructions and their properties

Speech reports are by far the most frequent clause type in Manambu discourse, and especially in conversations. Even the small textual sample at the end of this grammar contains speech reports in just about every third sentence.

Speech reports are extremely versatile: besides reporting actual speech events, they are employed to express internal speech and thought, desire and intention of third person, reason and purpose, and a few other related meanings. Multifunctional speech reports are a feature Manambu shares with a number of Papuan languages: speech reports often express thinking, desire, intention, and cognition. See Aikhenvald (2008) for an overview, and a summary of typological parameters relevant for the analysis of speech reports.

Manambu has three verbs of speech—*bla-* (allomorph *bəl-*) 'say/tell (something)', *yi-* 'say X, speak (a language)', and *wa-* 'say, tell'. Of these, only the verb *wa-* occurs with speech reports of any kind. The verb *yi-* occurs with just a few interjections as speech reports, as in *ay yi-da-d* (INTERJ say-3plSUBJ.VT-3masc.sgBAS.VT) 'they shouted' (lit. they said ay) (T1.29). A comparison of the three verbs of speech in terms of their further properties is in §21.1.3 (Table 21.1).

Speech reports in Manambu are multiclausal (Manambu has no reported evidentials). Speech reports can be coextensive with a clause, or a sentence. They may be less than a clause, containing just a vocative, as in 19.49, or an interjection, as in 19.50:

19.49 [gra-n] [ata wa-na]   [wun-a   ñan-eee]
      cry-SEQ then say-ACT.FOC+3fem.sgBAS.VT I-LK+fem.sg child-VOC
      'She said crying: 'Oh my chiiiild!'

19.50 [[mm] wa-ku]   [ada   ya:d]
      INTERJ say-COMPL:SS DEM.DIST.REACT.TOP+masc.sg go+3masc.sgBAS.P
      'Having said "mm" (an "up-to-no-good" interjection), he went off'

Or they may consist of several sentences, as in T2.40, and T3.22–5. Speech reports can be discontinuous—as in T1.33. Discontinuity only occurs on clause boundaries.

Speech reports do not have any special segmental markers other than the verb of speech itself in a framing clause. There is an optional pause between the speech report and the preceding framing clause. Speech reports do not have the falling intonation contour of medial clauses, or the rising contour of juxtaposed clauses.

Speech reports can precede or follow the framing clause containing the speech verb, with a slight preference for the former. Clear examples of speech reports preceding the framing clause are at T1.4, T1.11, T1.12, T1.16, T1.22, T1.24, T1.28, T2.5, T2.27, T3.8, T3.13, T3.16, T3.37, T3.40–1, T3.44, T3.47, and T3.50. Clear examples of speech reports following the framing clause are at T1.8, T1.13, T1.18, T1.19, T1.21, T1.23, T1.24, T1.26, T1.28, T2.40, T2.57, T2.58, T3.22, and T3.41. If a speech report follows the framing clause, another framing clause is often added at the end of the speech report. This is frequently cast as a medial clause—as in T1.33 and T2.7. This results in what looks like a speech framing construction: 'they said [Speech Report] having said'. A similar example is at 19.51. The speech report is in curly brackets, and the framing verb of speech is underlined:

19.51 [ada   wa:d],   {ya:kya, val-a:m
      DEM.DIST.REACT.TOP+masc.sg say+3masc.sgBAS.P OK   canoe-LK+LOC
      kə-da-kə-tua
      eat-go.downstream-FUT-1sgSUBJ.VT+3fem.sgBAS.VT
      adakw   ñab-a:m}   [wa-ku],
      DEM.DIST+masc.sg+AWAY.FROM.RIVER Sepik.river-LK+LOC say-COMPL.SS
      [a   kəbi   kamna:gw kar-da-n]   [val-a:m
      DEM.DIST.fem.sg basket food   bring-DOWN-SEQ canoe-LK+LOC
      kraku-taka-ku]   [waku-d   ñab-a:m]
      bring+AWAY.FROM.RIVER-put-COMPL.SS go.out-3masc.sgBAS.P river-LK+LOC
      'After it (the fish) stayed, that one (man) said, OK, I will eat it as I go downstream,
      out there on the Sepik River. Having said this, bringing that basket (with) food down,
      loading the canoe, he went out into the Sepik River'

A speech report can itself contain a speech report. Examples are at T1.33 (where the main character is quoting what he himself had said prior to going off to fight the moon), and T3.43.

We will now discuss further properties of speech reports in Manambu, including direct speech reports (§19.5.2), reported commands as indirect speech reports (§19.5.3), and semi-direct speech reports (§19.5.4). The syntactic role of speech reports is addressed at §19.5.5. Polysemous patterns in speech reports are analysed in §19.5.6.

19.5.2 Direct speech reports

An overwhelming majority of speech reports in Manambu are direct speech reports. These tend to reproduce what has been said without any shift in personal, temporal, or spatial deixis. Direct speech reports are often quotations. And more often than not they convey not just the words, but the intonation, the look, the gestures, the particular tone of voice, and so on. As Clark and Gerrig (1990: 772) put it, 'the internal structure of quotation is really the structure of what is being depicted, and that can range from the raging of a person to the racket of a machine'. Examples of direct speech reports with interjections and vocatives are at T1.3, and T3.40–2 and T3.50.

Reported questions are cast as direct speech reports: see 19.52 and T2.26:

19.52 [[ñə kas]   wa-ku]   [bas sa:d]
      sun how.much say-COMPL:SS first plant+3masc.sgBAS.P
      'He asked (saying) what time it is'

What looks like a reported question can be used as a complementation strategy, as in 19.103–4. A constituent within a speech report can be questioned, as in 10.113.

Narratives frequently consist of dialogues. The change of speaker is signalled by an intonation break, and a change in a tone of voice; then the actual verb of speech may be mentioned once at the beginning of a dialogue and subsequently omitted. This is the case in T1.6–7, T.1.11–12 and T1.23–4.

The verb *wa-* is the only speech verb which consistently introduces speech reports. A few other verbs denoting speech acts (most of which are intransitive: see §19.5.5), such as *gra-* 'cry', *ga:m sə-* 'call; serenade', *wa-taka-* (say-put) 'order', *wa-jali-* (say-?) 'call', can occur in a dependent medial clause preceding a clause with *wa-* 'say' and then following a direct speech report, as in 19.49. If the verb of speech is recoverable from the context, it can be omitted.

Then, a verb such as 'cry' in T3.16 can precede or follow the direct speech report on its own (but note that *wa-* 'say' has to be stated either in the preceding, or in the following sentence or clause).

19.5.3   Reported commands as indirect speech reports

Reported commands can be cast as direct speech reports. Examples are at 19.53 and T2.26. We will see, at §19.5.6, that commands cast as direct speech reports are often used in a variety of other meanings which do not necessarily imply a speech act. A prime example is the last clause of T2.34 where a reported command is in fact a causative strategy (also see §16.2.2, and example 16.80).

The direct speech reports are preferred in reported commands if the speaker chooses to preserve the exact words of the 'commander'. In 19.53, a speaker reminded me of her mother's command to me to hit her younger sister if she becomes too annoying:

19.53 [lə-kə-k   avi!]   [aka   wa-na]
     she-LK-DAT   IMPV+hit   DEM.DIST.REACT.TOP.fem.sg   say-ACT.FOC+3fem.sgBAS.VT
     'She said: "Hit her!"'

Other, similar examples include T1.5, T1.9, and T1.24. An alternative is to cast a command as an indirect speech report. Then, the exact words of the actual command are not preserved. The predicate in reported commands appears in the different-subject purposive modality (see §13.4.2 and examples 13.49–50), if the 'reporter' is not involved in the activity. The person shift in the verb 'consume' in 19.54 is indicative of an indirect speech report.

19.54 [[kə-di   mən-a-di   bal-a-wa   na:gw   kə-mən-kəkək]
     DEM.PROX-pl   you.masc-LK-PL   pig-LK-COM   sago   consume-2masc.sg-PURP.DS
     wa-tuə-k]   [war-na-dəmən-ək]
     say-1sg-COMPL.DS   go.up-ACT.FOC-2masc.sgBAS.VT-CONF
     'You have gone up, because/after I told you to eat these sago with pork of yours'

However, in generic statements containing indirect commands, and if the reporter is involved in the required activity, then the same-subject purposive is used, as in 13.45 and 19.55:

19.55 [apwi   vya-k]   [wa-da-l]
     cassowary.people   hit-PURP.SS   say-3plSUBJ.P-3fem.sgBAS.P
     '(At that time) they told (the village people) to fight the cassowary people (all together)'

The idea of 'telling (someone) not to do something' is rendered with the general negator *ma:* as a complement of the verb *wa-* 'say', as shown in 9.5, 13.78, and 14.42. That the command forms a dependent clause is corroborated by the use of the uninflected form *titiya:n* with a support verb *tə-* (see §17.2).

We will see, in §19.8, that a purposive clause as a complement of the verb *wa-* 'say' is the only way of forming a different-subject complement for the concept of 'wanting'.

In summary, indirect commands marked with purposive modality have the properties of indirect speech reports—there is person shift in the speech report, and a special verbal form is employed. We will now turn to speech reports of a different nature.

19.5.4 Semi-direct speech reports

A number of languages have a speech report construction which occupies middle ground between direct and indirect speech report (see Jackson 1987, Wiesemann 1990, and further discussion in Aikhenvald 2008). While in all indirect speech reports the person reference 'shifts' to the perspective of the reporter, there is no such shift in direct speech. In semi-direct speech, the reference for some participants is shifted, while for others it is not. Semi-direct speech reports share further properties with direct speech—for instance, vocative phrases occur in both, and not in indirect speech. This is hardly surprising, since vocatives 'refer' to the addressee, whose marking is the same in direct and in semi-direct reports.

Constructions of this kind have been documented for numerous African languages. In New Guinea, this phenomenon is found in a few Papuan languages (mostly from the Highland regions of New Guinea). In Papuan languages, semi-direct speech only occurs (a) if the reporter is first person narrator, and (b) if the reporter is involved in the speech report, often, but not necessarily, as an addressee (see Aikhenvald 2008, and references there).

Consider the following example. Before the two brothers left the house, they said 19.56a to their sister. This is cast as direct speech report within the narrative. The imperative is underlined, and the fact that it refers to second person reflected in the gloss.

19.56a [ñən   ata   wiya:m   <u>adakw</u>   an   ma: kami:k   yi-tək]
       you.sg then house+LOC stay:2sgIMPV we.two again fish+DAT go-1duIMPV
       [wa-ku]   ata   yi-bər
       say-COMPL:SS then go-3duBAS.P
       ' "You stay at home, let us two go fishing again", having said (this) the two went off'

Later in this story, the girl was kidnapped by a stranger. This is how she reports what her brothers had told her to do:

19.56b [wun   wiya:m   adakw]   wa-bər-kəkəb
       I:IND.SP.REP house+LOC stay:2pIMPV:**DIR.SP.REP** say-3du-AS.SOON.AS
       wiya:b   kwa-kwana-wun-ək   wun
       house+LOC stay-HAB:ACT.FOC-1fem.sgBAS.VT-CONF I
       'Since the two told me to stay (lit.**I you-stay**) in the house I am staying in the house'

The speech report in 19.56b contains a feature of direct speech: the second person imperative form of the verb (we can recall, from §13.2, that this is used only with second person). It also contains one feature of indirect speech—shift to first person 'I', to fit in with the perspective of the reporter—the kidnapped girl. This is a typical instance of semi-direct speech with an incomplete deictic shift.

A speech report containing an uninflected verb, e.g. a same-subject purposive or a desiderative clause, presents an additional problem if the narrator is involved in the activity reported. An example like 19.57 allows two interpretations. Note that, unlike 19.55 above, this example does not mean 'they told (other people) to fight us (all together)', in the given context.

19.57 [an-a:k   vya-k]   [wa-na-di]
      1du-LK+DAT hit-PURP.SS say-ACT.FOC-3plBAS.VT
      (a) 'They said that they were intending to hit us two'
      (b) 'They said "(We two) intend to hit them (that is, 'us' meaning the speaker)" '

What they HAD actually said was *ñan brə-kə-k vya-k* (we 3du-OBL-DAT hit-PURP.SS) 'we intend to hit those two'. The subject of the verb of speech is the same as that of the speech report, and the reference of the object, 'we two', has been changed to fit in with the perspective of the first person narrator. That is, this can be interpreted as indirect speech (option (a)). Alternatively, this can be interpreted as a semi-direct speech, by analogy with 19.56: the person shift in the object pronoun 'those two' to 'us two' attests to that.

The interpretation of the desiderative is even more problematic. Three options are available for 19.58a:

19.58a [lə-kə   mamək   ata   wa-lə-l]
        she-LK+fem.sg elder.sibling+LK+DAT then say-3fem.sgSUBJ.P-3fem.sgBAS.P
        [[a-də   du   **an-a:m**   kə-kər] wa-na-d]
        DEM.DIST-masc.sg man 1du-LK+ACC/LOC eat-DES say-ACT.FOC-3masc.sgBAS.VT
        (a) 'She then said to her elder sister: "That man said: '(I) want to eat **us**" ' or
        (b) 'She then said to her elder sister: "That man said (he) wanted to eat us" ' or
        (c) 'She then said to her elder sister: "That man wants to eat us" '

What the man actually said in the preceding stretch of discourse was 19.58b:

19.58b wun nəbə kə-kə-tua-digur-ək
        I   able eat-FUT-1sgSUBJ.VT-2plBAS.VT-CONF
        'I am capable of eating you up'

The girl did not quote the man's speech—she recast it in her own words.

The option (a) suggests interpreting this as an instance of indirect speech, given the person shift of the object pronoun to fit in with the reporter's perspective. Note that the verbal form has also been changed: the man did not use a desiderative form at all. Option (b) suggests interpreting this example as an instance of semi-direct speech, by analogy with 19.57. We will see in §19.5.6 that the verb 'say' accompanied by a speech report with a desiderative verb form is the conventional way of talking about a non-first person's wishes (as in 13.57–8); hence option (c). For the actual example, each option is equally valid.

The only potential problem with interpreting 19.57–8 as instances of indirect speech is the fact that such person shift is restricted to the context where the narrator (in each case first person) is involved in the speech report. That is, whatever way we look at these examples, a fact remains: person shift only occurs if the narrator is involved. This is very similar to the conditions under which semi-direct speech occurs in many Papuan languages (see Aikhenvald 2008): the shift of the person of narrator is a mark of his or her intense involvement in the reported activity.

19.5.5 Syntactic role of speech reports

The role of direct and of indirect speech report in multiclausal speech report constructions depends on the transitivity of the reporting verb. A reporting verb may be intransitive, transitive, or even ditransitive (see Munro 1982: 304–5, and discussion in Aikhenvald 2008).

The verb *wa-* 'say' is the only verb in Manambu consistently used to introduce and frame speech reports. This verb is rather unusual in its transitivity patterns. Unlike any other verb (including the other two verbs of speech, *bla-* and *yi-*, discussed in §21.1.3) it appears in a variety of frames.

A. *wa-* 'SAY' AS A DITRANSITIVE VERB can appear in two frames.

First, the verb *wa-* can take two NP objects meaning 'telling someone something', or 'telling someone about something'. Its second argument is an addressee. The object (as in 19.1) or the addressee (as in 19.59) can be cross-referenced in the second position if appropriate.

19.59 ñan-a   təp-a-maːj wa-kə-tua-digur-ək
  we-LK+fem.sg village-LK-story say-FUT-1sgSUBJ.VT-2plBAS.VT-CONF
  'I will tell you (many) our village tale'

A similar example is in T2.67. We will see, in §19.8, that *wa-* in this usage can occur with a headless relative clause in the O slot used as a complementation strategy. The object is questioned with *agwa jaːp* 'what?' (see §10.4) used to question direct objects of any kind (cf. example 10.84). The verb *wa-* can also mean 'promise', and is then used ditransitively. The thing 'promised' is the object, which can also be questioned with *agwa jaːp* 'what?'

19.60 [lə-kə-k   wa-tu-di   jaːp]
  she-OBL-DAT say-1sgSUBJ.P-3plBAS.P thing
  kədika-n-adika
  DEM.PROX.REACT.TOP+pl-PRED-REACT.TOP+pl
  'Here are the things I promised her'

Secondly, the verb *wa-* as ditransitive verb can occur with a name in what looks like an object slot, and the object or person named as a second argument, as in T2.3 ('those whom we call Gala') and in T2.18 (this (man) by that name of Kamkudi), 19.12, and 19.76. In 19.61, it is used with a reciprocal *awarwa* in the meaning of 'address each other as (name)'.

19.61 ñamus   maːm   awarwa wa-na-bər
  younger.sibling elder.sibling REC say-ACT.FOC-3plBAS.VT
  'They two address each other as siblings' (lit. say younger sibling elder sibling to each other)

The object or person named can be cross-referenced on the verb, and questioned either with *agwa jaːp* 'what?', or *sə* 'who?' (see §10.4). In contrast, the name is never cross-referenced on the verb. It is questioned with *ata* 'how?', just like NP objects in the examples discussed at B below, and direct speech reports.

B. *wa-* 'SAY' AS A TRANSITIVE VERB can take an NP object if the NP is something being said, e.g. 'verse' in 10.113, or a wrong word in 19.62a. A young girl instructed an older speaker not to use a Tok Pisin word:

19.62a *lukautim* wa-tukwa
  lukautim say-PROH.GEN
  'Do not say *lukautim*!'

It can also be used in describing ways of pronouncing a word, as in 19.62b:

19.62b [nəkə-di taːkw sajagalavi wa-kwa-na-di]   [nəkə-di taːkw sagəlawi
  other-pl woman sajagalawi say-HAB-ACT.FOC-3plBAS.VT other-pl woman sagəlawi
  wa-kwa-na-di]   wun sawəngalawi wa-kwa-na-un
  say-HAB-ACT.FOC-3plBAS.VT I sawəngalawi say-HAB-ACT.FOC-3plBAS.VT
  'Other women pronounce (lit. say) sajagalawi, other women say sagəlawi, I say sawəgalawi'

The word for language, *kudi*, as the object of *wa-* refers to a typical sound made by a non-human, e.g. *kudi aka wa-na* (language DEM.DIST.REACT.TOP.fem.sg speak-ACT.FOC+3fem.sgBAS.VT) 'she (the pot with water boiling) is making a sound', or *təb kudi wa-na* (sky language speak-ACT.FOC+3fem.sgBAS.VT) 'thunder is sounding' (lit. sky speaks language). Alternatively, the sound itself can be reproduced, as in 19.63:

19.63 tapwuk [pəkaka:u]   ada   wa:d
      rooster cockadoodledoo DEM.DIST.REACT.TOP+masc.sg say+3masc.sgBAS.P
      'The rooster said: "cock-a-doodle-doo" ', or 'The rooster sang'

In this use, the verb *wa-* allows for cross-referencing the addressee, or the time, or the manner as appropriate, and also the object NP referring to what's being said. What is being said can be questioned with *ata* 'how'. This is similar to direct speech reports—see C below.

The verb *wa-* forms a number of idiomatic collocations with interjections and adverbs, e.g. *ay wa-* (ay say-) 'let know', *ya:k wa-* or *ya:kya wa-* (OK say) 'agree, accept; say OK'. The combination *vyakəta wa-* (good say) means 'approve', and *ma: wa-* means 'refuse; reject'. These are lexicalized: the meaning of the whole is not easily deducible from the meanings of the parts. And the component in the speech report slot cannot be questioned.

A reported command cast as purposive indirect speech report is a purposive clause, of the type discussed in §19.4 above (see 19.54). It occupies the object slot of the verb *wa-* as a transitive verb. If the content of a reported command has to be questioned, *ata* is used. Alternatively, a constituent within a purposive clause can be questioned as appropriate (see §10.4). The first person imperative-permissive *wa:u* 'may I talk?' is used intransitively, as a turn-taking device.

C. *wa-* 'SAY' WITH A DIRECT SPEECH REPORT: TRANSITIVE OR DITRANSITIVE?

A direct speech report cannot be considered a direct object of the verb *wa-* since it can never be cross-referenced on this verb, and has to be questioned with the adverbial interrogative *ata* 'how' or its reduplicated version *ata ata*. The question at 19.64 can be answered with 19.61, 19.62a–b, or 19.53:

19.64 ata (ata) wa-na?
      how   say-ACT.FOC+3fem.sgBAS.VT
      'What did she say?'

The same question word can be used to question the sound made by a rooster in 19.63.

An adverbial demonstrative 'thus' is used to anaphorically refer to a speech report:

19.65 [mæy, mæy] kətawa wa-na
      come, come like.this say-ACT.FOC+3fem.sgBAS.VT
      ' "Come, come", this is what she said' (lit. like this she said)

Addressee, time, manner can be cross-referenced on the verb of speech accompanied by a direct speech report, as in T1.23, T2.7, and T1.26 (see §3.1, for the discussion of cross-referencing). The speech report can never be cross-referenced.

We can thus conclude that direct speech report is not a prototypical object. However, it is obligatory, and therefore is to be considered a core argument of the verb 'say'. It is best considered a special grammatical relation.

The transitivity patterns described in this section only apply to the underived verb *wa-*. When accompanied by directionals, or when used as first component in verb compounds, *wa-* can be used either transitively or ditransitively, like any other verb which displays this transitivity alternation (see §4.2.2 and Chapters 15 and 16).

19.5.6 Polysemous patterns in speech reports

In many languages, especially in the New Guinea area, speech reports express a variety of meanings beyond mere reporting of what someone else had actually said (see the survey in Aikhenvald 2008). The following meanings are expressed by direct speech reports.

I. INTERNAL SPEECH AND THOUGHT are cast as direct speech reports, as in T3.28 ('think, hope'). An alternative is to use the expression *mawəla:m wa-* (inside+LK+LOC say) 'think, say to oneself'. The semantics of *mawul* is discussed in §21.4.

19.66 [kə   ta:kw   kra-kə-tua]
     DEM.PROX+fem.sg woman marry/bring-FUT-1sgSUBJ.VT+3fem.sgBAS.VT
     [məwulam   ada   wa-na-d]
     inside+LK+LOC DEM.TOP+masc.sg say-ACT.FOC-3masc.sgBAS.VT
     'He said to himself (lit. in his mind/inside), "I will marry this woman" '

II. DESIRES AND INTENTIONS OF NON-FIRST PERSON are expressed as direct speech reports. A speech report typically contains a same-subject purposive, as in 19.67, or a desiderative, as in 13.57–8 (also see 19.58a).

19.67 [kayik   kurək]   [wa-na]
     picture/image do/get+PURP.SS say-ACT.FOC+3fem.sgBAS.VT
     'She wants or intends to take pictures'

If intention is expressed with a loan from Tok Pisin (*pait* 'hit'), it appears uninflected, as in 19.68—a threat to a naughty baby to make her stop crying lest Tedison whom she was thought to be afraid of might hit her.

19.68 Tedison [*pait*] [wa-k-na-d]
     Tedison hit   say-FUT-ACT.FOC-3masc.sgBAS.VT
     '(Calm down), Tedison intends to hit you'

An alternative is employing an inflected clause as a speech report, as in 19.69, or a noun in the dative case as in 19.70.

19.69 pusi væn   tə-na-d   [papər
     cat   see+SEQ stand-ACT.FOC-3masc.sg.BAS.VT later
     kə-kə-tua]   wa-na-d
     eat-FUT-1sgSUBJ.VT+3fem.sgBAS.VT say-ACT.FOC-3masc.sgBAS.VT
     'The cat is and has been looking (at the duckling), he wants to eat her later (lit. he says "I will eat her later" '

19.70 diya:k   wa-na
     shit+LK+DAT say-ACT.FOC+3fem.sgBAS.VT
     'She wants to have a shit' (said about a 1-year-old baby who could not talk yet, but whose intentions were clear)

None of these examples involves an actual speech act. As I was coming downstairs with a loaded camera (without saying anything), 19.67 was said by a speaker to make sure the girls whose pictures I was to take were ready. Tedison (mentioned in 19.68) had no idea that his name had been used to cajole the little baby into behaving herself. The baby mentioned in 13.67 could not talk yet—so her desire to have a poo could not have been expressed verbally.

And cats do not talk—the cat's intentions in 19.69 were clear from the way it looked at the duckling.

III. REASON, CAUSE, AND PURPOSE are expressed as direct speech reports. Example 19.71 did not involve any speech acts. This was an answer to a child's question about why her mother had gone out:

19.71 [wus-a:k   wa-ku]   [aka
      pee-LK+DAT say-COMPL:SS DEM.DIST.REACT.TOP.fem.sg
      waku-na]
      go.out-ACT.FOC+3fem.sgBAS.VT
      'She has gone out because of (desire to) pee' (lit. 'saying "because of pee" she went out')

And 16.81 explains the intentions of 9-month-old baby who could not yet talk.

We saw, at §16.2.2, that speech reports are one of the biclausal causative strategies; examples are at 16.84, 13.24–5, and T2.34.

IV. APPREHENSIVES can be expressed as direct speech reports. In 19.72 a speech report with an apprehensive meaning contains an irrealis form meaning 'might' (see §13.3):

19.72 [aw yaga-di]   [a-di   du-aba:b aw [a-di   a:s
      then be.scared-3plBAS.P DEM.DIST-pl man-TOO then DEM.DIST-pl dog
      vya-kə-dana-dian]   wa-ku]
      hit-IRR-3plSUBJ.VT-1plBAS.VT say-COMPL:SS
      'So they were afraid, men too, lest the dogs might hit them (lit. having said "Those dogs might hit us")'

V. THE END RESULT OF COUNTING is usually expressed as direct speech report, as in 19.73 and T2.21. Neither of these contains an actual speech report: the child we were talking about in 19.73 did not speak Manambu and was too shy to speak in the presence of a white woman anyway.

19.73 nabi a:li wa:d
      year four say+3masc.sgBAS.VT/P
      'He is 4' (lit. 'he says four')

We have seen that speech reports do not have to imply a speech act. However, there are two major differences between speech reports which do not imply an actual speech act and those reports that do.

First, a direct speech report can precede or follow the reporting verb (as we saw in §19.5.1 above) only if the actual speaking took place. If a speech report is used to express any of the meanings detailed in I–V in this section, it always has to precede the verb 'say'. Reported commands as indirect speech reports also have to precede the verb of speech.

Secondly, speech reports which do not imply an actual speech act tend not to be introduced by a speech introducer *ata* 'then' (see Aikhenvald 2008).

An additional way of making clear that a speech act has actually taken place is by using a 'framing' construction illustrated in 19.51. Then, if a speech report follows the framing clause, another framing clause is often added at the end of the speech report of the kind 'they said [Speech Report] having said'. A typical example is at 19.74:

19.74 [wa:l ja-k-na-d]   [wa-tuə-l]   [wa-ku],
rain rain-FUT-ACT.FOC-3masc.sgBAS.VT say-1sgSUBJ.P-3fem.sgBAS.P say-COMPL:SS
[ata wa:d],   [ma:] [jə ma:] [wa-ku]
then say+3masc.sgBAS.P no rain NEG say-COMPL:SS
' "It will rain", I said saying, then he said, "No, it won't rain", having said'

A speech report which does not imply a speech act cannot be used in such a 'framing' construction. Neither can the verb *wa-* in any of its ditransitive or transitive usages without a direct speech report; nor if it is used in one of the lexicalized collocations, such as *ma: wa-* 'refuse, reject' or *ya:kya wa-* 'agree'.

Framing constructions are very frequent. They also appear in speech reports in the local Tok Pisin: one frequently hears a dialogue being reported using a quote frame *na em i tok olsem na em i tok* (and he said thus and he said). This apparent redundancy serves a purpose: it distinguishes speech acts as speech acts from their metaphorical extensions.

19.6 CLAUSE LINKING INVOLVING CONNECTIVES

Connectives involved in linking clauses occupy clause-initial position. Connectives do not occur in any of the medial clauses discussed in Chapter 18, or dependent clauses in this chapter. The connective *a-lə-k* 'because; this is why' is an exception: it can occur in a causal clause (as in 19.75). This connective derives from *that-fem.sg-DAT* 'for that' and is employed only if explicit statement of reason is appropriate:

19.75 [lə wukəmar-la]   [alək ma:
she forget-3fem.sgSUBJ.P+3fem.sgBAS.P this.is.why again
wa-tua,   a ma:j]
say-1sgSUBJ.VT+3fem.sgBAS.VT DEM.DIST+fem.sg story
'She forgot (it), this is why I am telling it again, the story'

A similar example is at 4.16. Alternatively, the connective *alək* can be used within a causal clause, as in 19.76. This is an explanation as to why there is no men's road and women's road in Malu village.

19.76 [alək məya numa-di kəp rə-ma:r-da-lək]   [[du-a-ya:b
so real big-pl ground sit-NEG.SUB-3pl-BECAUSE man-LK-road
takwa-ya:b wa-n] kwasa kwa-ku] [bə suan
woman+LK-road say-SEQ small+fem.sg stay-COMPL.SS already hard
yi-na]
go-ACT.FOC+3fem.sgBAS.VT
'So since they do not occupy really big territory, since what is called men's and women's road is small, it is difficult (to have them)'

In T1.16 *alək* occurs after the subject *wun* 'I', since the subject is fronted as part of a topicalization strategy (see §20.2). This connective can link sentences as well as clauses as in 18.25, and T1.22. It often occurs in a main clause preceded by a medial causal clause, as in 18.49 and 19.77, or by another medial clause, as in 18.52.

19.77 [də da-də-lək],   [(alək) wi waku-dian]
he go.down-3masc.sg-BECAUSE this.is.why house go.out-1plBAS.P
'Since it (plane) went down, [this is why] we left our houses'

We recall, from §18.7, that the connective *alək* and the causal medial clause marker *-lək* share their etymology: both come from a dative-marked feminine form of the functionally unmarked distal demonstrative *a-*.

We saw in §18.3 that the medial clause form *tə-ku* (stand-COMPL.SS) operates almost like a conjunction 'thus, and so' when it follows another medial clause (see 18.28). This form is indeed in the process of grammaticalization as part of a conjunction: *alək tə-ku* (DEM.DIST.fem.sg+DAT stand-COMPL.SS) is used as a clause linker meaning 'and so, as a result'. It is pronounced as one phonological word. This connective does not occur with causal clauses. An example is in 19.78:

19.78 [sana:k   karabə   ja:p kui-taka-dana-di]
      money+LK+DAT men's.house+LK thing give.to.third.p-put-3plSUBJ.VT-3plBAS.VT
      [alək   tə-ku   ma: tə]
      this.is.why be-COMPL.SS NEG have.NEG
      'They (the neighbouring group) gave away the things from men's house for money, this is why they do not have (them anymore)'

The connective *aw* 'and then; so; but' links clauses and sentences. Its meaning may involve contrast, as in 19.79:

19.79 [vyakəta-d],   [aw   wun ñan ma: tə],   [a-də-rəb
      nice-3masc.sgNOM CONTRAST I   child NEG have:NEG DEM.DIST-masc.sg-FULLY
      lukauti-tək]
      look.after-1duIMPV
      'He (the foundling) is nice, and (surprise, surprise: unlike any normal woman) I don't have a child, (so) let's look right after this one'

It occurs as a sentence linker in T2.5–6, and T2.8–9. Also see 19.72 for its sequential meaning. When repeated, it refers to alternating actions, as in *aw yi-n aw ya-n* (and.then go-SEQ and.then come-SEQ) 'on the one hand coming, on the other hand going' (T3.18). A similar example, *aw war-ən aw da-n* (then go.up-SEQ then go.down-SEQ) 'alternately going up and coming down' is in T2.8. This same form can link noun phrases, e.g. *aw kami: aw lau-lap* (then fish then ripe-banana) '(we eat) sometimes fish sometimes banana' (or both).

The connective *a* 'then, as a result' has a sequential meaning, as in T2.3 and 19.4. It can link dependent clauses, as in T3.18 where it is similar to *aw*. It may have an adversative meaning, roughly translatable as 'but', as in 10.22b. The form *a* probably comes from the feminine distal demonstrative 'that'.

Connectives which link sentences within a paragraph are *ata* 'then', and *atawata:y* (from *ata wa-ta:y* 'then say-COTEMP') 'and so then, in summary, this is why'. The latter is a result of a recent grammaticalization of *ata* and a medial clause form of 'say'. The semantic development is congruent with the use of *wa-* 'say' to express reason (see §19.5.6). The connective *atawata:y* is often used without reference to an actual speech act, as in 18.33 where the speaker talks about how the Avatip people lived during the Second World War when they had to hide from the Japanese invaders. Or it may refer cataphorically or anaphorically to an actual speech report, as in 19.80:

19.80 [atawata:y takwa-sua:l   taka-ya-da-d]   [ta:kw
      thus/so   woman+LK-lie put-come-3plSUBJ.P-3masc.sgBAS.P woman
      kra-kə-məna]   [mən
      get-FUT-2masc.sgSUBJ.VT+3fem.sgBAS.VT you.masc
      nəbə-takwa-ñan-a
      young-woman+LK-child-3fem.sgNOM

kwatiya-kə-bana]   [atawata:y
give.to.nonthird.p-FUT-1plSUBJ.VT+3fem.sgBAS.VT thus
wa-da-d]
say-3plSUBJ.P-3masc.sgBAS.P
'Thus/this way they lied to him about women (lit. put woman-lie to him), "You will marry a woman, we will give you a young woman", thus they said to him'

The connective *ata* often introduces speech reports which imply actual speech, as can be seen throughout the texts at the end of this grammar. It typically precedes the verb and never occurs on the first sentence in a text (see examples 4.12 and T1.1, T1.8, T1.10, and T1.12). In the third clause of T1.12 the connective *ata* is placed after the imperative verb 'go'; this adds to the urgency of the command.

Ata can intervene between parts of numerous multiword constituents involving verbs (for instance, complex predicates: see §17.1–5, and negative constructions: see Chapter 14).

The question of whether the form *ata* meaning 'how; thus' and *ata* as a negator of desiderative and same-subject purposive (see §14.3.2) are related to each other and to the connective *ata* remains open. Several instances of *ata* in its different meanings do not occur; we can recall, from §10.4, that a repeated form *ata ata* has just the interrogative meaning 'how?'

When used in the predicate slot or as part of predicate focus, *ata* 'connective' and *ata* 'thus, how' take the predicate marker -*n* (see §10.2.3 on its occurrence with reactivated topic-marking demonstratives), as in 4.79 and 10.103. No other connective can be focused or head a predicate.

The connective *kəpa:b* 'in case' introduces dependent conditional clauses discussed at §13.7 and §18.8 (examples 13.88, and 18.52). This connective is most probably a terminative case form of *kəp* 'just' (§21.2.2). Just like any other connective, *kəpa:b* occupies a clause-initial position.

19.7 JUXTAPOSITION OF MAIN CLAUSES

Several main clauses can be juxtaposed to one another. Such juxtaposed main clauses do not have a special rising intonation contour characteristic of dependent juxtaposed clauses discussed at §19.1. There is usually a short pause between the clauses. Juxtaposition of clauses has the following semantic effects.

I. A subsequent clause offers a comment or a clarification to the preceding clause, elaborating on it. Examples include 19.79, and also 19.9, 19.29, 14.11, 14.12, 14.53, 14.95, 14.97, 14.104, and T1.9, T1.19–20, T1.22, and T1.28. A similar example is at 19.81: Kukəlyabau was explaining that she was a little girl when the Second World War broke out. The fourth clause provides additional information to the third clause.

19.81 [wun a   *taim* numa   ñan ma: tə]   [*war*
       I   DEM.DIST.fem.sg time big+fem.sg child NEG be:NEG war
       ya-də-l]   [numa   ñan ma: tə]   [kwasa
       come-3masc.sgSUBJ.P-3fem.sgBAS.P big+fem.sg child NEG be:NEG small+fem.sg
       ñan tə-lwun-ək]   [*war* ata ya:d]
       child be-1fem.sgBAS.VT-CONF war then come+3masc.sgBAS.P
       'I was not a big child that time, (time when) the war came. I was not a big child, I was a small child, then the war came'

A subsequent clause often rephrases the preceding clause, as in 14.50. This serves as a rhetorical device, to make sure the hearer understands the point made. Similar examples come from beginnings and endings of stories—this can be seen in T1.35, T2.68, and T3.1.

II. A subsequent clause offers an alternative, or a correction, to the preceding clause, as in 14.102 and 14.105. If the subsequent clause is cast in irrealis (see §13.3), it acquires an apprehensive meaning—that is, is understood as a warning against something negative. Examples are at 13.43 and 19.82.

19.82 [a   *plet*   akayblak]   [sa:r
      DEM.DIST.fem.sg plate   IMPV+CAUS+overturn   fly
      rə-kə-k-la]
      sit-IRR-IRR+3fem.sgSUBJ.VT-3fem.sgBAS.VT
      'Turn that plate upside down, or else a fly would sit (on it)'

A juxtaposed irrealis clause can be negated with the dependent negator *-ma:r-*, as shown in 19.83 (the meaning is that of possible negative consequence). This is unlike irrealis in main clauses which is negated with the particle *akəs* (see §14.3.1); also see 13.35. This suggests that juxtaposed irrealis clauses could well be treated as a subtype of dependent clauses.

19.83 [kə-di   *plet*   ajan]   [a   kamna:gw
      DEM.PROX-pl plate   IMPV+wash DEM.DIST+fem.sg food
      kə-mar-k-na-ñən]
      eat-NEG.SUB-IRR-ACT.FOC-2fem.sgBAS.VT
      'Wash these plates, (or else) you will not eat the food'

III. If one of the clauses is negated, the relationship between juxtaposed clauses is that of contrast, as in 14.41, 14.135, and 14.156. Juxtaposition of a positive and a negative clause can be used as a means of clausal disjunction, as in 7.23.

IV. The subsequent clause marks consequence or reason if it contains an imperative or a desiderative, as in 13.12, 13.20, 13.23–4, 13.58, 14.31, 14.90, 14.108, and 19.48. Both clauses can contain either an imperative or a desiderative, as in 19.84.

19.84 [væk akrawul]   [səkulək yi-kər]
      pot IMPV+bring+INSIDE cooking do-DES
      'Bring the pot inside (the house), (because) I want to cook'

V. A clause juxtaposed to another clause has a simultaneous temporal meaning if the verb cross-references time in the second position. This is the case in 19.81 (second clause: '(time when) the war came') and 9.33. This illustrates the anaphoric or cataphoric function of cross-referencing time in the second position on the verb, which acts as an additional clause-linking device.

VI. Juxtaposition of clauses may also reflect a sequence of actions, as in T1.27. Juxtaposition of two clauses with positional verbs has a similar effect, e.g. 19.85:

19.85 [wun-a-də   warag   nagwəm   war-ən   kwa:d]
      I-LK-masc.sg ancestor   sago+LK+LOC go.up-SEQ stay+3masc.sgBAS.P
      [ra:d]
      sit+3masc.sgBAS.P
      'My ancestor kept going up the sago (fields) (and) settled down (lit. sat) (there)'

We will see in §20.1.4 that there are no pivot restrictions on coreferential deletion of arguments in clause juxtaposition, with just one exception: if juxtaposition of clauses reflects a sequence of actions the subjects are always shared.

19.8 COMPLEMENTATION STRATEGIES

Manambu has no complement clauses as a separate clause type. Existing clause types are used in lieu of complement clauses depending on verb type, the semantics of complement clause (whether fact or activity, or potential), and the relative tense of the complement clause (see Dixon 2006, for the basic principles for a typological approach to complementation). A clausal complement can be in S or O function (but never in A function). These correlations are summarized in Table 19.4.

We discuss the existing complementation strategies one by one.

I. COMPLETIVE MEDIAL CLAUSES (discussed at §18.3) are used as clausal complements exclusively in O function, with the verbs of perception such as 'see/look' and 'hear/listen/obey' (and compounds and directional forms involving these: see Chapters 15 and 16). They indicate that the action of the clausal complement precedes that of the main clause. The semantics of clausal complement is activity or fact. If the subject of the main clause and of the clausal complement are different, different subject forms are employed. Examples are at 19.86–7; also see T2.4, T3.20, and T3.48.

19.86 [amæy wa-lə-k]   [awuk]
      mother see-3fem.sg-COMPL.DS IMPV+hear/listen/obey
      'Listen to/obey what mother said' (lit. mother having said, listen/obey)

19.87 [[a-də   wajək   akətawa kur-lə-k]   væn
      DEM.DIST-masc.sg eel+LK+DAT like.this do-3fem.sg-COMPL.DS see+SEQ
      tə-ku]
      stand-COMPL.SS
      'After he'd seen that she'd done this because of the eel (her husband killed this eel)'

II. JUXTAPOSITION OF MAIN CLAUSES (also see §19.7) is used for a clausal complement in O function with the same verbs of perception. Juxtaposition is used if the action of the complement is either simultaneous or subsequent to the main clause—in contrast to the completive medial clauses in I above. Examples of simultaneous action are at 19.48, 19.88–9, 19.93a–b, 19.94, and also T1.11 and T3.16.

19.88 [wa-tua]   [awuk]
      say-1sgSUBJ.VT+3fem.sgBAS.VT IMPV+hear/listen/obey
      'Listen to/obey what I am saying' (lit. having said, listen/obey)

19.89 [a   takwa-ñan   kətu   və-lə-l]   [du
      DEM.DIST woman+LK-child look.up see-3fem.sgSUBJ.P-3fem.sgBAS.P man
      kə-da-wur   adəka   rə-na-d]
      DEM.PROX-masc.sg-UP DEM.DIST.REACT.TOP+masc.sg sit-ACT.FOC-3masc.sgBAS.VT
      'That young woman looked up and saw: the up-there-man was sitting there'

If the action of the clausal complement is subsequent to that of the main clause, it can be cast in future tense, as in 19.90. Such constructions are polysemous, in that they can denote

TABLE 19.4   Complementation strategies in Manambu

STRATEGIES	VERB TYPES	SEMANTICS	RELATIVE TENSE	SYNTACTIC FUNCTION
I. Completive medial clause	perception		preceding	O
II. Juxtaposition	perception refuse/agree mental processes finishing	activity/fact	simultaneous/subsequent	S (finishing verbs; verbless clauses) O (all other verb types)
III. Relative clause	mainly perception		no restrictions	S/O
IV. Purposive SS	speaking, ordering			S
V. Desiderative	wanting			O, S (verbless clauses)
VI. Purposive DS	speaking, asking, ordering wanting	potential	subsequent	O, head of predicate resulting from desubordination
VII. Direct speech reports	speaking, asking, ordering	activity, fact, potential		Direct speech report as a special relation
VIII. Reported questions	knowledge			O
IX. Deverbal nominalizations	mental processes wanting forbidding, fearing, negative ordering difficulty finishing	activity/fact: Ø marked potential: dative-aversive case-marked	no restrictions	O, S of deverbal clauses and verb 'be difficult'
X. Sequencing medial clause	perception speaking teaching	fact	simultaneous	O
XI. Medial clause 'as soon as'	perception	activity		

activity or fact (reading (a)) or refer to a potential happening (reading (b)). The reason for this is morphological—we can recall, from §13.3, that future morphology is homophonous with irrealis.

19.90 [*kamapu*-k-na]   [və-kə-tua]
      appear-FUT/IRR-ACT.FOC+3fem.sgBAS.VT see-FUT/IRR-1sgSUBJ.VT+3fem.sgBAS.VT
      (a) 'I will see her appear' (lit, she will appear I will see)
      (b) 'I will see if she appears'

The sentence in 19.90 could also be understood as consisting of a juxtaposed dependent clause and a main clause (see §19.1), if it had a characteristic intonation contour with sharp rise on the last word of the juxtaposed clause. Then the reading would have been 'If she had appeared I would have seen her/it'. This highlights the importance of intonation.

A juxtaposed main clause can be used in lieu of a clausal complement of verbs *ma: wa-* (no say) 'refuse' and *ya:kya wa-* (OK say) 'agree', when they refer to a fact or activity and involve different subjects. We will see, at IV below, that if their subjects are the same, the same-subject purposive or dative-aversive-marked nominalization will be preferred. Potential meaning entails the use of either different-subject purposive or a dative-aversive-marked nominalization. In 19.91, a fact complement expressed with a juxtaposed clause (clause 1) is contrasted to a potential complement expressed with a dative-aversive-marked nominalization.

19.91 [yi-tua]   [ma: wa-na-di]   [kə-di   təp-a
      go-1sgSUBJ.VT+3fem.sgBAS.VT NEG say-ACT.FOC-3plBAS.VT DEM.PROX-pl village-LK
      du   [a-də   na:gw nagwu-gara:m   vəl-vələk]   ma:
      man DEM.DIST-masc.sg sago   sago+LK-field+LK+LOC cut-RED+DAT NEG
      wa-na-di]
      say-ACT.FOC-3plBAS.VT
      'They objected to the fact that I went (hunting), these village men refused me (the permission) to cut sago in the sago field'

Juxtaposition is also used if the clausal complement is in S function of the verb *kusə-* 'finish'. The clause which corresponds to the complement often cross-references time or manner in second position. The main clause takes feminine singular cross-referencing as a default option (see §5.2.3).

19.92 [warya-n   tə-ya-da-l]   [aka
      fight+come-SEQ stand-come-3plSUBJ.P-3fem.sgBAS.P DEM.DIST.REACT.TOP.fem.sg
      bə   kusə-l]
      already finish-3fem.sgBAS.P
      'Their fighting was already over' (lit. they kept fighting (it) was already over)

Juxtaposition of a main clause can also be used in lieu of a clausal argument in the O slot of mental processes: knowing, as in 19.93a–b, and forgetting, as in 19.94. The juxtaposed clause as a complementation strategy can be preposed or postposed to the clause containing the verb of mental process:

19.93a [barək   wa-mənə-l]   [wun ma: la:kw]
       fever+LK+DAT say-2masc.sgSUBJ.P-3masc.sgBAS.P I   NEG know:NEG
       'I did not know (that) he'd said he was sick' (lit. He said he was sick (lit. of sickness) I did not know)

19.93b [dəy ma: la:kw]   [ñan-ugw kurə-n kə-dana]
  they NEG know:NEG child-PL   get-SEQ eat-3plSUBJ.VT+3plBAS.VT
  'They do not know that their children get and eat (other people's sweet potatoes)' (lit.
  they do not know, children getting eat)

19.94 [wukəmar-tua]   [wun taka-tua-l]
  forget-1sgSUBJ.VT+3fem.sgBAS.VT I   put-1sgSUBJ.VT+3fem.sgBAS.VT-3fem.sgNOM
  'Then I forgot that I put (the hair cream on top of the mosquito net)' (lit. I forgot it-was-
  the case that I put (it there))

Finally, one main clause juxtaposed to another may be used in lieu of a clausal argument
marking an activity in the S function in a verbless clause, as in 19.95.

19.95 [vyakət-a]   [væra-məna]
  good-3fem.sgNOM come.toward-2masc.sgSUBJ.VT+3fem.sgBAS.VT
  'It is good you came/are coming' (lit. it is good—you came/are coming)

In each case, the clause boundary is signalled by an intonation break (less than a second
duration).

III. A RELATIVE CLAUSE with or without an overtly stated head noun can be used to express
clausal complement referring to a fact, as in 19.96a–b. The way of saying 'tell me why you
came' is 'tell me the reason for which you came'.

19.96a [ya-məna   maw]
  come-2masc.sgSUBJ.VT+3fem.sgBAS.VT reason/base
  [wa-məna]   [wukəu]
  say-2masc.sgSUBJ.VT+3fem.sgBAS.VT listen+1sgIMPV
  'You tell why you came, so that I listen'

Another way of saying essentially the same thing is 19.96b. The difference is that in 19.96a
the speaker is requesting the full story concerning the reason of the other person's coming,
while 19.96b presupposes a simpler statement—a 'thing' fought about:

19.96b [warya-bra   ja:p] [ma: la:kw]
  fight+come-3duSUBJ.P+3fem.sgBAS.P thing NEG know:NEG
  'I do not know why (lit. thing) they fought about'

Headless relative clauses, like the one at 19.25 (and 19.23a), can also be interpreted as
complementation strategies. They can express fact or activity. The syntactic context in 19.25
makes it clear that we are dealing with a headless relative clause: the common argument has
been omitted, but the adjective referring to it remains in its position in the noun phrase.
However, we saw above that a headless relative clause can be almost indistinguishable from
a main clause (cf. 19.26). And clause juxtaposition as a complementation strategy may also
be homonymous with a headless relative clause. So, 19.97a is inherently ambiguous between
reading (a), with a juxtaposed clause as a complementation strategy, and reading (b) as a
headless relative clause.

19.97a [kəlayir   rə-na]
  DEM.PROX.fem.sg+DIST+ALL sit-ACT.FOC+3fem.sgBAS.VT
  [və-ñəna]
  see-2fem.sgSUBJ.VT+3fem.sgBAS.VT
  (a) 'Do you see that she is sitting here further away?'
  (b) 'Do you see the one (female) sitting here further away?'

The ambiguity disappears if the second clause is negated: a relative clause would take the dependent clause negator *-ma:r-*, and the juxtaposed clause would be negated like any main clause (§14.5). The negated relative clause is at 19.97b, and a juxtaposed main clause at 19.97c:

19.97b [kəlayir   rə-ma:r-na]
       DEM.PROX.fem.sg+DIST+ALL   sit-NEG.SUB-ACT.FOC+3fem.sgBAS.VT
       [və-ñəna]
       see-2fem.sgSUBJ.VT+3fem.sgBAS.VT
       (a) 'Do you see the one (female) not sitting here further away?'

19.97c [kəlayir   ma: rə]   [və-ñəna]
       DEM.PROX.fem.sg+DIST+ALL   NEG   NEG:sit   see-2fem.sgSUBJ.VT+3fem.sgBAS.VT
       (a) 'Do you see that (she) is not sitting here further away?'

A similar example, with a verb of knowledge and understanding, is at 19.98, an angry shout at a naughty and disobedient child:

19.98 [laku-ñəna]   [wa-tua]
      know/understand-2fem.sgSUBJ.VT+3fem.sgBAS.VT   say-1fem.sgSUBJ.VT+3fem.sgBAS.VT
      (a) 'Did you understand that I was telling you (what to do)?'
      (b) 'Did you understand what I was telling you?'

IV. SAME-SUBJECT PURPOSIVE marks a purpose complement of any verb if semantically appropriate, as shown in 7.76 and 19.43 (see §19.4.1). Same-subject purposive can also be used as a complementation strategy with the verb 'say' if the subject of the verb expressing purpose or intention is coreferential with the subject of 'say'—see 13.45, 19.57 (§19.5.4), and 19.99:

19.99 [kwasa   ñan   tə-tuə-k]   [wun-a:k   krak
      small+fem.sg   child   stay-1sg-COMPL.DS   I-LK+DAT   take+PURP.SS
      wa-mənə-l]
      say-2masc.sgSUBJ.P-3fem.sgBAS.P
      'When I was a small girl you spoke of marrying me'

V. DIFFERENT-SUBJECT PURPOSIVE clauses can mark a purpose complement of any verb (see §19.4.1 and §13.4.2, and 13.54–5). This is also used in indirect commands, as in 19.54 and 13.49. A purposive clause as a complement of the verb *wa-* 'say' is the only way of forming a different-subject complement clause for the concept of 'wanting': 19.100 is ambiguous between 'we told them to go to the house' and 'we wanted them to go to the house'. This ambiguity can only be resolved by context.

19.100 [wiya:r   yi-bər-kəkək]   [wa-bana-bər]
       house+LK+ALL   go-3du-PURP.DS   say-1plSUBJ.VT-3duBAS.VT
       (a) 'We told them two to go to the house'
       (b) 'We wanted them two to go to the house'

In 13.51, only the 'wanting' reading is appropriate, since there was no speech act involved.

In different subject 'wanting' constructions, the verb 'say' can be omitted, as in 19.101. Then, there is no ambiguity between 'telling someone to do something' and 'wanting someone to do something'. Similar examples are at 13.55, and 14.70.

19.101 wun-aba:b   kə-də   ñan   kəta-bə   tə-də-kəkək
       I-TOO   DEM.PROX-masc.sg   child   now-already   stand/be-3masc.sg-PURP.DS
       'I too want this child to be like this now' (lit. I too so that this child be like this now)
       *I too tell this child to be like this'

The subject of the matrix clause can also be omitted—and then a sentence *kə-də ñan kəta-bə tə-də-kəkək* means '(speaker wants) this child to be like this now'. This use of the different-subject purposive may be interpreted as an instance of desubordination—whereby the erstwhile dependent clause becomes a main clause. Different-subject purposive clauses are also used as complementation strategies with verbs of asking, as in 13.52. An alternative is a direct speech report, or a reported question, in VI below.

VI. DESIDERATIVE clause can mark a purposive complement of any verb—see §19.4.2 and §13.5 and 19.47. Desideratives in dependent clauses in O function can be used as complementation strategies with potential meaning involving verbs of negative desire, such as 'be unwilling' in 19.102:

19.102 [wun tapwuk ba:d kə-kər] [kwasək   yi-na-dəwun-ək]
　　　　I   chicken egg   eat-DES unwilling go-ACT.FOC-1masc.sgBAS.VT-CONF
　　　　'I am unwilling to eat chicken egg'

A desiderative clause in the direct speech report slot of the verb *wa-* is the only way of reporting non-first person's desire—see 19.58 and 13.57. A desiderative clause can be in the S slot of a verbless clause—see 13.65.

VII. DIRECT SPEECH REPORTS framed by the verb *wa-* 'say' can be used as complementation strategies. We saw in §19.5 above that a direct speech report is a special grammatical relation. The meanings of direct speech reports range from fact/activity to potential, and can involve statements, questions, and commands.

VIII. REPORTED QUESTIONS can be used as complementation strategies in the O slot of the verb of knowledge/understanding:

19.103 [wun-aba:b ma: la:kw]   [agwa-mi də-kə-di   təkə-mi-a-di]
　　　　I-TOO   NEG know:NEG what-tree he-OBL-pl seed-tree-LK-3plNOM
　　　　'I, too, do not know what tree they are seeds of'

19.104 [wun ma: la:kw]   [kas   du-ta:kw   tə-na-di]
　　　　I   NEG know:NEG how.many man-woman be/have-ACT.FOC-3plBAS.VT
　　　　'I do not know how many people they have (in Malu)'

In 19.104, the interrogative quantifier *kas* is postposed to the noun 'people' which is its normal position (see 10.109–10 in §10.4). Reported questions typically refer to fact or activity. They are rather rare in discourse of any sort, and may have been calqued from Tok Pisin or even English.

IX. NOMINALIZATIONS are widely used as complementation strategies. We can recall, from §9.1.1, that deverbal nominalizations with Ø-case marking in O function are employed as complementation strategies, with the verb 'know', as in 9.2, and 'finish', as in 4.8. A deverbal nominalization in S function can also serve as a complementation strategy, as in 9.3. A nominalization can be a complement of a verb 'be difficult', as in 4.7, 9.9, 19.43, and T3.20, T3.33, and T3.35. An action nominalization can occur in the predicate slot, as in T3.34 (where it is negated). These nominalizations always refer to activity or fact.

Deverbal nominalizations marked with dative-aversive case *-Vk* are used in the O slot of verbs to do with not wanting, refusing, forbidding, feeling shame, as in 9.5–6, 13.78, and 13.81, waiting as in 9.4, forgetting as in 13.79, being afraid of doing something, as in 13.82, and in the sense of 'for fear of', as in 9.7 and 13.83, or ordering not to do something, as in 15.111.

There are no restrictions on subject coreferentiality—in 19.105a the subjects of the matrix clause and of the complementation strategy are the same, and in 19.105b they are different:

19.105a [barək   kwa-kwa-k] [ma: wa-na-wun]
       sick+LK+DAT stay-RED-DAT NEG say-ACT.FOC-1fem.sgBAS.VT
       'I don't want to become sick' (lit. to becoming sick I say no)

19.105b [ñən   barək   kwa-kwa-k] [ma: wa-na-wun]
       you.fem sick+LK+DAT stay-RED-DAT NEG say-ACT.FOC-1fem.sgBAS.VT
       'I don't want you to become sick' (lit. to you becoming sick I say no)

In all these cases a dative-aversive nominalization used as a clausal complement has a 'potential' meaning, that of future projection, similarly to 9.8. This is in contrast to a zero-marked nominalization—see 4.7 and 9.9. A dative-aversive nominalization can never occupy the S slot of any verb, except for verbs of difficulty.

X. SEQUENCING MEDIAL CLAUSES can mark clausal complements of a transitive verb (as in 18.12 and 19.106–7) or of a ditransitive verb (18.13), as complementation strategies. The meaning is that of an accomplished fact rather than a prolonged activity. They have been attested with the verb *wa-* 'speak' (18.12 and 19.106), 'teaching' as in 18.13, and perception, as in 19.107.

19.106 [na:gw ka:n   rapə-n]   [wa-kəkə-tua]
       sago eat+SEQ grow.up-SEQ say-FUT-1sgSUBJ.VT+3fem.sgBAS.VT
       'I will tell of (their) eating sago (and) growing up'

19.107 [[a-bər   ñidi   waku-n]   və-ku]   [[akətawa rə-na-bər]
       DEM.DIST-du child:DU go.out-SEQ see-COMPL.SS like.this   sit-ACT.FOC-3duBAS.VT
       wa-ku]   [vya-də-bər]
       say-COMPL.SS hit-3masc.sgSUBJ.P-3duBAS.P
       'Having seen the fact that the two children went out, having said, "This is how they are", he hit them two'

They can also be used with a verb denoting 'difficulty', in the S function (see 20.65).

XI. MEDIAL CLAUSES MARKED WITH -*kəb* 'AS SOON AS' can be occasionally used as clausal complements in the O slot of verbs of perception, if the speaker wishes to emphasize the temporal overlap between the perception and the activity (see §18.6).

19.108 [atawa sa:d tə-də-kəkəb]   [akəs
       thus   way stand-3masc.sg-AS.SOON.AS NEG.HAB
       və-kwa-bana-d]
       see-HAB-1plSUBJ.VT-3masc.sgBAS.VT
       'We usually do not see it (the rainbow) standing like this'

The meaning of the clausal complement is always that of activity simultaneous with perception; however, such examples are rare.

Table 19.4 shows that, of all the complementation strategies, the juxtaposition strategy and deverbal nominalization are the most versatile in terms of verb types they occur with. The verbs of perception and knowledge allow the greatest number of options in terms of types of complementation strategies they occur with.

19.9 DESUBORDINATION OF DEPENDENT CLAUSES

What is an essentially dependent clause can come to be used as a main clause through regular ellipsis of the erstwhile main clause. This phenomenon known as 'desubordination' has been described for numerous languages, including English (see Stirling 1998). Desubordination and the change of status of clauses can result in the creation of new tense-aspect-mood paradigms (as in Australian languages: Dixon 2002a: 148–9), or evidentiality (as in Estonian: Aikhenvald 2004a: 281–3).

Just three of the medial dependent clause types in Manambu are used on their own (see §18.2–4). In each case, this can be considered ellipsis; however, each use has its own semantic overtones and can be analysed as a new clause type 'in the making'.

Sequencing medial clauses with the verb marked with *-n* (§18.2) appear as strong commands, as shown in 16.96, and 19.109—an annoyed order to a naughty child to be seated:

19.109 jupwi   taka-n
        backside put.down-SEQ
        'Put your backside down!' (lit. putting your backside down!)

A medial completive same-subject form on its own can also be used as a command, an even stronger one. The illocutionary force is comparable to German participle commands, e.g. *hingesessen!* 'sitting here!' An example is at 19.110—the mother was even more annoyed than when she shouted 19.109:

19.110 təkər-ə-m   da-ku
        chair-LK-LOC sit-COMPL:SS
        'Sit down on the chair immediately!' (lit. Having sat on the chair!)

These command strategies fill what can be conceived of as a 'gap' in the system. We saw in §14.4.1 that Manambu has three prohibitive forms: a general prohibitive and two strong prohibitives. But there is only one positive imperative (§13.2). The different degrees of strength of command corresponding to the degree of strength of prohibition are expressed through command strategies employing desubordinated clauses. Rough correspondences, with numbers of example sentences, are in Table 19.5.

A medial sequencing clause can be used as a complete sentence if it states the result of an activity, as in 19.111. A pause of less than a second's duration signals a sentence boundary. There is no pause between the two sequential verb forms in the second sentence.

TABLE 19.5 Negative commands and desubordinated clauses as command strategies

SEMANTICS	POSITIVE	NEGATIVE
simple command	imperative: *awuk* 'listen!'	general prohibitive 'don't do it' (14.92a)
strong command	desubordinated sequencing clause (19.109)	strong prohibitive: 'don't you dare do it' (14.92b)
very strong command	desubordinated completive medial clause (19.110)	extra-strong prohibitive: 'don't you dare do it (or else)' (14.92c)

19.111 [[də-kaba:b gu   kə-də-k]   ata yi-bər   ya] [yi:n
       he-OBL+TOO water consume-3masc.sg-COMPL.DS then go-3duBAS.P EMPH go+SEQ
       waku-n   təp-a:m]
       go.out-SEQ village-LK+LOC
       'After he too had drunk water, then they two went. As a result they went and arrived in
       the village' (lit. going going out in the village)

Manambu does not have a morphological resultative derivation—desubordinated medial
sequencing clauses play the part of 'resultative' strategies.

Medial completive clauses, typically same-subject ones, can be used on their own, with a
completive meaning. A speaker came into the house and showed us a fish, commenting on
how she had obtained it:

19.112 [sa:n   yapi-ku]
       money buy/pay-COMPL.SS
       'I have paid money (for it)' (lit. having paid money (for it))

This completive use is semantically close to the meaning of the anterior complex predicate
with the auxiliary *tə-* discussed at §17.1.1. Yet, it is different inasmuch as the focus is on the
completion of the action and the result achieved.

Desubordination has its roots in ellipsis. Yet the two are different. Consider 19.113b, an
answer to the question in 19.113a:

19.113a akə   səkər væra-k-ñəna
        what.fem.sg time   come.back-FUT-2fem.sgSUBJ.VT+3fem.sgSUBJ.VT
        'What time will you come back?'

19.113b [na:gw yapi-ku]
        sago   buy-COMPL.SS
        'After I had bought sago' (lit. having bought sago)

This has a clear overtone of sequencing and of relative tense: 'I will come back after I've
bought sago'. Not so with 19.112 which simply focuses on the completion of an action. (An
additional way of focusing on the completion of one action before the start of another is
through using *ya:kya* 'OK' or its Tok Pisin equivalent *orait* in lieu of a main clause. We return
to this in §20.4.2.)

Along similar lines, a cotemporaneous clause can be used on its own, to express prolonged
action that started before the moment of speech and goes on and on. An example is at
19.114—a mother was exhausted by her baby daughter's drinking and peeing non-stop. Similar
examples are at 4.33 and 18.35.

19.114 [gu   kə-ta:y]   [wus yi-ta:y]
       water consume-COTEMP pee   go-COTEMP
       'All she does is drink and pee' (lit. having drunk water having peed)

Desubordinated cotemporaneous clauses typically occur in pairs, as in 19.114, 4.33, and
18.35, referring to continuous alternate or simultaneous actions. Since Manambu does not
have a dedicated verbal form to cover this meaning, once again a desubordinated verb can be
said to fill in a gap.

Desubordination of the three dependent clause types discussed here goes hand in hand with
grammaticalizing the most frequent desubordinated forms into connectives. We saw in §18.3
that the form *tə-ku* (stand-COMPL.SS) operates almost like a conjunction 'thus, and so' (18.28).

This form is indeed in the process of grammaticalization as part of a complex connective: *alək tə-ku* (DEM.DIST.fem.sg+DAT stand-COMPL.SS) is used as a clause linker meaning 'and so, as a result' (§19.6 and 19.78). Fixed combinations [*akəm tə-ku*] (where+LOC stay-COMPL.SS) or [*akəb tə-ku*] (where+TERM stay-COMPL.SS) meaning 'where from?' (as in 7.29 and 7.55) are frequently used as an interrogative on their own: we can recall, from §10.4, that Manambu does not have a dedicated interrogative form meaning 'where from' (there is one meaning 'where to', and another one meaning 'where (location)'). A desubordinated verb is again used to fill a gap: *akəm tə-ku* can be considered a new interrogative form. Desubordinated sequencing forms containing *-n* are on the way towards being reinterpreted as adverbs; see 18.7–8 in §18.2 (also see §4.4). Unlike corresponding verbal forms, they cannot be negated separately.

We can recall, from 18.8, that *səbənə-n* (return-SEQ) can be used as a verbal modifier meaning 'back', and can also be used as a medial verb 'returning'. The two usages can be distinguished: the verb in a dependent clause can have its own arguments and obliques and can be negated, and the verbal modifier cannot.

The dependent clause verb *səbən-ən* in its negative and positive form is illustrated in 19.115. The relevant forms are underlined.

19.115 [lə   wiya:r   s<u>əbən-ən</u>]   [ñan-ugw-a:k   kamna:gw
       she   house+LK+ALL   return-SEQ   child-PL-LK+DAT   food
       kui-k-la]   [<u>səbən-ma:r-ən</u>]   kui   ma:
       give.to.3p-FUT-3fem.sgSUBJ   return-NEG.DEP-SEQ give.to.third.pNEG NEG
       'On returning to the house (or: by returning to the house) she will give children food, on not returning (or: by not returning) she won't give (it to them)'

The same form *səbənən* reanalysed as a verbal modifier in 18.8 cannot be negated, since negation is a clausal category in Manambu, and a verbal modifier cannot be negated.

A cotemporaneous form of *wa-* 'say' in the form *ata-wa-ta:y* (then-say-COTEMP) has developed into a connective 'and so then, in summary, this is why'—see §19.6 (especially example 19.80). And the verb *yi-* with a sequencing medial clause marker *-n* is often employed as a marker of continuing action, as in 18.9 and 19.116.

19.116 [kwasa-kwasa-di sa:s   yin]   [numa-di kuyak tə-na-di]
       small-small-pl   boil/bubble go+SEQ big-pl   wound be/stand-ACT.FOC-3plBAS.VT
       'Tiny tiny boils gradually become big wounds'

In 19.116, little boils or bubble-like spots on the skin do not go anywhere: as they develop on and on, they grow into big wounds. It is this process of gradually and continually changing state that is captured by *yi:n* 'going'.

In summary: desubordination of dependent clauses and subsequent grammaticalization of the most frequently used desubordinated forms is an ongoing process in Manambu.

Clause Types and Discourse-Pragmatic Devices

We now turn to further issues in Manambu syntax, starting with a discussion of the structure of major constituents and order of words within them. We then summarize the properties of clause types and criteria for determining core grammatical relations (§20.1). We then discuss the pragmatic motivations behind the ordering of constituents within clauses (§20.2). Highlighting focus constructions are discussed in §20.3. The devices used for linking sentences in discourse, including turn taking, and marking of topicality, are addressed in §20.4. There we also deal with the principles of ellipsis—a prominent feature of Manambu discourse.

20.1 MAJOR CONSTITUENTS, CLAUSE TYPES, AND GRAMMATICAL RELATIONS

20.1.1 The structure of noun phrases

A noun phrase in Manambu is composed of a head—usually, a noun—and one or more modifiers. If the noun head is omitted, a modifier can be used in headless noun phrases. Closed classes differ in terms of whether they can occur as NP heads—this is summarized in Table 10.11 in §10.7. If a noun phrase is headed by a pronoun, no further modifiers can be used.

Inflected verbs within relative clauses, nouns, adjectives, and a number of closed classes (personal pronouns, indefinite pronoun *nəkə-* 'other, another', quantifiers, and numbers) can all be modifiers in a noun phrase. We recall (§4.1.1) that prehead modifiers take a linker which is only partially predictable. The most frequent order of modifiers in a noun phrase is in Scheme 20.1.

As shown in §10.2.1, a spatio-temporal demonstrative and a 'current relevance' demonstrative can occur together in one NP, as in 10.40–1. The current relevance demonstrative with no gender or number specification occurs first and the spatio-temporal one follows, providing further specification. The two complement each other, since the 'current relevance' demonstrative does not convey information about the gender of the noun or its additional distance from either the speaker or the addressee. And a spatio-temporal demonstrative can provide supplementary directional specification.

Consider 20.1. Combining two demonstratives in one noun phrase allows the speaker to be specific about the location of the village which is both upstream and inland, that is, away from the river from where he is. The location 'away from the river' is expressed with a demonstrative which follows the one stating the location 'upstream':

20.1 kə-na-wur kə-də-wul təp-ad
 DEM.PROX-CURR.REL-UP DEM.PROX-masc.sg-INLAND village-3masc.sgNOM
 'It is this-previously mentioned village upstream, this-away from the river big village'

That the village is big is clear from the masculine gender assignment (§5.2.1).

1. Third person pronoun in article-like function (§10.1) or an interrogative[a] (§10.4)
2a. Demonstrative denoting current relevance (§10.2.1)
2b. Demonstrative specified for distance and/or direction (§10.2.1)[b]
3. Possessor noun phrase (§8.1)
4. Relative clause with an inflected verb (§19.2.1)
5. Quantifier or numeral (§10.5–6)
6. Indefinite pronoun *nəkə-* (§10.3)
7. Agreeing adjective (§4.3.1)
8. Non-agreeing adjective (§4.3.1)
9. Noun, or a noun phrase, as a modifier
10. Head noun
11. Generic noun *məwi* 'things like this, this and other things'
12. Quantifier or numeral (§10.5–6)

SCHEME 20.1   The most frequent order of modifiers in a noun phrase

[a] An interrogative modifier is not compatible with any other modifier.
[b] A noun phrase can contain two demonstratives.

Alternatively, a spatio-temporal demonstrative can be preceded by the distal demonstrative in its anaphoric function, or if it is used to mark a previously mentioned definite referent. An example is *a-də kə-də təp* (DEM.DIST-masc.sg DEM.PROX-masc.sg village) 'definite/previously mentioned this-proximate village'—literally, 'that this village', used to refer to the Avatip village which has just been discussed in detail. That is, demonstratives in their different meanings complement each other. No other demonstratives can occur together in one noun phrase.

We will now look at further features of noun phrases. We start with (A) appositional noun phrases (where a noun modifies another noun), and then address (B) headship of a noun phrase, (C) noun phrase coordination and disjunction, and (D) the order, and types, of modifiers in noun phrases. Further problems in defining the boundaries of noun phrases are discussed in (E).

A. APPOSITIONAL NOUN PHRASES. A head noun can be modified by another noun which then takes a linker (most often *-a-*: see §4.1.1), as in *apawul-a du* (evil.spirit-LK man) 'male evil spirit'. The head noun itself can consist of a compound—see §9.3. Or it can consist of two nouns in apposition to each other. Appositional constructions are of four types. The order of components is fixed in types A.I–III.

A.Ia. A KINSHIP TERM FOLLOWED BY A PERSONAL NAME, as in 20.2. Note the absence of the linker on the first noun.

20.2 Lumawadəm   [də-kə-də   kə-də   ñamus   Kainuwa:k]
     Lumawandem   he-OBL-masc.sg   DEM.PROX-masc.sg   younger.sibling Kainu+LK+DAT
     ata   wa-də-d
     then   say-3masc.sgSUBJ.P-3masc.sgBAS.P
     'Lumawandem then said to Kainu, this younger brother of his'

A kinship term can be followed by the name of a kind of animal or reptile, as in *amæy karaki* (mother death.adder) 'death adder the mother' throughout Text 3 and *ñan kabay* (child snake) 'snake the child' in T3.8 (also see *amæy məd* 'mother cassowary' and *ñan məd* 'child cassowary' in 20.9). A name of an animal can be followed by a kinship term, and then a noun phrase can have two readings: *məd amæy* may mean 'cassowary's mother' or 'mother cassowary'. The two readings can be differentiated only by context.

A pronoun can also be followed by a personal name, as in *wun Walinum* 'me Walinum' and 20.11 (which contains three appositional NPs similar to those in 20.2).

A.Ib. ADDITIONAL MEANINGS OF KINSHIP TERMS *asa:y* 'FATHER' AND *amæy* 'MOTHER' IN APPOSITIONAL NOUN PHRASES. These have somewhat idiosyncratic meanings. We can recall, from §5.3 and 5.14, that the noun *asa:y* 'father' can be used with or without the adjective 'big' as a kind of augmentative, e.g. *numa-də asa:y wuk* (big-masc.sg father tooth) 'very big tooth', or simply *asa:y wuk* 'very big tooth'. The noun *amæy* is also used as a kind of augmentative in *amæy ta:b* (mother hand) 'thumb'. The combination *amæy ta:kw* (mother wife) refers to the first, elder wife (the term for non-first wife is *gəña ta:kw* 'last+LK wife' (or tail+LK wife), as in T2.50).

A.II. A name of an object (typically, a ritually important one) followed by the word denoting this object, e.g. *Makəmawi nəbək* 'Makemawi mountain' (Manambu name for Ambunti mountain), *Kəbənwali kara:b* 'men's house called Kebenwali'. The first noun takes the linker (see §4.1.1), e.g. *Pakanəbra kara:b* (Pakaneber+LK men's.house) 'men's house called Pakaneber', *Waikab-ə kara:b* 'men's house called Waikab'.

A.III. An appositional construction denoting extension of class consists of a noun followed by the generic *məwi* 'things like that'. This generic noun is not used anywhere else in the language (and cannot occur on its own). It is semantically comparable to the associative non-singular discussed at §6.2.2. And the two are in complementary distribution: we can recall that the associative non-singular can only be formed on personal names, e.g. *Nelma-bər* (Nelma-ASS) 'Nelma and others associated with her' (6.29). The generic noun *məwi* can be used with any noun, except personal names, definite nouns, and nouns with a uniquely identifiable referent. A noun phrase containing *məwi* is indefinite, and usually has no other modifiers (including quantifiers), as in 18.14 (*ñapwi məwi* 'firewood and things like that', *gu məwi* 'water and things like that'), T3.24 and 14.155 ('children and things like that'), and 20.3:

20.3 [[də a-də   kabay] adəka   yi-ta:y]   [[bal
     he DEM.DIST-masc.sg snake DEM.DIST.REACT.TOP+masc.sg go-COTEMP pig
     məwi]   vya-n] [karya-d   lə-kə-k]   [kamək
     things.like.that kill-SEQ bring-3masc.sgBAS.P she-OBL-DAT hunger+LK+DAT
     rə-kə-na   wa-ta:y]
     sit-FUT/IRR-ACT.FOC+3fem.sgBAS.VT say-COTEMP
     'That very one (previously mentioned) (topical) snake having gone (and) killed pigs and things like that brought (them) to her, so that she should not be hungry' (lit. having said 'she might be hungry')

A noun phrase containing *məwi* is one NP and not two coordinated ones, for three reasons. First, it is pronounced as one intonation unit without any pause. Secondly, no other constituent can intervene between the two. And thirdly, it takes one case marker at the end of the NP—see 20.4 (these criteria are addressed at E, at the end of the section).

20.4 [væs məwi:k]-a:b   yi   ma:
     grass things.like.that+DAT-TOO go:NEG NEG
     '(One) mustn't go to get grass and things like that' (lit. for grass and things like that)

The form *məwi* can be used to modify a component of a lexicalized complex predicate (see §17.3), as in 20.5. This shows that at least some such components are essentially nominal in nature:

20.5 [wi   kulapu-ta:y] [səkulək məwi   yi-ta:y]   [[nəkə   ja:p]
house clean-COTEMP cooking things.like.that 'go'-COTEMP other+fem.sg thing
[nəkə   ja:p] jan-ta:y]   [wiya:b
other+fem.sg thing wash-COTEMP house+LK+TERM
kwa-ba:gu-l]
stay-DO.INCESSANTLY-3fem.sgBAS.P
'Cleaning the house, cooking and doing things like that, washing one thing and another,
she kept staying in the house'

If a mass noun occurs in a noun phrase with the generic *məwi* 'things like this, things of similar
nature', the noun phrase requires plural agreement on the verb and on the reactivated topic
demonstrative, as in 6.21.

A.IV. Synonymous noun phrases consist of two near-synonyms (without a linker). These are
rare and are employed as a stylistic device for rhetorical purposes. Unlike the types A.I–III,
the order does not appear to be fixed. In 20.6, '(paternal) grandfather' and 'ancestor' refer to
the same person. These terms are almost synonymous: *gwa:l* on its own can be used to refer to
any paternal ancestor.

20.6 [aləm   rə-ku]   [kətay   kəti
DEM.DIST+fem.sg+LOC stay-COMPL.SS around around
və-də-l   wun-a-də   gwa:l   warag]
see-3masc.sgSUBJ.P-3fem.sgBAS.P I-LK-masc.sg grandfather ancestor
'Having stayed there, he looked around, my grandfather-ancestor'

A similar example is *karaki kabay* (death.adder snake) 'the snake death adder' in T3.3. Both
components of the NP acquire a plural form if they have one, as in 20.7.

20.7 [ñan-a-di gwalugw   waraga:gw] [ya-n]   [kar-da-l]
we-LK-pl grandfather+PL ancestor+PL come-SEQ bring-DOWN-3fem.sgBAS.P
[də-kə-l-a]
he-POSS-3fem.sgNOM-3fem.sgNOM
'This is the story of how our ancestors (lit. our grandfathers ancestors) brought (the
people) down by coming'

Appositional noun phrases of this type are very similar to synonymous compounds discussed
under §9.3 (type 4). However, unlike compounds, synonymous appositional NPs form two
grammatical and phonological words.

B. RECOGNIZING THE HEAD OF A NOUN PHRASE. The head of a noun phrase is generally easy to
recognize: it determines number and gender agreement on each of the agreeing modifiers (see
§4.3 and §§10.2–3), and cross-referencing on the verb. In 20.2, *Kainu* is the head of the NP and
is cross-referenced with the masculine singular throughout the noun phrase in brackets, and as
addressee on the verb of speech. As shown in Chapter 7, case markers go onto the head noun
which in most cases is also the last word in a noun phrase. Only the coordinating comitative
behaves differently: it occurs on each of the coordinands, or just the last one (see §7.9). If the
postposed modifier is a number or a quantifier, the case marking remains on the head noun as
in 7.50 and 10.142 (*asa:k viti* (dog+LK+DAT two) 'of two dogs').

C. NOUN PHRASE COORDINATION AND DISJUNCTION. Noun phrase coordination can be achieved
with a coordinating comitative case -*wa* (see §7.9), the argument elaboration (inclusory)
construction, or both (§6.2.3). A participant marked with the comitative or its equivalent

(postposition *wukən*) has a lesser role in the joint activity. An alternative is the coordinating connective *wa* (§4.5.3 and §7.9). This implies that the conjoined participants are equal, as in 20.8.

20.8 ata   war-bər   [Lumawadəm wa Parmali]
     then go.up-3duBAS.P Lumawandem and Parmali
     'Lumawandem and Parmali then went up(stream)'

The connective can also be used in an argument elaboration construction, as in 20.9. This appears in the speech of those who are highly proficient in Tok Pisin and English, and may well be a calque.

20.9 bər [[amæy məd]   wa [a-də   [ñan məd]]] bə   yara
     3du mother cassowary and DEM.DIST-masc.sg child cassowary already well
     a-də   kaw sar-ən   væki-brə-d
     DEM.DIST-masc.sg hole jump-SEQ cross-3dusUBJ.P-3masc.sgBAS.P
     'They two mother and son cassowary crossed the hole jumping' (lit. they two mother cassowary and child cassowary already crossed the hole well by jumping over it)

The connective *wa* can occur in a double comitative construction, as an additional mark of joint activity of both participants, as in 7.79.

There may be a historical connection between the comitative *-wa*, and the connective *wa*. This requires further investigation, as soon as further information on Ndu languages becomes available. The connective is much rarer in texts and in conversations than any other coordinating device. It is never used to coordinate clauses.

If more than two participants are coordinated, several techniques may be employed. In 20.10, there are five coordinands (plus the speaker). The noun phrase contains a coordinating comitative, and the rest of the participants are in apposition to each other. The adverb *nakamib* 'together' (see 6.39 on its use in lieu of argument elaboration constructions) is placed between the complex noun phrase and the verb which is marked for first person plural: the speaker was among the participants.

20.10 [[[wun-a-di ñan-ugw dəy-a-kə   kwasa   gwa:l]   Abasadu]
       I-LK-PL   child-PL they-LK-POSS+fem.sg little.fem.sg granddaughter Abasadu
       Dəmiyawi-wa   Gabəlmæg Yapikudi asa:y] nakamib yi-ba-l
       Demiyawi-COM Gabelmag Yapikudi father   together go-1plsUBJ.P-3fem.sgBAS.P
       'Abasadu, the little classificatory granddaughter of my children with Demiyawi, Gabelmag, Yapikudi (and) father, together we went (that time)'

And in 20.11, the connective *wa* is placed between the last two coordinands. This pattern is very similar to Tok Pisin and English (in which the speaker was highly proficient). That is, this may well be a calque from either of these contact languages:

20.11 [[mən   Yuasəsəg] [wun Yuanəg] wa [lə Ñamamayrata:kw] ñan gwalugw
       you.masc Yuasəsəng I   Yuanəng and she Ñamamayratakw   we clan
       nak] [Maliau-adian]
       one Maliau-1plNOM
       'You Yuasəsəng, I Yuanəng, and she Ñamamayratakw we (belong to) one clan, we are Maliau'

The coordinands themselves are complex noun phrases, each consisting of a pronoun followed by a personal name.

The suffix -*a:b*, -*aba:b* 'too' is also used as a way of coordinating noun phrases—see 20.13 below, and the discussion in §9.2.

Juxtaposition of noun phrases is used for two additional purposes. First, a juxtaposed noun can provide additional information to the preceding noun phrase, as in T2.63, *kə-di Sabrayi-bər Vali:k* (DEM.PROX-pl Sabray-ASS.PL Vali:k) 'these relatives of Sabrayi, the Vali:k clan'. We can recall, from §19.7, that juxtaposed clauses can be employed in a similar function (see 19.81).

Secondly, two noun phrases or two modifiers within a noun phrase can be juxtaposed as a means of expressing disjunction, e.g. 20.12–13. Lengthy noun phrases like the one in 20.13 are not very frequent in discourse.

20.12 [a-də   ñan bə   numa-d]   [[[nabi mugul a:li] kətək]
      DEM.DIST-masc.sg child already big-3masc.sgNOM year   three   four like
      ta:d]
      become+3masc.sgBAS.P
      'That child was already big, he was approximately (lit. like) three or four years old'

20.13 [ñan-a   təp   mugul *o* təp   a:li] [Malu Avatip Yuanab Yawabak
      we-LK+fem.sg village three or village four Malu Avatip Yuanab Yawabak
      kə-di-a:b]
      DEM.PROX-pl-TOO
      'Our villages (are) three or four, Malu, Avatip, Yuanab, and Yawabak, these too'

The first noun phrase in 20.13 illustrates an additional strategy used for disjunction—the Tok Pisin loan conjunction *o*. This is now used by speakers of all generations, to conjoin noun phrases, as in 20.13, or modifiers, as in 20.14, or even clauses, as in 10.82. The speaker who asked 20.14 was among the few old ladies whose Tok Pisin was rather fractured; this did not stop her from using the Tok Pisin import *o*.

20.14 [kwasa   *o* numa]   gu   yaku-na-ñən
      little.fem.sg or big.fem.sg water wash-ACT.FOC-2fem.sgBAS.VT
      'Have you washed a little bit or all over?' (lit. have you water-washed a little or a lot?)

This conjunction can link sentences, as in 20.15 (continuation of 10.82). There is a pause between the two sentences, the second of which is introduced with *o*. The character was trying to find out whether the owner of the house was a man or a woman:

20.15 [du kwa-na-d-ə   wi-ad]   PAUSE [*o* ta:kw
      man stay-ACT.FOC-3masc.sgBAS.VT-LK house-3masc.sgNOM PAUSE or woman
      kwa-na-d-ə   wi-ad]
      stay-ACT.FOC-3masc.sgBAS.VT-LK house-3masc.sgNOM
      'Is it a house where a man stays (lives)? Or is it a house where a woman stays (lives)?'

If there are more than two alternatives, the loan disjunction *o* occurs between the last two, e.g. *Telefomən Oksapmən o Vanimo-a:m* (Telefomin Oksapmin or Vanimo-LK+LOC) 'in Telefomin, Oksapmin, or Vanimo'. Once again, this is a Tok Pisin pattern replicated in Manambu.

Another option is to use the repeated conjunction *aw* 'then' (see §19.6) which then refers to alternating actions or marks alternatives, as in <u>*aw* kami:</u> <u>*aw* lau-lap</u> (then fish then ripe-banana) '(we eat) sometimes fish sometimes banana (or both)'.

D. THE ORDER, AND TYPES, OF MODIFIERS IN NOUN PHRASES. No noun phrases have all the positions filled, for semantic and phonological reasons. The longest noun phrase in the corpus contains six modifiers: *a-d-ə nəkə-d-ə [wiy-a-m sə kwa-na-d-ə] nəma-d-ə gla-ka-gəl du-a ñan* (DEM.DIST-masc.sg-LK other-masc.sg-LK house-LK-LOC sleep lie-ACT.FOC-3masc.sgBAS.VT-LK big-masc.sg-LK black-INT-black man-LK child) 'that other very black boy (male child) lying asleep in the house'. An average noun phrase is likely to contain two to three modifiers, e.g. *brə-brə-kə nəkə kapab-a wi* (3du-3du-POSS+fem.sg other+fem.sg separate-LK house) 'another separate house of well and truly their own'.

A modifier can itself be a noun phrase, as in *[[Yuajan kukəb]-a du]* (Yuajan behind+TERM-LK man) 'son who followed Yuajan' (lit. man after Yuajan).

The article-like third person pronouns do not combine with the inherently indefinite noun *məwi* 'things like this'. There can be just one quantifier or a numeral in a noun phrase, and not more than two adjectives. Typically, in a complex noun phrase only one of the coordinands is a long possessive NP—as in 20.10. In everyday conversations, speakers avoid long noun phrases—this is in contrast to long clause chains which nobody (except for children under 10) seems to mind using under any circumstances. In T1.23 a demonstrative precedes a possessive modifier (*a-də lə-kə-də ñamus* (DEM.DIST-masc.sg she-OBL-masc.sg younger.sibling) 'that younger brother of hers'). In T1.14, a demonstrative precedes a relative clause (*kə sə kwa-na bap* (DEM.PROX.fem.sg sleep stay-ACT.FOC+3fem.sgBAS.VT moon) 'this sleeping moon'). A noun phrase with three modifiers ('he this son of ours', that is, 'this previously mentioned child of ours') is at 20.70.

Alternatively, an NP containing modifiers can occupy the possessor slot, or both as in T3.34 *[[a:bab-a du ta:kw] dəy-a-kəya:m]* (all-LK man woman they-LK-POSS+fem.sg smell) 'the smell of all the people', and in *[[amæy karaki] lə-kə-də [a-də numa-də wiya:m]]* (mother death.adder she-OBL-masc.sg DEM.DIST-masc.sg big-masc.sg house+LK+LOC) 'in that big house of mother death adder'. A relative clause can contain a noun with a modifier, as in T3.40 (*[[a-l-ay ñan] səki-la-də sə]* (DEM.DIST-fem.sg-DIST youngster call.name-3fem.sgSUBJ.VT-3masc.sgBAS.VT name) 'the name that young lady there called'). An example of a complex noun phrase with a relative clause in both possessor and possessee is in 20.22.

A noun phrase of any length can occur with a postposition: see §4.5.2. A possessee—the head of the noun phrase—can be modified by a demonstrative, as in T3.5 (*[a-di [karaki lə-kə-di ñan-ugw]]* (DEM.DIST-pl death.adder she-OBL-pl child-PL) 'those children of a death adder'). An NP with modifiers can be in apposition to, say, a pronoun, as in T1.32 (*ñan [kə-di kəpa-kə-di ta:kw]* (we DEM.PROX-pl earth+LK-POSS-pl woman) 'we these women of this earth').

The order of modifiers in an NP tends to be fixed. Agreeing modifiers (third person pronoun in article-like function and demonstratives) precede the non-agreeing ones, and the third person pronoun in an article-like function always precedes all other agreeing modifiers, e.g. *[də a-də nəkə-də du]* (he DIST.DEM-masc.sg other-masc.sg man) 'that very one (previously mentioned important participant) other man' (also see 10.3).

A noun phrase cannot contain a sequence of two agreeing adjectives (see §4.3.1). If two agreeing adjectives occur together one of them has an adverbial meaning, e.g. *kwasa nəma-pək-a ñan* (small+fem.sg big+fem.sg-COMPAR-LK child) 'a child that is a little bigger (than another child)'.

A noun phrase usually contains no more than two adjectives. An agreeing adjective precedes the non-agreeing one (as shown in §4.3.1). In a sequence of non-agreeing adjectives, a dimension term precedes a colour term, as in *gərgər ñikiñiki ñan* (tiny red:RED child) 'tiny pink baby' (said ironically to a 3-year-old crying as if she were a baby). This is similar to many languages, including English. A non-agreeing value adjective precedes another non-agreeing adjective, as in *vyakata-yakə kula pətaka:u* (good-VERY new ladder) 'a good new ladder'. Only once did I register a noun phrase with three adjectives: the agreeing adjective preceded the sequence of non-agreeing ones: *kwasa-kwasa gərgər ñikiñiki ñan* (small-RED+fem.sg tiny red:RED child) 'little tiny pink baby'.

There are just two instances of variable word order within a noun phrase, which is determined by pragmatic parameters. First, a demonstrative and a pronominal possessive marker may occur in either order. In 20.16, the demonstrative precedes the possessive marker and in 20.2 it follows.

20.16 [lə kamnagw-a:b ma: kray]   [gu-a:b   ma: kray   [a-də
      she food-TOO   NEG bring+NEG water-TOO NEG bring+NEG DEM.DIST-masc.sg
      lə-kə-də   ñənək-a:b]]
      she-OBL-masc.sg child+LK+DAT-TOO
      'She did not bring the food either, did not bring the water either for that (previously mentioned) child of hers either'

The reason for the different positions of demonstratives lies in the status of the head noun. In 20.2, the new participant, Kainu, has just been introduced, while Lumawandem, the possessor, is an established referent. In 20.16, the child has been introduced some time ago (also see §20.2, for an explanation of a non-verb-final constituent order here); the demonstrative here has a distinctly anaphoric function.

Numerals (other than 'one') and quantifiers can either precede or follow the head noun. We saw in §§10.5–6 that a newly introduced or a non-topical referent is followed by a quantifier, and once the referent is established it is preceded by a quantifier. In 20.17, the characters ate any old three bananas, and so the numeral follows the noun.

20.17 [[laulap mugul] kan   napa-da-k]   [ada
      banana three   eat+SEQ COMPL.VB-3pl-COMPL.DS DEM.DIST.REACT.TOP+masc.sg
      wa:d]
      say+3masc.sgBAS.P
      'After they'd eaten three bananas, he then said'

In contrast, in 20.18 the children are definite, and so the numeral precedes the head noun. A preposed quantifier or a numeral takes a linker.

20.18 [[kə-di   mugul-a ñan-ugw] kur-ku]   [ata ya:l]
      DEM.PROX-pl three-LK child-PL get-COMPL.SS then go+3fem.sgBAS.P
      'Having taken these three children she then went'

Similar examples are at 10.116–17. This goes hand in hand with the general principle of ordering words and constituents in Manambu: a new and less established participant comes first. We return to this in §20.2.

We will see, in the next chapter, that many speakers code-switch with Tok Pisin. The code-switches behave in somewhat peculiar ways—which justify their treatment as 'foreign morphology'. The complex issue of how such code-switches are assigned to word classes in Manambu was mentioned in §4.5.6. Code-switches are equally foreign with respect to their syntactic position: as predicted by Moravcsik (1978), they occupy the same position in a Manambu constituent as they would in Tok Pisin, despite the fact that such a position would have been unthinkable in 'proper' Manambu (see §22.4).

So, *wanpela ta:kw* (one:TP woman) is a spontaneously produced variant of *ta:kw nak* 'one woman', and *wanpela liklik ma:j* (one:TP small:TP story) or *wanpela kwasa ma:j* (one:TP small+fem.sg story) both correspond to *kwasa ma:j nak* (small+fem.sg story one) 'one little story'. Such noun phrases with foreign forms in a foreign order are marginal in that they are rare, and speakers have a pejorative attitude towards them.

Only two such foreign elements have been observed in the domain of complex predicates, or clauses. One is a Tok Pisin modal *mas* 'must' which can occur with third person imperative in the meaning of strong obligation (13.22). The other is Tok Pisin *nogut* which was once used by a speaker as a nonce code-switch accompanied by a dependent negative clause (14.125), mirroring a corresponding structure in Manambu.

E. THE LIMITS OF A NOUN PHRASE. A few more questions remain. First, how do we determine the boundaries of a noun phrase? The relevant criteria include having one case per noun phrase (see §7.1). So, for instance, the allative case form of an appositional noun phrase *Makəmawi nəbək* 'Makemawi mountain' is *Makəmawi nəbəkər*. This is in contrast to 16.55 where *[adaki nəbəkər] [pause] [Makəmawir]* (DEM.DIST.masc.sg.ACROSS.AWAY hill+LK+DAT, Makemawi+DAT) 'to (that) hill across (away from us), to Makemawi' corresponds to two noun phrases. This brings us to the next criterion—that of prosodic cohesion. The insertion of a pause between the two allative-marked constituents indicates that these are indeed two noun phrases.

Also, if a noun phrase appears in a highlighting focus construction it is focused as a whole: a part of an NP cannot be focused separately. This explains why no constituent can be focused in relative clauses, as shown in Table 19.1. That is, focalization is another criterion which helps us determine the boundaries of an NP. Non-word class-changing suffixes detailed in §9.2 appear once per noun phrase. And the emphatic enclitic *-ya* always goes onto the last word in a noun phrase.

And, in addition to all this, we saw that the word order in a noun phrase is mostly fixed—except for the two instances of variable order in D above. For instance, an adjective followed by a demonstrative belong to different noun phrases, even if pronounced without a pause. An example is in 20.19:

20.19 [wun kwasa   tə-lwun-ək]   [kwasa]
      I   small+fem.sg be/stand-1fem.sgBAS.P-CONF small+fem.sg
      [[kəlaki   Kudaway] lə-kə   ñənpək]
      DEM.PROX+fem.sg+ACROSS Kudaway she-OBL+fem.sg child+LIKE
      'I was little (when the war started), little, like the daughter (lit. feminine child) of this Kudaway across away'

This example contains two noun phrases: one is an adjective 'small' (feminine singular) used headlessly, and the other is a possessive construction accompanied with the suffix *-pək* 'like' with the possessor modified by a demonstrative. The speaker, Kukelyabau, spoke very fast, and there were no pauses between the two. The placement of the demonstrative is indicative of an NP boundary.

But are noun phrases in Manambu always contiguous? They are not. However, instances of split noun phrases are limited to noun phrases with numerals and quantifiers as modifiers. The numeral or the quantifier can be split from the rest of the NP and postposed to the verb, as a clarification (see §20.2). An example is in 20.20: the two women were staying together; this togetherness is emphasized by positioning the numeral modifier after the verb. There is no pause before 'two'—as would have been expected, if this were an afterthought.

20.20 [a-bər   ta:kw] PAUSE abra   kwa-bər   [viti]
      DEM.DIST-du woman PAUSE DEM.DIST.REACT.TOP+du stay-3duBAS.P two
      'Those women stayed (topical) two (of them together)'

We return to the functions of this postposed numeral in §20.2.

If a relative clause contains an additional argument or oblique, it can be placed into a sentence-initial position as a means of focalizing it. We can recall, from Table 19.1, that no constituent of a relative clause can be focused independently. That is, removing an argument or an oblique from within the relative clause and preposing it is the only available means of focusing on it. Note that in such cases a relative clause—but not the whole noun phrase—is discontinuous:

20.21a [gwa:r   a-də   yi-d-ə   kwasa-də   ñan]
       water+ALL DEM.DIST-masc.sg go-3masc.sgBAS.P-LK small-masc.sg child
       tayib   waku-d
       before+TERM go.out-3masc.sgBAS.P
       'That little boy who <u>drowned</u> (lit. to water that one which went) left home before (his mother)'

The order of words without such preposition would have been:

20.21b [a-də   gwa:r   yi-d-ə   kwasa-də   ñan]
       DEM.DIST-masc.sg water+ALL go-3masc.sgBAS.P-LK small-masc.sg child
       tayib   waku-d
       before+TERM go.out-3masc.sgBAS.P
       'That little boy who drowned (lit. went to water) left home before (his mother)'

We saw in §10.2.3 that reactivated topic demonstratives do not form one NP with the noun they refer to (typically an O, an S, or a location). They agree with this noun in gender and number, but can never take any cases or suffixes or be arguments of postpositions. There can be an intonation break between a demonstrative and an NP it refers to (as in 10.66 and in 20.20)— something atypical for an NP. Within a clause, they tend to occur immediately preceding the verb, as in 20.20 and 20.22.

20.22 [[a-də   [kə-laki   ta:kw]
       DEM.DIST-masc.sg DEM.PROX-fem.sg+ACROSS woman
       suku-lə-d-ə   kwa:y gabu-ma:j]   [a-di
       write-3fem.sgSUBJ.P-3masc.sgBAS.P-LK shrimp traditional-story DEM.DIST-pl
       kurpatəktəka-lə-di   ma:j]] PAUSE [adiya
       leave.out+INCOMPL:RED-3fem.sgSUBJ.P-3plBAS.P story   PAUSE DEM.DIST.REACT.TOP+pl
       suku-kə-tua-di]
       write-FUT-1sgSUBJ.VT-3plBAS.VT
       'I will tell those stories about the shrimp which that woman across there got wrong' (lit. I will tell those (topical) stories of that traditional story of the shrimp written by this woman-across from here that she'd left out fully)'

That is, reactivated topic demonstratives are not modifiers to a noun within a noun phrase, even though they get translated as such, for want of a better equivalent in English.

20.1.2 The structure of complex predicates

Manambu has complex predicates containing polyfunctional verbs—these were discussed in Chapter 17. Table 17.1 summarizes the differences between complex predicates with auxiliaries (where the polyfunctional verbs provide aspectual or modal meanings: see §17.1.1), complex predicates containing polyfunctional verbs as support verbs (§17.2), lexicalized complex predicates (§17.3), and body part constructions (§17.4). Of these, only lexicalized complex predicates allow variation in the order of components.

Another type of complex predicate with temporal meaning is restricted to dependent clauses only and consists of a verb marked with the sequential *-n* and the generic completive verb *napa-* accompanied by the appropriate clause-chaining marker(s) (see §18.9). The order of components is fixed. Modal complex predicates consist of one of the two modal verbs (see §4.5.1, and examples 4.64–6 and 15.53) both meaning 'be able to, can' followed by an inflected verb. These complex predicates cannot be negated, questioned, or occur in a command. The order of components is also fixed.

All the complex predicates consist of two independent grammatical and phonological words. The components of complex predicates containing polyfunctional verbs (§§17.1–4) tend to be contiguous. Unlike noun phrases, however, they are not strictly contiguous. Constituents such as *ata* 'then', reactivated topic demonstratives, and adverbs can intervene between them, as in 12.81, 17.44, and 20.23.

20.23 day   vakər-ək   ata   kur-di
       they fall-PURP.SS then do/get-3plBAS.VT/P
       'They then were about to fall down'

In contrast, in 17.23, *ata* precedes the whole complex predicate. The difference is in the degree of its topicality: the closer the constituent is to the beginning of the clause the more likely it is to be a newly introduced topic.

And we can recall, from §14.1.3, that aspectual and positional complex predicates allow the negator to precede the whole predicate, as in 14.29 and 20.24a, as a means of focusing on the lexical verb. We were talking about various places in Australia, and the speaker was telling us that he had never seen Melbourne with his own eyes.

20.24a wun Melburnam   ma: væn   tə
       I   Melbourne+LK+ACC/LOC NEG see+SEQ 'stand'+NEG
       'I haven't seen Melbourne'

Alternatively, the negator can precede the auxiliary, and there is no focusing effect, as in 20.24b—an answer to a question as to whether anyone had seen the little boy.

20.24b wun də-kə-m   væn   ma: tə
       I   he-OBL-ACC/LOC   see+SEQ NEG 'stand'+NEG
       'I haven't seen him'

Aspectual complex predicates contain the sequencing verb form in *-n* (see §18.2) also used to link clauses. However, the negator can have such an effect only in complex predicates, and never in linked clauses. This demonstrates the differences in the synchronic status of the *-n* forms within monoclausal complex predicates and within multiclausal structures.

In contrast, complex predicates with *napa-* 'generic completive verb' and with the two modal verbs are always contiguous. They are also restricted in their use: neither can be negated, or appear in any other clause types.

We can recall that the lexical verb which appears with *napa-* is always marked with the sequential *-n* (see §18.9), while modal verbs allow for two options. The inflected verb can take third person feminine past tense cross-referencing (as in 4.64–6 and 20.25a), and the resulting construction has impersonal overtones and never occurs with first person subject.

20.25a mən   [nəbə wakwə-l]   ma:
       you.masc able   go.out-3fem.sgBAS.P again
       'You can go out again'

Or the inflected verb can be marked for person, number, and gender of the subject (as in 4.64, 15.53, and 20.25b). Then, there are no restrictions as to the person of the subject. The inflected verb itself can appear in the future form, as in 4.64, 15.53, 20.25b, and 20.58, in the versatile tense form, as in 19.58b, or in the past tense form, as in 20.25a. The choice is determined by the presence of a future projection: 15.53, 19.58b, and 20.25b contain a threat, while 20.58 is a question.

20.25b nəbə kiya-k-na-ñən-ək   ya
       can   die-FUT-ACT.FOC-2fem.sgBAS.VT-CONF EMPH
       'You can die (if you come near the broken ladder)'

In contrast, 20.25c is a statement about what is to be done with the leftovers from that day's meal:

20.25c sər   nəbə kə-da-l
       tomorrow can   eat-3plSUBJ.P-3fem.sgBAS.P
       'They can eat (this food) tomorrow'

No other forms of inflected verbs have been attested in the corpus. This suggests that clauses containing the two modal verbs have a realis–irrealis type distinction not attested anywhere else in the language. That is, they constitute a special clause type, albeit rare and restricted. This takes us to the next issue—the clause types and their properties.

20.1.3   Clause types and their properties

The major clause types in Manambu are (A) declarative, (B) imperative, and (C) interrogative. Exclamatory clauses have the same structure as declarative clauses; they differ from them in their sharply falling intonation (§2.7). The imperative is only used in imperative main, or independent, clauses. Other clauses can be either dependent or independent.

A. DECLARATIVE CLAUSES. The major distinguishing features of independent, or main, clauses and dependent clauses of various types were summarized in Table 19.1. The most prominent features include:

- Constituent order is not necessarily fixed in main clauses (see §20.2) but is almost always fixed in dependent clauses;
- Any word class can head a predicate of main clause, while only verbs can head the predicate of a dependent clause; non-verbs have to occur as copula complements in dependent clauses;
- The use of uninflected modal and aspectual forms is allowed only in main clauses; these same forms require support verbs when used in dependent clauses;
- Main clauses distinguish future negation, past negation, habitual negation (and also see Chapter 14), while all the dependent clauses are negated with *-ma:r-* 'dependent clause negator'.

That uninflected modal and aspectual forms require support verbs when used in dependent clauses indicates that they are less 'verbal' and more noun-like than inflected verbs. This is a property they share with non-verbs as predicate heads: in order to be used in dependent clauses, non-verbs have to occur as copula complements of the verb *tə-* which is also used as the most frequent support verb (see §17.2)—an example is at 20.26.

The first clause is an independent clause with a non-agreeing adjective in the predicate slot. This is an example of a non-verbal clause. The second clause is a medial dependent clause which contains a copula *tə-* and the same adjective in the copula complement slot. There is no other way in which an adjective can appear in the predicate slot in a dependent clause (a similar example is at T3.23). The third clause is a main clause, of the verbless type.

20.26 [vyakat-ad]   [vyakat tə-ku]   [ya:kya]
      good-3masc.sgNOM good   stand-COMPL.SS OK
      'It (masculine) was/is good. As it was good, (this was) OK'

As expected, main declarative clauses distinguish more grammatical categories than dependent clauses. However, as we will see shortly, not all main clauses distinguish all categories.

Main declarative clauses divide into three types: VERBAL, NON-VERBAL, and VERBLESS. VERBAL CLAUSES can be headed by a fully inflected, a partially inflected, or an uninflected verb (see §11.1.1). The number of inflectional positions depends on the category—for instance, positive indicative verbs are always fully inflected, while imperatives (see B below) are partially inflected, and negative indicative verbs are uninflected (unless they are in the habitual aspect)—see Table 11.1. Verbal clauses express the full set of tense, aspect, mood, and modality distinctions (detailed in Chapters 13–14), and can be headed by intransitive, transitive, ambitransitive, and ditransitive verbs—see §4.2.1. Or they can be headed by a copula—see under B §4.2.2.

COPULA CLAUSES in Manambu contain polyfunctional verbs in their predicate slot. There are ten such verbs, and they can each be used as copula verbs, as support verbs, and also as auxiliaries. In addition, five of them are also used as lexical verbs. A summary of these verbs and their functions is in Table 4.1.

When used as COPULA VERBS, they head the predicate of copula clauses which involve two arguments but cannot be considered transitive or intransitive (see Dixon 2002b for a typological overview of copulas; also see §17.1).

The relationship between the two arguments of a copula clause—the copula subject and the copula complement—covers identity, attribution, location, and possession. Their choice depends on (a) the meaning of the copula construction, and (b) the semantic type of copula complement.

We saw, both in Table 4.1 and examples 4.16–19, that copula clauses containing copulas *tə-* 'be, stand', *rə-* 'sit', and *kwa-* 'stay' are used to express location and existence (also see T1.32, T2.67, and T3.43, for *tə-*; T2.4 and T2.7 for *rə-*; and T1.11 and T1.14 for *kwa-*). A similar example is at 20.30.

The copula *tə-*—the most versatile in terms of its semantics—can also imply 'coming into existence'. The stative existential meaning and the more dynamic meaning of 'appearing' can only be distinguished by context.

Consider 20.27. Its first clause (which is a relative clause) contains the existential copula *rə-* 'sit (overtone of horizontal position)'. This copula never has any overtone of 'coming into existence'. It is used here because living or staying in an area is typically associated with a horizontal location and treated as 'sitting'. This is reminiscent of classificatory verbs found in some New Guinea languages—we saw, in §17.1.1, that despite some classificatory overtones, positional verbs in Manambu cannot really be considered classificatory.

The second clause of 20.27 contains the copula *tə-* meaning 'become, come into being'. This same clause may also mean 'a lake was (there)', but this is not the reading implied by the context of the story.

20.27 [ta:y   rə-ba-l   tami:] [ata   ar   ta:l]
    before sit-1plSUBJ.P-3fem.sgBAS.P area   then lake become+3fem.sgBAS.P
    'In the area where we used to be (lit. sit) a lake came into being'

The copula *tə-* is also used in the meaning of 'become', as in 3.8–9 and 20.28–9. These examples show that the copula complement of 'become' can be a noun (as in 20.28 and T2.42), or an adjective (as in 20.29). In T1.8, the copula complement is a deictic adverb, *atawa* 'like that'.

20.28 də adəka   lə-kə-də   la:n
    he DEM.DIST.REACT.TOP+masc.sg she-OBL-masc.sg husband
    tə-kə-k-na-d
    become-FUT-FUT-ACT.FOC-3masc.sgBAS.VT
    'He (topical) will become her husband'

20.29 kə-də   təp   alək   numa-də   tə-na-d
    DEM.PROX-masc.sg village that.is.why big-masc.sg become-ACT.FOC-3masc.sgBAS.VT
    'That is why this village has become big'

It is also used in the meaning of 'have' with any kind of possessum, as in 4.18, 8.16, and 14.33. In T1.4 a clause with *tə-* can be interpreted either as existential ('the sickness which exists on/to us-our village women') or as possessive ('the sickness we-our village women have'). The verb *tə-* is not used to express identity or equation; neither are the two other postural verbs. The verb *kwa-* 'stay' can be used in the meaning of 'become and remain', as shown in the last clause in 20.30:

20.30 [[ta:y   waku-na-di]   yibunmi-a:b a:li tə-na-di]   [samasa:m
    before go.out-ACT.FOC-3plBAS.VT chief-TOO   four be-ACT.FOC-3plBAS.VT many
    kwa-bana-lək]
    stay-1plSUBJ.VT+3fem.sgBAS.VT-BECAUSE
    'There are also four chiefs (lit. chiefs who go out first), because we remain numerous'

This is consistent with its lexical meaning of 'staying' and the way it is used in aspectual complex predicates to express prolonged durative meaning.

Other polyfunctional verbs used as copulas express identity and attribution. Their choice depends on the copula complement and in fact is only partly predictable.

As mentioned at B in §4.2.2, the copula verbs *na-* 'be (of physical states; natural phenomena)', *tay* -'be (of climatic states)', *yasa-/yasə-* 'be (of physical states, e.g. hunger, thirst)', and *say-* 'be (of some states, e.g. shame or pins and needles)' allow an additional option. They can take third person feminine cross-referencing, with the experiencer optionally added if appropriate. Examples are at 20.31a–34a. Or the experiencer can be cross-referenced on the copula verb. Examples are at 20.31b–34b. There are no restrictions on the person of the experiencer.

Each of the examples at (a) in 20.31–2 allows for two interpretations, no matter whether the overt experiencer is present or not (see §20.4.3 on ellipsis): they either refer to a general state of affairs, or to the feelings or state of an experiencer participant. Examples at (b) only refer to the state of the experiencer. As always in Manambu, the overt NP can be omitted. The two readings (i) and (ii) are equally frequent, and only context provides the clue. The person does not have to be 'I'—there are no restrictions on the person choice.

20.31a (wun) bwiyabwi na-na
    (I)   hot   BE:NAT-ACT.FOC+3fem.sgBAS.VT
    (i) 'It is hot'
    (ii) 'I am hot'

20.31b (wun) bwiyabwi na-na-wun
    (I)   hot   BE:NAT-ACT.FOC-1fem.sgBAS.VT
    'I am hot'

20.32a (wun) nəkər <u>tay-na</u>
    (I)   cold   BE:CLIM-ACT.FOC+3fem.sgBAS.VT
    (i) 'It is cold'
    (ii) 'I am cold'

20.32b (wun) nəkər <u>tay-na-wun</u>
    (I)   cold   BE:CLIM-ACT.FOC-1fem.sgBAS.VT
    'I am cold'

The preferential reading for example 20.33a is (i)—that is, these sentences refer to the feelings of a particular experiencer (not necessarily first person).

20.33a (wun) bag   <u>say-na</u>
    (I)   pins.and.needles BE:FEEL-ACT.FOC+3fem.sgBAS.VT
    (i) 'I feel pins and needles'
    (ii) 'It gives one a feeling of "pins and needles"; there is a feeling of "pins and needles" '

20.33b (wun) bag   <u>say-na-wun</u>
    I   pins.and.needles BE:FEEL-ACT.FOC-1fem.sgBAS.VT
    '<u>I</u> feel pins and needles'

And example 20.34a has only one reading—it can only refer to hunger (or other physical feelings: see 4.26a–d):

20.34a (wun) ka:m   <u>yasa-na</u>
    I   hunger BE:DESIRE-ACT.FOC+3fem.sgBAS.VT
    'I am hungry'

20.34b (wun) ka:m   <u>yasa-na-wun</u>
    I   hunger BE:DESIRE-ACT.FOC-1fem.sgBAS.VT
    '<u>I</u> am hungry'

In contrast, the meaning of the (b) examples at 20.31–4 is pretty uniform: first, they always imply the presence of an experiencer—cross-referenced on the verb—and secondly, the speaker is focusing on the state of the experiencer—who is also topical. This is why it is underlined in the translations.

This is very similar to the alternations in cross-referencing we already saw in 'body part constructions' many of which use the copula or polyfunctional verbs discussed here—see §17.4, and especially examples 17.57–9. A similar example, with the word *mawul* 'insides; feelings', appears in 14.87. Along similar lines, a normal way of saying 'I am angry' is 20.35a. This is another example of a body part construction.

20.35a (wun) ya:l gra-na
    (I)   belly cry-ACT.FOC+3fem.sgBAS.VT
    'I am angry'

If I want to focus on my anger, to make sure people understand that I am well and truly angry, I would say:

20.35b (wun) ya:l gra-na-wun
    (I)   belly cry-ACT.FOC-1fem.sgBAS.VT
    '<u>I</u> am angry'

In each of these cases, the choice of a pattern—whether to cross-reference an experiencer or not—has repercussions on the use of switch-reference in clause chaining. We recall, from §18.3, that body part constructions and copula clauses with these four verbs usually trigger different subject medial markers even if the experiencer is the same as the subject of a subsequent clause, as in 18.24 and 20.36a:

20.36a [wus   yasa-lə-k]   [a-wa-jəwi]
     urine BE:DESIRE-3fem.sg-COMPL.DS IMPV-say-be.awake
     'If you feel like peeing wake (me up)'

The independent clause alternative for the first clause in 20.36a is 20.36b, where the experiencer is not cross-referenced on the copula verb.

20.36b (ñən)   wus   yasa-na
     you.fem urine BE:DESIRE-ACT.FOC+3fem.sgBAS.VT
     'You feel like peeing'

This clause was used as a juxtaposed dependent clause in (i), a version of 20.36a:

20.36c [wus   yasa-na]   [a-wa-jəwi]
     urine BE:DESIRE-ACT.FOC+3fem.sgBAS.VT IMPV-say-be.awake
     'If you feel like peeing wake (me up)'

However, as we saw in §18.3 (18.25–6), if the subject is topical, it can be treated as 'same' with respect to switch-reference even within a body part construction. Such examples also occur with copula verb structures illustrated in 20.31–4 above, but they are less frequent. Another example is in 20.37.

20.37 [abakapi ata   ka:m   yasa-d]   [ka:m   yasa-ku,]   [ya:k]
     hawk   then hunger BE:DESIRE-3masc.sgBAS.P hunger BE:DESIRE-COMPL.SS OK
     'The hawk then felt hunger, after he felt hunger, it was OK'

As we saw in 17.60, even if the experiencer is cross-referenced on the polyfunctional copula verb *yasə-/yasa-* 'be (of desires)' in a main clause, it may not be cross-referenced on an adjacent dependent clause. Another rare example of the experiencer cross-referenced on copula verb within a dependent clause is at 20.63. We return to this phenomenon—rather pervasive in Papuan languages—in §20.1.4.

Unlike the four copula verbs discussed above, the verb *yæy-* 'be: of smell' does not refer to a feeling by any particular experiencer; typical examples are at 4.28 and 20.38.

20.38 du-a-jigərəpa   ya:m yæy-na
     man-LK-bodysmell+LK smell BE:SMELL-ACT.FOC+3fem.sgBAS.VT
     'There is a smell of human body'
     *'I smell human body', *'I emit a smell'

We already mentioned in §4.5 that the copula subject behaves like any other subject. In contrast, the copula complement of any copula verb is different from any other type of argument. It can never be cross-referenced on the copula verb. A copula complement cannot be case marked, or independently focused in a highlighting focus construction (§20.3).

None of the copula clauses can form an imperative. The verbs *tə-*, *rə-*, and *kwa-* do form imperatives when used in their positional senses ('stand', 'sit', and 'stay' respectively). The copula *na-* 'be: of physical states, natural phenomena' can occur in a command phrased as a sequencing clause chain only if used as a support verb (see §17.2.3 and example 17.36a). Other than that, copula clauses have all the properties of verbal clauses.

We now turn to NON-VERBAL CLAUSES, that is, clauses which have a member of a word class other than a verb in their predicate slot. We saw in §3.1 that non-verbs in the predicate slot require nominal cross-referencing enclitics cross-referencing their subject (see Table 3.4). This cross-referencing is not tense sensitive—that is, the tense distinctions expressed in verbs are not marked for non-verbal predicates.

As mentioned in §12.1, to express tense, aspect, or any other further categories, non-verbs have to be used as complements of a support verb (most frequently, *tə*- 'be, have, stand'). Also, if a non-verbal clause is to be used in a depedent clause, the non-verbal predicate has to occur with the support verb—see further discussion in §17.2.3.

Non-verbal predicates are negated differently from verbs—see §14.1.2, and especially Scheme 14.2. The negator *ma:* is postposed to the non-verb, and the person, number, and gender cross-referencing enclitics are suppressed. We can recall that, to negate a non-future declarative non-habitual verb, the same negator is preposed to a special negative verb form stripped of any cross-referencing. And to negate a future declarative non-habitual verb, the negator is postposed to the verb root (which is often different from the negative non-future form: see §14.1.1). These tense distinctions in negative declarative verbs are irrelevant for negative non-verbs. Example 20.39 recapitulates these correlations: 20.39a is an example of a non-future declarative negative verbal clause; 20.39b is the same example cast in the future; and 20.39c is a non-verbal negative clause. The only feature declarative negative verbal and non-verbal clauses share is the lack of personal cross-referencing.

20.39a ñan   ma: tə
       child NEG have+NEG
       '(I/you/we/they etc.) do not/did not have a child'

20.39b ñan   tə   ma:
       child have+NEG   NEG
       '(I/you/we/they etc.) will not have a child'

20.39c vyakət ma:
       good   NEG
       '(I/you/we/they/it etc.) is not/was not/will not be good'

In 20.39d–e, *vyakət* occurs with *tə*- as a support verb or as a copula (with the meaning of 'become')—and this support verb behaves as a normal verb, with all the appropriate tense and other distinctions:

20.39d vyakat ma: tə
       good   NEG SUP.VB+NEG
       (a) '(I/you/we/they/it etc.) is not/was not good'—support verb
       (b) '(I/you/we/they/it etc.) does not/did not become good'—copula clause

20.39e vyakat tə   ma:
       good   SUP.VB+NEG NEG
       (a) '(I/you/we/they/it etc.) will not be good'—support verb
       (b) '(I/you/we/they/it etc.) will not become good'—copula clause

We can recall, from §14.1.2 (also see the discussion above), that 20.39d–e are ambiguous in yet another way: the verb *tə*- with a non-verb may also be understood as a copula, 'become'.

Hence the reading (b) for each of 20.39d–e. Nothing but context can help us decide. Just like copula clauses, non-verbal clauses are not used in commands.

The subject of both copula and non-verbal clauses can occur in the highlighting focus construction, just like any subject of an intransitive clause (S)—see §20.3.

Cross-linguistically speaking, the meanings expressed with non-verbal clauses in Manambu are, in the majority, associated with copula clauses—see Dixon (2002). We discuss them one by one.

I. IDENTITY AND EQUATION are illustrated in 20.40, and in T1.6, T1.16, T2.8, T2.24, and the second clause of T2.27.

20.40 kə-di   du-adi
      DEM.PROX-pl man-3plNOM
      'These (ones) were/are people'

The subject can be omitted, as in 20.41.

20.41 wagi-adi
      eel-3plNOM
      'They are eels'

We can recall from §8.2 that an alternative to a construction with 'have' is what can be called identification construction whereby the possessor is the subject of a non-verbal clause, and the possessed noun occupies the predicate slot. These constructions tend to be employed if the possessive relationship is conceived of as a permanent one, as, for instance, belonging to a clan, as in 8.21–5, clauses 6 and 7 of T2.27, and 20.42. In the last clause of T2.26 an 'identification construction' is cast as a question.

20.42 wun gabak-adəwun-ək
      (I) Gabak.clan-1masc.sgNOM-CONF
      'I am a member of Gabak clan'

This is akin to predicative possession, further illustrated at 20.43–4.

II. PREDICATIVE POSSESSION AND PURPOSE are illustrated in 20.43–5. In 20.43, a headless possessive marked with -kə- (see §8.1) heads the predicate; a similar example is at 8.14. The 'double' gender marking is discussed in §8.1.

20.43 də-kə-l-al
      he-POSS-fem.sg-3fem.sgNOM
      'She is his (wife)'

A predicative possessive construction can be used as an alternative to a clan-identification construction, with little semantic difference. The only difference is pragmatic: in 20.42 the speaker fully identifies with the clan, while 20.44 simply states the fact of the clan membership.

20.44 yabun kwalgudəmi də sablap gwalugw-ə-kə-d-ad
      (name) (name)   he Sablap clan-LK-POSS-masc.sg-3masc.sgNOM
      'Yabun Kwalgudəmi, he is of Sablap clan'

We recall, from 8.24, that the identification construction is a preferred rhetorical device in a name debate, where clan membership and the ensuing name ownership are of vital importance.

In 20.45, a dative form, 'for you', heads the predicate:

20.45 kə   na:gw mən-a:k-al
    DEM.PROX+fem.sg sago   you.masc-LK+DAT-3fem.sgNOM
    'This sago is for you/yours'

III. NAMING illustrated in 20.46 can also be expressed with a non-verbal clause:

20.46 wun-a-də   sə   ma: Sepaywus-ad
    I-LK-masc.sg name again Sepaywus-3masc.sgNOM
    'My name, again, is Sepaywus'

Agreement is with the 'owner' of the name. Unlike possessive noun phrases (§8.1.1), possessor and not the possessee can be considered 'head' here.

IV. ATTRIBUTION is consistently expressed through non-verbal clauses with an adjective, a number or a quantifier in the predicate slot, as in 20.47, 20.26, and 20.39c above.

20.47 du   viti-abər
    man two-3duNOM
    'Men were/are two'

V. SIMILARITY is also expressed with non-verbal clauses. Any word class marked with the suffix -pək 'like' or -rəb 'fully like' (see §9.2) or a noun followed by the postposition kətək 'like, as' (§4.5.2) can occupy the predicate slot, as in T1.5 and 20.48.

20.48 lə-kə   amæy-pək-al
    she-POSS+fem.sg mother-LIKE-3fem.sgNOM
    'She is like her mother'

The suffix -rəb does not necessarily require nominal cross-referencing: as shown in 9.29, a noun with -rəb can occupy the predicate slot without any marking. Consider 20.49a and b which are almost synonymous. The difference is slight: 20.49a was used as a general statement pronounced after a lengthy discussion of what the Gala language is like. In contrast, 20.49b was an immediate reaction to a few rather striking cognates between Gala and Manambu:

20.49a ñan-a kudi-rəb-a
    we-LK language-FULLY-3fem.sgNOM
    'This is fully like our language' (a general statement based on a lengthy discussion)

20.49b ñan-a kudi-rəb
    we-LK language-FULLY
    'This is fully like our language' (a spontaneous statement based on a couple of cognates)

These two examples represent different structures: 20.49b and 9.29 are verbless clauses—see below.

Non-verbal clauses can also be used for pointing, as in T1.14, *bap ka* (moon DEM.PROX+3fem.sgNOM) 'This is the moon'. This is only possible if a nominal demonstrative is in the predicate slot. Otherwise a verbless clause is the preferred option.

Non-verbal clauses feature prominently in highlighting focus constructions—see §20.3.

A special subtype of NON-VERBAL CLAUSES is clauses whose predicate is a manner adverbial demonstrative or a reactivated topic demonstrative. As we saw in §§10.2.2–3, each of these takes the predicative marker -n(-). The adverbial demonstrative takes -n- accompanied by third person feminine singular nominal cross-referencing, as in *akatawa-n-a* (like.this.ANAPH-PRED-3fem.sgNOM) 'this is it, this is how it is'. And a reactivated topic demonstrative takes *-n* accompanied with its copy marked for number and gender, e.g. *aka-n-aka* (DEM.DIST.REACT.TOP.fem.sg-PRED-REACT.TOP.fem.sg) 'that is it'. Another example is at 20.52b.

If a clause with an adverbial demonstrative is negated, the predicative marker is omitted, e.g. *akatawa ma:* ((like.this.ANAPH NEG) 'this is not like this'). To negate a clause with a reactivated topic in its predicate slot one uses a biclausal structure, with the pro-clause *ma:* 'it is not the case', as a separate clause, e.g. *aka-n-aka* [PAUSE] *ma:* (REACT.TOP.DEM.DIST.fem.sg-PRED-REACT.TOP.fem.sg NEG) 'that is it—no', meaning 'this is not at all the case'. This is very similar to how *ma:* was used in 14.152–4 (§14.6), also to negate clauses.

Neither the adverbial demonstratives nor the reactivated topic demonstratives can occur with a support verb. Nor can they occur in any dependent clause; or be used in the highlighting focus construction (§20.3). These properties are similar to those of verbless clauses—our next topic.

VERBLESS CLAUSES contain no verb and no cross-referencing. No tense-aspect distinctions can be expressed; these clauses cannot be employed in clause chaining, or as complement clauses. They are negated in the same way as non-verbal clauses: with postposed negator *ma:*. Unlike copula clauses, no constituent can be in highlighting focus.

The word classes employed in verbless clause are rather limited. The semantic types covered include:

i. NAMING AND IDENTITY can be expressed with a verbless clause, as in 20.50a–b, and T2.1.

20.50a wun Walinəm
　　　　 I　　 Walinum
　　　　 'I am Walinum'

20.50b wun-a　　　 sə　　 Walinəm
　　　　 I-LK+fem.sg name Walinum
　　　　 'My name is Walinum'

Identity expressed with a verbless clause involves a clan name (or associated totems) or a kinship name in the second position (as in the first clause of T2.1 and the third clause of T2.27, and 20.51). Using any other word class there would be awkward.

20.51 wun dəmakau　　　 kanukaraki
　　　　 I　　 brown.snake death.adder
　　　　 'I am brown snake, death adder' (that is, I belong to a clan whose totems are brown snake and death adder)

We saw in 20.46 above that a non-verbal clause can be used for naming. In fact, 20.46 ('my name, again, is Sepaywus') and the first clause of T2.1 ('I am father's brother, Sepay') were used by the same person, for different stories. Another possibility would be to use a non-verbal clause in the meaning of identity: *wun Səpaywus-adəwun* (I Sepaywus-1masc.sgNOM) 'I am Sepaywus'. Verbless clauses are statistically the most frequent choice for people introducing themselves as story tellers—a slightly unusual situation in itself, given that all the listeners normally already know who the people are. A non-verbal clause appears to be more appropriate if one says one's name to an unfamiliar audience. But this is hardly a steadfast rule.

ii. POINTING is expressed with non-verbal clauses only if a reactivated topic demonstrative appears in the predicate slot, to bring back a topical participant. The context is always that of an immediate reaction—this is it, here and now, as in T2.25 and 20.52a. In conversations the object is pointed at with a hand.

20.52a ñən-a   kamna:gw kəka
       you.fem-LK+fem.sg food   DEM.PROX.REACT.TOP.fem.sg
       'Here is your food' (pointing) (I have just put it here; it is here right now)

An alternative would be a predicative form of a reactivated topic demonstrative, as in 20.52b. The implication is that the food has been here for some time, and its place is here.

20.52b ñən-a   kamna:gw kəka-n-aka
       you.fem-LK+fem.sg food   DEM.PROX.REACT.TOP.fem.sg-PRED-REACT.TOP.fem.sg
       'Here is your food' (pointing)

We have already seen (20.49b) that a verbless clause may have an overtone of spontaneity. It appears to be also the case in instances like 20.52a.

iii. SUMMARIZING a preceding stretch of discourse can be achieved through using an adverbial demonstrative on its own, in a verbless clause (and without a predicative marker), as in 20.53a. An alternative is to use the word 'manner' in a similar structure—another verbless clause:

20.53a akatawa
       thus
       'This is how it is'

20.53b akatawa sa:d
       thus   way
       'This way (it is)'

An alternative for each of these would be either a predicative form of adverbial demonstrative (*akatawa-n-a* for 20.53a), or a non-verbal clause (*akatawa sa:d-a* for 20.53b). The verbless versions sound more spontaneous and informal.

iv. Verbless clauses are used in a PRESENTATIONAL function, as in T1.2.

v. Verbless clauses are used in QUESTIONS (see C below) which involve manner and are marked with the question words *ata ata* 'how how', as in 10.100, and *agula* 'what's up; what for; why', as in 10.98. Verbless clauses are also employed in questions involving naming, as in 10.102 and 20.54:

20.54 ata   maway sə?
       how flower   name
       'What's the name of the flower?'

Verbless clauses are also used in short questions used to enquire after someone: 20.55 is the way of asking a child about his or her mother and father—that is, where they are, are they OK, and so on:

20.55 amæy? asa:y?
       mother father
       '(What about) mother? Father?'

A similar example is at 20.58—this is a question addressed to unknown beings in order to find out what food they would be capable of eating.

The interrogative pronoun *akə-* 'where' (as in Table 10.7, example 10.90) is used in non-verbal clauses, since it requires non-verbal cross-referencing.

If negated, verbless clauses are indistinguishable from non-verbal ones: 20.56 is a negative version of both a non-verbal clause *lə Təkəta:y-a* (she Teketay-3fem.sgNOM) 'she is Teketay' and a verbless clause *lə Təkəta:y* 'she is Teketay':

20.56 lə   Təkəta:y   ma:
    she Teketay   NEG
    'She is not Teketay'

Table 20.1 summarizes the properties which differentiate between copula clauses, verbless clauses, and two types of clauses with non-verbal predicates—those involving demonstratives with the predicative marker -*n*- and the rest.

The arguments in favour of considering non-verbal clauses as a separate type of clauses headed by non-verbs are: (a) kind of cross-referencing markers used, or lack thereof; (b) negation; (c) tense distinctions expressed with cross-referencing; (d) occurrence in subordinate clauses and in non-indicative moods; (e) semantics; (f) use in highlighting focus constructions; and (g) constituent order.

Unlike copula clauses—which are similar to normal verbal clauses in all but their (lack of) capacity to form commands—they are negated in the same, non-verbal, way, and have a strictly subject-predicate order (see §20.2). Clauses with adverbial and reactivated topic demonstratives in the predicate slot share more properties with verbless clauses than they do with non-verbal clauses.

But how do we identify grammatical relations, especially in verbless clauses? This is to be taken up in §20.1.4.

B. IMPERATIVE CLAUSES are always independent, and contain partially inflected imperative-permissive forms discussed in §13.2. Copula clauses, clauses with non-verbal predicates, and verbless clauses cannot occur in imperative clauses. Some verbs—such as perception verbs—have a telic meaning when used in commands; that is, 20.57 can only mean 'you listen' rather than 'you hear' or 'you understand'. (A loan verb *understand* was used in a command urging a child to understand what the mother was saying and to act accordingly, in 17.26b.) We return to the ways in which 'see' and 'hear' are used in commands in §21.1.2.

The ways in which imperatives can be negated were addressed in §14.4. An imperative strategy can be used in lieu of an imperative-permissive form—see Table 19.5, to express additional overtones to do with strength of the command.

The constituent order in imperative clauses follows the same principles as that in declarative clauses (see §20.2): it is predominantly verb final, but a constituent can be postposed to the verb for disambiguation or if the participant is unexpected (see T1.16).

Imperative clauses have a rising intonation on the verb, if they imply a command, and even if used as a turn-taking device, as in 20.57.

20.57 bər   awuk
    you.du IMPV+listen
    'You (two) listen!'

Permissive forms (see §13.2.2), which are often used in turn taking, tend to be pronounced with an interrogative rising intonation—see C below.

C. INTERROGATIVE CLAUSES correspond to either polar or content questions. We mentioned in §10.4 that content questions are marked with a question word and slightly rising intonation, while polar questions are marked by intonation only. There is no structural difference between a positive polar question and a corresponding statement. Only the intonation and the context decides. Some examples are at 10.79 and further examples in §10.4, 20.14–15, the last clauses of T1.4 and T1.18, and the first clause of T1.14. The last clause of T2.26 contains an 'identification construction' cast as a question.

TABLE 20.1 Copula clauses, verbless clauses, and clauses with non-verbal predicates

PROPERTIES	COPULA CLAUSES	CLAUSES WITH NON-VERBAL PREDICATES		VERBLESS CLAUSES
		NOUNS, ADJECTIVES, NOMINAL DEMONSTRATIVES, NUMBERS, QUANTIFIERS	ADVERBIAL AND REACTIVATED TOPIC DEMONSTRATIVES	
(a) Cross-referencing	verbal cross-referencing	nominal cross-referencing	predicative marker *-n-*	none
(b) Negation	copula negated as any verb	non-verbal negation		
(c) Tense distinctions	as any verb	can be expressed on a support verb	none	none
(d) Subordinate clauses; non-indicative moods	as any verb	expressed on a support verb	none	none
(e) Semantics	identity, attribution, location, and possession	identity, equation, attribution, possession and identification, purpose, pointing, naming, similarity	summarizing; pointing	limited identity, naming, pointing (limited), summarizing; some questions
(f) Highlighting focus	only the subject	only the subject	none	none
(g) Constituent order	subject—copula complement—verb / copula complement—verb—subject	'subject'-predicate		

The only instances of positive clauses with exclusively interrogative reading are short one-noun-phrase-long questions cast as verbless clauses. These are used to enquire after someone, as in 20.55 and 20.58 (which contains a relative clause).

20.58 [[bər   nəbə kə-kə-bra]   [kəkəpa:t]]
       you.du able eat-FUT-2duSUBJ.VT+3fem.sgBAS.VT food
       '(What about) food you two will be able to eat?'

These clauses would not make sense as declarative verbless clauses, since—as we saw in A above—verbless declarative clauses contain at least two independent NPs.

Polar questions display the same patterns of constituent order as do declarative clauses: 13.56 is an example of an oblique, 'with them', placed after the verb (see §20.2). Content questions also display the same patterns.

A question word does not have a fixed position in a clause. It tends to gravitate towards the beginning of the clause or to appear immediately before the verb, as in 10.87–8, T1.5, T1.30, and T3.8. The only exceptions are verbless clauses involving the question word *ata ata* 'how how' as in 10.100–2, and *agula* 'what's up; what for; why' (10.98): here the constituent order is fixed.

The pronoun *sə* 'who?' is unlike other interrogative words in that it takes the linker *-kə-* in order to combine with case markers. It is obligatorily marked for highlighting focus if in the subject position. And if it is used as predicate head, as in 10.82, or is marked for focus, as in 10.83, and 20.59, its form is reminiscent of a headless associative NP (as illustrated in 8.14): it takes gender-number markers *-l-* 'feminine', *-d-* 'masculine', *-bra-* 'dual', and *-di-* 'plural', followed by a nominal predicate cross-referencing enclitic.

20.59 sə-kə-l-al   mən-a:k   kwatiya-l
       who-OBL-fem.sg-3fem.sgNOM you-LK+DAT give.to.nonthird.p-3fem.sgBAS.P
       'Who gave it to you?'

Examples like 20.59–60 can be interpreted as instances of obligatory grammaticalized focus, not infrequent in content interrogatives worldwide. We will see, at §20.3 below, that a focused constituent can only rarely be in the A function.

The interrogative 'who' can be marked for double focus; then the nominal cross-referencing is repeated. The meaning is highly contrastive: 'who is it really?' (see §20.3). In 20.60, the speaker is wondering whether the mysterious person who had entered his house is a man or a woman.

20.60 [sə-kə-d-ad-ad   kə-də   wun-a-də
       who-OBL-masc.sg-3masc.sgNOM-3masc.sgNOM DEM.PROX-masc.sg I-LK-masc.sg
       wiya:m   rə-na-dəmən]   [o rə-na-ñən]?
       house+LK+LOC sit-ACT.FOC-2masc.sgBAS.VT or sit-ACT.FOC-2fem.sgBAS.VT
       'Who is it really, you (man) (who) are staying in this house of mine? Or you (woman) who are staying?'

A clause may consist just of a question word, as in the last clause of T1.23. And any verbal form, including the permissive (13.10), can occur in a question.

When negated, both content and polar questions take the negative dependent clause marker *-ma:r-* if they contain a verb—see 14.127–30. However, as we saw in §14.5.2, this is not the only option. Many speakers (and especially young and innovative ones) use negative declarative forms in negative questions, as in 14.131 and 14.151. If a negative question contains a non-verbal or a verbless clause, it has the same structure as its positive counterpart:

20.61 kə   kamna:gw   vyakat ma:
       DEM.PROX.fem.sg food   good   NEG
       'Is this food not good?'

Further issues, including the patterns of response to negative questions, were discussed in §14.5.2.

20.1.4 Grammatical relations: an overview

Throughout this grammar we invoked the categories of subject—A and S—object and non-subject in general. We will now summarize the criteria for these core grammatical relations, and discuss a number of problems to do with identifying them.

A. THE CATEGORY OF SUBJECT: A AND S. Subjects—A and S—share the following features:

(i) Subjects are obligatorily cross-referenced on fully inflected and on partially inflected verbs—see §11.1.1 and §3.1.
(ii) All subjects are Ø-marked for case—see §7.2.
(iii) Switch-reference-sensitive medial clause-marking suffixes indicate whether adjacent clauses have the same, or different, subjects (see a summary in §18.1).

In addition, just as in the majority of the world's languages, subjects are targets of imperatives, they control reflexives, and there is a 'same-subject' requirement in constructions involving the two modal verbs (20.25a–c and 20.58)—see Dixon (1994: 111–42). There are no other pivot restrictions on coreferential deletion—as is to be expected in a language with switch-reference.

Given such robust grammatical criteria, there should not be any problem in identifying subjects in each particular case. And yet there are. Body part constructions, copula clauses referring to mental and physical states, and impersonal constructions are the cases in point. We saw in §17.4, §18.3, and §20.1.1 (A) above that such constructions have two cross-referencing patterns: the verb can either take third person feminine cross-referencing or it can cross-reference the actual experiencer. Examples are at 20.31–5, and also in §17.4. The cross-referencing depends on topicality: the experiencer is cross-referenced only if highly topical.

And when used in a dependent clause, such constructions are marked for different subjects even if the subjects have the same referent. Examples like 20.62 may sound nonsensical: 'they' are hungry and the same 'they' will come—and yet, the subject is marked as 'different'.

20.62 [ka:m   yasa-lə-k]   [ya-k-na-di]
       hunger BE:FEEL-3fem.sg-COMPL.DS come-FUT-ACT.FOC-3plSUBJ.VT
       'If/when they feel hungry, they will come' (lit. if/when hunger feels, they will come)

This is in fact the most frequent situation—also see 18.24 and 20.36a. So, is a body part or the noun referring to a bodily state the subject here? We return to this issue shortly.

It should be noted that, as we saw in §18.3 (18.26), if the experiencer is topical, the situation is different. Then, the experiencer can be treated as 'same subject' with respect to switch-reference even within a body part construction, if the subject is indeed the same. A rare example is at 20.37. Or if the subject is different, it is marked as different; but the experiencer remains cross-referenced on the polyfunctional verb referring to a bodily state. An example is at 20.63.

20.63 [ka:m   yasa-də-k]   [anay   aka
      hunger BE:FEEL-3masc.sg-COMPL.DS DEM.DIST.CURR.REL DEM.DIST.REACT.TOP.fem.sg
      yi-ku]   [[[sau-la   na:gw] aka
      go-COMPL.SS   fry-3fem.sgSUBJ.P+3fem.sgBAS.P sago   DEM.DIST.REACT.TOP.fem.sg
      yata-n]   ka-war-ku]   [ada
      carry-SEQ bring-UP-COMPL.SS DEM.DIST.REACT.TOP.masc.sg
      kui-la-d]
      give.to.third.p-3fem.sgSUBJ.P-3masc.sgBAS.P
      'After he'd felt hunger, she (mother) having gone to the previously mentioned place,
      having brought the sago she'd fried by carrying it gave it to him'

The man in 20.63 is the one who is hungry. Consequently, 'he' is cross-referenced with a
masculine singular marker on the polyfunctional copula verb *yasa-*, within a medial clause.
The subject of this clause is different from that in the subsequent clause: the work is done by
one of his mothers. That is, different-subject marking in 20.63 is sensible—it shows that one
person (man) was hungry and another person (woman) came, brought sago, and fed him.

   We can conclude that if the experiencer is cross-referenced and is topical it is the subject.
Otherwise it is not, even if it is overtly stated, because it does not trigger same-subject marking
or get cross-referenced on the verb. These constructions can also be considered impersonal.
This is plausible, given that third person singular cross-referencing is used in constructions
with no subject at all, such as sentences with modal verbs at 20.25a. Here, the body part or
the expression of bodily state such as 'hunger' cannot be considered the subject because it
behaves as a copula complement. A similar situation obtains with impersonal constructions
which include complex predicates such as *suan yi-* (difficult go-) 'be difficult' (see §4.1.2), and
a corresponding loan from Tok Pisin *hat* (used with the support verb *tə-*). In 20.64, 13.80, and
T3.33, the support verb *yi-* takes third person feminine cross-referencing. All these statements
have a generic meaning—one does not eat rotten bananas:

20.64 [bapi   tə-dana]   [suan   yi-k-na]
      rotten become-3plBAS.VT+3fem.sgSUBJ.VT difficult go-FUT-ACT.FOC+3fem.sgBAS.VT
      [kəka:k]
      consume+RED+DAT
      'If they (bananas) become rotten, it will be difficult to eat (them)'

   An experiencer cannot be added—but an S can. And it can be expressed with a nominalization as a complementation strategy, as in T3.20 and T3.33, or with a sequencing -*n* form:

20.65 [kəkəpa:t kurə-n] [kə   tami: suan   ya:l]
      food   get-SEQ DEM.PROX.fem.sg area   difficult go+3fem.sgBAS.P
      'It was difficult to get food in this area'

   A clause used as a complementation strategy can contain an object (*ya:m* 'smell' in T3.20
and *kəkəpa:t* 'food' in 20.65). But is the clause itself a subject? Presumably, yes—at least
based on formal reasons. First, the feminine singular cross-referencing on the verb is the
least functionally marked, and hence likely to be used in constructions with non-prototypical
subjects (see Aikhenvald 2000: 28–44).

   Secondly, as far as switch-reference-sensitive markers go, constructions like those in T3.20
and T3.33 are treated in the grammar as having different subjects from that in the main clause,
even if the experiencer of the difficulty is the same as the subject of the adjacent clause. An
example is at T3.35: the predicate of the dependent clause is cross-referenced for different
subject; and the snake is the main character and the subject of this whole sentence.

Another option is to cross-reference the experiencer on the verb—then the experiencer has to be overtly stated, as in 20.66. The experiencer is highly topical: the hawk is stressing the difficulty he has in entering the house without a key:

20.66 [wiya:r   wula-wula:k]   [suan   yi-na-dəwun-ək]
      house+LK+ALL enter-RED+DAT difficult go-ACT.FOC-1masc.sgBAS.VT-CONF
      'It is difficult for me to enter the house' (lit. I am difficult to enter the house)

Such a topical experiencer has yet another crucial subject property: it controls switch-reference. In 20.67, the same person experienced difficulties in talking and got into the hands of an evil man:

20.67 [wun yi-yə   suan   yi-ku]   [kuprap-ə du   taba:r
      I   talk-RED difficult go-COMPL.SS bad-LK   man hand+LK+ALL
      wula-lwun-ək]
      enter-1fem.sgBAS.P-CONF
      'As it was difficult for me to talk (lit. as I was difficult to talk), I got into the hands of a bad man'

Neither body part constructions, nor copula clauses or impersonal constructions, can form imperatives or reflexives, or be used in constructions with modal verbs—which means that these universal criteria for subjecthood are not applicable here.

Bodily and mental processes in Papuan languages are very often expressed with 'impersonal' constructions, which are problematic with respect to their subjecthood. The title of Pawley, Gi, Majnep, and Kias's (2000) 'Hunger acts on me...' speaks for itself: the problems we have just addressed for Manambu are pervasive in the whole area—also see Pawley (forthcoming), Roberts (2001), and Priestley (2002). Compared to other Papuan languages, body part and impersonal constructions in Manambu are fairly limited. And the experiencer is never marked as an object. There is also a strong correlation between the topicality of an experiencer and its potential subjecthood.

We conclude that in all such constructions in Manambu the topical participant has the formal properties of a subject. This is congruent with the idea that subjects tend to be grammaticalized topics (see, for instance, Keenan 1987: 103–4; and discussion in Dixon 1994: 11–30). It is interesting to note that subjecthood and topicality are closely intertwined just in this instance, so much so that one is tempted to say that subjecthood in body part and impersonal constructions is determined entirely by pragmatics.

Verbless clauses are also potentially problematic in terms of how their subjects are to be identified. Clauses with non-verbal predicates other than adverbial and reactivated topic demonstratives are pretty straightforward in this respect: we recall, from §20.1.3 above, that their subject is cross-referenced on the predicate itself with cross-referencing enclitics. When used in dependent clauses, non-verbal predicates have to be used with a support verb which then also cross-references the subject constituent.

But verbless clauses and clauses with adverbial and reactivated topic demonstratives have no subject cross-referencing. Neither can they be used in dependent clauses.

Since the predicate is marked with the suffix *-n-* in both clauses with adverbial and reactivated topic demonstratives (see 20.52b), the other obligatory constituent can be safely identified with the subject. This other constituent—e.g. 'food' in 20.52b—triggers gender and number agreement on the demonstrative in the predicate slot, which makes it similar to a subject (A/S). The order of constituents is fixed: the predicate always comes last. We thus conclude that the non-predicate noun phrase in non-verbal clauses with adverbial and reactivated topic demonstratives as predicates is subject-like enough to be considered on a par with other subjects.

The situation in verbless clauses is less clear. In clauses of the naming type, there is semantic agreement between the first and the second noun phrase. The order is fixed; and the choice of the second NP depends on the first. And if a 'naming' verbless clause is rephrased as a non-verbal clause, the 'name' is in the predicate slot and the person named is the subject. This allows us to hypothesize that the 'name' occupies the predicate slot, and the person named is the subject.

The same line of argument holds for verbless clauses with a reactivated topic demonstrative in the second position—such as 20.52a. There is also some grammatical agreement between the two constituents: so, in a verbless clause *apawul ada* (spirit DEM.DIST.REACT.TOP+masc.sg) 'that is a (masculine) spirit' the masculine form is determined by the first noun phrase. We can thus suggest that the first noun phrase is subject-like, and the second is not. Following the principles of analogy with similar clauses, we can stipulate that the question word heads the predicate in 20.54, 10.98, 10.100–2. The situation with verbless clauses of other subtypes is just as murky: the notion of subject does not appear to be applicable at all to the one-word clauses like those in 20.53a and 20.55.

The category of a syntactic subject—A and S—is highly relevant for Manambu (despite its limited applicability to verbless clauses). What about other grammatical relations?

B. THE CATEGORY OF OBJECT (O). We saw in §7.3 that the direct object (O) is often marked with accusative case. An O can also be cross-referenced on the verb in the second position—see §3.1—and it can be referred to with a reactivated topic demonstrative (§3.3 and §10.2.3). The O is added to an intransitive verb as a result of applying the morphological causative *kay-* (see §16.2.1). But while accusative marking is just about exclusive to a direct object, the other two properties are not. In particular, any non-subject constituent—with the exception of speech reports and copula complements—can be cross-referenced on the verb in the second position, provided it is topical. Then, an 'object' is just a part of a more general category which can be negatively defined as 'non-subject'. This 'non-subject' shares a number of properties with S—the subject of an intransitive verb: see below.

C. LINKING TOGETHER S, O, AND 'NON-SUBJECTS'. All or most languages of the world display a number of links between S (= subject of an intransitive verb) and O (= object of a transitive verb) (see Dixon 1994: 55; and Aikhenvald and Dixon forthcoming). These links have nothing whatever to do with ergativity of any kind. They are expected to be found in languages with every pattern of syntactic and morphological alignment—that is, nominative/accusative, absolutive/ergative, and so on. So, if a language marks quantification on verbs, it is highly likely that the number expressed will be that of S or O. And this is indeed the case with the marker of complete involvement *-tu-* (see §12.4), e.g. *kiya-tu-di* (die-MANY-3plBAS.P) 'They$_S$ all died' and *vya-tu-di* (kill-MANY-3plBAS.P) 'They killed (all) of them$_O$ (all over the place)'; and not *They (all) killed them' (see 12.22–4 and 12.72).

Besides this expected correlation between S and O, Manambu has a number of less obvious ones. We saw in §3.3 and then in §10.2.3 that reactivated topic demonstratives can only refer to an S, or an O, or, somewhat more rarely, to another non-subject participant—for instance, recipient, location, and time. (That a demonstrative should operate on an absolutive basis is hardly surprising—in Dyirbal and a few other languages, an NP including a nominal demonstrative may only occur in S or O function which is the pivot function in Dyirbal: Dixon 2003: 83, 94–9.) These non-subject participants are the ones cross-referenced on the second position—provided they are topical.

This S/O, or, better, non-A, basis for reactivated topic markers has a pragmatic basis. It agrees with a cross-linguistic tendency for a correlation between the non-A function (typically, an S/O function) and introducing a new participant (Du Bois 1987). To put it simply: new participants tend to be introduced in S/O function, but hardly ever in the A function.

This principle in Manambu has interesting repercussions for the variations in constituent order, and for the highlighting focus construction. There is a strong preference for non-As to occur in a postverbal position reserved for unexpected and relatively new information and clarification (see §20.2). An A constituent hardly ever occurs in highlighting focus constructions reserved for new information (see §20.3).

20.2 CONSTITUENT ORDER: ITS SYNTACTIC AND PRAGMATIC MOTIVATIONS

Constituent order in Manambu is predominantly verb final in main clauses, and almost exclusively so in dependent clauses (see Tables 19.1 and 20.1). This is consistent with a verb-final tendency advocated as typical of languages with clause chaining and switch-reference.

However, this is not a steadfast rule. One Sunday in early 2002 Ken Nayau, the major consultant working with SIL missionaries Robin and Marva Farnsworth, was visiting his native Avatip. He burst into Yuamali's house where we were having a mid-afternoon snack to ask me an urgent question: 'What is a verb-final order?' I explained, using a mixture of Manambu, Tok Pisin, and English, what this is supposed to mean (it is not an easy task to say 'verb' in Manambu, or to talk about linguistics in general). 'You put your verb at the end of what you say.' 'Yes', replied Ken, 'this is what Robin told me it means. But we do not speak like that.'

And indeed, not all clauses in Manambu end with a verb. (In the corpus, about 15–20 per cent do not.) There are a number of principles which allow for non-verb-final orders in the language.

The general principle of ordering words and constituents in Manambu involves placing new and less topically established participants first. Participants tend to be introduced as O (as can be seen in T1.1 and T2.1), or in a verbless clause (as in T1.3 which may be translated as '(There was) a young man and a woman'), or as an S of a non-verbal clause (as in T2.3). In a transitive clause, the order is typically AOV, as in 20.68a. An overt A does not have to be expressed at all; but it is likelier to be expressed if the predicate is a non-inflecting verb as in 20.68a–b (also see 7.5).

20.68a wun mən-a:m   vi   ma:
       I   you.masc-LK+ACC/LOC hit+NEG NEG
       'I will not hit you'

An OAV order implies that the O is contrastive, new, and unexpected, as in 20.68b:

20.68b mən-a:m   wun vi   ma:
       you.masc-LK+ACC/LOC I   hit+NEG NEG
       'I will not hit <u>you</u>' (implying that I may hit someone else)

Placing an O before an A is so unusual that if the clause is to be repeated in a 'head-tail' bridging structure (see §20.4), the A is also repeated. Note that the O is not case marked, despite being a personal name: this O is a new participant never mentioned in the story again, and case marking is associated with topicality—see §7.3.

20.69 [də-kə-di ñan-ugw kur-taka]   [wula-taka]   [Apur_O Iraman_A
      he-OBL-pl child-PL get-IMM.SEQ enter-IMM.SEQ Apur   Iraman
      vya-də-d]   [Iraman_A vya-də-k]   [a
      hit-3masc.sgSUBJ.P-3masc.sgBAS.P Iraman   hit-3masc.sg-COMPL.DS DEM.DIST.fem.sg
      təp   atawa wapa-da-l]   [aka   Apatəp
      village thus   leave-3plSUBJ.P-3fem.sgBAS.P DEM.DIST.REACT.TOP.fem.sg Avatip
      kur-da-l]
      make-3plSUBJ.P-3fem.sgBAS.P
      'Having taken his children, having entered (the battlefield), Iraman hit Apur (not anyone
      else), after Iraman had hit him, they left the village that time, that is when/how they made
      Avatip'

A conventional way of marking 'head-tail' bridging linkage would have been to say *vya-də-d vya-də-k* (hit-3masc.sgSUBJ.P-3masc.sgBAS.P hit-3masc.sg-COMPL.DS), literally, 'he hit him, having hit' (see §20.4.1). But since there is potential ambiguity as to who did the hitting and who was hit, 'Iraman' is repeated again.

A fronted O in OAV clauses often appears in a highlighting focus construction:

20.70 alək   [klada   ta:kw-a]_O in focus   [də kə-də
      that.is.why DEM.PROX+fem.sg+DOWN woman-3fem.sgNOM he DEM.PROX-masc.sg
      ñan-a-də   ñan_A kra-kwa-d]
      we-LK-masc.sg child marry-IMPV.3p-masc.sg
      'That is why it is this woman down there (that) he this son of ours may marry'

Obliques also tend to be placed at the beginning of the clause if contrastive—see further discussion in §20.3.

The postverbal position is reserved for noun phrases, or sometimes parts thereof, which provide unexpected supplementary information which is partly new and partly confirms what we already know. We saw in 20.20 that a numeral can be extracted from a noun phrase postposed to the verb: in this case it emphasizes the 'togetherness' of the action.

Only a small fraction of such postverbal elements are separated from the verb with a pause, as one would have expected if it had been an afterthought. Consider 20.16: the woman did not bring water even for her own child, and this latter, oblique constituent, is postposed to the verb, as surprising information. This information is not fully new—we already know that the child accompanied her, and that she did not bother to bring either food or water for either of them. The postverbal position for the beneficiary, the child, stresses how remiss she was.

Similarly, in 20.6, the speaker reintroduces his ancestor in S function as the one who was looking around. A similar example is 13.56: the comitative 'with them' is supplied after the verb because it is unexpected, and needs to be reiterated. In T1.16, the S is postposed to the imperative form since it is conceived as a means of 'chasing away' an unexpected guest. And in T2.16 the tree finally falls down—this unexpected and surprising result is expressed via postposing the S to the verb. A similar example is at 20.71—a command by a mother to her daughter urging her to be less greedy and share some of the tiny Malay apples with her baby sister:

20.71 lə-kə-k   akui   mugul-a-jagwəs
      she-OBL-DAT IMPV+give.to.third.p three/few-LK-tiny.Malay.apple
      'Give her (guess what) a few tiny Malay apples!' (something you do not expect to give
      her)

A postverbal oblique often has a similar function, as in 10.3, 20.3 ('to her'), and 20.72 (where the postverbal noun phrase contains a relative clause). We already know where the mother and her brother had gone; that the child decides to follow them right there is unexpected.

20.72 kwapək ada   ya:d   [amæy wa
 next.day DEM.DIST.REACT.TOP+masc.sg go+3masc.sgBAS.P mother and
 away   yi-bra   tamiya:k]
 mother's.brother go-3duBAS.P+LK area+LK+DAT
 'Next day he (child) went (guess where) to the area where mother and uncle had gone'

As a result of this unexpected turn of events, the child discovers the existence of yams—this is the beginning of the story about the origin of yams. A similar example is at T3.26—the snake's entering the house (postposed to the verb) is unexpected: snakes are not supposed to enter houses.

Alternatively, a postverbal NP may provide additional clarification, as in 20.8: the speaker wanted to make sure the audience understands exactly who went up the river. A similar example is at 20.73: the postverbal oblique makes it clear that the speaker is urging his sister to return to the house:

20.73 səbənən   yi-tək   wiya:r
 return+SEQ go-1duIMPV house+LK+ALL
 'Let's go back, (that is) home'

When a little boy got drowned in the village, the whole family was involved in mourning him; 20.74a specifies that his mother was also among those who cried at that time:

20.74a [ata wukə-ku]   [gra-dian   də-kə   amæy wukən]
 then hear-COMPL.SS cry-1plBAS.P he-OBL+3fem.sg mother with
 'Then having heard (the news) we cried together with his mother'

Similarly, in T2.59 the possessor in a non-verbal possessive clause is postposed to the predicate, as a means of clarification. An NP which provides clarification is more likely to be separated from the rest of the clause with a pause than an NP which supplies unexpected information. An example of a clarifying afterthought is at T3.41.

Not every syntactic function allows for a postverbal position with equal ease. The number of transitive subjects in this position is remarkably limited. One such rare example is at 20.74b. The participant sucking the breast was—according to the speaker—a rather unexpected one:

20.74b a   ta:kw məñ ka:d   a-də   wa:j
 DEM.DIST.fem.sg woman breast eat+3masc.sgBAS.P DEM.DIST-masc.sg eel
 'That eel (guess who!) was sucking that woman's breast'

Another example is in the last clause of 16.29. This is an example of clarification stating exactly which members of the opposite clan group (that is, the wife's relatives) were conducting a debate about the man's mortuary festival.

Two noun phrases can be postposed to the verb, albeit rarely. In 20.75a two NPs (an oblique and an S) clarify a statement which would otherwise have appeared obscure. The adverb 'already' is also postposed to the verb—this emphasizes the unexpectedness of the fact that the plane (and Jager with it) is already going away, in the direction of Wewak:

20.75a væki-na-d   bə   Wewak-a:r   Jagər
 go.across-ACT.FOC-3masc.sgBAS.VT already Wewak-LK+ALL Jager
 'Jager is already going across to Wewak!' (lit. (He) is already (surprise!) going across to Wewak Jager)

The English translation presents this clause as if it contained afterthoughts—the Manambu clause does not, because there are no pauses intervening between the constituents.

A rare example of VOA order is at 20.75b: that I (the addressee) had not yet had the chance to go to the market and see Walinum ('her') again was surprising to the speaker:

20.75b ma: nəbay və   lə-kə-m   ñən
    NEG yet   see+NEG she-OBL-ACC/LOC you.fem
    'You (not anyone else: surprise) haven't yet seen (guess who) her'

An unusual constituent order, such as OVAO in 20.76, tends to involve repetition of one of the constituents. In 20.76, *bal* 'pig' (O) is repeated twice: once before and once after the verb:

20.76 [abra   {war-bər]   [war-ku]}   [bal$_O$
    DEM.DIST.REACT.TOP+du go.up-3duBAS.P go.up-COMPL.SS pig
    ada   vya-bra-d]   [amæy asa:y]$_A$
    DEM.DIST.REACT.TOP+masc.sg kill-3dusUBJ.P-3masc.sgBAS.P mother father
    [pətakaum kwa-d-ə   bal]$_O$
    ladder+LOC stay-3masc.sgBAS.VT-LK pig
    'The two went up, having gone up; killed the pig mother (and) father the pig that was on the ladder'

The second postposed constituent can be an afterthought, as in 20.77. It is separated from the rest of the clause by a pause:

20.77 [a-də   wi   ada   yi:n
    DEM.DIST-masc.sg house DEM.DIST.REACT.TOP+masc.sg go+SEQ
    səmaka-yi-də-d   du-a-ñan] PAUSE [a-di   *rum*-a:b]
    show-go-3masc.sgSUBJ.P-3masc.sgBAS.P man-LK-child PAUSE DEM.DIST-pl room-TOO
    'The boy (guess who) kept on showing that house on and on, those rooms too'

Speakers vary as to the frequency of postposed NPs and adverbs. Postposition for clarification purposes is more frequent with older women as story tellers, accustomed to explaining and spelling out things for their grandchildren as their audience. During my first stay at Avatip, speakers such as Yipawal, Yuawalup, and the late Wimali would use such postposed noun phrases (S, O, obliques, and even As) with much more frequency than later on, after I'd become much less of a novice (or a novelty), and was expected to understand a story like any other adult.

Postposing an NP to the verb in a command may have additional repercussions to do with its illocutionary force. This is shown in the three contrasting examples below. In 20.78a, the mother tells the elder child to give a doll to a younger child who is crying:

20.78a *dolly* nak lə-kə-k   akui
    dolly one she-OBL-DAT IMPV+give.to.third.p
    'Give her one dolly!'

The elder girl ignores the command, and the younger child continues crying. The mother, mildly annoyed, repeats the command as 20.78b:

20.78b *dolly* nak akui   lə-kə-k
    dolly one IMPV+give.to.third.p she-OBL-DAT
    'Give her one dolly' (lit. one dolly give to her)

The girl ignores it again, and the younger child cries more and more. The mother shouts:

20.78c akui PAUSE *dolly* nak lə-kə-k
IMPV+give.to.third.p PAUSE dolly one she-OBL-DAT
'Give her one dolly!!!' (Give (pause) one dolly to her)

In this last example, the noun phrases are separated from the verb with a short pause. However, it appears counterintuitive to treat them as 'afterthoughts'—rather, the mother sets the NPs off from the verb as a way of reminding the naughty girl what she is to do, unless she wants to face the consequences. (The child did not, and opted to run away.)

Order within dependent clauses tends to be verb final. However, there are exceptions—as in T1.3, and 20.79. These exceptions serve a didactic purpose—that of reminding the audience of an S, or an O, or an oblique (but hardly ever an A). The man was mentioned a few lines before; so the speaker chose to repeat a reference to him, just in case:

20.79 [və-kətakəp tə-ku du-a:k] [adiya səbənadi]
see-FR 'stand'-COMPL.SS man-LK+DAT DEM.DIST.REACT.TOP+pl return+3plBAS.P
'Having tried to see the man in vain, they returned'

There is never any pause between the predicate of the dependent clause and the postposed NP.

A dependent clause can be postposed to the main clause, as a means of providing supplementary information, as in 14.115, 14.116, and T1.34. This information is not new—the function of a postposed dependent clause is to remind the listener of something they are already supposed to know. Consider T1.34: all the postposed medial completive clause tells us is that the main character was married—something we have known from the very start of the story.

A similar example is at 20.80. The girl is very angry with her uncle who had mistreated her in the past. This is what the preceding paragraph is about. The uncle understands this and says to the girl's brother (for whom the fact that the girl is angry is also no news):

20.80 [lə [lə-kə sə kwa:l-a tamiya:b] kwa:l
she she-OBL+fem.sg sleep stay+3fem.sgBAS.P-LK area+LK+TERM stay+3fem.sgBAS.P
aka] [wun-a:k warsama-ku]
DEM.DIST.REACT.TOP.fem.sg I-LK+DAT be.angry-COMPL.SS
'She is in the place where she sleeps, having got angry at me'

A dependent medial clause postposed to the main clause with same-subject marking may have a recapitulative function. Then they form one intonation unit. Examples are in 18.19 and 18.28, 20.76, T2.23, and the penultimate clause of T2.40. We saw, in §19.5, that such recapitulating constructions are particularly frequent in speech reports, as in 19.74. An additional function of this is to stress that a speech act actually took place: speech report constructions in Manambu are used in a wide variety of meanings not all of which involve a speech act. Alternatively, the same-subject form of the verb *tə*- 'stand, be' can be used in the meaning of 'after that', literally, 'having been (like that)', as in 18.24 and 18.28, and T2.62.

We saw in §13.7, and especially examples such as 13.79–81 and 20.64, that a dative-aversive marked nominalization can precede or follow the main (inflected) verb. A postverbal position is reserved for an unexpected piece of information, as in 13.82 (people are normally not afraid of going into a house).

The position of the reactivated topic demonstrative *aka* (DEM.DIST.REACT.TOP.fem.sg) before or after the verb depends on what the demonstrative refers to. If it refers to a participant (typically in S, O or oblique function), it precedes the verb, as in 10.41 and T2.1. If it refers to the action itself, it can be placed either before or after the verb.

It appears after the verb if the whole action and its extent is somewhat unexpected. Consider the final lines of the three texts: in T2.69, *aka* precedes the verb, and in T1.35 and T3.53 it follows. In the latter instances, the end of a story is stated as being 'that topical one': neither story is a traditional one, and consequently does not have an ending that everyone would be aware of. In contrast, T2.69 is the ending of a traditional story which finishes in due course; and so *aka* precedes the verb. Along similar lines, in the first clause in 20.80 the fact that the girl is sleeping in her house and her uncle is left outside is somewhat unexpected and contrary to convention—this explains the postverbal position of *aka*.

In summary: constituent order in Manambu is both syntactically and pragmatically based. In particular, the fact that A (transitive subject) hardly ever appears postposed to the verb reflects its pragmatic function closely associated with its syntactic role.

We will see, in §20.4.1 (example 20.90) that having a non-verb-final constituent order does not affect the basics of 'head-tail' linkage between sentences.

20.3   HIGHLIGHTING FOCUS CONSTRUCTIONS

Highlighting focus constructions (mentioned in §3.1 and then in §11.1.1, and example 11.8) involve marking a noun phrase or a fully inflected verb as if it were a non-verbal predicate, in order to contrast it with another constituent, or another clause. A noun phrase or a verbal form in highlighting focus takes nominal cross-referencing enclitics. Gender and number specifications agree with the head of predicate. That is, if the predicate head is masculine singular, as in the first clause in 20.81, cross-referencing is masculine singular. And if the predicate head is feminine singular, so is the cross-referencing, as in the second clause in 20.81. If the whole inflected verb is in highlighting focus (examples 20.87–8), the agreement is third person feminine singular; this is in line with this being the least functionally marked choice. Highlighting focus constructions are highly frequent in conversations and narratives. They involve contrasting a constituent to another constituent; or 'stressing' a constituent as important for the discourse.

As mentioned in §20.1.1, parts of a noun phrase cannot be focused independently: only an NP as a whole can. The same principle applies to complex predicates. A clause cannot contain two constituents each in a focus construction. A constituent in focus tends to occupy a clause-initial position.

A highlighting focus construction does not appear to produce a cleft sentence: the non-focused part of the clause has the make-up of an independent clause. We would expect a cleft to split a clause into two clauses: one copula-like, and the other marked as a relative clause (see Matthews 1997). We return to this issue further below.

There is no intonation break or pause between the form in highlighting focus, which has to obligatorily precede the predicate. A story or a conversation never starts with a highlighting focus simply because a highlighting focus implies contrast to something previously mentioned. A constituent in highlighting focus does not have to be definite; but it has to have been mentioned previously in discourse.

Highlighting focus overwhelmingly involves S (intransitive subject), as in T1.3, T1.13, penultimate clause of T3.16, T3.25, and 20.81, or the object, as in T2.59, T3.3, and 20.82. Constituents in highlighting focus are in braces, and so are their translations into English:

20.81 [{jəpwas-ad}   təkər-əm   rə-kwa-na-d]
          initiated.man-3masc.sgNOM stool-LK+LOC sit-HAB-ACT.FOC-3masc.sgBAS.VT
          [{ta:kw-al}   təkər-əm   rə-rə   ma:]
          woman-3fem.sgNOM stool-LK+LOC sit-RED NEG

'{An initiated man} used to sit on a stool, {as for a woman}, there is no sitting on a stool' (lit. {It is an initiated man} used to sit on a stool,{it is a woman} there is no sitting on a stool)

An object in highlighting focus construction is never case marked. This is in line with the semantics of object case marking (see §7.3): only definite and topical, rather than focal, objects are case marked. This also agrees with a general tendency of not having case-marked constituents in the highlighting focus constructions.

20.82 {du də-kə-də   kui-ad}   kə-da-d
  man he-OBL-masc.sg meat-3masc.sgNOM eat-3plSUBJ.P-3masc.sgBAS.P
  '{It is man's flesh} they ate'

The S of a non-verbal clause can be in highlighting focus, as in T1.7 ('as for this one'), T2.27 (*ka* 'this is it (that I am)'), T3.40 (*kad bə numa-də ga:n-ad* 'this is that it is a big masculine night') and 20.83.

20.83 {a-də   *masalay*-ad}   kabay-ad
  DEM.DIST-masc.sg spirit-3masc.sgNOM snake-3masc.sgNOM
  '{It is that spirit} (who) is a snake' (lit. {It is a spirit} is a snake)

So can a time adverb as in T3.42 ('today'), and an addressee, as in 20.84.

20.84 {a-də   Kainu-ad}   wa-ñəna-d
  DEM.DIST-masc.sg Kainu-3masc.sgNOM say-2fem.sgSUBJ.P-3masc.sgBAS.P
  '{It is that Kainu} (that) you spoke to' (lit. {it is that Kainu} you spoke to)

If a location or an instrument is focused, it tends to appear without any case marking, as in 20.85a (this is also a possible alternative interpretation for the first clause of T2.8). A rare example of a case-marked oblique in highlighting focus is at 20.85b.

20.85a {gu-a}   ya-bər
  water-3fem.sgNOM come-3duBAS.P
  '{It is to water} (that) they came'

20.85b wiyar-a   yi-na-di
  house+LK+ALL-3fem.sgNOM go-ACT.FOC-3plBAS.VT
  '{It is to the house} (that) they went'

We mentioned in §10.2.2 that *ata* 'thus' has a predicative focus form *ata-n*, e.g. *ata-n au* (thus-PRED IMPV+talk) 'speak now' (lit. 'it is now that you are commanded to speak'). This marker also appears when *ata* heads the predicate (see §20.1.3). An example of *ata* in a highlighting focus construction is at 20.86 (the O, 'ceremony', is postposed to the verb as a clarification).

20.86 {ata-n-adi}   tə-da-di   ba:gw
  thus-PRED-3plNOM have-3plSUBJ.P-3plBAS.P ceremony
  '{This was the way} they had ceremonies' (lit. {Thus was} they had (what we already know, that is) ceremonies)

A constituent within a dependent clause can rarely occur in a highlighting focus construction unless there is a break (a rare example is at T2.35). A dependent clause (except for an -*n*-marked sequential clause) cannot be in highlighting focus.

We saw, at §20.1.3 above, that the interrogative pronoun *sə* 'who' is obligatorily marked for focus if it occurs in subject function. This is the only instance of grammaticalized focus whose occurrence is limited to S and A.

Highlighting focus constructions involving arguments and obliques cannot be negated separately. This is hardly surprising: we can recall that a constituent cannot be negated separately, without the whole clause being negated.

We now turn to a rather unusual construction whose function is to contrast an action, or a state, to other actions or states. Such 'predicate focus' constructions involve marking a fully inflected verb as if it were a non-verbal predicate. Note that they cannot involve a predicate already marked for action focus (§12.2). (If the predicate in 'predicate focus' contains an uninflected verb, it requires a support verb—see §17.2.) In 20.87, the speaker is saying that what they were going to do was to cut the pig, and not anything else. This is framed as predicate focus—that is, the whole clause is within the scope of the focus. A similar example is at 11.8.

20.87 [au {kə-də   bal ra-kə-bana-l}-a]
      then DEM.PROX-masc.sg pig cut-FUT-1plSUBJ.VT-3fem.sgBAS.VT-3fem.sgNOM
      'It is that {we are going to cut the pig}' (rather than doing something else)

'Predicate focus' structures produced spontaneously often provide an explanation for an unusual event or state. When we returned to Avatip from an exhausting trip to Swakap, people would look askance at my bandaged arms. The answer—provided by Yuaneng—was:

20.88 [{Swakapa:r   yi-ba-l}-a]
      Swakap+LK+ALL go-1plSUBJ.P-3fem.sgBAS.P-3fem.sgNOM
      'It is that {we went to Swakap}' (and got sunburnt and tired)

A distal demonstrative as head of non-verbal predicate can be put in a focus construction, as a form of a strong statement: *a-l-al* (DEM.DIST.fem.sg-3fem.sgNOM-3fem.sgNOM) 'this is it'. It is also used as a conversation sustainer, and as a summarizing statement indicating that the speaker has finished one point, and may well start on something else.

Such predicate focus constructions cannot contain reactivated topic demonstratives. Neither do they occur with a non-predicate-final constituent order. This is to do with their pragmatic organization: the event or the resulting state is viewed as a whole, and is thus contrasted to another event, the participants being of secondary importance.

The difference between the English translational equivalents in 20.87–8 and 11.8 and the Manambu structures is that there is no overt subordination marker in Manambu.

If the predicate in a highlighting focus construction is negated, it takes the subordinate negator *-ma:r-*. We can recall, from §14.5.3, that this is indeed the most frequent context under which a predicate of what looks like an independent clause may occur with *-ma:r-*. This involves focusing a negated clause. Examples are at 14.134–5, and 20.89a. What makes life in Swakap unbearable for the people from Avatip and Malu is that:

20.89a [{kwasa   wi   tə-ma:r-dana-l}-a]
       small+fem.sg house have-NEG.SUB-3plSUBJ.VT-3fem.sgBAS.VT-3fem.sgNOM
       'It is that {they do not have toilet (small house)}'

This brings us back to the issue of whether highlighting focus involves a cleft or not. In many languages, focus constructions are expressed via cleft clauses which, in their turn, involve marking part of a clause as a dependent clause. That a dependent clause negator is used in focused clauses shows that such clauses may be considered underlyingly dependent. That is, at least predicate focus constructions may be considered clefted, but the evidence only becomes apparent if they are negated. And this should not come as a surpise—it is also the case in relative and juxtaposed dependent clauses whose status as dependent clauses is fully revealed under negation. Highlighting focus constructions do not involve relative clauses (see §19.2): the rearrangement of participants typical for possessor relative clauses does not occur in highlighting focus constructions.

If a constituent in highlighting focus is contrastive, an option is to employ double focus. This involves adding another nominal cross-referencing marker, as in 20.89b. Here, the fact that they do not have a toilet is contrasted to the fact that other, more 'cultured' people do:

20.89b [{kwasa wi
small+fem.sg house
tə-ma:r-dana-l}-a]-al
have-NEG.SUB-3plSUBJ.VT-3fem.sgBAS.VT-3fem.sgNOM-3fem.sgNOM
'It is that {they **do not really have** toilet (small house)}'

The existence of double focus structures demonstrates that focus constructions are different from verbless clauses with non-verbal predicate heads: no non-verbal predicate would take double cross-referencing, outside the focus construction. Unlike 20.60, where a double focus structure is obligatory, in 20.89b it is pragmatically determined.

Are highlighting focus constructions monoclausal or biclausal? The evidence goes both ways. A noun phrase in highlighting focus has the appearance of a full verbless clause, since it includes non-verbal cross-referencing markers. On the other hand, it is not a full clause because it cannot be negated separately. It occupies the argument slot of the predicate. And if it is to be questioned, the question word also has to be cast as a focused constituent. We conclude that highlighting focus constructions combine features of biclausal and monoclausal constructions, and, just like transitivity-neutralizing constructions involving clause chaining (§17.5), are an additional instance of grammar-in-the-making. A similar construction in Iatmul was described by Jendraschek (2006b): their status as bi- or monoclausal is equally ambiguous.

20.4 FURTHER ISSUES IN DISCOURSE ORGANIZATION

Manambu clauses form sentences which contain one main clause, and sentences combine to form a paragraph. A paragraph—or a coherent stretch of discourse—is defined as having a topic of its own, and is normally separated from the next paragraph by a significant pause. As we saw above, a topic usually appears preposed to the predicate. A reactivated topic—that is, a topic mentioned in a previous stretch of discourse and known to the speaker and to the addressee, but not mentioned for some time—is marked with reactivated topic demonstratives (see §10.2.3 and §3.3). This is a powerful device which allows speakers to handle more than one topic at a time. The ways sentences can be linked together within a paragraph, or across paragraphs, are addressed in §20.4.1. In §20.4.2 we discuss the function of 'boundary-marking' clauses consisting of *ya:kya* 'all right' and its Tok Pisin equivalent *orait* (§20.4.2).

We saw in §20.2 above that constituent order plays its role in identification of topical participants. Narratives tend to be elaborate in stating participants, while conversational discourse is highly elliptical, and heavily relies on context. Some of the recurrent principles of ellipsis in the Manambu discourse are discussed in §20.4.3.

A typical turn-taking device is the first person permissive form of the verb *wa-* 'speak': *wau* 'May I speak? Shall I speak now?' A distal demonstrative as head of non-verbal predicate in a focus construction *a-l-al* (DEM.DIST.fem.sg-3fem.sgNOM-3fem.sgNOM) 'this is it' signals the end of what someone has to say, indicating that at least one point is finished, just like a verbless clause *akatawa* 'this is how it is' (see 20.53a).

Expressions like *a-l-al* and the interjection *ay* are used as conversation sustainers, supplying feedback from the listener and urging the speaker to go on talking. The expression *ma:j ma:* (speech NEG) 'there is nothing to say; talk is over' (very similar to Tok Pisin *nogat tok*) is a signal that there is nothing much else to add to the conversation.

20.4.1   Linking sentences

The most frequent way of putting sentences together within a paragraph is via a connective, e.g. *ata* 'then' and *atawata:y* 'and so then, in summary, this is why' (and also *aw* 'then' which involves contrast). These were discussed in §19.6. Sentences linked with these refer to events which follow each other and may, or may not, overlap.

LINKING SENTENCES often involves repetition, of a variety of subtypes. The last verb of a main clause is repeated as a completive medial clause at the start of the next sentence (or clause chain) (this bridging repetition is often called head-tail linkage, or tail-head linkage, see de Vries 2005 for a cross-linguistically based definition of this device across Papuan languages). A typical example is at T1.8: the third clause—a completive medial clause—repeats the predicate of the second, main, clause. The subject marking is preserved. Since the subjects of the third and the fourth clauses are different, the medial clause is marked for different subject. Similar examples are at T1.10 ('he came ashore. After he'd come ashore . . . '), T1.13, T1.17, T2.18–19, T2.19–20, T2.24, T2.50–1, T2.61–2, T2.63, and T3.16–17.

If the subject of a medial clause is the same as that of the subsequent clause, it is marked as same subject (as in T1.18, linked to T1.17 by 'head-tail' linkage). 'Head-tail' linkage may involve medial clauses other than completive type, as in T1.3 (which contains an immediate sequence clause marked with -*taka* in the same function).

In all such cases only the verb is repeated, rather than a full clause, or part thereof. In T1.18, only the first component of the compound is repeated. We saw in 15.14, 15.50, and 15.121 that the second part of the compound or the whole compound may be repeated. The choice depends on which aspect of the action expressed with a compound a speaker decides to focus on. If a main clause contains a compound with -*yakə-* 'fully' as a second component (see §15.3.1), there is no such choice: the whole compound is repeated in 'head-tail' linkage, as in T2.17. If a main clause contains a complex predicate containing an auxiliary, only the auxiliary gets repeated in the next clause—as in T2.20 and T2.21.

The main clause may have a non-main-predicate-final order. This does not impinge upon the way in which 'head-tail' linkage operates. Consider T2.23–4: a dependent clause 'having smelt his smell' is postposed to the main clause ('they barked in upward direction') in T2.23. This sentence is joined to the next sentence, T2.24, via head-tail linkage. But only the predicate of the main clause ('they barked in upward direction') is repeated in T2.24—as if the postposition of a dependent clause were invisible for the operation of 'head-tail' repetition. Noun phrases and adverbs which happen to be postposed to the predicate of a main clause are also irrelevant for 'head-tail' linkage—see T2.52–3, and 20.90. Only the verb itself is repeated:

20.90 [ata ma: warə-d nəkə-də numa-də miya:r]
then again go.up-3masc.sgBAS.P other-masc.sg big-masc.sg tree+LK+ALL
[war-ku] [ata [kətay kəti væn] və-də-l]
go.up-COMPL.SS then around around see+SEQ see-3masc.sgSUBJ.P-3fem.sgBAS.P
'Then he went up again onto another big tree, having gone up, he then looked around looking'

'Head-tail' linkage is quite frequent, but far from pervasive. This can be seen even in the short selection of texts at the end of this grammar. Unlike some Papuan languages (discussed in de Vries 2005), not every sentence is linked to every other sentence this way.

A close look at the corpus reveals a pattern. Texts containing pervasive 'head-tail' linkage usually describe close sequences of actions, and the linkage itself is a way of signalling the fact that one action has finished so that the other one can begin. The actions do not overlap. This is the case in 20.90, and even more so in T2.17. In this case, a *ya:kya* or an *orait* clause is the main clause of the sentence containing the 'head-tail' construction—and we will see, in §20.4.2, that *ya:kya* clauses are a way of finalizing a paragraph, or a stretch of narrative describing a connected set of events.

This brings us to the functions of 'head-tail' linkage. According to de Vries (2005: 378), this device has three functions for those languages where clause chaining is involved: 'processing ease, referential coherence, and thematic continuity'. What Manambu adds to this is an over-tone of completion of the action involved, and the lack of overlap between the action marked within the 'head-tail' linkage and a subsequent one.

We can also recall that a sequence of a verb in a main clause followed by the same verb in a medial completive clause has a recapitulating function (see §18.3); the two form one intonation unit and there is no pause between them. This makes sequences such as *kamapu-d kamapu-ku* in T2.63 and *səbənə-l səbən-ku* in T3.21 different from the ordinary linkage which involves repeating the final verb in a medial clause: here the focus is plainly on the completion of a process.

If two sentences are put together, the predicate of a previous clause can be repeated as an independent clause. The meaning is that of emphasis: 'this is what happens'. No wonder the repeated verb is often cast in the 'predicate focus', as in 20.91:

20.91 [wun kamna:gw kwatiya-tua] [mən-a
I food give.to.nonthird.p-1sgSUBJ.VT+3fem.sgBAS.VT you-LK+fem.sg
kamna:gw kwatiya-tua-l-a]
food give.to.nonthird.p-1sgSUBJ.VT-3fem.sgBAS.VT-3fem.sgNOM
'I give food (to you), it is that I give your food (to you)'

Repetition of a clause, as in T1.17 ('after he'd come ashore going on having come ashore') iconically reflects a prolonged repetitive action, in accordance with the general meaning of repetition (see §12.8.3). Repeating the same verb in different forms many times, as in T2.9–10, provides additional elaboration to a narrative.

20.4.2 Finalizing a paragraph and taking a break

We mentioned in §18.3 that a clause chain can be interrupted by *ya:kya* or *ya:k* 'all right, OK', or its Tok Pisin equivalent *orait*. A major function of such interruptions followed by a significant pause is to indicate that a certain time has elapsed between the actions of the two adjacent clauses, as in T1.27, T2.10, T2.16, T2.28, T2.30, T2.35, T2.38, T2.41, T2.49, T2.55, and T2.57. Such interruption also allows the speaker to regain their breath if a sentence they are producing turns out to be rather long. The more elaborate the speaker is, the less frequent are *ya:kya* clauses: the overuse of *ya:kya* clauses implies that the speaker has not really planned what they want to say.

A clause containing *ya:kya* or its Tok Pisin equivalent *orait* often occupies the slot of a main clause, and the last clause in a sentence, or a paragraph. Then, it implies that one action or set of actions is finished, and something else will now start—as in T1.24, T1.26, T2.9, T2.11, T2.24, T2.31, T2.33, T2.41, T2.42, T2.45, T2.49 (last clause), and T2.53. In T2.17, a *ya:kya* clause occurs together with 'head-tail' linkage signalling the end of a paragraph. (The linkage via repetition here also indicates that the action of 'fully hitting' is completed.) Another paragraph, with its own sequence of actions, will start in T2.18.

By themselves, *ya:kya* clauses are a subtype of verbless clauses. They are never negated or questioned. They can hardly be considered an instance of ellipsis since it is impossible to supply what could have conceivably been elided.

Ya:kya has an additional function: it signals the end of a paragraph, or a stretch of discourse, or a start of a new passage. This is how it is used in T1.1: we were talking about various Manambu stories, and as soon as Gaiawalimæg was ready she stopped all this talk by saying *ya:kya* and started her very own story (Text 1). *Ya:kya* is also a way of signalling agreement, as in T1.12 and T2.43. This use is reflected in a fixed expression *ya:kya wa-* (OK say) 'agree' (see T1.34).

20.4.3   Ellipsis

Being elaborate and precise is a skill highly appreciated for story tellers and orators in the Manambu speech communities. In contrast, day-to-day speech is highly elliptical. If a noun phrase is recoverable from the context, it won't be overtly mentioned. In 20.36a and 20.36b the referents of the full pronouns were obvious ('me' and 'you feminine'), so they did not have to be stated. And we saw that in 20.41 the subject was omitted—also because it is clear from the context. In 8.4 only the gender agreement shows that the possessed noun 'house' has been omitted. This was Yipawal's answer to my question 'Where is your house?' The reply was, literally, 'I this one (masculine)'. Further possibilities of ellipsis are illustrated with the following snippets of dialogue.

Consider 20.92–3. The sentence under a is a question, and b is an answer to it. The question in 20.92a is itself elliptical: we were talking about some women going to Maprik to sell fish, so this part is not stated:

20.92a sə-kə-dadi   yi-k-na-di?
       who-OBL-3pl+3plNOM go-FUT-ACT.FOC-3plBAS.VT
       'Who is going (to Maprik to sell fish)?' (lit. Who are going?)

The idea of the answer in 20.92b is that the speaker was going to find out who was going and then give them money to buy her some hair cream:

20.92b kwakə-ku   kui-kə-tua-di
       find-COMPL.SS give.to.third.p-FUT-1sgSUBJ.VT-3plBAS.VT
       'Having found (them), I will give (it: money) to them'

In 20.93a, the speaker asks the guest whether he'd come from Yawabak on foot. Note the absence of the overt pronoun: it is omitted, since the cross-referencing on the inflected verb conveys who the subject is:

20.93a nəbə-say ya-na-dəmən?
　　　 dry.ground+LK-TRANSP come-ACT.FOC-2masc.sgBAS.VT
　　　 'Have you come on foot?' (lit. via dry ground)

The addressee replies, omitting the main verb. The dependent clause is postposed to the elliptical main clause (which consists just of the instrument, 'with a canoe'), as a clarification: the speaker wants the audience to know that he came all the way just paddling (and therefore is tired and wouldn't mind refreshments).

20.93b [vala-rəb] [gus kan]
　　　 canoe+LK-FULLY paddle paddle+SEQ
　　　 'Straight with a canoe, paddling a paddle'

The main verb can only be omitted if it has been introduced in the preceding discourse. For instance, if A says *wali-kamna:gw akəs kə-kwa-na* (white.people-food NEG.HAB eat-HAB-ACT.FOC+3fem.sgBAS.VT) 'she never eats white people's food', B is likely to add *wun-aba:b akəs* (I-TOO NEG.HAB) 'I too never'. The latter clause would not make sense on its own, taken out of context. In 20.94—an example of a desubordinated clause, similar to 19.113b—both object and verb have been omitted from the second clause:

20.94 də-kə　　　 *buk* alə-da:m　　　　　　　 taka-ku　　 wun api:m
　　　 he-POSS+fem.sg book DEM.DIST+fem.sg-DOWN+LOC put-COMPL.SS I top+LOC
　　　 'I have put his notebook underneath, and mine on top' (lit. having put)

Elliptical clauses are very frequent in informal interaction. We saw in §19.9 how desubordinated clauses—which can be considered the result of conventionalized ellipsis—are employed as command strategies. An elliptic clause can be used as a command, with a particularly strong illocutionary force (similar to desubordinated medial clauses in Table 19.5), e.g. *ap kəka* (bone DEM.PROX.REACT.TOP.fem.sg) 'This bone!' meaning 'Put this bone here (or put it down) (or else)!'

Instead of producing a full clause, as in 7.29, people would just shout: *akəm tə-ku?* (where+LOC stay-COMPL.SS) 'where (are you/(s)he/they) coming from?' And we can recall that just one word, marked with dative, is enough to verbalize an impending threat: Tanina would shout *diya:k* (shit+LK+DAT) '(beware) of (dog's) shit', and I would know to watch my step. Along similar lines, a reciprocal marker was omitted in 14.114, since the sentence can only have a reciprocal reading.

If a support verb, or an auxiliary, is easy to supply, it can also be omitted, as in 20.95–6, and in 17.49–50—this latter was uttered by an angry speaker immediately on entering our house one Saturday. The context was clear; and the form *luku* only occurs with the verb *kur-*—so no ambiguity could possibly arise. A similar example is at 20.95a: the support verb which occurs with *sua:l* is either *kur-* or *taka-*; so it appears to be easily omissible in a quick dialogue (from a story):

20.95a [ñən　　 sua:l kur-ñən-ək]　　　　　　 [wa-lə-k]　　　　　 [ka
　　　 you.fem lie　 do-2fem.sgBAS.VT-CONF say-3fem.sg-COMPL.DS DEM.PROX.fem.sg
　　　 wun sua:l ma:]
　　　 I　 lie　 NEG
　　　 ' "You are lying (lit. doing a lie)", she having said, (the other said), "no! (lit. this!), I am not lying (lit. I a lie not)" '

The last clause without ellipsis would be rendered as in 20.95b (the ellided word is underlined, here and in the further examples in this section):

20.95b wun sua:l ma: kwa:r
    I   lie   NEG do+NEG
    'I am not lying' (lit. I am not doing a lie)

Along similar lines, *makən* 'be in mourning' can be omitted from a complex predicate with *kwa-ya-* (stay-come), as in 20.96a. This verb is typically used in combination with 'mourning'. The affected participant is overtly expressed and the context states that he or she had indeed died. This makes 'mourning' recoverable from the context, and thus dispensable.

20.96a [kiya-də-k]   [ya:kya] [də-kə-k   kwa-ya-di]
    die-3masc.sg-COMPL:DS OK   he-OBL-DAT stay-come-3plBAS.P
    'After he'd died, OK, (his relatives) stayed (in mourning) for him'

The full clause, without ellipsis, would be:

20.96b [kiya-də-k]   [ya:kya] [də-kə-k   makən   kwa-ya-di]
    die-3masc.sg-COMPL:DS OK   he-OBL-DAT in.mourning stay-come-3plBAS.P
    'After he'd died, OK, (his relatives) stayed in mourning for him'

If a support verb is omitted from the main clause, and the clause takes part in the bridging repetition (or 'head-tail') linkage, only the support verb gets repeated in the following medial clause. This is a frequent feature of any narrative, not just of a conversation. An example is at 20.97a. A pause indicates that there is a clause boundary.

20.97a [yi:n   gan   kusəm]   [PAUSE] [na-lə-k]   [ya:k]
    go+SEQ night finish+COMPL PAUSE BE:NAT-3fem.sg-COMPL.DS OK
    [ada   kwa-na-d]
    DEM.DIST.REACT.TOP+masc.sg stay-ACT.FOC-3masc.sgBAS.VT
    'As it went on and on, the night finished completely. It having finished, OK, he remained'

The same sentence without ellipsis is at 20.97b.

20.97b [yi:n   gan   kusəm   na:l]   [PAUSE] [kusəm
    go+SEQ night finish+COMPL BE:NAT+3FEM.SGBAS.P PAUSE finish+COMPL
    na-lə-k]   [ya:k] [ada
    BE:NAT-3fem.sg-COMPL.DS OK   DEM.DIST.REACT.TOP+masc.sg
    kwa-na-d]
    stay-ACT.FOC-3masc.sgBAS.VT
    'As it went on and on, the night finished completely. It having finished, OK, he remained'

The support verb here is uniquely identifiable because this is the only one that can occur with uninflected completive aspect (see §17.2)—so there is no need to state it in the main clause. Neither is there any need to repeat the complement of the support verb since it has just been mentioned.

Any support verb can be omitted in the same way. We recall, from 17.39–40, that a nominal *makəmak* 'silent' takes a support verb *rə-* 'sit' or *tə-* 'stand, be'. In narratives of any kind it often occurs on its own, without a support verb, as in 20.98a:

20.98a [ada   da-na-d]   [məkəmək]

       DEM.DIST.REACT.TOP+masc.sg   go.down-ACT.FOC-3masc.sgBAS.P silent

       'He went down, (being) silent'

A version without ellipsis is at 20.98b:

20.98b [ada   da-na-d]   [məkəmək

       DEM.DIST.REACT.TOP+masc.sg   go.down-ACT.FOC-3masc.sgBAS.P silent

       tə-ku]

       'stand'-COMPL.SS

       'He went down, (being) silent'

This is the only type of ellipsis pervasive in any type of discourse.

A lexical verb can be omitted from clauses with the generic completive *napa-* (see §18.9) if understood within the given context. The fact that the child had finished staying there is understood—there is nothing else the child was supposed to do after he'd been put there. The elliptical clause is underlined. Its unelided form would have been *kwa-n napa-də-k* (stay-SEQ COMPL.VB-3masc.sg-COMPL.DS).

20.99 [a   ñan   nakamib ata   yata-kwa-bana-d]

       DEM.DIST.fem.sg child together then carry-HAB-1plSUBJ.VT-3masc.sgBAS.VT

       [yata-ku]   [karda-n]   [taka-ba-k]   [ya:kya]

       carry-COMPL.SS bring.down-SEQ put-1pl-COMPL.DS OK

       <u>[napa-də-k]</u>   [ada   [yata-n]

       COMPL.VB-3masc.sg-COMPL.DS DEM.DIST.REACT.TOP+masc.sg carry-SEQ

       kawar-taka-bana-d]

       bring.up-put-1plSUBJ.VT-3masc.sgBAS.VT

       'We then used to carry that child together, having carried (him), we put him down (lit. having put her by carrying down), OK, after he'd completed (staying there), we take him and put him (there) carrying (him)'

Switch-reference (different subject marking in the clause with *napa-*) helps track the referents. Note that this is an example of a mismatch in gender agreement (see §5.2.2). The masculine child is small, and so is referred to with the feminine form of the demonstrative; but it is male, and so is cross-referenced with the masculine singular on the verb.

Even a part of a fixed expression can be omitted, if the speaker chooses to do so. As can be seen from the endings of the three texts at the end of this grammar (T1.35, T2.69, and T3.53), when a story finishes, it 'goes inside the base'. One very long story that the speaker chose to tell several times ended with:

20.100a gabu-maj   wula-d   aka

        traditional-story come.inside-3masc.sgBAS.P DEM.PROX.REACT.TOP+fem.sg

        'The (long) traditional story is over' (lit. goes inside)

What he could have said, had he not chosen to be elliptical, is:

20.100b gabu-ma:j   mawər   wula-d

        traditional-story base+LK+ALL come.inside-3masc.sgBAS.P

        aka

        DEM.PROX.REACT.TOP+fem.sg

        'The (long) traditional story is over' (lit. goes inside the base)

Such omissions are indicative of speakers who are less careful in how they lay out their narratives. And it is perhaps not a coincidence that speakers who tend to be elliptical are not among the most eloquent orators. That is, Manambu discourse presents a curious combination of both explicitness and ellipsis. This is comparable to the structure and use of the lexicon— which also combines a high degree of precision with the ever-present option of using a generic term. This is the topic of our next chapter.

Issues in Semantics and Features of Lexicon

Throughout this grammar we have dwelt upon the semantic content of various word classes, including nouns (§4.1.2), verbs (§4.2.2), the two classes of adjectives (§4.3.3), and adverbs (§4.4). This chapter focuses on a number of salient features of the Manambu lexicon in general.

Speakers often conceive of their languages in terms of lexicon, putting primary value on the knowledge of words. In the Manambu tradition, knowledge—viewed in terms of lexicon, especially the totemic names—is tantamount to monetary riches. In other words, the more names one knows the richer one is: these include personal names, terms of address, and denominations of culturally important items owned by different clans in general. The issue of name ownership acquires particular importance at name debates (*saki*). A man's oratorical skill plainly depends not so much on his eloquence but on his knowledge of names—in other words, nouns par excellence. Knowledge of totemic names belonging to a clan (and of their 'shadowy' equivalents: see §22.3) plays a role for both men and women when it comes to songs. Laments of foiled marriages, *namay* and *sui*, are sung by both men and women. The mourning songs *gra-kudi* (cry-language) are the prerogative of women. The quality of a song and the proficiency of a singer are judged by the richness of totemic names associated with the clan of the deceased. Such proficiency in a woman is comparable to the eloquence of a male orator in name debates—except that a good orator wins at a debate (and his clan acquires a name), while singing a mourning song does not result in winning anything, except prestige and respect. Multiple 'names'—each belonging to a different clan—create a situation of multiple synonymy (see §21.5), mostly for nouns.

The Manambu lexicon is large—especially where nouns are concerned. Very precise distinctions can be expressed. On the other hand, there is a high degree of 'generality'—one always has the option of using a generic noun or a generic verb if for some reason one chooses to do so. This is reminiscent of the organization of Manambu discourse: at the end of the preceding chapter we saw a curious combination of both explicitness and ellipsis. Manambu also has a large number of homonyms (partly resulting from a variety of phonological mergers in its history). A view from other Ndu languages may sometimes help—we return to this in §22.1.

We start with a discussion of a number of prominent semantic subclasses of verbs (§21.1). We then turn to the problem of generic, and specific, notions in the Manambu lexicon (§21.2). A general noun and a general verb meaning 'whatever' and 'do whatever' respectively are discussed in §21.3. Body part constructions and the expression of emotions are discussed in §21.4 (see §17.4 and §20.1.4 for grammatical relations in body part constructions). Their semantics is discussed in §21.4. In §21.5, we address speech formulae, especially the ways of addressing and farewelling each other, and touch upon multiple synonyms and name ownership.

21.1 VERB SEMANTICS

Roughly the same set of semantic distinctions is coded in the verbal lexicons of all the languages of the world. Language-specific concepts tend to include items relating to beliefs, cultural practices, and social organization. The range of meanings of a lexeme can be expected to vary from language to language. In this section, we briefly summarize a few of the semantic subclasses of Manambu verbs which appear to be cross-linguistically unusual.

One such instance in Manambu is ingestive verbs, to do with consuming food or drink—see §21.1.1. Verbs of perception display rather unusual patterns of polysemy, and may be considered a special semantico-grammatical subclass within the verbal lexicon—see §21.1.2. Verbs of speech, one of which was discussed at some length in §19.5, show an interesting distribution and a number of cross-linguistically unusual differences one from another—see §21.1.3.

21.1.1 'Eating', 'drinking', and 'chewing': ingestive verbs

Most of the world's languages distinguish lexemes for 'eating' (solid foods) and 'drinking' (liquid) (see Newman forthcoming, for an overview). However, this distinction itself is not universal.

Manambu has one verb *kə-* which covers consumption of any substance (independently of its consistency) that involves swallowing or going down the person's throat. That is, it covers drinking (as in 21.1a), eating (21.1b), and smoking (21.1c).

21.1a gu   kə-na-wun
    water consume-ACT.FOC-1fem.sgBAS.VT
    'I am drinking water' (lit. I am consuming water)

21.1b kamna:gw kə-na-wun
    food   consume-ACT.FOC-1fem.sgBAS.VT
    'I am eating food' (lit. I am consuming food)

21.1c yaki   kə-na-wun
    tobacco consume-ACT.FOC-1fem.sgBAS.VT
    'I am smoking tobacco' (lit. I am consuming tobacco)

Further examples of *kə-* in the sense of 'consuming food' are at 18.6, 18.12, 18.22, and 18.31b, and 'consuming drink' are at 19.111 and 18.22. The same verb is used with the meaning 'suck', as in *məñ kə-* (breast consume) 'be breastfeeding' (of a baby) (as in 7.80) and in the term for 'last child', *kə-təp-ə-məñ* (eat-be.closed-LK-breast) lit. 'eating breast for the last time'.

The verb *kə-* in combination with *gu* as its formally unmarked direct object may also mean 'drown', as in 18.17, 'after his son had died by drowning' (lit. 'after his son had died having consumed water'). In this case it is clear that 'consuming water' involved drowning because the verb 'die' is overtly mentioned. In fact, the context may be sufficient, as in a warning in 21.2:

21.2 gu   kə-k-ñəna!
    water consume-IRR-2fem.sgSUBJ.VT+3fem.sgBAS.VT
    'You might drown (since you can't swim, and the river is deep!)'

And the expression *yi kə-* (fire_A consume) is a way of referring to fire devouring something.

This verb has an additional culturally salient metaphorical extension, to do with 'consumption' of a payment. When a sister's child dies, their mother's agnatic kin people receive a large payment (usually of cash and/or shell valuables) which is supposed to repay them for their gifts and other services to the dead person (including payments for bride price). The payments are distributed as a follow-up to the mortuary feast, *Kəkə-təp* (eat:RED-be.closed), lit. 'eating for the last time' (see §15.3.1, and 16.29). This is not a coincidence: the feast is conceptualized as ritual 'eating' of a relative (see further discussion in Harrison 1990a: 35).[1] The bride price, *takwa-yu* (woman+LK-greensnail.shell (used as shellmoney)), or simply *yu-*, is also 'eaten', that is consumed, by the recipient. We can recall, from §1.3.1, that the mortuary ritual occupies a central role in Manambu society, providing a 'social glue' for the Manambu within the villages and away from them. This is undoubtedly due to the monetary exchange and potential gain for the participants.

One talks about 'consuming' a relative as a metaphor for the mortuary feast, as in 21.3a.

21.3a nakaləb kə-kwa-na-dian   gabəraw-ñan-ugw
      together consume-HAB-ACT.FOC-1plBAS.VT sister's.child-child-PL
      'We consume sister's children all together'

This is also a useful way of describing a kinship relationship between people, without going into too much detail. A store owner in Avatip said to me:

21.3b [kusə-ñən-ək]   [ñən-a:m   kə-k-na-dəwun]
      finish-2fem.sg-COMPL.DS you-LK+ACC/LOC consume-FUT-ACT.FOC-1masc.sgBAS.VT
      'When you die, I will consume you'

This was said instead of going into a lengthy explanation of what clan he belongs to and what makes me count among his sister's children. There are no more anthropophagical implications to such means of expression than there are to the Christian tradition of holy communion, whereby Christ's flesh and blood are metaphorically 'consumed'.

One also talks about 'consuming' money and valuables at the mortuary feast, as in 21.4.

21.4 [nak-a-na   nak-a-na   ja:p   *mani*   æm   san]   [kə-da-di]
      one-LK-one one-LK-one 'thing' money share plant+SEQ consume-3plSUBJ.P-3plBAS.P
      'They consume valuables (lit. thing) (and) money, sharing them'

The verb *kə-* 'consume' also applies to offenders against yams and fish (Harrison 1993: 49): they are said to run the danger of falling sick and dying as a result of being consumed by these foods they have misused.

The verb *kə-* is not used with directionals. It appears in the first slot of a few verb compounds, *kə-kəta-* (consume-try) 'taste, try, and consume' and *kə-kusə-* (consume-finish) 'finish consuming, eat/drink up'—see §15.3.1, and 15.33 and 15.40. Note that 'eating' and 'drinking' are always distinguished by the context: this explains the translations of 15.33 and 15.40 as 'eating'. The component *kə-* in *kə-marki-* 'swallow' (as in T2.31) is most probably related to *kə-*.

If the food is only chewed and not swallowed, the verb *jə-* is used, as in 21.5. All the ingestive verbs are S=A ambitransitive.

21.5 ma:s   akəs   jə-kwa-na
      betelnut NEG.HAB chew-HAB-ACT.FOC+3fem.sgBAS.VT
      'She never chews betelnut'

Nowadays, *jə-* also applies to such Western innovations as chewing gum (chewed, but not swallowed). In T2.31—a story told by a man—this verb describes the action of chewing food to facilitate its consumption by someone who is too weak to chew it himself. The same action for the same purpose is described using the verb *ñam* 'chew food (to feed the baby)' in another version of the same story of the origin of the Vali:k clan, told by a woman:

---

[1] The alternative term for 'mortuary feast' is *maja:n*.

21.6 [adəka   ñam-ta:y]
    DEM.DIST.REACT.TOP+masc.sg chew.food.in.mouth-COTEMP
    [kui-də-d]
    give.to.third.p-3masc.sgSUBJ.P-3masc.sgBAS.P
    'He (Sesawi) gave him (Kamkudi) (food) having chewed it in his mouth'

The verb *ñam-* refers to the way in which the Manambu women used to chew the food
before it was put into a baby's mouth, a typical woman's activity. Such babyfood is called *ñam-
kamna:gw* (chew.for.baby-food). And this brings us to an apparent asymmetry in the Manambu
lexicon. While there is no dedicated term for 'eating' rather than 'drinking', there are several
terms for 'food'.

The term *kamna:gw* or its phonetic variant *kamna:* refers to food prepared for eating. The
term *kami-kamna:gw* ('fish-food') is used to refer to provisions, or foodstuffs, to be stored, or
procured. The term *məy-a-kamna:gw* (real-LK-food) 'real food' refers to traditional Manambu
foods rather than the opposite, *wali-kamna:gw* (white.person-food) 'white people's food', typically store bought. (This is similar to how traditional thread is referred to as *məy-a-mæj*, and
store-bought thread as *wali-mæj*.) Saying *kamna:gw ma:* (food NEG) implies the lack of protein
food (on several occasions, this was said when there was plenty of sago, rice, and bananas in
the house, but no meat or fish).

The etymology of *kamna:gw* is unclear: this form bears a striking similarity to Iatmul
compound *kami-nau* (fish-sago) 'fish and sago'. The noun *nau* 'sago' in Iatmul is used in a
more general meaning of 'food' (e.g. *gabi-nau* 'morning food', 'breakfast'), while its Manambu
cognate *na:gw* is not. (Both *nau* and *na:gw* can refer to baked goods involving flour, e.g. Iatmul
waliniba-nau 'white.people-sago', Manambu *wali-na:gw*.[2])

The term for 'raw food' is *kəkəpa:t* (see 20.58 and 20.65). Synchronically, this form is not
segmentable. However, it has a cognate in Iatmul (Gerd Jendraschek, p.c.), *ki-ki-va:k* (eat-eat-
DER) 'food' (Iatmul *v* corresponds to the Manambu *p* whose intervocalic allophone is *v*; and
the word-final Iatmul *k* corresponds to Manambu *t*). While the Iatmul *-va:k* is a productive
derivational suffix, its Manambu cognate *-pa:t* is found only in this term.

The term *kəja:p* refers to protein food, such as game or fish. Speakers conceive of this word
as unsegmentable. Etymologically it may be a compound (*kə-* 'consume', *ja:p* 'thing'). If this is
so, this form would be structurally reminiscent of Iatmul *ki-ki-da* (eat-eat-thing) 'food'. Unlike
Manambu, in Iatmul *ki-ki-da* (eat-eat-thing) 'food' and *ki-ki-va:k* (eat-eat-DER) 'food' appear
to be full synonyms.

Manambu has no general word for a drink—the word *gu* 'water' covers all liquids, including
beer and wine, and even petrol. An alternative term for alcoholic drink is either *wali-gu*
'white person's water' or *kuprapə gu* 'bad water', or even *kuprapə-saprap gu* 'really bad water',
depending on the speaker's attitude. (Also see §21.2.3, on value terms in Manambu.)

The polysemy of *kə-* 'consume' in Manambu is not an innovation. Most Ndu languages
use the cognate to refer to both eating and drinking, e.g. Iatmul *ki-* (Gerd Jendraschek,
p.c.), Ambulas-Wosera *ka* (Kundama, Wilson, and Sapai 1987), Boiken (Kwusaun dialect) *kʌ*
(Laycock 1965: 165). Boiken (Yengoru dialect) has a form *ti ho* (Freudenburg 1975) which
translates as both 'eat' and 'drink'. (Laycock 1965 gives the form *kʌ* for this dialect.) This same
form means 'smoke' in Iatmul and Ambulas-Wosera (we have no information about other
languages).

---

[2] I am grateful to Gerd Jendraschek for providing the information on Iatmul. The forms quoted here are not found
in Staalsen and Staalsen (1973).

Along similar lines, Kwoma (which has been in contact with Manambu for a long time) has one verb *a* 'ingest' to refer to eating and drinking (Bowden 1997) (there is, however, a different root for 'smoke').

Gala distinguishes 'eat' (*kə-* or *kəkə-*) and 'drink' *(dugə-/duga-)* (*pace* Laycock 1965: 165). During my brief stay at Swakap in the company of my Manambu family (with whom my language of communication was Manambu), Gala speakers commented on the fact that, unlike Manambu, they do distinguish between 'eat' and 'drink'. The Kwoma expression *uku a* (lit. water ingest) 'drink' looks suspiciously similar to the Gala verb meaning 'drink'. We can recall, from §1.4.1, that there probably was a considerable amount of contact between the Gala and the Kwoma prior to the Gala wars (whose outcome is described in Text 2). The Gala form may well be a borrowing.[3] See further discussion in Aikhenvald (forthcoming h).

21.1.2 'Seeing' and 'hearing'

Every language has a way of referring to two basic sources of sensory perception: seeing and hearing. Polysemy patterns, basic meanings, and syntactic properties of terms referring to seeing and hearing vary across languages. Basic terms for perception in Manambu appear to be *və-* 'see' and *wukə-* 'hear, listen'. We now discuss each of them, and then summarize their properties.

A. 'SEEING'

The verb *və-* means 'see', 'look', and also 'try (often by taste or touch)' and 'experience'. This verb has a somewhat unusual argument structure. We can recall, from §7.3, that in its meaning 'see, look', it is transitive, and its O is unmarked for case if indefinite or not 'seen' completely. If the object is fully seen and the action is volitional and/or telic (meaning 'look (at)', or 'see well'), the object is marked with accusative-locative, as in 7.21. But in the meanings 'look around for' and 'see, notice', the object is marked with dative, as in 7.22 and 7.28.

The O in the meaning of non-volitional and uncontrolled experience is unmarked, as in 7.16 and 21.7. This was an answer to 7.23, a question about the age of Duamakwa:y, the oldest man in the Manambu communities, at the time when he had met Dangwan (one of the Manambu interpreters for Behrmann's 1912–13 expedition to the Ambunti area).

21.7 wun wasa-yuwi bə və-dəwun, bə və-dəwun
I cheek+LK-hair already see-1masc.sgBAS.P already see-1masc.sgBAS.P
'I already shaved, already shaved' (lit. I already experienced beard)

The same meaning of *və-* occurs in T2.56 ('experience body/skin' means 'have sex').

The expression *yigən və-* refers to dreaming—it can be understood either as 'seeing a dream' or 'experiencing a dream'. The polysemy of *və-* as 'see, look' and 'experience' is what makes Text 1 hilarious for Manambu speakers: it is centred around the expression *bap və-* (moon see/look/experience) which is a conventional way of referring to women's menstruation as 'experiencing the moon sickness'. A stupid young man—the main character of Text 1—does not know this, and understands this expression literally, as 'looking at the moon', or 'seeing the moon'.

---

[3] According to Laycock (1965: 165), only Yelogu has *kʌ* for 'eat' and *rə* for 'drink' (there are no forms for these in the SIL survey lists, so I was not able to check this).

Unlike in, say, Indo-European languages such as English (also see an overview in Evans and Wilkins 2000), 'see' does not cover the meanings of 'know' or 'understand' (these are expressed with *laku-* 'know, understand', and partly with *wukə-* —see below).

In its meaning 'try', *və-* typically describes trying something by taste or touch. The manner of 'trying' is specified with a sequencing *-n* form of a verb, as in 21.8:

21.8 ka:n   və-tua
      eat+SEQ see/try-1sgSUBJ.VT+3fem.sgBAS.VT
      'I am trying (the new food) by eating'

An imperative of *və-*, *ap*, can mean 'look!' or 'try!' As is typical for imperatives, it has to have a telic and volitional meaning—that is, *ap* does not mean *'see!' or *'experience!' However, a permissive form remains polysemous—21.9 has both meanings 'may I see/may I look' and 'may I try'. It does not mean 'may I experience', because 'experiencing' denoted by *və-* is beyond asking for permission—this is something that just happens no matter what.

21.9 vau
      see/try+1sgIMPV
      'May I see/look'; 'may I try?'

To avoid the ambiguity, one can use a verb compounding construction involving the bound root *-kəta* 'try' (discussed under A3 in §15.3.1; see 15.40). Forms with the bound root *-kəta* have no imperative.

21.10a [kə-kəta-n] [vau]
       eat-TRY-SEQ see/try+1sgIMPV
       'May I try and eat' (lit. try by eating)
       *May I see and eat

Yet another alternative is a biclausal construction with a sequencing *-n*:

21.10b [ka:n] [vau]
       eat+SEQ see/try+1sgIMPV
       'May I try by eating'
       *May I see and eat

If the verb *və-* is used in such a biclausal construction and is marked with *-n*, the resulting meaning is 'try and see, try and look', and not *'see looking':

21.11 [væn]   [ap]
      see/try+SEQ IMPV+see/try
      'Try and see, try and look'

If the verb *və-* appears with a completive medial clause as its clausal complement in O function (see §19.8), it can only mean 'see', as in T2.4, T3.20, T3.48, and 21.12.

21.12 [waku-də-k]   [və-lə-d]
      go.out-3masc.sg-COMPL.DS   see-3fem.sgSUBJ.P-3masc.sgBAS.P
      'She saw that he went out'
      *She tried for him to go out

We saw in §16.1.1 that the form *-kəta-* takes the directional markers to provide directional specifications for *və-* 'see/look'. Since directionals make the verb telic (see §16.1.3), the translation 'look', and not 'see', is the only one appropriate for *və-* with a directional (see 14.95, 16.7,

16.55, and 19.89). The directional forms of verbs of perception, 'see/look' and 'hear/listen', indicate the direction of the gaze or listening. The directional suppletive forms of 'look' are used adverbially, as modifiers, but never as verb roots. This is how 'look' differs from all other intrinsically directional verbs (see Table 16.2). If used with a directional, the verb *və-* cannot mean 'try', e.g. *kətu və-* (LOOK.UP see/look-) can only mean 'look upwards', and not *'try and look upwards'.

A recent extension of the verb *və-* is 'read'. The accusative-locative often marks the object of 'see' in this meaning, but does not have to (see §7.3):

21.13a a   lə-a:b   *buk*   ma: və,   də-kə-dəka   və-də-l
      then she-TOO book   NEG see+NEG he-OBL-ONLY   see-3masc.sgSUBJ.P-3fem.sgBAS.P
      'She did not read the book, only he read it'

21.13b *buka:m*   və-na
      book+LK+ACC/LOC   see-ACT.FOC+3fem.sgBAS.VT
      'She is reading a (specific) book'

We can also recall, from §17.4, that a formally unmarked body part *məl* 'eye' can be used in a body part construction with the verb *və-*. Its effect is to stress the perceptual meaning 'see; look', as in 17.65 and 21.14. In 17.65 a child is instructed to look properly at what she is doing, and in 21.14 the speaker was recounting her own experience:

21.14 kətabək-a   ja:p   məl   və-tua
      this.way+PRED+LIKE-LK   thing   eye   see-1sgSUBJ.VT+3fem.sgBAS.VT
      'I saw this kind of thing with my (own) eye'

We saw in §7.3 that occasionally *məl* 'eye' can take accusative-locative case if seeing with 'one's own eyes' is focused, as in *kəp-a məla:m və-k-na-ñən* (own-LK eye+LK+LOC see-FUT-ACT.FOC-2fem.sgBAS.VT) 'you will see (the Swakap people and their ways) with your own eyes (as opposed to hearing about them)'. (No such examples have been attested for 'ear' with 'hear'—see below.)

It was seen in §4.5 that the form *kukə-* 'back' appears in a few modifier-noun compounds, including a partially predictable one *kukə-məl*, in *kukə-məl və-* (back-eye see) meaning 'look back' (see §4.5.2). If repeated, it can be used ironically to describe someone looking over and admiring themselves, as in 21.15. This is how Kerryanne was supposed to react to a traditional Papua New Guinea style female dress 'meriblaus' which I was instructed to buy for her:

21.15 kukə-məl   kukə-məl   və-k-na
      back-eye   back-eye   see/look-FUT-ACT.FOC+3fem.sgBAS.VT
      'She will look at herself admiringly' (lit. eye to the back eye to the back she will see)

The body part does not affect the verb's transitivity: the object can be understood from the context, as in 21.15, or it can be overtly stated, as in 21.16:

21.16 kəp   məl   və-tua-d   kara:b
      just   eye   see-1sgSUBJ.VT-3masc.sgBAS.P   men's.house
      'It is that I saw the man's house with my (own) eyes'

The verb *və-* appears in a number of formations which marginally involve vision as a means of perception, e.g. *və-səməl-* (see-?-) 'look for', *və-səməl-səməl-* 'look for something very carefully' (see §15.3.1), *və-kəka-n tə-* (see-?-SEQ have-) 'look after' (15.27), and *və-və-ka-* (see-see-'move'?-) in *və-və-ka-taka-* (see-see-?-put-) 'watch carefully' (15.28). An additional irregular form *və-və-ka-* means 'see, watch' in the following lexicalized complex predicate. A synonymous expression is given in 20.17b:

21.17a məl və-və-kan   kwa-na
        eye see-RED-?+SEQ   stay-ACT.FOC+3fem.sgBAS.VT
        'She is watching (us talking) (not doing anything else)'

21.17b məl væn   kwa-na
        eye see+SEQ   stay-ACT.FOC+3fem.sgBAS.VT
        'She is watching (us talking) (not doing anything else)'

In none of these cases can the verb *və-* accompanied by *məl* have the meaning of 'try' or 'experience'. In just one instance does *və-* combine with a directional form of the verb *kar-/kra-* 'carry, bring': *və-kraki-* (see-carry.across-) means 'recognize by seeing'. It also combines with *-sapwi-* 'open', meaning *və-sapwi-* (see-open-) 'discover by seeing something' (see below on *wukə-sapwi-* 'discover by hearing').

B. 'HEARING'

The verb *wukə-* means 'hear, listen', and also 'understand, think about, smell, be missing (someone), worry (about someone), be sorry for, obey'. It is always transitive. The ways in which its object can be marked help differentiate its meanings.

In the meanings of 'hear', 'listen', 'obey', and 'think about', this verb requires an O marked with the accusative-locative case, as in 7.24 ('listen, obey'), and T2.51 ('think about'). This implies that something was fully heard, or listened to, or obeyed. If the object is unmarked, *wukə-* tends to mean 'hear (unintentionally), overhear', as in T3.17, or 'smell', as in T2.23 and T3.18–20. If the object is *ma:j* 'speech' (in the object case, or the terminative case), *wukə-* means 'listen, obey':

21.18 [majəb   wukə-ku]   [akətawa kurə-d]
       speech+LK+TERM listen-COMPL.SS like.this do-3masc.sgBAS.P
       'Having obeyed (his) words exactly, he acted this way'

If the object is marked with dative, *wukə-* is likely to have the meaning of 'worry (about someone), be missing (someone)', as in 21.19. This use of the dative case is congruent with its general meaning—to do with something negative (see §7.4).

21.19 [ma: amæy-wa   asayik   wukə-ku]   [yawi ma: kwa:r]
       again mother-COM father+DAT worry-COMPL.SS work NEG do+NEG
       'Having worried about mother and father, (I) did not work'

Or *wukə-* can mean 'listen so as to try and hear something' (as in T3.27–8). This is congruent with the purposive meaning of the dative case which often implies future projection.

When used in commands, *wukə-* always refers to controlled telic activities—'listen', 'obey', or 'smell' (especially if accompanied with *ya:m* 'smell'), as in 21.20–1 and 18.51. A third person command form may also have the meaning of 'know', as in 13.21 ('the father must know').

21.20 lə-kə-k   awuk
       she-OBL-DAT IMPV+listen
       'Listen to her, obey her!'

21.21 ya:m awuk
       smell IMPV+listen
       'Smell the smell!'

Accompanied by a complementation strategy, *wukə-* also has the meaning of 'listen', as in 19.96a and 19.86. It may also have the meaning of 'understand' in exactly the same contexts; to differentiate 'listen, obey' and 'understand', a speaker may opt for an English code-switch *understand*, as in 17.26b, or for a Tok Pisin code-switch, as in 21.22. This example also illustrates a parallel use of Manambu and Tok Pisin synonymous pairs as a means of 'pressing the point'. We return to code-switching in Manambu discourse in §22.4.

21.22 [ñən awuk] [*harim tok* ada]
  you.fem IMPV+listen listen speech 'stand'+IMPV
  'You listen! Listen to speech!'

The imperative *awuk!* is used as an attention-getting device, both in day-to-day life and in name debates. With the object *yanu* 'magic', *wukə-* means 'know, understand', as in *yanu wukə-d-ə du* (magic know/understand-3masc.sgBAS.VT-LK man) 'a man who understands magic; sorcerer'. We will see in §21.4 that *wukə-* in combination with *mawul* 'inside, mind' refers to 'understanding'—see 21.69–70.

Often just the context helps work out the exact meaning of *wukə-*. A little boy went missing and later it turned out that he had drowned—this, and the fact that we cried, provides the background for reading *wukə-* in 21.23 as 'be sorry (about someone), be missing (someone)':

21.23 [ata wukə-ku] [gra-dian]
  then be.sorry-COMPL.SS cry-1plBAS.P
  'Then being sorry we cried'

Speakers who tend to code-switch with Tok Pisin use *wori* instead of *wukə-* in the meaning of 'worry, be sorry'—see §22.4.

The verb *wukə-* in emphatic nominalizations (discussed under V in §9.1.1) typically means 'understand', as in 9.15–16; and so does the reduplicated *wukə-* (as in 12.61). A nominalization with a support verb *tə-* means 'listen', as in 21.24. (Its synonym is *wa:n tə-na* (ear have-ACT.FOC+3fem.sgBAS.VT) 'she is listening'.)

21.24 wukə-wuk tə-kwa-na
  listen-RED 'stand'-HAB-3fem.sgBAS.VT
  'She keeps listening'

A question *wukə-ñana* or *wukə-məna* 'do you (fem or masc) hear, understand?' is used as a conversation sustainer, to make sure the audience is following what is being said. It cannot possibly mean *'are you sorry?' or *'are you thinking?'

We saw above that the verb *və-* in its strictly perceptual meaning 'see' can appear with 'eye' in a body part construction. The verb *wukə-* appears in a similar construction, accompanied by 'ear'—see 21.25. The expression *wa:n wukə-* can mean 'listen', 'obey', or 'understand':

21.25 wa:n awuk
  ear IMPV+hear/listen
  'Listen/understand/obey!' (lit. ear listen)

Unlike 'eye', *wa:n* 'ear' cannot be case marked in this construction. The 'ear listen' construction remains polysemous—this is in contrast to the 'eye see' construction whose meaning is only perceptual.

The verb *wukə-* can combine with the full set of directional bound roots. Then its meaning is telic—as is expected for a directional compound. Such compounds refer to listening to a sound coming from a direction expressed with the bound root. For instance, in T3.31 *wukə-su-* (hear/listen-UP-) describes the snake sitting on the ground and listening to what was happening up there in the house. In 16.29 *wukə-saku-* (listen-OUTWARD-) and *wukə-səwəla-* (listen-INSIDE-) refer to listening to what is happening outside and inside respectively.

When *wukə-* combines with the directional *-tay-* 'sideways away', the resulting form has an idiomatic meaning 'miss, be longing for (someone)'. The directional can be reduplicated, and the result is *wukə-tay-tay-* 'worry a lot (about)' (see §16.1.4).

The verb *wukə-* also has idiomatic meanings when used with verbs meaning 'carry, bring', as in *wukə-n karya-* (hear-SEQ bring-), which means 'remember', and in combination with a directional form of the verb *kər-* 'carry, bring': *wukə-kraki-* (hear-carry.across) means 'recognize by hearing'. This is reminiscent of *və-kraki-* (see-carry.across-) 'recognize by seeing'.

The root *wukə-* combines with *-təp* 'be closed' as a second component, and the resulting compound is idiomatic—*wukə-təp(ə)-* (think/hear-be.closed) means 'forget (completely)' (this differs from *wukə-mar* (think/hear-NEG?) 'forget (not necessarily completely)')—see 15.94. The form *wukə-mar-* 'forget' is also idiosyncratic (see §14.6 on the component *-mar-* which may, or may not, be linked to the dependent negator *-ma:r-*). The compound *wukə-taka-* (hear/listen?-put-) means 'provide'. And *wukə-sapwi-* (hear-open-) means 'discover by hearing' (see above on *və-sapwi-* (see-open) 'discover by seeing something').

C. PATTERNS OF POLYSEMY FOR THE PERCEPTION VERBS: A SUMMARY

The polysemous patterns of *və-* 'see, look, try' can be easily disambiguated by grammatical contexts. This is much less so for *wukə-* 'hear, listen, understand, obey, be sorry for': the meanings 'obey, listen, and understand' are hard to disentangle in Manambu, just as they are in Tok Pisin. The range of meanings identified for *və-* suggests that 'seeing' is primary and 'experience' is secondary.

With respect to *wukə-* there is hardly any strong language-internal evidence favouring the oft-quoted development from perception to cognition. Many speakers try and use English to disambiguate the polysemous *wukə-*. Unlike many other verbs in the language, neither *və-* nor *wukə-* can ever be replaced with the generic verb *məgi-* 'do whatever'—see §21.3. Neither can the speech verbs—see the next section.

21.1.3   Speech verbs

We saw in §19.5 that speech reports are by far the most frequent clause type in Manambu discourse, and especially in conversations. Speech reports are normally introduced with one speech verb *wa-* 'say, speak' which has a variety of polysemous extensions discussed at length in §19.5.6. In addition to this verb, Manambu has two other verbs of speech—*bla-* (with an allomorph *bəl-*) 'say/tell (something)', and *yi-* 'say X, speak (a language)'. The three verbs of speech differ in their syntax, their meanings in a variety of constructions, the ways in which they combine with directionals, and the nature of object noun phrases they may occur with.

A comparison of the three verbs of speech is in Table 21.1. The major parameters of variation are discussed below.

I. OCCURRENCE WITH A SPEECH REPORT. The verb *wa-* is the only one to freely occur with speech reports (as a special grammatical relation—see §19.5.5). The verb *yi-* occurs with just a few interjections as speech reports, as in *ay yi-da-d* (INTERJ say-3plSUBJ.VT-3masc.sgBAS.VT) 'they shouted' (lit. they said 'ay') (T1.29).

TABLE 21.1 Comparison of three speech verbs

	bla-	*yi-*	*wa-*
(i) Occurrence with speech reports	no	limited	yes
(ii) Transitivity patterns	S=A ambitransitive	transitive	ditransitive (two frames) transitive
(iii) Types of noun phrases in O function	*kudi* 'language', *ma:j* 'talk', *yanu* 'witchcraft'	*kudi* 'language', *yarək* 'news, announcement'	various NPs, including types of *kudi* 'language'
(iv) Formation of directional compounds	yes lexicalized combination with *-saki-sala* 'across-inside'	no	combines with all directionals; lexicalized combination with *-saki* 'across'
(v) Formation of other verb compounds	few; one special combining form	hardly any	a few, most of them lexicalized
(vi) Patterns of grammaticalization	none	possible	yes
(vii) Idiomatic usage in prohibitions	none		possible
(viii) Polysemy/homonymy	none	some	

II. TRANSITIVITY PATTERNS of the verb *wa-* were discussed in §19.5.5. This verb is different from any other verb in the language in that it appears in two ditransitive frames:

(a) with two NP objects meaning telling someone something, as in 19.59–60; and
(b) with a name in what looks like an object slot, and the object or person named as a third argument, as in T2.3: 'those whom we call Gala'.

It can also be used as a transitive verb with an NP object if this is something being said, as in 19.62a–b. And it frequently occurs with a speech report (a special grammatical relation) and an optional addressee which can be cross-referenced. The only context in which *wa-* can be used intransitively is the permissive form *wau* 'may I speak?', a typical turn-taking device.

These transitivity patterns only apply to the underived verb *wa-*. When accompanied by directionals, or when used as first component in verb compounds, *wa-* can be used either transitively or ditransitively (see §4.2.2 and Chapters 15 and 16). And see IV and V below.

In contrast, the verb *yi-* is always used with an object, while *bla-* can be considered S=A ambitransitive, e.g.:

21.26a ma:j   aka   bla-na
speech DEM.DIST.REACT.TOP.fem.sg talk-ACT.FOC+3fem.sgBAS.VT
'She is speaking' (lit. she is talking speech)

21.26b abəl
IMPV+talk
'Talk!'

Any non-subject argument—provided it is more topical than the subject—can be cross-referenced on both *bla-* and *yi-*, in agreement with the general pattern of cross-referencing in Manambu (see §3.1). The only exceptions are short speech reports framed by *yi-* which cannot be cross-referenced.

The difference between *bla-* and *yi-* and other transitive and ambitransitive verbs lies in the nature and in the marking possibilities of the NP O: only a limited number of NPs can be used, and their reference is always generic. As a consequence, they can never be case marked.

III. TYPES OF NOUN PHRASES IN O FUNCTION. We saw in §19.5.5 that *wa-* can occur with a variety of noun phrases in O function, depending on the frame it is used in. It can also be used with *kudi* 'language' in the O slot, to refer to a sound made by a non-human (or a baby). If the sound itself is reproduced it occupies the O slot, as in 19.63 and 21.27:

21.27 məd   [kədran kədran kədran] aka   wa:l
cassowary sound   DEM.DIST.REACT.TOP.fem.sg say+3fem.sgBAS.P
'The cassowary said kəndran kəndran kəndran'

The verb *bla-* takes a limited number of noun phrases as an O: *kudi* 'language', *ma:j* 'talk', and *yanu* 'witchcraft'. The expression *yanu bla-* refers to performing sorcery, rather than to a particular speech act. None of these can be case marked; their meaning is generic.

The verb *yi-* occurs with *kudi* 'language' and *yarək* 'news, announcement' as O. A frequent command from mothers to children is 21.28a or 21.28b. Sadly, it is often ignored.

21.28a təp-a   kudi   ay
village-LK language IMPV+speak
'Speak Manambu!' (lit. village language)

21.28b təp-a   kudir   ay
village-LK language+INSTR IMPV+speak
'Speak Manambu!' (lit. village language)

The two are synonymous. Of all the speech verbs, this case alternation has been observed only for *yi-*.

The verb *wa-* forms a number of idiomatic collocations with interjections and adverbs, e.g. *ay wa-* (ay say-) 'let know', *ya:k wa-* or *ya:kya wa-* (OK say-) 'agree, accept; say OK'. There are no such idiomatic expressions involving *yi-* or *bla-*.

IV. DIRECTIONAL COMPOUNDS can be formed on *wa-*. Their meanings are often transparent, e.g. *wa-su-* 'say (something) or call in upward direction' (as in 16.10, 18.51), *wa-sada-* (16.6) 'say or call (something) in downward direction', *wa-saku-* 'say (something) or call in an outward direction' (16.36). One combination is lexicalized. The form *wa-saki-* contains a directional bound root *-saki-* meaning 'across away from the speaker'. It can have a transparent meaning 'call across', as in 16.25. More frequently, however, it refers to telling a traditional story transmitted across generations, as in T2.68. The expression *wa-saki ma:j* (speak-ACROSS.AWAY story) refers to a traditional account of true events, different from a *blajaya ma:j* (speak+come story) 'legend, story'.

The verb *bla-* combines with two directionals in an idiomatic expression *bla-saku-sala-* 'debate; perform ceremonial talk in men's house', as in 16.29 (last line), and is rarely used with any other directionals. The verb *yi-* is not used with directionals at all.

V. FORMATION OF OTHER VERB COMPOUNDS is limited for all the speech verbs. The verb *wa-* occurs as the first component in a number of lexicalized compounds, e.g. *wa-tək-* (say-break-) 'accuse', *wa-yakə-* (say-throw-) 'order', *wa-jali-* (say-?) 'call', *wa-kəta-* (say-try-) 'ask carefully, nicely' (§15.3), and also in *wa-karay-kur-* (say-bring-do-) 'be hospitable (to someone)' and *wa-təp-* (say-be.closed-) 'forbid, deprive', as in 15.92–3.

Only those compounds which involve *wa-* followed by a verb of motion are semantically predictable: *wa-yi-* 'say-go-' can mean either 'say and go', or 'speak while going', or 'keep saying (or repeating same thing many times over)' (as in 15.45), and *wa-ya-* 'say-come-' can only mean 'keep saying/talking (without repetition)'.

This verb also occurs as V₁ in cause-effect compounds involving four verbs in V₂ slot: *yaga-* 'be scared' as in *wa-yaga-* 'scare', *jəwi-* 'be awake' as in *wa-jəwi-* 'wake someone up' (15.59), *la:kw-* 'know' as in *wa-laku* 'give advice', and *buti-* 'fold' as in *wa-buti-* 'fold forcefully or with care; fold a full length of something, e.g. a long sheet'. In three of these the actual meaning of 'saying' is bleached: 'scaring', 'wakening', and especially 'folding' do not have to involve a speech act. The element *wa-* in these four verbs (and a few others discussed at B1 in §15.3.2) could be a mere homonym of the verb of speech.

The verb *yi-* 'say' does not occur in any compounds as second component. It appears to be used as a first component in one compound, *yi-pakw-* 'hide (something)', where it could act as a transitivizer (B2 in §15.3.2). However, whether the component *yi-* in *yi-pakw-* is indeed related to the verb 'say' or the two forms *yi-* are simple homonyms remains an open question.

The verb *bla-* occurs in one aspectual compound as the first component (see §15.3.1): *bla-təp-* (speak-be.closed-) means 'speak for the last time'. It has an idiosyncratic combining form *blaja-* which only occurs with *-ya-* as a durative marker: *blaja-ya-* (speak-come-), as in *blaja-ya-bana ma:j* (speak-come-1plSUBJ.VT+3fem.sgBAS.VT talk) 'our conversation, what we talk about' (see §9.3).

VI. PATTERNS OF GRAMMATICALIZATION of *wa-* may or may not involve its usage as a putative causative marker in the four verbs mentioned above. The verb *wa-* has grammaticalized into a connective *atawata:y* (from *ata wa-ta:y* 'then say-COTEMP') 'and so then, in summary, this is why' (see §19.6). The verb *yi-* may have grammaticalized into a transitivizing morpheme in *yi-pakw-* 'hide something'—however, this is just a hypothesis. The verb *bla-* shows no tendency towards grammaticalization.

VII. IDIOMATIC USAGE IN PROHIBITIONS is an exclusive property of the verb *wa-*: *wa-tukwa* (say-PROH.GEN) means either 'don't say it, don't talk (this way)', or something like 'say it again, I can't agree more with what you are saying'. The frequency of this expression in this meaning in Manambu is such that some local teenagers transfer this into their English, saying 'don't say' in lieu of 'say it again'.

No such idiomatic uses have been attested for *bla-* and *yi-*: *bla-tukwa* means 'shut up, do not talk (this way)', and *yi-tukwa* means 'don't say it, do not talk (this way)'. The two strong prohibitives (see §14.4.1) have no such idiomatic extensions with any of the speech verbs.

VIII. PATTERNS OF POLYSEMY/HOMONYMY differentiate the three speech verbs in a rather dramatic manner. The verb *bla-* is the most straightforward: it has no meanings other than those to do with speaking, and no homonyms. (Its origins could well be onomatopoeic.) The verb *yi-* 'say' is homophonous with the verb *yi-* 'go' in all forms but the second person imperative: we can recall, from §13.2.1, that the verb 'go' has a suppletive imperative *ma:y* (cognate to Ambulas *me*) while the verb *yi-* 'say' has a straightforward imperative *a-y* 'say!' The form *yi-* is also used as a support verb for some nominals—see §4.2.2 and §§17.2.3–4 (e.g. 17.38). Whether it is the same polyfunctional verb as the one meaning 'say' is an open question.

The verb *wa-* is the most versatile of all: we saw, in §19.5.6, that it effectively covers a variety of meanings to do with internal speech, thought, fear, reason, intention, desire, and so on. And we will see, in §21.4, how it appears with nouns expressing emotions: the person's inside, *mawul*, 'speaks' (*wa-*) if a person has an opinion about something.

In summary: the three verbs of speech differ in terms of their syntactic and semantic properties—despite the fact that they cover pretty similar semantic ground and are fairly general in their meanings.

21.2 POLYSEMY, SPECIFICITY, AND DISAMBIGUATION: FURTHER FEATURES OF THE MANAMBU LEXICON

We will now discuss a few further features of Manambu lexical semantics, focusing on a number of unusual patterns of polysemy.

21.2.1 Specific notions in the Manambu lexicon

Languages vary in how much detail can be expressed in the lexicon, both nominal and verbal. Manambu lacks special verbs for certain notions—such as 'want, desire, covet'. This is expressed with the desiderative or optative suffix (§13.2.3 and §13.5), or with a speech report (§19.5.6). There is no special root meaning 'refuse', or 'refute'—the only way of saying this is *ma: wa-*, lit. 'say no'. The notion of 'agree, accept' is expressed through *ya:kya wa-*, 'say OK'.

In other semantic fields, Manambu is highly specific. To properly say 'carry', one needs to know the manner in which the action was performed: if something is carried on the head the term is *tiya-*; if it is carried hanging from a shoulder, it is *kalu-*; if one carries a big bundle in one's arms, it is *tapu-* (or *kay-tapu-*: see §16.2); and carrying under the arm is referred to as *səkət-*. If the object is carried with hands and arms but is not too big, the appropriate term is *yata-*. Each of these verbs can occur with a directional. And the generic verb, *kar-/kra-/*ka-* 'bring, carry' (see §16.1.1, and Table 16.2), allows the speaker to remain vague as to the manner in which the object was carried. This intrinsically directional verb does not occur without a directional specification—except for the allomorph *kar/kra-* which means 'marry (of a man)' when accompanied with unmarked object *ta:kw* 'woman, wife' (*ta:kw kra-* 'marry', as in T1.3).

The choice of a term for 'putting' depends on the manner and the object: *kalu-* involves putting something on a shoulder and carrying it, *væga-* means putting something inside something (a bag, a basket, or a pocket), *taw-* means putting something spread out (e.g. clothes on a line), or erecting something, and *saka-* refers to putting something over the fire. A more general verb is *taka-* 'put' (also used as a second component of a variety of compound verbs, marking what looks like an applicative, among other things—see §15.3.1). And there is also an intrinsically directional generic verb *ku-* 'put, move', as in *ku-su-* (put/move-UP) 'move up; put upwards', *ku-sada-* (put/move-DOWN) 'move or put downwards', *ku-saki-* 'put, move across away from speaker', *ku-səwəla-* 'put inside'. Two of these directional forms have evolved metaphorical extensions—*ku-su-* (put/move-UP) also means 'put on (clothes)', and *ku-səwəla-* also means 'put on (shoe), put spear in, or spear someone'. See §16.1.1.

The set of verbs of breaking is another example of lexical sophistication, e.g. *wi:-* 'break into the open (a boil or a sore, an egg); breaking up (e.g. a ceremony)', *pərki-* 'tear, break (clothes, paper)', *vya-prapi-* 'break by hitting', *vya-wut(a)-* 'break small thin things in two (e.g. firewood)', *kay-pisa-* 'break in half', *kay-rətu-* 'break with hands', *kay-səgəl-* 'snap off, break off (as one does the leaves of a leafy vegetable)', *kay-təkwi-* 'split, break (bigger pieces of firewood, tree)'. However, unlike for 'carrying', there is no generic verb 'break' which could be used if the speaker chooses not to be specific.

Some lexical distinctions appear unusual for an observer from a European (and especially English-speaking) background. There is no general verb 'wash': the verb *jan-* refers to washing small things (like clothes or plates), or individual body parts (teeth or hands), and the verb *yaku-*, frequently in combination with *gu* 'water' (*gu yaku-* 'water wash'—see §7.2 on this construction), refers to washing the whole of something—such as one's whole body. To express the notion of 'pulling', one says *lagu-* if it involves a big object, such as a plank; *gwa-* if it involves something small, such as weeds or sticky seeds on plants or one's clothing; and *kuryak-* if it involves pulling out biggish thorns.

Some polysemous verbs can be disambiguated. The verb *rəp* means 'be enough', 'be equal' (in its reduplicated form *rəpərəp* 'equal, identical': 4.47–8), 'be fine' (as in 12.30), and 'be full', as in *ya:l rəpə-na* (belly be.enough-ACT.FOC+3fem.sgBAS.VT) 'I am full' (lit. belly is full), or *wun rəpə-na-wun* (I be.enough-ACT.FOC-1fem.sgBAS.VT) 'I am full'. The latter meaning can also be expressed with its partial synonym, the verb *wapruku-*. Its meaning—only subtly different from that of *rəp*—is 'be enough and more than enough, overflow, be overfull', as in *ya:l wapruku-na* (belly overflow-ACT.FOC+3fem.sgBAS.VT) 'I am very full' (lit. belly overflows) (see also 17.62a–b) and 21.29, from a hilarious story told by Gaiawalimæg (cf. 3.11).

21.29 nəkə *rum* sa:n-a-dəka wapruku-l
other+fem.sg room money-LK-ONLY overflow-3fem.sgBAS.P
'Another room was overflowing with money'

Both verbs can be used intransitively, or as extended intransitives (as in 21.29).

In contrast to many languages of the New Guinea area, there is no single term covering natural growth (hair, bodily hair, and grass). Instead, Manambu distinguishes *nab* 'head hair', *aba rə* 'grey hair', *yuwi* 'body hair (including facial hair), feathers, fur', and *væs* 'grass'. All of these correspond to *gras* in Tok Pisin: no wonder many language-conscious speakers of Manambu complain that Tok Pisin is nothing but a 'shortcut' (see §22.4).

A fair degree of specificity is notable in most word classes. Several terms for 'food' were discussed in §21.1.1. We can recall, from Chapter 1, that names are considered an item of wealth—there is little wonder that different types of 'names' are distinguished lexically: *ap-a-sə*, literally 'bone name', refers to the person's main name they are known by (which is usually the name given before other names); *ta:y-sə* (before-name) is another term for the name which was given first; and *səgliak* is a term for any additional name (also see Harrison 1990a: 60–1). Each of these contains the root *sə* 'name' (there is also a separate term for 'namesake', *wasali*, which does not contain the root 'name', but may contain the root *wa-* 'say, speak').

Time words are another area of high precision: with respect to *nəbəl* 'today', one distinguishes two terms for future: *sər* 'tomorrow' and *mu* 'the day after tomorrow', and five for the past: *na:l* 'yesterday', *nagəs* 'the day before yesterday', *dəbəñə* 'three days before today', *pasəta:kw* 'four days before today' and *wakənay* 'five days before today, remote past'. If one chooses not to be precise, one may just say *nagəs* to refer to the recent past, and *wakənay* or *ta:y, ta:yir* 'before' to say 'a long time ago'. This is the major feature of the Manambu discourse and lexicon: one can be highly specific, or choose to go for a highly general term.

A general term in frequent use may coexist with a variety of synonyms or near-synonyms, not so widely used. Of all the terms for 'being silent', *kaigən* 'be silent' is the most frequent. Its numerous synonyms or near-synonyms include an echo compound *kaygən saygən* 'be really silent' (see 7 at §9.3), *məkəmək* 'silent, quiet (without motion), very low' (also used in *məkəmək-ə ma:j* (silent-LK speech) 'quiet nagging, grumble, complain'), *kərkəm* 'completely silent' (17.36a–c), *kərnəm* 'completely silent' (as in *kərnəm na-n rə-* (completely.silent BE.NAT-SEQ sit) 'sit in complete frozen silence'), *wiləñ* 'silent', and *kaurak* 'be/become silent' (cf. *kaurak-* 'stop').

21.2.2   How grammar helps disambiguate polysemy

We saw above that Manambu shows an interplay of specific detail and overwhelming generality throughout its lexicon. One example is the kinship system (of Omaha type) which is rather complex. However, some distinctions are not made—at least not overtly. One word, *ta:kw*, covers 'wife' and 'woman'. In contrast, there are two distinct words for 'man' and 'husband'.

The terms for husband (*la:n*) and man (*du*) are only partly interchangeable: referring to a husband as *du* is considered highly informal. When sisters-in-law (one's brother's wives or co-wives) who are in a joking relationship tease each other (as illustrated in 4.56), one is expected to say to the other *wun ñən-a la:n-adəwun* 'I (masculine) am your husband (feminine)' (see 5.16). Replacing *la:n* with *du* would be inappropriate. But there is no word for 'wife' other than *ta:kw* 'woman'.

A distinction between 'wife' and 'woman' can be made if desired. We can recall, from Chapter 6, that only kinship terms form plurals, as does the word for husband, *lanugw*. The word *ta:kw* forms a plural only if it has the meaning 'wife': *takwa:gw* can usually only mean 'wives', as in 6.1 (just occasionally can it be used jokingly to refer to a group of women, with an ironic overtone of an 'old girls' club'). There is no **duagw* because *du* is not a kinship term. This is how different grammatical possibilities can differentiate polysemous nouns.

We saw above (§16.1.1) that the expression *ta:kw kra-* (woman get-) is used to refer to man's marriage. Here, *ta:kw* means 'wife'. When a woman gets married, this is called *du-a:k rə-* (man-LK+DAT sit-), or, occasionally, *lanək rə-* (husband+LK+DAT sit-), or *la:n rə-*. And again, here *du* means 'husband'. Using a noun as a verb's argument restricts its reference and limits its polysemy—we return to this further below.

The highly polysemous noun *kudi* is another case in point. It may refer to 'speech, language, noise' and '(the outside of) the mouth'. We saw in §6.1 that this second meaning is very restricted: it appears in compounds, e.g. *səp-a-kudi* (skin-LK-mouth) 'lip', *kudiy-ə-gu* (mouth-LK-water) 'saliva', and in fixed expressions, e.g. *kudi nak* (mouth one) 'one mouthful, a little bit'. (A general term for mouth is *day.*) The plural *kudi-ugw* only occurs in the first sense, with a collective meaning ('lips and mouth') and has an archaic feel to it (see 6.2).

In combination with the verb of speech *wa-*, *kudi* may refer to a sound made by a non-human (or a baby): *təb kudi wa-na-d* (sky language/noise say-ACT.FOC-3masc.sgBAS.VT) means 'there is a noise of thunder', literally, 'sky says language/noise'. If modified by an adjective, *kudi* often refers to 'voice': 21.30 is an alternative to 5.13:

21.30 numa-də   kudi   aw
       big-masc.sg language/noise IMPV+speak
       'Speak loudly!' (lit. speak big-masculine language/noise)

In compounds, *kudi* refers to different languages, or different speech genres. So, *Manabə kudi* means 'Manambu language', *Ñaula kudi* means 'Iatmul language', *Kum kudi* 'Kwoma language', and *wali-kudi* (white.man-language) 'Tok Pisin' (and, just occasionally, English). A general term for indigenous language is *təp-a kudi*, 'village language', as in 21.28 above. The term *gra-kudi* (cry-language) is the term used for mourning songs.

In all these instances, the possibility of forming a plural helps disambiguate a polysemous noun. For the high-frequency adverb *kəp* this works only partly. The form *kəp* has the following meanings:

1. 'Just, for nothing', as in 21.31a–b:

21.31a kəp kwa-na-d
      just stay-ACT.FOC-3masc.sgBAS.VT
      'He stays doing nothing, just stays (without anything to do)'

21.31b ma: kər,   kəp rə-na-d
      NEG itch+NEG just sit-ACT.FOC-3masc.sgBAS.VT
      '(The wound) is not itching, it just stays there'

2. 'Intensifier', as in 21.31c:

21.31c ma:j ma: kəp
      story NEG just
      'There is really nothing else to say'

3. 'For no reason', as in 21.31d.

21.31d kəp karkwas   kur-na
      just quarrelsome do/make-ACT.FOC+3fem.sgBAS.VT
      'She is just quarrelsome, for no reason'

4. Delimitative meaning 'only, nothing else', as in 21.31e:

21.31e kəp asəkət,   kə-də   gak
      just IMPV+move.away DEM.PROX-masc.sg side
      'Just move away, to this side (of the canoe)'

5. 'One's own', as in 21.31f (also see 21.16 above and discussion there). An alternative to *kəp məl* would be *kəp-a məl* (just-LK eye):

21.31f ma: və   kəp məl
      NEG see+NEG just eye
      'She cannot see with her own eyes' (meaning: she is not paying attention)

6. The general 'goodwill' address term of the same form *kəp*, plural *kəpugw* 'my dear', was mentioned in §4.1.2. This is used in commands and farewells, often clause-finally, as in 21.32a (also see §21.5 below, on greetings and farewells). *Kəp* optionally cliticizes to the verb.

21.32a maya   kəp
      go.IMPV+VOC dearie
      'Go, my dear'

The expression *yara kəp* (fine dear) 'let everything be fine, my dear' is used similarly to 'thank you', or just to say 'everything is OK'. The form *kəp* implies either a singular, or a generic referent. If the speaker wants to address explicitly plural referents, *kəp* as an address term can be pluralized with the suffix *-(V)gw* (see §6.1), as shown in 21.32b–c. This form tends to be used to refer to plural addressees as a mark of respect. In 21.32b, Duamakwa:y was addressing a largish audience which included a number of big men. In 21.32c (from a story), a young man who had just appeared in the house and was caught stealing food is explaining to his uncles that he was in fact their relative, and had a right to get food in their house:

21.32b al   kəpugw
     DEM.DIST.fem.sg+3fem.sgNOM ADDRESS.PL
     'This is it, dear respected ones'

21.32c [wun-adəwun] [kəpugw]
     I-1masc.sgNOM ADDRESS.PL
     'It is me, dear respected ones'

7. The form *kəp* appears in the conjunction *kəpa:b* 'in case' (see §14.5.1 and §19.5).

The question arises: should these uses of *kəp* be considered simple homonyms or instances of one, polysemous form? The address form *kəp*, plural *kəpugw* could be considered as separate from the others on formal grounds. As far as the rest are concerned, the question remains open. Only in some cases can etymology help distinguish what looks like the same morpheme—we return to this in §22.1.

A polysemous root may acquire an additional meaning when reduplicated. The non-agreeing adjective *kula* means 'new', as in *kula-ma:j* 'new word, new story', 'fresh', as in *kula-kija:p* 'fresh protein food', and 'raw', as in *kula-kami:* 'raw, uncooked fish'. It also appears in combination with *gu* 'water' as *kul-gu* 'fresh or cool water, flowing water (in contrast to stagnant water)' (the lack of the linker is puzzling; Pauline Laki suggested that this combination could have been influenced by Tok Pisin *kol wara* 'cold water'). When reduplicated, *kula-kul* means 'lacking previous knowledge, ignorant, newcomer'. We will see, in §21.2.3 below, how the root 'bad, poor' has just the meaning 'bad' when used in an echo compound.

21.2.3   The polysemy of value terms

Most value terms in Manambu are polysemous. The major meaning of *vyakət* (variant: *vyakat*) is 'good', or 'appropriate', as in *vyakat-a ya:b* (good-LK road) 'appropriate, correct road' (as contrasted to a wrong road), and 'good-looking', especially if intensified with *-yakə* 'throw' as a second component, as in *vyakəta-yakə ta:kw* (good-FULLY/'throw' woman) 'very beautiful woman'. It can also refer to 'good' in terms of good physical health, as in the last clause of 21.35.

Its synonym in the meaning 'well done' is the adverb *rəka:rək* 'properly'. The adverb *jaujay* 'in a sloppy way, not properly' can be considered the antonym of *rəka:rək*.

The antonym of *vyakat*, *kuprap*, can mean 'bad', especially with an inanimate referent, as in 21.33.

21.33 kuprap-ə-ja:p wi-ad
     bad-LK-thing house-3masc.sgNOM
     'It was a bad house'

A similar meaning of *kuprap* appears in 16.80 ('you yourself made him himself (be) in a bad way') and 16.99 ('village people are bad to each other'). Similar examples are 14.46, 14.59, and 14.62. Note that in all of these *kuprap* is part of the predicate.

Or it can mean 'wrong, incorrect', as in *kuprap-ə ya:b* (bad-LK road) 'wrong road' (as opposed to the 'good, correct' road). In T2.34 *kuprap-ə gu* 'bad water' is contrasted with *məya gu* 'real water'. With a human referent, *kuprap* can mean 'ugly', as in 21.34.

21.34 [də-kə-dəka   ta:kw   ma:] [kuprap-ad]
  he-OBL-he+OBL+fem.sg wife/woman NEG bad/ugly-3masc.sgNOM
  'He himself had no wife, he was ugly'

Here *kuprap* is the opposite of *vyakət* in its meaning 'good-looking'. However, the most frequent meaning of *kuprap* with human referents is that of 'poor old thing', with somewhat endearing overtones. In 21.35, the speaker is sorry for the poor little boy who was hungry:

21.35 [ata ka:d   kuprap-ə ñan] [kə-ku]   [ata vyakət
  then eat+3masc.sgBAS.P bad/poor-LK child eat-COMPL.SS then good
  ta:d]
  become+3masc.sgBAS.P
  'Then he ate, poor boy. Having eaten, he became fine'

The person referred to with *kuprap* does not have to have done anything wrong; one just feels slightly sorry for them, for whatever reason. The late Wimali was referred to as *kuprapə Wimali*, and 21.36 was said about a little boy who was sick with malaria:

21.36 a   kə   kuprap-ə kləm   kwa-k-na-d
  then DEM.fem.sg poor-LK DEM.PROX+fem.sg+LOC stay-FUT-ACT.FOC-3masc.sgBAS.VT
  'Then this poor one will stay here (rather than go home)'

The blind Ñatabi referred to herself and the story she'd just told as follows:

21.37 kə   kuprap-ə Ñatabi-al,   *stori* tə-na
  DEM.PROX+fem.sg poor-LK Ñatabi-3fem.sgNOM story have-ACT.FOC+3fem.sgBAS.VT
  'This is poor Ñatabi, she has a story'

An inanimate object, and even a time period, can occasionally be referred to with *kuprap* meaning 'poor old thing'. In 21.38, a speaker was explaining what she was doing: looking for her poor old hat which had been irrevocably lost:

21.38 wun-a   kuprap-ə *hat* kwakə-na-wun
  I-LK+fem.sg bad-LK   hat look.for-ACT.FOC-1fem.sgBAS.VT
  'I am looking for my poor old hat'

And 21.39 was a comment by Gemaj who had just realized the 'poor old today' was almost gone (about 2.30 p.m.):

21.39 a   kuprap-ə nəbəl bə   kusə-na
  DEM.DIST.fem.sg poor-LK today already finish-ACT.FOC+3fem.sgBAS.VT
  'That poor old day of today is already finished'

The meaning 'poor old thing' is restricted to the use of *kuprap* as a modifier to an argument. And then, an ambiguity may arise between 'bad man' and 'poor old man'. In one of her stories, Ñatabi resolved the ambiguity by adding explicitly that her father was not a good man (second clause), and then by putting the NP, *kuprapə asa:y* (poor/bad father), into the predicate slot where only the meaning 'bad, not good, evil' is appropriate:

21.40 [asa:y adiya   wa-saki-də-di-ya,
      father DEM.DIST.REACT.TOP+pl say-ACROSS.AWAY-3masc.sgSUBJ.P-3plBAS.P-EMPH
      kuprap-ə   asa:y] [vyakat-ə asa:y ma:n] [kuprap-ə du-ad]
      poor/bad-LK father good-LK   father NEG bad-LK   man-3masc.sgNOM
      'Father told those (stories), poor/bad father, he was not a good man, he was a bad man'

In some combinations *kuprap* has just one meaning—that of bad, or evil. The expression *kuprapə ja:p* 'bad thing' is a euphemistic way of referring to much feared 'sangguma' sorcery (a specific alternative term is *way*). The expression *kuprapə gu* 'bad water' is used to talk about alcoholic drinks. An alternative is an alliterative compound *kuprapə-saprap* 'really bad', *kəp kuprap* 'just/really bad', or *məy-a kuprap* (real-LK bad) 'really bad'. And this takes us to the notion of 'real'.

21.2.4   The notion of 'real'

A highly versatile, and highly frequent, term in Manambu is the adjective *məy* 'real, very' (also see §4.3.2, point 11, on how it provides an additional criterion for distinguishing between the major word classes in Manambu). When preposed to nouns and adjectives, it means 'real, really', as in *məy-a vyakət* 'really good/beautiful', *məy-a ma:j* 'real or true story', *məy-a ta:kw* 'real woman, human woman' (as opposed to a woman who is in fact a bird of paradise, or a cassowary in disguise), and *məy-a ñan* 'real child, human child' (as opposed to a cassowary's child).

It also has the meaing of 'genuine Manambu', as opposed to a store-bought equivalent. Examples are *məy-a mæj* 'natural fibre', lit. 'real thread' as opposed to *wali-mæj* (white.man-thread) 'store-bought thread or wool', and *məy-a kamna:gw* 'genuine Manambu food (e.g. sago, fish, etc.)' as opposed to *wali-kamna:gw* (white.man-food) 'store-bought food'.

The adjective *məy* helps disambiguate 'lie' and 'truth'. The noun *sua:l* refers to 'lie', or 'story (often, but not necessarily, fictitious)'.[4] As expected, the opposite of *sua:l ma:j* (lie story) 'a story which is a lie or fiction' is *məy-a ma:j* 'real story, true story'. Another option is *məy-a sua:l* which means 'real truth' (rather than *real lie). This usage indicates the versatility of the notion of *sua:l*, and obvious difficulties in finding a one-word translation for it since it is highly context dependent. But when *sua:l* occurs as an unmarked O of either *taka-* 'put' or *kur-* 'do, make', *sua:l* can only refer to a total lie. The lexicalized complex predicates *sua:l taka-* or *sua:l kur-* are two synonymous ways of saying 'tell a lie, deceive'. The verbs *taka-* and *kur-* have a broad range of meanings which appear bleached in lexicalized complex predicates. And this takes us to the issue of the numerous verbs in Manambu which behave in a similar manner, and whose generic semantics is hard to capture.

21.2.5   Generic verbs

We saw in §4.2.2 (under B) that Manambu has ten verbs which can each be used in two or three of the following functions—as copula verbs, as support verbs, and also as auxiliaries. In addition, five of them, including the three posture verbs 'sit', 'stand', and 'stay', are also

---

⁴ Other words meaning 'lie, trickery' are *guyuk* and *gwəyip*; they are less frequent than *sua:l.*

used as lexical verbs. We saw, in §17.1.1, that despite some correlations with the shape of the referent, posture verbs in Manambu cannot be considered classificatory verbs. A summary of these verbs and their functions is in Table 4.1. Further discussion is in Chapter 17 which deals with the ways in which these, and other generic verbs, form complex predicates.

Having a closed class of verbs with fairly general semantics and a wide range of polysemy is a feature of a few Papuan languages, among them Kalam (Kalam-Kobon: Pawley 1993). Unlike Manambu, Kalam has about 130–40 verb roots, of which 30 roots are most frequent. Each of these has numerous senses, and the verbs combine together in serial verb constructions consisting 'of a generic verb preceded by one or more verb stems and one or more nominal or adverbial complements' (Pawley 1993: 96). Unlike Kalam, Manambu has a large open class of verbs, and is not averse to adopting new ones (see §22.4). But a smallish subclass of generic verbs (some of them polyfunctional) behaves in a manner similar to Kalam: different semantic overtones for these verbs are achieved through the choice of a nominal complement, or a directional, or a part of a verb compound. The list of generic verbs in Manambu is given in Table 21.2 which also includes some examples. If a verb has already been mentioned in any of the previous chapters, a reference is supplied. All generic verbs are high in frequency.

A few more generic verbs could be postulated. The root component *v-* of the inherently directional verb (see §16.1.1, item I) *væki-* 'go across (away from the speaker)' can be considered a generic bound verb of movement, given that *-aki* is a directional suffix with other verbs. So can the component *w-* of the inherently directional verb *waku-* 'go out (including motion in the direction away from the Sepik River)', since *-aku* exists as a directional suffix with other verbs (see further discussion in §16.1.1).

Some generic verbs have a clear-cut meaning when used on their own—for instance, *taka-* means 'put', and *sə-* means 'plant'. However, we have no way of determining whether *sə-* 'plant', *sə-* 'move' accompanied with a directional, and *sə-* in lexicalized predicates are the same verb or homonymous forms. The same applies to the allomorphs *kar-/kra-/*ka-* 'bring, carry' which are only partially in complementary distribution with each other (see §16.1.1). The verb *væ-* 'dig' has the same form as *væ-* used in a restricted number of complex predicates, but is it the same verb? Speakers vary widely in their judgements concerning this. The question remains open.

The generic verbs occur in numerous lexicalized complex predicates. They are hardly ever mutually interchangeable—having two synonyms for 'lying', 'lie put' (*sua:l taka-*) and 'lie do' (*sua:l kur-*), is a rare instance.

In addition to this, many specific verbs can be replaced with a general one. This is the topic of our next section.

21.3 GENERAL NOUN AND GENERAL VERB

The general noun *ma:gw* 'whats-its-name, whatever', and the general verb *məgi-* 'do whatever, (whatever) happen' can replace most nouns, and most verbs respectively. The roots of these two are perceived by speakers as related. So far, no cognates have been found for either *ma:gw* or *məgi-*. A functional parallel comes from Ambulas, which has a few 'neutral nouns' with generic meaning: *mun* 'thingumajig, whats-its-name' called 'memory lapse neutral noun'; *kwabu* 'thing, person' called 'definitive neutral noun' which 'co-occurs with animate or inanimate nouns or replaces them', and *ban* 'one person, one thing' termed 'general neutral noun' (Wilson 1980: 52).

TABLE 21.2   Generic verbs in Manambu

VERB AND APPROXIMATE MEANINGS	FUNCTIONS AND USE
1. *tə-* 'become', 'be', 'exist (vertical position) (in a location)', 'have'	auxiliary verb, support verb, copula verb, and lexical verb (Table 4.1); in lexicalized complex predicates (§17.3)
2. *rə-* 'be in/at', 'exist (horizontal position)'	
3. *kwa-* 'be in/at', 'exist (in general, or in multiple locations)'	
4. *yi-* 'do, be (with some abstract terms)'	
5. *kur-* 'do, get, become (fully)'	
6. *na-* 'be (of physical states; natural phenomena)'	as support verb with various nominals; ideophones and onomatopoeia; uninflected completive aspect (Table 4.1)
7. *tay-* 'be (of climatic states)'	with nominals denoting climatic states (Table 4.1)
8. *yasa-/yasə-* 'be (of physical states: hunger, thirst)'	with nominals denoting physical states (Table 4.1)
9. *say-* 'be (of some states: shame, pins and needles)'	with nominals denoting some states (shame, pins and needles: Table 4.1)
10. *yæy-* 'be (of smells)'	with 'smell' (Table 4.1)
11. *sə-* 'plant, put, call'	lexical verb 'plant'; 'move' (with some directionals, e.g. *sə-tay-tay-* 'move back and forth': Chapter 16); component of bound directionals: Chapter 16; in lexicalized complex predicates, e.g. *bas sə-* (first plant) 'ask', *wayepi sə-* 'call address term', *ga:m sə-* 'sing, serenade' (see §17.3)
12. *kar-/kra-/*ka-* 'bring, carry'	lexical verb *kər/kra-* 'marry' (with object *ta:kw* 'wife'); intrinsically directional verb 'bring, carry' (§16.1.1); 'get' (allomorph *ka-* with *sapwi-* 'disclose something' (§16.1.1; §15.2.4))
13. *ku-* 'put'	only with bound directionals, e.g. *ku-su-* (put-upwards) 'wear, put on (clothing)' (§16.1.1)

TABLE 21.2 *Continued*

VERB AND APPROXIMATE MEANINGS	FUNCTIONS AND USE
14. *ta-* 'hit, move'	only with bound directionals, e.g. *ta-saku-* (hit/move-outward) 'appoint, elect someone' (§16.1.1)
15. *væ-*	only in complex predicates: *agur væ-* 'snore'
16. *taka-* 'put'	lexical verb 'put' (a cover term for various specific terms of 'putting') in complex predicates, e.g. *aban taka-* 'conspire', *api taka-* 'yawn'

21.3.1   The general noun *ma:gw*

The general noun *ma:gw* has a number of functions. It occurs at the beginning, or in the middle, of a clause if a speaker is searching for a right way to start, or to continue, their discourse. An example is at 21.41: the speaker announces that she is going to tell a story, and then hesitates as to exactly how to start it. The form *ma:gw* is used as a mark of such hesitation. It is underlined throughout this section.

21.41 [ada ma: suku-kə-tua-d]   [ma:gw]
DEM.DIST.REACT.TOP+masc.sg again 'carve'-FUT-1sgSUBJ.VT-3masc.sgBAS.VT whatever
[bər takwa-ñidi amæy asa:y məgi-də-k]   [kurən
3du woman+LK-child.du mother father do.whatever-3masc-COMPL.DS get+SEQ
tə-brə-d ñan-ad]
'stand'-3dusUBJ.P-3masc.sgBAS.P child-3masc.sgNOM
'I will record (lit. carve) another (long story) again, whatever, the two young women, after mother-father "whatevered" (i.e. died), there was a child the two looked after'

A young girl started telling a story without prior planning, and used *ma:gw* twice. The lack of planning is also reflected in the excessive repetition:

21.42 *wanpela* ta:kw ma:gw lə-kə-bər na: viti *twins*-abər
one woman whatever she-OBL-du daughter's.child two twins-3duNOM
takwa-ñidi-abər ata ma:gw ata kwa-bər, kwa-di, day
woman+LK-child.du-3duNOM then whatever then stay-3duBAS.P stay-3plBAS.P they
'One woman, whatever, her two grandchildren were twins, they were girls, then whatever, then they (two) stayed, they (many) stayed, they'

In this function, *ma:gw* is separated by a pause from the rest of the clause, and is never case marked. Alternatively, *ma:gw* can be used as an argument within a clause, or as the head of a verbless clause in the function of a placeholder for any noun (except for a noun with a human referent) if the speaker cannot remember the exact term. During our trip to Swakap, I asked Dameliway for a name of a fungus on a tree trunk. She immediately answered *ma:gw-ad* (whatever-3masc.sgNOM) 'it is whatever (I know that it has a name but can't remember it)', and readdressed my question to her husband Yuamuk.

The referent of *ma:gw* can be clear from the context, as in 21.43—the exact noun (*rami:m* 'on a branch') was supplied for my benefit, and only after I'd asked for it.

21.43 <u>mugum</u>   kaykətəwən tə-k-na-wun
       whatever+LK+LOC hang+SEQ   'stand'/stay-FUT-ACT.FOC-1fem.sgBAS.VT
       'I will be hanging on whatever' (said the flying fox)

If a speaker ends up mentioning the exact term, *ma:gw* is likely to be followed by a noun, as in 21.44. The two belong to different noun phrases since they may be separated with a pause. As a placeholder of an argument, *ma:gw* can take any appropriate case marker and be modified.

21.44 [kabay numa-də   kaba:y jəpis   paba:n]   [a-di
        snake   big-masc.sg snake   small.black.ant large.black.red.ant DEM.DIST-pl
        nəkəm   nəkəm   <u>mugur</u>   kwarba:r   yi-da-k]
        other+LOC other+LOC whatever+LK+ALL   bush+LK+ALL   go-3pl-COMPL.DS
        [a-di   və-kə-ñəna-di]
        DEM.DIST-pl see-FUT-2fem.sgSUBJ.VT-3plBAS.VT
        'Snake, big snake, small black ants, large black and reddish ants, after all these have gone wherever, to the bush, you will see them'

Ma:gw can also be used in a generic meaning of 'whatever else', as in 21.45. In this meaning it is similar to *məwi* 'things like that' (see A.III in §20.1.1):

21.45 na:gw <u>muguk</u>   ma:y   gur
       sago   whatever+LK+DAT go.IMPV you.pl
       'You (plural) go to fetch sago and whatever else'

In 21.45, *ma:gw* forms one noun phrase with the noun it follows because the case marking occurs just once, on the second component. The difference between *ma:gw* and *məwi* lies in the degree of specificity of associated items: saying *na:gw məwi:k yi-ku* (sago things.like.that+DAT go-COMPL.SS) means 'having gone to fetch sago and things associated with it', while the combination *na:gw ma:gw* (as in 21.45) refers to sago and anything else one can think of. A similar example is at 21.46, 'women (and) whatever else'.

21.46 war-ən   ta:kw   <u>ma:gw</u>   jau   kurən   kur-kwa-di-ya
       go.up-SEQ woman   whatever let.it.be get+SEQ get-IMPV.3p-PL-EMPH
       'After they'd gone up let them get women and whatever else'

We can recall, from §20.1.1, that *məwi* cannot form one noun phrase with nouns with a human referent. This does not apply to *ma:gw* which can occur in juxtaposition to any noun.

Ma:gw can be used in one noun phrase with *məwi*, if the speaker chooses to be non-specific, as in *a-di ma:gw məwi məjəl vya-dian* (DEM.DIST-pl whatever things.like.that small.bird kill-1plBAS.VT) 'we kill those whatever they are and similar things, small birds'.

And finally, *ma:gw* can refer to an 'unspecified type of thing' with a particular property, as in 21.47—an explanation of an unusual ornament on Yuawalup's stringbag:

21.47 [nabəsəm   ada   rə-na-d-ə]
        beach+LK+LOC   DEM.DIST.REACT.TOP+masc.sg sit-ACT.FOC-masc.sg-LK
        <u>ma:gw</u>   kəbay-a
        whatever small.shell.type-3fem.sgNOM
        'It is a small shell, a kind (lit. a whatever) that is found (lit. sits) on the beach'

In summary: *ma:gw* can be considered a pause filler, or a hesitation marker. At the same time it fulfils the role of replacement 'universal' noun, and of a cover term, with a rough meaning 'type, kind'. Overusing *ma:gw* does not create a good impression—it is looked upon as a mark of a not-very-eloquent speaker. In its functions and use, it is only partly similar to the general verb.

21.3.2 The 'lazy' verb

The general verb *məgi-* 'do whatever, happen (whatever)' is unusual in a number of ways. One of these is its versatile transitivity.

We saw in §16.1.3 that it is S=O=A ambitransitive (its transitive use was exemplified in 16.58a, T2.30–1, T2.34, and T3.50; its S=A ambitransitive use appeared in 16.58b and 21.41 above; and its S=O ambitransitive use was shown in 16.58c). If accompanied by a bound directional, *məgi-* has to be telic and transitive. And if used with the prefix *kay-* 'causative-manipulative', *kay-məgi-* 'do whatever with a special effort' is strictly transitive (see 16.71).

Its grammatical possibilities were discussed in Chapters 15 and 16. It freely combines with bound directionals and with directional suffixes, and takes part in some verb compounding structures. It occurs as a second component of a cause-effect compound *vya-məgi-* (hit-do.whatever) 'hit and break in whatever way' (15.22), and as a first component of compounds involving *-yakə-* '(do) fully', as in 15.109 (*məgi-yakə-ku* (do.whatever-FULLY-COMPL.SS) 'having done whatever fully') and *-taka* 'put', in *məgi-taka-* 'do whatever with respect to extended surface' (for instance, peeling pawpaw onto a mat), or 'do whatever and put it down' (e.g. pulling a lever down). It has not been attested in any other compounds, and any attempts to use it in such structures have been emphatically rejected by the speakers.

The general verb *məgi-* can replace just about any verb of affect and process. It cannot replace verbs of speech, any verb referring to emotion and mental process, any of the ditransitive verbs, or a stative verb. Its major function was captured by Teketa:y and Yuaneng who independently called it, in English, a 'lazy' verb—that is, a verb used when one cannot, or is unwilling to, think of a specific, more precise term.

The verb *məgi-* is often used as a placeholder for a verb of affect or of happening if the speaker cannot think of an appropriate specific verb. An example is at 21.48 (also see 16.58a). A specific verb can be supplied: *væga-ku* (put.inside-COMPL.SS) was used by the same speaker as a correction to *məgi-ku*:

21.48 [ñan wa-də   wurəm
    child DEM.PROX.ADDR-masc.sg big.string.bag+LK+LOC

    məgi-ku]   [akaytak]
    do.whatever-COMPL.SS IMPV+hang
    'Having "whatevered" (that is, "put") this child close to you in the stringbag, carry it (lit. hang)'

Speakers are often conscious of the 'lazy' nature of *məgi*—we can recall Teketa:y's instructions to use the exact verb in its stead, in 16.72 ('Having "whatevered" this coconut, (it is) to say like this: "I shall split it by hitting" ').

Alternatively, the exact meaning of *məgi-* can be easily recoverable from the context, as in 21.41. In stories about orphaned children their parents usually die—so, the verb *məgi-* in 21.41 is understood as referring to 'dying'.

A similar example is in T3.43: Oselo tells the story about how he killed all the snakes, and then states that there would not be any more snakes because he'd already 'whatevered' them. Then, he goes on to specify that he'd fully killed them all (*vya-yakə-tua-di* kill/hit-FULLY-1sgSUBJ.VT-3plBAS.VT), and that he'd killed them by smashing them with a knife (*vya-təpul-tua-di wali-baga:r* kill-'hit'-1sgSUBJ.VT-3plBAS.VT white.man-knife+LK+INSTR). A similar example is 16.58b: the context makes it obvious that thunder had 'struck' (this is what it usually does).

Məgi- can be used in lieu of a more complex verbal form, if the type of affect is obvious. A mother told a little girl to turn her skirt the right way round, using a full verb:

21.49a a-kay-blakə-saki
   IMPV-CAUS-be.turned-ACROSS.AWAY
   'Turn (it) the right way round' (away from speaker)

Later on, the same command was repeated using the 'lazy verb', with just the directional specification:

21.49b a-məgi-saki
   IMPV-do.whatever-ACROSS.AWAY
   'Whatever it the right way round!'

This same verb can be used if the speaker decides not to specify the kind of affect, as in 15.109, or the kind of movement involved. In 21.50–1, *məgi-* refers to a general movement inside and up respectively.

21.50 atawa *skirt* məgi-saula-ku   kwau
   thus skirt do.whatever-INSIDE-COMPL.SS sit+1sgIMPV
   'I will sit (lit. may I sit) having whatevered (that is, tucked) my skirt underneath'

21.51 a-məgi-su
   IMPV-do.whatever-UP
   'Whatever it upwards!' (that is, pull the mat upwards)

Or it can be used if there is no exact verb which would describe the situation, as in T2.30 and T2.31 ('do whatever to and fro'), T2.34, and 16.58c. In this last example, *məgi-* is used to refer to something adverse happening to the girl's leg. No one has any idea what exactly had happened—so the generic *məgi-* is appropriate. Here, it could be called a 'vague verb', not just a 'lazy' one. A similar example is T3.50 (the last line), *lə-kə-m məgiməgi ma:* (she-OBL-ACC/LOC do.whatever:RED NEG) 'there was no way they (people) could "whatever" her (the snake) (lit. there was no whatevering her)'. Here 'do whatever' is a vague way of referring to some kind of (negative) affect. Jacklyn Yuamali who helped me transcribe this story suggested that *məgiməgi ma:* could be replaced by *vyavi ma:* 'no killing', but then added that the author may have meant some other way of punishing the snake. Along similar lines, in 21.52 *məgi-* refers to something adverse flies were doing to a wound:

21.52 bə   ji-na,   sa:r məgi-lalək
   already tie-ACT.FOC+3fem.sgBAS.VT fly do.whatever-3fem.sg+BECAUSE
   'She already tied (the bandage) because flies (as a small group) were "whatevering" it'

The verb *məgi-* provides an option of not being precise—this is what makes it 'lazy'. We saw above that certain semantic fields in the Manambu lexicon are remarkably rich, but a general term is lacking. If the speaker does not wish to specify the exact manner of hitting, breaking, or mixing, they can use *məgi-* as in 15.22, 16.71, and in 21.53–4.

21.53 gu-a-wa   məgi-ta:y   ata
water-LK-COM do.whatever-COTEMP then
kui-də-d
give.to.third.p-3masc.sgSUBJ.P-3masc.sgBAS.P
'Having mixed (lit. "whatevered") (magic powder) with water, he gave it to him'

21.54 væt   yi-ku   məgi-la-d
heavy go-COMPL.SS do.whatever-3fem.sgSUBJ.VT-3masc.sgBAS.VT
'Because of weight (lit. having been heavy), it (the branch of a mango tree) whatevered (that is, broke)'

Məgi- can also be used as a generic pro-verb in a summarizing function, and can then be roughly translated as 'do; act', as in 21.55:

21.55 [*orait*] [yanu bla-ku]   [kədika-n-adika
alright magic speak-COMPL.SS DEM.PROX.REACT.TOP+pl-PRED-REACT.TOP.pl
məgi-da-di]   [aka
do.whatever-3plSUBJ.P-3plBAS.P DEM.PROX.REACT.TOP.fem.sg
kusə-na]
finish-ACT.FOC+3fem.sgBAS.VT
'OK, having done (lit. spoken) magic, they "whatevered" them (that is, did what was described above: eliminated the village), here (the story) finishes'

In this function, a more frequent and established alternative is the verb *kur-* 'do',—not infrequently employed as a summarizing verb, in the sense of 'this is what (characters) were doing', as in 19.87, 18.12, T2.8, T2.13, and T2.16. A similar example is at 21.56; the speaker used *məgi-* as a generic pro-verb ('this is what they were doing'). When transcribing the story, Yuamali suggested that it would be more appropriate to use *kur-*. The clause offered as 'replacement' is in braces.

21.56 [dəya-kə   yawi aka]   [atawa
they-OBL+3fem.sg job DEM.DIST.REACT.TOP.fem.sg thus
məgi-da-k]   {atawa kur-ya-da-k}
'do.whatever'-3pl-COMPL.DS thus   do-come-3pl-COMPL.DS
'That was their job (to feed the child), after they'd done that ("whatevered") (that man already grew up'

The 'lazy verb' is much more frequent in informal conversations than in carefully planned stories. It appears to be rare in ritual discourse: during a full day of name debate, I did not hear it used once. Speakers who know that they tend to code-switch and are trying to avoid this are likely to frequently use *məgi-* instead of Tok Pisin verbs. This is the reason why *məgi-* occurs in Texts 2 (three times) and 3 (twice): both speakers are proficient story tellers, but, similarly to other men, especially 'big men', they tend to use a fair bit of Tok Pisin. This was their way of avoiding a Tok Pisin term. The following example illustrates such auto-repair fortunately captured on a tape:

21.57 du   *bagarapim*, ka!   du   məgi-da-l
man hurt   DEM.PROX.fem.sg man do.whatever-3plSUBJ.P-3fem.sgBAS.VT
'They hurt the man (Tok Pisin), no!, they "whatevered" the man'

We now provide a brief comparison of the general noun and the general verb.

21.3.3   Similarities and differences between the general noun and the 'lazy' verb

The general verb *məgi-* shares some similarities with its nominal counterpart, *maːgw*. The latter never appears in planned discourse—this can be seen in its absence from the Texts at the end of the grammar. Both *maːgw* and *məgi-* can be used as 'replacement' noun and verb respectively if the speaker cannot remember the exact term, or the exact term is obvious from the context. But while *maːgw* can replace any noun, *məgi-* can only replace a verb of affect or process.

The noun *maːgw* can be generic—that is, meaning 'whatever else similar to the referent of the preceding noun', and 'unspecified type of thing with a particular property' (examples 21.46–7). The verb *məgi-* in its generic meaning can refer to a non-specified affect or process. And, unlike *maːgw*, it can have a summarizing function, similar to *kur-* 'do'.

Unlike *maːgw*, *məgi-* is never used as a pause filler, and never occurs uninflected (which is consistent with its being a regular verb).

The examples above may create an impression that *məgi-* often refers to negative actions or events. But this is not always the case, as can be seen in 16.58a,16.58d, 21.49b, and 21.55–6. The general verb *məgi-* is a versatile device which offers speakers an option of being vague, and also highlights the role of context in Manambu discourse.

21.4   'BODY' IN THE EXPRESSION OF EMOTIONS AND MENTAL PROCESSES

Languages of New Guinea—and of all over the world—utilize body part expressions to describe emotional states and mental processes (see Priestley 2002 for body parts and emotions in Koromu, a Madang language, and Lindström 2002, for body parts in expressing emotions in Kuot, the only non-Austronesian language of New Ireland). Body parts 'chosen' for expressing emotions vary from language to language. Manambu employs nine such items. We discuss them one by one, and then briefly look at polysemous extensions of a few other body parts.

I. STOMACH, *yaːl*, appears in the expression for 'anger', *yaːl gra-*, lit. 'stomach cry' (see 20.35a–b). This is a body part construction (§17.4), and the experiencer could be cross-referenced or not, depending on its prominence. This expression is synonymous with the Tok Pisin *bel hat* (belly hard), illustrated in 21.58a. This is an instance of lexical parallelism, which involves native and borrowed forms appearing together (see Hajek 2006; Aikhenvald 2006b and forthcoming c):

21.58a [də *bel* *hat* yaːl]   [yaːl   graːl]
       he belly hard go+3fem.sgBAS.P stomach cry+3fem.sgBAS.P
       'He is angry (lit. his belly is hard), he is angry (lit. his belly cried)'

The term *yaːl* is used as a body part term, as in 21.58b, where it means 'stomach', and in 7.16 (*yala-wa tə-* (belly+LK-COM stay) 'be pregnant').

21.58b [yaːl kagəl] [yi-k-na-ñən]
       belly be.sore go-FUT-ACT.FOC-2fem.sgBAS.VT
       'If your stomach is sore, will you go?'

Its other metaphorical extension is to do with 'belonging to one womb', that is, sharing maternal relatives: *yaːl nak* (belly one) is the term used to refer to one's maternal kin. Saying *yaːl rə-dian* (belly sit-1plBAS.VT) 'we sit in one belly' is a way of stressing 'uterine' connections across clans referring to each other as 'sisters' children' (also see 21.3a). This type of link prohibits sexual relations between people (see Harrison 1990a: 34). Then *yaːl* is treated as an inherently locational noun (and thus does not have to be overtly marked for the locative case: §4.1.2).

II. BLOOD, *ñiki*, is used to describe the feeling of being reckless, in the expression *ñiki yasə-na* (blood BE:DESIRE-ACT.FOC+3fem.sgBAS.NP), as in 4.26d, 'feel reckless enough to be going to die' (that is, to risk one's life in a stupid way). This same term, *ñiki*, is also used metaphorically to describe matrilineal links, as in *amæy ñiki lagu-da-dian* (mother blood pull-3plSUBJ.P-1plBAS.P) 'mother blood is pulling us (together)' (also see Harrison 1990a: 34).

III. BONE, *ap*, has a broad meaning of 'strength, strong, main', as in *ap-a-sə* (bone/main-LK-name) 'main name', *ap-a-du* (bone/main-LK-man) 'chief, head of the place or institution', and *ap-a-təp* (bone/main-LK-village) 'main village, Avatip'. A very thin person would be described as *ap-a-ka-ap* (bone-LK-INT-bone) 'very thin, bony' (see Table 4.3).

The construction *ap tə-* is inherently polysemous. If we are talking about a fish, it will be understood as fish which is full of bones. If we are talking about a person or a piece of wood, it would imply that the person is strong, and the wood is hard, as in *samasam-a ap tə-na-d-ə mi* (a.lot-LK bone/strength 'stand'/have-ACT.FOC-3masc.sgBAS.VT-LK wood) 'very hard wood'. The opposite, *ap ma: tə*, with the negator *ma:*, would mean 'be weak or meek' (of a person), 'be soft (of a piece of wood)', or 'have no bones' (of a fish). In idiomatic collocations, *ap* has an implication of 'resistance', as in *wun-a ya:l ap taka-na* (I-LK+fem.sg belly bone put-ACT.FOC+3fem.sgBAS.VT) 'I have no appetite' (lit. my belly puts bone), and in *ap krapə-na-wun* (bone lift-ACT.FOC-1fem.sgBAS.VT) 'I put up (with something)' (lit. I lift bone). (Whether the same root appears in *apan* 'old (male)' and *apau* 'old (female)' is an open question. The form *apar*, as in *apar ñan* 'main person', may well be related to *ap*.)

IV. SKIN, *səp*, is a term referring to bodily and emotional feelings of fatigue and being fed up, especially in body part constructions, e.g. *səp ji-na* (skin tired/fed.up-ACT.FOC+3fem.sgBAS.VT) and its synonym *səp sakwi-na* (skin tired/fed.up-ACT.FOC+3fem.sgBAS.VT). The expression *səp wiyaw na:d* (skin light.and.dry BE:NAT+3masc.sgBAS.VT/P) means 'be relieved, as if a burden had been taken off the soul'. In contrast, *səp væt yi-na* (skin heavy go-ACT.FOC+3fem.sgBAS.VT) means 'having difficult thoughts or emotional difficulties, feeling physically tired or unwell'. *Səp yaga-* (skin be.afraid) means 'be scared, timid'. The expression *səp kui-* (skin give.to.third.p) means 'be used to'.

This same term often refers to body (as in T2.50 and T3.49, glossed as 'skin'), e.g. *səp səlkə-* (skin/body diminish) 'lose weight'. In T2.56, *səp və-* (skin/body see/experience) is a euphemism for sexual intercourse. Most bodily feelings are experienced through *səp*, as in *səp bwuyabwi na-na* (skin very.hot BE.NAT-ACT.FOC+3fem.sgBAS.VT) 'skin is very hot' (to say that the experiencer is hot), or *səp kuku na-na* (skin lukewarm BE.NAT-ACT.FOC+3fem.sgBAS.VT) 'skin is lukewarm' (to say that the experiencer is just warm enough). *Səp* can be used as a descriptor of a person: *rək-a-səp* (dry-LK-skin) implies 'old person'. Also see 21.72, with *səp* used to enquire about a person's well-being.

The formation *səp-ə-ka-səp* (skin-LK-INT-skin) means 'skinny (of a person), thin (of a piece of wood)', and also, with a spatial extension, 'flat'.

V. HEAD, *ab*, may refer to 'thinking' or 'understanding': *ab ma: tə* (head NEG stand/have+NEG) means 'he/she/they are stupid, do not think'. We can recall, from §7.4, that *aba:k tə-* (head+LK+DAT be/stand/have) means 'be not quite right in one's head'.

VI. EAR, *wa:n*, has an overtone of 'aural attention' and also 'understanding', as in *wa:n tə-* (ear have-) 'listen, pay attention', or its synonyms *wa:n taka-* (ear put-) and *wa:n kui-* (ear give.to.third.p) (see §21.1.2). This is especially obvious in commands which have a telic reading, such as 21.25 'obey, listen!', literally, 'ear listen'. (This is similar to the extension of 'ear' in other Papuan languages, e.g. Karawari (Lower Sepik family: Telban 1998: 56–60).) This same term typically refers to hearing as a human capacity, e.g. *wa:n təp(ə)-* (ear be.closed) 'be deaf'.

VII. EYE, *məl*, has an overtone of 'visual attention', for instance, in commands *məl ap!* (eye IMPV+see) 'look!' and statements like *məl ma: və* (eye NEG see+NEG) 'she/he/they is/are not paying attention' (see §21.1.2). The term 'eye' typically refers to vision, as in *məl kusə-* (eye finish-) 'be blind'.

VIII. BREATH, *ya:p*, can refer to 'rest', as in 21.59, and also 'worry', as in 21.60 (used to describe young cassowaries playing around with nothing to worry about):

21.59 kwasa   ya:p   ada
      little+fem.sg breath   sit.IMPV
      'Have a rest, give it a rest'

21.60 agwa ya:p   sə-da-kəkək
      what breath   plant-3pl-PURP.DS
      'Why should they worry and think about things?'

An example of *ya:p* meaning 'breath' is in T3.50 (Oselo was squeezed by the snake to such an extent that he could not breathe). This same term *ya:p* is used to refer to asthma (as in 19.17b), and to any breathing-related disease (including angina).

IX. MAWUL 'something inside something else, bone marrow, core, pith (of a tree)' is the major body part associated with emotional and mental states. (A phonetic variant is *məwul*; it is occasionally translated as 'liver'; an alternative and preferred term for 'liver', 'spleen', and also 'lung' is *wurəpi*; see Lindström 2002, on a similar polysemy in Kuot.) *Mawul* may roughly correspond to 'mindset', as in *suguya-mawul ma: tə* (help+LK-'inside' NEG have+NEG) 'she does not have a mindset of helping (people)', *suku-mawul* (carve-'inside') 'mindset of a carver, patience'. A compound *wukə-mawul* (hear/listen-'inside') refers to instinct, or thinking. One 'thinks' or 'worries' in one's *mawul*, as in *mawul wukə-na-wun* ('inside' hear/listen-ACT.FOC-1fem.sgBAS.VT) 'I am thinking, worrying', and also in 14.86 (*mawul wukə-tukwa* inside worry-PROH.GEN) 'don't you worry'. *Mawul* can also refer to liking, as in *məwula ja:p* ('inside'+LK thing) 'whatever one likes, things to one's liking'—see 21.61, a statement about the shopping centre in Maprik:

21.61 a [Maprika:r   yi-na-di]   *stoam*   məwula
         then Maprik+LK+ALL go-ACT.FOC-3plBAS.VT   store+LOC   'inside'+LK
         ja:p yapi-na-di
         thing buy-ACT.FOC-3plBAS.VT
         'Those who go to Maprik buy whatever they like'

If something is taken in and remembered, it 'stays' in the *mawul*, as in 19.28 (*məwula:m kwa-*). The collocation *mawul kwa-* can also mean 'like', as can the expression *mawul taka-* ('inside' put)—see 21.62 which contains three synonymous expressions, one of them a borrowing from Tok Pisin:

21.62 agwajapək   *laiki*-na-dəmən   mawul
      what+thing+LK+DAT like-ACT.FOC-2masc.sgBAS.VT 'inside'
      taka-na-dəmən   mawul kwa-na-dəmən
      put-ACT.FOC-2masc.sgBAS.VT 'inside' stay-ACT.FOC-2masc.sgBAS.VT
      'What (thing) do you like, what appeals to you, what do you feel like?'

Another alternative would be *vyakat-a mawul taka-* (good-LK 'inside' put), 'like, enjoy'. The expression *mawul taka-* can also mean 'think, put one's mind to something'. Or, in an appropriate context, it can refer to an action performed willingly, as in 21.63a.

21.63a mawul taka-n kwatiya-k-na-di
'inside' put-SEQ give.to.nonthird.p-FUT-ACT.FOC-3plBAS.VT
'They will give me (the ancestral words) willingly'

A synonym is 21.63b—an action performed willingly is performed with 'light' *mawul*:

21.63b mawul wiyau na-n kwatiya-k-na-di
'inside' light.and.dry BE.NAT-SEQ give.to.nonthird.p-FUT-ACT.FOC-3plBAS.VT
'They will give me (the ancestral words) willingly'

Secrets, including secret knowledge, 'sit' in the *mawul*, as in *məwula:m rə-na-di ja:p* ('inside'+LK+LOC sit-ACT.FOC-3plBAS.VT thing) 'things which stay unspoken'. If people agree, they are said to have one *mawul*: *mawul nak tə-na-di* ('inside' one have-ACT.FOC-3plBAS.VT) 'they agree, are of the same mind'. 'Opening up' one's *mawul*, *mawul kaja-*, refers to the process of educating children and 'opening them up' for socialization. The same expression is used to describe breaking open the husk or the rind of a fruit, exposing the soft flesh inside.

'Internal speech' and thoughts are often phrased as *məwula:m wa-* 'say in the inside', as shown in §19.5.6 (example 19.66). *Mawul* may be associated with fond memory and nostalgia, as in 21.64a–b:

21.64a məwula:m wukə-n rə-kə-bana
'inside'+LK+LOC hear/listen-SEQ sit-FUT-1plSUBJ.VT+3fem.sgBAS.VT
'We will remember and miss (you)' (lit. 'we will sit listening in our inside')

21.64b [yi-kə-gura] [ñan-a mawul
go-FUT-2plSUBJ.VT+3fem.sgBAS.VT we-LK+fem.sg 'inside'
kray-kə-gura]
take-FUT-2plSUBJ.VT+3fem.sgBAS.VT
'When you go, we will miss you' (lit. 'you will carry away our inside')

In 21.65, Kawidu indicated that his thoughts were with R. M. W. Dixon, whom he'd never met, but toward whom he had developed warm family feelings:

21.65 wun-a mawul də-kə-wa tə-na
I-LK+fem.sg 'inside' he-OBL-COM 'stand'-ACT.FOC+3fem.sgBAS.VT
'I keep thinking about him' (lit. 'my "inside" is with him')

Mawul often appears in body part constructions, such as *mawul war-* 'be excited, develop a desire for' (lit. ' "inside" go up') illustrated in 14.87a–c and 21.66—a comment on Kerryanne's spontaneous rush to perform a household chore:

21.66 lə mawul war-kwa-na væs kapək
she 'inside' go.up-HAB-ACT.FOC+3fem.sgBAS.VT grass cut+PURP.SS
'She typically develops a desire to cut grass'

Depending on the context, *mawul war-* can mean 'get angry, annoyed'. Either *mawul* or the experiencer can be cross-referenced on the verb, as is typically the case in such constructions (see §20.1.4). If it is in the object function, *mawul* is never case marked. It is never cross-referenced on the verb either: but this may be the effect of its feminine gender since the feminine gender in Manambu is formally unmarked (see §5.1.2), e.g. *mawul nəma kui-* ('inside' big+fem.sg give.to.third.p) 'be happy'.

Mawul may appear to be agentive: *wun-a mawul ata wa-na* (I-LK+fem.sg 'inside' then say-ACT.FOC+3fem.sgBAS.VT) 'my inside says thus' refers to a decision-making process. An alternative expression, also with *mawul*, is *mawul kur-* ('inside' do/get) 'make a decision, make up one's mind', as in 21.67:

21.67 [[kuprap wa-tua-d-ə   ñan] [wa-ku]]
      bad   say-1sgSUBJ.VT-3masc.sgBAS.P-LK child say-COMPL.SS
      [lə-ka   mawul kur-lə-l]
      she-OBL+fem.sg+DEM.DIST.fem.sg 'inside' do/get-3fem.sgSUBJ.P-3fem.sgBAS.P
      'She decided that she had ruined the child' (lit. 'this is a child that I have ruined, having said this, she had decided')

An example of *mawul* in S function in a fairly idiomatic construction is in 21.68. The speaker hears people calling her and suspects that something must have happened to her husband (who in fact had been attacked by a crocodile):

21.68 wun-a-kə   mawul ata-n   draku-l
      I-LK-OBL+fem.sg 'inside' then-PRED unglue-3fem.sgBAS.P
      'It was then that I had a presentiment' (lit. my 'inside' unglued)

A synonymous expression is *wun-a-kə mawul aka draku-n waku-na* (I-LK-OBL+fem.sg 'inside' DEM.DIST.REACT.TOP.fem.sg unglue-SEQ go.out-ACT.FOC+3fem.sgBAS.VT) 'I have a presentiment', lit. 'my "inside" goes unglued'.

Having a good *mawul* (*vyakat-a mawul*) implies being good-hearted and even-tempered. Having a bad *mawul* (*kuprapə mawul*) implies having a bad temper and a nasty character. A way of saying that a person is happy is *mawul rakrak ta:d*, lit. ' "Inside" became happy'. Saying *mawul tugwam na-na* ('inside' clear BE.NAT-ACT.FOC+3fem.sgBAS.VT) means that one has a clear idea of something. And if *mawul* feels hot (*mawul kuku na-na* ('inside' hot BE:NAT-ACT.FOC+3fem.sgBAS.VT), the person feels excited and potentially ready to fight. If a person feels injured or upset, this is phrased as *mawul pukam na-na* ('inside' rot+COMPL BE:NAT-ACT.FOC+3fem.sgBAS.VT) 'The inside has rotted' (or *mawul puka-na* 'the inside rots') (a synonym is *mawul pəka-na* (lit. 'inside' rot-ACT.FOC+3fem.sg.BAS.VT)).

An alternative to saying *ya:l gra-na* (stomach cry-ACT.FOC+3fem.sgBAS.VT) for being angry is *mawul ya:l gra-na* (inside belly cry-ACT.FOC+3fem.sgBAS.VT). (According to Harrison 1993: 101, *ya:l* in this expression is a synecdoche for *mawul*; this is a matter of interpretation.) Here, *mawul* appears as a bona fide location of an emotion.

And someone who has no sense is said to have no *mawul* (*mawul ma: tə*). For those who are stupid, *mawul* does not 'hear', or 'listen' (see §21.1.2, B). A speaker described himself as having been young and stupid, and not interested in learning the Manambu traditional lore:

21.69 tayir   wun mawul ma:n wa:k
      before I   'inside' NEG hear/listen+NEG
      'Before I was stupid' (lit. I inside did not hear/listen)

A parent scolding a disobedient child would use a similar expression:

21.70 mən-a   mawul ma: wa:k   kwam
      you.masc-LK+fem.sg 'inside' NEG hear/listen+NEG crazy
      tə-na-dəmən
      stand-ACT.FOC-2masc.sgBAS.VT
      'Are you stupid? Are you crazy?'

Harrison (1993: 98) reports that 'an orator disputing in debate with a political rival', may say the same thing.

This brief discussion does not exhaust the wealth of expressions involving *mawul*. Other body part terms occur in a limited number of expressions to do with emotional, physical, or mental states. In contrast, the number of expressions in which *mawul* occurs is open-ended, and often depends on the speaker's creative ability to produce metaphors. This is a topic for an extensive lexicographically oriented study.

Harrison (1990a: 89–90; 1993: 97–8; 106–9; 1990b) analyses *mawul* as 'the aspect of personality' which he calls 'Understanding'. Its counterpart and in some respects its opposite would be *kayik* which he interprets as 'Spirit'. The term *kayik* is polysemous: it refers to image, picture, reflection (in water), shadow (but not shade which is termed *la:gw*), and nowadays also photographs, videos, and films (see §22.6.2). Painted designs and carvings are referred to as *kayik* or *məy-a-kayik* (real-LK-spirit/image). When a person dies, *kayik* leaves the body; *kayik* may threaten living people as a ghost does, and may appear as the person's 'double'. An 8-year-old girl was afraid of sleeping in her own mosquito net, and when I asked her mother why, the reply was *kayka:k yaga-na* (spirit+LK+DAT be.scared-ACT.FOC+3fem.sgBAS.VT) 'she is afraid of ghosts'.

We saw in §13.2 that a traditional blessing can be accompanied by asking the blesser's spirit to ensure the addressee is cured if they are sick, and saying 13.20 ('my spirit (*kayik*) may the illness end, may he (the patient) be well'). *Kayik* is conceptualized as the source of people's 'health, growth and vitality' (Harrison 1993: 106), and sometimes as their 'inner self', invoking of which may be embarassing.

When giving my consultants money or presents for telling stories or helping me transcribe them, I was instructed to say *ñən-a kaykak* (you-LK+fem.sg spirit+LK+DAT) lit., 'for your self, for your soul, for your personal enjoyment', as a way of making sure this is understood as a gesture of particular friendship, and not as a payment. A reply would be either *agwa kayka:k* (what spirit+LK+DAT) 'for what self/soul?', or *wun kayik ma: tə* (I spirit NEG have+NEG) 'I do not have a soul'—as if mockingly refusing a present. The present was then usually accepted with obvious gratitude.

The pattern of polysemy of *kayik* is remarkably similar to that of *mayi* in Kwoma, defined by Bowden (1997: 124) as including: 'soul (of a person), entity seen in a dream, spiritual or supernatural power that vivifies a ceremonial sculpture depicting a clan spirit', and also 'shadow', 'reflection (in a stream or mirror)', and picture or portrait. This may be one of the numerous examples of contact-induced similarities between Kwoma and Manambu discussed in §22.2.3.

Returning to the concept of *mawul*, it is somewhat unusual from a typological perspective. In many languages of the world, and of New Guinea, emotions and mental processes are 'located' in the stomach, liver, or lungs (see Lindström 2002, for Kuot), or 'heart' (as in Iatmul: Gerd Jendraschek, p.c.). According to Laycock (1986), the heart is 'the seat of emotions' in Momoona (Central and South New Guinea) and Foe (Kutubuan), and the 'lungs' in Buin (Bougainville). Tok Pisin utilizes *lewa* 'liver' and *bel* 'stomach'. Alternatively, emotions and mental processes can be located in the 'insides', that is, 'a space inside of something', as in Koromu (Priestley 2002).

An even closer analogy to *mawul* comes from Karawari (Lower Sepik: Telban 1998: 59): here the term *wambung* roughly translated as 'heart' denotes the insides of plants, animals, and even the moon and the sun; and, just like *mawul*, it refers to the soft pith and the middle of a plant. And it also applies to sense and knowledge. (A similar term exists in the neighbouring Awiakay, from the unrelated Arafundi family: Darja Hoenigman, p.c.) The opposition of *mawul* and *kayik* suggested by Harrison for Manambu is paralleled by the opposition of 'inside' and 'spirit' in Kawarari.

Many more in-depth studies of body part expressions in reference to emotions and mental states are needed before we can make any attempt at explaining why these three unrelated languages spoken within the Sepik area share their location of emotions and knowledge. For now, it remains a curious fact.

A word on other body part terms and their semantic extensions. We saw in §19.2.2 that *wus* 'urine, penis' is employed in the term for 'blood father', as in *kui-wus asa:y* (give.to.third.p-penis father) (also see 19.32). The term *kwa:l* 'neck, throat' is used in the expression for 'being thirsty': *kwa:l yasa-*, lit. 'neck BE:DESIRE'; and also *kwa:l wurdəp-*, both characteristic of the Yambon variety.

We saw in §8.1.1 that body parts acquire spatial meanings in part–whole constructions. So, *ya:l* 'stomach, belly' is associated with the 'inside', as in *yala-wi* (belly+LK-house) 'inside the house', and *yala-ta:b* (belly+LK-hand) 'the inside of the hand'. And *mutam* 'face' is associated with the front of any object, e.g. *mutam-a-wi* (face-LK-house) 'in front of the house', *mutam-a-su* (face-LK-shoe) 'front part of a shoe', *kukəm mutəma:m* (back+LOC face+LK+LOC) 'back to front'. The noun *ma:d* 'testicles' is used to refer to a lower part of, or a location underneath, an object, e.g. *mad-a ya:l* (under-LK belly) 'lower part of abdomen', *na:gw ma:d* 'underneath the sago'. The word for 'tail', *gəñ*, is used in the meaning 'last, non-first', as in *gəñ-a-ta:kw* (tail-LK-wife) 'non-first wife' (see T2.60; the opposite is *amæy-ta:kw* (mother-wife) 'first wife'). The word for 'head' has two spatial extensions. It may refer to the top part of an object, as in *ab-a-wa:n* (head-LK-ear) 'top part of the ear' and *ab-a-wuk* 'upper tooth'. Or it may refer to the edge of something, as in *ab-a-gəñ* (head-LK-last) 'last of all', *ab-a-talək* 'last house', and *ab-a-war* 'last boundary'. None of the body part terms shows any sign of grammaticalization as an adposition.

21.5 SPEECH FORMULAE, GREETINGS, AND FAREWELLS

Speech formulae are an important—and frequently neglected—part of the language. They may be considered marginal from a grammarian's perspective; and yet they are indispensable tokens of language knowledge, without which successful communication cannot be achieved (cf. Pawley 1993). In Manambu, speech formulae—especially those to do with greetings and farewells—offer a curious combination of the old and the new. We start with a few examples of Manambu 'small talk' (§21.5.1), and then turn to imperatives in greetings (§21.5.2), and other markers of speech etiquette, including the old greeting *kəpəyay* and a variety of Western imports (§21.5.3). In §21.5.4 we briefly look at address terms whose choice depends on clan membership.

21.5.1 Manambu 'small' talk

A typical small talk-type interaction in Manambu involves a formulaic question-answer pattern: 'are you OK?'—'yes, I am OK' shown in 21.71a–b:

21.71a ñən   yara (kwa-na-ñən)
       you.fem.sg well stay-ACT.FOC-2fem.sgBAS.VT
       'Are you OK?'

21.71b wun yara (kwa-na-wun)
     I   well stay-ACT.FOC-1fem.sgBAS.VT
     'I am OK'

The verb 'stay' can be omitted. To continue the same kind of conversation, the interlocutor may add *ñəna:k* (you.fem+LK+DAT) lit. 'for you', meaning 'how about you, it is you I am asking/worrying about'. We can recall, from 20.55, that verbless clauses are also used in short questions to enquire after someone's location or well-being in general. As an alternative way of enquiring after someone's health and well-being, a verbless clause or a copula clause can be used:

21.72 də-kə   səp yara vyakət tə-na-d
     he-OBL+fem.sg skin fine good   stand/be-ACT.FOC-3masc.sgBAS.VT
     'Is he OK (lit. is his skin fine?)? Is he well?'

When the speaker decides that they have no more questions to ask, or nothing else to add, they come up with the conversation stopper *ma:j ma:* (talk NEG) 'no more talk'—an exact equivalent, and maybe a calque, of Tok Pisin *nogat tok* (cf. 21.31c).

21.5.2 Imperatives in greetings

In Manambu, as in many languages of the world, greetings to the addressee often contain imperatives (§13.2). A suppletive form of the verb *yi-* 'go' is used in the departure formula.

21.73a yara <u>ma:y</u>
     well go.IMPV
     'Go well, good-bye'

An answer to this involves a suppletive imperative of the verb *kwa* 'stay'.

21.73b yara <u>adakw</u>
     well stay.IMPV
     'Stay well'

If you pass someone on the road, you may greet them saying:

21.73c yara kwa:n   <u>a-nay</u>
     well stay+SEQ IMPV-play
     'Staying well, play!'

If they are working, a proper thing to say is:

21.73d yara kwa-n   yawi <u>akur</u>
     well stay-SEQ work IMPV+do
     'Staying well, do work'

If one is sitting in a house and wants to greet a passer-by, they would use a second person imperative, encouraging them to move on in the direction they are already going. The direction could follow the course of the Sepik River (the major orientation point in Avatip). Example 21.74a would be used if the person's direction of movement follows the river upstream, and 21.74b if the person's direction of movement follows the river downstream. In each case, a vocative form can be used in lieu of a non-vocative one (*maya* instead of *ma:y*) if the addressee is sufficiently far away.

21.74a maya   a-war
      go.IMPV+VOC IMPV-go.up
      'Off you go upstream'

21.74b maya   adi:d
      go.IMPV+VOC go.down.IMPV
      'Off you go downstream'

Saying 21.74c has an additional overtone of 'go away', if trying to get rid of someone:

21.74c maya   a-væki
      go.IMPV+VOC IMPV-go.across
      'Off you go across'

A face-to-face greeting is usually accompanied by shaking hands, and a 'reminder'—either *ta:b kuru* (hand get+1sgIMPV) 'May I take (your) hand?', or *tab-a-dəka* (hand-LK-ONLY), lit. 'just hand'. (Speakers with a proclivity to code-switch would use the Tok Pisin alternative *sek han*, especially if one of the people involved in shaking hands is a child—see §22.4.)

Orait (sometimes replaced with Manambu *ya:kya*) can also be used as a token of the fact that the person is about to leave. Normally, leave-taking is preceded by announcing:

21.75 wapa-kə-tua-ñən-ək
     leave-FUT-1sgSUBJ.VT-2fem.sgBAS.VT-CONF
     'I will leave you'

This is followed by the formula 'you go!', and the answer 'you stay!' Address terms and greetings employed with these are discussed in the next sections.

21.5.3 Further greetings and tokens of 'speech etiquette'

Manambu greetings combine the old, and the new. Nowadays, it is customary to start one's greetings with *vyakata ganəb* 'good morning', *vyakata ñə* 'good day (or good afternoon)', and *vyakata gra:b* 'good afternoon'. To wish someone good night, one says *vyakata ga:n* 'good night'. These expressions—new calques from Tok Pisin and English—are used alongside Tok Pisin code-switches, e.g. *moning tru*, *apinun tru*, and suchlike.

The customary greeting *kəpəyay* used to be accompanied by a gesture involving touching the addressee's nose and then sliding the hand to their navel (also described by Behrmann 1922: 178). As explained by Leo Kalangas, and Waliaundemi, this often was used together with the traditional blessing (*wurəbasawul-*) which consisted in slight blowing onto the person to be blessed and uttering a spell.[5] Nowadays, *kəpəyay* is employed somewhat differently, especially in Avatip.

Traditionally, this greeting—typically from male to male—was employed as an expression of acceptance and goodwill, and was accompanied by touching the interlocutor's nose, upper body, and navel (Leo Kalangas, p.c.). Nowadays, only a few speakers are aware of its use as a greeting of 'goodwill' and to express warm feelings. Some speakers claim that it is only used to someone higher up in status than the speaker (e.g. older, or belonging to a senior generation than oneself). In actual fact, it is often used ironically to a child who has done something

---

[5] Waliaundemi performed this on me, Yuaneng, and her daughters on our visit to Malu village, 30 September 2004, saying that this should protect us from disasters and illnesses.

unusually naughty or smart; or to anyone as a sign of endearment and appreciation. Hardly anyone remembers the gesture that used to go with it.

First, it is a somewhat honorific way of addressing an older person, or a person higher in status than onself (that is, a relative belonging to a senior generation, no matter what their actual age is). Secondly, one often hears *yara kəpəyay* (fine greeting) 'hello, farewell' addressed to an elder kinsman. And it also has an ironic use, as a sign of joking admiration. When a baby wandered off and brought a towel back, a relative who happened to be in the house exclaimed *kəpəyay!* admiring the baby's intelligence. And when a little girl sat down and wrapped herself in a shawl, as if she were an old woman, her mother's ironic reaction was:

21.76 apaw   ta:kw   *kol*   tə-na-ñən   kəpəyay
      old.fem   woman   cold   have-ACT.FOC-2fem.sgBAS.VT   greeting
      '(You) old woman, are you cold, hello?'

This is similar to the way *hello* is employed in English to attract attention to something unusual. It points to the erosion of an ancient customary greeting, and goes together with the loss of the practice of 'blessing'. That this meaning of *kəpəyay* is not all that recent is reflected in the way it is translated in Farnsworth, M. (n.d.) ('an expression meaning hello, thank you, sorry'). The ironic use of *kəpəyay* is looked upon by Manambu purists as a sign of 'corrupting' the language.

There are no terms for 'thank you', or 'you are welcome'. And this perceived gap is readily filled with a Tok Pisin import *tenkyu*, or *tenkyu tru*. A special way of thanking someone is *nəma apau tenkyu* 'big(feminine) old(feminine) thankyou' (see §5.2.3). Traditional speakers prefer to say *yara kəp* (fine good.will) 'it is fine, my dear' or *ya:kya kəp* (OK good.will). The general 'goodwill' address term *kəp*, plural *kəpugw* 'my dear', stands apart from all other address terms—see §4.1.2, and examples 21.32a–c above on how it is used.

Another important term to do with etiquette is *excuse*—typically used when going in front of a big man or anyone one respects. *Plis* does not mean 'please'—rather, it is an ironic exclamation showing incredulity at something outrageous or strange. After having done something wrong one says *sori*. And the ubiquitous Tok Pisin *maski* is gradually replacing the traditional Manambu hortative *jau* 'let it be, don't worry, you may do it' (discussed in §13.2.2).

Despite all these Western imports, Manambu speech etiquette retains one—highly valued—traditional feature: the address terms, which typically accompany an appropriate kinship term, or a personal name.

21.5.4   How to address each other

Addressing each other in Manambu involves a variety of techniques, including kinship terms and personal names. In a society with a classificatory kinship system, everyone's relationship to everyone else is defined through kinship links—which may vary, given that many children are adopted, and thus may be called brothers and sisters when in fact they are not so by blood. For instance, Yuaneng addresses Yuamali's mother Lowai as *ma:m* 'elder sibling' because Yuaneng's father Lumawandem had adopted the young Lowai and treated her as his daughter. Every such instance has a story behind it: calculating kinship relationships to one another is part of day-to-day routine, with a lot of gossip involved.

Personal names are an object of value among the Manambu. The more names a person has, the richer, and more respected, they are. People are typically addressed by the main name (*apasə*, 'bone name'), and only on particular occasions by their other names (*səgliak*). The main name can be shortened: for instance, the full name *Yuamali-mæg* or *Yuamali-wæg* is often shortened to *Yuamali*, or simply to *Mali*. Most people also have a 'white man's' name (*wali sə*): such as Jacklyn, Pauline, Patricia, Paul, or James. Some, however, do not: Gemaj is one of these. And some do not like their white names: Damel, or Dameliway, let me know immediately that her white man's name, Leona, meant nothing to her. Some people are typically referred to by their white names: many call Badaibæg simply 'Paul'. This appears to reflect personal preferences, rather than any steadfast rule. Some children and teenagers, even if they are good speakers of Manambu, do not know their 'village name' (when asked what it was, some used to ask their parents, or even me—since I was supposed to 'keep track' of the language).

Disentangling the multitude of names can be quite a puzzle for an outsider. It took me a few days to work out that the lady who first introduced herself to me as Jacklyn is actually the same person as Mali, Yuamali, Yuamali-mæg, and Yuamali-wæg; that Patricia is also Walup or Yuawalup; that Rex prefers to be addressed as Kawidu or Kawi; and the now late Wimali often called herself Yabukwi. This is reminiscent of the multitude of variants and abbreviations of the same name which baffle Western readers of Russian novels—except that in the Manambu culture most names cannot be easily derived from one another. But this is not the full story as far as addressing people goes.

Linguistic knowledge is tantamount to material wealth among the Manambu (see §1.3). Being well versed in totemic names belonging to different clans, as well as personal names, is valued most of all. In day-to-day life, this knowledge is reflected in the correct and creative use of 'address terms' (*wayəpi*, *wa:y*), a typologically unusual subclass of nouns (see §4.1.2).

In the Manambu tradition, every clan possesses a set of terms for culturally important objects, alongside the clan's 'own' personal names. Natural objects, flora, and fauna are also divided between clans as their totems. The names of entities which belong to a particular clan are used for addressing and farewelling members of this clan (also see discussion in Harrison 1990a: 76–7). Examples were given in 4.5–6. An address term can be used as a mode of clan identification, as illustrated in T2.27: Sesawi asks Kamkudi what clan he belongs to, and Kamkudi replies 'I am brown snake, death adder': these are the totems of the clan group *Gla:gw*, to which the Vali:k clan founded by Kamkudi belongs.

In greeting and farewelling people, it is highly important to use the correct address terms which reflect the clan of the addressee (that is, the clan of their father): this is known as *wayəpi sə-* 'address.term call'. Mentioning an address term of their mother's clan is a sign of particular endearment and respect. The beginning of a conversation, or of a letter (as in 21.77), is more often than not accompanied by one or more address terms.

21.77 wun-a   ñamus   yara yabənay   kwa-na-ñən
      I-LK+fem.sg younger.sibling well Maliau.ADDR.FEM stay-ACT.FOC-2fem.sgBAS.VT
      'Are you OK, my younger sister, woman of Maliau clan?'

From the form of the greeting it is obvious that the person to whom it is addressed is a woman belonging to the Maliau clan (part of the *Wulwi-Ñawi* clan group: see Table 1.1). The same applies to a farewell:

21.78 yara ma:y   yabənay   makajəwi   ga:j   tapwuk
      well go.IMPV Maliau.ADDR.FEM Maliau.ADDR small.pelican hen
      'Off you go (goodbye), you woman of Maliau clan, daughter of a woman of Sablap clan'

The address forms here reflect the fact that the addressee is a woman belonging to the Maliau clan, but that her mother's clan is Sablap (part of the Nabul-Sablap clan group): since *ga:j* 'small pelican-like white bird' and *tapwuk* 'chicken' are the totems of this clan.

We saw in §4.1.2 that some of the address terms are words in Manambu. So, *bap* 'moon'—a totem of the Maliau, Ñakau, and other clans for the Wulwi-Ñawi group—is an address term for their members. *Wapi* 'bird' is an address term for the Nagudau subclan of the Wulwi-Ñawi group, and *wudəb* 'spirit, dead people' is the term for the Nabul clan, while *wa:m* 'white cockatoo' is used for the Wapanab, Makem, and Wargab clans of the Gla:gw clan group. The name of a clan itself can be used as an address term, as in *yimal* 'address term for someone from the Yimal clan'. The term *mana:b*—the denomination of the Manambu— appears in the address term *apwi mana:b*, for the Maliau clan. A compound can be used as an address term, e.g. *amnəbi* 'bow and arrow', for members of the Wapanab clan.

The address term *gəñap* used for members of the Yimal clan (Gla:gw clan group) is puzzling: this is the name of a bush people whom Manambu had exterminated in the past. Stories of the Gəñap wars are widespread (see their description by Harrison 1993: 67–9; some of them are reminiscent of the descriptions of the Gala: see Chapter 1). Harrison hypothesizes that the Gəñap could have been speakers of the Sawos language or some variant of it. These people are referred to as either *gəñap* or *gəñap-kwalap* (*kwalap* is the 'shadowy' equivalent of *gəñap*— see §22.3). We can recall, from Text 2, that a Gala man was adopted into one of the clans of the Gla:gw group. This clan group is associated with dark things and bush in general. It is perhaps no wonder that the term *gəña*, also used to refer to the original 'bush people', has been 'reused' as an address term for a clan group associated with bush, earth, and all things 'dark'.

Numerous address terms are not used for any other purpose—*apwi* 'address term for Sarak clan', to do with a totemic term for 'cassowary', is one such example. (We will see in §22.2.3 that *apwi* appears as a farewell term in Kwoma-Manambu pidgin (Bowden 1997), no doubt due to the fact that the Kwoma (*Kum*) are associated with cassowaries in the Manambu stories (as told by John Sepaywus).)

Other examples include *ñirvi*, *makajəwi* 'address terms for Maliau clan', *maguni* for Gla:gw clan group, *kaligab* for the Wapanab clan, and so on. The term *makati* is used to address members of Gla:gw clan group; this term also appears to be used to address women of the Maliau clan by members of the Gla:gw.

That is, successful communication is grounded in the knowledge of the addressee's and their family's clan membership. This knowledge comes naturally to most Manambu people—given the importance of one's paternal and maternal relatives—for bride price, mortuary payment, and various obligations. But being proficient in a variety of address forms is a highly valued asset.

The address forms are used by adults of all generations and religious affiliations (even devout Christians—many of whom condemn 'heretic customs' such as the mortuary payment— appreciate their use and knowledge). To get them wrong is shameful; and discussing the appropriate address forms for various clans is one of the favourite topics of conversation. In stories, address terms are used between protagonists of all sorts, including animals (e.g. turtles). The speakers use address terms when spontaneously talking to pet animals: for instance, a tree kangaroo (*yayi:b*), a totem of the Gla:gw clan group, was spontaneously addressed as *makati*— a member of the Gla:gw clan.

Address terms are just one aspect of the general principle which permeates the Manambu language, and culture—name ownership and multiple synonymy (see §1.3).

Besides owning their own, particular totems, each Manambu subclan 'owns' one or more special totemic names for culturally salient items, such as crocodile (general term *mu*), totemic trees and crotons (*kwalami*), stone (*kabak*), dog (*a:s*), slit drum (*ra:b*), spirit (*apawul*), totemic haze (*mali*), house (*wi*), ceremonial house (*kara:b*, *sa:y*), residential area (*yarəg*), spear (*væy*), ceremonial mound (*təpwi*), grass skirt (*kwa:r*), canoe (*val*), wind (*ma:r*), mountain (*nəbək*), food storing basket (*kəbi*), and many more. This creates multiple synonymy, restricted just to nouns. Not too many people know the full set of terms nowadays. The terms themselves are a potential matter for dispute ultimately resulting in name debates (*saki*). A full analysis and a list of these names is currently being compiled by Pauline Yuaneng Luma Laki, with the assistance of such knowledgeable elders as John Sepaywus (a major *səbək*, office holder of a ceremonial division in Avatip) and old ladies including Gemaj, Maguniway, Sawsəpali, and Walinəm. Going into the structure and ownership of these names (a potentially sensitive issue) lies beyond the scope of this grammar.

Name ownership goes hand in hand with ownership of landmarks and areas (*waːgw* 'area'). The term for 'owned valuable thing' is *jaːb*. For instance, the Ambunti mountain, which towers over the settlement itself and can be seen from Avatip on a fine day, is said to belong to the Ñakau clan. Yet its name in Manambu, Makəmawi, is said to have been bestowed upon it by the Yimal clan, as was explained to me:

21.79 Ñakau dəy-a-di   jaːp   Yimal saki-taka-da-l
       Ñakau they-LK-pl thing Yimal bestow.name-put-3plSUBJ.P-3fem.sgBAS.P

    'It (the Ambunti mountain) is the property of Ñakau clan, the Yimal clan bestowed the name (Makəmawi) onto it'

The name *Ambunti* is believed to be a name of a totemic ceremonial house, ultimately belonging to the Ñakau:

21.80 Ambunti karab-ə   saːd,   Ñakau dəy-a-di   nəbək
       Ambunti ceremonial.house-LK name+3masc.sgNOM Ñakau they-LK-pl mountain
       dəy-a-də   saːd
       they-LK-masc.sg name+3masc.sgNOM

    'Ambunti is a name of a ceremonial house, it is the name of a mountain belonging to the Ñakau'

Knowledge of the multitude of totemic names, synonyms, and address terms is affected by encroaching obsolescence. This is one of the signs of language endangerment, and culture loss, among the younger generation of the Manambu lamented by the older generation in their 'discourse of nostalgia'. We address this in the next chapter.

Genetic and Areal Relationships, and New Developments in the Language

We will discuss genetically inherited and areally diffused features of the Manambu lexicon and grammar, before addressing code-switching with Tok Pisin and English, and further new developments in the language.

22.1 MANAMBU AS A NDU LANGUAGE

All languages of the Ndu family show uniformity in their pronominal paradigms (see Appendix 22.1), and in a large part of their nominal and verbal lexicon. All the Ndu languages have cases for core and peripheral arguments. Verbal categories vary in their marking and semantics.

The Ndu languages are predominantly suffixing, with few prefixes, such as the imperative *a-*, and the causative-manipulative *kay-*, both attested in Manambu. They are strictly nominative-accusative, with pronominal cross-referencing for A/S recently evolved out of pronouns. Only Manambu and Gala cross-reference more than one argument. A reconstruction of Proto-Ndu phonology and morphology is in Aikhenvald (forthcoming b).

In terms of grammatical complexity and richness of forms, Manambu and Gala (or Ngala) exceed other Ndu languages. Gala is unusual in a number of further ways, such as the pronominal system (see below), pervasive prefixing, complex vowel system, and lack of prenasalization of stops. When, on my visit to the Swakap village, I first enquired after the name of the language, I was told that it was /gala duṕ/, and not /*ᵑgala/—the latter was condemned as a way the Manambu refer to this language. (We can recall, from §1.4.1, that the old enmities between the Gala and the Manambu dating back to the Gala wars are still alive in people's memories: the Avatip people recall recent hostile attacks by the Gala.)

Distinguishing two genders, roughly defined as 'masculine' and 'feminine', is a pervasive feature of the Ndu languages. In terms of its semantics, gender assignment is sex based for human referents. It is shape and size based for referents of other groups (see Chapter 5 above), at least in Manambu, Iatmul, and Gala. In the Yangoru dialect of Boiken, the assignment is based on size and also hardness or softness of the referent (hard objects, such as ironwood and hard-textured yam varieties, are assigned masculine gender and soft objects, such as soft tuber varieties, are female: Paul Roscoe, p.c.). Gender marking is overt in personal pronouns and in verbs, and covert in numerous other contexts (such as adjectival agreement).

Gender marking is uniform across the Ndu family. Cognates of the Manambu masculine singular *-d* (cf. masculine singular pronoun *də*) are found in Iatmul *di* 'he; 3masc.sg agreement marker', Hanga Kundi (West Wosera) *dé* 'personal pronoun; subject agreement suffix' (Wendel 1993: 59), Ambulas *dé* (Kundama, Wilson, and Sapai 1987) 'he', and Boiken (Yangoru) *də* (Freudenburg 1979).

TABLE 22.1   Personal pronouns in Gala compared with Manambu

PERSON/GENDER	SG		DU		PL	
	Gala	Manambu	Gala	Manambu	Gala	Manambu
1 masculine	*wun*	*wun*	*æn*	*an*	*nan*	*ñan*
1 feminine	*ñin*					
2 masculine	*min, mən*	*mən*	*bən*		*gun*	*gwur*
2 feminine	*yin*	*ñən*		*bər*		
3 masculine	*kəl, kər*	*də*	*(na)bəl*		*lar, lal*	*dəy*
3 feminine	*ki*	*lə*				

Note: Based on my notes 2004; correction of Laycock (1965: 133). In his list of Gala personal pronouns, Laycock erroneously interpreted second feminine form as having third feminine reference.

Cognates of the Manambu feminine singular *-l* are attested in Iatmul *li* 'she; 3fem.sg agreement marker', Hanga Kundi *lé* 'personal pronoun; subject agreement suffix' (Wendel 1993: 59), Ambulas *lé* 'she', and Boiken (Yangoru) *lə* (Laycock 1965). Also see Appendix 22.1.

A ø-marked feminine could be a Manambu-Gala innovation, cf. Gala *a* 'third person singular feminine bound pronoun' (Laycock 1965: 133), and third person feminine singular free pronoun *ki* 'she' as opposed to third person masculine singular *kəl, kər* 'he'.

Cognates to the Manambu second person masculine pronoun and agreement marker *mən* are found throughout the family. And so are the cognates to the Manambu second person feminine *ñən*. The only partial exception to this pattern is found in Gala—see Table 22.1. Personal pronouns in Manambu are added for comparison (repeated from Table 3.3).

A striking feature of this paradigm is the gender distinction in first person. The Proto-Ndu *ñən(ə)* 'second person singular feminine' was reinterpreted as first person singular feminine, and *yin* co-opted as second person feminine. The form *yin* is cognate with the second person feminine *yine* in Boiken (Freudenburg 1979; also see Aikhenvald forthcoming b). The third person pronoun contains the stem *kə-* cognate to the Ndu proximate demonstrative (e.g. Manambu *kə-*). The third person feminine form is formally less marked than the masculine form *kər/kəl*. The latter contains the masculine marker *-l* which is a regular correspondent of Proto-Ndu *d*, as in Manambu *du* versus Gala *lu* 'man'.

Manambu also shares a considerable amount of nominal, and of verbal, lexicon with other Ndu languages. Structural and formal similarities between Manambu and Iatmul may have been enhanced by constant contact (see below, §22.3, on the loans from Iatmul). A number of innovations are shared with the Abelam-Wosera group. We can recall, from §4.2.2, that Manambu shares the formal distinction and the marking of 'give to third person' and 'give to non-third person' with Abelam-Wosera. This distinction is absent from all other Ndu languages, and is not reconstructible for Proto-Ndu.

Historically, Manambu must have undergone a strong diffusional impact from non-Ndu sources (such as Kwoma—see §22.2.3). This may explain why it is morphologically more complex than most other Ndu languages. For instance, Manambu has more case forms, modalities, directionals, and negators than any other Ndu language. At the same time, certain morphemes

non-singular ⟶ dual 3rd person/2nd person (A;B)
      ↓   ↓
plural marker on kinship terms(C)   associative plural(D)

CHART 22.1   Putative semantic development of the polysemous morpheme *-bər* in Manambu

found in other Ndu languages have been lost in Manambu. We saw in §21.1.1 that the cognate of a nominalizing suffix *-va:k*, highly productive in Iatmul as a word class-changing device, and as a complementation strategy, survives in Manambu in just one formation: *kə-kə-pa:t* (eat-eat-DER) 'raw food' (see 20.58 and 20.65). Synchronically, this form is no longer segmentable.

Manambu underwent a number of phonological processes and mergers. We saw in §4.1.1 that Manambu lost the final vowels of Proto-Ndu disyllabic nouns whose final syllable ends in a stop. In each case, the lost vowel surfaces as the linker when a noun occurs with a case marker, or as a modifier (cf. *takwa:k* 'to woman', *ñəga:k* 'to leaf', etc.). Some of the forms Manambu shares with the unrelated Kwoma maintain the final vowel in at least one Kwoma dialect (Bangwis, documented by Bowden 1997: see §22.2.3). This may indicate that the early Kwoma–Manambu contact pre-dated the Manambu final vowel loss.

A number of Proto-Ndu distinctions in word-final stops are neutralized in Manambu. Not surprisingly, this has created numerous homonymous morphemes. Consider the suffix *-bər*, which has four meanings in Manambu:

(A) second person dual basic and subject cross-referencing marker (see Chapter 3);
(B) third person dual number agreement marker on agreeing modifiers (see Chapter 5) and in verbal basic and subject cross-referencing paradigms (see Chapter 3);
(C) plural marker on a limited number of kinship terms (see §6.1); and
(D) marker of associative non-singular with personal names only (see §6.1).

Synchronically speaking, this can be described as an instance of polysemy of a marker with a general meaning of 'non-singular'. An inventive analyst could invoke the widespread polysemy of second and third person dual marking in New Guinea languages (and elsewhere)—this would account for a link between (A) and (B).

Non-singular marking on a personal name often has an associative reading, as it does in English (e.g. *The Smiths*, understood as 'Smith and his associates', rather than ?'many Smiths': see Moravcsik 2003). And it is well known that nouns with high animate and human referents are more likely to be overtly marked for plural than nouns of other groups (see Smith-Stark 1974; Stebbins 1997; and Aikhenvald 2000). That is, (C) and (D) are also connected.

One can thus establish the semantic chain of Manambu-internal development for a putative 'non-singular' suffix *-bər* as in Chart 22.1.

However, cognates with other Ndu languages tell us a different story. The four synchronically distinguishable morphemes (A–D) with the phonological shape *-bər* go back to three distinct markers:

(A) *bər* '2du' goes back to Proto-Ndu **bən(e)* 'second person dual' (cf. Wosera *beni*, Abelam *béné*, Gala *ben* (Table 22.1 above) (also see Laycock 1965: 152); Iatmul *bit* (Staalsen n.d.b), *bi'k* (Jendraschek, p.c.), Boiken *ple* (Freudenburg 1979)) (just as Manambu *gwur* '2pl' corresponds to Wosera, Abelam *guni*, *guné*, Gala *gun*, Iatmul *guk*, Boiken *kle*, from Proto-Ndu **gun(e)*). (These correspondences are regular—see Aikhenvald forthcoming b.)

(B) *-bər* '3du; dual agreement marker' goes back to Proto-Ndu **bəd* (cf. Abelam *bét*, Wosera *ber* (also see Laycock 1965: 152), Gala *bəl*; Iatmul *bit* (Staalsen and Staalsen 1973), *bik*

(Jendraschek, p.c.), Boiken *ple*). The second–third person syncretism in dual forms is found in Iatmul, Manambu, and also in Boiken.

The morpheme **bən(e)* 'second person dual' could be further analysed into *-*bə*- 'dual' and *-*n(e)* 'second person'. Along similar lines, **gun(e)* 'second person plural' could be analysed as *-*gu*- 'plural' and *-*n(e)* 'second person'. The morpheme -*gu* 'plural' is found in restricted contexts, in Manambu -*Vgw* (see §6.1), and also in Wosera -*(n)gu*, Abelam -*gu* (Wilson 1980: 46), where it is restricted to kinship nouns.

This analysis presupposes that number marking is followed by person marking. This is indeed the case in Ndu, as can be seen from Manambu cross-referencing markers -*də-wun* (-masc.sg-1sg) 'first person singular basic set versatile tense', or -*di-gwur* (-pl-2pl) 'second person plural basic set versatile tense' (see further forms in Chapter 3). The morpheme **-bəd* 'third person dual' can be analysed as consisting of *-*be* 'dual' and -**d* 'third person'.

(C) -*bər* 'plural marker with kin terms' goes back to Proto-Ndu **-bere*, attested in Abelam -*béré* 'pluralizer' (Wilson 1980: 36). This marker also survives in irregular plural marker -*mbri* in West Wosera (Wendel 1993: 57–8: all examples are with kin terms).

It is likely to have developed an additional meaning (D), that of associative plural, when used with personal names. The development of a reflex of **-bere* into a marker of associative plural is attested in Abelam (Wilson 1980: 36). This is analogous to the way Manambu marks associative non-singular with -*bər* (and also consistent with typologically well-attested patterns of development of associative plural: Moravcsik 2003). In addition, this illustrates another shared innovation of both Manambu and Ambulas-Wosera.

This is an example of how the existing cognates can help trace the linguistic history of several markers, and disentangle the problem of polysemy and homonymy in Manambu from a historical perspective. In other cases, we are less lucky. The form *ata* in Manambu corresponds to five morphemes:

  (i)   question word 'how?' (near-synonyms: *ata ata*, *atəta*)—see §10.4;
  (ii) manner adverbial demonstrative 'thus' used for textual anaphora and cataphora, with a near-synonym *atawa*—see §10.2.2;
  (iii) a marker introducing a speech report—see §19.5;
  (iv) connective 'then, and then'—see §19.6; and
  (v)   negator for purposives and desideratives—see §14.3.2.

Meanings (ii)–(iv) can be linked together: in these three instances the marker *ata* can be seen as having a general sequential marker which acquires a special overtone when used in different constructions. However, *ata* can be in predicative focus (and then take the predicative marker -*n*) only when used as (ii) and (iv)—this may be indicative of synchronically different form–function correlations.

When used as a manner adverbial demonstrative, *ata* appears to contain the distal demonstrative *a*- and is in paradigmatic opposition to similar adverbial formations containing the proximal demonstrative *kə*- (see Table 10.6). This is indicative of the special status of *ata* in its meaning (ii).

Whether *ata* 'how' (meaning (i)) and *ata* 'thus' (meaning (ii)) are connected or not is an open question: a link between a manner interrogative and a manner demonstrative is tempting, but hard to prove.

And finally, can a plausible connection between functions (i)–(iv) and function (v) be established? Perhaps it can if a typologist allows their imagination to run wild. But this is hardly scientific. Unfortunately, comparative evidence from other Ndu languages provides little help.

A potential cognate for *ata* 'negator for purposives and desideratives' is Gala *woda*; however, this requires further study. We are thus left with a problem for which no adequate solution can at present be provided.

Negation in Manambu is particularly problematic for morphological reconstruction. The marking and wealth of forms are quite unusual for a Ndu language (see Chapter 14). In particular, the negator *ma:* (or its variant *ma:n*) has few easily identifiable cognates in other languages. One of these is *-man* in Iatmul subordinate negator *-lapman*; cf. also Gala *map* 'negative imperative'.

Most Ndu languages other than Manambu employ the formative *-ka-* as a negator (e.g. Gala *kafá* 'not, there is not'; Abelam *kaapuk* 'no, not', and Iatmul *kay* 'no'). We can recall, from §14.6, that Manambu has an inherently negative adverb *kapi sapi* 'no way' used as a negative response and a negative pro-clause. This could well be an alliterative compound based on the root *kapi* cognate to these negators (its variants are *sapi kapi* or just *kapi*). In addition, a proximate demonstrative *kə* in contrastive focus (*ka, kal* (DEM.PROX+3fem.sgNOM) or *kad* (DEM.PROX+3masc.sgNOM)) can be used as an emphatic negator, as in 10.24, 18.26, 14.41, and 14.148. Speakers consistently translate this as a demonstrative, but we cannot rule out that this form is in fact a remnant of a Proto-Ndu negator with a velar in the first syllable, ultimately cognate with *kapi*. Once again, we are faced with a puzzle.

As in most language families of the world, some parts of the lexicon and grammar are more stable than others. A particularly stable feature of Ndu languages is numbers: a form *na(k)* attested in Manambu and Gala *nə/na-* 'one' reconstructs to Proto-Ndu (see §10.6.1). So does number 'two'. Reflexes of Proto-Ndu *vət-* 'two' are found in every Ndu language.

In all the Ndu languages, number five contains the root for 'hand', *ta:ba*, accompanied by 'one', e.g. Abelam *nak-taba*, Wosera *na-tamba*, Iatmul *taba nak* (Gerd Jendraschek, p.c.), and Gala *nə wajan* 'one hand'. Manambu displays a slightly different pattern: the form *taba:b* 'five' consists of *taba-* 'hand+LK' accompanied by the formative *-a:b*, which could be cognate to *-ab* 'too', or to *-a:bab* 'all'. In the neighbouring Kwoma (Bowden 1997) numbers from five upwards contain a body part followed by *abo* 'all' (the number 'five' *yatii abo* in Kwoma translates as 'leg all'). The structure of 'five' in Manambu is likely to have been influenced by Kwoma. This takes us to areal diffusion patterns, and the question of the nature of similarities between Kwoma and Manambu.

22.2 DISCERNING THE EFFECTS OF LANGUAGE CONTACT: THE KWOMA–MANAMBU RELATIONSHIP

22.2.1 Linguistic diversity in the Sepik area of New Guinea

The extreme genetic diversity among the non-Austronesian languages in New Guinea, with numerous families interspersed with isolates, remains a puzzle for comparative linguists. Languages of New Guinea have suffered—perhaps, more than any other area in the world—at the hands of 'lumpers', with their attempts to put languages together into 'stocks', 'macro-stocks', 'micro-phyla', and 'macro-phyla' based on just a few lookalikes. Laycock and Z'graggen (1975) postulated their 'Sepik-Ramu phylum' based on a number of typological similarities, and a few dubious lexical similarities (including terms for 'child' and 'pig'), for which 'cognate' sets were not provided.

The Sepik River Basin (which includes East Sepik and Sandaun Provinces) is the most complex linguistic area within New Guinea. It contains about 200 languages, an extreme language density unparalleled anywhere else in the world. The Sepik River Basin displays cultural as well as linguistic diversity and fragmentation, perhaps more so than any other area of New Guinea. Reasons for this include geographic diversity, inaccessible terrains, patterns of language contact, and language attitudes (see Foley 1986, 1988: 167–8; Aikhenvald 2004b; Aikhenvald and Stebbins 2007), and also frequent migrations in search of further hunting and fishing grounds and sago fields (Paul Roscoe, p.c.). The average size of language communities is significantly lower than in the New Guinea Highlands.

Established families in the Sepik area include the Lower Sepik family, the Lower Ramu family, the Ndu family, the Sepik Hill family, the Ram family, and the Tama family (Aikhenvald and Stebbins 2007). An attempt has been made to establish genetic links between the latter four families, and other languages of the Sepik area, such as Wogamusin, Chenapian, Kwoma-Nukuma, Kwanga, and Abau (Foley 2000, 2005a), grouping them into a larger Sepik family. Though some similarities (including some in pronouns) appear suggestive, there are hardly any shared paradigms, or any regular correspondences.[1] Much more comparative analysis is required, including low-level reconstructions for individual language families, before any definitive conclusion can be reached.

A major problem with comparative linguistics in the New Guinea area is the misguided idea that any linguistic similarity should be indicative of a genetic link. This is not the case.

22.2.2 Motivations for linguistic similarities

What are the reasons for similarities between languages? Linguistic categories can be similar because they are universal—for instance, every language has some way of asking a question or framing a command. Occasionally, two languages share a form and meaning combination by pure coincidence. Goemai (Angas-Goemai subgroup of Chadic, Afroasiatic family: Birgit Hellwig, p.c.) and Manambu happen to use *a:s* for 'dog'. Kwoma, a neighbour of Manambu, has a similar form, *as(a)*—see below. And numerous languages of the world have a negator *ma:*, just like Manambu. Similarities due to universal properties of a language are of interest for general linguistics, while chance coincidences are no more than curious facts. These two kinds of similarities tell us nothing about the history of languages or their speakers. This is in contrast to other types of similarities: those due to genetic inheritance and those due to contact, and interactions thereof.

A shared feature may be based on common linguistic origin. The languages can then be shown to have descended from the same ancestor (this is achieved by using the rigorous procedures of historical and comparative linguistics). Aikhenvald (forthcoming b) is such a study for Ndu languages.[2]

It is known that related languages 'will pass through the same or strikingly similar phases': this 'parallelism in drift' (Sapir 1921: 171–2) accounts for additional similarities between related languages, even for those 'long disconnected'. This is another option for explaining why related languages share a feature—for instance, why the Proto-Ndu plural marker **bəd* developed a meaning of 'associative plural' in Manambu, and in Abelam-Wosera.

Alternatively, shared features may result from geographic proximity, contact, and borrowing. If two or more languages are in contact, with speakers of one language having some knowledge

---

[1] Readers should be warned that Foley's (2005a) lists of forms in Ndu languages are replete with errors, and, in consequence, the subsequent reconstructions require revision.

[2] Laycock's (1965) attempt at Proto-Ndu reconstruction is flawed, as it is based on scanty data.

of the other, they come to borrow linguistic features and forms of all kinds. The extent of this varies; but no feature is absolutely borrowing proof (see Aikhenvald 2006b).

Languages which are not in contact with each other may have borrowed the same form—or the same pattern—from some common source, or from different sources (see Tosco 2000 on the notion of shared substrata). The fact that numerous languages of the Sepik area share the term *yaki* for tobacco (Yimas *yaki*, Arafundi Pidgin *yaki*, Alamblak Pidgin *yagi* (Foley 2005b), Karawari, Awiyakay *yaki*) does not imply that they were in actual contact with Iatmul, the ultimate source for this form. The form *yaki* could have been borrowed into Yimas and Karawari independently from Iatmul-based pidgin(s) (given the importance of Iatmul as a trade language). Awiyakay may have borrowed this form from Karawari (Darja Hoenigman, p.c.), from a Iatmul-based pidgin, or from another, unidentifiable, source. Manambu has the same form, shared with Iatmul—and this could be either a common inheritance or, again, a loan from some shared source. (Also see Riesenfeld 1951, for another hypothesis.[3])

A commonality can be due to the interaction of all these features. An additional process may involve reinforcement, or lexico-grammatical accommodation, whereby a form existing in a language is adjusted to one found in a neighbouring language (Aikhenvald 2006b provides examples of such processes). One such instance could be the term for 'dog' in Manambu and in Kwoma. We return to this in §22.2.3.

Teasing apart similarities due to genetic inheritance and those due to borrowings of varied kinds is one of the hardest problems in comparative linguistics. As Dench (2001: 113–14) put it, 'it may not be possible to show conclusively for any particular innovation that it results from genetic inheritance rather than that it is motivated by contact with another language. If enough such cases occur, then the suspicion we might attach to any putative inherited innovation will mount and we should become increasingly sceptical of any suggested genetic classifications.' In Dench's words, 'we should leave open the possibility that all questions may turn out to be undecidable'. We will now turn to the putative connections between Manambu and Kwoma.

22.2.3   Manambu and Kwoma

We saw in §1.4 that Kwoma and Manambu must have been in contact for a few hundred years. No wonder that the two languages share numerous features. An important indicator of the intensity of contact between the Kwoma and the Manambu is a Kwoma–Manambu mixed 'lingua franca', illustrated by Bowden (1997: 337–8). This was 'occasionally used by Kwoma and Manambu speakers when communicating with each other for such purposes as arranging intervillage barter markets'. A few old people in the Manambu villages speak Kwoma (§1.4.1); but no one today appears to be familiar with the Kwoma–Manambu pidgin.

A text in Kwoma-Manambu pidgin provided by Bowden (1997: 338) is instructive in the way this mixed language is organized. The personal and demonstrative pronouns appear to be of Ndu origin (the forms could be Manambu or Iatmul). Some nouns are Manambu (such as *kami:* 'fish', a kind of trade goods supplied by the Manambu, the river people), and some are Iatmul (*gay* 'village'), while the verbs are mostly Kwoma. The verbs which are said to be Manambu have been adjusted to Kwoma phonology, and are only partly recognizable.

---

[3] Riesenfeld (1951: 90) suggests that the word for tobacco—Iatmul and Manambu *yaki*—could be 'a gradually corrupted derivation of the word *tobacco*'; he does not say exactly how. It appears that tobacco as a crop was indeed a European import (see arguments in Riesenfeld 1951: 90) which is corroborated by its lack of integration into the traditional rituals (also see Mead 1938; the practice of planting tobacco on the Sepik River, and its significance as a crop in the Malu village, was described by Behrmann 1922: 192–3).

TABLE 22.2   Subject pronouns in Kwoma

PERSON/NUMBER	FIRST PERSON	SECOND PERSON	THIRD PERSON
singular masculine ⎱ feminine ⎰	*ada, an*	***miita, mii*** *nija, **nicha, ni***	*riita, rii* *siita, sii*
dual	*sicha, si*	*kicha, ki*	*piiriita, piir*
plural	*nota, no*	***kwota, kwo***	*yecha, ye*

The pidgin appeared to employ the ubiquitous *ya:kya*, 'all right', from Manambu, and also an adjusted version of the Manambu expression *ma:j ma:* (talk NEG) 'there is nothing else to say' (cf. 21.31c) in the form of *maji* (Kwoma 'word, sentence, expression, statement': Bowden 1997: 113–14) *ma'a* (NEG, a Manambu form). The similarity between the Manambu form *ma:j* and the Kwoma *maji* could be due to borrowing whose direction is unknown. The pronunciation of the negator with a glottal stop rather than a long vowel indicates a somewhat archaic variety of Manambu (see §2.1.2 on the use of identical vowel sequences with glottal stop by older speakers, where younger speakers would use long vowels).

The greeting 'goodbye' at the end is particularly interesting: it contains the Manambu form *apwi* 'greeting for members of the Sarak clan' (whose totem is the cassowary which appears in Manambu stories as an animal from which the Kwoma had descended), and the conventional Manambu greeting *yaramay* (*yara* 'well', *ma:y* 'go.IMPV'), literally 'go well' (see §21.5.2, on the greetings and departure formulae in Manambu).

One thing is certain. Kwoma (which appears to form a separate small family with the closely related Nukuma) is not demonstrably related to Manambu. Consider the paradigm of subject pronouns in Kwoma (Kooyers 1974: 14) in Table 22.2.

The formatives in bold have a 'Ndu-like' feel to them. The second person masculine *m-* looks similar to the Proto-Ndu *mən(ə)* (see Appendix 22.1). Similar, but not identical—so we cannot exclude the possibility of a coincidence.

The formative *r-* in third person singular looks very similar to third person formative *-r-* in Gala (and we can recall that there was a considerable amount of contact, and conflict, between the Gala and the Kwoma prior to the Gala wars). Gala *-r-* in pronouns is a reflex of Proto-Ndu *-d-* (e.g. Manambu *də* 'he'). But as we will see below, in none of the numerous words Manambu and other Ndu languages 'share' with Kwoma does the Kwoma *r* correspond to *d* or *t*. So, again, this similarity in third person pronouns could be a mere coincidence. Along similar lines, the formative *kwo-* in second person plural is similar to the formative *gu-* in Proto-Ndu **gun(e)* (which is arguably an exponent of number and not of person: see §22.1 above).

Suggestive as these similarities may appear to be for those desperate to lump languages into 'stocks', they do not amount to much in terms of real evidence for genetic relationship. Importantly, there are no regular correspondences between Ndu and Kwoma, and no reconstructible paradigms. There are no further similarities in any inflectional or derivational morphology, or in any closed classes (interrogatives, demonstratives, or numbers).

There are, however, a few dozen forms shared by Manambu and Kwoma. Some of these may have been borrowed from Manambu into Kwoma, and some from Kwoma into Manambu. The absence of regular phonological correspondences between these suggests that either the borrowing took place at different times, or the similarities are due to pure coincidence.

We can recall, from the preceding section, that Manambu has lost the final vowels of nouns (which surface as a linker: see §4.1.1). The equivalents of the Manambu forms in the Bangwis dialect of Kwoma (Bowden 1997) often preserve the final vowel. The final vowel in Manambu (lost in citation forms and retrievable from the linker: see §4.1.1) is supplied in brackets.

An example of a potential borrowing from Manambu or from Iatmul into Kwoma is *tapa* 'arm (including hand), handprint, branch, wing of a bird' (Bowden 1997: 209); the Manambu form is *ta:b(a)* 'hand, arm', and the Iatmul form is *ta'ba* (Jendraschek 2007), from Proto-Ndu *ta:ba*.

Kwoma *me* 'tree, wood, plank of wood, wood carving, hollow log, slit drum' (Bowden 1997: 125) is likely to be borrowed from Manambu *mi* 'tree, wood, stick, upward direction', or, more likely, from Iatmul *mi* 'tree, stick, wood, slit drum' (Proto-Ndu *mi:*; the Manambu term does not mean 'slit drum').

Manambu *ta:m(a)* 'nose, edge' (possibly Proto-Ndu *ta:ma*) is a likely source for Kwoma *tam* 'outer edge or periphery' (Bowden 1997: 208). That this is a loan from Manambu and not from any other Ndu language (e.g. Iatmul *dama*, Gala *domo* 'nose') is corroborated by the absence of the final vowel in Kwoma. Further examples are in Aikhenvald (forthcoming i).

Further potential loans in Kwoma from Manambu or from Iatmul (for which reconstructions are not available, but some of which have a cognate in Abelam-Wosera) include Manambu *jub, jəb* 'design, drawing, letter, painting' (cf. Iatmul *ji'vwa*, Abelam *jébaa* 'work'), Kwoma *jebwa* 'design' (Bowden 1997: 78); Manambu *yayi:b* 'tree kangaroo' (cf. Wosera *yepiné* 'tree kangaroo'), Kwoma *yobo* 'tree kangaroo' (Bowden 1997: 259), and a few others.

The Kwoma noun *mayira* 'object of ritual or cultural significance given by one tribe to another in exchange for a similar object for the purpose of cementing peace between the two groups' (Bowden 1997: 124–5) could be a loan from Manambu *Mayir(a)* 'powerful spirit' (cf. Abelam *mayéra* 'carved figure'; whether this term goes back to Proto-Ndu or not requires further study). The Kwoma form *apokibi* 'flying fox' (Bowden 1997: 13) may consist of *apo* 'bird' and *kibi* 'flying fox', the latter suspiciously similar to Manambu *kəbwi* (also attested in some sources for the Tambunum dialect of Iatmul (Roesicke 1914)), and the former similar to Manambu *wapi*, Gala *apwi* 'bird'.

The quantifier *aba:b* 'all' in Manambu is suspiciously similar to Kwoma *abo* 'all' (Bowden 1997: 1; Kooyers 1974: 19). Both forms appear in the word for 'five' (whose structure is 'body.part-all': see §10.6.1).

A number of words could be borrowings from Kwoma into Manambu since they are not attested in any other Ndu languages. These include:

- Manambu *mu* 'crocodile', Kwoma *mo* 'crocodile' (Bowden 1997: 135);
- Manambu *kara:b(ə)* 'ceremonial house', Kwoma *korobo* 'ceremonial house' (Bowden 1997: 96–7);
- Manambu *Yabunay* 'address term for a woman from Maliau clan, a term for the Iatmul', Kwoma *Yabunay* 'term for the Iatmul' (Bowden 1997: 243);
- Manambu *ma:j(i)* 'word, talk, speech, story', Kwoma *maji* 'word, sentence, expression, statement' (Bowden 1997: 113–14);
- Manambu *apwi* 'address term for members of Sarak clan, including the Kwoma people', Kwoma *apo* 'greeting' (Angela Filer, p.c.).

Kwoma *asa* 'dog' (Bowden 1997: 15) is very similar to Manambu *a:s(a)*. The form *waasa* for 'dog' is found in Abelam; it appears to be cognate with Manambu *a:s(a)*. However, the loss of *w* in Manambu is irregular. The form *asa* in Kwoma looks suspiciously similar: we can hypothesize that Manambu may have had a form *was(a)* which was later 'adjusted' to the form in Kwoma.

Further lookalikes include Manambu *taka-* 'put' and Kwoma *taka* 'bandage, dress a wound, opening', Manambu *gu* 'water' and Kwoma *uku* 'water', Manambu *gwa:m* 'earthworm' and Kwoma *gwoyibi* 'earthworm', Manambu *tə-* 'stand, be' and Kwoma *ta-* 'be' (Kooyers 1974: 65). These numerous similarities and the potential lexical loans exemplified above are indicative of intensive language contact—but cannot be used to demonstrate any kind of genetic relationship.

Kwoma and Manambu share a number of structural features indicative of diffusion of patterns, alongside diffusion of forms. These include the similative *-ga* 'like' reminiscent of Manambu *-pək* 'like' (see §9.2), and the form 'back and forth' used for reciprocal (Bowden 1997: 16–17; note that the form itself, *awasen*, is somewhat similar to Manambu *awarwa* 'reciprocal, back and forth', Iatmul *awat*: Staalsen and Staalsen 1973: A.7). In addition, Manambu shares two features of speech report constructions with Kwoma, rather than with Ndu languages. These are the use of anaphoric 'thus' (Manambu *ata*, Kwoma *eecha*: Kooyers 1974: 59) to introduce a speech report, and indirect speech reports used in reported commands (see §19.5.3 for Manambu and Kooyers 1974: 60 for Kwoma).

22.3   LOANS FROM WESTERN IATMUL AND ELSEWHERE

Manambu and Western Iatmul, or Nyaura, have been in contact for a long period of time (see Harrison 1990a, 1993; Bragge 1990; and a summary in Chapter 1). The fact that they share numerous structural similarities can be explained as a consequence of genetic inheritance. One cannot exclude a 'parallelism in drift' characteristic of genetically related languages, or a contact-induced change—see §22.2.2.

The most salient structural similarities between Western Iatmul and Manambu include (see Jendraschek 2006a, 2006b):

- grammaticalization of *tika* (from *ti-* 'stay' and *-ka* 'sequencing') as a clause linker 'because' (see §19.6, on *təku* (*tə-* 'stand, be', *-ku* 'completive same subject') as part of a newly formed connective 'this is why');
- the use of *agiyabak* 'that's all' to signal the end of one clause within a sequence, similar to *ya:kya* clauses (§20.4.2);
- the structure and often the form of various lexicalized complex predicates, e.g. Iatmul *sudu kwa-* (sleep lie-), Manambu *sə kwa-* (sleep stay-) 'sleep'; Iatmul *gu yaku-*, Manambu *gu yaaku-* (water wash-) 'wash';
- different negation patterns for main clause predicates (*ana* in Iatmul, *ma:(n)*, *akəs*, or *ata* in Manambu: see §14.1–3) and for dependent clauses (*-lapman* in Iatmul, *-ma:r-* in Manambu: see §14.5);
- polysemous speech reports referring to reason, intention, desire, etc. (see §19.5.6);
- contrastive focus constructions involving copula clauses—see Jendraschek (2006b) and §20.3.

In addition to shared structural features, Manambu has a few lexical loans from Iatmul. The Manambu, similarly to many other Sepik groups, have an overwhelmingly 'importing culture'. This implies an emphasis on exchange and value assigned to outside goods, both material and non-material (Mead 1938). In many Sepik societies, language was traditionally considered on a par with material goods—spells, incantations, and even names and individual words being traded and bought (see Harrison 1990a: 20–3).

In Harrison's (1990a: 20) words, 'from an historical perspective, the circulation of ritual forms in the regional trading system seems to have been a key formative influence on Manambu society . . . , because the most valued scarce resources among the Manambu, and the items of strategic prestige value in the political system of their villages, were rights in ritual property, much of which the Manambu acquired from the Iatmul. Manambu ritual and cosmology seem, in fact, to be not only a kind of patchwork of the ritual and cosmological traditions of neighbouring societies, but a largely *bought* patchwork, acquired piecemeal through trade.' Trading ownership of names and cults is a feature of numerous Sepik cultures—including the Kwoma (Bowden 1983: 67), the Abelam, and the Iatmul (Bateson 1958).

These 'acquisitions' used to surface in various speech styles, many of them effectively lost in modern days. Harrison (1990a: 78) reports that shamanic spirits used to speak 'through their human mediums in a special, arcane language, intelligible only to those with many years of experience of shamanic séances, which is actually a kind of Manambu-based jargon with exaggerated *outré* Iatmul features'. Harrison stresses that in Manambu, 'all specifically "religious" forms of speech borrow heavily from Western Iatmul'. We will see, in §22.6.1, that due to the encroaching influence of Western culture (including the virtual obsolescence of initiation) most of the religious registers are rapidly falling into oblivion, and with them the 'Iatmulized' forms of speech.

Some Iatmul imports are still actively used in poetic register, and are identified by speakers themselves as being originally Iatmul. The songs of foiled marriages and love affairs, known as *namay* and *sui*, and also mourning songs (*gra-kudi*) are a case in point. These poetic literary forms (improvised by performers) consist of two parallel stanzas, each referred to either as *apək* 'side, part', or *agək* 'side, counterpart (one of two)'. Such songs typically consist of a string of not-too-complex sentences interspersed with totemic address terms and names (often relating to the clan of the addressee or the 'character' of the song). The second stanza restates the first one in different wording using what the Manambu speakers call 'shadowy' register, or 'the other side' (*agəkem* 'on the (other) side of two'). This reflects the binarism, or 'parallelism', a pervasive feature of the Sepik culture—in Bateson's (1958: 239) words, 'the idea that everything in the world has its equal and opposite counterpart' (also see Harrison 1983: 20, on binarism in the song styles).

While *gra-kudi*, the mourning songs, are the prerogative of women (typically, old and knowledgeable ones), *namay* and *sui* can be sung by both men and women. Harrison (1983) put together a collection of *namay* sung by men (also see his comment on the role of mythological setting and secret knowledge in the creation of *namay*). Women also compose *namay* and *sui*, and sing them—traditionally, on women-only fishing expeditions or anywhere where men would not be able to overhear them. I recorded over twenty *namay* sung by women (most of them over 50); but was told not to share them with anyone since they discuss the foiled loves, suitors, and nostalgic feelings for men other than their husbands, and if I disclosed them, this might get these women into trouble.

My estimate is that the 'other side' register may have traditionally contained several hundred words. At present, few people have complete knowledge of it. A number of kinship terms and items from other semantic groups have a 'shadowy' equivalent, while most do not. The kin terms which are the same in both 'sides' include *gwa:l* 'father's father', *yæ:y* 'father's mother' (similarly to the 'Mother-in-law' language in some Australian languages: Dixon 1990), *kagrəs* 'son's wife', and *kajal* 'brother's wife', as well as numerous body part terms, such as *məl* 'eye', and verbs, e.g. *vækər* 'fall', *və-* 'see'. Many clan address names have a shadowy equivalent—for instance, the equivalent of *gəñap* 'address term for Yimal clan' is *kwalap*.

Table 22.3 illustrates a sample of words which have an equivalent in the 'other side' (or 'shadowy') register. Loans from Iatmul—shown in bold—include five kinship terms and one body part term. The kinship terms—all except one of which (*waw*) were recognized by the authors of the songs as being Iatmul imports—have the same meaning in Manambu as in Iatmul.

The body part term *da:m* 'nose' in the 'shadowy' register is a Iatmul form adapted to Manambu (the real Iatmul form is *da:ma*, cf. the Manambu form *ta:m* 'nose'; most probably Proto-Ndu *da:ma 'nose'). The term *da:m* is used as the equivalent of another body part, 'ear'.

And this takes us to at least three principles discernible for the correspondences between 'everyday' items and their 'shadowy' counterparts. First, the choice of a 'shadowy' counterpart may involve the opposite—as is the case for 'hand, arm' and 'foot, leg'; and also 'fingers' and 'toes' (these are switched). This is somewhat reminiscent of the 'upside-down Warlbiri', 'spoken by guardians in the presence of junior novices', that is, by initiated men in the Warlbiri men's rituals (Hale 1971: 473). The principle of the 'upside-down Warlbiri' is: 'replace each noun, verb and pronoun of ordinary Warlbiri by an "antonym".'

Secondly, a distinction in the everyday terms may be neutralized in the 'shadowy' register— as is the case for 'sun' and 'moon' (from a mythological, or totemic, point of view this makes sense inasmuch as 'sun' and 'moon' are totems of the same clan group). And finally, a more general term may be used to subsume a more specific one—this is the case with 'child, youngster (a term also used for uninitiated men)' and 'young (person) in general', and perhaps also 'nose' and 'face' (as its generic location).

In the limited data available, verbs seem to be replaced by other verbs, with somewhat similar meanings (see the last three rows in Table 22.3).

If only a part of a word has a counterpart in the 'shadowy' register, and the other part does not, then only the first part will change. Many of the names of the Maliau clan start with *Yu-a* (shell.valuable-LK); their shadowy counterparts start with *Rama* (see Table 22.3), e.g. the names *Yua-nəg*—shadowy register *Rama-nəg*; *Yua-muk*—shadowy register *Rama-muk*. (*Yu* as an object is a totem of the Maliau clan; the origin of *Ram(a)* is unknown.)

Little more can be said at this stage about the semantics and the forms in the 'shadowy' register. An additional complication lies in the nature of the knowledge associated with this register: an outsider's attempts to gain unjustified knowledge of this run the danger of being treated as attempts to unlawfully appropriate a valuable. And in addition, fewer and fewer people still have this knowledge.

There is little evidence of loans into Manambu from other Ndu sources. The only loan from Abelam-Wosera is the mixed origin term *gai-du*, *gai-ta:kw* 'address term for the Abelam people, or the people of the Maprik area'. This consists of an adjusted version of Abelam-Wosera *gayé* 'village' and Manambu *du* 'man', *ta:kw* 'woman'. An alternative is simply *gai*. The Abelam-Wosera people do not figure among the traditional trade partners of any of the Manambu clans (the major partners include the Chambri, the Sawos, the Iatmul, the Kaunga, the Kwoma, the Yessan-Mayo, and the Yerikai-Garamambu: see Harrison 1990a: 23, 70–2). Yet, there is an ongoing trade relationship between the Abelam-Wosera and the Manambu: even nowadays, the Manambu women routinely go to Maprik to sell their dried fish to the locals who pay them with stringbags, other goods, and money. According to my consultants, these trade links are of a considerable antiquity. This explains the existence of a special address term for the Abelam-Wosera.

The term *Ñaura*, *Ñaula* used by the Manambu for the Iatmul in general comes from Iatmul itself (it is an autodenomination of the Western Iatmul), and the term *Kum* for the Kwoma is a loan from the Kwoma autodenomination *kwow ma* 'hill people' (Bowden 1997: xv, 105).

Table 22.3 'The other side' lexicon in Manambu: a sample

Everyday use	Meaning	'Other side' counterpart	Origin
ñab	Sepik River	*təmgun*	—
amæy	mother	***ñaməy***	**Iatmul**
asay	father	***ñas***	**Iatmul**
ma:m	elder sibling	***ñamun***	**Iatmul**
ñamus	younger sibling	***suab***	**Iatmul**
ñan	child, youngster	*badi* 'young'	Manambu
away	maternal uncle	***wau***	**Iatmul**
ñə	sun, day	*ba:p*	Manambu
ba:p	moon		
gu	water, river	*ka:r*	?
nab	Sepik River	*gubi* 'be wet; wet area'	Manambu
sual	story, lie	*kama:l*	?
ta:m	nose	*muta:m* 'face'	Manambu
ta:b	hand, arm	*ma:n* 'foot, leg'	Manambu
ma:n	foot, leg	*ta:b* 'hand, arm'	Manambu
jigərta:b	finger	*jigərma:n* 'toe'	Manambu
jigərma:n	toe	*jigərta:b* 'finger'	Manambu
mu	crocodile	*rukwi*	?
yu	valuable	*ra:m*	?
wa:n taka-	listen (ear put)	***da:m*** *taka-* (nose:Iatmul put: Manambu)	**Iatmul**/Manambu
vætəka-n	putting upright	*tau-n tə-na-d* 'putting up (e.g. post) he stands'	Manambu
sarən	jumping	*pəkən* 'getting up'	Manambu
væsən	walking, stepping	*wapan* 'leaving'	Manambu

An alternative term for the Kwoma is *Apo*, an address form in Kwoma also used as a greeting (Bowden 1997: 12–13).

There is no evidence for any other loans, except for a few curious similarities with Oceanic. One such similarity is the Manambu irregular imperatives of the verb *ya-* 'come', *mæy*, and of the verb *yi-* 'go', *ma:y* (see Table 13.2). The form *mæy* 'come' looks very much like Proto-Oceanic **mai* 'come' (see, for instance, Lynch, Ross, and Crowley 2002: 47). Could this be a borrowing, or is it a simple coincidence? A potential cognate to either *mæy* or *ma:y* is the Abelam imperative marker *mé* (Wilson 1980: 165), which does not preclude the possibility of the form being borrowed from coastal Oceanic languages in northern New Guinea. And we can recall, from §1.5.3, that at least one clan group of the Manambu claims to have come from the coast.

The term for 'dog', *a:s(a)*, is especially intriguing in light of this. It bears a similarity to Proto-Austronesian **asu* 'dog', reconstructed on the basis of reflexes in the languages of Taiwan, the Philippines, western Indonesia, and others, but hitherto unattested in any Oceanic language with which a Papuan language could have come in contact. A number of Oceanic languages of Bougainville have a form for 'dog' reconstructible as ***kasu*; however, positing a reconstruction higher than Proto-North-Bougainville appears to be dubious (Andrew Pawley, p.c.). The dog was introduced to New Guinea through coastal areas, and perhaps through maritime coastal trade into the Sepik-Ramu area, and the date given is circa 5500 BC. The archaeological data indicate that the introduction of the dog in New Guinea may have been consistent with the Lapita/Austronesian culture (Jack Golson, p.c.). If the dog was indeed introduced by Austronesians in the coastal areas, and then spread further inland, it would not be surprising that the name for dog could have been of Austronesian descent. The word *wa:sa* 'dog' in Abelam may indicate that if the term for 'dog' was indeed borrowed, the borrowing could have occurred at the Proto-Ndu stage. This, however, is pure speculation.

Manambu (and other Ndu languages) have a number of further lookalikes with Oceanic and Austronesian. Proto-Oceanic **manuk* 'bird' (with its variants *manu*, *ma:n*, or *ma:n* in coastal New Guinea languages: Andrew Pawley, p.c.) is similar to Manambu *ma:n*, Iatmul *ma:n*, and Kwoma *manu* 'bird of paradise'. And Proto-Oceanic **taw* 'man' could be compared to the Proto-Ndu **du(e)* 'man, male' (cf. Boiken *tuo* 'man' which earned Boiken the name *Tuo-language* by Kirschbaum 1922). However, these are likely to be mere coincidences.

Curious 'foreign language' insertions occur in the stories which comprise my Manambu corpus. Gemaj, a highly qualified story teller, quoted an evil character who, according to her, was speaking 'dry-land man's language' (*nəbə-du kudi wa:d* dry.land-man language speak+3masc.sgBAS.P). Examples 22.1 and 22.2 come from essentially the same story told on two different occasions. Insertions in the unidentified language are in italics.

22.1 wus *sakura-məni*, au wus *sakura-wəni* nəb-ə   du kudi   wus
     pee ?-2masc.sg? ?   pee ?-1sg   dry.land-LK man language pee
     yi-k-na-dəmənək,   ayey, yi-k-na-dəwunək   gwarabi
     go-FUT-ACT.FOC-2masc.sgBAS.VT yes go-FUT-ACT.FOC-1masc.sgBAS.VT mango
     sakura-məni sakura-wəni atawada   ata wa-yi-d   wa-yin
     ?-2masc.sg? ?-1sg?   thus+ONLY then say-go-3masc.sgBAS.P say-go+SEQ
     wa-yin   wa-yin
     say-go+SEQ say-go+SEQ
     ' "*You will go to* pee, *yes, I will go to* pee", dry-land man's language: "you will go to pee, yes, I will go to pee", "*to get* mango *you will go, to get* mango *I will go*". Just like that he went on talking, talking, talking, talking'

In 22.2, the character of the story engages in a dialogue with the stranger speaking a strange language. The form *sakurawəni* was again explained as 'dry-land man's language'. In this example, the stranger uses the Manambu *ayey* 'yes' rather than *au* as in 22.1.

22.2 [atawa tə-də-kəkəb]   [ada   yi-ta:y
      thus   stand-3masc.sg-AS.SOON.AS DEM.DIST.REACT.TOP+masc.sg go-COTEMP
      wusa:k]   [wun wus-a:k   wula-kə-na-dəwun]   [wus
      pee+LK+DAT I   pee-LK+DAT enter-FUT-ACT.FOC-1masc.sgBAS.VT pee
      sakura-məni?] [ayey, *sakura-wəni*] [ada
      ?-2masc.sg   yes   ?-1sg   DEM.DIST.REACT.TOP+masc.sg
      yi-na-d]
      go-ACT.FOC-3masc.sgBAS.VT
      'As soon as he stayed like this, as he'd gone inside (the bush) to have a pee, (he said), "I am going inside the jungle to have a pee, *are you going* for a pee? Yes, *I am going*"'

So far, I haven't been able to identify these inserts. It is obvious that they come from the same language. Judging by the person marking, it appears to be a Ndu language (but not Gala). The obvious source is Kaunga (the closest 'dry-land people' who speak a Ndu language: see Harrison 1993: 33–4 on the Manambu–Kaunga relations). This needs to be verified when more Kaunga data become available.

It is possible that some examples of 'animal talk' are in fact insertions from other languages, e.g. *sakatelo* 'sound made by man transformed into a victoria pigeon'.

Very few grammatical descriptions, and dictionaries, are as yet available for most languages of the Sepik area. At the present time, we have many more questions than answers as to why some of the Sepik languages share rather unusual, 'exotic' features. Can it be a simple coincidence that shape-based gender assignment is attested in Ndu languages, and in Alamblak and Sare, or Kapriman (both Sepik Hill) (Bruce 1984; Sumbuk 1999)? And that the unusual patterns of cross-referencing in Manambu (§3.1) are so strikingly similar to those in Alamblak? What is the nature of the areal diffusion of patterns within the Sepik area? These questions are undecidable—until well-founded facts can be provided.

Nowadays, the major agents of foreign influence on Manambu are Tok Pisin and English, the two lingua francas of Papua New Guinea as a whole.

22.4 INFLUENCE OF TOK PISIN AND OF ENGLISH: BORROWING AND CODE-SWITCHING

At present, all the Manambu people are proficient in Tok Pisin: there are no Manambu monolinguals. As mentioned in Chapter 1, just a few old ladies are more comfortable speaking Manambu than Tok Pisin. I was told that two children in Avatip (one 4, one 6 years of age, in 2004) speak nothing but Manambu; but no one seemed to know exactly where they lived, or how to find them. Schooling is conducted in Papua New Guinea English (see §1.4.2 on the incipient Manambu 'tok ples' programmes in primary schools in Yawabak and Avatip). The result is not really a balanced triglossia: Tok Pisin and English tend to dominate many domains, such as village council, churches, and parent–teacher meetings. The latter is not so surprising given that of a dozen or so teachers at the Avatip school, two or three are usually not Manambu, and even those teachers who are Manambu prefer communicating in English or Tok Pisin to make sure they do not exclude the outsiders or those children whose Manambu is halting.

Even the meetings accompanying the mortuary ritual *Kəkətəp* involve a large amount of interaction in Tok Pisin. This is to do with their major topic which concerns the distribution of material wealth between the parties and power relationships in general. The powerful 'big' men (*numa-də du*) intersperse their speech with Tok Pisin inserts, even during the name debate ceremony. We will see below that Tok Pisin and, even more so, English are the languages of authority. This, and also the fact that men are exposed to the outside world more than women, explains why men of all generations code-switch more than women.

The encroaching dominance of Tok Pisin is speeded up by the number of outsiders living in the villages, especially in Avatip, mostly as the result of mixed marriages. A few non-Manambu women do speak the language (for instance, Nelma, Iatmul herself, is a very proficient speaker; and so is Jagər, Yuamali (Jacklyn's) husband), but even they often communicate with their children in Tok Pisin.

We start with the status of Tok Pisin and English 'inserts' as borrowings, or code-switches (§22.4.1), and then look at their morphological and syntactic integration into the language (§22.4.2). We also mention the issue of syntactic calques in Manambu. Then, in §22.4.3, we discuss the functions of these 'inserts'.

22.4.1   Borrowings or code-switches?

Distinguishing code-switches and borrowings in Manambu presents a problem.

Borrowings and code-switches are usually considered extremes on a continuum (see the glossary in Aikhenvald and Dixon 2006). They can be potentially distinguished by (i) frequency of occurrence (code-switches are often one-off occurrences); (ii) phonological integration; (iii) morpho-syntactic integration; and (iv) a number of lexical criteria:

(a) Does an equivalent exist in the other language?
(b) If so, is it in use in the community?
(c) Is the equivalent known to the speaker?
(d) To which language does the individual regard the word as belonging?
(e) Is it in use by monolingual speakers?

Most Tok Pisin insertions are high in frequency. There are no monolinguals in Manambu, and most 'inserts' can be provided with a Manambu equivalent. Even ad hoc and one-off occurrences of Tok Pisin—and of Papua New Guinea English—words tend to be phonologically and morphosyntactically integrated.

The absence of full phonological integration may provide a partial clue. The phoneme *f*, shared by Tok Pisin and PNG English but absent from Manambu, is realized either as *f* or as *p*; the two are in free variation, as in *faivpela du, paipela, faipela du* (five:TP man) 'five men'. The English *tʃ* appears in code-switches as a foreign import, as in *tatʃi-tukwa* (touch-PROH.GEN) 'don't touch!' Borrowings and code-switches may contain consonant clusters absent from Manambu, e.g. *faivpela* 'five:TP', *intrestin tə-na* (interesting:E stand/be-ACT.FOC+3fem.sgBAS.VT) 'it is interesting', and the vowel *e*. Loans and code-switches may display variability atypical of Manambu forms: for instance Tok Pisin loan, or code-switch, *sekan* 'shake hands' is often pronounced in a somewhat Anglicized way *sekhan*. However, all these can be considered tokens of loan phonology in Manambu. Borrowings, and code-switches, may also present a problem in terms of how they are assigned to word classes—see §22.4.2, and §4.5.6.

Here is an example of how an ad hoc English import can quickly become morphologically integrated. At the start of a whole-night working session with John Sepaywus, Pauline Yuaneng

Laki presented him with a lengthy list of totemic terms for various important objects she had previously compiled (see the end of §21.5.3). She then asked me, in English, to 'tick' the forms she had got right as we would go through each of them one by one. John Sepaywus tuned in immediately, and, whenever the term was right, kept telling me *a-tik* (IMPV-tick) 'tick (it)'. No one in the Manambu community used this verb in their Manambu before or after. So, this could be considered a one-off code-switch—yet it was highly morphologically integrated. And that night it exceeded any other verb in its frequency.

Other foreign imports are more frequent than *tik-*, but less morphologically integrated. For instance, some never occur with the imperative prefix: one says *sekan*, or *sekhan* 'shake hands!', but never **a-sekan*, or **a-sekhan*—yet this is the term spontaneously used by most people (see §21.5.3 on its Manambu equivalents). Alternatively, *sekhan* could be considered an interjection, or an unsegmentable one-word command.

The only bona fide borrowings could be the ones for which there is no Manambu equivalent, and which are considered part of the language by at least some speakers. The problem is that speakers vary in their judgements. Consider the term for 'peanuts', nowadays a major cash crop for Manambu women. I asked one highly proficient speaker how to say 'peanut' in Manambu. Her response was *kasan*—which is one of the two Tok Pisin terms for 'peanut'. Her husband, one of the Manambu 'purists' (we return to this in §22.6), told her off for using a Tok Pisin import; what he suggested instead was *galip*—which is also a loan from Tok Pisin *galip* 'peanut'. He did not seem to be aware of the Tok Pisin provenance for this word.

The expression *mən-a waya:m* (you.masc-LK+fem.sg *way*+LK+LOC) '(let it be done in) your way' was considered good enough Manambu by one speaker; where another one rejected it as a blatant foreignism (he suggested *mən-a-rəb* (you.masc-LK-FULLY) instead). Both speakers rejected *laiki-* as a term for 'like' as an obvious Tok Pisin form (*laikim*), suggesting *mawul kwa-na* (inside stay-ACT.FOC+3fem.sgBAS.VT, lit. inside stay), or *məyakw kwa-na* instead. The fact remains that *laiki-* is used very frequently by all generations of speakers, even by those whose Tok Pisin is not 100 per cent.

These examples show that Tok Pisin and English code-switches and borrowings in Manambu form a hard-to-parse continuum. Borrowings and code-switches span all the open and semi-open word classes. They include:

- nouns, e.g. *ailan* (T1.11), *ailand* (T1.10) 'island', *mani* 'money' (21.4), *bus* 'bush' (T1.21), *stori* 'story' (21.37), *taim* 'time' (T2.54), *pas* 'letter' in 22.6, and *taul* 'towel' and *beg* 'bag' in 22.32a, c;
- non-agreeing adjectives, e.g. colour adjectives *grin* 'green', *blu* 'blue', dimension adjectives such as *liklik* 'small', *bigpela* 'big', physical property adjectives, such as *strongpela* 'strong', and indefinite adjective *sampela* 'some';
- adverbs, e.g. *hariap* 'quickly', from Tok Pisin *hariap* 'quickly', *olsem* 'thus, like this', from Tok Pisin *olsem* 'thus', *ken* 'again', from Tok Pisin *ken* 'again', the negator *nogat* 'no, this is not the case', from Tok Pisin *nogat* 'there is not';
- numerals, e.g. *wanpela* 'one', *tupela*, *tu* 'two' (also see T2.21);
- quantifiers, e.g. *planti* 'plenty', from Tok Pisin *planti* (22.36);
- conjunctions, e.g. *sapos* 'if, suppose', from Tok Pisin *sapos* 'if' (22.8) and *tasol* 'only, contrastive linker', from Tok Pisin *tasol* 'only, but' (T2.3, 22.7), *o* 'or' (T2.50), and even clause-chaining markers *nau* 'then, as soon as' (Tok Pisin *nau* 'then') and *pinis* 'completive' (Tok Pisin *pinis* 'completive aspect marker').

We now turn to the morphological and syntactic integration of such forms.

22.4.2   Morphological and syntactic integration of Tok Pisin and English code-switches and calques

Foreign nouns and other non-verbs often occur in their root form. They can be fully inflected. Nouns ending in a consonant can take the linker *a*, as does *beg* 'bag' in 22.32c, *ailand* in T1.10, *kar* 'car'; or *ə*, as does *ailan* 'island' in T1.11; or *i*, as does *bus* 'bush' in T1.21.

The behaviour of verbs in code-switching deserves special mention. A code-switch consisting of a verb plus its object cannot be inflected, and has to occur with a support verb, as in 21.22. Loan verbs can be treated as parts of complex predicates with support verbs (see examples in §17.2.2), e.g. *stati tə-* 'start', *pinisi tə-* 'finish', *andestand tə-* 'understand'. Or they can be inflected, as in 22.3, from a speech by an orator at the name debate (8 October 2004). In the examples, English forms are underlined and Tok Pisin forms are in italics.

22.3 <u>witness</u> *em nau kamapu-n*   *streti*-kə-bana
      witness it   now come.up-SEQ correct/settle-FUT-1plSUBJ.VT+3fem.sgBAS.VT
      'As the witness/evidence is appearing, we will correct (the information)'

Or this may be uninflected, as in 22.4:

22.4 wun *askim* aka   kəp *olsem* wun *askim*
      I   ask   DEM.DIST.REACT.TOP.fem.sg only just I   ask
      'I am *asking*, I am *just asking*'

The same 'code-switched' verb can occur without either inflection or support verb, and then occur inflected, within one sentence. Example 22.5, also from the name debate, illustrates this:

22.5 wun aka   *stretim streti*-ku   ya:kya
      I   DEM.DIST.REACT.TOP.fem.sg correct correct-COMPL.SS OK
      'I am now *correcting* (the statements by previous orators), after I have *corrected* (this), it will be OK'

This is not restricted to a spontaneous oral discourse. Kulanawi, Simon Harrison's classificatory father, dictated me a letter which I was to send to Simon Harrison (whose Manambu name is Yuasəsəg). Simon Harrison lives in Belfast, and Kulanawi was worried that he might have been affected by what Kulanawi saw as the ongoing warfare in Ireland:

22.6 Yuasəsəg [*sali*-tuə-l   *pas* au   ma: *beki*]   [*alək*
      Yuasəsəg send-1sgSUBJ.P-3fem.sgBAS.P letter CONTRAST NEG answer:NEG this.is.why
      wun *wori* tə-na-dəwun]   [*pas* kwar-ma:r-tu-lək]
      I   worry be/have-ACT.FOC-1masc.sgBAS.VT letter get:NEG-NEG.SUB-1sg-BECAUSE
      [kə-də   warya-da-d-ə   <u>war</u> bə
      DEM.PROX-masc.sg fight+come-3plSUBJ.P-3masc.sgBAS.P-LK war already
      bagarapi-da-d]   [*alək*   wun-a:k *pas*
      ruin-3plSUBJ.P-3masc.sgBAS.P this.is.why I-LK+DAT letter
      suku-ma:r-na-d]   [*alək*   asa:y *wori*
      write-NEG.SUB-ACT.FOC-3masc.sgBAS.VT this.is.why father worry
      tə-na-d]
      be/have-ACT.FOC-1masc.sgBAS.VT
      'Yuasəsəg, you did not *reply* to the *letter* I *sent*, this is why I am *worried*, as I did not receive the *letter*, this *war* that is being fought *ruined* him, this is why it is that he has not written me a *letter*, this is why father is *worried*'

Verbs *sali* 'send' (TP *salim*), *beki* 'answer' (TP *bekim*), and *bagarapi* 'ruin' (TP *bagarapim*) are inflected. *Wori* 'be worried' appears with a support verb.

This variability in the treatment of code-switches and borrowings is indicative of their uncertain status as marginal—albeit dangerously frequent—insertions into 'proper' Manambu.

We will now turn to the issue of the linear position of borrowings and code-switches in Manambu, and to the question of morphological and syntactic calques from Tok Pisin.

The position of borrowings and code-switches in a sentence, clause, and noun phrase in Manambu presents a researcher with a number of puzzles. Moravcsik (1978) suggested that a grammatical word can only be borrowed if the linear order with respect to its head is also borrowed—that is, if a preposition is borrowed from language X into language Y, it has to be borrowed as preposition, even if the language Y has nothing but postpositions. (Also see Curnow 2001: 430–1 on a potential counterexample from Basque.) Manambu partly follows Moravcsik's prediction, and partly goes against it (also see Aikhenvald forthcoming c).

In agreement with her prediction, borrowed or code-switched conjunctions keep the same place in Manambu as they have in the source language—Tok Pisin. This is the case with *o* 'or' in T2.50, *tasol* 'but' in T2.3 and 22.7, and *sapos* 'if' in 22.8.

22.7 [Yawabak təp ra-bana kəka] [*tasol*
Yawabak village sit/live-1plSUBJ.VT+3fem.sgBAS.VT DEM.PROX.REACT.TOP.fem.sg but
ñan Avatip-adian]
we Avatip-1plNOM
'We live in this Yawabak, *but* we are Avatip people'

22.8 [*sapos* vitiyay-ad] [ma:]
if second-3masc.sgNOM NEG
'*If* it is the second one (second child), this is no good (first child is more important)'

The language-internal motivation behind this is that the few connectives Manambu has occupy exactly the same position. The same applies to *nau* 'then' which occurs in the same place in Manambu clauses as it does in the Tok Pisin spoken by the Manambu. This clause-chaining insert accompanies the sequencing marker, and *nau* forms one phonological word with the verb:

22.9 [Ya-tataka-*nau*] ata wa-di
come-IMM.SEQ-then then say-3plBAS.P
'On having come, they then said'

Within a noun phrase, non-agreeing adjectives of Tok Pisin extraction occupy the same place as they would in Tok Pisin, and in Manambu, as shown in 22.17, and 22.10.

22.10 a *liklik* ma:j wa-kə-tua
then little story say-FUT-1sgSUBJ.VT+3fem.sgBAS.VT
'Then I will tell a *little* story'

A Tok Pisin indefinite pronoun *sampela* 'some' or *narapela* '(an)other' precedes a Tok Pisin adjective, as would its Manambu equivalent *nəkə-* '(an)other, some'; it also precedes a Manambu adjective, as in 22.11:

22.11 *narapela*   ma:j   wa-kə-tua   *sampela* kwasa   ma:j
       (an)other story say-FUT-1sgSUBJ.VT+3fem.sgBAS.VT some   little+fem.sg story
       'I will tell *another* story, *some* little story (or other)'

A quantifier *planti* 'many' precedes the noun, just like its Manambu equivalent *samasa:m* (see 22.36); and a quantifier *olgeta* 'all' follows the noun, just like Manambu *aba:b* 'all'; 22.12b was the speaker's correction of his spontaneous code-switch in 22.12a.

22.12a ñan *olgeta* atawa kwa-na-dian
        we   all   thus   stay-ACT.FOC-1plBAS.VT
        'We *all* stay like this'

22.12b ñan aba:b atawa kwa-na-dian
        we   all   thus   stay-ACT.FOC-1plBAS.VT
        'We all stay like this'

In all the instances so far, the linear position of a Tok Pisin item was the same as that of its Manambu counterpart. Not so for the numerals. We can recall, from §10.6.1, that numerals in Manambu follow the head noun. In Tok Pisin, they precede it. When Tok Pisin *wanpela* 'one, a' appears in Manambu speech, it precedes the noun, following Moravcsik's predictions that if a term is borrowed, so is its linear order. *Wanpela* is quite frequent (and uniformly condemned as 'bad language'). It appears with Tok Pisin nouns, as in 22.13–14, and with Manambu nouns, as in 22.15–16 and 21.42 (where *wanpela ta:kw* (one:TP woman) is repeated as *ta:kw nak* (woman one)).

22.13 gabu-ma:j   adəka   suku-kə-tua-d,
       traditional-story DEM.DIST.REACT.TOP.masc.sg 'carve'-FUT-1sgSUBJ.VT-3masc.sgBAS.VT
       wanpela stori
       one   story
       'I will tell (lit. carve) a traditional story, *a story*'

22.14 *wanpela taim* Wəjiməur-ad   kar-da-də-d
       one   time Wenjimeur-3masc.sgNOM bring-DOWN-3masc.sgSUBJ.P-3masc.sgBAS.P
       '*Once* it was Wenjimeur (water spirit) who took him down'

22.15 *wanpela* du   ya:d
       one/a   man go+3masc.sgBAS.P
       'A man went (off)'

22.16 *wanpela* tepam   a-də   təp   du viti kwa-bər
       one/a   village+LK+LOC   DEM.DIST-masc.sg village man two stay-3duBAS.P
       'In *a* village, in that village, there were two men'

The Tok Pisin form *wanpela* precedes any adjective in a noun phrase; it is more often found with Tok Pisin adjectives than with those from Manambu:

22.17 *wanpela liklik* ma:j aka   wa-kə-tua
       one/a   little story DEM.DIST.REACT.TOP.fem.sg say-FUT-1sgSUBJ.VT+3fem.sgBAS.VT
       'I will tell *one little* story'

Occasionally, *wanpela* and *nak* 'one' occur in one noun phrase, reinforcing each other (as in 21.42). We return to this in § 22.5.4. In all these instances, *wanpela* has nothing to do with counting; it is an indefinite introducer for a new referent. A story in Tok Pisin would start with *wanpela* plus a participant—so this use of *wanpela* in Tok Pisin is an obvious consequence of a tendency to 'match genres' in languages in contact (see Aikhenvald 2006b: 27), that is, sharing pragmatic patterns and the ways of organizing discourse structures.

Other borrowed numerals do not behave this way. They always precede foreign nouns, as in T2.21 and T2.40 *tu wik* 'two weeks' (from English). Code-switching in numbers is considered a mistake—in T2.40 the speaker corrected himself by saying *wik* (TP, E) *viti* 'two weeks'; in T2.41 he used *sande viti* 'two weeks', lit. 'two Sundays'.

If used with a Manambu noun, Tok Pisin numerals typically follow them, just as a Manambu numeral would, thus going against Moravcsik's prediction. These numbers are used for counting, and often occur accompanied by Manambu terms, in 'parallel' structures:

22.18 nəkə-di   tənəb   *foa faiv* aːli tabaːb kwa-na-di
      other-PL household four five four five   stay-ACT.FOC-3plBAS.VT
      'Other (clan) households are *four (or) five*, four (or) five'

English and Tok Pisin terms are often used for numbers bigger than ten (as in T2.65)—see §22.4.3 below, on the motivation for this.

The Tok Pisin preposition and adverb *wantaim* occurs in Manambu as a postposition, replacing the postposition *wukən* 'together, with' (see §4.5, and 4.68–9). The postposition *wantaim* is used by younger speakers, and is considered highly substandard. An example spontaneously produced is in 22.19:

22.19 mən-a   *wantaim* yi-k-na-bran
      you.masc-LK   with   go-FUT-ACT.FOC-1duBAS.VT
      'We will go together *with* you; you and I will go together'

Other numerous code-switches involve pro-clauses, e.g. *orait* 'OK' often used similarly to Manambu *yaːkya* 'OK' (see §20.4.2) (also see T2.50, T2.60, T2.65), *em nau* 'this is it', and *em tasol* 'this is it, just this'. They are not morphologically or syntactically integrated. The question about whether they can be assigned to a Manambu word class remains open.

As we saw at the end of §4.5, the word class assignment for a number of Tok Pisin inserts is problematic (this may justify considering them as code-switches rather than borrowings). One such problematic word is the modal *mas* 'must' (from Tok Pisin *mas*) which—unlike any other modal—can occur with an imperative-marked verb as in 13.22. Another one is *tabu*, from Tok Pisin *tambu*, 'be prohibited'. This form never occurs inflected. It can head a predicate, as in 22.20:

22.20 Apatəpa-wa   gəñər warya-wari *tabu*
      Avatip+LK-COM later fight-RED   forbidden
      'Later on it was *forbidden* to fight with Avatip'

Or it may form one constituent with an inflected verb in non-future or in future, in what superficially looks like a complement clause construction, as in 22.21–2:

22.21 abra-wur   bəyib ñan *tabu*   rə-bana
      DEM.DIST+du-UP stream we   forbidden sit-1plSUBJ.VT+3fem.sgBAS.VT
      aka-n-aka
      DEM.DIST.REACT.TOP.fem.sg-PRED-REACT.TOP.fem.sg
      'It is that it is *forbidden* for us to live (lit. sit) on the two streams up there'

22.22 [dəyam   vyavi]   [ma]: [wun *tabu*
      they+LK+ACC/LOC hit+RED   NEG   I   forbidden
      vya-kə-tua]
      hit-FUT-1sgSUBJ.VT+3fem.sgBAS.VT
      'There is no hitting them, it is *forbidden* for me to hit (them)' (lit. I am forbidden I will
      hit)

In terms of its synchronic status, *tabu* forms a subclass of its own.

The Tok Pisin completive marker *pinis* also behaves in an unusual way when it occurs in
Manambu speech. It can head a predicate (and be modified by *olgeta* 'altogether', also from
Tok Pisin), as in 22.23, or form a whole clause, as in 22.24 (where it is preceded by a pause):

22.23 ata   Səruali *pinis* *olgeta*   ata   kusə-taka-d
      then   Seruali COMPL   altogether then   finish-PUT-3masc.sgBAS.P
      adiya
      DEM.DIST.REACT.TOP+pl
      'Then the Seruali (i.e. Gala: see §1.4) *finished altogether*. Then he put an end to them'

22.24 ka-n   napa-ku   rapə-da:-l   PAUSE *pinis*
      eat-SEQ COMPL.VB-COMPL.SS   get.up-3plSUBJ.P-3fem.sgBAS.P   COMPL
      'After they had eaten they got up, and it was all over'

If accompanied by an inflected verb, as in 22.25, it may be interpreted as an aspect marker: its
position is the same as that of the Tok Pisin *pinis*.

22.25 vya-da-k   *olgeta*   *pini*s
      hit-3pl-COMPL.DS altogether COMPL
      'Having *completely* killed all . . .'

Mas, *tabu*, and *pinis* may be interpreted as tokens of incipient 'loan' morphology in Manambu
(see §4.5.6).

Syntactic and morphological calques from Tok Pisin are difficult to identify because of the
nature of Tok Pisin as a Creole language. Any structural similarity between Tok Pisin and
Manambu may well be due to the indigenous substratum in Tok Pisin itself rather than its
influence on Manambu. Such similarities include some compounds, e.g. Manambu *mæn-ta:b*
(leg-hand), Tok Pisin *lekhan* 'hands and feet', the polysemy of Manambu *vya-* 'hit, kill' and
Tok Pisin *kilim*, and numerous others.

If the Manambu patterns used by frequent code-switchers into Tok Pisin (most, but not
all, of whom are younger than 40–50) differ from those employed by traditional speakers and
display striking structural similarity to Tok Pisin, we can suspect that calquing is at work. For
instance, code-switchers tend to use the postposition *wukən* in many contexts where a comitative would be expected (see §7.9), and even replace it with *wantaim* (see above). This reflects a
tendency towards analytic constructions possibly developed under Tok Pisin influence. Code-
switchers display more frequent verb-medial order than traditional speakers, which may again
be due to the Tok Pisin influence (traditional speakers have a pronounced verb-final tendency
in their constituent order).

The more Tok Pisin the person uses, the more impoverished their Manambu sounds—such
speakers would prefer series of juxtaposed clauses to clause chains (see Chapters 18–19), and
would rarely use certain clause-chaining markers, such as *-taka* 'immediate sequence'. This
takes us to the issue of incipient language obsolescence—taken up in §22.6.1.

22.4.3   Functions of code-switches and borrowings

When children and teenagers speak among themselves, they use hardly any Manambu. Some use Manambu to talk to their parents, and some to talk to their grandparents. In actual fact, however, a lot of parent–child communication involves Tok Pisin, or even English. Typical examples include 21.22 and 17.26b. Similar examples are 22.26–8. In these cases, the most topical NP is in Tok Pisin—this goes together with Tok Pisin used as a way of getting the child to do things. Tok Pisin inserts are in italics both in Manambu and in the English translations:

22.26 *nem   bilong yu*   aw
  name of you IMPV+speak
  'Say *your name!*'

22.27 dan   ada *long graun*
  go.down+SEQ sit.IMPV on ground
  'Sit, *on the ground!*'

22.28 *wara   bilong* yæy   kusə-k-ñəna
  water of paternal.grandmother finish-IRR-2fem.sgSUBJ.VT+3fem.sgBAS.VT
  'You might finish off granny*'s water!*' (a warning not to drink too much)

All these examples involve commands. This takes us to a major function of Tok Pisin, as a language of authority. This is also known as 'DIRECTIVE' function.

Consider the following interaction. The mother was getting more and more annoyed with the little girl trying to pull bits off the stringbag the mother was knitting. She starts telling her off in Manambu (22.29a), and then switches to a mixture of English and Tok Pisin (22.29b): this makes the threat real and immediate.

22.29a kur-tukwa da-n   ada
   do-PROH.GEN go.down-SEQ sit.IMPV
   'Don't do (it), sit down'

22.29b <u>naughty</u> *yu* <u>stupid idiot</u> *bai mi pait-im yu nogut tru*
   naughty you stupid idiot FUT I hit-TRANS you bad/strong really
   'Naughty, stupid idiot, *I will hit you really strongly*'

And the threat was fulfilled, too: the mother hit the girl, the girl cried, and the mother soothed her saying—in Tok Pisin—*sori, mi sori.* The incident was over. An alternative would have been for the child to run away; and this was indeed her reaction to her mother's shouting the following:

22.30 kal   kiya-kiya-kə-tua-ñən-ək   *nogut mi*
  DEM.PROX+3fem.sgNOM kill-kill-FUT-1sgSUBJ.VT-2fem.sgBAS.VT-CONF bad/lest I
  brukim lek han bilong yu
  break leg hand of you
  'It is this one, I will kill you, beware *I might break your legs and hands*'

The first clause is an interesting example of the verb *kiya-* 'die' used transitively meaning 'make die, kill'. I was told that this usage is not quite grammatical.

This kind of language socialization is strongly reminiscent of the situation in Gapun village analysed by Kulick (1987). In both cases, code-switching and language mixing varies depending on speech genre, and has a special illocutionary force. We will see in §22.6.1 that the sheer number of Tok Pisin inserts may be indicative of the fact that language shift from Manambu to Tok Pisin and English is imminent.

English is also in the process of becoming an even stronger 'power-talk', especially for those for whom Tok Pisin is the major language anyway. A group of young boys gathered around Yuakalu's house were obviously up to no good. Yuamali went up to them to enquire about their intentions, and addressed them as 'Hello boys, what are you doing here?' The boys muttered something unintelligible and disappeared. Using English was Yuamali's way of asserting her authority over the wayward youngsters. This is very similar to the ways in which the majority languages—be it Spanish, or Portuguese, or English—are used throughout the world by minority speakers to claim power over others (see discussion, and references, in Aikhenvald 2002a: 187–211 and Hill and Hill 1986: 364–86). The motivation for this is fairly straightforward: speakers of the majority language are the ones in the position of authority, and so those who speak minority languages employ these same languages to acquire the air of authority; this may happen consciously, or not.

Children also code-switch when they talk to adults. A girl was trying to tell a story, and forgot the name of the main character. In the question addressed to her mother, the possessor (and the topic) was referred to in Tok Pisin. This agrees with the pattern illustrated in 22.26–8 above—the central, topical constituent, appears in Tok Pisin:

22.31 ta:kw-al   lə-kə   təp-a   sə   Maimwi-al
      woman-3fem.sgNOM she-OBL+fem.sg village-LK name Maimwi-3fem.sgNOM
      du-ad   *mama* təp-a   sə   *bilong dispela man?*
      man-3masc.sgNOM mama village-LK name of   this   man
      'There is a woman, her village name is Maimwi, there is a man...*Mummy*, what's the village name *of this man?*'

But, more often than not, a child would spontaneously address an adult in Tok Pisin. One girl (11 years of age), herself a highly sophisticated speaker of Manambu, was told to get her mother's towel (22.32a), using the Tok Pisin word *taul*. Her spontaneous reaction was 22.32b; the mother answered 22.32c (note the English loan *beg* rather than the Tok Pisin *bek*):

Mother:

22.32a wun-a   *taul*   akray
       I-LK+fem.sg   towel   IMPV+bring
       'Bring my *towel*!'

Daughter:

22.32b *i   stap   we?*
       PRED   stay   where
       '*Where is it?*'

Mother:

22.32c wuka   bega:m   kwa-na
       DEM.PROX.ADDR.REACT.TOP.fem.sg bag+LK+LOC   stay-ACT.FOC+3fem.sgBAS.VT
       'This here (next to you) is in the <u>bag</u>'

The trigger for the code-switch in this case could be the fact that the mother herself used a Tok Pisin word (see Clyne 1987, on potential triggers for code-switching). This type of interaction is highly frequent—and there is always enough Tok Pisin around to provide a trigger.

'Power-talk' is not the only function of Tok Pisin: it can be used as a sort of baby talk. All the children address their mothers and fathers in Tok Pisin (see *mama* as in 22.31). A speaker lovingly said to her little niece: *sindaun na kaikai* 'sit and eat'. This is also reflected in frequent parallel Manambu–Tok Pisin structures, as shown in 22.33. Here, the mother was trying to placate a crying baby, and said the same thing twice—in Manambu and in Tok Pisin:

22.33 yata-u   *mama i   karim yu*
      carry-1sgIMPV mama PRED carry you
      'Shall I carry you? *Shall Mummy carry you?*'

In 22.34, another mother was trying to convince her baby to go and wash hands together with her other children:

22.34 yi-nak   *mipela i   was   han*
      go-1plIMPV we   PRED wash hand
      'Let's go, *we wash hands*'

Speakers have an explanation for this function of Tok Pisin, saying that it is easier than Manambu for small children. And indeed, the fact is that most children acquire Tok Pisin first. Little Joana (about 3 in 2004) was quite good at Tok Pisin, and did not speak any Manambu at all. And no wonder: her carers talked to her almost exclusively in Tok Pisin. Her mother was not concerned about this in the slightest, saying, on various occasions, 'she will speak, (in) the village language together with the white people's language' (cf. 4.73). We return to this in §22.6.2.

Some relatives are always addressed with a Manambu term; then this is like a personal name, and there is no code-switching. The child addressed in 22.28 always calls this grandmother *yæy* ('paternal grandmother'). This explains why the mother used this term within the noun phrase containing a Tok Pisin code-switch.

In summary: the major function of code-switching between Tok Pisin, English, and Manambu is asserting one's authority—that is, both Tok Pisin and English are used as 'power-talk'; nowadays, English is rapidly monopolizing this function. At the same time, Tok Pisin (but not English) plays a special role in language socialization: it is considered 'easier' than Manambu and is employed as a 'baby talk'.

Another function of Tok Pisin is FILLING A PERCEIVED GAP in the language. Manambu does not have a dedicated contrast marker, so *tasol* comes in as in 22.7 and T2.3. A similar explanation would hold for the introduction of *sapos* 'if' in 22.8 (Manambu has a fairly elaborate system of conditionals, but not a word for 'if'), and for the disjunction *o* (as in T2.50). There is no special word for 'everything'—no wonder an exasperated mother exclaimed about her baby daughter trying to grab everything: *everfing kurə-k*! (everything get-PURP.SS) 'She is going to grab everything!'

Similar examples abound for lexical items. Filling a lexical gap accounts for the use of *mas* 'must', *tabu* 'forbidden', and the verb *laik* 'like'. The concepts of 'liking' and 'wanting' can be expressed through using the desiderative modality, a speech report construction, a complex predicate with the form *məyakw kwa-*, or a body part construction with the noun *mawul* 'insides'. But each of these constructions is rather complex, and fraught with additional overtones. Most speakers find it easier to say *wun laiki-na-wun* 'I like' or *wun ma: laik* (I NEG like) 'I don't like' rather than *wun ma: wa-na-wun* (I NEG say-PRES-1sgBAS) 'I am saying no'. Note that the latter form is in fact ambiguous between 'I don't want', 'I don't like' and 'I refuse' (to say 'no' to). Here, the introduction of Tok Pisin results in a resolution of potential ambiguity. And this takes us to the next point.

We saw in Chapter 21 that Manambu abounds in polysemous terms. Tok Pisin helps DISAM-BIGUATE POLYSEMY. We can recall that *wukə-* can mean 'hear, listen, smell, obey, and worry'. By using a Tok Pisin term *wori* 'worry, miss someone' to replace *wukə-* a speaker avoids a potential misunderstanding.

The same word *suku-* is used for 'write, carve, record'—to disambiguate these, one often says *raitim* and *rikodim*, keeping *suku-* just for 'carve'. The Manambu word *ñəg* means 'leaf, mosquito net, paper, letter'—but the Tok Pisin word *pas* only means 'letter', and its use makes communication more efficient (see 22.6 and 22.37). We can recall, from §21.1.1, that *kə-* means 'eat, drink, consume (e.g. smoke)'. Tok Pisin distinguishes *kaikai* 'eat' and *dringim* 'drink'—and some speakers, especially mothers, use these words when urging children to eat or to drink, to ensure that the distinction is made. Along similar lines, *laku* means 'know' and 'understand'. And one frequently hears *wun save ma: tə* (I know NEG have:NEG) 'I don't know, I have no knowledge' rather than *wun laku-n ma: tə* (I know/understand-SEQ NEG have:NEG) 'I don't know/understand, I have no knowledge/understanding'. The compound *gabə-ma:j* refers to a traditional story (e.g. Texts 1 and 3) and to a teacher; many people choose unambiguous *stori* and *ticha*, to avoid potential confusion.

Traditional Manambu had the same word meaning 'truth' and 'lie' (*sua:l*); the two meanings can be disambiguated with a special construction (see Chapter 21). But it is quicker and easier to say *giaman* 'lie' (originally from English *gammon*) and *tru* 'true', or *tru stori*. And this takes us to yet another function of Tok Pisin code-switches—that of a 'shortcut'.

The Manambu speakers themselves often lament that Tok Pisin is a 'SHORTCUT'—a language where *brukim* means 'break', no matter what sort of breaking we are talking about, *karim* 'carry' covers all sorts of carrying, and *kukim* 'burn' does not allow one to distinguish different types of 'burning'. (I heard similar complaints from Gala speakers who plainly stated that Tok Pisin is not a language at all, only a 'shortcut'.)

However, the lure of a quick-and-easy shortcut is strong. It is easier to say *stori* 'story' than to choose an exact term—*gabu-ma:j* 'traditional story', or *wa-saki-ma:j* 'true story' (21.37). A short term *hat* 'hat' is easier than *aba-wapi* (head+LK-clothing) (see 21.38). A lengthy *ap tə-na-d-ə mi* (bone/strength 'stand'/have-ACT.FOC-3masc.sgBAS.VT-LK wood) 'hard wood' is liable to be replaced with short *strongpela* (TP) *mi* (M), with the same meaning. Same for higher numerals: we can recall, from §10.6.2, that numbers higher than ten in Manambu are complex in structure. As a result, Tok Pisin and English numbers are preferred, as an 'easy' option (see T2.65).

Manambu has several ways of saying 'I am lazy, fed up, unwilling (to do something)'. Body part constructions *səp* (skin) *jina, sakwina* (lit. skin is tired) mean 'I am tired and fed up' and *səp væt yina* (lit. skin goes heavy) means 'I am very tired, unwell' (see §21.4). A complex predicate *kwasək yinawun* means 'I am unwilling (to do something)' (cf. 13.81). Tok Pisin has one word, *les* 'tired, unwilling, dislike', which covers all these distinctions. Young people and children often use *les* in combination with the functionally unmarked auxiliary *yi-* 'go, say': one hears *les yinawun* instead of any of the four combinations above. This construction has the same syntax as *kwasək yi-* (it requires a dative-aversive-marked nominalization, as in 9.8 and 13.81). The following example comes from a spontaneous conversation: a thirty-something speaker refused to drink any more water (for fear of having to go down to pee at night):

22.35 *les*   yi-na-wun   gu   kəka:k   wus-a:k
       tired go-ACT.FOC-1fem.sgBAS.VT water eat/drink+RED+DAT urine-LK+DAT
       'I don't want to drink water (or 'I am *fed up* with drinking water') for fear of urine'

And using *brukim* for 'break' means that one does not have to be specific—we can recall that Manambu has numerous verbs for breaking, but no generic term. This is similar to the ways in which some speakers use the general verb *məgi-* if explicitly asked to avoid excessive code-switching, as we saw in §21.3.2.

Speakers are aware of the fact that using Tok Pisin involves simplification—and this attitude is indeed reflected in how Tok Pisin appears to be used as 'baby talk'. Along similar lines, speakers of inflectionally complex languages—such as Bilingual Navajo—borrow 'easy-to-process' words from English (Schaengold 2004: 52–7; Aikhenvald 2006b: 34). Using a Tok Pisin word, or a whole phrase, results in levelling distinctions obligatorily made in Manambu.

A further function of Tok Pisin inserts is GETTING THE POINT ACROSS; this is similar to 'reiteration' as one of the functions of code-switching recognized by Gumperz (1982). A frequent technique here involves parallelism, whereby native and borrowed forms appear together (see Hajek 2006; Aikhenvald 2006b), as in 21.22, 21.57, 22.9, 22.25, T2.54, and 22.36–7. Such parallelism may involve repetition of a whole clause, as in 21.22, 21.57, and 21.42, or a noun phrase, as in 22.36, or a noun, as in 22.37, or just a modifier, as in 22.18.

22.36 *planti man meri*   samasama du   ta:kw   tə-na-di
      many man woman   many+LK   man woman   have-ACT.FOC-3plBAS.VT
      'There are *many people*, many people'

22.37 ñən-a:k   ñəg *pas* suku-kə-tua
      you.fem-LK+DAT letter letter write/carve-FUT-1sgSUBJ.VT+3fem.sgBAS.VT
      raiti-kə-tua
      write-FUT-1sgSUBJ.VT+3fem.sgBAS.VT
      'I will carve, *write* you leaf, *letter*'

Such parallelism has additional functions for different speakers. Examples 22.36 and 22.37 were produced by relatively young men (around 40) who consider themselves knowledgeable in the traditional lore. They typically code-switch with Tok Pisin, but are acutely aware of this 'deficiency', and insert the Manambu forms whenever they can, as a sort of afterthought. The parallelism in 22.33 had another additional function: stressing the point, and making the speech more expressive. Note that the order of Tok Pisin and Manambu parallel forms in 22.37 differs from that in 22.36 and 22.18. Example 13.22 also illustrates such a parallelism: the Tok Pisin *mas* 'must' is accompanied by the third person command form of the verb 'know' (which already has a deontic meaning of obligation: see §13.2.2). The function is to make sure the addressee understands the importance of this obligation.

In addition to this, code-switching may be used to stress a particular point (see Hill and Hill 1986: 377). Tok Pisin forms often sound more expressive than their Manambu equivalents. If someone really approves of something, they are likely to exclaim *Nambawan!* rather than *Vyakat-a-məy* (good-LK-very) 'very good'; or *tru-al!* (true-3fem.sgNOM) 'it is true!' rather than *məy-a sual-a* 'it is really a true story!' During the *Saki* (name debate) ceremony, such exclamations were accompanied with an often unanimous sound of appreciation (sounding like a very loud AAA↗-iii↘). And a negative *Nogat!* reflects a much stronger rejection than a simple Manambu *ma:* or even *ka* (see 10.24). This difference in illocutionary force between Tok Pisin and Manambu can be linked together with the role of Tok Pisin as a 'power-talk'.

We will see in §22.6 that Manambu is currently threatened by the encroachingly dominant Tok Pisin and English. As a consequence, many speakers have word retrieval problems. And this is where Tok Pisin insertions come into play—a Tok Pisin equivalent is the one they remember first. This is perhaps the saddest function of Tok Pisin, and the one speakers lament most. For them, mixing Tok Pisin with Manambu results in a 'rubbish talk'.

22.5   NEW DEVELOPMENTS IN THE MANAMBU LEXICON

Despite extensive code-switching, there is a marked tendency to extend the meanings of Manambu words to refer to newly introduced items and activities. The maintenance of these items is ensured by language purists (see §22.6) concerned with the survival of Manambu, and those speakers who prefer to avoid 'rubbish talk'—Manambu peppered with Tok Pisin inserts. In public places outside the Manambu-speaking villages, many of these words serve the function of 'secret talk'—everyone would understand *mani* (Tok Pisin for 'money'), but hardly anyone would make any sense of *kabak* (lit. 'stone') or *sa:n* (lit. shell valuable).[4]

For instance, a rifle is called *jarkañ* (a term for bamboo shoot originally used as a storing tube), and *jarkañ lə-kə væy* (bamboo.tube 3fem.sg-POSS+3fem.sg spear, lit.'bamboo tube's little spear') is the word for 'bullet'. A term for a long piece of bamboo *kañgu* is used to refer to a policeman (by reference to policemen carrying a long bamboo-like rifle on their shoulder).

The word *kabak* 'stone' is used to refer to large sums of money, and *sa:n* 'shell valuable' is used to refer to money (any quantity). The word *jələg* 'ten shell valuables strung together' is used for a ten-kina note. *Kabasək* 'seed' now means 'rice', *tək-ə-mi* (seed/little.fruit-LK-tree) 'seed, little fruit of a tree' is a term for 'medicine'; *wali-na:gw* (white.man-sago) refers to 'biscuit', and *wali-gus* (white.man-paddle) means 'outboard motor'. Few people say *kar* for 'car'—most prefer *val* 'canoe', and hardly anyone says *umbrella*—*aba-ñəg* (head+LK-leaf) is used instead. The term for a plane is *mi val* (high canoe); though many do switch to *balus*, a Tok Pisin term. *Telefon* is in competition with *mi ma:j* (high talk). The term *jəb* 'design, drawing' is also used for 'letter, literacy'; its major competitor is English *letter*. And the term *taba-ñə* (hand+LK-sun) is used in the meaning of 'watch' more than the English word *watch*.

Some new developments in the Manambu lexicon result in creating further patterns of polysemy. An example of a newly evolving polysemy is *kayik* 'image, picture, reflection (in water), shadow, ghost' (see §21.4), and nowadays also 'photographs, pictures' and 'films'. (Examples 16.107 and 19.20 illustrate *kayik* in the sense of 'photographs'.) A noun phrase *kayik və-bana tami:* (image see-1plSUBJ.VT+3fem.sgBAS.VT area) can be understood as 'area where we see films', and 'area where we see ghosts'. This is, of course, easy to disambiguate in a context of real life. Another option, as we saw above, is to use a Tok Pisin or an English word instead—neither *film* nor *piksa* evoke any implications of 'ghosts'.

The noun *ñəg* 'leaf, mosquito net', also used for 'letter' (but hardly ever for 'book'), presents a similar problem. We saw in 22.6 and 22.37 that it is in stiff competition with Tok Pisin *pas*.

As mentioned above, *suku-* means 'carve, write, record (on a tape-recorder)'. This polysemy posed unexpected problems for a fieldworker as well as for the speakers, since it does not allow one to easily distinguish between 'writing' and transcribing a story, and 'recording it'. The only way out appears to be a Tok Pisin code-switch (see §22.4.2 above). Another new pattern of polysemy involves the verb *və-* 'see, look' in the meaning of 'read' (see 21.13a, b). It is difficult to distinguish between 'look at a book' (as a child or an illiterate person would do), and 'read a book'—so Tok Pisin *ridim* 'read' comes to the rescue.

---

[4] This category also includes terms for people from areas of Papua New Guinea other than the Sepik area, e.g. *məg-a lap* (unripe-LK banana) for the Tolai, and *bal* (pig) for Highlanders.

Manambu purists go even further in suggesting lexically 'pure' innovations covering edu-
cational, financial, and religious terminology, e.g. *suku-mawul* (carve-insides) 'patience, that
is, the mindset of a carver', *kalipa-də du* (teach-3masc.sg man) 'male teacher', *saːn warapwi-
dana tamiy* (money change-3pl area) 'stock exchange', *du-awa kwa-mar-na taːkw* (man-COM
lie-NEG.SUB-PRES+3fem.sg woman, lit. 'woman who does not lie with men') 'virgin', *God maːj
krayin kalpa-di* (God speech carry+SEQ teach-3plBAS.VT, lit. 'teachers carrying God's speech')
'disciples', and even *Nəma-də Du* (big-masc.sg man) 'The Christian God'.

It is too early to evaluate the effects of language engineering by this group of purists.
Conservative attitudes toward loanwords are known to have hampered efforts to maintain
endangered languages; 'unrealistically severe older-speaker purism can discourage younger
speakers' (Dorian 1994; similar points were raised by Hill and Hill 1986: 140–1). And Hamp
(1989) suggested that if a minority language survives next to a larger dominant language, it has
to allow for a certain amount of borrowing of morphemes. On the other hand, some degree of
purism may stop otherwise unlimited borrowing and code-switching with Tok Pisin.

There appears to be a certain amount of language consciousness and resistance to borrowings among some young villagers. One of the urban Manambu, when she visited Malu village,
asked a 10-year-old boy to tie her canoe for her, using a Tok Pisin verb *pas* 'be closed, stuck':

22.38 val   a-*pas*
      canoe IMPV-tie
      'Tie the canoe!'

The boy corrected her, saying:

22.39 a-*pas*   maː atawtak   aw
      IMPV-tie NEG IMPV+tie+put IMPV+say
      'Not "apas", say "tie"'

Since this urban Manambu is known to be a purist and an authority on Manambu culture,
the boy could have just been trying to get his own back, demonstrating that he knows enough
to correct the 'authority'. But opportunities like this no doubt enhance the language awareness
of speakers.

We now turn to the effects of language obsolescence, and the perspectives for the survival of
the language in its current setting.

22.6   INCIPIENT LANGUAGE OBSOLESCENCE AND
PERSPECTIVES FOR SURVIVAL

22.6.1   Signs of language obsolescence

The difference between language change in 'healthy' and in endangered or obsolescent languages very often lies not in the SORTS of change, which are often the same. Rather, it lies
in the QUANTITY of change, and in the SPEED with which the obsolescent language changes
(see Aikhenvald 2002a: 243–60; 2004b). Language obsolescence frequently entails a general
breakdown in language structure resulting in allophonic and morphological variation, regu-
larization, and even new allomorphs. Stylistic, rhetorical, and expressive loss in language shift
results in lexical and even in grammatical reduction (cf. Woodbury 1998).

As we saw in Chapter 1, outside the domestic environment, Manambu is used in ritual
discourse, and sometimes in village- or clan-level meetings. Even then, it is often replaced

with Tok Pisin, or English, and just about always appears interspersed with Tok Pisin and English code-switches.

The types of changes observed in modern Manambu follow the general principles of change in language obsolescence summarized by Campbell and Muntzel (1989), Dixon (1991), Sasse (1992), and Aikhenvald (2002a: 243–60). VARIABILITY OF PHONOLOGICAL PROCESSES is a sign of language disintegration. The process of rhotic dissimilation (§2.6, A1) is violated by urban speakers of Manambu, as well as those villagers whose major language of communication within their homes is Tok Pisin.

NEW MORPHOLOGICAL VARIABILITY, a frequent consequence of language obsolescence, has been noticed for kinship terms which have overt number markers (§6.1). Younger speakers whose knowledge of the kinship system appears to be incomplete freely oscillate between such forms as sg. *ñap*, pl. *ñap-a-bər*, *ñap-agw* 'mother's elder sister'; sg. *ñasap*, pl. *ñasap-bər*, *ñasap-agw* 'father's elder brother'; sg. *gwal*, pl. *gwalugw-bər*, *gwal-ugw* 'grandchild, father's father'; sg. *babay*, pl. *babay-bər*, *babay-ugw* 'mother's parent', and a few others. In one case double plural marking was given as an alternative: sg. *ma:m*, pl. *mam-əgw*, *mam-ugw-bər* 'elder sibling'. The lack of confusion in marking dual on kinship terms is due to an obvious link between the dual marker *-vəti* and the number '2' (*viti*). Not so for the irregular dual of *ñan* 'child', *ñədi* (plural *ñanugw*). Younger speakers regularize this form, by adding *-vəti* 'dual, two' to it: *ñədi-vəti*, lit. 'child:DU-two' 'two children'. Older and more traditional speakers frown at this.

Stylistic reduction and obsolescence of traditional knowledge affects the frequency of number marking. The archaic plurals *takwa:gw* (woman/wife+PL) 'women', from *ta:kw* 'woman, wife', *lanugw* 'husbands' (*la:n* 'husband'), and *tidigw* (*ti:d* 'co-wife, woman of same generation') 'co-wives' only occur in *namai* 'foiled love songs'; and they are not known to younger people (or people who have lived outside the Manambu-speaking area for a long time). Non-kinship terms which contain the plural marker *-əgw* tend to fall into disuse. Speakers who speak more Tok Pisin than Manambu tend not to use some sequencing forms, such as *-taka* 'immediate sequence', or *-ga:y* 'conditional'.

DIALECT MIXING AND DIALECT LEVELLING is another feature of obsolescent languages. When a language becomes restricted in its use, speakers often spontaneously mix forms from what were previously distinct dialects, without realizing that they belong to different linguistic systems. Sometimes speakers may not even be able to tell which form comes from which dialect.

In the Manambu context, dialect mixture is reinforced by the mobility of speakers. In particular, those Manambu who live in towns freely mix with each other, and often 'pick up' one another's speech habits. Dialect variation in the Manambu-speaking communities is not great. The language is spoken in five villages; of these, Yawabak is considered an 'extension' of Avatip, and there are hardly any differences; similarly, Apa:n is an 'extension' of Malu. Yuanab (or Yambon) stands apart. In spite of being further away from the government station Ambunti, it has always been more open to outside influences than the other villages. It appears to have had a strong influx of Iatmul migrants and Iatmul influence (see discussion by Harrison 1990a), and also perhaps some Gala substratum (according to Paul Badaibæg Kat). Yuanab was the only Manambu village to have welcomed SIL missionaries in the early 1960s.[5]

The Yuanab dialect has a number of marked differences from Avatip and Malu. One difference between this and other varieties lies in the *r/l* distinction: the Yuanab variety does not distinguish *r* and *l* (that is, *l* in other Manambu varieties corresponds to *r*); so *Ñaula* 'Iatmul' is pronounced as [Ñauɾa]; and *salyakən* 'stretching out' comes out as [saɾyakən]. This difference

---

[5] Most Manambu speakers maintain that a major drawback of the first version of the Bible in Manambu, published in 1979, was its bias towards the Yuanab variety; the revision of the translation is currently in progress.

is the only one that appears to be consistently maintained; and is also held to be emblematic for those who come from Yambon. However, in the speech of the Yuanab Manambu who live outside the Manambu-speaking villages area the two sounds *r* and *l* tend to become allophones in free variation. There used to be minor lexical and grammatical differences, which are nowadays difficult to retrieve. For instance, the word for 'dark' is *gɾa-gəɾ* (black+LK-black) in Yuanab, and *gla-ka-gəl* (black+LK-INT-black) in the Avatip and Malu varieties; in actual fact one hears both forms in Avatip and in Malu.

The varieties spoken in Malu and in Avatip are very similar; minor lexical differences include:

- Avatip *ba:g*, Malu *arəp* 'bush knife';
- Avatip *saku*, Malu *sapwi* 'give birth';
- Avatip *ya:l bə rəpə-na* (belly already be.full/enough-PRES+3fem.sgBAS), Malu *ya:l bə kapə-na* (belly already full-ACT.FOC+3fem.sgBAS) '(I) am full'. An alternative expression in Avatip is *ya:l bə waprukə-na* (belly already overflow/overfull-ACT.FOC+3fem.sgBAS.VT) 'I am very full indeed'.

In actual fact, these items are used interchangeably by those living in Avatip and in Malu (though at least some Manambu purists, most of whom reside outside the villages, make it a point to never use expressions from a different dialect). For instance, an Avatip man spontaneously said: *arəp ka:w tə-na-d* (bush.knife sharpness have-PRES-3masc.sgBAS) 'the knife is sharp', using the form *arəp*, from the Malu variety.

As a result of ongoing levelling of dialectal differences, speakers are often unable to distinguish which form belongs to which dialect. There are several ways of referring to being thirsty. Avatip speakers reject *kwa:l yas-* (throat feel-) as being either Malu or Yuanab; *gu yasa-* (water EXIST-) is judged to be better, but still not quite right (it is said that this form must be Malu). I was advised to say *gu kə-kəɾ* (water eat-DES) 'I want to drink water' or, with a somewhat different meaning, *kwa:l gu-a:k wurtəpə-na* (throat water-LK+DAT long-ACT.FOC+3fem.sgBAS.VT) 'I am very thirsty', to avoid any confusion. The speakers themselves used the first three forms interchangeably.

Dialect levelling does not always imply language attrition—it is, for instance, a well-known fact that the spread of radio and television results in the levelling of dialect differences in just about every language, including English. Neither does dialect levelling necessarily imply the 'death' of a particular dialect—it may imply the creation of a new system incorporating features of several dialects, and thus be similar to 'koineization' (a similar situation for Koiari, a not-yet-endangered Papuan language, was reported by Tom Dutton, p.c.). But with incipient language attrition already in place, dialect mixture and dialect merging may lead to disruption of lexical and grammatical rules, and thus to the development of new variability.

The major feature of Manambu language attrition lies in STYLISTIC REDUCTION AND LOSS OF TRADITIONAL KNOWLEDGE. Such stylistic reduction has been noted for numerous languages of Papua New Guinea. For instance, the knowledge of a ritual 'pandanus' language used by a number of peoples of the Southern Highlands Province during the harvest of pandanus nuts has decreased during the past thirty to forty years, as Franklin and Stefaniw (1992) report for Kewa and Imbongu (Kewa has about 25,000 speakers, and Imbongu has 16,000; neither of these languages is in any immediate danger of becoming extinct). Stylistic reduction often pre-dates language obsolescence (as was the case with Dyirbal 'Mother-in-law' language: Dixon 1990). For instance, the oratorical style *sesade kwanif* associated with the ritual food exchange in Abuʼ Arapesh was dying out in the 1960s, long before children stopped acquiring the language (Nekitel 1985: 182). Tuzin (1976) made similar observations for Ilahita Arapesh.

In the case of Manambu, stylistic reduction goes along several lines. First, the breakdown in the transmission of traditional knowledge and in the continuation of rituals brings about a lack of access to certain genres. One such genre is name debating, *sə saki*. The fact that at least some industrious people go off to towns to pursue a career of European-based education means that, even if they have traditional knowledge themselves, they do not transmit it to their children. Neither do many of those who remain in the village. Two traditional speech styles, songs of foiled love affairs (*namay* and *sui*) and funerary laments (*gra-kudi*), involve the deployment of Iatmul-based 'shadowy' lexicon and of totemic terms relating to the clan of the man or the woman mourned. Simon Harrison, during his work with old men in the 1980s, managed to get them to sing *namay* without any hesitation. My own experience with older women singing *namay* and *sui* in 2001–2 and 2004 was that many of them showed signs of hesitation in the choice of appropriate terms. During various mortuary feasts (*Kəkətəp*) held at the village at this time, only a few very old women knew how to sing *gra-kudi* properly, which was a cause of worry to some members of the community.

These genres require the use of totemic equivalents for numerous words, referred to as 'other side', or 'shadowy' lexicon (see §22.3). Knowledge of this is virtually non-existent among younger people; and this results in drastic lexical reduction. While one could possibly argue that the knowledge of the 'other side' lexicon implied a certain amount of diglossia, this diglossia is at present on its way out.

Younger speakers and those speakers who employ mostly Tok Pisin in their day-to-day life frequently face problems of word retrieval and incipient lexical obsolescence. This involves time words, numerals, and especially Manambu personal names (and also terms for flora and fauna). Most speakers of Manambu can count up to ten in the language; younger speakers find it hard to count beyond ten; only a few can count up to twenty. But those who do count further tend to somewhat regularize the system, as shown in Table 10.9. Needless to say, younger speakers were much more comfortable counting in Tok Pisin than in Manambu—which is a source of chagrin to their parents, and to themselves; we can recall, from §10.6, that speakers of Manambu are 'number-proud'.

Younger people are often ill at ease with kinship terms: it is easier for them to say *brata* (Tok Pisin 'brother'), *susa* (Tok Pisin 'sister'), or *anti* (from English 'auntie'), rather than be more precise and distinguish siblings in terms of age, or different types of 'aunties' depending on whether paternal or maternal. Word-retrieval problems result in increased frequency of the catch-all *maːgw* 'what's its name', and the 'lazy' general verb *məgi-* (see §21.3.1–2; and 21.42). Many young speakers do not know their own Manambu names, let alone those of their peers. In a culture where personal names are an important part of one's knowledge and are considered on a par with material wealth such obsolescence is tragic. Problems in word retrieval result in a growing INSECURITY OF YOUNGER SPEAKERS, another common consequence of language obsolescence. Urban Manambu, who have lost their fluency, and village teenagers, who are unsure of themselves, prefer to answer in Tok Pisin when addressed in Manambu, to avoid potential communication problems, and also for fear of being ridiculed for their mistakes (similar tendencies are reported for Abu' Arapesh by Nekitel 1998).

Code-switching within a multilingual context comes in a variety of guises (see Clyne 1987; Gumperz 1982 on types, functions, and constraints on code-switching). Code-switching may obey strict rules, as is often the case in situations of di- and polyglossia, which imply stable functional differentiation of languages in distinct domains. Code-switching may depend on the communicative situation without involving diglossia as such (Aikhenvald 2002a: 187–209).

In situational code-switching, the domain determines the language used—so, in the context of the Sepik area, Tok Pisin would be expected at meetings of the local council, and Manambu during discussions concerning mortuary rituals. Alternatively, code-switching may be unrestricted (Landweer 2000: 7): the language choice may change without any functional differentiation or consistency, simply because speakers are more proficient in one language than in the other. Similar patterns were discussed by Kulick (1987) for Taiap (and also see Nekitel 1992: 56 on extensive code-switching in Abu' Arapesh as indicative of the growing lack of language proficiency).

Unrestricted code-switching is thus concomitant with lexical obsolescence and insecurity of those speakers who do not have sufficient exposure to the vernacular. In the Manambu context, frequent unrestricted code-switching is an indicator of speakers effectively losing allegiance to their ancestral language (Landweer 2000: 7), and is in itself disquieting.

We now turn to the perspective of Manambu language survival.

22.6.2 The 'Manambu revival' movement and perspectives for language survival

A notable feature of the language attitude among many Manambu is the discourse of 'nostalgia'. When I first arrived in the village and started explaining what I was doing, the general response was: yes, we do need a linguist, because our language might die (*ñan-a kudi kusə-k-na* (we-LK+fem.sg language finish-IRR-ACT.FOC+3fem.sgBAS.VT)). This attitude, which goes together with strong preference for 'the old ways' of speech, has some similarities to what Hill (1998) described as the 'discourse of nostalgia', for the bilingual communities around the Malinche volcano in central Mexico. Like speakers of Nahuatl, speakers of Manambu contrast the linguistic 'purity' of 'long ago' with 'the language mixing' of 'today'; they also strive to be as close as possible to the 'long ago' ideal in their language monitoring. The discourse of nostalgia among many city-dwelling Manambu speakers extends to Tok Pisin (*wali kudi*, lit. 'white people language'). They lament that not only do their children have no knowledge of Manambu (and little desire to acquire this knowledge); they do not even speak or understand Tok Pisin.

Obsolescence of the true Manambu language is an object of concern for most senior people in the village, and also a few younger people in their thirties and forties. A number of purists—most of whom are successful middle-class urban-dwellers—are trying their best to exclude Tok Pisin and English loans and instead invent indigenous terms. We saw numerous examples in §22.5 above.

Discourse of nostalgia could be a dangerous sign—it often indicates that the language is well and truly on its way out. There are, however, indications that speakers do value Manambu and are not prepared to just let it go. Within the urban communities, Manambu is employed as a sort of 'secret language' and an in-group means of communication emblematic in itself. In the village context, one frequently hears mothers shouting at children 'Say this in the village language, don't speak white language (Tok Pisin)!' (see 21.28a, b). Children who are proficient in Manambu feel valued. It was a matter of particular pride for 11-year-old Tanina to be able to correct her mothers and grandmothers whenever they let slip a Tok Pisin word. No matter how much Tok Pisin she uses herself, she is a language revivalist in the making.

Manambu remains an emblematic language for the people it 'belongs' to. Hardly any young people know as many totemic terms as they could be expected to; but many make it a point to learn at least some correct greetings: this is seen to enhance their status in the community. Even ardent Christians who otherwise reject traditional rituals as 'heretical' adhere to these traditional patterns as emblematic of their Manambu identity and their place in the village clan and kinship system.

People vary in the extent of their concern about the fact that children tend to speak Tok Pisin. Some are convinced—and perhaps rightly so—that their children will acquire proficiency in Manambu. See Janet's observation that her daughter—whose first language is Tok Pisin—will be speaking Manambu and Tok Pisin together in no time at all (4.73).

And despite the disquieting fact that little Joana spoke only Tok Pisin as her first language, Janet's predictions may well come true. Joana is frequently left in the care of Janet's mother Lowai and elder sister Dora—both elaborate and proficient speakers of Manambu, just like Janet herself. That Tanina, Kerryanne, Celestin, and Stevie are good at Manambu, and that Tanina has already grown to be an excellent story teller, is in large part due to the fact that the children live in the same house with Gemaj, one of the best speakers and connoisseurs of lore. The survival of the language lies in the hands of these mature-age women and their charges.

A number of cultural and economic trends in modern-day Papua New Guinea could also be favourable to slowing down the process of impending language shift, and improving the perspective for language survival.

The sheer prestige of Manambu speakers—such as Paul Badaibæg Kat, Eric Yuamalen, John Sepaywus, Kulanawi, and others—in a larger Sepik context helps maintain the high prestige of the language and of the traditional knowledge. Avatip is lucky in having Leo Yabwi Luma, a highly knowledgeable and respected man and an elaborate connoisseur of the language and of the tradition, as the headmaster of its primary school.

Within a broader context, the fact that many members of the urban elite in the cities are Manambu provides further appreciation of those who know the language and the lore. Just a few examples. Lieutenant-Colonel James Laki is a major expert on security issues in Papua New Guinea and worldwide; Colonel David Takendu is an ex-High-Commissioner to New Zealand; Joel Yuakalu Luma occupies a high position in the government. The current Ambassador to the Philippines and the Chief of Staff of Papua New Guinea army are Manambu. A growing number of the Manambu acquire higher degrees overseas and return to their country to work in universities and various companies.

These people create role-models for the new generation—those who want to be 'like uncle Leo', or 'like uncle Joel', would try and learn at least some Manambu to maintain their status in the village and outside it.

Some of the retiring urban elite go back to the village. This has already brought another influx of interest and culture revival into the village. The activity of an overseas linguist and an overseas anthropologist each working with highly respected Manambu speakers boosts the prestige of the language as a means of day-to-day communication; this has already initiated a community-based project of Manambu language and culture documentation and teaching (see Hornberger and King 2000: 185 on the importance of such activities in the context of Quechua language maintenance). The 'revival' of Manambu school programme is now under way, under the leadership of Leo Luma. Despite dangerous signs of obsolescence, one should not be pessimistic: the language may well live on.

APPENDIX 22.1 PERSONAL PRONOUNS IN NDU LANGUAGES

A reconstruction of Proto-Ndu personal pronouns is given in Table A22.1 below; correspondences are discussed in Aikhenvald (forthcoming b), which also contains a discussion of bound pronouns in Ndu languages.

TABLE A22.1   Personal pronouns in Proto-Ndu

PERSON/GENDER	SG	DU	PL
1 masculine	*wun*	*an(e)*	*nan(e)*
1 feminine			
2 masculine	**mən(ə)*	**bən(e)*	**gun(e)*
2 feminine	**ñən(ə)*		
3 masculine	**də*	**bər(e)*	
3 feminine	**lə*		

Source: Aikhenvald (forthcoming b).

TABLE A22.2   Personal pronouns in Iatmul

PERSON/GENDER	SG	DU	PL
1 masculine	*wun*	*an*	*nin*
1 feminine			
2 masculine	*min*		*guk/gut*
2 feminine	*nyin*	*bit* (Staalsen 1965) *biʼk* (Jendraschek, p.c.)	
3 masculine	*di*		*di*
3 feminine	*li*		

Sources: Staalsen (1965: 29); Gerd Jendraschek (p.c.). Both represent different varieties of the Nyaula dialect (mostly Brugnowi in Staalsen 1965; Korogo, or Koloko, from Gerd Jendraschek).

TABLE A22.3   Personal pronouns in Wosera-Abelam

PERSON/GENDER	SG	DU	PL
1 masculine	*wuné* - Abelam *wuni* -West Wosera	*ané* - Abelam *ani* - West Wosera	*naané* - Abelam *nani, me* - West Wosera
1 feminine			
2 masculine	*mené* - Abelam *méni* - West Wosera	*béné* - Abelam *béni* - West Wosera	*guné* - Abelam *guni* - West Wosera
2 feminine	*nyéné* - Abelam *nyéni* - West Wosera		
3 masculine	*dé*	*bét* - Abelam *bér* - West Wosera	*de* - Abelam *di* - West Wosera
3 feminine	*lé*		

Sources: See Wilson (1980: 53) for Abelam; Wendel (1993: 59) for West Wosera.

TABLE A22.4   Personal pronouns in Boiken (Yangoru dialect and Kwusaun dialect)

PERSON/GENDER	SG	DU	PL
1 masculine	*wune* - Yangoru *nwʌ* - Kwusaun	*nane* - Yangoru *nʌnə*	*nine* - Yangoru *nanə*
1 feminine			
2 masculine	*mine* - Yangoru *mənə* - Kwusaun	*ple* - Yangoru *bərə* - Kwusaun	*kle* - Yangoru *gwrə* - Kwusaun
2 feminine	*yine* - Yangoru *ñənə* - Kwusaun		
3 masculine	*ti, ri* - Yangoru *də* - Kwusaun		*tie* - Yangoru *dy* - Kwusaun
3 feminine	*yi* - Yangoru *ny* - Kwusaun		

Note: These forms of 'regular pronouns' in Yangoru dialect are from Freudenburg (1979: section 4); the forms in Kwusaun dialect are from Laycock (1965: 106).

TABLE A22.5   Personal pronouns in Yelogu

PERSON/GENDER	SG	DU	PL
1 masculine	*wny*	*any*	*ñany*
1 feminine			
2 masculine	*məny*	*bəny*	*gwny*
2 feminine	*ñəñy*		
3 masculine	*də*	*bərə*	*jy*
3 feminine	*lə*		

Source: Laycock (1965: 140).

Tables A22.2–5 contain independent personal pronouns in Iatmul, Wosera-Abelam, Boiken (Yangoru and Kwusaun dialects), and Yelogu. Tables 3.3 and 22.1 contain pronouns in Manambu and in Gala.

Texts

Most texts recorded and analysed (approximately 190 in all) are rather long. These texts include traditional tales (genre termed *gabu-ma:j*), traditional stories about historical events which are passed on from one generation to another (*wa-saki-ma:j* and *blajaya-ma:j*), and various songs (mourning songs *gra-kudi,* and laments about foiled marriages *namai* and *sui*). I have chosen three shorter texts, each from a different speaker, so as to provide as broad a picture as possible. Texts were recorded, transcribed, glossed, and provided with an explanation by me. Jacklyn Yuamali Benji Ala assisted me with transcribing Texts 1 and 2, and Jennie Kudapa:kw helped with Text 3.

Text 1 was told by a highly knowledgeable lady, Gaiawalimæg (in her fifties). It is a funny story based on a word game: 'see the moon' or 'look at the moon' is an expression used to refer to menstruating women. A naive husband decides to go and punish the moon for frivolously looking at his wife. As a result, he suffers and repents. This is a *gabu-ma:j*, a traditional fairy tale type story.

Text 2 was told by John Səpaywus, the esteemed leader (*yibunmi*) of Avatip, formerly the member of the provincial Council (now in his seventies). The story is about the origin of Vali:k clan (one of the clans of the Gla:gw group: see §1.3), based on the encounter of Səsawi and Kamkudi (Kamkundi). The origin of the Vali:k is connected with the wars with the Gala (Swakap). I have recorded and transcribed at least ten different versions of this same story (another version was published in Takendu 1977; also see Harrison 1993). The Gala wars were discussed in §1.4.1. This is a typical example of a *wa-saki ma:j* (say-ACROSS story), a traditional story about a historical event.

Text 3 was told by James Katalu Angi Balangawi, a highly proficient story teller in his fifties, and is a *gabu-ma:j* about an unfortunate and somewhat stupid man Oselo who had tried to exterminate all the snakes.

The texts below are given in phonological transcription. They are divided in sentences (and are referred to accordingly throughout the grammar). Comments on interesting or unusual linguistic phenomena within these sentences and references to the relevant sections of the grammar are provided after each sentence when necessary. Within each sentence, clauses are in square brackets. Smaller complex constituents (noun phrases and auxiliary constructions) are in braces. Loans from Tok Pisin and English are in italics.

TEXT 1. A MAN WHO WENT TO FIGHT THE MOON, NARRATED BY GAIAWALIMÆG; RECORDED 17 OCTOBER 2004 (APPROXIMATE LENGTH 7 MINUTES)

T1.1 [ya:kya] [nəkə-də   gabu-ma:j   ata   ma:
     OK   other-masc.sg   traditional-story   then   again
     suku-kə-ta-d]
     write/carve-FUT-1duSUBJ.VT-3masc.sgBAS.VT
     'OK, another traditional tale then again we two will record'

This was the third story Gaiawalimæg (commonly addressed as Gaia) volunteered to tell that day; this is why she started it with *ya:kya*. Note the alternative phonetic realization of *gabu-ma:j* is *gama:j* (see A7 at §2.6). The story is considered sufficiently 'long' to warrant masculine agreement on the agreeing modifier *nəkə-* 'other' (see §5.1). The verb *suku-* can mean 'carve, write down, record', so the second clause is ambiguous as to whether we two (Gaia and myself) will record the story, or write it down.

T1.2 [wun Gaia] [ada   ma: suku-kə-tua-d]
     I   Gaia,   DEM.DIST.REACT.TOP+masc.sg   again   write/carve-FUT-1sgSUBJ.VT-3masc.sgBAS.VT
     'I am Gaia, I will write/record one (story) again'

The first clause is a typical verbless naming clause (see §20.1.3). The reactivated topic demonstrative refers to the topical object, the story itself.

T1.3 [{naubadi du-a-wa}   ta:kw]   [də ta:kw kra-d   a-də   du]
young   man-LK-COM woman he wife   get-3masc.sgBAS.P DEM.DIST-masc.sg man
[kra-taka]   [tə-ta-taka   a-də   du]   [tə-brə-k]   [nəkə-də
get-IMM.SEQ have-EP-IMM.SEQ DEM.DIST-masc.sg man stay-3du-COMPL.DS other-masc.sg
du-ad   ya:d]   [ya-ku]   [ada
man-3masc.sgNOM come+3masc.sgBAS.P come-COMPL.SS DEM.DIST.REACT.TOP+masc.sg
wa:d]   [sa!]
say+3masc.sgBAS.P hey!
'(There was) a young man and a woman, he got married (lit. got wife) that man, on having married, having been (that way), that man, that man, on having married, having stayed, that man, after they'd stayed together, there is another man (he) came, after he'd come, he said "Hey!"'

The first clause is verbless; it contains an instance of the coordinating comitative (see §7.9). In the second clause the A ('that man') is postposed to the verb as a clarification (see §19.7). Two 'medial' clauses (each marked with same-subject immediate sequence) are postposed to the main clause; the second medial clause has a summarizing function. The next clause is a rare example of a dependent clause with a non-verb-final order. The next clause—a medial completive clause—contains the same verb as the preceding clause. This is a typical example of bridging 'head-tail' clause or sentence linkage (as is the third clause in this sentence: see §20.4.1). Within the second clause, the nominal clause 'there is another man' is an instance of contrastive focus (see §20.3). The last clause is a speech report consisting of the attention getter 'hey'.

T1.4 [[wa-məna   ta:kw]   bap   və-k-la]
say-2masc.sgSUBJ.VT+3fem.sgBAS.VT woman moon see-FUT-3fem.sgSUBJ.VT+3fem.sgBAS.VT
[wa:d]   [wa-də-l]   [[[a ñan-a-kə   ta:kw
say+3masc.sgBAS.P say-3masc.sgSUBJ.P-3fem.sgBAS.P then we-LK-POSS+fem.sg woman
a]   tə-kwa-bana   sik]   bə
DEM.DIST.fem.sg stand/have-HAB-1plSUBJ.VT+3fem.sgBAS.VT sickness already
laku-ñəna]?
know-2fem.sgSUBJ.VT+3fem.sgBAS.VT
' "The wife you talk about (or to) will menstruate (lit. see moon)", he said, he said to her, "Do you already know the sickness we-our village women (not anyone else) have?"'

The first clause contains a relative clause (see §19.2). The speech verb *wa-* is repeated in the second and third clauses, with different cross-referencing (the addressee, 'woman', is cross-referenced on the verb 'say' in the second position). The fourth clause contains a relative clause with *sik* (a Tok Pisin loan) as a common argument. The subject (A) of the relative clause ('our village woman') is in contrastive focus (see §20.3). Throughout the story we see the polysemy of man and husband (note that there is a separate word for husband, *la:n*: see Chapter 8). Note that the verb of perception *və-* means both 'see' and 'look'. 'See/look at moon' is the way of saying 'menstruate'.

T1.5 [a   sik-a-pək-a   mm]   [wa-də-k]   [a
DEM.DIST.fem.sg sickness-LK-LIKE-3fem.sgNOM mm say-3masc.sg-COMPL.DS then
wa:d   {a   ta:kw a-də   lə-kə-də   du}]
say+3masc.sgBAS.P DEM.DIST.fem.sg woman DEM.DIST-masc.sg she-OBL-masc.sg man
[a-də   du takwa:m   ay]   [ka   wun-a
DEM.DIST-masc.sg man woman+LK+OBJ IMPV+speak DEM.PROX+3fem.sgNOM I-LK+fem.sg
ta:kw-a]   [bap   agwa-japək   və-k-la]
woman-3fem.sgNOM moon what-thing+LK+DAT see-FUT-3fem.sgSUBJ.VT+3fem.sgBAS.VT
' "It is like a sickness, mm", after he'd said this, then (the other man) said, the husband of that woman (said), "You speak to that man's wife, as for this one it is my wife, why will she see the moon?"'

The third clause has a VS-Direct Speech report order, since the S ('that husband of that woman') has been reintroduced again for clarification (see §20.2). A complex NP is in braces. The following speech report contains a rare instance of another speech report introduced by the speech verb *yi-* 'go, say' (see §21.1.3).

T1.6 [a,   day ta:kw day-a-kə   ja:p-a]   [day ta:kw akətawa bap
     then   they woman they-LK-OBL+fem.sg thing-3fem.sgNOM they woman like.this moon
     və-kwa-na-di]
     see-HAB-ACT.FOC-3plBAS.VT
     ' "Ah, it is their, women's, business, they women see moon like this" (said the other man)'

Here and in T1.7 the verb of speech has been omitted since it is clear from the context. The speaker made a slight change in her tone of voice, to show that it is a different character speaking.

T1.7 [ah ma:] [[ka]   wun-a   ta:kw-a]   [lə-kə-k   bap
     Ah NEG DEM.PROX+3fem.sgNOM I-LK+fem.sg woman-3fem.sgNOM she-OBL-DAT moon
     və-və   ma:]
     see-RED NEG
     ' "Oh, no, as for this one it is my wife, moon is not to look at her" '

The form *ka* is in contrastive focus. In the last clause the negated nominalization 'seeing/looking' (marked with full reduplication of *və-* 'see, look' (§9.1.1)) has a prescriptive meaning.

T1.8 [və-ku]   [ata warsama-də-d]   [warsama-də-k]   [ata
     see-COMPL.SS   then be.angry-3masc.sgSUBJ.P-3masc.sgBAS.P   be.angry-3masc.sg-COMPL.DS   then
     wa:d]   [sa!] [Miyawa ta:kw   atawa   tə-kwa-na-di]
     say+3masc.sgBAS.P Hey! all   woman like.that stay-HAB-ACT.FOC-3plBAS.VT
     [wa-də-k]   [ma:] [bap-a:m   vya-k]
     say-3masc.sg-COMPL.DS NEG   moon-LK+OBJ kill-PURP.SS
     [yi-k-na-dəwun-ək]   [ata wa:d]
     go-FUT-ACT.FOC-1masc.sgBAS.VT-CONF then say+3masc.sgBAS.P
     'Having seen (this happen) he got angry, after he'd got really angry, he (the other man) said, "Hey! All women become like that", after he'd said that, "No, I will go to kill the moon", thus he (the husband) said'

In the second clause, the 'object' of anger is cross-referenced in the second position. The third clause contains an instance of head-tail linkage. Switch-reference indicates change in subject(s) throughout this sentence.

T1.9 [wa-də-k]   [ah ah ma:y] [yin   ap]   [wa-də-k]   [ñan
     say-3masc.sg-COMPL.DS ah ah go   go+SEQ IMPV+see say-3masc.sg-COMPL.DS we
     kə-di   takwaba:b   kra-bana-di]   [ta:kw bap
     DEM.PROX-pl woman+LK+TOO get-1plSUBJ.VT-3plBAS.VT woman moon
     və-kwa-la-di]   [oh ma: ma:] [wa-ku]   [kədəka
     see-HAB-3fem.sgSUBJ.VT-3plBAS.VT oh no no   say-COMPL.SS DEM.PROX.REACT.TOP+masc.sg
     ya:d]
     go+3masc.sgBAS.P
     'After he'd said this, "Ah, ah, go (and) have a look (lit. going see)", after he'd said, "we also marry these women, moon sees the women", having said "oh, no, no", this one (the husband) went off'

Switch-reference indicates change in subject(s) throughout this sentence. The third clause translates as 'go and look'; literally it is 'going look'. The fourth and fifth clause are juxtaposed without any connective (see §19.7). In the last clause, the husband is referred to with a reactivated topic demonstrative, to make sure his identity is clear to the hearer (he has not been referred to with a full NP for a while). The proximal demonstrative is used to distinguish him as more important for the story than the other man.

T1.10 [val   kur-ku]   [nəkə   *ailandar*   ata ya:d]   [*ailandar*
canoe get-COMPL.SS   other+fem.sg island+LK+ALL then go+3masc.sgBAS.P island+LK+ALL
yin   yin   yin   yin   yin]   [təp-a:m   ata
go+SEQ go+SEQ go+SEQ go+SEQ go+SEQ village-LK+LOC then
kawid]   [kawi-də-k]   [kwasa-ñan-ugw {waku-n
come.ashore+3masc.sgBAS.P come.ashore-3masc.sg-COMPL.DS small-child-PL   go.out-SEQ
kwa-n}] [gwa:m   nayi-di]
stay-SEQ water+LK+LOC play-3plBAS.P
'Having taken a canoe, he then went to another island, going going going going going to the
island, he came ashore in a village, after he'd come ashore, small children were playing in water
keeping going out (away from shore)'

The second clause contains a code-switch with English *island* and not Tok Pisin *ailan*—this form occurs
in the last clause of T1.11. Repetition of the sequencing form *yin* (five times) in the third clause iconically
reflects the lengthy character of the action. Clause 5 contains head-tail linkage. The next clause contains
a durative complex predicate with the auxiliary *kwa-* 'stay' in a sequencing clause (see §17.1.1).

T1.11 [ay] [kəlawurəm   və-gura]   [bap
hey DEM.PROX+fem.sg+UP+LK+LOC see-2plSUBJ.VT+3fem.sgBAS.VT moon
kwa-na]   [wa-də-k]   [oh, bap   ma: ku]   [bap
stay-ACT.FOC+3fem.sgBAS.VT say-3masc.sg-COMPL.DS oh   moon NEG stay+NEG moon
anay   al-ay   *ailanəm*   kwa-na]
DEM.DIST.CURR.REL DEM.DIST.fem.sg-DIST island+LK+LOC stay-ACT.FOC+3fem.sgBAS.VT
' "Hey, do you see that up here moon lives", after he'd said that, "oh, moon does not live (here),
moon lives there (previously mentioned), there in the distance, on an island" '

The third clause contains a juxtaposed main clause used as a complementation strategy (§19.8). The
speech verb is omitted in the last clause, as it is in T1.12: the dialogue is rendered by the speaker's
modulation of voice.

T1.12 [a   ya:kya] [wun lə-kə-wa   warya-k   yi-k-na-dəwun-ək]   [ah,
then OK   I   she-OBL-COM fight-PURP.SS go-FUT-ACT.FOC-1masc.sgBAS.VT-CONF ah
ma:ya ata] [wa-da-k]   [ata ya:d]
go   then say-3pl-COMPL.DS then go+3masc.sgBAS.P
' "Then OK, I will go to fight with her" (he said), "ah, go then", after they'd said (this), he then
went'

In the third clause, the connective *ata* is placed after the imperative verb 'go'; this adds to the urgency of
the command (the children do not want to have anything to do with the man who is behaving strangely).

T1.13 [yin   yin   yin]   [nəkə   təp-a:m   ata kawid]
go+SEQ go+SEQ go+SEQ other+fem.sg village-LK+LOC then come.ashore+3masc.sgBAS.P
[kawi-də-k]   [[du viti-abər]   waku-bər]   [waku-brə-k]
come.ashore-3masc.sg-COMPL.DS man two-3duNOM go.out-3duBAS.P go.out-3du-COMPL.DS
[ata wa:d]   [sa!]
then say+3masc.sgBAS.P hey
'Going, going, going, he then came ashore in another village, after he'd come ashore, two men
went out, after they'd gone out, he said, "Hey!" '

Repetition of the sequencing form of 'go' (three times) reflects how far the man went. The third and fifth
clauses contain head-tail linkage. Within the fourth clause, the noun phrase 'two men' (lit. there are two
men) is in contrastive focus (see §20.3).

T1.14 [gur-a-gur-a   təp-a:m   bap   kwa-na?]   [Ata-n
you.pl-LK-you.pl-LK+fem.sg village-LK+LOC moon stay-ACT.FOC+3fem.sgBAS.VT thus-PRED
bap   ka]   [{kə   bap}   {kə   [sə
moon DEM.PROX+3fem.sgNOM DEM.PROX.fem.sg moon DEM.PROX.fem.sg sleep
kwa-na]   bap}   {wun-a   takwa:m}   və-kwa-lalək]
stay-ACT.FOC+3fem.sgBAS.VT moon I-LK+fem.sg wife+LK+OBJ see-HAB-3fem.sg+BECAUSE
[wun lə-kə-wa   warya-k   ya-na-dəwun-ək]
I   she-OBL-COM fight-PURP.SS come-ACT.FOC-1masc.sgBAS.VT-CONF
[və-kwa-lalək]
see-HAB-3fem.sg+BECAUSE
' "Does the moon live in your village? Thus it is, this is the moon, this moon, because this
sleeping moon keeps looking at my wife, I have come to fight with her, because she keeps looking
(at her)" '

The third clause contains a relative clause within a noun phrase. Note the repetition of the causal clause.
This repetition is characteristic of casual speech.

T1.15 [oh, mən-a   bap-al]   [lə-kə-wa   warya-wari ma:]
oh   you.masc-LK+fem.sg moon-3fem.sgNOM she-OBL-COM fight-RED   NEG
[takwa:m   akətawa və-kwa-na]
woman+LK+OBJ like.this see-HAB-ACT.FOC+3fem.sgBAS.VT
'Oh, it is your moon, there is no fighting with her, she usually looks at women like this'

Note the omission of the verb of speech, typical in a dialogue. In the last clause the negated nominalization 'fighting' (marked with full reduplication: §9.1.1) has a prescriptive meaning (compare T1.7 above).

T1.16 [ma: ma: ma:] [wun-a   ta:kw-a]   [wun alək   lə-kə-m   vya-k]
no no no   I-LK+fem.sg wife-3fem.sgNOM I   this.is.why she-OBL-OBJ hit-PURP.SS
[wa-də-k]   [a   ma:ya   ata mən]   [wa-də-k]
say-3masc.sg-COMPL.DS then go.IMPV+VOC then you.masc say-3masc.sg-COMPL.DS
[wa-ku]   [rapə-ku]   [ata ya:d]
say-COMPL.SS get.up-COMPL.SS then go+3masc.sgBAS.P
' "No, no, no, it is my wife, this is why I am going to hit her (the moon)", after he'd said this,
"then you go", after (the other man) had said this, having said; having got up (the husband)
then went off'

The negative pro-clause *ma:* in the first clause is repeated three times. This is pronounced as one
phonological phrase. In the third clause, the connective *alək* 'this is why' is placed after the A (it usually
occupies the sentence- or clause-initial position—see §19.6). The V-connective-S order in the fifth clause
emphasizes the urgency of the command: everyone is happy to get rid of the crazy man.

T1.17 [yin   yin   yin]   [nəkə   təp-a:m   ata kawid]
go+SEQ go+SEQ go+SEQ other+fem.sg village-LK+LOC then come.ashore+3masc.sgBAS.P
[kawi-də-k]   [yi:n]   [kawi-də-k]   [{{{kə
come.ashore-3masc.sg-COMPL.DS go+SEQ come.ashore-3masc.sg-COMPL.DS DEM.PROX.fem.sg
bap}   lə-kə-də   ñamus}   də-kə-də   sə]   Yalawi-ad]   [ata
moon she-OBL-masc.sg younger.sibling he-OBL-masc.sg name Yalawi-3fem.sgNOM then
waku-d]   [bap bə   [yi:n]   kwarbam   ta:l]
go.out-3masc.sgBAS.P moon already go+SEQ jungle+LK+LOC stand+3fem.sgBAS.P
[tə-lə-k]   [də ata waku-də-k]   [də ata
stand-3fem.sg-COMPL.DS he   then go.out-3masc.sg-COMPL.DS he   then
kawi-yi-d]   kə-də   du]
come.ashore-go-3masc.sgBAS.P DEM.PROX-masc.sg man
'Going, going, going, he came ashore in another village, after he'd come ashore, going on having
come ashore, the name of the younger brother of this moon was Yalawi, he then went out, the

moon already went off and was in the bush, after she (the moon) had been in the bush, after he (the brother) had gone out, he then kept going ashore, this man (the husband)'

This sentence contains a number of instances of head-tail linkage. Clause 6 contains a complex NP ('the name of the younger brother of this moon'). The last clause contains S in the clause-final position of an afterthought (separated from the verb by a short pause).

T1.18 [kawi-ku]   [ata wa-də-d]   [mən bap
come.ashore-COMPL.SS then say-3masc.sgSUBJ.P-3masc.sgBAS.P you   moon
laku-məna?]
know-2masc.sgSUBJ.VT+3fem.sgBAS.VT
'Having come ashore, then he said to him, "You know the moon?"'

This sentence is connected to the preceding one by head-tail linkage. Note that only the first component of the compound in the last clause of T1.17 (*kawi-yi-* (come.ashore-go) (see §15.3.1)) is repeated in the first clause of this sentence—see §20.4.1 on head-tail linkage.

T1.19 [ata wa-də-d]   [a?]   [wun bapa-wa
then say-3masc.sgSUBJ.P-3masc.sgBAS.P what? I   moon+LK-COM
kwa-na-dəwun-ək]   [a   wun-a   ma:m-a]
stay-ACT.FOC-1masc.sgBAS.VT-CONF DEM.DIST.fem.sg I-LK+fem.sg elder.sibling-3fem.sgNOM
'Then he said, "What? I live with the moon, that is my elder sister"'

The third and fourth clauses are juxtaposed to each other without any connective: the fourth clause provides explanation for the third clause (see §19.7).

T1.20 [lə akə-l]   [wun lə-kə-m   vya-k   ya-na-dəwun-ək]   [lə
she where-fem.sg I   she-OBL-OBJ hit-PURP.SS come-ACT.FOC-1masc.sgBAS.VT-CONF she
wun-a   takwa:m   və-lalək]
I-LK+fem.sg wife+LK+OBJ see-3fem.sg+BECAUSE
' "Where is she? I have come to hit her, because she looks at my wife"'

The first and second clauses are juxtaposed without any connective: the second clause provides explanation for the first (see §19.7). The causal clause is postposed to the main clause as a way of backgrounding it (see §20.2).

T1.21 [wa-də-k]   [ata wa-də-d]   [ooh!] [lə bə
say-3masc.sg-COMPL.DS then say-3masc.sgSUBJ.P-3masc.sgBAS.P ooh   she already
yi-na   *busir*]
go-ACT.FOC+3fem.sgBAS.VT bush+ALL
'After he's said this, he then said, "Ooh, she is already gone, to the bush"'

The Tok Pisin code-switch *busir* 'to the bush' was replaced with the Manambu equivalent *kwarbar* (bush+LK+ALL) by Yuamali when transcribing the story. As is typical for Manambu, loans and code-switches are inflected in the same way as native forms. The form *busir* is postposed to the inflected verb and separated from it with a small pause, as an afterthought—see §20.2.

T1.22 [mən   atəta   vya-kə-məna]   [wa-də-k]   [ma:]
you.masc how/why hit-FUT-2masc.sgSUBJ.VT+3fem.sgBAS.VT say-3masc.sg-COMPL.DS no
[lə wun-a   takwa:m   agwa-japək   və-kwa-la?]
she I-LK+fem.sg wife+LK+OBJ what-thing+LK+DAT see-HAB-3fem.sgSUBJ.VT+3fem.sgBAS.VT
[alək   vya-na-dəwun-ək]   [vya-k   alək
this.is.why hit-ACT.FOC-1masc.sgBAS.VT-CONF hit-PURP.SS this.is.why
ya-na-dəwun-ək]   [lə-kə-m   vya-k]   [wa-də-k]
come-ACT.FOC-1masc.sgBAS.VT-CONF she-OBL-OBJ hit-PURP.SS say-3masc.sg-COMPL.DS

[wa-də-k]   [a!] [ata adakw] [ya-k-na]
say-3masc.sg-COMPL.DS a! then stay.IMPV come-FUT-ACT.FOC+3fem.sgBAS.VT
[wa-də-k]   [ata kwa:d]
say-3masc.sg-COMPL.DS then stay+3masc.sgBAS.P
' "Why will you hit her?", after he'd said this, "no, for what purpose does she keep looking at
my wife? This is why I will hit her, this is why I have come to hit her", after he'd said this, after
he'd said "Ah! wait (lit. then stay), she will come", after he'd said this, he then stayed'

The husband's speech is highly repetitive. Note the placement of the connective *alək* 'this is why' in clause
6. Clause 11 contains a speech formula meaning 'wait'. The next clause is juxtaposed without a connective
and provides a comment to it (see §19.7).

T1.23 [kwa-də-k]   [ata ya:l]   [ya-lə-k]   [ata
       stay-3masc.sg-COMPL.DS then come+3fem.sgBAS.P come-3fem.sg-COMPL.DS then
       wa-də-l]   [a-də   lə-kə-də   ñamus   ata
       say-3masc.sgSUBJ.P-3fem.sgBAS.P DEM.DIST-masc.sg she-OBL-masc.sg younger.sibling then
       wa-də-l]   [kə-də   du   ñən-a-wa   warya-k
       say-3masc.sgSUBJ.P-3fem.sgBAS.P DEM.PROX-masc.sg man you.fem-LK-COM fight-PURP.SS
       ya-na-d]   [wa-də-k]   [ah] [agwa-japək?]
       come-ACT.FOC-3masc.sgBAS.VT say-3masc.sg-COMPL.DS ah   what-thing+LK+DAT
       'After he'd stayed, then she came, after she'd come, then he said to her, that younger brother of
       hers then said to her, "This man has come to fight with you", after he'd said thus, "ah, why?"
       (she said)'

Note the extensive use of switch-reference-sensitive completive medial clause marker for disambiguating
who said what. The last two clauses are part of a speech report with an omitted verb of speech (recoverable
from the context). The last clause consists of just one interrogative—this is an example of ellipsis.

T1.24 [ma:]   [də-kə   takwa:m   və-kwa-ñənalək]   [ata
       no   he-OBL+fem.sg wife+LK+OBJ see-HAB-2fem.sg+BECAUSE then
       da-kwa-d]   [ata warya-tək]   [wa-ku]   [ya:n]
       go.down-IMPV.3p-masc.sg then fight-1duIMPV say-COMPL.SS come+SEQ
       [waku-lə-k]   [ya:kya]
       go.out-3fem.sg-COMPL.DS OK
       ' "No, (it is) because you keep looking at his wife". "May he come down then, then let's fight",
       after she'd said thus coming out, she did go out'

The first and second clauses are part of what the brother said; the speech verb is omitted. The negative
pro-clause is used in the meaning of 'it is not what you expect' (see Chapter 14). The third and fourth
clauses contain connective *ata* marking temporal sequence of the suggested events. The last clause
contains just *ya:kya* 'OK': this is a typical strategy used to emphasize that the action of the preceding
clause did take place.

T1.25 [kəbra   ata   {warya-k kur-bər}]   [kur-də-k]   [lə
       DEM.PROX.REACT.TOP+du then fight-PURP do/get-3duBAS.P do/get-3masc.sg-COMPL.DS she
       bəta:y bap   yi-səwul-ku]   [kwala:b   kətəkə-lə-d]
       already moon go-turn-COMPL.SS neck+LK+TERM cut-3fem.sgSUBJ.P-3masc.sgBAS.P
       'The two were then about to fight, after he was about to fight, she already turned into the moon
       and cut him right on his neck'

The first clause contains a construction of imminent modality with an auxiliary *kur-* 'be about to' (see
§17.1.2).

T1.26 [kətəkə-lə-k,]   [{kə-də   lə-kə-də   du-a-ma:gw} ata
       cut-3fem.sgSUBJ.P-COMPL.DS DEM.PROX-masc.sg she-OBL-masc.sg man-LK-sibling then
       wa-də-l]   [way] [mən-a:k   wa-tua]
       say-3masc.sgSUBJ.P-3fem.sgBAS.P oh.dear you.masc-LK+DAT say-1sgSUBJ.VT+3fem.sgBAS.VT

[kə   bap   akəs   du   ta:kw   warya-kwa-dana]
DEM.PROX.fem.sg   moon NEG.HAB   man   woman   fight-HAB-3plSUBJ.VT+3fem.sgBAS.VT
[kal   bap-a]   [[kə-də   kəpa:m
DEM.PROX.fem.sg   moon-3fem.sgNOM   DEM.PROX-masc.sg   earth+LK+OBJ
səsi-yi-kwa-na]   bap-al]   [akəs   du   ta:kw
shine+RED-go-HAB-ACT.FOC+3fem.sgBAS.VT   moon-3fem.sgNOM   NEG.HAB   man   woman
warya-kwa-dana]   [wa-tu-l-al]   [ya:kya]
fight-HAB-3plSUBJ.VT+3fem.sgBAS.VT   say-1sgSUBJ.P-3fem.sgBAS.P-3fem.sgNOM   OK
'After she'd cut (him), this younger brother of hers said, "Oh dear, I have told you, people never
fight with this moon, this is the moon who keeps shining all over this earth, it is the moon,
people never fight (with her), this was what I told (you), OK" '

In the second clause, the second argument cross-referenced on the verb 'say' is time (and not the addressee,
since the addressee is a man and not a woman). In clause 5, the subject (A) is placed after the habitual
negator *akəs* (see §14.2). Clause 7 contains a relative clause. The predicate in the penultimate clause is
focused (see §20.3). The form *ya:kya* marks the end of a stretch of discourse.

T1.27 [vya-lə-k]   [vækər-ku]   [ya:kya] [rapə-ku]   [ata   səbən-ən
       hit-3fem.sg-COMPL.DS   fall-COMPL.SS   OK   get.up-COMPL.SS   then   return-SEQ
       ya:d]   [a-di   təp-a-təp   ata   kwa-ya-d]
       go+3masc.sgBAS.P   DEM.DIST-pl   village-LK-village   then   stay-come-3masc.sgBAS.P
       'After she'd hit him, after he'd fallen down, OK, he got up, then he went back, he stayed in each
       of those villages'

Clauses 5 and 6 are juxtaposed without any connective, in a sequential meaning (see §19.7).

T1.28 [ya:n]   [waku-da-k]   [təp-a-kə-di   ata   wa-da:-d]
       come+SEQ   go.out-3pl-COMPL.DS   village-LK-POSS-pl   then   say-3plSUBJ.P-3masc.sgBAS.P
       [yi-mənə-l]   [bap   vya-mənə-l]   [wa-da-k]
       go-2masc.sgSUBJ.P-3fem.sgBAS.P   moon   hit-2masc.sgSUBJ.P-3fem.sgBAS.P   say-3pl-COMPL.DS
       [oh!]
       oh
       'Going, having gone out, the villagers then said to him, "As you went, you hit the moon", after
       they'd said this, "Oh" ' (he said)

The addressee of 'say' is cross-referenced in the third clause. The fourth and fifth clauses are juxtaposed
without any connective, with one clause providing a comment to the other (see §19.7). In both cases, time
is cross-referenced in the second position.

T1.29 [aw   vya-lə-k]   [ya-dəwun-ək]   [rapə-ku]
       then   hit-3fem.sg-COMPL.DS   come-1masc.sgBAS.VT-CONF   get.up-COMPL.SS
       [ya-na-dəwun-ək]   [wa-də-k]   [ata   ay
       come-ACT.FOC-1masc.sgBAS.VT-CONF   say-3masc.sg-COMPL.DS   then   INTERJ
       yi-da-d]   [samasama   du   ta:kw]   [waji-ta:y   waji-ta:y]   [ata
       say-3plSUBJ.P-3masc.sgBAS.P   many+LK   man   woman   laugh-COTEMP   laugh-COTEMP   then
       ay   yi-da-d]
       INTERJ   say-3plSUBJ.P-3masc.sgBAS.P
       ' "Then after she'd hit me, I came, having got up I have come", after he'd said (this), many people
       shouted, laughing and laughing then they shouted'

Clause 6 contains the verb *yi-* 'go, say' with the interjection *ay* as a speech report (see §19.5). The next
clause provides elaboration of clause 6. The cotemporaneous dependent clause *waji-ta:y* is repeated twice;
and the two instances are pronounced as one phonological phrase.

T1.30 [agwa-japək   [yi-kər]   yi-mənə-l-a?]
       what-thing+LK+DAT   go-DES   go-2masc.sgSUBJ.VT-3fem.sgBAS.VT-3fem.sgNOM
       'Why was it the case that you went, to go for what purpose?'

This clause is focused (focus being marked with nominal cross-referencing on the main inflected verb—see §20.3).

T1.31 [{kə-də   kəpa:m}   {kə-di   {kwa-na-di}   du   ta:kw} bap
      DEM.PROX-masc.sg earth+LK+OBJ DEM.PROX-pl stay-ACT.FOC-3plBAS.VT man woman moon
      və-kwa-na-dian]
      see-HAB-ACT.FOC-1plBAS.VT
      ' "We, these people (lit. man woman) who stay on this earth, we menstruate (lit. see the moon)" '

This sentence contains a relative clause whose common argument is the S of the relative clause and the A of the main clause.

T1.32 [al]   [{ñan} {kə-di   kəpa-kə-di   ta:kw} {ñan-a   ma:j}-a]
      this.is.it we   DEM.PROX-pl earth+LK-POSS-pl woman we-LK+fem.sg story-3fem.sgNOM
      [ñan-a:m   tə-kwa-na   sik-a]   [{ñan ta:kw}
      we-LK+LOC stand-HAB-ACT.FOC+3fem.sgBAS.VT sickness-3fem.sgNOM we woman
      [ñan-a:m   tə-kwa-na]   ja:p-a]
      we-LK+LOC stand-HAB-ACT.FOC+3fem.sgBAS.VT thing-3fem.sgNOM
      ' "This is it, we these women of this earth, it is our story. It is a sickness that stays on us, us women, it is the thing that stays on" '

The noun phrase in the second clause contains the pronoun ('we') in apposition to a complex noun phrase ('these village women'). The last clause contains two relative clauses.

T1.33 [və-la-dian]   [wa-n]   [wa-kwa-bana   ma:j-a]
      see-3fem.sgSUBJ.VT-1plBAS.VT say-SEQ say-HAB-1plSUBJ.VT+3fem.sgBAS.VT story-3fem.sgNOM
      [aba:b ta:kw   ata   wa-da-k]   [wa-lə-k]   [ata wa:d]
      all   woman then say-3pl-COMPL.DS say-3fem.sg-COMPL.DS then say+3masc.sgBAS.P
      [ayəy] [wun [aka   bə   du-ad]   wa-ku]   [yin]
      yes   I   DEM.DIST.REACT.TOP.fem.sg already man-3masc.sgNOM say-COMPL.SS go+SEQ
      [warya-u]   [wa-ku]   [yi-na-dəwun-ək]
      fight-1sgIMPV say-COMPL.SS go-ACT.FOC-1masc.sg.BAS.VT-CONF
      ' "She sees us", it is the story we usually tell (lit. it is the story we usually tell telling)", after all women had said this, after she'd said this, then he said, "Yes, I have gone (to fight the moon), having said, "Here is a man", having said "Let me go and fight" '

Note a speech report within a speech report in clause 8.

T1.34 [ya:kya wa-ku]   [ata kwa:d]   [a   ta:kw kra-ku]
      OK   say-COMPL.SS then stay+3masc.sgBAS.P DEM.DIST.fem.sg woman get-COMPL.SS
      'Having settled this (lit, having said "OK"), then he remained, having married that woman'

The first clause contains a fixed expression, *ya:kya wa-* (OK say) meaning 'agree, settle'. The third clause is a medial clause following the main clause, as a way of backgrounding it (see §20.2).

T1.35 [adəka   kusə-na-d]   [mawər
      DEM.DIST.REACT.TOP+masc.sg finish-ACT.FOC-3masc.sgBAS.VT base+LK+ALL
      wula-d   aka]
      go.inside-3masc.sgBAS.VT DEM.PROX.REACT.TOP+fem.sg
      'This (long story) is finished; it is over' (lit. goes inside the base)

The two clauses are juxtaposed without a connective: the second one is an elaboration of the first one (see §19.7). The second clause contains a typical expression used in endings of story, literally '(the story) enters its base'.

TEXT 2. THE ORIGIN OF THE VALI:K CLAN, NARRATED BY JOHN SəPAYWəS,
RECORDED 18 JANUARY 2002 (APPROXIMATE LENGTH 12 MINUTES)

This story, told by John Səpaywəs, Yuaneng's and my classificatory paternal uncle (father's brother), is one of the major narratives of the Manambu relating to the Gala wars (see §1.5) and the origin of the Vali:k clan. John Səpaywəs was the indicated person to narrate the story, given his high status in the Manambu community as one of the most knowledgeable 'big men' in terms of totemic lexicon and names (see §1.5 and the discussion of totemic terms in §4.1.2 and §21.5.4). The story is addressed to both Yuaneng and myself; hence the second person dual pronoun in T2.1.

Like most big men in the Manambu-speaking villages nowadays, John Səpaywəs often code-switches with Tok Pisin. Occasionally, he corrects himself.

T2.1 [wun ñaj]   [kə   ma:j aka   kə   *stori*
     I   father's.brother this+fem.sg story DEM.PROX.REACT.TOP+fem.sg this+fem.sg story
     aka   kui-kə-tua]   [wun
     DEM.PROX.REACT.TOP+fem.sg give.to.third.p-FUT-1sgSUBJ.VT+3fem.sgBAS.VT I
     ñaj   Səpay] [kə   *stori* aka   bra:k
     father's.brother Sepay this+fem.sg story DEM.PROX.REACT.TOP+fem.sg 2du+LK+DAT
     kwatiya-kə-tua]
     give.to.non.third.p-FUT-1sgSUBJ.VT+3fem.sgBAS.VT
     'I am father's brother, this very story, this story, I will give, I am father's brother, I will give this story to you two'

The first clause is a verbless clause used for introducing participants in discourse and for naming (also see the third clause). The second clause employs the third person recipient form of the verb 'give' with second person recipients (see under C at §4.2.2). This could either be a mistake or the result of a tendency to use the third person recipient form as a generic one. The last clause employs the non-third person recipient form of 'give'.

T2.2 [kə   [kakəl-ba-l]   ma:j aka wa-kə-tua
     this+fem.sg win-1plSUBJ.VT-3fem.sgBAS.VT story here tell-FUT-1sgSUBJ.VT+3fem.sgBAS.VT
     ya   kəp] [*orait*] [kakəl-ba-l   aka]
     EMPH only all.right win-1plSUBJ.P-3fem.sgBAS.P DEM.PROX.REACT.TOP+fem.sg
     'I will tell the story of how we won, just, all right, this is how we won'

The first clause contains a relative clause with the object relativized, 'a story of how we won'. In the first clause, John Səpaywəs said *wini-ba-l* (win:Tok Pisin-1plSUBJ.VT-3fem.sgBAS.VT) instead of *kakəl-ba-l* and then corrected himself. In the last clause the reactivated topic demonstrative refers to the way in which 'we won' cross-referenced in the second position of *kakəl-* 'win, exceed'.

T2.3 [kə-di gala-di]   [gala wa-bana-di]   [a   kəta
     this-PL Gala-3plBAS Gala tell-1plSUBJ.VT-3plBAS.VT then now
     wuka   Vali:k wa-bana]   [*tasol*   ma:]
     DEM.PROX.ADDR.REACT.TOP+fem.sg Valik tell-1plSUBJ.VT+3fem.sgBAS.VT but/because no
     [gala-di]
     Gala-3plBAS
     'These are Gala, those whom we call Gala, now this one here close to addressee we call Vali:k, but no, they are Gala'

John Səpaywəs was adamant that the Vali:k were not the real Manambu but actually the Gala (also known as Ngala), that is, the group called Gala (we saw, in §1.4.1, that the question of the identity between the Gala discussed here and the Gala currently living in Swakap may still be open). He used the 'proximate to addressee' demonstratives, because there were at least two representatives of the Vali:k clan in the audience, one of them Jennie Kudapa:kw.

The second and third clauses are examples of ditransitive use of *wa-* 'say' (see §19.5.5). The negative pro-clause forms a full clause in clause 4; clause five is a typical verbless clause with a noun in the predicate slot. The Tok Pisin word *tasol* 'but' is occasionally used as a marker of contrast linkage.

T2.4 [ya-ku]   [kələm   kə-də   du a:s kray-ku]
come-COMPL.SS DEM.PROX+fem.sg+LOC DEM.PROX-masc.sg man dog bring-COMPL.SS
[və-də-di]   [ap-a-kwuim   rə-da-k]   PAUSE [[ja:b
see-3masc.sgSUBJ.P-3plBAS.P bone-LK-tree.species+LK+LOC sit-3pl-COMPL.DS PAUSE floor
saki-ku]   [wi   kur-ku   rə-da-k]]   [rə-da:k]
put.together-COMPL.ss house get-COMPL.ss sit-3pl-COMPL.DS sit-3pl+COMPL.DS
[aka   yi-ku]   [a:s kray-ku,   kədiya
DEM.DIST.REACT.TOP+fem.sg go-COMPL.ss dog bring-COMPL.ss DEM.PROX.REACT.TOP.pl
və-də-di]
see-3masc.sgSUBJ.P-3plBAS.P
'Having come, having brought a dog here this man saw them, as they sat on big (lit. bone) kway tree having put a tree house together, having made a house they sat, as they sat, having gone, having brought a dog, he saw them'

This is a typical clause chain. The second clause is an example of a medial completive clause used as a complementation strategy with the verb of perception 'see'. So is the next clause (postposed to the main clause). A pause after it indicates that the next clause is a complement of the second occurrence of 'see'.

This relates to the part of the story omitted by John Səpaywəs since this is something everyone knows: the people who made a *ja:b* 'floor' (also raft, tree house) are the Gala who had already been defeated by the Manambu (or the Kwoma: see §1.4.1) and escaped.

The lengthened vowel in the form *rə-da:k* 'as they sat' reflects the prolonged period of time the Gala spent hiding in their tree houses.

T2.5 [və-də-k]   [a:s kəka   {saula-su-l]
see-3masc.sg-COMPL.DS dog DEM.PROX.REACT.TOP.pl bark-UP-3fem.sgBAS.P
[saula-su-lə-k]}   [kətu və-ku]   [[oh, kə-di   du-adi]
bark-UP-3fem.sg-COMPL.DS look.UP see-COMPL.ss oh DEM.PROX-pl man-3plNOM
wa-ku]   [vyatəkul-ku]   [kəda   ya:d
say-COMPL.ss spy-COMPL.ss DEM.PROX.REACT.TOP+masc.sg go+3masc.sgBAS.P
kə-də   Səsawi]
DEM.PROX-masc.sg Sesawi
'After he'd seen (them), this very dog barked in the upward direction, after she'd barked in the upward direction, after he'd looked up, having said, "Oh, these are men", having spied (on them), this one went off this Sesawi'

This is another example of a lengthy clause chain. The braces in the second line show that the two occurrences of the verb 'bark upwards' form one phonological phrase; the second one summarizes the first one (see §18.3). The form *kəda* is a fast speech register version of *kədəka* (see A3 in §2.6). The S is postposed to the verb in the last clause as an afterthought: John Səpaywəs remembered the name of the character.

T2.6 [aw Səsawi ya-ku]   [ma: ra:b   vya-d   Apatəp-a:m]
then Sesawi go-COMPL.ss again slit.drum hit-3masc.sgBAS.P Avatip-LK+LOC
[vya-də-k]   [yin]   [du ata   vægru-di]
hit-3masc.sg-COMPL.DS go+SEQ man then get.together-3plBAS.P
'After Sesawi had gone off, he struck the slit gong in Avatip, after he'd struck (it), going on and on men came together'

This is another example of a lengthy clause chain. The locational form, 'in Avatip', in the second clause follows the verb (see §20.2). The form *yin* 'going' is used in an adverbial meaning 'on and on'—see §18.2 and §19.9.

T2.7 [Vægru-da-k]   [wa-də-di]   [və-tua-di   gala
   get.together-3pl-COMPL.DS say-3masc.sgSUBJ.P-3plBAS.P see-1sgSUBJ.VT-3plBAS.P Gala
   kə-nay   apakuim   rə-na-di]   [wa-ku]   [day
   DEM.PROX-CURR.REL+DIST tree.sp+LK+LOC sit-ACT.FOC-3plBAS.VT say-COMPL.SS they
   rə-da-l   aka]
   sit-3plSUBJ.P-3fem.sgBAS.P DEM.PROX.REACT.TOP.pl
   'After they'd got together, he said to them, "The Gala that I saw are here (previously mentioned
   place) at a distance on apakway-tree", having said, "This is where they are sitting"'

The speech report is framed with two occurrences of the verb *wa-* 'speak, say' (see §19.5.2). This is also
an example of a discontinuous speech report.

T2.8 [*orait*] [ya:p-ad]   [a-bər   ya:p viti aw   warə-n   a-də
   OK   rope-3masc.sgNOM DEM.DIST-du rope two then go.up-SEQ DEM.DIST-masc.sg
   wiya:m]   [aw da-n   kəp-a:m]   [atawa kur-ku]   [na:gw
   house+LK+LOC then go.down-SEQ ground-LK+LOC thus   get-COMPL.SS sago
   yaku-yaku-ək] [yipər   ña:m   a   ñapwi   kur-ta:y]   [ya:kya]
   wash-RED-DAT gnetum.gnemon edible.green DEM.DIST.fem.sg firewood get-COTEMP OK
   'OK, there was a rope, with two ropes alternately going up to that house and coming down to
   the ground, to wash sago, they used to get (lit. having got) "gnetum gnemon" (a type of leafy
   vegetable), edible greens, firewood, OK'

In the first clause, *orait* is used to introduce a new paragraph. An alternative interpretation of *ya:p-ad*
could be that of a contrastive focus; note that there is no pause after it—see §20.3. A series of dependent
clauses is used to describe a sequence of actions performed by the Gala hiding in their tree houses. Clauses
consisting just of *ya:kya* 'OK' are discussed in §20.4.2.

T2.9 [aw war-da-l]   [a-də   ya:p pətəkaum war-ta:y]
   then go.up-3plSUBJ.P-3fem.sgBAS.P DEM.DIST-masc.sg rope ladder+LOC go.up-COTEMP
   [warə-n   ap-a-miya:m   a   wiya:m]   [ya:k] [a-də
   go.up-SEQ main-LK-tree+LK+LOC DEM.DIST.fem.sg house+LK+LOC OK   DEM.DIST-masc.sg
   pətəka:u yata-ta:y] [ka-war-da-d]   [ka-war-ən   a-də
   ladder   tie-COTEMP carry-UP-3plSUBJ.P-3masc.sgBAS.P carry-UP-SEQ DEM.DIST-masc.sg
   wiya:m]
   house+LK+LOC
   'Then this is how they got up, having gone up using rope as a ladder, going up the mature tree, to
   that house, OK, having tied that ladder they carried it up, carrying it up to that house'

The last clause is an example of a dependent clause postposed to the main clause.

T2.10 [rə-da-k]   [ya:kya] [lagu-ta:y]   [ka-war-da-d]
   sit-3pl-COMPL.DS OK   pull-COTEMP carry-UP-3plSUBJ.P-3masc.sgBAS.P
   'They having stayed, OK'.

Clauses consisting just of *ya:kya* 'OK' are discussed in §20.4.2. The next sentence (T2.11) is linked to the
preceding one (T2.10) via repetition (see §20.4.1).

T2.11 [lagu-ta:y]   [ka-warə-n]   [a-də   wiya:m   taka-da-d]
   pull-COTEMP carry-UP-SEQ DEM.DIST-masc.sg house+LK+LOC put-3plSUBJ.P-3masc.sgBAS.P
   [ya:kya]
   OK
   'Having been pulling it, by carrying (things up), they put them into the house. OK'

T2.12 [aw {da-kər   tə-ta:y}]   [ata ma: yakə-sada-da-d]
   then go.down-DES 'stand'-COTEMP then again throw-DOWN-3plSUBJ.P-3masc.sgBAS.P
   'Then as they were going down, then again they threw (the rope) down'

The connective *aw* is employed here to link sentences. The constituent in braces is a complex predicate with the meaning of imminent modality (see §17.1.2).

T2.13 [akatawa-dəka kur-da-k]   [Səsawi kədəka   yi-ku]   [[a:s
    like.that-ONLY do-3pl-COMPL.DS Sesawi DEM.PROX.REACT.TOP+masc.sg go-COMPL.SS dog
    saula-da-k]   [və-ku]]   [ya-ku]   [ra:b   vya-n
    bark-3pl-COMPL.DS see-COMPL.SS come-COMPL.SS slit.drum strike-SEQ
    napa-də-k]   [ya-n] [væegru-da-k]   [kwapək
    COMPL.VB-3masc.sg-COMPL.DS go-SEQ get.together-3pl-COMPL.DS next.day
    kədika   yi-di]
    DEM.PROX.REACT.TOP+masc.sg go-3plBAS.P
    'After they'd done thus, this Sesawi having gone, having seen the dogs bark, having come, after
    he'd struck the slit gong, after they'd got together coming, next day they went'

Another example of a lengthy clause chain with switch-reference-sensitive markers indicating the change of subjects of adjacent clauses. The third clause contains a complementation strategy. The following clause contains an instance of the generic completive verb *napa-* (see §18.9).

This sentence recapitulates what was said in T2.5–6.

T2.14 [kədəka   {kadawa   vi:wa}   {a-də   kabak
    DEM.PROX.REACT.TOP+masc.sg shield+LK+COM spear+LK+COM DEM.DIST-masc.sg stone
    kul-a-wa}   kur-ku]   [kədiya   yi-di]
    axe-LK-COM get-COMPL.SS DEM.PROX.REACT.TOP+pl go-3plBAS.P
    'With this shield with spear having grabbed axe and stone these (people: topical) went'

The constituents in braces are NPs with two nouns coordinated with comitatives. The first one is a double comitative (§7.9), referring to shield and spear as an 'inseparable' unit.

T2.15 [yi-ku]   [{vələ-n tə-da-kəkəb}]   [væy kwar-sada-ta:y]
    go-COMPL.SS cut-SEQ 'stand'-3pl-AS.SOON.AS spear throw-DOWN-COTEMP
    [vya-da-di   kada:m]
    hit-3plSUBJ.P-3plBAS.P shield+LK+LOC
    'Having gone, as soon as they (the Avatip people) cut (the tree), having thrown the spear, they
    (the Gala) hit the shield(s)'

The second clause contains an aspectual complex predicate with anterior meaning (§17.1.1). In the last clause the object (shield) is postposed to the verb, in agreement with the tendency described in §20.2.

T2.16 [kur-da-k]   [kur-da-k]   [ya:kya] [{vələ-n tə-da-k}]   [yi:n]
    do-3pl-COMPL.DS do-3pl-COMPL.DS OK   cut-SEQ 'stand'-3masc.sg-COMPL.DS go+SEQ
    [aka   væekrə-l   a   kway]
    DEM.DIST.REACT.TOP+fem.sg fall-3fem.sgBAS.P DEM.DIST.fem.sg tree.sp
    'After they have done this, done this, OK, cutting (the tree) on and on, that one (tree) fell'

The first clause is repeated twice, iconically reflecting repetition of the action. The second clause contains an aspectual complex predicate with anterior meaning (§17.1.1). The form *yi:n* is used adverbially to refer to the action going on and on (see §19.9). An alternative pronunciation for *væekrə-l* could be *væekərə-l*—this is the result of an optional loss of schwa in *k-r* sequences. See §20.2 on the VS order in the last clause.

T2.17 [væekərək]   [kədika   vya-yakə-da-di]
    fall+3fem.sg+COMPL.DS DEM.PROX.REACT.TOP+pl hit-FULLY-3plSUBJ.P-3plBAS.P
    [vya-yakə-da-k]   [orait]
    hit-FULLY-3pl-COMPL.DS OK
    'After that tree fell, they fully hit these (Gala) this (time). Having fully hit (them), OK'

The form *væekərək* (fall+3fem.sg+COMPL.DS) is underlyingly *væekər-lə-k* fall-3fem.sg-COMPL.DS); this alternative pronunciation is possible, but many speakers simplify the sequence of *r-l* to just *r*. The first, second, and third clauses contain head-tail linkage.

T2.18 [{kə-də   a-də   wa-bana-d-ə   sə   Kamkudi}
      DEM.PROX-masc.sg DEM.DIST-masc.sg say-1plSUBJ.VT-3masc.sgBAS.VT-LK name Kamkudi
      kədəka-n-adəka]   [də-də-kə Səsawi
      DEM.PROX.REACT.TOP+masc.sg-PRED-REACT.TOP+masc.sg he-he-OBL Sesawi
      adəka   vya-də-d]
      DEM.DIST.REACT.TOP+masc.sg hit-3masc.sgSUBJ.P-3masc.sgBAS.P
      'Then this (man) by that name of Kamkudi here he is, Sesawi himself hit him'

The constituent in braces is a complex NP (§20.1). The reduplicated form of the third person pronoun in
the last clause has an emphatic reading, 'himself' (see §10.1). The reactivated topic demonstrative in the
last clause refers to Kamkudi, as part of a reintroduced topic.

T2.19 [vya-də-k]   [kədəka   væy kaygrəpə-ku]
      hit-3masc.sg-COMPL.DS DEM.PROX.REACT.TOP+masc.sg spear break-COMPL.SS
      [kədəka   tabu-d]
      DEM.PROX.REACT.TOP+masc.sg escape-3masc.sgBAS.P
      'After he'd hit him, having broken his spear this one (Kamkudi) escaped'

The first clause contains head-tail linkage with the previous sentence. Since Kamkudi is the most topical
participant in this stretch, he is being referred to with a reactivated topic demonstrative.

T2.20 [tabu-ku   yi-ku]   [dəpu-nagwum   vya-prapi-ku]
      escape-COMPL.SS go-COMPL.SS inside.hollow+LK-sago+LK+LOC hit-be.hollow-COMPL.SS
      [{wulan   ta:d}]
      enter+SEQ 'stand'+3masc.sgBAS.P
      'Having escaped (and) gone, having broken the hollow part (of a sago palm) he had entered the
      hollow inside of a sago palm'

The first clause contains head-tail linkage with the previous sentence. The form *yi-ku* in the first clause is
pronounced as one intonation unit with *tabu-ku* (see §18.3) in a recapitulating function. The constituent
in braces in the third clause is a complex predicate with an anterior meaning (§17.1.1).

T2.21 [tə-də-k]   [*tu wik*   bə   wa:l]
      'stand'-3masc.sg-COMPL.DS two weeks   already say+3fem.sgBAS.P
      'After he'd entered (it), two weeks already went' (lit. two weeks already says)

The first clause contains head-tail linkage with the previous sentence; note that only the auxiliary *tə-* is
repeated here. The second clause contains an instance of the metaphorical use of *wa-* 'say', in the meaning
of 'count' (see V at §19.5.6). The functionally unmarked third person feminine cross-referencing may refer
to time (given that time is always feminine: see Chapter 5).
      Jennie Kudapa:kw suggested *sande viti* (Sunday two) as a more authentic version of *tu wik* used by
John Səpaywəs.

T2.22 [wa-lə-k]   [a-də   Səsawi ya:b ma: ada
      say-3fem.sg-COMPL.DS DEM.DIST-masc.sg Sesawi road again DEM.DIST.REACT.TOP+masc.sg
      yi-na-d]
      go-ACT.FOC-3masc.sgBAS.VT
      'After (two weeks) had finished, that Sesawi again is going on the road'

The first clause contains head-tail linkage with the previous sentence. The second clause contains an
inherently locational noun *ya:b* 'road' unmarked for case (see §7.2). The form *ada* is a fast register form
of *adəka*. The action focus marker is used in the second clause as a way of focusing on a new activity.

T2.23 [a:s kur-ku]   [yi-ku]   [ada   ma: a-di   a:s
      dog get-COMPL.SS go-COMPL.SS DEM.DIST.REACT.TOP+masc.sg again DEM.DIST-pl dog
      adəka   saula-na-di]   [də-kə   ya:m wukə-ku]
      DEM.DIST.REACT.TOP+masc.sg bark-ACT.FOC-3plBAS.VT he-OBL+fem.sg smell hear-COMPL.SS

'Having got (dogs) and gone, again those dogs are barking (at) that one (Sesawi) having smelt his smell'

The two medial verbs in two adjacent clauses are pronounced without intonation break, since the actions occurred close to each other. The last medial clause is postposed to the main clause, since it contains backgrounded information already stated previously (we can recall that the dogs have already done exactly the same thing in T2.5 and T2.13: see §20.2).

T2.24 [saula-su-da-k]   [də Səsawi adəka   wa-na-d]
      bark-UP-3pl-COMPL.DS he Sesawi DEM.DIST.REACT.TOP+masc.sg say-ACT.FOC-3masc.sgBAS.P
      [ay yayi:b-ad]   [ay] [kəpanay-ad]   [ay] [wiyəw-ad]
      ay? tree.kangaroo-3masc.sgNOM ay? wallaby-3masc.sgNOM ay? lizard.sp-3masc.sgNOM
      [wa-ku   ya:kya]
      say-COMPL.SS OK
      'After they'd barked in upward direction, that Sesawi says, "Hey, this is a tree kangaroo (or) hey, this is a wallaby, (or) hey, this is a lizard", having said this, OK'

The first clause contains head-tail linkage with the previous sentence; the repeated verb is that of the main clause from T2.23, and not the actual final verb which happens to be the predicate of a dependent clause. Note a speech report framing construction (§19.5.1) consisting of two instances of *wa-* 'say', one preceding the report and the other following it.

T2.25 [adəka   vya-prapi-da-d]
      DEM.DIST.REACT.TOP+masc.sg hit-be.hollow-3masc.sgSUBJ.VT-3masc.sgBAS.VT
      [a-də   na:gw vya-prapi-də-k]   [wa!   du
      DEM.DIST-masc.sg sago hit-be.hollow-3masc.sg-COMPL.DS SURPRISE man
      kədəka]
      DEM.DIST.REACT.TOP+masc.sg [məl pukə-puk pukə-puk na-ku]   [aw wuk
                                  eye bulge-RED bulge-RED BE:NAT-COMPL.SS then tooth
      sər   sər   sər   na-ku]   [ada
      EXPR:white EXPR:white EXPR:white BE:NAT-COMPL.SS DEM.DIST.REACT.TOP+masc.sg
      {tə-kətaku-n   tə-na-d}]   [tə-də-k]
      stay/be-look.OUTWARDS-SEQ 'stand'-ACT.FOC-3masc.sgBAS.VT/P stand-3masc.sg-COMPL.DS
      'He hit it (palm) hollow, having hit the sago palm hollow, "Wow! It is a man!" His eyes bulging out, having been white-white-white (in his) tooth he has been standing facing outwards'

The third clause contains a speech report with the verb of speech omitted. It is not clear whether the remainder of this sentence is a speech report or not. The fourth clause contains an instance of reduplicated verb 'bulge' with *na-* as support verb (see §17.2). The fifth clause contains an expressive referring to the intensity of white colour of teeth in the dark sago trunk. In the next clause, *tə-kətaku-n tə-* is an anterior complex predicate (§17.1.1) (the form *tə-kətaku-n* contains a directional only used with verb 'see': see Chapter 16). The last clause is an instance of recapitulating the essence of the penultimate clause (see §18.3); the two verbs *tə-na-d* and *tə-də-k* form one intonation group.

T2.26 [adəka   wa-da-d]   [mæy]   [avi
      DEM.DIST.REACT.TOP+masc.sg say-3masc.sgSUBJ.VT-3masc.sgBAS.VT come.IMPV IMPV+kill
      ya   wun-a:m] [aw Səsawiya:k   ada
      EMPH I-LK+OBJ then Sesawi+LK+DAT DEM.DIST.REACT.TOP+masc.sg
      wa-da-d]   [avi-ya   jau   wun-a:m] [wa-ku]
      say-3masc.sgSUBJ.VT-3masc.sgBAS.VT IMPV+kill-EMPH let.it.be I-LK+OBJ say-COMPL.SS
      [wa-də-k]   [Səsawi ada   wa-na-d]
      say-3masc.sg-COMPL.DS Sesawi DEM.DIST.REACT.TOP+masc.sg say-ACT.FOC-3masc.sgBAS.P
      [mən   atətawa gwalugw-adəmən]
      you.masc how   clan-2masc.sgNOM

'After he'd been (standing), he (Kamkudi) said to him (Sesawi), "Come, do hit (me)", that (man) said to Sesawi, "Do hit me, let it be", after he'd said this, Sesawi said, "What clan do you belong to?" '

The first clause introduces a direct speech report. The fourth clause is a clarification, to make sure the audience understands that it was Kamkudi who spoke to Sesawi. Note the difference in the treatment of the emphatic clitic *ya* in the third clause and in the fifth clause. The speech report in the fifth clause is framed by two occurrences of the speech verb *wa-* (§19.5.1). The form *wa-də-k* has a recapitulating function and forms one intonation unit with the preceding *wa-ku*. In the last clause, 'belonging to a clan' is expressed via identification construction, literally 'you what clan?' (see §20.1.3).

T2.27 [wa-də-k]   [ka]   [wun kal
       say-3masc.sg-COMPL.DS DEM.PROX.fem.sg+3fem.sgNOM I   DEM.PROX.fem.sg+3fem.sgNOM
       dəmakau   kanukaraki] [wa-də-k]   [oh, mæy]   [wun
       brown.snake death.adder say-3masc.sg-COMPL.DS oh   come.IMPV I
       kəka   wun-adəwun]   [wun dəmakau-adəwun   wun-a:bab]
       DEM.PROX.REACT.TOP.fem.sg I-1masc.sgNOM I   brown.snake-1masc.sgNOM I-TOO
       [wa-ku]   [kədəka   waku-d]
       say-COMPL.SS DEM.PROX.REACT.TOP+masc.sg go.out-3masc.sgBAS.P
       'After he'd said this, "This is it, I am this, 'brown snake', 'death adder' (totems of the Gla:gw clan group)", after he'd said that, "Oh, come, I am this (clan) (lit. this is that that I am), I am 'death adder', me too", having said, this here (Kamkudi) went out'

The first clause introduces a speech report which follows it. The speech report consists of two verbless clauses. The switch-reference markers reflect the change of subjects. The second clause of the second speech report contains an identification construction (see §8.2, §10.1) with the notional possessor as the subject of a verbless clause, and the possessed noun in the predicate slot. In the next clause the pronoun is repeated as an afterthought.

Both brown snake and death adder are totems of the clan group Gla:gw, to which the Vali:k clan founded by Kamkudi also belong. Clan association is equated with totems. It is on the basis of this clan association that Sesawi recognizes Kamkudi as his brother. Exactly why this is so is not clear to me. My hypothesis is that the Manambu (themselves river people) consider the Gala as belonging to the broad class of *nəbə-du* 'jungle/dry-land-dwellers'. Since everything associated with the ground and earth is identified with the 'dark' Gla:gw group (even the term *gla:gw* translates as (dark/black+PL) 'dark ones'), the dry-land-dwellers are assigned to this clan group.

T2.28 [waku-ku   ya:kya] [taka-də-k   ra:d]
       go.out-COMPL.SS OK   put-3masc.sg-COMPL.DS sit+3masc.sgBAS.P
       'After he'd gone out, OK. After he (Sesawi) put him down, he stayed in a sitting position'

The second clause can be understood as the functional equivalent of a passive (see §16.2.3): 'he was put into a sitting position'.

T2.29 [bə   {kusə-k   tə-də-k}]   [taka-də-k]
       already finish-PURP.SS 'stand'-3masc.sg-COMPL.DS put-3masc.sg-COMPL.DS
       [rə-də-k]   [ya:kya] [lau-lap   viti kray-də-bər
       sit-3masc.sg-COMPL.DS OK   ripe-banana two bring-3masc.sgSUBJ.P-3duBAS.P
       lau-lap]
       ripe-banana
       'As he (Kamkudi) was about to die (lit. finish), he (Sesawi) having put him (down), he (Kamkudi) having sat, OK, he (Sesawi) brought him (Kamkudi) two ripe bananas'

The first clause contains a complex predicate with the meaning of imminent modality (§17.1.2). The compound noun *lau-lap* (ripe-banana) is repeated as a clarification in the last clause. The gift (and not the recipient) is cross-referenced on the verb 'bring'.

T2.30 [taːy nak kui-də-l]   [kui-də-k]
first one give.to.third.p-3masc.sgSUBJ.P-3fem.sgBAS.P give.to.third.p-3masc.sg-COMPL.DS
[yaːkya] [məgi-saki-sala-n]   [məgi-saki-sala-n]
OK   do.whatever-ACROSS.AWAY.INSIDE-SEQ do.whatever-ACROSS.AWAY.INSIDE-SEQ
[kə-bər   wuk-aːb   bə   warku-bər]
DEM.PROX-du tooth-TOO already close.up-3duBAS.P
'He gave (him) ripe bananas, first one, after he'd given it, OK. Turning in and out turning in and out (trying to get banana in) his teeth already closed up'

In the first clause, the gift (banana) is cross-referenced on the verb 'give'. The fourth and fifth clauses contain the general verb *məgi-* here referring to a general kind of movement back and forth for which it is difficult to find an appropriate term in the language (see §21.3.2 on this and other meanings of the verb *məgi-* 'do whatever').

'Closing up' of teeth most probably refers to rigor mortis of Kamkudi who was about to die.

T2.31 [məgi-saki-sala-n]   [məgi-saki-sala-n]   [gu-gu
do.whatever-ACROSS.AWAY.INSIDE-SEQ do.whatever-ACROSS.AWAY.INSIDE-SEQ water-water
jan   jan   jan   jan]   [yiːːn]   [al   ata
chew+SEQ chew+SEQ chew+SEQ chew+SEQ go+SEQ DEM.DIST+3fem.sgNOM then
kəmarkí-də-l]   [kəmarki-də-k]   [yaːkya]
swallow-3masc.sgSUBJ.P-3fem.sgBAS.P swallow-3masc.sg-COMPL.DS OK
'Turning in and out turning in and out pushing (the food) so as it became like water, pushing pushing pushing on and on, this is it (that) then he swallowed it, after he'd swallowed it it was OK'

The first two clauses are pronounced as separate intonation units. The repetition of the verb has to do with the way the action was repeated. In the third clause, the four instances of *jan* form one intonation unit to transmit the impression of intensive and repetitive action (see §12.8.3 for similar further examples and their discussion). The long vowel in the form *yiːːn* in the meaning of 'on and on and on' iconically reflects the length of time spent feeding the man. The distal demonstrative in contrastive focus (*al* 'this is it') shows that the result was achieved.

T2.32 [nak ata   kui-də-l]   [wabwi-ku]
one   then give.to.third.p-3masc.sgSUBJ.P-3fem.sgBAS.P peel-COMPL.SS
[kui-də-k]   [al]
give.to.third.p-3masc.sg-COMPL.DS DEM.DIST+3fem.sgNOM
'He gave him one (other banana), having peeled it, having given it, so it was'

The gift is again cross-referenced on the verb 'give'. The distal demonstrative pronoun in the last clause has a recapitulating meaning.

T2.33 [kan   napa-ku]   [*orait*]
eat+SEQ COMPL.VB-COMPL.SS OK
'He has really eaten (lit. he having eaten, OK)'

Note the emphatic meaning of the sentence containing *orait* (or its Manambu equivalent *yaːkya*) as its final clause—see §20.4.2.

T2.34 [a   kuprap-ə gu, [məy-a gu   maː] [bal rəpa-taka-da-l]
DEM.DIST.fem.sg bad-LK   water real-LK water NEG pig dig-put-3pisUBJ.P-3fem.sgBAS.P
kuprap-ə gu]   [məy-a gu   maː] [ñəg-aːm   məgi-ku]
bad-LK   water real-LK water NEG leaf-LK+LOC do.whatever-COMPL.SS
[kui-də-d]   [a-də-da   kwaːl gubi
give.to.third.p-3masc.sgSUBJ.P-3fem.sgBAS.P DEM.DIST-masc.sg-DOWN throat wet
kwa-kwa-d]   [wa-ku]
stay-IMPV.3p-masc.sg say-COMPL.SS

'(That was) bad water, it was not real water, (it was water) dug up by pigs, bad water, it was not real water, having captured (lit. whatevered) it on a leaf he gave it to him, so that his throat down there should be wet' (lit. saying may his throat down there be wet)

The insertions *[məya gu ma:]* in the first clause are clause-like; this is the only way of negating a constituent and saying 'not real water'. Note the general verb *məgi-* used in the sense of 'get, capture', for want of a more precise term that the speaker could not think of. The verb 'give' cross-references the recipient ('to him') in the second position. The last clause contains a speech report which does not imply any speech act—this is one of the syntactic causative strategies described in §16.2 and §19.5.

T2.35 [kui-də-k]   [ya:kya] [də-ad   kan   napa-ku]
       give.to.third.p-3masc.sg-COMPL.DS OK   he-3masc.sgNOM eat+SEQ COMPL.VB-COMPL.SS
       [rə-də-k]   [ada   wa-də-d]
       sit-3masc.sg-COMPL.DS DEM.DIST.REACT.TOP+masc.sg say-3masc.sgSUBJ.P-3masc.sgBAS.P
       'After he'd given him (water), OK. After he (not anyone else) had eaten, having sat, then he (Sesawi) said to him'

In the third clause, the subject 'he' is in contrastive focus—see Chapters 11 and 20. The verb of speech in the last clause cross-references the addressee in the second position (see §19.5.5).

T2.36 [mən   ata   ada]   [wun aka
       you.masc then sit/stand.IMPV I   DEM.DIST.REACT.TOP.fem.sg
       yi-k-na-dəwun   təp-a:r]
       go-FUT-ACT.FOC-1masc.sgBAS.VT village-LK+ALL
       'You stay here, I will go to that, to the village'

This is the speech report introduced by *wa-* in the previous sentence. The two clauses are linked by juxtaposition (§19.7), where the second clause provides justification for the first one. In the second clause, the form *aka* refers to the direction, 'village'. The oblique, 'village', is postposed to the verb—see §20.2.

T2.37 [yi-ku]   [wun-a-bər takwa   viti wa-tu-ək]   [səkulək yi:n
       go-COMPL.SS   I-LK-du   wife+LK   two say-1sg-COMPL.DS cooking 'go'+SEQ
       napa-brə-k]   [ya:k] [ata ya-k-na-dəwun]   [sər
       COMPL.VB-3du-COMPL.DS OK   then go-FUT-ACT.FOC-1masc.sgBAS.VT   tomorrow
       ya-k-na-dəwun   ma: [PAUSE] səbən-ən]
       come-FUT-ACT.FOC-1masc.sgBAS.VT again [PAUSE] return-SEQ
       'Having gone, after I'd told my two wives, after the two have done the cooking, OK, then I will come, tomorrow I will come again, back'

This is the continuation of the speech report. The first three clauses represent a clause chain with change of subject signalled by switch-reference-sensitive markers. In the second clause, the addressee ('two wives') is formally unmarked since its function is obvious from the context. The third clause contains the generic completive verb *napa-* which ensures the temporal reading of the clause (see §18.9). The fourth clause consists just of 'OK'. The two following clauses are juxtaposed (see §19.7): the last clause elaborates on the penultimate clause. The adverb 'again' is postposed to the verb. The adverb 'back' (grammaticalized sequential form of the verb 'return'—see §18.2) is separated from the rest of the clause by a pause indicating that this is an afterthought.

T2.38 [wa-də-k]   [a   ya:k] [ma:y] [wa-ku]   [ya:kya] [də Səsawi ata
       say-3masc.sg-COMPL.DS then OK   go.IMPV say-COMPL.SS OK   he Sesawi then
       səbənə-d]
       go.back-3masc.sgBAS.P
       'After he'd said that, "Then OK, you go", he having said, OK. This Sesawi then went back'

The first clause contains the verb of speech which frames the speech report in T2.36–7 above.

T2.39 [səbən-ku]   [wula-d   {kə-də-wula   təp-a:m}
go.back-COMPL.SS enter-3masc.sgBAS.P DEM.PROX-masc.sg-INLAND village-LK+LOC
{kə-də-wula   Apatəp-a:m}]
DEM.PROX-masc.sg-INLAND Avatip-LK+LOC
'Having gone back he came into this village away from the river, the Avatip away from the river'

The noun phrases in braces are postposed to the verb (see §20.2). The Avatip village is referred to as 'this big (masculine) village inland': at the time referred to in the story the village was on the river; however, since the river had changed its course, the old location had become a swamp away from the river, and was subsequently abandoned (§1.2).

T2.40 [[kra-də-bər   takwa:k]   abra
get-3masc.sgSUBJ.P-3duBAS.P woman+LK+DAT DEM.DIST.REACT.TOP.du
wa-də-bər]   [bər sər   səkulək ay]   [wun akatawa
say-3masc.sgSUBJ.P-3duBAS.P 2du tomorrow cooking IMPV+'go' I   like.this
yi-k-na-dəwun   *tu wik*, oh! *wik* viti] [də-kə-m ma: səkulək
go-FUT-ACT.FOC-1masc.sgBAS.VT two week oh week two he-OBL-OBJ again cooking
ay]   [{wa-ku   wa-də-k}]   [səkulək yi-ku]
IMPV+'go' say-COMPL.SS say-3masc.sg-COMPL.DS cooking 'go'-COMPL.SS
[wa-də-k]   [nəma-də   wurəb   væga-brə-k]   [ata
say-3masc.sg-COMPL.DS big-masc.sg string.bag+LK+TERM put.inside-3du-COMPL.DS then
ya:d   PAUSE səbənə-n]   [a-di   kamna:gw kur-ku]   [yi-ku]
go+3masc.sgBAS.VT PAUSE go.back-SEQ DEM.DIST-pl food   get-COMPL.SS go-COMPL.SS
ya:k
OK
'He said to the two wives he'd married, "Tomorrow you two cook! I will go like this for two weeks, oh, two weeks, do the cooking for him", having said this, after he'd said this, after they'd cooked, after he'd said, having put (the food) into a big stringbag, then he went back, having got those foods and gone, OK'

The very first clause is a relative clause (the common argument, 'women', is O of the relative clause and addressee of the matrix clause). The addressee is cross-referenced on the verb of the second clause. The third, fourth, and fifth clauses are part of the speech report within the framing construction with three occurrences of *wa-* 'say'. The third clause contains a command with a non-singular addressee marked with dual pronoun. In the fourth clause, John corrected himself, changing Tok Pisin *tu wik* to more Manambu-like *wik viti*. The next clauses represent a chain where subject change is marked with switch-reference.

T2.41 [adiya   *sandə* viti {kurə-n kwa-də-d}]   [kwarbab
DEM.DIST.REACT.TOP.pl Sunday two get-SEQ stay-3masc.sgSUBJ.P-3duBAS.P bush+LK+TERM
{kurə-n kwa-də-k}]   [a-di   kamna:gw kui-də-k]
get-SEQ stay-3masc.sg-COMPL.DS DEM.DIST-pl food give.to.third.p-3masc.sg-COMPL.DS
[kui-də-k]   [kui-də-k]
give.to.third.p-3masc.sg-COMPL.DS give.to.third.p-3masc.sg-COMPL.DS
[kui-də-k]   [ya:kya] [də-kə   du   ata
give.to.third.p-3masc.sg-COMPL.DS OK   he-OBL+fem.sg man/body then
səbənə-l]   [ata katapwi-də-k]   [ya:kya]
go.back-3fem.sgBAS.P then get.body.back-3masc.sg-COMPL.DS OK
'He stayed looking after him for those two weeks, having looked after him in the bush, having given him these foods, given given given, OK. His (Kamkudi's) body got back to normal (lit. his body then returned), after he got his body back, it was OK'

The Tok Pisin word *sande* is used in the meaning of 'week'. Constituents in braces in the first and second clauses are aspectual complex predicates (see §17.1.1). Repetition of the word 'having given' in the following clauses iconically reflects the prolonged character of the action. There is a short break between each occurrence of this verb, indicative of clause boundaries. The functions of *ya:kya* clauses are described in §20.4.2. In the third clause, 'bush' is used in a locative meaning without the locative case, since this is an inherently locational noun.

T2.42 [bər   rəp-ə-rəp-ə-du   tə-ku]   ya:k
they.two equal-LK-equal-LK-man become-COMPL.SS OK
'The two have become two equal men' (lit. two having become equal men, OK)

See §20.4.2, for the functions of *ya:kya* clauses.

T2.43 [ata wa:d]   [ya:kya] [sər   yi-k-na-bran]   [wa-ku]
then say+3masc.sgBAS.P OK   tomorrow go-FUT-ACT.FOC-1duBAS.VT say-COMPL.SS
'He said, "OK, we will go tomorrow", having said'

This is a typical example of a speech report framing construction—see §19.5.1.

T2.44 [nəkə   *sandi*-a-yay   aka   viti-a-yay
another+fem.sg week-LK-ORD DEM.DIST.REACT.TOP.fem.sg two-LK-ORD
aka-n-aka]   [kəka   səbənə-n
DEM.DIST.REACT.TOP.fem.sg-PRED-REACT.TOP DEM.DIST.REACT.TOP.fem.sg go.back-SEQ
səbən-brə-l]
go.back-3dusUBJ.P-3duBAS.P
'On the other Sunday, the second (Sunday) there was, then this time the two returned back'

The first and second clauses are linked via juxtaposition: the second clause is the consequence of the first. The first clause illustrates the use of the cardinal number marker -*yay* to mark sequence (as in 'second week')—see §10.6. In the second clause, the time of the action is cross-referenced in the second position on the verb. The form *səbənə-n* (go.back-SEQ) is used as an adverb 'back'—see §18.2 and §19.9.

T2.45 [bər glabadi   a-l-ayib   kur-bər] [də-kəba:b   krəkiya:p]
3du decoration DEM.DIST-fem.sg-DIST+TERM get-3duBAS.P he-OBL+TOO ornament
[də-kəba:b   krəkiya:p] [də-kəba:b   gəl   yi-ku]   [də-kəba:b   gəl
he-OBL+TOO ornament he-OBL+TOO black.paint go-COMPL.SS he-OBL+TOO black.paint
yi-ku]   [də ma:pw ji-ku]   [də ma:pw ji-ku]   [ata ya-ku
go-COMPL.SS he possum tie-COMPL.SS he possum tie-COMPL.SS then come-COMPL.SS
ya:kya]
OK
'The two got the decoration there at a distance, one (lit. he) (got) ornaments, the other (lit. he) (got) ornaments, one (lit. he) went in black paint, the other (lit. he) went in black paint, one (lit. he) tied possum fur, the other (lit. he) tied possum fur, they then went (lit. having then gone, OK)'

The first clause summarizes the ways in which Sesawi and Kamkudi adorned themselves. The next three pairs of clauses describe the two men each doing the same thing. The second and third clauses are elliptical (see §20.4.3). 'Putting on black paint' (lit. going black) refers to the custom of painting black the face of a man who had killed someone (and can thus be considered a true man—see §1.4.1, and Harrison 1993). The last clause contains *ya:kya*—see §20.4.2, for the functions of *ya:kya* clauses.

T2.46 [karya-ku]   [kawi-ku]   [{Səsawi ta:y də gañ} ata   yi-bər] [ma:s
bring-COMPL.SS go.ashore-COMPL.SS Sesawi first he last then go-3duBAS.P betelnut
ata ji-bər]
then chew-3duBAS.P
'Having brought (Kamkudi), having gone ashore, Sesawi first, he last they went, then they chewed betelnut'

The subject of the first clause is Sesawi. The subject of the second clause is both Sesawi and Kamkudi; these are treated as the same subject as in the next main clause. This agrees with the semantics of same-subject marking in completive medial clauses (§18.3) whereby if the subject of the first clause is part of a (non-singular) subject of the subsequent clause, the two subjects tend to be treated as the same (see 18.22).

The third clause contains a coordinated NP (via juxtaposition): see §20.1.

T2.47 [adəka   Səsawi ata   wa:d]
      DEM.DIST.REACT.TOP+masc.sg Sesawi then   say+3masc.sgBAS.VT
      [kədəka   karya-tua-dəmən]   [[vya-k   wa-ku]
      DEM.DIST.REACT.TOP+masc.sg bring-1sgSUBJ.VT-2masc.sgBAS.VT kill-PURP.SS say-COMPL.SS
      [ta:y wun-a:b   vya-gur-ək]]   [wun kiau   ta:y] [də kukər
      first I-LK+TERM kill-2pl-COMPL.DS I   die+1sgIMPV first he after
      vya-kə-gura-d]   [vya-gur-ək]   [kiya-k-na-d]
      kill-FUT-2plSUBJ.VT-3masc.sgBAS.VT kill-2pl-COMPL.DS die-FUT-ACT.FOC-3masc.sgBAS.VT
      [atawa-dəka   wa-yi-bər]
      like.that-ONLY say-go-3duBAS.P
      'That Sesawi then said, "I have brought you (Kamkudi), if you people intend to kill (him) (lit. saying "We intend to kill"), after you killed me first, let me die first, you will kill him after; after you kill him he will die", like that only the two went on talking'

The first clause introduces a speech report by Sesawi. In the second clause the object is cross-referenced and also referred to with the reactivated topic demonstrative. The next clause is directed at the men from Avatip, for whom Kamkudi remains an enemy. It contains a speech report in the meaning of 'intend to do something' ('say kill-purposive') (see §19.5.6, for metaphorical meanings of speech reports). In the fifth clause, the adverb is postposed to the verb (in first person permissive). The last clause anaphorically refers to the speeches above.

T2.48 [wa-yi-də-d]   [yi::n]   [warən   wiya:m]
      say-go-3masc.sgSUBJ.P-3masc.sgBAS.P   go:REP+SEQ go.up+SEQ house+LK+LOC
      'He went on saying this to him (or about him), on and on, going up into the house'

Either the addressee or the topic of conversation is cross-referenced on the verb of speech (see §19.5.5). The verb form *yi:n* shows iconic lengthening of the vowel to reflect the prolonged action; it has an adverbial meaning 'on and on'.

T2.49 [rə-ku]   [ya:kya] [ata wa-də-d   ma:j]   [ya:kya]
      sit-COMPL.SS OK   then say-3masc.sgSUBJ.P-3masc.sgBAS.P word/story OK
      'Having stayed (there), OK. Then he said a word to him, OK'

The object in the third clause is postposed to the verb, as an afterthought. The verb 'say' cross-references the addressee (see §19.5.5).

T2.50 [mən   sər   *o* mu   kwa-ku]   [ata kə
      you.masc tomorrow or day.after.tomorrow stay-COMPL.SS then DEM.PROX.fem.sg
      gəña-ta:kw kur-ku]   [nagwuk   ma:y]   [*orait*] [yi-ku]   [*orait*] [akatawa
      last+LK-wife get-COMPL.SS sago+LK+DAT go.IMPV alright go-COMPL.SS alright like.this
      lə-kə   səp-a:m   kwa:r   a-rali]   [wa-də-k]   [*orait*] [ata
      she-OBL+fem.sg skin-LK+OBJ grass.skirt IMPV-untie say-3masc.sg-COMPL.DS alright then
      ya:d]
      go+3masc.sgBAS.P
      ' "You having stayed tomorrow or the day after, having taken this younger wife (of mine) go to fetch sago, all right, having gone, all right, untie the grass skirt on her skin", after he'd said this, alright, then he (Kamkudi) went'

The verb 'say' introduces a lengthy speech report consisting of seven clauses. This is a command from Sesawi to Kamkudi to take his younger wife and go to fetch sago, so as to have sex (the expression 'untie grass skirt' is a euphemism for sex). The loan disjunction *o* occurs in the first clause.

T2.51 [yi-ku]   [yi-də-l]
go-COMPL.SS go-3masc.sgSUBJ.P-3fem.sgBAS.P then again they-LK+OBJ   [a ma: dəy-aːm
wukə-d]   [oh! wun amæy-viti-abər] [wa-ku]
think/hear-3masc.sgBAS.P oh I mother-du-3duNOM say-COMPL.SS
[wa-də-k]   [aw yi-də-k]   [ada
say-3masc.sg-COMPL.DS then go-3masc.sg-COMPL.DS DEM.DIST.REACT.TOP+masc.sg
jikə-də-d]
curse-3masc.sgSUBJ.P-3masc.sgBAS.P
'Having gone, he went this time, then again he thought about them. Having thought (lit. said), "Oh, these two are my mothers", having said this, then after he'd gone, he (Sesawi) cursed that one (Kamkudi)'

The first clause is linked to the preceding sentence via head-tail linkage. The predicate of the second clause cross-references time in the second position. The repetition of the verb *wa-* is typical of speech reports—see §19.5.1.

T2.52 [{vya-k   kur-də-d}   viːr   ma:]
hit-PURP.SS do/get-3masc.sgSUBJ.P-3masc.sgBAS.P spear+LK+INSTR again
'He was about to hit him again with a spear'

The constituent in braces is a purposive complex predicate—see §17.1.2. The instrument and the adverb 'again' are postposed to the verb—see §20.2.

T2.53 [kur-də-k]   [vya-k   kur-də-k]
do/get-3masc.sg-COMPL.DS hit-PURP.SS do/get-3masc.sg-COMPL.DS
[ada   wa:d]   [wa-ku]   [ya:kya]
DEM.DIST.REACT.TOP+masc.sg say+3masc.sgBAS.VT say-COMPL.SS OK
'After he'd (Sesawi) been about (to hit Kamkudi), after he'd been about to hit (him), that (Kamkudi) said, having said, "OK" '

This sentence is linked to the previous one via head-tail linkage (§20.4.1). Repetition of *wa-* is typical of speech reports. It has a function: the last clause, *ya:kya*, is a genuine speech report: Kamkudi had said 'OK'. If the verb *wa-* had not been repeated the sentence would have been ambiguous between the actual speech report and a fixed expression *ya:kya wa-* 'agree, accept'.

T2.54 [{nəkə   *taim*} {nəkə   ñə} aka
another+fem.sg time another+fem.sg day DEM.DIST.REACT.TOP.fem.sg
kray-də-l-ya]
take-3masc.sgSUBJ.P-3fem.sgBAS.P-EMPH
'Another time, another day he took her'

The second of the two noun phrases (in braces) is a correction: John Səpaywəs decided not to use a Tok Pisin word after all.

T2.55 [kray-ku]   [ya:kya] [kwa:r   ata rali-də-l]
take-COMPL.SS OK   grass.skirt then untie-3masc.sgSUBJ.P-3fem.sgBAS.P
'He had taken her (lit. having taken her, OK), he then untied her grass skirt'

See §20.4.2, for the functions of *ya:kya* clauses.

T2.56 [rali-ku]   [lə-kə   səp   ata   və-də-l]
     untie-COMPL.SS she-OBL+fem.sg body then see/experience-3masc.sgSUBJ.P-3fem.sgBAS.P
     [və-ku]   [ya:k] [miya-ñəg   sə-ku]   [a-də   miya-ñəg
     see/experience-COMPL.SS OK   tree+LK-leaf plant-COMPL.SS DEM.DIST-masc.sg tree+LK-leaf
     sə-ku]   [ata ya:d]
     plant-COMPL.SS then go+3masc.sgBAS.P
     'Having untied (the grass skirt), then he experienced her body, having experienced, OK, having
     planted a leaf of a tree, having planted that leaf of a tree then he went (back)'

This is a typical clause chain with the same subject marked with switch-reference. See §20.4.2, for the
functions of *ya:k(ya)* clauses.

T2.57 [ya-bər]   [ya-brə-k]   [ya:kya] [{væn   rə-ku}]
     come-3duBAS.P go-3du-COMPL.DS OK   see+SEQ sit-COMPL.SS
     [ada   wa:d]   [Oh, ya:kya] [pusa-mi,
     DEM.DIST.REACT.TOP+masc.sg say+3masc.sgBAS.P oh,   OK   rot/be.broken-tree
     pusa-bæy   ay]   [akətawanək   wa-tua]
     rot/be.broken-limbum IMPV+say like.this+CONF say-1sgSUBJ.VT+3fem.sgBAS.VT
     [{wa-tu-l]   [wa-ku}]
     say-1sgSUBJ.P-3fem.sgBAS.P say-COMPL.SS
     'The two came back, after they'd come back, OK, as he (Sesawi) had been watching (them), he
     said, "Oh, OK, say say broken tree, broken limbum (mat), exactly like this I told him having
     told (to do)", he said'

The first clause contains a correction to the last clause of the preceding sentence (Kamkudi came back
together with the woman). The constituent in braces in the fourth clause is a complex predicate referring
to prolonged action (see §17.1.1). The next clause introduces a speech report, and is part of a speech
report framing construction (see §19.5.1). The last two clauses contain two occurrences of the verb of
speech *wa-* typical of colloquial register (see §19.5.6). The two occurrences of *wa-* form one intonation
group, and this is why they are in braces.

T2.58 [wa-ku]   [ya:kya] [aw ya:k {kurə-n   rə-ku}]   [ya:n]   [ya:k]
     say-COMPL.SS OK   then OK   look.after-SEQ sit-COMPL.SS come+SEQ OK
     [war-ku   PAUSE wiya:r]   [ada   wa:d]
     go.up-COMPL.SS PAUSE house+LK+ALL DEM.DIST.REACT.TOP+masc.sg say+3masc.sgBAS.P
     [ñən   də-kə-k   [na:gw sau-n] atak]
     you.fem he-OBL-DAT sago   fry-SEQ IMPV+put
     'He did say this (lit. having said (this), OK) after he'd been looking after him, OK, as he came,
     after he went up into the house, he said, "You (woman) put sago (out) for him as you fry (it)"'

The constituent in braces is an aspectual complex predicate (§17.1.1). In the sixth clause, the oblique 'to
the house' is postposed to the predicate as an afterthought (separated from the predicate by a pause). The
meaning of the *-n* 'sequencing' form in the last clause is that of concomitant action.

T2.59 [də-kə   {gəña-ta:kw-al}   kui-də-l]
     he-OBL+fem.sg last+LK-wife-3fem.sgNOM give.to.third.p-3masc.sgSUBJ.P-3fem.sgBAS.P
     [{amæy-ta:kw-al}   də-kə-l-al   Səsawi]
     mother-wife-3fem.sgNOM he-OBL-fem.sg-3fem.sgNOM Sesawi
     'It is his last wife (that) he gave, as for the first wife (lit. mother-wife) she is his, Sesawi('s)'

Constituents in braces in the first and second clauses are in contrastive focus—see §20.3 on the use of
nominal cross-reference markers in contrastive focus constructions. The verb 'give' in the first clause
cross-references gift ('woman') and not recipient in the second position. The second clause contains a
possessive pronoun 'his' in the predicate slot. See §20.2 on the possessor-final constituent order in this
clause.

T2.60 [*orait*] [Səsawi də-kə-l   gəña-ta:kw   kəka
      alright Sesawi he-OBL-fem.sg last+LK-wife DEM.PROX.REACT.TOP.fem.sg
      kui-də-l   PAUSE Kamkudiyik]
      give.to.third.p-3masc.sgSUBJ.P-3fem.sgBAS.P PAUSE Kamkudi+DAT
      'All right, Sesawi gave this (topical) his own last wife, to Kamkudi'

This sentence rephrases the previous sentence. The verb 'give' in the first clause cross-references gift ('woman') in the second position. The recipient, Kamkudi, is added as an afterthought: this is why it is separated from the verb with a pause.

T2.61 [kui-də-k]   [ya:kya, Kamkudi aka   {kra:n
      give.to.third.p-3masc.sg-COMPL.DS [OK   Kamkudi DEM.DIST.REACT.TOP.fem.sg get+SEQ
      tə-də-l}]
      'stand'-3masc.sgSUBJ.P-3fem.sgBAS.P
      'He'd given her (to him) (lit. after he'd given her, OK) Kamkudi had married (lit. got) her'

See §20.4.2 on the semantics of *ya:kya* clauses (like the second one here). The constituent in braces is a complex predicate with aspectual meaning (§17.1.1).

T2.62 [tə-ku]   [ta:y du-a-ñan-ad]   [bas wa-təpə-da-l]
      'stand'-COMPL.SS first man-LK-child-3masc.sgNOM first say-stop-3plSUBJ.P-3fem.sgBAS.VT
      [aka-n-aka]
      DEM.DIST.REACT.TOP.fem.sg-PRED-DEM.DIST.REACT.TOP
      'After he'd married her, OK, first (child) was a boy, first it was the case that they prohibited her (from working), that is what it was'

This sentence is linked to the preceding sentence via head-tail linkage. The second clause has a noun in its predicate slot. The last clause contains a recapitulative reactivated topic demonstrative, meaning 'that is what it was'. The second clause contains a reference to prohibition to work after the birth of the first offspring.

T2.63 [du-a-ñan   ata {*kamapu*-d]   [*kamapu*-ku}] [[a-də   ñan
      man-LK-child   then appear-3masc.sgBAS.VT appear-COMPL.SS DEM.DIST-masc.sg child
      də-kə   wa:ñ} aw   kədiya   kwa-na-di   PAUSE
      he-OBL+fem.sg line   then DEM.DIST.REACT.TOP+pl stay-ACT.FOC-3plBAS.VT PAUSE
      {kə-di   Sabrayi-bər} Vali:k]
      DEM.PROX-pl   Sabray-ASS.PL Valik
      'Then a boy appears, after he has appeared his line (lit. this boy his line) then are these ones (topical), these relatives of Sabrayi, the Vali:k clan'

The second clause forms one intonation unit with the preceding main verb; this is an instance of a completive medial clause in a recapitulating function. Constituents in braces are noun phrases. 'These relatives of Sabrayi' is expressed with an associative plural—see §6.2.2. The subject of the last clause is an afterthought, separated from the predicate with a pause.

T2.64 [kədiya   Vali:k kəka   kwa-dana]
      DEM.DIST.REACT.TOP+pl Vali:k DEM.DIST.REACT.TOP.fem.sg stay-3plSUBJ.VT+3fem.sgBAS.VT
      'These Vali:k stay here'

The reactivated topic demonstrative refers to the location (Avatip) where the members of Vali:k clan who are present live during the story telling.

T2.65 [dəy-a-kə   *generation*, gwalugw aw   kəta
      they-LK-OBL+fem.sg generation   ancestors then now
      aka-n-aka]   [*tu handred   seventy*] [*orait*] [a
      DEM.DIST.REACT.TOP.fem.sg-PRED-DEM.DIST.REACT.TOP two hundred seventy alright then

tu hundred seventy   bəta:y   kakəl-na   {a
two hundred seventy already surpass-ACT.FOC+3fem.sgBAS.VT DEM.DIST.fem.sg
dəy-a   wa:ñ}]
they-LK+fem.sg line
'Their generations, their clans now are here, here it is, two hundred seventy, all right, their line
(of descendants) has already surpassed two hundred seventy'

In the first clause the narrator corrected himself replacing the English word *generation* with the Manambu
term *gwalugw* meaning 'ancestors; clans'. The second clause is a verbless clause. In the last clause, a noun
phrase is in braces. The subject appears after the verb—see §20.2.

T2.66 [kakəl-ku]   [a   war-na]
        surpass-COMPL.SS then go.up-ACT.FOC+3fem.sgBAS.VT
        'Having surpassed, then it goes up'

T2.67 [{a-di   Gal-adi}   kə   təp-a:m   bə   ma:] [a-di
        DEM.DIST-pl Gala-3plNOM DEM.PROX.fem.sg village-LK+LOC already NEG DEM.DIST-pl
        [wuka   wa-bana]   [kə-di
        DEM.PROX.ADDR.fem.sg say-1plSUBJ.VT+3fem.sgBAS.VT DEM.PROX-pl
        dəpu-nagwum   tə-di]]
        inside.hollow+LK-sago+LK+LOC stay-3plBAS.P
        'As for those Gala, there are none (left) in this village, those we were talking about close to you,
        those staying inside the hollow sago palm'

The constituent in braces is in contrastive focus (see §20.3); the second and third clauses are headless
relative clauses (see §19.2.1).

T2.68 [a-l-a]   [lə-kə   wa-saki-ma:j-al]
        DEM.DIST-fem.sg-3fem.sgNOM she-OBL+fem.sg say-ACROSS.AWAY-story-3fem.sgNOM
        [[kə   kəp   *wini*-tuə-l   *stori*]
        DEM.PROX.fem.sg ground win-1sgSUBJ.P-3fem.sgBAS.P story
        aka-n-aka]
        DEM.DIST.REACT.TOP.fem.sg-PRED-DEM.DIST.REACT.TOP
        'This is it, this is the traditional story, the story of how I got this land here it is'

The clauses are linked via juxtaposition. The first clause contains a distal demonstrative used anaphorically in its predicate slot. The second clause contains a compound noun in the predicate slot. The third
clause contains a reactivated topic demonstrative (distal) in the predicate slot, and includes a relative
clause. Note that the first person reference is not just to the narrator—he subsumes the whole Manambu
people under 'I'.

T2.69 [ya:kya] [mawər   aka   wula-na]
        OK   base+LK+ALL DEM.DIST.REACT.TOP.fem.sg go.inside-ACT.FOC+3fem.sgBAS.VT
        'OK, it is finished (lit. goes inside the base)'

There is a second-long pause between the two clauses. The last clause contains a typical ending: when a
story finishes it is understood as 'going back to where it came from'.

TEXT 3. HOW OSELO WANTED TO KILL ALL THE SNAKES, NARRATED
BY JAMES KATALU ANGI BALANGAWI, RECORDED 15 OCTOBER
2004 (APPROXIMATE LENGTH 10.5 MINUTES)

T3.1 [kə-də   gabu-ma:j-ad]   [{Osəlo də-kə-də
       DEM.PROX-masc.sg traditional-story-3masc.sgNOM Oselo he-OBL-masc.sg
       gabu-ma:j}-ad]
       traditional-story-3masc.sgNOM
       'This is a traditional story, it is a traditional story of Oselo'

The name Osəlo (phonetic variant: Osolo) is rather unusual in that it contains the sound *o* which is highly marginal in Manambu (see §2.1.2). The two clauses are linked via juxtaposition; one constitutes a comment to the other. In the second clause, an NP is in braces.

T3.2 [du   sa-dəka   Osəlo] [ñə nak ada   kwarba:r
      man name+LK-ONLY Oselo day one DEM.DIST.REACT.TOP.masc.sg jungle+LK+ALL
      ya:d]
      go+3masc.sgBAS.VT
      'It is exactly the man's name Oselo. One day he went to the jungle'

The suffix *-dəka* has the meaning of 'just, exactly'. The first clause is a typical example of verbless naming clause (§20.1). The second clause comments on Oselo's activities, and is juxtaposed to the first one.

T3.3 [kwarba:r   yi-də-l]   [aka   {karaki
      jungle+LK+ALL go-3masc.sgSUBJ.P-3fem.sgBAS.P DEM.DIST.REACT.TOP.fem.sg death.adder
      kabay lə-kə-di   ñan-ugw-adi}   və-də-di]
      snake she-OBL-pl child-PL-3plNOM see-3masc.sgSUBJ.P-3plBAS.P
      'That (time) he went to the jungle (and) what he saw were the children of death adder the snake'

The two clauses are linked via juxtaposition (§19.7), indicating sequence of actions. Time is cross-referenced in the second position of the predicate of the first clause. The constituent in braces is in contrastive focus construction (see §20.3).

T3.4 [yin]   [a-də   kwarba:r   yi-n]   [yi-ta-taka]   [a-də
      go+SEQ DEM.DIST-masc.sg jungle+LK+ALL go-SEQ go-EP-IMM.SEQ DEM.DIST-masc.sg
      təbur   waku-də-l]
      clearing+ALL go.out-3masc.sgSUBJ.P-3fem.sgBAS.P
      'Having gone, as soon as he went to the jungle, he went out onto a clearing (that time)'

The predicate of the last clause cross-references time in the second position.

T3.5 [{a-di   {karaki   lə-kə-di   ñan-ugw} } adika   ata gəpi-ya-n
      DEM.DIST-pl death.adder she-OBL-pl child-PL   DEM.DIST.REACT.TOP+pl then run-come-SEQ
      gəpi-ya-di]
      run-come-3plBAS.VT
      'Those children of a death adder were running around a lot'

The braces indicate the internal structure of a complex noun phrase (see §20.1.1). Repetition of the complex verb *gəpi-ya-* (run-come) 'run around' in sequencing form was discussed at A in §12.8.3; this denotes a repeated action. The verbs 'run around' in the sequencing form and in its inflected form constitute one intonation unit; there is no intonation break or pause between them (which would be indicative of a clause boundary).

T3.6 [də-kə-m   və-ku]   [gəpi-yi-n   gəpi-ya-da]
      he-OBL-OBJ see-COMPL.SS run-go-SEQ run-come-3plSUBJ.P+3fem.sgBAS.P
      'Having seen him, they ran back and forth'

The repetition of 'run-go' 'run-come' is an example of the 'go-come' construction discussed at A6 in §15.3.1 (see 15.60). The construction has the meaning of erratic movement to and fro, back and forth and every way.

T3.7 [Osəlo ada]   [ooh [vætəkə-tukwa ñən-a
      Oselo DEM.DIST.REACT.TOP.masc.sg ooh bite-PROH.GEN you.fem.sg-VOC
      aka]   nəbəl ya   kiya-k-na-digur-ək]   [gur-a
      DEM.DIST.REACT.TOP.fem.sg today EMPH die-FUT-ACT.FOC-2plBAS.VT-CONF 2pl-LK+fem.sg
      amæy akrəl   yi-na]   [wa-ku]   [ata wa:-d]
      mother where.to go-ACT.FOC+3fem.sgBAS.VT say-COMPL.SS then say+3masc.sgBAS.P
      'That (topical) Oselo, "It is you (feminine), don't you bite! Today you will die, where is mother gone?", having said this, he said'

A speech report intervenes between the constituents of the clause. The first clause of the speech report contains a mock command: 'you just try and bite me.' The second clause of the speech report contains an interrogative clause; the constituent order in an interrogative clause is the same as in a declarative clause. Repetition of the verb of speech is characteristic of speech report framing constructions.

T3.8 [wa-də-k]   [wa-ku] [wali-bag kur-də-l]
  say-3masc.sg-COMPL.DS say-COMPL.SS white.man-knife get-3masc.sgSUBJ.VT-3fem.sgBAS.VT
  [jip jip jip jip jip ata kətəkə-yi-də-di]   [na kətəkə-n] [na kətəkə-n] [na
  sound.of.cutting then cut-go-3masc.sgSUBJ.P-3plBAS.VT one cut-SEQ one cut-SEQ one
  kətəkə-n] [na kətəkə-n] [na kətəkə-n] [a-di ñan kabay kətəkə-yakə-taka] [wun
  cut-SEQ one cut-SEQ one cut-SEQ DEM.DIST-pl child snake cut-FULLY-IMM.SEQ I
  Osəlo-adəwun-ək] [və-gura-dəwun-ək]   [wun-a:m vætəkə-tukwa
  Oselo-1masc.sgNOM-CONF see-2plSUBJ.VT-1masc.sgBAS.VT-CONF I-LK+OBJ bite-PROH.GEN
  gur-a] [aka   vya-tua-digur-ək   ya] [amæy
  you.pl-VOC DEM.DIST.REACT.TOP.fem.sg kill-1sgSUBJ.VT-2plBAS.VT-CONF EMPH mother
  akrəl yi-na]   [lə-kəba:b kətawa kətəkə-kə-tua]   [wun
  where.to go-ACT.FOC+fem.sg she-OBL+TOO like.this cut-FUT-1sgSUBJ.VT+3fem.sgBAS.VT I
  Osəlo] [wa-ta:y-kəkəb]   [ata vya-də-di]
  Oselo say-COTEMP-AS.SOON.AS then hit-3masc.sgSUBJ.P-3plBAS.P
  'Having said, he said (this); he got the white man's knife, jip-jip-jip-jip-jip he went on cutting (the snake's children), cutting one, cutting another, cutting another, cutting another, cutting another, immediately after he fully cut up all the snake's children, as soon as he said "I am Oselo, you see me, do not you bite me, I am about to kill you, mother where is she gone, her too I will cut like this, I Oselo", he then hit them'

Repetition of the verb of speech in the first and second clauses is characteristic of colloquial speech reports (see §19.5.6). In the third clause, time is cross-referenced in the second position (the knife is usually masculine). In the fourth clause, an expressive referring to the sound of a knife cutting snakes is repeated five times. The next five clauses consist of a sequencing form marked with -n and the reduced form na of the numeral nak 'one' (see §10.6.1), in the meaning of 'one another yet another etc.'. The form kətəkə-n is pronounced as kətə-n following the intervocalic velar elision rule (§2.6). The next clause has the proper name, Oselo, in the predicate slot ('I am Oselo'). The subject of the imperative, 'you', appears in a focus construction, since this is a very strong command, 'don't you (not anyone else) bite me'.

T3.9 [vya-yakə-də-k]   [{ñan kabay nak} yaga-ku]   [ta:yib
  hit-FULLY-3masc.sg-COMPL.DS child snake one be.scared-COMPL.SS before+TERM
  və-ma:r-də-k]   [aka-bə
  see-NEG.SUB-3masc.sg-COMPL.DS DEM.DIST.REACT.TOP.fem.sg-already
  alədar   varla-ku]   [yi::n
  DEM.DIST.fem.sg+DOWN+ALL go.underneath-COMPL.SS go:REP+SEQ
  alədar   varla-ku]   [yi::n] [api-məy-a-ñəg
  DEM.DIST.FEM.sg+DOWN+ALL go.underneath-COMPL.SS go:REP+SEQ top-real-LK-mosquito.net
  rə-da:-k] [a-də   məy-a-ñəg-a:m   wula-ku]
  sit-3PL-COMPL.DS DEM.DIST-masc.sg real-LK-mosquito.net-LK+LOC go.inside-COMPL.SS
  [kaypakwvakwa-ku] [yi-n] [kwasa-məy ata ra:l]
  coil-COMPL.SS   go-SEQ little-real then sit+3fem.sgBAS.P
  'After he'd hit (them), one little snake (lit. snake child) being scared, as he did not see it, after it (the snake) had already gone underneath, as they (other snakes) stayed on top of a mosquito net, it, having entered the net (and) coiled there sat there for a little while on and on'

This example illustrates a lengthy clause chain where the change of subject is signalled by switch-reference-sensitive markers. The form yi:n 'go:REP+SEQ' undergoes expressive lengthening iconically reflecting the length of time of the action. This form can be interpreted either as referring to the actual 'going' or as meaning 'on and on'—see §18.2. The inherently locational possessive construction 'top of real mosquito net' (pronounced as one phonological word: §2.5) is not marked for locative case.

T3.10 [[amæy karaki]   aka-bə   kwarba:r   ya:l]
mother death.adder DEM.DIST.REACT.TOP.fem.sg-already jungle+LK+ALL go+3fem.sgBAS.P
'The death adder mother had already gone to the jungle'

The adverb *bə* 'already' is cliticized to the reactivated topic pronouns *aka*. The constituent in brackets is an appositional noun phrase (see §20.1.1).

T3.11 [[amæy karaki]   kwarba:r   yi-lə-l
mother death.adder jungle+LK+ALL go-3fem.sgSUBJ.P-3fem.sgBAS.P
aka]   [[ñəgañam   ata   kur-ku]
DEM.DIST.REACT.TOP.fem.sg leafy.vegetable then   get-COMPL.SS
karya-lə-di]
bring-3fem.sgSUBJ.P-3fem.sgBAS.P
'The time when the mother death adder went to the jungle, having got leafy vegetables she brought them'

The first clause contains a reactivated topic pronoun placed after the verb (see §20.2). The first clause is linked to the rest of the sentence via juxtaposition (see §19.7).

T3.12 [a-di   ñan-ugw-a:k   kui-lə-k]   [kə-da-kəkək]
DEM.DIST-pl child-PL-LK+DAT give.to.third.p-3fem.sg-COMPL.DS eat-3pl-PURP.DS
[[kə-kwa-di] wa-ku]   [yi-ku]   [ata væytu-ya-l]
eat-IMPV.3p-pl say-COMPL.SS go-COMPL.SS then whistle-come-3fem.sgBAS.P
'Having given them to those children for them to eat, having said, "May they eat", having gone, she whistled for a long time'

The second clause contains a different-subject purposive. The change of subjects between the second and the third clauses explains the different subject on the first clause (which is the same as that of the third, fourth, and fifth clauses). The third clause has causative overtones—this is the only idiomatic way of expressing the idea of getting them to eat, or making them eat. The predicate of the last clause contains an aspectual compound (§15.3.1) with durative meaning.

T3.13 [atawa væytu-ya-lə-l   aka]   [[a-di
thus   whistle-come-3fem.sgSUBJ.P-3fem.sgBAS.P DEM.DIST.REACT.TOP.fem.sg DEM.DIST-pl
ñan-ugw waku-k-na-di]   wa-ku]   [və-lə-l]   [ma:]
child-PL go.out-FUT-ACT.FOC-3plBAS.VT say-COMPL.SS see-3fem.sgSUBJ.P-3fem.sgBAS.P NEG
'Thus she whistled for a long time, having said, "Those children will go out", she looked (that time), nothing (lit. no)'

The first clause contains a reactivated topic pronoun placed after the verb (see §20.2). The second clause contains a speech report expressing the snake's thoughts or internal speech. The predicates of the first and third clauses cross-reference time in the second position. The last clause consists of a negative pro-clause, expressing the negative result—no children came out to welcome their mother.

T3.14 [ah? [ña-ñə   væytu-ya-kwa-tua]
ah   day+LK-day whistle-come-HAB-1sgSUBJ.VT+3fem.sgBAS.VT
[waku-kwa-na-di]   [nakaməy ma: kləm   rə]
go.out-HAB-ACT.FOC-3plBAS.VT one.fem.sg NEG DEM.PROX.fem+LOC sit:NEG
wa-lə-l]
say-3fem.sgSUBJ.P-3fem.sgBAS.P
' "Ah? Every day I used to whistle for some time, they used to go out, not one is here", she said at that time'

This sentence contains a speech report. The speech report consists of three juxtaposed main clauses (§19.7). The third clause in the speech report contains a negative construction where an adverb intervenes between negation and the verb—see §14.1.

T3.15 [ma:] [nakaməy aka   alədar
NEG   one.fem.sg DEM.DIST.REACT.TOP.fem.sg   DEM.DIST.fem.sg+DOWN+ALL
varla-ku]   [yi-ku]   [ñəg   sapu-sada-ku]   [ra:l]
go.underneath-COMPL.SS go-COMPL.SS mosquito.net put-DOWN-COMPL.SS sit+3fem.sgBAS.P
'No, one was sitting having gone underneath, having crawled under the mosquito net (lit. having
put itself under)'

The first clause is a negative pro-clause, negating the preceding T3.15. In the second clause, the reactivated
topic demonstrative is used to remind the speaker that this is a familiar participant—the little snake who
managed to escape Oselo and was the protagonist of T3.9. The next two clauses are part of the clause
chain (all marked for same subject) describing a sequence of actions by the little snake.

T3.16 [aba-dəka   ku-saku-ku]   [ku-saku-taka]   [kaigən] [kwasa-kwasa
head+LK-ONLY put-OUTSIDE-COMPL.SS put-OUTSIDE-IMM.SEQ silent   little-little
mæy   ñən]   [kwasa-kwasa kə-də   rə-ku]
come.IMPV you.fem little-little   DEM.PROX-masc.sg sit-COMPL.SS
[rə-na-d]   [və-ñəna-d]   [wa-ku]   [[eh ata
sit-ACT.FOC-3masc.sgBAS.VT see-2fem.sgSUBJ.VT-3masc.sgBAS.VT say-COMPL.SS eh   how
yi-na-di]   [sə   vya-na-di]]   [wa-ku]   [ya:kya] [yi:n] [[ee
go-ACT.FOC-3plBAS.VT who hit-ACT.FOC-3plBAS.VT say-COMPL.SS OK   go+SEQ ee
karakiyee]   [wun-a-di ñan-ugw-adiyee   bə   kiya-na-diyee]]
death.adder+VOC I-LK-pl   child-PL-3plNOM+VOC already die-ACT.FOC-3plBAS.VT+VOC
[ata gra:l]
then cry+3fem.sgBAS.P
'Having thrust only the head out, immediately having thrust (it) out, (she was) silent. (The
mother said), "Come a little closer, you saw what happened around you (lit. you saw this stayed
having stayed a little)", having said (this), "Oh, how did they go, who killed them", after she'd
said this, OK, (she went) on, "Oh, death adder, it is my children who already died!", thus she
cried'

The first and the second clause describe the actions by the little snake (the verb *ku-* 'put' can only occur
with directionals—see §16.1.2). The predicate of the third clause is omitted (see §20.4.3). The next four
clauses form a speech report by the snake mother. In the first clause in the speech report, the subject
(S) follows the imperative form of the verb (see §20.2). The third clause within the speech report is
juxtaposed to the fourth clause as a complementation strategy. The next speech report consists of two
juxtaposed clauses. Note the plural agreement on the verb 'kill': the snake mother is assuming that many
offenders were involved in killing her children. The speech verb is followed by *ya:kya* 'OK', and *yi:n*
'go+SEQ' in its adverbial meaning 'on and on', and then another speech report framed by the verb 'cry'.
The speech report contains two vocative forms—one of an argument, and the other of the predicate
(see §2.1.3).

T3.17 [gra-lə-k   [ñan aka   wa:l]
cry-3fem.sg-COMPL.DS child DEM.DIST.REACT.TOP.fem.sg say+3fem.sgBAS.P
[[maya   gra-tukwa]   [[ñən   wukə-taka]
come.on.IMPV+VOC cry-PROH.GEN you.fem hear-IMM.SEQ
ya-kə-k-na-d]   [a-də   du sə   bə
come-FUT-FUT-ACT.FOC-3masc.sgBAS.VT DEM.DIST-masc.sg man name already
wukə-tua-d]   [də-kə-də   sə   Osəlo-ad]]   wa-ku]
hear-1sgSUBJ.VT-3masc.sgBAS.VT he-OBL-masc.sg name Oselo-3masc.sgNOM say-COMPL.SS
[ata wa-lə-l]
then say-3fem.sgSUBJ.P-3fem.sgBAS.P
'After she'd cried, the child said, "Come on, don't cry." "As soon as he hears you he will come,
I already heard this man's name, his name is Oselo", she said to her (lit. she said to her having
said)'

T3.17 is linked to T3.16 via head-tail linkage (see §20.4.1). The speech report by the little snake is framed with two occurrences of the speech verb *wa-* 'speak' (§19.5.1). In the second clause of the speech report, the object, 'you feminine', appears without any case marking (see §7.2), as its function is clear from the context. In the next clause, the name of the man is cross-referenced in the second position (with masculine gender)—see Chapter 5.

T3.18 [aa,   ya:kya] [a   karaki   aw   [kətawa yi-n]   [aw kətawa
       agreement OK   DEM.DIST.fem.sg death.adder then this.way go-SEQ then this.way
       ya:n]   [a kətawa yi-n]   a   təp   wukə-lə-l]
       come+SEQ then this.way go-SEQ DEM.DIST.fem.sg village smell-3fem.sgSUBJ.P-3fem.sgBAS.P
       ' "Yes, OK" (said the mother). That death adder smelt that village every way (lit. this way going
       this way coming this way going)'

The speech verb which would introduce mother snake's response is omitted. The second clause contains sequential forms of verbs 'come' and 'go', indicating the snake's movements every which way.

T3.19 [wukə-l]   [gəp-ə-rəb   a-də   [yi-də-d-ə]
       smell-3fem.sgBAS.P   run-LK-FULLY DEM.DIST-masc.sg go-3masc.sgSUBJ.P-3masc.sgBAS.VT-LK
       yabə-rəb]   [ata gəpəl   amæy   karaki   yama:b   yama:b]
       road+LK-FULLY then run+3fem.sgBAS.P mother death.adder smell+LK+TERM smell
       [sam   karya-lə-l]   [ya-n]   [ya-n]   [təp-a:r
       hornet bring-3fem.sgSUBJ.P-3fem.sgBAS.P come-SEQ   come-SEQ   village-LK+ALL
       waku-lə-l]
       go.out-3fem.sgSUBJ.P-3fem.sgBAS.P
       'She smelt (and) ran fully straight by the road he went on, then she ran, the mother death adder
       by the smell, by the smell, the one a hornet brought, coming and coming she (mother) went out
       (of the jungle) into the village'

The first and the second clauses are linked via juxtaposition (see §19.7). The second clause contains an uninflected verb marked with the suffix *-rəb* 'straight, fully' (see §9.2). The predicate is followed by an oblique, a location modified by a relative clause (a road he went on), with the common argument in locative function. The S and the oblique ('by the smell') of the following clause are postposed to the verb (see §20.2). The word 'by the smell' is repeated twice; the next clause is a headless relative clause.

T3.20 [ma:] [ababa du   ta:kw ya:n]   [a-di   yi-n]
       NEG   all+LK man woman come+SEQ   DEM.DIST-pl go-SEQ
       [ya-kwa-dana]   [ya-da-k]   [və-ku]   [ya:m
       come-HAB-3plSUBJ.VT+3fem.sgBAS.VT go-3pl-COMPL.DS see-COMPL.SS smell
       aka   bə   də-kə   ya:m aka
       DEM.DIST.REACT.TOP.fem.sg already he-OBL+fem.sg smell DEM.DIST.REACT.TOP.fem.sg
       bə   dəy-a-kə   yamawa   yin   rasagwa-də-lək]   [aw ma:]
       already they-LK-OBL+fem.sg smell+LK+COM go+SEQ mix.up-3masc.sg-BECAUSE then NEG
       [də-kə   ya:m wukəwuk suan   ata ya:l]
       he-OBL+fem.sg smell smell:RED difficult then go+3fem.sgBAS.P
       'No, all people kept coming and going, as she saw them come, since the smell already, his smell
       had mixed up together with their smell, it was hard for her to smell his smell'

The first clause consists of a negative pro-clause indicating that the snake's efforts were all in vain. The repetition of the verbs *ya-* 'come' and *yi-* 'go' in sequential forms reflect the idea of coming and going back and forth (obscuring the smells). The sixth clause is a medial completive clause used as a complementation strategy with the verb *və-* 'see' in the following clause. The last clause contains a nominalization (*wukəwuk* 'smelling') as a complementation strategy with the verb 'be difficult'. The latter cross-references the subject, 'snake' (see §20.1.4).

T3.21 [yi-ku]   [ata {səbənə-l]   [səbən-ku}]   [a   gra:b   ata
go-COMPL.SS then return-3fem.sgBAS.P return-COMPL.SS DEM.DIST.fem.sg afternoon then
kwa:l   ya]
stay+3fem.sgBAS.VT EMPH
'Having gone, then she came back, that afternoon she did stay'

The two occurrences of the verb 'return' in third and fourth clauses are pronounced as one intonation unit (this is why they are in braces); the second occurrence has a summarizing function rather than being used for head-tail linkage (see §18.3 and §20.4.1).

T3.22 [gan kusə-lə-k]   [ata wa-lə-l   a
night fall-3fem.sg-COMPL.DS then say-3fem.sgSUBJ.P-3fem.sgBAS.P DEM.DIST.fem.sg
ñənək]   [ñən   adakw]   [kwa-ñənə-k]   [wun aka
child+LK+DAT you.fem stay.IMPV stay-2fem.sg-COMPL.DS I   DEM.DIST.REACT.TOP.fem.sg
yi-k-na-wun-ək]   [kə   gan
go-FUT-ACT.FOC-1fem.sgBAS.VT-CONF DEM.PROX.fem.sg night
yi-kə-tua   aka]
go-FUT-1sgSUBJ.VT+3fem.sgBAS.VT DEM.DIST.REACT.TOP.fem.sg
'After night had fallen, she said to her, to that child, "You stay, as you stay, I will go, this night I will go" '

The addressee of the second clause (cross-referenced on the verb of speech) is postposed to the verb—see §20.2. The last clause contains a reactivated topic pronoun (referring to the time, 'this night') in clause-final position.

T3.23 [vyakat tə-kə-tua]   [aka
good   be-FUT-1sgSUBJ.VT+3fem.sgBAS.VT DEM.DIST.REACT.TOP.fem.sg
ya-k-na-wun-ək]   [kuprap tə-kə-tua]   [ah,
come-FUT-ACT.FOC-1fem.sgBAS.VT-CONF bad   be-FUT-1sgSUBJ.VT+3fem.sgBAS.VT ah
ya: ma:]
go/come no
' "If I am fine, I will come, if I am in a bad way, ah, (I) will not come" '

The first clause is an example of a juxtaposed dependent clause with a conditional reading (see §19.1): it is pronounced with a characteristic rising intonation. The same for the third clause. The last clause contains an example of future declarative negation (see §14.1).

T3.24 [ñən   ma:] [adakw] [[ñan-ugw məwi]   saku-n]   [adakw]
you.fem NEG stay.IMPV child-PL   things.like.that produce-SEQ stay.IMPV
' "You no, you stay, stay producing children and things like that" '

The first clause is elliptical (see §20.4.3); the three clauses are juxtaposed (see §19.7). The noun phrase in brackets is an appositional noun phrase with the generic noun 'things like this' (see §20.1.1).

T3.25 [wun-a:m vya-kə-dana]   [a   kiya-k-na-wun-ək]
I-LK+OBJ kill-FUT-3plSUBJ.VT+3fem.sgBAS.VT then die-FUT-ACT.FOC-1fem.sgBAS.VT-CONF
[wun-a   aka   yi-na-wun-ək]   [wa-ku]
I-3fem.sgNOM DEM.DIST.REACT.TOP.fem.sg go-ACT.FOC-1fem.sgBAS.VT-CONF go-COMPL.SS
[kəka   ya:l]
DEM.PROX.REACT.TOP.fem.sg go+3fem.sgBAS.P
' "If (or when) they kill me, then I will die, it is me who is going to go", having said (this) she here went off'

The first clause is a juxtaposed dependent clause with a conditional or a temporal reading.

T3.26 [ga:n aka   a-də   yabə-rəb   yi::n]   [ta:y
      night DEM.DIST.REACT.TOP.fem.sg DEM.DIST-masc.sg road+LK-FULLY go:REP+SEQ first
      waku-l   wiya:r]
      go.out-3fem.sgBAS.P house+LK+ALL
      'At night she having gone straight on the road first entered the house'

The temporal noun *ga:n* in the first clause is unmarked for case (as expected: §7.2). An unusually long vowel in the sequential form *yi::n* iconically reflects the distance travelled. In the last clause the oblique appears after the verb—see §20.2.

T3.27 [aka   yi::n]   [a   gapum   [ata wukə-su
      DEM.DIST.REACT.TOP.fem.sg go:REP+SEQ then big.post+LK+LOC then listen-UP
      kui-n]   ra:l]
      give.to.third.p-SEQ sit+3fem.sgBAS.P
      'Having gone to another house, she sat on the big post listening to what was above'

An unusually long vowel in the sequential form *yi::n* iconically reflects the distance. The directional form of the verb 'hear' is used adverbially, just as in 16.59 (see the discussion there).

T3.28 [a-də   sa:k]   [[aw Osəlo səki-kə-dana-d]
      DEM.DIST-masc.sg name+LK+DAT then Oselo call.name-FUT-3plSUBJ.VT-3masc.sgBAS.VT
      wa-ku]   [wukə-n]   [rə-lə-l]
      say-COMPL.SS listen-SEQ sit-3fem.sgSUBJ.P-3fem.sgBAS.P
      'She sat listening for that name, thinking (lit. having said), "They will call the name of Oselo" '

The argument of the verb 'listen', a noun phrase 'for that name' is split off from the verb by a completive medial clause expressing internal speech or thinking of the snake (with the verb of speech: see §19.5.6).

T3.29 [rə-p rə-p rə-p rə-p tə-ku]   [nəkə   wiya:r   ma: ata
      sit-FR sit-FR sit-FR sit-FR be-COMPL.SS other+fem.sg house+LK+ALL again then
      ya:l]
      go+3fem.sgBAS.P
      'Having sat and sat and sat and sat in vain, she then went again to another house'

The first clause contains a durative frustrative (§13.6). Repetition of the frustrative form reflects the length of 'sitting'.

T3.30 [nəkə   wiya:r   yi-ku]   [a   gapum   wukə-su
      other+fem.sg house+LK+ALL go-COMPL.SS then big.post+LK+LOC listen-UP
      kui-n]   [aka   ra:l]
      give.to.third.p-SEQ DEM.DIST.REACT.TOP.fem.sg sit+3fem.sgBAS.P
      'Having gone to another house, she sat on the big post listening to what was above'

The directional form of the verb 'hear' is used adverbially, just as in 16.59 (see the discussion there) and in T3.27.

T3.31 [wukə-su:n]   [rə-lə-l]   [rə-p rə-p rə-p rə-p] [ma: səki]
      listen-UP+SEQ sit-3fem.sgSUBJ.P-3fem.sgBAS.P sit-FR sit-FR sit-FR sit-FR NEG call:NEG
      'She sat listening in the upward direction (that time), she sat and sat and sat and sat, (they) did not call the name'

The first clause contains a sequencing form of the verb 'listen' accompanied by a directional (in contrast to an adverbial use of the same form in T3.27, and T3.30). Time is cross-referenced in the second position of the predicate of the second clause. The next clause contains a durative frustrative (§13.6).

T3.32 [yi-ku]   [nəkə   wiya:r   ata ya:l]
      go-COMPL.SS other+fem.sg house+LK+ALL then go+3fem.sgBAS.P
      'Having gone she then went to another house'

T3.33 [yi-lə-l]   [aw də-kə   ya:m-ab   wukəwuk   samasama
     go-3fem.sgSUBJ.P-3fem.sgBAS.VT then he-OBL+fem.sg smell-TOO smell:RED a.lot+LK
     suan   ya:l]
     difficult go+3fem.sgBAS.P
     'She went that time, but his smell too was very difficult to smell'

Time is cross-referenced in the second position of the predicate of the first clause. The next clause is linked to the preceding one with the connective *aw* (see §19.6) which has a contrastive meaning. The last clause contains a nominalization (*wukəwuk* 'smelling') as a complementation strategy with the verb 'be difficult'.

T3.34 [[a:bab-a du   ta:kw] dəy-a-kə   ya:m] [də-kə-wa   rasəgwa-də-lək]
     all-LK   man woman they-LK-OBL+fem.sg smell he-OBL-COM mix.up-3masc.sg-BECAUSE
     [wukəwuk ma:]
     smell:RED   NEG
     'Since the smell of all the people mixed up with him, there was no possibility of smelling (it)'

The first clause is a causal clause (see §18.7). It contains a complex possessive noun phrase (see §20.1.1). The second clause contains a negated nominalization (§14.3.3) in the meaning of 'absolute' negation.

T3.35 [ya-n]   [wukəwuk suan   yi-lə-k]   [aka   kəp
     come-SEQ smell:RED difficult go-3fem.sg-COMPL.DS DEM.DIST.REACT.TOP.fem.sg just
     yi-ku]   [mugul-a-wiya:r   ata   ya:l]
     go-COMPL.SS three-LK-house+LK+ALL then go+3fem.sgBAS.P
     'Having come, as it was difficult to smell, having gone just like that she went to a third house'

The second clause cross-references third person which could well be the mother snake. However, the predicate of this clause is cross-referenced for different subject; and the snake is the main character and the subject of this whole sentence. This indicates that the second clause contains a 'body part construction' or that the nominalization is in the S function (see §17.4 and §20.1.4). In the next clause, *kəp* 'just' has an overtone of 'for nothing'—see Chapter 21 on its other meanings. The form *mugul-a-wi* could also mean 'three houses' (see §20.1.1); here it means 'number three house'.

T3.36 [[a   mugul-a-yay wiya:r]   yi-lə-l
     DEM.DIST.fem.sg three-LK-ORD house+LK+ALL go-3fem.sgSUBJ.P-3fem.sgBAS.VT
     aka]
     DEM.DIST.REACT.TOP.fem.sg
     'She went (that time) to a third house'

The constituent in brackets in the first clause is a noun phrase with two modifiers (see §20.1.1). The reactivated topic demonstrative referring to time (cross-referenced in the second position on the verb) is postposed to the verb—see §20.2.

T3.37 [rə-lə-k   rə-lə-k   rə-lə-k]   [yi::n]   [ga:n
     sit-3fem.sg-COMPL.DS sit-3fem.sg-COMPL.DS sit-3fem.sg-COMPL.DS go:REP+SEQ night
     kusə-yakə-lə-k]   [[oh ma!] wa-ku]   [nəkə   wiya:r   ata
     finish-FULLY-3fem.sg-COMPL.DS oh   NEG say-COMPL.SS other+fem.sg house+LK+ALL then
     ya:l]
     go+3fem.sgBAS.P
     'As she sat, as she sat, as she sat, on and on, the night had completely fallen, she having said, "Oh, no (or nothing)", went to another house'

The three occurrences of *rə-lə-k* are pronounced as one intonation unit (without a break). The repetition iconically reflects the length of the action. The next clause consists of *yi:n*, literally, 'going', used adverbially in the meaning 'on and on' (see §18.2), and lengthened to reflect the amount of time the snake spent sitting. The speech report consists of just an interjection and a negative pro-clause which can be translated as 'no' or as 'nothing'.

T3.38 [nəkə   wiya:r   yi::n]   [wula-ku   [a   gapəm   ata
other+fem.sg house+LK+ALL go:REP+SEQ enter-COMPL.SS then big.post+LK+LOC then
rə-kətəwun] ra:l]
sit-LOOK   sit+3fem.sgBAS.P
'As she went and entered another house she sat on the post looking'

The penultimate clause contains the verb 'sit' accompanied by a special directional form of 'look'—see §15.2.1.

T3.39 [rə-kətəwun rə-lə-k]   [də-kə   ta:kw karabur   ata
sit-LOOK   sit-3fem.sg-COMPL.DS he-OBL+fem.sg woman men's.house+LK+ALL then
væsə-lə-l]
step-3fem.sgSUBJ.P-3fem.sgBAS.P
'As she sat looking, his wife then stepped into the men's house'

The reference is to Oselo's wife. In the last clause, time is cross-referenced in the second position.

T3.40 [Osəloee]   [mən   [warən]   kamna:gw ak   ya]
Oselo+VOC   you.masc   go.up+SEQ food   IMPV+consume EMPH
[kad   bə   numa-də   ga:n-ad]   [ñan ñan-ugwa-wa
DEM.PROX+3masc.sgNOM   already big-masc.sg night-3masc.sgNOM   we   child-PL+LK-COM
sə   kwa-kwa:k]   [wa-lə-k]   [a   amæy   karaki
sleep stay-RED+DAT say-3fem.sg-COMPL.DS DEM.DIST.fem.sg mother death.adder
aka   wa:l]   [mm, [a-l-ay   ñan
DEM.DIST.REACT.TOP.fem.sg say+3fem.sgBAS.P mm   DEM.DIST-fem.sg-DIST youngster
səki-la-də   sə]   adəka]   [ya:k] [nəbəl
call.name-3fem.sgSUBJ.VT-3masc.sgBAS.VT name DEM.DIST.REACT.TOP+masc.sg OK   today
kiya-kə-na-dəmən-ək]   [a   wun-a-di ñan-ugw
die-FUT-ACT.FOC-2masc.sgBAS.VT-CONF then I-LK-pl   child-PL
vya-məna-yæy]   [wun-aba:b aka
kill-2masc.sgSUBJ.VT+3fem.sgBAS.VT-SUBST I-TOO   DEM.DIST.REACT.TOP.fem.sg
ya-na-wun-ək]   [wa-ku]   [ya:kya]
come-ACT.FOC-1fem.sgBAS.VT-CONF say-COMPL.SS OK
'After she said, "Oselooo, you do go up and eat, it is that it is already very late (lit. this is that it is big masculine night), the children and I (lit. we with children) are about to go to sleep", mother death adder then said, "Mm, this is the name that young lady there called, OK, today you will die, in exchange for you killing my children, I too have come here", after she'd said this, OK'

The first word in the first clause of the speech report is in a vocative form (marked by lengthening the vowel of the last syllable: §2.1.3). In the next clause, a very dark night is referred to as a big-masculine night: see §5.2.1. The next clause contains an inclusory construction ('we with children' meaning 'children and I'). The dative-aversive nominalization in this clause refers to an intention—see §13.7. The next speech report is by the snake. It starts with the interjection *mm* (see §2.1.3)—a marker of 'warning', indicating that the speaker is up to no good. The constituent in brackets is a lengthy noun phrase—see §20.1.1. The next clause contains a threat which sounds almost like a prediction, due to the confirmation marker: 'today you will die'. The use of substitutive case as a clause-linking device was discussed in §19.3. And see §20.4.2, for the functions of *ya:kya* clauses.

T3.41 [Osəlo ata warə-d   PAUSE wiya:r]   [wun aka
Oselo   then   go.up-3masc.sgBAS.P PAUSE house+LK+ALL I   DEM.DIST.REACT.TOP.fem.sg
war-kə-tua-ley   [wa-ku]   [Osəlo warə-n   wiya:m]
go.up-FUT-1sgSUBJ.VT-3fem.sgBAS.VT+VOC say-COMPL.SS Oselo   go.up-SEQ house+LK+LOC
[wiya:m   rə-ku]   [ada   wa:d]   [ŝa!]
house+LK+LOC sit-COMPL.SS DEM.DIST.REACT.TOP+masc.sg say+3masc.sgBAS.P hey
'Oselo then went up, into the house, having said, "I will go up!!!", Oselo having gone up into the house, having stayed in the house, he (topical) said, "Hey!"'

In the first clause, the oblique 'into the house' is postposed to the verb; a short pause between the verb and this constituent shows that this is an afterthought (see §20.2). The second clause contains a vocative form of the final verb (§2.1.3). The dependent medial clause following the clause with the verb of speech *wa-* contains a locational constituent postposed to the verb (see §20.2). The last clause is the beginning of a new speech report.

T3.42 [ñan-ugway   [wukə-n] ada]   [nəbəl-a   kwarbar
      child-PL+VOC listen-SEQ sit.IMPV today-3fem.sgNOM jungle+LK+ALL
      yi-tua]
      go-1sgSUBJ.VT+3fem.sgBAS.VT
      'Children-ey, sit and listen, it is today (that) I went to the jungle'

The first clause contains a vocative form of the irregular plural noun 'children'. The last clause is juxtaposed to the rest of the sentence; this is an example of juxtaposition employed as a complementation strategy (see §19.8).

T3.43 [yi-tua]   [a-d-ay   təbur   [yi::n]
      go-1sgSUBJ.VT+3fem.sgBAS.VT DEM.DIST-masc.sg-DIST clearing+ALL go:REP+SEQ
      waku-tua]   [[ñan kabay] [ñan karaki]   sama-ja:p
      go.out-1sgSUBJ.VT+3fem.sgBAS.VT child snake child death.adder lot+LK-thing
      vya-ta:y]   [ata wa-tua-di-a-wa]   [wun Osəlo-adəwun-ək]   [aw
      kill-COTEMP then say-1sgSUBJ.VT-3plBAS.VT-LK-COM I   Oselo-1masc.sgNOM-CONF so
      a   wun-a:k ap]   [və-kə-gura]   [wa-ta:y] [ata
      then I-LK+DAT see+IMPV see-FUT-2plSUBJ.VT+3fem.sgBAS.VT say-COTEMP then
      kətəkə-tua-di]   [a-na-y   bə   miyawa səmərab kabay
      cut-1sgSUBJ.VT-3plBAS.VT DEM.DIST-CURR.REL-DIST already all   never.ever snake
      tə   ma:] [bə   məgi-tu-di]   [vya-yakə-tua-di]
      have:NEG NEG already do.whatever-1sgSUBJ.P-3plBAS.P kill/hit-FULLY-1sgSUBJ.VT-3plBAS.VT
      [vya-təpul-tua-di   wali-baga:r]   [wa-də-k]   [ñan-ugw
      kill-'hit'-1sgSUBJ.VT-3plBAS.VT white.man-knife+LK+INSTR say-3masc.sg-COMPL.DS child-PL
      ata   waji-di]
      then laugh-3plBAS.P
      ' "As I went, I came out there onto a clearing, as I kept killing snake's children, many children of a death adder, with those (the words which) I was saying, 'I am Oselo, look at me, you will see', as I kept saying I cut them, there already in all that place never ever there will be any snakes, I already 'whatevered' them, hit them all, killed them with a white man's knife", after he'd said thus, the children laughed'

The first clause is a juxtaposed clause with a temporal meaning—see §19.1. Constituents in brackets in the third clause are appositional noun phrases—see §20.1.1. The next clause contains a headless relative clause with comitative marking on it (see §19.2.1). Clause 11 contains the generic verb *məgi-* 'do whatever' used as a cover term for a variety of possible verbs of hitting and killing (see §21.3.2). The next two clauses are juxtaposed to this clause, providing further specification of the action. In the last clause of the speech report the oblique 'with a white man's knife' follows the verb (see §20.2).

T3.44 [aah, Osəlo [mən   ya]   mən   du-adəmən-ək]   [bə
      aah   Oselo you.masc EMPH you.masc man-2masc.sgNOM-CONF already
      vya-məna-di]   [wa-ku]   [yi-kə-bana-l-a:b]   [yara
      kill/hit-2masc.sgSUBJ.VT-3plBAS.VT say-COMPL.SS go-FUT-1plSUBJ.VT-3fem.sgBAS.VT-TOO well
      yi:n] [ya-k-na-dian]   [wa-ku]   [ya:k]
      go+SEQ come-FUT-ACT.FOC-1plBAS.VT say-COMPL.SS OK
      ' "Oh, Oselo, you really, you are a man, you already killed them", having said, "it is that we will go too, well going we will come", having said (thus), OK'

The bracketed clause within the first clause is elliptical—see §20.4.3. This is an example of a discontinuous speech report; note that the speech verb *wa-* intervenes between clausal constituents. The first clause after the speech verb *wa-* contains an instance of the predicate in a contrastive focus construction (see §20.3). The last clause consists just of *ya:k*—see §20.4.2 on the function of *ya:k(ya)* clauses.

Oselo's children are now saying that it is safe for them to go to the bush now that there are no more snakes there.

T3.45 [kamna: kan   napa-ku]   [ñan-ugw ta:kw [sə   kwa-kər]
       food   eat+SEQ COMPL.VB-COMPL.SS child-PL woman sleep stay-DES
       wula-da:-k]   [də-kaba:b Osəlo ata   wula:d]
       go.inside-3pl-COMPL.DS he-OBL+TOO Oselo then go.inside+3masc.sgBAS.P
       'Having eaten food, after children (and) wife went inside (their mosquito nets) to sleep, Oselo, he too, went inside'

The first clause contains the generic completive verb *napa-* (see §18.9) denoting that the process of eating food was completed. The first word in this clause, *kamna:*, is a variant of *kamna:gw* (see A3 in §2.6). The second clause has a complex structure: it consists of a matrix clause and a desiderative clause indicating the intention ('to sleep'). A desiderative rather than same-subject purposive is used here because presumably neither the wife nor the children got much sleep that night—see below. The verb *wula-* in this context means 'go inside the mosquito net'.

T3.46 [Osəlo ñəg-a:r   wula-də-l]   [agur   ata
       Oselo mosquito.net-LK+ALL go.inside-3masc.sgSUBJ.P-3fem.sgBAS.P snoring then
       væd   ya   fiR fiR fiR]
       snore+3masc.sgBAS.P   EMPH fiR fiR fiR
       'The time Oselo went inside the mosquito net, he then snored, fiR fiR fiR'

Time is cross-referenced on the predicate of the first clause. The second clause contains a lexicalized complex predicate *agur væ-* 'snore' (see §17.3). The last word in this clause is an expressive imitating the sound of the man snoring.

T3.47 [aka   amæy karaki   aka
       DEM.DIST.REACT.TOP.fem.sg mother death.adder DEM.DIST.REACT.TOP.fem.sg
       wa:l]   [nəbəl kiya-kə-na-dəmən-ək]   [nəbəl
       say+3fem.sgBAS.P   today die-FUT-ACT.FOC-2masc.sgBAS.VT-CONF today
       kiya-kə-na-dəmən-ək]   [aka
       die-FUT-ACT.FOC-2masc.sgBAS.VT-CONF DEM.DIST.REACT.TOP.fem.sg
       war-k-na-wun-ək]   [wa-ku]   [ya:kya] [a   gapu
       go.up-FUT-ACT.FOC-1fem.sgBAS.VT-CONF say-COMPL.SS OK   then big.post+LK
       təpurəb war-lə-l]   [aka   warəən]
       top+FULLY go.up-3fem.sgSUBJ.P-3fem.sgBAS.P DEM.DIST.REACT.TOP.fem.sg go.up.REP+SEQ
       'The mother death adder said, "Today you will die, today you will die, I will climb up", having said (this), OK, she climbed up straight on top of the big post, going up and up'

In her speech introduced by the verb *wa-*, the mother snake makes a prediction which sounds like a threat. The verb of speech is used twice, as is typical for a speech report framing construction (see §19.5.1). Time is cross-referenced on the predicate of the next clause. The sequencing medial clause is postposed to it (see §20.2). The prolonged final vowel iconically reflects slow and lengthy movement by the snake.

T3.48 [Osəlo agur   væ-də-k]   [və-ku]   [yi:n] [[tə-kəta-n]
       Oselo snoring snore-3masc.sg-COMPL.DS see-COMPL.SS go+SEQ stand-LOOK-SEQ
       [da-l]]
       go.down-3fem.sgBAS.P
       'After she saw that Oselo was snoring, she went down going looking'

The first clause is a medial completive clause used as a complementation strategy with the verb 'see' in the next clause (see §19.8). The last clause contains a special compounding verb of the verb 'see'—see §15.2.1.

T3.49 [[tə-kəta-n]　　　[da-ku]]　　　　　[a-də　　　　　də-kə-də
stand-LOOK-SEQ　go.down-COMPL.SS　DEM.DIST-masc.sg　he-OBL-masc.sg
ñəg-aːr　　　　vǽki-n]　　　　[ata [warbutə-n　　tə-ku]]　　　　[də-kə
mosquito.net-LK+ALL　go.across-SEQ　then　bend.over-SEQ　'stand'-COMPL.SS　he-OBL+fem.sg
səp-aːr　　　agək-ər　　　da-ku]　　　　[də-kə-bər taːb　akətawa yi-n]
skin-LK+ALL　side-LK+ALL　go.down-COMPL.SS　he-OBL-du　hand　like.this　go-SEQ
[rə-brə-k]　　　　[ata　miyawa　kay-rətu-lə-d　　　　　　　ya]
sit-3du-COMPL.DS　then　all　　　CAUS-break/split-3fem.sgSUBJ.P-3masc.sgBAS.P　EMPH
'Having come down looking, having gone across to that mosquito net of his, having bent over, having descended onto his body (lit. skin) from the side, as his arms stayed like this (showing that the hands were apart), she then fully squeezed him to the point of breaking'

The constituent in brackets in the third clause is a complex predicate with anterior meaning—see §17.1.1. In the last clause, the form *miyawa* (which contains a comitative marker *-wa* in its derivational meaning: see §7.9) means 'fully, altogether'.

T3.50 [kay-rətu-lə-k]　　　　　　　[də ya:p　səsə-aːb　　ma:]
CAUS-break/split-3fem.sg-COMPL.DS　he　breath　'put':RED-TOO　NEG
[ada　　　　　　　　bə　　kay-rətu-yakə-lə-k]　　　　　　[kiya-k
DEM.DIST.REACT.TOP.masc.sg　already　CAUS-break/split-FULLY-3fem.sg-COMPL.DS　die-PURP.SS
tə-ku]　　　　[ata ooo,
be:SUP.VB-COMPL.SS　then　ooo
kay-rətu-lee-dəwun-əkoo]　　　　　　　　　　　　　　　　[kabay
CAUS-break/split-3fem.sgSUBJ.P+VOC-1masc.sgSUBJ.P-CONF+VOC　snake
kay-rətu-la-dəwun-əkoo]　　　　　　　　　　　[wa-də-k]　　　　[du
CAUS-break/split-3fem.sgSUBJ.P-1masc.sgSUBJ.P-CONF+VOC　say-3masc.sg-COMPL.DS　man
taːkw　yi-daː-l]　　　　　[lə-kə-m　　məgiməgi　　ma:]
woman　go-3plSUBJ.P-3fem.sgBAS.P　she-OBL-OBJ　do.whatever:RED　NEG
'After she squeezed him to the point of breaking, he too could not breathe, he, after she squeezed him really fully, as he was about to die, then after he said, "Ooo, she is squeezing me-eee, snake is squeezing me-eee", people came that time, there was no way they could "whatever" her (lit. there was no whatevering her)'

The second clause contains a negated nominalization in its predicate slot. The fourth clause contains a complex predicate with the meaning of imminent modality, 'be about to' (§17.1.2). The next two clauses contain vocative forms of the predicate (see §2.1.3). The last clause contains a negated nominalization in the predicate slot.

Jacklyn Yuamali suggested that *məgiməgi ma:* be replaced by *vyavi ma:* 'no killing'.

T3.51 [Osəlo kiya-də-k]　　　　　　[lə-kabaːb　　aka
Oselo　die-3masc.sg-COMPL.DS　she-OBL+TOO　DEM.DIST.REACT.TOP.fem.sg
aləb　　　　　　　kətəkə-da-l]
DEM.DIST+fem.sg+TERM　cut-3plSUBJ.P-3fem.sgBAS.P
'After Oselo died, her too they cut into pieces right there'

The predicate of the second clause cross-references the object (snake) in the second position; the object is also expressed with the pronoun 'she' (which is not marked for object case because case marking is not compatible with non-word class-changing suffixes, such as *-aba:b* 'too' (see §9.2)).

T3.52 [[[Osəlo-wa kabay-wa] bər]　　viti-kərəb　　a　　　　　ga:n　kiya-bər]
Oselo-COM　snake-COM　they.two　two-TOGETHER　DEM.DIST.fem.sg　night　die-2duBAS.P
'Oselo and the snake the two together died that night'

The constituent in brackets is an argument elaboration (inclusory) construction which contains a coordinating structure with a double comitative (see §7.9) to indicate that the two characters participated in the action together.

T3.53 [gabu-maːj   mawər   wula-l   aka]
       traditional-story base+LK+ALL go.inside-3fem.sgBAS.P DEM.DIST.REACT.TOP.fem.sg
       'Here the story is finished'

This last clause of the story contains a typical ending: when a story finishes it is understood as 'going back to where it came from'. Note a slight difference in the form of the verb and constituent order (whereby the reactivated topic demonstrative is postposed to the verb: see §20.2) between this ending and T2.69: here the speaker had felt that his story had gone on for too long, and in this sentence the fact of its finally coming to an end is in the sentence-final position marking its 'unexpectedness' (see §20.2). Not so in T2.69 which was a traditional story and, according to the speaker, finished in due course.

Vocabulary

Only words occurring in the examples and texts above are listed here. Each root is specified for its word class, and transitivity (in the case of verbs). Roots which require suffixes (that is, verbs) have a hyphen (-) at the end. Verb roots are given in their positive declarative root form (e.g. *wukə*- 'hear, listen' or *wa*- 'say, speak'). For nominal components of complex verbs, we include the support verb used (in brackets). A morphologically complex word is divided into morphemes. Different meanings of homophonous lexemes are separated with a semicolon (;), as in *kapə*- 'cut grass; wait'. Different meanings of polysemous lexemes are separated with a comma, as in *ñan* 'child, youngster (in terms of age and status group), child of someone (n)'. The following abbreviations are used:

adj	adjective
adv	adverb (including time words)
conn	connective
cp	complex predicate
interj	interjection
n	noun
ncv	nominal component of complex verbs
part	particle
q	quantifier
vitr	intransitive verb
vp	polyfunctional verb (which can function as a support, auxiliary, and copula verb)
vtr	transitive and ambitransitive verb

I have not included here grammatical markers and members of closed classes discussed elsewhere in the grammar, such as pronouns or postpositions. Neither have productive or semi-productive derivations (such as nominalizations or causatives) been included. Affixes are included in the list of affixes. Loanwords and code-switches in Tok Pisin and English have not been included. A list of kinship terms is in Table 6.1.

Entries are translated with one or two English words that give some indication of the most central meaning of the Manambu word. A fuller statement of the meanings of the Manambu lexicon will be in the dictionary of Manambu (currently in preparation, by Pauline Laki and Aikhenvald). All the entries are in the Avatip variety, unless the Malu variety is explicitly indicated.

The alphabetical order is: a, a:, æ, æ:, b, d, ə, g, i, i:, j, k, l, m, n, ñ, p, r, s, t, u, u:, w, y.

a then (conn)
ab head (n)
abakapi hawk (n)
aban taka- conspire (cp)
aba-ñəg umbrella (n)
aba rə grey hair (n)
aba-wapwi headdress, hat (n)
agək one of two sides (q)
agur væ- snore (cp)
aki-ta:b left hand (n)
alək this is why (conn)
am bow (n)
am measure (n)
amæy mother (n)

amæy-ta:kw (mother-wife) first wife (n)
aməy basket of a fish-trap type (n)
ankəl nettle (n)
ap bone, strength (n)
ap-a-du (bone/main-LK-man) chief, head of the place or institution (n)
ap-a-ka-ap very thin (adj)
apar adult, main (n/adj)
ap-a-sə (bone/main-LK-name) main and first given name (n)
apan old (masculine) (adj)
apaw old (feminine) (adj)
apawul, apawəl spirit (n)
apa:n old (masculine) (adj)

api taka- yawn (cp)
api top (n)
apwi address term for the Sarak clan (n)
apwi mana:b address term for the Maliau
    clan (n)
ar lake (n)
arəp bush knife (Malu) (n)
asa:y father (n)
asə-kami: catfish (n)
asəki bad cold (n)
ata then (conn)
atawa thus (conn)
atawata:y and so then, in summary, this is why
    (conn)
aw then (conn)
awar side, sideways (n)
awarəb in turn (adv)
awa:y mother's brother (n)
ayey yes (proform)
ayvul hot water (n)

a:s dog (n)

æm share (n)
æywan some, a few (q)

babay maternal grandparent (n)
badi young (man) (n), young (adj)
bag (say-) pins and needles (feel) (cp)
baga wi back part of the house, backyard (n)
bagul ankle (n)
bak crowd (q)
bal, ba:l pig (n)
balay tail (e.g. of a crocodile) (n)
bap moon, month, address term for the
    Wulwi-Ñawi group (n)
bapi rotten, very soft (adj/ncv)
bas first (adv)
bas sə- ask (cp)
batay mother's brother's wife (n)
baw ashes, haze (n)
ba:b wasp (n)
ba:d egg (n)
ba:g bush knife (n)
ba:gw dance, ceremony, music, performance (n)
ba:n back (n)
ba:p line (of people) (q)
ba:r fever, malaria, sickness (n)
ba:u, bau scaly mudgroper (n)
bæy flat bundle, used for mats and limbum (q);
    limbum leaf (n); mat (n); feast (n)
bæy yi- be tasty (cp)
bəkəs yi- quarrel (cp)

bəməy- discover (cp)
bənak capable, possible (modal)
bənawi-yi- bənawi-ya- dive all over the place,
    back and forth (vitr)
bəta:y already (adv)
bətuku- pump by itself, be blown like a balloon
    (vitr)
bəutagər croton (n)
bəyib stream (n)
bibir dragonfly (n)
bi:r foam (n)
bla- talk (vtr/vitr)
blakə- overturn (vitr)
bla-saku-sala- debate; perform ceremonial talk
    in men's house (vtr)
bra- scrape (e.g. coconut) (vtr)
buti- fold, be folded (vtr/itr)
bwi hot to the point of boiling (ncv)
bwiyabwi (na-) very hot (ncv)

da- go down (vitr)
dab layer, generation (n)
dakul spirit (n)
damda:m spider (n)
dapu- be wrapped (vitr)
da:m spider (n)
dəb fence, ritual enclosure (n)
dəbəñə three days before today (adv)
dəbrəm (na-) perfect (ncv)
dəg beak, nose (of an animal) (n)
dəmakau brown snake (n)
dəpugwəl hiccup, burp (n)
dəpu-na:gw inside sago tree (n)
di excrement, shit (n)
draku- unglue (vitr)
du man (n)
duama:gw brother (of female ego) (n)

gabəraw-ñanugw sisters' children (n)
gabi creeper plant, edible vine (n)
gabu-ma:j traditional story, fairy tale (n)
gai-du, gai-ta:kw address term for the Abelam
    people, or the people of the Maprik area (n)
gaji- rub something, wipe (vtr)
gak side (n)
galab-a ta:kw nanny, woman who looks after
    children (n)
galab kur- take care of someone (cp)
gala-mæn forked area between toes (n)
gala-ta:b forked area between fingers (n)
ganəb morning (n)
gañ last (n/adj)

gapu big post of a house (n)

gawi white-breasted eagle (n)

gawun narrow (adj)

ga:j small pelican-like white bird, address term for the Sablap clan (n)

ga:l twig, fork-like part of tree (n)

ga:m song, shout (n)

ga:m sə- sing, serenade, call, shout (cp)

ga:n night (n)

ga:r sago field, sago patch (n)

gəl blackness, black paint, dark cloud (n), black (adj)

gəm first pregnancy (n)

gəngən (na-) tremble, cherish (ncv)

gəñ last (adj), tail (n)

gəñap address term for members of the Yimal clan (n)

gəña-ta:kw last wife, non-first wife (n)

gəñər later (adv)

gəp(ə)- bury (vtr); run (vitr)

gər tiny (adj)

gər- establish, found (e.g. a village); scratch (vtr)

gərgər tiny (adj)

gərpaw wild cat (n)

glabadi decoration (n)

glajəpis little black ant (n)

glu- be settled down (vitr)

gra- cry (vtr)

gra-kudi mourning song (n)

gra-maki- cry inconsolably (vitr)

gra:b afternoon (n)

gu water, drink (n)

gubi wet (adj)

gu-jabər water-raft (n)

gus paddle (n)

gu yaku- wash oneself, bathe (cp)

guyuk lie (n)

gwa- pull out weeds or sticky seeds on plants or one's clothing, pluck (vtr)

gwaj(ə)- spin, turn (the handle), turn (by itself) (vtr/itr)

gwalugw clan (n)

gwar ointment (n)

gwarabi mango (n)

gwas a big string or bundle (n)

gwa:l paternal grandfather, ancestor; grandchild (n)

gwa:s turtle (n)

gwəyip lie (n)

ja- fall (of rain) (vitr)

jabər ship, big boat (n)

jagər garfish (n)

jaguy yam soup (n)

jagwəs small Malay apple (n)

jama-saku- (extinguish.fire-OUTWARDS) light up the fire which is almost extinguished (vtr)

jan- wash part of body or small things (vtr)

japal bigger bat (n)

japuka:p location underneath the house (n)

jar- put hand inside to take something out (vtr)

jarkañ bamboo shoot originally used as a storing tube; rifle (n)

jataw small bat (n)

jau, ja:u let it be, don't worry, you may do it (part)

jaujay, jauja:y in a sloppy, incorrect way (adv)

jay stick (n)

jayib moment (n)

ja:m a set of hereditary magical and ritual powers (n)

ja:p thing (n)

jə- chew (vtr)

jəb design, drawing; letter, literacy (n)

jələg ten shell valuables strung together; ten-kina note (n)

jəpis small black ant (n)

jəpwas initiated man (n)

jəwi- be awake, wake up (vitr)

ji- (with səp skin) sick and tired (cp)

ji- tie (vtr)

jibəl arrangement of fish on a string (q)

jigər (na-) go up (ncv)

jigərəp body smell (n)

jigər-mæn toe (n)

jigər-ta:b finger (n)

jijap various things (n)

jikinəbi growth on skin, pimple (n)

jukwar sister (of male ego) (n)

jupwi backside, buttocks (n)

juwi type of tree with reddish-brownish berries (n)

ka- paddle; plant (vtr)

kabak stone, large sums of money (n)

kabasək seed; rice (n)

kabay snake (n)

kabəl- surround (vtr)

kagəl (yi-) be sore, painful (ncv)

kagər daughter-in-law (son's wife) (n)

kagrəs father's sister's child (n)

kagul- leave (vtr)

kaigən be silent (ncv/adv)

kaigən saigən very quiet (ncv/adv)

kaja- open by moving apart, disperse (vtr/itr)
kajal husband's sister, brother's wife (n)
kakəl- win, surpass (vitr/tr)
kakəlka:u competition (n)
kalakw- stop (vitr)
kalipa-, kaləpa- teach (vtr)
kaligab address term for the Wapanab clan (n)
kalu- put and carry on shoulder (vtr)
kamal- come back, reverse direction (vitr)
kami-kamna:gw (fish-food) foodstuff (n)
kami: fish (n)
kamkaw hairy yam (n)
kamna:gw, kamna: food (n)
kanukaraki death adder (n)
kanu taipan (n)
kaña- be stuck, glue, mend (vtr/itr)
kañgu policeman; piece of bamboo (n)
kapawi friend, member of peer group (n)
kapayawi sweet potato (n)
kapə- be full (Malu) (vitr)
kapə- cut (grass); wait (vtr/itr)
kapi flat-sided fish (n)
kar-/kra-/*ka- bring, carry (vtr)
karaki death adder (n)
kara:b ceremonial men's house (n)
karkar quietly (adv)
karki mud (n)
karkwas angry, quarrelsome (adj), (yi-) squabble
    (ncv)
karu mudgroper (n)
karya- bring (vtr)
karyam na- dawn (cp)
kasapwi- open (vtr/itr)
katəlam na- dawn (cp)
kau- be deep (vitr)
kaula- carry inside (vtr)
kaurak- stop; be/become silent (vitr/ncv)
kaw hole (n)
kawami cemetery (n)
kawar- take up, carry up (vtr)
kawi- disembark, come ashore (vitr)
kay-bətuku- pump (vtr)
kay-blakə- turn (vtr)
kay-buti- fold (vtr)
kay-dapə- wrap (vtr)
kaygən saygən be really silent (adv/ncv)
kay-gəpə- hold in hand, hug (vtr)
kay-grəpə- break (vtr)
kay-gwaj- wrap (vtr)
kayik spirit, image, picture, reflection (in water),
    ghost, shadow (n)
kaykətək(ə)- hold onto (vtr)

kay-kwa- pour, spill, capsize (vtr/vitr)
kaykwap lazy (adj)
kaykwapa-ta:b left hand (n)
kaylapə- get dark (vitr)
kay-napwi- open (e.g. a parcel) (vtr)
kay-pəsə- go around something, turn around
    something (vtr/vitr)
kay-pisa- break in half (vtr)
kay-puti- take off (e.g. clothing or skin) (vtr)
kay-rali untie (with force) (vtr)
kay-rətu- break or split with hands (vtr)
kay-səgəl- snap off, break off (as one does the
    leaves of a leafy vegetable) (vtr)
kay-tapu- carry a bundle in one's arms (vtr)
kay-təkwi- split, break (bigger pieces of
    firewood, tree) (vtr)
kay-wər- lift off the top layer of a log (vtr)
kay-wi:- break by hand (e.g. nuts) (vtr)
ka:b (tə-; yi-) be selfish (ncv)
ka:d shield (n)
ka:gw slit drum (n)
ka:l mayfly (n)
ka:m (yasa-/yasə-) hunger (ncv)
ka:m breadfruit (n)
ka:ñ bamboo flute, bamboo (n)
ka:p on its own, alone, reflexive (adv)
ka:u platoon, group (n/q)
ka:w sharpness (n)
kə- consume (eat, drink, smoke) (vtr/vitr)
kəbay small shell type (n)
kəbi food-storing basket (n)
kəbwi flying fox (n)
kədran kədran imitating a cassowary speaking,
    or summoning a cassowary (interj)
kəkəpa:t food (n)
Kəkətəp mortuary ritual (n)
kəl(ə)- become dry (of water), go down (of
    water) (vitr)
kə-marki- swallow (vtr)
kəp goodwill address term (n)
kəp ground (n)
kəp just; on one's own; greeting (n)
kəpanay wallaby (n)
kəpa:b in case (conn)
kəpəyay traditional greeting (greeting/n)
kəpi mosquito (n)
kər-/kra- (ta:kw) marry (for a man marrying a
    woman) (vtr)
kərkəm (na-) completely silent (ncv)
kərnəm (na-) completely silent (ncv)
kəsək- shake (vtr)
kəta now (adv)

kətək like (postposition)

kətək- cut (vtr)

kətəka- snap (something) (vtr)

kə-təp-ə-məñ (eat-be.closed-LK-breast) last child (n)

kija:p protein food (n)

kisa-ñədi twins (n)

kiya- die (vitr)

kraku- carry across (vtr)

kraku-taka- (carry.across-put) get and put (e.g. when loading a canoe) (vtr)

krəjan crackling noise, screeching sound (interj)

krəsakrəs (yi-) scratchy (ncv)

kru fat (adj), fatness (n)

ku- put (vtr)

kudi language, lip, mouth (n)

kugab owl (n)

kugar star (n)

kui meat (n)

kui- give to third person (vtr)

kui-taka- (give.to.3rd.p-put) spread, send around, distribute, put on display in a store (vtr)

kukə- back (n)

kukər behind (postposition)

kuku warm (ncv)

kul axe (n)

kula new, fresh, raw (adj)

kulakul new, innocent, newcomer (adj/n)

kulapu- clean, arrange (vtr)

kulkul needle (n)

kunay spear grass (n)

kuprap bad, ugly (adj)

kuprapə-saprap really bad (adj)

kur- do, make, get, become (fully) (vp/vtr)

kurju- mix together (vtr)

kurpatəktəka- leave out, forget (vtr)

kur-saku- (do/get-OUTWARD) do a job incompletely (vtr)

kur-taka- (do-put) do for other people, take things out (e.g. of a stringbag) and spread on a surface, assemble (e.g. a canoe) (vtr)

kuryak- pull out biggish thorns (vtr)

kusə- fall (of night) (vitr)

kusə- finish, be finished, die (vtr/vitr)

ku-su- (put-UPWARD) wear, put on (clothing) (vtr/vitr)

kuyak wound (n)

kwa- be in/at, exist (in general, or in multiple locations) (vp/vitr)

kwakə- look for, find (vtr)

kwakuli orphan (n)

kwalami tree, stick (n)

kwam, kwa:m crazy, mad, unthinking, unintentional (adj)

kwapək next day (adv)

kwarəb bush (n)

kwasa small (adj)

kwasabi stringbag (n)

kwasək (yi-) be unwilling (ncv)

kwati knee (n)

kwatiya- give to non-third person (vtr)

kwatu island (n)

kwayugw wet season (n)

kwa:j bat (n)

kwa:l neck, throat (n)

kwa:r grass skirt (n)

kwa:s salt, type of pheasant (n)

kwa:t post (in a house) (n)

kwa:y shrimp (n)

lagu- pull a big object (such as a plank) (vtr)

lakati- sort things out (vtr)

laki ginger (n)

laki-ka-laki green (adj)

laku- know, learn, understand (vtr/vitr)

lama- burn, light (vitr)

lap banana (n)

lapa-ñəg letter (n)

lapi- take off (clothing, skin) (vtr)

lau ripe (adj)

lau-lap ripe banana (n)

la:gw shade (n)

la:n husband (n); headache (n)

ləkiləki soft (adj)

ləpa-way- break, tear (something) (vtr)

luku kur- steal (cp)

madək madək especially, namely (adv)

maguni address term for the Gla:gw clan group (n)

maja:n mortuary ritual (n)

makajəwi address term for the Maliau clan (n)

makati address term for members of the Gla:gw clan group (n)

makaw telopia fish (n)

makən rə- stay (lit. sit) in mourning (cp)

makwər sakwər very happy (adj/adv)

mali totemic haze (n)

mama-du enemy (n)

maməy mother's younger sister (n)

mapa-jəpis little red ants (n)

mapa-ta:b right hand (n)

mapi breast (n)

maw base (n)

maway flower (n)

mawul something inside something else, bone marrow, core, pith (of a tree), feelings (n)

mayir(a) powerful spirit (n)

mayka:r openly, visibly (adv)

ma: negation, again (adv)

ma: wa- refuse, disapprove (vitr)

ma:d testicle; underneath (n)

ma:gw generic noun, whatever (n)

ma:j story (n)

ma:k in person, face to face, oneself (adv)

ma:l side, stern (of canoe) (n)

ma:m elder sibling (n)

ma:n bird of paradise (n)

ma:pw yellowish possum (n)

ma:r wind (n)

ma:s betelnut (n)

mæm enemy, quarrel (n)

mæn leg, foot (n)

mæ:j rope (n)

mæ:r plate (n)

məd cassowary (n)

məgi- do whatever (vtr/vitr)

məj, mij fork spear (n)

məjəl small bird (n)

məkəmək silent, quiet (without motion), very low (ncv)

məl eye (n)

məl kusə- (eye finish-) be blind (cp)

məl sray-taka- (eye ?-put) look with great attention (cp)

məñ breast (n)

məñər- chip, break off (like a tooth chips off) (vitr)

məy real, very (adj)

mi, mi: tree (n)

mij fish spear (n)

mijma:j chit-chat (n)

mi ma:j (high talk) telephone (n)

mi val (high canoe) plane (n)

miyawa together (adv)

mi:r upwards (adv)

mu crocodile (n)

mu, mu: the day after tomorrow (n)

mutam face (n)

na daughter's child (n)

na- be (of physical states, natural phenomena) (vp)

nab head hair (n)

nabəs beach (n)

nabi year (n)

nagər fishing net (n)

nagəs the day before yesterday, not long ago (n)

nagw tree trunk (n)

namay lament about foiled marriages (n)

nan (nən-) smoking grid (n)

nana:u earthquake (n)

nap strap (n)

napa- completive generic verb (no transitivity value: §18.9)

napwi- be unwrapped (vitr)

narək narək (tə-) rock, be rocking (ncv)

narkə- shake (vitr)

nas(ə)- count, enumerate (vtr)

naubadi young (man) (n/adj)

nawidu mate, man from same peer group (n)

nawi-ta:kw mate, woman from same peer group (n)

nawul- be stretched, line up (vitr)

nay- play (vitr)

na:gw sago (n)

na:l yesterday (n)

nəb dry land, stranger, enemy (n)

nəbay yet (n)

nəbə be able to (modal)

nəbək hill, mountain (n)

nəbəl today (adv)

nəbə-ta:kw young woman (n)

nəbi arrow (n)

nəkər (tay-) cool, cold (ncv)

nəma, numa big (adj)

nəmnəm (tə-, na-) tired, itchy (ncv)

nugu- collect (e.g. fruit) (vtr)

ñab Sepik River (n)

ñaj father's brother (n)

ñakamali dry season (n)

ñam, ñigañam edible greens (n)

ñam- chew the food before putting it into a baby's mouth (vtr)

ñamus, ñaməs younger sibling (n)

ñan child, youngster (in terms of age and status group), child of someone (n)

ñan red yam (n)

ñap mother's elder sister (n)

ñapwi firewood (n)

ñasap father's elder brother (n)

ñauñau (tə-) smash (ncv)

ña:p tusk (n)

ñə sun (n)

ñəd middle (n)

ñəg mosquito net, leaf, letter (n)
ñiki blood (n)
ñikiñiki red (adj)
ñirvi address term for the Maliau clan (n)

paba:n large black ant (n)
paki number (n)
pakwur pakwur in a secretive way (adv)
papər later (adv)
pasəta:kw four days before today (adv)
patəp- cut (e.g. rope) (vtr)
patiaku-, patiyaku- turn into something (vitr)
pa:kw- be hidden (vitr)
pa:m na- be empty (ncv)
pa:p shortness (n), short (refers to both animates
    and inanimates) (adj); wound (n)
pa:t youngster (n)
pəkaka:u cock-a-doodle-doo (interj)
pəkə- jump (vitr)
pəp wing (n)
pəpli loud noise (n)
pərəgabi a small string of things, especially
    fish (n)
pərki- be torn, tear (clothes, paper) (vtr/itr)
pəsəp rubbish (n)
pətaka:u, pətəkau ladder (n)
pəu sound of explosion (interj)
piñu- slip (e.g. in the mud), slide (vtr)
prapi- be hollow (vitr)
prəm prəm, brəm brəm sound of a drum (interj)
pui parcel (n/q)
puka- break (vitr)
pukə-puk- bulge (vitr)
pusa- rot (vitr)
pusəp rubbish (n)
puti- fall off, come off by itself (e.g. a shoe which
    is too big), throw away, take off (vitr/vtr)
pwipwi pig's bladder (n)

ra- cut (vtr)
rabə-taka- cover (vtr)
rak fish scale (n)
rakrak happy (adj)
rali- untie (something), untie (by itself), roll
    (vtr/vitr)
rami: branch (n)
rapya- twist (something) (vtr)
rasagwa- mix up (vtr)
rasə- get up, stand up, grow (vitr)
raw- peel (vtr)
ra:b slit drum (n)
ra:w mother's brother's child (n)

rə- be in/at, exist (horizontal position), marry (a
    woman marrying a man) (vp/vitr)
rəbə-jay drumstick (n)
rək dry (adj); joke (n)
rək-a-səp (dry-LK-skin) old person (n)
rəka:rək carefully (adv)
rəp- be enough (vitr)
rəpa- dig, scrape (vtr)
rəpərəp equal, identical (adj/ncv)
rou rou rou roaring sound (interj)

sa, ča, śa, ša hey (attention getter); don't do it,
    stop! (interj)
sajagalavi, sawəgalawi, sagəlawi tree seeds used
    in children's games (n)
saka- light (fire), put something over fire (vtr)
saka-taka- put on light (vtr)
sakə- smoke (food) (vtr)
sakibag wild taro (n)
saki-taka- bestow name (vtr)
saku- lay an egg, give birth to a child, have
    children, push outside, open (vtr)
sakwar happy, proud (adj)
sakwar sakwar happy, proud (adj/adv)
sakwi- (with səp 'skin') sick and tired (cp)
salyakə- stretch out (e.g. legs) (vtr/vitr)
sam hornet (n)
samasa:m a lot (q)
sapəyakə- open mouth (vtr/vitr)
sapu- cover (vtr)
sapu-taka- (cover-put-) put a headdress on
    someone else's head, cover a large surface
    (vtr)
sapwi- give birth (Malu) (vtr)
sar fowl (n)
sar(ə)- jump, step up(wards) (vitr)
sarmabap destitute (n/ncv)
sau- fry (e.g. sago) (vtr)
saula- bark (vitr)
saulǝy paulǝy (yi-/tǝ) be in great numbers (ncv)
saun, sawən white pelican (n)
sawəl- become transformed (vitr)
saw-taka adorn, decorate (vitr)
say- be (of some states: shame, pins and needles)
    (vp); go until (vitr)
sa:d fashion, way, manner (n)
sa:gw shoulder (n)
sa:l (yi-) be lacking something, be short of
    something (ncv)
sa:m bee (n)
sa:n money, shell valuable (n)
sa:p character, image (n)

sa:r fly (n)

sa:s boil, bubble (n)

sa:y bundle (of leaves) (q); ceremonial house for uninitiated men (n)

sə name (n); bundle (as of banana) (q)

sə- plant, put, call, move (vtr/vitr); shine (of sun) (vitr)

səbək, səbuk ritual officer (n)

səbən- return (vitr)

səgliak names other than the first one (n)

sək far (adj/adv)

səkər time (n)

səkət- carry under arm; move away (vtr/vitr)

səki- call (name) (vtr)

sək-sək-sək (na-) (be) very black (ncv)

səkulək yi- cook (cp)

səkwara- scrape earth (vitr)

səlkə- diminish (vitr)

səlki- surround, tie around (vtr)

səluku- forget something, be forgotten (vtr/vitr)

səmaka- show (vtr)

səmərab, səma:b, səmsəma:b never ever (adv)

səmi long, tall (about a person) (adj), length (n)

səp skin (n)

səpakudi mouth (n)

səp-ə-ka-səp skinny (of a person), thin (of a piece of wood), flat (adj)

səpər- be dry (vitr)

səpər- snap something (vtr)

səpisəpi drizzle, drizzly (adj/ncv)

sər tomorrow (n)

sərr sound of making canoe fall into water (interj)

sər-sər-sər (na-) (be) very white (ncv)

səwəl-, səwul- turn into (vitr)

stakra- meet (vtr/vitr)

suan (yi-) be difficult (ncv)

sua:l true story, lie (n)

suguya- help (vtr)

sui laments about foiled marriages (n)

suku- carve, write, record (vtr)

sukulək, sikulək yi- cook (cp)

su: edible cane, pitpit (n)

ta- hit, move (vtr)

taba-ñə (hand+LK-sun) wrist watch (n)

tabək side, half (n/q)

tabu- escape (vitr)

taga wi front part of the house (n)

tagər type of croton (n)

tak seed (n)

taka- put down (vtr)

taka-yi-taka-ya- be very angry, be raging all over the place (vitr)

takətap door (n)

takutakw (na-) dawn (cp)

takw market (n)

takw- clear garden (vitr)

takwa-ñan (woman+LK-child) girl (n)

tala:b before (adv)

tama:y, tamay promontory, cape (n)

tami: area (n)

tan measure, bundle (q)

tapu- carry a bundle in one's arms (vtr)

tapwuk, tapwək chicken, address term for the Sablap clan (n)

ta-saku- (put/cut-OUTWARDS-) appoint, choose, elect (vtr)

taw- put up (e.g. a post), erect, spread out (vtr)

taw-taka- put out or up on a large surface (vtr)

taw-təpə- prevent from seeing, stand in the way (vtr/vitr)

tay- be (of climatic states) (vp)

taykət- join two pieces (vtr)

ta:b hand (n)

ta:k tip (n)

ta:kw woman, wife (n)

ta:l in the past, past (adv)

ta:m nose (n)

ta:y first, in front, before, a long time ago (adv)

ta:yir before, a long time ago (adv)

tə- become, be, exist (vertical position) (in a location), have (vp/vitr)

təb sky (n)

təkə-mi tree seed, medicine (n)

təkər stool, chair (n)

təməl- roll (vitr); make noise (vitr)

tənəb fireplace (n)

təp coconut; village (n)

təp(a)- sew (vtr)

təp(ə)- close, be closed (vtr/vitr); dive (vitr)

təpə-taka- (identical to that of taka-təp-) prevent from seeing, block (vtr)

təpwi ceremonial mound (n); wide (adj)

tikal tongue (n)

titiya:n tə- walk about (cp)

ti:- carry on one's head (vtr)

ti:d co-wife (n)

tu- burn (vtr)

tugwam (na-) clear (ncv)

tukura- cover; heap up (something) (vtr)

tukwi heap, pile (q)

tu-taka- (?-put) tie (vtr)

tu:- fetch water (vtr)

va- fall (of night) (vitr)

vakər-, væker- fall (vitr)

val canoe, car (n)

va:l taboo, prohibition (n)

væ- dig (vtr/vitr)

væga- put inside (bag or basket) (vtr)

vægru- meet, get together (vitr)

væj frying pan (n)

væk pot (n)

væki- go across (vitr)

væra-, vara- go across towards the speaker (vitr)

væs grass (n)

væs(ə)- step on (vtr/vitr); store (vitr)

væt heavy (adj/ncv)

væt(ə)- bite (vtr)

vætəka- put something standing up (vtr)

væy spear (n)

væytu- whistle (vitr)

və- see, look, experience (vtr/vitr)

və-kraki- (see-carry.across-) recognize by seeing (vtr/vitr)

vəl- cut (vtr)

vər lake (n)

vər- burn (of fire) (vitr)

vərvər- be shallow (adj)

və-sapwi- (see-open-) discover by seeing something (vtr/vitr)

və-səməl- (see-?-) look for (vtr)

vya- hit (vtr/vitr)

vyakanaku- improve, correct (vtr)

vyakət, vyakat good, beautiful (adj)

vya-ləpa- smash (vtr)

vyapra- shoot, kill, spear (vtr)

vya-prapi- break by hitting, split open (vtr)

vya-səp(a)- kill, hit to death (vtr)

vya-taka (ta:b) wave a hand (vitr)

vya-təpul- smash (vtr)

vyavya-ta:b right hand (n)

vya-wuta- break small thin things in two (e.g. firewood) (vtr)

vyæj- put in line (vtr)

wa- say, speak (vtr/vitr)

wa-buti- fold forcefully or with care, fold a full length of something (e.g. a long sheet) (vtr)

wabwi- peel (banana) (vtr)

wagrəb curse (n)

wa-jali- (say-?) call (vtr)

wa-jəwi wake someone up (vtr)

waji- laugh (vitr)

wa-karay-kur- (say-bring-do-) be hospitable (to someone) (vtr/vitr)

wakənay five days before today, remote past (adv)

wa-kəta- (say-try-) ask carefully, nicely (vtr/vitr)

waku- go out (vitr)

wakuli mouse, rat (n)

wa-laku- give advice (vtr)

walba:b near (adv/adj)

walba:b kalba:b very close (adv)

waləb close (adv)

waləb kaləb very close (adv)

wali east; non-indigenous people (n)

wali- walk around (vitr)

wali-bag knife (n)

wali-gus (white.man-paddle) outboard motor (n)

wali-kamna:gw (white.man-food) store-bought food (n)

walimaudi rainbow (n)

wali-mæj (white.man-thread) store-bought thread or wool (n)

wali-na:gw (white.man-sago) biscuit (n)

wam shell (n)

wama white (n/adj)

wamən bay (n)

wanəb noise (n)

wap (say-) shame (feel) (n/ncv)

wapa- leave (vtr)

wapi bird, address term for the Nagudəu subclan of the Wulwi-Ñawi (n)

wapruku- be enough and more than enough, overflow, be overfull (vitr)

wapu- push (vtr)

wapu-taka- (?-put-) light a fire (vtr/vitr)

wapwi clothing (n)

war- go up (vitr)

warag ancestor (n)

warapwi- change (vitr)

warbutə- bend over (vitr)

warku- close up (vitr)

warsam(a)- be angry (vitr)

warya- fight (vtr/vitr)

wasali namesake (n)

wasupu- gossip (vitr)

wa-sway- postpone (vtr)

wa-tək- (say-break-) accuse (vtr/vitr)

wa-təp- (say-be.closed-) forbid, deprive (vtr/vitr)

waw blue fly (n)

wawəs wife's brother (n)

way address term (n)

wayab very recently, moments ago (n)

wa-yaga- scare (vtr)

wa-yakə- (say-throw-) order (vtr)

wayəpi address term (n)

wayəy, wayay oh dear, oh God (interj)
waygər (wa-) complain (ncv)
waygər saygər complain a lot (ncv)
wayik trace, footprint (n)
wayway maybe (adv)
wa:gw totemic area (n)
wa:j medium-sized eel (n)
wa:l rain (n)
wa:m white cockatoo, address term for the
    Wapanab, Makəm, and Wargab clans (n)
wa:n ear (n)
wa:ñ line (especially in genealogy) (n)
wa:ñ- be alive (vitr)
wa:r big stringbag (n)
wa:s cheek (n)
wa:y magic, address term (n)
wəlpəm (na-) completed, finished (ncv)
wər- move (vtr/vitr)
wər-saki- (move-ACROSS) turn, translate, pour
    water (from a bucket to a bucket) (vtr)
wər-taka- move downwards onto a larger surface
    (e.g. fish from pot to plate) (vtr)
wi house (n)
wiləñ silent (adj)
wiy- be broken, break into the open (a boil or a
    sore, an egg), breaking up (e.g. a ceremony)
    (vitr)
wiyaw (na-) light and dry (ncv)
wiyəw lizard (n)
wiyugw door (n)
wudəb spirit, dead people; address term for the
    Nabul clan (n)
wuk tooth (n)
wuk(ə)- hear, listen (vtr/vitr)
wuka- drop or spill unintentionally, fall (vtr/vitr)
wukə-kraki- (hear-carry.across) recognize by
    hearing (vtr/vitr)
wukə-mar- forget (not necessarily completely)
    (vtr/vitr)
wukən together, with (postposition)
wukə-sapwi- (hear-open-) discover by hearing
    (vtr/vitr)
wukə-taka- (hear-put-) provide (vtr)
wukə-tay- worry (vtr/vitr)
wukə-təp- (think/hear-be.closed) forget
    (completely) (vtr/vitr)
wul- be swollen (vitr)
wula- come inside, enter, make enter, go inside,
    away from the Sepik River (vtr/vitr)
wulək lightning (n)
wuli- multiply (vitr)
wuliñ fingernail (n)

wulpi- close up (vitr)
wur- pour (vtr), fly (vitr)
wurəbasawul- bless in a traditional way (see
    §21.5.3) (vtr/vitr)
wurəbi large mosquito (n)
wurəpi liver, spleen, lung (vtr/vitr)
wus urine, penis (n)
wusabwi water (in childbirth) (n)
wusau- itch (vitr)
wuta- break (as a coconut falling from a tree)
    (vitr)
wuti spoon (n)
wu: ton fruit (n)
wu::: sound of person crying (interj)

ya- come (vitr)
yabənay address term for the Maliau clan (n)
yabər- fan (someone) (vtr/vitr)
yabi:b quickly (adv)
yabrəkay fan (n)
yaga- be scared, afraid (vitr)
yakə- throw (vtr)
yaki tobacco (n)
yakraw thunder (n)
yaku- wash whole body (vtr/vitr)
yakwiya- adopt (a child) (vtr/vitr)
yana- burn (vitr)
yanan grandchild (n)
yanu magic (n)
yap string, rope, objects strung on a string (n)
yapi- buy, shop, pay (vtr/vitr)
yapwur yapwur quickly (adv)
yara fine, well, well-behaved (adj/adv)
yarakara well (adv)
yarəg enclave, residential area (n)
yarəp fence (n)
yasə-/yasa- be (of physical states: hunger,
    thirst) (vp)
yata- carry with hands and arms (vtr)
yata-vəl- carry off (vtr)
yati- knit (vtr/vitr)
yawəl husband's mother (n)
yawi work (n)
yawus father's sister (n)
yayi:b tree kangaroo, wallaby (n)
ya:b road (n)
ya:kya OK (adv)
ya:kya wa- say OK, agree, accept, approve
    (cp)
ya:l womb, belly (n)
ya:m smell (n)
ya:p, ya:pw breath, asthma, rest (n)

ya:w husband's mother's brother (n)
yæj frying pan (n)
yæy appendix (n)
yæy- be (of smells) (vp)
yæ:p cane (n)
yæ:y, yæy grandmother (paternal) (n)
yi, yi: fire (n)
yi- do, be (with some abstract terms), go, say,
    speak (vp/vtr/vitr)
yibən port (n)
yibun-mi chief (n)

yi-gaji- rub something onto something (vtr)
yigən dream (n)
yimal address term for the Yimal clan (n)
yi-pa:kw- hide something (vtr)
yipayip (na-) be cool (ncv)
yipər gnetum gnemon tree and edible leaf (n)
yi-sawəl- transform, become transformed
    (vitr/vtr)
yu green snail shell (n)
yuwi body hair (including facial hair), feathers,
    fur (n)

List of Affixes

This list of affixes includes all the bound grammatical morphemes (suffixes, two prefixes, and one infix) discussed in this grammar. Each affix is accompanied by an abbreviated English translation. Sections or chapters where the marker is discussed are indicated after the translation. The list does not include components of verbal compounds (see §15.2.4 and §15.3), or reduplication as a derivational device (see §9.1.1; §12.8.2).

a- 'second person imperative' (§13.2)
-a- 'linker'
-aba:b, a:b 'too' (§9.2)
-aki(-) 'directional marker with demonstratives: across' (§10.2.1); 'directional marker with intrinsically directional verbs: across away from speaker' (§16.1)
-aku(-) 'directional marker with demonstratives: outwards' (§10.2.1); 'directional marker with intrinsically directional verbs: outwards from speaker' (§16.1)
-(a)pra-/-(a)par 'directional marker with intrinsically directional verbs: across towards speaker' (§16.1)
-awi 'distance suffix on demonstratives: very far from speaker/hearer' (§10.2.1)
-ay 'distance suffix on demonstratives: further from speaker/hearer' (§10.2.1)

-ba- 'third person negative imperative' (§14.4); 'non-productive possession marker' (§8.1.1)
-bər 'second and third person dual'; 'plural' (kinship terms); 'associative plural (personal names)' (Chapters 3, 6; §22.1)

-d(-) 'singular masculine' (Chapters 3, 5, 11–13)
-d(a) 'directional marker with demonstratives: down' (§10.2.1); 'directional marker with intrinsically directional verbs: down' (§16.1)
-dəka 'only' (§9.2)

-ək 'confirmation marker' (§12.5)
-əka 'suffix in reactivated topic demonstratives' (§10.2.3)
-əu 'optative modality' (§13.2.3)

-ga:y 'unlikely condition clause marker' (§18.8)

-ja:y 'collective' (§9.2)
-jəbər 'customary aspect' (§12.7)

-ka- 'intensive' (accompanied by root reduplication) (§9.1.2; §4.3.2)
-kara 'non-productive derivational suffix' (§9.2)
kay- 'causative-manipulative prefix' (§16.2.1)
-kay 'non-productive object nominalization' (§9.1.2)
-ka:u 'action nominalization' (syllable weight sensitive) (§9.1.2)
-kə- 'future' (§12.2) (syllable weight sensitive: see §2.4.2)
-kə- 'irrealis' (§13.3)
-kə- 'possessive marker' (Chapter 8); 'linker with third person non-plural pronouns and the interrogative "who"' (§4.1.1)
-kəb/-kəkəb 'medial clause marker as soon as' (DS; syllable weight sensitive) (§18.6; §2.4.2)
-kəkl-kəkək 'different-subject purposive' (syllable weight sensitive) (§13.4.2; §2.4.2)

-*kər* 'desiderative' (§13.5)
-*kər əb* 'derivational suffix "together" with numbers' (§10.6.1)
-*kul-k* 'completive medial clause SS/DS markers' (switch-reference sensitive) (§18.3)
-*kwa-* 'habitual aspect non-past' (§12.3)
-*kwa(-)* 'third person imperative' (§13.2)

-*l* 'singular feminine' (Chapters 3, 5, 11–13)
-*lək* 'causal medial clause marker' (§18.7)

-*m* 'predicate marker in demonstratives' (§10.2)
-*ma:r-* 'negator used in non-main clauses' (§14.5)

-*n* 'sequencing medial clause marker' (§18.2)
-*n(-)* 'predicate marker in demonstratives and some interrogatives' (§10.2.2–3; §10.4).
-*na-* 'action focus marker on verbs' (§12.1)
-*na-* 'current relevance marker with demonstratives' (§10.2.1)
-*nak* 'first person plural imperative' (§13.2)
-*naral* 'non-productive derivational suffix' (§9.1.2)

-*p* 'durative frustrative' (§13.6)
-*pək* 'more or less'; 'comparative' (with adjectives) (§9.2)

-*rəb* 'fully' (§9.2)

-*sada-* 'bound directional with optionally directional verbs: down' (§16.1)
-*saki-* 'bound directional with optionally directional verbs: across away from speaker' (§16.1)
-*saki-sala* 'bound directional with optionally directional verbs: to and fro, across away-towards' (§16.1)
-*saku-* 'bound directional with optionally directional verbs: outside, outward' (§16.1)
-*sap* 'transportative case' (§7.7); 'non-productive derivational suffix' (§9.1.2)
-*sapra-/sapar* 'bound directional with optionally directional verbs: across towards speaker' (§16.1)
-*say* 'transportative case' (§7.7)
-*səwəl(a)/-sawəl*; -*sula/-sul-*; *saula-* 'bound directional with optionally directional verbs: inside, away from the Sepik River' (§16.1)
-*su* 'bound directional with optionally directional verbs: up' (§16.1)

-*taka* 'immediate sequence medial clause marker' (SS; syllable weight sensitive: §18.5)
-*tay-* 'directional marker with intrinsically directional verbs and bound directional with optionally directional verbs: sideways away from speaker' (§16.1)
-*ta:y* 'cotemporaneous medial clause marker' (§18.4)
-*tæy-* 'directional marker with intrinsically directional verbs and bound directional with optionally directional verbs: sideways towards speaker' (§16.1)
-*tək* 'first person dual imperative' (§13.2)
-*tu-* 'complete involvement of S/O' (§12.4)
-*tukwa* 'general negative imperative' (§14.4)

-*u* 'first person singular imperative' (§13.2)
-*u-/-war* 'directional marker with intrinsically directional verbs: up' (§16.1)

-*wa* 'comitative case' (§7.9)
-*way* 'strong negative imperative' (§14.4)
-*wayik* 'extra-strong negative imperative' (§14.4)
-*wula* 'directional marker with demonstratives: inside, away from the Sepik River' (§10.2.1)

-wula-/-wəla-/-wul 'directional marker with intrinsically directional verbs: towards speaker or inland' (§16.1)
-wur 'directional marker with demonstratives: up' (§10.2.1)

-yakəp 'non-durative frustrative' (§13.6)
-yay 'ordinal number marker' (§10.6.1)
-yæy 'substitutive case: instead of, rather than' (§7.8; §19.3)
-yikwa- 'habitual aspect past' (§12.3)

-Vb 'terminative case' (§7.6)
-Vk 'dative-aversive case' (§7.4)
-Vk 'same subject purposive' (§13.4.1)
-Vm 'locative-accusative case'; 'completive aspect' (§12.6)
-Vr 'allative-instrumental case' (§7.5)

References

AIKHENVALD, A. Y. 1986. 'On the reconstruction of syntactic system in Berber-Lybic.' *Zeitschrift zur Phonetik, Sprachwissenschaft und Kommunikationsforschung* 39: 527–39.

—— 1994. 'Grammatical relations in Tariana.' *Nordic Journal of Linguistics* 17: 201–18.

—— 2000. *Classifiers: A Typology of Noun Categorization Devices.* Oxford: Oxford University Press.

—— 2002a. *Language Contact in Amazonia.* Oxford: Oxford University Press.

—— 2002b. 'Traditional multilingualism and language endangerment', pp. 24–33 of *Language Maintenance for Endangered Languages: An Active Approach*, edited by David Bradley and Maya Bradley. London: Curzon Press.

—— 2002c. 'Typological parameters for the study of clitics, with special reference to Tariana', pp. 42–78 of *Word: A Cross-linguistic Typology*, edited by R. M. W. Dixon and Alexandra Y. Aikhenvald. Cambridge: Cambridge University Press.

—— 2003. *A Grammar of Tariana, from Northwest Amazonia.* Cambridge: Cambridge University Press.

—— 2004a. *Evidentiality.* Oxford: Oxford University Press.

—— 2004b. 'Language endangerment in the Sepik area of Papua New Guinea', pp. 97–142 of *Lectures on Endangered Languages: 5—From Tokyo and Kyoto Conferences 2002*, edited by O. Sakiyama and F. Endo. The project 'Endangered languages of the Pacific Rim'. Suita, Osaka: ELPR.

—— 2006a. 'Serial verb constructions in typological perspective', pp. 1–68 of *Serial Verb Constructions: A Cross-linguistic Typology*, edited by Alexandra Y. Aikhenvald and R. M. W. Dixon. Oxford: Oxford University Press.

—— 2006b. 'Grammars in contact: a cross-linguistic perspective', pp. 1–66 of Aikhenvald and Dixon (eds.).

—— 2007. 'Typological distinctions in word-formation', pp. 1–65 of *Language Typology and Syntactic Description*, iii: *Grammatical Categories and the Lexicon*, edited by T. Shopen. Cambridge: Cambridge University Press.

—— 2008. 'Semi-direct speech: Manambu and beyond.' *Language Sciences* 30: 383–422.

—— Forthcoming a. *Imperatives and Other Commands.* Oxford: Oxford University Press.

—— Forthcoming b. 'Reconstructing Proto-Ndu phonology and morphology.'

—— Forthcoming c. 'Multilingual fieldwork, and emergent grammars'. To appear in the *Proceedings of BLS 33*.

—— Forthcoming d. 'Versatile case.' *Journal of Linguistics* 45.

—— Forthcoming e. 'Reciprocals in the making: multiple grammaticalization in Manambu', to appear in *Festschrift for Christian Lehmann*, edited by Johannes Helmbrecht et al. Berlin: Mouton de Gruyter.

—— Forthcoming f. 'Causatives which do not "cause".'

—— Forthcoming g. 'The semantics of clause linking in Manambu.'

—— Forthcoming h. 'Eating, drinking and smoking: a generic verb and its semantics in Manambu.' In *The Linguistics of Eating and Drinking*, edited by John Newman. Amsterdam: John Benjamins.

—— Forthcoming i. 'Language contact along the Sepik river.'

—— and R. M. W. DIXON. 1998. 'Dependencies between grammatical systems.' *Language* 74: 56–80.

—— —— (eds.). 2006. *Grammars in Contact: A Cross-linguistic Typology.* Oxford: Oxford University Press.

—— —— Forthcoming. 'Explaining associations between intransitive subject (S) and transitive object (O).' *Word.*

—— and P. Y. L. LAKI. 2006. 'Manambu', pp. 475–6 of *Encyclopaedia of Language and Linguistics.* 2nd edition. Oxford: Elsevier.

—— and T. STEBBINS. 2007. 'Languages of Papua New Guinea', pp. 239–66 of *Vanishing Languages of the Pacific*, edited by O. Miyaoka, O. Sakiyama, and M. E. Kraus. Oxford: Oxford University Press.

ALLEN, B. J. ET AL. 2002. *Agricultural Systems of Papua New Guinea*. Working Paper No. 2. Canberra: Australian National University.

ALLEN, J. D. and P. W. HURD. 1972. 'Manambu phonemes.' *Te Reo* 15: 37–44.

AMHA, A. and G. I. DIMMENDAAL. 2006. 'Verb compounding in Wolaitta', pp. 319–57 of *Serial Verb Constructions: A Cross-linguistic Typology*, edited by Alexandra Y. Aikhenvald and R. M. W. Dixon. Oxford: Oxford University Press.

AUSTIN, P. 1981. 'Switch-reference in Australia.' *Language* 57: 309–34.

BASS, J. n.d. 'Essentials for translation. Part 1. Grammar. Wosera.' MS. Ukarumpa.

BATESON, G. 1958. *Naven*. 2nd edition. Stanford, Calif.: Stanford University Press.

BEHRMANN, W. 1917. *Der Sepik (Kaiserin-Augusta-Fluss) und sein Stromgebiet: Mitteilungen aus den deutschen Schutzgebieten Ergänzungsheft* XII. Berlin: Mittler and Sohn.

—— 1922. *Im Stromgebiet des Sepik*. Berlin: August Scherl.

—— 1924a. 'Die Stammessplitterung im Sepikgebiet (Neuguinea) und ihre geographischen Ursachen.' *Petermanns Geographische Mitteilungen* 70: 61–5, 121–3.

—— 1924b. 'Das westliche Kaiser-Wilhelms-Land in Neu Guinea.' *Zeitschrift der Gesellschaft für Erdkunde Ergänzungsheft* 1.

—— 1950–1. 'Die Versammlunghäuser (Kulthäuser) am Sepik in Neu-Guinea.' *Die Erde* 3–4: 304–27.

BLAKE, BARRY J. 1993. 'Verb affixes from case markers.' *La Trobe University Working Papers in Linguistics* 6: 33–58.

—— 1999. 'Nominal marking on verbs: some Australian cases.' *Word* 50: 299–317.

BOWDEN, R. 1983. *Yena: Art and Ceremony in a Sepik Society*. Oxford: Pitt Rivers Museum.

—— 1987. 'Sorcery, illness and social control in Kwoma society', pp. 183–208 of *Sorcerer and Witch in Melanesia*, edited by M. Stephen. Melbourne: Melbourne University Press.

—— 1997. *A Dictionary of Kwoma, a Papuan Language of North-East New Guinea*. Canberra: Pacific Linguistics.

BRAGGE, L. 1990. 'The Japandai migrations', pp. 36–49 of Lutkehaus et al. (eds.).

—— ULRIKE CLAAS, and PAUL ROSCOE. 2006. 'On the edge of empire: military brokers in the Sepik "Tribal Zone".' *American Ethnologist* 33: 110–13.

BRUCE, L. 1984. *The Alamblak Language of Papua New Guinea (East Sepik)*. Canberra: Pacific Linguistics.

—— 1988. 'Serialization: from syntax to lexicon.' *Studies in Language* 12: 19–49.

CAMPBELL, L. and M. MUNTZEL. 1989. 'The structural consequences of language death', pp. 181–96 of *Investigating Obsolescence: Studies in Language Contraction and Death*, edited by N. Dorian. Cambridge: Cambridge University Press.

CHAPPELL, J. 2005. 'Geographic changes of coastal lowlands in the Papuan past', pp. 525–40 of Pawley et al. (eds.).

CLAAS, ULRIKE. 2007. *Das Land entlang des Sepik: Vergangenheitsdarstellungen und Migrationsgeschichte im Gebiet des mittleren Sepik, Papua New Guinea*. Göttinger Studies, zur Ethnologie 17. Berlin: LIT-Verlag.

CLARK, H. H. and R. J. GERRIG. 1990. 'Quotations as demonstrations.' *Language* 66: 764–805.

CLUNE, FRANK. 1951. *Somewhere in New Guinea: A Companion to Prowling through Papua*. Sydney: Angus and Robertson.

CLYNE, M. 1987. 'Constraints on code-switching: how universal are they?' *Linguistics* 25: 739–64.

COMRIE, B. 2003. 'Recipient person suppletion in the verb "give"', pp. 265–81 of *Language and Life. Essays in Memory of Kenneth L. Pike*, edited by Mary Ruth Wise, Thomas N. Headland, and Ruth M. Brend. Dallas: Summer Institute of Linguistics International and the University of Texas at Arlington.

CURNOW, T. J. 2001. 'What language features can be "borrowed"?', pp. 412–36 of *Areal Diffusion and Genetic Inheritance: Problems in Comparative Linguistics*, edited by A. Y. Aikhenvald and R. M. W. Dixon. Oxford: Oxford University Press.

CURTAIN, R. 1978. 'Labor migration from the Sepik.' *Oral History* 6: 1–114.

DENCH, A. 2001. 'Descent and diffusion: the complexity of the Pilbara situation', pp. 105–33 of *Areal Diffusion and Genetic Inheritance: Problems in Comparative Linguistics*, edited by A. Y. Aikhenvald and R. M. W. Dixon. Oxford: Oxford University Press.

DIXON, R. M. W. 1972. *The Dyirbal Language of North Queensland.* Cambridge: Cambridge University Press.

—— 1977. *A Grammar of Yidiny.* Cambridge: Cambridge University Press.

—— 1982. *Where Have All the Adjectives Gone? And Other Essays in Semantics and Syntax.* Berlin: Mouton.

—— 1988. *A Grammar of Boumaa Fijian.* Chicago: University of Chicago Press.

—— 1990. 'The origin of "Mother-in-law vocabulary" in two Australian languages.' *Anthropological Linguistics* 32: 1–56.

—— 1991. 'A changing language situation: the decline of Dyirbal, 1963–1989.' *Language in Society* 20: 183–200.

—— 1994. *Ergativity.* Cambridge: Cambridge University Press.

—— 1997. *The Rise and Fall of Languages.* Cambridge: Cambridge University Press.

—— 2000. 'A typology of causatives: form, syntax and meaning', pp. 30–83 of *Changing Valency: Case Studies in Transitivity,* edited by R. M. W. Dixon and Alexandra Y. Aikhenvald. Cambridge: Cambridge University Press.

—— 2002a. *Australian Languages: Their Nature and Development.* Cambridge: Cambridge University Press.

—— 2002b. 'Copula clauses in Australian languages: a typological perspective.' *Anthropological Linguistics* 44: 1–36.

—— 2003. 'Demonstratives: a cross-linguistic typology.' *Studies in Language* 27: 61–112.

—— 2004. 'Adjective classes in typological perspective', pp. 1–49 of *Adjective Classes: A Cross-linguistic Typology,* edited by R. M. W. Dixon and Alexandra Y. Aikhenvald. Oxford: Oxford University Press.

—— 2005. *A Semantic Approach to English Grammar.* Oxford: Oxford University Press.

—— 2006. 'Complement clause types and complementation strategies in typological perspective', pp. 1–48 of *Complementation: A Cross-linguistic Typology,* edited by R. M. W. Dixon and Alexandra Y. Aikhenvald. Oxford: Oxford University Press.

—— Forthcoming. *Basic Linguistic Theory.*

—— and A. Y. AIKHENVALD. 2002. 'Word: a typological framework', pp. 1–41 of *Word: A Cross-linguistic Typology,* edited by R. M. W. Dixon and Alexandra Y. Aikhenvald. Cambridge: Cambridge University Press.

DORIAN, N. 1994. 'Purism vs. compromise in language revitalisation and language revival.' *Language in Society* 23: 479–94.

DU BOIS, J. 1987. 'The discourse basis of ergativity.' *Language* 63: 805–55.

EVANS, N. 1995. *A Grammar of Kayardild, with Historical-Comparative Notes on Tangkic.* Berlin: Mouton de Gruyter.

—— and D. WILKINS. 2000. 'In the mind's ear: the semantic extensions of perception verbs in Australian languages.' *Language* 76: 546–92.

FARNSWORTH, M. 1971. *Nyana Maaj.* Ukarumpa: Summer Institute of Linguistics.

—— n.d. 'Manambu dictionary.' MS.

FARNSWORTH, R. 1966. 'Manambu pronouns and demonstratives.' MS. Ukarumpa: Summer Institute of Linguistics.

—— 1975. 'Manambu phrases and clauses.' MS. Ukarumpa: Summer Institute of Linguistics.

—— 1976. 'Developing a "plain language" style.' *Read* 11: 71–3.

—— and M. FARNSWORTH. 1966. 'Grammar sketch. Manambu. Part 1. Morphology.' MS. Ukarumpa: Summer Institute of Linguistics.

—— —— 1975. 'Request for established orthography.' MS. Ukarumpa: Summer Institute of Linguistics.

—— —— 1981 (?). 'Organized phonology data. Manambu language.' MS. Ukarumpa: Summer Institute of Linguistics.

—— n.d. 'Essentials for translation.' MS. Ukarumpa: Summer Institute of Linguistics.

FOLEY, W. A. 1986. *The Papuan Languages of New Guinea.* Cambridge: Cambridge University Press.

—— 1988. 'Language birth: the processes of pidginisation and creolisation', pp. 162–84 of *Language: The Socio-cultural Survey.* Vol. IV of *Linguistics: The Cambridge Survey,* edited by F. J. Newmeyer. Cambridge: Cambridge University Press.

FOLEY, W. A.1991. *The Yimas Language of New Guinea*. Stanford, Calif.: Stanford University Press.

—— 2000. 'The languages of New Guinea.' *Annual Review of Anthropology* 29: 357–404.

—— 2005a. 'Linguistic prehistory in the Sepik-Ramu basin', pp. 109–44 of Pawley et al. (eds.).

—— 2005b. 'Personhood, identity, purism and variation.' Paper presented at ALS meeting, Melbourne, September 2005.

FRANKLIN, K. J. and R. STEFANIW. 1992. 'The "pandanus languages" of the Southern Highlands Province, Papua New Guinea: A further report', pp. 1–6 of *Culture Change, Language Change: Case Studies from Melanesia*, edited by T. E. Dutton. Canberra: Pacific Linguistics.

FREUDENBURG, ALLEN. 1970. 'Grammar essentials, Boiken language.' MS. Ukarumpa.

—— 1975. 'Survey list (standard): Boiken (Yengoru)'. MS. Ukarumpa: Summer Institute of Linguistics.

—— 1976. 'The dialects of Boiken', pp. 80–90 of *Surveys in Five Papua New Guinea Languages*, edited by Richard Loving. Workpapers in Papua New Guinea Languages, 16. Ukarumpa: Summer Institute of Linguistics.

—— 1979. 'Grammar sketch: Boiken language. Yangoru Dialect.' MS. Ukarumpa: Summer Institute of Linguistics.

GEWERTZ, D. B. 1983. *Sepik River Societies: A Historical Ethnography of the Chambri and their Neighbors*. New Haven: Yale University Press.

—— and F. K. ERRINGTON. 1999. *Emerging Class in Papua New Guinea: The Telling of Difference*. Cambridge: Cambridge University Press.

GOLSON, J. 2005. 'Introduction to the chapters on archaeology and ethnology', pp. 221–34 of Pawley et al. (eds.).

GUMPERZ, J. J. 1976. 'The sociolinguistic significance of conversational code-switching.' *Working Papers of Language Behavior Research Laboratory* 16: 1–45.

—— 1982. *Discourse Strategies*. Cambridge: Cambridge University Press.

HAHL, A. 1980. *Governor in New Guinea*. Edited and translated by P. G. Sack and D. Clark. Canberra: Australian National University Press.

HAIG, G. 2001. 'Linguistic diffusion in present-day Anatolia: from top to bottom', pp. 195–224 of *Areal Diffusion and Genetic Inheritance: Problems in Comparative Linguistics*, edited by Alexandra Y. Aikhenvald and R. M. W. Dixon. Oxford: Oxford University Press.

HAIMAN, J. 1983. *Hua: A Papuan Language of the Eastern Highlands of New Guinea*. Amsterdam: John Benjamins.

—— and P. MUNRO. 1983. 'Introduction', pp. ix–xv of *Switch-Reference and Universal Grammar*, edited by J. Haiman and P. Munro. Amsterdam: John Benjamins.

HAJEK, J. 2006. 'Language contact and convergence in East Timor: the case of Tetun Dili', pp. 163–78 of Aikhenvald and Dixon (eds.).

HALE, K. 1971. 'A note on a Warlbiri tradition of antonymy', pp. 472–82 of *Semantics: An Interdisciplinary Reader in Philosophy, Linguistics and Psychology*, edited by D. D. Steinberg and L. A. Jakobovits. Cambridge: Cambridge University Press.

HAMP, E. 1989. 'On signs of health and death', pp. 197–210 of *Investigating Obsolescence: Studies in Language Contraction and Death*, edited by N. Dorian. Cambridge: Cambridge University Press.

HARRISON, S. J. 1983. *Laments for Foiled Marriages: Love Songs from a Sepik River Village*. Boroko: Institute of Papua New Guinea Studies.

—— 1985a. 'Concepts of the person in Avatip religious thought.' *Man* NS 20: 115–20.

—— 1985b. 'Ritual hierarchy and secular equality in a Sepik River village.' *American Ethnologist* 12: 413–26.

—— 1985c. 'Names, ghosts and alliance in two Sepik River societies.' *Oceania* 56: 138–46.

—— 1987. 'Cultural efflorescence and political evolution on the Sepik River.' *American Ethnologist* 14: 4491–507.

—— 1990a. *Stealing People's Names: History and Politics in a Sepik River Cosmology*. Cambridge: Cambridge University Press.

—— 1990b. 'Concepts of the person in Avatip religious thought', pp. 351–63 of Lutkehaus et al. (eds.).

—— 1993. *The Mask of War: Violence, Ritual and the Self in Melanesia*. Manchester: Manchester University Press.

HATANAKA, S. and L. W. BRAGGE. 1973–4. 'Habitat, isolation and subsistence economy in the Central Range of New Guinea.' *Oceania* 44: 38–57.

HEINE, B. 2001. 'Grammaticalization chains across languages: an example from Khoisan', pp. 177–99 of *Reconstructing Grammar: Comparative Linguistics and Grammaticalization*, edited by S. Gildea. Amsterdam: John Benjamins.

—— and T. KUTEVA. 2002. *World Lexicon of Grammaticalization*. Cambridge: Cambridge University Press.

HILL, J. 1998. ' "Today there is no respect": nostalgia, "respect" and oppositional discourse in Mexicano (Nahuatl) language ideology', pp. 68–86 of *Language Ideologies: Practice and Theory*, edited by Bambi B. Schieffelin, Kathryn A. Woolard, and Paul V. Kroskrity. New York: Oxford University Press.

—— and K. C. HILL. 1986. *Speaking Mexicano: Dynamics of Syncretic Language in Central Mexico*. Tucson, Ariz.: The University of Arizona Press.

HORNBERGER, N. H. and K. A. KING. 2000. 'Reversing Quechua language shift in South America', pp. 166–94 of *Can Threatened Languages Be Saved? Reversing Language Shift, Revisited: A 21st Century Perspective*, edited by J. Fishman. Clevedon: Multilingual Matters.

HOUSEMAN, MICHAEL and CARLO SEVERI. 1998. *Naven, or the Other Self: A Relational Approach to Ritual Action*. Leiden: Brill.

JACKSON, E. 1987. 'Direct and indirect speech in Tikar.' *Journal of West African Languages* 17: 98–109.

JENDRASCHEK, G. 2006a. 'The semantics of clause linking in Iatmul.' Presentation at RCLT Local Workshop on the Semantics of Clause Linking.

—— 2006b. 'Clause fusion in Iatmul: from cleft sentences to highlighting constructions.' Seminar presented at RCLT.

—— 2007. Iatmul–English dictionary. Draft edition. RCLT.

—— Forthcoming. *A Grammar of Iatmul*.

KEENAN, E. 1987. 'Towards a universal definition of "subject of" ', pp. 89–120 of his *Universal Grammar: 15 Essays*. London: Croom Helm.

—— and B. COMRIE. 1977. 'NP accessibility and universal grammar', *Linguistic Inquiry* 8: 63–100.

KIRSCHBAUM, F. 1922. 'Sprachen- und Kulturgruppierungen in Deutsch-Neuguinea.' *Anthropos* 16/17: 1052–3.

KLUGE, T. 1938. *Die Zahlbegriffe der Australier, Papua und Bantuneger, nebst einer Einleitung über die Zahl*. Berlin.

—— 1942. 'Völker und Sprachen von Neu-Guinea.' *Petermanns Geographische Mitteilungen* 88: 241–55.

KOOYERS, O. 1974. 'Washkuk grammar sketch.' *Work Papers in Papua New Guinea Languages* 6: 5–74.

—— 1975. 'Hierarchy of Washkuk (Kwoma) clauses.' *Linguistics* 147: 5–14.

—— M. KOOYERS, and D. BEE. 1971. 'The phonemes of Washkuk.' *Te Reo* 14: 37–41.

KULICK, D. 1987. 'Language shift and language socialisation in Gapun: a report on fieldwork in progress.' *Language and Linguistics in Melanesia* 17: 125–50.

—— 1992. *Language Shift and Cultural Reproduction: Socialisation, Self, and Syncretism in a Papua New Guinean Village*. Cambridge: Cambridge University Press.

KUNDAMA, J., P. WILSON, with A. SAPAI. 1987. *Kudi Kupuk: Ambulas (Maprik Dialect) Tok Pisin English*. Ukarumpa: Summer Institute of Linguistics.

LANDWEER, M. L. 2000. 'Endangered languages: indicators of ethnolinguistic vitality.' *Notes on Sociolinguistics* 5: 5–22.

LARSON, M. L. 1984. *Meaning-Based Translation: A Guide to Cross-language Equivalence*. Lanham, Md.: University Press of America.

LAYCOCK, D. C. 1965. *The Ndu Language Family (Sepik District, New Guinea)*. Canberra: Linguistic Circle of Canberra Publications.

—— 1973. *Sepik Languages: Checklist and Preliminary Classification*. Canberra: Pacific Linguistics.

—— 1974. 'The Torricelli Phylum', pp. 767–80 of *New Guinea Area Languages and Language Study, i: Papuan Languages and the New Guinea Linguistic Scene*, edited by S. A. Wurm. Canberra: Pacific Linguistics.

LAYCOCK, D. C. 1986. 'Papuan languages and the possibility of semantic classification', pp. 1–10 of *Papers in New Guinea Linguistics* 24. Canberra: Pacific Linguistics.

——1991. 'Three vowels, semivowels, and neutralisation: orthographic and other problems of Sepik languages', pp. 107–13 of *Papers in Papuan Linguistics*, edited by Tom Dutton. Canberra: Pacific Linguistics.

——and J. Z'GRAGGEN. 1975. 'The Sepik-Ramu phylum', pp. 731–64 of *New Guinea Area Languages and Language Study*, i: *Papuan Languages and the New Guinea Linguistic Scene*, edited by S. A. Wurm. Canberra: Pacific Linguistics.

LEHMANN, C. 1988. 'Towards a typology of clause linkage', pp. 181–225 of *Clause-Combining in Grammar and Discourse*, edited by J. Haiman and S. A. Thompson. Amsterdam: John Benjamins.

LEVINSON, STEPHEN C. 2003. *Space in Language and Cognition: Explorations in Cognitive Diversity.* Cambridge: Cambridge University Press.

LEWIS, A. 1923. *The Use of Sago in New Guinea.* Chicago: Field Museum of Natural History.

LICHTENBERK, F. 2000. 'Inclusory pronominals.' *Oceanic Linguistics* 39: 1–32.

LINDSTRÖM, E. 2002. 'The body in expressions of emotion: Kuot.' *Pragmatics and Cognition* 10: 159–84.

LOUKOTKA, Č. 1957. *Classification des langues papoues.* Lingua Posnaniensis 6. Nadbitka.

LUSCHAN, VON F. 1911. 'Zur Ethnographie der Kaiserin Augusta Flüsses.' *Bässler-Archiv* 1: 103–17.

LUTKEHAUS, N., C. KAUFMANN, W. E. MITCHELL, D. NEWTON, L. OSMUNDSEN, and M. SCHUSTER (eds.). 1990. *Sepik Heritage: Tradition and Change in Papua New Guinea.* Durham, NC: Carolina Academic Press.

LYNCH, J., M. D. ROSS, and T. CROWLEY. 2002. *The Oceanic Languages.* London: Curzon Press.

MCCARTHY, J. K. 1963. *Patrol into Yesterday: My New Guinea Years.* Melbourne: F. W. Cheshire.

MCGREGOR, D. E. and A. R. F. MCGREGOR. 1982. *Olo Language Materials.* Canberra: Pacific Linguistics.

MANABE, T. 1981. 'Sociolinguistic survey of West Wosera.' MS. Ukarumpa: Summer Institute of Linguistics.

MATTHEWS, P. H. 1997. *The Concise Oxford Dictionary of Linguistics.* Oxford: Oxford University Press.

MEAD, M. 1931. 'Talk-Boy.' *Asia* 31: 144–51, 191.

——1935. *Sex and Temperament in Three Primitive Societies.* New York: Morrow.

——1938. 'The Mountain Arapesh: an importing culture.' *American Museum of Natural History, Anthropological Papers* 36: 139–349.

MITHUN, M. 1984. 'The evolution of noun incorporation.' *Language* 60: 847–94.

MORAVCSIK, E. 1978. 'Language contact', pp. 93–123 of *Universals of Human Languages*, vol. i, edited by Joseph H. Greenberg, Charles A. Ferguson, and Edith A. Moravcsik. Stanford, Calif.: Stanford University Press.

——1983. 'On grammatical classes: the case of "definite objects" in Hungarian', pp. 75–107 of *Working Papers in Linguistics*, vol. 15–1. Honolulu: University of Hawaii.

——2003. 'A semantic analysis of associative plurals.' *Studies in Language* 27: 469–503.

MUNRO, P. 1982. 'On the transitivity of "say" verbs', pp. 301–19 of *Syntax and Semantics.* Volume 15. *Studies in Transitivity*, edited by P. J. Hopper and S. A. Thompson. New York: Harcourt Press.

NEKITEL, O. 1985. 'Sociolinguistic aspects of Abuʹ: a Papuan language of the Sepik area, Papua New Guinea.' Ph.D. thesis. Australian National University.

——1992. 'Culture change, language change: the case of Abuʹ Arapesh, Sandaun Province, Papua New Guinea', pp. 49–58 of *Culture Change, Language Change: Case studies from Melanesia*, edited by T. E. Dutton. Canberra: Pacific Linguistics.

——1998. *Voices of Yesterday, Today and Tomorrow: Language, Culture and Identity.* New Delhi: UBS, Publisher Distributors Ltd.

NEWMAN, J. Forthcoming. 'A cross-linguistic overview of "eat" and "drink".' In *The Linguistics of Eating and Drinking*, edited by John Newman. Amsterdam: John Benjamins.

NEWTON, D. 1971. *The Crocodile and the Cassowary: Religious Art of the Upper Sepik River, New Guinea.* New York: Museum of Primitive Art.

NIKOLAEVA, I. 1999. 'Object agreement, grammatical relations, and information structure.' *Studies in Language* 23: 331–76.

OSBORNE, C. R. 1974. *The Tiwi Language.* Canberra: Australian Institute of Aboriginal Studies.

PAWLEY, A. K. 1993. 'A language which defies description by ordinary means', pp. 87–129 of *The Role of Theory in Language Description*, edited by W. A. Foley. Berlin: Mouton de Gruyter.

—— Forthcoming. 'On the argument structure of complex predicates in Kalam.' *Berkeley Linguistics Society* 32.

—— S. P. GI, I. S. MAJNEP, and J. KIAS. 2000. 'Hunger acts on me: the grammar and semantics of bodily and mental process expressions in Kalam', pp. 153–85 of *Grammatical Analysis: Morphology, Syntax and Semantics. Studies in Honor of Stanley Starosta*, edited by V. P. De Guzman and B. W. Bender. Honolulu: University of Hawai'i Press.

—— R. ATTENBOROUGH, J. GOLSON, and R. HIDE (eds.). 2005. *Papuan Pasts: Cultural, Linguistic and Biological Histories of Papuan-Speaking Peoples*. Canberra: Pacific Linguistics.

PAYNE, DORIS L. and I. BARSHI. 1999. 'External possession: what, where, how and why', pp. 3–29 of *External Possession*, edited by D. L. Payne and I. Barshi. Amsterdam: John Benjamins.

PAYNE, J. and DAVID PAYNE. 2005. 'The pragmatics of split-intransitivity in Asheninca.' *Revista Latinoamericana de estudios etnolingüísticos. Lingüística arawaka* 10: 37–56.

PIKE, E. V. 1964. 'The phonology of New Guinea Highlands languages.' *American Anthropologist*. Special Publication, no. 4, pt. 1, 121–32.

PRIESTLEY, C. 2002. 'Insides and emotion in Koromu.' *Pragmatics and Cognition* 10: 243–70.

RAY, S. H. 1919. 'The languages of Northern Papua.' *Journal of the Royal Anthropological Institute of Great Britain and Ireland* 49: 317–41.

—— 1927. 'The Papuan languages', pp. 377–85 of *Festschrift Meinhof*. Hamburg: Kommisionsverlag von L. Friederichsen.

RECHE, O. 1910. 'Eine Bereisung des Kaiserin Augusta Flusses.' *Globus* 97: 285–8.

REESINK, G. 1983. 'Switch reference and topicality hierarchies.' *Studies in Language* 7: 215–46.

RIESENFELD, A. 1951. 'Tobacco in New Guinea and the other areas of Melanesia.' *Journal of the Royal Anthropological Institute of Great Britain and Ireland* 81: 69–112.

ROBERTS, J. 1988. 'Switch-reference in Papuan languages: a syntactic or extrasyntactic device?' *Australian Journal of Linguistics* 8: 75–117.

—— 1997. 'Switch-reference in Papua New Guinea: a preliminary survey', pp. 101–241 of *Papers in Papuan Linguistics* 3. Canberra: Pacific Linguistics.

—— 2001. 'Impersonal constructions in Amele', pp. 201–50 of *Non-canonical Marking of Subjects and Objects*, edited by A. Y. Aikhenvald, R. M. W. Dixon, and M. Onishi. Amsterdam: John Benjamins.

ROESICKE, A. 1914. 'Mitteilungen über ethnographische Ergebnisse der Kaiserin Augusta-Fluss-Expedition.' *Zeitschrift für Ethnologie* 46: 507–22.

ROSCOE, P. 1994. 'Who are the Ndu? Ecology, migration, and linguistic and cultural change in the Sepik Basin', pp. 49–84 of *Migrations and Transformations: Regional Perspectives on New Guinea*, edited by A. J. Strathern and G. Stürzenhofecker. Pittsburgh: University of Pittsburgh Press.

—— 1996. 'War and society in Sepik New Guinea.' *Journal of the Royal Anthropological Institute* NS 2: 645–66.

—— 2005. 'Foraging, ethnographic analogy, and Papuan pasts: contemporary models for the Sepik-Ramu past', pp. 555–84 of Pawley et al. (eds.).

ROSENBAUM, P. 1967. *The Grammar of English Predicate Complement Constructions*. Cambridge, Mass.: MIT Press.

ROWLEY, CHARLES DUNFORD. 1958. *The Australians in German New Guinea, 1914–1921*. Carlton: Melbourne University Press.

RYAN, P. (ed). 1972. *Encyclopaedia of Papua New Guinea*. Melbourne: Melbourne University Press in association with the University of Papua New Guinea.

SANDS, A. K. 2000. 'Complement clauses and grammatical relations in Finnish.' Ph.D. dissertation. ANU, Canberra.

SAPIR, E. 1921. *Language*. New York: Harcourt, Brace & World.

SASSE, H.-J. 1992. 'Language decay and contact-induced change: similarities and differences', pp. 59–80 of *Language Death: Factual and Theoretical Explorations with Special Reference to East Africa*, edited by M. Brenzinger. Berlin: Mouton de Gruyter.

Saun, E. and J. Nate. 1975. 'Gaikunti dictionary.' MS. Ukarumpa.

Schaengold, C. C. 2004. 'Bilingual Navajo: mixed codes, bilingualism, and language maintenance.' Ph.D. dissertation. Ohio State University.

Schanely, L. 1965. 'The phonemes of Gaikunti.' MS. Ukarumpa.

Schmidt, W. 1901. 'Die sprachliche Verhältnisse von Deutsch-Neuguinea.' *Zeitschrift für afrikanische und ozeanische Sprachen* 5: 355–84.

—— 1902. 'Die sprachliche Verhältnisse von Deutsch-Neuguinea'. *Zeitschrift für afrikanische und ozeanische Sprachen* 6: 1–99.

Smith-Stark, S. 1974. 'The plurality split'. *Papers from the Annual Regional Meeting of the Chicago Linguistic Society* 10: 657–71.

Staalsen, P. 1963(?). 'Big Sepik (Iatmul) phonemes.' MS. Ukarumpa.

—— 1965. 'Iatmul grammar sketch.' MS. Ukarumpa.

—— 1966. 'The phonemes of Iatmul', pp. 69–76 of *Papers in New Guinea Linguistics* 5. Canberra: Pacific Linguistics.

—— 1969. 'The dialects of Iatmul', pp. 68–84 of *Papers in New Guinea Linguistics* 10. Canberra: Pacific Linguistics.

—— 1972. 'Clause relationships in Iatmul', pp. 45–69 of *Papers in New Guinea Linguistics* 15. Canberra: Pacific Linguistics.

—— 1975. 'The languages of the Sawos region (New Guinea).' *Anthropos* 70: 6–16.

—— 1992. 'Organised phonology data: Iatmul (Big Sepik) language.' MS. Ukarumpa.

—— n.d.a. 'Iatmul verbs.' MS. Ukarumpa.

—— n.d.b. 'Essentials for translation: grammar section. Iatmul language.' MS. Ukarumpa.

—— and L. Staalsen. 1973. 'Iatmul–English Dictionary.' MS. Ukarumpa.

Stebbins, T. 1997. 'Asymmetrical nominal number marking: a functional account.' *Sprachtypologie und Universalienforschung* 50: 5–47.

—— Forthcoming. *A Grammar of Mali Baining*. Canberra: Pacific Linguistics.

Stirling, L. 1998. 'Isolated *if*-clauses in Australian English', pp. 273–94 of *The Clause in English: In Honour of Rodney Huddleston*, edited by P. Collins and D. Lee. Amsterdam: John Benjamins.

Sumbuk, K. M. 1999. 'Morphosyntax of Sare.' Ph.D. thesis. University of Waikato.

Swadling, P. and R. Hide. 2005. 'Changing landscape and social interaction: looking at agricultural history from a Sepik-Ramu perspective', pp. 289–328 of Pawley et al. (eds.).

Takendu, D. 1977. 'Avatip village, Ambunti sub-province, East Sepik.' *Oral History* 5(5): 2–53.

Telban, B. 1998. *Dancing Through Time: A Sepik Cosmology*. Oxford: Clarendon Press.

Tosco, M. 2000. 'Is there an "Ethiopian Linguistic area"?' *Anthropological Linguistics* 42: 329–65.

Townsend, G. W. L. 1968. *District Officer: From Untamed New Guinea to Lake Success 1921–46*. Sydney: The Sydney and Melbourne Publishing Company.

Tuzin, D. 1976. *The Ilahita Arapesh: Dimensions of Unity*. Berkeley and Los Angeles: University of California Press.

Vallauri, E. L. 2004. 'Grammaticalization of syntactic incompleteness: free conditionals in Italian and other languages.' *SKY Journal of Linguistics* 17: 189–215.

Vries, L. J. de. 2005. 'Towards a typology of head-tail linkage in Papuan languages.' *Studies in Language* 29: 363–84.

Wassmann, J. 1988. *Der Gesang an das Krokodil: Die rituellen Gesänge des Dorfes Kandingei am Land und Meer, Pflanzen und Tiere (Mittelsepik, Papua New Guinea)*. Basel: Ethnologisches Seminar der Universität und Museum für Völkerkunde.

Wendel, T. D. 1993. 'A preliminary grammar of Hanga Hundi.' MA thesis. University of Texas at Arlington.

Whitehead, C. R. 1991. 'Tense, aspect, mood and modality: verbal morphology in Menya', pp. 245–311 of *Papers in Papuan Linguistics*, edited by Tom Dutton. Canberra: Pacific Linguistics.

Wiesemann, Ursula. 1990. 'A model for the study of reported speech in African languages.' *Journal of West African Languages* 20(2): 75–80.

Wilson, P. 1973. 'Ambulas sentences.' *Work Papers in New Guinea Linguistics* 1: 21–164.

—— 1976. 'Ambulas dialect survey', pp. 51–79 of *Surveys in Five Papua New Guinea Languages*, edited by R. Loving. Work Papers in Papua New Guinea Languages 16. Ukarumpa: Summer Institute of Linguistics.

—— 1980. *Ambulas Grammar*. Ukarumpa: Summer Institute of Linguistics.

WOODBURY, A. 1998. 'Documenting rhetorical, aesthetic, and expressive loss in language shift', pp. 234–58 of *Endangered Languages: Current Issues and Future Prospects*, edited by L. A. Grenoble and L. J. Whaley. Cambridge: Cambridge University Press.

YIP, MOIRA. 1998. 'Identity avoidance in phonology and morphology', pp. 216–46 of *Morphology and its Relation to Phonology and Syntax*, edited by Steven G. Lapointe, Diane K. Brentari, and Patrick M. Farrell. Stanford, Calif.: CSLI Publications.

ZÖLLER, H. 1890. 'Untersuchungen über 24 Sprachen aus dem Schutzgebiet der Neuguinea-Compagnie.' *Dr. A. Petermanns Mitteilungen aus Justus Perthes Geographischer Anstalt* 36: 122–52.

—— 1891. *Deutsch New-Guinea*. Stuttgart: Union Deutsche Verlagsgesellschaft.

Index of Authors, Languages, and Subjects

Examples from Texts (pp. 627–64) are marked with T before page numbers.